Central Europe

Paul Smitz

Aaron Anderson, Brett Atkinson, Becca Blond, Lisa Dunford, Steve Fallon,
Sarah Johnstone, Vesna Maric, Tim Richards, Ryan Ver Berkmoes

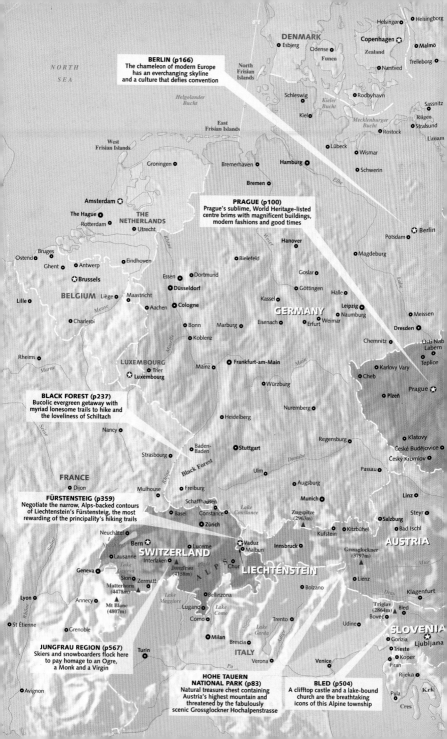

BERLIN (p166)
The chameleon of modern Europe has an everchanging skyline and a culture that defies convention

PRAGUE (p100)
Prague's sublime, World Heritage-listed centre brims with magnificent buildings, modern fashions and good times

BLACK FOREST (p237)
Bucolic evergreen getaway with myriad lonesome trails to hike and the loveliness of Schiltach

FÜRSTENSTEIG (p359)
Negotiate the narrow, Alps-backed contours of Liechtenstein's Fürstensteig, the most rewarding of the principality's hiking trails

JUNGFRAU REGION (p567)
Skiers and snowboarders flock here to pay homage to an Ogre, a Monk and a Virgin

HOHE TAUERN NATIONAL PARK (p83)
Natural treasure chest containing Austria's highest mountain and threatened by the fabulously scenic Grossglockner Hochalpenstrasse

BLED (p504)
A clifftop castle and a lake-bound church are the breathtaking icons of this Alpine township

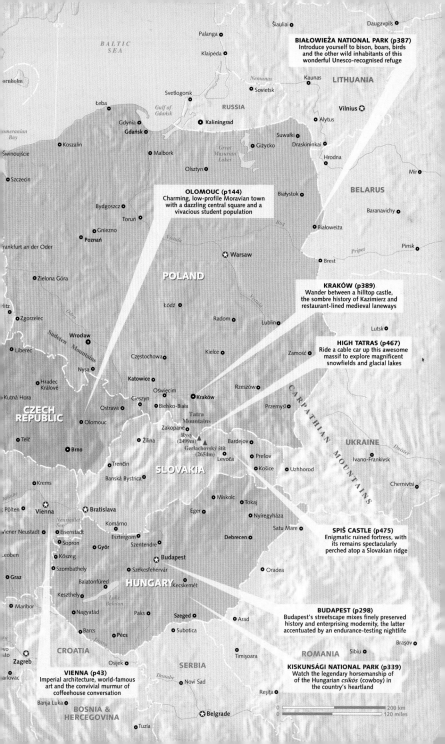

BIAŁOWIEŻA NATIONAL PARK (p387)
Introduce yourself to bison, boars, birds
and the other wild inhabitants of this
wonderful Unesco-recognised refuge

OLOMOUC (p144)
Charming, low-profile Moravian town
with a dazzling central square and a
vivacious student population

KRAKÓW (p389)
Wander between a hilltop castle,
the sombre history of Kazimierz and
restaurant-lined medieval laneways

HIGH TATRAS (p467)
Ride a cable car up this awesome
massif to explore magnificent
snowfields and glacial lakes

SPIŠ CASTLE (p475)
Enigmatic ruined fortress, with
its remains spectacularly
perched atop a Slovakian ridge

BUDAPEST (p298)
Budapest's streetscape mixes finely preserved
history and enterprising modernity, the latter
accentuated by an endurance-testing nightlife

VIENNA (p43)
Imperial architecture, world-famous
art and the convivial murmur of
coffeehouse conversation

KISKUNSÁGI NATIONAL PARK (p339)
Watch the legendary horsemanship of
of the Hungarian *csikós* (cowboy) in
the country's heartland

Destination Central Europe

The patchwork of countries that makes up Central Europe is remarkable for its shared history: filled with the ebb and flow of empires, quickfire revolts and the collaborative genius of composers, writers and painters. But the region is equally remarkable for the defiant individuality of its member nations, which offer travellers the chance to savour vibrant folk traditions, exuberant city-centre street parties, the architectural legacies of fallen dynasties and a beautiful diversity of landscapes that stretch from the snowy heights of the Alps through misty forests to Baltic beaches.

Before the raising of the Iron Curtain, the simplistic separation of Europe into an 'East' and a 'West' denied the existence of a culturally rich heartland where ideologies, ethnic heritage and artistry intermingled. Modern-day travellers can see the results for themselves when they taste the borderless cuisines of Berlin's restaurants and learn how those mild-mannered Swiss invented the acid trip. They may share a bench in a Prague *pivnice* (pub) with working-class guzzlers and fashionista sippers, wander down Venetian-inspired laneways in a Slovenian town, or revel in the echoes of the fabulous convergence of European composers in 19th-century Vienna. They may sample world-famous Hungarian wine in a mythical valley and ponder the Gothic lifestyle of Liechtenstein's super-wealthy monarch. Or they may join Wrocław's vivacious student population as they roam a baroque streetscape, or feast on a gourmet internationalist meal in Bratislava before strolling by the city's communist-era New Bridge.

Getting under the chameleonic skin of Central Europe is the prize for those who explore this wonderful region.

GRANT

Iconic Sights

JAN STROMME

Soak up the atmosphere of Hradčany (p107) with its Prague Castle backdrop, Prague, Czech Republic

JONATHAN SMITH

Get a bird's eye view of Vienna while riding the Riesenrad (p51), Austria

Look out over Berlin through the iconic glass-domed Reichstaggebäude (p172), Germany

NEIL SETCHFIELD

CRAIG PERSHOUSE

Kick back at an open-air café on Long Market, Royal Way (p425), Gdańsk, Poland

WITOLD SKRYF

Watch water shoot at 200km/h at the Jet d'Eau fountain (p540), Geneva, Switzerland

Stroll along Triple Bridge (p498) towards Franciscan Church of the Annunciation, Ljubljana, Slovenia

RICHARD I'ANSON

Enjoy some alfresco dining (p458) in Bratislava's old town, Slovakia

Wander among the medieval buildings of Budapest's Castle Hill (p305), Hungary

Great Outdoors

GARETH MCCORMACK

Cycle along the scenic Grossglockner Hochalpenstrasse (p83), Hohe Tauern National Park, Austria

Explore the Adršpach-Teplice Rocks (p139), Czech Republic

NEIL WILSON

CHRISTIAN ASLUND

Get some air while snowboarding (p584) in Central Europe

RICHARD NEBESKY

Get your fix of outdoor activities at Zejmarska Gorge (p477), Slovenský raj National Park, Slovakia

DAVID TOMLINSON

Take in some incredible views, Jungfrau (p567), Switzerland

Trek through Berchtesgaden (p227), while enjoying endless views of the Bavarian Alps, Germany

MARTIN MOOS

History & Culture

Snap a photo of picturesque Vaduz Castle (p357), Vaduz, Liechtenstein

Visit the chilling remains of Birkenau concentration camp (p398), Oświęcim, Poland

See how royalty used to spend their summers, Schloss Schönbrunn (p50), Vienna, Austria

Catch an opera performance at the famous Semperoper (p187), Dresden, Germany

Look for the abudance of Art-Nouveau architecture, Budapest (p298), Hungary

Explore Château de Chillon (p547) on Lake Geneva, Montreux, Switzerland

Take a tour of the impressive Český Krumlov Castle (p136), Český Krumlov, Czech Republic

Entertainment & Nightlife

Check out the vibrant dance scene at Bern's many clubs and bars (p536), Switzerland

Make the beer lover's pilgrimage to Oktoberfest (p215), Munich, Germany

Take your pick from many of Budapest's bars to enjoy a drink (p312), Hungary

Contents

Regional Map Contents

Germany
p159

Poland
p362

Czech Republic
p94

Slovakia
p449

Liechtenstein
p356

Switzerland
p527

Austria
p41

Hungary
p293

Slovenia
p491

The Authors

PAUL SMITZ
Introductory chapters, Regional Directory, Transport in Central Europe

Paul has made several forays into Central Europe over the years (make that decades), starting with his first backpacking trip to celebrate the end of his teens, when he sledded into the side of a house near Interlaken, spent entire days in German train stations, and curled up inside the Olympic rings in Innsbruck. He has coordinated and contributed to a dozen Lonely Planet guidebooks, including *Prague Condensed*, for which he forced himself to develop a lasting appreciation of Pilsner and jazz, and a *Matrix*-esque ability to avoid umbrella tips in Old Town laneways.

My Favourite Trip

My favourite Central European trip (so far) was centred on my two-month stint in the Czech Republic researching Lonely Planet's *Prague Condensed*. I rented an apartment in a 15th-century building on the Royal Way, right in the heart of the Old Town (p108), and from here took long walks down to Vyšehrad (p109), Prague's other legendary castle; to the boarded-up Ukrainian church hidden on the wooded slopes of Petřín Hill; and through the enigmatic backstreets of Malá Strana (p114) at twilight, when the lights of Staré Město would reflect off the languid waters of the Vltava. Memorable excursions into the Czech countryside included visits to the amazing ossuary in Kutná Hora (p122) and the medieval majesty of Karlštejn Castle (p121).

AARON ANDERSON
Austria

Aaron was first drawn to Austria when his Western Europe travels were temporarily suspended by an extended stopover in Mayrhofen, Tirol. He became so happy with the alpine lifestyle and serenity that he took on a part-time job wrenching on bikes to help make the experience last longer. A month quickly turned into a year of living it up and garnering an appreciation for everything Austrian. He is based in Boulder, Colorado, and enjoys Saturdays at home with his girlfriend (also a Lonely Planet author), and dog (not an LP author...yet), loves anything outdoors, wears a mohawk in the summertime, and isn't afraid to sport a handlebar moustache. When not travelling the world, he works part-time in a friend's microbrewery as a professional brewer.

LONELY PLANET AUTHORS

Why is our travel information the best in the world? It's simple: our authors are independent, dedicated travellers. They don't research using just the internet or phone, and they don't take freebies in exchange for positive coverage. They travel widely, to all the popular spots and off the beaten track. They personally visit thousands of hotels, restaurants, cafés, bars, galleries, palaces, museums and more – and they take pride in getting all the details right, and telling it how it is. For more, see the authors section on www.lonelyplanet.com.

RYAN VER BERKMOES   Germany

Ryan Ver Berkmoes once lived in Germany. He spent three years in Frankfurt, during which time he edited a magazine until he got a chance for a new career with Lonely Planet. One of his first jobs was working on the Germany chapter of the 4th edition of this very book. Since then he's travelled the world as a writer for LP and others, but was more than happy to return to Germany for this book. Fortunately he won't have to worry about withdrawal from German beer as he lives in Portland, Oregon – one of the world's great beer cities.

SARAH JOHNSTONE   Germany

Sarah Johnstone is a freelance journalist based in London. She hates author bios and wishes the editors would stop asking for them. Having studied German (and journalism) at university, worked for employers from news agency Reuters to business travel magazines, and done an MSc at the London School of Economics, she's spent the last few years dutifully traipsing back and forth across Europe for Lonely Planet.

BECCA BLOND   Switzerland & Liechtenstein

Becca and Switzerland became acquainted at an early age – she was born in Geneva. Although she moved to the States as a toddler, her American parents didn't let her forget the country. She has slightly embarrassing childhood memories of wearing traditional Swiss alpine dresses to holiday functions and fonder ones of feeding local goats during family vacations in the Swiss Alps. These early holidays inspired Becca's desire to travel. When she realised the monotony of a nine-to-five job was not something she could live with, she swapped newspaper reporting on rock stars and homicides for wandering the world for Lonely Planet. When not on the road she calls Boulder, Colorado home.

BRETT ATKINSON   Czech Republic

Brett's first experiences of Eastern Europe were Bulgaria and Yugoslavia, when the Iron Curtain was still pulled tightly shut. He's since returned to write about Hungary's communist legacy, island hopped in Croatia and honeymooned in Sarajevo. During eight weeks of research in the Czech Republic, he furthered his hobby of beer appreciation, especially while watching Friday night ice hockey at the local *pivnice* (pub). When he's not travelling for Lonely Planet, Brett lives with Carol in Auckland, New Zealand, about as far from Eastern Europe as possible. He advises never to drive a Skoda Fabia across a narrow castle drawbridge, especially if there's no room to turn around on the other side.

VESNA MARIC   Hungary
Vesna loved researching Hungary in below-zero January temperatures, spending a lot of time warming her bones in thermal baths, eating hot goulash, drinking wine and dancing in smoky clubs. Her first visit to Hungary was some years ago: after an overnight train from Sarajevo, she emerged into a springtime Budapest so full of beans and birds and bees, and she kept longing to go back for more. Vesna will never forget the joy of skating on a frozen lake, along with residents of a whole Hungarian village.

TIM RICHARDS   Poland
Tim spent a year teaching English in Kraków, Poland, in 1994–95, having transferred with an international teaching organisation from a two-year stint in Egypt. He was fascinated by the massive post-communism transition affecting every aspect of Polish life, and by surviving remnants of the Cold War days. As a result, he jumped at the chance to return for this assignment more than a decade later, and was delighted by his intense reacquaintance with this beautiful, complex country. When he's not on the road for Lonely Planet, Tim is a freelancer living in Melbourne, Australia, writing on topics such as travel, lifestyle, the arts, technology and pets.

LISA DUNFORD   Slovakia
A fascination with Eastern Europe gripped Lisa from childhood, probably because her grandfather came from the Carpathian region that was Hungary, then Czechoslovakia and is now in the Ukraine. She studied in Budapest and arrived in Bratislava, Slovakia, after graduation looking for work; various projects led to a job at the US Agency for International Development. She danced with the country as it became an independent nation, learned the language and made life-long friends. Lisa now lives in Houston, Texas, but projects and travel take her back to the region often; she always makes sure she spends as much time as possible on the trip in Slovakia. It still feels like home.

STEVE FALLON   Slovenia
Steve has been travelling to Slovenia since the early 1990s, when a well-known publishing company refused his proposal to write a guidebook to the country because of 'the war going on' (it had ended two years earlier) and an influential American daily newspaper told him that their readers weren't interested in 'Slovakia'. Never mind, it was his own little secret for a good 10 years. Though he still hasn't reached the top of Mt Triglav, Steve considers at least part of his soul Slovenian and returns to the country as often as he can for a glimpse of the Julian Alps in the sun, and a dribble of *bučno olje* (pumpkinseed oil).

Getting Started

To some travellers the act of 'planning' is the antithesis of independent travel, an exercise that merely restricts the on-the-road experience. However, to plan your trip does not have to mean chiselling your itinerary – or your expectations – in stone. It simply makes sense to give consideration to your priorities before boarding your plane/boat/train/camper van. If you want your trip to last as long as possible, for example, you'll want to minimise travel in the more-expensive countries. Alternatively, if you're a fan of cosmopolitana, you'll probably want to spend most of your time sauntering around a couple of choice urban destinations. And for those keen on specific festivities or activities, the timing of their trip will obviously be of utmost importance. The good news for those intending to explore Central Europe is that this is a sizeable, easily navigable and wonderfully choice-ridden region that can accommodate most of the scenarios any travel-conscious mind can dream up.

WHEN TO GO

Every Central European country has seasonal attractions that conspire to keep visitors engaged year-round and encourage special-interest groups to favour some periods of the calendar over others. If skiing is your thing, be it atop the continent's most dramatic peaks (Switzerland) or at some of its most affordable ski resorts (Slovenia, Slovakia), the wintry months from December to April are for you. To smell the spring flowers and avoid the tourist congestion during summer, try visiting in May.

Summer throughout the region is in full swing from June through August. July and August are the hottest months and also the busiest in terms of tourists and the range of activities, events and services on offer. In general, prices go up during summertime, with some notable differences: in Slovakia, for example, accommodation prices are much lower in its cities than in its jam-packed mountain resorts. The onset of winter obviously sees prices soar in the snowfields.

See Climate Charts (p585) for more information.

While some prefer a lake dip in June, for others it's an autumn tipple of wine. September is another great time to visit the region, with still-warm temperatures and shadow patterns across the many vineyards of the area.

COSTS & MONEY

This wide swathe of Europe encompasses an equally wide range of costs and prices; whatever holes Switzerland burns in your wallet can be stitched up in Slovakia. This stretch of the continent will surely leave you scratching your head over the vagaries of capitalism – just how can the same item differ in price over a few hundred kilometres? *Vive la différence* indeed! That said,

---

DON'T LEAVE HOME WITHOUT...

You can buy almost anything in the countries of Central Europe that you might have left at home, but some things may be prohibitively expensive and others are better left unforgotten. If you require any specific medicines, it's best to stock up on these before your departure. If you're taking a digital camera, handheld computer or the like, consider whether you might need any specialised or brand-specific electronic equipment that will be hard to obtain in the region. It's also worth double-checking visa regulations, though most visitors will be able to travel visa-free. It was once *de rigueur* for travellers to pack their own Swiss army knife, but if you really need one you can just buy it in its home country.

although it was once a truism that eastern European countries were cheaper than those in the west of the continent, the rise of the EU has certainly challenged this assertion.

A bare-bones day of hostels and store-bought food can usually be had for €30 to €45. To allow for stays in medium- to upper-range accommodation, restaurant-cooked meals and regular visits to museums and bars, plan on spending from €70 per day in less-expensive destinations and a minimum of €100 per day elsewhere. Accommodation is likely to make up the bulk of your daily expenditure but some excursions and travel fares (most noticeably in Switzerland) can munch through a daily budget in a trice.

ATMs are easy to find throughout most of the region, the exception being remote rural areas. The most popular currencies are the euro, US dollar and British pound; other currencies are possible to change, though probably only in the capitals and large cities. Credit cards (in particular Visa and Master-Card) are widely accepted, although you won't be able to rely on these in parts of the region's eastern countries. Travellers cheques are also widely accepted but are a dying breed.

A satirical travel guide and deft Lonely Planet send-up, *Molvania: A Land Untouched by Modern Dentistry* (by Santo Cilauro et al) creates a fictitious land in Eastern Europe that's the 'next big thing'.

READING UP
Books

- *Between Past and Future: The Roma of Central and Eastern Europe* (2002), by Will Guy, comprises essays examining the fate, and speculating on the future of, one of Europe's most maligned and fascinating ethnic groups.
- *Central Europe: Enemies, Neighbors, Friends* (2001), by Lonnie R Johnson, may well be the definitive work about the culture and politics of the region and its position in world history.
- *Court, Cloister & City* (1997), by Thomas Kaufmann, takes the reader on a ride through Central European art and culture between 1450 and 1800, providing a multilayered context for all those museums, castles and monasteries.
- *Jewish Heritage Travel: A Guide to East-Central Europe* (1999), by Ruth Ellen Gruber, is the perfect companion piece for anyone travelling in the area in search of lost and remaining Jewish culture.
- *Kaffeehaus* (2002), by Rick Rodgers, is a delightful look at Prague, Vienna and Budapest, only from inside their splendid coffeeshops. Recipes galore are included in this sweetest of travelogues.
- *Longman Companion to Central and Eastern Europe since 1919* (2002), by Adrian Webb, should help clear the cobwebs of confusion over the ever-changing borders of Central Europe throughout the turbulent 20th century.
- *Stealing From a Deep Place* (1989), by Brian Hall, details the author's two-year journey across communist Central Europe by bicycle at a time when change was inevitable but not yet understood and accepted.
- *Vanished Empire* (1990), by Stephen Brook, crankily compares Prague, Vienna and Budapest – three cities shaped by the Habsburg Empire but radically different in outlook – just before the fall of the Iron Curtain.

The acclaimed *Stalin's Nose* (1992) by Rory MacLean is the surreal and darkly funny tale of the author's travels through Germany, Czechoslovakia, Hungary and Poland mere weeks after the toppling of the Berlin Wall.

Websites

Central Europe Online (www.centraleurope.com) The region's main news headlines, updated daily.

Gemut.com (www.gemut.com) Dedicates itself to travel features on Austria, Germany and Switzerland.

In Your Pocket (www.inyourpocket.com) A snappily written, up-to-date compendium of events and listings in Germany, Poland, Hungary and the Czech Republic.

Lonely Planet (www.lonelyplanet.com) Check out the Thorn Tree for the latest tips and opinions about the area you're heading to.

Real Beer (www.realbeer.com/edu/central_europe) There's a Central European page here for those of you who have your priorities straight.

Transitions Online (www.tol.cz) Czech Republic-based website with lots of locally-sourced news and cultural commentary on the host country, Hungary, Slovenia, Poland and Slovakia.

MUST-SEE MOVIES

The European Vintage Computer Festival (www.vcfe.org/E), held in early May in Munich, Germany, brings together techno-geeks who get excited over old Commodores and Olivettis.

- *Goodbye Lenin* (2003) Set in East Berlin (p166) at the fall of the Iron Curtain, this crowd-pleasing comedy speaks for an entire generation in all the ex-communist countries. A young woman falls into a coma just before the onslaught of capitalism and when she wakes up, her family shields her from the shock and hilariously goes about restoring the old communist ways.

- *Heidi* (1968) You'll want to re-enact scenes from this classic groaner about poor orphan Heidi while skipping though the Swiss Alps (p548). 'Grandpa – wherefore art thou'! Follow sweet (sickly sweet) Heidi on her quest to be reunited with her beloved grandfather in this most popular version of the pigtailed legend.

- *Kafka* (1991) Not much to do with the real Kafka, but Prague and its castle (p105) never looked so beautiful in black-and-white surrealism. Jeremy Irons plays the role of an insurance clerk with a secret passion for writing. He seeks to uncover a dastardly plot in the bowels of the castle.

- *Latcho Drom* (1993) Tony Gatlif's unforgettable and beautiful musical travelogue follows present-day Roma culture across Eastern and Central Europe. Eschewing dialogue, Gatlif lets his subjects sing and dance their history, persecution and values.

- *The Pianist* (2002) Your trip to Poland won't be the same after this stirring film featuring Oscar-winner Adrian Brody as the last pianist to play live on Polish radio before the Nazis arrive – and who survives the Warsaw Ghetto (p381). This touching masterpiece by Roman Polański doesn't glorify its protagonist as a hero; he is but a lucky and wilful survivor.

Andrzej Warda's classic *Ashes and Diamonds* (1961) is about a young member of the resistance in post-war Poland who's hired to assassinate a communist secretary. The film doesn't feel dated in its dealings of politics, allegiances, nationalism – and ever-elusive freedom. It stars the 'Polish James Dean', Zbigniew Cybulski.

- *Schindler's List* (1993) Considered *the* film made about the Holocaust, its haunting images will sensitise you to what millions faced in the region not so long ago… Steven Spielberg's film is considered one of the greatest of all time for the skilful and noncontrived way it tells the tale of one man who saved hundred of Jews from certain death.

- *The Sound of Music* (1965) Sure, you've seen it 14 times already, but you need to practise your lines before prancing along in Salzburg's Schloss Mirabell gardens (p67). C'mon, all together now: 'you are sixteen, going on seventeen…'

- *The Third Man* (1939) Trying to find some remnants of post-WWII Vienna (p43) will become an obsession after this great film noir by Carol Reed. Joseph Cotton is an alcoholic author of pulp novels who falls into the pit of intrigue and suspicion that the shattered city has become. It begins with the line, 'I knew the old Vienna, before the war…'

- *Zentropa* (1991) Lars von Trier's mesmerising film captures the engulfing creepiness in the air in post-WWII Germany. The action takes place in the subconscious, or perhaps in a dream, as we follow Jean-Marc Barr as a second generation German-American who arrives in war-torn Germany and finds himself over his head in unfathomable intrigue.

TOP 10 FESTIVALS

- Budapest Spring Festival (Hungary; March) – welcome spring in style in this cornucopia of light, breezy art; the accent is on popular opera, classical music and ballet. Mainly held in glorious concert halls and open-air spaces in Budapest, in recent years the festival has spilled over into other towns throughout Hungary.
- Prague Spring (Czech Republic; May) – also welcoming spring with the top names in the world of classical music is this festival, which transforms Prague into a European cultural champ. It's been going strong since 1946. The festival begins with a parade from Smetana's grave at Vyšehrad to the Smetana Hall, where his *Má vlast* is performed.
- Christopher Street Day (Berlin and other towns, Germany; June) – founded in 1978, this is one of the oldest gay and lesbian festivals in the world, and one of the biggest, with over half a million participants from around the globe. While there are some social marches included, the emphasis is on carefree fun and frolicking.
- Bratislava Cultural Summer Festival (Slovakia; June to September) – ensuring that Slovakia's capital has its cultural dance card filled all summer long, this festival encompasses a whole range of concerts, performances and exhibitions.
- Montreux Jazz Festival (Switzerland; July) – Europe's premier jazz event, this famously fabulous festival has a distinct air of glamour to it, as the world's biggest names in the jazz scene play to rapt audiences.
- Salzburg Festival (Salzburg, Austria; July to August) – some 250,000 people crowd into quaint Salzburg for this world-renowned classical music and theatre festival, born in 1920. Performances are held in various places throughout the city, which is a shrine to baroque architecture.
- St Dominic's Fair (Gdańsk, Poland; August) – talk about tradition: this festival, one of Poland's largest, has been going strong since 1260. Craftspeople and artists exhibit their wares while orchestras, street performers, cabarets and a fireworks show round out the party atmosphere.
- Zürich Street Parade (Switzerland; August) – where else but in this Swiss city can you take part, along with a million other people, in a festival of, well, life, love and techno music. Love-mobiles cruise the street while ravers and revellers lap up the fun – and each other.

WORLD HERITAGE SIGHTS

Speaking of responsibility, Unesco has undertaken to protect many of Central Europe's historic, cultural and natural gems by including them on its World Heritage list – at last count the region had 85 destinations on this prestigious register.

In Poland, the nominations include Warsaw's magnificent **Old Town** (p377) and the European bison refuge of **Białowieża National Park** (p387). Slovakia boasts the well-preserved 15th-century town of **Bardejov** (p478) and the eerie fortress of **Spiš Castle** (p475), while Hungary is justifiably proud of **Pannonhalma Abbey** (see boxed text on p323) in Győr and the wine-friendly **Tokaj region** (p345). The Unesco roll call continues in Slovenia with the **Škocjan Caves** (p512); in Austria with **Salzburg's historic centre** (p67) and the mountain-backed village of **Hallstatt** (p75); and in Germany with the **Wartburg castle** (p197) in Eisenach and the rococo **Schloss Sanssouci** (p184) in Potsdam.

Not to be outdone, the Czech Republic gets a gong for the medieval townscape of **Kutná Hora** (p122) and the **Lednice-Valtice Cultural Landscape** (p149), as does Switzerland for **Bern's Old Town** (p532) and a trio of fairytale castles in **Bellinzona** (p550). However, poor Liechtenstein has failed (so far at least) to garner a World Heritage vote.

- Oktoberfest (Munich, Germany; September) – this is touted as the biggest public festival in the world: some six million people guzzle five million litres of beer and 400,000 sausages each year, while music and madness abound. The burping has been going on for over 170 years.
- Ars Electronica Festival (Linz, Austria; September) – definitely the winner in the 'cool' category, this festival emphasises science, technology and electronica in all its variations. Conferences, interactive displays and dazzling presentations make this a must-see.

RESPONSIBLE TRAVEL

Central Europe contains vast areas of pristine alpine landscape, thick forests and delicate ecosystems. The countries in the western part of the region have reasonably well-established systems of ecological protection in place; follow the directions often signposted throughout the national parks. In the eastern countries, while there is a deep bond felt with nature, systemic eco-awareness is only budding. While amid nature, use common sense and even if you see litter, do not contribute to it.

As everywhere, sensitivity to local customs as well as to locals' sensitivity about their stereotypes will go a long way towards making and maintaining friends on the road – not all Swiss will appreciate your Heidi and yodelling jokes, for example. For tips regarding your health, see p610.

General travel tips include the following:

- When there's a choice, don't stay in accommodation that dumps sewage into any water systems – and tell them why you made your choice.
- Wherever possible, buy locally made souvenirs and day-to-day necessities.
- Avoid purchasing goods made from endangered species, and resist the temptation to souvenir local flora or artefacts.
- While camping in the countryside, carry out all your rubbish, use a kerosene stove, don't use detergents or toothpaste near water sources (even if they are biodegradable) and bury human waste in holes at least 15cm deep and at least 100m from any nearby water.
- In Germany, look out for ecologically responsible camping grounds sporting the Green Leaf award from the ADAC motoring association.
- Visit websites such as www.climatecare.org or www.carbonneutral.com to find out how you can help compensate for the increase in global warming caused by aeroplane and motor vehicle carbon emissions.

The region's major cities can get intolerably crowded in peak season. Traffic congestion on the roads is a major problem, and visitors will do themselves and residents a favour if they forgo driving and use public transport.

Itineraries
CLASSIC ROUTES

A CAPITAL TOUR
Two Weeks

Spend the first few days of your tour in the dynamic, delightfully idiosyncratic city of **Berlin** (p166), former capital of Prussia, the German Republic and Nazi Germany, and current capital of a reunited Germany, the economic powerhouse of Central Europe. Then head to the magnificently reconstructed Old Town of **Warsaw** (p375), which became a capital after the creation of the Commonwealth of Poland-Lithuania in the mid-16th century. Next, travel south to indulge in the architectural beauty (not to mention the amber fluids) of **Prague** (p100), the Czech seat of power and once a major player in the Habsburg Empire for some 400 years – it was even its capital for a while. Your next stop is **Vienna** (p43), the long-term throne of the mighty, opulent Habsburg Empire of Austria-Hungary, and capital of Austria since the early 20th century. After overloading your senses with Viennese art and the city's grandiose buildings, journey west into the jumble of cultures that makes Switzerland such a fascinating microcosm of Europe. **Bern** (p531) is the charming, modern capital of the land once overrun by the Holy Roman and Habsburg empires, as well as by the French Republic – it's so beautiful that it's no wonder everyone wanted a piece of it.

This tour will introduce you to the region's contemporary urban life and at the same time give you a feel for its grand and often imperial history. Over the last 1000 years, numerous power-mongers and their followers have tramped over this land, so why shouldn't you?

Go with the flow and follow the course of the Danube – the continent's second-longest river – as it surges from the southern forests of Germany eastwards through Austria and Slovakia to Hungary's Great Plain. Medieval townships, thriving modern cities and diverse Central European landscapes compete for your attention along the way.

BLUE DANUBE
Three Weeks

Build on Johan Strauss' classical attempt to capture the mood of the Danube River by conducting a firsthand exploration of the Central European terrain this wide and wonderful watercourse passes through. Begin your cruising in Germany's splendid **Black Forest** (p237), where several smaller rivers conspire to create the Danube, then visit the Bavarian city of **Regensburg** (p225), replete with historic constructions that include a Gothic church hewn from limestone. Before forging eastwards into Austria, consider detouring north to the stunning Czech town of **Český Krumlov** (p135), its fine architecture arrayed along the Vltava River. In Austria, make straight for the castle- and vineyard-crowded section of the **Danube Valley** (p59) between Krems an der Donau and **Melk** (p60), the latter township dominated by an intimidating Benedictine monastery. Meander to **Vienna** (p43) to battle crowds in the Schloss Schönbrunn and maybe have a splash in the Old Danube, then continue to the Slovakian capital of **Bratislava** (p452) to marvel at some strikingly ugly communist real estate and gaze down on the Danube from the city's signature hilltop castle. Follow the Danube east as it marks out the border between Slovakia and Hungary before sweeping south in a grand arc called the **Danube Bend** (p316). Prime sights here include **Esztergom's** (p319) awesome basilica and the ruined citadel in **Visegrád** (p318). From here the Danube flows south to **Budapest** (p298) where you can end your Danube adventure with a well-deserved soak in Széchenyi Fürdő (baths).

Boat, train and bicycle are some of the available transport options for this itinerary. For details, browse the Transport chapter (p596).

CROSSING ALL BORDERS   One Month

Well and truly get your bearings in Central Europe by making forays into every country packed into this fascinating region. Many travellers get their first taste of German culture in the transport hub of **Frankfurt-am-Main** (p249), so assume this will be your first base. Travel into the Rhineland for some wine tasting in the pretty **Moselle Valley** (p245) before savouring the eclectic attractions of **Berlin** (p166) and checking out lively **Leipzig** (p191). Beer lovers will heed the call of Bohemian Pilsner in **Plzeň** (p130), while everyone else will fall in love with the gorgeous cityscape of **Prague** (p100) and the spectacular sandstone formations of the **Adršpach-Teplice Rocks** (p139). Visit charming **Kraków** (p389) to cycle along the Vistula River, then wander south to **Zakopane** (p400) and hike or ski in the **Tatras** (p402). History is up next in neighbouring Slovakia in the magical medieval towns of **Levoča** (p474) and **Bardejov** (p478). After exploring vibrant **Bratislava** (p452), head to the enigmatic contrasts of **Budapest** (p298) via the Catholic splendour of **Esztergom** (p319). Get active around **Lake Balaton** (p327) and overnight in pleasant **Ljubljana** (p493) before spelunking in the magnificent **Škocjan Caves** (p512). Now visit **Salzburg** (p66) and find out what it takes to solve a problem like Maria, then enter one of the world's greatest ice caves at **Werfen** (p72) before sending postcards to your friends from Liechtenstein's tiny capital, **Vaduz** (p357). Finally, travel west into Switzerland where the Jungfrau area near **Interlaken** (p564) and the **Lake Geneva region** (p545) will take your breath away.

For information on border crossings and transport, see the Transport chapter (p596).

This challenging route, which covers every country in the region, is best done in a roughly clockwise direction. Art, culture, history, rest and fun are all on a programme that will get you intimately acquainted with the heartland of continental Europe.

ROADS LESS TRAVELLED

Despite having 'opened up' since the early 1990s, Eastern Europe is still off-the-beaten path for most visitors to continental Europe. This trip offers the uninitiated a rewarding array of pleasant surprises and plenty of enticements for return trips. Beware: there's plenty of charm in them thar hills.

EASTWARD BOUND   Two Weeks

Avoid the tourist hordes by taking this tour into lovely, little-populated areas in the eastern stretches of several countries. Start off in **Leipzig** (p191) and find out why Bach, Wagner and Goethe wanted to live here. Make a brief stop in the reconstructed baroque city of **Dresden** (p186) before slipping into the Czech Republic. Stopover in the monumental city of **Prague** (p100) and then make for the bustling university town of **Brno** (p140) to sample contemporary Czech life away from the Czech capital's crowds. From here, travel south to Mikulov and the marvellous, Unesco-protected **Lednice-Valtice Cultural Landscape** (p149). Backtrack to Brno and then point yourself towards Poprad in Slovakia. Don't dwell here, though. Take the electric railway north to the **Tatra National Park** (p467) for several days of blissful communing with nature. Skip over to beautiful **Zakopane** (p400) in Poland for some more fine hiking and isolation. The ancient village of **Levoča** (p474) is a worthwhile stop on your way to the foothills of the Carpathians in northeastern Hungary. Consider the sugar content of wines in **Tokaj** (p345) and go south via historic **Eger** (p342) and beautiful **Budapest** (p298) to **Kecskemét** (p336) and the nearby **Kiskunság National Park** (p339). Another option is to head southwest to **Lake Balaton** (p327) – heavily touristed yes, but at 77km long, there are lots of mostly deserted spots along the shores to call your own.

TAILORED TRIPS

CASTLES

Anyone harbouring a fortress fetish will love Central Europe, where a mixture of monarchic egoism and a centuries-old siege mentality has resulted in an abundance of impressive – if not downright intimidating – castle architecture.

Start with the biggest, not just the biggest in the region but the biggest in the world – the magnificent, 1100-year-old bulk of **Prague Castle** (p105). Once you've finished marvelling at St Vitus Cathedral and strolling down Golden Lane, check out the stunning confines of **Wawel Castle** (p389) in Poland's capital, Kraków, and the World Heritage-listed **Wartburg castle** (p197) in Germany. For a more whimsical experience, have a look at the Bavarian follies of **Neuschwanstein** and **Hohenschwangau** (p226) near the town of Füssen. The magnificent ruins of Slovakia's **Spiš Castle** (p475) cover several hectares, while the remains of **Devín Castle** (p461) outside Bratislava are also worth a look. In Slovenia, look no further than the medieval, clifftop **Bled Castle** (p505). **Eger Castle** (p342) offers fine views of the surrounding Hungarian countryside, while a similarly grand vista is offered from **Schloss Vaduz** (p357) in Liechtenstein. Wrap up by visiting Montreux's lovely **Château de Chillon** (p457) in Switzerland and Salzburg's **Festung Hohensalzburg** (p67) in Austria, all lit up at night.

STAYING ACTIVE

Central Europe's beautiful countryside accommodates numerous exhilarating activities, from hikes under forest canopies and slow paddles down wide rivers to snowboarding down steep, powdery slopes.

Hikers can stride through **Bohemian Switzerland National Park** (p126) in the Czech Republic or follow challenging trails across the sublime valleys and peaks of the **High Tatras** (p467) in Slovakia. More spectacular cliffs and gorges are revealed to walkers in **Slovenský Raj** (p477), which also pleases climbers with several ladder-assisted ascents. Speaking of climbing, those who love hauling themselves up sheer rock faces should head for the **Adršpach-Teplice Rocks** (p139) in the Czech Republic, while mountaineers should try their hands at scaling the **Bavarian Alps** (p227) in Germany. Water sports in the region include kayaking around the glacier-gouged **Great Masurian Lakes** (p436) in Poland and swimming at Hungary's **Lake Balaton** (p327), one of Europe's largest lakes – when it freezes over in winter, skating becomes the activity of choice. Cyclists can spin their wheels around Germany's **Rügen Island** (p210). The more adventurous can try caving at **Škocjan Caves** (p512), canyoning or mountain biking at **Bovec** (p509), both in Slovenia, or skydiving or night sledding at **Interlaken** (p564) in Switzerland. Skiing and snowboarding is offered at **Stubai Glacier** (p77) near Innsbruck, Austria, but life can't go downhill any faster than it does in Switzerland's **Jungfrau region** (p567) or in the shadow of the Matterhorn at **Zermatt** (p548).

LIQUID DELIGHTS

A sipping and slurping tour of the region doesn't have to mean the continuous elimination of brain cells and a throbbing head each morning. Conducted with a sense of moderation and an awareness of the consequences of over-indulgence, a tipple tour of Central Europe will instead initiate you into some memorable local social customs.

Pivo (beer) is the mother of all drinks in the Czech Republic. Pay your respects to this fine fluid by visiting **Plzeň** (p130), the birthplace of Pilsner, and **České Budějovice** (p133), home of the Budweiser Budvar Brewery. For another beery treat, visit Munich at the end of September to chug your way through **Oktoberfest** (p215). Germany's **Moselle Valley** (p245) makes a different but just as pleasing impression on the palate

with its trademark wines. The stand-out drop in Poland is vodka and the place to sample it is **Warsaw** (p375), which abounds in convivial pubs and bars. In Hungary you can acquire a taste for Bull's Blood, the full-bodied red wine produced in **Eger** (p342). Meanwhile, a trip to the Slovenian plateau of **Karst** (p511) will leave your lips stained with Terna wine and a visit to lovely **Mayrhofen** (p81) will require a ritualistic sip of Austrian schnapps. Up the alcoholic ante in Switzerland by downing absinthe in **Val de Travers** (p538), where the potent, original version of the liqueur is now being distilled after the recent lifting of a 100-year-old embargo.

TIME TRAVEL

Transport yourself back in time to significant events and periods in Central European history by tackling the following history-soaked itinerary.

To most visitors **Bad Ischl** (p73) is simply a relaxing spa resort in Austria's Lake District, but it was here in 1914 that WWI was declared by a holidaying emperor. Another place with a strong WWI connection is **Kobarid** (p510), a town that bore witness to the fierce fighting in Slovenia's Soèa Valley. The

second instalment in the World War series reached its nadir in the concentration camp at **Terezín** (p124) in the Czech Republic where 35,000 people died, most of them Jews. A less grim historical episode can be reimagined in Bern's **Einstein Museum** (p532), where a guy by the name of Albert decided that some things are relative. In the outer Kraków suburb of **Nowa Huta** (p364) you can get a glimpse of a communist-era version of paradise, and in **Malá Fatra National Park** (p464) you can learn all about Slovakia's 18th-century version of Robin Hood, Juraj Jánošik. The most recent momentous event in the region's history can be invoked by tracing the collapse of the notorious **Berlin Wall** (p175).

Snapshots

CURRENT EVENTS

The ongoing expansion of the European Union is one of the big, ongoing topics of conversation in Central Europe, not least because five of the nations in the region – the Czech Republic, Hungary, Poland, Slovakia and Slovenia – were accepted into the EU's bureaucratic fold as recently as 2004 and are still coming to terms with the economic and social ramifications of their respective memberships.

In January 2007 Slovenia became the first of the aforementioned countries (and the first former communist country) to put a stop to the circulation of its own currency, the tolar, and adopt the euro in its place. Slovenia's inhabitants have subsequently braced themselves for a large increase in the number of euro-wielding tourists, not to mention exposure to the unpredictable judgements, whims and spending habits of all those extra visitors to their small country. Many Slovenians also debate the effect that the currency changeover will have on the cost of local goods, although the government has vowed to keep a close eye on retailers to ensure that fair pricing rather than overpricing is the norm in the country's shops.

In other newish EU member countries, people have been talking as much about politics as they have about economic matters, particularly with the increasing prominence of nationalist parties that some believe has been prompted (at least in part) by the growing influence and perceived agendas of pan-European institutions. On the streets of Warsaw and Kraków, for example, you might find yourself debating local views on the coalition of ultra-conservative parties that constitute the government in staunchly Catholic Poland. This coalition includes the League of Polish Families, which has campaigned vigorously against foreign investment, gays and EU membership. Another talking point in Poland has been the recent domination of national politics by a pair of identical twins – in mid-2006, in what appeared to be a rather nepotistic move, President Lech Kaczynski appointed his twin brother Jaroslaw as the country's prime minister.

Citizens of Slovakia have also been debating the politics of the right, specifically since midway through 2006 when the then-newly elected, left-wing Smer party chose to create a governing coalition with two right-wing and equally populist parties. Around the same time, the Hungarian government loudly criticised its Slovakian counterpart for failing to denounce attacks on members of Slovakia's large ethnic Hungarian minority, which numbers over a half-million people. Tensions between the two countries have only grown since then.

In late 2006, Czech residents were still struggling to understand their own political landscape after mid-year elections failed to produce a clear winner. Three months after the June elections, the country still didn't have a functional government and this was one of the issues dominating conversations in beer halls and cafés. Another issue that kept Czech tongues wagging was a controversial proposal to build a US anti-missile base in the country, a plan that was still being debated at the time of writing.

Some Central European residents have been giving consideration to some profound social issues in recent times. Austria, a country that for years has been engrossed in the emergence of home-grown anti-immigration sentiments, turned its attention inwards after it was discovered that a man in the small village of Strasshof had abducted a Viennese schoolgirl and kept her prisoner in his home for eight years. And it isn't just the ordeal of Natascha

The EU's newest members are doing well economically, with GDP increases of between 5% and 7% in the Czech Republic, Slovakia, Poland, Slovenia and Hungary between the first quarters of 2005 and 2006.

Kampusch at the hands of a fellow countryman that is certain to fascinate Austrians for some time to come. Soon after her escape and some preliminary psychiatric treatment, Kampusch acquired a public relations agent and a media advisor to help her deal with the lucrative sensationalism of cheque-book journalism, something that may be common elsewhere in Europe but which Austria has apparently never confronted before.

Switzerland also had cause to examine its national character in mid-2006 when famous Swiss skier Corinne Rey-Bellet was shot dead by her husband soon after their estrangement. Domestic murders are becoming disturbingly common in what is generally regarded as one of Europe's most orderly societies, and they invariably involve one of the military firearms kept at home by Swiss men after they serve their obligatory stint in the national army. Switzerland's strong gun culture and the interpersonal stresses in a country where it's often assumed life will always go according to plan have been widely discussed since Rey-Bellet's death.

Terrorism is a topic of conversation that is unfortunately resonating more and more in Central Europe. Soon after the fanfare of the World Cup had died down and only a few weeks before a plot to blow up planes departing London for the US was foiled, German police were called to two local trains (bound for Dortmund and Koblenz) and discovered a pair of bombs that had failed to detonate. Security at German train stations and airports was subsequently stepped up.

HISTORY

Central Europe has never been an officially recognised entity with well-established borders and as such does not have an easily traceable history. Rather, it began life as a vague geographic area that took on identifiable characteristics due to the regional dominance of a succession of empires and which, for much of last century, was often treated as the borderland between an increasingly liberal Western Europe and an increasingly conservative Eastern Europe.

'In the beginning, there was no Europe', writes Professor Norman Davies in *Europe: A History*. In the beginning, all that existed was an unpopulated peninsula attached to the western edge of the world's largest landmass (Asia). But after humanoid settlers arrived between 850,000 and 700,000 BC, Europe's temperate climate and nonthreatening environment would make it the cradle of agriculture and the birthplace of great civilisations such as Greece and Rome.

The outline of Central Europe began to take shape with the creation of the Holy Roman Empire under Charlemagne, who was crowned Roman emperor in AD 800. The official death of the Empire eventually took place over 1000 years later in 1806, but it took to its sick bed at least several centuries beforehand. A particularly influential family that occasionally took charge of the Empire from the 13th century – and oversaw its dissolution – was the Austrian Habsburgs, whose original seat of power was a town sited in present-day Switzerland.

Europe began to undergo enormous social upheaval in the 15th century, beginning with the Renaissance and continuing through the Reformation and the French Revolution. The Renaissance fomented mainly artistic expression and ideas. The key issue of the Reformation, however, was religion. Challenging Catholic 'corruption' in 1517, German theologian Martin Luther established a breakaway branch of Christianity called Protestantism. The ongoing struggle between Catholics and Protestants came to a terrible head during the Thirty Years' War (1618–48) which devastated continental Europe.

The powerful Austrian Empire ruled by the Habsburgs joined forces with the well-established Kingdom of Hungary in 1867 to create the Austro-

The Thirty Years' War was sparked by the defenestration (the act of throwing someone out of a window) of two Catholic councillors in Prague by the Protestant leaders of the Bohemian Revolt.

Hungarian Empire, which encouraged economic growth throughout the region. During this period Central Europe was also dominated both politically and culturally by Germany and the region became known for a time as Mitteleuropa (Middle-Europe).

In 1914 Serbia was accused of backing the assassination of the heir to the Austria-Hungarian throne and the resulting conflict between the two states erupted into what became known as WWI. Crippled by a huge bill for reparations imposed at the war's end in 1918, Austria's humbled ally, Germany, proved susceptible to politician Adolf Hitler's nationalist rhetoric during the 1930s. The international community stood by as Nazi Germany annexed Austria and parts of Czechoslovakia, but its invasion of Poland in 1939 was one land-grab too much and sparked WWII. During the final liberation of Europe in 1945, Allied troops from Britain, France, the USA and the USSR uncovered the full extent of the genocide that had occurred in Hitler's concentration camps for Jews, Roma (gypsies) and other 'degenerates'.

The Allies carved out spheres of influence on the continent and Germany was divided to prevent it from rising up again militarily. However, long-standing differences in ideology between the Western powers and the communist USSR soon led to a stand-off. The USSR closed off its assigned sectors – East Germany, East Berlin and much of Eastern Europe – behind the figurative Iron Curtain. This 'Cold War' consolidated a perception of Europe that had strengthened since WWI: that the continent consisted of a western region that pursued democracy and an eastern region that pursued authoritarianism. Lost in this battle of so-called east–west ideologies was the existence of a central region with its own relatively distinctive political and social leanings.

The Cold War lasted until 1989 when the Berlin Wall fell. Germany was unified in 1990 and a year later the USSR was dissolved, prompting Czechoslovakia, Hungary and Poland, among others, to grasp multiparty democracy. The end of the Cold War brought a sense of peace to Europe and reintroduced the idea of a Central Europe, a region that perhaps didn't embrace change as much as Western Europe but was arguably more open to suggestions than Eastern Europe.

The raising of the Iron Curtain also allowed for great expansion of the European Union. The EU was formed in 1951 as a trade alliance and by mid-2006 its member count had climbed to 25; the only two Central European nations that are not yet EU members are Switzerland and Liechtenstein.

PEOPLE

Over 83 million people call Germany home, which makes it the most populous country in Central Europe. No prizes for guessing that the region's least populous nation is tiny Liechtenstein, the residents of which number a mere 33,000.

Many generalisations have been made about the people of the region, but travellers will quickly find out that the locals seem to delight in defying any attempts at stereotyping. The Swiss, for example, appear to be imbued with a tireless formality and an enthusiasm for rule following, but no rules apply during Zürich's huge annual techno-fest, the Street Parade. Austrians are famous for their exterior sternness and a seeming lack of vivacity, which utterly fails to explain why so many Viennese practically live in local bars and coffeehouses. Czechs can also seem brusque and not very welcoming, yet are possessed of a remarkably sly sense of humour and deep pockets when it comes to buying complete strangers drinks in crowded beer halls.

Central Europe contains a myriad of thoroughly modern places, from the cosmopolitan streetscape of Berlin to the worldly finances of Geneva. But throughout the area there are native enclaves that strive to maintain aspects of their traditional cultures. Folk traditions are in evidence in the lifestyles of Slavonic Sorbs in east Germany; occupants of some Alpine regions of Switzerland; mainstream Slovakian society, where family heritage is strongly nurtured, and among the country's Rusyn communities; and the Roma people (gypsies) who are concentrated in the Czech Republic, Hungary and Slovakia, where their transient lives are the subject of much suspicion, if not downright hostility.

Around 0.7% of Central Europe's population is Muslim. As a percentage of national population, Austria hosts the most Muslims (4.7%) and Slovakia the least (0.05%).

Thanks to the legacy of the Holy Roman Empire, Central Europe is dominated by practising Catholics, with countries such as Poland and Slovakia remaining deeply Christian. Over half of Hungary's population is Roman Catholic, with a reasonable representation of Protestants as well, while in Germany and Switzerland the Catholics and the Protestants are almost equally represented. In some former communist countries, religion has struggled to regain a foothold – the Czech Republic, for instance, is distinguished by a high number of atheists, amounting to almost 40% of the population.

ARTS

Lovers of the arts will be in seventh (if not eighth) heaven in Central Europe as they trace the origins and accomplishments of famous local artists by visiting their birthplaces, drinking in their favourite haunts and enjoying their output in concert halls, cinemas, bookshops and galleries.

For a taste of literary claustrophobia and paranoia, you can't go past the Czech writing duo of Franz Kafka and Milan Kundera. Contemporary Hungarian writers such as Tibor Fischer use their creativity to chaotic effect in stories such as *The Thought Gang* or, in the case of Imre Kertész, to recreate the horrors of Nazi death camps, while Slovenians still pay their respects to 19th-century poet France Prešeren whenever they recite their national anthem. Budding philosophers can while away the hours, or the years if they so desire, by mulling over the scribblings of Swiss thinker Jean-Jacques Rousseau or the Faustian complexities sketched by Johann Wolfgang von Goethe. Another brilliant German writer is Günter Grass, though his moral authority was somewhat undermined by his admission in late 2006 that he had been a member of Nazi Germany's infamous SS.

2007 should see the release of a US-produced remake of *Funny Games*, again directed by Michael Haneke and starring Naomi Watts and Tim Roth.

Though a much younger artistic form, Central European cinema has in some ways been just as thought-provoking as the region's literary traditions. *Funny Games*, a late-1990s effort from Austrian director Michael Haneke, challenged its audience's taste for violence with relentless torture scenes, and was arguably the most confronting European film since Belgium's serial-killer mockumentary, *Man Bites Dog*, released five years earlier. Haneke went on to make the much-acclaimed 2005 thriller, *Hidden*.

And few films have commanded the emotional impact of *The Pianist*, Polish director Roman Polański's depiction of Holocaust atrocities. Similar historical subject matter (can you sense a pattern here?) was tackled in the big-budget 2005 Hungarian film, *Fateless*, based on the book by Imre Kertész, and in German director Marc Rothemund's *Sophie Scholl: The Final Days*, released to much acclaim in 2006. The region's cinema even eschews the feel-good approach in its interpersonal efforts, as epitomised by Krzysztof Kieślowski's *Three Colours: Blue/White/Red* trilogy.

In terms of music, Central Europe can lay claim to an astonishing roll call of classical composers. Johann Strauss Jr devoted himself to the waltz in Vienna and fellow Austrian, Wolfgang Amadeus Mozart pumped out more than 600 compositions before dying at the youthful age of 35. Antonín Dvořák concocted symphonies and operas in what is now the Czech Republic. Franz Liszt composed his way into history in 19th-century Hungary, while Frédéric Chopin simultaneously did likewise in Poland (well, he attempted to – Liszt ultimately outlived him by 36 years). Germany gets the most kudos in this category, however, as it nursed numerous household names such as Ludwig van Beethoven, Richard Wagner and Johann Sebastian Bach into classical legend. Traditional folk music has been kept alive in the countryside of several Central European countries, including in the villages of eastern Slovakia, while in countries such as Slovenia there has been a skilful and highly successful appropriation of folk music by modern-day musicians. Dance music rules the roost across much of the region today, however, encompassing everything from Slovenian techno to Austrian electronica and German trance.

Superb practitioners of painting also abound in the region's history. Gustav Klimt was one of Austria's most renowned painters and his artistic value has not diminished since his death in 1918. Probably the best-known Swiss painter was Paul Klee, who was fond of abstraction, and Art-Nouveau maestro Alfons Mucha is cherished in Prague due to the trademark decorations he left throughout the city. Other famous local forms of visual art include the wonderful ceramic constructions of Hungarian artist Margit Kovac, and the beautiful amber and garnet jewellery that adorns wrists and necks across Poland and the Czech Republic respectively.

In 2006, Gustav Klimt's portrait of Adele Bloch-Bauer was snapped up by a New York gallery for the measly sum of US$135 million.

SPORT

Football fever is rife enough in Central Europe, as it is pretty much everywhere else in Europe, but in June/July 2006 it became a pandemic when Germany hosted the 18th FIFA World Cup. Germany was generally congratulated for doing an excellent job of staging the world's biggest sporting event, although its tournament motto, 'A time to make friends', had little influence on the conduct of Italian Marco Materazzi and Frenchman Zinedine Zidane in the final. The host nation fared the best out of the four participating Central European teams, finishing third. Switzerland was next best, making it through to the 'Round of 16'. The Czech Republic and Poland finished third in their respective groups and so did not progress past the group stage of the tournament.

The dust had barely settled on the World Cup campaign when preparations began for the next high-profile football event in the region. The finals of the UEFA (Union of European Football Associations) Euro 2008 tournament, for which all Central European countries have a chance to qualify, will be held in stadiums across Austria and Switzerland.

Ice hockey comes close to rivalling football for popularity in several countries in the region, particularly in the Czech Republic and Slovakia. In terms of international competition, the Czech Republic's men's team had a particularly good year in 2006 when it came third in the Winter Olympics in Turin, Italy, and second in the Ice Hockey World Championship held in the Latvian capital, Riga. Slovakia finished fifth in the men's competition of the Winter Olympics, while Switzerland came sixth and Germany came 10th; placings in the women's competition included fifth place to Germany and seventh place to Switzerland. Central Europe will have a brief monopoly on the staging of the Ice Hockey World Championship from 2009 (when it will be hosted by Switzerland) through 2010 (hosted by Germany) and 2011 (hosted by Slovakia).

Good websites for info on popular sports include:

www.uefa.com – Union of European Football Associations

www.uci.ch – Union Cycliste Internationale

www.iihf.com – International Ice Hockey Federation

Slovenia's contribution to major winter sporting events comes in the form of the ski jumping (also called ski flying) championships held in the alpine valley of Planica, where the world record mark of 239m was set in 2005.

Other hugely popular sporting events in Central Europe include the Formula One Hungarian Grand Prix, staged at the Hungaroring track north of Budapest, the German Grand Prix held at Hokeinheim and the Nürburgring, and the Czech Republic's Motorcycle Grand Prix (or MotoGP), held outside the Moravian city of Brno. Several countries also indulge aficionados of long-distance running, including Slovenia via its Ljubljana Marathon and Austria with its Vienna Spring Marathon.

ENVIRONMENT

An enormous diversity of landscapes exists in the geopolitical region known as Central Europe, from the high-altitude Alpine area that makes a formidable natural barrier in the south, down to the vast lowlands that characterise the north. Intimidating peaks such as Switzerland's famous Matterhorn, Germany's glorious forests and the flow of the Danube River, as it sweeps from near the French border with Germany eastwards to Austria and down through Hungary, are all prominent landmarks of this central slice of the European continent.

The smallest country in Central Europe is Liechtenstein, which covers 150 sq km of undulating terrain. The biggest is Germany, which claims 356,866 sq km of real estate, and not far behind it in second place is the 312,677-sq-km expanse of Poland. Every nation except for Germany, Poland and Slovenia is landlocked – a significant stretch of Poland's northern border is washed by the Baltic Sea, while northern Germany sinks into the depths of both the Baltic and North Seas, and just a tiny stretch of southwestern Slovenia dips itself into the Adriatic.

Staked out in the physical heart of the region is the Czech Republic, which has common borders with four other Central European countries; the winner of the 'most borders' competition, however, is Austria, which has seven immediate neighbours. The Czech Republic comprises the twin river basins of Bohemia and Moravia, each encircled by hills and separated by forested plains. North of here are the enormous plains and other low-lying areas of Poland and northern Germany. In the south, Germany raises itself into a series of low mountain ranges that stretch ever skywards until they eventually become the Alps, the glacier-speckled mountains that define almost three-quarters of Switzerland and which mirror the landscape in the western swathe of Austria and across Slovenia. East of Austria is Slovakia, which is snuggled up against the Carpathian Mountains and whose centre is occupied by the High Tatras. Also lying east of Austria is Hungary, the dominant landscape of which can be deduced from the name given to the country's chief feature, the Nagyalföld (Great Plain).

Flora- and fauna-rich national parks are scattered mainly across the central and southern parts of Central Europe. Around 20% of Slovakia and 15% of the Czech Republic is preserved within the boundaries of national parks; at the other end of the scale, only around 3% of Austrian territory and a mere 1% of Poland has national park status. Switzerland only manages a single, tiny national park. The wildlife that calls these areas home includes rarely glimpsed species of eagle, bat, wild cat, bison and ibex (mountain goat).

Most of Central Europe's 85 World Heritage sites are predominantly man-made, but this status has been awarded to several profoundly significant nature-made areas, including Poland's Białowieża National Park (p387), Slovenia's Škocjan Caves (p512) and Hungary's Hortobágy National Park. For more information on World Heritage sites in the region, see the 'World Heritage Sights' boxed text (p25).

The region faces some severe environmental problems, not least of which is the pollution from all manner of poorly maintained, energy-inefficient motor vehicles and the burning of low-grade coal by local industries – in the Czech Republic this has resulted in the devastation of some eastern forests by acid rain. The global warming attributable to CO_2 emissions is seen as a particular problem in Switzerland due to the country's numerous Alpine glaciers. Fortunately, not all the news is bad on this front. The environmental-impact regulations imposed by the European Union on its member states have begun to have an impact, and environmentally friendly measures such as waste recycling and the reduction of CO_2 emissions are taken very seriously in countries such as Austria, Germany and Switzerland.

The 2006 session of the World Heritage Committee added Centennial Hall in Wrocław, Poland, and the Old Town of Regensburg, Germany, to its esteemed list.

Austria

It sounds clichéd to say, but this country really is alive with the sound of music. Mozart's symphonies waft through the cobbled streets of Salzburg like Julie Andrews floating around the picturesque Austrian countryside. The story of Austria is surely an opera, a concerto, a work in progress, complete with elaborate sets and a plot that's as bloody as it is beautiful. Monarchs, political instability, assassinations and the Great War narrate just one side of the story, however. Juxtaposed against them is incredible natural beauty blanketed in an edifying patchwork of depth and character like no other. Gorgeous enough to make you gasp in awe, its snow-capped peaks stare back at you with jagged smiles. Its verdant valleys, strewn with summer wildflowers, make the perfect outdoor playground. Graceful old cities exude genteel airs of times long past and even the smallest rural villages are cultural reservoirs rich in history. In Austria the past is as pertinent as the present and the country surprises with its ability to change without sacrificing its time-honoured heritage and traditions.

FAST FACTS

- **Area** 83,855 sq km
- **Capital** Vienna
- **Currency** euro (€); A$1 = €0.60; ¥100 = €0.67; NZ$1 = €0.50; UK£1 = €1.48; US$1 = €0.78
- **Famous for** apple strudel, Wiener schnitzel, Adolf Hitler, Arnold Schwarzenegger, Freudian psychoanalysis
- **Official Language** German (Slovene, Croat and Hungarian are also official languages in some southern states)
- **Phrases** *Grüss Gott* (hello); *Servus!* (hello and goodbye); *Ba Ba* (bye bye)
- **Population** 8.2 million
- **Telephone Codes** country code ☎ 43; international access code ☎ 00

HIGHLIGHTS

- Take in art from a completely different standing (literally) at the popular **Kunst HausWien** (p49) by Friedensreich Hundertwasser in Vienna.
- Relive scenes from *The Sound of Music* while singing along on a fabulously kitsch tour in the picture-postcard city of **Salzburg** (p66).
- Experience Tyrolean culture with plenty of recreation opportunities and nightlife on the side in **Innsbruck** (p77) or **Mayrhofen** (p81).
- Road-trip through the Hohe Tauern National Park along one of the world's most scenic highways, the **Grossglockner Hochalpenstrasse** (p83).
- Gaze at what locals have dubbed 'the friendly alien', the spaceship-shaped **Kunsthaus Graz** (arts centre; p63) in Graz.

ITINERARIES

- **Two days** Spend this entire time in Vienna, making sure to visit the Habsburg palaces and the Riesenrad before cosying up in a *Kaffeehaus* (coffee house). At night check out the pumping bar scene or catch a Vienna Boys' Choir concert.
- **One week** Spend three days in Vienna, plus one day on a wine tour in the Wachau, a day each in Salzburg and Innsbruck, and one day visiting the Salzkammergut lakes district to hike or ski (depending on the season).

CLIMATE & WHEN TO GO

Austria has a typical central European climate, with Vienna enjoying an average maximum of 2°C (35°F) in January and 25°C (77°F) in July. Some people find the *Föhn* – a hot, dry wind that sweeps down from the mountains in early spring and autumn – rather uncomfortable. For more information, see p586.

Austria hangs out its *Zimmer frei* (rooms vacant) signs year-round, but its high seasons are from July to August and Christmas to New Year. Christmas to late February is the peak skiing time. Alpine resorts can be pretty dead between seasons, ie May, June and November.

HISTORY

Austria is a little nation with a big past. It may be hard to believe that this diminutive,

HOW MUCH?

- **1L milk** €0.95
- **Loaf of bread** from €1.20
- **Bottle of house white wine market/ restaurant** from €3/10
- **Newspaper** €0.80 to €1.45
- **Short taxi ride** €5

LONELY PLANET INDEX

- **1L petrol** €1
- **1L bottled water** €0.40 to €2.50
- **Bottle of beer** from €2.50
- **Souvenir T-shirt** €15
- **Street snack (wurst)** €3

landlocked Alpine country, bordering eight other states (Germany, Switzerland, Liechtenstein, Italy, Slovenia, Hungary, Slovakia and the Czech Republic) was once the epicentre of the mighty Habsburg empire and, in the 20th century, a pivotal player in the outbreak of WWI. For centuries the Habsburgs used strategic marriages to maintain their hold over a territory now encompassing parts of today's Bosnia-Hercogovina, Croatia, Poland, Romania, the majority of the aforementioned proximate nations and, for a period, even Germany. But defeat in WWI brought that to an end, when the small republic of Austria was formed in 1918.

There had been military and political struggles before. Twice the neighbouring Ottoman Empire reached Vienna, in 1529 and 1683. In 1805 Napoleon defeated Austria at Austerlitz. Austrian Chancellor Metternich cleverly reconsolidated Austria's power in 1815 after Waterloo, but in the 1866 Austro-Prussian War the country (hampered by an internal workers' revolution in 1848) lost control of the German Confederation. At this point the empire's Hungarian politicians asserted themselves and forced the formation of Austria-Hungary.

However, these setbacks pale beside Archduke Franz Ferdinand's assassination by Slavic separatists in Sarajevo on 28 June 1914. When his uncle, the Austro-Hungarian emperor Franz Josef, declared war on Serbia

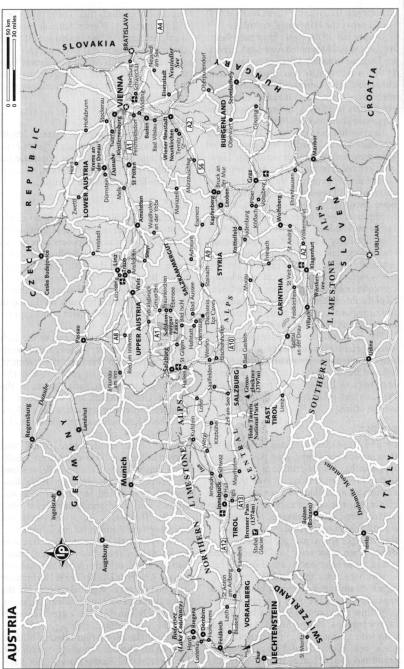

AUSTRIA

in response, the ensuing 'Great War' (WWI) would prove the Habsburgs' downfall.

During the 1930s Nazis from neighbouring Germany assassinated Austrian Chancellor Dolfuss, installing a puppet regime. With Hitler, a native Austrian, also as German chancellor, the German troops met little resistance when they invaded recession-hit Austria in 1938. A national referendum supported the *Anschluss* (union).

Heavily bombed during WWII, Austria has since worked hard to be a good global citizen by maintaining its neutrality. However, echoes of its fascist past have regularly come back to haunt it. In the 1980s rumours surfaced that President Kurt Waldheim had been involved in war crimes in WWII. In the late 1990s other European nations briefly imposed sanctions when the far-right Freedom Party (FPÖ) and its controversial leader, Jörg Haider, joined the national government. Joining the EU in 1995, Austria has persevered despite political setbacks and currently holds the Presidency of the Council of the European Union and the headquarters or regional centre of many international organisations, including the UN.

The new Alliance for Austria's Future elected Haider as its leader in Salzburg. After a split in the Freedom Party he once led and the defection of the majority conservatives to Haider's new political party, the far-right politician looks confident to stay in office.

PEOPLE

By and large, Austrians are shrugging off their controversial right-wing past, a stereotype that has lost its grip since the collapse of the Iron Curtain along the country's eastern border more than 15 years ago. At first glance, Austrians can seem reserved and even slightly suspicious of strangers. Not generally regarded for outward displays of friendliness, this changes when you get to know them better. Then most are friendly and exhibit genuine interest in sharing a multifaceted culture with the rest of the world. Politeness and formality are highly esteemed and expected, especially among the older generation.

Within the country, Vienna has always been a paradox, mixing Austrian conservatism with a large dollop of decadence. The scene you might get at Viennese balls of grand old society dames flirting with drag queens aptly reflects this. The capital's pervading humour, *Wiener Schmäh*, is quite ironic and cutting, but is also meant to be charming. In essence, it's very camp.

Nearly one-fifth of the population lives in Vienna, but other cities are small, so more than two-thirds live in small towns or in rural areas.

RELIGION

Although Vienna once had a sizable Jewish population, Austria today is a largely Christian nation. Some 80% of the population is Catholic. The rest is Protestant, concentrated in Burgenland and Carinthia.

ARTS

Austria's musical heritage tends to elbow most of its other artistic achievements off the page. European composers were drawn to the country by the Habsburgs' generous patronage during the 18th and 19th centuries: Beethoven, Brahms, Haydn, Mozart and Schubert all made Vienna their home during this period. The waltz originated in the city, perfected by Johann Strauss junior (1825–99).

However, Vienna at the end of the 19th century was also a city of design and painting. The Austrian Secessionist movement, the local equivalent of Art Nouveau *(Jugendstil)*, turned out such talents as the painter Gustav Klimt and architect Otto Wagner. Expressionist painters Egon Schiele and Oskar Kokoschka and modernist architect Adolf Loos followed.

While Austrian literature is not well known in the outside world, Arthur Schnitzler's *Dream Story (Traumnovelle)* inspired the Stanley Kubrick film *Eyes Wide Shut*. Football fans should be familiar with one famous work by Carinthian novelist Peter Handke, *The Goalie's Fear of the Penalty Kick (Der Angst des Tormanns beim Elfmeter)*.

Today Austria's fine musical tradition has moved in the wholly different direction of chilled, eclectic electronica and dub lounge. Celebrity DJs Kruder & Dorfmeister have had the greatest global success, but the scene is loaded with other talent, including Pulsinger & Tunakan, the Vienna Scientists and the Sofa Surfers.

Meanwhile, expert film director Michael Haneke has also been creating a splash with his controversial *Funny Games* (1997) and the twisted romance of the much-lauded *The Piano Teacher* (2001). The country's most famous TV export is the detective series *Inspector Rex (Kommisar Rex)*. As well as being big in Germany and Australia, Rex, a German shepherd dog who regularly proves invaluable to his police owners, apparently has a cult following in some 93 countries. In recent times perhaps the most noteworthy Austrian imprint to be stamped on the world (and particularly the USA) is former professional bodybuilder/actor turned politician, and current governor of the state of California, Arnold Schwarzenegger, who was born near Graz.

ENVIRONMENT

More than half of Austria's 83,855 sq km is mountainous. Three chains run west to east: the Northern Limestone Alps, the Central (or High) Alps, which have the tallest peaks in Austria, including the 3797m Grossglockner, and the Southern Limestone Alps. They are banded around the middle and the south of the country, occupying most of its western half, and leaving flats around the Danube Valley and Vienna in the northeast and Graz to the southeast.

Meadows and forests cover much of the country. Although Austria is home to Europe's largest national park, Hohe Tauern, only 3% of its landmass is national park. These protected wilderness areas are good places to spot wildlife, such as marmots. Hohe Tauern itself has many species of alpine wildflower, and the bearded vulture and lyre-horned ibex were reintroduced in recent years.

Austria is highly environmentally conscious and no one wants to spoil the pristine landscape by littering. Recycling and biocompost bins are ubiquitous throughout the country.

FOOD & DRINK
Staples & Specialities

There's more to Austrian cuisine than *Wiener schnitzel* (a veal or pork cutlet coated in breadcrumbs). Traces of the country's wider historical reach endure in the Hungarian paprika used to flavour several dishes, including *Gulasch* (beef stew), and in the Styrian polenta and pumpkinseed oil popular in Italian and Slovenian cuisine respectively. Some staples like wurst (sausage)

and regional dishes, such as *Tiroler Bauernschmaus* – a selection of meats served with sauerkraut, potatoes and dumplings – can be very fatty and stodgy. However, hearty soups often include *Knödel* (dumplings) or pasta.

Besides *Strudel* (filo pastry filled with a variety of fruits, poppy seeds or cheese), *Salzburger Nockerl* (a fluffy soufflé) is a popular Austrian dessert.

Known for its lager beer – from brands like Gösser, Schwechater, Stiegl and Zipfer to *Weizenbier* (wheat beer) – Austria also produces some white wines in its east. *Heuriger* wine is the latest vintage, and is avidly consumed, even in autumn while still semi-fermented (called *Sturm*).

Where to Eat & Drink

A traditional Austrian inn is called a *Beissl* or *Stüberl*. A *Beissl* (from the Hebrew word for 'house') tends to be more about meeting friends and having a drink, with food a necessary but ancillary pastime, whereas the emphasis is usually more on the food itself in a *Stüberl* (from the word *Stube,* meaning 'cosy living room'). Not all *Beissl* or *Stüberl* will be 100% traditional; however, only a few of them in the middle of Vienna are touristy enough to be wary of.

Of course, lots of Asian restaurants and pizzerias dot the countryside. These, in addition to the dumplings in local cuisine, mean that vegetarians shouldn't have any trouble finding satisfying meals.

For cheap food, try *Mensens* (university canteens). The main meal is at noon, when many restaurants provide a good-value *Tagesteller* or *Tagesmenu* (set meal).

VIENNA

☎ 01 / pop 1.6 million

The Ottomans referred to Vienna (Wien) as the city of the 'golden apple', but this crossroads of Eastern and Western Europe is more akin to a big wedding cake; a vivacious, multilayered concoction, stuffed full with galleries, museums and exhibitions, and a sensation of resuscitated times past. The demarcation between antiquity and contemporary is hazily represented here. Take the time to absorb the copious vestiges of grandiose marzipan-like buildings filling the streets, and the many ornate

AUSTRIA

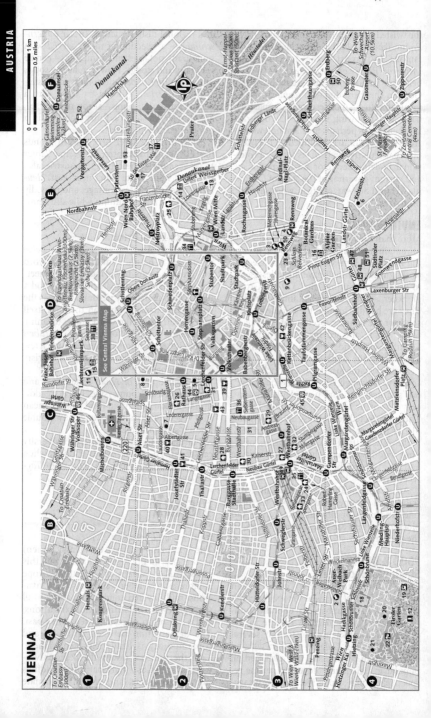

VIENNA

baroque edifices decorating the city's inner circular road, the Ringstrasse. But these are only the proverbial icing on this beguiling marvel. The flavour of this city is as elaborate as its heritage and is many centuries in the making. The colourful narrative of the Habsburg dynasty can be traced through the rooms of the Hofburg palace or Schloss Schönbrunn, while the legacy of Art Nouveau artists Gustav Klimt and Egon Schiele is on show at the Secession Building, Schloss Belvedere and at the Leopold Museum.

This busy intersection of ethnicities, beliefs and cultural facets has always percolated with creative energy. It was here that Johann Strauss invented the waltz and where Sigmund Freud developed his psychoanalytic theories. And it was not too long ago that Vienna's artisans, musicians and academia flocked to coffee houses (chiefly as a respite from their drafty, more often than not, unheated flats) to embrace and disseminate ideas. So, if this city's rich diet of music, art and philosophy starts to feel a bit stodgy, ease up and relax in one of the many cafés, or take to the top of the *Riesenrad* (the Ferris wheel featured in the film *The Third Man*) for a panorama 65m aloft.

ORIENTATION
Many of the historic sights are in the old city, the Innere Stadt. The Danube Canal (Donaukanal) is located to the northeast

and a series of broad boulevards called the Ring or Ringstrasse encircle it.

Most of the attractions in the city centre are within walking distance of each other. Stephansdom (St Stephen's Cathedral), in the heart of the city, is the principal landmark.

In addresses, the number of a building within a street *follows* the street name. Any number *before* the street name denotes the district, of which there are 23. District 1 (the Innere Stadt) is the central region, mostly within the Ring. Generally, the higher the district number, the further it is from the city centre. The middle two digits of postcodes refer to the district, hence places with a postcode 1010 are in district 1, and 1230 means district 23.

The main train stations are Franz Josefs Bahnhof to the north, Westbahnhof to the west and Südbahnhof to the south; transferring between them is easy. Most hotels and *pensions* (B&Bs) are in the city centre and to the west.

INFORMATION
Bookshops
British Bookshop (Map p48; ☎ 512 19 45; 01, Weihburggasse 24-6) Stocks English-language titles.
Freytag & Berndt (Map p48; ☎ 533 86 85; 01, Kohlmarkt 9) Sells maps and guidebooks.
Reisebuchladen (Map p48; ☎ 317 33 84; 09, Kolingasse 6) Specialises in guidebooks.
Shakespeare & Co Booksellers (Map p48; ☎ 535 50 53; 01, Sterngasse 2) Sells new and second-hand books.

WHAT'S ON A COFFEE DRINKER'S MIND?

From the way customers linger over their cappuccino, *Grosser Brauner* or *Melange* in a Viennese *Kaffeehaus* (coffee house), it's easy to believe Austrians have always been born with a coffee spoon in their mouths. But those great tea drinkers, the English, opened their first coffee house before the Austrians ever did, so how did the tradition take such a hold here?

Local schoolchildren are taught that the beverage entered their country after the Ottoman Empire's siege of Vienna in 1683. Polish merchant Georg Kolschitzky smuggled a message out of his adopted city to the Polish king, who eventually came to Vienna's rescue; and Kolschitzky asked to be rewarded with the sacks of coffee beans abandoned by Kara Mustafa's retreating army. As historian Simon Schama put it, Austria managed to 'resist the Turkish siege but (was) defenceless against the coffee bean'.

Only much later, from the 18th century, did the tradition of spending long hours in coffee houses really became entrenched. To escape Vienna's mostly unheated apartments, impoverished artists and intellectuals would set up shop at their coffee-house tables, writing and holding meetings and debates. Sigmund Freud and Leon Trotsky spent hours at Café Central (p55), plotting, playing chess and running up a tab for hot drinks. When the Russian revolution started, Trotsky left Vienna (much to the chagrin of the head waiter) without paying his bill.

Today coffee drinking remains a central part of Viennese, and to a lesser extent Austrian, life. It goes beyond a simple Starbucks culture (but surprisingly that chain now exists here, too). The true coffee house is still a place for music, exhibitions and cultural events; see what's on at the **Viennese Coffee House** (www.wiener-kaffeehaus.at). Above all, in the birthplace of psychoanalysis, it's somewhere to offset the stresses of the everyday. As the owner of a Viennese coffee shop once theorised to the *Guardian* newspaper, 'The coffee is the medicine, the waiters, the therapists'.

Internet Access

Bignet (Map p48; ☎ 503 98 44; Kärntner Strasse 61; per 30 min €3.90)

Speednet Café (Map p44; ☎ 892 56 66; 15 Europlatz 1, Westbahnhof; per 30 min €3.30) Conveniently located inside the train station.

Surfland Internetcafé (Map p48; ☎ 512 77 01; Krugerstrasse 10; initial charge €1.50, per extra min €0.08)

Medical Services

Allgemeines Krankenhaus (general hospital; Map p44; ☎ 40 400; 09, Währinger Gürtel 18-20; ☼ 24hr)

Dental Treatment (☎ 512 20 78; ☼ 24hr) German-speaking only.

Post

Main Post Office (Map p48; 01, Fleischmarkt 19; ☼ 24hr) Other post offices open long hours are at Süd-bahnhof, Franz Josefs Bahnhof and Westbahnhof.

Tourist Information

Tourist offices and hotels sell the Vienna Card (€16.90), which provides admission discounts and a free 72-hour travel pass.

Information & Hotel Reservation Counters West-bahnhof (☼ 8.30am-9pm); Airport arrivals hall (☼ 7am-10pm) Opposite the baggage-claim areas.

Jugend-Info Wien (Vienna Youth Information; Map p48; ☎ 17 99; 01, Babenbergerstrasse 1; ☼ noon-7pm Mon-Sat) Offers various reduced-price tickets for 14- to 26-year-olds.

Tourist-Info Zentrum (Map p48; ☎ 24 555; www .wien.info; 01, cnr Am Albertinaplatz & Maysedergasse; ☼ 9am-7pm) Near the state opera house, with loads of regional information.

Travel Agencies

Amex (Map p48; ☎ 5124 0040; Kärntner Strasse 21-23; ☼ 9am-5.30pm Mon-Fri, 9am-noon Sat)

STA Travel Vienna (Map p44; ☎ 40 148-0; 09, Garnison-gasse 7; ☼ 9am-5.30pm); Central Vienna (Map p48; ☎ 40 148-7000; 09, Türkenstrasse 6B; ☼ 9am-6pm); Central Vienna (Map p48; ☎ 50 243-0; 04, Karlsgasse 3; ☼ 9am-6pm)

SIGHTS

Vienna's ostentatious buildings and beauti-fully tended parks make it a lovely city just to stroll through. If you catch tram 1 or 2 around the Ringstrasse (the road circling the city centre) you'll acquire a taste of the city, passing the neo-Gothic **Rathaus** (city hall; Map p48), the Greek Revival-style **Parliament** (Map p48) and the 19th-century **Burgtheater** (Map p48), among others. You can even glimpse the baroque **Karlskirche** (St Charles' Church; Map p48) from the tram.

Strolling along the pedestrian-only tree-lined **Kärntner Strasse** (Map p48) will take you past plush shops, cafés and street entertainers. The main point of interest in Graben is the knobbly **Petsäule** (Plague Column; Map p48), designed by Fischer von Erlach and built to commemorate the end of the Plague. There's also a concrete **Holocaust memorial** (Map p48) by Rachel Whiteread in Judenplatz, Austria's first monument of its kind. Look closely and you'll notice that the sides are constructed of cement books facing open-end out, perhaps to convey a lack of closure coupled with an enduring remembrance for the victims of the holocaust.

Interesting buildings in the city centre include **Loos House** (Map p48), now a Raiffeisen bank, across from the Hofburg. The Art Nouveau **Postsparkasse** (Savings Bank; Map p48; Georg Coch Platz) and **Stadtbahn Pavilions** (train station pavilions; Map p48; Karlsplatz) are both by architect Otto Wagner.

Stephansdom

The prominent latticework spire of **St Stephen's Cathedral** (Map p48) makes this 13th-century Gothic masterpiece one of the city's key points of orientation, and the geometric pattern of its roof tiles is also striking. Bearing in mind the significance of the church in daily medieval commerce, run your fingers across over-200-year-old rudimentary circular grooves on the cathedral's face (right side of front), once used for standardising and regulating exact measurements of bread loaves, and over two horizontally fastened iron bars at one time utilised for gauging proper lengths of cloth.

Inside, you can take the lift up the north tower (€4) or the stairs up the higher south tower (€3) – but travellers are sometimes disappointed by the fairly mediocre views. Some of the internal organs of the Habsburgs reside in urns in the church's **Katakomben** (catacombs; admission €3).

Hofburg

The **Hofburg** (Imperial Palace; Map p48) was the Habsburgs' city-centre base. Added to many times since the 13th century, resulting in a mix of architectural styles, the palace continues to be a seat of power, housing the office of the president of Austria and a major congress centre. Wander around a bit and admire the exterior before venturing inside. While not as ornate as Schönbrunn's rooms, the **Kaiserappartements & 'Sissi' Museum** (Map p48; ☎ 535 75 75; Hofburg; admission €7.50; ☼ 9am-5pm; U-Bahn Herrengasse) are worth seeing because they relate the unusual life story of Empress Elisabeth (Sissi). You don't particularly have to be a fan to enjoy the experience: the empress' 19th-century gym and her obsession with her looks are attention-grabbing enough. Plus, the museum helps explain why Sissi's face still adorns shop windows in Vienna today. A ticket to the Kaiserappartements includes entry to the **Silberkammer** (silver chamber).

Among several other points of interest within the Hofburg you'll find the Burgkapelle (Royal Chapel), where the Vienna Boys' Choir performs (see p57), and the Spanish Riding School (p57).

Kaisergruft

Also known as the Kapuzinergruft, the **Imperial Vault** (Map p48; 01, Tegetthofstrasse/Neuer Markt; admission €4; ☼ 9am-5pm; U-Bahn Stephansplatz) offers another weirdly compelling take on the cult of 'Sissi'. Stabbed by an Italian anarchist on the waterfront in Geneva in 1898, Empress Elisabeth was brought back here as her final resting place. Her coffin, still strewn with flowers by fans, lies alongside that of her husband, the penultimate emperor Franz Josef, and other Habsburgs. It's as bizarre as anything on TV's *Six Feet Under*.

VIENNA IN TWO DAYS

Starting at the **Stephansdom** (above), head via Graben and the Kohlmarkt to the **Hofburg** (above). Drop by the **Kaisergruft** (above), before finding a coffee house and settling into a long break. After lunch, hop on tram 1 around the Ringstrasse. Do one circuit and a half, just taking in the sights, before alighting near the **Museums Quartier** (p49). Try to get tickets to the **opera** (p56) for the evening or head to a club like **Flex** (p56).

Choose a few galleries or a museum and explore them in-depth on your second morning. If it's a warm afternoon, laze in the gardens at **Schloss Schönnbrunn** (p50). At night venture into the suburbs for delicious wine in Vienna's *Heurigen* (wine taverns; p55).

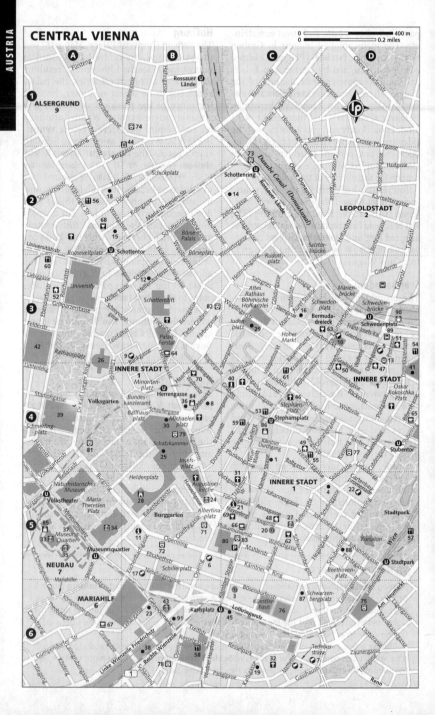

CENTRAL VIENNA

Museums Quartier

Small guidebooks have been written on the popular **Museums Quartier** (Map p48; ☎ 523 04 31; 07, Museumsplatz 1; Ⓡ U-Bahn Museumsquartier), so only a taster can be given here. The highpoint is undoubtedly the **Leopold Museum** (Map p48; ☎ 525 700; adult/senior/student €9/7/5.50; ☽ 10am-7pm Wed-Mon, 10am-9pm Fri; Ⓡ U-Bahn Museumsquartier), which houses the world's largest collection of Egon Schiele paintings, with some minor Klimts and Kokoschkas thrown in.

Schloss Belvedere

This **palace** (Map p44; ☎ 79 557-134; www.belvedere.at; combined admission €7.50; ☽ 10am-6pm Tue-Sun Apr-Oct, 10am-5pm Nov-Mar; Ⓡ tram D to Schloss Belvedere) consists of two main buildings. One is the **Oberes Belvedere & Österreichische Galerie** (Upper Belvedere & Austrian Gallery; Map p44; 03, Prinz Eugen Strasse 37; adult/student €6/3; ☽ 10am-6pm Tue-Sun Apr-Oct, 10am-5pm Nov-Mar), where you'll find instantly recognisable works, such as Gustav

Klimt's *The Kiss*, accompanied by other late-19th to early-20th-century Austrian works. The other is the **Unteres Belvedere** (Lower Belvedere; Map p44; 03, Rennweg 6A; admission €6; ☽ 10am-6pm Tue-Sun Apr-Oct, 10am-5pm Nov-Mar), which contains a baroque museum. The buildings sit at opposite ends of a manicured garden.

Secession Building

This popular Art Nouveau 'temple of art' **building** (Map p48; ☎ 587 53 07; 01, Friedrichstrasse 12; adult/student €5.50/3; ☽ 10am-6pm Tue-Sun, 10am-8pm Thu; Ⓡ U-Bahn Karlsplatz) was built in 1898 and bears an intricately woven gilt dome that the Viennese say looks like a 'golden cabbage' – and it definately does. The highlight inside is the 34m-long *Beethoven Frieze* by Klimt.

KunstHausWien

This formerly inconspicuous factory building, now fairy-tale **art gallery** (Map p44; ☎ 712

04 91; 03, Untere Weissgerberstrasse 13; admission €9, half-price Mon; ☾ 10am-7pm; ⊕ tram N or O to Radetzkyplatz) designed and transformed by Friedensreich Hundertwasser into a repository for his art, is redolent of Antonio Gaudi's buildings in Barcelona. Irregular elements, like uneven floors, misshapen windows, amalgamations of glass, metal, brick and ceramic tile, almost literally sweep you off your feet. Down the road there's a block of residential flats by Hundertwasser, the **Hundertwasser-shaus** (Map p44; cnr Löwengasse & Kegelgasse). To the west, heading towards the town of Dürnstein, another spectacle arises that would make Willy Wonka proud. Visible by its towering, golden-tiled smoke stack, this is Vienna's architecturally unique rubbish incinerator that also heats water for homes in the surrounding area.

Albertina

Simply reading the highlights among its enormous rotating collection – several Michelangelos, some Raphaels and Albrecht Dürer's *Hare* – might give a misleading impression of this reopened **gallery** (Map p48; ☎ 53 483-540; www.albertina.at; 01, Albertinaplatz 1A; adult/senior/student €9/7.50/6.50; ☾ 10am-6pm Thu-Tue, 10am-9pm Wed; ⊕ U-Bahn Karlsplatz or Stephansplatz). When we visited, the exhibitions ranged from pop art to Rembrandt and included two fascinating photography displays, making it feel quite modern. The curators do a superb job, so keep an eye out for what's on here.

In addition to the mostly temporary exhibitions, a series of Habsburg staterooms are always open.

Schloss Schönbrunn

The single attraction most readily associated with Vienna is the Habsburgs' **summer palace** (Map p44; ☎ 81 113-0; 13, Schönbrunner Schlossstrasse 47; self-guided 22-/40-room tour €8/10.50; ☾ 8.30am-5pm Apr-Oct, 8.30am-4.30pm Nov-Mar; ⊕ U-Bahn Schönbrunn). However, the sumptuous 1440-room palace is so vast, crowded and out of the way that you'll need to put aside at least half a day to see it, and it won't be to everyone's taste. Students get a slight discount.

Inside this mini-Versailles you'll traipse through progressively more luxurious apartments. The most impressive, the **Audience Rooms**, are only included in the 40-room grand tour.

The grounds are more enjoyable and are home to the world's oldest zoo, the **Tiergarten** (adult/senior/student/child €12/10/5/4), founded in 1752. Highlights include the formal gardens and fountains, the **maze** (admission €2.10), the **Palmenhaus** (greenhouse; admission €3.30) and the **Gloriette Monument** (admission €2.10), whose roof offers a wonderful view over the palace grounds and beyond.

Liechtenstein Museum

The collection of Duke Hans-Adam II of Liechtenstein is now on show at Vienna's new **museum** (Map p44; ☎ 319 57 67-0; 09, Fürstengasse 1; adult/senior/student €10/8/5; ☾ 9am-8pm Wed-Mon; ⊕ U-Bahn Friedensbrücke or Franz Josefs Bahnhof), located in a refurbished, frescoed, baroque palace. There are classical paintings, including some by Rubens.

Kunsthistorisches Museum

A huge range of art amassed by the Habsburgs is showcased at the **Museum of Fine Arts** (Map p48; ☎ 52 524-0; www.khm.at; 01, Maria Theresien Platz; admission €10; ☾ 10am-6pm Tue-Sun, 10am-10pm Thu; ⊕ U-Bahn Volkstheater or Museumsquartier). Included are works by Rubens, van Dyck, Holbein and Caravaggio. Paintings by Peter Brueghel the Elder, including *Hunters in the Snow*, also feature. There is an entire wing of ornaments, clocks and glassware, and Greek, Roman and Egyptian antiquities.

Other Museums

Vienna has so many museums you might overlook the superlative **Haus der Musik** (House of Music; Map p48; ☎ 51 648-51; www.haus-der-musik -wien.at; Seilerstätte 30; admission €10; ☾ 10am-10pm; ⊕ U-Bahn Karlsplatz or Stephansplatz). Try not to. Interactive electronic displays allow you to create different forms of music through movement and touch, and to connect with something a lot deeper than just your inner child.

Some former homes of the great composers, including one of Mozart's, are open to the public; ask at the tourist office. There is also the fairly low-key **Sigmund Freud Museum** (Map p48; ☎ 319 15 96; 09, Bergasse 19; admission €5; ☾ 9am-6pm Jul-Sep, 9am-5pm Oct-Jun; ⊕ U-Bahn Rossauer or Schottentor).

Cemeteries

Beethoven, Schubert, Brahms and Schönberg have memorial tombs in the **Zentralfriedhof** (Central Cemetery; 11, Simmeringer Hauptstrasse

232-244), about 4km southeast of the city centre. Mozart also has a monument here, but he is actually buried in the **St Marxer Friedhof** (Cemetery of St Mark; 03, Leberstrasse 6-8).

Naschmarkt

Saturday is the best day to visit this **market** (Map p48; 06, Linke Wienzeile; ✆ 6am-6pm Mon-Sat; ✆ U-Bahn Karlsplatz or Kettenbrückengasse) when the usual food stalls and occasional tatty clothes stall are joined by a proper flea market. Curios and trinkets sit beside produce from Austrian farms, plus there are cafés for an alfresco breakfast, lunch or refuelling stop.

ACTIVITIES
Riesenrad

In theory, riding the **Riesenrad** (giant wheel; Map p44; admission €7.50; ✆ U-Bahn Praterstern) in the Prater amusement park allows you to relive a classic film moment: when Orson Welles ad-libbed his immortal speech about peace, Switzerland and cuckoo clocks in *The Third Man*. In practice, you'll be too distracted by other passengers and by the views as the Ferris wheel languidly takes you 65m aloft. It's fun, but not quite the London Eye.

Water Sports

You can swim, sailboard, boat and windsurf in the stretches of water known as the Old Danube, northeast of the Donaustadt island and the New Donau, which runs parallel to and just north of the Donaukanal (Danube Canal). There are stretches of river bank with unrestricted access. Alternatively, visit the **Schönbrunn baths** (Map p44; Schönbrunner Schlossstrasse 47; full day/afternoon incl locker €9.50/6.50; ✆ 8.30am-5pm May-Sep; ✆ U-Bahn Schönbrunn), within the Schloss Schönbrunn grounds.

TOURS

The tourist office publishes a monthly list of guided walks, called *Wiener Spaziergänge*. **Vienna Walks** (✆ 774 89 01; www.viennawalks.tix.at) organises **Third Man tours** (tour €16; ✆ 4pm Mon & Fri), including through the city's sewers, and a tour of **Jewish Vienna** (tour €11; ✆ 1.30pm Mon).

FESTIVALS & EVENTS

The **Vienna Festival**, from mid-May to mid-June, has a wide-ranging arts programme. Contact the **Wiener Festwochen** (Map p48; ✆ 58 922-22; www.festwochen.or.at; Lehárgasse 11; ✆ Jan–mid-Jun; ✆ U-Bahn Karlsplatz) for details.

The extremely popular **Vienna Spring Marathon** is held in April/May and Vienna's **Summer of Music** runs from mid-July to mid-September; contact **KlangBoden** (Map p44; ✆ 40 00-8410; 01, Stadiongasse 9; ✆ U-Bahn Rathaus).

Look out for free rock, jazz and folk concerts during the **Donauinselfest**, held at the end of June. The free open-air **Opera Film Festival** on Rathausplatz runs throughout July and August.

Each year Vienna's traditional **Christmas market** *(Christkindlmarkt)* takes place in front of the Rathaus between mid-November and 24 December.

SLEEPING
Budget

Vienna has lots of budget choices, although rooms fill quickly in summer, so try to book ahead when possible.

Wien West (✆ 914 23 14; www.wiencamping.at; Hüttelbergstrasse 80; camp site per adult/tent Sep-Jun €5/3.50, Jul-Aug €6/3.50, 2-/4-person cabin Apr-Oct €27/37; ✆ closed Feb) On the edges of the Wiener Wald (Vienna Woods), but just 20 minutes from the city centre, this well-equipped

---

GRAPE GRAZING

Cycle, sit, swirl, sip, cycle, slurp, savour, then cycle again, your way from winery to winery and let your taste buds reap the rewards of one of Austria's best wine regions. Expert guides and a lovely path along the Danube river make **Mitch's Tours Grape Grazing Tour** (✆ 699-1882 0155; www.mitchstours.com; Grangasse 4, 1150 Vienna; adult/student €55/45) a great choice for the authentic Vienna countryside excursion.

You'll spend a day touring the breathtakingly beautiful scenery and old medieval villages of the Wachau by bike. Wander through the fortress ruins in Durnstein, where England's King Richard the Lion-Heart was imprisoned, perhaps the most historically infamous stop on the route. Learn how Austrian schnapps is made. You can also go swimming, play beach volleyball or relax while enjoying a barbecue. Tours depart 9.30am daily (except Monday and Wednesday) and hotel pick-up is available.

camping ground has modern facilities, and even a wi-fi hotspot. Take U4 or the S-Bahn to Hütteldorf, then bus 148 or 152.

Jugendgästhaus Wien Brigittenau (☎ 332 82 94; jgh1200wien@chello.at; 20, Friedrich Engels Platz 24; dm from €15) This large Hostelling International (HI) hostel is popular with school groups. Take the U6 to Handelskai and then bus 11A one stop to Friedrich Engels Platz.

Wombat's (Map p44; ☎ 897 23 36; www.wombats.at; 15, Grangasse 6; dm/d €18/24; 🖳) Top-flight cleanliness and comfort fuse with a gregarious party bar to make Wombat's immensely popular. The mixed-gender dorms have secured entry, wooden bunk beds and modern bathrooms. It's where the hip kids stay – if they remember to do something as terminally un-hip as book ahead. Rates include breakfast.

Westend City Hostel (Map p44; ☎ 597 67 29; www.westendhostel.at; 6, Fügergasse 3; dm €18, s/d €41/49; 🗶 🖳) The weirdest thing behind the pale purple façade isn't the knowledge that this was once a *bordello*. It's the particle board–encased en suite bathrooms in some of the mixed dorms; these bathrooms have extra mattresses on their mezzanine roof. Still, the place is well located and friendly.

Pension Kaffeemühle (Map p44; ☎ 523 86 88; www.kaffeemuhle.at; 07, Kaiserstrasse 45; s/d from €48/60; 🅿 🗶) Family-run *pension* offering comfortable clean rooms and a central location not far from the Westbahnhof. It's a good place to rest up before another day in the city.

Pension Hargita (Map p44; ☎ 526 19 28; www.hargita.at; 07, Andreasgasse 1; s/d €55/66, with shared bathroom from €38/53) One of the cleanest and most charming budget *pensions* in Vienna. Rooms have aqua blue or sunny yellow features, the friendly Hungarian owner keeps things spotless and breakfast is included in the rates.

Midrange

There are lots of charming guesthouses and small hotels in this price bracket.

Hotel Urania (Map p44; ☎ 713 17 11; www.hotel-urania.at; 03, Obere Weissgerberstrasse 7; s/d/tr/q from €55/70/95/115) This hotel is tacky, but fun. Episodes of various Austrian TV series (eg *Inspector Rex*) have been filmed here, and as a guest you'll feel you're in one, too. Not all of the eclectic rooms will be to everyone's taste (a knight's boudoir with animal skins on the floor, anyone?). Others, as in the Hundertwasser and Japanese rooms, are

actually quite chic. The hotel is quiet, but central.

Pension Residenz (Map p48; ☎ 406 47 86-0; www.pension-residenz.co.at; 01, Ebendorferstrasse 10; s/d €60/90; 🅿) This *pension* is a model of restraint. Traditionally decorated, with white, light-coloured fittings, it has a pleasant, if not overly personal, feel. Its location near the university is also handy.

Lauria (Map p44; ☎ 522 25 55; www.lauria-vienna.at; 3rd fl, 07, Kaiserstrasse 77-8; d/tr/q from €62/78/96, with shared bathroom €48/66/84) A good place for young couples or small groups of travellers staying a couple of nights – you get your own homy quarters, your own keys and access to a fully equipped kitchen. There is a €7 surcharge for single-night stays.

Pension Dr Geissler (Map p48; ☎ 533 28 03; www.hotelpension.at; 01, Postgasse 14; s/d from €65/88, with shared bathroom from €39/50; 🅿) Don't let the slow lift deter you: when you do make it to your floor, you'll find rooms are an eclectic mix of faux baroque and 1950s retro. The airport bus to Schwedenplatz almost brings you to the door, making it handy for jet-lag rehab.

Pension Wild (Map p44; ☎ 406 51 74; www.pensions-wild.com; 08, Langegasse 10; s/d €65/90, with shared bathroom from €37/45) Most of the rooms at this gay-friendly *pension* have been recently renovated, but some cheaper accommodation remains, with showers and toilets outside the rooms. All guests can prepare snacks in the small kitchenette on each floor.

Hotel-Pension Zipser (Map p44; ☎ 40 454-0; www.zipser.at; 08, Langegasse 49; s/d from €69/109; 🅿) This

---

AUTHOR'S CHOICE

Hostel Ruthensteiner (Map p44; ☎ 893 42 02; www.hostelruthensteiner.com; 15, Robert Hamerling Gasse 24; dm/d from €12.50/25; 🗶 🖳) If stars were given out for hostels, this place would be a 5. The first truly independent backpackers in central Europe, the über-friendly owners, Erin and Walter, have been catering to travellers for 34 years strong. Start with a quirky low-key vibe then add an immaculate, modern facility with more renovations in progress, mix in a strong dose of personality and options galore, and you'll have a feel for this place. A beautifully handmade wooden bar, music/lounge room and a lovely garden area also enhance the surroundings.

place has elegant contemporary furnishings and some rooms have balconies facing a garden.

Hotel Post (Map p48; ☎ 51 583-0; www.hotel-post -wien.at; 01, Fleischmarkt 24; s/d €75/115, with shared bathroom €44/70; P) The strongest feature of this hotel is its location, right in the heart of things. With its parquet flooring in the rooms, long, carpeted hallways and decorative cast-iron lift, it feels like a grand, if somewhat faded, 19th-century boarding house.

Kärtnerhof (Map p48; ☎ 519 19 23; www.kartnerhof .com; 01, Grashofgasse 4; s/d from €80/105; P) Tucked away in a cul-de-sac in the city centre, Kärtnerhof is a terrific find with quietly elegant rooms, many of them with bathtubs. It has a policy of not accepting tour groups.

Hotel zur Wiener Staatsoper (Map p48; ☎ 513 12 74; www.zurwienerstaatsoper.at; 01, Krugerstrasse 11; s/d from €85/126; P) Famous for its appealing façade, this hotel's rooms are small, but its prices are great value for the central location.

Top End

Vienna has a glut of four- and five-star hotels. Every major chain is represented and even the city's most recognisable names now belong to one of these groups.

InterCity Hotel (Map p44; ☎ 52 585-0; www .intercityhotel.de; 07 Mariahilfer Strasse 122; s/d €121/205; P X ☺) Located on a major shopping thoroughfare, with soundproof modern rooms and tasteful décor, this place is a fine choice for convenience and comfort. Use of local transport included in the rate means you won't fret about getting around the city.

Kaiserin Elisabeth (Map p48; ☎ 51 526-0; www .kaiserinelisabeth.at; 01, Weihburggasse 13; s/d €175/200; P X ☺) The central Kaiserin, with its mix of chandeliers, red velvet, wooden floors and rugs, is a plush option.

EATING

The city's signature dish, *Wiener schnitzel*, is widely available and Vienna is renowned for its excellent pastries. You can buy groceries outside normal shopping hours at Franz Josefs Bahnhof and Westbahnhof.

Restaurants

Schnitzelwirt Schmidt (Map p44; 07, Neubaugasse 52; schnitzel from €5.50; ☺ Mon-Sat) With fabulously grumpy waiters – who'll shout at you if you get in their way – and huge *Wiener schnitzels*,

this buzzing place lets you experience the authentic Vienna of today.

OH Pot, OH Pot (Map p48; ☎ 319 42 59; 09, Währinger Strasse 22; hotpots lunch/dinner €6.50/8.50) Painted in warm Mediterranean colours, this sweet boho restaurant has decent ethnic stews (or hotpots) on the menu. Whether African, Asian, central European or South American, they all come with either soup or salad. The best deal is from 3pm to 6pm, when prices drop to €5.

Ra'an (Map p48; ☎ 319 35 63; 09, Währinger Strasse 6-8; lunch €6, dinner €6.50-13) Ra'an is a cool noodle bar and has what listings magazine *Falter* has decreed the 'cutest cardboard lunch boxes in town'. The menu ranges from sushi and rice dishes at lunch to more elaborate Thai and Vietnamese in the evening.

Vegetasia (Map p44; ☎ 523 10 91; 07, Kaiserstrasse 45; mains €6.50-22) Flavourful and eclectic combinations of fresh vegetables, Asian spices and pure vegetable-based home-made dishes will bring gastric delight to anyone wanting to avoid *Fleisch* (meat) in their diet. Every item on the menu is vegetarian.

Immervoll (Map p48; ☎ 5135 2288; 01 Weihburggasse 17; mains €9-14.50) Run by a famous Austrian actor, Immervoll (literally, 'always full') attracts an arty crowd to its uncluttered small room. The menu changes daily, but the delicious food often has Hungarian and Italian influences.

Stomach (Map p44; ☎ 310 20 99; 09, Seegasse 26; mains €9-15; ☺ dinner Wed-Sat, lunch & dinner Sun) Many vegetarian dishes have dropped off

AUTHOR'S CHOICE

1516 Brewing Company (Map p48; ☎ 961 15 16; 01, Schwarzenbergstrasse 2) Flaunting exposed copper and stainless-steel piping, wine-barrel tables and a long bar extending along the front room, this hip brewpub is an awesome place to go for a drink while you're in the city centre. Unfiltered ales and lagers, an unpretentious ambience and friendly staff are all on tap here. Specifically named after the year of one of the oldest 'consumer protection' laws (the *Reinheitsgebot*), beer enthusiasts will imbibe with glee knowing that their pint is made exactly the same as it was in the year 1516, using only water, malt, hops and yeast.

the menu at Styrian-style Stomach, but some remain, and the quaint, ramshackle rooms and the courtyard create a rustic outpost in the big city.

Schweizerhaus (Map p44; ☎ 319 35 63; 02, Strasse des Ersten Mai 116; mains €10-20; ⏰ Mon-Sat Mar-Oct) In the Prater park, this place serves *Hintere Schweinsstelze* (roasted pork hocks) and the like to a rowdy crowd of international travellers who wash it all down with huge mugs of beer.

Wrenkh (Map p48; ☎ 533 15 26; 01, Bauernmarkt 10; mains €11) Quiche, mung beans and nut roast are *not* on the menu at this vegetarian restaurant. Instead, this is an upmarket affair, with sleek customers and lip-smacking Mediterranean, Austrian and Asian fare – from risotto to tofu.

Indochine 21 (Map p44; ☎ 513 76 60; 01, Stubenring 18; mains €12.50-38; ⏰ lunch & dinner) This is one of Vienna's hotter, newer eateries, having been named the best Asian restaurant in the city a few years back. The food is trendy French/Vietnamese, while red-lacquered umbrellas hang on the walls and exotic potted plants evoke a vaguely colonial ambience.

DO & CO (Map p48; ☎ 535 39 69; 01, Haas Haus, Stephansplatz 12; mains €15-24) The food and the views from seven floors above Stephansplatz keep this elegant restaurant in business. Contemporary Viennese dishes are highlighted, but it also serves Austrian classics, Uruguayan beef and Asian specialities. The service is flawless. Booking ahead is advised.

Steirereck (Map p48; ☎ 713 31 68; 03, Heumarkt 2a-Stadtpark; mains €22.50-30; ⏰ lunch & dinner) This

long-standing gourmet temple's name means 'corner of Styria' and is famous for traditional Viennese fare and new Austrian selections. Try the Styrian roast beef with red-pepper risotto. Patrons can examine the vast wine cellar, which holds some 35,000 bottles, or choose from 150 different types of cheese. Reservations are required.

Cafés

Trzesniewski (Map p48; ☎ 512 32 91; 01, Dorotheergasse 1; sandwiches €1) You can really feel like one of the Austrian emperor's minions on the way home from the factory at this stand-up café. It sells tiny open sandwiches, usually featuring egg or fish of some description, which you wash down with a tiny *Pfiff* (125mL) beer.

Sato Turkish Café-Restaurant (Map p44; ☎ 897 58 54; 15, Mariahilferstrasse 151; mains €3-13; ⏰ 8am-midnight) This restaurant entices clientele with generous portions of bona fide Turkish cuisine, an easy atmosphere, and inexpensive *Tagesmenus* sure to satisfy every taste and budget. Live traditional music on the weekends is also worth checking out.

Quick Eats & Self-Catering

Cheap student cafeterias include **Technical University Mensa** (Map p48; 04, Resselgasse 7-9; mains €3.50-5; ⏰ 11am-2pm Mon-Fri) and **University Mensa** (Map p48; 7th fl, 01, Universitätsstrasse 7; mains €4.50-5; ⏰ 11am-2pm Mon-Fri). Though the latter is closed in July and August, its adjoining **café** (⏰ 8am-3pm Mon-Fri) remains open year-round.

DRINKING
Bars

The area around Ruprechtsplatz, Seitenstettengasse and Rabensteig near Schwedenplatz is dubbed the Bermudadreieck (Bermuda Triangle; Map p48) for the way drinkers disappear into its numerous pubs and clubs, but you'd have to seriously overindulge to become lost here. Venues are lively and inexpensive, and draw a mix of crowds.

Crossfield's Aussie Pub (Map p48; ☎ 241 000; 01, Maysedergasse 5) There's a saying on some of the touristy T-shirts – 'there's no kangaroos in Austria'. Well, this pub proves the contrary, with upstairs and downstairs bar areas serving Australian, import and local beers, plus enough outback charm to make you forget what country you're in. Grub like crocodile, ostrich fillet, grilled grasshoppers and plenty of roo any way you like it, makes this place one of our favourites.

Shebeen (Map p44; ☎ 524 79 00; 07, Lerchenfelder Strasse 45-47) This African-inspired pub remains a popular evening spot for English-speaking travellers, expats and internationals alike. Major football matches, decent music and activities, like nightly quizzes of the Trivial Pursuit variety, all create a lively atmosphere.

Das Möbel (Map p44; ☎ 524 94 97; 07, Burggasse 10) The interior is never dull at this bar near the Museums Quartier. It's remarkable for its funky décor and furniture – cube stools, assorted moulded lamps, plus a round ping-pong table.

Café Stein (Map p48; ☎ 3197 2419; 09, Währinger Strasse 6-8; 🖳) This trendy, student café/bar-cum-diner offers a smoke-free environment in which to curl up with a good book or surf the Net. It also hosts poetry slams and modern art exhibitions.

Also recommended:

Die Wäscherei (Map p44; ☎ 409 23 75-11; 08, Albertgasse 49) Lots of draught beers.

Rhiz (Map p44; ☎ 409 25 05; Lechenfelder Gürtel 37-38) A mecca for Vienna's electronic music scene; it's near the U-Bahn arches.

Schikanader (Map p44; ☎ 585 58 88; 04, Margaretenstrasse 22-4) In the foyer of a cinema.

Coffee Houses

Vienna's famous *Kaffeehäuser* (coffee houses) are like economic forecasts; ask two people for a recommendation and you'll get four answers. Following are a few local favourites – a full-sized coffee will cost roughly €3 to €3.50, but you can take as long as you like to drink it without being moved on.

Café Sacher (Map p48; ☎ 151 45 69; 01, Philharmoniker strasse 4; ☽ 8am-noon) Arguably home to the world's most famous chocolate cake – the Sacher Torte, fastidiously baked in-house. Savour a slice of this exquisite speciality that has been a well-kept secret since 1832. Wash it all down with an Original Sacher Café coffee and enjoy the conservatory, which faces the Staatsoper (State Opera) and in summer is transformed into a huge terrace.

Café Central (Map p48; ☎ 533 37 63; 01, Herrengasse 14; ☽ Mon-Sat) A lot more commercialised than when Herrs Trotsky, Freud and Beethoven drank here, we dare say, but still appealing with vaulted ceilings, palms and baroque architecture.

Café Prückel (Map p48; ☎ 512 61 15; 01, Stubenring 24) This 1950s-style café is the epitome of shabby chic. A traditional Viennese coffee house, it's been around some 100 years.

Heurigen (Wine Taverns)

Vienna's *Heurigen* are a good way to see another side of the city. Selling 'new' wine produced on the premises, they have a lively atmosphere, especially as the evening progresses. Outside tables and picnic benches are common. There's usually buffet food, and often strolling piano-accordion musicians entertaining with folk songs.

Because *Heurigen* tend to be clustered together, it's best just to head for the wine-growing suburbs to the north, south and west of the city and look for the green wreath or branch hanging over the door that identifies a *Heuriger*. Opening times are approximately 4pm to 11pm, and wine costs less than €2.50 a *Viertel* (250mL).

The *Heurigen* areas of Nussdorf and Heiligenstadt are near each other at the terminus of tram D, north of the city centre. In 1817 Beethoven lived in at 19, Pfarrplatz 3, Heiligenstadt in what is now know as Beethovenhaus. Down the road (bus 38A from Heiligenstadt or tram 38 from the Ring) is Grinzing, an area favoured by tour groups.

Reinprecht (☎ 320 14 71; 19, Cobenzlgasse 22) This is the best option in the row of *Heurigen* where Cobenzlgasse and Sandgasse meet. It's in a former monastery and boasts a large paved courtyard and a lively, if somewhat touristy, atmosphere.

Sirbu (☎ 320 59 28; 19, Kahlenberger Strasse 210; ☽ Mon-Sat Apr-Oct) This spot has great views of the Danube. Catch bus 38A east to the final stop at Kahlenberg, from where it is a 15-minute walk.

Esterházykeller (Map p48; ☎ 533 34 82; Haarhof 1; ☺ 11am-11pm Mon-Fri, 4-11pm Sat & Sun) If you don't have time to venture out into the suburbs, you can get a genuine taste of the *Heurigen* experience here. After descending sharply down a steep stairwell, aromas of dank air, hints of pipe and cigar smoke combined with mugs of wine and food befall olfactory senses in this truly 'underground' *Heurigen* that's as authentic as it gets. Dating from 1683, it was also allegedly used as a way for Viennese to gather provisions during the unsuccessful Turkish siege by tunnelling under the wall that enclosed the city.

ENTERTAINMENT

Check listings magazine *Falter* (€2.05) for weekly updates. The tourist office has copies of *Vienna Scene* and produces monthly events listings.

Cinemas & Theatre

Burgkino (Map p48; ☎ 587 84 06; 01, Opernring 19; admission €6-8) Screens *The Third Man* every Friday evening and Sunday afternoon, if you want to revisit this classic movie while in Vienna. Otherwise, check local papers for listings. Seats are cheapest on Monday.

There are performances in English at the **English Theatre** (Map p44; ☎ 402 82 84; www .englishtheatre.at; 08, Josefsgasse 12) and the **International Theatre** (Map p48; ☎ 319 62 72; 09, Porzellangasse 8).

Classical Music

The state ticket office, **Bundestheaterkassen** (Map p48; ☎ 51 444-7880; www.bundestheater.at; 01, Goethegasse 1), sells tickets without commission for both the Staatsoper and Volksoper. In the hut by the Staatsoper, **Wien Ticket** (Map p48; ☎ 58 885; Linke Wienzeile 6, 1060 Wien) also charges little or no commission for cash sales.

The cheapest deals are the standing-room tickets that go on sale at each venue an hour before performances. However, you may need to queue three hours before that for major productions. An hour before the curtain goes up, unsold tickets also go on sale at cheap prices to students under 27 years (from €3.70; home university ID plus international student card necessary).

Staatsoper (State Opera; Map p48; ☎ 51 444-2960; 01, Opernring 2; standing room €4, seats €5.50-220) Performances are lavish, formal affairs, where people dress up.

Volksoper (People's Opera; Map p44; ☎ 51 444-3670; 09, Währinger Strasse 78; standing room €1.50-24, seats €17-75) Productions are more modern here and the atmosphere is a little more relaxed.

Musikverein (Map p48; ☎ 505 18 90; www.musik verein.at; 01, Bösendorferstrasse 12; standing room €5-7, seats €16-110) The opulent and acoustically perfect (unofficial) home of the Vienna Philharmonic Orchestra. You can buy standing tickets three weeks in advance at the box office to hear this world-class orchestra.

There are no performances in July and August. Ask at the tourist office for details of free concerts at the Rathaus or in churches.

Nightclubs

Flex (Map p48; ☎ 533 75 25; Donaukanal/Augartenbrücke) The stairwell leading from the U-Bahn stop to its doors constantly reeks of urine and the circling dealers are an annoyance, but Flex is still the finest club in the city. Time after time this uninhibited shrine to music (it has one of the best sound systems in Europe) puts on great live shows and features the top DJs from Vienna and abroad. Each night is a different theme, with dub club on Monday and London Calling on Wednesday among the most popular.

Porgy n Bess (Map p48; ☎ 512 88 11; 01, Riemergasse 11; ☺ 8am-4am Mon-Sat, 7pm-4am Sun) Vienna's best spot to catch modern, local and international jazz acts. It has a relaxed and sophisticated atmosphere that attracts a professional crowd. DJs are a ruling feature on weekends and Wednesday night sees impromptu jam sessions.

Volksgarten (Map p48; ☎ 533 05 18; 01, Burgring 1) In the middle of the park of the same name, this place is very popular. There's modern dance and an atmospheric 1950s-style salon that was once a former *Walzer Dancing* venue. Friday and Saturday are the big nights, although it's open other evenings, too.

Roxy (Map p48; ☎ 961 88 00; 04, Operngasse 24; ☺ Tue-Sat) Often leading the way, or at least keeping pace, with Vienna's progressive clubbing scene. Its tiny dance floor is therefore regularly bursting at the seams. The sounds range from jazz to world music.

Club U (Map p48; ☎ 505 99 04; 04, Karlsplatz; ☺ Tue-Sun) In the ornate Otto Wagner Stadtbahn

Pavilions café, Club U is a bit like a squat party and plays indie/alternative music.

Why Not? (Map p48; ☎ 535 11 58; 01, Tiefer Graben 22; ☯ Wed-Sun) A popular gay and lesbian bar/disco; on Wednesday night it's men only.

Rosa Lila Villa (Map p44; ☎ 586 81 50; 06, Linke Wienziele 102) This pink-and-purple building is another favourite spot with alternative lifestyles types. Along with the on-site bar, it also has an information centre. It's a good place to link up with like-minded locals.

Spanish Riding School

The famous Lipizzaner stallions strut their stuff at the **Spanish Riding School** (Map p48; tickets@srs.at; Michaelerplatz 11010; standing room €24-25, seats €45-145) behind the Hofburg. Performances are sold out months in advance, so write to the Spanische Reitschule, Michaelerplatz 1, A-1010 Wien, or ask in the office about cancellations (unclaimed tickets are sold 45 minutes before performances); there's no phone. Travel agents usually charge commission on top of the listed prices.

You need to be pretty keen on horses to pay the high admission price, although a few tricks, such as a stallion bounding along on its hind legs like a demented kangaroo, do tend to stick in the mind. Same-day **tickets** (€11.50, or with entry to the Lipizzaner Museum €15; ☯ 10am-noon Tue-Sat Feb-Jun & Sep-Dec) can be bought to watch the horses train. The best riders go first and queues disappear by 11am. Watching the weekly final **rehearsal** (tickets €20; 7pm Fri & Sat) is also an option.

Vienna Boys' Choir

Never mind bands like Take That and Nsync; the Vienna Boys' Choir (*Wiener Sängerknaben*) is *the* original boy band. The first troupe was put together back in 1498 and the latest bunch of cherubic angels in sailor suits still holds a fond place in Austrian hearts.

The choir performs weekly at the **Burgkapelle** (Music Chapel; Map p48; ☎ 533 99 27; hofmusikkapelle@asn-wien.ac.at; Hofburg, Rennweg 1; standing free, seats €5.50-30, tickets Fri & 8.15am Sun) at 9.15am on Sunday, except from July to mid-September. Concerts are routinely sold out and there's often a crush of fans to meet the choir afterwards. The group also performs regularly in the **Konzerthaus** (Map p48; ☎ 242 002; 03, Lotheringerstrasse 20) at 3.30pm on Friday in May, June, September and October.

SHOPPING

Stephansplatz (Map p48; ☎ 514 130; Kärntner Strabe 19; ☯ 9.30am-7pm Mon-Fri, 9.30am-5pm Sat) Set along the famous plaza by the same name, the Stephansplatz is filled with all the stores a good mall needs.

Österreiche Werkstätten (Map p48; Kärntner Strasse 6) Good for Art Deco–type jewellery and household objects in the Viennese tradition; other local specialities include lamps, handmade dolls, and wrought-iron and leather goods.

Café Demel (Map p48; ☎ 535 17 17-0; 01, Kohlmarkt 14) Lavish Café Demel has the old-world atmosphere that makes for the perfect landmark coffee house, but it's usually too crowded. Instead, pop in to buy some fantastic cakes, pastries or sandwiches here.

GETTING THERE & AWAY
Air

Regular scheduled flights link Vienna to Linz, Salzburg, Innsbruck, Klagenfurt and Graz. Check with **Austrian Airlines** (code OS; Map p48; ☎ 051 789; www.aua.com; 01, Kärntner Strasse 11, Vienna). There are also daily nonstop flights to all major European destinations. For further details, see p90.

Boat

Between April and November, fast hydrofoils travel eastwards to Bratislava (one-way/return €23/35, bike extra €7, 1½ hours, Wednesday to Sunday June to September) and Budapest (one-way/return €76/100, bike extra €19, 5½ hours, daily). Bookings can be made through **DDSG Blue Danube** (Map p48; ☎ 58 880-0; www.ddsg-blue-danube.at; 01, Friedrichstrasse 7) or **G Glaser** (Map p44; ☎ 726 08 20; www.members.aon.at/danube; 02, Handelskai 265).

Heading west, a series of boats plies the Danube between Krems and Passau (in Germany), with a handful of services originating in Vienna. Two respectable operators include DDSG Blue Danube and **Brandner** (☎ 07433-25 90; www.brandner.at; Ufer 50, Wallsee). Both run trips from April through October that start at around €17 one-way.

Bus

Bus company Eurolines operates from two locations. At least daily, buses leave from its terminal at **Südbahnhof** (Map p44; ☎ 79685 52; 03, Arsenal strasse; ☯ 7am-7pm) heading to Belgrade (one-way/return €40/60, nine hours), to Budapest (one-way/return €26/40, 3½ hours), to Ljubljana (one-way/return €36/60, 15 hours 20 minutes), to Warsaw (one-way/return €34/62, 13½ hours) and to Zagreb (one-way/return €26/42, 4¾ hours).

Services to Bratislava (one-way/return €4/8, 1½ hours) leave from outside Euroline's **city office** (Map p44; ☎ 798 29 00; 03, Erdbergstrasse 202; ☽ 7am-7pm).

Euroline's services to Prague depart from 01, Rathausplatz 5 (Map p48; one-way/return €22/36, five hours. Call ☎ 93 000-34305 for details.

Car & Motorcycle

The Gürtel is an outer ring road that joins up with the A22 on the north bank of the Danube and the A23 southeast of town. All the main road routes intersect with this system, including the A1 from Linz and Salzburg, and the A2 from Graz.

Train

International trains leave from Westbahnhof (Map p44) or Südbahnhof (Map p44). Westbahnhof has trains to northern and Western Europe, and western Austria. Services to Salzburg leave roughly hourly; some go on to Munich and terminate in Paris (14½ hours total). To Zürich there are two trains during the day (€80, nine hours) and one night train (€80, plus charge for fold-down seat/couchette). Eight trains daily go to Budapest (€39, 3½ hours).

Südbahnhof has trains to Italy (inlcuding to Rome, via Venice and Florence), Slovakia, the Czech Republic, Hungary and Poland, and southern Austria. Five trains daily go to Bratislava (€17, 1½ hours) and four to Prague (€41, five hours), with two of those continuing to Berlin (10 hours in total).

Wien-Mitte Bahnhof handles local trains only, and Franz Josefs Bahnhof has local and regional trains.

For train information, call ☎ 05-17 17.

GETTING AROUND
To/From the Airport

It is 19km from the city centre to **Wien Schwechat airport** (VIE; ☎ 70 07-0; www.viennaairport.com). The **City Airport Train** (☎ 25 250; www.cityairporttrain.com) takes 15 minutes between Schwechat and Wien Mitte (one-way €9). The S-Bahn (S7) does the same journey (single €2.90, 25 minutes).

Buses run every 20 or 30 minutes, 24 hourly, from the airport (single €6). Services include to Südtiroler Platz, Südbahnhof and Westbahnhof, and another direct to Schwedenplatz in the city centre.

Taxis cost about €32. **C&K Airport Service** (☎ 44 444) charges €22 one-way for shared vans.

Bicycle

There's a system of **Vienna city bikes** (☎ 0810-500 500; www.citybikewein.at/; deposit €2, 1st hr free, 2nd hr €2, 3rd hr €3, per hr thereafter €2). You'll need a Maestro debit card, Austrian visa or city bike card to be able to use the payment machines. Check its website for locations.

The rather steeply priced **Pedal Power** (Map p44; ☎ 729 72 34; 02, Ausstellungsstrasse 3; hire per half-/full day €18/28) is the city's dominant operator, but the tourist office should be able to point to others near your hostel or hotel. *Tips für Radfahrer*, available from the tourist office, shows circular bike tours.

Car & Motorcycle

Parking is difficult in the city centre and the Viennese are impatient drivers. Blue parking zones allow a maximum stop of 1½ or two

---

HAPPY SNAPS

Want to give your holiday photos extra pizzazz? Want to be able to put on a slide show back home that won't send friends and family to sleep? Well, as Vienna is the home of Lomo – inventor of the ActionSampler – it's the perfect place to rediscover your love of photography.

Of course, Lomo cameras – plastic compacts that, for example, put nine identical images in one frame or that capture a sequence of four actions in one picture – are a worldwide cult. Although originally a Russian brand, they are now designed in Vienna, which also hosts the Lomographic World Archive at **Lomography Society International** (www.lomography.com). The **Lomo Shop** (Map p48; ☎ 521 890; Museums Quartier; ☽ 10am-7pm; ⓐ U-Bahn Volkstheater), next to the Kunsthalle, is eminently browsable, as you can just admire the artistic photos on its walls.

hours from 9am to 8pm (to 7pm in the Innere Stadt) on weekdays.

Parking vouchers (€0.40 per 30 minutes)
for these times can be purchased in *Tabak*
(tobacconist) shops and banks. The cheapest parking garage in the city centre is at
Museumsplatz.

Fiakers

Before hiring a *Fiaker* (horse-drawn carriage)
by the Stephansdom for a ride around the
city, it's worth asking yourself whether these
are pony traps or tourist traps. Sure, they're
kind of cute, but at around €65/95 for a 30-/
60-minute ride…well, you do the maths.

Public Transport

Vienna has a unified public transport network that encompasses trains, trams, buses,
and underground (U-Bahn) and suburban
(S-Bahn) trains. Routes are outlined on the
free tourist office map.

Before use, all advance-purchase tickets
must be validated at the entrance to U-Bahn
stations or on trams and buses. Tickets are
cheaper to buy from ticket machines in U-
Bahn stations or from *Tabak* shops, where
single tickets cost €1.50. On board, they
cost €2. Singles are valid for an hour, and
you may change lines on the same trip.

Daily passes *(Stunden-Netzkarte)* cost
€17 (valid 24 hours from first use); a three-
day pass costs €12 (valid 72 hours); and an
eight-day multiple-user pass *(8-Tage-Karte)*
costs €24 (validate the ticket once per day
per person). Weekly tickets (valid Monday
to Sunday) cost €12.50.

Children under six years travel free;
those under 16 travel free on Sunday, public
holidays and during Vienna school holidays (photo ID necessary). Senior citizens
should ask about discounts.

Ticket inspections are not very frequent,
but fare dodgers pay an on-the-spot fine of
€62. Austrian and European rail passes (see
p607) are valid on the S-Bahn only. Public
transport finishes around midnight, but
there's also a comprehensive night bus service, for which all train tickets are valid.

Taxi

Taxis are metered for city journeys and cost
€2 or €2.10 flag fall, plus from €1.09 per kilometre. There is at least another €2 surcharge
for phoning a radio taxi.

THE DANUBE VALLEY

Cruise along the country's most picturesque
stretch of the Danube River between Krems
an der Donau and Melk. The beautiful valley is filled with terraced vineyards, ruined
castles and medieval towns.

KREMS AN DER DONAU

☎ 02732 / pop 23,000

Quaint as it is, Krems is unlikely to be
more than a stopover on a boat or bike trip
through the Danube Valley. There's riverside camping at **ÖAMTC Camping Krems** (☎ 84
455; Wiedengasse 7; camp site per person/car/tent €5/4/4;
◷ Apr-Oct) and an HI **Jugendherberge** (☎ 83 452;
Ringstrasse 77; dm from €15; ◷ Apr-Oct) with basic
facilities. Otherwise try the atmospheric
Gästehaus Einzinger (☎ 82 316; fax 82 316-6; Steiner
Landstrasse 82, Krems-Stein; s/d €36/52), which has individually designed rooms around a leafy
sunken courtyard (watch out for the rather
precarious stairs).

The **tourist office** (☎ 82 676; www.tiscover.com/
krems; Kloster Und, Undstrasse 6; ◷ 9am-6pm Mon-Fri,
10am-noon & 1-5pm Sat, 10am-noon & 1-4pm Sun Apr-
Oct) can offer more accommodation details.

The *Schiffsstation* (boat station) is a 20-
minute walk west from the train station
along Donaulände. Between three and five
buses leave daily from outside the train
station to Melk (€8.50, one hour and five
minutes). Trains to Vienna (€10.50, one
hour, multiple daily) arrive at Franz Josefs
Bahnhof.

DÜRNSTEIN

☎ 02711 / pop 1000

This pretty town, on a curve in the Danube,
is not only noted for its beautiful buildings but also for the castle above the town,
which at one time imprisoned English king
Richard I (the Lion-Heart) in 1192. His
unscheduled stopover on the way home
from the Crusades came courtesy of Austrian archduke Leopold V, whom he had
insulted.

There's not much left of **Künringerburg castle** today. It's basically just a pile of rubble.
Still, it's worth snapping a picture and the
views from the top are rather breathtaking.

For more about Dürnstein, contact the
Rathaus (town hall; ☎ 219; www.duernstein.at; Hauptstrasse 25; ◷ 9am-5pm Mon-Fri).

AUSTRIA

MELK

☎ 02752 / pop 6500

The sheer size and majesty of Melk's imposing abbey-fortress, rising above the Danube and the small town, is stunning. Featured in the epic medieval German poem *Nibelungenlied* and Umberto Eco's best-selling novel *The Name of the Rose*, the impressive Benedictine monastery endures as a major Wachau landmark. It's an essential stop along the Danube Valley route, however, so be prepared to fight through loads of tourists to explore the place.

Orientation & Information

The train station is 300m from the town centre. Walk straight ahead from the train station along Bahnhofstrasse, turning right into Abt Karl Strasse if you're going to the hostel or continuing ahead for the town. The quickest way to the central Rathausplatz is through the small Bahngasse path (to the right of the cow's-head mural at the bottom of the hill), rather than veering left into Hauptplatz.

Turn right from Bahngasse into Rathausplatz and right again at the end, following the signs to the **tourist office** (☎ 52 307-410; www .tiscover.com/melk; Babenbergerstrasse 1; ☉ 9am-noon & 2-6pm Mon-Fri, 10am-2pm Sat Apr-Jun & Sep-Oct, 9am-7pm Mon-Sat, 10am-2pm Sun Jul & Aug, closed Nov-Mar).

Sights & Activities

On a hill overlooking the town is the ornate golden abbey **Stift Melk** (☎ 555 232; www .stiftmelk.at; adult/student €7/4.10; guided tours extra €1.80; ☉ 9am-6pm May-Sep, 9am-5pm Oct-Apr, guided tours only Nov-Mar). Home to monks since the 11th century, the current building was erected in the 18th century after a devastating fire. Consequently, it's an elaborate example of baroque architecture, most often lauded for its imposing marble hall and beautiful library, but just as unforgettable for the curved terrace connecting these two rooms. The **Abbey Museum** on the grounds outlines the history of the building and the church with its exhibition topic entitled 'The Path from Yesterday to Today – Melk in its Past and Present'. Various rooms using computer animation, sound and multimedia accurately narrate the 910-year-plus Benedictine monastic history of Melk.

Useful explanatory booklets (€4) for the whole building are available in various languages, or phone ahead if you want a tour in English, which works out cheaper.

Sleeping & Eating

Camping Melk (☎ 53 291; Kolomaniau 3; camp site per person/tent/car €4/3/2; ☉ Mar-Oct) Located on the west bank of the canal that joins the Danube, this camping ground is a tranquil spot. If you get hungry, there is an attached restaurant, where you'll also find reception.

Jugendherberge (☎ 52 681; Karl Strasse 42; dm €17; ☉ Mar-Oct, check-in 5-9pm) This HI hostel is modern and comfy, although it often plays host to large groups. Call ahead to see if it's full.

Gasthof Goldener Stern (☎ 52 214; Sterngasse 17; s/d from €22/44; P) When the friendly owners renovated recently, they decided to keep some cheaper 'student' rooms for budget travellers – they share bathrooms but are clean and excellent value. At the other end are the so-called 'romantic' rooms, all individually decorated. The place has a welcoming feel and a secluded location above the main square. It also has a fine restaurant.

Pasta e Pizza (☎ 53 686; Jakob Prandtauerstrasse 4; pizza €6-8) Tucked away from the main tourist trail, this eatery offers heaps of pizza and pasta dishes in cheerful environs.

Self-caterers should stock up at the **Spar supermarket** (Rathausplatz 9).

Getting There & Away

Boats leave from the canal by Pionierstrasse, 400m behind the monastery. Multiple daily trains to Vienna's Westbahnhof (€12, 75 to 90 minutes) are direct or via St Pölten.

LINZ

☎ 070 / pop 218,000

Austria's second-largest city is essentially industrial by nature and largely overlooked by tourists. It was discovered years ago that its small, old-town centre couldn't compete with Vienna or Salzburg. Linz's biggest claims to 'fame' were being Adolf Hitler's favourite town and having a type of cake – the Linzer torte – named after it. So the city carved a niche for itself by becoming technologically industrial as well. Its world-leading cybercentre, stunning first-rate contemporary art gallery and appealing attractions for kids prove that Linz certainly has the ability to please and interest.

Orientation

Most of the city is on the south bank of the Danube. The main square, Hauptplatz, is reached from the train station on tram 3. To walk here, turn right (northeast) out of the station forecourt, Bahnhofplatz, and continue straight ahead until you come to a park on the left. Turn left here into Landstrasse and continue for 10 minutes to get to Hauptplatz.

Information

Ars Electronica Center (☎ 72 720; www.aec.at; Hauptstrasse 2; ⊙ 9am-5pm Wed & Thu, 9am-9pm Fri, 10am-6pm Sat & Sun) Offers free Internet access.

Main Post Office (Bahnhofplatz 11-13; ⊙ 7am-9pm Mon-Fri, 7am-6pm Sat, 7am-1pm Sun)

Tourist Office (☎ 707 017-77; www.linz.at; Hauptplatz 1; ⊙ 8am-7pm Mon-Fri, 10am-7pm Sat & Sun May-Oct, 10am-6pm Nov-Apr) Has the Linz City Ticket (€20), which offers free public transport, sightseeing discounts and a free €10 meal.

Sights & Activities

Architecturally eye-catching and artistically impressive, the riverside **Lentos Kunstmuseum Linz** (☎ 7070 3600; www.lentos.at; Ernst Koref Promenade 1; admission €7; ⊙ 10am-6pm Wed-Mon, 10am-8pm Thu) is an important new addition to the Linz scene. It's built a little like an asymmetric tray table, with legs on either side. Behind its partially reflective glass façade lie works by artists such as Klimt, Schiele, Picasso, Kokoschka, Matisse, Haring and Warhol. Lit up at night, the building looks spectacular.

Across the Danube lies an older art and technology centre that will help you indulge your childhood superhero fantasies, without having to jump off the garage roof and graze your knee. At the **Ars Electronica Center** (☎ 72 72-0; www.aec.at; Hauptstrasse 2; adult/student €6/3; ⊙ 9am-5pm Wed & Thu, 9am-9pm Fri, 10am-6pm Sat & Sun) you'll be given a virtual-reality headset, then strapped to the ceiling and sent 'flying' over Linz and into the future. If you like this, you'll also love the world's only public 'cave', a virtual environment where you can travel through space and time.

A ride on the **Pöstlingbergbahn** (funicular railway; ☎ 7801 7002; one-way/return €2/3.20, children half-price; ⊙ 5.20am-8pm Mon-Sat, 11.40am-8pm Sun) offers great views and is bound to keep kids of all ages happy. It looks like a quaint street trolley from a movie and climbs slowly to the ornate twin-spired church and **children's**

grotto railway (☎ 3400 7506; www.linzag.at; adult/child €4/2; ⊙ 10am-5pm Oct-Apr, 10am-6pm May-Sep) atop the Pöst-lingberg hill. To reach the Pöstlingbergbahn take tram 3 to Bergbahnof Urfahr.

Festivals & Events

The **Ars Electronica Festival** (☎ 72 72-0; www.aec.at) in early September showcases cyberart, computer music, and other marriages of technology and art. This leads into the **Brucknerfest** (Bruckner Festival; ☎ 775 230; www.brucknerhaus.at; Brucknerhaus Kasse, Untere Donaulände, A-4010 Linz), which pays homage to native son Anton Bruckner with a month of classical music between mid-September and mid-October. For this, you should book early.

In July there's the **Pflasterspektakel street performers' festival**.

Sleeping

The tourist office offers a free accommodation booking service for visitors, but only face-to-face and not over the phone.

Jugendgästehaus (☎ 664 434; www.oejhv.or.at; Stanglhofweg 3; dm/s/d €18.50/28.50/41) Modern and comfortable, even if it's a little way from the centre of town; take bus 17, 19 or 27. Half- and full-board options are available.

Wilder Mann (☎ 656 078; wilder-mann@aon.at; Goethestrasse 14; s/d/tr from €36/60/77, with shared bathroom from €26/44/53) Despite first impressions at this boarding house–style place, the rooms are reasonably comfy and the bathrooms clean. Try to avoid the top floor, where frosted-glass door panels let in hall light.

Goldener Anker (☎ 771 088; Hofgasse 5; s/d from €42/70) A tastefully decorated family-run *Gasthof* (guesthouse) inside Linz's oldest pub, rooms are comfortable and conveniently located.

Novotel Linz (☎ 347 28 10; www.accorhotels.com /novotel_linz.htm; Wankmüllerhofstrasse 37; s/d €69/84; ⓟ ⊠ ⊠ ⊠ ⊠) Packed with all sorts of amenities, including a sauna and tennis courts, this place is popular with business travellers as well families on weekends or holidays. Rooms are modern and efficient, and there's a playground for the kids.

Hotel Wolfinger (☎ 773 291-0; www.austria-classic -hotels.at/wolfinger; Hauptplatz 19; s/d €83/115, with shared bathroom from €44/65; ⊠) A central option, this hotel is in a wonderful former cloister renovated in baroque style and with unique flair. It has a very limited number of cheaper rooms.

Eating & Drinking

Café Traximayr (☎ 773 353; Promenadestrasse 16; snacks from €5; ☻ Mon-Sat) An elegant coffee house, with only a few snooker tables breaking up the formal environment of white walls, marble, mirrors and chandeliers. Try the Linzer torte – this heavy, nutty-tasting sponge filled with strawberry jam isn't on the menu but it is on the cake trolley, so just ask.

p'aa (☎ 776 461; Altstadt 28; mains €8-12; ☻ 11am-midnight Mon-Sat) Serving mainly vegan cuisine in an elegant interior, the menu is an eclectic mix of Tibetan, Indian and Mexican. Sit on the cobblestones outside or inside under low arched ceilings.

Stiegelbräu zum Klosterhof (Landstrasse 30; mains €11-17.50) A huge beer garden and a fine gastronomic reputation, it's as popular for business lunches as it is for tourist outings.

Sky Loft Media Bar (Ars Electronica Center, Hauptstrasse 2; ☻ 9am-5pm Wed & Thu, 9am-2am Fri & Sat) This glassed-in bar is a great place for a beer or cocktail overlooking the Danube and the Lentos museum.

Getting There & Around

Low-cost Ryanair flies in daily from London Stansted to **Linz airport** (LNZ; ☎ 600-0; www .flughafen-linz.at), which provides a shuttle bus (€2.20, 20 minutes) to the main train station.

Linz is halfway between Salzburg and Vienna on the main road and rail routes. Trains to Salzburg (€17.70) and Vienna (€23.50) take between 1¼ and two hours. Trains leave approximately hourly.

City transport tickets are bought before you board: €0.70 per journey or €3 for a day card. Some of the bus services stop early in the evening. The suburban **Lilo train station** (☎ 654 376; Coulinstrasse 30) offers bike hire for €7 per day.

THE SOUTH

Austria's two main southern states, Styria (Steiermark) and Carinthia (Kärnten), often feel worlds apart from the rest of the country, both in climate and attitude. Elements of Italian, Slovenian and Hungarian culture are present here, and residents have historical connections with each of those countries. Styria is a blissful amalgamation of genteel architecture, rolling green hills, vine-covered slopes and soaring mountains. Its capital, Graz, is one of Austria's most attractive cities (with some of the highest standards of living in Europe).

A jet-setting, fashion-conscious crowd heads to sun-drenched Carinthia for summer holidays. The region (right on the border with Italy) exudes an atmosphere that's as close to Mediterranean as this staunch country gets.

GRAZ

☎ 0316 / pop 250,000

European Capital of Culture in 2003 and recently included in the list of world cultural heritage sites, this provincial capital of Styria offers a little something for everyone. Funky and laid-back at the same time, the futuristic, bluish-bloblike Kunsthaus Graz will make you think that aliens have landed nearby. There's so much to see and do in Graz that it's fair to say your hotel room will not enjoy much use. Experience the unique blend of Mediterranean and medieval atmosphere of the Old Town and see why it leaves such an indelible impression on other travellers.

Orientation

Austria's second-largest city is dominated by its *Schlossberg* (castle hill) looming above the city centre. The River Mur runs in a north–south path in front (west) of the hill, separating the city centre from the main train station (Hauptbahnhof). Trams 3, 6 and 14 all run from the train station to the central Hauptplatz. Several streets radiate from this square, including café-lined Sporgasse and the primary pedestrian thoroughfare, Herrengasse. This thoroughfare leads to Jakominiplatz, which is a major transport hub.

Information

Graz Tourismus (☎ 80 75-0; www.graztourismus.at; Herrengasse 16; ☻ 9am-6pm Mon-Sat, 10am-6pm Sun)

Main Post Office (Neutorgasse 46; ☻ 7.30am-8pm Mon-Fri, 8am-noon Sat)

Medien.kunstbar (Kunsthaus Graz, Lendkai 1; ☻ 10am-6pm Tue-Sun, 10am-8pm Thu) Offers free Internet access.

Speednet-café (Hauptbahnhof Europaplatz 4; per hr around €6; ☻ 8am-10pm Mon-Sat, 9am-9pm Sun) Offers Internet access.

Tourist Information Counter (☎ 80 75-21; Hauptbahnhof; ☻ 8.30am-1pm & 2-5.30pm Mon-Wed & Fri, to 6.30pm Thu)

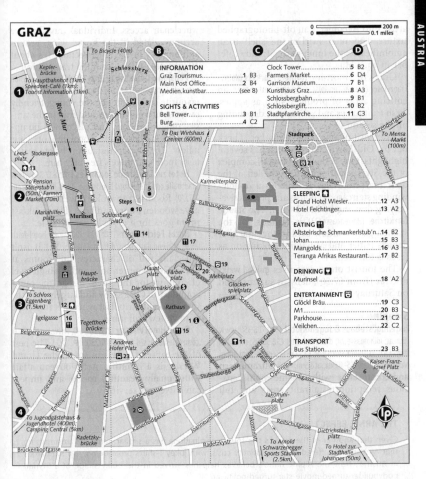

GRAZ

INFORMATION	
Graz Tourismus	1 B3
Main Post Office	2 B4
Medien.kunstbar	(see 8)

SIGHTS & ACTIVITIES

Bell Tower	3 B1
Burg	4 C2
Clock Tower	5 B2
Farmers Market	6 D4
Garrison Museum	7 B1
Kunsthaus Graz	8 A3
Schlossbergbahn	9 B1
Schlossberglift	10 B2
Stadtpfarrkirche	11 C3

SLEEPING

Grand Hotel Wiesler	12 A3
Hotel Feichtinger	13 A2

EATING

Altsteirische Schmankerlstub'n	14 B2
Iohan	15 B3
Mangolds	16 A3
Teranga Afrikas Restaurant	17 B2

DRINKING

Murinsel	18 A2

ENTERTAINMENT

Glöckl Bräu	19 C3
M1	20 B3
Parkhouse	21 C2
Veilchen	22 C2

TRANSPORT

Bus Station	23 B3

Sights & Activities

Here you'll find a plethora of museums, galleries, grandiose architecture, churches and unusual surprises. Most visitors head first for the **Schlossberg** to get an overview of the city and explore what remains of its fortress. This includes the medieval **clock tower**, plus a **bell tower**, **bastion** and **garrison museum** (827 348; adult/concession €1.50/0.85; 10am-5pm Tue-Sun Apr-Oct). There are three main ways to ascend: the glass **Schlossberglift**, hewn through the hill; the **Schlossbergbahn** funicular railway (both requiring a Zone 1 transport ticket, €1.70); and the 260 steps near the lift (free).

From this vantage point, you can't help but notice the bubble-shaped **Kunsthaus Graz** (8017 9200; www.kunsthausgraz.at; Lendkai 1; adult/

senior/student €6/4.50/2.50; 10am-6pm Tue, Wed & Fri-Sun, 10am-8pm Thu). Notice anything extraterrestrial? This creation by UK architects Colin Fournier and Peter Cook is referred to as the 'friendly alien'. It has also been compared to a mutant bladder and a spaceship, but there's general agreement that it's one of Europe's leading modern buildings. Whatever the temporary exhibitions – and these are often very good – it's the structure that's the star.

Likewise, the **Murinsel** (24hr), an artificial island in the River Mur that's connected to both banks, north of the Kunsthaus and Hauptbrücke (main bridge). Designed in the form of an open seashell, the glass, concrete and steel construction, by New York

AUSTRIA

artist Vito Acconic, is an oft-photographed fixture. The outer swirl of the 'shell' is an amphitheatre; the inner part, a trendy café/bar in aqua blue.

Graz's two morning **farmers markets** (Kaiser-Franz-Josef Platz & Lendplatz; ☽ Mon-Sat) offer an enticing array of produce, such as apples, fresh fruit juices and schnapps – depending on the season.

After visiting one of these markets, check out the Old Town centre, which has several highlights. One is the **Burg** (Hofgasse) complex of the Styrian parliament; to the left of the door marked 'Stiege III' there's a double-winding staircase as good as any perspective-defying drawing by MC Escher. The **Stadtpfarrkirche** (Herrengasse 23) is famous for the stained-glass window behind the altar that depicts Hitler and Mussolini looking on as Jesus is tortured.

The tourist office organises **guided walks** of Graz (from €7.50), daily in summer and on Saturday in winter.

Sleeping

Jugendgästehaus & Jugendhotel (☎ 708 350; www .jfgh.at; Idlhofgasse 74; dm/d in hostel €18.50/55, r in hotel from €47, 1st-night surcharge €3; ☽ reception 7am-10pm Mon-Fri, 7-10am & 5-10pm Sat & Sun; **P**) Ultramodern and comfortable, with en suite rooms, spacious reception/restaurant areas and full wheelchair access. Individual travellers are accommodated in the hostel wing, groups and families in the hotel section. It's about 10 minutes on foot from the train station.

Pension Steierstub'n (☎ 716 855; www.pension -graz.at; Lendplatz 8; s/d/tr from €39/70/100; **P**) A favourite choice of ours, the young, friendly owners put fresh flowers and fruit in the simple, modern rooms, and place local pumpkinseeds, rather than chocolates, on your pillow. The Styrian restaurant below serves tasty food, and there's free bike hire.

Hotel zur Stadthalle Johannes (☎ 837 766; www .stadthalle.co.at; Münzgrabenstrasse 48 & 87; s/d from €47/70) Rooms at this older, well-kept hotel have wooden floors and beds. The breakfast room goes for a more Italianate style.

Hotel Feichtinger (☎ 724 100; www.hotel-feich tinger.at; Lendplatz 1A; s/d from €50/94; ✗) It isn't especially full of character, but rooms at one of Graz's newer hotels offer a high level of comfort for the price. It's on the outer boundary of Graz's tiny and largely inoffensive red-light strip, but when it's this close to town few will mind.

Grand Hotel Wiesler (☎ 70 66-0; www.hotelwiesler .com; Grieskai 4; s/d from €170/230; **P** ✗) The best of the top-end hotels in town, the Grand Wiesler is a beautiful Art Nouveau affair with equally beautiful rooms and impeccable five-star service.

THE ARNIE EFFECT

Given that another of the world's top tourist destinations has a similar name, it's unsurprising that Austria has suffered from an identity crisis, with jokey T-shirts proclaiming, 'No Kangaroos in Austria'. Now the Alpine nation believes help has arrived in the bulky shape of a Styrian bodybuilder-turned-movie-star-turned-politician.

Arnold Schwarzenegger, locals hope optimistically, will help even the most geographically ignorant American schoolchild locate their tiny country on a map.

When the Terminator became the Californian 'Gubernator' in late 2003, even left-wing Austrians put aside their reservations for the evening. Bar-goers in Graz, just a few miles from Schwarzenegger's boyhood home of Thal, erupted in cheers.

'Mozart is no longer the world's most famous Austrian', Dieter Hardt-Stremayr of the Graz tourist office told AFP.

While Californians have since been welcomed in Austria like long-lost members of the family, there's little Arnie memorabilia for them, or anyone else, to see. Two Russian artists have been trying to erect a huge Terminator statue in Graz's Stadtpark. However, they've met with resistance because, ultimately, Arnie is a controversial figure in Austria.

In fact, in 2005 it appeared the Governor was actually trying to sever ties with his hometown. A museum exhibiting training equipment used by the former bodybuilder closed in 2005 due to money woes. Museum officials say they reached out to Schwarzenegger for financial help to save it but were ignored. Now all that marks his presence in Graz is the Arnold Schwarzenegger Sports Stadium. The stadium is to the southwest of the city centre; take tram 4.

Eating

With green, leafy salads dressed in delicious pumpkinseed oil, lots of polenta, fish
specialities and *Pfand'l* (pan-grilled) dishes,
Styrian cuisine feels lighter and healthier
than most regional Austrian cooking.

Mangolds (Griesgasse 11; salad per 100g from €1.05;
⊙ 11am-8pm Mon-Fri, 11am-4pm Sat) An ultra-
healthy and reasonably cheap vegetarian
buffet, with loads of salads to choose from.

Mensa Markt (Schubertstrasse 2-4; menus €4-4.50)
This spot by the university has a range of
inexpensive takeaway.

Altsteirische Schmankerlstub'n (☎ 823 211; Sackstrasse 10; mains €7.50-16.50) Hidden in a passageway off Sackstrasse, this rustic restaurant
serves Styrian staples, such as *Bauernschmaus*
(roast pork with blood sausage, sauerkraut
and dumplings), *Ochsenfetzen* (beef strips
with sour cream and roast potatoes) and
Vogerlsalat (green salad) with roast potatoes,
egg, tomatoes and pumpkinseed oil.

Iohan (☎ 821 312; Landhausgasse 1; mains from €18;
⊙ dinner Tue-Sat) Locals come here for a treat.
In the former cold-storage room of the city
hall, it has formal white tablecloths, draped
white canvas chairs and a cool, somewhat
more relaxed, bar. The select menu might
include saddle of lamb with black lentils or
veal with polenta and mushrooms.

Drinking & Entertainment

Graz, like Vienna, has a 'bar zone' known
as the Bermudadreieck. It's located between
Sporgasse, Färbergasse and Stempfergasse,
where you will find venues ranging from the
humble **Glöckl Bräu** (☎ 814 781; Glockenspielplatz 2-
3) to the 3rd-floor **M1** (☎ 811 233; Färbergasse 1),
favoured by the beautiful people. There are
other clusters of hip bars at the top of Sporgasse and behind the Kunsthaus Graz.

Murinsel (☎ 818 669; ⊙ café/bar 9am-11pm Sun-
Wed, 9am-2am Thu-Sat) You'll never again drink
anywhere quite like the Murinsel, so at
least start the evening in this shimmering,
fluorescent-lit platform in the middle of the
river. There are DJs on some evenings.

Parkhouse (☎ 827 434; Stadtpark 2) Join the
crowd at this atmospheric and friendly
place in the city park if you're looking to
party minus any type of pretentious vibe.

Veilchen (☎ 8277 3416; Stadtpark 1) Near the
Parkhouse, this can be an interesting venue.
It's an art gallery and community centre
that usually has DJs on Saturday.

Getting There & Away

Ryanair has flights daily from London Stansted to **Graz airport** (GRZ; ☎ 29 02-0; www.flughafen
-graz.at, in German). Direct Intercity (IC) trains
to Vienna's Südbahnhof depart every two
hours (€30, 2¾ hours). Trains depart every
two hours to Salzburg (€40, 4¼ hours), either direct or changing at Bischofshofen.
Two daily, direct trains depart for Ljubljana
(€38, four hours), and every hour or two to
Budapest (€63, 6½ hours) via Szentgotthard
and Szombathely. Trains to Klagenfurt (€30,
three hours) go via Bruck an der Mur. The
A2 autobahn from Vienna to Klagenfurt
passes a few kilometres from the city.

Getting Around

Public transport tickets cover trams, buses,
the Schlossbergbahn and the Schlossberglift.
Tickets cost €1.60 each. The 24-hour/weekly
passes cost €3.20/7.50. Buses 600, 630 and
631 connect the airport with the train station, Hauptplatz or Jakominiplatz (€1.60);
the same journey by taxi costs about €15.

You can hire a bike from **Bicycle** (☎ 821 357-
0; Körösistrasse 5) from €7.50/42 per day/week.

KLAGENFURT

☎ 0463 / pop 87,000
In a salacious location on the water, this
sunny provincial capital makes a handy base
for exploring the Wörthersee's lakeside villages and elegant medieval towns to the

AUSTRIA

north. The town is not hugely interesting, but gets buzzing in summer when Austrians on weekend holiday flock here.

Orientation

The heart of the city is Neuer Platz, which is 1km north of the main train station. Walk straight down Bahnhofstrasse and turn left into Paradiesergasse to get there, or take bus 40, 41 or 42 to Heiligengeistplatz, just around the corner from Neuer Platz.

Information

Gates Cafebar (Waagplatz 7; per 10 min €1; 9am-1am Mon-Fri, 7pm-1am Sat & Sun) Offers Internet access.

Main Post Office (Dr Hermann Gasse 4; 7.30am-6pm Mon-Fri, 8-11am Sat)

Tourist Office (537 22 23; www.info.klagenfurt.at; Rathaus, Neuer Platz; 8am-8pm Mon-Fri, 10am-5pm Sat & Sun May-Sep, 8am-6.30pm Mon-Fri, 10am-3pm Sat & Sun Oct-Apr)

Sights & Activities

The **Wörthersee**, 4km west of the city centre, is one of the region's warmer lakes, thanks to subterranean thermal springs: the average water temperature between June and September is 21°C (69°F). Events from go-kart rallies to avant-garde festivals of tattoo and body painting ensure you'll never be left without something to see. The 50km **cycle path** around the lake is one of the 'Top 10' in Austria. There is a *Fahrad Verleih* (Hire a Bike) scheme in summer; hire a standard bicycle at one of several outlets around the lake and return it at any other outlet (five hours/24 hours/one week €5/9/35). Mountain and road bikes are available, and you can also arrange to return the bike to the same location, although it costs a few euros more.

Also near the lake, Europa Park has various attractions, including the theme park **Minimundus** (21 194-0; Villacher Strasse 241; adult/student €10/4.50; Apr-Oct), which displays more than 150 models of famous international buildings on a 1:25 scale.

Sleeping & Eating

When you check into your accommodation in Klagenfurt, ask for a copy of your *Gästekarte* (guest card), which entitles you to a range of discounts on local attractions and public transport.

Jugendherberge (230 020; jgh.klagenfurt@oejhv .or.at; Neckheimgasse 6; dm €17.50, dm as d €42; reception 7-11am & 5-10pm;) Modern and clean, this HI hostel is near the university and Europa Park. Take bus 12 to get there. Book ahead, as it's often full with school groups.

Hotel Liebetegger (56 935; www.liebetegger.com, in German; Völkermarkterstrasse 8; s/d from €28/60) The décor is modern, with interesting touches like cast-iron door handles and Gustav Klimt prints on the walls, making this three-star hotel quite a good deal. There's an inviting café/bar (mains €7 to €10) attached, and breakfast is available for an extra €7.50.

Hotel Geyer (57 886; www.hotelgeyer.com; Priesterhausgasse; s/d €55/95;) Everyone's favourite Klagenfurt hotel, the public areas are quite funky with loads of modern art on the walls. Rooms were recently renovated, and although they're compact, they're still comfortable. A generous breakfast buffet is included.

Zum Augustin (513 992; Pfarrhofgasse 2; mains €7-16) A smoky brewery that makes its own beer – it has eight different ales on tap. It is popular with the after-work crowd, serves a decent range of regional food and has a pleasant cobblestone patio.

Getting There & Around

Flights are available with Ryanair from London daily, with a bus running to the city centre. Trains to Graz (€28, five hours) go via Bruck an der Mur and depart every two hours. Trains to western Austria, Italy and Germany go via Villach, 40 minutes away.

Bus drivers sell single tickets (€1.50), while a strip of 10 costs €12 from ticket machines. Daily/weekly passes cost €3.30/13. For the Europa Park vicinity, take bus 10, 11, 12, 20, 21 or 22 from Heiligengeistplatz in the city centre. To the airport, take bus 42 or a taxi (about €16). Bikes can be hired from **Zweirad Impulse** (516 310; 24hr hire adult/child €10/7).

SALZBURG

0662 / pop 145,000

The joke 'if it's baroque, don't fix it' would make a perfect maxim for Salzburg; the tranquil Old Town burrowed in below steep hills looks as much as it did when Mozart lived here 250 years ago. Second only to Vienna in numbers of visitors, ornate 17th-century buildings still shadow the narrow, cobbled streets, while gorgeous manicured grounds surround the baroque Schloss Mirabell.

By night, the medieval Hohensalzburg fortress hovers in an arc of lights above the city. By day, the warren of courtyards, fountains and churches below is fully revealed. And visitors still tour film locations used for *The Sound of Music* in and around Salzburg, Austria's charming capital of kitsch.

ORIENTATION

The pedestrianised Old Town is on the south bank of the River Salzach, wedged between the river and Mönchsberg behind it. Many attractions and the shopping street of Getreidegasse are here. On the north bank is Mozart's Wohnhaus and Schloss Mirabell, as well as the new city centre, with most of the cheaper hotels. Buses 1, 6, 51 and 55 will take you from the main train station (Hauptbahnhof) to the city centre. To walk, turn left out of the train station into Rainerstrasse and follow it (taking the second, not the first tunnel under the railway) to Mirabellplatz.

INFORMATION

Tourist offices and hotels sell the Salzburg Card (€21/28/34 for 24/48/72 hours), which provides free museum entry and public transport, and offers various reductions. Students get a 10% discount. The tourist office's commission for hotel reservations is €2.20 or €4 for three or more people.

Amex (☎ 80 80; Mozartplatz 5; ☺ 9am-5.30pm Mon-Fri, 9am-noon Sat) For travel agency information.

Cybar (☎ 844 822; Mozartplatz 5; per 10 min €1.50-1.80; ☺ 9am-10pm) Offers Internet access.

Main Post Office (Residenzplatz 9; ☺ 7am-7pm Mon-Fri, 8-10am Sat)

Main Tourist Office (☎ information 88-987 330, hotel reservations 88-987 314; www.salzburg.info; Mozartplatz 5; ☺ 9am-6pm May-Jun & Sep-Oct, 9am-7pm Dec, Jul & Aug, 9am-6pm Mon-Sat Nov & Jan-Apr)

Piterfun (Ferdinand-Porsche-Strasse 7; per 10 min €1.50-1.80; ☺ 10am-10pm) Offers Internet access.

St Johanns-Spital (☎ 44 82-0; Müllner Hauptstrasse 48) For medical treatment.

STA Travel (☎ 458 733; Fanny-von-Lehnert Strasse 1; ☺ Mon-Fri)

Tourist Information Counter (Platform 2A, Hauptbahnhof; ☺ 9.15am-8pm) Opening hours vary.

Train Station Post Office (Hauptbahnhof; ☺ 7am-8.30pm Mon-Fri, 8am-2pm Sat, 1-6pm Sun)

SIGHTS & ACTIVITIES

A Unesco World Heritage site, Salzburg's Old Town centre is equally entrancing whether viewed from ground level or from the hills above.

Residenzplatz is a good starting point for a wander. The **Dom** (cathedral), just to the south, is worth checking out for the three bronze doors symbolising faith, hope and charity. From here, head west along Franziskanergasse and turn left into a courtyard for **St Peterskirche**, an abbey dating from AD 847. Among lovingly tended graves in the abbey's grounds you'll find the entrance to the **Katakomben** (catacombs; adult/student €1/0.70; ☺ 10.30am-5pm summer, 10.30am-3.30pm winter). The western end of Franziskanergasse opens out into Max Reinhardt Platz, where you'll see the back of Fisher von Erlach's **Universitätskirche** (Universitätsplatz), an outstanding example of baroque architecture. The **Stift Nonnberg** (Nonnberg Abbey), where *The Sound of Music* first encounters Maria, is back in the other direction, to the east of the Festung Hohensalzburg.

Festung Hohensalzburg

This **castle fortress** (☎ 842 430-11; www.salzburg burgen.at; Mönchsberg 34; admission €4, for interior & audioguide €7.50; ☺ 9am-6pm 15 Mar-14 Jun, 9am-7pm 15 Jun-14 Sep, 9am-5pm 15 Sep-14 Mar), built in 1077, was home to many archbishop-princes (who ruled Salzburg from 798). Inside are the impressively ornate staterooms, torture chambers and two museums.

It takes 15 minutes to walk up the hill to the fortress, or you can catch the funicular **Festungsbahn** (☎ 849 750; Festungsgasse 4; adult/concession one-way incl admission to fortress grounds €5.60/5; ☺ 9am-9pm May-Sep, 9am-5pm Oct-Apr).

Schloss Mirabell

The formal gardens of **Schloss Mirabell** (☺ dawn-dusk), with their tulips, crocuses and Greek statues, are the main attraction at this palace built by the archbishop-prince Wolf Dietrich for his mistress in 1606. The view from the western end (looking east towards the fortress) is one of Salzburg's most attractive. The gardens were featured in *The Sound of Music*, and are now popular with wedding parties. Concerts are often held in the palace, and there are sometimes open-air performances in the garden. Parts of the garden are off limits in winter.

Museums

Although Mozart is now a major tourist drawcard, the man himself found Salzburg

SALZBURG

0 ____ 300 m
0 ____ 0.2 miles

INFORMATION
Amex..............................(see 2)
Cybar.............................(see 2)
Main Post Office................1 C5
Main Tourist Office.............2 C5
Piterfun........................3 B2
STA Travel......................4 B1
Tourist Information Counter.....5 B2
Train Station Post Office........6 C1

SIGHTS & ACTIVITIES
Dom (Cathedral)..................7 C5
Festung Hohensalzburg............8 C6
Festungsbahn.....................9 C6
Fraülein Maria's Bicycle
  Tours..........................10 B4
Kapuzinerkloster Lookout........11 C4
Mausoleum of Wolf Dietrich......12 C4
Mönchsberg Lift.................13 A5
Mozart Sound & Film
  Museum.......................(see 15)
Mozart's Geberthaus.............14 B5
Mozart's Wohnhaus...............15 B4
Museum der Moderne
  Rupertinum....................16 A5
Panorama Tours..................17 B3
Residenz........................18 B5
St Peterskirche &
  Katakomben....................19 B6
Salzburg Sightseeing Tours......20 B4
Schloss Mirabell................21 B4
Stift Nonnberg..................22 C6
Universitätskirche..............23 B5

SLEEPING 🛏
Blaue Gans......................24 B5
Centro Hotel....................25 B3
Hotel Wolf......................26 C5
Institut St Sebastian...........27 C4
International Youth Hotel........28 C3
Jugendgästehaus.................29 D6
Naturfreundehaus................30 A5
Pension Bergland................31 D3
Pension Elisabeth...............32 D1

EATING 🍴
Ahrlich.........................33 C4
Bio Bistro Spicy Spices.........34 C4
Café Konditorei Fürst...........35 C5
Eurospar Supermarket............36 B1
Fruit & Vegetable Market........37 B4
Gablerbräu......................38 B4
Stadtalm......................(see 30)
Stiftskeller St Peter...........39 B6
Wilder Mann.....................40 B5
Zum Mohren......................41 C5

DRINKING 🍷
Augustiner Bräustübl............42 A3
Bar Flip........................43 A4
Humboldt........................44 A5
Republic........................45 A5

TRANSPORT
Buses to Kitzbühel..............46 B1
Buses to Salzkammergut..........47 B2
Salzach Insel...................48 B4
Top Bike........................49 B5
Top Bike........................50 B2

stifling and couldn't wait to leave. Consequently, Mozart's **Geburtshaus** (birthplace; ☎ 844 313; Getreidegasse 9; adult €5.50; ☿ 9am-6pm Sep-Jun, 9am-7pm Jul & Aug, last entry 30 min before closing) and his **Wohnhaus** (residence; ☎ 874 227-40; Makartplatz 8; adult €5.50; ☿ 9am-6pm Sep-Jun, 9am-7pm Jul & Aug, last entry 30 min before closing) cover only his early years as a prodigy and young adult, until he left town in 1780 at 24 years of age. A combined ticket to both houses is €9 (students and seniors €7). The Wohnhaus is more extensive, and houses the **Mozart Sound and Film Museum** (admission free).

In the **Residenz** (☎ 80 42-2690; www.salzburg -burgen.at; Residenzplatz 1; adult/student €7.30/5.50; ☿ 10am-5pm, gallery closed Wed Oct-Mar) you can visit the archbishops' baroque staterooms and a gallery housing fine 16th- and 17th-century Dutch and Flemish paintings.

The **Museum der Moderne Rupertinum** (☎ 8042 2541; www.museumdermoderne.at; Mönchsberg; prices vary; ☿ 10am-6pm Tue-Sun, 10am-9pm Wed) adds a contemporary touch to historic Salzburg. Ask at the tourist office about other museums.

Mausoleum of Wolf Dietrich

In the **graveyard** (Linzer Gasse; ☿ 9am-7pm Apr-Oct, 9am-4pm Nov-Mar) of the 16th-century St Sebastian's Church sits Wolf Dietrich's not-so-humble **memorial** to himself. Both Mozart's father and his widow are also buried in the graveyard.

TOURS
Sound of Music Tours

Although these are the tours that interest the greatest number of visitors, how much fun you have depends on whether your fellow passengers enter into the necessary kitsch, tongue-in-cheek attitude. If you can, try to get together your own little posse. Otherwise, hope to find yourself among manic Julie Andrews impersonators flouncing in the fields, screeching 'the hills are alive' or some such thing.

Tours take three to four hours and usually spend most time in neighbouring Salzkammergut, rather than Salzburg itself. Following are some recommended operators:

Fraülein Maria's Bicycle Tours (☎ 0646-342 62 97; Makartplatz; adult €16; ☿ 9.30am mid-May–Sep) At the entrance to Mirabellgarten, behind Hotel Bristol.

Panorama Tours (☎ 874 029; Mirabellplatz; adult €33; ☿ 9.30am & 2pm)

Salzburg Sightseeing Tours (☎ 881 616; Mirabellplatz; adult €33; ☿ 9.30am & 2pm)

River Tours

Boats operated by **Salzburg Schiffahrt** (☎ 825 769-12) cruise along the Salzach (adult/child €11/7, 40 to 50 minutes) leaving half-hourly to hourly from 10am to 6pm May to September. Others go to Schloss Hellbrunn (adult/child €14/10), departing at 12.45pm from September to June, and 9.30am and 12.45pm from July to August. The company also has atmospheric tours by night in late July and August.

Boats leave from the Salzach Insel, on the city side of the Makart bridge.

FESTIVALS & EVENTS

Austria's most renowned classical music festival, the **Salzburg Festival** (www.salzburgfestival .at), attracts international stars from late July to the end of August. Book on its website before January, or ask the **Festspielhäuser ticket office** (☎ 80 45; Herbert von Karajan Platz 11; ☿ 9.30am-6.30pm during the festival, 9.30am-3pm during the few weeks before) about cancellations during the festival.

SLEEPING

Ask for the tourist office's hotel brochure, which gives prices for hotels, *pensions,* hostels and camping grounds. Accommodation is at a premium during festivals.

Budget

Naturfreundehaus (☎ 841 729; Mönchsberg 19; dm €13.50; ☿ mid-Apr–mid-Oct) The rooms are little more than glorified shoeboxes, but the hostel is atop the Mönchsberg hill and you soon forget the cramped conditions when you wake up to such amazing views. There is a 1am curfew. To get here, take the Mönchsberg lift (€2.60 return) from Anton Neumayr Platz or the stairs from Toscaninihof, behind the Festival Halls.

International Youth Hotel (YoHo; ☎ 879 649; www .yoho.at; Paracelsusstrasse 9; dm with shared bathroom from €16, s/d/tr €28/21/19; **P**) If you're hankering after a lively bar scene with cheap beer, friendly staff and regular events, including daily screenings of *The Sound of Music*, this hostel is for you. Book ahead on its website – phone reservations are accepted only one day in advance for its spartan, but spotless, rooms. Reception doesn't close during the day.

Jugendgästehaus (☎ 842 670-0; jgh.salzburg@jgh .at; Josef Preis Allee 18; dm from €18, d €36, with shared bathroom from €14, 1st-night surcharge €2.50; check-in from 11am, access to rooms from 1pm; P) Lots of Austrians and families stay at this comfy HI hostel that is also popular with backpackers. The eight-bed dorms feel a bit like boarding school, but the en suite four-bed dorms and doubles on the floors above could belong to a nice budget hotel.

Institut St Sebastian (☎ 871 386; www.st-sebastian -salzburg.at; Linzer Gasse 41; dm €18, s/d €36/57, with shared bathroom €31/51) Just a few minutes walk from the bridge, through the gate marked 'Feuerwache Bruderhof', on Linzer Gasse, Institut St Sebastian is closer to the action than any other Salzburg hostel-style accommodation. In fact, when the church bells ring next door, you might find this student abode is almost too close to the action. Don't expect much of a social atmosphere, as there is no bar or comfortable lounge; however, there is a roof terrace and kitchen.

Haus Lindner (☎ 456 681; info@haus-lindner.at; Panoramaweg 5; d/tr €30/45) The largest and one of the most popular private-room options in the city, with comfortable rooms and a homy atmosphere. Breakfast is provided, but there are kitchen facilities, too.

Try the following camping recommendations:

Camping Kasern (☎ /fax 450 576; campingkasern@aon .at; Carl Zuckmayer Strasse 4; camp site per adult/car/tent €4.50/3/3; Apr-Oct) Just north of the A1 Nord exit.

Camping Nord-Sam (☎ 660 494; www.camping-nord -sam.com; Samstrasse 22A; camp site per adult/car & tent €5.50/8; Easter & May-Sep) Slightly closer to the city.

Midrange & Top End

Salzburg has a fair number of options in these price brackets.

Pension Elisabeth (☎ 871 664; Vogelweiderstrasse 52; s/d from €44/66, with shared bathroom from €35/42; P) A small, friendly budget hotel; bright rooms come with white duvets, coloured upholstered chairs and wooden floors. It's near the Breitenfelderstrasse stop of bus 15, which heads into the city every 15 minutes. Beware there can be price increases during the high season for single-night stays.

Pension Bergland (☎ 872 318; www.berglandhotel .at; Rupertgasse 15; s/d/tr/f €56/86/102/120; P) Austrian rustic collides with '70s retro in the folksy rooms at this friendly, family-run *pension*. It's about a 15-minute walk from the Old Town.

Centro Hotel (☎ 882 221; www.centro-hotel.com; Auerspergstrasse 24; s/d €68/104; P) Slightly minimalist décor, the well-proportioned rooms have wooden furniture offset with touches of green. Ask for one with a private balcony.

Hotel Wolf (☎ 843 453-0; www.hotelwolf.com; Kaigasse 7; s/d from €70/100) With its neat living room set off from the main entrance hall, this family-owned hotel immediately feels like a real home. Austrian country-style bedrooms have been reconstructed in this 500-year-old abode, which has none of the mustiness of most buildings its age.

Blaue Gans (☎ 842 491-0; www.blauegans.at; Getreidegasse 41-43; s/d from €120/170) One of Salzburg's oldest inns converted into a trendy 'art hotel', it combines modern luxury with its historic setting.

EATING
Restaurants

If you wish to eat cheaply in Salzburg, it's worth following the Austrian tradition of making lunch your main meal, because some cheaper restaurants open only during daylight hours on weekdays.

Bio Bistro (☎ 870 712; Wolf-Dietrich-Strasse 1; mains €5.50) Vegetarian and vegan food is prepared

---

HANG(AR)TIME AT THE SALZBURG AIRPORT

Whether you have time to kill and want to get out of the airport or Salzburg is your final stop, it's worth a trip to check out the **Hangar-7** (☎ 662 2197; www.hangar-7.com; Wilhelm-Spazier-strasse 7A, Salzburg airport; admission free). This huge, clear plexi-enclosed airplane hangar is large enough to house a Douglas DC6 jumbo jet, a B-52 bomber, a plethora of assorted Red Bull Team Formula One racing cars, motorcycles and other cool historical aircraft. There's also a café where you can recharge your engine with a snack and, of course, a can of the silver and blue elixir that 'Gives you Wiiings'. Red Bull's founder and motorsports/aviation enthusiast, Dietrich Mateschitz, came up with the idea for his energy drink in 1984, after drinking a locally brewed tonic in Thailand. He is now one of the most successful businessmen in Austria.

fresh daily, along with Eastern 'holistic' specialities and salads.

Wilder Mann (☎ 841 787; Getreidegasse 20; mains €5.50-12; Mon-Fri) Traditional Austrian food in a friendly, bustling environment, located in the passageway off Getreidegasse. Tables, both inside and out, are often so packed it's almost impossible not to get chatting with fellow diners.

Zum Mohren (☎ 484 23 87; Judengasse 9; mains €9-16) This cellar restaurant offers traditional food in a cosy environment. Dishes include roast pork, Hungarian goulash and Tirolean calf's liver with bacon.

Ährlich (☎ 871 275-60; Wolf-Dietrich-Strasse 7; mains €11-17; dinner Tue-Sat, lunch Jul & Aug, closed Feb & Mar) If you've had enough of wurst and *Tafelspitz* (boiled beef with apple and horseradish sauce), this organic restaurant provides relief, with a brief, seasonal menu of international veggie and meat mains. It does sometimes have a bit of a weird health-farm vibe, but the food is tasty.

Gablerbräu (☎ 88 965; Linzer Gasse 9; mains €12) Low-key and pleasant, choose from homemade pasta and lip-smacking Styrian specialities served in four atmospheric rooms with a stained-glass arch, tiled oven and other rustic features.

Stiftskeller St Peter (☎ 841 268-34; St Peter Bezirk I/4; mains €12.50-20) Be prepared to play the tourist when you visit the much advertised Austrian specialist. Environs are in a huge dining complex. The baroque main salon is worth a peek even if you don't stay for the food.

Cafés

Café Konditorei Fürst (☎ 843 759; Brodgasse 13 in Alter Markt; confections from €3) Café Konditorei Fürst boasts that its *Mozartkugeln* chocolates – wrapped in blue and silver paper instead of the usual red and gold – are the original 'Mozart's Balls'. They're still made here from the same recipe.

Stadtalm (☎ 841 729; Mönchsberg 19C; mains €6-10; 10am-5pm Tue-Sun Apr-Oct) The meals are standard Germanic fare – wurst, *Wiener schnitzel* and *Züricher Geschnetzeltes* (veal in cream sauce). You won't care, though, with such fantastic views.

Quick Eats & Self-Catering

Salzburg has no shortage of markets, with a **fruit and vegetable market** (Mirabellplatz) on Thursday morning, and market stalls and fast-food stands on Universitätsplatz and Kapitelplatz. There's a **Eurospar supermarket** (Mon-Sat) opposite the train station.

DRINKING

Salzburg's most famous stretch of bars, clubs and discos remains Rudolfskai, but it's largely patronised by teenagers. Those who've already hit their 20s (or beyond) will probably prefer the scene around Anton Neumayr Platz, where things keep going until 4am on weekends.

Augustiner Bräustübl (☎ 431 246; Augustinergasse 4-6; 3-11pm Mon-Fri, 2.30-11pm Sat & Sun) It's Oktoberfest year-round here. Well, perhaps it's not *quite* so boisterous, but this hillside complex of beer halls and gardens is not to be missed. The local monks' brew keeps the huge crowd of up to 2800 humming.

Bar Flip (☎ 843 643; Gstättengasse 17) This is a dark, low-ceilinged student bar serving cocktails and cheap beer.

Humboldt (☎ 843 171; Gstättengasse 4-6) Slightly more upmarket, with jellybean dispensers, a video projection of the Mirabellgarten on one wall and a pair of traditional antelope's horns…painted purple.

Republic (☎ 841 613; Anton Neumayr Platz 2) A hip, American bar/brasserie, it is liable to have MTV DJs in for its regular club nights.

GETTING THERE & AWAY
Air

The **airport** (SZG; ☎ 85 80-100; www.salzburg-airport.at) handles regular scheduled flights to Amsterdam, Brussels, Frankfurt, London, Paris and Zürich, and charter flights to the Mediterranean. Contact **Austrian Airlines** (☎ 854 511-0) or no-frills Ryanair, which has two flights daily (three on Saturday) from London.

Bus

Services to the Salzkammergut region leave from just to the left of the main train-station exit. Destinations include Bad Ischl (€7.60, 1¾ hours), Mondsee (€5, 50 minutes) and St Wolfgang (€7, 1½ hours).

Buses to Kitzbühel (€13, 2¼ hours, at least three daily) go via Lofer; they depart from Südtiroler Platz, across from the train station post office.

There are timetable boards at each departure point and a bus information office in the train station. Alternatively, call ☎ 46 60-333 for information.

Car & Motorcycle

Three autobahns converge on Salzburg and form a loop around the city: the A1 from Linz, Vienna and the east – the A8/E52 from Munich and the west; and the A10/E55 from Villach and the south. Heading south to Carinthia on the A10, there are two tunnels through the mountains; the combined toll is €10 (€7 for motorcycles).

Train

Fast trains leave for Vienna (€37, 3¼ hours) via Linz hourly. The express service to Klagenfurt (€28, three hours) goes via Villach. The quickest way to Innsbruck (€30, two hours) is by the 'corridor' train through Germany via Kufstein; trains depart at least every two hours. There are trains every hour or so to Munich (€26, two hours), and hourly trains to Salzburg (€7.40) via St Gilgen.

GETTING AROUND

Salzburg airport is 4km west of the city centre. Bus 2 goes there from the main train station (€1.70). A taxi costs about €12.50.

Bus drivers sell single bus tickets for €1.70. Other tickets must be bought from the automatic machines at major stops, *Tabak* shops or tourist offices. Day passes cost €3.20 and weeklies €10. Children aged six to 15 years travel half-price; those under six travel free.

Most of the Old Town is pedestrianised. The nearest central parking area is the Altstadt Garage under the Mönchsberg. Attended car parks cost €1.40 to €2.40 per hour. On streets with automatic ticket machines (blue zones), a three-hour maximum applies (€0.50 for 30 minutes) during specified times – usually shopping hours.

Bicycle hire is available from **Top Bike** (☎ 0676-476 72 59; www.topbike.at; 2hr/4hr/day €6/10/15), which has two locations: just outside the train station and on the bridge.

For a taxi, call ☎ 81 11, or go to the ranks at Hanuschplatz, Residenzplatz or the train station.

AROUND SALZBURG

Four kilometres south of Salzburg's Old Town centre is the popular **Schloss Hellbrunn** (☎ 820 372-0; www.hellbrunn.at; Fürstenweg 37; adult/student €7.50/5.50; ⊗ 9am-10pm Jul & Aug, 9am-5.30pm May, Jun & Sep, 9am-4.30pm Apr & Oct). Built by bishop Markus Sittikus, this 17th-century castle is known for its ingenious trick fountains and

water-powered figures. When the tour guides set them off, expect to get wet! Admission includes a tour of the **baroque palace**. Other parts of the garden (without fountains) are open year-round and free to visit.

City bus 55 runs to the palace every 30 minutes from Salzburg's main train station, via Rudolfskai in the Old Town. Salzburg tickets are valid.

Werfen

☎ 06468 / pop 3000

The world's largest accessible ice caves are in the mountains near Salzburg. These **Eisriesenwelt Höhle** (Giant Ice Caves; ☎ 56 46; www.eisriesenwelt.at; adult/student with cable car up €17/15, without cable car €8/7; ⊗ 1 May-26 Oct) house elaborate and beautiful ice formations; take warm clothes because it gets cold inside and the tour lasts 1¼ hours – you also need to be reasonably fit.

The **Hohenwerfen Fortress** (adult/student €9/7.50; ⊗ Apr-Nov) stands on the hill above the village. It was originally built in 1077, although the present building dates from the 16th century. Admission includes an exhibition, a guided tour of the interior and a dramatic falconry show, in which birds of prey swoop low over the heads of the crowd. The walk up from the village takes 20 minutes.

Both attractions can be visited in one day if you start early (tour the caves first and be at the castle by 3pm for the falconry show). The **tourist office** (☎ 53 88; www.werfen.at; Markt 24; ⊗ 9am-7pm Mon-Fri, 5-7pm Sat mid-Jul–mid-Aug, 9am-5pm Mon-Fri mid-Aug–mid-Jul) is in the village's main street.

Werfen can be reached from Salzburg along the A10. By train it takes 50 minutes and costs €8. The village is a five-minute walk from Werfen train station. Getting to the caves is a bit more complicated, though scenic. A minibus service (€6.50 return) from the train station operates along the steep, 6km road to the car park, which is as far as cars can go. A 15-minute walk then brings you to the cable car (admission €9 return), from where it is a further 15-minute walk to the caves. Allow four hours return from the train station, or three hours from the car park (keep in mind that peak-season queues may add an hour). The whole route can be hiked, but it is a very hard four-hour ascent, rising 1100m above the village.

SALZKAMMERGUT

A picture-perfect wonderland of glassy blue lakes and tall craggy peaks, Austria's Lake District is a longtime favourite holiday destination attracting visitors in droves from Salzburg and beyond – including Habsburg emperors and their hangers-on. The waters in this salt-mining region (mining has taken place in the area since Celtic times) are rich in minerals, and believed to have medicinal value. In fact, Emperor Franz Josef once declared the region to be 'an earthly paradise' and spent a large part of every summer at Bad Ischl, whose healing waters were credited with his conception.

Whether you're looking for a way to entertain the kids or hoping to just commune with nature, the area is big on variety. The peaceful lakes offer limitless opportunities for boating, fishing, swimming, or just sitting on the shore and chucking stones into the water. Favourite waterside beauty spots include the picturesque villages of Hallstatt and St Wolfgang, and the Riviera-style port of Gmunden. You can also tour the salt mines that made the region wealthy or plunge into the depths of the fantastic Dachstein caves, where glittering towers of ice are masterfully illuminated in the depths of a mountain.

Getting There & Around

The major rail routes bypass the heart of Salzkammergut, but regional trains cross the area north to south. You get on this route from Attnang-Puchheim on the Salzburg–Linz line. The track from here connects to Bad Ischl, Hallstatt and Obertraun in one direction, as well as to Gmunden in another. When you're travelling from a small, unstaffed station (*unbesetzter Bahnhof*), you buy your ticket on the train; no surcharge applies.

After Obertraun, the railway continues eastwards via Bad Aussee before connecting with the main Bischofshofen–Graz line at Stainach-Irdning.

Attersee can also be reached via Vöcklamarkt, the next stop on the Salzburg–Linz line before Attnang-Puchheim.

Regular buses connect the region's towns and villages, though less frequently on weekends. Timetables are displayed on stops, and tickets can be bought from the driver.

Passenger boats ply the waters of the Attersee, Traunsee, Mondsee, Hallstätter See and Wolfgangsee.

To reach Salzkammergut from Salzburg by car or motorcycle, take the A1 or Hwy 158.

BAD ISCHL

☎ 06132 / pop 13,000

A longtime favourite of the imperial family, Bad Ischl also has the dubious distinction of being the birthplace of WWI, or at least the concept of it (Emperor Franz Josef was enjoying his annual holiday here in 1914 when troubles with Serbia arose). It's hard to picture the Bad Ischl of today as the conception point for such brutality, given it's a spa resort devoted to rather more holistic pursuits.

Many of Bad Ischl's dignified buildings still wear an imperial aura. It's a handsome-looking place and makes a good base for visiting the region's five main lakes.

Orientation

The town centre rests within a bend of the Traun River. To head into town, turn left into the main road as you come out of the train station; you'll pass the tourist office and post office.

Information

Post Office (Aübockplatz 4; ☷ 8am-6pm Mon-Fri, 9am-noon Sat)

Salzkammergut Touristik (☎ 24 000-0; www .salzkammergut.co.at; Götzstrasse 12; ☷ 9am-8pm) Has Internet access.

Tourist Office (Kurdirektion; ☎ 27 757-0; www.badischl .at, in German; Bahnhofstrasse 6; ☷ 8am-6pm Mon-Fri, 9am-3pm Sat, 10am-1pm Sun Jul-Sep, 8am-5pm Mon-Fri, 8am-noon Sat Oct-Jun)

Sights & Activities

The **Kaiservilla** (☎ 23 241; www.kaiservilla.at; Kaiserpark; ☷ May–mid-Oct) was Franz Josef's summer residence and shows he loved huntin', shootin' and fishin' – it's decorated with an obscene number of animal trophies. It can be visited only by guided tour (€12; in German but with written English translations), during which you'll pick up little gems, like the fact that Franz Josef was conceived in Bad Ischl after his mother, Princess Sophie, took a treatment to cure her infertility in 1828. There are several 40-minute tours daily (main season) and only three on Wednesday (noon, 2pm and 3pm) from January to April.

SALZKAMMERGUT

The teahouse of Franz Josef's wife, Elisabeth, is now a **photo museum** (admission €3). Admission to the grounds alone costs €4.20/3.50 per adult/child.

Free *Kurkonzerte* (spa concerts) are held regularly during summer; the tourist office has venues and times. An **operetta festival** takes place in July and August; for details and advance reservations call ☎ 23 839.

Bad Ischl has downhill skiing from **Mt Katrin** (winter day pass €21); however, there are only three trails. It also has various cross-country skiing routes. In summer the Mt Katrin cable car costs €12.50 return.

The tourist office has information on **health treatments** in Bad Ischl.

Sleeping & Eating

Jugendgästehaus (☎ 26 577; www.oejhv.or.at; Am Rechensteg 5; dm €13, s/d €27/38; ⏰ reception 8am-1pm & 5-7pm) Rooms are standard hostel fare, but comfortable enough for a night or two. The exterior is rather nondescript. Look for it in the town centre behind Kreuzplatz.

Haus Rothauer (☎ 23 628; Kaltenbachstrasse 12; s/d €25/55) You'll feel as if you're staying with longtime family friends when spending a few days at this immaculately clean, super-friendly guesthouse. Do phone ahead, however, to make sure there's space and someone is around to let you in.

Hotel Garni Sonnhof (☎ 23 078; www.sonnhof.at; Bahnhofstrasse 4; s/d €45/90; Ⓟ) Nestled into a leafy glade of maple trees next to the train station, this is an excellent option – it has cosy, traditional décor, a lovely garden (complete with a pond), a sunny conservatory, and large bedrooms with interesting old furniture and wooden floors. There's a billiard room, sauna and a steam bath on-site.

Café Zauner (☎ 23 013; Pfarrgasse 7; snacks from €5) This café has changed little since imperial times, retaining its glittering chandeliers, marble floors and fantastical displays of confectionary. Founded in 1832, it was Franz Josef's bakery of choice – his mistress ordered their morning pastries here when he was in residence. Its summer pavilion on the Esplanade by the river is equally atmospheric.

Blue Enzian (☎ 28 992; Wirerstrasse 2; mains €7-14; ⏰ Mon-Sat) The laid-back Enzian does a variety of pastas, salads, and regional and seasonal dishes with solid results. It's an informal place set back from the main street. When you've finished eating, check out the popular Hofbeisl (open 9am to 4pm), almost next door. It's an atmospheric spot with baroque décor.

Weinhaus Attwenger (☎ 23 327; Lehárkai 12; mains €7-20) High-quality Austrian food is served at this quaint chalet with a relaxing garden next to the river. The menu changes seasonally, with wines to match. Ask about set-course meals.

Getting There & Around

Trains from Salzburg (€17, two hours) arrive via Attnang-Puchheim. Trains on to Hallstatt depart roughly hourly between 6am and 6pm (€4, 50 minutes); however, be aware that you need to catch a ferry from this train station to the actual village (see p76).

Buses arrive and depart from in front of the train station. They run hourly to Salzburg (€7.40, 1¾ hours) via St Gilgen between 5am and 8pm. To St Wolfgang (€3.10), you generally need to change at Strobl (although you can buy one ticket straight through). Buses depart for Hallstatt every couple of hours (€3.60, 50 minutes), arriving in the village itself.

Salzkammergut Touristik (☎ 24 000-0; www.salzkammergut.co.at; Götzstrasse 12; ☼ 9am-8pm) has bikes for hire. Call ahead for reservations and rates as they change periodically.

HALLSTATT
☎ 06134 / pop 1150
With pastel-hued homes, swans and towering mountains on either side of a glassy green lake, breathtakingly beautiful Hallstatt looks like some kind of greeting card for tranquillity. Boats chug lazily across the water from the train station to the village itself, which clings precariously to a tiny bit of land between mountain and shore. So small is the patch of land occupied by the village that its annual Corpus Christi procession takes place largely in small boats on the lake.

There's evidence of human settlement at Hallstatt as long as 4500 years ago, and the village has been classified as a Unesco World Heritage site. Mining salt in the peak above the village was the main activity for thousands of years. Today tourism is the major money-spinner. Fortunately, the crowds of summer day-trippers only stay a few hours, then calm returns.

TIP!
Throughout the year resorts have a holiday/guest card (Gästekarte) offering region-wide discounts; ask at your hotel, hostel or camping ground. Alternatively, buy the Salzkammergut Card (€4.90; available May to October), which provides a 25% discount on sights, ferries, cable cars and some buses.

Orientation & Information
Seestrasse is the main street. Turn left from the ferry to reach the **tourist office** (☎ 82 08; hallstatt@inneres-salzkammergut.at; Seestrasse 169; ☼ 9am-noon & 1-5pm Mon-Fri year-round, 10am-5pm Sat May-Oct, 10am-2pm Sun Jul-Aug). The **post office** (Seestrasse 160) is around a bend in the road.

Sights & Activities
Hallstatt is rich with archaeological interest. Near the mine, 2000 graves were discovered, dating from 1000 to 500 BC. Don't miss the macabre **Beinhaus** (Bone House; ☎ 82 79; Kirchenweg 40; admission €1; ☼ 10am-6pm 1 May-27 Oct) near the village parish church; it contains rows of stacked skulls painted with flowery designs and the names of their former owners. These human remains have been exhumed from the too-small graveyard since 1600 in a practice that recalls the old Celtic pagan custom of mass burial. The last skull in the collection was added in 1995. Gross.

Around the lake at Obertraun are the intriguing **Dachstein Rieseneishöhle** (Giant Ice Caves; ☎ 8400 1830; www.dachstein.at; tours adult/child €9/5; ☼ early May-late Oct, tours 9.20am-4pm).

The caves are millions of years old and extend into the mountain for nearly 80km in places. The ice itself is no more than 500 years old, but is increasing in thickness each year – the 'ice mountain' is 8m high, twice as high now as it was when the caves were first explored in 1910. Ask at the ticket office about tours in English – if none are available you can take a sheet of printed information around the caves with you.

Above the village are the **Salzbergwerk** (Saltworks; ☎ 84 00; admission €20; ☼ 9am-4pm late Apr-26 Oct, 9am-3.30pm from mid-Oct). Riding the funicular up adds €5 to the salt mine ticket, or costs €7.50 return if you just want to get up the mountain. Ask the tourist office about the two scenic hiking trails you could take to get there.

Sleeping

Some private rooms are available during the busiest months of July and August only; others require a minimum three-night stay. The tourist office will telephone around for you without charge.

Campingplatz Krausner-Höll (☎ 83 22; Lahnstrasse 7; per adult €8; ☯ 15 Apr-15 Oct) This camping ground is conveniently located south of the town centre.

Gasthaus zur Muhle (☎ 83 18; www.toeroe.f@magnet.at; Kirchenweg 36; dm €13) On the Hallstatt hillside and overlooking the lake, this place is popular with independent travellers. Dorms are rather basic, however.

Jugendherberge (☎ 82 12; Salzbergstrasse 50; dm €15; ☯ May-Oct, check-in 5-6pm) Some dorms in this hostel have lots of beds and can be cramped. Phone ahead as reception hours are irregular. It is usually full with groups in July and August.

Gasthof Hallberg (☎ 82 86; www.pension-hallberg.at.tf; Seestrasse 113; s/d from €45/60; **P**) An excellent-value guesthouse, the best rooms are light and airy, furnished with pale wood and boasting superb lake views on both sides. Even the more ordinary rooms are still great quality, with many featuring quaintly sloping ceilings and mountain views.

Eating

Hallstatt's steep footpaths certainly help you work up an appetite. The following eateries are open for lunch and dinner.

Pferdestall (☎ 20 00; Seestrasse 156; mains €7.50-20) A one-time stable, tables are built into the old horse stalls complete with wooden partitions and iron bars. This small bar and trattoria turns out cheap pizza and pasta, along with some pricier meat dishes.

Bräu Gasthof (☎ 20 012; Seestrasse 120; mains €8-20; ☯ May-Nov) Served in vaulted rooms or on tables by the lake, the menu promises hearty local fare and turns out dishes like sirloin steak with onions (€13) or game goulash (€12), as well as a few salads.

Getting There & Away

There are six buses daily to/from Bad Ischl. You alight at 'Lahn', just south of the road tunnel. Beware, as services finish very early and the last guaranteed departure from Bad Ischl is 4.10pm. There are at least nine train services daily from Bad Ischl (€4, 50 minutes). The train station is across the lake

from the village, but the ferry captain waits for trains to arrive before making the short crossing (€2). Though trains run later, the last ferry departs from the train station at 6.30pm (leaving Hallstatt just after 6pm). Parking in the village is free if you're staying the night and therefore have a guest card.

WOLFGANGSEE

You can swim or go boating on this lake, climb the mountain above it, or just sit on the shore, gazing at the scenery. The only downside is that its proximity to Salzburg means it can become crowded in summer.

The Schafberg peak on the northern shore dominates the lake. Next to it is the resort of St Wolfgang. St Gilgen, on the western shore, provides easy access to Salzburg, 29km away. The **St Wolfgang tourist office** (☎ 06138-22 39-0; info@stwolfgang.at; ☯ 8am-8pm Mon-Sat, noon-6pm Sun Jul & Aug, 9am-noon Mon-Sat & 2-5pm Mon, Tue, Thu & Fri Sep-Jun) has regional tourist information.

Some people like to climb mountains because they're there; others prefer the less-strenuous train ride to the top. The former will love the four-hour hike to the peak of the **Schafberg** (1783m). The rest need to get there between early May and the end of October, when the Schafberg cog-wheel railway operates. It runs approximately hourly during the day and costs €13 to the top or €22 return. There is also a stop halfway up.

The village of St Wolfgang's 14th-century **Pilgrimage Church** (☯ 9am-6pm) still attracts pilgrims interested in viewing this highly ornate church.

On the lakefront, **Camping Appesbach** (☎ 06138-22 06; Au 99; adult/tent & car €5/6; ☯ Easter-Oct), 1km from St Wolfgang heading south towards Strobl, is a favourite with Austrians on holiday.

The **Jugendgästehaus Schafbergblick** (☎ 236 575; www.oejhv.or.at; Mondseestrasse 7; dm/d from €13/16; ☯ reception 8am-1pm & 5-7pm Mon- Fri, 8-9am & 5-7pm Sat & Sun) is in nearby St Gilgen. It's an up-market hostel with a great position near the town's swimming beach. Some of the rooms have lake views. There's no lock-out.

Both St Wolfgang and St Gilgen have numerous *pensions*, starting from about €20. Ask at the local tourist office for details and bookings.

A ferry operates from Strobl to St Gilgen, stopping at various points en route, including St Wolfgang. Services are from late April to 26 October, but are more frequent from early July to early September. The ferry journey from St Wolfgang to St Gilgen takes 45 to 50 minutes (€4.50), with boats sailing during the high season approximately twice hourly between 8am and 8pm.

Buses from St Wolfgang to St Gilgen and Salzburg go via Strobl on the east side of the lake. From St Gilgen the bus to Salzburg (€4.80, 50 minutes) departs hourly until at least 8.30pm.

NORTHERN SALZKAMMERGUT

West of Attersee is **Mondsee**, a lake whose warm water makes it a favourite swimming spot. Mondsee village has an attractive church that was used in the wedding scenes of *The Sound of Music*.

East of Attersee is another lake, **Traunsee**, and its three main resorts: Gmunden, Traunkirchen and Ebensee. **Gmunden** is famous for its twin castles, linked by a causeway on the lake, and its ceramic manufacturing.

TIROL

With converging mountain ranges behind lofty pastures and tranquil meadows, Tirol (also Tyrol) captures a quintessential Alpine panorama view. In the northeast and southwest are superb ski resorts. In the southeast, separated somewhat from the main state since part of South Tirol was ceded to Italy at the end of WWI, lies the protected natural landscape of the Hohe Tauern National Park, and the country's highest peak, the Grossglockner (3797m). Back further west, in the middle of the main state, Innsbruck is the region's jewel.

INNSBRUCK

☎ 0512 / pop 140,000

Sandwiched between majestic snow-capped mountains dominating your periphery, it's hard to resist the urge to get up high when in Innsbruck. Whether you're visiting the reopened winter Olympics stadium and the Bergisel ski-jump tower or partaking in an all-day hiking adventure, the region around this gorgeous Alpine town embodies just about everything a good skiing mecca should. In fact, on the Stubai Glacier (Austria's largest), 40km to the south, you can ski or snowboard at any time of the year.

Orientation

Innsbruck, in the valley of the River Inn, is scenically squeezed between the northern chain of the Alps and the Tuxer mountains to the south. The city centre is compact, with the main train station (Hauptbahnhof) only a 10-minute walk from the pedestrian-only Old Town centre (Altstadt). The main street in the Old Town is Herzog Friedrich Strasse.

Information

Bubble Point Waschsalon (☎ 565 007; www.bubble point.com; Brixner Strasse 1; per 30 min €1.50) Internet café and laundrette combined.

Internetcafé Moderne (☎ 584 848; Maria Theresien Strasse 16; per min €2) Offers Internet access.

Landeskrankenhaus (University Clinic; ☎ 504-0; Anichstrasse 35) For medical treatment.

Main Post Office (Maximilianstrasse 2; ۞ 7am-9pm Mon-Fri, 7am-3pm Sat, 8am-7.30pm Sun) There is another branch in the main train station.

Main Tourist Office (☎ general information 59 850, tickets & packages 53 56, hotel reservations 562 000-0; www .innsbruck.info; Burggraben 3; ۞ 9am-6pm) There is a €3 booking fee for hotel reservations. Check out the tourist office's free newspaper *Innsbruck Hallo!* for a map and lots of useful information.

Tourist Counter (main train station, lower concourse; ۞ 7am-7pm)

Sights

OLD TOWN

Innsbruck's atmospheric, medieval Old Town is ideal for a lazy stroll. The famous **Goldenes Dachl** (Golden Roof; Friedrich Herzog Strasse), built by Emperor Maximilian I in the 16th century as a display of wealth, is a good starting point. Comprised from 2657 gilded copper tiles, Maximilian used it to observe street performers from the balcony beneath.

The **Hofkirche** (Imperial Church; ☎ 584 302; Universitätsstrasse 2; adult/student under 27yr €2.20/1.45, admission free Sun & holidays; ۞ 9am-5pm Mon-Sat, before 8am, noon-3pm & after 5pm Sun) is another favourite (and worthwhile) attraction. It contains a memorial to Maximilian, and although his 'sarcophagus' has been restored, it's actually empty. Perhaps more memorable are the 28 giant statues of Habsburgs lining either side of the cask. You're now forbidden to touch the statues, but numerous inquisitive hands have already polished parts of the dull bronze, including Kaiser Rudolf's codpiece!

BERGISEL TOWER

If you've ever wondered what it feels like to stand on top of an Olympic-sized ski jump, you'll leave the **Bergisel tower** (☎ 589 259; adult/child €7.90/3.90; ☺ 9am-6pm Jun-Nov, 9am-5pm Dec-May) with a better idea. And if you've never been curious about such death-defying feats, you'll still be rewarded with truly fantastic views; the tower sits 3km south of the city centre on the crest of the refurbished Winter Olympics ski-jump stadium, overlooking Innsbruck. (Some wag has built a cemetery over the lip of the hill, directly in line with the end of the ski jump.)

The tower evinces the curving design typical of its designer – Iraqi-born, British-based celebrity architect Zaha Hadid. For the full experience, stop for coffee in the Café im Turm (meals €8.50 to €16.60), whose panorama windows give a whole new meaning to the term 'caffeine high'.

To get here, take tram/bus 1 (direction Bergisel) or tram 6 (direction Igls) from Museumstrasse. At the stop, follow the signs to Bergisel, up a fairly steep path for 15 minutes. The stadium is still used for ski-jumping in June and January, so ring ahead to check that it's OK to visit.

SWAROVSKI KRISTALLWELTEN

To get to the heart of Swarovski you must visit the mind-blowing **Crystal Worlds** (☎ 05224-51 080; www.swarovski.com/kristallwelten; Kristallwelten-strasse 1; adult/child €8/free; ☺ 9am-6pm). Enter behind sparkling crystalline eyes and the waterfall-spewing mouth (frozen in winter) of a giant cranium, and an interactive exhibition awaits further inside. It features the works of Eno, Warhol and Dali. Navigate your way through numerous black curtains and into ambient sound rooms, trippy interactive exhibits, and one-of-a-kind fusions of crystals, lights, sounds and mirrors. The centre is in Wattens and best reached by bus (€8.50 return, 30 minutes).

ALPENZOO

The **Alpine Zoo** (☎ 292 323; www.alpenzoo.at, in German; Weiherburggasse 37; adult/student/child €7/5/3.50; ☺ 9am-6pm) houses a comprehensive collection of alpine animals, including ibexes, bears, an eagle and a bearded vulture. Walk up the hill to get there or take the Hungerburgbahn, which is free if you buy your zoo ticket at the Hungerburgbahn station.

OTHER SIGHTS

The **Landesmuseum Ferdinandeum** (☎ 59 489; Museumstrasse 15) has a massive collection of Gothic statues and altarpieces. The **Alpenverein Museum** (Alpine Club Museum; ☎ 59 547-19; Wilhelm Greil Strasse 15; adult/child €2.20/1.10; ☺ 10am-5pm Mon, Tue, Thu & Fri, noon-7pm Wed, 10am-1pm Sat May-Oct) has a collection of Alpine art and relief maps.

A new 'hop on, hop off' **Sightseer bus** (adult/concession day ticket €8/5.60; ☺ services every half-hour btwn 9am-5.30pm May-Oct, 10am-5pm Nov-Apr) does make getting to some of the more remote sights a little easier. Pick up a brochure at the tourist office.

Activities

HIKING

Those staying in Innsbruck are entitled to the Club Innsbruck card, available at your hostel or hotel, which includes free guided mountain hikes. This is a fantastic deal, offering remarkable views for nothing more than the cost of your own food and water. The hiking programme runs from June to September, with most of the 40-odd diverse hikes leaving at 9am from the **Congress Centre** (Rennweg 3). The popular sunrise hikes leave at 4.45am Friday and you'll need to book by 4.30pm the previous day. Night-time lantern walks depart at 7.45pm Tuesday.

SKIING

The ski region around Innsbruck is constantly improving with new runs added each year. A one-day ski pass is around €26. Downhill equipment hire starts at €15.

You can ski or snowboard year-round at **Stubai Glacier**. A one-day pass costs €36 (€25 in summer). Catch the white IVB Stubaltalbahn bus, departing hourly from near the main train station. The journey takes 80 minutes and the last bus back is at 5.30pm. Several places offer complete packages to the glacier, which compare favourably with going it alone. The **tourist office** (☎ 53 56) has a package for €49, including transport, passes and equipment hire. This works out to be a good deal in summer. In winter, however, there's a free ski bus leaving from various hotels, so compare going it alone with taking a tourist office package first.

Sleeping

The tourist office has lists of private rooms in Innsbruck from €20 per person. If you're

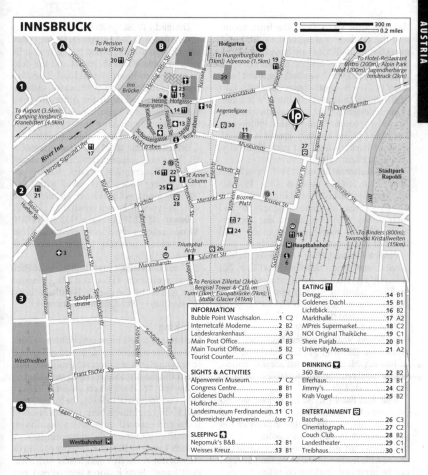

INNSBRUCK

| 0 | 300 m |
| 0 | 0.2 miles |

INFORMATION
Bubble Point Waschsalon	1	C2
Internetcafé Moderne	2	B2
Landeskrankenhaus	3	A3
Main Post Office	4	B3
Main Tourist Office	5	B2
Tourist Counter	6	C3

SIGHTS & ACTIVITIES
Alpenverein Museum	7	C2
Congress Centre	8	B1
Goldenes Dachl	9	B1
Hofkirche	10	B1
Landesmuseum Ferdinandeum	11	C1
Österreicher Alpenverein	(see 7)	

SLEEPING
| Nepomuk's B&B | 12 | B1 |
| Weisses Kreuz | 13 | B1 |

EATING
Dengg	14	B1
Goldenes Dachl	15	B1
Lichtblick	16	B2
Markthalle	17	A2
MPreis Supermarket	18	C2
NOI Original Thaiküche	19	C1
Shere Purjab	20	B1
University Mensa	21	A2

DRINKING
360 Bar	22	B2
Elferhaus	23	B1
Jimmy's	24	C2
Krah Vogel	25	B2

ENTERTAINMENT
Bacchus	26	C3
Cinematograph	27	C2
Couch Club	28	B2
Landestheater	29	C1
Treibhaus	30	C1

staying at a hostel or hotel, ask for the complimentary Club Innsbruck card. It provides various discounts and benefits.

Camping Innsbruck Kranebitten (☎ 284 180; www.campinginnsbruck.com; Kranebitter Allee 214; adult/tent/car €5/3/5) In an idyllic location 5km from the Old Town centre, under the mountains, this camping ground is open year-round. It has a restaurant and bike hire, and offers a shuttle service into the city.

Jugendherberge Innsbruck (☎ 346 179; www .jugendherberge-innsbruck.at; Reichenauerstrasse 147; dm from €15.60, d with shared bathroom €46; ☼ closed 10am-3pm summer, 10am-5pm rest of year, curfew 11pm; ☐) Seen from afar, this hostel resembles a building from the former USSR – a huge, concrete monstrosity. Up close the picture

is a bit prettier – its dorms are actually quite modestly sized. Prices include breakfast. To get here, take bus O (direction Olympisches Dorf/Josef Kerschbaumer Strasse) from Museumstrasse.

Nepomuk's Bed & Breakfast (☎ 584 118; Kiebachgasse 16; dm/d with shared bathroom €25/30) At the time of research this was the newest kid in one of the oldest buildings on the block. The staircase has been around since the year 1800, but the charming rooms are newly remodelled (only 10), and the breakfast in the wonderful attached patisserie downstairs will get your day going.

Pension Paula (☎ 292 262; www.pensionpaula .at; Weiherburggasse 15; s/d €36/58, with shared bathroom €29/49; P) This hilltop *pension* looks out over the city, with views from the front rooms and the outdoor seating next to the buffet breakfast room. Rooms are fairly humble, although bathrooms are better than average.

Binders (☎ 33 436-0; www.binders.at; Dr Glatz Strasse 20; s/d €45/70, with shared bathroom €40/54; (P)) East of the main train station, Binders is a rare thing: a designer hotel for those on a budget. Brightly coloured lampshades, pillows or armchairs create a splash against a neutral, modern background. Just east of the city, this is excellent value for money.

Hotel-Restaurant Bistro (☎ 346 319; www.tiscover .at/hotel-bistro; Pradler Strasse 2; s/d €42/84; (P)) This small family-run hotel won't win any interior-design awards; it's plain, businesslike and unassuming. However, rooms are comfortable and offer good value for money, and the staff is welcoming and friendly.

Pension Zillertal (☎ 582 129; www.pensionzillertal .com; Fritz Konzert Strasse 7; s/d/tr from €54/85/128; (P) (✗)) A family-run B&B in a converted apartment building, south of the city and close to the Bergisel tower. The recently renovated rooms are spotless, and have TVs and phones.

Weisses Kreuz (☎ 59 479; www.weisseskreuz.at; Herzog Friedrich Strasse 31; s/d from €62/96, with shared bathroom from €35/66; (P) (✗)) It's had the honour of hosting Mozart, and this creaky, atmospheric hotel remains comfortable to this day. Parking costs €10.

Alpin Park Hotel (☎ 346 172; alpinpark@innsbruck -hotels.at; Pradler Strasse 28; s/d €82/120; (P)) New and modern, this place has all the slick amenities you'd expect from a classy hotel – minus the super-high prices. Rooms are small but clean, with fluffy white duvets. Ski packages can be arranged. Parking costs €8.

Eating

University Mensa (Herzog Siegmund Ufer 15; mains €4-5; (✓) 11am-2pm Mon-Thu, 11am-1.30pm Fri) Enjoy great views of the Alps while lunching here. The food is cheap, but just OK.

NOI Original Thaiküche (☎ 589 777; Kaiserjäger-strasse 1; mains €4-11; (✓) lunch & dinner Mon-Fri, dinner Sat) Serves delicious Thai staples, such as soups, noodle dishes and curries. It's small, but in summer there are lots of outdoor tables with brightly coloured chairs.

Shere Purjab (☎ 282 755; Innstrasse 19; mains €6-10) Innstrasse is lined with cheap eats, including this cut-price Indian restaurant, which has a daily menu and, naturally, lots of veggie food.

Lichtblick (☎ 566 550; 7th fl, Maria Theresien Strasse 18; daytime snacks €6.50-9, evening menu €30-40; (✓) Mon-Sat) This is the city's hot ticket, and little wonder, given both the views and the delicious modern international food. The Alps rise up along one side of this small, glassed-in restaurant, while in the other direction you can see the Bergisel tower. It's a romantic setting at night. After dinner grab a drink across the foyer in the 360 Bar (below).

Goldenes Dachl (☎ 589 370; Hofgasse 1; mains €10-15) The menu features Tirolean specialities, such as *Bauerngröstl*, a pork, bacon, potato and egg concoction served with salad (€9.90), along with *Wiener schnitzel* and various types of *Braten* (roasts).

Dengg (☎ 582 347; Riesengasse 11-13; mains €13-18) An upmarket eatery, it serves everything from Thai coconut curry soup to international fish and meat dishes.

There is an **MPreis Supermarket** ((✓) 6am-9pm) in the main train station and a large indoor food market by the river in **Markthalle** (Herzog Siegmund Ufer; (✓) 8am-4pm Mon-Fri, Sat morning).

Drinking

Elferhaus (☎ 582 875; Herzog-Friedrich Strasse 11) Tunnelling into a slab of rock, this cool *Bierhaus* (beerhouse) has a vibe that gets lively late when the mostly college crowd shows up.

Jimmy's (☎ 570 473; Wilhelm Greil Strasse 17) Very cool, very industrial looking, the hub of Innsbruck's hip nightlife is here. It features lots of metal and exposed stone, and a Buddha on the wall that oversees the proceedings.

Krah Vogel (☎ 5801 4971; Anichstrasse 12) Red-walled, festive, Krah Vogel is a favourite student haunt. Stop in for a beer after 10pm when it gets busy.

360 Bar (☎ 566 550; 7th fl, Maria Theresien Strasse 18; (✓) Mon-Sat) Like the name says, it's all about the views. This hip wine bar across from Lichtblick has perhaps the best views of the city. Relax in the plush surroundings and lounge in style swathed in ultramodern comfort with excellent service.

Entertainment

The tourist office sells tickets for 'Tirolean evenings' (€32 for alpine music, folk dancing, yodelling and one drink), classical concerts and performances in the **Landestheater** (Rennweg 2). For more entertainment options, pick up a copy of *Innsider*, found in cafés across town.

Bacchus (☎ 940 210; Salurnerstrasse 14) A mixed/gay club that attracts what German speakers succinctly call *ein gemischtes Publikum* (all ages, all tastes and all looks).

Cinematograph (☎ 578 500; Museumstrasse 31) Screens independent films in their original language.

Couch Club (Anichstrasse 7; ☾ Thu-Sat) Come to the hip Couch Club for clubbing.

Treibhaus (☎ 586 874; Angerzellgasse 8) The arty, community-minded Treibhaus hosts live music ranging from urban groove to ska, short-film festivals and the like. On Sunday there's a 'jazz breakfast' from 10.30am and 'five o'clock tea'.

Getting There & Away

Austrian Airlines has three flights a week from London Gatwick to **Innsbruck airport** (INN; ☎ 22 525). Tyrolean Airways flies daily to Amsterdam, Frankfurt, Paris, Vienna and Zürich.

The A12 and the parallel Hwy 171 are the main roads to the east and west respectively. Hwy 177 heads north to Germany and Munich. The A13 motorway is a toll road (€8) southwards through the Brenner Pass to Italy; it includes the impressive Europabrücke (Europe Bridge), several kilometres south of the city. Toll-free Hwy 182 follows the same route, passing under the bridge.

Fast trains depart seven times daily for Bregenz (€25.10, 2¾ hours) and every two hours to Salzburg (€29.50, two hours). Connections are hourly to Kitzbühel (€12.20, 1¼ hours). On many trains to Lienz, people travelling on Austrian rail passes must pay a surcharge for travelling through Italy. Ask before boarding or call ☎ 05-17 17, available 24 hours.

Getting Around

The airport is 4km west of the city centre. To get there, take bus F, which departs from opposite the main train station half-hourly (hourly on Saturday afternoon and Sunday) and passes through Maria Theresien Strasse. A taxi from the main train station to the airport costs around €10.

Single bus tickets, including to the airport, cost €1.80. A 24-hour pass is €3.50.

Street parking is very limited in the city centre. Parking garages (eg under the Old Town) cost €10 and upwards per day.

MAYRHOFEN

☎ 05285 / pop 4000

Run barefoot in meadows and inhale the purified, brisk mountain air surrounded by the beautiful Zillertal (Ziller) Valley, where unspoilt landscapes and the power of the piste dominate your periphery. Old farmhouses alongside elegant hotels make for a quaint contrast in this mountain chalet village. Have a glass of schnapps when you arrive – it has been a symbol of hospitality welcoming visitors to the Ziller for centuries. There's also a little test in this: how you drink it may foretell your experience in Mayrhofen. Gulp it and your holiday may be action packed and exhilarating, or sip it and enjoy a more relaxed and serene alpine paradise.

The **Europa House tourist office** (☎ 67 60; www .mayrhofen.at; Europahaus; ☾ 8am-6pm Mon-Fri, 9am-noon & 2-6pm Sat, 10am-noon Sun) has loads of comprehensive information, basically from A-Z for both summer and winter. It's free and written in English. There are good **walks** originating from the village; ask at the tourist office for maps or about guided trips. Mayrhofen is home to the steepest piste in Austria, known as the HariKari. There is year-round **skiing** on the Hintertux Glacier. A pass costs €33/29 per day in winter/summer; inquire at the tourist office.

To work your taste buds instead of your legs, visit **Erlebnis Sennerei** (☎ 62 713; www.cennerei -zillertal.at; Hollenzen 116; adult/child €11/free; ☾ 10am-3pm), a grass-roots dairy. See how local cheeses are made on the production facility tour and then enjoy the chance to taste them.

For sleeping, try the **Hotel Neue Post** (☎ 62 131; www.neue-poast.at; Hauptstrasse 400; s/d from €51/86; P ☒ ☒). It's a lavish affair that's surprisingly well priced – although rates vary with the season and are higher in winter. It has a fabulous indoor swimming pool, and a great spa, sauna and solarium.

Our favourite local eating and drinking spot is **Mo's** (☎ 63 435; Hauptstrasse 417; mains €6-20), on the town's main street. The food is quite good, although the mix of cuisines is a bit strange – it encompasses the Mediterranean, Caribbean and American South. It also showcases live music.

To reach Mayrhofen catch a train to Jenbach from Innsbruck (€10, 1½ hours, hourly). From Jenbach (€5, 45 minutes) there are multiple trains daily to Mayrhofen, which is the last stop on the rail line.

AUSTRIA

KITZBÜHEL

☎ 05356 / pop 8600

Kitzbühel began life in the 16th century as a silver and copper mining town and today continues to preserve a charming medieval centre despite its other persona – as a fashionable and prosperous winter resort. It's renowned for the white-knuckled Hahnenkamm downhill ski race in January and the excellence of its slopes.

Orientation & Information

From the main train station to the town centre is 1km. You emerge from the train station onto Bahnhofstrasse and walk straight ahead and then turn left into Josef Pirchl Strasse; take the right fork (no entry for cars), which is still Josef Pirchl Strasse, and continue past the post office. Following this road will eventually take you to the **tourist office** (☎ 62 155-0; www.kitzbuehel.com; Hinterstadt 18; ☪ 8.30am-6pm Mon-Fri, 9am-6pm Sat).

Activities

SKIING

In winter there is good intermediate skiing on Kitzbüheler Horn to the north and Hahnenkamm to the south of town. A one-day ski pass costs around €35, though some *pensions*/hotels offer 'Ski Hit' reductions before mid-December or after mid-March.

HIKING

Dozens of summer hiking trails surround the town; the tourist office gives free maps and free guided hikes. Get a head start to the heights with a one- or three-day cable-car pass for €15/35.

There is an alpine flower garden (free) on the slopes of the Kitzbüheler Horn (a toll road for drivers). The scenic Schwarzsee is a fine location for summer swimming.

Sleeping

Prices quoted for *pensions* and hotels are for the winter high season.

Pension Hörl (☎ /fax 63 144; Josef Pirchl Strasse 60; s/d €20/40, with shared bathroom €18/36) Conveniently close to the train station, this *pension* is cheap, friendly and more comfortable than the jumble-sale décor first suggests.

Pension Schmidinger (☎ 63 134; Ehrenbachgasse 3; s/d from €35/70) The spotless rooms here are decorated in a pleasant country style and have new bathrooms.

Pension Mühlbergerhof (☎ 62 835; fax 64 488; Schwarzseestrasse 6; s/d from €35/70) The colour scheme in the public areas of this *pension* is somewhat darker than Schmidinger, but the rooms are light and airy. The owners serve breakfast featuring fresh produce from their farm.

Eating

Asia Markt (Josef Pirchl Strasse 16; meals €4.50-6.50; ☪ Mon-Sat) This grocery store serves light weekday lunches and early evening meals.

La Fonda (☎ 73 673; Hinterstadt 13; mains €5-12; ☪ dinner) The kitschy Tex-Mex décor makes this place a popular choice, plus the kitchen is open until midnight for those wanting to dine late.

Huberbräu Stüberl (☎ 65 677; Vorderstadt 18; mains €6.50-12.50) This is a Kitzbühel 'must', although so many diners come for the Austrian food and beer that the service is sometimes rather off-hand.

Zinnkrug (☎ 62 613; Bichlstrasse 9; mains €6-17.50) A typically Austrian inn, Zinnkrug is known for its pork spare ribs and fondue (€15.60).

For self-caterers, there's a **Spar supermarket** (☪ Mon-Sat) on Bichlstrasse (corner of Ehrenbachgasse).

Getting There & Away

Direct trains to Innsbruck (€12.20, one to two hours, depending on the service) only leave Kitzbühel every two hours or so, but there are hourly services to Wörgl, where you can change for Innsbruck. Trains to Salzburg (€20.80, two hours) leave roughly hourly. Slower trains stop at Kitzbühel-Hahnenkamm, which is closer to the town centre than the main Kitzbühel stop.

Getting to Lienz by public transport is awkward. The train is slow and the bus is infrequent (€12.50, two hours). There are four bus departures Monday to Friday and two each on Saturday and Sunday.

Heading south to Lienz, you pass through some marvellous scenery. Hwy 108 (the Felber Tauern Tunnel) and Hwy 107 (the Grossglockner mountain road; closed in winter) both have toll sections.

LIENZ

☎ 04852 / pop 13,000

The piste-filled outline of the Dolomite mountain range engulfing the southern skyline beckons visitors to the capital of East

Tirol. Lienz serves mostly as a stopover for skiers and hikers passing through or on the way to the Hohe Tauern National Park, which is Europe's largest national park.

Orientation & Information

The town centre is within the junction of the Isel and Drau Rivers. To reach Hauptplatz from the train station cross the road (or take the 'Zur Stadt' exit) and follow the street past the post office. The **tourist office** (☎ 65 265; www .lienz-tourismus.at; Europaplatz 1; ☺ 8am-6pm Mon-Fri, 9am-noon Sat, 9am-noon Sun summer & winter high season) will find rooms free of charge, or you can use the hotel board (free telephone) outside.

Sights & Activities

There is downhill skiing on the nearby **Zettersfeld** and **Hochstein** peaks. A one-day ski pass covering both is €30. However, the area around Lienz is more renowned for its cross-country skiing; the town fills up for the annual **Dolomitenlauf** cross-country skiing race in mid-January.

In summer there's good hiking in the mountains. The cable cars are closed during the low season (April, May, October and November).

Sleeping & Eating

There are ADEG supermarkets on Hauptplatz and Tiroler Platz.

Comfort-Camping Falken (☎ 64 022; Eichholz 7; camp site without/with electricity €8/10.50, adult €6; ☺ mid-Dec–Oct) Just south of town, this camping ground has good washing facilities, a restaurant and mountain views.

Altstadthotel Eck (☎ 64 785; altstadthotel.eck@ utanet.at; Hauptplatz 20; s/d from €55/110) Atmospheric and spacious, it provides all the comfort you'd expect from one of the town's leading hotels.

Pick Nick Ossi (☎ 71 091; Europaplatz 2; snacks €3-7) Salads, pizza and other fast food are on offer here.

Adlerstüberl (☎ 62 550; Andrä Kranz Gasse 5; mains from €8) Daily specials are featured at this eatery, which does the usual assortment of Austrian dishes with varying results.

Getting There & Away

Except for the 'corridor' route through Italy to Innsbruck, trains to the rest of Austria connect via Spittal Millstättersee to the east. Trains to Salzburg (€26.90) take at least three hours. Villach, between Spittal and Klagenfurt, is a main junction for rail routes to the south. To head south by car, you must first divert west or east along Hwy 100.

HOHE TAUERN NATIONAL PARK

You wouldn't guess from its small stature, but little Austria actually contains the largest national park in the Alps. Straddling Tirol, Salzburg and Carinthia, the Hohe Tauern National Park stretches over 1786 sq km. At the heart of this protected oasis of flora and fauna (including marmots and some rare ibexes) lies the **Grossglockner** (3797m), Austria's highest mountain. The Grossglockner towers over the 10km-long Pasterze Glacier, which is best seen from the outlook at **Franz Josef's Höhe**.

Although camping is not allowed in the park, there are mountain huts and hiking trails. Ask the tourist office in Lienz (left) for details. If you're on foot, the most direct public transport into the park from Lienz is by bus to Franz Josef's Höhe. This goes via Heiligenblut, where you'll find the **Hotel Senger** (☎ 22 15; www.romantic.at; Hof 23; s/d from €40/80; **P** ☒ ☐). Located in a charming old farmhouse, it lends a real feel for being up in the mountains (think stone floors, open fireplaces, and plenty of nooks and crannies in which to relax). The whole place has the friendly, sociable atmosphere of a ski chalet.

Buses run from mid-June to late September, but infrequently and on a very complicated and confusing schedule, so ask the Lienz tourist office *and* your bus driver before boarding in front of the train station. The return fare from Lienz is €10.20, plus a park toll of €2.70.

The portion of the **Grossglockner Hochalpenstrasse** (Hwy 107; www.grossglockner.at, in German) running through the park is considered one of the most scenic in the world. It winds upwards 2000m past waterfalls, glaciers and Alpine meadows. The highway runs between Lienz and Zell am See, and if you catch a bus from Lienz to Franz Josef's Höhe, you'll be traversing the southern part of this route. If you want to travel further north, ask your driver, or the **Kärnten tourist office** (☎ 04824-200 121) just up the road from the bus stop in Heiligenblut about current bus schedules.

If you have your own vehicle, you'll have more flexibility. However, beware that the road is open only between May and mid-

AUSTRIA

September, and you must pay tolls (at least €26/17 for a car/motorcycle, but more if you take a circular route).

At the northern end of the park, turn west along Hwy 168 (which becomes Hwy 165) to reach the spectacular, triple-level **Krimml Falls**.

VORARLBERG

Vorarlberg is Austria's 'wild west', occupying the country's furthest western reaches and separated from it by the Arlberg massif. Over the centuries its isolation has helped cultivate an individual identity (right down to the language) and it still often associates itself more with neighbouring Switzerland than Vienna.

Alluringly beautiful, this region is an aesthetic mix of mountains, hills and valleys. Trickling down from the Alps to the shores of Lake Constance (Bodensee), Vorarlberg is a destination in its own right, attracting everyone from classical-music buffs to skiers. It's also a gateway, by rail or water, to Germany, Liechtenstein or Switzerland.

BREGENZ
☎ 05574 / pop 27,500
Ritzy Bregenz sits pretty on the shores of Lake Constance and emits a decidedly posh vibe – go window shopping for Dior and Louis Vuitton at one of the designer shops gracing its quaint Old Town streets. Visit in summer, during the annual Bregenzer Festspiele (Bregenz Festival), to catch this provincial capital at its most boisterous.

Orientation
Bregenz is on Lake Constance's eastern shore. Turn left at the main train station exit and take Bahnhofstrasse to the city centre (five minutes). Buses for the city leave from outside the train station.

Information
Cockpit Café (Seegalerie, Bahnhofstrasse 10; per 15 min €1.20; ☼ 5pm-midnight) Offers Internet access.
Post Office (Seestrasse 5; ☼ 7am-7pm Mon-Fri, 8am-noon Sat)
Tourist Office (☎ 49 59-0; www.bregenz.at, in German; Bahnhofstrasse 14; ☼ 9am-noon & 1-5pm Mon-Fri, to noon only Sat, to 7pm Mon-Sat during the Bregenz Festival) Also offers free Internet access.

Sights & Activities
Most tourists who arrive in Bregenz are drawn almost instinctively to the **Bodensee**, a major summer holiday destination for Austrians, Swiss and Germans, all of whom take advantage of the many water sports and attractions lining its banks.

Other highlights around the Bodensee include the **Zeppelin Museum** (Friedrichshafen), Meersburg's picturesque half-timbered houses built in classical German style and its two castles, the **Cathedral of St Nicholas** (Überlinge), the **flower island** of Mainau and the Gothic cathedral of Konstanz.

Bregenz offers spectacular views from its **Pfänder** mountain; a **cable car** (☎ 421 600; www .pfaenderbahn.at, in German; admission €10; ☼ 9am-7pm, closed 2 weeks in Nov) carries you up and back. There are hiking trails at the top.

Bregenz is also of interest to architecture fans. The most notable modern building is the shimmering art-gallery block, the **Kunsthaus**, by award-winning Swiss architect Peter Zumthor.

Festivals & Events
A feature that makes the **Bregenzer Festspiele** (Bregenz Festival) in July and August so remarkable is its setting. During the four-week programme, operas and classical works are performed from a floating stage on the lake's edge. For tickets, contact the **Kartenbüro** (☎ 407-6; www.bregenzerfestspiele.com; Postfach 311, A-6901) about nine months beforehand, or ask about cancellations on the day.

Sleeping & Eating
The tourist office has a list of private homes that let rooms for €20 to €30 per person if none of the following options sound appealing. Expect prices during the festival to be higher than those quoted here.

Jugendgästehaus Bregenz (☎ 42 867; www.jgh.at /bregenz; Mehrerauerstrasse 5; dm from €20; ⓟ ▣) In a former needle factory, this HI hostel is a lively place, with larger than average dorms boasting only six beds plus en suite. There's also a decent restaurant on the premises. The hostel is near the skateboard park; take the 'Zum See' exit from the train station and pass the casino.

Pension Sonne (☎ 42 572; Kaiserstrasse 8; s/d from €35/66) This family-run *pension* is rather basic (the wooden floors can feel a little cold), but it is the most central accommodation option around. Ask to see a few rooms; some have nicer décor than others. The cheapest rooms share bathrooms.

Gästehaus am Tannenbauch (☎ 44 174; Im Gehren 1; s/d €40/80; ☺ May-Oct; ℗) Travellers with a taste for something different might prefer this quirky guesthouse. From the outside it looks like a normal house; inside it explodes into an ornate display of baroque kitsch. The highlight is the regal breakfast room.

Deuring-Schlössle (☎ 47 800; www.deuring-schloessle .com; Ehregutaplatz 4; s/d €135/210; ℗) Bregenz's best rooms are found in this fabulously renovated old castle. Each one is decorated differently, but all have loads of medieval charm and grace. Its restaurant (mains from €20) is also the best in Bregenz, with a sophisticated look and a gourmet menu.

Gösserbräu (☎ 42 467; Anton Schneider Strasse 1; mains €8-12; ☺ 9am-1pm Tue-Sun) Solid Austrian fare, simple and hearty, but not too stodgy, is served in a number of uniquely decorated dining rooms. The vegetarian mushroom goulash with dumplings is divine.

Getting There & Away

Trains to Munich (€36, 2½ hours) go via Lindau. There are also regular departures to St Gallen and Zürich. Trains to Innsbruck (€27, 2¾ hours) depart every two hours.

Boat services operate from late May to late October, with a reduced schedule from early March. For information, call ☎ 42 868. Bregenz to Lake Constance by boat via Friedrichshafen takes about 3½ hours and there are about seven departures daily. Special boat passes offer discounts.

ARLBERG REGION

The Arlberg region, shared by Vorarlberg and neighbouring Tirol, has some of the best skiing in Austria. Summer is less busy and many bars are closed.

St Anton am Arlberg is the largest resort, where you're are likely to hear a cheery antipodean 'G'day' or Scandinavian *God dag*, as you are to hear an Austrian *Grüss' Di*. There are good intermediate to advanced runs here, as well as nursery slopes on Gampen and Kapall. The **tourist office** (☎ 05446-22 690; www.stantonamarlberg.com; ☺ 9am-5pm Mon-Fri), on the main street, has details. Head diagonally left from the train station to find it.

A ski pass valid for 83 ski lifts in St Anton and neighbouring St Christoph Lech, Zürs

and Stuben costs €45 for one day and €180 for six days (reductions for children and seniors).

There are nearly 600 accommodation options in and around St Anton, 80% of which are open during summer. Even with all this choice, it can be hard to find somewhere to stay over winter without booking ahead (note that short stays of a couple of days will usually incur a surcharge).

Haus Wannali (☎ 05446-23 50; Arlberg Strasse 509; s/d €40/80) is a central spot, with a friendly atmosphere and entertaining regulars. Some of the best views in town are enjoyed from the relatively spick-and-span **Pension Strolz Christian** (☎ 05446-30 119; Ing Gomperz Strasse 606; s/d €40/80).

When hunger hits, there is a Spar supermarket on the main road, and decent pizza and pasta dishes at **Pomodoro** (☎ 33 33; Fussgängerzone 70; mains from €8; ☺ dinner Dec-Apr). The food isn't great but the atmosphere is lively.

Loud, bawdy and very English, **Piccadilly** (☎ 221 32 76; Fussgängerzone 55) often has live music. For an après-ski cocktail or two head to **Krazy Kanguruh** (☎ 26 33), a longtime favourite bar on the lower slopes.

Getting There & Away

St Anton is on the main railway route between Bregenz (€14.50) and Innsbruck (€13.60), less than 1½ hours from both cities. St Anton is close to the eastern entrance of the Arlberg Tunnel, the toll road connecting Vorarlberg and Tirol. The tunnel toll is €9.45/7.25 for cars/motorcycles. You can avoid the toll by taking the B197, but no vehicles with trailers are allowed on this winding road.

AUSTRIA DIRECTORY

ACCOMMODATION

Reservations are recommended at Christmas, Easter and during summer. They are binding on both parties, so if you don't take a reserved room, the price could still be deducted from your credit card. Hostels tend to be more flexible; however, small groups booking into hostels might find their reservation for a four-bed room translated into four separate beds on arrival.

Tourist offices can supply lists of all types of accommodation and will generally make reservations – sometimes for a small fee.

Many resort towns hand out a *Gästekarte* (guest card) to people staying overnight. This card is funded by a resort tax of around €1 to €2 per night, added to the accommodation tariff, and it offers useful discounts on transport, sporting facilities and museums. Check with the tourist office if you're not offered one at your resort accommodation. In smaller towns, the first night's accommodation can cost slightly more than subsequent nights.

There are more than 500 camping grounds in Austria, but most close in winter. If you pitch a tent outside an established camping ground you need the property owner's approval; on public land it's illegal. Outside Vienna, Tirol and protected areas, free camping is allowed in a campervan, but only if you don't set up equipment outside the van. The **Austrian Camping Club** (Österreichischer Camping Club; Map p48; ☎ 01-71 199-1272; Schubertring 1-3, A-1010 Vienna) has information.

In the mountains, hikers can take a break from camping by spending the night in an alpine hut. See below for further details.

Two HI-affiliated hostelling associations operating within the country are **Österreichischer Jugendherbergsverband** (Map p48; ☎ 01-533 53 53; www.oejhv.or.at; 01, Schottenring 28, A-1010 Vienna) and **Junge Hostels Austria** (Map p48; ☎ 01-533 18 33; www.jungehotels.at; 01, Helferstorferstrasse 4, Vienna). Prices are generally €13 to €20 per night.

It's quite common for house owners to rent out rooms in their home (€15 to €30 per person, per night). Look out for the ubiquitous *Zimmer frei* (room vacant) signs.

The cheapest budget hotels start at around €25/40 for singles/doubles with a shared bathroom, and €35/60 for those with private facilities. Most midrange hotels start at around €50/80 for rooms with private facilities.

For this chapter we've defined places costing less than €40 as budget, while midrange options cost €40 to €80 and top-end hotels start at €80 per person.

Accommodation prices quoted in this chapter are for the high summer season (or winter in ski resorts) and include all taxes. Unless otherwise stated, all rooms have private facilities and breakfast is included.

ACTIVITIES
Hiking & Mountaineering
Walking and climbing are popular with visitors and Austrians alike, and most tourist offices sell maps of hiking routes. Mountain paths have direction indicators and often markers indicating their level of difficulty. Those with a red-white-red marker mean you need sturdy hiking boots and a pole; a blue-white-blue marker indicates the need for mountaineering equipment. There are 10 long-distance national hiking routes, while three European routes pass through Austria. Options include the northern Alpine route from Lake Constance to Vienna, via Dachstein, or the central route from Feldkirch to Hainburger Pforte, via Hohe Tauern National Park.

Don't try mountaineering without the proper equipment or experience. The **Österreichischer Alpenverein** (ÖAV; Austrian Alpine Club; Map p79; ☎ 0512-587 828; office@alpenverein-ibk.at; Wilhelm Greil Strasse 15, A-6010 Innsbruck) has touring programmes and also maintains a list of alpine huts in hill-walking regions. These provide inexpensive accommodation and often have meals or cooking facilities. Members of the club take priority but anyone can stay. It's a good idea to book huts. Listing your next intended destination in the hut book on departure provides you with an extra measure of safety, as search-and-rescue teams will be alerted should a problem arise.

Skiing & Snowboarding
Austria has some of the world's best skiing and snowboarding. The most popular regions are Vorarlberg and Tirol, but Salzburg province and Carinthia offer cheaper possibilities. Unusually, skiing is possible year-round at the famous Stubai Glacier near Innsbruck.

The skiing season starts in December and lasts well into April at higher-altitude resorts. Count on spending €20 to €38 for a daily ski pass (to ride the ski lifts). Rental generally starts at €16 for downhill equipment or €14 for cross-country skis; rates drop for multiple days.

Spa Resorts
There are spa resorts throughout the country, identifiable by the prefix *Bad* (bath), eg Bad Ischl. While perfect for the self-indulgent pampering that stressed-out city-dwellers today so often crave, they also promise more traditional healing cures for respiratory, circulatory and other ailments. The **Austrian National Tourist Office** (www.austria-tourism.at) can provide details, as can the **Österreichischer**

Heilbäder & Kurortverband (Austrian Thermal Baths & Spa Association; ☎ 01-512 19 04; oehkv@newsclub.at).

BOOKS

Lonely Planet has guides to both *Austria* and *Vienna*, as well as the *German Phrasebook*.

Graham Greene's evocative spy story *The Third Man* is set in Vienna, as is John Irving's *Setting Free the Bears*. Numerous travel writers, from the masterful Patrick Leigh Fermor (*A Time of Gifts*) to the amusing Bill Bryson (*Neither Here Nor There*), have passed through the city.

BUSINESS HOURS

Shops usually open 9am to 6pm Monday to Friday, and 9am to 1pm or 5pm on Saturday. However, grocery stores might open as early as 6am, and other shops don't close their doors until 7.30pm. In smaller cities, there's sometimes a two-hour closure over lunch.

Banks keep short hours, usually 9am to 12.30pm and 1.30pm to 3pm Monday to Friday, with 'late' (5.30pm) closing on Thursday. Information offices are generally open from 9am to 5pm Monday to Saturday. Restaurants generally open around 11am and stop serving food around 10pm. Most bars open sometime around noon, while clubs don't start rocking until after 10pm.

EMBASSIES & CONSULATES
Austrian Embassies & Consulates

Following is a list of Austrian diplomatic missions abroad.

Australia (☎ 02-6295 1533; www.austriaemb.org.au; 12 Talbot St, Forrest, Canberra, ACT 2603)

Canada (☎ 613-789 1444; www.austro.org; 445 Wilbrod St, Ottawa, ON K1N 6M7)

France Embassy (☎ 01 40 63 30 63; www.aussen ministerium.at/paris; 6, rue Fabert, 75007 Paris); Consulate (☎ 01 40 63 30 90; 17, ave de Villars, 75007 Paris) Visas only at the consulate.

Germany (☎ 30-202 87-0; www.oesterreichische -botschaft.de; Stauffenbergstrasse 1, D-10785 Berlin)

Ireland (☎ 01-269 4577; dublin-ob@bmaa.gv.at; 93 Ailesbury Rd, Dublin 4)

Netherlands (☎ 070-324 54 70; den-haag-ob@bmaa.gv .at; van Alkemadelaan 342, 2597 AS Den Haag)

New Zealand (☎ 04-499 6393; diessl@ihug.co.nz, Level 2, Willbank House, 587 Willis St, Wellington)

UK (☎ 020-7235 3731; www.austria.org.uk; 18 Belgrave Mews West, London SW1X 8HU)

USA (☎ 202-895 6700; www.austria.org; 3524 International Court NW, Washington, DC 20008)

Embassies & Consulates in Austria

Only *Botschaften* (embassies) and *Konsulate* (consulates) in Vienna issue visas. In case of an emergency, you might be redirected to a limited-hours consulate in a nearer city. The following diplomatic missions are located in Vienna unless otherwise stated:

Australia (Map p48; ☎ 01-50 674-0; www.australian -embassy.at; 04, Mattiellistrasse 2-4)

Canada (Map p48; ☎ 01-53 138-3000; www.kanada.at; 01, Laurenzerberg 2)

Croatia (☎ 01-484 87 83-0; 17, Heubergg 10)

Czech Republic (Map p44; ☎ 01-894 37 41; 14, Penzingerstrasse 11-13)

France (Map p48; ☎ 01-50 275-0; www.ambafrance-at .org; 04, Technikerstrasse 2)

Germany (Map p44; ☎ 01-71 154-0; 03, Metternich- gasse 3)

Hungary (Map p48; ☎ 01-53 780-300; 01, Bankgasse 4-6)

Ireland (Map p48; ☎ 01-715 42 46-0; 01, Rotenturm- strasse16-18)

Italy (Map p44; ☎ 01-712 51 21-0; 03, Rennweg 27)

Netherlands (Map p48; ☎ 01-58 939; 01, Opernring 5)

New Zealand (☎ 01-318 85 05; Salesianergasse 15/3)

Slovakia (☎ 01-318 90 55-200; 19, Armbrustergasse 24)

Slovenia (Map p48; ☎ 01-586 13 09; 01, Niebelungen- gasse 13)

Switzerland (Map p44; ☎ 01-79 505-0; 03, Prinz Eugen Strasse 7)

UK (Map p44; ☎ 01-71 613-0; www.britishembassy.at; 03, Jaurèsgasse 12)

USA Embassy (Map p44; ☎ 01-31 339-0; www.usembassy .at; 09, Boltzmanngasse 16); Consulate (Map p48; ☎ 512 58 35; 01, Gartenbaupromenade 2) Visas at the consulate only.

FESTIVALS & EVENTS

The Austrian National Tourist Office Vienna (ANTO; www.austria-tourism.at) has a list of annual and one-off events on its website; just click on 'Events'. Following is a list of major festivals.

February

Fasching This Shrovetide carnival before Lent involves parties, waltzes and a parade; celebrated countrywide.

May/June

Festwochen (Vienna) The Vienna Festival focuses on classical music, theatre and other performing arts.

Lifeball (Vienna; www.lifeball.org) One of the final balls of the season, this is a huge gay/straight AIDS fundraising gala attracting celebrity guests.

July

Bregenzer Festspiele (Bregenz) Opera with a difference – performed on a floating stage on Lake Constance.

Salzburger Festspiele (Salzburg) Austria's leading classical music festival attracts major stars, like Simon Rattle and Placido Domingo.

Love Parade (Vienna) Austria hosts its own version of the popular techno street parade.

September

Ars Electronica Festival (Linz) This is a celebration of weird and wonderful technological art and computer music.

Bruckner Fest (Linz) This highbrow classical music festival pays homage to native Linz son Bruckner.

November

Christmas Markets (particularly Vienna and Salzburg) Quaint stalls selling traditional decorations, foodstuffs, mulled wine and all manner of presents heralding the arrival of the festive season.

December

Krampus (Innsbruck and elsewhere) St Nicholas, his friend Krampus (Black Peter) and an array of masked creatures cause merriment and mischief in a parade that harks back to pagan celebrations.

Kaiserball (Vienna) The Imperial Ball kicks off Vienna's three-month season of balls, combining glamour and high society with camp decadence.

GAY & LESBIAN TRAVELLERS

Public attitudes to homosexuality are less tolerant than in most other Western European countries, except perhaps in Vienna. A good information centre/meeting point in Vienna is **Rosa Lila Villa** (Map p44; ☎ 01-586 81 50; 06, Linke Wienzeile 102). The age of consent for gay men is 18; for everyone else it's 14. Vienna has a Pride march, the Rainbow Parade, on the last Saturday in June.

HOLIDAYS

New Year's Day 1 January
Epiphany 6 January
Easter Monday March/April
May Day 1 May
Ascension Five and a half weeks after Easter
Whit Monday Seven weeks after Easter
Corpus Christi 10 days after Whit Monday
Assumption of the Virgin Mary 15 August
National Day 26 October
All Saints' Day 1 November
Immaculate Conception 8 December
Christmas Day 25 December
Boxing Day 26 December

INTERNET RESOURCES

The **Austrian National Tourist Office** (ANTO; www .austria-tourism.at) is a comprehensive starting point, with general information and details on different attractions and types of holidays.

Train times and fares are available from **Österreiche Bundesbahnen** (ÖBB; Austrian Railways; www.oebb.at).

Herold (www.herold.at) maintains an online telephone book. Budget travellers might also find quite useful the *Mensa* (university canteen; www.mensen.at, in German) listing.

LANGUAGE

Although Austrians understand Hochdeutsch ('high' or received German), they use different words and some even speak a dialect. Apart from using the expressions *Grüss Gott* (hello), *Servus!* (hello and goodbye) and *Ba Ba* (bye bye), they join their Bavarian cousins in forming the diminutive with 'erl' instead of the northern German 'chen'. Therefore when Austrians say *ein Bisserl*, they mean *ein Bisschen* (a little), and they use the word *Mäderl* (girl) instead of *Mädchen*.

Some expressions of time are also unique. *Heuer* means 'this year' and Austrians talk not of the German *Januar* but of *Jänner* (January).

MONEY

The currency is the euro, although you will still hear some references to its Austrian predecessor, the Schilling. Straight conversion of prices from Schilling to euro is the reason for occasionally strange prices – eg €3.63 for a phone card or €2.91 for a cup of coffee.

Major train stations have currency offices, and there are plenty of banks, *bureaux de change* and *Bankomats* (ATMs) across the country.

Costs

Expenses in Austria are average for Western Europe, with prices highest in big cities and ski resorts. Budget travellers can possibly scrape by on €40 a day, after rail-card costs; double this amount if you intend to avoid self-catering or staying in hostels. The minimum you can expect to pay per person is €13/25 for a hostel/hotel and €5/10 for a lunch/dinner.

Taxes & Refunds

Value-added tax (*Mehrwertsteuer* or MwSt) is charged at either 10% (eg travel, food and museum entry) or 20% (drinks and luxury goods). Prices always include taxes. For purchases over €75, non-EU residents can reclaim the MwSt either upon leaving the EU or afterwards. (Note that one-third of your refund will be absorbed in charges.) Ensure the shop has the forms to be filled out at the time of purchase, and present the documentation to customs on departure for checking and stamping.

The airports at Vienna, Salzburg, Innsbruck, Linz and Graz have counters for instant refunds, as do some land crossings. You can also reclaim by post.

Tipping & Bargaining

Austrian waiters aren't renowned for friendly or speedy service, but it's still rude not to round off the bill so that it includes a 10% tip. Pay it directly to the server; don't leave it on the table. Taxi drivers will also expect tips of 10%. Bargaining is unheard of.

POST

Post office hours vary: typical hours in smaller towns are 8am to noon and 2pm to 6pm Monday to Friday (money exchange to 5pm), and 8am to 11am Saturday, but a few main post offices in big cities are open daily until late, or even 24 hours. Stamps are also available in *Tabak* (tobacco) shops. Postcards and standard letters (up to 20g) cost €0.55 both within Austria and to Europe.

TELEPHONE

Don't worry if a telephone number you are given has only four digits, as many as nine digits, or some odd number in between. The Austrian system often adds direct-dial (DW) extensions to the main number after a hyphen. Thus, say ☎ 12 345 is a main number, ☎ 12 345-67 will be an extension, which could be a phone or fax. Generally, a -0 will give you the switchboard operator.

From a public phone, it costs €0.12 per minute to call anywhere in Austria, be it next door or across the country.

Mobile Phones

Mobile phones in Austria operate on GSM 900/1800, which is compatible with other European countries and Australia, but not with the North American GSM 1900 system or the system used in Japan.

If you're staying for a while, it's possible to get a prepaid phone in Austria, or strike a deal where you pay for calls and line rental but get your handset free. Try **Max.Mobil** (Map p44; ☎ 0676-20 00; 03, Kelsenstrasse 5-7) or **Mobilkom** (☎ 0800-664 300).

Phonecards

The minimum tariff in phone boxes is €0.20. Some boxes will only accept phonecards (Telefon-Wertkarte), which can be bought from post offices in two denominations – €3.60 and €6.90.

TIME

Austria operates on Central European Time (GMT/UTC plus one hour). Clocks go forward one hour on the last Saturday night in March and back again on the last Saturday night in October.

TOURIST INFORMATION

Tourist offices (usually called *Kurverein, Verkehrsamt* or *Tourismusverband*) tend to adjust their hours from one year to the next, so the hours listed in this chapter are a guide only and may have changed slightly by the time you arrive.

The **Austrian National Tourist Office** (ANTO; www.austria-tourism.at) has a number of overseas offices, including those in the following list. Some of these offices are not open to personal callers, so phone first. There is a comprehensive listing on the ANTO website.

Australia (☎ 02-9299 3621; info@antosyd.org.au; 1st fl, 36 Carrington St, Sydney, NSW 2000)

UK (☎ 020-7629 0461; info@anto.co.uk; 14 Cork St, London W1S 3NS)

USA (☎ 212-944 6880; info@oewnyc.com; PO Box 1142, New York, NY 10108-1142)

VISAS

Visas are not required for EU, US, Canadian, Australian or New Zealand citizens. Visitors may stay a maximum of three months (six months for Japanese citizens). There are no time limits for European Union and Swiss nationals, but they should register with the police before taking up residency. Most African and Arab nationals require a visa.

TRANSPORT IN AUSTRIA

GETTING THERE & AWAY

Air

The national carrier, Austrian Airlines, has an excellent safety record and specialises in linking numerous Eastern European cities to the West via Vienna.

Low-cost airlines also serve Austria. Ryanair flies from London to Graz, Klagenfurt, Linz and Salzburg; Air Berlin flies to Vienna from Germany; and German Wings has limited services from Düsseldorf and Stuttgart. Central European low-cost carrier Sky Europe flies to many destinations, including Croatia, France, Hungary, Italy and Poland. Be warned, however, that its 'Vienna' airport is far from the city – in Slovakia, actually.

Following are the key international airports in Austria:

Graz (GRZ; ☎ 0316-29 02-0; www.flughafen-graz.at, in German)

Innsbruck (INN; ☎ 0512-22 525-0; www.innsbruck-airport.com, in German)

Klagenfurt (KLU; ☎ 0463-41 500; www.klagenfurt-airport.com)

Linz (LNZ; ☎ 07221-600-0; www.flughafen-linz.at)

Salzburg (SZG; ☎ 0662-85 80-100; www.salzburg-airport.com, in German)

Vienna (VIE; ☎ 01-7007 22333; www.viennaairport.com)

Major international airlines, reputable regional carriers and low-cost airlines flying to and from Austria include:

Air Berlin (code AB; ☎ 0820-400 011; www.airberlin.com)

Air France (code AF; ☎ 01-50 222-2400; www.airfrance.com)

Alitalia (code AZ; ☎ 01-505 17 07; www.alitalia.com)

Austrian Airways (code OS; ☎ 05-17 66; www.aua.com)

British Airways (code BA; ☎ 01-79 567-567; www.ba.com)

Croatia Airlines (code OU; ☎ 01-70 07-36163; www.croatiaairlines.com)

CSA (code OK; ☎ 01-512 38 05-0; www.czechairlines.com)

German Wings (code 4U; ☎ 01-50 291-0070; www.germanwings.com)

Iberia (code IB; ☎ 01-795 67 61-2; www.iberia.com)

KLM (code KL; ☎ 0900-359 556; www.klm.com)

LOT Polish Airlines (code LO; ☎ 01-961 08 85; www.lot.com)

Lufthansa (code LH; ☎ 0810-1025 8080; www.lufthansa.com)

Ryanair (code FR; ☎ 0900-210 240; www.ryanair.com)

SAS Scandinavian Airlines (code SK; ☎ 01-68 055-4466; www.scandinavian.net)

SkyEurope Airlines (code NE; ☎ 01-9985 5555; www.skyeurope.com)

Swiss International Air Lines (code LX; ☎ 0810-810 840; www.swiss.com)

Land

BORDER CROSSINGS

There are many entry points from the Czech Republic, Hungary, Slovakia, Slovenia and Switzerland; main border crossings are open 24 hours. There are usually no border controls to/from Germany and Italy.

BUS

Buses leave Austria for as far afield as England, the Baltic countries, the Netherlands, Germany and Switzerland. But most significantly, they provide access to Eastern European cities small and large – from the likes of Belgrade, Sofia and Warsaw, to Banja Luka, Mostar and Sarajevo.

Services operated by **Eurolines** (www.eurolines.at) leave from Vienna (see p57) and from several regional cities.

CAR & MOTORCYCLE

Austria levies fees for its entire motorway network. Therefore tourists need to choose between a 10-day pass (motorcycle/car €4.30/7.60), a two-month pass (€10.90/21.80) or a yearly pass (€29/72.60) and then clearly display the chosen toll label (*Vignette*) on their vehicle. Passes are available at borders, on freeways or from service stations. Without one, you will face an on-the-spot fine of up to €220 or, if you don't pay up immediately, a €2180 fine. See **Asfinag** (www.oesag.at, in German) for details .

TRAIN

The main rail services in and out of the country include the route from Vienna's Westbahnhof to Munich, via Salzburg and Bregenz. Trains to the Czech Republic leave from Südbahnhof in Vienna. Express services to Italy go via Innsbruck or Villach; trains to Slovenia are routed through Graz.

For Austrian rail passes that extend into other countries, see p607.

River & Lake

Hydrofoils run to Bratislava and Budapest from Vienna (see p57). Germany and Switzerland can be reached from Bregenz (see p85).

GETTING AROUND
Air
Austrian Airlines and its subsidiary, Tyrolean Airlines, operate regular internal flights, but train, bus and car travel usually suffices in such a small country.

Bicycle
Private operators and hostels hire bikes; expect to pay anything from €7 to €10 per day. Vienna has cut-price city bikes (p58).

You can pay separately to take your bike on slow trains (€2.90/7.50/22.50 for a daily/weekly/monthly ticket); on fast trains it costs €6.80 per day, if space allows. Booking is advisable, because if there's no space in the passenger carriages, you will have to send your bike as registered luggage (€21.40). If a group of you are travelling with bikes, ask about the '1-Plus Freizeitticket' (passenger plus bike).

Boat
Services along the Danube are mainly scenic pleasure cruises, but provide a leisurely way of getting from A to B. For more information on boat services along the river, see p57.

Bus
Both *Postbuses* and *Bahnbuses* are now operated by the railways, ÖBB. Bus services are generally limited to less-accessible regions, such as the Salzkammergut or Hohe Tauern National Park. Between major cities in environmentally friendly Austria, only train services exist.

Buses are single class, clean, efficient and run on time. Generally you can only buy tickets from the drivers. Call ☎ 01-71 101 for inquiries.

Car & Motorcycle
AUTOMOBILE ASSOCIATIONS
The **Austrian Automobile Club** (Map p48; Österreichischer Automobil, Motorrad und Touring Club; ÖAMTC; ☎ 01-71 199-0; Schubertring 1-3, A-1010 Vienna) provides emergency breakdown assistance via its **24-hour phone line** (☎ 120). It charges nonmembers an initial call-out fee of €95/135 per day/night, on top of other service charges.

> **EMERGENCY NUMBERS**
>
> ▪ Alpine Rescue ☎ 140
> ▪ Ambulance ☎ 144
> ▪ Fire ☎ 122
> ▪ Police ☎ 133

BRING YOUR OWN VEHICLE
Cars can be transported on trains; Vienna is linked by a daily motorail service to Innsbruck, Salzburg and Villach.

DRIVING LICENCE
Visitors from the EU and the USA can drive using their home driving licence; those from elsewhere require an International Driving Permit.

FUEL & SPARE PARTS
Motorway service stations are found at regular intervals. Basic spare parts are widely available. Ordering more specialised parts, especially for non-European models, takes time and can be costly.

HIRE
Multinational car-hire firms **Avis** (www.avis.at), **Budget** (www.budget.at), **Europcar** (www.europcar.co.at) and **Hertz** (www.hertz.at) all have offices in major cities; ask at tourist offices for details. The minimum age for hiring small cars is 19 years, or 25 years for larger, 'prestige' cars. Customers must have held a driving licence for at least a year. Many contracts forbid customers to take cars outside Austria, particularly into Eastern Europe.

ROAD CONDITIONS
Roads are generally good, but care is needed on difficult mountain routes. Snow chains are highly recommended in winter. There are tolls (usually €2.50 to €10) for some mountain tunnels.

ROAD RULES
Vehicles drive on the right-hand side, and you must give way to traffic on the right. On mountain roads, buses always have priority; otherwise, priority lies with uphill traffic. The usual speed limits are 50km/h in towns, 130km/h on motorways and 100km/h on other roads. There's a steep on-the-spot fine for drink-driving (over 0.05% blood-alcohol

content) and your driving licence may be confiscated. If you plan to drive on motorways, you must pay a tax and affix a *Vignette* to your windscreen (see p90).

Many city streets have restricted parking (called 'blue zones') during shopping hours. Parking is unrestricted on unmarked streets.

Motorcyclists must have their headlights on during the day, and crash helmets are compulsory for riders and passengers.

Hitching

It's illegal to hitchhike on Austrian motorways (and for minors under 16 years of age to hitch anywhere in Burgenland, Upper Austria, Styria and Vorarlberg).

Train

The efficient state network, ÖBB, is supplemented by a few private lines. Eurail and Inter-Rail passes (see p608) are always valid on the state network, but only valid sometimes on private lines. There is no supplement on Eurail and Inter-Rail passes for national travel on faster EC (Eurocity) and IC (Intercity) trains. Tickets purchased on the train cost about €3 extra. Fares quoted in this chapter are for 2nd-class tickets.

Before arriving in Austria, EU residents can buy a Eurodomino Pass (see p608) for Austria for €104 for three days and €10 for each extra day for up to eight days in total.

Available to non-EU residents are the Austrian rail pass (US$119 for three days; US$18 for each extra day up to eight days in total) and the European Eastpass (US$158 for five days; US$23 for each extra day up to 10 days in total) for travel within Austria, the Czech Republic, Hungary, Poland and Slovakia. Both are valid for a month. The Austria & Switzerland Pass (US$270/228 over/under 26 years for four days, and $32/27 for each extra day up to 10 days in total) is valid for two months.

Within Austria, anyone can buy a Vorteils-card (adult/under 26 years/senior €99.90/19.90/26.90), which reduces fares by 45% and is valid for a year.

Nationwide train information can be obtained by dialling ☎ 05-17 17 (local rate) or by going online at **ÖBB** (www.oebb.at).

Czech Republic

For a country that's only been around since 1993, the Czech Republic does a fine job of showcasing a thrilling history. Castles and chateaux abound, illuminating the stories of powerful families and individuals whose influence was felt well beyond the nation's current borders. Unravel the history of Bohemia and Moravia and you're delving into the legacy of Europe itself.

Experience beautifully preserved Renaissance towns, but include a 21st-century spin by sharing a chilled Pilsner lager in street-side cafés with a forthright population confidently taking its place in a united Europe. And if the architectural splendour overwhelms, explore some of Europe's most idiosyncratic landscapes and spectacular forests, which are making a comeback after the industrial sabotage and neglect of the communist era.

The impact of 1989's Velvet Revolution is most obvious in Prague, a stunning melange of high culture, architectural achievement and modern Europe, but spend time in the rest of the country as well. Take in the audacious cliff-top chateau and improbably arcing river at Český Krumlov, the discreetly confident Moravian university town of Olomouc, and the energetic blue-collar Bohemian beer towns of Plzeň and České Budějovice.

You'll soon discover that the Czech Republic is as much about the future as the past.

FAST FACTS

- **Area** 78,864 sq km
- **Capital** Prague
- **Currency** Czech crown (Kč); A$1 = 16.55Kč; €1 = 28.45Kč; Ą100 = 19.47Kč; NZ$1 = 13.56Kč; UK£1 = 41.48Kč; US$1= 22.29Kč
- **Famous for** beer, ice hockey, Kafka, Dvořák
- **Official Language** Czech
- **Phrases** Dobrý den/ahoj (hello/informal), na shledanou (goodbye), děkuji (thank you), promiňte (excuse me)
- **Population** 10.2 million
- **Telephone codes** country code ☎ 420; international access code ☎ 00; there are no telephone codes in the Czech Republic
- **Visas** Citizens of Australia, Canada, Israel, Japan, New Zealand, Switzerland and the USA can stay for up to 90 days without a visa (see p153)

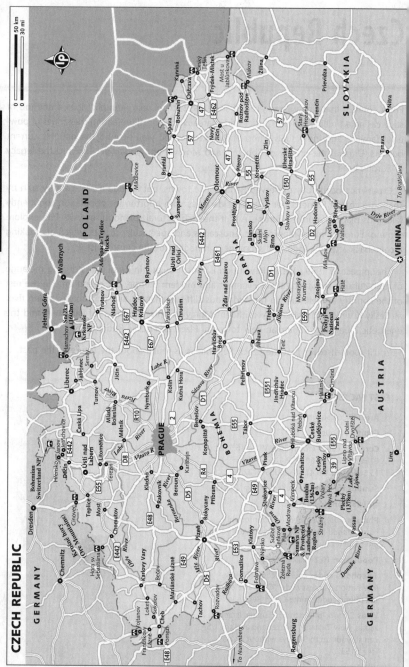

CZECH REPUBLIC

HIGHLIGHTS

- Tune out the tourist crowds in **Prague** (p100) and immerse yourself in the city's legacy of art, architecture and existential angst.
- Conduct your own taste test of two of the world's finest beers at **Plzeň** (p130) and **České Budějovice** (p133).
- Navigate through the spectacular rock formations and hidden river valleys of the **Bohemian Switzerland National Park** (p126).
- Keep the gorgeous old town square of **Olomouc** (p144) and its relaxed student ambience as your own special secret.

ITINERARIES

- **One week** Give Prague its best chance to grab your heart – it's worth at least three days. Mix it up with day trips to Kutná Hora and Terezín, and then head south to Český Krumlov for a couple of days riverside R&R.
- **Two weeks** Begin by sampling the spa waters at Karlovy Vary, and then balance the ledger with beer tasting at Plzeň. Continue to Prague and discover it's actually worth at least five days. If you're not all walked out, divert northeast to hike through the Adršpach-Teplice Rocks. More relaxed souls should head south to Český Krumlov for riverside cafés and lazy meandering down the Vltava. Continue east to Telč's Renaissance grandeur and Brno's cosmopolitan galleries and museums. Squeeze in a day trip to the nearby Moravian Karst caves, and continue to underrated Olomouc to admire the Holy Trinity Column.

CLIMATE & WHEN TO GO

The Czech climate is temperate, with cool, humid winters, warm summers and distinct spring and autumn seasons. While summer has the best weather, July and August are very busy so it's better to visit in May, June or September. Winter has its charms, but Easter, Christmas and New Year are also busy. During the Prague Spring festival (in May), accommodation in Prague can be scarce.

Also see Climate Charts (p586).

HISTORY

Czech history is the story of a people doing whatever they can to survive occupation, and Czechs are more interested in the stories of their rebels and heretics than they are of the kings, emperors and dictators who oppressed them.

Sited in the middle of Europe, the Czechs have been invaded by the Habsburgs, the Nazis, the Soviets, and now by tour groups. Many see EU membership as just another occupation. The Czechs' location has meant none of their local upheavals has stayed local for long. Their rejection of Catholicism in 1418 resulted in the Hussite Wars. The 1618 revolt against Habsburg rule ignited the Thirty Years' War, and the German annexation of the Sudetenland in 1938 helped fuel WWII. The liberal reforms of 1968's Prague Spring led to tanks rolling in from across the Eastern Bloc, and the peaceful ousting of the government during 1989's Velvet Revolution is a model for freedom-seekers everywhere.

Bohemian Beginnings

Ringed by hills, the ancient Czech lands of Bohemia and Moravia have formed natural territories since earliest times. A Celtic tribe called the Boii gave Bohemia its name, while Moravia comes from the Morava River, a Germanic name meaning 'marsh water'.

Slavic tribes from the east settled these territories, and they united from 830 to 907 in the Great Moravian Empire. Christianity was adopted after the arrival in 863 of the Thessalonian missionaries Cyril and Methodius, who created the first Slavic (Cyrillic) alphabet.

CZECH REPUBLIC

HOW MUCH?

- **Night in hostel** 400Kč
- **Double room in pension** 1000Kč
- **Spa Wafer** 5Kč
- **Shot of Becherovka** 45Kč
- **Postcard home** 11Kč

LONELY PLANET INDEX

- **Litre of petrol** 30Kč
- **Litre of bottled water** 35Kč
- **Half-litre of beer** 35Kč
- **Souvenir T-shirt** 300Kč
- **Street snack (sausage & mustard)** 15Kč

In the 9th century the first home-grown dynasty, the Přemysls, erected some huts on a hill in what was to become Prague. This dysfunctional clan gave the Czechs their first martyred saints – Ludmila, killed by her daughter-in-law in 874, and her grandson, the pious Prince Václav (or Good 'King' Wenceslas; r 921–29), murdered by his brother Boleslav the Cruel.

The rule of the Přemysls ended in 1306, and in 1310 John of Luxembourg came to the Bohemian throne through marriage, and annexed the kingdom to the German Empire. The reign of his son, Charles IV (1346–78), who became Holy Roman Emperor, saw the first of Bohemia's two 'Golden Ages' – Charles founded Prague's St Vitus Cathedral, built Charles Bridge, and established Charles University. The second was the reign of Rudolf II (1576–1612), who made Prague the capital of the Habsburg Empire and attracted artists, scholars and scientists to his court. Bohemia and Moravia remained under Habsburg dominion for almost four centuries.

Under the Habsburg Thumb

In 1415 the Protestant religious reformer Jan Hus, rector of Charles University, was burnt at the stake for heresy. Hus led a movement that espoused letting the congregation taste the sacramental wine as well as the host (the Hussites' symbol was the communion chalice). The religious and nationalist Hussite movement, which plunged Bohemia into civil war between 1419 and 1434 was inspired by his ideas.

When the Austrian – and Catholic – Habsburg dynasty ascended the Bohemian throne in 1526, the fury of the Counter-Reformation was unleashed on 23 May 1618 when a group of Protestants threw two Habsburg councillors from a Prague Castle window. The squabble escalated into the Catholic–Protestant Thirty Years' War (1618–48), which devastated much of central Europe and shattered Bohemia's economy.

The defeat of the Protestant uprising at the Battle of White Mountain in 1620 marked the start of a long period of forced re-Catholicisation, Germanisation and oppression of Czech language and culture. The baroque architectural style, which flourished in the 17th and 18th centuries, was the outward symbol of Catholic victory over the Protestant heretics.

National Reawakening

The Czechs began to rediscover their linguistic and cultural roots at the start of the 19th century, during the so-called Národní obrození (National Revival). Overt political activity was banned, so the revival was culturally based. Important figures of the time included historian Josef Palacký and composer Bedřich Smetana. A distinctive neo-Renaissance architecture emerged, exemplified by Prague's National Theatre and National Museum.

The drive towards an independent Czech and Slovak state was realised after WWI, when the Habsburg Empire's demise saw the creation of the Czechoslovak Republic on 28 October 1918. The first president was Tomáš Garrigue Masaryk. Three-quarters of the Austro-Hungarian empire's industrial power was inherited by Czechoslovakia, as were three million Germans, mostly in the border areas of Bohemia (the pohraniči, known in German as the Sudetenland).

The Czechs' elation was to be short-lived. Under the Munich Pact of September 1938, Britain and France accepted the annexation of the Sudetenland by Nazi Germany, and in March 1939 the Germans occupied the rest of the country (calling it the Protectorate of Bohemia and Moravia).

The rapid occupation ensured the country's historic buildings suffered minimal damage, but most of the Czech intelligentsia and 80,000 Jews died at the hands of the Nazis. When Czech paratroopers assassinated the Nazi governor Reinhardt Heydrich in 1942, the entire town of Lidice was wiped out in revenge.

Communist Coup

After the war, the Czechoslovak government expelled 2.5 million Sudeten Germans – including antifascists who had fought the Nazis – from the Czech borderlands and confiscated their property. During the forced marches from Czechoslovakia many were interned in concentration camps, and it is estimated that tens of thousands died. In 1997 Czech Prime Minister Václav Klaus and German chancellor Helmut Kohl signed a declaration of mutual apology, but many Sudeten Germans are still campaigning for the restitution of lost land and houses.

In 1947 a power struggle began between the communist and democratic forces, and in early 1948 the Social Democrats withdrew from the postwar coalition. The result was the Soviet-backed coup d'état of 25 February 1948, known as *Vítězný únor* (Victorious February). The new communist-led government established the dictatorship of the proletariat, and communist leader Klement Gottwald became the country's president.

The industrial sector was nationalised and the government's economic policies nearly bankrupted the country. The 1950s were repressive years and thousands of noncommunists fled the country. Many were imprisoned and hundreds were executed or died in labour camps for no more than believing in democracy or religion. A series of Stalinist purges were organised, and many, including top party members, were executed.

Prague Spring & Velvet Revolution

In April 1968 the new first secretary of the Communist Party, Alexander Dubček, introduced liberalising reforms to create 'socialism with a human face' – known as the 'Prague Spring'. Censorship ended, political prisoners were released and economic decentralisation began. Moscow was not happy, but Dubček refused to buckle. Soviet tanks entered Prague on 20 August 1968, and Czechoslovakia was subsequently occupied by 200,000 Soviet and Warsaw Pact soldiers.

Around 14,000 Communist Party functionaries were expelled, and 500,000 party members lost their jobs after the dictatorship was re-established. Dissidents were summarily imprisoned and educated professionals were made manual labourers.

The 1977 trial of the rock group The Plastic People of the Universe inspired the formation of the human-rights group Charter 77. (The communists saw the musicians as threatening the status quo, but others viewed the trial as an assault on human rights.) Charter 77's group of Prague intellectuals, including the playwright/philosopher Václav Havel, continued their underground opposition throughout the 1980s.

By 1989 Gorbachev's perestroika was sending shock waves through the region and the fall of the Berlin Wall on 9 November raised expectations of change in Czechoslovakia. On 17 November an official student march in Prague was smashed by police. Daily demonstrations followed, and the protests grew to a general strike on 27 November. Dissidents led by Havel formed the anti-Communist

Civic Forum and negotiated the resignation of the Communist government on 3 December.

A 'Government of National Understanding' was formed, with Havel elected president on 29 December. With no casualties, the days after 17 November became known as *Sametová revoluce* (the 'Velvet Revolution').

Velvet Divorce

Following the dissolution of the communists' central authority, antagonisms between Slovakia and Prague re-emerged. The federal parliament tried to stabilise the situation by granting both the Czech and Slovak Republics full federal status within a Czech and Slovak Federated Republic (ČSFR), but failed to satisfy Slovak nationalists. The Civic Forum split into two factions: the centrist Civic Movement and the Civic Democratic Party (ODS).

Elections in June 1992 sealed Czechoslovakia's fate. Václav Klaus' ODS took 48 seats in the 150-seat federal parliament; while 24 went to the Movement for a Democratic Slovakia (HZDS), a left-leaning Slovak nationalist party led by Vladimír Mečiar.

In July, goaded by Mečiar's rhetoric, the Slovak parliament declared sovereignty. The two leaders could not reach a compromise and splitting the country was seen as the best solution. On 1 January 1993 Czechoslovakia ceased to exist for the second time. Prague became capital of the new Czech Republic, and Havel was elected its first president.

Thanks to booming tourism and a solid industrial base, the Czech Republic started strongly. Unemployment was negligible, shops were full and, by 2003, Prague enjoyed Central Europe's highest living standards. Capitalism also meant a lack of affordable housing, rising crime and a deteriorating health system.

In 2003, Václav Havel was replaced by former prime minister Klaus - it took three elections for Czechs to settle on a new president, and the uncharismatic and conservative Klaus is far from the popular leader Havel was. Further government instability followed inconclusive elections in June 2006 that left the Czech Republic's lower house equally divided between the left and the right.

Left-leaning Social Democrat leader Jiri Paroubek finally resigned as Prime Minister in August 2006, and was replaced by right-leaning Civic Democrats leader Mirek

CZECH REPUBLIC

MIND YOUR MANNERS

It is customary to say *dobrý den* (good day) when entering a shop, café or quiet bar, and *na shledanou* (goodbye) when leaving. If you are invited to a Czech home, bring fresh flowers and remember to remove your shoes when you enter the house.

Topolanek in an attempt to form a minority government. The country's next general election is planned for 2009, but at the time of writing an early election was looking far more likely due to the impasse in the Czech Republic's lower house.

The Czech Republic became a member of NATO in 1999, and joined the EU on 1 May 2004. With EU membership, greater numbers of younger Czechs are working and studying abroad, seizing opportunities their parents didn't have. The Czech Republic is scheduled to adopt the euro in 2010.

PEOPLE

The population of the Czech Republic is 10.2 million, and fairly homogeneous: 95% of the population are Czech and 3% are Slovak. Only 150,000 of the three million Sudeten Germans evicted after WWII remain, comprising about 1.5% of the current population. A significant Roma population (0.3%) is subject to hostility and racism, and suffers from poverty and unemployment.

RELIGION

Most Czechs are either atheist (39.8%) or nominally Roman Catholic (39.2%), but church attendance is low. There are small Protestant (4.6%) and Orthodox (3%) congregations, while the Jewish community (1% of the population in 1918) today numbers only a few thousand. Religious tolerance is accepted and the Catholic Church does not involve itself in politics.

ARTS
Literature

Franz Kafka was one of Bohemia's greatest writers, and his circle of German-speaking Jewish writers strongly influenced Prague's literary scene in the early 20th century.

After WWI Jaroslav Hašek devoted himself to lampooning the Habsburg empire and its minions; his folk masterpiece *The Good Sol-*dier Švejk is a riotous story of a Czech soldier during WWI.

Bohumil Hrabal (1914–97), one of the finest Czech novelists of the 20th century, wrote *The Little Town Where Time Stood Still*, a gentle portrayal of the machinations of small-town life.

Milan Kundera (b 1929) is the most renowned Czech writer internationally, with his novel *The Unbearable Lightness of Being* having been made into a film. His first work *The Joke* is a penetrating insight into the communist era's paranoia.

An interesting contemporary Czech writer is poet and rock-lyricist Jáchym Topol, whose stream-of-consciousness novel *Sister City Silver* is an exhilarating exploration of postcommunist Prague.

Cinema

Ceský Sen (Czech Dream, 2004) is a recent feature documentary showing the hoax launch of a new Czech department store. With a fake marketing campaign, fake advertising and even a massive fake façade to the new hypermarket, *Ceský Sen* is a timely observation of the postcommunist expectations of Czech society in the months leading to their entry into the EU.

Music

Bedřich Smetana (1824–84), the first great Czech composer and an icon of Czech pride, created a national style by incorporating folk songs and dances into his classical compositions. His best-known pieces are the operas *Prodaná Nevěsta* (The Bartered Bride) and *Dalibor a Libuše* (Dalibor and Libuše, named after the two main characters), and the symphonic-poem cycle *Má vlast* (My Homeland). Prague Spring (p151), the country's biggest festival, is dedicated to Smetana and begins with a parade from the composer's grave at Vyšehrad to the Smetana Hall, where *Má vlast* is then performed.

Antonín Dvořák (1841–1904) is perhaps everyone's favourite Czech composer. His most popular works include his symphony *From the New World* (composed in the USA while lecturing there for four years), his *Slavonic Dances* of 1878 and 1881, the operas *The Devil & Kate* and *Rusalka*, and his religious masterpiece *Stabat Mater*.

Visual Arts

Think Art Nouveau and you're probably thinking Alfons Mucha (1860– 1939). Though he lived mostly in Paris and is associated with the French Art Nouveau movement, Mucha's heart remained at home in Bohemia and much of his work visits and revisits themes of Slavic suffering, courage and cross-nation brotherhood. The most outstanding of his works is a series of 20 large, cinematic canvasses called the *Slav Epic*, which are presently in Moravský Krumlov (p144), and his interior decoration in the Municipal House in Prague (see p108), but his design and print work can be seen all over the Czech Republic.

David Černý (b 1967) is a controversial contemporary Czech sculptor. His work includes the statue of St Wenceslas riding an upsidedown horse in Prague's pasáž Lucerna, and the giant babies crawling up the Žižkov TV tower in Prague. See www.davidcerny.cz.

ENVIRONMENT

The Czech Republic is a landlocked country bordered by Germany, Austria, Slovakia and Poland. The land is made up of two river basins: Bohemia in the west, drained by the Labe (Elbe) River flowing north into Germany; and Moravia in the east, drained by the Morava River flowing southeast into the Danube. Each basin is ringed by low, forestclad hills, notably the Šumava range along the Bavarian–Austrian border in the southwest, the Krušné hory (Ore Mountains) along the northwestern border with Germany, and the Krkonoše mountains along the Polish border east of Liberec. The country's highest peak, Sněžka (1602m), is in the Krkonoše. In between these ranges are rolling plains mixed with forests and farm land. Forests – mainly spruce, oak and beech – still cover one-third of the country.

The South Bohemian landscape is characterised by a network of hundreds of linked fish ponds and artificial lakes. The biggest lake in the republic, the 4870-hectare Lake Lipno, is also in South Bohemia. East Bohemia is home to the striking 'rock towns' of the Adršpach-Teplice Rocks (p139).

National Parks

Though numerous areas are set aside as national parks and protected landscape areas, the emphasis is on visitor use as well as species and landscape protection. National parks and protected areas make up approximately 15% of the Czech Republic, including the Bohemian Switzerland (p126) and Šumava (p138) national parks, as well as the Adršpach-Teplice Protected Landscape Area (p139).

Environmental Issues

The forests of northern Bohemia and Moravia have been devastated by acid rain created by the burning of poor-quality brown coal at factories and thermal power stations. The most affected region is the eastern Ore Mountains where most of the trees are dead. In recent years sulphur dioxide levels in Prague have declined, while carbon monoxide pollution from cars and trucks has increased. Industrial emissions have been cleaned up in recent years following the entry of the Czech Republic into the EU in 2004. Local industries are being forced to adopt stringent environmental codes which are further alleviating domestic pollution.

Following the entry of the Czech Republic into the EU in 2004, local industries are being forced to adopt EU environmental codes, which should further alleviate domestic pollution.

FOOD & DRINK

On the surface, Czech food seems very similar to German or Polish food: lots of meat served with *knedlíky* (dumplings) and cabbage. The little differences make the food here special – eat a forkful of *svíčková* (roast beef served with a sour-cream sauce and spices) sopped up with fluffy *knedlíky* and you'll be wondering why you haven't heard more about this cuisine.

Staples & Specialities

Traditional Czech cuisine is strong on meat, *knedlíky* and gravy, and weak on fresh vegetables; the classic Bohemian dish is *knedlo-zelo-vepřo* – bread dumplings, sauerkraut and roast pork. Other tasty homegrown delicacies to look out for include *cesneková* (garlic soup), *svíčková na smetaně* (roast beef with sour cream sauce and cranberries) and *kapr na kmíní* (fried or baked carp with caraway seed). *Ovocné knedlíky* (fruit dumplings), with whole fruit, are served as a dessert with cottage cheese or crushed poppy seeds and melted butter.

The Czech Republic is a beer-drinker's paradise – where else could you get a 500mL glass of top-quality Pilsner for less than a dollar? One of the first words of Czech you'll

CZECH REPUBLIC

CZECH REPUBLIC

TOP FIVE BEERS

Czech beer is not just about Pilsner Urquell and Budvar. Watch out for these interesting brews:

■ Černá Hora (Black Mountain) Brewery's honey-flavoured Kvasar lager.

■ Bernard's special *cerne pivo* (dark beer), which uses five different malts.

■ The wheat beer with lemon at Pivnice Pegas in Brno.

■ The champagne beer at Pivovarský Dům in Prague.

■ Zlatý Bažant (Golden Pheasant) lager from Slovakia.

---

learn is *pivo* (beer). The Czechs serve their draught beer with a high head of foam.

Bohemian *pivo* is probably the best in the world – the most famous brands are Budvar (see p133) and Pilsner Urquell (p130). The South Moravian vineyards (p148) produce reasonable *bílé víno* (white wines).

Special alcoholic treats include Becherovka (see p126) and *slivovice* (plum brandy). *Grog* is rum with hot water and sugar. *Limonáda* often refers to any soft drink, not just lemonade.

Where to Eat & Drink

A *bufet* or *samoobsluha* is a self-service, cafeteria-style place with *chlebíčky* (open sandwiches), salads, *klobásy* (spicy sausages), *špekačky* (mild pork sausages), *párky* (frankfurters), *guláš* (goulash) and of course *knedlíky*. Some of these places are tucked to the side of *potraviny* (food shops). A *bageteria* serves made-to-order sandwiches and baguettes.

A *pivnice* is a pub without food, while a *hospoda* or *hostinec* is a pub or beer hall that serves basic meals. A *vinárna* (wine bar) may have anything from snacks to a full-blown menu. The occasional *kavárna* (café) has a full menu but most only serve snacks and desserts. A *restaurace* is any restaurant.

Restaurants start serving as early as 11am and carry on till midnight; some take a break between lunch and dinner. Main dishes may stop being served well before the advertised closing time, with only snacks and drinks after that.

Vegetarians & Vegans

In Prague and other main cities there is a growing range of vegetarian restaurants, but options in the smaller towns remain more limited. Vegans will find life very difficult. There are a few standard *bezmasá jídla* (meatless dishes) served by most restaurants: the most common are *smažený sýr* (fried cheese) and vegetables cooked with cheese sauce. The pizza joints that you'll find in almost every town make for a good standby option.

Habits & Customs

Most beer halls have a system of marking everything you eat or drink on a small piece of paper that is left on your table, then totted up when you pay (say *zaplatím, prosím* – I'd like to pay, please). Waiters in all Czech restaurants, including the expensive ones, often whisk away empty plates from under your nose before you manage to swallow the last of your *knedlíky*.

In a pub, always ask if a chair is free before sitting down (*Je tu volno?*). The standard toast involves clinking together first the tops, then the bottoms of glasses, then touching the glass to the table; most people say *Na zdraví* (To health).

PRAGUE

pop 1.19 million

It's the perfect irony of Prague. You are lured there by the past, but compelled to linger by the present and the future. Fill your days with its artistic and architectural heritage – from Gothic and Renaissance to Art Nouveau and Cubist – but after dark move your focus to the here and now in the form of lively bars, cutting-edge galleries and innovative jazz clubs. And if the frantic energy of post-communist Prague and its army of tourists wears thin, that's OK. Just drink a glass of the country's legendary premium Bohemian lager, relax and be reassured that quiet moments still exist in one of Europe's most exciting cities: a private dawn on Charles Bridge; a chilled beer in Letná as you gaze upon the surreal cityscape of Staré Město; or getting reassuringly lost in the intimate streets of Malá Strana. You'll then be ready to dive once more into this thrilling collage of past and future.

ORIENTATION

Central Prague nestles in a bend of the Vltava River, which separates Hradčany (the medieval castle district) and Malá Strana (Little Quarter) on the west bank from Staré Město (Old Town) and Nové Město (New Town) on the east.

Prague Castle, visible from almost everywhere in the city, overlooks Malá Strana, while the twin Gothic spires of Týn Church dominate the wide open space of Staroměstské nám (Old Town Square). The broad avenue of Václavské nám (Wenceslas Square) stretches southeast from Staré Město towards the National Museum and the main train station.

You can walk from Praha-hlavní nádraží (Prague's main train station) to Staroměstské nám in 10 minutes. From Praha-Holešovice, take the metro (also 10 minutes) to Staroměstské nám. There's a metro station at Florenc bus station too; take Line B (yellow) two stops west to Můstek for the city centre.

Maps

Lonely Planet's plastic-coated *Prague City Map* is convenient and detailed. Other good maps include Marco Polo's *Praha – centrum* (1:5,000) and SHOCart's GeoClub *Praha – plán města* (1:15,000). PIS offers a free *Welcome to the Czech Republic* pamphlet with a map of the city centre.

INFORMATION
Bookshops

Anagram (Map pp110-11; ☎ 224 895 737; www .anagram.cz; Týn 4, Staré Město; ☽ 10am-8pm Mon-Sat, 10am-7pm Sun) An excellent range of history and culture books.

Big Ben Bookshop (Map pp110-11; ☎ 224 826 565; www.bigbenbookshop.com; Malá Štupartská 5, Staré Město; ☽ 9am-6.30pm Mon-Fri, 10am-5pm Sat & Sun) Prague's biggest range of English-language books, magazines and newspapers.

Globe (Map pp110-11; ☎ 224 934 203; www.globebook store.cz; Pštrossova 6, Nové Město; ☽ 10am-midnight) Has new and secondhand books in English and German, a good range of magazines and Prague's biggest gay and lesbian interest section.

Kiwi (Map pp110-11; ☎ 224 948 455; Jungmannova 23, Nové Město; ☽ 9am-6.30pm Mon-Fri, 9am-2pm Sat) A specialist travel bookshop with a huge range of maps and guidebooks.

Neo Luxor (Map pp110-11; ☎ 221 111 364; Václavské nám 41, Nové Město; ☽ 8am-8pm Mon-Fri, 9am-7pm

Sat, 10am-7pm Sun) Books and magazines in English, German and French and internet access (1Kč per minute).

Emergencies

If your passport, wallet or other valuables have been stolen, obtain a police report and crime number from the **State Police Station** (Map pp110-11; Vlašská 3, Malá Strana; ☽ 24hr). You will need this to make an insurance claim. Unless you speak Czech, forget about telephoning the police, as you will rarely get through to an English speaker.

Internet Access

An increasing number of hotels, bars, fast-food restaurants and internet cafés in Prague provide wi-fi hotspots where can use your own laptop.

Bohemia Bagel (per min 1.50Kč) Malá Strana (Map pp110-11; ☎ 257 310 694; Újezd 16; ☽ 7am-midnight); Staré Město (Map pp110-11; ☎ 224 812 560; Masná 2; ☽ 7am-midnight). Also provides low-cost international phone calls.

Globe (Map pp110-11; ☎ 224 934 203; www.globebook store.cz; Pštrossova 6, Nové Město; per min 1.50Kč, no minimum; ☽ 10am-midnight) Also has ethernet sockets where you can connect your own laptop (same price; cables provided, 50Kč deposit).

Mobilarium (Map pp110-11; ☎ 221 967 327; Rathova Pasaž, Na příkopě 23, Nové Město; per min 1.50Kč; ☽ 10am-8pm Mon-Fri, 11am-8pm Sat & Sun)

Planeta (Map pp102-3; ☎ 267 311 182; Vinohradská 102, Vinohrady; per min 0.40-0.80Kč; ☽ 8am-11pm) Cheap rates before 10am and after 8pm Monday to Friday, and 8am to 11pm Saturday and Sunday.

Praha Bike (Map pp110-11; ☎ 732 388 880; Dlouhá 24; Staré Město; per min 1Kč; ☽ 9am-7pm Mar-Nov, noon-6pm Oct-Feb) Wi-fi at same cost.

Internet Resources

Dopravní podnik (www.dp-praha.cz) Information about public transport in Prague.

Prague Information Service (www.prague-info.cz) Official tourist office site.

Prague Post (www.praguepost.cz) Keep up-to-date with news, events and visitor information with this English-language website.

Prague TV (www.prague.tv) Highlights Prague's best events, arts and nightlife.

Laundry

Most self-service laundrettes will charge around 160Kč to wash and dry a 6kg load of laundry.

Laundry Kings (Map pp102-3; ☎ 233 343 743; Dejvická 16, Dejvice; ☽ 7am-10pm Mon-Fri, 8am-10pm Sat & Sun)

CZECH REPUBLIC

PRAGUE

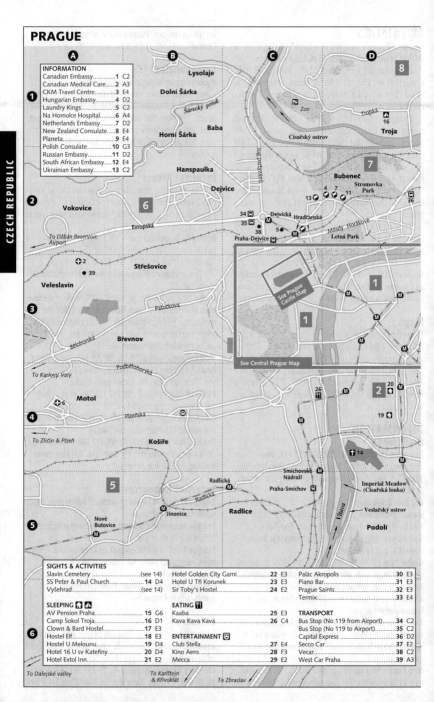

INFORMATION
Canadian Embassy	1	C2
Canadian Medical Care	2	A3
CKM Travel Centre	3	E4
Hungarian Embassy	4	D2
Laundry Kings	5	C2
Na Homolce Hospital	6	A4
Netherlands Embassy	7	D2
New Zealand Consulate	8	E4
Planeta	9	E4
Polish Consulate	10	G3
Russian Embassy	11	D2
South African Embassy	12	E4
Ukrainian Embassy	13	C2

SIGHTS & ACTIVITIES
Slavín Cemetery	(see 14)	
SS Peter & Paul Church	14	D4
Vyšehrad	(see 14)	

SLEEPING
AV Pension Praha	15	G6
Camp Sokol Troja	16	D1
Clown & Bard Hostel	17	E3
Hostel Elf	18	D3
Hostel U Melounu	19	D4
Hotel 16 U sv Kateřiny	20	D4
Hotel Extol Inn	21	E2

EATING
Kaaba	25	E3
Kava Kava Kava	26	C4

ENTERTAINMENT
Club Stella	27	E4
Kino Aero	28	F3
Mecca	29	E2

Hotel Golden City Garni	22	E3
Hotel U Tří Korunek	23	E3
Sir Toby's Hostel	24	E2

Palác Akropolis	30	E3
Piano Bar	31	E3
Prague Saints	32	E3
Termix	33	E4

TRANSPORT
Bus Stop (No 119 from Airport)	34	C2
Bus Stop (No 119 to Airport)	35	C2
Capital Express	36	D2
Secco Car	37	E2
Vecar	38	C2
West Car Praha	39	A3

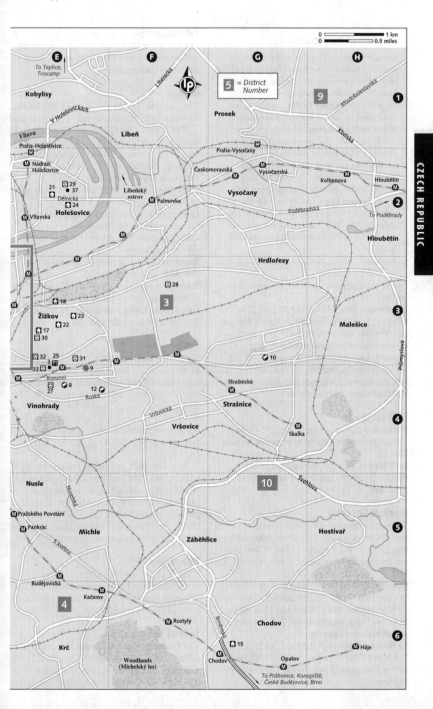

CZECH REPUBLIC

PRAGUE IN TWO DAYS

Beat the tourist hordes with an early-morning stroll across **Charles Bridge** (p107) and continue uphill to Hradčany and the eclectic **Strahov Library** (p107). Move on to grandiose **Prague Castle** (opposite) and then head down the hill to the compelling **Franz Kafka Museum** (p107).

On day two continue exploring Kafka's heritage in **Josefov** (p108), Prague's original Jewish quarter, and then visit the hilltop fortress at **Vyšehrad** (p109). Be sure to savour a glass or two of tasty Czech beer: try **U Zlatého Tygra** (p116) for tradition, or sample the innovative brews at **Pivovarský Dům** (p116). After dark check out the jazz vibe at the coolly sophisticated **Dinitz Café** (p115).

Expat-run place with a bulletin board, newspapers and internet (1.50Kč per minute).

Laundryland (Map pp110-11; ☎ 221 014 632; Na příkopě 12, Nové Město; ☺ 9am-8pm Mon-Fri, 9am-7pm Sat, 11am-7pm Sun) On the 1st floor of Černá Růže shopping centre, above the Panská entrance.

Prague Cyber Laundromat (Map pp102-3; ☎ 222 510 180; Korunní 14, Vinohrady; ☺ 8am-8pm) Near Nám Míru metro station. Friendly place with internet café (1.50Kč per minute) and kids' play area.

Left Luggage

Florenc bus station (per bag per day 25Kč; ☺ 5am-11pm) Halfway up the stairs on the left beyond the main ticket hall.

Main train station (per small/large bag per day 15/30Kč; ☺ 24hr) On Level 1. There are also lockers (60Kč coins).

Medical Services

There are several 24-hour pharmacies in the centre of town, including **Praha lékárna** (Map pp110-11; ☎ 224 946 982; Palackého 5, Nové Město); for emergency service after hours, ring the bell.

Canadian Medical Care (Map pp102-3; ☎ 235 360 133, after hours 724 300 301; Veleslavínská 1, Veleslavín; ☺ 8am-6pm Mon, Wed & Fri, 8am-8pm Tue & Thu) Expat centre with English-speaking doctors, 24-hour medical aid, physiotherapist and pharmacy.

Na Homolce Hospital (Map pp102-3; ☎ 257 271 111, after hours 257 272 527; www.homolka.cz; 5th fl, Foreign Pavilion, Roentgenova 2, Motol) Prague's main casualty department.

Polyclinic at Národní (Map pp110-11; ☎ 222 075 120; 24hr emergencies 720 427 634; www.poliklinika.narodni .cz; Národní třída 9, Nové Město) With English-, French- and German-speaking staff.

Money

The major banks – Komerční banka, Živnostenská banka, Česká spořitelna and ČSOB – are the best places for changing cash, but using a debit card in an ATM gives a better rate of exchange. Avoid *směnárna* (private exchange booths), which advertise misleading rates and have exorbitant charges.

Amex (Map pp110-11; ☎ 222 800 237; Václavské nám 56, Nové Město; ☺ 9am-7pm)

Česká spořitelna (Map pp110-11; Václavské nám 16, Nové Město; ☺ 8am-5pm Mon-Fri)

ČSOB (Map pp110-11; Na příkopě 14, Nové Město; ☺ 8am-5pm Mon-Fri)

Komerční banka (Map pp110-11; Václavské nám 42, Nové Město; ☺ 8am-5pm Mon-Fri)

Travelex (Map pp110-11; ☎ 221 105 276; Národní třída 28, Nové Město; ☺ 9am-1.30pm & 2-6.30pm)

Živnostenská banka (Map pp110-11; Na příkopě 20, Nové Město; ☺ 8am-4.30pm Mon-Fri)

Post

To use the **main post office** (Map pp110-11; Jindřišská 14, Nové Město; ☺ 2am-midnight), collect a ticket from one of the automated machines just outside the main hall (press button No 1 for stamps and parcels; No 4 for EMS). Wait until your *lístek číslo* (number) comes up on the electronic boards inside; these tell you which window to go to for *přepážka* (service).

You can pick up poste restante mail at window No 1 and buy phonecards at window No 28. Parcels weighing up to 2kg, as well as international and Express Mail Service (EMS) parcels, are sent from window Nos 7 to 10. (Note that these services close at noon on Saturday and all day on Sunday.)

Telephone

There's a 24-hour telephone centre to the left of the right-hand entrance to the post office. Bohemia Bagel (p101) has phones for making low-cost international calls.

Tourist Information

The **Prague Information Service** (Pražská infor mační služba, PIS; ☎ 12 444, in English & German 221 714 444; www.prague-info.cz) provides free tourist information with good maps and detailed brochures (including accommodation and historical monuments).

There are three PIS offices:

Main train station (Praha hlavní nádraží; Map pp110-11; Wilsonova 2, Nové Město; 🕑 9am-7pm Mon-Fri, 9am-6pm Sat & Sun Apr-Oct; 9am-6pm Mon-Fri, 9am-5pm Sat & Sun Nov-Mar)

Malá Strana Bridge Tower (Map pp110-11; Charles Bridge; 🕑 10am-6pm Apr-Oct)

Old Town Hall (Map pp110-11; Staroměstské nám 5, Staré Město; 🕑 9am-7pm Mon-Fri, to 6pm Sat & Sun Apr-Oct; 9am-6pm Mon-Fri, to 5pm Sat & Sun Nov-Mar)

Travel Agencies

Čedok (Map pp110-11; ☎ 224 197 699, 800 112 112; www.cedok.cz; Na příkopě 18, Nové Město; 🕑 9am-7pm Mon-Fri, 9.30am-1pm Sat) Tour operator and travel agency. Also books accommodation, concert and theatre tickets, rents cars and exchanges money.

CKM Travel Centre (Map pp102-3; ☎ 222 721 595; www.ckm.cz; Mánesova 77, Vinohrady; 🕑 10am-6pm Mon-Thu, 10am-4pm Fri) Books air and bus tickets, with discounts for those aged under 26. Sells youth cards.

Eurolines-Sodeli CZ (Map pp110-11; ☎ 224 239 318; Senovážné nám 6, Nové Město; 🕑 8am-6pm Mon-Fri) Agent for Eurolines buses.

GTS International (Map pp110-11; ☎ 222 211 204; www.gtsint.cz; Ve Smečkách 33, Nové Město; 🕑 8am-8pm Mon-Fri, 11am-4pm Sat) Youth cards and air, bus and train tickets.

DANGERS & ANNOYANCES

Prague's crime rate is low by Western standards, but beware of pickpockets who regularly work the crowds at the astronomical clock, Prague Castle and Charles Bridge, and on the central metro and tram lines, especially tourists getting on or off crowded trams 9 and 22.

Being ripped off by taxi drivers is another hazard. Most taxi drivers are honest, but a sizable minority who operate from tourist areas greatly overcharge their customers (even Czechs). Try not to take a taxi from Václavské nám, Národní třída and other tourist areas. It's better to phone for a taxi (see p121) or walk a couple of streets before hailing one.

The park outside the main train station is a hang-out for drunks and dodgy types and should be avoided late at night.

Scams

We've had reports of bogus police approaching tourists and asking to see their money, claiming that they are looking for counterfeit notes. They then run off with the cash. If in doubt, ask the 'policeman' to go with you to the nearest police station; a genuine cop will happily do so.

SIGHTS

All the main sights are in the city centre, and are easily reached on foot; you can take in the castle, Charles Bridge and Staroměstské nám in a day.

Prague Castle
INFORMATION

Dominating Prague's skyline like a vast, beached battleship is **Prague Castle** (Pražský hrad; Map p106; ☎ 224 373 368; www.hrad.cz; 🕑 9am-5pm Apr-Oct, 9am-4pm Nov-Mar; grounds 5am-midnight Apr-Oct, 6am-11pm Nov-Mar; ♿). The biggest castle complex in the world feels more like a small town than a castle. It is the seat of Czech power, both political and symbolic, housing the president's office and the ancient Bohemian crown jewels.

Among many ticket options, **Ticket B** (adult/child 220/110Kč) is the best value, giving access to St Vitus Cathedral (choir, crypt and tower), Old Royal Palace and Golden Lane. **Ticket A** (350/175Kč) includes all of these plus the Basilica of St George, Powder Tower and Story of Prague Castle exhibit. Buy tickets at the **Castle Information Centre** in the Third Courtyard and at the entrance to the main sights. Most areas are wheelchair accessible.

SIGHTS

The main entrance is at the western end. The **changing of the guard**, with stylish uniforms created by Theodor Pistek (costume designer for the film *Amadeus*) takes place every hour, on the hour. At noon a band plays from the windows above.

The **Matthias Gate** leads to the second courtyard and the **Chapel of the Holy Cross** (concert tickets on sale here). On the north side is the **Prague Castle Gallery** (adult/child 100/50Kč; 🕑 10am-6pm), with a collection of European baroque art.

The third courtyard is dominated by **St Vitus Cathedral**, a French Gothic structure begun in 1344 by Emperor Charles IV, but not completed until 1929. Colour from stained-glass windows created by early-20th-century Czech artists floods the interior, including one by Alfons Mucha (3rd chapel on the left as you enter the cathedral)

CZECH REPUBLIC

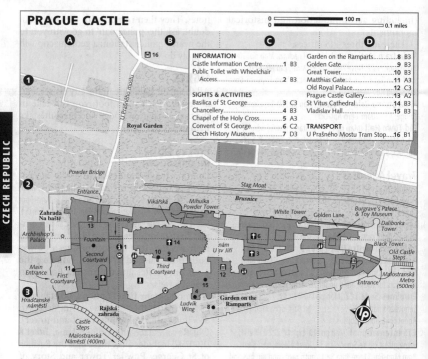

PRAGUE CASTLE

0 ———— 100 m
0 ———————— 0.1 miles

INFORMATION
Castle Information Centre............**1** B3
Public Toilet with Wheelchair
   Access.....................................**2** B3

SIGHTS & ACTIVITIES
Basilica of St George.................**3** C3
Chancellery..............................**4** B3
Chapel of the Holy Cross...........**5** A3
Convent of St George.................**6** C2
Czech History Museum.............**7** D3

Garden on the Ramparts............**8** B3
Golden Gate.............................**9** B3
Great Tower.............................**10** B3
Matthias Gate..........................**11** A3
Old Royal Palace......................**12** C3
Prague Castle Gallery...............**13** A2
St Vitus Cathedral...................**14** B3
Vladislav Hall..........................**15** B3

TRANSPORT
U Prašného Mostu Tram Stop....**16** B1

---

featuring SS Cyril and Methodius. In the apse is the massive **tomb of St John of Nepomuk** – two tonnes of baroque silver watched over by hovering cherubs.

The 14th-century chapel on the cathedral's southern side with the black imperial eagle on the door contains the **tomb of St Wenceslas**, the Czechs' patron saint and the Good King Wenceslas of Christmas carol fame. Wenceslas' zeal in spreading Christianity and his submission to the German King Henry I saw him murdered by his brother, Boleslav I. According to legend he was stabbed to death clinging to the Romanesque lion's-head handle that graces the chapel door. The smaller door on the far side, beside the windows, leads to the Bohemian crown jewels (not open to the public).

On the other side of the transept, climb the 287 steps of the **Great Tower** (✪ 9am-4.15pm Apr-Oct) for views over the city.

On the southern side of the cathedral's exterior is the **Golden Gate** (Zlatá brána) a triple-arched doorway topped by a 14th-century mosaic of the Last Judgment: to the left, the righteous are raised into heaven; to the right, sinners are cast into hell.

Opposite is the entrance to the **Old Royal Palace** with the elegantly vaulted **Vladislav Hall**, built between 1486 and 1502. Horsemen used to ride into the hall up the ramp at the far end for indoor jousts. Two Catholic councillors were thrown out the window of the adjacent **Chancellery** by irate Protestant nobles on 23 May 1618. This infamous Second Defenestration of Prague ignited the Thirty Years' War.

Leaving the palace, the Romanesque **Basilica of St George** (1142) is in front of you, and in the nearby **Convent of St George** (adult/child 100/50Kč; ✪ 10am-6pm Tue-Sun) is the National Gallery's collection of Czech art from the 16th to 18th centuries.

Beyond, the crowds surge into Golden Lane, a 16th-century tradesmen's quarter of tiny houses in the castle walls. It's a souvenir-laden tourist trap you can safely miss, though Kafka fans should note his sister's house at No 22, where he lived and wrote in 1916–17.

On the right, before the castle's exit, is the Lobkowicz Palace, housing the **Czech History Museum** (adult/child 40/20Kč; ✪ 9am-5pm Tue-Sun). From the castle's eastern end, the Old Castle Steps lead to Malostranská metro station, or turn sharp right to wander back through the lovely **Garden on the Ramparts** (admission free; ☺ 10am-6pm Apr-Oct).

Forgoing an uphill hike, get to the castle by tram 22 or 23 from Národní třída on Staré Město's southern edge, Malostranské nám in Malá Strana, or Malostranská metro station to the U Prašného mostu stop. To wander through Hradčany first, stay on the tram until the Pohořelec stop.

Hradčany

The lanes and stairways of Hradčany are perfect for wandering. The area extending west from Prague Castle is mainly residential, with a single strip of shops and restaurants (Loretánská and Pohořelec). Before it became a borough of Prague in 1598, Hradčany was almost levelled by Hussites and fire. The 17th-century palaces were built on the ruins.

The 18th-century Šternberg Palace outside the castle entrance houses the main branch of the **National Gallery** (Map pp110-11; ☎ 220 514 598; www.ngprague.cz; adult/child 150/70Kč; ☺ 10am-6pm Tue-Sun), the country's principal collection of 14th- to 18th-century European art.

A passage at Pohořelec 8 leads to the **Strahov Library** (Map pp110-11; ☎ 233 107 718; www.strahovsky klaster.cz; adult/child 80/50Kč; ☺ 9am-noon & 1-5pm), the country's largest monastic library, built in 1679. The Philosophy and Theological Halls feature gorgeous frescoed ceilings. The collection of natural curiosities in the connecting corridor includes books on tree growing bound in the bark of the trees they describe. The long, brown, leathery things beside the model ship are actually whales' penises, despite the prudish attendants claiming they're tanned elephants' trunks.

The exuberantly baroque **Sanctuary of Our Lady of Loreta** (Map pp110-11; ☎ 220 516 789; www .loreta.cz; Loretánské nám 7; adult/child 90/70Kč; ☺ 9.15am-12.15pm & 1-4.30pm) is a place of pilgrimage famed for its treasury of precious religious artefacts. The cloister houses a 17th-century replica of the Santa Casa from the Italian town of Loreta, said to be the house of Virgin Mary in Nazareth, miraculously transported to Italy by angels in the 13th century.

Malá Strana

Head downhill from the castle to the beautifully baroque back streets of Malá Strana (Little Quarter), built in the 17th and 18th centuries by victorious Catholic clerics and nobles on the foundations of their Protestant predecessors' Renaissance palaces. Today it's an upmarket neighbourhood with embassies and government offices.

Near the café-crowded main square of Malostranské nám is **St Nicholas Church** (Map pp110-11; www.psalterium.cz; admission 60/30Kč; ☺ 9am-5pm Mar-Oct, 9am-4pm Nov-Feb), one of the city's greatest baroque buildings. If you visit only one church in Prague, this should be it. Take the stairs to the gallery to see the 17th-century *Passion Cycle* paintings and the doodlings of bored 1820s tourists.

To the east, along Tomášská, is the impressive **Wallenstein Palace** (Map pp110-11; Valdštejnský palác; admission free; ☺ 10am-4pm Sat & Sun), built in 1630 and home to the Czech Republic's Senate. Albrecht von Wallenstein, a notorious general in the Thirty Years' War, started on the Protestant side but defected to the Catholics, and built this palace with his former comrades' expropriated wealth. In 1634 the Habsburg Emperor Ferdinand II learned that Wallenstein was about to switch sides again and had him assassinated. The ceiling fresco of the palace's baroque hall shows Wallenstein glorified as a chariot-driving warrior.

Enter the adjacent **Wallenstein Gardens** (Map pp110-11; admission free; ☺ 10am-4pm Apr-Oct) via the palace or from Letenská, a block to the east. These beautiful gardens boast a giant Renaissance loggia, a fake stalactite grotto full of hidden animals and grotesque faces, bronze (replica) sculptures by Adrian de Vries (the Swedish army looted the originals in 1648 and they're in Stockholm) and a pond full of giant carp.

Malá Strana is linked to Staré Město by the elegant **Charles Bridge** (Karlův most). Built in 1357, and graced by 30 18th-century statues, until 1841 it was the city's only bridge. Stroll leisurely across, but first climb the **Malá Strana bridge tower** (Map pp110-11; adult/child 50/30Kč; ☺ 10am-6pm Apr-Nov) for a great view of bridge and city. In the middle of the bridge is a bronze statue (1683) of St John of Nepomuk, a priest thrown to his death from the bridge in 1393 for refusing to reveal the queen's confessions to King Wenceslas IV. Crammed with tourists, jewellery stalls, portrait artists and the odd busker, try and visit the bridge at dawn before the hordes arrive.

North of Charles Bridge is the modern **Franz Kafka Museum** (☎ 420 221 333; www.kafkamuseum.cz; Cihelná 2b; adult/child 120/60Kč; ☺ 10am-6pm), which has 'come home' after time in Barcelona and New York. Kafka's diaries, letters and a wonderful collection of first editions provide a poignant balance to the T-shirt cliché the writer has become in tourist shops.

On a hot summer afternoon escape the tourist throngs on the funicular railway (20Kč tram ticket, every 10 to 20 minutes from 9.15am to 8.45pm) from Újezd to the rose gardens on **Petřín Hill**. From here climb up 299 steps to the top of the iron-framed **Petřín Tower** (Map pp110–11; adult/child 50/40Kč; 10am-7pm Apr-Oct, 10am-5pm Sat & Sun Nov-Mar), built in 1891 in imitation of the Eiffel Tower, for one of the best views of Prague. Behind the tower a staircase leads to picturesque lanes taking you back to Malostranské nám.

Staré Město

On the Staré Město (Old Town) side of Charles Bridge narrow and crowded Karlova leads east towards **Staroměstské nám**, Prague's Old Town Square, dominated by the twin Gothic steeples of **Týn Church** (Map pp110–11; 1365), the baroque wedding cake of **St Nicholas Church** (Map pp110–11; 1730s), (not to be confused with the more famous St Nicholas Church in Malá Strana; p107) and the Old Town Hall's **clock tower** (Map pp110–11; 224 228 456; Staroměstské nám 12; adult/child 50/40Kč; 11am-6pm Mon, 9am-6pm Tue-Sun Apr-Oct, to 5pm Nov-Mar). Climb to the top (or take the lift), and spy on the crowds below watching the **astronomical clock** (Map pp110–11; 1410), which springs to life every hour with its parade of apostles and a bell-ringing skeleton. In the square's centre is the **Jan Hus Monument**, erected in 1915 on the 500th anniversary of the religious reformer's execution.

The shopping street of Celetná leads east from the square to the gorgeous Art Nouveau **Municipal House** (Obecní dům; Map pp110–11; www.obecni-dum .cz; nám Republiky 5; guided tours 150Kč; 10am-6pm), a cultural centre decorated by the early 20th-century's finest Czech artists. Included in the guided tour are the impressive Smetana Concert Hall and other beautifully decorated rooms.

South of the square is the neoclassical **Estates Theatre** (Stavovské divadlo; Map pp110–11; 1783), where Mozart's *Don Giovanni* was premiered on 29 October 1787 with the maestro himself conducting.

Josefov, the area north and northwest of Staroměstské nám, was once Prague's Jewish Quarter. It retains a fascinating variety of

monuments, which form the **Prague Jewish Museum** (222 317 191; www.jewishmuseum.cz; adult/child 300/200Kč; 9am-6pm Sun-Fri Apr-Oct, to 4.30pm Nov-Mar). The museum's collection of artefacts exists because in 1942 the Nazis gathered objects from 153 Jewish communities in Bohemia and Moravia, planning a 'museum of an extinct race' after completing their extermination programme.

The oldest still-functioning synagogue in Europe, the early Gothic **Old-New Synagogue** (Map pp110–11; Červená 1; 200Kč), dates from 1270. Opposite is the Jewish town hall with its picturesque 16th-century clock tower. The 1694 **Klaus Synagogue** (Map pp110–11; U Starého hřbitova 1) houses an exhibition on Jewish customs and traditions. The **Pinkas Synagogue** (Map pp110–11; Široká 3) is now a holocaust memorial, its interior walls inscribed with the names of 77,297 Czech Jews, including Franz Kafka's three sisters.

The **Old Jewish Cemetery** (entered from the Pinkas Synagogue) is Josefov's most evocative corner. The oldest of its 12,000 graves date from 1439. Use of the cemetery ceased in 1787 as it was becoming so crowded that burials were up to 12 layers deep. Look at the cemetery through an opening in the wall north of the **Museum of Decorative Arts** (224 811 241; 17 listopadu 2; adult/concession 80/40Kc; 10am-6pm, closed Monday) or from outside the 1st-floor public toilets in the museum.

Tucked away in the northern part of Staré Město's narrow streets is one of Prague's oldest Gothic structures, the magnificent **Convent of St Agnes** (Map pp110–11; 221 879 111; www.ngprague .cz; U Milosrdných 17; adult/child 100/50Kč; 10am-6pm Tue-Sun) housing the National Gallery's collection of Bohemian and Central European medieval art, dating from the 13th to the mid-16th centuries.

Nové Město

Nové Město (New Town) is new only compared with Staré Město, being founded in 1348! The broad, sloping avenue of **Václavské nám** (Map pp110–11; Wenceslas Sq), lined with shops, banks and restaurants, is dominated by a **statue of St Wenceslas** on horseback. Wenceslas Sq has always been a focus for demonstrations and public gatherings. Beneath the statue is a shrine to the victims of communism, including students Jan Palach and Jan Zajíc, both of whom burned themselves alive in 1969 protesting against the Soviet invasion.

At the southeastern end of the square is the imposing, neo-Renaissance **National Museum** (Map pp110-11; ☎ 224 497 111; www.nm.cz; Václavské nám 68; adult/child 100/50Kč; ☯ 10am-6pm May-Sep, 10am-5pm Oct-Apr, closed first Tuesday of every month). The ho-hum collections cover prehistory, mineralogy and stuffed animals (captions in Czech only), but the grand interior is worth seeing for the pantheon of Czech politicians, writers, composers, artists and scientists.

Fans of artist Alfons Mucha, renowned for his Art Nouveau posters of garlanded Slavic maidens, can admire his work at the **Mucha Museum** (Map pp110-11; ☎ 221 451 333; www.mucha.cz; Panská 7; adult/child 120/60Kč; ☯ 10am-6pm), including an interesting video on his life and art. See also Moravský Krumlov (p144).

The **City of Prague Museum** (Map pp110-11; ☎ 224 227 490; www.muzeumprahy.cz; Na Poříčí 52; adult/child 80/30Kč; ☯ 9am-6pm Tue-Sun), housed in a grand, neo-Renaissance building near Florenc metro station, charts Prague's evolution from prehistory to the 19th century, culminating in a huge scale model of Prague in 1826–37. Among the intriguing exhibits are the silk funeral cap and slippers worn by astronomer Tycho Brahe when he was interred in the Týn Church in 1601 (they were removed in 1901).

The **Museum of Communism** (Map pp110-11; ☎ 224 212 966; www.muzeumkomunismu.cz; Na příkopě 10; adult/child 180/140Kč; ☯ 8am-9pm) is tucked ironically behind Prague's biggest McDonald's. The introductory rooms covering communism's origins are a tad wordy, but the exhibition is fascinating through its use of simple everyday objects to illuminate the restrictions of life under communism. The display ends poignantly detailing 1989's Velvet Revolution.

Vyšehrad

To escape the tourist crowds, pack a picnic and take the metro to the ancient hilltop fortress **Vyšehrad** (Map pp102-3; www.praha-vysehrad.cz; admission free; ☯ 9.30am-6pm Apr-Oct, to 5pm Nov-Mar), perched on a cliff top above the Vltava on Nové Město's southern edge. Dominated by the twin towers of **SS Peter & Paul Church** (Map pp102-3) and founded in the 11th century, Vyšehrad was rebuilt in neo-Gothic style between 1885 and 1903. Don't miss the Art Nouveau murals inside. The **Slavín Cemetery** (Map pp102-3), beside the church, contains the graves of many distinguished Czechs, including the composers Smetana and Dvořák. The view from the citadel's southern battlements is superb.

TOURS

City Walks (☎ 608 200 912; www.praguer.com; per person 300-450Kč) Guided walks ranging from 90 minutes to four hours. Tours include a Literary Pub Tour and Ghost Trail.

Prague Venice (☎ 603 819 947; www.prague-venice .cz; adult/child 270/135Kč; ☯ 10.30am-11pm Jul & Aug, to 8pm Mar-Jun & Sep-Oct, 10.30am-6pm Nov-Feb) Runs 45-minute cruises in small boats under the arches of Charles Bridge and along the Čertovka mill stream in Kampa. Jetties are at the Staré Město end of Charles Bridge, on the Čertovka stream in Malá Strana, and at the west end of Mánes Bridge, near Malostranská metro station.

Prague Walks (☎ 608 339 099; www.praguewalks .com; per person 300-390Kč) Small group walks ranging from Franz Kafka to micro-breweries to communism.

Wittman Tours (☎ 603 426 564; www.wittman-tours .com; per person from 500Kč) Specialises in tours of Jewish interest, including day trips to the Museum of the Ghetto (p124) at Terezín.

FESTIVALS & EVENTS

Prague Spring (www.festival.cz) From 12 May to 3 June, classical music kicks off summer.

United Islands (www.unitedislands.cz) World music in mid-June.

Loveplanet (www.loveplanet.cz) Outdoor rock festival in August.

Prague Autumn (www.pragueautumn.cz) Celebrates summer's end from 12 September to 1 October.

Prague International Jazz Festival (www.jazzfestival praha.cz) Late October.

Christmas Market 1 to 24 December.

New Year's Eve *Pivo*-fuelled crowds in Staroměstské nám, and castle fireworks on 31 December.

SLEEPING

If you're visiting at New Year, Christmas or Easter, or from May to September, book accommodation in advance. Prices quoted are for the high season, generally April to October. These rates can increase up to 15% on certain dates, notably at Christmas, New Year, Easter and weekends during the Prague Spring festival. Some hotels have slightly lower rates in July and August. High season rates normally decrease by 20% to 40% from November to March.

Consider an apartment for stays longer than a couple of nights. Many one- to

CZECH REPUBLIC

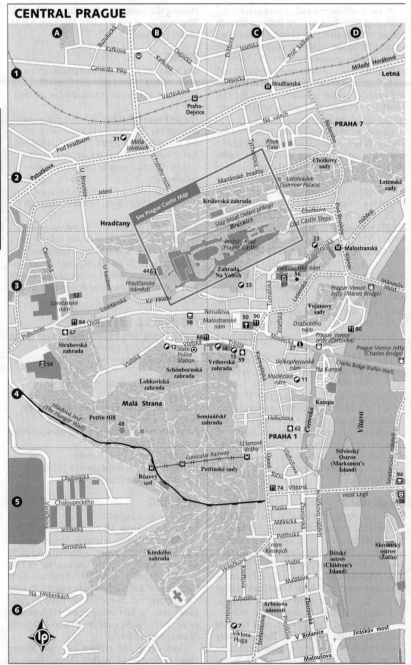

CENTRAL PRAGUE

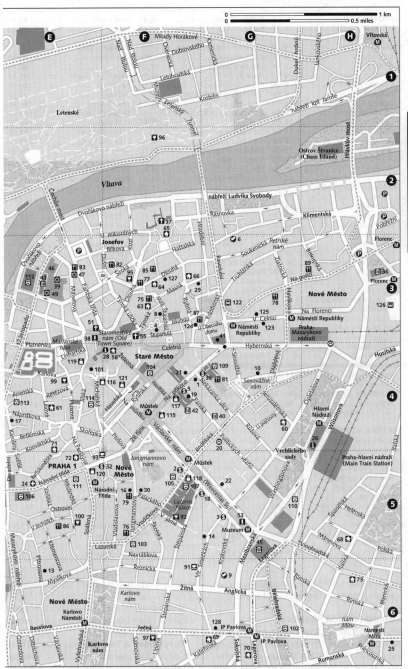

six-person apartments are available for even a single night, offering excellent value.

Accommodation Agencies

AVE (☎ 251 551 011; www.avetravel.cz; Praha-hlavní nádraží, Nové Město; ☼ 6am-11pm) Offices at the airport, main train station and Praha-Holešovice train station. The main train station branch specialises in last-minute accommodation.

Hostel.cz (☎ 415 658 580; www.hostel.cz) Website database of around 60 hostels, with a secure online booking system.

Mary's Travel & Tourist Service (Map pp110-11; ☎ 222 253 510; www.marys.cz; Italská 31, Vinohrady; ☼ 9am-9pm) Private rooms, hostels, *pensions*, apartments and hotels in Prague and surrounding areas across all price ranges.

Prague Apartments (☎ 323 641 476; www.prague-apartments.com) Web-based service with a range of smartly furnished flats. Availability displayed online.

Stop City (Map pp110-11; ☎ 222 521 233; www.stopcity.com; Vinohradská 24, Vinohrady; ⏰ 10am-9pm Apr-Oct, 10am-8pm Mon-Sat Nov-Mar) Apartments, private rooms and *pensions* in the city centre, Vinohrady and Žižkov areas.

Budget

Clown & Bard Hostel (Map pp102-3; ☎ 222 716 453; www.clownandbard.com; Bořivojova 102, Žižkov; dm 300-380Kč; d 1000Kč, apt 2400Kč; P ▣) Just maybe Prague's most full-on hostel – party hard in the basement bar, and recharge at the all-you-can-eat breakfast any time until 1pm. The self-catering apartments offer slightly more seclusion.

Hostel Elf (Map pp102-3; ☎ 222 540 963; www.hostelelf.com; Husitská 11, Žižkov; dm 320-360Kč, s/d 1000/1200Kč; ▣) Have the best of both worlds at this hip hostel near Žižkov's pub district. Swap travellers' tales in the compact beer garden or grab some quiet time in the nooks and crannies.

Hostel U Melounu (Map pp102-3; ☎ 224 918 322; www.hostelumelounu.cz; Ke Karlovu 7, Vinohrady; dm/s/d 390/700/1000Kč; P ▣) An attractive hostel in an historic building on a quiet street, U Melounu also features a sunny barbecue area, and shared kitchen and laundry facilities.

Sir Toby's Hostel (Map pp102-3; ☎ 283 870 635; www.sirtobys.com; Dělnická 24, Holešovice; dm 340-400Kč, s/d 1000/1350Kč; P ✕ ▣) In an up-and-coming suburb a quick 10-minute tram ride from the city centre, Sir Toby's is in a refurbished apartment building on a quiet street. The staff are friendly and helpful, and there is a shared kitchen and lounge.

Hostel Sokol (Map pp110-11; ☎ 257 007 397; post@sokol-cos.cz; Tyršův dům, Nosticova 2, Malá Strana; dm 390Kč; ✕) Set in a converted riverside mansion you can't beat the location, but the dorms can get crowded (and hot) in summer; a worthwhile backup though.

Hostel Týn (Map pp110-11; ☎ 224 808 333; www.tyn.prague-hostels.cz; Týnská 19, Staré Město; dm/d/tr 400/1200/1350Kč; ✕) In a quiet lane metres from Old Town Square, you'll struggle to find better-value central accommodation. The 14 two-to-six bed rooms are very popular so book ahead.

Camp Sokol Troja (Map pp102-3; ☎ 233 542 908; www.camp-sokol-troja.cz; Trojská 171a, Troja; camp site per person/car 125/90Kč; P ▣) This riverside camping ground, with kitchen and laundry, is one of six in the suburb of Troja, 15 minutes north of the centre via tram 14 or 17.

Midrange

Hotel Extol Inn (Map pp102-3; ☎ 220 876 541; www.extolinn.cz; Přístavní 2, Holešovice; s/d from 790/1350Kč; P ✕ ▣) The reader-recommended rooms here are all excellent value. The cheapest rooms with shared bathrooms are no-frills but spick and span, while the three-star rooms with private bathroom include use of the sauna and spa. The city centre is just 10 minutes by tram.

Miss Sophies (Map pp110-11; ☎ 296 303 530; www.miss-sophies.com; Melounova 3; dm 440Kč, s/d from 1500/1700Kč, apt from 2100Kč) 'Boutique hostel' sums up this tasty spot in a converted apartment building on the southern edge of the New Town. Polished concrete blends with oak flooring and coolly neutral colours, and the basement lounge is all bricks and black leather.

Pension Březina (Map pp110-11; ☎ 296 188 888; www.brezina.cz; Legerova 39-41; s/d economy 1100/1300Kč, luxury 2000/2200Kč; P) A friendly *pension* in a converted Art Nouveau apartment block with a small garden. Ask for a quieter room at the back. The economy rooms are great value for budget travellers.

Dasha (Map pp110-11; ☎ 602 210 716; www.accommodation-dasha.cz; Jeruzalémská 10; s/d from €30/40, apt €50-110) A restored apartment building 200m from the main train station conceals a variety of private rooms and apartments that can accommodate up to 10 people. With kitchen facilities the apartments are a good choice for larger groups or families. Forward bookings by phone or on the website are essential.

AV Pension Praha (Map pp102-3; ☎ 272 951 726; www.pension-praha.cz; Malebná 9; d with/without bathroom 2000/1500Kč; P 🐾) This garden villa with bright rooms and breakfast on the patio in the southeastern suburbs comes reader recommended. It's a five-minute walk east of Chodov metro station.

Pension Unitas (Map pp110-11; ☎ 224 211 020; www.unitas.cz; Bartolomějská 9; dm per person 350-510Kč, s/d 1280/1580Kč; P ✕) This former convent has an interesting past – the rooms were once prison cells (ex-president Havel did time here). A generous breakfast is included and bathrooms are shared. Choose between cramped dorms or more spacious *pension* rooms.

Hotel Golden City Garni (Map pp102-3; ☎ 222 711 008; www.goldencity.cz; Táboritská 3, Žižkov; s/d/tr

1900/2700/2900Kč; P X Q) Golden City is a converted 19th-century apartment block with crisp and clean IKEA-furnished rooms, grand buffet breakfasts and easy access to the city centre on tram 5, 9 or 26.

Dům U Krále Jiřího (Map pp110-11; ☎ 221 466 100; www.kinggeorge.cz; Liliová 10; s/d 2250/3550Kč) 'King George's House' combines old-world *pension* charm with crisply modern rooms just metres from Old Town Square. The attic rooms (only accessible by steep stairs) are the most attractive with exposed wooden beams.

Penzión U Medvídků (Map pp110-11; ☎ 224 211 916; www.umedvidku.cz; Na Perštýně 7, Staré Město; s/d 2300/3500Kč) 'At the Little Bear' is a traditional pub and restaurant with several attractive rooms upstairs. Romantic types should choose an historic attic room with exposed wooden beams. Just mind your head after having a few in the micro-brewery downstairs.

Hotel 16 U sv Kateřiny (Map pp102-3; ☎ 224 920 636; www.hotel16.cz; Kateřinská 16, Nové Město; s/d incl breakfast from 2800/3500Kč; P Q) Near the Botanic Gardens and five minutes' walk from Karlovo nám metro station, you're more likely to wake to birdsong than honking cars at this family-run spot with a quiet garden and cosy bar.

Hotel U Tří Korunek (Map pp102-3; ☎ 222 781 112; www.3korunky.cz; Cimburkova 28; Žižkov; s/d from 2480/3380Kč) Rambling across three buildings in Žižkov, the 'Three Crowns' has 78 comfy and clean rooms. It's worth upgrading to a superior room with wooden floors and designer furniture (300Kč extra), and don't be put off by the down-at-heel-looking neighbourhood. It's safe and quiet and the city centre is just a few tram stops away.

Hotel Antik (Map pp110-11; ☎ 222 322 288; www .hotelantik.cz; Dlouhá 22; s/d 3590/3990Kč) The Antik shares a 15th-century building (no lift) with a delightfully jumbled antique shop. It's a great area for bars and restaurants, so ask for one of the more quiet back rooms with a balcony. Breakfast is served in a garden courtyard.

Apostolic Residence (Map pp110-11; ☎ 221 632 222; www.prague-residence.cz; Staroměstké nám 26; s/d 4600/5700Kč) Right on Old Town Square, this hotel positively reeks understated class with antique furniture and Oriental rugs. Yes, you are paying more for the supercentral location, but it's still good value compared with other more expensive hotels in the city.

Top End
Hotel Josef (Map pp110-11; ☎ 221 700 111; www .hoteljosef.cz; Rybná 20, Staré Město; s/d from €149/173;

P X Q &) Sleekly modern in old-world Staré Město, this boutique hotel was designed by London-based Czech architect Eva Jiřičná. Descend the playful suspended staircase to surf the web in the lobby's wi-fi hotspot. Two rooms are wheelchair accessible.

Hotel Casa Marcello (Map pp110-11; ☎ 222 310 260; www.casa-marcello.cz; Řásnovka 783; d/ste/apt from €130/185/215) Housed in two medieval buildings that were once part of the Covent of St Agnes, Casa Marcello is one of Prague's most intimate and romantic hotels. In a quiet but central area near the Old Town Sq, surprise your loved one with room 104 with its king-size bed and preserved medieval archway.

Hotel Questenberk (Map pp110-11; ☎ 220 407 600; www.questenberk.cz; Úvoz 5, Hradčany; s/d €160/200; P X Q) Spacious and sunny rooms now fill Strahov Monastery's former hospital just minutes from the castle. Old and new blends seamlessly with antique pine furnishings and internet access amid the baroque splendour.

Aria Hotel (Map pp110-11; ☎ 225 334 111; www.aria hotel.net; Tržiště 9, Malá Strana; d from €250; P X Q) Choose your favourite composer or musician and stay in a themed room with a selection of their music. Not at all tacky – just pure five-star class with 21st-century touches like music databanks and flat-screen computers.

EATING
Prague has restaurants offering all kinds of cuisines and price ranges. Take your pick from good-value Czech beer halls with no-nonsense pork-and-*knedlíky* fare, or enjoy a riverside view in a chic Italian restaurant with a high-flying clientele and prices. In between, there's everything from Afghani to Argentinean, and Thai to Tex-Mex.

Eating in Prague's tourist areas can be pricey, but considerably cheaper eats are available just a block or two away. Pubs offer both snacks and full meals, and there are stands in Václavské nám selling street snacks such as *párek* (hot dog) or *bramborák* (potato pancake).

Prague has an increasing number of vegetarian restaurants, and most restaurants feature at least one or two veggie options. Most restaurants are open from 11am to 11pm.

Hradčany & Malá Strana
Bohemia Bagel (Map pp110-11; ☎ 257 310 694; Újezd 18, Malá Strana; mains 90-270Kč; 🕑 7am-midnight Mon-Fri, from 8am Sat & Sun) Expat heaven with bagel

sandwiches, soups and coffee. There's another Bohemia Bagel at Masná 2 in Staré Město – both are good spots for breakfast.

Malý Buddha (Map pp110-11; ☎ 220 513 894; Úvoz 46, Hradčany; mains 60-120Kč; ☻ noon-10.30pm Tue-Sun) Vietnamese-owned Malý ('Little') Buddha is an incense-infused haven atop Hradčany hill. If the castle's crowds wear you down, restore your chi with restorative wines, healing tea and crab spring rolls. Credit cards are not accepted.

Hergetova Cihelna (Map pp110-11; ☎ 257 535 534; Cihelná 2b, Malá Strana; mains 200-550Kč; ☻ 9am-2am) A restored *cihelná* (brickworks) is now a hip space with a riverside terrace looking back to Charles Bridge and Staré Město. Come for steak, seafood or pizza and linger for the sublime view – 'one more *pivo prosím*'.

Also check out the Moorish flavours (think baklava and spicy *merguez* sausages) at **Sha-harazad** (Map pp110-11; ☎ 257 913 046; Vlasská 6, Malá Strana; mains 100-200Kč; ☻ noon-midnight), and the thoroughly modern **Square** (Map pp110-11; ☎ 257 532 109; Malostranské nám 5, Malá Strana; tapas 3 for 275Kč, 7 for 455Kč; ☻ 9am-12.30am) with interesting tapas like saffron *arancini* (rice balls).

Staré Město

Kolkovna (Map pp110-11; ☎ 224 819 701; Kolkovně 8; meals 160-400Kč; ☻ 9am-midnight) This contemporary spin on the traditional Prague beer hall serves up classy versions of heritage Czech dishes like goulash and roast pork. And because it's owned by the Pilsner Urquell brewery, guess what beer accompanies most of the huge meals?

Country Life Nové Město (Map pp110-11; ☎ 224 247 280; Jungmannova 1; ☻ 9.30am-6.30pm Mon-Thu, 9am-6pm Fri); Staré Město (Map pp110-11; ☎ 224 213 366; Melantrichova 15; mains 75-150Kč; ☻ 9am-8.30pm Mon-Thu, 9am-6pm Fri, 11am-8.30pm Sat & Sun) This all-vegan cafeteria offers inexpensive salads, sandwiches, pizzas, soy drinks, sunflower-seed burgers etc.

Orange Moon (Map pp110-11; ☎ 222 325 119; Rámová 5; mains 165-230Kč; ☻ 11.30am-11.30pm) The world's best beer (no doubt) combines with (probably) the world's best cuisines. Expats and locals are transported to Asia by authentic flavours of Thailand and India.

Dahab (Map pp110-11; ☎ 224 837 375; Dlouhá 33; mains 200-400Kč; ☻ noon-1am) Morocco meets the Middle East amid the softly lit ambience of this North African souk. Relax with a mint tea and a hookah (hubble-bubble pipe). If you've got the munchies there's everything

from baklava to *tagine* (meat and vegetable stew) with couscous.

Red Hot & Blues (Map pp110-11; ☎ 222 314 639; Jakubská 12; mains 180-480Kč; ☻ 8am-midnight) This jumping jive, jazz and jambalaya spot is a long way from 'N'awlins', but the eggplant creole and cajun shrimp have travelled well. There's live jazz night, and breakfast is available until 4pm at the weekend – just maybe the best way to resurrect yourself after a big night.

Les Moules (Map pp110-11; ☎ 222 315 022; Pavížská 19; mains 300-500Kč; ☻ 8.30am-midnight Mon-Fri, 9am-midnight Sat & Sun) Another modern update of a European drinking establishment, Les Moules is a traditional Belgian-style brasserie, dishing up comfort food like *moules* (mussels) with crispy (Belgian!) fries. The Leffe and Hoegaarden on tap prove that Belgian beer travels well – even to the home of Pilsner.

Nové Město

Pizzeria Kmotra (Map pp110-11; ☎ 224 934 100; V Jirchářích 12; pizza 95-145Kč; ☻ 11am-midnight) More than 30 varieties are on offer at this cellar pizzeria that gets really busy after 8pm. With over 50 additional toppings you can get really creative.

Kaaba (Map pp102-3; ☎ 224 254 021; Mánesova 20; snacks 50-80Kč; ☻ 8am-10pm Mon-Sat, 10am-10pm Sun) Vinohrady's hipsters park themselves on 1950s-style furniture and recharge with snappy espressos, terrific teas and tasty snacks. After dark Belgian beers provide the entrée to nearby clubs.

Siam Orchid (Map pp110-11; ☎ 222 319 410; Na poříčí 21; mains 160-280Kč; ☻ 10am-10pm) The waiter may be from Cambodia, but that doesn't stop the Thai food in this tiny restaurant from being Prague's most authentic Asian cuisine. Try the fiery *laap kai* (spicy chicken salad).

Café FX (Map pp110-11; ☎ 224 254 776; Bělehradská 120, Vinohrady; mains 100-200Kč; ☻ 11.30am-2am) Café FX is shabbily chic, draped in hippy-trippy chiffon, with Prague's best vegetarian flavours from Mexico, India and Thailand. Relax at weekend brunch and lose yourself in the eclectic CD store across the arcade.

Dinitz Café (Map pp110-11; ☎ 222 313 308; Na poříčí 14; mains 200-400Kč; ☻ 9am-3am) Art Deco heaven is this cool homage to 1920s café society. The kitchen delivers elegant Mediterranean-style meals until 2am, and live jazz is dished up every night from 9pm. Try and get a mezzanine table overlooking the stage.

Kogo (Map pp110-11; ☎ 224 451 259; Slovanský dům; Na příkopě 22; pizzas 150-250Kč, mains 200-450Kč;

CZECH REPUBLIC

9am-midnight) Prague's business community chooses from a diverse wine list to accompany Kogo's classy pizza, pasta, steak and seafood. There is another stylish branch at Havelská 27.

DRINKING

Bohemian beer is probably the world's best. The most famous brands are Budvar, Plzeňský Prazdroj (Pilsner Urquell), and Prague's own Staropramen; and there's no shortage of opportunities to imbibe. An increasing number of independent micro-breweries also offer a more unique drinking experience.

Avoid the tourist areas, and you'll find local bars selling half-litres for 30Kč or less (compared with over 65Kč around Malostranské nám and Staroměstské nám). Traditional pubs open from 11am to 11pm. More stylish modern bars open from noon to 1am, and often stay open till 3am or 4am on Friday and Saturday.

If you want to avoid stag parties, stay away from the Irish and English pubs in the Old Town, and the sports bars on and around Ve Smečkách in the New Town.

Cafés

Before the communist coup Prague had a thriving café scene, and since 1989 it has returned strongly. The summer streets are crammed with outdoor tables, and good-quality tea and coffee are widely available. Keep an eye out for funky teahouses with a diversely global range of brews.

U zeleného čaje (Map pp110–11; ☎ 257 530 027; Nerudova 19, Malá Strana; ☺ 11am–10pm; ✗) Linger at this tiny tea-haven on the way to the castle. There are only four tables so maybe grab a speciality tea to go for the final push up the hill.

Café Vesmírna (Map pp110–11; ☎ 222 212 363; Ve Smečkách 5, Nové Město; ☺ 9am–10pm Mon-Fri, 1-8pm Sat, closed Sun; ✗) The friendly Vesmírna provides training and opportunities for people with special needs. The wait staff are warm and professional, and the menu features healthy snacks like savoury crepes and a 'how do I choose?' selection of teas and coffees. It's a special place making a real difference.

Káva.Káva.Káva Nové Město (Map pp110–11; ☎ 224 228 862; Národní třída 37; ☺ 7am–10pm Mon-Fri, 9am-10pm Sat & Sun); Smíchov (☎ 257 314 277; Lidicka 42; ☺ 7am–10pm) Hidden away in the Platýz courtyard, this café offers huge smoothies and tasty nibbles like carrot cake and chocolate brownies. Access the internet (2Kč per minute or 15 minutes

free with a purchase) on their computers or hitch your laptop to their wi-fi hotspot.

Kavárna Slávia (Map pp10–11; ☎ 224 220 957; Národní třída 1, Nové Město; mains 130–260Kč; ☺ 8am–midnight Mon-Fri, 9am-midnight Sat & Sun) Before or after the theatre savour the cherry wood and onyx Art Deco elegance of Prague's most famous old café.

Pubs

U Zlatého Tygra (Map pp110–11; ☎ 222 221 111; Husova 17, Staré Město; ☺ 3-11pm) The 'Golden Tiger' is an authentic Prague pub where President Havel took President Clinton to show him a real Czech *pivnice*. You'll need to be there at opening time for any chance of a seat, but we're sure Václav and Bill had no problems.

Jáma (Map pp110–11; ☎ 224 222 383; V jámě 7, Nové Město; ☺ 11am-1am) Spot your favourite band on the posters covering the walls of this popular American-themed bar. Expats, tourists and locals come for the burgers'n'Budvar and free wi-fi internet.

Velryba (Map pp110–11; ☎ 224 912 484; Opatovická 24, Nové Město; ☺ 11am-midnight Sat-Thu, 11am-2am Fri) The 'Whale' is the café-bar that finally fulfils your expectations of 'Bohemian' with smoky and intense conversations between local students and a basement art gallery. Bring your own black polo-neck jumper.

Kozička (Map pp110–11; ☎ 224 818 308; Kozí 1, Staré Město; ☺ noon-4am Mon-Fri, 6pm-4am Sat & Sun) The 'Little Goat' (look for the iron sculpture outside) rocks in standing-room-only fashion until well after midnight in a buzzing basement bar. Your need for midnight munchies will be answered by the late-night kitchen.

Pivovarský Dům (Map pp110–11; ☎ 296 216 666; cnr Ječná & Lipová, Nové Město; ☺ 11am-11.30pm) The 'Brewery House' micro-brewery conjures up interesting tipples from a refreshing wheat beer to coffee and banana flavoured styles – even a beer 'champagne' served in champagne flutes. If you're more of a traditionalist, the classic Czech lager is a hops-laden marvel.

U Medvídků (Map pp110–11; ☎ 296 216 666; cnr Ječná & Lipová, Nové Město; ☺ 11.30am-11pm, beer museum noon-10pm) A microbrewery with the emphasis on 'micro', 'At the Little Bear' specialises in X-Beer, an 11.8% 'knocks-your-socks-off' dark lager. You can't drink too many without falling over, so the usual range of Budvar brews is available to make your evening last longer than a couple of hours.

Letenské sady (Map pp110–11; Letna Gardens, Bubeneč) This outdoor garden bar provides sublime views across the river to the Old Town and southwest to the castle. In summer it's packed with young Praguers enjoying cheap beer and grilled sausages. Sometimes the simple things in life are the best.

ENTERTAINMENT

From clubbing to classical music, puppetry to performance art, there's no shortage of entertainment in Prague. The city has long been a centre of classical music and jazz, and is now also famed for its rock and postrock scenes. The scene changes quickly, and it's possible places listed here will have changed when you arrive. For current listings, see *Culture in Prague* (available from PIS offices; see p104), the 'Night & Day' section of the weekly *Prague Post* (www .praguepost.cz), and the monthly free *Provokátor* magazine (www.provokator.org), from clubs, cafés, arthouse cinemas and backpacker hostels. For online listings see www.prague.tv.

For classical music, opera, ballet, theatre and some rock concerts – even the most 'sold-out' *vyprodáno* (events) – you can often find tickets on sale at the box office around 30 minutes before the performance starts. There are also many ticket agencies selling the same tickets at a high commission.

Although some expensive tickets are set aside for foreigners, non-Czechs normally pay the same price as Czechs at the box office. Tickets can cost as little as 50Kč for standing-room only to over 950Kč for the best seats; the average price is about 550Kč. Be wary of touts selling concert tickets in the street. They often offer good prices, but you may end up sitting on stacking chairs in a cramped hall listening to amateur musicians, rather than the grand concert hall that was implied.

Ticket Agencies

FOK Box Office (Map pp110-11; ☎ 222 002 336; www.fok .cz; U obecního domu 2, Staré Město; ☺ 10am-6pm Mon-Fri) For classical concert tickets.

Ticketpro (Map pp110-11; ☎ 296 333 333; www.ticket pro.cz; pasáž Lucerna, Štěpánská 61; Nové Město; ☺ 9am-12.30pm & 1-5pm Mon-Fri) Sells tickets for all kinds of events. Also has branches in PIS offices (see p104).

Bohemia Ticket International (☎ 224 227 832; www.ticketsbti.cz); Nové Město (Map pp110-11; Na příkopě 16, ☺ 10am-7pm Mon-Fri, 10am-5pm Sat, 10am-3pm Sun); Staré Město (Map pp110-11; Malé nám 13; ☺ 9am-5pm Mon-Fri, 9am-1pm Sat) Sells tickets to all kinds of events.

Ticketstream (www.ticketstream.cz) An internet-based agency covering events in Prague and the Czech Republic.

Classical Music & Performance Arts

Around Prague you'll see fliers advertising concerts and recitals for tourists. It's a good chance to relax in atmospheric old churches and stunning historic buildings, but unfortunately many performances are of mediocre quality. The programme changes weekly, and prices begin around 400Kč.

Rudolfinum (Map pp110-11; ☎ 227 059 352; www .rudolfinum.cz; nám Jana Palacha, Staré Město; ☺ box office 10am-12.30pm & 1.20-6pm Mon-Fri plus one hour before performances) One of Prague's main concert venues is the Dvořák Hall in the neo-Renaissance Ruldolfinum, and home to the Czech Philharmonic Orchestra.

Smetana Hall (Municipal House; Obecní dům; Map pp110-11; ☎ 222 002 101; www.obecni-dum.cz; nám Republiky 5, Staré Město; ☺ box office 10am-6pm Mon-Fri) Another main concert venue is Smetana Hall in the Art Nouveau Municipal House. A highlight is the opening of the Prague Spring festival.

Prague State Opera (Státní opera Praha; Map pp110-11; ☎ 224 227 266; www.opera.cz; Legerova 75, Nové Město; ☺ box office 10am-5.30pm, 10am-noon & 1-5pm Sat & Sun) Opera, ballet and classical drama (in Czech) are performed at this neo-Renaissance theatre.

National Theatre (Národní divadlo; Map pp110-11; ☎ 224 901 377; www.narodni-divadlo.cz; Národní třída 2, Nové Město; ☺ box office 10am-6pm) Classical drama, opera and ballet are also performed at the National Theatre.

Laterna Magika (Map pp110-11; ☎ 224 931 482; www .laterna.cz; Nová Scéna, Národní třída 4, Nové Město; tickets from 680Kč; ☺ box office 10am-8pm Mon-Sat) Beside the National Theatre is the modern Laterna Magika, a multimedia show combining dance, opera, music and film.

Estates Theatre (Stavovské divadlo; Map pp110-11; ☎ 224 902 322; Ovocný trh 1, Staré Město; ☺ box office 10am-6pm) Every night during summer (mid-July to the end of August) **Opera Mozart** (☎ 271 741 403; www.mozart-praha.cz) performs *Don Giovanni*. The opera premiered in the same theatre in 1787.

Clubs & Live Music

Mecca (Map pp102-3; ☎ 283 870 522; www.mecca.cz; U Průhonu 3, Holešovice; admission 90-390Kč, free Wed & Thu; ☺ 10pm-6am Wed-Sat) Prague's most fashionable club attracts film stars, fashionistas and fab types attracted by the classy restaurant (11am to 11pm) and the pumping dance floor action.

Lucerna Music Bar (Map pp110-11; ☎ 224 217 108; www.muiscbar.cz; Lucerna pasaž, Vodičkova 36, Nové Město; ☺ 8pm-4am) Lucerna features local bands and the occasional up-and-coming international act. Leave your musical snobbery in the cloak room at the popular '80s nights on Friday and Saturday with everything from The Human League to Soft Cell.

Palác Akropolis (Map pp102-3; ☎ 296 330 911; www .palacakropolis.cz; Kubelikova 27, Žižkov; ☺ club 7pm-5am) Get lost in the labyrinth of theatre, live music, clubbing, drinking and eating that makes up Prague's coolest venue. Hip-hop, house, reggae and world music – anything goes. Even a few touring acts like the Strokes and the Flaming Lips.

Club Radost FX (Map pp110-11; ☎ 224 254 776; www .radostfx.cz; Bělehradská 120, Vinohrady; admission 100-250Kč; ☺ 10pm-6am) Prague's most stylish, self-assured club remains hip for its bohemian-boudoir décor and its popular Thursday hip-hop night FXBounce (www.fxbounce.com).

Jazz

Prague has dozens of jazz clubs ranging from the traditional to the avant-garde.

Reduta Jazz Club (Map pp110-11; ☎ 224 912 246; www .redutajazzclub.cz; Národní třída 20, Nové Město; admission 300Kč; ☺ 9pm-3am) Founded in 1958 and one of the oldest clubs in Europe. Bill Clinton jammed here in 1994.

USP Jazz Lounge (Map pp110-11; ☎ 603 551 680; www .jazzlounge.cz; Michalská 9, Staré Město; ☺ 9pm-3am) A less traditional venue with modern (and sometimes uncompromising) live jazz and a DJ session from midnight onwards.

Theatre

Black Theatre of Jiří Srnec (Map pp110-11; ☎ 257 921 835; www.blacktheatresrnec.cz; Reduta Theatre, Národní 20, Nové Město; tickets 490Kč; ☺ box office 3-7pm Mon-Fri) See the uniquely Czech 'black light theatre' shows at various venues. The performances combine mime, ballet, animated film and puppetry. Jiří Srnec's Black Theatre is the original and the best.

Theatre on the Balustrade (Divadlo na zábradlí; Map pp110-11; ☎ 222 868 868; www.nazabradli.cz; Anenské nám 5, Staré Město; ☺ box office 2-7pm Mon-Fri, 2 hrs before show Sat & Sun) Plays by former president Václav Havel are often staged (in Czech, of course) here.

Divadlo Minor (Map pp110-11; ☎ 222 231 351; www .minor.cz; Vodičkova 6, Nové Město; ☺ box office 9am-

1.30pm & 2.30-8pm Mon-Fri, 11am-6pm Sat & Sun) If the kids are all castled out, consider the puppets'n'pantomime shows at 9.30am and in the afternoon.

Gay & Lesbian Prague

Termix (Map pp102-3; ☎ 222 710 462; www.club-termix .cz; Třebízkého 4A, Vinohrady; ☺ 8pm-5am Wed-Sun) A friendly mixed gay-and-lesbian scene with an industrial/high-tech vibe. You'll need to queue for Thursday's popular techno party.

Club Stella (Map pp102-3; ☎ 224 257 869; Lužicka 19, Vinohrady; ☺ 8pm-4pm Mon) A narrow and intimate bar (just wider than a bar stool) opens out into a candlelit lounge filled with armchairs and friendly locals. Ring the doorbell to get in.

Piano Bar (Map pp102-3; ☎ 222 727 496; Milešovská 10, Žižkov; ☺ 5pm-midnight or later) This cellar bar, cluttered with bric-a-brac and unpretentious locals, is a good spot for a quiet drink. The background beats usually consist of kitschy '70s and '80s Czech pop.

Downtown Café Praha (Map pp110-11; ☎ 724 111 276; Jungmannovo nám 21, Nové Město; ☺ 8.30am-midnight) A Prague institution since 1999, the Downtown Café reopened in April 2006 seemingly even more impossibly hip. Chill until late in the LookBetterNaked Lounge, and then ease into the following day with the all-day breakfast and free wi-fi.

Prague Saints (Map pp102-3; ☎ 222 250 326; www .praguesaints.cz; Polska 32) An excellent source of information on Prague's gay scene.

Cinemas

Most films are screened in their original language with Czech subtitles (*české titulky*), but Hollywood blockbusters are often dubbed into Czech (*dabing*); look for the labels 'tit.' or 'dab.' on listings.

Kino Aero (Map pp110-11; ☎ 271 771 349; www.ki noaero.cz; Biskupcova 31, Žižkov) Prague's best-loved art-house cinema, with themed weeks and retrospectives; often with English subtitles.

Kino Světozor (Map pp110-11; ☎ 224 946 824; www .kinosvetozor.cz; Vodičkova 41, Nové Město) Your best bet for seeing Czech films with English subtitles, this place is under the same management as Kino Aero but is more central.

Palace Cinemas (Map pp110-11; ☎ 257 181 212; www .palacecinemas.cz; Slovanský dům, Na příkopě 22, Nové Město) Central Prague's main popcorn palace – a modern 10-screen multiplex showing first-run Hollywood films.

SHOPPING

Prague's main shopping streets are in Nové Město – Václavské nám, Na příkopě, 28.října and Národní třída – and there are many tourist-oriented shops on Celetná, Staroměstské nám, Pařížská and Karlova in Staré Město. Prague's souvenir specialities include Bohemian crystal, ceramics, marionettes and garnet jewellery.

Tesco Department Store (Map pp110-11; ☎ 222 003 111; Národní třída 26, Nové Město; ⊗ 8am-9pm Mon-Fri, 9am-8pm Sat, 10am-7pm Sun) With four floors of clothes, electrical and household goods, plus Prague's best-stocked **supermarket** (⊗ 7am-10pm Mon-Fri, 8am-8pm Sat, 9am-7pm Sun).

Crystal

Moser (Map pp110-11; ☎ 224 211 293; Na příkopě 12, Nové Město; ⊗ 10am-8pm Mon-Fri, 10am-7pm Sat & Sun) Founded in 1857, Moser specialises in top-quality Bohemian crystal.

Rott Crystal (Map pp110-11; ☎ 224 229 529; Malé nám 3, Staré Město; ⊗ 10am-8pm) Housed in a beautiful neo-Renaissance building, Rott is worth a look even if you're not buying.

Handicrafts, Antiques & Ceramics

Manufaktura (Map pp110-11; ☎ 221 632 480; Melantrichova 17, Staré Město; ⊗ 10am-7.30pm) Branches of Manufaktura around the city centre sell traditional Czech handicrafts, wooden toys and handmade cosmetics.

There are good antique and bric-a-brac shops along Týnská and Týnská ulička, near Staroměstské nám. For ceramics in traditional Moravian folk designs, see **Tupesy lidová keramika** (Map pp110-11; ☎ 224 210 728; Havelská 21, Staré Město; ⊗ 10am-6pm).

Music

Philharmonia (Map pp110-11; ☎ 224 247 291; Pasáž Alfa, Václavské nám 28; ⊗ 10am-7pm Mon-Fri, 11am-6pm Sat) For music by Dvořák, Smetana or Janáček. Also stocks Czech folk music and Jewish music.

Bontonland (Map pp110-11; ☎ 224 473 080; Václavské nám 1, Nové Město; ⊗ 9am-8pm Mon-Sat, 10am-7pm Sun) A megastore stocking music genres ranging from classical, jazz, folk, rock, metal, dance and Czech pop, Bontonland also sells DVDs and has an internet café and a Playstation arena.

GETTING THERE & AWAY

See also p153.

Bus

The main terminal for international and domestic buses is **Florenc Bus Station** (ÚAN Florenc; Map pp110-11; ☎ 12 999; Křižíkova 4, Karlín), 600m northeast of the main train station (ÚAN is short for *Ústřední autobusové nádraží*, or 'central bus station'). Some regional buses depart from near metro stations Anděl, Dejvická, Černý Most, Nádraží Holešovice, Smíchovské Nádraží and Želivského. Find online bus timetables at www.idos.cz.

At Florenc get information at **window No 8** (⊗ 6am-9pm), or use the touch-screen computer.

Short-haul tickets are sold on the bus. Long-distance domestic tickets are sold at the station from AMS windows 1 to 4 in the central hall or direct from Student Agency. Tickets can be purchased from 10 days to 30 minutes prior to departure.

More buses depart in the mornings. Buses, especially if full, sometimes leave a few minutes early, so be there at least 10 minutes before departure time. If you're not seated five minutes before departure, you may lose your reservation. Many services don't operate at weekends, so trains can often be a better option.

There are direct services from Florenc to Brno (150Kč, 2½ hours, hourly), České Budějovice (125Kč, 2¾ hours, four daily), Karlovy Vary (130Kč, 2¼ hours, eight daily), Litoměřice (61Kč, 1¼ hours, hourly) and Plzeň (80Kč, 1½ hours, hourly).

Most buses from Prague to České Budějovice (120Kč, 2½ hours, 16 daily) and Český Krumlov (140Kč, three hours, seven daily) depart from Ná Knížecí bus station, at Anděl metro's southern entrance, or from outside Roztyly metro station.

Bus companies include the following:

Capital Express (Map pp102-3; ☎ 220 870 368; www.capitalexpress.cz; I výstaviště 3, Holešovice; ⊗ 8am-6pm Mon-Thu, 8am-5pm Fri) Daily service between London and Prague via Plzeň.

Eurolines-Bohemia Euroexpress International (Map pp110-11; ☎ 224 218 680; www.bei.cz; ÚAN Praha Florenc Bus Station, Křižíkova 4-6, Karlín; ⊗ 8am-6pm Mon-Fri) Buses to all over Europe.

Eurolines-Sodeli (Map pp110-11; ☎ 224 239 318; www.eurolines.cz, in Czech; Senovážné nám 6, Nové Město; ⊗ 8am-6pm Mon-Fri) Links Prague with cities in Western and Central Europe. There is another Eurolines office in Florenc.

Student Agency Central Prague (Map pp110-11; ☎ 224 999 666; Ječná 37; ⊗ 9am-6pm Mon-Fri); Florenc (☎ 224

894 430; www.studentagency.cz; 9am-6pm Mon-Fri) Linking major Czech cities; services throughout Europe.

Train

Prague's main train station is **Praha-hlavní nádraží** (Map pp110-11; 221 111 122; Wilsonova, Nové Město). International tickets, domestic and international couchettes and seat reservations are sold on level 2 at even-numbered windows from 10 to 24, to the right of the stairs leading up to level 3. Domestic tickets are sold at the odd-numbered windows from 1 to 23 to the left of the stairs. Note that Praha-hlavní nádraží is undergoing a major redevelopment between 2006 and 2009 and the station layout may alter.

There are three other major train stations in the city. Some international trains stop at Praha-Holešovice station on the northern side of the city, while some domestic services terminate at Praha-Masarykovo in Nové Město, or Praha-Smíchov south of Malá Strana. Study the timetables carefully to find out which station your train departs from or arrives at. Check train timetables online at www.idos.cz.

You can also buy train tickets and get timetable information from the **ČD Centrum** (6am-7.30pm) at the southern end of Level 2 in Praha-hlavní nádraží, and at the **České drahy** (Czech Railways; Map pp110-11; 972 223 930; www.cd.cz; V Celnici 6, Nové Město; 9am-6pm Mon-Fri, 9am-noon Sat) travel agency.

There are direct trains from Praha-hlavní nádraží to Brno (294Kč, three hours, eight daily), České Budějovice (204Kč, 2½ hours, hourly), Karlovy Vary (274Kč, four hours, three daily), Kutná Hora (98Kč, 55 minutes, seven daily) and Plzeň (140Kč, 1½ hours, eight daily). There are also daily departures to Brno, Bratislava and Vienna from Praha-Holešovice.

GETTING AROUND
To/From the Airport

Prague's Ruzyně airport is 17km west of the city centre. To get into town, buy a ticket from the public transport (Dopravní podnik; DPP) desk in arrivals and take bus 119 (20Kč, 20 minutes, every 15 minutes) to the end of the line (Dejvická), then continue by metro into the city centre (another 10 minutes; no new ticket needed). Note that you'll also need a half-fare (10Kč) ticket for your backpack or suitcase (if it's larger than 25cm x 45cm x 70cm).

Alternatively, take a **Cedaz minibus** (220 114 296; www.cedaz.cz) from outside arrivals; buy your ticket from the driver (90Kč, 20 minutes,

every 30 minutes 5.30am to 9.30pm). There are city stops at Dejvická metro and at **Czech Airlines** (Map pp110-11; V Celnici 5) near nám Republiky. You can also get a Cedaz minibus to your hotel or any other address (480Kč for one to four people; 960Kč for five to eight). Phone to book a pick-up for the return trip.

Airport Cars (220 113 892) taxi service, with prices regulated by the airport administration, charges 650Kč (20% discount for return trip) into central Prague (a regular taxi fare *from* central Prague should be about 450Kč). Drivers speak some English and accept Visa cards.

Bicycle Rental

City Bike (Map pp110-11; 776 180 284; www.citybike-prague.com; Královská 5, Staré Město; 9am-7pm May-Sep) Two-hour tours cost from 480Kč, departing at 11am, 2pm and 5pm. Rental includes helmet and padlock.
Praha Bike (Map pp110-11; 732 388 880; www.prahabike.cz; Dlouhá 24, Staré Město; 4/8hr 360/500Kč; 9am-7pm 15 Mar-15 Nov) Good, new bikes with lock, helmet and map, plus free luggage storage, student discounts and group tours.

Car & Motorcycle

Driving in Prague is no fun. Challenges include trams, lunatic drivers and pedestrians, one-way streets and police looking for a little handout. Try not to arrive or leave on a Friday or Sunday afternoon or evening, when most of Prague seems to head to and from their weekend houses.

Central Prague has many pedestrian-only streets, marked with Pěší Zoná (Pedestrian Zone) signs, where only service vehicles and taxis are allowed; parking can be a nightmare. Meter time limits range from two to six hours at around 40Kč per hour. Parking in one-way streets is normally only allowed on the right-hand side. Traffic inspectors are strict, and you could be clamped or towed. There are several car parks at the edges of Staré Město, and Park-and-Ride car parks around the outer city (most are marked on city maps), close to metro stations.

Public Transport

All public transport is operated by **Dopravní podnik hl. m. Prahy** (DPP; 296 191 817; www.dpp.cz), which has **information desks** (7am-10pm) at Ruzyně airport and in four metro stations — **Muzeum** (7am to 9pm), **Můstek** (7am to 6pm), **Anděl** (7am to 6pm) and **Nádraží Holešovice**

(☻ 7am to 6pm) – where you can get tickets, directions, a multilingual system map, a map of *Noční provoz* (night services) and a detailed English-language guide to the whole system.

Buy a ticket before boarding a bus, tram or metro. Tickets are sold from machines at metro stations and major tram stops, at newsstands, Trafiky snack shops, PNS and other tobacco kiosks, hotels, all metro station ticket offices and DPP information offices.

A *jízdenka* (transfer ticket) is valid on tram, metro, bus and the Petřín funicular and costs 20Kč (half-price for six- to 15-year-olds); large suitcases and backpacks (anything larger than 25cm x 45cm x 70cm) also need a 10Kč ticket. Kids under six ride free. Validate (punch) your ticket by sticking it in the little yellow machine in the metro station lobby or on the bus or tram the first time you board; this stamps the time and date on it. Once validated, tickets remain valid for 75 minutes from the time of stamping, if validated between 5am and 8pm on weekdays, and for 90 minutes at other times. Within this period, you can make unlimited transfers between all types of public transport (you don't need to punch the ticket again).

There's also a short-hop 14/7Kč adult/concession ticket, valid for 15 minutes on buses and trams, or for up to five metro stations. No transfers are allowed with these, and they're not valid on the Petřín funicular nor on night trams (51 to 58) or night buses (501 to 512). Being caught without a valid ticket entails a 400Kč on-the-spot fine (50Kč for not having a luggage ticket). The inspectors travel incognito, but will show a badge when they ask for your ticket. A few may demand a higher fine from foreigners and pocket the difference, so insist on a *doklad* (receipt) before paying.

You can also buy tickets valid for 24 hours (80Kč) and three/seven/15 days (200/250/280Kč). Again, these must be validated on first use only; if a ticket is stamped twice, it becomes invalid.

On metro trains and newer trams and buses, an electronic display shows the route number and the name of the next stop, and a recorded voice announces each station or stop. As the train, tram or bus pulls away, it says: *Příští stanice* (or *zastávka*)… meaning 'The next station (or stop) is…', perhaps noting that it's a *přestupní stanice* (transfer station). At metro stations, signs point you towards the *výstup* (exit) or to a *přestup* (transfer to another line).

The metro operates from 5am to midnight daily. There are three lines: Line A runs from the northwestern side of the city at Dejvická to the east at Skalka; line B runs from the southwest at Zličín to the northeast at Černý Most; and line C runs from the north at Nádraží Holešovice to the southeast at Háje. Line A intersects line C at Muzeum, line B intersects line C at Florenc and line A intersects line B at Můstek.

After the metro closes, night trams (51 to 58) and buses (501 to 512) rumble across the city about every 40 minutes. If you're planning a late evening, check if one of these services passes near where you're staying.

Taxi

Prague taxi drivers are notorious for overcharging tourists – try to avoid getting a taxi in tourist areas such as Václavské nám. To avoid being ripped off, phone a reliable company such as **AAA** (☎ 14 014) or **ProfiTaxi** (☎ 844 700 800). If you feel you're being overcharged ask for an *účet* (bill). The Prague City Council has a website detailing legitimate fares (http://panda.hyperlink.cz/taxitext/etaxiweb .htm), and has increased the maximum fine for overcharging to one million Kč.

AROUND PRAGUE

The following places can easily be visited on day trips using public transport.

Karlštejn

Fairy-tale **Karlštejn Castle** (☎ 274 008 154; www .hradkarlstejn.cz; Karlštejn; ☻ 9am-6pm Tue-Sun Jul & Aug; 9am-5pm May, Jun & Sep; 9am-4pm Apr & Oct; 9am-3pm Nov-Mar) perches above the Berounka River, 30km southwest of Prague. Erected by the Emperor Charles IV in the mid-14th century, it crowns a ridge above the village, a 20-minute walk from the train station.

The castle's highlight is the **Chapel of the Holy Rood**, where the Bohemian crown jewels were kept until 1420, with walls covered in 14th-century painted panels and precious stones. The 45-minute guided tours (in English) on Route I cost 200/120Kč for adult/child tickets. Route II, which includes the chapel (June to October only), are 300/150Kč adult/child per person and must be prebooked. Trains from Praha-hlavní nádraží station to Beroun stop at Karlštejn (46Kč, 45 minutes, hourly).

Konopiště

The assassination in 1914 of the heir to the Austro-Hungarian throne, Archduke Franz Ferdinand d'Este, sparked off WWI. For the last 20 years of his life he avoided the intrigues of the Vienna court, hiding away southeast of Prague in what became his country retreat, **Konopiště Chateau** (☎ 274 008 154; www .zamek-konopiste.cz; Benešov; ☺ 9am-5pm Tue-Sun May-Aug; 9am-4pm Tue-Fri, 9am-5pm Sat & Sun Sep; 9am-3pm Tue-Fri, 9am-4pm Sat & Sun Apr & Oct; 9am-3pm Sat & Sun Nov)

Three guided tours are available. **Tour III** (adult/child 300/200Kč) is the most interesting, visiting the archduke's private apartments, unchanged since the state took over the chateau in 1921. **Tour II** (in English adult/child 180/100Kč) takes in the **Great Armoury**, one of Europe's most impressive collections.

The castle is a testament to the archduke's twin obsessions: hunting and St George. Having renovated the massive Gothic and Renaissance building in the 1890s, and installed all the latest technology (electricity, central heating, flush toilets, showers and a lift), Franz Ferdinand decorated his home with his hunting trophies. His game books record that he shot around 300,000 creatures during his lifetime, from foxes and deer to elephants and tigers. About 100,000 of them adorn the walls, marked with when and where it was killed. The **Trophy Corridor** and antler-clad **Chamois Room** (both on Tour III) are truly bizarre sights.

The archduke's collection of St George related art and artefacts relating is also impressive, with 3750 items, many of which are displayed in the **Muzeum sv Jiří** (adult/child 25/10Kč) at the front of the castle. From June to September weekend concerts are held in the castle's grounds.

There are frequent direct trains from Prague's hlavní nádraží to Benešov u Prahy (64Kč, 1¼ hours, hourly). Buses depart from Florenc and Roztyly metro station to Benešov on a regular basis (37Kč, 1¼ hours)

Konopiště is 2.5km west of Benešov. Local bus 2 (9Kč, six minutes, hourly) runs from a stop on Dukelská, 400m north of the train station (turn left out of the station, then first right on Tyršova and first left) to the castle car park. Otherwise it's a 30-minute walk. Turn left out of the train station, go left across the bridge over the railway, and follow Konopištská street west for 2km.

Kutná Hora

In the 14th century Kutná Hora rivalled Prague as Bohemia's most important town, growing wealthy on the silver ore that laced the rocks beneath it. The silver *groschen* that were minted here at that time represented the hard currency of Central Europe. The good times ended when the silver ran out. Mining ceased in 1726, leaving the medieval townscape largely unaltered. It's an attractive place with several fascinating and unusual historical attractions, and was added to Unesco's World Heritage List in 1996.

ORIENTATION & INFORMATION

Kutná Hora hlavní nádraží (the main train station) is 3km northeast of the old town centre. The bus station is more conveniently located on the northeastern edge of the old town.

The easiest way to visit Kutná Hora on a day trip is to arrive on a morning train from Prague, then make the 10-minute walk from Kutná Hora hlavní nádraží to Sedlec Ossuary. From there it's another 2km walk or a five-minute bus ride into town.

The helpful **information centre** (☎ 327 512 378; http://infocentrum.kh.cz; Palackého nám 377; ☺ 9am-6.30pm Apr-Oct; 9am-5pm Sat & Sun, 9am-5pm Mon-Fri Oct-Mar) books accommodation, provides internet access (1Kč per minute), and rents bicycles (220Kč per day).

SIGHTS

Walk 10-minutes south from Kutná Hora hlavní nádraží to the remarkable **Sedlec Ossuary** (Kostnice; ☎ 327 561 143; adult/child 45/30Kč; ☺ 8am-6pm Apr-Sep, 9am-noon & 1-5pm Oct, 9am-4pm Nov-Mar). When the Schwarzenberg family purchased Sedlec monastery in 1870 they allowed a local woodcarver to get creative with the bones of 40,000 people, which had lingered in the crypt for centuries. Garlands of skulls and femurs are strung from the vaulted ceiling like macabre Christmas decorations. The central chandelier contains at least one of each bone in the human body. Four giant pyramids of stacked bones squat in the corner chapels, and crosses of bone adorn the altar. There's even a Schwarzenberg coat of arms made from bones.

From Sedlec it's another 2km walk (or five-minute bus ride) to central Kutná Hora. **Palackého nám**, the town's main square is unremarkable, but the interesting old town lies to its south.

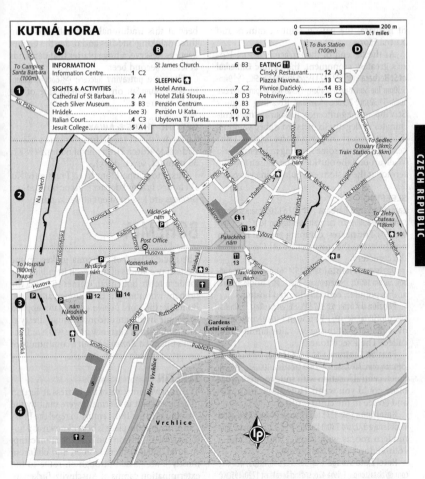

KUTNÁ HORA

0   200 m
0   0.1 miles

INFORMATION
Information Centre..............**1** C2

SIGHTS & ACTIVITIES
Cathedral of St Barbara.........**2** A4
Czech Silver Museum............**3** B3
Hrádek................................(see 3)
Italian Court.......................**4** C3
Jesuit College.....................**5** A4

St James Church..................**6** B3

SLEEPING
Hotel Anna.........................**7** C2
Hotel Zlatá Stoupa................**8** D3
Penzión Centrum..................**9** B3
Penzión U Kata...................**10** D2
Ubytovna TJ Turista.............**11** A3

EATING
Čínský Restaurant...............**12** A3
Piazza Navona....................**13** C3
Pivnice Dačický..................**14** B3
Potraviny..........................**15** C2

From the western end of the square a narrow lane called Jakubská leads to **St James Church** (1330), east of which lies the **Italian Court** (Vlašský dvůr; ☎ 327 512 873; Havlíčkovo nám 552; adult/child 80/50Kč; ۝ 9am-6pm Apr-Sep, 10am-5pm Mar & Oct, 10am-4pm Nov-Feb), the former Royal Mint; Florentine craftsmen began stamping silver coins here in 1300. It now houses a mint museum, and a 15th-century **Audience Hall** with two impressive 19th-century murals depicting the election of Vladislav Jagiello as king of Bohemia in 1471 and the Decree of Kutná Hora being proclaimed by Wenceslas IV and Jan Hus in 1409.

From the southern side of St James Church a cobbled lane, Ruthardská, leads to the **Hrádek** (Little Castle), a 15th-century palace housing the **Czech Silver Museum** (České Muzeum Stříbra; ☎ 327 512 159; www.cms-kh.cz; adult/child 60/30Kč; ۝ 10am-6pm Jul & Aug, 9am-6pm May, Jun & Sep, 9am-5pm Apr & Oct, 10am-4pm Sat & Sun Nov, closed Mon year-round). The exhibits celebrate the mines that made Kutná Hora wealthy, including a huge wooden device used to extricate 1000kg of rock from the 200m-deep shafts. Don a miner's helmet and lamp to join a 45-minute **tour** (adult/child 110/70Kč) through 500m of medieval mine shafts beneath the town.

Beyond the Hrádek is a 17th-century former **Jesuit college**, with a front terrace featuring 13 baroque sculptures of saints, inspired by those on Prague's Charles Bridge. The second one along of a woman holding a chalice with a stone tower at her side, is

St Barbara, the patron saint of miners and Kutná Hora.

At the far end of the terrace is Kutná Hora's greatest monument, the Gothic **Cathedral of St Barbara** (☎ 327 512 115; adult/child 30/15Kč; ⏰ 9am-5.30pm Tue-Sun May-Sep, 10am-11.30am & 1-4pm Apr & Oct, 10am-11.30am & 2-3.30pm Nov-Mar). Rivalling Prague's St Vitus in magnificence, its soaring nave culminates in elegant, six-petalled ribbed vaulting. The ambulatory chapels preserve original 15th-century frescoes, some showing miners at work. Walk around the outside of the church too; the terrace at the eastern end enjoys fine views.

SLEEPING

Camping Santa Barbara (☎ 327 512 051; santabarbara .com@worldonline.cz; camp site per person 100Kč; ⏰ Apr-Oct; **P**) The nearest camping ground is 800m northwest of the town centre off Česká, near the cemetery.

Ubytovna TJ Turista (☎ 327 514 961; nám Národního od-boje 56; dm 160Kč; ⏰ reception 5-6pm; **P**) Book ahead at this popular, centrally located hostel.

Penzión U Kata (☎ 327 515 096; www.ukata.cz; Uhelná 596; s/d 450/600Kč; **P**) You won't lose your head over the rates at this great value family hotel called 'The Executioner'.

Penzión Centrum (☎ 327 514 218; www.centrum .penzion.com; Jakubská 57; d incl breakfast 1000Kč; **P**) A quiet, central location with snug rooms – what more could you want? How about pancakes and coffee in the courtyard?

Hotel Anna (☎ 327 516 315; www.sweb.cz/hotel.anna; Vladislavova 372; s/d 730/1150Kč; **P**) The Anna has modern rooms with shower and TV, and a 16th-century cellar restaurant.

Hotel Zlatá Stoupa (☎ 327 511 540; http://web.tele com.cz/zlatastoupa; Tylova 426; s/d incl breakfast 1220/1950Kč; **P**) Treat yourself with an intriguing combination of mahogany period furniture and full-size bottles of wine in the minibar.

EATING & DRINKING

Piazza Navona (☎ 327 512 588; Palackého nám 90; mains 100-140Kč; ⏰ 9am-midnight May-Sep, 9am-8pm Oct-Apr) Have authentic pizza by an authentic Italian on Kutná Hora's main square. Finish with gelati in summer and hot chocolate in winter.

Čínský Restaurant (☎ 327 514 151; nám Národního odboje 48; mains 80-220Kč; ⏰ closed Mon) The food is Chinese but the stately building is pure Czech. With dishes like rabbit *gung-po*, the menu is still making its mind up. Try the duck with mushrooms.

Pivnice Dačický (☎ 327 512 248; Rakova 8; mains 80-2200Kč; ⏰ 11am-11pm) Try Kutná Hora's dark beer at this traditional beer hall. Rustle up three drinking buddies and order the Game-keepers Reserve, a huge platter that demands at least a second beer.

There's a **potraviny** (grocery; ⏰ 6am-5pm Mon-Fri, 7am-11.30am Sat) on the eastern side of the main square.

GETTING THERE & AWAY

There are direct trains from Prague's hlavní nádraží to Kutná Hora hlavní nádraží (98Kč, 55 minutes, seven daily).

Buses to Kutná Hora from Prague (64Kč, 1¼ hours, hourly) depart Florenc bus station; services are less frequent at weekends.

BOHEMIA

The ancient land of Bohemia makes up the western two-thirds of the Czech Republic. The modern term 'bohemian' comes to us via the French, who thought that Roma came from Bohemia; the word *bohémien* was later applied to people living an unconventional lifestyle. The term gained currency in the wake of Puccini's opera *La Bohème* about a community of poverty-stricken artists in Paris.

TEREZÍN

The massive ramparts of the fortress at Terezín (Theriesenstadt in German) were built by the Habsburgs in the 18th century to repel the Prussian army, but the place is better known as a notorious WWII prison and concentration camp. Around 150,000 men, women and children, mostly Jews, passed through en route to the extermination camps of Auschwitz-Birkenau: 35,000 of them died here of hunger, disease or suicide; only 4000 survived. From 1945 to 1948 the fortress served as an internment camp for the Sudeten Germans who were expelled from Czechoslovakia after the war.

The **Terezín Memorial** (☎ 416 782 576; www .pamatnik-terezin.cz) consists of two main parts – the Museum of the Ghetto in the Main Fortress, and the Lesser Fortress, a 10-minute walk east across the Ohře River. Admission to one part costs 160/130Kč; a combined ticket for both (also including the Madeburg Barracks) is 180/140Kč. At the ticket office, ask about the historical films in the museum's cinema.

The **Museum of the Ghetto** (Muzeum ghetta; ⏰ 9am-6pm Apr-Oct, 9am-5.30pm Nov-Mar) records daily life in the camp during WWII through moving displays of paintings, letters and personal possessions; the Nazi documents recording the departures of trains to 'the east' chillingly illustrate the banality of evil.

Around 32,000 prisoners, many of them Czech partisans, were incarcerated in the **Lesser Fortress** (Malá pevnost; ☉ 8am-6pm Apr-Oct, 8am-4.30pm Nov-Mar). Take the grimly fascinating self-guided tour through the prison barracks, workshops, morgues and mass graves, before arriving at the bleak execution grounds where more than 250 prisoners were shot.

At the **Magdeburg Barracks** (Magdeburská kasárna; cnr Tyršova & Vodárenská), the former base of the Jewish 'government', are exhibits on the rich cultural life – music, theatre, fine arts and literature – that flourished against this backdrop of fear. Most poignant are the magazines containing children's stories and illustrations.

Terezín is northwest of Prague and 3km south of Litoměřice; buses between Prague and Litoměřice stop at both the main square and the Lesser Fortress. There are frequent buses between Litoměřice bus station and Terezín (8Kč, 10 minutes, at least hourly).

LITOMĚŘICE
pop 25,100
The cheerful town of Litoměřice offers relief from the horrors of nearby Terezín. Founded by German colonists in the 13th century, it prospered in the 18th century as a royal seat and bishopric. The old town centre has many picturesque buildings and churches, some designed by the locally born baroque architect Ottavio Broggio.

The old town lies across the road to the west of the train and bus stations, guarded by the remnants of the 14th-century town walls. Walk along Dlouhá to the central square, Mírové nám.

The **information centre** (☎ 416 732 440; www .litomerice.cz; Mírové nám 15/7; ☉ 8am-6pm Mon-Sat, 8am-4pm Sun May-Sep; 8am-4pm Mon-Fri, 8-11am Sat Oct-Apr) in the town hall, books accommodation and run tours from April to October.

Sights
The main square is lined with Gothic arcades and pastel façades, dominated by the tower of **All Saints Church**, the step-gabled **Old Town Hall** and the distinctive **House at the Chalice** (Dům U Kalicha), housing the present town hall – the green copper artichoke sprouting from

the roof is actually a chalice, the traditional symbol of the Hussite church. The delicate slice of baroque wedding cake at the square's elevated end is the **House of Ottavio Broggio**.

Along Michalská on the square's southwest corner you'll find another of Broggio's designs, the **North Bohemia Fine Arts Gallery** (☎ 416 732 382; Michalská 7; adult/child 32/18Kč; ☉ 9am-noon & 1-6pm Tue-Sun Apr-Sep, 9am-5pm Oct-Mar) with the priceless Renaissance panels of the Litoměřice Altarpiece.

Turn left at the end of Michalská and follow Domská towards tree-lined Domské nám on Cathedral Hill, passing **St Wenceslas Church**, a baroque gem, along a side street to the right. At the top of the hill is the town's oldest church, **St Stephen Cathedral**, from the 11th century.

Follow the arch on the cathedral's left and descend a steep cobbled lane called Máchova. At the foot of the hill turn left then first right, up the zigzag steps to the **old town walls**. Follow the walls to the right as far as the next street, Jezuitská, then turn left back to the square.

Sleeping & Eating
Autocamp Slavoj (☎ 416 734 481; kemp.litomerice@post .cz; per tent/bungalow 70/200Kč; ☉ May-Sep; P 🖵) South of the train station, this pleasant camping ground is on an island called Střelecký ostrov (Marksmen Island).

U Svatého Václava (☎ 416 737 500; www.upfront .cz/penzion; Svatovaclavská 12; s/d incl breakfast 600/1000Kč) Beside St Wenceslas Church, this haven has well-equipped rooms, hearty cooked breakfasts, and owners whose English is better than they think.

Pension Prislin (☎ 416 735 833; www.pension.cz; Na Kocandě 12; s/d incl breakfast 700/1200Kč; P) On a busy road near the train station, Pension Prislin conceals a quiet garden with river views.

Hotel Salva Guarda (☎ 416 732 506; www. salva -garda.cz; Mírové nám 12; s/d 990/1450Kč; P ☺) With interesting old maps in reception, it's a shame they keep the lights so low. The spotless rooms, however, are well-lit in this classy hotel that's housed in a *sgraffito* building built in 1566.

Music Club Viva (☎ 606 437 783; Mezibrani; mains 90-220Kč) Shared wooden tables ensures conversation flows as naturally as the drinks in this hip spot in the old town bastion. The posters feature everyone from Frank Sinatra to Bob Marley.

Radniční sklípek (☎ 416 731 142, Mírové nám 21; mains 80-170Kč) Keep your head down in this labyrinth of underground cellars. It should be easy because you'll be tucking into great value grills accompanied by a good wine list.

Pizzeria Sole (☎ 416 737 150; Na Valech 56; pizza 75Kč) This no-frills Italian café has cheap pizzas and good-value soup, pasta and dessert combos.

Pekárna Kodys & Hamele (Novobranská 18) Head here for baked goodies.

Getting There & Away
Direct buses from Prague to Litoměřice (61Kč, 1L hours, hourly) depart from station No 17 at Florenc bus station (final destination Ústí nad Labem).

BOHEMIAN SWITZERLAND NATIONAL PARK
The main road and rail route between Prague and Dresden follows the fast-flowing Labe (Elbe) River, gouging a sinuous, steep-sided valley through a sandstone plateau on the border between the Czech Republic and Germany. The landscape of sandstone pinnacles, giddy gorges, dark forests and high meadows that stretches to the east of the river is the **Bohemian Switzerland National Park** (Národní park České Švýcarsko), named after two 19th-century Swiss artists, who liked the landscape so much they settled here.

A few hundred metres south of the German border, **Hřensko** is a cute village of pointy-gabled, half-timbered houses crammed into a narrow sandstone gorge where the Kamenice River flows into the Labe. It's overrun with German day-trippers at summer weekends, but a few minutes' walk upstream peaceful hiking trails begin.

A signposted 16km circular hike takes in the main sights; allow five to six hours. From the eastern end of Hřensko a trail leads via ledges, walkways and tunnels through the mossy chasms of the **Kamenice River Gorge**. There are two sections – **Edmundova Soutěska** (Edmund's Gorge; ☼ 9am-6pm May-Aug; Sat & Sun only Apr, Sep & Oct) and **Divoká Soutěska** (Savage Gorge; ☼ 9am-5pm May-Aug; Sat & Sun only Apr, Sep & Oct) – that have been dammed. Continue by punt, poled along by a ferryman through a canyon 5m wide and 50m to 150m deep. Each ferry trip costs adult/child 50/25Kč.

A kilometre beyond the end of the second boat trip, a blue-marked trail leads uphill to the Hotel Mezní Louka. Across the road, a red-marked trail continues through the forest to the spectacular rock formation **Pravčická Brána** (www.pbrana.cz; adult/child 50/30Kč; ☼ 10am-

6pm Apr-Oct, 10am-4pm Sat & Sun Nov-Mar), the largest natural arch in Europe. In a nook beneath the arch is the **Falcon's Nest**, a 19th-century chateau housing a national park museum and restaurant. From here the red trail descends westward back to Hřensko.

Sleeping & Eating
Pension Lugano (☎ 412 554 146; fax 412 554 156; Hřensko; s/d incl breakfast 540/1080Kč; ℗) A cheerful place in the centre of Hřensko serving terrific breakfasts.

Restaurace U Raka (☎ 412 554 157; Hřensko 28; mains 100-220Kč; ☼ 10am-9.30pm) Near Pension Lugano is a pretty half-timbered cottage offering Czech specialities. Try the local *pstruh* (trout).

In hills, **Hotel Mezní Louka** (☎ 412 554 220; Mezní Louka 71; s/d 700/1050Kč; ℗) is a 19th-century hiking lodge with a decent restaurant (mains 90Kč to 170Kč). Across the road is **Camp Mezní Louka** (☎ 412 554 084; per tent/bungalow 60Kč/450Kč; ℗).

If you have your own transport, base yourself in the pretty villages of Janov and Jetřichovice. In Janov **Pension Pastis** (☎ 142 554 037; www.pastis .cz; Janov 22; s/d incl breakfast 550/1100Kč; ℗) has an excellent restaurant; in Jetřichovice try **Pension Dřevák** (☎ 412 555 015; www.cztour.cz/drevak; s/d incl breakfast 700/1050Kč ℗), which is housed in a pretty 19th-century wooden building.

Getting There & Away
There are frequent local trains from Dresden to Schöna (€5.20, 1¼ hour, every half hour), on the German (west) bank of the river opposite Hřensko. From the station, a ferry crosses to Hřensko (€0.85 or 12Kč, three minutes) on demand.

From Prague, take a bus (84Kč, 1¾ hours, five daily) to Děčín, then another to Hřensko (14Kč, 20 minutes, four daily). Alternatively, catch a Dresden-bound train and get off at Bad Schandau (184Kč, two hours, eight daily), then a local train back to Schöna (€1.80, 12 minutes, every half hour).

On weekdays there are three buses a day (year-round) between Hřensko and Mezní Louka (8Kč, 10 minutes), and two a day at weekends (July to September only).

KARLOVY VARY
pop 60,000

If you've been hiding a designer dog or an ostentatious pair of sunglasses in your backpack, then Karlovy Vary (Karlsbad in German) is

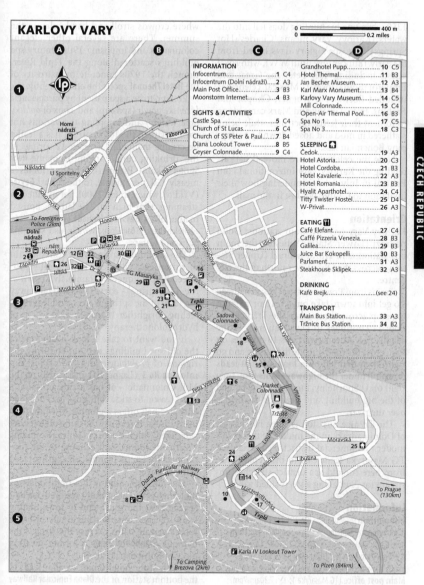

KARLOVY VARY

INFORMATION	
Infocentrum	1 C4
Infocentrum (Dolní nádraží)	2 A3
Main Post Office	3 B3
Moonstorm Internet	4 B3

SIGHTS & ACTIVITIES	
Castle Spa	5 C4
Church of St Lucas	6 C4
Church of SS Peter & Paul	7 B4
Diana Lookout Tower	8 B5
Geyser Colonnade	9 C4

Grandhotel Pupp	10 C5
Hotel Thermal	11 B3
Jan Becher Museum	12 A3
Karl Marx Monument	13 B4
Karlovy Vary Museum	14 C5
Mill Colonnade	15 C4
Open-Air Thermal Pool	16 B3
Spa No 1	17 C5
Spa No 3	18 C5

SLEEPING	
Čedok	19 A3
Hotel Astoria	20 C3
Hotel Cordoba	21 B3
Hotel Kavalerie	22 A3
Hotel Romania	23 B3
Hyalit Aparthotel	24 C4
Titty Twister Hostel	25 D4
W-Privat	26 A3

EATING	
Café Elefant	27 C4
Caffé Pizzeria Venezia	28 B3
Galilea	29 B3
Juice Bar Kokopelli	30 B3
Parlament	31 A3
Steakhouse Sklipek	32 A3

DRINKING	
Kafé Brejk	(see 24)

TRANSPORT	
Main Bus Station	33 A3
Tržnice Bus Station	34 B2

CZECH REPUBLIC

your chance to give them both an airing. The fashionable town is the closest the Czech Republic has to a glam resort, but Karlovy Vary is definitely glam with a small 'g'. Well-heeled hypochondriacs from Germany, Austria and Russia make the pilgrimage and try to enjoy courses of lymphatic drainage and hydrocolon-otherapy and other such cleansing wonders.

If Russian matrons walking canine 'bling-on-a-string' doesn't appeal, there's good hiking in the surrounding hills, or just have a drink at a riverside café. It will taste infinitely better than the sulphurous spa water everyone else is drinking.

According to legend, Emperor Charles IV discovered the hot springs accidentally in

1350 when one his hunting dogs fell into the waters (Karlovy Vary means 'Charles' Hot Springs). The spa's glory days lasted from the early 18th century until WWI, with royal guests including Tsar Peter the Great and Emperor Franz Josef I. Musical celebrities included Beethoven, Wagner, Chopin and Brahms. Even Tolstoy and Marx came along to foment their leftist doctrines while being slathered in mud and hosed down by a strapping Bohemian lass.

Now the celebrities are more B-list, attending the Karlovy Vary International Film Festival in July, while wondering how their invitation to Cannes got lost in the mail.

Orientation

Karlovy Vary has two train stations: Dolní nádraží (Lower Station), beside the main bus station, and Horní nádraží (Upper Station), across the Ohře River north of the city centre.

Trains from Prague arrive at Horní nádraží. To get into town, take bus 11, 12 or 13 from the stop across the road to the Tržnice station; 11 continues to Divadelní nám in the spa district. Alternatively, it's 10 minutes on foot: cross the road outside the station and go right, then first left on a footpath that leads downhill under the highway. At its foot, turn right on U Spořitelny, then left at the far end of the big building and head for the bridge over the river.

The Tržnice bus stop is three blocks east of Dolní nádraží, in the middle of the town's modern commercial district. Pedestrianised TG Masaryka leads east to the Teplá River; from here the old spa district stretches upstream for 2km along a steep-sided valley.

Information

Infocentrum Dolní nádraží (☎ 353 232 838; www .karlovyvary.cz; Západní; ☯ 9am-5pm Mon-Fri, 10am-4pm Sat & Sun); Lázeňska (☎ 353 224 097; Lázeňska 1; ☯ 9am-7pm Mon-Fri, 10am-6pm Sat & Sun) Stocks maps, books accommodation and gives transport advice.

Main post office (TG Masaryka 1; ☯ 7.30am-7pm Mon-Fri, 7am-1pm Sat, 7am-noon Sun) Includes a telephone centre.

Moonstorm Internet (TG Masaryka 31; per 15 min 12Kč; ☯ 9am-9pm)

Sights

At the heart of the old spa district is the neoclassical **Mill Colonnade** (Mlýnská Kolonáda),

where crowds stroll and bands play in the summer. There are several other elegant colonnades and imposing 19th-century spa buildings scattered along the Teplá River, though the 1970s concrete monstrosity of the **Hotel Thermal** spoils the effect slightly.

Pretend to be a spa patient by purchasing a *lázeňské pohár* (spa cup) and a box of *oplátky* (spa wafers) and sampling the various hot springs (free); the Infocentrum has a leaflet describing them all. There are 12 springs in the 'drinking cure', ranging from the **Rock Spring** (Skalní Pramen), which dribbles a measly 1.3L per minute, to the robust **Geyser** (Vřídlo), which spurts 2000L per minute in a steaming, 14m-high jet. The latter is housed in the 1970s **Geyser Colonnade** (Vřídelní Kolonáda; admission free; ☯ 6am-7pm), which also sells spa cups and wafers.

The sulphurous spring waters carry a whiff of rotten eggs. Becherovka, a locally produced herbal liqueur, is famously known as the '13th spring' – a few shots will take away the taste of the spring waters, and leave you feeling sprightlier than a week's worth of hydrocolonotherapy.

If you want to take a look inside one of the old spa buildings without enduring the rigours of *proktologie* and *endoskopie*, nip into **Spa No 3** (Lázně III) just north of the Mill Colonnade – it has a café upstairs, a good reason to stick your nose in. The faded entrance hall offers a glimpse of white-tiled institutional corridors stretching off to either side, lined with the doors to sinister-sounding 'treatment rooms' and echoing to the flip-flopped footsteps of muscular, grim-faced nurses. Shiver.

The most splendid of the traditional spa buildings is the beautifully restored **Spa No 1** (Lázně I) at the south end of town, dating from 1895 and once housing Emperor Franz Josef's private baths. Across the river is the baroque **Grandhotel Pupp**, a former meeting place of European aristocrats.

North of the hotel, a narrow alley leads to the bottom station of the **Diana Funicular Railway** (single/return 36/60Kč; ☯ 9am-6pm), which climbs 166m to great views from the **Diana Lookout Tower** (admission free). It's a pleasant walk back down through the forest.

If you descend north from Diana towards the **Karl Marx Monument** and Petra Velikého (Peter the Great Street), visit the Russian Orthodox **Church of SS Peter & Paul** (kostel sv Petra a

Pavla; 1897), amid an enclave of elegant villas and spa hotels. Its five golden onion domes and colourful exterior were modelled on the Byzantine Church of the Holy Trinity in Ostankino near Moscow. It and the Anglican **Church of St Lucas** along the road are reminders of the town's once-thriving expat communities.

Rainy-day alternatives include the **Karlovy Vary Museum** (Nová Louka 23; adult/child 30/15Kč; 9am-noon & 1-5pm Wed-Sun), which has displays on local history, and the **Jan Becher Museum** (353 170 156; TG Masaryka 57; adult/child 100/50Kč; 9am-5pm), dedicated to the 18th-century inventor of the local liqueur.

Activities

Although the surviving traditional *lázně* (spa) centres are basically medical institutions, many of the town's old spa and hotel buildings have been renovated as 'wellness' hotels catering for more hedonistic tastes, with saunas, cosmetic treatments, massages and aromatherapy. **Castle Spa** (Zámecké Lázně; 353 225 307; Zámecký vrch; basic admission €20; 7.30am-7.30pm) is a modernised spa centre, complete with a subterranean thermal pool, and retains an atmospheric heritage ambience. Basic admission gets you one hour loafing about in the pool; a four-hour session (€70) adds a full-body massage and spa treatments such as hydro-massage and electro-aerosol inhalation.

If all you want is a quick paddle head for the **open-air thermal pool** (bazén; admission per hr 40Kč; 8am-8.30pm Mon-Sat, 9am-9.30pm Sun, closed every 3rd Mon) on the cliff above the Hotel Thermal. There's also a sauna (open 10am to 9.30pm) and a fitness club here.

Festivals & Events

Karlovy Vary International Film Festival (www .kviff.com) Early July.
International Student Film Festival (www.fresh filmsfest.net) Late August.
Karlovy Vary Folklore Festival Early September.
Jazzfest Karlovy Vary Early September; international jazz festival.
Dvořák Autumn September; classical music festival.

Sleeping

Accommodation is pricey, and can be tight during weekends and festivals; book ahead. Agencies **Čedok** (353 227 837; Dr Bechera 21; 9am-6pm Mon-Fri, 9am-noon Sat) and **W-Privat** (353 227 768; nám Republiky 5; 8.30am-5pm Mon-Fri, 9.30am-1pm

Sat) can book private rooms from 400Kč per person. Infocentrum (opposite) can find hostel, *pension* and hotel rooms.

Camping Březova (353 222 665; www.brezovy -haj.cz; tent/bungalow per person 90/150Kč; Apr-Oct;) Beside a quiet river valley, this camp site is 3km south of town. Catch a bus from Tržnice bus station to the village of Březova.

Titty Twister Hostel (353 239 071; www.hosteltt .cz; Moravská 44; per person from 390Kč) In a town where cheap sleeps aren't bubbling over, this hostel with a silly name rises to the top. Accommodation is in apartments with two, four or six beds; all with separate kitchens.

Hotel Kavalerie (353 229 613; www.kavalerie.cz; TG Masaryka 43; s/d incl breakfast from 950/1225Kč) Friendly staff abound in this cosy spot above a café, located near the bus and train stations, and away from the spa district's high restaurant prices.

Hotel Romania (353 222 822; www.romania.cz; Zahradní 49; s/d incl breakfast 1000/1750Kč;) Don't be put off by the ugly Hotel Thermal dominating the views from this good-value, reader-recommended spot. Just squint a little, because the rooms are spacious and the English-speaking staff very helpful.

Hotel Astoria (353 335 111; www.astoria-spa.cz; Vřídelní 92; s/d incl breakfast from €40/80;) A riverside location opposite the Mill Colonnade completes this classy spot offering a full range of treatments. A leafy lobby relaxes you as soon as you walk in.

Hyalit Aparthotel (353 229 638; www.hyalit.cz; Stará Luka 62; d from 1900Kč;) With stylish décor and kitchens, these five apartments are recommended for self-caterers. Children under 15 stay free.

Hotel Cordoba (353 200 255; www.hotel-cordoba .com; Zahradní 37; d incl breakfast 1800Kč) A worthwhile backup.

Eating & Drinking

Caffe Pizzeria Venezia (353 229 721; Zahradní 43; pizza 120Kč) After a strong espresso and tasty pizza, blur your eyes through your designer sunnies, and see if you can spot any gondoliers from this pretty-in-pink spot looking out on the Teplá River.

Galilea (353 221 183; TG Masaryka 3A, Pasáž Alfa; mains 130-180Kč) Try the creamy dips and Turkish bread at this authentic Middle Eastern spot. Downstairs grab a felafel kebab (65Kč) and relax by the river. Both the restaurant and the kebab shop have good vegetarian options.

Steakhouse Sklipek (☎ 353 229 197; Zeyerova 1; steaks 180Kč) With red-checked tablecloths this place looks like a hangout for Tony Soprano and his mates. The huge steak meals are big enough to feed your entire mob too.

Parlament (☎ 353 586 155; Zeyerova 5; ☽ closed Sun) With outdoor tables on the edge of the bustling TG Masaryka pedestrian mall, this is a favoured drinking place for locals. And the food's pretty good too.

Also recommended:

Café Elefant (☎ 353 223 406; Stará Louka 30; coffee 45Kč) Classy old-school spot for coffee and cake.

Juice Bar Kokopelli (☎ 353 236 254; Bulharská 9; juice & smoothies 20-37Kč) For fruit smoothies that are probably healthier than sulphur-laden spa water.

Kafé Brejk (Stará Louka 62; coffee 35Kč, baguettes 50Kč; ☽ 9am-5pm) Trendy new-school spot for takeaway coffees and design-your-own baguettes.

Getting There & Around

Direct buses to Prague (130Kč, 2¼ hours, eight daily) and Plzeň (76Kč, 1½ hours, hourly) depart from the main bus station beside Dolní nádraží train station.

There are direct (but slow) trains from Karlovy Vary to Prague (274Kč, four hours). Heading west from Karlovy Vary to Nuremberg, Germany (980Kč, three hours, two a day), and beyond, you'll have to change at Cheb (Eger in German). A slow but scenic alternative is a trundle north through the hills and forests to Leipzig (890Kč, 4½ hours, 10 daily); there are several routes, involving two or three changes of train – check the online timetables for these routes at www.idos.cz or www.bahn.de.

Local buses cost 10Kč; there are ticket machines at the main stops. Bus 11 runs hourly from Horní nádraží to Tržnice in the commercial district, and on to Divadelni nám. Bus 2 runs between Tržnice and Grandhotel Pupp (Spa No 1) every half hour or so from 6am to 11pm daily.

LOKET

Wrapped snugly in a tight bend of the Ohre River, the village of Loket is a pretty little place that has attracted many famous visitors from nearby Karlovy Vary. A plaque on the façade of the Hostinec Bílý Kůň on the chocolate-box town square commemorates Goethe's seven visits. The forbidding **castle**

(☎ 352 684 104; adult/child with English guide 90/60Kč, with English text 80/45Kč; ☽ 9am-4.30pm May-Oct, 9am-3.30pm Nov-Apr), perched high above the river, houses a museum dedicated to locally produced porcelain, but the village's main attraction is just wandering around admiring the views.

Have lunch at **Pizzeria na Růžka** (☎ 606 433 282; cnr TG Masaryka & Kostelni; pizza 110Kč) with a sunny Mediterranean ambience and thin-crust wood-fired pizzas.

You can walk from Karlovy Vary to Loket along a 17km blue-marked trail, starting at the Diana lookout; allow three hours. Otherwise, buses from Karlovy Vary to Sokolov stop at Loket (21Kč, 30 minutes, hourly).

PLZEŇ

pop 175,000

You'll never forget your first authentic Pilsner beer, and that's why brew aficionados from around the world flock to this city where lager was invented in 1842. Plzeň (Pilsen in German) is the home town of Pilsner Urquell (Plzeňský prazdroj), the world's first lager beer, which is now imitated all around the world. 'Urquell' (in German; *prazdroj* in Czech) means 'original source' or 'fountainhead', and the authentic hoppy marvel concocted by the town's brewery puts all pretenders firmly in the shade.

The capital of West Bohemia is a sprawling industrial city, but at its heart lays an attractive old town wrapped in a halo of tree-lined gardens. Plzeň's industrial heritage includes the massive Škoda Engineering Works. These armament factories were bombed heavily at the end of WWII and now make machinery and locomotives.

These days Plzeň is known as a university town, and the town's many pubs showcase its history as the original fountain of eternal golden froth.

Orientation

The main bus station is west of the centre on Husova, opposite the Škoda Engineering Works. Plzeň-hlavní nádraží, the main train station, is on the eastern side of town, 10 minutes' walk from nám Republiky, the old town square. Tram 2 goes from the train station to the centre of town and on to the bus station.

There are left-luggage facilities at the **bus station** (per small/large bag 12 Kč/25Kč; ☽ 8am-8pm Mon-

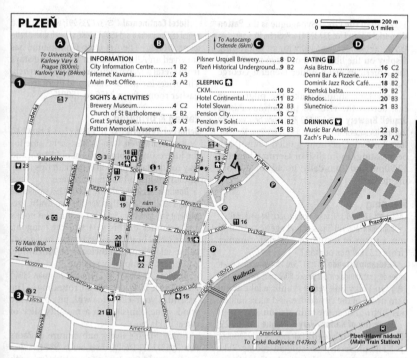

PLZEŇ

CZECH REPUBLIC

Fri) and the **train station** (per small/large bag 12/25Kč; 24hr).

Information
City Information Centre (www.plzen-city.cz) nám Republiky (městské informační středisko; ☎ 378 035 330; nám Republiky 41; 9am-6pm); train station (☎ 972 524 313; 9am-5pm) Charges 1Kč per minute for internet access.**Internet Kavarna** (☎ 377 222 146; Tylova 6, 1st fl; per hr 40Kč; 8am-10pm Mon-Thu, 8am-7.30pm Fri, noon-8pm Sat & Sun)
Main post office (Solní 20; 7am-7pm Mon-Fri, 8am-1pm Sat, 8am-noon Sun) Includes a telephone centre.

Sights
In summer people congregate at the outdoor beer bar in nám Republiky, the broad and sunny old town square, beneath the glowering, Gothic **Church of St Bartholomew** (adult/child 20/10Kč; 10am-6pm Wed-Sat Apr-Sep, 10am-6pm Wed-Fri Oct-Dec). Inside the soaring 13th-century structure there's a Gothic *Madonna* (1390) on the high altar and fine stained-glass windows. On the exterior, around the back, is an iron grille – touch the angel and make a wish. Climb the 102m church **tower** (adult/child 30/10Kč; 10am-

6pm weather dependent), the highest in Bohemia, for great views.

The **Brewery Museum** (☎ 377 235 574; www.prazdroj.cz; Veleslavínova 6; adult/child 80/50Kč, with text 120/60Kč; 10am-6pm Apr-Dec, 10am-5pm Jan-Mar) is a block east of the square in an authentic medieval malt house. Enjoy a tasty unfiltered beer in the museum's pub.

In previous centuries beer was brewed, stored and served in the tunnels beneath the old town. The earliest were dug in the 14th century and the latest date from the 19th century; some 500m of passages are now open, and you can take a 30-minute guided tour at the **Plzeň Historical Underground** (☎ 377 225 214; Perlová 4; adult/child 45/25Kč; 9am-5pm Tue-Sun Jul-Sep, Wed-Sun Apr-Jun, Oct & Nov). The temperature is a constant 10°C, so take a jacket.

The **Great Synagogue** (☎ 377 223 346; Sady Pětatřicátníků 11; adult/child 45/30Kč; 11am-6pm Sun-Fri Apr-Sep, 11am-5pm Sun-Fri Jun, 11am-4pm Sun-Fri Oct, closed Nov-Mar), west of the old town, is the third largest in the world – only those in Jerusalem and Budapest are bigger. It was built in the Moorish style in 1892 by the 2000 Jews who lived here then. English tours cost 50Kč extra.

North of the Great Synagogue is the **Patton Memorial Pilsen** (☎ 377 320 414; Podřežni 10; adult/child 45/25Kč; 🕑 9am-5pm Tue-Sun), with an interesting display on the liberation of Plzeň in 1945 by the American army under General George Patton.

Beer fans should make the pilgrimage east across the river to the famous **Pilsner Urquell Brewery** (☎ 377 062 888; www.beer world.cz; tour adult/concession 120/50Kč; 🕑 10am-9pm Mon-Sat, 10am-8pm Sun). One-hour guided tours (with beer tasting) in English or German begin at 12.30pm and 2pm daily; no advance booking needed.

Sleeping

CKM (☎ 377 236 393; info@ckmplzen.cz; Dominikánská 1; 🕑 9am-6pm Mon-Fri) This travel agency can find you a room in a student hostel in summer (from 225Kč per person).

Autocamp Ostende (☎ 377 520 194; www.cbox.cz/atc -ostende; tent/bungalow per person 80/200Kč; 🕑 May-Sep; 🅿) On Velký Bolevecký rybník, a lake about 6km north of the city centre, and accessible by bus 20 from near the train station.

University of Karlovy Vary & Prague (☎ 377 259 381; www.webpark.cz/bolevecka; Bolevecká 34; s/d 250/500Kč; 🅿) The university has student rooms. Take tram 4 two stops north from the Great Synagogue. There is a similar operation at Bolevecká 30. Phone ahead.

Penzion v Solní (☎ 377 236 652; www.volny.cz/pension solni; Solní 8; s/d 600/1020Kč) The best deal in town is this friendly spot sandwiched between a butchery and a clothes shop. With only three rooms, it's essential to book ahead.

Sandra Pension (☎ 377 325 358; sandra.101@seznam .cz; Kopeckého sady 15; s/d incl breakfast 990/1260Kč; 🅿) This *pension* has three clean rooms above a friendly park-side restaurant with off-street parking. The staff speak good English.

Pension City (☎ 377 326 069; fax 377 222 976; Sady 5 kvetna 52; s/d incl breakfast 1000/1390Kč; 🅿) On a quiet street near the river, the City is popular with both local and overseas guests. The English-speaking staff are a good source of information.

Hotel Slovan (☎ 377 227 256; http://hotelslovan.pilsen .cz; Smetanovy sady 1; s/d 1450/2100Kč, s/d with shared bathroom 530/810Kč; 🅿) Centrally located opposite a park, the Slovan's old-world glamour is now faded but the rooms are functional, and it's just a matter of time before it is redeveloped to luxury status. Stay there while you can still afford it.

Hotel Continental (☎ 377 235 292; www.hotelconti nental.cz; Zbrojnicka 8; s/d 1580/2150Kč, s/d with shared bathroom 860/1460Kč) The Art Deco Continental has survived an Allied bomb in WWII and stays from Gerard Depardieu and John Malkovich. The prices include breakfast and there are also flasher rooms from 2450 to 4500Kč

Eating & Drinking

Denní Bar & Pizzerie (☎ 377 237 965; Solní 9; pizza 75Kč; 🕑 8am-10pm Mon-Fri, 11am-10pm Sat-Sun) Come for the interesting photographs of old Plzeň, and stay for the tasty pizza and pasta in this lively restaurant just off the main square.

Dominik Jazz Rock Café (☎ 377 323 226; Dominikánská 3; mains 100Kč; 🕑 9am-11pm Mon-Thu, 9am-1am Fri, 3pm-midnight Sat, 3pm-10pm Sun) Get lost in the nooks and crannies of this vast student hangout. There's cool beats all day everyday, and good-value salads and sandwiches at lunchtime. After dark is enjoyably raucous.

Rhodos (☎ 736 677 344; Bezručova 20; mains 130Kč) Has Greek fare in leafy surroundings. The 'assemble yourself' gyros with pita bread are good value. Finish with a naughty slice of sweet baklava.

Enjoy Plzeň's lively pub culture at **Zach's Pub** (☎ 377 223 176; Palackého nám 2; 🕑 1-9pm Mon-Thu, 1pm-2am Fri, 5pm-2am Sat, 5pm-midnight Sun), with live music, tasty food and a suitably student atmosphere, and **Plzeňská bašta** (☎ 377 237 262; Riegrova 5) with wooden beams making it a quaint and rustic spot for your first (and maybe your best) Pilsner Urquell.

By day **Music Bar Anděl** (☎ 377 323 226; Bezručova 7) is a coolly hip café, but after dark it's a rocking live venue featuring the best of touring Czech bands.

Also recommended:

Asia Bistro (Pražská 31; mains 70Kč; 🕑 11am-11pm) Tasty Vietnamese fare including good spring rolls.

Slunečnice (Jungmanova 10; baguettes 50Kč; 🕑 7.30am-6pm) For fresh sandwiches on the go.

Getting There & Away

All international trains travelling from Munich and Nuremberg to Prague stop at Plzeň. There are fast trains that run from Plzeň to Prague (140Kč, 1½ hours, eight daily) and České Budějovice (162Kč, two hours, five daily).

If you're heading for Karlovy Vary, take a bus (76Kč, 1¾ hours, five daily). There are also express buses to Prague (80Kč, 1½ hours, hourly).

ČESKÉ BUDĚJOVICE
pop 100,000

After Plzeň, conduct the ultimate Bohemian beer taste test at České Budějovice (Budweis in German), the home of Budweiser Budvar lager. The regional capital of South Bohemia is also a picturesque medieval city. Arcing from the town square are 18th-century arcades leading to bars that get raffishly rowdy on weekends – all fuelled by the town's prized export of course.

Orientation

From the adjacent bus and train stations it's a 10-minute walk west down Lannova třída, then Kanovnická, to nám Přemysla Otakara II, the main square.

Information

Internet Café Babylon (5th fl, nám Přemysla Otakara II 30; ☽ 10am-10pm Mon-Sat, 1-9pm Sun)

Kanzelsberger (☎ 386 352 584; Hroznová 17) Bookshop with English-language books upstairs.

Left luggage (per small/large bag 12/25Kč) bus station (☽ 7am-7pm Mon-Fri, 7am-2pm Sat); train station (☽ 2.30am-11pm)

Municipal Information Centre (Městské Informarční Centrum; ☎ 386 801 413; www.c-budejovice.cz; nám Přemysla Otakara II 2; ☽ 8.30am-6pm Mon-Fri, 8.30am-5pm Sat, 10am-4pm Sun) Books tickets, tours and accommodation.

Sights

The broad expanse of **Nám Přemysla Otakara II**, centred on the **Samson Fountain** (1727) and surrounded by 18th-century arcades, is one of the largest town squares in Europe. On the western side stands the baroque **town hall** (1731), topped with allegorical figures of the cardinal virtues: Justice, Wisdom, Courage and Prudence. On the hour a tune rings out from its tower. On the square's opposite corner is the 72m-tall **Black Tower** (adult/child 25/15Kč; ☽ 10am-6pm Tue-Sun Apr-Oct), dating from 1553 and providing great views.

The streets around the square, especially Česká, are lined with old burgher houses. West near the river is the former **Dominican monastery** (1265) with another tall tower and a splendid pulpit. Adjacent is the **Motorcycle Museum** (☎ 723 247 104; Piaristické nám; adult/child 40/20Kč; ☽ 10am-6pm Tue-Sun), with its fine collection of Czech Jawas and some wonderful WWII Harley-Davidsons. The **Museum of South Bohemia**

ČESKÉ BUDĚJOVICE

CZECH REPUBLIC

(Jihočeské muzeum; ☎ 387 929 328; adult/child 50/20Kč; ⏲ 9am-12.30pm & 1-5.30pm Tue-Sun) has an extensive collection on history, books, coins, weapons and wildlife; it's southeast of the centre.

Just as beer from Pilsen (see p130) is called Pilsner, so beer from Budweis is called Budweiser. Indeed, the founders of US brewer Anheuser-Busch chose the brand name Budweiser in 1876 because it was synonymous with good beer. Since the late-19th century, both breweries have used the name, and a legal arm wrestle over the brand continues. There is no debate over which beer is superior: one taste of Budvar and you'll be converted.

The **Budweiser Budvar Brewery** (☎ 387 705 341; www.budweiser.cz; cnr Pražská & K Světlé; adult/child 100/50Kč; ⏲ 9am-4pm) is 3km north of the main square. Group tours run every day and the 2pm tour (Monday to Friday only) is open to individual travellers; beer tasting costs 22Kč extra. Afterwards taste what all the fuss is about at the brewery's **beer hall** (⏲ 10am to 10pm).

Sleeping

The Municipal Information Centre and **CKM** (☎ 386 351 270; Lannova třída 63; ⏲ 9am-5pm Mon-Thu, 9am-3.30pm Fri) travel agency can arrange dorm accommodation from 150Kč per person. Small private *pensions* are a better deal than hotels.

Pension U výstaviště (☎ 387 240 148; trpakdl@email .cz; U výzstaviště 17; r per person 270Kč; ℗) The city's closest thing to a travellers hostel. It's 30 minutes from the city centre on bus 1 from the bus station to the fifth stop (U parku); the *pension* is 100m up the street (Čajkovského) on the right.

Kolej jihočeské univerzity (☎ 387 774 201; Studentská 13-19; d 440Kč; ℗) This student block, 2km west of the centre, offers beds from July to September

AT Pension (☎ 603 441 069; Dukelská 15; s/d 500/800Kč; ℗) Don't hold your breath for stunning (or even 20th-century) décor, but this convenient spot is mighty friendly with mighty big breakfasts (50Kč).

Penzión Centrum (☎ 387 311 801; www.penzion centrum.cz; Biskupská 130/3; s/d incl breakfast 900/1200Kč) Huge rooms with queen-size beds and crisp white linen make this an excellent reader-recommended spot right near the main square.

Hotel Bohemia (☎ 386 354 500; www.hotel-bohemia .cz; Hradební 20; s/d incl breakfast 1490/1790Kč; ℗) Carved wooden doors open to a restful interior in two old burghers' houses down a quiet street. The restaurant comes recommended by the local tourist information office.

Hotel Malý Pivovar (☎ 386 360 471; www.malypivo var.cz; Karla IV 8-10; s/d incl breakfast 2300/3300Kč; ☒ ☒) With sports trophies and elegant leather sofas, the lobby is like a flash gentleman's club. However, the smartly elegant rooms will please both the men and the ladies, and it's a short stroll to the Budvarka beer hall downstairs (11am to 11pm).

Eating & Drinking

pizza/grill (Panská 17; pizzas 100Kč; ⏲ closed Sun) Just maybe where the phrase 'hole-in-the-wall' came from, pizza/grill fits a wood-fired oven, a vintage espresso machine and seating for five diners into a tiny space. Grab takeaway pivo'n'pizza and dine al fresco.

U Tři Sedláku (☎ 387 222 303; Hroznová 488; mains 100-160Kč) Locals celebrate that nothing much has changed at U Tři Sedláku since opening in 1897. Tasty meat-filled dishes go with the Pilsner Urquell that's constantly being shuffled to busy tables.

Indická (Gateway of India; ☎ 386 359 355; 1st fl, Chelčického 11; mains 100-150Kč; ⏲ closed Sun) From Chennai to České comes respite for travellers wanting something different. Be sure to request spicy because the kitchen is used to dealing with timid Czech palates.

Singer Pub (Česká 55) With Czech and Irish beers, and the city's cheapest and strongest cocktails, don't be surprised if you get the urge to rustle up something on the Singer sewing machines on every table. If not, challenge the regulars to a game of *foosball* with a soundtrack of noisy rock.

modrý dveře jazz & blues (☎ 386 359 958; Biskupská 1; ⏲ 10am-midnight) By day modrý dveře is a welcoming bar–café with vintage pics of Sinatra. At dusk the lights dim for regular jazz piano gigs on Wednesdays (from 7pm) and live blues and jazz on Thursdays (from 8pm). Tell them Frank sent you.

For bracing coffee and decadent hot chocolate head to **Caffé Bar Piccolo** (Ná Mlýnské stoce 9; coffee 35Kč, hot chocolate 40Kč; ⏲ 7.30am-7pm Mon-Thu, to 10pm Fri & Sat).

Getting There & Away

There are fast trains from České Budějovice to Prague (204Kč, 2½ hours, hourly) and Plzeň (162Kč, two hours, five daily). Heading for Vienna (780Kč, four hours, two daily) you'll have to change at Gmünd, or take a direct train to Linz (410Kč, 2¼ hours, one daily) and change there.

WORTH A TRIP

It's time to lose the black polo-neck jersey and discover the true meaning of bohemian. Perched on a precarious bluff, the old town of **Tábor** was (and still is) a formidable natural defence to invasion. Six centuries ago, the Hussite religious sect founded Tábor as a military bastion in defiance of Catholic Europe. Based on the biblical concept that 'nothing is mine and nothing is yours, because everyone owns the community equally', all Hussites participated in communal work, and possessions were allocated equally in the town's main square. This exceptional non-conformism gave the word 'bohemian' the connotations we associate with it today. The unconventional Taborites further enhanced the location's natural defences by constructing their town as a maze of narrow lanes and protruding houses; all designed to defeat an enemy attack. Religious structures dating from the 15th century line the town square, and it's possible to visit the 650m stretch of underground tunnels the Hussites used for refuge in times of war.

Now the town square is bordered by lively bars like **Kafe & Bar Havana** (☎ 381 253 383; Žižkovo nám 17; mains 60-200Kč). If you're staying overnight, **Penzión Alfa** (☎ 381 256 165; www.pensionalfa .zde.cz; Klokotská; s/d/tr 500/800/1200Kč) occupies a cosy corner just metres from the main square. Downstairs you can get your Geronimojo back at the funky Native American–themed café. If that doesn't work there is a groovily hip massage place across the lane that's doing its best to keep the bohemian spirit alive in its original hometown.

The annual **Hussite Festival of Tábor** is held on the second weekend in September. Expect medieval merriment with lots of food, drink and colourfully dressed locals celebrating their Hussite heritage.

Travel to Tábor by bus, either from Prague (80Kč, 1½ hours, 15 daily) or České Budějovice (56Kč, one hour, 18 daily).

The bus to Brno (210Kč, 3½ to 4½ hours, four daily) travels via Telč. Twice a week there's a direct Eurolines bus to Linz (430Kč, 2½ hours) and Salzburg (750Kč, 4½ hours) in Austria.

HLUBOKÁ NAD VLTAVOU

Hluboká nad Vltavou's neo-Gothic **chateau** (☎ 387 843 911; ☼ 9am-6pm Jul & Aug, 9am-5pm Tue-Sun May-Jun, 9am-4.30pm Apr, Sep & Oct), was rebuilt by the Schwarzenberg family in 1841–71 with turrets and crenellations supposedly inspired by England's Windsor Castle; the palace's 144 rooms remained in use right up to WWII. There are two guided tours to choose from. Tour 1 (adult/child with an English-speaking guide 160/80Kč) takes in the main attractions, while Tour 2 (adult/child 150/80Kč) includes the chateau's kitchen. The surrounding park is open throughout the year. The **information centre** (☎ 387 966 164; Masarykova 35) can help with accommodation.

Hluboká is 10km north of České Budějovice by local bus (16Kč, 20 minutes, two hourly).

ČESKÝ KRUMLOV

pop 14,600

Crowned by a spectacular castle, and centred on an elegant old-town square, Český Krumlov is a pocket-sized Prague. Renaissance and Baroque buildings enclose the meandering arc of the Vltava river, housing riverside cafés and bars. Like Prague the town's no stranger to tourists. During summer Český Krumlov may feel like a Middle Europe theme park, but visit a few months either side of July and August and the narrow lanes and footbridges will be (slightly) more subdued and secluded. Winter is an enchanting time to visit with the castle blanketed in snow and pine smoke from chimneys wafting across the river.

The town's original Gothic fortress was rebuilt as an imposing Renaissance chateau in the 16th-century for the lords of Rožmberk, the richest landowners in Bohemia. Since the 18th century the town's appearance is largely unchanged, and careful renovation and restoration has replaced the architectural neglect of the communist era. In 1992 Český Krumlov was added to Unesco's World Heritage List.

Orientation

The bus station is east of the town centre, but if you're arriving from České Budějovice get off at the Špičák bus stop (the first in the town centre, just after you pass beneath a road bridge). The train station is 1.5km north of the town centre; buses 1, 2 and 3 go from the station to the Špičák bus stop. From the bridge

LOCAL VOICES

Oldřiška Baloušková's family has lived in Český Krumlov for six generations. Since returning to the town after living in San Francisco for 11 years, she's uniquely qualified to know why living in the town on the Vltava is better than living in the city on the bay.

- 'A feeling of *pohoda*, (peace of mind), permeates Český Krumlov.'
- 'There are no traffic jams – Krumlov is built for people, not for cars.'
- 'We've got a rich history, with buildings over 800 years old.'
- 'We get fog in winter, not in summer.'
- 'It's easier to survive a flood than an earthquake.'

over the main road beside the bus stop, Latrán leads south into town.

Don't take a car into the centre of the old town; use one of the car parks around the perimeter. The one on Chvalšinská, north of the old town, is the most convenient for the castle.

Information

Infocentrum (☎ 380 704 622; www.ckrumlov.cz; nám Svornosti 1; 🕑 9am-8pm Jul-Aug; 9am-7pm Jun & Sep; 9am-6pm Apr, May & Oct; 9am-5pm Nov-Mar) Transport and accommodation information, books and maps, plus internet access (5Kč per five minutes).

Shakespeare & Sons (☎ 380 711 203; Soukenická 44; 🕑 11am-7pm) Good for interesting English-language paperbacks. Cult movies screen in a cinema downstairs, and co-owner Oldřiška Balouškovás (☎ 737 920 901) conducts interesting walking tours.

Unios Tourist Service (☎ 380 725 110; tourist. servic@unios.cz; Zámek 57; 🕑 9am-6pm) Tourist information, accommodation booking and internet café with international calls.

Sights

The old town, almost encircled by the arcing Vltava River, is watched over by **Český Krumlov Castle** (☎ 380 704 721; 🕑 9am-6pm Tue-Sun Jun-Aug, 9am-5pm Apr, May, Sep & Oct), and its ornately decorated fairytale **Round Tower** (35/20Kč). Three different guided tours are on offer: Tour I (adult/child 160/80Kč) takes in the lavish Renaissance and baroque apartments that the aristocratic Rožmberk and

Schwarzenberg families once called home; Tour II (adult/child 140/70Kč) concentrates on the Schwarzenbergs and visits the apartments used by the family in the 19th-century; and the Theatre Tour (adult/child 180/90Kč) explores the chateau's remarkable rococo theatre, complete with original stage machinery. Wandering through the courtyards and gardens is free.

The path beyond the fourth courtyard leads across the spectacular **Most ná Plášti** to the castle gardens. A ramp to the right leads to the **former riding school**, now a restaurant. The relief above the door shows cherubs offering the head and boots of a vanquished Turk – a reference to Adolf von Schwarzenberg, who conquered the Turkish fortress of Raab in the 16th-century. From here the Italian-style **Zámecká zahrada** (castle gardens) stretch away towards the **Bellarie summer pavilion**.

Across the river is nám Svornosti, the old town square, ringed by pleasant cafés and overlooked by the Gothic **town hall** and a baroque **plague column** (1716). Above the square is the striking Gothic **Church of St Vitus** (1439), and nearby is the **Regional Museum** (☎ 380 711 674; Horní 152; adult/child 50/25Kč; 🕑 10am-6pm Jul-Aug; 10am-5pm May-Jun & Sep; 9am-4pm Tue-Fri, 1-4pm Sat & Sun, Mar-Apr & Oct-Dec), with an interesting collection including an interactive model of the town as it was in 1800.

Activities

The big attraction in summer is messing about on the river. Rent canoes, rafts and rubber rings from **Maleček** (☎ 380 712 508; www.malecek .cz; Rooseveltova 28; 🕑 9am-5pm), where a half-hour splash in a two-person canoe costs 350Kč, or **Vltava Tourist Services** (☎ 380 711 988; Kájovská 62; 🕑 9am- 7pm), which also rents bikes (320Kč a day) and arranges horse riding (250Kč an hour). Maleček also has sedate river trips through Český Krumlov on giant wooden rafts seating up to 36 people (45 minutes; 280Kč).

Festivals & Events

Infocentrum sells tickets to most festivals.

Five-Petalled Rose Festival In mid-June; features two days of street performers, parades and medieval games (expect a small admission fee).

Chamber Music Festival Late June to early July.

International Music Festival (www.czechmusic festival.com) August.

Jazz at Summer's End Festival End of August.

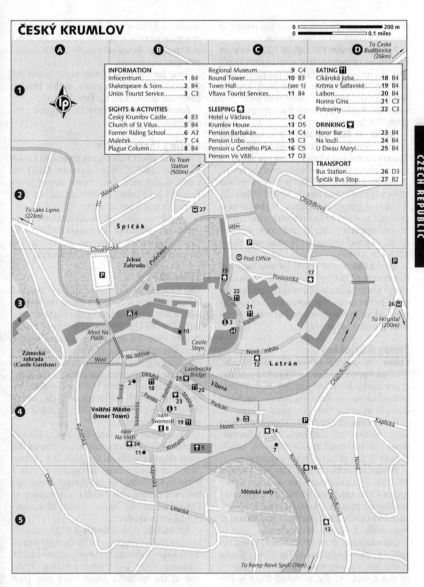

ČESKÝ KRUMLOV

INFORMATION
Infocentrum...........................1 B4
Shakespeare & Sons............2 B4
Unios Tourist Service...........3 C3

SIGHTS & ACTIVITIES
Český Krumlov Castle...........4 B3
Church of St Vitus................5 B4
Former Riding School...........6 A3
Maleček................................7 C4
Plague Column....................8 B4

Regional Museum.................9 C4
Round Tower.......................10 B3
Town Hall......................(see 1)
Vltava Tourist Services........11 B4

SLEEPING
Hotel u Václava...................12 C4
Krumlov House....................13 D5
Pension Barbakán...............14 C4
Pension Lobo......................15 C3
Pension u Černého PSA.......16 C5
Pension Ve Věži..................17 D3

EATING
Cikánská jizba.....................18 B4
Krčma v Šatlavské...............19 B4
Laibon...............................20 B4
Nonna Gina.......................21 C3
Potraviny...........................22 C3

DRINKING
Horor Bar..........................23 B4
Na louži............................24 B4
U Dwau Maryí....................25 B4

TRANSPORT
Bus Station........................26 D3
Špičák Bus Stop..................27 B2

Sleeping

Kemp Nové Spolí (☎ 380 728 305; camp site per person 65Kč; ☼ Jun-Aug; 🅿) Located on the east bank of the Vltava River about 2km south of town, the facilities here are basic but the location is idyllic. Take bus 3 from the train or bus station to the Spolí mat. šk. stop (eight a day on weekdays); it's a half-hour walk from the old town.

Krumlov House (☎ 380 711 935; www.krumlovhostel .com; Rooseveltova 68; dm/d 300/650Kč) Perched above the river, Krumlov House is friendly and comfortable, and has plenty of books, DVDs and local info to feed your inner backpacker. Lots of fun day trips are also on offer.

Pension Lobo (☎ 380 713 153; www.pensionlobo.cz; Latrán 73; d incl breakfast 1100Kč) Pension Lobo offers more than just spotless and central rooms. It also has a convenient laundromat.

Pension u Černého PSA (☎ 380 712 366; www.pension-cerny-pes.cz; Rooseveltova 36; d incl breakfast 1200Kč; P) The name means 'Place of the Black Dog', and the black labrador in the photo outside just begs you to stay. Follow your heart and make the dog happy at this friendly spot with retro '70s furniture.

Penzión Ve Věži (☎ 380 711 742; www.ckrumlov.cz/pensionvevezi; Pivovarská 28; d incl breakfast 1200Kč; P) Spartan rooms, but where else can you sleep in a Gothic tower with a brewery across the road?

Pension Barbakán (☎ 380 717 017; www.barbakan.cz; Horní 26; d incl breakfast from 1700Kč; P) Originally the town's gunpowder arsenal, Barbakán now creates fireworks of its own with supercomfy rooms featuring bright and cosy wooden décor. A good restaurant is attached (mains 120Kč to 200Kč).

Hotel u Václava (☎ 380 715 094; www.uvaclava.cz; Nové Město 25; d 2500Kč; P) Four-poster beds create a romantic atmosphere that's perfect for that first (or second) honeymoon. Not recommended for single travellers, but you won't go wrong with a loved one.

Eating & Drinking

Laibon (☎ 728 676 654; Parkán 105; mains 80-160Kč; ☼ 11am-11pm) Candles and vaulted ceilings create a great boho ambience in the best vegetarian teahouse in Bohemia. Try the blueberry dumplings or the tasty couscous.

Nonna Gina (☎ 380 717 187; Klášterini ul 52; pizza 110Kč; ☼ 11am-11pm) Authentic Italian flavours from the authentic Italian Massaro family feature in this pizzeria down a quiet lane.

Krčma v Šatlavské (☎ 380 713 344; Horní 157; mains 100-150Kč; ☼ noon-midnight) Nirvana for meatlovers – this medieval barbecue cellar serves sizzling platters in a funky labyrinth illuminated by candles and the flickering flames of open grills. Be sure to book ahead.

Cikánská jizba (☎ 380 717 585; Dlouhá 31; mains 100-200Kč; ☼ 3pm-midnight Mon-Sat) The Gypsy Room is the best spot in town to try the flavours of the Roma. At the weekend there is live Roma music.

Na louži (☎ 380 711 280; Kájovská 66; mains 120-180Kč; ☼ 11am-11pm) Nothing's changed in this wood-panelled *pivo* parlour for almost a century. Locals pack Na louži for tasty dark beer from the local Eggenberg brewery and huge meals.

U Dwau Maryí (☎ 380 717 228; Parkán 104; mains 80-175Kč; ☼ 11am-midnight) Dive into the authentic medieval interior and emerge onto a sunny riverside terrace. Inside or outside, the food and drink go down very easily in this enjoyably raucous tavern.

Horor Bar (☎ 728 682 724; Masná 22; ☼ 6pm-late) Occasional live gigs surface in this kitschy labyrinth celebrating the (un)dead.

Potraviny (supermarket; Latrán 55) For good self-catering.

Getting There & Away

There are direct buses from Prague to Český Krumlov (140Kč, three hours, six daily) via České Budějovice; some buses depart from Prague's Ná Knížecí bus station, near Anděl metro, others from Florenc.

Local buses (26Kč, 50 minutes, seven daily) and trains (46Kč, one hour, eight daily) run to České Budějovice, where you can change for onward travel to Brno, Plzeň or Austria.

ŠUMAVA

The Šumava is a range of thickly forested hills stretching for 125km along the border with Austria and Germany; the highest summit is Plechý (1378m), west of Horní Planá. Before 1989 the range was divided by the Iron Curtain: a line of fences, watchtowers, armed guards and dog patrols between Western Europe and the communist East; many Czechs made a bid for freedom by creeping through the forests at night. Today the hills are popular for hiking, cycling and cross-country skiing.

The **Povydří trail** along the Vydra (Otter) River in the northern Šumava is one of the most popular walks in the park. It's an easy 7km hike along a deep, forested river valley between Čeňkova Pila and Antýgl. Buses run between Sušice and Modrava, stopping at Čeňkova Pila and Antýgl. Plenty of accommodation is available.

Around the peak of **Boubín** (1362m), the 46-hectare *prales* (virgin forest) is the only part of the Šumava forest that is largely untouched by human activity. The trailhead is 2km northeast of the zastávka Zátoň train stop (not Zátoň town train station) at Kaplice, where there is car parking as well as basic camping facilities. From here it's an easy 2.5km to U pralesa Lake on a blue and green marked trail. Remain on the blue trail for a further 7.5km to reach the summit of Boubín. Return by following the trail southwest. The complete loop takes about five hours.

CZECH REPUBLIC

If you'd rather use wheels, the **Šumava Trail** is a week-long ride through dense forests and past mountain streams from Český Krumlov to Domažlice. Top Bicycle (p148) hires out bikes from April to October and also runs organised rides in summer.

If lying in the sun sounds more fun, head to **Lake Lipno**, a 30km-long reservoir south of Český Krumlov. Known as 'the Czech Riviera', it's lined with camping grounds, swimming areas and water-sports centres; there's even a yacht marina at Lipno nad Vltavou.

Infocentrum in Český Krumlov (see p136) has full details.

Getting There & Away

Up to eight trains a day run from České Budějovice and Český Krumlov to Volary (120Kč, three hours), calling at Horní Planá and Nová Pec on Lake Lipno. From May to September, buses cover a similar route (80Kč, two hours).

From Volary, trains continue north to Strakonice via Zátoň (28Kč, 30 minutes, four daily).

The Povydří trail is best approached from Sušice, which can be reached by direct bus from Prague (105Kč, 2½ hours, two daily). Another bus links Sušice with Čeňkova Pila and Antýgl (44Kč, one hour, two or three daily).

ADRŠPACH-TEPLICE ROCKS

The Czech Republic's most extraordinary scenery lies near the Polish border, in a protected landscape region known as the Adršpach-Teplice Rocks (Adršpašsko-Teplické skály). Thick layers of stratified sandstone have been eroded and fissured by water and frost to form giant towers and deep, narrow chasms. Discovered by mountaineers in the 19th century, the region is popular with rock climbers and hikers. Sandy trails lead through pine-scented forests, loud with the drumming of woodpeckers, and loop through the pinnacles, assisted occasionally by ladders and stairs.

There are two main formations – **Adršpach Rock Town** (Adršpašské skalní město) and **Teplice Rock Town** (Teplické skalní město). They now comprise a single state nature reserve, about 15km east of Trutnov. At the entrance to each rock town there's a **ticket booth** (adult/child 50/20Kč; ☉ 8am-6pm Apr-Nov) where you can pick up a handy 1:25,000 trail map. Outside the official opening hours you can enter for free.

There's a small **information office** (☎ 491 586 012; www.skalyadrspach.cz; ☉ 8.30am-6pm Apr-Oct) near Adršpach train station. In summer the trails are busy and you should book accommodation at least a week ahead; in winter (snow lingers to mid-April) you'll have this stunning landscape mostly to yourself, though some trails may be closed.

If you're pushed for time, walk the green loop trail (1½ hours), starting at Adršpach and progressing through deep mossy ravines and soaring rock towers to the **Great Lookout** (Velké panorama). Admire the view of pinnacles escalating above the pines, before threading through the **Mouse Hole** (Myší dírá), a vast vertical fissure barely a shoulder-width wide.

The blue loop trail (2½ hours), starting at Teplice, passes a metal staircase leading strenuously to **Střmen**, a rock tower once occupied by an outlaw's timber castle, before continuing through the area's most spectacular pinnacles to the chilly ravine of **Siberia** (Sibiř). An excellent day hike (four to five hours), taking in the region's highlights, links the head of the Teplice trail, beyond Sibiř, to Adršpach via the **Wolf Gorge** (Vlčí rokle). Return from Adršpach to Teplice by walking along the road (one hour) or by train (10 minutes).

Sleeping & Eating

In Teplice nad Metují-Skály the **Hotel Orlík** (☎ 491 581 025; www.orlik.hotel-cz.com; s/d incl breakfast 500/1000Kč; **P**) is a good place to recharge and relax with a popular bar. Nearby **Pension Skály** (☎ 491 581 174; www.adrspach-skaly.cz; Střmenské Podhradí 132; s/d incl breakfast 500/1000Kč; **P** ✕) has cosy rooms for post-hike relaxation.

The modern **Penzion Adršpach** (☎ 491 586 102; www.adrspach-skaly.cz; s/d incl breakfast 500/1000Kč; **P**) in Adršpach overcomes a lack of old-world charm with comfortable rooms, an excellent restaurant and a friendly border collie.

In a quiet setting between Teplice and Adršpach, the **Skalní Mlýn** (☎ 491 586 961; www .skalni-mlyn.cz; s/d incl breakfast 580/1060Kč; **P**) has rustic rooms and more friendly dogs in a restored river mill; it's best if you have your own transport.

Getting There & Away

There are direct buses from Prague's Černý Most metro station to Trutnov (125Kč, 2¾ hours, hourly).

CZECH REPUBLIC

Single-car trains rattle along from Trutnov to Adršpach (40Kč, one hour) and Teplice nad Metují (46Kč, 1¼ hours, eight daily).

Frequent trains run from Teplice nad Metují station to Týniště nad Orlicí (76Kč, 1½ hours, eight daily), where there is an early evening train to Wrocław in Poland (224Kč, 4¼ hours, one daily).

MORAVIA

Away from the tourist commotion of Prague and Bohemia, Moravia provides a quietly authentic experience. Olomouc and Telč are two of the country's prettiest towns, and bustling Brno delivers Czech urban ambience, but without the tourists. Active travellers can explore the stunning landscapes of Moravian Karst region, and everyone can celebrate with a good vintage from the Moravian wine country.

BRNO
pop 387,200

Brno, the Czech Republic's second-largest city and the capital of Moravia, might seem a tad buttoned-down after the buzz of Prague. Stay a while though, because that traditional Moravian reserve melts away in the old town's bars and restaurants, and a cosmopolitan array of galleries and museums lets you experience modern Czech life away from the touristy commotion of the capital.

Orientation

The main train station is at the southern edge of the old town, with a major tram stop outside. Opposite the station is the beginning of Masarykova, which leads north to nám Svobody, the city's main square. The main bus station (Brno ÚAN Zvonařka) is 800m south of the train station, beyond Tesco department store. Go through the pedestrian tunnel under the train tracks, and follow the crowd through the Galerie Vankovka shopping centre. Brno's Tuřany airport is 7.5km southeast of the train station.

Information

Geokart (☎ 542 216 561; Vachova 8) Maps and guidebooks.
Internet Centrum (Masarykova 22; per hr 40Kč; ☼ 8am-midnight) internet café.
Knihkupectví Literární Kavárna (☎ 542 217 954; nám Svobody 13; ☼ 10am-7pm) English-language

books with a good café upstairs.**Left luggage** train station (ground fl; per day 26Kč, ☼ closed 11pm-4am); bus station (per day 25Kč; ☼ 5.15am-10.15pm Mon-Fri, 6am-10.15pm Sat & Sun)
Lékárna Koliště (☎ 545 424 811; Koliště 47) A 24-hour pharmacy.
Netbox (☎ 542 210 174; Jezuitská 3; per hr 50Kč; ☼ 9am-1am Mon-Sat, 2pm-1am Sun) internet café.
Tourist information office (Kulturní a Informační Centrum; KIC; ☎ 542 211 090; www.ticbrno.cz; Radnická 8; ☼ 8am-6pm Mon-Fri, 9am-5.30pm Sat & Sun Apr-Sep; 9am-5pm Sat, 9am-3pm Sun Nov-Mar) Sells maps and books accommodation.
Tourist police station (☎ 974 626 100; Bartošová 1)
Úrazová nemocnice (☎ 545 538 111; Ponávka 6) Main hospital.

Sights & Activities

Heading north on Masarykova from the train station, the second turn on the left leads to the gruesomely compelling **Capuchin Monastery** (☎ 542 213 232; Kapucínské nám 5; adult/child 40/20Kč; ☼ 9am-noon & 2-4.30pm Tue-Sat, 11-11.45am & 2-4.30pm Sun, closed Dec & Jan) with a dry, well-ventilated crypt allowing the natural mummification of dead bodies. On display are the desiccated corpses of 18th-century monks, abbots and local notables, from a nameless 12-year-old ministrant to chimney-sweeper Barnabas Orelli, still wearing his boots. In the glass-topped coffin in a separate room is Baron von Trenck – soldier, adventurer, gambler and womaniser, who bequeathed loads of cash to the monastery.

Opposite the monastery, the lane leads into the sloping square of **Zelný trh** (Cabbage Market), the heart of the old town, and where live carp were sold from the baroque **Parnassus Fountain** (1695) at Christmas. The fountain is a symbolic cave encrusted with allegorical figures. Hercules restrains three-headed Cerberus, watchdog of the underworld, and the three female figures represent the ancient empires of Babylon (crown), Persia (cornucopia) and Greece (quiver of arrows). The triumphant lady on top (arrogantly) symbolises Europe.

From the top of the Cabbage Market take Petrská to Petrov Hill, site of the gargantuan **Cathedral of SS Peter & Paul**. Climb the **tower** (adult/child 35/30Kč; ☼ 10am-5pm Tue-Sun) for great views or descend into the **crypt** (adult/child 15/10Kč; ☼ as per tower).

Nám Svobody, the city's main square, is rather drab and mostly 19th century but there are a few older monuments. The **plague column** dates

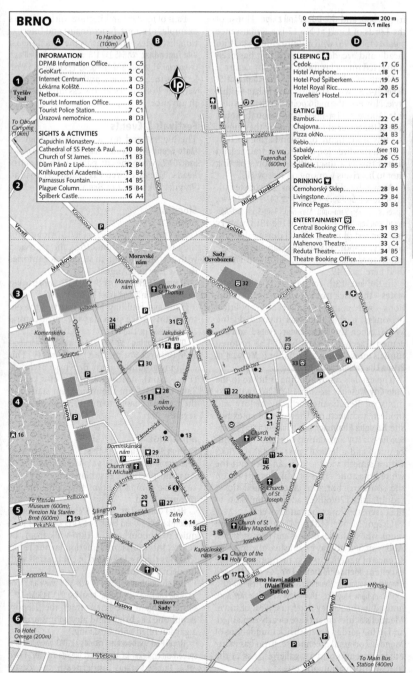

BRNO

0 _____ 200 m
0 _____ 0.1 miles

INFORMATION
DPMB Information Office....................1 C5
GeoKart...................................2 C4
Internet Centrum..........................3 C5
Lékárna Koliště...........................4 D3
Netbox....................................5 C3
Tourist Information Office.................6 B5
Tourist Police Station....................7 C1
Úrazová nemočnice.........................8 D3

SIGHTS & ACTIVITIES
Capuchin Monastery........................9 C5
Cathedral of SS Peter & Paul.............10 B6
Church of St James.......................11 B3
Dům Pánů z Lipé..........................12 B4
Knihkupectví Academia....................13 B4
Parnassus Fountain.......................14 B5
Plague Column............................15 B4
Špilberk Castle..........................16 A4

SLEEPING
Čedok....................................17 C6
Hotel Amphone............................18 C1
Hotel Pod Špilberkem.....................19 A5
Hotel Royal Ricc.........................20 B5
Travellers' Hostel.......................21 C4

EATING
Bambus...................................22 C4
Chajovna.................................23 B5
Pizza okNo...............................24 B3
Rebio....................................25 C5
Sabaidy..............................(see 18)
Spolek...................................26 C5
Špalíček.................................27 B5

DRINKING
Černohorský Sklep........................28 B4
Livingstone..............................29 B4
Pivnice Pegas............................30 B4

ENTERTAINMENT
Central Booking Office...................31 B3
Janáček Theatre..........................32 C3
Mahenovo Theatre.........................33 C4
Reduta Theatre...........................34 B5
Theatre Booking Office...................35 C3

CZECH REPUBLIC

from 1680, and the **Dům Pánů z Lipé** (House of the Lords of Lipá) at No 17 is a Renaissance palace (1589–96) with a 19th-century sgraffito façade and arcaded courtyard that has been converted into a boutique shopping centre.

North of nám Svobody is the **Church of St James** (1473), with a soaring nave in late-Gothic style. However the main point of interest is outside. Above the 1st-floor window on the south side of the tower at the west end of the church, is a tiny stone figure of a man baring his buttocks in the direction of the cathedral. Legend claims this is a disgruntled mason's parting shot to his rivals working on Petrov Hill.

Above the old town looms the sinister silhouette of **Špilberk Castle** (☎ 542 215 012; www.spilberk.cz; ⊙ 9am-6pm May-Sep, 9am-5pm Oct-Apr, closed Mon Sep-Jun). Founded in the 13th century and converted into a citadel during the 17th century, opponents of the Hapsburgs were imprisoned here until 1855. Baron von Trenck died here in 1749.

In the late-18th century parts of the **casemates** – the brick tunnels within the fortifications – were converted into cells for political prisoners, a role that was revived during WWII when the Nazis incarcerated and executed Czech partisans here. The restored tunnels now house a forbidding **Museum of Prison Life** (adult/child 60/30Kč).

The castle's main building is home to the **Brno City Museum** (adult/child 100/50Kč), with exhibits on Renaissance art, city history and modern architecture. There is also an exquisite **Baroque Pharmacy** (adult/child 20/10Kč; ⊙ 9am-6pm Tue-Sun May-Sep), dating from the mid-18th century, and a **lookout tower** (adult/child 20/10Kč) with a superb view – you can pick out the white limestone crags of Mikulov (p149) on the southern horizon. A combined ticket (adult/child 120/60Kč) allows admission to the casemates, museum and tower.

Gregor Mendel (1822–84), the Augustinian monk whose studies of peas and bees at Brno's Abbey of St Thomas established the modern science of genetics, is commemorated in the excellent **Mendel Museum** (☎ 543 424 043; www.mendel-museum.org; Mendlovo nám 1; adult/child 80/40Kč; ⊙ 10am-6pm May-Oct, 10am-4pm Wed-Sun Nov-Apr), housed in the Abbey itself, just west of town. Mendel's achievements are clearly explained, and in the garden are the brick foundations of Mendel's original greenhouse. Brno has many other museums and art galleries. Ask at the tourist information office.

Fans of modern architecture will love Brno's examples of cubist, functionalist and Internationalist styles. The finest is the functionalist **Vila Tugendhat** ☎ 545 212 118; www.tugendhat-villa.cz; Černopolni 45; adult/child 120/60Kč; ⊙ 10am-6pm Wed-Sun), northeast of town, and designed by Mies van der Rohe in 1930. It's essential to book in advance.

Festivals & Events

The biggest and noisiest event is August's **Moto Grand Prix** (www.motograndprix.com; admission from 700Kč), when the city packs out with petrol heads. The race circuit is off the D1 road to Prague, 10km west of Brno.

Sleeping

BUDGET

Čedok (☎ 542 321 267; Nádražní 10/12) Along with the tourist information office, they can help with accommodation in student dormitories during July and August.

Travellers' Hostel (☎ 542 213 573; www.travellers.cz; Jánská 22; dm incl breakfast 290Kč; ⊙ Jul-Aug) Set in a grand old building in the heart of the old town, this place provides the most central cheap beds in the city.

Obora Camping (☎ 546 223 334; www.autocampobora.cz; tent per person 80Kč, dm 200Kč; ⊙ May-Sep; P) This camping ground is at the Brněnská přehrada (Brno dam), northwest of the city centre. Take tram 1 from the main train station to the zoo and change to bus 103. Get off at the seventh stop.

MIDRANGE

Penzion Na Starém Brně (☎ 543 247 872; www.pension-brno.com; Mendlovo nám 1a; s/d incl breakfast 850/1050Kč) An atmospheric Augustinian monastery conceals five compact rooms that come reader-recommended.

Hotel Omega (☎ 543 213 876; www.hotelomega.cz; Křídloviská 19b; s/d incl breakfast 890/1350Kč; P) In a quiet neighbourhood, a 1km walk from the centre, this tourist information favourite has spacious rooms decorated in cool pastels with modern pine furniture.

Hotel Amphone (☎ 545 428 310; www.amphone.cz; třída kpt Jaroše 29; s/d incl breakfast 990/1490Kč; P) On an elegant tree-lined street, the friendly Amphone has bright and airy rooms around a garden filled with birdsong.

Hotel Pod Špilberkem (☎ 543 235 003; www.hotelpodspilberkem.cz; Pekařská 10; s/d incl breakfast 1100/1450Kč; P) Tucked away underneath the castle are quiet rooms clustered around a central courtyard.

TOP END

Hotel Royal Ricc (☎ 542 219 262; www.romantichotels .cz; Starobrněnská 10; s/d incl breakfast 3500/3900Kč; ☒ ☒ ▣) An utterly captivating mix of traditional and modern, this intimate hotel with 29 rooms would be right at home in Paris or Venice.

Eating

Spolek (☎ 542 213 002; Orli 22; mains 70-100Kč; ☼ 10am-10pm Mon-Sat) The service is unpretentious at this coolly bohemian (yes, we are in Moravia) haven with interesting salads and soups, and a diverse wine list.

Sabaidy (☎ 545 428 310; trída kpt Jaroše 29; mains 100-220Kč; ☼ 5pm-11pm Mon-Fri) With décor incorporating Buddhist statues and a talented Laotian chef conjuring authentically spicy flavours, Sabaidy delivers 'ommm…' and 'mmmm…'.

Rebio (☎ 542 211 110; Orli 16; mains 60-90Kč; ☼ 8am-8pm Mon-Fri, 10am-3pm Sat) Who says vegetarian food can't taste great? Healthy risottos, veggie pies and tasty desserts stand out in this popular self-service spot.

Špaliček (☎ 542 215 526; Zelný trh 12; mains 140-300Kč; ☼ 11am-11pm) Brno's oldest (and just maybe its 'meatiest') restaurant sits on the edge of the Cabbage Market. Ignore the irony and dig into the huge Moravian meals.

Also recommended:

Bambus (Kobližná 13; mains from 70Kč) Tasty Asian snacks and light meals.

Čhajovna (Dominikánské nám 6/7; tea 30Kč) Forty different types of tea and cruisy world music.

Haribol (Lužanecká 4; mains 70Kč; ☼ 11am-4pm Mon-Fri) Wholesome veggie feasts with Hare Krishna hospitality.

Pizza okNo (Solniční 8; pizza by the slice 15Kč) Hole-in-the-wall and eat-on-the-run pizza.

Drinking

Livingstone (Dominikánské nám 5; ☼ until 1am) Think raucous Irish pub meets funky world discoverer and you're part-way there. There's an adventure travel agency on hand if you get inspired.

Pivince Pegas (Jakubská 4) *Pivo* melts that old Moravian reserve as the locals become pleasantly noisy. Try the wheat beer with a slice of lemon.

Černohorský Sklep (nám Svobody 5; ☼ closed Sun) Try the Black Hill aperitif beer or the honey infused Kvasar brew at the Black Mountain Brewery's Brno outpost.

Entertainment

Brno has an excellent theatre and classical music, and you're expected to put your glad rags on. You can find entertainment listings (mostly in Czech) in the free monthly *Metropolis*.

Theatre Booking Office (předprodej; ☎ 542 321 285; Dvořákova 11; ☼ 8am-5.30pm Mon-Fri, 9am-noon Sat) Buy tickets for performances at the Reduta, Mahenovo and Janacek Theatres at this office behind the Mahenovo Theatre.

Central Booking Office (Centrální předprodej; ☎ 542 210 863; Běhounská 17; ☼ 9am-1pm & 2-6pm Mon-Fri) Tickets to rock, folk and classical concerts at many venues.

Janáček Theatre (Janáčkovo divadlo; Sady Osvobození) Opera and ballet are performed at the modern theatre, named after composer Leoš Janáček.

Mahenovo Theatre (Mahenovo divadlo; Dvořákovo 11) The neobaroque Mahenovo Theatre was designed by the Viennese theatrical architects Fellner and Hellmer, and presents classical drama in Czech and operettas.

Reduta Theatre (Reduta divadlo; Zelný trh 4) Newly restored, the Reduta has an emphasis on Mozart's work (he played there in 1767).

Getting There & Away

There are frequent buses from Brno to Prague (130Kč, 2½ hours, hourly), Bratislava (110Kč, 2¼ hours, hourly) and Vienna (200Kč, 2½ hours, two daily). The departure point is either the bus station or near the railway station opposite the Grand Hotel. Check your ticket.

There are trains to Prague (160Kč, three hours) every two hours. Direct Eurocity trains from Brno to Vienna (575Kč, 1¾ hours, five daily) arrive at Vienna's Südbahnhof.

ČSA (www.csa.cz) has scheduled flights to Prague and **Ryan Air** (www.ryanair.com) flies daily from London.

Getting Around

Buy public transport tickets from tram-stop vending machines, hotels, newsstands or at the **DPMB Information Office** (☎ 543 174 317; www .dpmb.cz; Novobranská 18; ☼ 6am-6pm Mon-Fri, 8am-3.30pm Sat). Tickets are valid for 40/60 minutes, cost 13/19Kč and allow unlimited transfers; 24-hour tickets are 50Kč. A 10-minute, no-transfer ticket is 8Kč.

You can order a cab from **City Taxis** (☎ 542 321 321).

Around Brno

SLAVKOV U BRNA

Slavkov u Brna is better known to history by its Austrian name – **Austerlitz**. On 2 December 1805 the Battle of the Three Emperors was fought over the rolling countryside between Brno and Slavkov, and Napoleon Bonaparte's Grande Armée defeated the combined forces of Emperor Franz I (Austria) and Tsar Alexander I (Russia). The battle was decided at **Pracký kopec**, a hill 12km west of Slavkov, now marked by the **Cairn of Peace** (Mohyla míru; adult/child 75/35Kč; ◷ 9am-6pm Jul-Aug, 9am-5pm May, Jun & Sep, 9am-5pm Tue-Sun Apr, 9am-3.30pm Tue-Sun Oct-Mar) with a museum detailing the horrors of the conflict, which claimed 20,000 lives. Re-enactments of the battle take place annually around December 2.

Pracký kopec is awkward to reach by public transport. Take a local train from Brno to Ponětovice (28Kč, 25 minutes, 10 daily), and walk 3.5km southeast through Prace.

MORAVIAN KARST

The limestone plateau of the Moravian Karst (Moravský kras), 20km north of Brno, is a speleologist's delight, riddled with caves and canyons carved by the subterranean Punkva River. There's a car park at Skalní Mlýn, at the end of the public road from Blansko, with an information desk and ticket office. A **mini-train** (adult/child 50/40Kč return) travels along the 1.5km between the car park and the cave entrance. You should be able to walk there in 20 minutes.

The first part of the tour through the **Punkva Caves** (Punkevní jeskyně; ☎ 516 418 602; www.cavemk.cz; adult/child 100/50Kč; ◷ 8.20am-3.50pm Apr-Sep; 8.40am-2pm Mon-Fri, 8.40am-3.40pm Sat & Sun Oct; 8.40am-2pm Nov-Mar; ♿) involves an amazing 1km walk through caverns draped with stalactites and stalagmites before you emerge at the bottom of the Macocha Abyss. You then board a small, electric-powered boat to cruise along the underground river back to the entrance.

At weekends and in July and August, tickets for cave tours can sell out up to a week in advance, so book ahead.

Beyond the Punkva Caves entrance a **cable car** (adult/child 60/50Kč return, combined tourist train and cable-car ticket 90/70Kč) whisks you to the upper rim of the spectacular **Macocha Abyss**, a 140m-deep sinkhole. If you're feeling energetic, hike to the top on the blue-marked trail (2km).

The comfortable **Hotel Skalní Mlýn** (☎ 516 418 113; www.smk.cz; s/d 980/1320Kč; Ⓟ) and its res-

taurant (mains 70Kč to 180Kč) is beside the car park. Near the top of the Macocha Abyss is **Chata Macocha** (dm 260Kč), a hikers hostel and restaurant (mains 80Kč); book through Hotel Skalní Mlýn.

From Brno there are frequent trains to Blansko (34Kč, 30 minutes, hourly). Buses depart from Blansko bus station (across the bridge from the train station) to Skalní Mlýn (12Kč, 15 minutes, five daily April to September). Check times at the Tourist Information Office in Brno before setting off. You can also hike an 8km trail from Blansko to Skalní Mlýn (two hours).

MORAVSKÝ KRUMLOV

If you have been impressed by the works of Art Nouveau artist Alfons Mucha in Prague's Municipal House (p108) and Mucha Museum (p109), then you should visit this obscure town near Brno where his greatest achievement is on display (Mucha was born in the nearby village of Ivančice). The **Slav Epic** (Slovanská epopej; ☎ 515 322 789; adult/child 60/30Kč; ◷ 9am-noon & 1-4pm Tue-Sun Apr-Oct), painted between 1919 and 1926, is housed in a slightly down-at-heel Renaissance chateau 300m off the main square, the only venue big enough to accommodate it. Twenty monumental and cinematic canvases – total area around 1000 sq metres – depict events from Slavic history and mythology. Though different from the Art Nouveau style of the artist's famous Paris posters, these canvases retain the same mythic, romanticised quality, full of wild-eyed priests, medieval pageantry and battlefield carnage, all rendered in symbolic shades. In the artist's own words, 'black is the colour of bondage, blue is the past, yellow the joyous present, orange the glorious future'.

Moravský Krumlov lies 40km southwest of Brno. There are frequent local trains from Brno's hlavní nádraží to Moravský Krumlov (46Kč, 50 minutes, 10 daily); it's a 2.5km walk west from the station to the chateau.

OLOMOUC

pop 105,000

As countless tourists embrace the overt charms of Prague and Český Krumlov, Olomouc (pronounced 'Olla-moats'), exudes a subdued charm to emerge as the travellers' equivalent of a special restaurant that is your own little secret. An old town square rivalling Prague for scale and beauty combines with the youthful

OLOMOUC

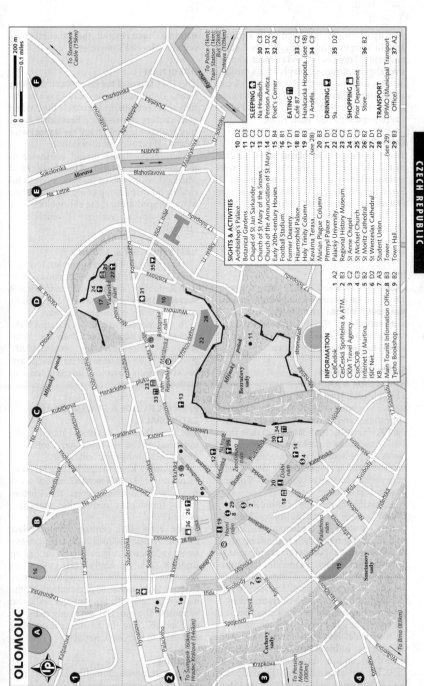

CZECH REPUBLIC

INFORMATION		
CedCedok............................	1	A2
CesCeská Spořitelna & ATM......	2	B3
CKM Travel Agency.................	3	C2
CsoCSOB.............................	4	C3
Internet U Martina.................	5	B2
ISIC Net..............................	6	D2
KB.....................................	7	A3
Main Tourist Information Office..	8	B3
Tycho Bookshop....................	9	B2

SIGHTS & ACTIVITIES		
Archbishop's Palace................	10	D2
Botanical Gardens..................	11	D3
Chapel of St Jan Sarkander......	12	C2
Church of St Mary of the Snows..	13	C3
Church of the Annunciation of St Mary..	14	C3
Early 20th-century Houses........	15	B4
Football Stadium....................	16	B1
Former Deanery....................	17	D1
Hauenschild Palace.................	18	B3
Holy Trinity Column...............	19	B3
Kavárna Terasa.....................	(see 28)	
Marian Plague Column............	20	B3
Přemysl Palace.....................	21	D1
Palacký University.................	22	D2
Regional History Museum........	23	C2
St Anne Chapel....................	24	D1
St Michael Church.................	25	C2
St Moritz Cathedral...............	26	B2
St Wenceslas Cathedral..........	27	D1
Student Union......................	28	D2
Tower................................	(see 29)	
Town Hall...........................	29	B3

SLEEPING		
Na Hradbach.......................	30	C3
Pension Antica.....................	31	D2
Poet's Corner......................	32	A2

EATING		
Café 87.............................	33	C2
Hanácká Hospoda.................	(see 18)	
U Anděla............................	34	C3

DRINKING		
9a.....................................	35	D2

SHOPPING		
Prior Department Store...........	36	B2

TRANSPORT		
DPMO (Municipal Transport Office)..	37	A2

To Šternberk Castle (15km)

To Police (1km); Train Station (1km); Bus Station (2km); Ostrava (109km)

To Šumperk (60km); Hradec Králové (146km)

To Pension Moravia (300m)

To Brno (83km)

0 200 m
0 0.1 miles

vivacity of a modern student town amid the graceful campus of the country's second-oldest university. Some of Moravia's most impressive religious structures play host to a thrilling history, and the youthful population looks ahead with a quiet confidence. And with tourist numbers a mere trickle, Olomouc is one of the Czech Republic's best-value cities.

Orientation

The main train station (hlavní nádraží) is 2km east of the old town, over the Morava river and its tributary the Bystřice (take tram 1, 2, 5 or 6 heading west). The bus station is 1km further east (take tram 4 or 5).

The old town comprises the two linked squares of Horní (Upper) and Dolní (Lower) nám. The Přemysl Palace is along Ostružinická and třída 1.máje.

Information

Internet U Martina (Ostružnická 29; internet & Skype per min 1Kč; ☻ 9am-midnight) internet and international calls.
Main tourist information office (Olomoucká informační služba; ☎ 585 513 385; www.olomouc-tour ism.cz; Horní nám; ☻ 9am-7pm) Located in the town hall and sells maps and books accommodation.

Sights & Activities

HORNÍ NÁM & AROUND

The splendid, **town hall** in the middle of the square was built in 1378, though its present appearance and needle-like **tower** (věž; admission 15Kč; ☻ tours at 11am & 3pm Mar-Oct) date from 1607. Don't miss the **astronomical clock** on the north side, remodelled in communist style so that each hour is announced by ideologically pure workers instead of pious saints. The best display is at midday.

Across the square is the beautiful **Holy Trinity Column** (Sousoší Nejsvětější trojice). Built between 1716 and 1754, the baroque mélange of gold and grey is remarkably reminiscent of the Buddhist shrine of Borobudur in Indonesia. A delightful nun explains the meaning of the interior sculptures in a variety of languages. In 2000 the column became part of Unesco's World Heritage list. The square's surrounded by a jaw-dropping line-up of historic façades and has two of the city's six baroque fountains.

Down Opletalova is the immense and overwhelmingly Gothic **St Moritz Cathedral** (chrám sv Mořice), built methodically from 1412 to 1530. The cathedral's amazing island of peace is shattered every September with an International Organ Festival (the cathedral's own organ is Moravia's mightiest).

DOLNÍ NÁM

The 1661 **Church of the Annunciation of St Mary** (kostel Zvěstování Panny Marie) has a beautifully sober interior. In contrast is the opulent 16th-century Renaissance **Hauenschild Palace** (not open to the public), and the **Marian Plague Column** (Mariánský morový sloup).

Picturesque lanes thread northeast to the green-domed **St Michael Church** (kostel sv Michala), with a robust baroque interior, including a rare painting of a pregnant Virgin Mary. Draped around the entire block is an active Dominican seminary (Dominikánský klášter).

NÁM REPUBLIKY & AROUND

The original Jesuit college complex, founded in 1573, stretched along Universitní and into nám Republiky, and includes the **Church of St Mary of the Snows** (kostel Panny Marie Sněžné), with an interior full of fine frescoes.

In a former convent across the road is the **Regional History Museum** (Vlastivědné muzeum; ☎ 585 515 111; www.vmo.cz; nám Republiky 5; adult/child 40/20Kč, free on Wed; ☻ 9am-6pm Tue-Sun Apr-Sep, 10am-5pm Wed-Sun Oct-Mar) with historical, geographical and zoological displays.

PŘEMYSL PALACE & ST WENCESLAS CATHEDRAL

The pocket-sized Václavské nám, to the northeast of the old town, has Olomouc's most venerable historic buildings.

Originally a Romanesque basilica first consecrated in 1131, **St Wenceslas Cathedral** (dóm sv Václava) was rebuilt several times before having thoroughly 'neo-Gothic' makeover in the 1880s.

The early 12th-century **Přemysl Palace** (Přemyslovský palác; adult/child 20/10Kč; ☻ 10am-6pm Tue-Sun Apr-Sep), was originally built for Bishop Jindřich Zdík. An English text guides you through a cloister, with 15th- and 16th-century frescoes, to the archaeological centrepiece, the bishops' rooms with Romanesque walls and windows. The quarters were only rediscovered in 1867, and the artistry is unequalled elsewhere in the Czech Republic.

Sleeping

The tourist information office can book private and hotel rooms.

AUTHOR'S CHOICE

Pension Antica (☎ 731 560 264; www.pension
.antica.cz; Wurmova 1; apt 1600-2000Kč; **P**) If
you're travelling by yourself then don't read
this. But if you're looking for a romantic stay
in a quietly romantic city then read on. With
antique furniture, crisp white duvets and
Oriental rugs covering polished wooden
floors, there's every chance you won't be
outside for long enough to enjoy the easy
going Renaissance charm of Olomouc. But
when you do slip the shackles of luxury, kick
the night off in the snug café-bar downstairs before moving on to a cosy restaurant
in the old town.

Poet's Corner (☎ 777 570 730; www.hostelolomouc
.com; 3rd fl, Sokolská 1; dm/tw 300/800Kč) Aussie owner
Greg is a wealth of local information at this
friendly and well-run hostel. Bicycles can be
hired for 100Kč per day.

Pension Moravia (☎ 585 416 403; www.pension-moravia
.com; Dvořá kova 37; s/d 500/800Kč; **P** 🖳) A 10-minute
walk from the centre, this *pension* provides
good value in a quiet residential street without
the parking hassles of the old town. If arriving
by public transport, catch bus 19 from the
railway station to the Dvořákova stop.

Na Hradbach (☎ 585 233 243; nahradbach@quick
.cz; Hrnčířská 3; s/d 600/800Kč) On a pretty street
sits Olomouc's best-value *pension* with two
good restaurants across the lane. Be sure to
book ahead.

Eating & Drinking

Café 87 (Denisova 87; chocolate pie 30Kč, coffee 25 Kč;
🕑 7.30am-8pm) Locals flock to this funky café
beside the Museum of Art for coffee and their
famous chocolate pie. You be the judge – dark
chocolate or white chocolate?

Hanácacká Hospoda (☎ 582 237 186; Dolní nám 38;
mains 70-100Kč) In the same building as the Hauenschild palace, the menu lists everything in
the local Haná dialect. It's worth persevering
though because the Moravian meals are robust, tasty and supreme value.

U Anděla (☎ 585 228 755; Hrnčířská 10; mains 130-
395Kč) Have a wander round and look at the
seriously intriguing memorabilia. Don't be
too tardy because the service is prompt and
the Moravian food very good.

9a (☎ 608 122 993; Nábřeží Premyslovcú 9; 🕑 noon-
midnight Mon-Fri, 3pm-midnight Sat & Sun) Wood and

bricks combine in a spot that's a cut above
Olomouc's other grungier student bars. Try
your hand(s) and feet on the climbing wall.

Getting There & Away

From Brno, there are about 15 buses (60Kč,
1¼ hours) and five direct fast trains (120Kč,
1½ hours) a day. The best connection from
Prague (294Kč, 3¼ hours) is by fast train from
Praha hlavní nádraží.

TELČ
pop 6000

Telč is a quiet town, with a gorgeous old centre
ringed by medieval fish ponds and unspoilt
by modern buildings. It is also a good spot to
unwind with an engrossing book and a glass
of Moravian wine.

The bus and train stations are a few hundred metres apart on the eastern side of town.
A 10-minute walk along Masarykova leads
to nám Zachariáše z Hradce, the old town
square.

The **information office** (☎ 567 243 145; www.telc
-etc.cz; nám Zachariáše z Hradce 10; 🕑 8am-5pm Mon-Fri,
11am-4pm Sat & Sun) is in the town hall; you can
check email here (1Kč per minute).

Sights

In a country full of picturesque old town
squares, Telč's World Heritage–listed and
cobblestoned **nám Zachariáše z Hradce** outshines
the lot. In the evening, when the tour groups
have gone, the Gothic arcades and elegant
Renaissance façades are a magical setting.

At the square's northwestern end is the
Water Chateau (☎ 567 243 821; tours in Czech adult/child
70/35Kč, in English adult/child 140/70Kč; 🕑 9am-11.45am &
1-5pm Tue-Sun May-Aug, 9am-4pm Apr, Sep & Oct), a jewel
of Renaissance architecture. Tour 1 (adult/
concession 80/40Kc, in English 160Kc, one
hour) is through some of the country's loveliest Renaissance halls, while Tour 2 (adult/
concession 70/35Kc, in English 140Kc, 45
minutes) visits the private apartments, inhabited by the aristocratic owners until 1945.

At the castle's entrance gaze into the **Chapel
of All Saints**, where trumpeting angels stand
guard over the tombs of Zacharias of Hradec,
the castle's founder, and his wife. The local
historical museum (adult/child 20/10Kč; 🕑 9am-11.45am
& 1-5pm Tue-Sun May-Aug, 9am-4pm Apr, Sep & Oct), in
the courtyard, has a scale model of Telč from
1895 showing just how little the townscape
has changed.

CZECH REPUBLIC

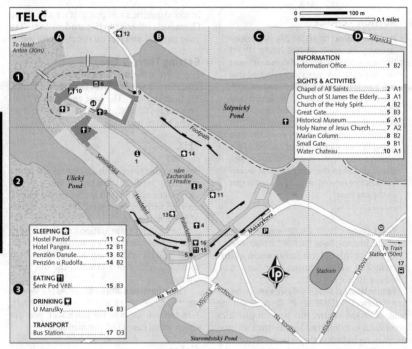

TELČ

INFORMATION
Information Office......................1 B2

SIGHTS & ACTIVITIES
Chapel of All Saints.....................2 A1
Church of St James the Elderly.....3 A1
Church of the Holy Spirit............4 B2
Great Gate...............................5 B3
Historical Museum.....................6 A1
Holy Name of Jesus Church.........7 A2
Marian Column..........................8 A2
Small Gate................................9 B1
Water Chateau..........................10 A1

SLEEPING
Hostel Pantof............................11 C2
Hotel Pangea............................12 B1
Penzión Danuše.........................13 B2
Penzión u Rudolfa......................14 B2

EATING
Šenk Pod Věží...........................15 B3

DRINKING
U Marušky................................16 B3

TRANSPORT
Bus Station...............................17 D3

Sleeping & Eating

Hostel Pantof (☎ 776 887 466; www.pantof.cz; nám Zachariáše z Hradce 42; dm/d 300/800Kč; ☯ Jul-Aug; P) A relaxed atmosphere and rooms overlooking the square add up to one of the country's best hostels.

Penzión u Rudolfa (☎ 567 243 094; www.volny.cz /libuse.javurkova; nám Zachariáše z Hradce 58; s/d 300/600Kč) A pretty merchant's house on the main square conceals a friendly *pension* with shared kitchen facilities.

Penzión Danuše (☎ 567 213 945; www.telc-etc.cz/cz /privat/danuse; Hradebni 25; s/d 450/900Kč, 4-bed apt 2000Kč; P) Discreet wrought-iron balconies and wooden window boxes provide a touch of class on this quiet corner just off the main square.

Hotel Pangea (☎ 567 213 122; www.pangea .cz; Na Baště 450; s/d incl breakfast 1200/1600Kč; P X X 🖥 📷 🔧) Huge buffet breakfasts and loads of facilities make this slightly functional spot very good value. Rates drop by up to 30% outside July and August.

Hotel Anton (☎ 567 223 315; www.hotel-anton.cz; Slavatovská 92; s/d incl breakfast 1350/1800Kč; P 🖥) Designer furniture and private balconies com-

bine in Telč's best accommodation. This new hotel has been recommended by readers.

Šenk Pod Věží (☎ 603 526 999; Palackého 116; mains 100-180Kč; ☯ 11am-3pm & 6-9pm Mon-Sat, 11am-4pm Sun) Sizzling grills, tasty pizza and occasional live music are the big drawcards at this cosy restaurant tucked under the tower.

U Marušky (☎ 605 870 854; Palackého) Telč's hipper younger citizens crowd this buzzy bar for cool jazz and tasty eats.

Getting There & Away

There are five buses per day from Prague to Telč (120Kč, 2½ hours). Buses between České Budějovice and Brno also stop at Telč (90Kč, two hours, two daily).

MORAVIAN WINE COUNTRY

If you're heading south from Brno to Vienna, the Moravian wine country lies en route. Bohemian beer is famous worldwide, but until recently the wines of South Moravia were little known internationally.

Czech wine has improved greatly since the fall of communism in 1989, with small producers concentrating on the high-quality end of the market. Czech red wines, such as the local speciality Svatovavřinecké (St Lawrence), are mediocre, but local whites can be very good.

There are lots of *vinné sklepy* (wine cellars), *vinoteky* (wine shops) and *vinárny* (wine bars) to explore, as well as some spectacular chateaux. The Tourist Information Office in Brno (p140) sells maps and guides covering the wine country. The terrain of the wine country is relatively flat, so cycling is a nice and leisurely way to get around.

Mikulov

The picturesque town of Mikulov lies at the heart of the Moravia's largest wine-growing region, which specialises in dry, fruity whites like Veltlínské Zelené, Vlašský Ryzlink and Müller-Thurgau.

The **tourist information office** (☎ 519 510 855; www.mikulov.cz; Nám 30; ☺ 8am-6pm Mon-Fri, 9am-6pm Sat & Sun Jun-Sep, 8.30am-noon & 1-5pm Mon-Fri Oct-May) is on the main square, beneath the impressive Renaissance **chateau** (☎ 519 510 255; adult/child 60/30Kč; ☺ 9am-5pm Tue-Sun May-Sep, 9am-4pm Apr & Oct), seat of the Dietrichstein and Liechtenstein families. Bicycles and cycle-touring information are available from **Top Bicycle** (☎ 519 513 745; www.topbicycle.com; Nám 24/27).

There are plenty of buses from Brno to Mikulov (52Kč, one hour, 14 daily), and less frequent buses between Mikulov and Vienna (165Kč, two hours, two daily).

Lednice & Valtice

A few kilometres east of Mikulov, the **Lednice-Valtice Cultural Landscape** consists of 200 sq km of woodland, streams, artificial lakes and tree-lined avenues dotted with baroque, neoclassical and neo-Gothic chateaux. Effectively Europe's biggest landscaped garden, it was created over several centuries by the dukes of Liechtenstein, and is now a Unesco World Heritage site.

The town's main attraction is the massive neo-Gothic pile of **Lednice Chateau** (☎ 519 340 128; ☺ 9am-6pm Tue-Sun May-Aug, 9am-5pm Tue-Sun Sep, 9am-4pm Sat & Sun only Apr & Oct), the Liechtensteins' summer palace. Embellished with battlements, pointy pinnacles and dog-shaped gargoyles, it gazes across a vast, island-dotted artificial lake to a minaret-shaped folly. Tour 1 (adult/concession 80/40Kč, 45 minutes) takes you through a selection of the major rooms, while Tour 2 (adult/concession 100/50Kč, 45 minutes) concentrates on the Liechtenstein apartments. Wander through the gardens for free.

The huge baroque chateau at Valtice houses the **National Wine Salon** (Národní salon vín; ☎ 519 352 072; www.salonvin.cz; Zámek 1; ☺ 9.30am-5pm Tue-Sat), where you can choose from various wine-tasting sessions costing from 99Kč to 399Kč per person (minimum five people). Next door is the **Zámecké vinoteka** (☺ 10am-6pm), a wine shop where you can get a free tasting before you buy.

There are five buses a day from Mikulov to Lednice (25Kč, 40 minutes), and one a day from Brno (65Kč, 1¾ hours).

CZECH REPUBLIC DIRECTORY

ACCOMMODATION

Accommodation reviews in this chapter are listed in order of price, from cheapest to most expensive. In the Prague section, budget means less than 1200Kč for a double, midrange is 1200Kč to 4000Kč, and top end is more than 4000Kč.

You usually have to show your passport when checking in at accommodation in the Czech Republic; some places might insist on keeping it for the duration of your stay, but you can demand to get it back as soon as your details are registered. If they keep it, don't forget to ask for it before you leave!

There are several hundred camping grounds spread around the Czech Republic; most are open from May to September only and charge around 60Kč to 100Kč per person. Camping on public land is prohibited.

Klub mladých cestovatelů (KMC Young Travellers Club; Map pp110-11; ☎ 222 220 347; www.kmc.cz; Karolíny Světlé 30, Prague 1) is the HI affiliate in Prague, and can book hostel accommodation throughout the country. In July and August many student dormitories become temporary hostels, and some in Prague are also year-round backpacker hostels. Prague and Český Krumlov are the only places with a solid choice of backpacker-oriented hostels. Dorm beds costs around 400Kč in Prague and 300Kč to 350Kč elsewhere; it's best to book ahead. An HI-membership card is not usually needed, although it will often get you a reduced rate. An ISIC, ITIC, IYTC or Euro26 card may also get you a discount.

Another category of hostel accommodation is *turistické ubytovny* (tourist hostels), which provide very basic dormitory accommodation (175Kč to 300Kč); rooms can usually be booked through the local tourist information office or KMC branch. Look for signs advertising private rooms (*privát* or *Zimmer frei* – like B&Bs without the breakfast). Most tourist information offices can book them for you. Expect to pay from 300Kč to 500Kč per person outside Prague. Some have a three-night minimum-stay requirement.

Pensions (penzióny) are a step up: small, homely, often family-run, but offering rooms with private bathroom, often including breakfast. Rates range from 1000Kč to 1500Kč for a double room (1750Kč to 2500Kč in Prague).

Hotels in central Prague and Brno are expensive, but smaller towns are usually significantly cheaper. Two-star hotels offer reasonable comfort for 800Kč to 1000Kč for a double, or 1000Kč to 1400Kč with private bathroom (50% higher in Prague).

ACTIVITIES

There is good hiking among the hills of the Šumava (p138) south of Český Krumlov, in the forests around Karlovy Vary (p126), in the Moravian Karst (p144) and in the Adršpach-Teplice Rocks (p139). Climbing is also excellent in the Moravian Karst and the Adršpach-Teplice Rocks. Canoeing and rafting are popular on the Vltava River around Český Krumlov (p135), and the whole country is ideal for cycling and cycle touring. Especially good for cycling are the Sumava region (p138) and the Moravian Wine Country (p148). A recent introduction are beer and wine tours. We do not recommend you combine these with cycling.

The following companies provide activities-based tours:

Ave Bicycle Tours (☎ 251 551 011; www.bicycle-tours .cz) Cycle touring specialists.

E-Tours (☎ 572 557 191; www.etours.cz) Nature, wildlife and photography tours.

Greenways Travel Club (☎ 519 512 603; www.gtc .cz) From cycling and walking to beer and wine, Czech glass and Czech music tours.

BUSINESS HOURS

Outside Prague, almost everything closes on Saturday afternoon and all day Sunday. Most restaurants are open every day; most museums, castles and chateaus are closed on Mondays year round.

Banks 8am to 4.30pm Monday to Friday

Bars 11am to midnight daily

Post offices 8am to 6pm Monday to Friday, 8am to noon Saturday.

Restaurants 11am to 11pm daily.

Shops 8.30am to 5pm or 6pm Monday to Friday, 8.30am-noon or 1pm Saturday

COURSES

The **Institute for Language & Preparatory Studies** (Ústav jazykové a odborné přípravy; ☎ 224 990 411; www.ujop.cuni.cz) runs six-week Czech language courses for foreigners.

The **PCFE Film School** (☎ 257 534 013; www.prague -center.cz) runs four-week intensive film-making workshops in summer, covering screenwriting, directing, cinematography, editing and sound design.

The **International Partnership for Service, Learning & Leadership** (www.ipsl.org) provides longer-term (up to one year) opportunities for volunteering in the Czech Republic. Participants stay with local families and combine study with volunteer work. Opportunities for volunteering include teaching English to blind students and working with special-needs children.

CUSTOMS

Customs officers can be strict about antiques and will confiscate goods that are questionable There is no limit to the amount of Czech or foreign currency that can be taken into or out of the country, but amounts exceeding 500,000Kč must be declared.

DANGERS & ANNOYANCES

Pickpocketing can be a problem in Prague's tourist zone, and there are occasional reports of robberies on overnight international trains. There is intense racism towards the local Roma population, which occasionally results in verbal abuse (and even assault) directed at darker-skinned visitors.

DISABLED TRAVELLERS

Ramps for wheelchair users are becoming more common, but cobbled streets, steep hills and stairways often make getting around difficult. Public transport is a major problem as most buses, trains and trams don't have wheelchair access. Major tourist attractions such as Prague Castle do have wheelchair access though – anything described as *bez-barierová* is 'barrier-free'.

Prague Wheelchair Users Organisation (Map pp110-11; Pražská organizace vozíčkářů; ☎ 224 827 210; www.pov .cz in Czech; Benediktská 6, Staré Město) can organise a guide and transportation at about half the cost of a taxi, and has a CD-ROM guide to barrier-free Prague in Czech, English and German.

EMBASSIES & CONSULATES
Czech Embassies & Consulates

Australia (☎ 02-6290 1386; www.mzv.cz/canberra; 8 Culgoa Circuit, O'Malley, Canberra ACT 2606)

Canada (☎ 613-562 3875; www.mzv.cz/ottawa; 251 Cooper St, Ottawa, Ontario K2P 0G2)

France (☎ 01 40 65 13 00; www.mzv.cz/paris; 15 Ave Charles Floquet, 75007 Paris)

Germany (☎ 030-22 63 80; www.mzv.cz/berlin; Wilhelmstrasse 44, 10117 Berlin)

Ireland (☎ 031-668 1135; www.mzv.cz/dublin; 57 Northumberland Rd, Ballsbridge, Dublin 4)

Netherlands (☎ 070-313 0031; www.mzv.cz/hague; Paleisstraat 4, 2514 JA The Hague)

New Zealand (☎ 09-522 8736; auckland@honorary .mzv.cz; Level 3, BMW Mini Centre, 11-15 Great South Rd, Newmarket, Auckland) Postal address: PO Box 7488, Auckland.

UK (☎ 020-7243 1115; www.mzv.cz/london; 26 Kensington Palace Gardens, London W8 4QY)

USA (☎ 202-274 9100; www.mzv.cz/washington; 3900 Spring of Freedom St NW, Washington, DC 20008)

Embassies & Consulates in the Czech Republic

Most embassies and consulates are open at least 9am to noon Monday to Friday.

Australia (Map pp110-11; ☎ 296 578 350; www.emb assy.gov.au/cz.html; 6th fl, Klimentská 10, Nové Město) Honorary consulate for emergency assistance only; nearest Australian embassy is in Vienna.

Austria (Map pp110-11; ☎ 257 090 511; www.austria .cz in German & Czech; Viktora Huga 10, Smíchov)

Bulgaria (Map pp110-11; ☎ 222 211 258; bulvelv@mbox .vol.cz; Krakovská 6, Nové Město)

Canada (Map pp102-3; ☎ 272 101 800; www.canada.cz; Muchova 6, Bubeneč)

France (Map pp110-11; ☎ 251 171 711; www.france.cz in French & Czech; Velkopřerovské nám 2, Malá Strana)

Germany (Map pp110-11; ☎ 257 113 111; www.deutsch land.cz in German & Czech; Vlašská 19, Malá Strana)

Hungary (Map pp102-3; ☎ 233 324 454; huembprg@vol.cz; Českomalínská 20, Bubeneč)

Ireland (Map pp110-11; ☎ 257 530 061; pragueembassy@dfa.ie; Tržiště 13, Malá Strana)

Netherlands (Map pp102-3; ☎ 233 015 200; www .netherlandsembassy.cz; Gotthardská 6/27, Bubeneč)

New Zealand (Map pp102-3; ☎ 222 514 672; egermayer@nzconsul.cz; Dykova 19, Vinohrady) Honorary consulate providing emergency assistance only (eg stolen passport); the nearest NZ embassy is in Berlin.

Poland Consulate (Map pp102-3; ☎ 224 228 722; konspol@mbox.vol.cz; Vúžlabině 14, Strašnice); Embassy (Map pp110-11; ☎ 257 099 500; www.prague.polemb .net; Valdštejnská 8, Malá Strana) Go to the consular department for visas.

Russia (Map pp102-3; ☎ 233 374 100; embrus@tiscali .cz; Pod Kaštany 1, Bubeneč)

Slovakia (Map pp110-11; ☎ 233 113 051; www .slovakemb.cz, in Slovak; Pod Hradbami 1, Dejvice)

South Africa (Map pp102-3; ☎ 267 311 114; saprague@terminal.cz; Ruská 65, Vršovice)

Ukraine (Map pp102-3; ☎ 233 342 000; emb_cz@mfa .gov.ua; Charlese de Gaulla 29, Bubeneč)

UK (Map pp110-11; ☎ 257 402 111; www.britain.cz; Thunovská 14, Malá Strana)

USA (Map pp110-11; ☎ 257 022 000; www.usembassy .cz; Tržiště 15, Malá Strana)

FESTIVALS & EVENTS

Festival of Sacred Music (www.mhf-brno.cz) Easter; Brno.

Prague Spring (www.festival.cz) May; international music festival.

United Islands (www.unitedislands.cz) June; world music festival, Prague.

Five-Petalled Rose Festival June; medieval festival, Český Krumlov.

Karlovy Vary International Film Festival (www .kviff.com) July

Český Krumlov International Music Festival (www .auviex.cz) July to August

Loveplanet (www.loveplanet.cz) August; rock and hip-hop festival, Prague.

Dvořák Autumn September; classical-music festival, Karlovy Vary.

Prague Autumn (www.pragueautumn.cz) September; international music festival.

GAY & LESBIAN TRAVELLERS

Prague Saints (www.praguesaints.cz) is the most comprehensive online source for English-language information and has links to gay-friendly accommodation and bars. Homosexuality is legal in the Czech Republic (the age of consent is 15), but Czechs are not yet used to seeing public displays of affection; it's best to be discreet.

HOLIDAYS

New Year's Day 1 January
Easter Monday March/April

CZECH REPUBLIC

Labour Day 1 May
Liberation Day 8 May
SS Cyril and Methodius Day 5 July
Jan Hus Day 6 July
Czech Statehood Day 28 September
Republic Day 28 October
Struggle for Freedom and Democracy Day
17 November
Christmas 24 to 26 December

INTERNET RESOURCES

Czech Tourism (www.czechtourism.com) Official tourist information.

Czech.cz (www.czech.cz) Informative government site on travel and tourism, including visa requirements.

IDOS (www.idos.cz) Train and bus timetables.

Mapy (www.mapy.cz) Online maps.

Prague Information Service (www.prague-info.cz) Official tourist site for Prague.

PragueTV (www.praguetv.cz) Prague events and entertainment listings.

Radio Prague (www.radio.cz) Dedicated to Czech news, language and culture (in English, French, German, Spanish and Russian).

MONEY
Currency

The Czech crown (Koruna česká, or Kč), is divided into 100 hellers or *haléřů* (h). Banknotes come in denominations of 20, 50, 100, 200, 500, 1000, 2000 and 5000Kč; coins are of 10, 20 and 50h and one, two, five, 10, 20 and 50Kč.

Keep small change handy for use in public toilets, telephones and tram-ticket machines, and try to keep some small denomination notes for shops, cafés and restaurants – changing the larger notes from ATMs can be a problem.

Exchanging Money

There is no black market; anyone who offers to change money in the street is a thief.

There's a good network of *bankomaty* (ATMs). The main banks – Komerční banka, ČSOB and Živnostenská banka – are the best places to change cash and travellers cheques or get a cash advance on Visa or MasterCard. Amex and Thomas Cook/Travelex offices change their own cheques without commission. Credit cards are widely accepted in petrol stations, midrange and top-end hotels, restaurants and shops.

Beware of *směnárna* (private exchange offices), especially in Prague – they advertise misleading rates, and often charge exorbitant commissions or 'handling fees'.

Costs

Food, transport and admission fees are fairly cheap, but accommodation in Prague can be expensive. Staying in hostels and buying food in supermarkets, you can survive on US$20 a day in summer. Staying in private rooms or *pensions*, eating at cheap restaurants and using public transport, count on US$30 to US$35 a day.

Get out of the capital and your costs will drop dramatically. Some businesses quote prices in euros; prices in this chapter conform to quotes of individual businesses.

Tipping

Tipping in restaurants is optional, but increasingly expected in Prague. If there is no service charge you should certainly round up the bill to the next 10 or 20Kč (5% to 10% is normal in Prague). The same applies to tipping taxi drivers.

POST

General delivery mail can be addressed to Poste Restante, Pošta 1, in most major cities. For Prague, the address is Poste Restante, Jindřišská 14, 11000 Praha 1, Czech Republic. International postcards cost 11Kč.

TELEPHONE

All Czech phone numbers have nine digits – you have to dial all nine for any call, local or long distance. Make international calls at main post offices or directly from phonecard booths. The international access code is ☎ 00. The Czech Republic's country code is ☎ 420.

Payphones are widespread, some taking coins and some phonecards. Buy phonecards from post offices, hotels, newsstands and department stores for 150Kč or 1000Kč.

Mobile-phone coverage (GSM 900) is excellent. If you're from Europe, Australia

EMERGENCY NUMBERS

- Ambulance ☎ 155
- EU-wide Emergency Hotline ☎ 112
- Fire ☎ 150
- Motoring Assistance (ÚAMK) ☎ 1230
- Municipal Police ☎ 156
- State Police ☎ 158

or New Zealand, your own mobile phone should be compatible. It's best to purchase a Czech SIM card from any mobile-phone shop for around 450Kč (including 300Kč of calling credit) and make local calls at local rates. In this case you can't use your existing mobile number.

TOURIST INFORMATION

Czech Tourism (www.czechtourism.com) offices provide information about tourism, culture and business in the Czech Republic.

Austria (☎ 01-533 2193; info-at@czechtourism.com; Herrengasse 17, 1010 Vienna)

Canada (☎ 416-363 9928; info-ca@czechtourism.com; Czech Airlines Office, 401 Bay St, Suite 1510, Toronto, Ontario M5H 2Y4)

France (info-fr@czechtourism.com; Rrue Bonaparte 18, 75006 Paris)

Germany (info-de@czechtourism.com; Friedrichstrasse 206, 10969 Berlin).

Poland (☎ 22-629 29 16; info-pl@czechtourism.com; Al Róż 16, 00-555 Warsaw)

UK (☎ information line 207-631-0427; info -uk@czechtourism.com) Office not open to callers.

USA (☎ 212-288 0830; info-usa@czechtourism.com; 1109 Madison Ave, New York, NY 10028)

VISAS

Everyone requires a valid passport (or identity card for EU citizens) to enter the Czech Republic.

Citizens of EU and EEA countries do not need a visa for any type of visit. Citizens of Australia, Canada, Israel, Japan, New Zealand, Switzerland and the USA can stay for up to 90 days without a visa; other nationalities do need a visa.

Visas are not available at border crossings or at Prague's Ruzyně airport; you'll be refused entry if you need one and arrive without one.

Note that although the Czech Republic is now part of the EU, the visas issued by the Czech Republic are national and not Schengen visas. When the Czech Republic joined the EU, the country did not become part of the Schengen area. Therefore valid Schengen visas cannot be used for entering the Czech Republic. Note that the reverse of this is also true; Czech visas cannot be used to enter other EU Member States.

Visa regulations change from time to time, so check www.czech.cz or one of the Czech embassy websites listed on p151.

TRANSPORT IN THE CZECH REPUBLIC

GETTING THERE & AWAY

Air

The Czech Republic's main international airport is **Prague-Ruzyně** (☎ 220 113 314; www.csl .cz/en). The national carrier, **Czech Airlines** (ČSA; Map pp110-11; ☎ 239 007 007 www.csa.cz; V celnici 5, Nové Město), has direct flights to Prague from many European cities.

The main international airlines serving Prague:

Aer Lingus (EI; ☎ 224 815 373; www.aerlingus.ie)
Aeroflot (SU; ☎ 227 020 020; www.aeroflot.ru)
Air France (AF; ☎ 221 662 662; www.airfrance.com/cz)
Alitalia (AZ; ☎ 224 194 150; www.alitalia.com)
Austrian Airlines (OS; ☎ 227 231 231; www.aua.com)
British Airways (BA; ☎ 239 000 299; www.britishair ways.com)
Croatia Airlines (OU; ☎ 222 222 235; www.croatiaair lines.hr)
Czech Airlines (OK; ☎ 239 007 007; www.csa.cz)
EasyJet (EZY; www.easyjet.com)
El Al (LY; ☎ 224 226 624; www.elal.co.il)
FlyGlobespan (B4; ☎ 220 113 171; www.flyglobespan .com)
GermanWings (4U; www.germanwings.com)
JAT Airways (JU; ☎ 224 942 654; www.jat.com)
KLM (KL; ☎ 233 090 933; www.klm.com)
LOT (LO; ☎ 222 317 524; www.lot.com)
Lufthansa (LH; ☎ 224 422 911; www.lufthansa.com)
Malev (MA; ☎ 220 113 090; www.malev.com)
SAS (SK; ☎ 220 116 031; www.sas.se)
SkyEurope (NE; ☎ 900 14 15 16; www.skyeurope.com)
SmartWings (QS; ☎ 900 166 565; www.smartwings.net)
SN Brussels Airlines (SN; ☎ 220 116 352; www.flysn.com)
Turkish Airlines (TK; ☎ 234 708 708; www.turkishair lines.com)

Land

BUS

Prague's main international bus terminal is Florenc Bus Station, 600m north of the main train station. The peak season for bus travel is mid-June to the end of September, with daily buses to major European cities; outside this season, frequency falls to two or three a week.

The main international bus operators serving Prague:

Eurolines-Bohemia Euroexpress International (Map pp110-11; ☎ 224 218 680; www.bei.cz; ÚAN Praha

Florenc Bus Station, Křižíkova 4-6, Karlín; 🕙 8am-6pm Mon-Fri) Buses to destinations all over Europe.

Eurolines-Sodeli (Map pp110-11; ☎ 224 239 318; www .eurolines.cz, in Czech; Senovážné nám 6, Nové Město; 🕙 8am-6pm Mon-Fri) Links Prague with cities in Western and Central Europe. There is another Eurolines ticket office in Florenc bus station.

Capital Express (Map pp102-3; ☎ 220 870 368; www .capitalexpress.cz; I výstaviště 3. Holešovice; 🕙 8am-6pm Mon-Thu, 8am-5pm Fri) Daily bus service between London and Prague via Plzeň.

Student Agency (www.studentagency.cz) Central Prague (Map pp110-11; ☎ 224 999 666; Ječná 37; 🕙 9am-6pm Mon-Fri); Florenc bus station (Map pp110-11; ☎ 224 894 430; 🕙 9am-6pm Mon-Fri) Their big yellow buses link all major Czech cities and provide services to other cities in Western and Central Europe. Also have branches in major Czech cities.

Sample one-way fares from Prague include the following:

Bratislava 230Kč, 4¾ hours
Brno 130Kč, 2½ hours
Budapest 1250Kč, 7¼ hours
Frankfurt 1250Kč, 8½ hours
Salzburg 930Kč, 7½ hours
Vienna 300Kč, five hours
Warsaw 820Kč, 10½ hours
Wrocław 690Kč, 4¾ hours

CAR & MOTORCYCLE

Motorists can enter the country at any of the many border crossings marked on most road maps; see the map on p94 for all major 24-hour crossings.

You will need to buy a *nálepka* (motorway tax coupon) – on sale at border crossings, petrol stations and post offices – in order to use Czech motorways (100/200Kč for 10 days/one month).

TRAIN

International trains arrive at Prague's main train station (Praha-hlavní nádraží, or Praha hl. n.), or the outlying Holešovice (Praha Hol.) and Smíchov (Praha Smv.) stations.

Prague and Brno lie on the main line from Berlin and Dresden to Bratislava and Budapest, and from Hamburg and Berlin to Vienna. Trains from Frankfurt and Munich pass through Nuremberg and Plzeň on the way to Prague. There are also daily express trains between Prague and Warsaw via Wrocław or Katowice.

Sample one-way fares to Prague include the following:

Berlin €44, five hours
Bratislava €18, 4¾ hours
Frankfurt €61, 7½ hours
Kraków €28, 8½ hours
Salzburg €37, eight hours
Vienna €29, 4½ hours
Warsaw €36, 9½ hours

You can buy tickets in advance from Czech Railways (České dráhy, or ČD) ticket offices and various travel agencies. Seat reservations are compulsory on international trains. International tickets are valid for two months with unlimited stopovers. Inter-Rail (Zone D) passes are valid in the Czech Republic, but Eurail passes are not.

GETTING AROUND
Bicycle

The Czech Republic offers good opportunities for cycle touring. Cyclists should be careful as minor roads are often narrow and potholed. In towns cobblestones and tram tracks can be a dangerous combination, especially after rain. Theft is a problem, especially in Prague and other large cities, so always lock up your bike.

It's fairly easy to transport your bike on Czech trains. First purchase your train ticket and then take it with your bicycle to the railway luggage office. There you fill out a card, which will be attached to your bike; on the card you should write your name, address, departure station and destination.

The cost of transporting a bicycle is 40Kč to 60Kč depending on the length of the journey. You can also transport bicycles on most buses if they are not too crowded and if the bus driver is willing.

Bus

Within the Czech Republic buses are often faster, cheaper and more convenient than trains, though not as comfortable. Many bus routes have reduced frequency (or none) at weekends. Buses occasionally leave early, so get to the station at least 15 minutes before the official departure time.

Most services are operated by the national bus company **ČSAD** (☎ information line 900 144 444; www.csadbus.cz); you can check bus timetables online at www.idos.cz. Ticketing at main bus stations is computerised, so you can often book a seat ahead and be sure of a comfortable trip. Other stations are rarely computerised and you must line up and pay the driver.

The footnotes on printed timetables may drive you crazy. Note the following: crossed hammers means the bus runs on *pracovní dny* (working days; ie Monday to Friday only); a Christian cross means it runs on Sundays and public holidays; and numbers in circles refer to particular days of the week (1 is Monday, 2 Tuesday etc). *Jede* means 'runs', *nejede* means 'doesn't run' and *jede denne* means 'runs daily'. *V* is 'on', *od* is 'from' and *do* is 'to' or 'until'.

Fares are very reasonable; expect to pay around 80Kč for a 100km trip. Prague to Brno costs 130Kč, with Prague to Karlovy Vary around the same.

Car & Motorcycle

DRIVING LICENCE
Foreign driving licences are valid for up to 90 days. Strictly speaking, licences that do not include photo identification need an International Driving Permit as well, although this rule is rarely enforced – ordinary UK licences without a photo are normally accepted without comment.

FUEL
There are plenty of petrol stations, many open 24/7. Leaded petrol is available as *special* (91 octane) and *super* (96 octane), and unleaded as *natural* (95 octane) or *natural plus* (98 octane). The Czech for diesel is *nafta* or just *diesel*. *Autoplyn* (LPG gas) is available in every major town but at very few outlets. *Natural* costs around 30Kč per litre and diesel 25Kč.

HIRE
The main international car-rental chains all have offices in Prague. Small local companies offer better prices, but are less likely to have fluent, English-speaking staff; it's often easier to book by email than by phone. Typical rates for a Škoda Felicia are around 800Kč a day including unlimited kilometres, collision-damage waiver and value-added tax (VAT). Reputable local companies include the following:

Secco Car (Map pp102-3; ☎ 220 802 361; www.secco car.cz; Přístavní 39, Holešovice)

Vecar (Map pp102-3; ☎ 224 314 361; www.vecar.cz; Svatovítská 7, Dejvice)

West Car Praha (Map pp102-3; ☎ 235 365 307; www .westcarpraha.cz, in Czech; Veleslavínská 17, Veleslavín)

ROAD RULES
Road rules are the same as the rest of Europe. A vehicle must be equipped with a first-aid kit, a red-and-white warning triangle and a nationality sticker on the rear; the use of seat belts is compulsory. Drinking and driving is strictly forbidden – the legal blood alcohol level is zero. Police can hit you with on-the-spot fines of up to 2000Kč for speeding and other traffic offences (be sure to insist on a receipt).

Speed limits are 30km/h or 50km/h in built-up areas, 90km/h on open roads and 130km/h on motorways; motorbikes are limited to 80km/h. At level crossings over railway lines the speed limit is 30km/h. Beware of speed traps.

You need a motorway tax coupon (see opposite) to use the motorways; this is included with most rental cars.

Police often mount checkpoints, stopping vehicles for random checks. They are generally looking for locals driving without insurance or overloaded goods vehicles. If you are stopped, present your licence, passport and insurance or rental documents; as soon as the officer realises you're a tourist, you'll probably be waved on.

Local Transport
City buses and trams operate from around 4.30am to midnight daily. Tickets must be purchased in advance – they're sold at bus and train stations, newsstands and vending machines – and must be validated in the time-stamping machines found on buses and trams and at the entrance to metro stations. Tickets are hard to find at night, on weekends and out in residential areas, so carry a good supply.

Taxis have meters – ensure they're switched on.

Train
Czech Railways provides efficient train services to almost every part of the country. Fares are based on distance: one-way, 2nd-class fares cost around 64/120/224/424Kč for 50/100/200/400km. For travel within the Czech Republic only, the Czech Flexipass is available (from US$78 to US$138 for three to eight days travel in a 15-day period). The sales clerks at ticket counters rarely speak English, so write down your destination with the date and time you wish to travel.

Train categories include the following:

EC (EuroCity) Fast, comfortable international trains, stopping at main stations only, with 1st- and 2nd-class coaches; supplementary charge of 60Kč, reservations recommended.

Ex (express) As for IC (below), but no supplementary charge.

IC (InterCity) Long-distance and international trains with 1st- and 2nd-class coaches; supplement of 40Kč, reservations recommended.

Os (osobní) Slow trains using older rolling stock that stop in every one-horse town; 2nd-class only.

R (rychlík) The main domestic network of fast trains with 1st- and 2nd-class coaches and sleeper services; no sup-plement except for sleepers; express and *rychlík* trains are usually marked in red on timetables.

Sp (spěšný) Slower and cheaper than *rychlík* trains; 2nd class only.

If you need to purchase a ticket or pay a supple-ment on the train, advise the conductor *before* they ask for your ticket or you'll have to pay a fine. Some Czech train conductors may try to intimidate foreigners by pretending there's something wrong with their ticket. Don't pay any 'fine', 'supplement' or 'reservation fee' un-less you first get a *doklad* (written receipt).

Germany

The more you know about Germany the less you understand it. Think Germans only drink beer? Wait until you spend a week drinking nothing but excellent white wines in cute little wine bars. Think the food is all about sausage? Wait until you find your meal choices span the globe with nary a wurst in sight. Think Germans are closed minded and cold? Wait until one chats you up and you experience their good-natured humility and progressive world view.

What Churchill called Russia, 'a riddle wrapped in a mystery inside an enigma' could just have easily applied to Germany. Dismiss everything you think you know about it and start from scratch. As you travel Germany's regions you'll find that given all their differences they might as well be separate countries. And that's the real fun of visiting Germany – first having your stereotypes blown away and then trying to make sense of what you've found.

From the ongoing reinvention of Berlin to the celebration of tradition in Munich you will find contradictions everywhere. Your best course of action is to savour the richly financed museums and culture, revel in the nation's soul (the land) and join in the serious pursuit of consumption – be it beer, wine and yes, sausage, or something exotic. Through experience you'll relish one of Europe's richest cultures.

GERMANY

FAST FACTS

- **Area** 356,866 sq km (138 Luxembourgs, two-thirds of France)
- **Capital** Berlin
- **Currency** euro (€); A$1 = €0.60; ¥100 = €0.67; NZ$1 = €0.50; UK£1 = €1.48; US$1 = €0.78
- **Famous for** sausages, beer, culture, cars, history
- **Official Language** German
- **Phrases** *Guten Tag* (good day); *Auf Wiedersehen* (goodbye); *Ja/Nein* (yes/no); *Danke* (thank you); *Sprechen Sie Englisch?* (Do you speak English?)
- **Population** 83 million
- **Telephone Codes** country code ☎ 49; international access code ☎ 00

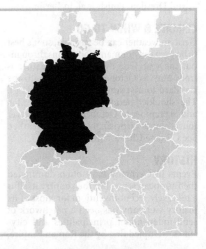

HIGHLIGHTS

- Party day and night in **Berlin** (p166); save sleep for somewhere else as there's no time with the clubs, museums, bars and mind-blowing culture.
- Time your journey for **Oktoberfest** (p215), Munich's big booze up, or just hang out in a beer garden.
- Seek out the villages less visited in the **Moselle Valley** (p245) home to the crisp white wine of the same name.
- Go cuckoo in the **Black Forest** (p237), discovering its chilly crags, misty peaks and endless trails.
- Get into the vibe of **Leipzig** (p191), the surprisingly vibrant star of the east.

ITINERARIES

- **One week** Starting in Berlin spend three days in and around the city, then head south through the wonderful little Bavarian town of Bamberg before ending up in Munich.
- **One month** Start in Munich for some Bavarian joy, then head up to the goofy castles in Füssen. Take in some of the Bavarian Alps and Lake Constance before the fun of Freiburg. Explore the Black Forest, soak up Baden-Baden and settle in for a boat voyage down the Rhine in Mainz. Detour up the Moselle to Trier and then hit Cologne. Pop up to Hamburg and Lübeck before heading back to Bavaria and Bamberg. Head north into the old East and Weimar and then enjoy Leipzig and Dresden. Finish it all in Berlin.

CLIMATE & WHEN TO GO

German weather can be variable, so it's best to be prepared for many conditions throughout the year. The most reliable weather is from May to October, coinciding with the standard tourist season (except for skiing). The shoulder periods (late March to May and September to October) can bring fewer tourists and surprisingly pleasant weather. See Climate Charts p585.

HISTORY

Events in Germany have often dominated the European stage, but the country itself is a relatively recent invention: for most of its history Germany has been a patchwork of semi-independent principalities and city-states, occupied first by the Roman Empire,

---

HOW MUCH?

- **Budget hotel room** €50
- **Tasty sausage meal** €6
- **Baden-Baden spa** €21
- **Bottle of Rhine wine** €6
- **U-Bahn ticket** €1.80

LONELY PLANET INDEX

- **1L petrol** €1.35
- **1L bottled water** €1
- **Beer (0.3L local Pils)** €2
- **Souvenir T-shirt** €15
- **Döner kebab** €2

---

then the Holy Roman Empire and finally the Austrian Habsburgs. Perhaps because of this, many Germans retain a strong regional identity, despite the momentous events that have occurred since.

The most significant medieval events in Germany were pan-European in nature – Martin Luther brought on the Protestant Reformation with his criticism of the Catholic Church in Wittenberg in 1517, a movement that sparked the Thirty Years' War. Germany became the battlefield of Europe, only regaining stability after the Napoleonic Wars with increasing industrialisation and the rise of the Kingdom of Prussia. In 1866 legendary Prussian 'Iron Chancellor' Otto von Bismarck brought the German states together, largely by force, and a united Germany emerged for the first time in 1871, under Kaiser Wilhelm I.

WWI & the Rise of Hitler

With the advent of the 20th century, Germany's rapid growth soon overtaxed the political talents of Kaiser Wilhelm II and led to mounting tensions with England, Russia and France. When war broke out in 1914, Germany's only ally was a weakened Austria-Hungary. Gruelling trench warfare on two fronts sapped the nation's resources, and by late 1918 Germany sued for peace. The kaiser abdicated and escaped to the Netherlands. Amid widespread public anger and unrest a new republic, which became known as the Weimar Republic, was proclaimed.

GERMANY

0 — 100 km
0 — 60 miles

DENMARK

SWEDEN

COPENHAGEN

Bornholm

NORTH SEA

Sylt Island

Amrum Island

North Frisian Islands

Schleswig

Heide

Kiel

BALTIC SEA

Rügen Island

Sassnitz

Binz

SCHLESWIG-HOLSTEIN

East Frisian Islands

Cuxhaven

Lübeck

Wismar

Warnemünde

Stralsund

Rostock

Wilhelmshaven

Hamburg

Schwerin

MECKLENBURG-WESTERN POMERANIA

HAMBURG

A24

A241

A19

A1

NETHERLANDS

BREMEN

Bremen

A7

Elbe River

A11

POLAND

A31

LOWER SAXONY

A1

SAXONY-ANHALT

BRANDENBURG

A19

BERLIN

Oder

Frankfurt/Oder

A30

A2

Hanover

Potsdam

A12

Hameln

A2

Magdeburg

A13

Badenwerder

Lötherstadt Wittenberg

River

NORTH RHINE-WESTPHALIA

Rhine

Goslar

Wernigerode

Dessau

A15

A44

Clausthal-Zellerfeld

Quedlinburg

A9

Dortmund

Göttingen

A7

Nordhausen

Halle

Leipzig

A13

Düsseldorf

Kassel

Meissen

Görlitz

Cologne

THURINGIA

Naumburg

Dresden

A4

Aachen

Marburg

Eisenach

Erfurt

Weimar

A45

A5

A4

SAXONY

Bonn

61

Rhine

HESSE

A9

A72

BELGIUM

Cochem

Koblenz

Frankfurt-am-Main

A7

PRAGUE

A48

A3

Wiesbaden

Hanau

RHINELAND-PALATINATE

Rüdesheim

Mainz

LUXEMBOURG

Trier

Moselle

Würzburg

Bamberg

Marktredwitz

A3

CZECH REPUBLIC

SAARLAND

Mannheim

Heidelberg

Nuremberg

Saarbrücken

A6

Rothenburg/Tauber

BAVARIA

Regensburg

A19

Karlsruhe

Dinkelsbühl

A3

Danube

Baden-Baden

Stuttgart

Nördlingen

River

Passau

A5

A8

A92

FRANCE

BADEN-WÜRTTEMBERG

Ulm

Augsburg

A81

A7

Munich

AUSTRIA

Freiburg

Donaueschingen

Constance

Lindau

A95

A8

Lake Constance

Füssen

Garmisch-Partenkirchen

Berchtesgaden

Oberstdorf

SWITZERLAND

LIECHTENSTEIN

GERMANY

The Treaty of Versailles in 1919 chopped huge areas off Germany and imposed heavy reparation payments. These were impossible to meet, and when France and Belgium occupied the Rhineland to ensure continued payments, the subsequent hyperinflation and miserable economic conditions provided fertile ground for political extremists. One of these was Adolf Hitler, an Austrian drifter, would-be artist and German army veteran.

Led by Hitler, the National Socialist German Workers' Party (or Nazi Party) staged an abortive coup in Munich in 1923. This landed Hitler in prison for nine months, during which time he wrote *Mein Kampf*.

From 1929 the worldwide economic Depression hit Germany hard, leading to unemployment, strikes and demonstrations. The Communist Party under Ernst Thälmann gained strength, but wealthy industrialists began to support the Nazis and police turned a blind eye to Nazi street thugs.

The Nazis increased their strength in general elections and in 1933 replaced the Social Democrats as the largest party in the Reichstag (parliament), with about one-third of the seats. Hitler was appointed chancellor and one year later assumed absolute control as *Führer* (leader).

WWII & the Division of Germany

From 1935 Germany began to re-arm and build its way out of depression with strategic public works such as the autobahns. Hitler reoccupied the Rhineland in 1936, and in 1938 annexed Austria and, following a compromise agreement with Britain and France, parts of Czechoslovakia.

All of this took place against a backdrop of growing racism at home. The Nuremberg Laws of 1935 deprived non-Aryans – mostly Jews and Roma (sometimes called Gypsies) – of their German citizenship and many other rights. On 9 November 1938, the horror escalated into *Kristallnacht* ('night of broken glass'), in which synagogues and Jewish cemeteries, property and businesses across Germany were desecrated, burnt or demolished.

In September 1939, after signing a pact that allowed both Stalin and himself a free hand in the east of Europe, Hitler attacked Poland, which led to war with Britain and France. Germany quickly occupied large parts of Europe, but after 1942 began to

suffer increasingly heavy losses. Massive bombing reduced Germany's cities to rubble, and the country lost 10% of its population. Germany accepted unconditional surrender in May 1945, soon after Hitler's suicide.

At the end of the war, the full scale of Nazi racism was exposed. 'Concentration camps', intended to rid Europe of people considered undesirable according to Nazi doctrine, had exterminated some six million Jews and one million more Roma, communists, homosexuals and others in what has come to be known as the Holocaust, history's first 'assembly line' genocide.

At conferences in Yalta and Potsdam, the Allies (the Soviet Union, the USA, the UK and France) redrew the borders of Germany, making it around 25% smaller than it had become after the Treaty of Versailles 26 years earlier. Germany was divided into four occupation zones.

In the Soviet zone of the country, the communist Socialist Unity Party (SED) won the 1946 elections and began a rapid nationalisation of industry. In September 1949 the Federal Republic of Germany (FRG) was created out of the three western zones; in response the German Democratic Republic (GDR) was founded in the Soviet zone the following month, with (East) Berlin as its capital.

From Division to Unity

As the West's bulwark against communism, the FRG received massive injections of US capital, and experienced rapid economic development (the *Wirschaftswunder* or 'economic miracle') under the leadership of Konrad Adenauer. The GDR, on the other hand, had to pay US$10 billion in war reparations to the Soviet Union and rebuild itself from scratch.

A better life in the west increasingly attracted skilled workers away from the miserable economic conditions in the east. As these were people the GDR could ill afford to lose, it built a wall around West Berlin in 1961 and sealed its border with the FRG.

In 1971 a change to the more flexible leadership of Erich Honecker in the east, combined with the *Ostpolitik* (East Politics) of FRG chancellor Willy Brandt, allowed an easier political relationship between the two Germanys. In the same year the four occupying powers formally accepted the division of Berlin.

Honecker's policies produced higher living standards in the GDR, yet East Germany barely managed to achieve a level of prosperity half that of the FRG. After Mikhail Gorbachev came to power in the Soviet Union in March 1985, the East German communists gradually lost Soviet backing.

Events in 1989 rapidly overtook the GDR government, which resisted pressure to introduce reforms. When Hungary relaxed its border controls in May 1989, East Germans began crossing to the west. Tighter travel controls resulted in would-be defectors taking refuge in the FRG's embassy in Prague. Meanwhile, mass demonstrations in Leipzig spread to other cities and Honecker was replaced by his security chief, Egon Krenz, who introduced cosmetic reforms. Then suddenly on 9 November 1989, a decision to allow direct travel to the west was mistakenly interpreted as the immediate opening of all GDR borders with West Germany. That same night thousands of people streamed into the west past stunned border guards. Millions more followed in the next few days, and the dismantling of the Berlin Wall began soon thereafter.

The trend at first was to reform the GDR but, in East German elections held in early 1990, citizens voted clearly in favour of the proreunification Christian Democratic Union (CDU). A Unification Treaty was drawn up to integrate East Germany into the Federal Republic of Germany, enacted on 3 October 1990. All-German elections were held on 2 December that year and, in the midst of national euphoria, the CDU-led coalition, which strongly favoured reunification, soundly defeated the Social Democrat opposition. CDU leader Helmut Kohl earned the enviable position of 'unification chancellor'.

Into the Millennium

In 1998 a coalition of Social Democrats, led by Gerhard Schröder, and Bündnis 90/die Grünen (the Greens party) took political office from Kohl and the CDU amid allegations of widespread financial corruption in the unification-era government.

Schröder and the SDP-Greens only narrowly managed to retain office in the 2002 general election. In 2004 things looked even worse. The slashing of university funding brought students out in protest for several weeks, and a botched reform of the public health insurance system was one of the most unpopular pieces of legislation ever, resulting in massive gains for the supposedly discredited CDU at subsequent local elections.

These advances paid off in September 2005 as a fumbling Schröder went down in national elections, although just barely. The winner by a very narrow margin was Angela Merkel and the CDU. Not only is Merkel the first woman chancellor in German history but she is also the first one who grew up in the old GDR.

A trained physicist who studied quantum chemistry, Merkel may find a use for her old training in her government. Because of the CDU's narrow victory it was forced into a 'grand coalition' with the SDP in which the latter gets half of the cabinet seats. Truly it's a situation where unexpected and unwanted reactions could be the norm.

Surprisingly, however, despite her tiny margin of victory, Merkel's popularity soared in the months after she took power. Perhaps it was her unusual background or her straight-talking style that had Germans of all stripes intrigued by what they saw. But with unemployment hitting 12% in 2006, Merkel and her unlikely coalition have their work cut out for them.

PEOPLE

Germany has a population of around 83 million, making it the most populous in Europe after Russia. Germany's main native minority is the tiny group of Slavonic Sorbs in the eastern states of Saxony and Brandenburg, who maintain their own folk traditions. In political and economic terms, Germany is Europe's most decentralised nation, but considerable variation in population density exists. The Ruhr district in the northern Rhineland has Germany's densest concentration of people and industry, while Mecklenburg-Western Pomerania in the northeastern corner is relatively sparsely settled. About one-third of the population lives in 84 cities, each with more than 100,000 people.

Immigration compensates for the extremely low birth rate among the established German population, and more than seven million foreigners now live in Germany. Most hail from Turkey, Italy, Greece and

GERMANY

the former Yugoslavia, and have arrived as 'guest workers' in the FRG since the early 1960s to work in lower-paid jobs. In 1999 archaic immigration laws dating back to 1913 were changed to make it easier for residents without German ancestry to gain citizenship. Integration is generally fairly successful, although larger immigrant communities tend to stick together.

RELIGION

The majority religions in Germany are Protestantism and Catholicism, which claim roughly equal numbers of followers. Some regions have higher concentrations of one branch – Bavaria is staunchly Catholic, for example.

The most significant minority religion is Islam, with about 1.8 million adherents, many of them immigrants. Around 60,000 Jews also live in Germany, little more than a tenth of pre-WWII numbers. Many are actually from the former Soviet Union, attracted by the relaxed immigration and citizenship deals offered around the time of reunification.

Germans who belong to a registered denomination have to pay a church tax on top of their income tax, usually around 10% of their salary. Unsurprisingly, fewer and fewer people are choosing to declare their religious affiliation!

ARTS

Germany's meticulously creative population has made major contributions to international culture, particularly during the 18th century when the Saxon courts at Weimar and Dresden attracted some of the greatest minds of Europe. With such rich traditions to fall back on, inspiration has seldom been in short supply for the new generations of German artists, despite the upheavals of the country's recent history.

Literature

The undisputed colossus of the German arts was Johann Wolfgang von Goethe: poet, dramatist, painter, politician, scientist, philosopher, landscape gardener and perhaps the last European to achieve the Renaissance ideal of excellence in many fields. His greatest work, the drama *Faust*, is the definitive version of the legend, showing the archetypal human search for meaning and knowledge.

Goethe's close friend Friedrich Schiller was a poet, dramatist and novelist. His most famous work is the dramatic cycle *Wallenstein*, based on the life of a treacherous general of the Thirty Years' War who plotted to make himself arbiter of the empire. Schiller's other great play, *William Tell*, dealt with the right of the oppressed to rise against tyranny.

On the scientific side, Alexander von Humboldt contributed much to environmentalism through his studies of the relationship of plants and animals to their physical surroundings. His contemporary, the philosopher Georg Wilhelm Friedrich Hegel, created an all-embracing classical philosophy that is still influential today.

Postwar literature in both Germanys was influenced by the politically focused Gruppe 47. It included writers such as Günter Grass, winner of the 1999 Nobel Prize for Literature, whose modern classic, *Die Blechtrommel* (The Tin Drum), humorously follows German history through the eyes of a young boy who refuses to grow up. Christa Wolf, an East German novelist and Gruppe 47 writer, won high esteem in both Germanys. Her 1963 story *Der geteilte Himmel* (Divided Heaven) tells of a young woman whose fiancé abandons her for life in the West.

A wave of recent novelists has addressed modern history in a lighter fashion. *Helden wie wir* (Heroes Like Us) by Thomas Brussig, an eastern German, tells the story of a man whose penis brings about the collapse of the Berlin Wall, while the GDR's demise is almost incidental to the eponymous barfly in Sven Regener's *Herr Lehmann* (Mr Lehmann). Also from Berlin is Russian-born Wladimir Kaminer, whose books document the stranger-than-fiction lives of his many friends and acquaintances in the capital. He's currently *the* hot author and *Russian Disco* has been translated into English. There's also acclaim for Robert Löhr's *Der Schachautomat* (The Chess Automat), a novel about a 19th-century puppet that plays chess.

Cinema & TV

Since the foundation of the UFA studios in Potsdam in 1917, Germany has had an active and successful film industry. Marlene Dietrich (1901–92) became the country's first international superstar and sex symbol, starting out in silent films and later moving to Hollywood. Director Fritz Lang also made a name for himself, with complex films like *Metropolis* (1926) and *M* (1931).

During the Third Reich, the arts were devoted mainly to propaganda, with grandiose projects and realist art extolling the virtues of German nationhood. The best-known Nazi-era director was Leni Riefenstahl (1902–2003) whose *Triumph of the Will* (1934), depicting the Nuremberg rallies, won great acclaim but later rendered her unemployable. The controversy surrounding her personal politics dogged her for much of her life.

The 1960s and 1970s saw a great revival of German cinema, spearheaded by energetic, politically aware young directors such as Rainer Werner Fassbinder, Wim Wenders, Volker Schlöndorff and Margarethe von Trotta.

Most recently, Wolfgang Becker's GDR comedy *Good Bye Lenin!* (2003) was a surprise smash hit worldwide. One of the most powerful recent movies has been Marc Rothemund's *Sophie Scholl: The Final Days* (2006). It's a harrowing true story about a woman who protested against the Nazis in Munich and paid the ultimate price.

Meanwhile, German TV still shows a real predilection for showing musical variety shows long on hokum and schmaltz. After a few beers they're a hoot.

Music

Forget brass bands and oompah music – few countries can claim the impressive musical heritage of Germany. Even a partial list of household names would have to include Johann Sebastian Bach, Georg Friedrich Händel, Ludwig van Beethoven, Richard Strauss, Robert Schumann, Johannes Brahms, Felix Mendelssohn-Bartholdy, Richard Wagner and Gustav Mahler, all of whom are celebrated in museums, exhibitions and festivals around the country.

These musical traditions continue to thrive: the Berlin Philharmonic, Dresden Opera and Leipzig Orchestra are known around the world, and musical performances are hosted almost daily in every major theatre in the country.

Germany has also made significant contributions to the contemporary music

scene. Internationally renowned artists include punk icon Nina Hagen, '80s balloon girl Nena, and rock bands from the Scorpions to Die Toten Hosen and current darlings Wir sind Helden. Gothic and hard rock are disproportionately well-followed in Germany, largely thanks to the success of death-obsessed growlers Rammstein.

For real innovation, though, the German dance music scene is second to none, particularly in Frankfurt-am-Main and Berlin. Kraftwerk pioneered the original electronic sounds, which were then popularised in raves and clubs such as Berlin's Tresor in the early '90s. Paul van Dyk was among the first proponents of euphoric trance, which pushed club music firmly into the commercial mainstream; DJs such as Ian Pooley, Westbam and Ellen Allien now play all over the world. Producers and remixers Jazzanova also have a great worldwide reputation on the more jazzy, down tempo side of things.

Meanwhile what's old is new. Max Raabe and his Palast Orchester have been touring the country to sold out performances of the classic Berlin cabaret-style music of the 1920s and 1930s. Less old but still new, many local groups such as Wir sind Helden, Silbermond, Tomte and Kettcar have attracted a loyal following by playing the festival circuit with German-language rock.

Architecture

The scope of German architecture is such that it could easily be the focus of an entire visit. The first great wave of buildings came with the Romanesque period (800–1200), examples of which can be found at Trier Cathedral, the churches of Cologne and the chapel of Charlemagne's palace in Aachen.

The Gothic style (1200–1500) is best viewed at Freiburg's Münster cathedral, Cologne's Dom (cathedral) and the Marienkirche in Lübeck. Red-brick Gothic structures are common in the north of Germany, with buildings such as Schwerin's Dom and Stralsund's Nikoliakirche.

For classic baroque, Balthasar Neumann's superb Residenz in Würzburg, the magnificent cathedral in Passau and the many classics of Dresden's old centre are must-sees. The neoclassical period of the 19th century was led by Karl Friedrich Schinkel, whose name crops up all over Germany.

In 1919 Walter Gropius founded the Bauhaus movement in an attempt to meld theoretical concerns of architecture with the practical problems faced by artists and craftspeople. The Bauhaus flourished in Dessau, but with the arrival of the Nazis, Gropius left for Harvard University.

Albert Speer was Hitler's favourite architect, known for his pompous neoclassical buildings and grand plans to change the face of Berlin. Most of his epic works ended up unbuilt or flattened by WWII.

Frankfurt shows Germany's take on the modern highrise. For a glimpse of the future of German architecture, head to Potsdamer Platz, Leipziger Platz and the new government area north of the Reichstag in Berlin, which are becoming glitzy swathes of glass, concrete and chrome.

Visual Arts

The Renaissance came late to Germany but flourished once it took hold, replacing the predominant Gothic style. The draughtsman Albrecht Dürer of Nuremberg was one of the world's finest portraitists, as was the prolific Lucas Cranach the Elder, who worked in Wittenberg for more than 45 years. The baroque period brought great sculpture, including works by Andreas Schlüter in Berlin, while romanticism produced some of Germany's most famous paintings, best exemplified by Caspar David Friedrich and Otto Runge.

At the turn of the 20th century, expressionism established itself with great names like Swiss-born Paul Klee and the Russian-born painter Wassily Kandinsky, who were also associated with the Bauhaus design school. By the 1920s, art had become more radical and political, with artists like George Grosz, Otto Dix and Max Ernst exploring the new concepts of Dada and surrealism. Käthe Kollwitz is one of the era's few major female artists, known for her social realist drawings.

The only works encouraged by the Nazis were of the epic style of propaganda artists like Mjölnir; nonconforming artists such as sculptor Ernst Barlach and painter Emil Nolde were declared 'degenerate' and their pieces destroyed or appropriated for secret private collections.

Since 1945 abstract art has been a mainstay of the German scene, with key figures like Joseph Beuys, Monica Bonviciniand and Anselm Kiefer achieving worldwide reputations. Leipzig has recently emerged as a hotspot for art. Figurative painters like Neo Rauch are generating much acclaim.

Theatre & Dance

In the 1920s Berlin was the theatrical capital of Germany; its most famous practitioner was the poet and playwright Bertolt Brecht (1898–1956). Brecht introduced Marxist concepts into his plays, aiming to encourage moral debate by detaching the audience from what was happening on stage.

Today Berlin once again has the most dynamic theatre scene in the country, as Volksbühne director Frank Castorf vies with Schaubühne head Thomas Ostermeier to capture the attention of young audiences neglected by the major stages, choosing mainly modern, provocative works. Dance, too, is undergoing a renaissance – although it is in Frankfurt. American William Forsythe has put together what is possibly the world's most innovative dance troupe, the Forsythe Company, which tours almost constantly.

SPORT

Football (soccer) is the number one spectator sport in Germany, as in most other European countries. Germany hosted the cup in 2006 in new or rebuilt stadiums all over the country. Although Germany finished third (Italy beat France in the final in Berlin), it was widely praised for hosting a fantastic series of matches and many Germans took great pride in their time on the world stage.

The German national team actually did better than many expected, even if it couldn't add another World Cup victory to its previous two. The Bundesliga is the top national league, with seasons running from September to June; notable top-flight teams include Bayern München, Borussia Dortmund and Hertha BSC (Berlin's major team). The DFB (www.dfb.de) is the national body responsible for all levels of the game.

International sports are also very well-attended, especially when the relevant national teams are in form; major tennis, athletics, Grand Prix, swimming, cycling and water polo events are all features of the German sporting calendar.

ENVIRONMENT
The Land
Germany covers 356,866 sq km and can be divided from north to south into several geographical regions.

The Northern Lowlands are a broad expanse of flat, low-lying land that sweeps across the northern third of the country from the Netherlands into Poland. The landscape is characterised by moist heaths interspersed with pastures and farmland.

The complex Central Uplands region divides northern Germany from the south. Extending from the deep schisms of the Rhineland massifs to the Black Forest, the Bavarian Forest, the Ore Mountains and the Harz Mountains, these low mountain ranges are Germany's heartland. The Rhine and Main Rivers, important waterways for inland shipping, cut through the southwest of this region. With large deposits of coal as well as favourable transport conditions, this was one of the first regions in Germany to undergo industrialisation.

The Alpine Foothills, wedged between the Danube and the Alps, are typified by subalpine plateaus and rolling hills, and moors in eastern regions around the Danube.

Germany's Alps lie entirely within Bavaria and stretch from the large, glacially formed Lake Constance in the west to Berchtesgaden in Germany's southeastern corner. Though lower than the mountains to their south, many summits are well above 2000m, rising dramatically from the Alpine Foothills to the 2962m Zugspitze, Germany's highest mountain.

Wildlife
Few species of flora and fauna are unique to Germany. Unique, however, is the importance Germans place on their forests, the prettiest of which are mixed-species deciduous forests planted with beech, oak, maple and birch. You'll find that many cities even have their own *Stadtwald* (city forest). Alpine regions bloom in spring with orchids, cyclamen, gentians, edelweiss and more; and the heather blossom on the Lüneburg Heath, north of Hanover, is stunning in August.

Apart from human beings, common mammals include deer, wild pigs, rabbits, foxes and hares. The chances of seeing these in summer are fairly good, especially in eastern Germany. On the coasts you will find seals and, throughout Germany, falcons, hawks, storks and migratory geese are a common sight.

National Parks
Berchtesgaden (in the Bavarian Alps), the Wattenmeer parks in Schleswig-Holstein, Lower Saxony and Hamburg, and the Unteres Odertal, a joint German-Polish endeavour, are highlights among Germany's 13 national parks. There are also a number of Unesco-listed sites in Germany, including the Wartburg castle in Eisenach.

Environmental Issues
Germans are fiercely protective of their natural surroundings. Households and businesses participate enthusiastically in waste-recycling programmes. A refund system applies to a wide range of glass bottles and jars, while containers for waste paper and glass can be found in each neighbourhood. The government is a signatory of the major international treaties on climate change and runs its own campaigns to save energy and reduce $CO2$ emissions domestically; a controversial 'eco-tax' was recently added to the price of petrol.

FOOD & DRINK
Staples & Specialities
Wurst (sausage), in its hundreds of forms, is by far the most universal main dish. Regional favourites include bratwurst (spiced sausage), *Weisswurst* (veal sausage) and *Blutwurst* (blood sausage). Other popular main dishes include *Rippenspeer* (spare ribs), *Rotwurst* (black pudding), *Rostbrätl* (grilled meat), *Putenbrust* (turkey breast) and many forms of schnitzel (breaded pork or veal cutlet).

Potatoes feature prominently in German meals, as *Bratkartoffeln* (fried), *Kartoffelpüree* (mashed), Swiss-style *Rösti* (grated then fried) or *Pommes Frites* (french fries); a Thuringian speciality is *Klösse*, a ball of mashed and raw potato that is then cooked into a dumpling. A similar Bavarian version is the *Knödel*. *Spätzle*, a noodle variety from Baden-Württemberg, is a common alternative.

Germans are keen on rich desserts. Popular choices are the *Schwarzwälder Kirschtorte* (Black Forest cherry cake) – one worthwhile tourist trap – as well as endless varieties of

GERMANY

Apfeltasche (apple pastry). In the north you're likely to find berry *mus*, a sort of compote. Desserts and pastries are also often enjoyed during another German tradition, the 4pm coffee break.

DRINKS

Beer is the national beverage and it's one cultural phenomenon that must be adequately explored. The beer is excellent and relatively cheap. Each region and brewery has its own distinctive taste and body.

Vollbier is 4% alcohol by volume, *Export* is 5% and *Bockbier* is 6%. *Helles Bier* is light, while *dunkles Bier* is dark. *Export* is similar to, but much better than, typical international brews, while the *Pils* is more bitter. *Alt* is darker and more full-bodied. A speciality is *Weizenbier,* which is made with wheat instead of barley malt and served in a tall, 500mL glass. Nonalcoholic beers such as *Clausthaler* are also popular.

Eastern Germany's best beers hail from Saxony, especially Radeberger from near Dresden and Wernesgrüner from the Erzgebirge on the Czech border. *Berliner Weisse* is a low-alcohol wheat beer mixed with woodruff or raspberry syrup, seen as a bit of a tourist drink by locals. The breweries of Cologne produce *Kölsch*, always served in 200mL glasses to keep it fresh; in Bamberg *Schlenkerla Rauchbier* is smoked to a dark-red colour.

German wines are exported around the world, and for good reason. They are inexpensive and typically white, light and intensely fruity. A *Weinschorle* or *Spritzer* is white wine mixed with mineral water. The Rhine and Moselle Valleys are the classic wine-growing regions.

The most popular nonalcoholic choices are mineral water and soft drinks, coffee and fruit or black tea. Bottled water almost always comes bubbly *(mit Kohlensäure)* – order *ohne Kohlensäure* if you're bothered by bubbles.

Where to Eat & Drink

Increasingly, German towns of any size have bright and modern bistro-type restaurants serving a wide range of fresh and creative food. In addition you'll find no shortage of ethnic foods; Italian, Turkish, Greek and Chinese are all popular. Most pubs serve basic German food. If you're on a low budget, you can get a feed at stand-up food stalls *(Schnellimbiss* or *Imbiss)*. The food is usually reasonable and filling, ranging from döner kebabs to traditional German sausages with beer.

Much of the German daily and social life revolves around daytime cafés, which often serve meals and alcohol as well as coffee. The late-opening variety are great places to meet people.

For self-caterers, supermarkets are inexpensive and have a decent range. Make a point of buying your drinks in supermarkets if your budget is tight.

Students can eat cheaply (though not always well) at university *Mensa* (caféterias). ID is not always checked.

Vegetarians & Vegans

Most German restaurants will have at least a couple of vegetarian dishes on the menu, although it is advisable to check anything that doesn't specifically say it's meat-free, as bacon and chicken stock both seem to be common undeclared ingredients in German cuisine. Asian and Indian restaurants will generally be quite happy to make vegetarian dishes on demand. Vegans may find themselves having to explain exactly what they do and don't eat to get something suitable.

Habits & Customs

Restaurants always display their menus outside with prices, but watch for daily or lunch specials chalked onto blackboards. Lunch is the main meal of the day; getting a main meal in the evening is never a problem, but you may find that the dish or menu of the day only applies to lunch.

Rather than leaving money on the table, tip when you pay by stating a rounded-up figure or saying '*es stimmt so*' (that's the right amount). A tip of 10% is generally more than sufficient.

BERLIN

☎ 030 / pop 3.45 million

Apologies to Samuel Johnson, who coined the compliment to London, but in the 21st century it's he, or she, who is tired of *Berlin* who is tired of life. Even the English capital can't currently compete with the pace of change in its reborn German counterpart.

Just two decades ago this was still a divided city, split between the rival Cold War blocs of communist east and capitalist west. Today it's the European Shanghai, where building cranes watch over the skyline, and world-beating architectural icons – Norman Foster's Reichstag dome, Daniel Libeskind's Jewish Museum and Peter Eisenman's Holocaust Memorial – pop up every few years.

Renowned for its diversity and tolerance, its alternative culture, its night-owl stamina and its affordability it might be. But the best thing about the German capital is the way it reinvents itself and isn't shackled by its powerful – and still palpable – history.

Tills ring in the halls of the gleaming Potsdamer Platz complex just down the road from Hitler's bunker, university stallholders sell novels opposite the site of a major book-burning and bits of the 'Berlin Wall' (they're not) are hawked everywhere alongside döner kebabs and Wurst.

Students rub shoulders with Russian émigrés, fashion boutiques inhabit monumental GDR buildings, and the nightlife has long left the American sector, as clubbers watch the sun rise in the city's east.

In short, all human life is here, and don't expect to get much sleep.

HISTORY

United, divided, united again, Berlin has a rollercoaster past. The merger of two medieval trading posts, it enjoyed its first stint as a capital when in 1701 it became the leading city of the state of Brandenburg-Prussia. Under Prussian King Friedrich I and his son, Friedrich II, it flourished culturally and politically.

The Industrial Revolution, when commercial giants like Siemens emerged, also boosted the city. As workers flooded to Berlin's factories, its population doubled between 1850 and 1870. 'Deutschland' was a latecomer to the table of nationhood, but in 1871 Berlin was again proclaimed a capital, this time of the newly unified Germany.

By 1900 the city was home to almost two million people, but it fell into decline after WWI. Defeated and left to pay heavy war reparations, Germany suffered economic crisis and hyperinflation. There was a brief, early communist uprising in the capital, led by Karl Liebknecht and Rosa Luxemburg (whose names now adorn East Berlin

streets). However, that was quickly quashed and during the following Weimar Republic (1919–1933) Berlin gained a reputation for decadence. Cabaret, the savage political theatre of Bertolt Brecht (see p181), expressionist art and jazz all flourished as Berliners partied to forget their troubles.

Worse horrors arose with Hitler and the Third Reich. Berlin became a showground for Nazi power from the mid-1930s – including during the 1936 Olympics – and so suffered heavily during WWII. During the 'Battle of Berlin' from August 1943 to March 1944, British bombers hammered the city nightly. The Soviets also shelled Berlin and invaded from the east.

In August 1945 the Potsdam Conference (see Schloss Cecilienhof, p184) split the capital into zones occupied by the four victorious powers – the USA, Britain, France and the Soviet Union. In June 1948 the three Western Allies introduced a separate currency and administration in their sectors. In response, the Soviets blockaded West Berlin. Only a huge airlift by the Allies managed to keep the city stocked with food and supplies. In October 1949 East Berlin became the capital of the GDR.

The Berlin Wall, built in August 1961, was originally intended to prevent the drain of skilled labour from the East, but soon became a Cold War symbol. For decades, East Berlin and West Berlin developed separately, until Hungarians breached the Iron Curtain in May 1989 and the Berlin Wall followed on 9 November. By 1 July 1990, when the western Deutschmark was adopted in the GDR, the Wall was being hacked to pieces. The Unification Treaty signed on 3 October that year designated Berlin the official capital of Germany, and in June 1991 the parliament voted to move the seat of government from Bonn back to Berlin. In 1999, that was finally achieved.

Not everything has been plain sailing since. Without the huge national subsidies provided during the decades of division, the newly unified Berlin has struggled economically. In 2001 the centre-right mayor resigned amid corruption allegations, leaving the city effectively bankrupt. Current centre-left mayor Klaus Wowereit is popular but has made few inroads into the crisis, and the city's public debts now exceed €58 billion. Wowereit tries to look on the bright

---

BERLIN IN TWO DAYS

Investigate the **Brandenburg Gate** (opposite) area, including the **Reichstag** (p172) and the **Holocaust Memorial** (p172). Walk east along Unter den Linden, stopping at the **Bebelplatz book-burning memorial** (p173). Veer through the **Museumsinsel** (p173) for window-shopping and café-hopping through **Hackescher Markt** (p173). In the evening, explore the bars of Prenzlauer Berg, along Kastanieanallee, Pappelallee and the 'LSD' triangle between Lette-, Stargarder- and Dunckerstrasse. Stop in **Wohnzimmer** (p182).

Start the next day at the **East Side Gallery** (p175) remnant of the Berlin Wall, before heading for **Checkpoint Charlie** (p175) and the nearby **Jewish Museum** (p175). Take the U-Bahn to **Kurfürstendamm** (p175) and catch a scenic bus 100 back to the **Fernsehturm** (p174). Later, explore Friedrichshain nightlife around Simon-Dach-Strasse and Boxhagener Platz and perhaps go clubbing – **Watergate** (p181) is good. Alternatively head for the **Philharmonie** (p181) or the **Berliner Ensemble** (p181).

---

side, once famously declaring, 'Berlin is poor, but sexy'. He got that right, at least.

ORIENTATION

Standing at Berlin's Brandenburg Gate, on the former east–west divide, you can see many major sights. Looking east, your eye follows the road Unter den Linden, past the Museumsinsel (Museum Island) and the Spree River, to the needle-shaped Fernsehturm (TV tower) at Alexanderplatz.

If you turn west, you face the golden Siegessäule (Victory Column) along the equally huge thoroughfare of Strasse des 17 Juni, which cuts through the middle of Berlin's central park, the Tiergarten. To your right, just near the Brandenburg Gate, is the glass-domed Reichstag (Parliament) and beyond that the new government district and even newer Hauptbahnhof (main train station). The cluster of skyscrapers diagonally off to the left, with the unusual, circus-tent roof, is Potsdamer Platz.

On the other, far west side of the Tiergarten, out of sight near Zoo station, lies the one-time centre of West Berlin, including the shopping street of the Kurfürstendamm (or 'Ku'damm').

Although wealthier, more mature Berliners still happily frequent the west, the eastern districts are the most vibrant. Even 'Mitte', or the centre, now lies east of the former Wall. As Mitte heads northeast, it merges into the trendy district of Prenzlauer Berg. Friedrichshain, another nightlife hotspot, is found several kilometres east of the centre, around Ostbahnhof.

Kreuzberg, south of Mitte, was the alternative hub of West Berlin and is still hanging in there, with some interesting restaurants and bars. So, too, are the better-heeled southwestern districts of Charlottenburg, Schöneberg and Wilmersdorf.

Maps

Excellent free maps of the centre are available from tourist offices and many hotels. If you're heading to the suburbs, newsagents and bookshops sell full-size maps from publishers Falk, Michelin and ADAC.

INFORMATION
Bookshops

Dussman (Map pp170-1; ☎ 205 1111; Friedrichstrasse 90; ⏰ 10am-10pm Mon-Sat; Ⓜ S-Bahn Friedrichstrasse) Books (including in English), CDs and DVDs over five huge floors.

Discount Card

Berlin-Potsdam Welcome Card (48/72hr card €16/22) Free public transport, plus museum and entertainment discounts.

Internet Access

@ Internet (Map p176; ☎ 2977 6270; 1st fl, main hall, Ostbahnhof; per 15 min €1; ⏰ 10am-10pm)

Al Hamra (Map pp170-1; ☎ 4285 0095; Raumerstrasse 16; per 15 min €1; ⏰ from 10am; Ⓜ Eberswalder Strasse)

easyInternetcafé (Map p177; ☎ 7870 6446; www .easyInternetcafe.com; Kurfürstendamm 224; ⏰ 6.30am-2am; Ⓜ Kurfürstendamm/Zoologischer Garten) One of several throughout the city.

Surf & Sushi (Map pp170-1; ☎ 2838 4898; Oranienburger Strasse 17; per 30 min €2.50; ⏰ from noon Mon-Sat, from 1pm Sun; Ⓜ Oranienburger Strasse/ Hackescher Markt)

GREATER BERLIN

Laundry

Schnell und Sauber (€5; ☺ 6am-11pm) Charlottenburg (Map p177; Uhlandstrasse 53); Mitte (Map pp170-1; Torstrasse 115)

Medical Services

Kassenärztliche Bereitschaftsdienst (Public Physicians' Emergency Service; ☎ 310 031) Phone referral service.

Post

Post office (Map pp170-1; Georgenstrasse 12; ☺ 8am-10pm) Inside Friedrichstrasse station.

Tourist Information

Berlin Tourismus Marketing (☎ 250 025; www.berlin -tourist-information.de) Europa-Center (Map p177; Budapester Strasse 45; ☺ 10am-7pm Mon-Sat, 10am-6pm Sun); Brandenburger Tor (Map pp170-1; ☺ 10am-6pm); Fernsehturm (Map pp170-1; ☺ 10am-6pm)
EurAide (Map p177; www.euraide.de; Zoo Station; ☺ 8.30am-noon Mon-Sat Jun-Oct, 1-4.45pm Mon-Fri Nov-May) English-language service.

DANGERS & ANNOYANCES

Berlin is generally safe and tolerant. Walking alone at night on city streets isn't risky.

Begging on the street and in the U-Bahn is increasing, but aggressive demands are rare. Take the usual precautions against theft in major stations.

SIGHTS

Unless otherwise indicated, where sights are grouped together they are all accessed by the same station listed at the beginning of the section.

Brandenburg Gate

Finished in 1791 as one of 18 city gates, the neoclassical **Brandenburger Tor** (Map pp170-1; Pariser Platz; Ⓜ S-Bahn Unter den Linden) became an east–west crossing point after the Wall was built in 1961. A symbol of Berlin's division, it was a place US presidents loved to grandstand. John F Kennedy passed by in 1963. Ronald Reagan appeared in 1987 to appeal to the Russian leader, 'Mr Gorbachev, tear down this wall!'. In 1989, more than 100,000 Germans poured through it, as the Wall fell. Five years later, Bill Clinton somewhat belatedly noted: 'Berlin is free'. The crowning Quadriga statue, a winged

MITTE & PRENZLAUER BERG

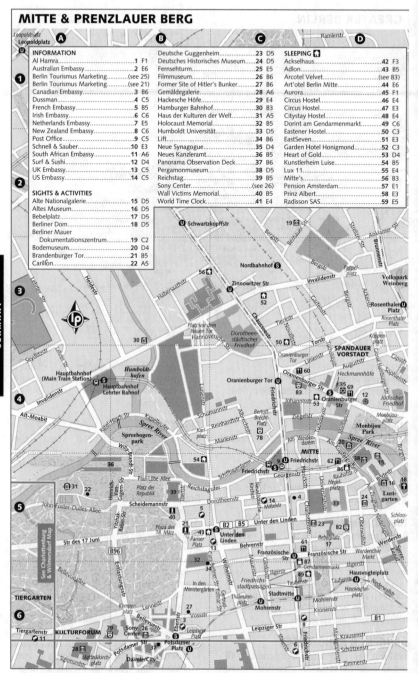

INFORMATION
Al Hamra.......................................1 F1
Australian Embassy.......................2 E6
Berlin Tourism Marketing..........(see 25)
Berlin Tourism Marketing..........(see 21)
Canadian Embassy........................3 B6
Dussman.......................................4 C5
French Embassy.............................5 B5
Irish Embassy.................................6 C6
Netherlands Embassy....................7 E5
New Zealand Embassy....................8 C6
Post Office....................................9 C5
Schnell & Sauber.........................10 E3
South African Embassy.................11 A6
Surf & Sushi................................12 D4
UK Embassy..................................13 C5
US Embassy..................................14 C5

SIGHTS & ACTIVITIES
Alte Nationalgalerie.....................15 D5
Altes Museum..............................16 D5
Bebelplatz....................................17 D5
Berliner Dom................................18 D5
Berliner Mauer
    Dokumentationszentrum...........19 C2
Bodemuseum................................20 D4
Brandenburger Tor.......................21 B5
Carillon.......................................22 A5

Deutsche Guggenheim.................23 D5
Deutsches Historisches Museum...24 D5
Fernsehturm.................................25 E5
Filmmuseum.................................26 B6
Former Site of Hitler's Bunker.....27 B6
Gemäldegalerie............................28 A6
Hackesche Höfe............................29 E4
Hamburger Bahnhof.....................30 B3
Haus der Kulturen der Welt..........31 A5
Holocaust Memorial.....................32 B5
Humboldt Universität...................33 D5
Lift...34 B6
Neue Synagogue..........................35 D4
Neues Kanzleramt........................36 B5
Panorama Observation Deck.........37 B6
Pergamonmuseum........................38 D5
Reichstag....................................39 B5
Sony Center.............................(see 26)
Wall Victims Memorial..................40 B5
World Time Clock.........................41 E4

SLEEPING
Acekselhaus................................42 F3
Adlon...43 B5
Arcotel Velvet.........................(see 83)
Art'otel Berlin Mitte....................44 E6
Aurora.......................................45 F1
Circus Hostel...............................46 E4
Circus Hostel...............................47 E3
Citystay Hostel............................48 E4
Dorint am Gendarmenmarkt.........49 C6
Eastener Hostel...........................50 C3
EastSeven...................................51 C3
Garden Hotel Honigmond.............52 C3
Heart of Gold.............................53 D4
Kunstlerheim Luise.......................54 B5
Lux 11.......................................55 E4
Mitte's.......................................56 B3
Pension Amsterdam......................57 E1
Prinz Albert................................58 E3
Radisson SAS..............................59 E5

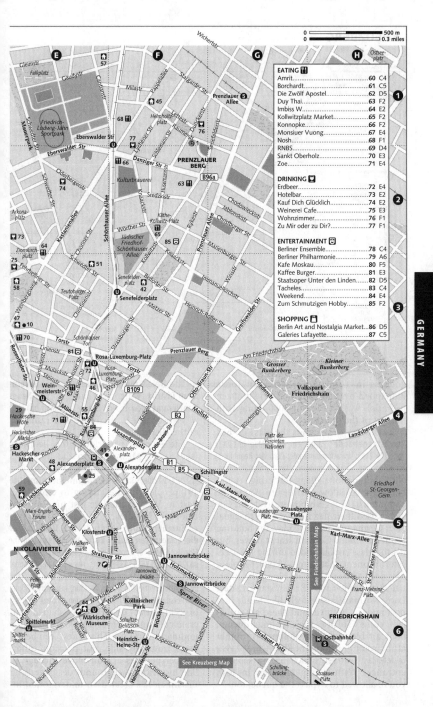

EATING
Amrit..60 C4
Borchardt...................................61 C5
Die Zwölf Apostel.....................62 D5
Duy Thai....................................63 F2
Imbiss W....................................64 E2
Kollwitzplatz Market.................65 F2
Konnopke...................................66 F2
Monsiuer Vuong........................67 E4
Nosh...68 F1
RNBS..69 D4
Sankt Oberholz..........................70 E3
Zoe...71 E4

DRINKING
Erdbeer.......................................72 E4
Hotelbar.....................................73 E2
Kauf Dich Glücklich...................74 E2
Weinerei Cafe.............................75 E3
Wohnzimmer..............................76 F1
Zu Mir oder zu Dir?...................77 F1

ENTERTAINMENT
Berliner Ensemble.......................78 C4
Berliner Philharmonie.................79 A6
Kafe Moskau...............................80 F5
Kaffee Burger.............................81 E3
Staatsoper Unter den Linden......82 D5
Tacheles......................................83 C4
Weekend.....................................84 E4
Zum Schmutzigen Hobby............85 F2

SHOPPING
Berlin Art and Nostalgia Market...86 D5
Galeries Lafayette........................87 C5

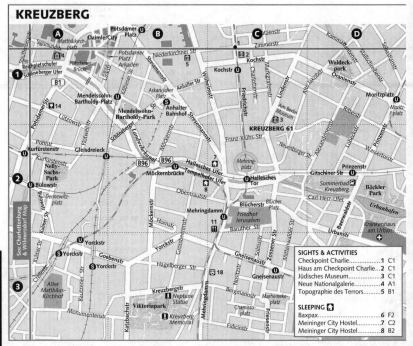

KREUZBERG

SIGHTS & ACTIVITIES	
Checkpoint Charlie	1 C1
Haus am Checkpoint Charlie	2 C1
Jüdisches Museum	3 C1
Neue Nationalgalerie	4 A1
Topographie des Terrors	5 B1

SLEEPING	
Baxpax	6 F2
Meininger City Hostel	7 C2
Meininger City Hostel	8 B2

goddess in a horse-drawn chariot (once kidnapped by Napoleon and briefly taken to Paris), was cleaned in 2000 along with the rest of the structure.

Just to the west stands the glass-domed **Reichstaggebäude** (Parliament Bldg; Map pp170-1; ☎ 2273 2152; www.bundestag.de; Platz der Republik 1; admission free; ☉ 8am-midnight, last admission 10pm), with four national flags fluttering. A fire here in 1933 allowed Hitler to blame the communists and grab power, while the Soviets raised their flag here in 1945 to signal Nazi Germany's defeat. Today, the building is once again the German seat of power, but it's the glass cupola added during the 1999 refurbishment that some 10,000 people a day flock to see. Walking along the internal spiral walkway by British star architect Lord Norman Foster feels like being in a postmodern beehive, and there are excellent vistas. To beat the one-hour queues, book a table for breakfast, lunch or dinner at the rooftop restaurant **Käfer** (☎ 2262 9935; www.feinkost-kaefer.de), which uses a separate entrance. With young children in tow, you're allowed to bypass the queue, too.

The Reichstag is part of the new **Government District**, which also includes the **Neues Kanzleramt** (New Federal Chancellery; Map pp170-1; Willy-Brandt-Strasse 1), the office and residence of the chancellor.

The Reichstag overlooks the **Tiergarten** (see p174). Meanwhile to the building's south stands the **Wall Victims Memorial** (Map pp170-1; Scheidemannstrasse), commemorating the 191 people who died trying to cross from East to West – the last just nine months before the Wall fell.

Further south again is the **Denkmal für die ermordeten Juden Europas** (Memorial to the Murdered Jews of Europe or Holocaust Memorial; Map pp170-1; ☎ 2639 4336/4311; www.stiftung-denkmal .de; Cora-Berliner-Strasse 1; admission free; field ☉ 24hr, information centre 10am-8pm Tue-Sun, last entry 7.15pm; Ⓜ Potsdamer Platz/S-Bahn Unter den Linden) a grid of 2711 'stelae' or differently shaped concrete columns set over 19,000m2 of gently undulating ground. This 'forest' can be entered from any side, but presents different perspectives as you move through it. For historical background, designer Peter Eisenman has created an underground in-

EATING

Amrit	9 F2
Café V	10 F2
Curry 36	11 C2
Hasir	12 E2
Weltrestaurant Markthalle	13 F1

DRINKING

Kumpelnest 3000	14 A1
Möbel Olfe	15 E2
Tabou Tiki Room	16 F3

ENTERTAINMENT

Schokofabrik	17 E2
SchwuZ	18 C3
SO36	19 E2

formation centre in the southeast corner of the site. Weekly **English tours** (€3; ⏱ 4pm Sun) meet near the **lift** (Map pp170-1) here.

Unter den Linden

Celebrated in literature and lined with lime (or linden) trees, the street **Unter den Linden** (Ⓜ S-Bahn Unter den Linden) was the fashionable avenue of old Berlin. Today, after decades of communist neglect, it's been rebuilt and regained that status. The thoroughfare stretches east from the Brandenburger Tor to the Museumsinsel, passing shops, embassies, operas, the **Deutsche Guggenheim** (Map pp170-1; ☎ 202 0930; www.deutsche-guggenheim.de; Unter den Linden 13-15; adult/concession €4/3, free Mon; ⏱ 11am-8pm, to 10pm Thu; Ⓜ Französische Strasse) and the **Humboldt Universität** (Map pp170-1; Ⓜ S-Bahn Friedrichstrasse).

Stop by **Bebelplatz** (Map pp170-1; Ⓜ Französische Strasse), opposite the university, where there's a **book-burning memorial** – a reminder of the first major Nazi book-burning, which occurred in May 1933. A transparent window tile in the stone pavement reveals empty bookshelves below.

Museumsinsel

The so-called **Museums Island** (Map pp170-1; ☎ all museums 2090 5577; www.smb.museum; adult/concession €8/4 each, or €12/6 all; ⏱ 10am-6pm Tue-Sun, to 10pm Thu; Ⓜ S-Bahn Hackescher Markt) lies in the Spree River. On it stands the **Pergamonmuseum** (Map pp170-1; Am Kupfergraben; Ⓜ S-Bahn Hackescher Markt), which is to Berlin what the British Museum is to London: a feast of Mesopotamian, Greek and Roman antiquities looted by archaeologists. The museum takes its name from the Pergamon Altar inside, but the real highlight of the collection is the Ishtar Gate from Babylon.

Meanwhile, the **Alte Nationalgalerie** (Old National Gallery; Map pp170-1; Bodestrasse 1-3; Ⓜ S-Bahn Hackescher Markt) houses 19th-century European sculpture and painting; the **Altes Museum** (Map pp170-1; Am Lustgarten; Ⓜ S-Bahn Hackescher Markt) has art from ancient Rome and Greece; and the reopened **Bodemuseum** (Map pp170-1; Monbijoubrücke; Ⓜ S-Bahn Hackescher Markt) houses sculpture, Byzantine art and painting from the Middle Ages to the 19th century. Watch for special exhibitions at each.

Overlooking the 'island' is the **Berliner Dom** (Berlin Cathedral; Map pp170-1; adult/concession/under 14 €5/3/free). The nearby **Deutsches Historisches Museum** (German History Museum; Map pp170-1; ☎ 203 040; www.dhm.de; Unter den Linden 2; admission €4, free Mon; ⏱ 10am-6pm) has a new permanent exhibition on national history, but is still arguably most notable for the glass-walled spiral staircase by modernist architect IM Pei (creator of the Louvre's glass pyramid).

Hackescher Markt

A complex of shops and apartments around eight courtyards, the **Hackesche Höfe** (Map pp170-1; Ⓜ S-Bahn Hackescher Markt) is Germany's largest live/work space and a major attraction

GERMANY

of 21st-century Berlin. Despite increasing commercialisation – Adidas, Puma and, gulp, Hugo Boss recently opened stores – the neighbourhood retains sufficient cutting-edge streetwear boutiques to woo savvy young consumers.

Shops, cafés and restaurants are the main draw here, but you'll also find the **Neue Synagogue** (Map pp170-1; ☎ 8802 8451; www.cjudaicum .de; Oranienburger Strasse 28-30; adult/concession €3/2; ⏰ 10am-8pm Sun & Mon, to 6pm Tue-Thu, to 5pm Fri, reduced hr Nov-Apr), with its history of local Jewish life. Plus, there's the counter-cultural cum shopping centre of **Tacheles** (Map pp170-1; ☎ 282 6185; Oranienburger Strasse 54-56) in a bombed-out department store.

Further north, the spectacular gallery of the **Hamburger Bahnhof** (Map pp170-1; ☎ 3978 3439; www.smb.museum; Invalidenstrasse 50, Mitte; adult/concession €6/3; ⏰ 10am-6pm Tue-Fri, 11am-6pm Sat & Sun; Ⓜ Hauptbahnhof/Lehrter Stadtbahnhof) showcases works by Warhol, Lichtenstein, Rauschenberg and Joseph Beuys.

TV Tower

Call it Freudian or call it *Ostalgie* (nostalgia for the communist East or *Ost*), but Berlin's once-mocked socialist **Fernsehturm** (Map pp170-1; ☎ 242 3333; www.berlinerfernsehturm.de; adult/ concession €7.50/3.50; ⏰ 10-1am; Ⓜ Alexanderplatz) is fast becoming its most-loved symbol. Originally erected in 1969 and the city's tallest structure, its central bauble was decorated as a giant football for the 2006 Fifa World Cup™, while its 368m outline still pops up in numerous souvenirs. That said, ascending 207m to the revolving (but musty) Telecafé is a less singular experience than visiting the Reichstag dome.

The Turm dominates **Alexanderplatz**, a former livestock and wool market that became the lowlife district chronicled by Alfred Döblin's 1929 novel *Berlin Alexanderplatz* and then developed as a 1960s communist showpiece.

Even in a city so often described as one big building site, today's Alexanderplatz is an unusual hive of construction activity as it is transformed into the next Potsdamer Platz-style development. However, its communist past still echoes through the retro **World Time Clock** (Map pp170-1) and along the portentous **Karl-Marx-Allee**, which leads several kilometres east from the square to Friedrichshain.

Tiergarten

From the Reichstag (see p172), the Tiergarten park's **carillon** (Map pp170-1; John-Foster-Dulles-Allee; bus 100 or 200) and the **Haus der Kulturen der Welt** (House of World Cultures; Map pp170-1; John-Foster-Dulles-Allee) are clearly visible. The latter was the US contribution to the 1957 International Building Exposition and it's easy to see why locals call it the 'pregnant oyster'.

Further west, the wings of the **Siegessäule** (Victory Column; Map p177; bus 100 or 200) were the *Wings of Desire* in that famous Wim Wenders film. This golden angel was built to commemorate Prussian military victories in the 19th century. Today, as the end point of the annual Christopher Street Parade, she's also a gay icon. However, there are better views than those at the column's peak.

A short walk south from here is a cluster of interesting embassy buildings and museums, including the **Bauhaus Archiv** (off Map pp172-3; ☎ 254 0020; www.bauhaus.de; Klingelhöferstrasse 14; adult/concession €6/3; ⏰ 10am-5pm Wed-Mon; Ⓜ Nollendorfplatz), with drawings, chairs and other Modernist objects from the famous Bauhaus school of design – as well as a very tempting shop. The school itself survives in Dessau (see p202).

The **Berliner Philharmonie**, founded in 1961, (see p181) and yet more museums are found a little east in the **Kulturforum** (Map pp170-1; Ⓜ S-Bahn Potsdamer Platz). These include the spectacular **Gemäldegalerie** (Picture Gallery; Map pp170-1; ☎ 266 2951; www.smb.museum; Matthäiskirchplatz 4-6; adult/concession €6/3; ⏰ 10am-6pm Tue-Sun, to 10pm Thu) showing European painting from the 13th to the 18th centuries. Nearby is the **Neue Nationalgalerie** (Map pp172-3; ☎ 266 2951; www.smb.museum; Potsdamer Strasse 50; adult/concession €6/3; ⏰ 10am-6pm Tue-Fri, to 10pm Thu, 11am-6pm Sat & Sun). Housing 19th- and 20th-century works by Picasso, Klee, Miró and many German expressionists, it was built by Bauhaus director Ludwig Mies van der Rohe.

Potsdamer Platz

The lid was symbolically sealed on capitalism's victory over socialism in Berlin when this postmodern temple to mammon was erected in 2000 over the former death strip. Under the big-top, glass-tent roof of the **Sony Center** (Map pp170-1; Ⓜ or S-Bahn Potsdamer Platz) and along the malls of the Lego-like **DaimlerCity** (Map pp170-1; Ⓜ or S-Bahn Potsdamer Platz), people swarm in and around shops, restaurants, offices, loft apartments, clubs, a cinema, a luxury hotel and a casino – all revitalising what was the busiest square in prewar Europe.

During the Berlin Film Festival (see p176), Potsdamer Platz welcomes Hollywood A-listers. In between, you can rub shoulders with German cinematic heroes – particularly Marlene Dietrich – at the **Filmmuseum** (Map pp170-1; ☎ 300 9030; www.filmmuseum-berlin.de; Potsdamer Strasse 2, Tiergarten; adult/concession €6/4; ☼ 10am-6pm Tue-Sun, to 8pm Thu). There's also 'Europe's fastest' lift to the **Panorama Observation Deck** (Map pp170-1; www.panoramapunkt.de; adult/concession €3.50/2.50; ☼ 11am-8pm).

But, as ever in Berlin, the past refuses to go quietly. Just north of Potsdamer Platz lies the former site of **Hitler's Bunker** (Map pp170-1). A little southeast lies the **Topographie des Terrors** (Map pp172-3; ☎ 2548 6703; www.topographie .de; Niederkirchner Strasse; admission free; ☼ 10am-8pm May-Sep, to dusk Oct-Apr), a sometimes shockingly graphic record of the Gestapo and SS headquarters that once stood here.

Jewish Museum

The Daniel Libeskind building that's the **Jüdisches Museum** (Map pp172-3; ☎ 2599 3300; www .juedisches-museum-berlin.de; Lindenstrasse 9-14; adult/concession €5/2.50; ☼ 10am-10pm Mon, to 8pm Tue-Sun, last entry 1hr before closing; Ⓜ Hallesches Tor) is as much the attraction as the Jewish-German history collection within. Designed to disorientate and unbalance with its 'voids', cul-de-sacs, barbed metal fittings, slit windows and uneven floors, this still-somehow-beautiful structure swiftly conveys the uncertainty and sometime terror of past Jewish life in Germany. It's a visceral experience, after which the huge collection itself demands your concentration. A highlight is the Garden of Exile, with tall concrete columns like trees and an uneven floor. The building's footprint is a ripped-apart Star of David.

Kurfürstendamm

West Berlin's legendary shopping thoroughfare, the Ku'damm has lost some of its cachet since the Wall fell, but is worth visiting. You will find the **Kaiser-Wilhelm-Gedächtniskirche** (Map p177; ☎ 218 5023; Breitscheidplatz; Memorial Hall ☼ 10am-4pm Mon-Sat, Hall of Worship ☼ 9am-7.30pm) here, which remains in ruins – just as British bombers left it on 22 November 1943 – as an antiwar memorial. Only the broken west tower still stands.

Stasi Museum

The one-time secret police headquarters now houses the **Stasi Museum** (Map p169; ☎ 553 6854; House 1, Ruschestrasse 103; adult/concession €3/2; 11am-6pm Tue-Fri, 2-6pm Sat & Sun; Ⓜ Magdalenenstrasse). It's largely in German, but worth it to see the cunning surveillance devices and communist paraphernalia.

Tours

Guided tours are phenomenally popular; you can choose Third Reich, Wall, bunker, communist, boat or bicycle tours, as well as guided pub-crawls. Most cost €10 to €12 each.

TRACING THE BERLIN WALL

Just as the infamous Wall snaked across Berlin, so today's remnants are scattered across the city. The longest surviving stretch is the so-called **East Side Gallery** (Map p176; www.eastsidegallery.com; Mühlenstrasse; Ⓜ S-Bahn Warschauer Strasse) in Friedrichshain. Panels along this 1.3km of graffiti and art include the famous portrait of Soviet leader Brezhnev kissing GDR leader Erich Hönecker and a Trabant car seemingly bursting through the (now crumbling) concrete.

Climbing the tower at the **Berliner Mauer Dokumentationszentrum** (Berlin Wall Documentation Centre; Map pp170-1; ☎ 464 1030; Bernauer Strasse 111; admission free; ☼ 10am-5pm; Ⓜ S-Bahn Nordbahnhof) you overlook a memorial across the street – an artist's impression of the death strip behind an original stretch of wall. Photos and eyewitness testimonies are also on show.

In Kreuzberg, the famous sign at **Checkpoint Charlie** (Map pp172-3) still boasts 'You are now leaving the American sector'. But it and the reconstructed US guardhouse are just a bit of fun now. To learn about the seriously tragic past, visit **Haus am Checkpoint Charlie** (Map pp172-3; ☎ 253 7250; www.mauer-museum.com; Friedrichstrasse 43-45; adult/concession €9.50/5.50; ☼ 9am-10pm; Ⓜ Kochstrasse/Stadtmitte). Tales of spectacular escape attempts include through tunnels, in hot-air balloons and even using a one-man submarine.

GERMANY

New Berlin (☎ 017-9973 0397; www.newberlintours .com) even offers free (yup, free) 3½-hour introductory tours. These leave at 11am and 1pm outside the Starbucks that's rather controversially located in Pariser Platz near the Brandenburg Gate. Guides are enthusiastic, knowledgeable… and accept tips.

Alternatively, you can beetle around Berlin in a Trabant car. **Trabi Safari** (☎ 275 2273; www .trabi-safari.de; €25-35) operates from Gendarmenmarkt.

Other operators include:

Brewer's Berlin Tours (☎ 017-7388 1537; www .brewersberlintours.com).

Insider Tours (☎ 692 3149; www.insidertour.com)

Original Berlin Walks (☎ 301 9194; www.berlin walks.com)

FESTIVALS & EVENTS

International Film Festival Berlin (☎ 259 200; www .berlinale.de) The Berlinale, held in February, is Germany's answer to the Cannes and Venice film festivals.

Christopher Street Day (☎ 017-7277 3176; www.csd -berlin.de) On the last weekend in June, this is Germany's largest gay event.

Love Parade (☎ 308 8120; www.loveparade.net) At the time of research, Berlin's huge techno street parade was making a comeback, hopefully sustainable.

SLEEPING
Mitte & Prenzlauer Berg
BUDGET

Berlin's independent hostels far outdo the DJH (www.jugendherberge.de) offerings in the city.

Circus Hostels (Map pp170-1; ☎ 2839 1433; www .circus-hostel.de; Rosa-Luxemburg-Strasse 39 & Weinbergsweg 1a; dm €15-20, s/d €32/48, 2/4-person apt €75/130; ⌨ ; Ⓜ U-Bahn Rosenthaler Platz) These two are widely regarded as the best hostels in town, with great central locations, efficient staff, good bars and upbeat, tastefully decorated rooms in cheerful colours.

Citystay Hostel (Map pp170-1; ☎ 2362 4031; www .citystay.de; Rosenstrasse 16; dm €15-20, s/d €34/48; ⌨ ; Ⓜ S-Bahn Alexanderplatz/Hackescher Markt) Tucked away on a quiet street between the Fernsehturm and Hackescher Markt, this loft-style establishment uses expensive finishes and bright colours to create an upbeat atmosphere. Showers (none ensuite) are clean, but the sparse rooms lack cupboards.

Heart of Gold (Map pp170-1; ☎ 2900 3300; www .heartofgold-hostel.de; Johannisstrasse 11; dm €14-19, s/d €40/60, apt €120-160, d without bathroom €48; ⌨ ; Ⓜ Oranienburger Tor) Even if you're not into the subtle *Hitchhiker's Guide to the Galaxy* theming, this new building in Mitte still offers comfortable accommodation and a convenient location. A nice touch is the stylish tiled niches with stainless-steel sinks.

EastSeven (Map pp170-1; ☎ 9362 2240; www.east seven.de; Schwedter Strasse 7; dm €17-23, s/d €35/55, bedding €3; ⌨ ; Ⓜ Senefelder Platz) It sounds like a boy band and this wonderful, cosy place *is* squeaky clean. Even the retro '70s look that emulates many nearby Prenzelberg bars has been achieved with the help of IKEA(!). The kitchen adjoins a lovely garden perfect for summer barbecues.

Aurora (Map pp170-1; ☎ 4699 5524; www.aurora-hostel .com; Pappelallee 21; s/d with bathroom €42/66, s/d/tr €26/48/64; ⌨ ; Ⓜ Eberswalder Strasse) The way of

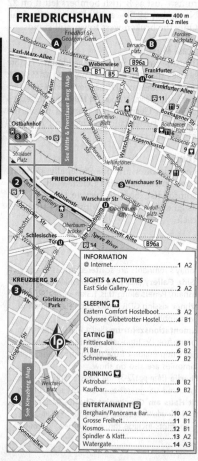

FRIEDRICHSHAIN

0 _____ 400 m
0 _____ 0.2 miles

the future, this sleek streamlined pad straddles the gulf between budget and boutique hotel. Decorated in neutral tones, it even has customisable coloured lighting, as in some famous Phillipe Starck abodes.

Pension Amsterdam (Map pp170-1; ☎ 448 0792; www.pension-amsterdam.de; Gleimstrasse 24; s €36.50, d €70-90, tr €75-120; 🖵; Ⓜ Schönhauser Allee) There's plenty to like about this contemporary *pension*: big apartments, full kitchens, rooms with four-poster beds and a buzzy downstairs café popular with a mixed gay crowd.

Other recommendations:

Eastener Hostel (Map pp170-1; ☎ 017-5112 3515; www.eastener-hostel.de; Novalisstrasse 15; dm €15-20, s/d €30/44; ✗) Small quiet, unassuming-looking hostel, where guests rave about the personal touch.

Mitte's (Map pp170-1; ☎ 2839 0965; www.backpacker .de; Chausseestrasse 102; dm €15-19, d €44-66; 🖵; Ⓜ Zinnowitzer Strasse) and **Baxpax** (Map pp172-3; ☎ 6951 8322; www.baxpax.de; Skalitzer Strasse 104; Ⓜ Görlitzer Bahnhof) These sister establishments are a bit ramshackle, especially Mitte's, but fun and funky, with rooms themed by nationality in Baxpax.

MIDRANGE

Arcotel Velvet (Map pp170-1; ☎ 278 7530; www.arcotel .at; Oranienburger Strasse 52; s €60-100, d €70-110; 🅿 ✗; Ⓜ Oranienburger Tor) Floor-to-ceiling windows give front rooms a bird's-eye view of the bustling street and, combined with bathrooms separated only by gauze curtains, create a feeling of loft living. Back rooms are more traditional.

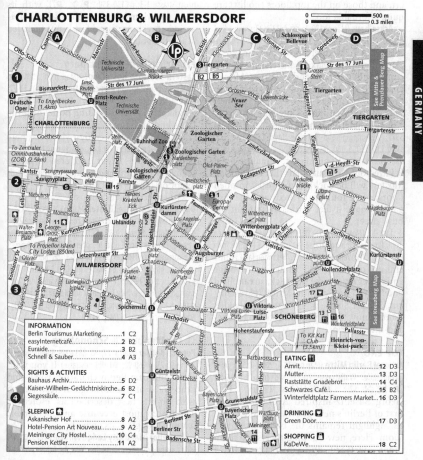

CHARLOTTENBURG & WILMERSDORF

0 ———— 500 m
0 ———— 0.3 miles

INFORMATION

Berlin Tourismus Marketing	1 C2
easyInternetcafé	2 B2
Euraide	3 B2
Schnell & Sauber	4 A3

SIGHTS & ACTIVITIES

Bauhaus Archiv	5 D2
Kaiser-Wilhelm-Gedächtniskirche	6 B2
Siegessäule	7 C1

SLEEPING 🛏

Askanischer Hof	8 A2
Hotel-Pension Art Nouveau	9 A2
Meininger City Hostel	10 C4
Pension Kettler	11 A2

EATING 🍴

Amrit	12 D3
Mutter	13 D3
Raststätte Gnadebrot	14 C4
Schwarzes Café	15 B2
Winterfeldtplatz Farmers Market	16 D3

DRINKING 🍷

Green Door	17 D3

SHOPPING 🛍

KaDeWe	18 C2

GERMANY

Prinz Albert (Map pp170-1; ☎ 293 833; www.prinz albert-berlin.de; Veteranenstrasse 10; s €65-85, d €90-110; ✗ ; Ⓜ Rosenthaler Platz) Although minutes from hipster-central Kastanienallee, this sweet, gay-friendly hotel has a neighbourhood feel. Six of the seven generously sized, neutrally decorated rooms overlook the pleasant Weinbergspark, and there's a restaurant downstairs.

Kunstlerheim Luise (Map pp170-1; ☎ 284 480; www.kuenstlerheim-luise.de; Luisenstrasse 19; s/d from €85/120, s/d without bathroom €50/80; Ⓟ ✗ ; Ⓜ Friedrichstrasse) A room with Andy Warhol-style bananas and golden crowns, another with a giant bed and yet another with Edward Hopper-style murals – every room in the wonderful Kunstlerheim Luise is a work of art, and those on the top floors (no lift) are quite affordable too.

Ackselhaus (Map pp170-1; ☎ 4433 7633; www.acksel haus.de; Belforter Strasse 21; s €85-120, d €95-160; Ⓜ Senefelder Platz) A Mediterranean oasis in Prenzlauer Berg, this relaxing and elegant terrace comes with a garden and Italian or African apartments (with kitchens). Its sister three doors down boasts various 'blue' themes, plus all-day restaurant Club del Mar.

Garden Hotel Honigmond (Map pp170-1; ☎ 2844 5577; www.honigmond-berlin.de; Invalidenstrasse 122; s €90-110, d €115-160; Ⓟ ✗ ; Ⓜ Zinnowitzer Strasse/S-Bahn Nordbahnhof) This classic, romantic hotel is kitted out with such flair that even urban hipsters will be enchanted. Creaky wooden floors, some four-poster beds and the lush garden make it feel worlds away from the busy street.

Lux 11 (Map pp170-1; ☎ 936 2800; www.lux-eleven .com; Rosa-Luxemburg-Strasse 9-13; r from €115, ste from €135; ✗ ; Ⓜ Weinmeisterstrasse/Alexanderplatz) A liberal use of white – off-white, cream, beige and light grey –make this slick, streamlined hotel a haven of calm in Mitte. Its restaurant, Shiro I Shiro, is also winning plaudits for its innovative cuisine and striking whiteand-blue interior.

TOP END

Art'otel Berlin Mitte (Map pp170-1; ☎ 240 620; www .arthotel.de; Wallstrasse 70-73; s/d from €130/260; Ⓟ ✗ ✗ ▣ ; Ⓜ Märkisches Museum) This Georg Baselitz-inspired Art'otel was the first of Berlin's new-generation hotels, and its highlight remains the breakfast/dining room. Here, new building meets old in an inner courtyard, and you realise what a

broad, but still cool, mix of people you're staying with.

Dorint am Gendarmenmarkt (Map pp170-1; ☎ 203 570; www.dorint.de; Charlottenstrasse 50-52; s/d from €160/190, breakfast €25; ✗ ; Ⓜ Französische Strasse) The Adlon notwithstanding, this is some people's Berlin favourite. Frosted glass, chocolate brown tones and a wonderful enclosed terrace in the top-floor spa area show real style. However, it's the sly hint of fun – the old gym rings, for example – that's always won us over.

Both the prestigious **Hotel Adlon** (Map pp170-1; ☎ 226 10; www.hotel-adlon.de, www.kempinski.com; Am Pariser Platz, Unter den Linden 77; s/d from €280/325; Ⓟ ✗ ✗ ▣) and the new **Radisson SAS** (Map pp170-1; ☎ 238 280; www.radissonsas.com; Karl-Liebnecht-Strasse 1-3; r €130-350; Ⓟ ✗ ▣), with its giant aquarium lobby, are themselves sightseeing attractions. Breakfast is not included at the Radisson.

Friedrichshain & Kreuzberg

Eastern Comfort Hostelboot (Map p176; ☎ 6676 3806; www.eastern-comfort.com; Mühlenstrasse 73-77; dm €14-18, s/d from €42/46, bedding €5; ▣ ; Ⓜ S-Bahn Warschauer Strasse) This floating hostel near the last standing bit of Wall is refreshingly unusual. Upper cabins enjoy river views here and there's a nicely designed bar at the back, where Captain Edgar and crew organise regular events and gigs. Campers can pitch a tent on the deck for €10 a night.

Other recommendations:

Odyssee Globetrotter Hostel (Map p176; ☎ 2900 0081; www.globetrotterhostel.de; Grünberger Strasse 23; dm €10-16, s/d from €29/39; ▣ ; Ⓜ S-Bahn Warschauer Strasse) Popular party hostel in bohemian Friedrichshain.

Meininger City Hostel (Map pp172-3; ☎ 6663 6100; www.meininger-hostels.de; Hallesches Ufer 30; dm €13.50-25, s/d €49/66; Ⓟ ✗ ▣) Dorms are clean but spartan, while cheerfully furnished doubles and singles stand out. Branches at Tempelhofer Ufer 10 (**Map pp172-3**) and Meininger Strasse 10 (**Map p177**).

Charlottenburg & Schöneberg

Pension Kettler (Map p177; ☎ 883 4949; Bleibtreustrasse 19; s €50-75, d €60-90; Ⓜ Uhlandstrasse) If you want quirk and true Berlin character, you'll find heaps of it at this nostalgic retreat, strewn with objects best described as 'esoterica'. The place's most eccentric and memorable feature, though, is its owner!

Propellor Island City Lodge (off Map p177; ☎ 891 9016; www.propeller-island.de; Albrecht-Achilles-Strasse

58; s €65-125, d €90-195; ✕ ; Ⓜ Adenauer Platz) Berlin's most eccentric hotel is the brainchild of artist/musician Lars Stroschen, who crafted these 30 unique environments. Here walls slant, beds seemingly hang above the floor, wardrobes hide showers, and there are other surreal features.

Hotel-Pension Art Nouveau (Map p177; ☎ 327 7440; www.hotelartnouveau.de; Leibnizstrasse 59; s €95-140, d €110-165; ✕ ; Ⓜ Adenauer Platz/S-Bahn Savignyplatz) A rickety bird-cage lift drops you off on the 4th floor in one Berlin's best *pensions*, with handpicked antiques and creative use of colour. The owners are its greatest asset, though, treating guests like family friends.

Askanischer Hof (Map p177; ☎ 881 8033; www .askanischer-hof.de; Kurfürstendamm 53; s €100-110, d €125-145; ✕ ; Ⓜ Adenauer Platz/S-Bahn Savignyplatz) Decorated in decadent 1920s style (with a few other eras thrown in), it's little surprise this became David Bowie's favourite hotel in the creative cradle of 1970s West Berlin. It's still an artistic meeting spot.

EATING

Berliners love eating out and you needn't walk far for a feed. Restaurants usually open from 11am to midnight, with varying *Ruhetage* or rest days; many close during the day from 3pm to 6pm. Cafés often close around 8pm, though equal numbers stay open until 2am or later.

Berlin is a snacker's paradise, with Turkish (your best bet), Wurst (sausage), Greek, Italian, Chinese, even Sudanese *Imbiss* stalls throughout the city.

Self-caterers will find Aldi, Lidl, Plus and Penny Markt discount supermarkets throughout Berlin. There's the excellent organic **Kollwitzplatz market** (Map pp170-1; 🕑 9am-4pm Sat & Sun) and the **Winterfeldtplatz farmer's market** (Map p177; 🕑 Wed & Sat).

Mitte & Prenzlauer Berg

Konnopke (Map pp170-1; Schönhauser Allee 44a; 🕑 5.30am-8pm Mon-Fri; Ⓜ Eberswalder Strasse) Even former chancellor Gerhard Schröder has eaten Wurst here under the S-Bahn tracks in Prenzelberg.

RNBS (Map pp170-1; ☎ 540 2505; Oranienburger Strasse 50; mains €2-4; Ⓜ Oranienburger Strasse/Hackescher Markt) We can't vouch for the 'beauty tea' (sadly didn't work for us), but the Asian soups and noodle dishes served up by this tiny orange-and-white outlet are as delicious as they are

healthy: no preservatives, no MSG, no artificial flavourings.

Sankt Oberholz (Map pp170-1; ☎ 2408 5586; Rosenthaler Strasse 72a; dishes €3.50-5; Ⓜ Rosenthaler Platz) Not so much a café as a hilarious social experiment, where Berlin's '*Urbanen Pennern*' (office-less, self-employed creatives) flock with their laptops for the free wi-fi access. The deli fare of soups, lasagne and savoury polenta cake is pretty good too.

Monsieur Vuong (Map pp170-1; ☎ 3087 2643; Alte Schönhauser Strasse 46; mains €6.50; Ⓜ Weinmeisterstrasse/Rosa-Luxemburg-Platz/Alexanderplatz) Because this Vietnamese is where everyone says you should eat, this is where everyone is. Arrive early to avoid queuing. Mr Vuong himself shakes regulars' hands in the red-lacquer room, and the soups are toothsome.

Nosh (Map pp170-1; ☎ 4404 0397; Pappelallee 77; mains €6-13; 🕑 dinner only in winter; Ⓜ Eberswalder Strasse) Relaxed diner style eatery, with a daily changing blackboard menu and staples of spring rolls, Asian and European dishes. Sunday brunch is a great time to come.

Zoe (Map pp170-1; ☎ 2404 5635; Rochstrasse 1; mains €8-18, 2-course lunch menus €6-7; Ⓜ Weinmeisterstrasse/ Alexanderplatz) The all-white fittings and trendy customers fortunately don't denote a case of style over substance here. Mediterranean and Asian flavours are skilfully mixed to create a piquant tang. Excellent lunch deals.

Borchardt (Map pp170-1; ☎ 8188 6250; Französische Strasse 47; mains €13-20; Ⓜ Französische Strasse) On every Berlin *promi*'s (celeb's) speed-dial list, this refined French-German bistro also tolerates ordinary civilians.

Other recommendations:

Imbiss W (Map pp170-1; ☎ 4849 2657; Kastanienallee 49; mains €3-6; Ⓜ Rosenthaler Platz) Canadian-run joint offering Southeast Asian food and naan pizzas.

Duy Thai (Map pp170-1; ☎ 4431 7116; Kollwitzstrasse 89; mains €5-14; Ⓜ Eberswalder Strasse) Dishes are made to order in this relaxed canteen.

Die Zwölf Apostel (The 12 Apostles; Map pp170-1; ☎ 201 0222; Georgenstrasse; mains €9-16; Ⓜ Friedrichstrasse) Ecclesiastical décor and huge pizzas, including a 'Judas'. Good weekday lunch deals.

Friedrichshain & Kreuzberg

Curry 36 (Map pp172-3; ☎ 881 4710; Mehringdamm 36; 🕑 9am-5pm; Ⓜ Mehringdamm) This is Kreuzberg's – some believe Berlin's – best sausage stand.

Frittiersalon (Map p176; Boxhagener Strasse 104; Ⓜ Frankfurter Tor) The enormous choice here includes Wurst, organic fries, tofu and even a Camembert burger.

Hasir (Map pp172-3; Adalbertstrasse 10; ⏰ 24hr; Ⓜ Kottbusser Tor) The birthplace (yes, really) of the döner kebab is a sit-down restaurant, too.

Café V (Map pp172-3; ☎ 612 4505; Lausitzer Platz 12; dishes €5.50-9.50; Ⓜ Görlitzer Bahnhof) Yellow, red and gilt trimmings greet you as you enter this old-school veggie/vegan café. Everything comes with a soya/caffeine-free/tofu alternative, although you can also choose straight-up dishes like pizza or Thai fish curry.

Schneeweiss (Map p176; ☎ 2904 9704; Simplonstrasse 16; day menu €5.50-11, dinner mains €13-20; ⏰ dinner only Mon-Fri, all day Sat & Sun; Ⓜ S-Bahn Warschauer Strasse) Subtly embossed vanilla wallpaper, rectangular glass lights along the long, central table and parquet flooring keep neutral 'Snow White' feeling more après-ski than icy. The vaguely Swiss/Austrian 'Alpine' food is a '70s throwback, but still enjoyable. Evenings here are megafashionable, so book.

Amrit Kreuzberg (Map pp172-3; ☎ 612 5550; Oranienstrasse 202; dishes €7-14.50; Ⓜ Görlitzer Bahnhof); Mitte (Map pp170-1; ☎ 2888 4840; Oranienburger Strasse 45; Ⓜ Oranienburger Tor); Schöneberg (Map p177; ☎ 2101 4640; Winterfeldtstrasse 40; Ⓜ Nollendorfplatz) One of three busy Amrits around town, that serve the same tasty pan-Indian cuisine.

Pi-Bar (Map p176; ☎ 2936 7581; Gabriel-Max-Strasse 17; mains €7-17; Ⓜ S-Bahn Warschauer Strasse) A salubrious Friedrichshain stalwart that has seen off countless pretenders, Pi continues to serve a tasty combination of vegetarian and fish-based cuisine, plus great breakfasts. The comfy sofas remain, but the walls have a new lick of red/tangerine paint.

Weltrestaurant Markthalle (Map pp172-3; ☎ 617 5502; Pücklerstrasse 34; mains €8-15; Ⓜ Görlitzer Bahnhof) This wood-lined, century-old pub draws a mixed clientele of ageing hipsters and neighbourhood folk with its relaxed vibe and simple no-nonsense food.

Charlottenburg & Schöneberg

Raststätte Gnadebrot (Map p177; ☎ 2196 1786; Marin-Luther-Strasse 202; mains €3.50-6; Ⓜ Victoria-Luise-Platz/Nollendorfplatz) An ironic, retro '70s take on a motorway roadhouse, this wins loyal fans for its friendly atmosphere (you share bench seats) and good, cheap food and drinks.

Schwarzes Café (Map p177; ☎ 313 8038; Kantstrasse 148; dishes €4.50-9; Ⓜ S-Bahn Zoo/Savignyplatz) Founded in 1978, this 24-hour food'n'booze

institution must have seen half of Berlin pass through it (or out in it) at some point. Interesting toilets, too.

Mutter (Map p177; ☎ 216 4990; Hohenstaufenstrasse 4; mains €4-14; Ⓜ Nollendorfplatz) Sushi, Thai soups and often wonderfully presented Asian dishes are complemented by a list of cocktails that includes coconut-flavoured *Muttermilch* (mother's milk) in this opulent, gold-bedecked café.

Engelbecken (off Map p177; ☎ 615 2810; Witzlebenstrasse 31; mains €8-16; ⏰ dinner only Mon-Sat, lunch & dinner Sun; Ⓜ Sophie Charlotte Platz) Come here for what many rate as Berlin's best Bavarian food, with Schweinsbraten, schnitzels, dumplings and sauerkraut. All meats are organic.

DRINKING

After dark, each Berlin district offers something different, but for the past decade, the hottest action has lain east. Prenzlauer Berg was the first GDR sector to develop a happening nightlife and still attracts student, creative and gay customers. Later, more clubs and bars sprang up in Mitte around Hackescher Markt, catering to a cool, slightly older and wealthier crowd. The area around Simon-Dach-Strasse and Boxhagener Platz in Friedrichshain is the latest to have emerged.

In the west, Kreuzberg remains alternative, becoming grungier as you move east. Charlottenburg and Winterfeldtplatz are fairly upmarket and mature, but liberal.

Bars without food open between 5pm and 8pm and may close as late as 5am (if at all).

Astrobar (Map p176; ☎ 2966 1615; Simon-Dach-Strasse 40; Ⓜ S-Bahn Warschauer Strasse) One of the first on the Friedrichshain scene and still going strong, the Astro offers the future as it looked in the 1960s, with spaceships, robots and classic computer games in the back room.

Erdbeer (Map pp170-1; Max-Beer-Strasse 56; Ⓜ Rosa-Luxemburg-Platz) A warren of interconnected rooms, this rambling cocktail bar derives its name not only from its red colour scheme, but also its customers' favourite brand of daiquiri (*Erdbeer*, or strawberry).

Kumpelnest 3000 (Map pp172-3; ☎ 8891 7960; Lützowstrasse 23; Ⓜ Kurfürstenstrasse) Once a brothel, always an experience – the Kumpelnest has been famed since the '80s for its wild, inhibition-free nights. Much of the original whorehouse décor remains intact. According to some locals, your bag may not (remain intact, that is) unless you keep a beady eye on it.

Hotelbar (Map pp170-1; ☎ 4432 8577; Zionkirchstrasse 5; Ⓜ Rosenthaler Platz) This cosy subterranean bar has a broad music policy, with jazz, latin beats and electropop to things like 'balkandub', 'Hammondorgel' and even spoken word.

Green Door (Map p177; ☎ 215 2515; Winterfeldtstrasse 50; Ⓜ Nollendorfplatz) Ring the doorbell to get them to open the namesake green door and let you into this tiny neighbourhood bar. Cocktails are on offer.

Other recommendations:

Möbel Olfe (Map pp172-3; ☎ 6165 9612; Reichenberger Strasse 177; Ⓨ closed Mon; Ⓜ Kottbusser Tor) Sparsely furnished beer hall good for Polish beer and table football.

Tabou Tiki Room (Map pp172-3; Maybuchufer 39; Ⓨ closed Mon; Ⓜ Schönleinstrasse) A slice of kitschy '60s Hawaii in Berlin. Exotic cocktails.

ENTERTAINMENT

Berlin's legendary nightlife needs little introduction. Whether alternative, underground, cutting-edge, saucy, flamboyant or even highbrow, it all crops up here.

Nightclubs

Clubs rarely open before 11pm (though earlier 'after-work' clubs and Sunday sessions are also popular) and stay open well into the early hours – usually sunrise at least. As the scene changes so rapidly, it's always wise to double-check listings magazines or ask locals. Admission charges, when they apply, range from €5 to €15.

Berghain/Panorama Bar (Map p176; www .berghain.de; Wrienzer Bahnhof; Ⓨ from midnight Thu-Sat; Ⓜ Ostbahnhof) Techno fans from across the world pump it up in a huge cathedral-like former railway workshop, or chill out in the quieter Panorama Bar upstairs. Cutting-edge sounds in industrial surrounds.

Café Moskau (off Map pp170-1; ☎ 2463 1626; www .das-moskau.com; Karl-Marx-Allee 34; Ⓜ Schillingstrasse) It doesn't really matter what's on, this one-time GDR restaurant is the epitome of retro Soviet kitsch and has to be seen. At the time of research, intermittent funk/reggae events were the order of the day, although the WMF techno/house evenings might return.

Kaffee Burger (Map pp170-1; ☎ 2804 6495; www .kaffeeburger.de; Torstrasse 60; Ⓜ Rosa-Luxemburg-Platz) A cornerstone of Berlin's so-bad-it's-good alternative scene, decked out in original GDR '60s wallpaper. Come here for indie, rock, punk and cult author Wladimir Kaminer's fortnightly *Russendisko* (Russian disco; www.russendisko.de).

Kosmos (Map p176; ☎ 4004 8130; www.kosmos -berlin.de; Karl-Marx-Allee 131a; Ⓨ from 10am; Ⓜ Frankfurter Tor) This monolithic GDR cinema has been reborn as one of Berlin's newest club/bar/bistros, with a huge main floor.

Spindler & Klatt (Map p176; ☎ 609 3702; www .spindlerklatt.com; Köpenicker Strasse 16-17; Ⓨ from 8pm Wed-Sun; Ⓜ Ostbahnhof/Schlesisches Tor) Unusually upmarket for Berlin, this club's combination of horizontal loungers and food service (hiccup!) has garnered plenty of headlines. In summer, there's a nice terrace.

Watergate (Map p176; ☎ 6128 0394; www.water -gate.de; Falckensteinstrasse 49a; Ⓨ from 11pm Fri & Sat; Ⓜ Schlesisches Tor) Watch the sun rise over the Spree River through the floor-to-ceiling windows of this fantastic lounge. The music is mainly electro, drum'n'bass and hip-hop.

Weekend (Map pp170-1; www.week-end-berlin.de; Am Alexanderplatz 5; Ⓨ from 11pm Thu-Sat; Ⓜ Alexanderplatz) Tear your eyes from the beautiful people and gaze through the 12th-floor windows, across the *Blade-Runner* landscape of dug-up Alexanderplatz and over Berlin. (Alexanderplatz 5 is the one with the Sanyo logo.)

Berlin also has a thriving scene of no-holds-barred sex clubs. The notorious **KitKat Club** (off Map p177; ☎ 7889 9704; Bessemerstrasse 14; Ⓜ Alt-Tempelhof) is the original and best.

Music & Theatre

Berliner Philharmonie (Map pp170-1; ☎ information 254 880, tickets 2548 8999; www.berliner-philharmoniker .de; Herbert-von-Karajan Strasse 1; Ⓜ Potsdamer Platz) Director Sir Simon Rattle has consolidated the orchestra's supreme musical reputation and the hall is praised for its acoustics, too.

Staatsoper Unter den Linden (Map pp170-1; ☎ information 203 540, tickets 2035 4555; www.staatsoper -berlin.de; Unter den Linden 5-7; Ⓜ S-Bahn Unter den Linden) This is the handiest and most prestigious of Berlin's three opera houses, where unsold seats go on sale cheap an hour before curtains-up.

Berliner Ensemble (Map pp170-1; ☎ information 284 080, tickets 2840 8155; www.berliner-ensemble.de; Bertolt-Brecht-Platz 1; Ⓜ Friedrichstrasse) *Mack the Knife* had its first public airing here, during the *Threepenny Opera's* premiere in 1928. Bertolt Brecht's former theatrical home continues to present his plays.

GERMANY

IN BERLIN'S LIVING ROOM

Berlin was once famous for its ramshackle squat bars. And while many snow-white nightlife venues are going upmarket, others have been trying to reclaim that anarchic legacy. A spate of new bars exists decorated like 1950s, 1960s or 1970s domestic living rooms. They feature flock wallpaper, bead curtains and mismatched, sometimes threadbare, sofas seemingly rescued from the rubbish tip.

The most famous exponent of this 'second-hand design' is the dimly lit pub/café called **Wohnzimmer** (Living Room; Map pp170-1; ☎ 445 5458; Lettestrasse 6; ☷ 10am-4am; Ⓜ Eberswalder Strasse). In hip Prenzlauer Berg, it combines styles from Louis XVI to, primarily, GDR c 1950.

Weinerei Cafe (Map pp170-1; ☎ 440 6983; cnr Veteranenstrasse & Fehrbellinerstrasse; ☷ 10am-midnight; Ⓜ Eberswalder Strasse) feels even more ad hoc, like stepping into someone's house. On Friday and Saturday nights, you simply rent a wine glass for €1, enjoy as many refills as you want and pay what you think is appropriate at the evening's end. (Be fair, otherwise they'll go broke!)

Zu Mir oder zu Dir? (Your place or mine?; Map pp170-1; Lychener Strasse 15; ☷ from 8pm; Ⓜ Eberswalder Strasse) is a slightly more plush and trendy bar, with a double bed and some eye-catching pop-art features.

In two venues, **Kaufbar** (Buy-Bar or Purchasable; Map p176; ☎ 464 1030; Gärtnerstrasse 4; ☷ 11am-1am; Ⓜ S-Bahn Warschauer Strasse) and the sunny ice-cream café **Kauf Dich Glücklich** (Shop Yourself Happy; Map pp170-1; ☎ 4435 2182; Oderberger Strasse 44; ☷ noon-midnight; Ⓜ Eberswalder Strasse), even the furniture is on sale. As you enjoy one of the latter's famous waffles, just pray someone doesn't come in and snap up the chair or table you're using.

SHOPPING

Department store **KaDeWe** (Map p177; Tauentzienstrasse 21; Ⓜ U-Bahn Wittenbergplatz) is Germany's most renowned retail emporium, equivalent to Harrods. The 6th-floor gourmet food halls are extraordinary, and the store is near the principal western shopping thoroughfare of Kurfürstendamm. Famous Parisian store **Galeries Lafayette** (Map pp170-1; ☎ 209 480; Friedrichstrasse 76-78; ☷ 10am-8pm Mon-Sat; Ⓜ S-Bahn Friedrichstrasse) also has a ritzy branch in Mitte.

While **Hackescher Markt** (p173) is increasingly commercial, plenty of cutting-edge boutiques are found in Prenzlauer Berg, especially along Kastanienallee (nicknamed 'casting alley' for its beautiful people) and Stargarder Strasse.

With flea markets across town, the **Berlin Art & Nostalgia Market** (Map pp170-1; Georgenstrasse, Mitte; ☷ 8am-5pm Sat & Sun; Ⓜ S-Bahn Friedrichstrasse) is heavy on collectibles, books, ethnic crafts and GDR memorabilia.

GETTING THERE & AWAY
Air

The plan is to turn Schönefeld into the city's main hub, Berlin-Brandenburg-International (BBI). That won't be for several years, however, and presently **three airports** (www.berlin-airport.de) operate.

Schönefeld (SXF) is the furthest from the centre but increasingly the busiest, with flights to/from Europe, Israel and North Africa, including easyJet (www.easyjet.com) services to the UK and Netherlands.

Tegel (TXL) has a similarly European focus and is the Air Berlin (www.airberlin.com) hub. Direct Delta Airlines (www.delta.com) services to/from New York also rotate out of here.

The landing hub for Allied airlifts during the Berlin blockade of 1948–49, **Tempelhof** (THF) today serves domestic and Danish destinations only.

Bus

Berlin is well connected to the rest of Europe by a network of long-distance buses. Most buses arrive at and depart from the **Zentraler Omnibusbahnhof** (ZOB; off Map p177; ☎ 302 5361; Masurenallee 4-6; Ⓜ Kaiserdamm/Witzleben), opposite the Funkturm radio tower. Tickets are available from travel agencies or at the bus station.

Car

Lifts can be organised by **ADM Mitfahrzentrale** (ride-share agencies; ☎ 194 40); Zoo station (Map p177; ☷ 9am-8pm Mon-Fri, 10am-6pm Sat & Sun); Alexanderplatz U-Bahn (Map pp170-1; ☷ 10am-6pm Mon-Fri, 11am-4pm Sat & Sun).

Train

Regular long-distance services arrive at the new Hauptbahnhof (also called Lehrter Bahnhof), with many continuing east to Ostbahnhof and Lichtenberg. You'll probably need to switch to local services to get to the former major terminus of Berlin Zoo (although local petitioning *might* change this). ICE and IC trains leave hourly to every major city in Germany and there are connections to central Europe. Sample fares include to Leipzig (€36, 1¼ hours), Hamburg (€48 to €58, 1½ to two hours), Stralsund (€32.30, three hours) and Prague (€53.80, five hours).

GETTING AROUND

Berlin's public transport system is excellent and much better than driving around the city. The comprehensive network of U-Bahn and S-Bahn trains, buses, trams and ferries covers most corners.

To/From the Airport

There are two principal ways of reaching Schönefeld. The half-hourly S9 travels through all the major downtown stations, taking 45 minutes from Friedrichstrasse. Faster 'Airport Express' trains (mainly RE4, RE5) travel the same route, also half-hourly, taking 31 minutes from the Hauptbahnhof, 21 minutes from Alexanderplatz and 15 minutes from Ostbahnhof. A taxi costs up to €35. The airport station is 400m from the terminal, linked by covered walkway.

Tegel airport is connected by bus 109 to Zoo station, via Kurfürstendamm and Luisenplatz. JetExpress Bus TXL (€4.10) goes via Unter den Linden, Potsdamer Platz and

the Reichstag. A taxi between Tegel airport and Zoo station will cost around €20.

Tempelhof airport is reached by the U6 (Platz der Luftbrücke) and by bus 119 from Kurfürstendamm via Kreuzberg. A taxi costs around €15.

Car & Motorcycle

Although garage parking is expensive (about €1.50 per hour), it makes sense to ditch your wheels as soon as possible in Berlin. Few hotels have their own garages.

Public Transport

One type of ticket is valid on all transport – including the U-Bahn, buses, trams and ferries run by **Berliner Verkehrsbetriebe** (☎ 194 49; www .bvg.de) as well as the S-Bahn and regional RE, SE and RB trains operated by **Deutsche Bahn** (www.bahn.de).

Three tariff zones exist – A, B and C. Unless venturing to Potsdam or the outer suburbs, you'll only need an AB ticket. The following are available:

Ticket type	AB	BC	ABC
Single	€2.10	€2.30	€2.60
Day Pass	€5.80	€5.70	€6
Group Day Pass (up to 5 people)	€14.80	€14.30	€15
7-Day Pass	€25.40	€26.20	€31.30

Most tickets are available from vending machines located in the stations, but must be validated before use. If you're caught without a validated ticket, there's a €50 on-the-spot fine.

GERMANY

GAY & LESBIAN BERLIN

Up there with Amsterdam as one of the gayest cities in Europe, Berlin boasts a wild scene reminiscent of the anything-goes 1920s. Venues are concentrated around Nollendorfplatz in Schöneberg and Schönhauser Allee station in northern Prenzlauer Berg. Consult gay and lesbian freebie *Siegessäule* to bone up (oo-er) on the scene.

Dance club SchwuZ (Map pp172–3; ☎ 693 7025; www.schwuz.de; Mehringdamm 61; ☿ from 11pm Fri & Sat; Ⓜ Mehringdamm) is one of the longest-running mixed institutions; there's a café here all week too.

SO36 (Map pp172–3; ☎ 6140 1307; Oranienstrasse 190; Ⓜ Kottbusser Tor) is a thrashy punk venue also popular with gays and lesbians.

Men cruise at **Grosse Freiheit** (Map p176; Boxhagener Strasse 114; ☿ from 10pm; Ⓜ Frankfurter Tor) and lesbians hang out at **Schokofabrik** (Map pp172–3; ☎ 615 1561; Mariannenstrasse 6; Ⓜ Kottbusser Tor).

A popular new bar, attracting a mixed crowd is **Zum Schmutzigen Hobby** (Map pp170–1; Rykestrasse 45; ☿ from 5pm; Ⓜ Eberswalder Strasse) run by well-known drag queen Nina Queer.

U-Bahn and S-Bahn services operate from 4am until just after midnight on weekdays, with many *Nachtbus* (night bus) services in between. At weekends, major U-Bahn lines run every 15 minutes all night, while most S-Bahns operate hourly.

Taxi

Taxi stands are located at all main train stations and throughout the city. Ring **TAXIfon** (☎ 0800-8001 1554) or **Funk Taxi** (☎ 0800-026 1026).

BRANDENBURG

Despite its proximity to Berlin, Brandenburg has suffered from a poor reputation since reunification. Many western Germans still think of Brandenburgers as archetypal Ossis, ambivalent about the demise of the GDR and perhaps even a touch xenophobic. However, even the most sneering Wessi will happily go to Potsdam on a day trip.

POTSDAM

☎ 0331 / pop 131,000

With ornate palaces and manicured gardens dotted around a huge riverside park, the Prussian royal seat of Potsdam is the most popular day trip from Berlin. Elector Friedrich Wilhelm of Brandenburg laid the ground for the town's success when he made it his second residence in the 17th century. But Friedrich II (Frederick the Great) commissioned most of the palaces in the mid-18th century.

In August 1945, the victorious WWII Allies chose nearby Schloss Cecilienhof for the Potsdam Conference, which set the stage for the division of Berlin and Germany into occupation zones.

In the suburb of Babelsberg is the site of a historic – and now once again functioning – film studio (with less historic theme park).

Orientation

Potsdam Hauptbahnhof is just southeast of the city centre, across the Havel River. As this is still quite a way – 2km – from Sansoucci Park, you might like to change here for a train going one or two stops to Charlottenhof (for Schloss Sanssouci) or Sanssouci (for Neues Palais). Some RB trains from Berlin stop at all three stations.

Information

Potsdam Information (☎ 275 580; www.potsdam tourismus.de; Brandenburger Strasse 3; ⏰ 9.30am-6pm Mon-Fri, 9.30am-4pm Sat & Sun Apr-Oct, 10am-6pm Mon-Fri, 9.30am-4pm Sat & Sun Nov-Mar) Near the Hauptbahnhof.

Sanssouci Besucherzentrum (☎ 969 4202; www.spsg .de; An der Orangerie 1; ⏰ 8.30am-5pm Mar-Oct, 9am-4pm Nov-Feb) Near the windmill and Schloss Sanssouci.

Sights

SANSSOUCI PARK

At the heart of **Sanssouci Park** (adult two-day pass incl all interiors €15; ⏰ dawn-dusk) lies a celebrated rococo palace, **Schloss Sanssouci** (☎ 969 4190; mandatory tour adult/concession €8/5; ⏰ 9am-5pm Tue-Sun Apr-Oct, to 4pm Nov-Mar). Built in 1747, it has some glorious interiors. Only 2000 visitors are allowed entry each day (a Unesco rule), so tickets are usually sold by 2.30pm, even in quiet seasons. Tours run by the tourist office guarantee entry.

The late-baroque **Neues Palais** (New Palace; ☎ 969 4255; adult/concession €5/4; ⏰ 10am-5pm Sat-Thu) was built in 1769 as the royal family's summer residence. It's one of the most imposing buildings in the park and the one to see if your time is limited. The tour takes in about a dozen of its 200 rooms.

The **Bildergalerie** (Picture Gallery; ☎ 969 4181; adult/concession €2.50/1.50; ⏰ 10am-5pm Tue-Sun 15 May-15 Oct) contains a rich collection of 17th-century paintings by Rubens, Caravaggio and other big names.

Many consider the **Chinesisches Haus** (Chinese Teahouse; ☎ 969 4222; admission €1; ⏰ 10am-5pm Tue-Sun 15 May-15 Oct) to be the pearl of the park. It's a circular pavilion of gilded columns, palm trees and figures of Chinese musicians and animals, built in 1757. Look out for a monkey with Voltaire's face!

NEUER GARTEN

When outgoing British PM Winston Churchill and his accompanying successor Clement Attlee arrived at **Schloss Cecilienhof** (☎ 969 4244; tours adult/concession €4/3; ⏰ 9am-5pm Tue-Sun) in 1945 they must have immediately felt at home. Located in the separate New Garden, northeast of the centre on the bank of the Heiliger See, this is an incongruously English-style country manor in rococo-heavy Potsdam.

Churchill and Attlee, along with US President Truman and Soviet leader Stalin, were

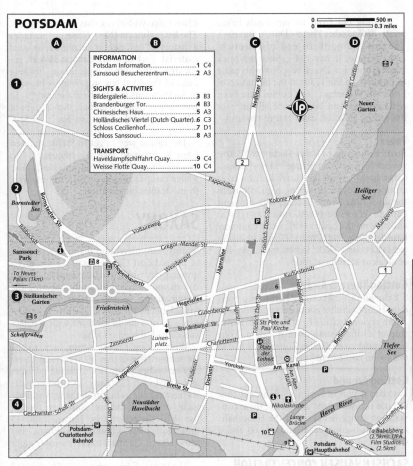

POTSDAM

INFORMATION
Potsdam Information.........................1 C4
Sanssouci Besucherzentrum...........2 A3

SIGHTS & ACTIVITIES
Bildergalerie....................................3 B3
Brandenburger Tor..........................4 B3
Chinesisches Haus............................5 A3
Holländisches Viertel (Dutch Quarter)..6 C3
Schloss Cecilienhof..........................7 D1
Schloss Sanssouci...........................8 A3

TRANSPORT
Haveldampfschiffahrt Quay.............9 C4
Weisse Flotte Quay........................10 C4

GERMANY

here for the Potsdam Conference on administering postwar Germany. Large photos of the participants are displayed inside.

FILMPARK BABELSBERG
Germany's small retort to Hollywood, the **UFA Film Studios** (☎ 721 2755; www.filmpark.de; Grossbeerenstrasse; adult/concession/child €17/15.50/12.50; ⏰ 10am-6pm 15 Mar-2 Nov) was where Fritz Lang's *Metropolis* was shot, FW Murnau filmed the first Dracula movie, *Nosferatu*, and Marlene Dietrich starred in *The Blue Angel*. Since a relaunch in 1999, it's helped Berlin regain its film-making crown, with Jean-Jacques Annaud's *Enemy at the Gates* and Roman Polanski's *The Pianist* also made here. However, the visitor experience

is not that thrilling – just par-for-the-course theme-park rides and a studio tour. The studios are east of the city centre.

ALTSTADT
In April 1945, Royal Air Force bombers devastated the historic centre of Potsdam, including the City Palace on Alter Markt. Fortunately some features – and the palaces of Sanssouci Park – survived undamaged.

The **Brandenburger Tor** (Brandenburg Gate) at the western end of the old town on Luisenplatz isn't a patch on that in Berlin but it is older, dating from 1770. From here, pedestrian Brandenburger Strasse runs due east, providing the town's main eating strip.

Standing out from its surrounds is the pretty **Holländisches Viertel** (Dutch Quarter). Towards the northern end of Friedrich-Ebert-Strasse, it has 134 gabled red-brick houses, built for Dutch workers who came to Potsdam in the 1730s at the invitation of Friedrich Wilhelm I. The homes have been well restored and now house all kinds of interesting galleries, cafés and restaurants.

Tours

Boats belonging to **Weisse Flotte** (☎ 275 9210; www.schiffahrt-in-potsdam.de; Lange Brücke 6; ☼ 8.45am-4.15pm Apr-Oct) cruise the Havel and the lakes around Potsdam, departing regularly from the dock near Lange Brücke, with frequent trips to Wannsee (€8/10 one way/return) and around the castles (€9). Sister company **Haveldampfschiffahrt** (☎ 275 9233; www.schiffahrt-in-potsdam.de; Lange Brücke 6; tours from €9.50) has equivalent steamboat tours.

Getting There & Away

S-Bahn line S7 links central Berlin with Potsdam Hauptbahnhof about every 10 minutes. Some regional (RB/RE) trains from Berlin stop at all three stations in Potsdam. Your ticket must cover Berlin Zones A, B and C (€2.60) to come here.

Getting Around

Potsdam is part of Berlin's S-Bahn network but has its own trams and buses; these converge on Lange Brücke near the Hauptbahnhof. A two-zone ticket costs €1.60 and a day pass €3.70.

SACHSENHAUSEN CONCENTRATION CAMP

In 1936 the Nazis opened a 'model' *Konzentrationslager* (concentration camp) for men in a disused brewery in Sachsenhausen, some 35km north of Berlin. By 1945 about 220,000 prisoners had passed through the gates – labelled, as at Auschwitz in Poland, *Arbeit Macht Frei* (Work Sets You Free). About 100,000 were murdered here.

After the war, the Soviets and the communist leaders of the new GDR set up Speziallager No 7 (Special Camp No 7) for political prisoners, ex-Nazis, monarchists and other 'misfits', jailing 60,000 and killing up to 12,000.

The **Sachsenhausen Memorial and Museum** (☎ 03301-200 200; ☼ 8.30am-6pm Tue-Sun Apr-Sep,

8.30am-4.30pm Oct-Mar) consists of several parts. The **Neues Museum** (New Museum) includes a history of anti-Semitism and audiovisual material. East of it are **Barracks 38 & 39**, reconstructions of two typical huts housing most of the 6000 Jewish prisoners brought to Sachsenhausen after Kristallnacht (9–10 November 1938). Number 38 was rebuilt after being torched by neo-Nazis in September 1992.

The easiest way to get to Sachsenhausen from Berlin is to take the frequent S1 to Oranienburg (€2.60, 50 minutes). The walled camp is a signposted 20-minute walk from Oranienburg station.

SAXONY

Saxony is in many ways the most successful of the old East German states. Leipzig is a growing city with a dynamic centre. Dresden is a major tourist draw and is nearing the culmination of decades of rebuilding. Linked to the latter by the fabled Elbe River, Meissen is a gem of a medieval town with a palace and cathedral high on a hill.

With a long history dating back to the Germanic tribes of over 1000 years ago, Saxony embodies many of the classic qualities associated with Germany. Its two main cities have a long tradition in the arts and are today centres of culture. And even though the local dialect can be impenetrable to those with mere schoolbook German, that same classic German traces its roots right back here.

The state is fairly compact and highspeed rail links make the region easily accessible from all corners of Germany.

DRESDEN

☎ 0351 / pop 483,000

In death, Dresden became even more famous than in life. In life, she was famous throughout Europe as 'Florence on the Elbe', owing to the efforts of Italian artists, musicians, actors and master craftsmen who flocked to the court of Augustus the Strong, bestowing countless masterpieces upon the city. Shortly before the end of WWII, Allied bombers blasted and incinerated much of the historic centre, a beautiful jewel-like area dating from the 18th century. More than 35,000 died and in bookstores throughout town you can you can see books showing the destruction (or read about it in Kurt Vonnegut's classic *Slaughterhouse Five*).

Rebuilding began under the communist regime in the 1950s and accelerated greatly after reunification. The city celebrated its 800th anniversary in 2006 and the event was capped by opening Frauenkirche, an icon that had been a pile of rubble for the previous decades. With a beautiful baroque centre and vibrant nightlife, Dresden is a major tourist attraction that's best enjoyed outside of the peak summer season.

Orientation

The Elbe River splits the town in a rough V-shape, with the Neustadt to the north and the Altstadt to the south.

Dresden has two main train stations: the Hauptbahnhof on the southern side of town, and the contemporary Dresden-Neustadt north of the river. Most trains stop at both. Dresden-Mitte is little more than a forlorn platform between the two.

From the Hauptbahnhof, pedestrian-only Prager Strasse leads north into the Altstadt. Here there's a mix of communist-era triumphalism and modern-day commercialism. The lovely Brühlsche Terrasse runs along the Elbe between the Albertinum and the Zwinger, with boat docks below.

In the Neustadt, home to much of the city's nightlife, the main attractions for visitors are the Albertplatz and Antonstadt quarters. In and around Louisenstrasse you'll find all manner of shops, galleries, funky boutiques and dozens of cafés, bars and clubs. Hauptstrasse is pedestrianised and connects Albert platz with the Augustusbrücke.

Information

Dresden Information Prager Strasse 21 (☎ 4919 2100; www.dresden.de); Theaterplatz 2 (✆ 10am-6pm Mon-Fri, 10am-4pm Sat & Sun) Discount cards from €19.

E@sy Internet (☎ 017-2579 5652; Pfarrgasse 1; per hr €4; ✆ 9am-midnight) Note that wi-fi access and Internet terminals are common in Dresden's cafés.

Haus Des Buches (☎ 497 369; Dr-Külz-Ring 12) Bookshop with huge selection on local history and culture.

Sights

MONUMENTS & LANDMARKS

One of Dresden's most beloved icons, the **Frauenkirche** (Church of Our Lady; ☎ 439 3934; www .frauenkirche-dresden.org; Neumarkt; ✆ 10am-6pm)

was rebuilt in time for city's 800th anniversary celebrations. Built between 1726 and 1743 under the direction of baroque architect George Bähr, it was Germany's greatest Protestant church until February 1945, when bombing raids flattened it. The communists decided to leave the rubble as a war memorial; after reunification, calls for reconstruction prevailed and the huge project began in 1992.

Look for the very few blackened stones on the exterior, these were salvaged from the rubble of the original. Otherwise – not surprisingly – the church feels brand new, especially inside. Most moving is the melted cross from the original. You can also climb to the top for good views. The surrounding Neumarkt is part of a massive redevelopment designed to evoke prewar Dresden.

The neo-Renaissance opera house, **Semperoper** (☎ 491 1496; www.semperoper.de; Theaterplatz; tour adult/child €6/3; ✆ varies), designed by Gustav Semper, *is* Dresden. The original building opened in 1841 but burned down less than three decades later. Rebuilt in 1878, it was pummelled in WWII and reopened in 1985 after the communists invested millions restoring it. The best way to appreciate it is through one of the many performances.

The **Schloss** (☎ 491 4619; Schlossplatz), a massive neo-Renaissance palace, has ongoing restoration projects. Its many features include the **Hausmannsturm** (Servants' Tower; adult/child €2.50/1.50; ✆ 10am-6pm Wed-Mon) and the baroque Catholic **Hofkirche** (✆ 9am-5pm Mon-Thu, 1-5pm Fri, 10am-5pm Sat, noon-4pm Sun), which contains the heart of Augustus the Strong. Outside, you'd need a really wide-angle lens to get a shot of Wulhelm Walther's amazing 102m-long tiled mural, the **Fürstenzug** (Procession of Princes; Augustusstrasse), on the wall of the former Stendehaus (Royal Stables). The scene, a long row of royalty on horses, was painted in 1876 and then transferred to some 24,000 Meissen porcelain tiles in 1906. The Schloss also houses museums, see below.

MUSEUMS

For information on most of Dresden's museums, see the website www.skd-dresden.de. Allow at least two full days for a sampling of what's on offer.

The imposing block, **Albertinum** (☎ 491 4619; Brühlsche Terrasse; adult/child €5/2.50; ✆ 10am-6pm Wed-Mon), houses many of Dresden's art treasures, including the **Münzkabinett** collection of antique coins and medals, and the **Skulpturensammlung**, which includes classical and Egyptian works. The **Galerie Neue Meister**, with renowned 19th- and 20th-century paintings from leading French and German impressionists, was closed during 2006 for expansion and renovation.

Dresden's elaborate 1728 fortress **Zwinger** (☎ 491 4622; Theaterplatz 1; ✆ 10am-6pm Tue-Sun) is an attraction in its own right, with a popular ornamental courtyard, and also houses six major museums. The most important are the **Rüstkammer** (armoury; adult/child €3/2), with its superb collection of ceremonial weapons, and the **Galerie Alte Meister** (adult/child €6/3.50,

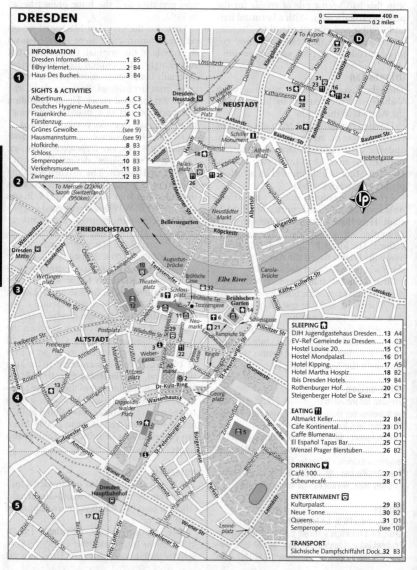

DRESDEN

0 ——————— 400 m
0 ——————— 0.2 miles

incl entry to Rüstkammer), which features masterpieces including Raphael's *Sistine Madonna*. The dazzling **Porzelansammlung** (Porcelain Collection; adult/child €5/3) is another highlight.

Located in the Schloss, the **Grünes Gewölbe** (Green Vault; adult/child €6/3.50; ☺ 10am-6pm Wed-Mon) is one of the world's finest collections of jewel-encrusted precious objects. Treasures include the world's biggest green diamond, tiny pearl sculptures and a stunning group of 137 gem-studded figures by Johann Melchior Dinglinger, court jeweller of Augustus the Strong.

Also in the Schloss, the **Verkehrsmuseum** (Transport Museum; ☎ 864 40; Augustusstrasse 1; adult/child €3/1.50; ☺ 10am-5pm Tue-Sun) is fittingly located in the Johanneum, the old stables. Motoring back towards the 20th century, this is a fascinating collection including penny-farthings, trams, dirigibles and carriages. Included in the admission is a great 40-minute film with original black-and-white footage of 1930s Dresden.

One of the oddest museums is the product of a mouthwash baron. The **Deutsches Hygiene-Museum** (☎ 484 6670; Lingnerplatz 1; adult/child €6/3; ☺ 10am-6pm Tue-Sun) is awash in displays relating to the ravages of venereal disease, the theory of eugenics and reasons to bathe.

Tours

Cruise the Elbe on the world's oldest fleet of paddle-wheel steamers with **Sächsische Dampfschiffahrt** (☎ 866 090; www.saechsische-dampfschiffahrt .de; adult/child €11/5.50). Ninety-minute tours leave from the Terrassenufer dock at 11am, 1pm, 3pm and 5pm daily. There's also service to villages along the river.

Sleeping

Accommodation in Dresden can be very expensive in the high season. Luckily, several good-value budget places can be found in the lively Neustadt. New luxury hotels are opening as the Altstadt is renovated.

BUDGET

DJH Jugendgästehaus Dresden (☎ 492 620; jgh dresden@djh-sachsen.de; Maternistrasse 22; dm €17; ☒ ☐) This tower block was once a Communist Party training centre; now it's a great hostel, with 480 beds in small dorms and a bistro (breakfast included). Take tram 7 or 10 to the corner of Ammonstrasse and Freiberger Strasse.

Hostel Louise 20 (☎ 889 4894; www.louise20.de; Louisenstrasse 20; dm/s/d €15/30/40; ☐) Rooms are divided between two buildings here. Basic ones are off a courtyard at the back while more expensive – and stylish – units are up front. Families can rent entire suites of rooms. There are kitchen facilities; most rooms share baths.

Hostel Mondpalast (☎ 804 6061; www.mondpalast .de; Louisenstrasse 77; dm/s/d €15/39/50; ☒ ☐) The Moon Palace has rooms decorated by theme (Australia, Greece, space travel – see the website) and a great bar/café. It's one of many good value places in this fun-filled neighbourhood.

EV-Ref Gemeinde zu Dresden (☎ 438 230; www.ev -ref-gem-dresden.de; Brühlscher Garten 4; s/d €45/70) Amazing value in a great location – right across from the Albertinum and on the river. This historic retirement home makes rooms available for travellers whenever a resident has permanently 'checked out'. Rooms have baths and TV and often great views, although obviously they'd prefer you keep quiet.

MIDRANGE

Hotel Kipping (☎ 478 500; www.hotel-kipping.de; Winckelmannstrasse 6; s/d from €75/90; ☒ ☐) Just south of the Hauptbahnhof, this is a family-run, family-friendly hotel that comes with 20 comfortable rooms in a house right out of the *Addams Family*. The bar and café are especially appealing and there's wi-fi.

Ibis Dresden Lilienstein (☎ 4856 6663; www.ibis hotel.com; Prager Strasse 13; r €50-120; ☒ ☒ ☐) Together with the adjoining Ibis Dresden Bastei and the Ibis Dresden Königstein, this huge communist-era complex has over 900 rooms. The décor has been redone in 'cheap and cheerful' and pluses include wi-fi and a good chance at a vacancy in summer. The breakfast buffet is vast.

Hotel Martha Hospiz (☎ 817 60; www.vch.de; Nieritzstrasse 11; r €54-120; ☒ ☐) Quiet reigns in this 50-room inn with country furnishings, built over 100 years ago by a church. The location is central and it has many amenities, including wi-fi.

Rothenburger Hof (☎ 812 60; www.rothenburger -hof.de; Rothenburger Strasse 15-17; r €75-140; ☒ ☐ ☒) In the middle of Neustadt you'll find this well-appointed 26-room place in a renovated 1865 mansion. It offers many health treatments in its spa and sauna.

TOP END

Steigenberger Hotel De Saxe (☎ 438 60; www.desaxe-dresden.steigenberger.com; Neumarkt 9; r from €200; ☒ ☒ ⬚) This 178-room grand hotel opened in 2006 on the site of a historic hotel of the same name. It's part of the scheme to recreate the prewar Neumarkt around the Frauenkirche. The hotel offers a spa, sauna, wi-fi and many more luxuries.

Eating

It's no problem finding somewhere to eat in the Neustadt, with oodles of cafés and restaurants found along Königstrasse and the streets north of Albertplatz. This is definitely the most interesting part of town at night. South of the river, look near the Altmarkt, and Münzgasse/Terrassengasse, between Brühlsche Terrasse and the Frauenkirche, for restaurants representing all kinds of local and international cuisine.

Cafe Kontinental (☎ 801 3531; Görlitzer Strasse 1; mains €5-15; ☽ 24hr; ⬚) A bustling place open around the clock, this trendy café caters to a broad swath of Neustadt characters.

Caffe Blumenau (☎ 802 6502; Louisenstrasse 67; mains €5-15; ☽ 8am-2am; ⬚) Flowers abound in this beautiful café and bar, which also has a sunny back patio. A long breakfast menu is served through the day as well as sandwiches, salads, pasta and cakes.

Wenzel Prager Bierstuben (☎ 804 2010; Königstrasse 1; mains €7-20; ☽ 11am-midnight) This busy beer hall serves up oceans of Czech lager under arched brick ceilings. Always crowded, the menu leans towards traditional meaty mains. The garlic soup is sublime, the cured pork with horseradish a delight.

El Español Tapas Bar (☎ 804 8670; An der Dreikönigskirche 7; meals €7-20; ☽ 11am-1am) On a leafy square overlooking the newly restored Three Kings Church, this tapas place glows with good seasoning and good cheer. When it's warm dine on the square, when it's cold settle into the woodsy interior. The tapas menu is long and varied.

Altmarkt Keller (☎ 481 8130; Altmarkt 4; mains €8-25; ☽ 11am-midnight) The foods of Saxony and neighbouring Bohemia (in the Czech Republic) are featured in this underground restaurant. Look for lots of hearty pork and beef dishes and as well as all manner of dumplings. On many nights there's live music that gets the tourist toes a-tapping.

Drinking & Entertainment

As elsewhere, many of the places listed under Eating above are also good just for a drink.

Dresden is synonymous with opera, and performances at the spectacular **Semperoper** (☎ 491 1496; www.semperoper.de; Theaterplatz) are brilliant. Tickets cost from €10, but they're usually booked out well in advance. Some performances by the renowned philharmonic are also held there, but most are in the communist-era **Kulturpalast** (☎ 486 60; www.kulturpalast-dresden.de; Schlossstrasse 2), which hosts a wide range of concerts and events.

Neue Tonne (☎ 802 6017; www.jazzclubtonne.de; Königstrasse 15; entry free-€15) This well-known place has live music almost nightly.

Scheunecafé (☎ 802 6619; Alaunstrasse 36-40; mains €7-12) Set back from the street, Indian food, a vast beer garden, live music and deejays all combine here for a fun and funky stew.

Café 100 (☎ 801 7729; Alaunstrasse 100) Off a courtyard, you'll pass hundreds of empty bottles on the way in, a foreshadowing of the lengthy wine list and delights that follow. Candles give the underground space a romantic yet edgy glow.

Queens (☎ 810 8108; Görlitzerstrasse 3) This hopping gay bar/lounge/disco is a good first stop to find out what's happening locally.

Getting There & Around

Dresden's **airport** (DRS; www.dresden-airport.de), served by Lufthansa, DBA, Air Berlin among others, is 9km north of the city centre, on S-Bahn line 2 (€1.70, 30 minutes). The Airport City Liner bus serves Dresden-Neustadt (€3) and the Hauptbahnhof (€4), with stops at key points in town. A taxi to the Hauptbahnhof is about €15.

Dresden is well linked to the regular service through the day to Leipzig (€26, 70 minutes), Berlin-Hauptbahnhof by IC/EC train (€30.20, 2¼ hours) and Frankfurt-am-Main (€76, 4½ hours).

Dresden's **public transport network** (www.dvbag.de) charges €1.70 for a single ticket; day tickets cost €4.50. Tram 3, 6, 7 and 8 provide good links between the Hauptbahnhof and Neustadt.

AROUND DRESDEN

Meissen

☎ 03521 / pop 29,000

Some 27km northwest of Dresden, Meissen is a compact, perfectly preserved old town and the centre of a rich wine-growing region. It makes for a good day trip out of Dresden by train or boat and beguiles with its red-tiled roofs and historic charm.

Meissen's medieval fortress, the Albrechtsburg, crowns a ridge high above the Elbe River and contains the former ducal palace and Meissen Cathedral, a magnificent Gothic structure. Augustus the Strong of Saxony created Europe's first porcelain factory here in 1710. The town celebrated its 1075th anniversary in 2004.

Like Dresden, Meissen straddles the Elbe River, with the old town on the western bank and the train station on the eastern. Both sides were struck by record flood levels in 2002, with water pushing quite a distance into the Altstadt; look out for plaques marking the highest points. Cafés line the streets and are popular on warm days.

The tourist office is at **Meissen-Information** (☎ 419 40; www.touristinfo-meissen.de; Markt 3; ☽ 10am-6pm Mon-Fri, to 4pm Sat & Sun, to 4pm Mon-Fri, to 3pm Sat Nov-Mar). Staff can help find accommodation.

Steep stepped lanes lead up to Meissen's towering 13th-century **Albrechtsburg Cathedral** (☎ 452 490; Domplatz 7; adult/child €3.50/2; ☽ 10am-6pm Mar-Oct, 10am-4pm Nov-Feb), which contains an altarpiece by Lucas Cranach the Elder.

Beside the cathedral is the remarkable 15th-century **palace** (☎ 470 70; Domplatz 1; adult/child €3.50/2.50; ☽ 10am-6pm Mar-Oct, to 5pm Nov-Feb), widely seen as the birthplace of Schloss architecture, with its ingenious system of internal arches. A combined ticket for both buildings costs adult/child €5/2.50.

Meissen has long been renowned for its chinaware, with its trademark insignia of blue crossed swords. The Albrechtsburg palace was originally the manufacturing site, but the factory is now 1km southwest of the Altstadt in an appropriately beautiful building, the **Porzellan Manufaktur** (Porcelain Factory; ☎ 468 700; Talstrasse 9; adult/child €8/4; ☽ 9am-6pm May-Oct, 9am-5pm Nov-Apr), which dates to 1916. There are often long queues for the workshop demonstrations, but you can view the porcelain collection upstairs at your leisure.

GETTING THERE & AWAY
Half-hourly S-Bahn trains run from Dresden's Hauptbahnhof and Neustadt train stations (€5.10, 45 minutes). To visit the porcelain factory, get off at Meissen-Triebischtal (one stop after Meissen).

A more interesting way to get here is by steamer (between May and September). Boats leave from the Sächsische Dampfschiffahrt (see p189) dock in Dresden at 9.45am and head back at 2.45pm (€16.10 return, two hours).

Saxon Switzerland
Sächsische Schweiz (Saxon Switzerland) is a 275 sq km national park 50km south of Dresden, near the Czech border. Its wonderfully wild, craggy country is dotted with castles and tiny towns along the mighty Elbe. The landscape varies unexpectedly and radically: its forests can look deceptively tropical, while the worn cliffs and plateaus recall the parched expanses of New Mexico or central Spain (generally without the searing heat).

The highlight of the park is the **Bastei** lookout, on the Elbe some 28km southeast of Dresden. One of the most breathtaking spots in the whole of Germany, it features towering outcrops 305m high and unparalleled views of the surrounding forests, cliffs and mountains, not to mention a magnificent sightline right along the river itself.

LEIPZIG
☎ 0341 / pop 498,000
Leipzig is the busiest city in Saxony, a livelier alternative to Dresden. Although it lacks the capital's bus-load of museums, Leipzig in many ways feels more vibrant in an everyday sense. It's not weighed down by the past and like its shopping passages, invites exploration.

Leipzig also has some of the finest classical music and opera in the country, and its art and literary scenes are flourishing. Once home to Bach, Wagner and Mendelssohn, and to Goethe (who set a key scene of *Faust* in the cellar of his favourite watering hole), it more recently earned the sobriquet *Stadt der Helden* (City of Heroes) for its leading role in the 1989 democratic revolution.

The city has a compact arts centre worth wandering and a growing arts scene. It's definitely worth a day or two of your travels.

Orientation
Leipzig's centre lies within a ring road that outlines the town's medieval fortifications. To reach the city centre from the Hauptbahnhof, cross Willy-Brandt-Platz and continue south along Nikolaistrasse for five minutes.

The central Markt (square), which was being redeveloped for a new station at the time of research, is a couple of blocks southwest, and east down Grimmiasche Strasse is the massive Augustusplatz, home to some of the city's most important (if not prettiest) GDR-era buildings and also the modern MDR Tower.

The Hauptbahnhof contains a modern mall with over 140 shops and (radically for Germany) it is open from 6am to 10pm daily. You'll find good bookshops, a post office, banks and much more. There's wi-fi in the DB Lounge.

Information

Internetcafé (☎ 993 9530; Reichsstrasse 18; per 15 min €1; ☷ 10am-10pm) A full service shop for CD burning and Internet.

Leipzig Tourist Service (☎ 710 4260; www.leipzig.de; Richard-Wagner-Strasse 1; ☷ 9am-7pm Mon-Fri, 9am-4pm Sat, 9am-2pm Sun) One of the most helpful in Germany, with discount cards from €7.40.

Sights

Don't rush from sight to sight – wandering around Leipzig is a pleasure in itself, with many of the blocks around the central Markt crisscrossed by old internal shopping passages. Four good ones: **Steibs Hof** (100-year-old blue tiles and classic cafés), **Specs Hof** (soaring atrium, bookshops, cafés), **Jägerhofpassage** (galleries, theatre, antiques) and the classic **Mädlerpassage** (grand design, the famous Auerbachs Keller, see p194).

MONUMENTS & LANDMARKS

Off the southern ring road is the 108m-high tower of the baroque **Neues Rathaus** (new town hall; ☎ 1230; Martin-Luther-Ring; ☷ 7am-4.30pm Mon-Fri). Though the origins date to the 16th century, its current manifestation was completed in 1905. The interior makes it one of the finest municipal buildings in Germany; the lobby houses rotating art exhibitions, mostly on historical themes.

Located 4km southeast of the centre, the **Völkerschlachtdenkmal** (Battle of Nations Monument; Strasse des 18 Oktober; adult/child €3/1.50; ☷ 10am-6pm Apr-Oct, to 4pm Nov-Mar) is a massive 91m-high monument commemorating the decisive victory here by the combined Prussian, Austrian and Russian forces over Napoleon's army in 1813. Climb the 500 steps for a view of the region. Take tram 15 from the station (direction Meusdorf).

MUSEUMS

Leipzig's finest museum, the **Museum der Bildenden Künste** (Museum of Fine Arts; ☎ 216 990; Grimmaische Strasse 1-7; adult/child €5/3.50; ☷ 10am-6pm Tue & Thu-Sun, 10am-8pm Wed), is housed in a stunning new building that provides both a dramatic – and echoey – backdrop to its collection, which spans old masters and the latest efforts of local artists.

Haunting and uplifting by turns, the **Zeitgeschichtliches Forum** (Forum of Contemporary History; ☎ 222 20; Grimmaische Strasse 6; admission free; ☷ 9am-6pm Tue-Fri, 10am-6pm Sat & Sun) tells the story of the GDR from division and dictatorship to resistance and reform. It does a good job of chronicling the 1989 revolution, which started here and it captures the tragic drama of the original Iron Curtain division.

Former headquarters of the East German secret police, the **Stasi Museum** (☎ 961 2443; Dittrichring 24; admission free; ☷ 10am-6pm) has exhibits on propaganda, amazingly hokey disguises, surveillance photos and other forms of 'intelligence'. There are also mounds of papier-mâché that were created when officers shredded and soaked secret documents before the fall of the GDR.

Opposite the Thomaskirche, is the **Bach Museum** (☎ 964 110; Thomaskirchhof 16; adult/child €3/2; ☷ 10am-5pm), where JS Bach worked from 1723 until his death in 1750. This collection focuses on the composer's busy life in Leipzig. There are portraits, manuscripts and other Bach memorabilia.

ART

Leipzig has a thriving art scene thanks to the Art Academy of Leipzig, a famous old school where figurative painting never went out of style. Now the efforts of its many local grads such as Neo Rauch, Tim Eitel and Tilo Baumgärtel are all the rage. You can see some of the best works at the Museum der Bildenden Künste (see above) or you can go out to the many **galleries** found along Spinnereisstrasse, 2km west of the centre (take tram 14 to stop S-Bf. Miltitzer Allee). The tourist office has useful gallery information.

Sleeping

Leipzig Tourist Service (see left) offers free booking in private homes near the centre. Average cost is €30 to €45.

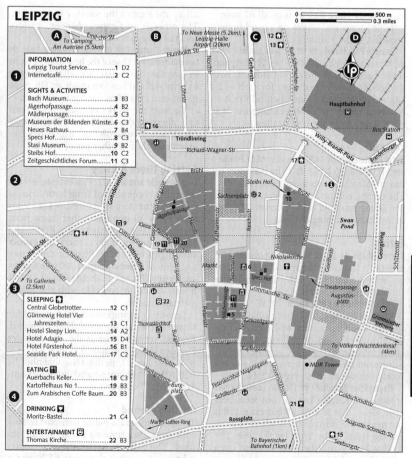

LEIPZIG

0 ──── 500 m
0 ──── 0.3 miles

BUDGET

Camping Am Auensee (☎ 465 1600; www.motel-auensee .de; Gustav-Esche-Strasse 5; camp sites per person from €3, cabins €28-35) This camping ground is in a pleasant wooded spot on the city's northwestern outskirts (take tram 10 or 28 to Wahren). The cabins are A-frame bungalows.

Central Globetrotter (☎ 149 8960; www.globetrotter -leipzig.de; Kurt-Schumacher-Strasse 41; dm €14, s/d €24/36; 🖳) In a busy location just north of the train station, this 80-room hostel offers bare-bones accommodation, although some rooms boast murals, albeit ones that won't win any scholarships to the Art Academy of Leipzig.

Hostel Sleepy Lion (☎ 993 9480; www.hostel-leipzig .de; Käthe-Kollwitz-Strasse 3; dm €15, s/d €28/40; ✕ 🖳)

All rooms have their own baths at this 59-room facility in a renovated building. Some come with fake trees as well.

MIDRANGE

Midrange accommodation in the centre is fairly unexciting and usually the preserve of the big chains (particularly the many Accor brands).

Hotel Adagio (☎ 216 699; www.hotel-adagio.de; Seeburgstrasse 96; r €72-95; ✕) The 32 rooms here are smartly decked out with a black-and-white theme. You can take breakfast in the garden and there's a certain intimate charm.

Günnewig Hotel Vier Jahreszeiten (☎ 985 10; www.gunnewig.de; Kurt-Schumacher-Strasse 23; r €60-130; ✕ 🖳) Close to the train station, this anonymous place has wi-fi in all 67 comfortable rooms and serves up a good buffet breakfast in the atrium.

Seaside Park Hotel (☎ 985 20; www.seaside-hotels .de; Richard-Wagner-Strasse 7; r €95-140; ⌘) Leipzig could hardly be further from the sea, but the Seaside makes a real name for itself with 288 well-furnished rooms. Behind the Art Nouveau façade is a modern interior. It's right across from the train station.

TOP END

Hotel Fürstenhof (☎ 1400; www.starwood.de; Tröndlinring 8; r €135-350; ⌘ ⌘ ⌘ ⌘ ⌘) The best place to stay in town has roots going back 200 years. The current edition has 92 rooms, a fine garden and reeks of old world elegance. It's part of the Starwood conglomerate.

Eating

Kartoffelhaus No 1 (☎ 960 4603; Barfussgässchen 12; mains €6-12) Kids love the spuds, and you can get 'em baked, fried, boiled, grilled and more (that's the tubers not the kids).

Zum Arabischen Coffe Baum (☎ 965 1321; Kleine Fleischergasse 4; mains €6-15) Leipzig's oldest coffee bar has a restaurant and café offering excellent meals over three floors, plus a free coffee museum at the top. Composer Robert Schumann met friends here, and if you ask nicely you can sit at his regular table.

Bayerischer Bahnhof (☎ 124 5760; Bayerischer Platz 1; mains €7-20) Leipzig has its own local beer style, Gose, that is sadly all but extinct. But not here at this microbrewery where you can get the light, herby brew by the litre. The food is hearty and the place remains open while the real train station is rebuilt next door. Take tram 9, 10 or 16.

Auerbachs Keller (☎ 216 100; www.auerbachs-keller -leipzig.de; Mädlerpassage; mains €14-22) Founded in 1525, Auerbachs Keller is one of Germany's classic restaurants, serving typically hearty fare. Goethe's *Faust – Part I* includes a scene here, in which Mephistopheles and Faust carouse with some students before they ride off on a barrel. The historic section of the restaurant includes the Goethe room and the Fasskeller; note the carved tree-trunk in the latter, depicting the whole barrel-riding adventure.

Drinking & Entertainment

Barfussgässchen and Kleine Flieschergasse, west of the Markt, form one of Leipzig's two 'pub miles', packed with outdoor tables that

fill up the second the weather turns warm. The other is on Gottschedstrasse, a wider cocktail strip just west of the Altstadt.

Moritz-Bastei (☎ 702 590; www.moritzbastei.de; Universitätsstrasse 9) One of the best student clubs in Germany, in a spacious cellar below the old city walls. It has live music or DJs most nights and runs films outside in summer.

To hear the works of native-born Bach and others, try the 18th-century **Thomaskirche** (☎ 212 4676; Thomaskirchhof 18), which has frequent recitals and other performances.

Getting There & Away

Leipzig-Halle airport (LEJ; www.leipzig-halle-airport .de), roughly equidistant from both cities, is served by the Airport Express (€4, 15 minutes) every 30 minutes. Other trains from the region also stop there. Air Berlin and Lufthansa are the main carriers, the former with flights to London. Ryanair serves tiny and remote **Altenburg airport** (ADC; www.flughafen -altenburg.de). There's a shuttle bus (€14, 1¾ hours) timed to coincide with the flights to/from London.

Leipzig is an important rail hub and fittingly has a monumental Hauptbahnhof. Regular service through the day includes Dresden (€26, 70 minutes), Munich by ICE (€74, five hours), Berlin-Hauptbahnhof by ICE (€36, 70 minutes) and Frankfurt-am-Main (€61, 3½ hours).

Getting Around

Trams are the main public transport option, with most lines running via the Hauptbahnhof. The S-Bahn circles the city's outer suburbs. A single ticket costs €1.70 and a day card €4.90. A vast project of building an S-Bahn line under the city centre is due for completion in 2009.

THURINGIA

Thuringa likes to trade on its reputation as the 'Green Heart' of Germany, an honour helped by the former GDR's dodgy economy, which limited development. These days its main towns of Erfurt, Weimar and Eisenach are popular for their historic centres and deserve visits, even if it's just a break in a train journey.

While the communist era may have been relatively benign, the previous decades were not. The Nazis had numerous concentration camps here including the notorious Buchenwald and the nightmare of Mittelbau Dora. But yet again, in contrast, Weimar was the place where Germany tried a liberal democracy in the 1920s and in previous centuries it was home to notables such as Bach, Schiller, Goethe, Thomas Mann and many more.

ERFURT
☎ 0361 / pop 202,000

Thuringia's capital was founded by St Boniface as a bishopric in 742. In the Middle Ages the city shot to prominence and prosperity as an important trading post. The Altstadt's many well-preserved 16th-century and later buildings attest to its wealth.

During WWII, damage was extensive, and the GDR regime did little to restore the city's former glories. Over the past decade, however, Erfurt has spiffed up what it has and a stroll through the old streets and across the rivers is a delight.

Orientation

Most of the car traffic is routed around the Altstadt via two ring roads, making it a pleasure to walk between the main sights. The train and bus stations are just beyond the southeastern edge of the town centre, and were undergoing a massive reconstruction at the time of research. It's a five-minute walk north along Bahnhofstrasse to Anger, the main shopping and business artery. The little Gera River bisects the Altstadt, spilling off into numerous creeks.

Information

Erfurt Tourismus (☎ 664 00; www.erfurt-tourist-info .de; Benediktsplatz 1; ☼ 10am-7pm Mon-Fri, to 4pm Sat & Sun) Has a discount card from €9.90.
Internettreff (☎ 262 3834; Ratskellerpassage, Fischmarkt 5; per hr €1.50; ☼ 1-8pm Mon-Sat) Has Internet access.

Sights

It's hard to miss Erfurt's cathedral, **Dom St Marien** (☎ 646 1265; Domplatz; tours adult/child €2.50/1.50; ☼ 9am-5pm Mon-Fri, to 4pm Sat, 1-5pm Sun, less in winter), which casts its massive shadow over Domplatz from an artificial hill built specially to hold it. Ironically, it was originally only planned as a simple chapel in 752; by the time it was completed it was the rather strange, huge amalgam you see today (if only

a divine hand could reach down and rearrange things a bit…). In July the stone steps leading up to the cathedral are the site of the **Domstufenfestspiele**, where operas are performed against the dramatic background.

Next to the cathedral, the 1280 **Severikirche** (☎ 576 960; ☼ 9am-12.30pm & 1.30-5pm Mon-Fri, less in winter) is an impressive five-aisled church hall boasting a stone Madonna (1345) and a 15m-high baptismal font (1467), as well as the sarcophagus of St Severus, whose remains were brought to Erfurt in 836.

The **Augustinerkloster** (☎ 576 600; Augustinerstrasse; adult/child €6/5; ☼ tours 10am-noon & 2-5pm Tue-Sat, 11am-2pm Sun), now a nunnery, has a strong pedigree: Martin Luther was a monk here from 1505 to 1511 and, after being ordained beneath the chapel's stained-glass windows, read his first mass. You can view Luther's cell and an exhibit on the Reformation. The grounds and church are free.

North of the Dom complex and west of Andreasstrasse, many of the city's lesser churches were demolished to erect the impressively tough-looking **Citadelle Petersberg** (Petersberg fortress; ☎ 211 5270) – hence the reason why Erfurt has so many steeples without churches attached. There is a fascinating series of subterranean tunnels within the thick walls, which can only be seen on a guided tour from the tourist office.

Unique in this part of Europe, the medieval **Krämerbrücke** (Merchants' Bridge) is an 18m-wide, 120m-long curiosity spanning the Gera River. Quaint houses and shops line both sides of the narrow road.

Sleeping

Jugendherberge Hochheimerstrasse (☎ 6013 2600; www.djh.de; Hochheimer Strasse 12; dm from €17; ☒ 🖳) This modern 200-bed hostel is 2km south of the city (take tram 5 to Steigerstrasse).

Pension am Dom (☎ 55048660; www.pension-am-dom -erfurt.de; Lange Brücke 57; r €29-69; ☒) True to its name, this friendly little central *pension* has superb views of the cathedral from the breakfast room and terrace. Rooms are light and airy with natural wood floors. It's located over some trendy stores.

InterCity Hotel (☎ 560 00; www.intercityhotel.com; Willy-Brandt-Platz 11; r €60-120; ☒ 🐾 🖳) Part of the new train station complex, this modern and comfortable abode has good views of the choo-choos and is convenient for the centre. It has wi-fi.

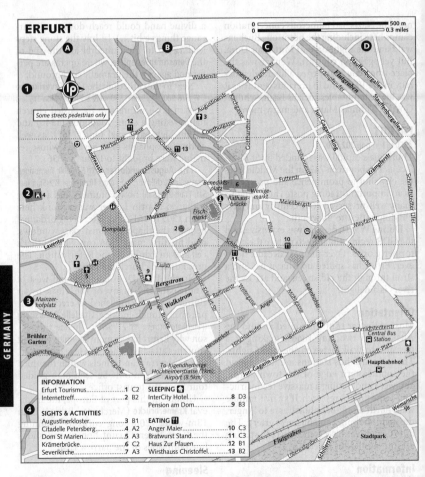

ERFURT

0 — 500 m
0 — 0.3 miles

Some streets pedestrian only

To Jugendherberge
Hochheimerstrasse (1km);
Airport (8.5km)

INFORMATION	
Erfurt Tourismus................1	C2
Internettreff....................2	B2
SIGHTS & ACTIVITIES	
Augustinerkloster..............3	B1
Citadelle Petersberg...........4	A2
Dom St Marien.................5	A3
Krämerbrücke..................6	C2
Severikirche....................7	A3

SLEEPING	
InterCity Hotel.................8	D3
Pension am Dom...............9	B3
EATING	
Anger Maier...................10	C3
Bratwurst Stand...............11	C3
Haus Zur Pfauen..............12	B1
Wirsthauss Christoffel.........13	B2

Eating

Look for interesting and trendy restaurants and cafés along Michaelisstrasse and Marbacher Gasse. For a quick treat, have a *Thuringer Bratwurst* hot off the grill from a **stand** (☎ 793 5250; Schlösserstrasse; meal €1.50) near a small waterfall.

Wirsthauss Christoffel (☎ 262 6943; Michaelisstrasse 41; mains €6-11) History oozes out of the wooden walls at this quaint little café. As the name implies, local sausage is a house specialty. On some nights films are shown in the basement.

Anger Maier (☎ 566 1058; Schlösserstrasse 8; mains €6-12) This tunnel-like restaurant is an Erfurt institution, with cheap, quality eats in a busy, smoky old warren.

Haus Zur Pfauen (☎ 211 5209; Marbacher Gasse 12; mains €7-10) An atmospheric microbrewery with a large beer garden and tasty brews. If you're reduced to crawling, you might just head upstairs to the simple rooms (accommodation from €45).

Getting There & Around

Erfurt's Hauptbahnhof is on a line with frequent service linking Leipzig (€25, one hour), Weimar (€7, 15 minutes) and Eisenach (€9 to €17, 30 to 50 minutes). Hourly ICE/IC service goes to Frankfurt (€46, 2½ hours) and Berlin-Hauptbahnhof (€47, 2¾ hours).

Public transport in the city centre costs €1.50 but you're likely to just walk.

AROUND ERFURT

Eisenach is home to the Wartburg, the only German castle to be named a Unesco World Heritage Site. Composer Johann Sebastian Bach was born here but he plays second fiddle to the amazing edifice in stone and half-timber high on the hill.

The small town has a good **tourist office** (☎ 792 30; www.eisenach.de; Markt 9; ☺ 10am-6pm Mon, 9am-6pm Tue-Fri, 10am-2pm Sat & Sun), which can help you find accommodation if your day trip gets extended.

The **Wartburg** (☎ 2500; www.wartburg-eisenach .de; tour adult/child €6/3; ☺ tours 8.30am-5pm), parts of which date to the 11th century, is perched high above the town on a wooded hill, is said to go back to Count Ludwig der Springer (the Jumper); you'll hear the story of how the castle got its name many times, but listen out for how Ludwig got his peculiar moniker as well.

The castle owes its huge popularity to Martin Luther, who went into hiding here from 1521 to 1522 after being excommunicated; during this time he translated the entire New Testament from Greek into German, contributing enormously to the development of the written German language. His modest, wood-panelled **study** is part of the guided tour (available in English), which is the only way to view the interior. The **museum** houses the famous Cranach paintings of Luther and important Christian artefacts from all over Germany. Most of the rooms you'll see here are extravagant 19th-century impressions of medieval life rather than original fittings; the re-imagined Great Hall inspired Richard Wagner's opera *Tannhäuser*. Between Easter and October, crowds can be horrendous; arrive before 11am.

Frequent direct trains run to Erfurt (€9 to €17, 30 to 50 minutes) and most continue on the short distance to Weimar.

WEIMAR

☎ 03643 / pop 64,000

The city of Goethe is not impressive on first glance. There are no vast cathedrals or palaces, nor are there any world-renowned museums. But spend a little time wandering its very attractive old streets and visiting its fascinating little museums and historic houses and soon you will understand the allure. You'll feel the presence of notables like Luther, Schiller and Liszt and you'll begin to understand the remarkable cultural accomplishments achieved in Weimar over the centuries.

Because of its historical significance, Weimar has received particularly large handouts for the restoration of its many fine buildings, and in 1999 it was the European Capital of Culture. While the city can sometimes feel like a giant museum teeming with tourists, it is one of Germany's most fascinating places and should not be missed.

Orientation

Weimar's compact and walkable centre is a 20-minute jaunt downhill from the station.

Information

There are scores of little book and music shops in town.

Tourist Information (☎ 240 00; www.weimar.de; Markt 10; ☺ 9.30am-6pm Mon-Fri, 9.30am-4pm Sat & Sun) Discount cards good for most admissions from €13.

Vobis (☎ 902 925; Schwanseestrasse; per hr €2; ☺ 10am-8pm) Internet access.

Sights

A good place to begin a tour is in front of the neo-Gothic 1841 **Rathaus** on the Markt. For in-depth museum information and high-end souvenirs try the **Stiftung Weimarer Klassik** (Weimar Classics Foundation; ☎ 545 401; www.swkk.de; Frauentorstrasse 4; ☺ 10am-6pm).

Those who visit the **Goethe Nationalmuseum** (☎ 545 347; Frauenplan 1; adult/child €6.50/5; ☺ 9am-6pm Tue-Sun) expecting to learn all about the great man of letters will probably be disappointed. Rather than focusing on Goethe himself, the museum offers a broad overview of German classicism, from its proponents to its patrons.

The adjoining **Goethe Haus**, where such works as *Faust* were written, focuses much more on the man himself. He lived here from 1775 until his death in 1832. Goethe's original 1st-floor living quarters are reached via an expansive Italian Renaissance staircase decorated with sculpture and paintings brought back from his travels to Italy. You'll see his dining room, study and the bedroom with his deathbed. Because demand often exceeds capacity, you'll be given a time slot to enter. Once inside, you can stay as long as you want. The **Faustina café** has a controversial Christoph Hodgson mural depicting Weimar's famous and infamous.

GERMANY

The Bauhaus school and movement were founded in Weimar in 1919 by Walter Gropius, who managed to draw top artists including Kandinsky, Klee, Feininger and Schlemmer as teachers. The exhibition at the **Bauhaus Museum** (☎ 545 961; Theaterplatz; adult/child €4.50/3.50; ☉ 10am-6pm) chronicles the evolution of the group, explains its innovations and spotlights the main players. In 1925 the Bauhaus moved to Dessau and in 1932 to Berlin, where it was dissolved by the Nazis the following year.

Housed in the **Stadtschloss**, the former residence of the ducal family of Saxe-Weimar, the **Schlossmuseum** (☎ 545 960; Burgplatz 4; adult/child €5/4; ☉ 10am-6pm Tue-Sun Apr-Oct, 10am-4pm Nov-Mar) displays encompass sculpture, paintings and arts-and-craft objects. Highlights include the Cranach Gallery, several portraits by Albrecht Dürer and collections of Dutch masters and German romanticists. Several restored residence rooms can also be seen.

Goethe's fellow dramatist Friedrich von Schiller lived in Weimar from 1799 until his early death in 1805; unlike his mentor, he had to buy his own house, now known as **Schiller Museum** (☎ 545 350; Schillerstrasse 12; adult/child €6.50/5; ☉ 9am-6pm Wed-Mon). The study at the end of the 2nd floor contains the desk where he penned *Wilhelm Tell* and other works, and also holds his deathbed.

Liszt Haus (☎ 545 388; Marienstrasse 17; adult/child €2.50/2; ☉ 10am-6pm Tue-Sun Apr-Oct) is on the western edge of **Ilm Park**. Composer and pianist Franz Liszt lived here in 1848 and again from 1869 to 1886, when he wrote *Hungarian Rhapsody* and *Faust Symphony*.

Sleeping

The tourist office can help find accommodation, especially at busy times. There are many *pensions* scattered about the centre, which is where you should try to stay.

Hababusch (☎ 850 737; www.hababusch.de; Geleitstrasse 4; dm €10, s/d €15/24) Get in touch with the town's past at this unrestored 19th-century house. Conditions are, well, historic, but if you're looking for atmosphere this is it. The charming fountain out front is dedicated to the city.

Jugendherberge Germania (☎ 850 490; www.djh .de; Carl-August-Allee 13; dm from €17; ☒ ☐) The 121-bed Germania, south of the station, is convenient for a quick getaway but a little far from the centre.

Hotel Fürstenhof (☎ 833 231; www.fuerstenhof -weimar.de; Rudolf-Breitscheid-Strasse 2; r €46-100; ☐) A nice modern alternative to the ubiquitous 'period' décor elsewhere, the 17 rooms boast abstract prints. There's a vivid yellow breakfast room.

Ringhotel Kaiserin Augusta (☎ 2340; www.hotel -kaiserin-augusta.de; Carl-August-Allee 17; r €66-140; ☒ ☐) Directly across from the train station, this 242-bed business hotel offers many services and well-equipped rooms with wi-fi. It has a good terrace and breakfast buffet.

Hotel Elephant (☎ 8020; www.starwood.com; Markt 19; r €100-250; ☒ ☐) A true classic, the marble Bauhaus-Deco splendour of the 99-room Elephant has seen most of Weimar's great and good come and go; just to make the point, a golden Thomas Mann looks out over the Markt from a balcony in front. Its **Elephantenkeller** restaurant is also a local institution. Was that Goethe you just saw stroll past? The terrace is a delight.

Eating

Residenz-Café (☎ 594 08; Grüner Markt 4; mains €5-15) Known as the 'Resi' by regulars, this is one of Weimar's most popular haunts and has been for more than 160 years. The food is hearty and local, look for filling, starchy treats. The Sunday brunch draws hordes.

Johanns Hof (☎ 493 617; Scherfgasse 1; mains €6-14) Large windows punctuate the maroon walls in this historic and stylish café. The long wine list specialises in German white wines. Creative dishes include a fine garlic soup.

Zum Zwiebel (☎ 502 375; Teichgasse 6; mains €7-13; ☉ dinner) Look for the cute statue and logo at this unassuming place with exposed brick walls. The menu combines potatoes, sausage and, of course, onions. Yum.

Köstritzer Schwarzbierhaus (☎ 779 337; Scherfgasse 4; mains €7-18) Fans of dark beer and substantial traditional Thuringian cooking are in exactly the right place here – the listed half-timbered house has been converted into a restaurant and *pension* (double €80).

Entertainment

Deutsches Nationaltheater (German National Theatre; ☎ 755 334; www.nationaltheater-weimar.de; Theaterplatz; ☉ closed Jul-Aug) This historic venue was used to draft the constitution of the ill-fated Weimar Republic in 1919. Expect a mix of classic and contemporary plays, plus ballet, opera and classical concerts.

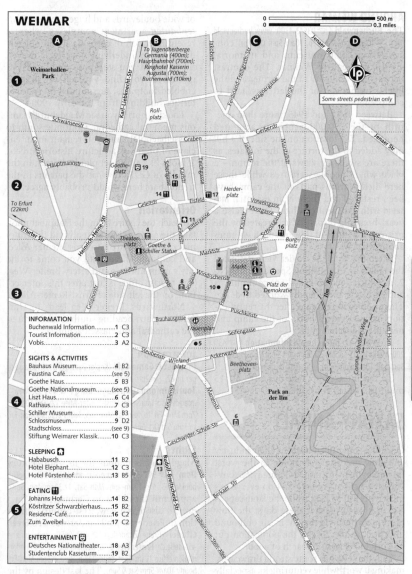

WEIMAR

GERMANY

Studentenclub Kasseturm (☎ 851670; www.kasse turm.de; Goetheplatz 10; ☽ 6pm-late) A classic, the Kasseturm is a historic round tower with three floors of live music, DJs and cabaret.

Getting There & Away

Weimar's Hauptbahnhof is on a line with frequent service linking Leipzig (€22, one hour) and Erfurt (€7, 15 minutes). Hourly ICE/IC services go to both Frankfurt (€49, 2½ hours) and Berlin-Hauptbahnhof (€44, 2½ hours).

The town centre is a 20-minute walk south of the Hauptbahnhof. Most buses serve Goetheplatz, on the northwestern edge of the Altstadt.

AROUND WEIMAR

The **Buchenwald** (☎ 03643-4300; www.buchenwald
.de; ☒ 10am-6pm May-Sep, 10am-5pm Oct-Apr) concentration camp museum and memorial
are 10km north of Weimar. The contrast
between the brutality of the former and the
liberal humanism of the latter is hard to
comprehend.

Between 1937 and 1945, more than one-
fifth of the 250,000 people incarcerated
here died. The location on the side of a hill
only added to the torture of the inmates, as
there are sweeping views of the region – a
place where people were free while those
here died. Various parts of the camp have
been restored and there is an essential **museum** with excellent exhibits. There's also a
heart-breaking display of art created by the
prisoners. Murals of flowers speak volumes
about what was lost.

After the war, the Soviet victors turned
the tables by establishing Special Camp No
2, in which 7000 so-called anticommunists
and ex-Nazis were literally worked to death.
Their bodies were found after the reunification in mass graves north of the camp and
near the Hauptbahnhof.

In Weimar, **Buchenwald Information** (☎ 430
200; Markt 10; ☒ 10am-12.30pm & 1-5pm Mon-Fri, 10am-
3pm Sat, 10am-2pm Sun) is a good resource.

To reach the camp, take bus 6 (€1.60, 15
minutes), which runs often.

SAXONY-ANHALT

Once the smog-filled heart of GDR industry
and now unfortunately home to the worst
unemployment in a united Germany, Saxony-
Anhalt (Sachsen-Anhalt) isn't on everyone's
must-visit list. In fact, while the landscape is
looking much greener these days, the flow
of human traffic is mainly in an outbound
direction, as the 25% of the population out
of work looks west in search of a job.

Still, the state has some strong drawcards,
making it worthwhile venturing in, especially
Dessau's Bauhaus legacy and the wonderful
bordering landscape of the Harz region.

MAGDEBURG

☎ 0391 / pop 228,000

Sometimes, just turning the corner in
Magdeburg can take you back 100 years.
Generally, Saxony-Anhalt's capital is a city
of wide boulevards and huge concrete *Plat-
tenbauten* apartment complexes, where a
recent injection of euros hasn't completely
disguised an underlying poverty. However,
the moment you step onto tree-lined He-
gelstrasse, you find yourself on pristine
cobbled footpaths, surrounded by restored
terrace buildings from the early 1900s.

Looking north, you see Magdeburg's famous medieval cathedral. Continue south to
Hasselbachplatz and you remain in an enclave of pretty-as-a-picture historic streets.
It looks like a film set plonked down in the
middle of GDR-town, as the patrons in the
trendy bars here would probably agree.

Orientation

To reach the centre from the Hauptbahnhof,
take the city exit, skirt left around the Cine-
maxx movie theatre into Ernst-Reuter-Allee,
and continue ahead until you come to the
city's main north–south artery Breiter Weg.
The tourist office is just after this intersection, on the left side of Ernst-Reuter-Allee.

Northwards, Breiter Weg leads to Universitätsplatz; heading south it takes you to
the cathedral and Hasselbachplatz.

Information

Internet & Game Café (Kepler Passage, Keplerstrasse 9;
per hr €2; ☒ 2pm-midnight)
Tourist Information Magdeburg (☎ 194 33; www
.magdeburg-tourist.de; Ernst-Reuter-Allee 12; ☒ 10am-
7pm Mon-Fri, to 4pm Sat May-Sep, 10am-6.30pm Mon-Fri,
to 3pm Sat Oct-Apr)

Sights

Magdeburg is famous for its 13th-century
Dom (☎ 543 2414; Domplatz; admission free, English
booklet €3; ☒ 10am-4pm Mon-Sat, 11.30am-4pm Sun),
apparently the oldest on German soil. However, it also has a new, 21st-century attraction in Friedensreich Hundertwasser's **Green
Citadel** (Grüne Zitadelle; ☎ 400 9650; www.gruene
-zitadelle.de; Breiter Weg 8-10; German tours €5; ☒ information office 10am-6pm, tours 11am, 3pm & 5pm Mon-Fri,
hourly 10am-5pm Sat & Sun). The last design by the
famous Austrian architect, this apartment
and shopping complex was completed in
2005, five years after his death. It evinces all
his signature features – irregular windows,
free-form walls and golden domes. The
building's pink, but derives its name from
its natural architecture and grass-covered
roof.

WORTH A TRIP: MITTELBAU DORA

From late 1943, thousands of slave labourers – mostly Russian, French and Polish prisoners of war toiled under horrific conditions to dig enormous tunnels in the chalk hills north of Nordhausen. From a 20km labyrinth of immense proportions, they produced the V1 and V2 rockets that rained destruction on London, Antwerp and other cities late in the war.

The camp, **Mittelbau Dora** (☎ 03631-495 820; www.buchenwald.de; 🕑 10am-6pm Tue-Sun May-Sep, 10am-4pm Oct-Apr), was created as a satellite of the Buchenwald concentration camp after British bombers destroyed the missile plants in far northeastern Germany. During the last two years of WWII, at least 20,000 prisoners died at Dora.

A museum with permanent exhibits of this horror opened in 2006. The grounds are open during daylight hours but to see the tunnels – many still filled with partially assembled rockets, you need to take a **tour** (🕑 11am & 2pm Tue-Fri, 11am, 1pm & 3pm Sat & Sun).

During the GDR era Dora mouldered away, with but a couple of small memorials to mark the site. Since reunification, recognition of what happened at Dora has been slowly growing, with visitors only allowed into the tunnels since 1995. The horrible truth of the place belies any need for extensive facilities and a visit to the camp may be among the most unforgettable experiences you have in Germany.

Getting There & Away

Mittelbau Dora is 5km north of Nordhausen, an unfortunate town you'll want to visit only to change trains. The Harzquerbahn (www.hsb-wr.de) train line links Nordhausen to Wernigerode (see 'Bewitching Harz' p202). The stop closest to Mittelbau Dora is Nordhausen-Krimderode, 11 minutes by almost hourly trains (€4) from tracks adjacent to the DB station. From the stop it is a 20-minute walk to the memorial.

Nordhausen is linked to Halle and Göttingen (both €15, 1½ hours) by frequent trains.

The historic area surrounding **Hasselbachplatz** is an attraction in its own right and full of bars, clubs and restaurants. Just wander or check listing magazine *Dates* for tips.

Sleeping & Eating

DJH Jugendherberge Magdeburg (☎ 532 101; www .jugendherberge.de; Leiterstrasse 10; dm junior/senior €18/21; P X 🖭) The smart, modern premises, generous space, good facilities and quiet but central location make this a winner. The staff are friendly and there's a late curfew.

Green Citadel (☎ 620 780; www.hotel-zitadelle.de; Breiter Weg 9; r from €105; P X) One of only two Hundertwasser hotels in the world and certainly the cheaper, this allows you to savour up-close the architect's penchant for uneven, organic forms. The attached café (dishes €3.50 to €4.50, 🕑 7am to 7pm) is open to the public, serving breakfast and light meals.

Bingöl 2 (☎ 744 8640; Breiter Weg 226; mains €2-8.50; 🕑 10am-midnight, to 6am Fri & Sat) This superior döner kebab shop has a large sit-down section and a menu that includes falafel, Turkish pizza, börek and dishes from the grill.

Liebig (☎ 555 6754; Liebigstrasse 1-3; snacks €3-9, meals €5-16; 🕑 10am-1am) Private alcoves and pleated curtains lining the walls create a feeling of warmth and privacy amid this trendy bar/café/restaurant. Mediterranean fare, curries and steaks are all served.

Getting There & Away

There are trains to/from Berlin (€22, one hour and 40 minutes, hourly), while regular IC and RE trains run to Leipzig (€19 to €23, 1¼ to two hours, twice hourly).

DESSAU

☎ 0340 / pop 79,500

'Less is more' and 'form follows function' – both these dictums were taught in Dessau, home of the influential Bauhaus school. Between 1925 and 1932, some of the century's greatest artists and architects breathed life into the ground-breaking principles of modernism here, among them Walter Gropius, Paul Klee, Wassily Kandinsky and Ludwig Mies Van der Rohe. Their legacy still stands proud, in the immaculate Bauhaus school building, the lecturers' purpose-built homes and other pioneering constructions.

GERMANY

GERMANY

BEWITCHING HARZ

The **Harz Mountains** constitute a mini-Alpine region straddling Saxony-Anhalt and Lower Saxony. Here, medieval castles overlook fairy-tale historic towns, while there are caves, mines and numerous hiking trails to explore.

The region's highest – and most famous – mountain is the Brocken, where one-time visitor Johann Wolfgang von Goethe set the 'Walpurgisnacht' chapter of his play *Faust*. His inspiration in turn came from folk tales depicting Walpurgisnacht as an annual witches' coven. Every 30 April to 1 May it's celebrated enthusiastically across the Harz region, particularly in Thale.

Goslar

Goslar is a truly stunning 1000-year-old city with beautifully preserved half-timbered buildings and an impressive **Markt**. The town's **Kaiserpfalz** is a reconstructed Romanesque 11th-century palace. Just below there's the restored **Domvorhalle**, which displays the 11th-century 'Kaiserstuhl' throne, used by German emperors.

One way to reach the **Brocken's summit** is to take a bus (810) or train (faster) from Goslar to Bad Harzburg and then a bus (820) to Torfhaus, where the 8km Goetheweg trail begins.

The **tourist office** (☎ 05321-780 60; www.goslar.de, in German; Markt 7; ᐧᐧᐧ 9.15am-6pm Mon-Fri, 9.30am-4pm Sat, to 2pm Sun May-Oct; 9.15am-5pm Mon-Fri, 9.30am-2pm Sat Nov-Apr) can help with accommodation, which includes a **DJH Hostel** (☎ 05321-222 40; www.jugendherberge.de; Rammelsbergerstrasse 25; dm junior/senior €16.50/19.50; P) and hotels **Die Tanne** (☎ 05321-343 90; www.die-tanne.de; Bäringerstrasse 10; s €40-65, d €65-100) and **Kaiserworth** (☎ 05321-7090; www.kaiserworth.de; Markt 3; s €70-100, d €120-180) .

As well as being serviced by buses (www.rbb-bus.de), Goslar is connected by train to Hanover (€13.40, one hour and 10 minutes) and Wernigerode (€7.60, 50 minutes).

Wernigerode

Flanked by the foothills of the Harz Mountains, Wernigerode boasts colourful half-timbered houses, many with uniquely distinctive features. A fairy-tale ducal castle – one of the most-visited in Germany – watches above. The town is the northern terminus of the steam-powered **Harzquerbahn railway** (☎ 03943-5580; www.hsb-wr.de), which chugs to the summit of the Brocken from here.

Wernigerode Tourismus (☎ 03943-633 035; www.wernigerode-tourismus.de; Nicolaiplatz 1; ᐧᐧᐧ 9am-7pm Mon-Fri, 10am-4pm Sat, 10am-3pm Sun May-Oct, slightly reduced hr winter) can provide more details.

The Bauhaus was born in Weimar in 1919, and it sought brief respite in Berlin (see p174) before being disbanded by the Nazis in 1933. But as the site of the movement's heyday and the 'built manifesto of Bauhaus ideas', Dessau is the true keeper of the flame.

Orientation

The leading Bauhaus sights are west of the Hauptbahnhof, clearly signposted and within easy walking distance. The town centre lies east, also reachable on foot.

Information

Bauhaus Foundation (☎ 650 8251; www.bauhaus -dessau.de; Gropiusallee 38; ᐧᐧᐧ 10am-6pm Mon-Fri) Has info on, and tours of, Bauhaus buildings, including in English.

Tourist office (☎ 204 1442, accommodation reservations 220 3003; www.dessau-tourismus.de; Zerbster Strasse 2c;

ᐧᐧᐧ 9am-6pm Mon-Fri, 9am-1pm Sat Apr-Oct, 9am-5pm Mon-Fri, 10am-1pm Sat Nov-Mar) Offers city tours and sells a three-day discount card.

Sights

Bauhaus founder Walter Gropius considered architecture the ultimate creative expression. So his first realised project, the **Bauhaus Building** (Bauhaus Gebäude; ☎ 650 8251; www .bauhaus-dessau.de; Gropiusallee 38; exhibition hall adult/concession €4/3, with Meisterhäuser €8/5, tours €4/3; ᐧᐧᐧ 10am-6pm, German tours 11am & 2pm, extra tours Sat & Sun), is extremely significant. Once home to the Institute for Design (Hochschule für Gestaltung) where the architect and colleagues taught, the recently renovated building today houses a postgraduate college but remains open to the public. You can visit the changing exhibitions and wander through a small section. However,

Accommodation options include a private **Jugendgästehaus** (☎ 03943-632 061; Friedrichstrasse 53; dm junior/senior €16.50/20; **P**) and **Altwernigeroder Aparthotel** (☎ 03943-949 260; www.appart-hotel .de, in German; Marktstrasse 14; s/d €45/75, apt from €85; **P** **X**)

Direct buses run to most major towns in the region. For trains to Quedlinburg (€7.60, 50 minutes) and Thale (€9.10, one hour and 10 minutes), change at Halberstadt.

Quedlinburg

Quedlinburg's spectacular castle district, perched on a 25m-high plateau above its historic half-timbered buildings, was established during the reign of Heinrich I, from 919 to 936. The present-day Renaissance **Schloss** dates from the 16th century. Its centrepiece is the restored baroque **Blauer Saal** (Blue Hall).

Contact **Quedlinburg-Tourismus** (☎ 03946-905625;www.quedlinburg.de;Markt2; ☉ 9am-7pm Mon-Fri, 10am-4pm Sat & Sun Apr-Oct; 9.30am-5.30pm Mon-Fri, to 2pm Sat Nov-Mar) for more information. Lodgings include a **DJH hostel** (☎ 03946-811 703; www.jugendherberge.de; Neuendorf 28; dm junior/senior €14/18, bedding €3; **P**) and the hotels **Zum Alten Fritz** (☎ 03946-704 880; Pölkenstrasse 18; s/d €45/65; **P**) and **Romantik Hotel Theophano** (☎ 03946-963 00; www.hoteltheophano.de; Markt 13-14; s/d from €70/100).

There are frequent trains to Thale (€1.80, 11 minutes) and Magdeburg (€11.70, one hour, hourly).

Thale

Two rugged outcrops, the **Hexentanzplatz** and **Rosstrappe**, flank the sensational **Bode Valley**, which is a hikers' favourite. There's a cable car to the rather overdeveloped Hexentanzplatz. Meanwhile, the Rosstrappe, reached by chairlift, bears a strange hoof imprint, supposedly left when the mythological Brunhilde jumped the gorge on horseback to escape her unloved husband Bode. (He fell to his death.) Both outcrops become bacchanalian party sites on Walpurgisnacht.

Thale Tourismus (☎ 03947-2597; www.thale.de; Rathausstrasse 1; ☉ 9am-5pm Mon-Fri, 10am-3pm Sat & Sun) can help with accommodation, which includes a **DJH Hostel** (☎ 03947-2881; www.jugendherberge .de; Bodetal-Waldkater; dm junior/senior €14.50/17.50, s/d from €19.50/24.50; **P**) and **Hoffmanns Gästehaus** (☎ 03947-2881; www.hoffmanns-gaestehaus.de; s €50-65, d €65-75, f €75-105).

There are trains and buses to Wernigerode and Quedlinburg, as well as trains from Magdeburg (€13.40, 1½ hours).

taking a tour is best; it gets you into otherwise closed rooms, even if you don't understand German.

Since a key Bauhaus aim was to 'design for living', the three white, concrete **Master Craftsmen's Houses** (Meisterhäuser; www.meister haeuser.de; Ebertallee 63-71; admission to all three adult/concession €5/3; ☉ 10am-6pm Tue-Sun summer, to 5pm winter), are a fascinating isnsight into the style. These villas were built by Gropius for senior institute staff, including himself, Klee, Kandinsky, Laszlo Moholy-Nagy and Lyonel Feiniger. In addition to this, Marcel Breuer – creator of the iconic steel frame chair – ocassionally meddled in the homes' interior design.

The many other Bauhaus buildings include the world's first housing estate **Törten**. Take tram 1 to Dessau Süd, alighting at Damashckestrasse.

Sleeping & Eating

In Dessau, you really can eat, drink and sleep Bauhaus. For a different diet, investigate the main thoroughfare of Zerbster Strasse.

Bauhaus dorms (☎ 650 8318; oede@bauhaus-dessau .de; Gropiusallee 38; r per person from €28; **P** **X**) Since the Bauhaus school was renovated in 2006, you can really live the modernist dream, by hiring the former students' dorms inside. If the main building's booked out, opt for a taste of the GDR instead, by reserving a cheaper bed (€15) in a 1970s *Plattenbau* apartment complex at Heidestrasse 33.

An den 7 Säulen (☎ 619 620; www.pension7saeulen .de, in German; Ebertallee 66; s €47-52, d €65-72; **P** **X**) This relaxed *pension* has a spa and a glass-fronted breakfast room overlooking the Master Craftsmen's Houses across the leafy street.

Bauhaus Klub (☎ 650 8444; Gropiusallee 38; dishes €3-7) Starting to see a pattern here? The occasional cool dude in black polo-neck jumper and horn-rimmed glasses can be seen among the broad mix of people in this basement bar of the Bauhaus school.

Kornhaus (☎ 640 4141; Kornhausstrasse 146; mains €7-13) Treat yourself to traditional local specialities and a refined evening in the curved Bauhaus dining room, with its striking 1930s carpet. Or, enjoy a light meal on the balcony overlooking the Elbe River.

Getting There & Away

IC and RE trains run to Berlin every two hours (€22, 1½ hours). Dessau is equidistant from Leipzig and Magdeburg (both €9.10, one hour), with frequent services to each.

MECKLENBURG-WESTERN POMERANIA

Mecklenburg-Vorpommern combines historic Hanseatic-era towns like Schwerin, Wismar and Stralsund with holiday areas such as Warnemünde and Rügen Island. It is off the path for many travellers but in summer it seems like half the country is here in some state of undress lolling on the sands. Outside of these somewhat mild times (this is a region where the beaches are dotted with large wicker beach baskets to provide shelter) the intrepid visitor is rewarded with journeys far from the maddening crowds.

SCHWERIN

☎ 0385 / pop 97,000

State capital Schwerin has a modest dignity befitting its status. The oldest city in Mecklenburg-Western Pomerania, it has numerous lakes, including one that is the town's centrepiece. Buildings are an interesting mix of 16th- to 19th-century architecture. It's small enough to explore on foot and if you're on the move, you can see it as part of a half-day break on a train journey. But Schwerin's beauty and charm are invariably infectious, and few people regret spending extra time here.

Orientation

The Altstadt is a 10-minute walk south from the Hauptbahnhof along Wismarsche Strasse.

A couple of blocks east of the Hauptbahnhof is the rectangular Pfaffenteich, a pretty artificial pond with the garish apricot-coloured 1840 Arsenal (now government offices) at its southwest corner. Heading east from here will take you to the central Markt.

Information

In-Ca Internet (☎ 500 7883; Wismarsche Strasse 123; per hr €3; ☼ 10am-midnight)

Schwerin-Information (☎ 592 5212; www.schwerin.de; Markt 14; ☼ 9am-7pm Mon-Fri, 10am-6pm Sat & Sun, reduced hr winter)

Sights

Southeast of the Alter Garten, over the causeway on the Burginsel (Burg Island), Schwerin's superb neo-Gothic palace, the **Schloss Schwerin** (☎ 525 2920; www.schloss-schwerin.de; adult/child €4/2.50; ☼ 10am-6pm 15 Apr-14 Oct, 10am-5pm Tue-Sun 15 Oct-15 Apr), was built in the mid-1800s around the chapel of a 16th-century ducal castle and is quite rightly the first attraction visitors head to upon arrival. The causeway is overlooked by a statue of **Niklot**, an early Slavic prince, who was defeated by Heinrich der Löwe in 1160. The huge, graphic picture of his death is a highlight of the castle's interior.

You don't get better examples of north German red-brick architecture than this 14th-century Gothic **Dom** (☎ 565 014; Am Dom 4; tower €1; ☼ 10am-5pm Mon-Fri, noon-5pm Sun), towering above the Markt. You can climb up to the platform in the 19th- century tower.

The enormous neoclassical building in the Alter Garten, the **Staatliches Museum** (☎ 595 80; Alter Garten 3; adult/child €6/4; ☼ 10am-8pm Tue, 10am-6pm Wed-Sun), couldn't really be anything other than a museum, and the contents fit the imposing exterior well: the permanent displays showcase old Dutch masters including Rembrandt, Rubens and Brueghel, as well as oils by Lucas Cranach the Elder and collections of more modern works by Marcel Duchamp and Ernst Barlach.

Sleeping & Eating

There are numerous cafés in the pedestrianised centre.

DJH Jugendherberge (☎ 326 0006; www.djh.de; Waldschulweg 3; dm from €17) This hostel is about 4km south of the city centre, just opposite the zoo. Take bus 14, which has stops at the Hauptbahnhof and Marienplatz.

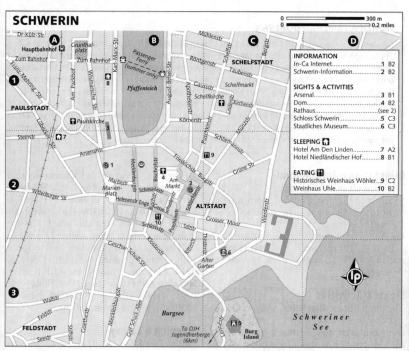

SCHWERIN

0 — 300 m
0 — 0.2 miles

INFORMATION
In-Ca Internet.............................1 B2
Schwerin-Information.................2 B2

SIGHTS & ACTIVITIES
Arsenal.....................................3 B1
Dom..4 B2
Rathaus...............................(see 2)
Schloss Schwerin.....................5 C3
Staatliches Museum.................6 C3

SLEEPING
Hotel Am Den Linden................7 A2
Hotel Niederländischer Hof.........8 B1

EATING
Historisches Weinhaus Wöhler...9 C2
Weinhaus Uhle......................10 B2

GERMANY

Hotel Am Den Linden (☎ 512 084; Franz-Mehring-Strasse 26; s/d €64/77) Close to the train station and the centre, this dignified 25-room hotel looks onto the impressive Paulskirche. Rooms are comfortable and there is a good breakfast.

Hotel Niederländischer Hof (☎ 591 100; www .niederlaendischer-hof.de; Karl-Marx-Strasse 12-13; s/d from €90/118; P) You can't beat the Pfaffenteich location or the swank rooms and marble bathrooms at this exceedingly classy hotel. There's even a library with an open fire for those contemplative German winters.

Historisches Weinhaus Wöhler (☎ 555 830; Puschkinstrasse 26; mains €8-16) The stained-glass windows framed in lead tell you that this place is indeed historic. Opened in 1895, the building dates to the 18th century. The food is classic German and on weekends you can enjoy live music. The beer garden is alluring and you can sleep it off in the comfortable rooms (€80 to €130) upstairs.

Weinhaus Uhle (☎ 562 956; Schusterstrasse 13-15; mains €9-24) This long-standing traditional family wine merchant (the building is from the 18th century) has vaulted ceilings in the

downstairs restaurant and a lovely *weinstube* upstairs. As you'd guess, the wine list is long.

Getting There & Away
Schwerin is on the line linking Hamburg (€23, one hour) with Stralsund (€28, two hours). Service to Rostock (€13.40 to €17, one hour) is frequent, as is that to Wismar (€6.20, 30 minutes). There are RE trains to Berlin-Hauptbahnhof (€29, 2½ hours).

WISMAR
☎ 03841 / pop 46,000
Wismar, a Hanseatic gem that's fast being discovered, is about halfway between Rostock and Lübeck. It joined the powerful trading league in the 13th century – the first town east of Lübeck to do so. For centuries it was in and out of Swedish control, and traces of that rule can still be seen, particularly in the 'Swedish heads' all over town. Quieter than Rostock or Stralsund, Wismar can fill up with visitors quickly in high season; it's definitely worth an overnight stay, and is also the gateway to **Poel Island**, a lovely little piece of green to the north.

WORTH A TRIP: BAD DOBERAN

For centuries the amazing 13th-century **Munster** (☎ 038203-627 16; Klosterstrasse 2; admission €3; ☷ 9am-6pm Mon-Sat, 11.30am-6pm Sun, reduced hr winter) slumbered away in a green pasture near the centre of the small town of Bad Doberan. In recent years it has been rediscovered and its 1.2 million bricks are getting a cleaning, while the nearby medieval monastery is getting a complete renovation. You can easily spend a few hours wandering this site that's at its best when the wind rustles though the surrounding trees. Inside look for the carved wood alter (1310) from Lübeck.

The Munster complex is a 15-minute walk from the train station, which has hourly service on the scenic branchline linking Rostock (€2.60, 20 minutes) and Wismar (€6.20, 45 minutes). From the station walk towards the mannered centre and look for the steeple.

Orientation & Information

The Altstadt is built up around the Markt, which is the largest medieval town square in northern Germany. The Bahnhof is at the northeastern corner of the Altstadt and the Alter Hafen port is in the northwest.

In the Altstadt you'll find **tourist information** (☎ 251 3025; www.wismar.de; Am Markt 11; ☷ 9am-6pm).

Sights & Activities

The old harbour, **Alter Hafen**, with old boats swaying in the breeze, evokes trading days from centuries ago. Featured in the 1922 film *Nosferatu* it is still a focal point of activity in Wismar. **Clermont Reederei** (☎ 224 646; www.reederei-clermont.de; adult/child €7/6) operates hour-long harbour cruises five times daily from April to October, leaving from Alter Hafen. Daily boats also go to Poel Island (€14/7 return). Various other companies run tours on historic ships during summer; contact the harbour for details.

Running through town, the **Grube** (channel) is the last artificial medieval waterway in the north and should be a part of any stroll through the historic quarter. The **Wasserkunst** is a 12-sided well from 1602 that anchors a corner of the attractive **Markt**.

The town's historical museum **Schabbellhaus** (☎ 282 350; www.schabbellhaus.de; Schweinsbrücke 8; adult/child €2/1, free Fri; ☷ 10am-8pm Tue-Sun May-Oct, to 5pm Nov-Apr) has taken over a former Renaissance brewery (1571), just south of the Nikolaikirche across the canal. The museum's pride and joy is the large tapestry *Die Königin von Saba vor König Salomon* ('The Queen of Sheba before King Solomon'; 1560–75).

CHURCHES

Wismar was a target for Anglo-American bombers just weeks before the end of WWII.

Of the three great red-brick churches that once rose above the rooftops only **St-Nikolai-Kirche** (St-Nikolai-Kirchhof; admission €1; ☷ 8am-8pm May-Sep, 10am-6pm Apr & Oct, 11am-4pm Nov-Mar), built from 1381 to 1487, remains intact. Massive **St-Georgen-Kirche** is being restored for use as a church, concert hall and exhibition space with a much-doubted completion date of 2010. Cars now park where 13th-century **St-Marien-Kirche** once stood, though its great brick **steeple**, (☷ 10am-8pm Apr-Oct), built in 1339, still towers above the city.

Sleeping & Eating

Pension Chez Fasan (☎ 213 425; www.pension-chez-fasan.de; Bademutterstrasse 20a; r €21-50) The best budget deal in town. Rooms in the three-building complex come with baths, satellite TV and a great central location.

Hotel Reuterhaus (☎ 222 30; www.hotel-reuterhaus.de; Am Markt 19; r €60-90) With views over the Wasserkunst from many of the 10 rooms, this family-run hotel makes for an atmospheric stay. The restaurant here is good and there are tables on the Markt when the sun shines.

Fischerklause (☎ 252 850; Fischerreihe 4; mains €7-13; ☷ lunch & dinner Tue-Sat) A small place popular with locals that serves up the catch brought into the nearby Alter Hafen. The place swims with character.

Brauhaus am Lohberg (☎ 250 238; Kleine Hohe Strasse 15; mains €7-13) Spread over a series of warehouses dating back to the 16th century, this popular spot is honouring Wismar's long tradition of brewing by once again making its own beer. There's a good seafood menu.

Getting There & Away

Trains travel the coastal branchlines to Rostock (€9.10, 65 minutes, hourly) and Schwerin (€6.20, 30 minutes, hourly).

ROSTOCK & WARNEMÜNDE

☎ 0381 / pop 198,000

Rostock, the largest city in sparsely populated northeastern Germany, is a major Baltic port and shipbuilding centre. Its chief suburb – and chief attraction – is Warnemünde, 12km north of the centre. Counted among eastern Germany's most popular beach resorts, it's hard to see it as a small fishing village these days, but the boats still bring in their catches, and some charming streets and buildings persist amid the tourist clutter.

First mentioned in 1161 as a Danish settlement, Rostock began taking shape as a German fishing village around 1200. In the 14th and 15th centuries, it was an important Hanseatic trading city; parts of the city centre, especially along Kröpeliner Strasse, retain the flavour of this period.

Orientation & Information

The city begins at the Südstadt (Southern City), south of the Hauptbahnhof, and extends north to Warnemünde on the Baltic Sea. Much of the city is on the western side of the Warnow River, which creates a long shipping channel due north to the sea.

The Altstadt is an oval area approximately 1.5km north of the Hauptbahnhof. Rosa-Luxemburg-Strasse runs north from the station to Steintor, which unofficially marks the southern boundary of the old town.

Tourist Information (☎ 381 2222; www.rostock.de; Neuer Markt 3; ☼ 10am-7pm Mon-Fri, 10am-4pm Sat & Sun May-Sep, closed Sun Oct-Apr)

Warnemünde-Information (☎ 548 000; www.warnemuende.de; Am Strom 59; ☼ 10am-6pm Mon-Fri, 10am-3pm Sat & Sun)

Sights

Lined with 15th- and 16th-century burghers' houses, Kröpeliner Strasse is a lively, cobbled pedestrian street that runs west from Neuer Markt to the **Kröpeliner Tor**, a 55m-high tower, which contains the **Regional History Museum** (☎ 454 177; adult/child €3/1.50; ☼ 10am-6pm Wed-Sun).

The mostly intact **Kloster Zum Heiligen Kreuz** (Holy Cross convent; ☎ 203 590; Klosterhof 18), was established in 1270 by Queen Margrethe I of Denmark; today it houses the **Cultural History Museum** (adult/child €3/1.50; ☼ 9am-6pm Tue-Sun), with an excellent and varied collection including sculptures by Ernst Barlach and large numbers of everyday items used by locals over the centuries.

Rostock's pride and joy, the **Marienkirche** (☎ 453 325; Am Ziegenmarkt; admission €2; ☼ 10am-4pm Mon-Sat, 11.15am-noon Sun), built in 1290, was the only one of Rostock's four main churches to survive WWII unscathed. The long north–south transept was added after the ceiling collapsed in 1398. Notable features include the 12m-high astrological clock (1470–72), the Gothic bronze baptismal font (1290), the baroque organ (1770) and some fascinating tombstones in the floor.

The crowded seafront promenade to the north at **Warnemünde**, lined with hotels and restaurants, is where the tourists congregate. Its broad, sandy beach stretches west from the **lighthouse** (1898) and the **Teepott** exhibition centre, and is chock-a-block on hot summer days with bathers.

Sleeping

Accommodation in Warnemünde can be like gold dust in summer. For private rooms, contact the tourist office. At other times – especially in the spring and fall – it is a lovely alternative to Rostock.

Baltic-Freizeit Camping und Ferienpark (☎ 04 544-800 30; www.baltic-freizeit.de; Dünenweg 27, Markgrafenheide; camp sites per person €9-17) On the east side of Warnow River, this enormous city-run affair has 1200 sites. Take tram 4 to Dierkower Kreuz, then bus 18 (45 minutes).

City-Pension (☎ 252 260; www.city-pension-rostock .de; Krönkenhagen 3; r €40-90) A small family *pension* occupying a lovely quiet street near the harbour, in the heart of the old-fashioned northern Altstadt. Rooms are simple but comfortable.

Hotel Kleine Sonne (☎ 497 3153; www.die-kleine -sonne.de; Steinstrasse 7; r €60-100; ✗ ▣) The bargain offshoot of the swanky Hotel Sonne across the street, this is actually a fine place in its own right, with a very modern style and art by landscape painter Nils Ausländer.

InterCity Hotel (☎ 495 00; www.intercityhotel.de; Herweghstrasse 51; r €85-120; ✗ ▣) Right by the train station, the InterCity has wi-fi and 174 comfortable modern rooms. Ask for one with a view other than the lightwell however.

Eating

On many mornings fish-smokers set up shop on the Neuer Markt, as well as Warnemünde's harbour. Kröpliner Strasse in Rostock is a good place to find cafés. Warnemünde abounds in stands selling fish and chips, ice cream and other gut-popping fare.

Krahnstöver Likörfabrik (☎ 252 3551; Grosse Wasserstrasse 30/Grubenstrasse 1; mains €5-12) This late-15th-century old liquor factory is an excellent example of late Gothic architecture. The wine bar has an inventive menu; around the corner, the Kneipe seems as old as the building and dishes up hearty fare.

Zum Alten Fritz (☎ 208 780; Warnowufer 65; mains €7-18) This locally popular pub/restaurant honours two Rostock traditions at its harbourside location: seafaring and brewing. Lucky sailor! The creative menu feature organic ingredients.

Seekist zur Krim (☎ 521 14; Am Strom 47, Warnemünde; mains €9-20) On a tree-shaded and quiet stretch of Am Strom, this restaurant serves steaks, schnitzel and seafood. Try a platter of the latter for €15. There's a nice patio.

Getting There & Around

Rostock is on the busy line linking Hamburg (€28 to €35, two hours) to Stralsund (€12, one hour). Services to Schwerin (€13.40 or €17, one hour) are frequent as is the branch line to Wismar (€9.10, 70 minutes, hourly). There are RE trains to Berlin Hauptbahnhof (€32, three hours, every two hours).

Various ferry companies operate from Rostock seaport. **Scandlines** (☎ 673 1217; www .scandlines.de) has daily services to Trelleborg in Sweden (€20, 5¾ hours) and Gedser in Denmark (€5 to €10, two hours). **TT-Line** (☎ 670 790; www.ttline.de) departs for Trelleborg several times daily (€20 to €30, three to six hours).

There's frequent S-Bahn service linking Rostock to Warnemünde (€1.40, 20 minutes). In Rostock tram lines 5 and 6 link the train station with the centre. The entire area lends itself to bike touring. **Radstation** (☎ 252 3990; Hauptbahnhof; per day from €15; ☺ 10am-6pm Mon-Fri, to 1pm Sat) is very convenient for rentals.

STRALSUND

☎ 03831 / pop 59,000

Possessing an unmistakable medieval profile, Stralsund was the second-most powerful member of the medieval Hanseatic League, after Lübeck. In 1648 Stralsund, Rügen and Pomerania came under the control of Sweden, which had helped in their defence. The

city remained Swedish until it was incorporated into Prussia in 1815.

An attractive town of imposing churches and elegant townhouses, Stralsund boasts more examples of classic red-brick Gothic gabled architecture than almost anywhere else in northern Germany. It has some good, growing museums and is great place if you want to feel the culture of the Baltic.

Orientation

The Altstadt is effectively on its own island, surrounded by lakes and the sea. Its main hubs are Alter Markt in the north and Neuer Markt in the south. The Hauptbahnhof is across the Tribseer Damm causeway, west of the Neuer Markt. The harbour is on the Altstadt's eastern side.

Information

Toffi's Web Cafe (☎ 309 385; Lobshagen 8a; per min €0.05; ☺ noon-10pm) This groovy place has a long list of coffees, tea and beers to help lubricate your surfing.

Tourismuszentrale (☎ 246 90; www.stralsundtourismus .de; Alter Markt 9; ☺ 9am-7pm Mon-Fri, to 2pm Sat, 10am-2pm Sun May-Sep, 9am-5pm Mon-Fri, 10am-2pm Sat Oct-Apr)

Sights

One of the two structures dominating the Alter Markt is the gorgeous 14th-century **Rathaus**, with its late-Gothic decorative façade. The upper portion has slender copper turrets and gables that have openings to prevent strong winds from knocking over the façade; this ornate design was Stralsund's answer to its rival city, Lübeck, which has a similar town hall. The sky-lit gallery overhanging the vaulted walkway is held aloft by shiny black pillars on carved and painted bases.

Exit through the eastern walkway to the main portal of the other dominant presence in the Alter Markt, the 1270 **Nikolaikirche** (☎ 299 799; Alter Markt; ☺ 10am-noon & 2-4pm). Modelled after the Marienkirche in Lübeck (p279) and bearing a fleeting resemblance to Notre Dame, it's filled with art treasures. Also worth a closer look are the **high altar** (1470), 6.7m wide and 4.2m tall, showing Jesus' entire life, and the mostly inaccurate **astronomical clock** (1394), allegedly the oldest in the world.

The Neuer Markt is dominated by the massive 14th-century **Marienkirche** (☎ 298 965; Neuer Markt; ☺ 10am-7pm May-Oct, 10am-noon, 2-4pm

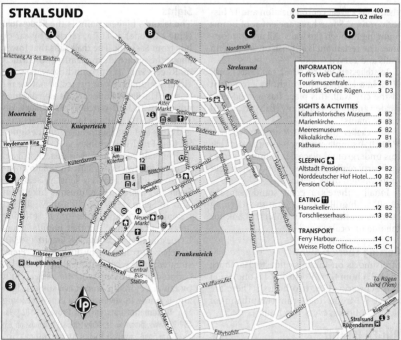

STRALSUND

0   400 m
0   0.2 miles

INFORMATION
Toffi's Web Cafe.................1 B2
Tourismuszentrale...............2 B1
Touristik Service Rügen.........3 D3

SIGHTS & ACTIVITIES
Kulturhistorisches Museum......4 B2
Marienkirche...................5 B3
Meeresmuseum...................6 B2
Nikolaikirche..................7 B1
Rathaus........................8 B1

SLEEPING
Altstadt Pension...............9 B2
Norddeutscher Hof Hotel....10 B2
Pension Cobi..................11 B2

EATING
Hansekeller..................12 B2
Torschliesserhaus............13 B2

TRANSPORT
Ferry Harbour................14 C1
Weisse Flotte Office.........15 C1

GERMANY

Nov-Apr), another superb example of north German red-brick construction. Check out the huge **F Stellwagen organ** (1659), festooned with music-making cherubs. You can climb the steep wooden steps up the **tower** (admission €1) for a sweeping view of the town and Rügen Island. Ongoing renovations through to 2010 are intended to restore the church to its original look.

MUSEUMS
North of Neuer Markt, a 13th-century convent church is now the **Meeresmuseum** (Oceanographic Museum; ☎ 265 010; www.meeresmuseum.de; Katharinenberg 14-20; adult/child €6.50/4.50; ☼ 10am-6pm Jun-Sep, 10am-5pm Oct-May). It has extensive displays on local sealife and the people who catch it. A major new addition opening in 2008 will focus on the Baltic and have several huge tanks of live fish.

Stralsund's cultural history museum, **Kulturhistorisches Museum** (☎ 287 90; Mönchstrasse 25-27; adult/child €3/1.50; ☼ 10am-5pm Tue-Sun), has a large historical collection, paintings by Caspar David Friedrich and Philipp Otto Runge, *faïence* (tin-glazed earthenware), playing

cards and Gothic altars, as well as various outlying exhibitions in restored houses.

Tours
Ferries operate seven times daily by **Weisse Flotte** (☎ 0180-321 2120; www.weisse-flotte.com; Fährstrasse 16; one way €2.30; ☼ May-Oct) to the scenic fishing village of Altefähr on Rügen. One-hour **harbour cruises** depart four times daily (€6) in summer.

Sleeping & Eating
Pension Cobi (☎ 278 288; www.pension-cobi.de; Jakobiturmstrasse 15; s/d €32/46) In the shadow of the Jakobikirche, this is a great location for exploring the Altstadt, and also offers bike hire to get a bit further afield. The 14 rooms are smart, clean and some have balconies.

Altstadt Pension (☎ 303 580; Tribseer Strasse 15; s/d €45/65; ☒) This 12-room inn is on the main drag into town and is popular with touring cyclists. The modern rooms contrast with the vintage building and precinct. There's a sunny terrace for breakfast or a drink.

Norddeutscher Hof Hotel (☎ 293 161; www.nd-hof.de; Neuer Markt 22; r €40-90) This maroon vision has a great central location and 13 historic rooms. Some have ancient roof beams plunging through the walls. All are comfortable. The restaurant is a stylish melange of tin walls and carved wood.

Torschliesserhaus (☎ 293 032; Am Kütertor 1; mains €7-16) In a 1281 building right by a fragment of the city wall, this place has a good beer garden and tasty local chow (fishy treats and meaty mains).

Hansekeller (☎ 703 840; Mönchstrasse 48; mains €7.50-13) A simple exterior belies the fact that this underground place lies within. It serves up hearty regional dishes at moderate prices in its vaulted brick cellar.

Finally, there's a great stand (sausage €1.50) with grilled sausages at the morning farmers market on Neuer Markt. Look for the line of locals.

Getting There & Away

Stralsund is on the busy line to Hamburg (€44, 3¼ hours) via Rostock (€12, one hour) and Schwerin (€28, two hours). There are direct IC trains to Berlin Hauptbahnhof (€42, 2¾ hours, every two hours).

RÜGEN ISLAND

Germany's largest island, Rügen has 574km of coast. It is at times hectic, relaxed, barren, windblown and naked. If you don't mind losing a little epidermis to the scouring sands, you can have a very German beach holiday here. Otherwise, it makes a good day trip out of Stralsund, especially if you have your own car.

The resort tradition here reflects all aspects of Germany's recent past. In the 19th century, luminaries such as Einstein, Bismarck and Thomas Mann came to unwind in the fashionable coastal resorts. Later, both Nazi and GDR regimes made Rügen the holiday choice for dedicated comrades.

From the bridge near Stralsund that links the mainland and Rügen, the island is easily traversed by numerous well-marked roads.

Information

Tourismus Rügen (☎ 03838-807 70; www.ruegen.de; Am Markt 4, Bergen) Has extensive accommodation listings.
Touristik Service Rügen (☎ 03831-285 70; www.insel-ruegen.de; Bahnhof Rügendamm, Werftstrasse 2; ⏰ 8am-9pm Mon-Fri, 9am-8pm Sat, 10am-7pm Sun) The place for information in Stralsund.

Sights

The island's highest point is the **Königsstuhl** (king's throne) at 117m, reached by car or bus from Sassnitz. The **chalk cliffs** that tower above the sea are the main attraction. Much of Rügen and its surrounding waters are either national park or protected nature reserves. The **Bodden** inlet area is a bird refuge popular with bird-watchers. **Kap Arkona**, on Rügen's north shore, is famous for its rugged cliffs and two lighthouses, one designed by Karl Friedrich Schinkel.

The main resort area is in eastern Rügen, around the towns of **Binz**, the main tourist town which boasts a lengthy seafront, **Sellin** and **Göhren**. A picturesque hike from Binz to Sellin skirts the cliffs above the sea through beech and pine forests, offering great coastal views. Another popular tourist destination is **Jagdschloss Granitz** (1834), which is surrounded by lush forest. **Prora**, situated up the coast from Binz, is the location of a 2km-long workers' retreat built by Hitler before the war. It is a surreal sight and is home to several museums including the **Dokumentationszentrum Prora** (☎ 038393-139 91; www.proradok.de; Objektstrasse 1; admission €3; ⏰ 10am-6pm), which looks at the huge construction's history.

Getting There & Around

Trains from Stralsund reach Sassnitz (€9.10, 50 minutes, hourly) and Binz (€12, 45 minutes, every two hours). Trains from the latter also serve Hamburg (€51, four hours).

To get around the island however and really appreciate it, you'll need a car.

Scandlines (☎ 0381 543 50; www.scandlines.de) car ferries run from Sassnitz Mukran, several kilometres south of Sassnitz, to Trelleborg in Sweden (one way €12 to €15, 3¾ hours, five daily). The port is linked to the train station by bus.

BAVARIA

For many, Bavaria (Bayern) is every German stereotype rolled into one. Lederhosen, beer halls, oompah bands and romantic castles are just some Bavarian clichés associated with Germany as a whole. But as any Bavarian will tell you, the state thinks of itself as Bavarian first and German second. And as any German outside of Bavaria will tell you, the *Bavarian* stereotypes aren't representative of the rest of Germany. It's a mostly Catholic place and the politics are often conservative (almost 90 years ago this was the land of beer hall putsches), even if people drink serious quantities of beer.

Bavaria was ruled for centuries as a duchy under the line founded by Otto I of Wittelsbach, and eventually graduated to the status of kingdom in 1806. The region suffered amid numerous power struggles between Prussia and Austria and was finally brought into the German empire in 1871 by Bismarck. The last king of Bavaria was Ludwig II (1845–86), who earned the epithet 'the mad king' due to his obsession with building fantastic fairy-tale castles at enormous expense. He was found drowned in Starnberger See in suspicious circumstances and left no heirs.

Bavaria draws visitors year-round. If you only have time for one part of Germany after Berlin, this is it. Munich, the capital, is the heart and soul. The Bavarian Alps, Nuremberg and the medieval towns on the Romantic Road are other important attractions.

MUNICH
☎ 089 / pop 1.25 million

Munich (München) is truly the capital of all things Bavarian. It's a heady mix of world-class museums, historic sites, cosmopolitan shopping, exhausting nightlife, trendy restaurants, roaring beer halls, vast parks and, of course, Oktoberfest.

It can easily occupy several days of your time and it will indeed be time well spent. The efficient public transport system can whisk you around town – although if you stay above ground you might be surprised at how compact the centre really is. Against all this urban life is the backdrop of the Alps, peaks that exude an allure that many locals – and visitors – find inescapable.

It is hard to imagine any visit to Germany feeling complete without at least some time spent in this vibrant city.

History
Originally settled by monks from the Benedictine monastery at Tegernsee in the 7th and 8th century, the city itself wasn't founded until 1158 by Henry the Lion. In 1255 Munich became the home for the Wittelsbach dukes, princes and kings who ruled for the next 700 years. The city suffered through the Black Plague first in 1348 and again in 1623, when two-thirds of the population died.

Munich has been the capital of Bavaria since 1503, but didn't really achieve prominence until the 19th century under the guiding hand of Ludwig I. Ludwig became more conservative and repressive, and carried on an affair with the actress and dancer Lola Montez. He was forced to abdicate in favour of his son, Maxmilian II, who started a building renaissance, promoting science, industry and education.

At the turn of the last century there were half a million residents, but in the aftermath of WWI Munich became a hotbed of right-wing political ferment. Hitler staged a failed coup attempt in Munich in 1923 but the National Socialists seized power only a decade later. WWII brought bombing and more than 6000 civilian deaths until American forces entered the city in 1945. Then, in 1972, the Munich Olympics turned disastrous when 11 Israeli athletes were murdered.

Today it is the centre of Germany's hi-tech industries, besides being the home of Siemens and BMW.

Orientation
The main train station is just west of the city centre. From the station, head east along Bayerstrasse, through Karlsplatz, and then along Neuhauser Strasse and Kaufingerstrasse to Marienplatz, the hub of Munich.

North of Marienplatz are the Residenz (the former royal palace), Schwabing (the famous student section) and the parklands of the Englischer Garten through which the Isar River runs. East of Marienplatz is the Platzl quarter for beer houses and restaurants, as well as Maximilianstrasse, a fashionable street that is ideal for simply strolling and window-shopping.

Information
For late-night shopping and services such as pharmacies and currency exchange, the Hauptbahnhof's multilevel shopping arcades cannot be beat.

BOOKSHOPS
Hugendubel Marienplatz (☎ 484 484; Marienplatz 22); Salvatorplatz (☎ 484 484; Salvatorplatz 2) Has a good selection of guides and maps and the Salvatorplatz outlet has all English titles.

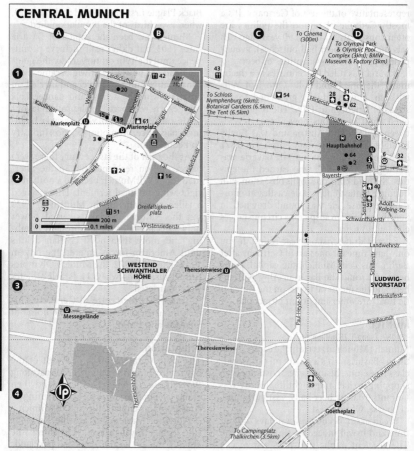

CENTRAL MUNICH

GERMANY

Max&Milian (☎ 260 3320; Ickstattstrasse 2) Gay bookshop and unofficial community centre.

INTERNET ACCESS
easyInternetcafé (☎ 5599 9696; Bahnhofplatz 1; per 80 min €2; ☒ 24hr) In the post office building, part of a chain of Internet cafés. Has hundreds of terminals and is normally packed with cyber surfers.
Internet Café (☎ 2070 2737; Tal 31; per 30 min €1; ☒ 24hr) Full service shop.
Times Square Internet Cafe (☎ 5126 2600; Hauptbahnhof; per 5 min €0.50; ☒ 7.30am-1am) Large bar and restaurant across from track 11.

LAUNDRY
City SB-Waschcenter (Paul-Heysestrasse 21; ☒ 7am-11pm; €4) Close to the Hauptbahnhof.

MEDIA
Expats in Bavaria (www.expats-in-bavaria.com) Quirky, colourful and useful site for all manner of local info.
Munich Found (www.munichfound.de; €3) Long-running English language local magazine with a good website. Good entertainment coverage.
Munich Transport (www.mvv-muenchen.de/en) Everything you need to know about Munich's transport system.
Municipal Website (www.muenchen.de) The city government's site is stuffed with useful info and links.
Toytown Munich (www.toytowngermany.com) Irreverent English-language recommendations from locals and expats. Good bar and club reviews.

POST
Main post office (Bahnhofplatz 1; ☒ 7.30am-8pm Mon-Fri, 9am-4pm Sat) The poste restante address is:

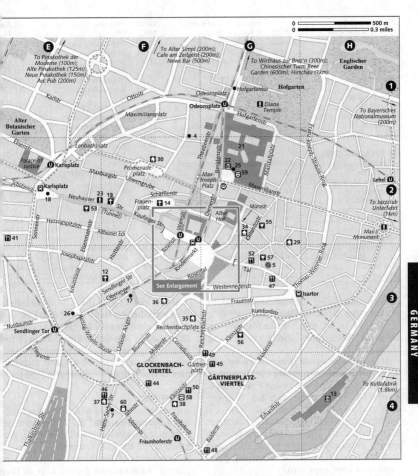

Hauptpostlagernd (Poste Restante), Bahnhofplatz 1, 80074 München.

TOURIST INFORMATION

EurAide (☎ 593 889; www.euraide.com; Hauptbahnhof; ⊗ 8am-noon & 1-4pm Jun) Next to platform 11 at the main train station, EurAide validates rail passes, sells train tickets and tours and dispenses savvy advice in English.

Tourist office (☎ 2333 6500; www.muenchen-tourist.de) Main tourist office (Hauptbahnhof; ⊗ 9am-8pm Mon-Sat, 10am-6pm Sun); branch office (Marienplatz; ⊗ 10am-8pm Mon-Fri, 10am-4pm Sat) Both offices sell the Munich Welcome Card (from €7.50), which allows one to three days unlimited travel on public transport, plus discounts for many museums, galleries and other attractions. The main tourist office is to the right as you exit the Hauptbahnhof via the eastern entrance; its room-finding service is free. The branch

office is beneath the Neues Rathaus. Be sure to ask for the excellent and free guide *Young and About in Munich*.

TRAVEL AGENCIES

DER Reisebüro (☎ 120 40; Hauptbahnhof)

Sights
PALACES

The huge **Residenz** (Max-Joseph-Platz 3) housed Bavarian rulers from 1385 to 1918 and features more than 500 years of architectural history. Apart from the palace itself, the **Residenzmuseum** (☎ 290 671; www.schloesser .bayern.de; Residenzstrasse 1; adult/child €6/5; ⊗ 9am-6pm Tue-Sun, to 8pm Thu Apr-Oct, 10am-4pm Tue-Sun Nov-Mar) has an extraordinary array of 100 rooms containing no end of treasures and artworks.

In the same building, the **Schatzkammer** (☎ 290 671; enter from Max-Joseph-Platz 3; adult/child €6/3; ☺ 9am-6pm Tue-Sun, to 8pm Thu Apr-Oct, 10am-4pm Tue-Sun Nov-Mar) exhibits jewels, crowns and ornate gold.

If this doesn't satisfy your passion for palaces, visit **Schloss Nymphenburg** (☎ 179 080; www .schloesser.bayern.de; adult/child museum €5/4, museum & gallery €10/8; ☺ 9am-6pm Tue-Sun, to 8pm Thu Apr-Oct, 10am-4pm Tue-Sun Nov-Mar), northwest of the city centre via tram 17 from the main train station (Hauptbahnhof). This was the royal family's equally impressive summer home. Parts date to the 17th century. The surrounding park deserves a long, regal stroll.

ART GALLERIES

A treasure-house of European masters from the 14th to 18th centuries, recently renovated **Alte Pinakothek** (☎ 238 052 16; www.alte-pinakothek .de; Barer Strasse 27; adult/child €5.50/4, €1 Sun; ☺ 10am-8pm Tue, 10am-5pm Wed-Sun), a stroll northeast of the city, includes highlights such as Dürer's Christ-like *Self Portrait* and his *Four Apostles*, Rogier van der Weyden's *Adoration of the Magi* and Botticelli's *Pietà*.

Immediately north of the Alte Pinakothek, the **Neue Pinakothek** (☎ 238 051 95; www.neue -pinakothek.de; Barer Strasse 29; adult/child €5.50/4, €1 Sun; ☺ 10am-8pm Wed, to 5pm Thu-Mon) contains mainly 19th-century works, including Van Gogh's *Sunflowers*, and sculpture.

One block east of the Alte Pinakothek, the **Pinakothek der Moderne** (☎ 2380 5360; www .pinakothek-der-moderne.de; Barer Strasse 40; adult/child €9/5, €1 Sun; ☺ 10am-5pm Tue & Wed, Sat & Sun, to 8pm Thu & Fri) displays four collections of modern art, graphic art, applied art and architecture in one suitably arresting building.

MUSEUMS

An enormous science and technology museum, **Deutches Museum** (☎ 217 91; www.deutsches -museum.de; Museumsinsel 1; adult/child €8.50/3, planetarium €2; ☺ 9am-5pm) celebrates the many achievements of Germans and humans in general. Kids become gleeful kids as they interact with the exhibits. So do adults. Many get a charge out of the shocking electrical displays. Take the S-Bahn to Isartor.

The **Bayerisches Nationalmuseum** (☎ 211 2401; www.bayerisches-nationalmuseum.de; Prinzregentenstrasse 3; adult/child €5/4; ☺ 10am-5pm Tue-Sun, to 8pm Thu), east of the Hofgarten, houses an impressive collection of Bavarian and southern German artefacts.

Tracing the lives of local Jews before, during and after the Holocaust, the **Jüdisches Museum** (☎ 2332 8189; www.juedisches-museum .muenchen.de; St Jakobsplatz 16) is moving to an impressive new space in March 2007. It promises to document a culture once important to Munich that was almost wiped out by the Nazis.

GERMANY

North of the city, auto-fetishists can thrill to the **BMW Museum** (☎ 3822 3307; www.bmwmobile tradition.de), adjacent to the BMW headquarters. As part of the recent corporate image arms race among German car-makers (see p230), BMW is opening a vast new celebration of its brand in mid-2007. Take the U3 to Olympiazentrum.

PARKS & GARDENS

One of the largest city parks in Europe, the **Englischer Garten**, west of the city centre, is a great place for strolling, especially along the Schwabinger Bach. In summer, nude sunbathing is the rule rather than the exception. It's not unusual for hundreds of naked people to be in the park during a normal business day, with their clothing stacked primly on the grass. If they're not doing this, they're probably drinking merrily at one of the park's three **beer gardens** (p220).

Munich's beautiful **Botanical Gardens** (☎ 1786 1350; adult/child €3/2; ☒ varies with season, generally 9am–6pm) are two stops past Schloss Nymphenburg on tram 17.

OLYMPIA PARK COMPLEX

If you like heights, then take a ride up the lift of the 290m **Olympiaturm** (tower) situated in the **Olympia Park complex** (☎ 672 750; www .olympiapark-muenchen.de; adult/child €4/3.50; ☒ tower 9am–midnight). And if you fancy a swim, then the **Olympic Pool Complex** (☎ 3067 2290; Olympic Park; admission €3.50; ☒ 7am–11.15pm) will have you feeling like Mark Spitz while you imagine seven gold medals around your neck – or just work on your breast stroke. Take the U3 to Olympia zentrum.

Tours

The hordes of visitors and plethora of sights mean there's lots of people willing to show you around – an excellent way to gain background and context on what you see.

Mike's Bike Tours (☎ 2554 3987; www.mikesbiketours .com; tours from €24) Enjoyable (and leisurely) city cycling tours in English. Tours depart from the archway at the Altes Rathaus on Marienplatz.

Munich Walk Tours (☎ 2070 2736; www.munichwalk tours; Tal 31; tours from €10) Walking tours of the city and a tour focused on 'beer, brewing and boozing'.

Original Munich Walks (☎ 5502 9374; www.radius munich.com; Hauptbahnhof near track 32; tours from €10) Runs English-language tours: a two-hour walk of the city heart and an excellent tour of Third Reich sites.

Festivals & Events

Hordes come to Munich for **Oktoberfest** (www .oktoberfest.de) running the 15 days before the first Sunday in October. Reserve accommodation well ahead and go early in the day so you can grab a seat in one of the hangar-sized beer 'tents'. The action takes place at the Theresienwiese grounds, about a 10-minute walk southwest of the Hauptbahnhof. While there is no entrance fee, those €7 1L steins of beer add up fast. Although its origins are in the marriage celebrations of Crown Prince Ludwig in 1810, there's nothing regal about this beery bacchanalia now; expect mobs, expect to meet new and drunken friends, expect decorum to vanish as night sets in and you'll have a blast.

Sleeping

Munich has no shortage of places to stay – except at Oktoberfest or during some busy summer periods, when the wise (meaning those with a room) will have booked. Many of the budget and midrange places can be found in the anonymous streets around the train station. There's no good reason to stay here if you can avoid it as you'll find more charm and genuine fun elsewhere.

BUDGET

Munich's youth hostels that are DJH and HI affiliated do not accept guests over age 26, except group leaders or parents accompanying a child.

Campingplatz Thalkirchen (☎ 7243 0808; www .camping-muenchen.de; Zentralländstrasse 49; camp sites per person/tent €4.50/4, heated cabin per person €11; ☒ mid-Mar–end Oct) To get to this camping ground, southwest of the city centre, take the U3 to Thalkirchen and then catch bus 57 (about 20 minutes).

The Tent (☎ 141 4300; www.the-tent.com; In den Kirschen 30; bed in main tent €9, camp sites per tent/person €5.50/5.50; ☒ Jun–Sep) Pads and blankets provided for the bagless, bring your own lock for the lockers. Take tram 17 to the Botanic Gardens then follow the signs to a legendary international party.

Euro Youth Hotel (☎ 5990 8811; www.euro-youth -hotel.de; Senefelderstrasse 5; dm €15-18, r €39-60; ☒) The party never stops at the friendly Euro Youth Hotel, where happy noncampers work on international relationships in the bar and lounge. Rooms and facilities in this classic old building are well maintained.

4 you München (☎ 552 1660; www.the4you.de; Hirtenstrasse 18; dm €17-25, r €34-54; 💻) The 4 you is proud of its ecofriendly practices (check out the virgin wool blankets). Dorms have four to 12 beds while the private rooms have their own baths.

Wombat's (☎ 599 8918; www.wombats-hostels.com; Senefelderstrasse 1; dm €19, d €62; 💻) Despite the name this 300-bed hostel is refreshingly free of Aussie shtick. Dorms have six to eight beds. There's a fun and relaxed vibe at this well-run place.

Easy Palace Station Hotel (☎ 558 7970; www .easypalace.com; Schützenstrasse 7; dm €20, r €29-69; 💻) This once-sedate midrange hotel has been converted into a budget haven (you can still see traces of its past stodgy life). Dorm rooms have four to six beds. Singles and doubles have both shared and private baths.

MIDRANGE

Pension Haydn (☎ 5440 4703; www.pension-haydn.de; Haydnstrasse 9; r €38-95) Not far from Goetheplatz U-Bahn station on a quiet residential street, the Haydn's rooms are tended with care. More money buys private bathrooms.

Hotel am Viktualienmarkt (☎ 225 014; www.hotel -am-viktualienmarkt.de; Utzschneiderstrasse 14; r €40-150; 💻) Near the Viktualienmarkt (duh!), the 27 renovated rooms have a nice, light feel. It's good value in a great location.

Creatif Hotel Elephant (☎ 555 785; www.munich -hotel.net; Lämmerstrasse 6; r €50-150; ✖ 💻) The Creatif is a delightful and friendly place bursting with flowers. Its 44 rooms are stylish and comfortable, in an Ikea sort of way and there's free wi-fi.

Hotel Alcron Garni (☎ 228 3511; www.hotel-alcron .de; Ledererstrasse 13; r €60-100; ✖ 💻) Nicely located near the Marienplatz, the 14 rooms here are furnished with vintage furniture. It's a good place to crash in the very middle of town.

Hotel Blauer Bock (☎ 231 780; www.hotelblauerbock .de; Sebastiansplatz 9; r €60-102, with shared bathroom €41-79; ✖) This hotel traces its hostelry roots back more than a century. The 75 rooms now are modern and comfortable and the location on a quieter side street is excellent.

Pension am Gärtnerplatztheater (☎ 202 5170; www.pension-gaertnerplatztheater.de; Klenzestrasse 45; r €65-180; 💻) An antique-filled classic just down the street from hip and happening Gärtnerplatz. The 10 rooms have a timeless air, although that scent is wood polish.

TOP END

Hotel Olympic (☎ 231 890; www.hotel-olympic.de; Hans-Sachs-Strasse 4; r €90-180; 💻) This hotel has classy yet with unfussy decor that highlights the many fine antiques and artworks. There are 38 very nice, spacious rooms and they have wi-fi. You can't beat the relatively quiet location.

Apartments & Hotel Maximilian (☎ 242 580; www .maximilian-munich.com; Hochbrückenstrasse 18; r €130-300; ✖ ✖ 💻) This new and stylish place has 54 studios and apartments in a great location. All units come with kitchen facilities and wi-fi. There's a garden out back and the staff are truly lovely. This is a great place for longer stays or for those sick of hotel rooms. Look for deals.

Bayerischer Hof (☎ 212 00; www.bayerischerhof .de; Promenadeplatz 2-6; r from €210; ✖ ✖ 💻 🛒) Opened in 1841, generations of world leaders have made the Bayerischer Hof their home in Munich. The beautiful glass domed atrium, marble and gold leaf details and bustling efficiency are just some of the exquisite details. Breakfast on the top-floor terrace is a sublime treat.

Eating

Clusters of restaurants can be found anywhere there's pedestrian life. The streets in and around Gärtnerplatz and Glockenbach-Viertel are the flavour-of-the-moment. You can always do well in and around Marienplatz and the wonderful Viktualienmarkt, while Schwabing is always full of eating delights.

RESTAURANTS

Riva Bar Pizzeria (☎ 220 240; Tal 44; mains €7-12) Straight from fashionable Milan, this authentic pizza place packs 'em in for wood-fired treats. Wait for a table inside or out at the long bar up front, toss a *ciao* or two to the cheery chefs.

Fraunhofer (☎ 266 460; Fraunhoferstrasse 9; mains €7-14; 💻) The always-crowded Fraunhofer serves up good Bavarian cuisine from a changing menu. The setting is old and the patrons young at this hip place.

Wirthaus zur Brez'n (☎ 390 092; Leopoldstrasse 72; mains €7-15) Tradition abounds at this Bavarian beer hall and restaurant. Of the many levels, go for the *keller* (basement) for real authenticity. There's season brews on tap and choice menu items like duck. Look for the bad jokes on the walls.

GERMANY

MUNICH WALKING TOUR

The pivotal **Marienplatz** is a good starting point for a walking tour of Munich. Dominating the square is the towering neo-Gothic **Neues Rathaus** (new town hall; Marienplatz), with its ever-dancing **Glockenspiel** (carillon), which performs at 11am and noon (also at 5pm from March to October), bringing the square to an expectant standstill (note the fate of the Austrian knight...). Two important churches are on this square: the baroque star **St Peterskirche** (Rindermarket 1; tower €1.50; ☺ 9am-7pm Apr-Oct, to 6pm Nov-Mar) and, behind the **Altes Rathaus**, the often forgotten **Heiliggeistkirche** (Tal 77; ☺ 7am-6pm). Head west along shopping street Kaufingerstrasse to the landmark of Munich, the late-Gothic **Frauenkirche** (Church of Our Lady; ☎ 423 457; Frauenplatz; tower adult/child €3/1.50; ☺ tower 10am-5pm Mar-Oct) with its then-trendy 16th-century twin onion domes. Go inside and join the hordes gazing at the grandeur of the place, or climb the tower for majestic views of Munich. Continue west to the large grey 16th-century **Michaelskirche** (☎ 609 0224; Neuhauserstrasse 52; ☺ 8am-7pm), Germany's earliest and grandest Renaissance church.

Further west is the **Richard Strauss Fountain** and the medieval **Karlstor**, an old city gate. Double back towards Marienplatz and turn right onto Eisenmannstrasse, which becomes Kreuzstrasse and converges with Herzog-Wilhelm-Strasse at the medieval gate of **Sendlinger Tor**. Go down the shopping street Sendlinger Strasse to the **Asamkirche** (Sendlinger Strasse 34), a flamboyant 17th-century church designed by brothers Cosmas Damian and Egid Quirin Asam. The ornate marble façade won't prepare you for the opulence inside, where scarcely an inch is left unembellished.

Continue along Sendlinger Strasse and turn right on Hermann-Sack-Strasse to reach the **Stadtmuseum** (☎ 233; St-Jakobs-Platz 1; adult/child €4/2; ☺ 10am-6pm Tue-Sun), where a mixed but good bag of exhibits cover beer brewing, fashion, musical instruments, photography and puppets (who *don't* get top billing).

Santini (☎ 202 2658; Fraunhoferstrasse 43; mains €8-15) Jaunty red-and-white checked tablecloths set the mood at this cheery pizzeria and pasta place. There are tables outside and candles providing a romantic glow inside.

Seven Fish (☎ 2300 0219; Gärtnerplatz 6; mains €8-20) Outside there's a stylish café, inside it's a higher-end stylish restaurant with blue accents on exposed brick walls. As the name implies, fish is the specialty here and the line-up depends on what's fresh.

Alhambra (☎ 5488 1741; Schwanthaler Strasse 13; meals €9-18) A great place near the Hauptbahnhof, this stylish tapas place serves up Mediterranean and Spanish treats that range from hummus to tortillas. There's a great long bar.

Weisses Brauhaus (☎ 290 1380; Tal 7; mains €9-20) The place for classic Bavarian fare in an ancient beer-hall setting. Everything from *weissewurst* (beloved local white sausage) to hearty traditional fare such as boiled ox cheeks is on offer.

CAFÉS

Two in One (☎ 2024 4595; Klenzestrasse 39; snacks €3-6; ☺ 10am-7.30pm Tue-Sat) That amazing smell may be the fresh cut flowers or the fine tea. It's hard to tell at this florist-cum-tea shop

near Gärtnerplatz. Have a cake at one of the tiny tables and try to decide.

News Bar (☎ 281 787; Amalienstrasse 55; sandwiches €5; ▣) Besides food and drinks, newspapers and magazines are available at this popular Schwabing hang-out. Enjoy the *Herald-Tribune* with a latte.

Café am Zeitgeist (☎ 2865 6873; Türkenstrasse 74; meals €6-12) This casual place stretches back off the street so you can enjoy an outside table without exhaust. There are toys for the kids and treats like *flammenkuchen* for one and all.

Nil (☎ 265 545; Hans-Sachs-Strasse 2; meals €7-12; ☺ 8am-4am) Right in trendy Glockenback-Viertel, this hip place draws a straight and gay crowd in the know. Tables outside are packed when the sun shines, inside it's packed all night long.

Interview (☎ 202 1646; Gärtnerplatz 1; mains €7-15) Patrons at this thriving and trendy café are more interested in eyeing each other than their food. Too bad, as the breakfasts served to 5pm (as well as the pastas, salads and more) are worth more than a glance.

SELF-CATERING

Viktualienmarkt, just south of Marienplatz, is a large open-air market open daily except

GERMANY

Saturday afternoon and Sunday, where you can put together a picnic feast to take to the Englischer Garten. The fresh produce, cheese and baked goods are hard to resist. Or relax here under the trees, at tables provided by one of the many beer and sausage vendors.

Alois Dallmayr (☎ 213 50; Dienerstrasse 14) One of the world's great delicatessens, behind the mustard-yellow awnings you'll find sparkling cases filled with fine foods. This is the place to come if you want a pet crayfish (see their fountain home).

Drinking

Apart from the beer halls and gardens, Munich has no shortage of lively pubs. Schwabing and Glockenback-Viertel are good places to follow your ears. Many serve food.

Alter Simpl (☎ 272 3083; Türkenstrasse 57) On a quieter Schwabing street than most, this historic pub exudes atmosphere. Thomas Mann hung out here 100 years ago and probably still would today.

Arc Pub (☎ 0178-3256423; Schraudolphstrasse 24) A popular sports bar with expats and travellers who want to catch live broadcasts of the action from home – wherever that may be. Popular and lively.

Klenze 17 (☎ 228 5795; Klenzestrasse 17) The extensive whisky selection is almost as large as Klenze 17's two small rooms, usually populated with young folks, many scarfing down nachos at midnight.

Entertainment
CINEMAS & THEATRE

Munich is one of the cultural capitals of Germany; the publications and websites listed on p212 can guide you to the best events. For tickets, try **Munchën Ticket** (☎ 5481 8154; www .muenchenticket.de).

Residenztheater (☎ 2185 1920; Max-Joseph-Platz 2) Home of the Bavarian State Opera (www .staatsoper.de) and the site of many cultural events (particularly during the opera festival in July).

Cinema (☎ 555 255; www.cinema-muenchen.com; Nymphenburger Strasse 31) Current films in English are screened here. Take the U1 to Stiglmaier Platz, exit at Nymphenburgerstrasse.

NIGHTCLUBS

Jazzclub Unterfahrt (☎ 448 2794; Einsteinstrasse 42-44) Near the Max-Weber-Platz U-Bahn station.

It has live music from 7.30pm nightly, and open jam sessions on Sunday night. Things often go until 3am.

Kultafabrik (www.kultafabrik.de; Grafingerstrasse 6; ☹ 8pm-6am or later) From potatoes to clubbing. This former spud factory has been reborn as a vast playground of clubs. There's over 25 that you can sample before you end up mashed or fried. The themes range from live rock to techno (of course) to post-Soviet squalor. It's close to the Ostbahnhof station.

GAY & LESBIAN VENUES

Much of Munich's gay and lesbian nightlife is around Gärtnerplatz and the Glockenback-Viertel. Any of the places in this area listed above (such as Nil) will have a mixed crowd. *Our Munich* and *Sergej* are monthly guides easily found in this neighbourhood. Another good resource is Max&Milian (p211).

Morizz (☎ 201 6776; Klenzestrasse 43) is a popular haunt for gay men that takes it cue from a classic Paris nightspot. It has a long wine and cocktail list and goes until dawn.

Shopping

All shoppers converge on the Marienplatz to buy designer shoes or kitschy souvenirs. The stylish department store **Ludwig Beck** (☎ 236 910; Marienplatz 11) has something for everyone. Bypass Calvin et al for more unusual European choices.

For the well-heeled, check out the *haute couture* shops on Maxmilianstrasse. Meanwhile Schwabing boasts its fair share of quirky, artistic boutiques, especially along Hohenzollernstrasse.

The edgy, trendy culture of Glockenback-Viertel is exemplified by **Fuckuall** (☎ 2323 1816; Jahnstrasse 6), a purveyor of German gangsta clothing and whose distinctive and declarative logo is pasted up all over town.

Christkindlmarkt (Marienplatz) in December is large and well stocked but often expensive, so buy a warm drink and just wander around. A huge flea market, the **Auer Dult** (Mariahilfplatz), has great buys and takes place during the last weeks of April, July and October.

Getting There & Away
AIR

Munich's sparkling white **airport** (MUC; www .munich-airport.de) is second in importance only to Frankfurt-am-Main for international and national connections. Flights will take you to all major destinations worldwide. Main German cities are serviced by at least half a dozen flights daily. easyJet and DBA are major budget carriers here.

BUS
Munich is linked to the Romantic Road by the popular **Deutsche-Touring** (☎ 889 895 13; www .deutsche-touring.com; Hirtenstrasse 14) Munich-Frankfurt service (see p220). Buses stop along the northern side of the train station on Arnulfstrasse.

CAR & MOTORCYCLE
Munich has autobahns radiating out on all sides. Take the A9 to Nuremberg, the A92 to Passau, the A8 east to Salzburg, the A95 to Garmisch-Partenkirchen and the A8 to Ulm or Stuttgart. The main rental companies have counters together on the second level of the Hauptbahnhof. For arranged rides, the **ADM-Mitfahrzentrale** (☎ 194 40; www.mitfahrz.org; Lämmerstrasse 6; ☒ 8am-8pm) is near the Hauptbahnhof. The cost is split with the driver and you can reach most parts of Germany for well under €40.

TRAIN
Train services to/from Munich are excellent. There are rapid connections at least every two hours to all major cities in Germany, as well as daily EC trains to other European cities such as Paris (€105, nine hours), Vienna (€68, four hours) and Zurich (€59, 4½ hours).

High-speed ICE services from Munich include Frankfurt (€75, 3¾ hours, hourly), Hamburg (€115, six hours, hourly) and Berlin (€96, six hours, every two hours).

Getting Around
TO/FROM THE AIRPORT
Munich's international airport is connected by the S8 and the S1 to Marienplatz and the Hauptbahnhof (€8.80). The service takes about 40 minutes and there is a train every 10 minutes from 4am until around 12.30am. The S8 route is slightly faster.

Taxis make the long haul for at least €60.

BICYCLE
Pedal power is popular in relatively flat Munich. **Radius Bike Rental** (☎ 596 113; www .radiusmunich.com; Hauptbahnhof near track 32; ☒ 10am-

6pm May-Sep) rents out two-wheelers from €17 per day.

CAR & MOTORCYCLE
It's not worth driving in the city centre – many streets are pedestrian only. The tourist office has a map that shows city parking places (€2 or more per hour).

PUBLIC TRANSPORT
Munich's excellent public transport network (MVV; www.mvv-muenchen.de) is zone-based, and most places of interest to tourists (except Dachau and the airport) are within the 'blue' inner zone (Innenraum; €2.20). MVV tickets are valid for the S-Bahn, U-Bahn, trams and buses, but they must be validated before use. The U-Bahn stops operating around 12.30am Monday to Friday and 1.30am on Saturday and Sunday, but there are some later buses and S-Bahns. Rail passes are valid exclusively on the S-Bahn.

Kurzstrecke (short rides) cost €1.10 and are good for no more than four stops on buses and trams, and two stops on the U- and S-Bahns. *Tageskarte* (day passes) for the inner zone cost €4.80, while three-day tickets cost €11.80, or €20 for two adults travelling together (partner ticket).

TAXI
Taxis are expensive (€2.80 flag fall, plus €1.50 per kilometre) and not much more convenient than public transport. For a radio-dispatched taxi dial ☎ 216 10.

DACHAU
The first Nazi concentration camp was **Dachau** (☎ 08131-669 970; www.kz-gedenkstaette-dachau .de; Alte-Roemerstrasse 75; admission free; ☒ 9am-5pm Tue-Sun), built in March 1933. Jews, political prisoners, homosexuals and others deemed 'undesirable' by the Third Reich were imprisoned in the camp. More than 200,000 people were sent here; more than 30,000 died at Dachau and countless others died after being transferred to other death camps. An English-language documentary is shown at 11.30am and 3.30pm. A visit includes camp relics, memorials and a very sobering museum. Take the S2 (direction Petershausen) to Dachau and then bus 726 or 724 to the camp. A Munich XXL day ticket (€6.50) will cover the trip.

ROMANTIC ROAD

The popular and schmaltzily named Romantic Road (Romantische Strasse) links a series of picturesque Bavarian towns and cities. It's not actually one road per se but rather a 353km route chosen to highlight as many quaint towns and cities as possible in western Bavaria.

From north to south it includes the following major stops:

- Würzburg – Starting point and featuring 18th-century artistic splendour among the vineyards.
- Rothenburg ob der Tauber – The medieval walled hub of cutesy picturesque Bavarian touring.
- Dinkelsbühl – Another medieval walled town replete with moat and watchtowers, a smaller Rothenberg. The town is best reached by the Romantic Road by bus or car.
- Augsburg – A medieval and Renaissance city with many good places for a beer.
- Wieskirche – This Unesco World Heritage **church** (☎ 08862 932 930; www.wieskirche.de; ⊙ 8am-5pm) is a truly amazing work of 18th-century rococo excess. It towers over

a tiny village 25km northeast of Füssen. The church is best reached by the Romantic Road bus or car.

- Füssen – The southern end of the route and the cute and over-run home of mad King Ludwig's castles.

In addition to these principal stops, more than a dozen more little towns clamour for attention – and your money.

Getting There & Around

The principal cities and towns listed above are all easily reached by train – see the individual listings for details. But to really explore the route, you are best off with your own transportation. The entire length is copiously marked with brown signs in German, English and Japanese. With a car, you can blow through places of little interest and linger at those that attract.

A popular way to tour the Romantic Road is the **Deutsche-Touring Romantic Road bus** (www .deutsche-touring.com). Starting in Frankfurt in the north and Munich in the south, a bus runs in each direction each day covering the entire route between Würzburg and Füs-

---

BEER HALLS & BEER GARDENS

Beer-drinking is not just an integral part of Munich's entertainment scene, it's a reason to visit. Germans drink an average of 130L of the amber liquid each per year, while Munich residents manage to drink much more. Locals will be happy to help ensure that you don't bring down the average.

Beer halls can be vast boozy affairs seating thousands or much more modest neighbourhood hang-outs. The same goes for beer gardens. Both come in all shapes and sizes. What's common is a certain camaraderie among strangers, huge litre glasses of beer (try putting one of those in your carry on) and lots of cheap food – the saltier the better. Note that in beer gardens tradition allows you to bring your own food, a boon if you want an alternative to pretzels, sausages and the huge white radishes served with, you guessed it, salt.

On a warm day there's nothing better than sitting and sipping among the greenery at one of the Englischer Garten's classic beer gardens. **Chinesischer Turm** (☎ 383 8730) is justifiably popular while the nearby **Hirschau** (☎ 369 942) on the banks of Kleinhesseloher See is less crowded.

Augustiner Keller (☎ 594 393; Arnulfstrasse 52) Only five minutes from the Hauptbahnhof, the Keller has a large and leafy beer garden and a fine cavernous hall when the weather keeps you indoors.

Augustiner Bierhalle (☎ 5519 9257; Neuhauser Strasse 27) What you probably imagine an old-style Munich beer hall looks like, filled with laughter, smoke and clinking glasses.

Zum Dürnbrau (☎ 222 195; Tal 21) Tucked into a corner off Tal, this is a great and authentic little alternative to the Hofbräuhaus. There's a small beer garden and drinkers of dark drafts enjoy pewter-topped mugs.

Hofbräuhaus (☎ 2901 3610; Am Platzl 9) The ultimate cliché of Munich beer halls. Tourists arrive by the busload but no-one seems to mind that this could be Disneyland (although the theme park wasn't once home to Hitler's early speeches, like this place was).

sen. However, seeing the entire route in one day is only for those with a love of buses and unusual fortitude. Stops are brief (15 minutes for Wieskirche, *Schnell!* 30 minutes for Rothenburg, *Schnell!* etc) so you'll want to choose places where you can break the trip for a day (stopovers are allowed). But of course this leads you to decide between a 30-minute visit and a 24-hour one.

The buses depart April to October from Frankfurt Hauptbahnhof at 8am and from Munich Hauptbahnhof at 8.15am and take about 13 hours. The total fare (tickets are bought on board) is a pricey €139. Railpass holders get a 60% discount and flexipass holders do not need to use a travel day for the discount. You can also just ride for individual segments (eg Rothenberg to Augsburg costs €27).

WÜRZBURG

☎ 0931 / pop 133,000

Nestled among river valleys lined with vineyards, Würzburg beguiles even before you reach the city centre. Three of the four largest wine growing estates in all of Germany are here and most of the delicate whites produced locally never leave the region – the locals will always reach for a wine glass first. Over 1300 years old, Würzburg was rebuilt after bombings late in the war (it took only 17 minutes to almost completely destroy the city). Today it's a centre of art, beautiful architecture and delicate wines.

The **tourist office** (☎ 372 335; www.wuerzburg .de; Oberer Markt; ⏰ 10am-6pm Mon-Fri, 10am-2pm Sat & Sun May-Oct, reduced hr & closed Sun other times), in the rococo masterpiece Haus zum Falken.

Sights

The magnificent, sprawling **Residenz** (☎ 355 170; www.schloesser.bayern.de; Residenzplatz 2; adult/child €5/4; ⏰ 9am-6pm Apr-Oct, 10am-4pm Nov-Mar), a baroque masterpiece by Neumann, took a generation to build and boasts the world's largest ceiling fresco (graphic artists take note: he didn't need no stinking Photoshop); the **Hofgarten** at the back is a beautiful spot. The interior of the **Dom St Kilian** (☎ 386 261; Kiliansplatz; admission €5; ⏰ 10am-7pm Tue-Sun Apr-Oct, to 5pm Tue-Sun Nov-Mar) and the adjacent **Neumünster**, an 11th-century church in the old town housing the bones of St Kilian – the patron Saint of Würzburg – continue the baroque themes of the Residenz.

Neumann's fortified **Alter Kranen** (old crane), which serviced a dock on the riverbank south of Friedensbrücke, is now the **Haus des Frankenweins** (☎ 390 1111; Kranenkai 1), where you can taste Franconian wines (for around €3 per glass).

The medieval fortress **Marienberg**, across the river on the hill, is reached by crossing the 15th-century stone **Alte Mainbrücke** (bridge) from the city and walking up Tellstiege, a small alley. It encloses the **Fürstenbau Museum** (☎ 438 38; admission €4; ⏰ 9am-6pm Tue-Sun Apr-Oct, 10am-4pm Tue-Sun Nov-Mar) featuring the Episcopal apartments, and the regional **Mainfränkisches Museum** (☎ 430 16; adult/child €3/1.50; ⏰ 10am-5pm Tue-Sun Apr-Oct, to 4pm Nov-Mar). See both on a combined card (€5). For a simple thrill, wander the walls enjoying the panoramic views.

Sleeping & Eating

Würzburg's many *Weinstuben* are excellent places to sample the local vintages. Look for crests of gilded grapes over entrances. Sanderstrasse has a good strip of lively bars.

Kanu-Club (☎ 725 36; Mergentheimer Strasse 13b; camp sites per person/tent €5/5; ⏰ Apr-Sep) A camping ground on the west bank of the Main; take tram 3 or 5 to Jugendbühlweg.

Hostel Babelfish (☎ 3040430; www.babelfish-hostel .de; Prymstrasse 3; dm/d from €16/45; 💻) Close to the centre, this new hostel is ultra-clean and well run. Dorms have four to 10 beds each. From the train station walk east 200m.

Pension Spehnkuch (☎ 547 52; www.pension -spehnkuch.de; Röntgenring 7; s/d from €29/60) Located by the train station, the seven simple rooms are kept spotless by the charming family.

Hotel Till Eulenspiegel (☎ 355 840; www.hotel -till-eulenspiegel.de; Sanderstrasse 1a; s/d from €63/85; ⌧) Oxygen-lovers celebrate: this is a non-smoking hotel. Run by the gregarious Johannes, the 18 rooms are comfortable and some have sunny balconies. There's also a small but good *weinstube* and a pub serving unusual Bavarian microbrews.

Karma X (☎ 329 4149; Kardinal-Fraulhaber-Platz 4; meals €4-8; ⏰ 7am-7.30pm Mon-Sat; ⌧) A kind of Danish modern café done up in creams and orange – sort of like fresh-squeezed orange juice (which you can order). This upscale deli offers breakfasts, soups, salads, sandwiches, desserts and picnics to go.

Weinstuben Juliusspital (☎ 540 80; Juliuspromenade 19; meals €8-20) This rambling place serves from a long list of wines. You can have a meal or just a drink at one of the many old wooden tables.

Zum Stachel (☎ 527 70; Gressengasse 1; mains €12-25) This cosy *weinstube* traces its roots back to the 15th century. The ambitious menu has numerous local specialities including excellent beef and seafood dishes. There's a garden seating area and the ceiling inside is decorated with murals showing a *stachel* (mace) in action. Book ahead.

Getting There & Away

Würzburg is served by frequent trains from Frankfurt (€21 to €28, one to two hours) and one hour from Nuremberg (€14 to €19, 40 minutes to one hour). It's a major stop for the ICE trains on the Hamburg–Munich line. It is also on the Deutsche-Touring Romantic Road bus route (€14, 2¼ hours to/from Rothenburg). The stop is in front of the train station.

BAMBERG

☎ 0951 / pop 70,000

Off the major tourist routes, Bamberg is celebrated by those in the know. It boasts an amazing and preserved collection of 17th- and 18th-century buildings, palaces and churches. It is bisected by a large canal and a fast-flowing river that are spanned by cute little bridges and it even has its own local style of beer. No wonder it has been recognised by Unesco as a World Heritage Site. Could it be the best town in Germany?

The **tourist office** (☎ 871 161; www.bamberg.info; Geyerswörthstrasse 3; ☯ 9.30am-6pm Mon-Fri, to 2.30pm Sat year-round & Sun May-Oct) is on an island in the Regnitz River.

Sights

Bamberg's main appeal is its fine buildings – their sheer number, their jumble of styles and the ambience this creates. Most attractions are spread either side of the Regnitz River, but the colourful **Altes Rathaus** (Obere Brücke; ☯ 9.30am-4.30pm Tue-Sun Apr-Sep, 10am-4pm Tue-Sun Oct-Mar) is actually precariously perched on its own islet.

The princely and ecclesiastical district is centred on Domplatz, where the Romanesque and Gothic **cathedral** (Domplatz; ☯ 8am-6pm Apr-Sep, 8am-5pm Oct-Mar), housing the statue of the chivalric king-knight, the *Bamberger Reiter*, is the biggest attraction. Across the

square, the imposing 17th-century **Neue Residenz** (☎ 519 390; Domplatz 8; adult/child €3/2; ☯ 9am-6pm Apr-Sep, 10am-4pm Oct-Mar) is filled with treasures and opulent décor.

Above Domplatz is the former Benedictine monastery of St Michael, at the top of Michaelsberg. The **Kirche St Michael** (Franziskanergasse 2; ☯ 9am-6pm) is a must-see for its baroque art and the herbal compendium painted on its ceiling. The garden terraces afford another marvellous overview of the city's splendour.

Sleeping & Eating

Bamberg's unique style of beer is called *Rauchbier*, which literally means smoked beer. With a bacon flavour at first, it is a smooth brew that goes down easy. Happily, many of the local breweries also rent rooms.

Campingplatz Insel (☎ 563 20; www.campinginsel .de; Am Campingplatz 1; camp sites per person/tent €3.50/6) A well-equipped place in a tranquil spot right on the river. Take bus 18 to Camping platz.

Jugendherberge Wolfsschlucht (☎ 560 02; www .djh.de; Oberer Leinritt 70; dm €15; ☯ closed mid-Dec–mid-Jan) On the river's west bank, take bus 18 to Rodelbahn, walk northeast to the riverbank, then turn left to this cute 92-bed hostel.

Brauerei Spezial (☎ 243 04; www.brauerei-spezial .de; Obere Königstrasse 10; r €20-55, meals €8-15) Across from Fässla, this half-timbered brewery has cosy drinking and dining areas featuring old tile stoves. The seven rooms are quite simple but comfortable.

Petrolthof Fässla (☎ 265 16; www.faessla.de; Obere Königstrasse 19-21; s/d €37/55) It's a dream come true – a bed in a brewery. The 21 rooms are large, clean and comfy. Look for the keg over the door.

Hotel Alte Post (☎ 980 260; Heiliggrabstrasse 1; r €38-100; ☐) A five-minute walk from the train station, this 40-room place has simple rooms that come with wi-fi.

Teegiesserei (☎ 297 2595; Pfahlplätzchen 2; meals €6-10; ☯ 11am-7.30pm Tue-Sun) Like an upscale home featured in a Sunday supplement, this stylish café at first seems all style over substance. But sample the many cakes and teas and you'll see the depths of its goodness.

Schlenkerla (☎ 560 60; Dominikanerstrasse 6; meals €7-15) This ancient half-timbered building is *the* place to sample Rauchbier. The traditional menu boasts many a porky platter and there's always seasonal specials.

GERMANY

Getting There & Away

There are hourly trains to/from both Würzburg (€15.50, one hour) and Nuremberg (€10, one hour). Bamberg is also served by ICE trains running between Munich (€48, 2½ hours) and Berlin (€69, four hours) every two hours.

ROTHENBURG OB DER TAUBER
☎ 09861 / pop 12,000

In the Middle Ages, Rothenburg's town fathers built strong walls to protect the town from siege; today they are the reason the town is under siege from tourists. The most stereotypical of all German walled towns, Rothenburg can't help being so cute.

Granted 'free imperial city' status in 1274, it's a confection of twisting cobbled lanes and pretty architecture enclosed by towered stone walls. The **tourist office** (☎ 404 92; www.rothenburg .de; Marktplatz 2; ⌚ 9am-noon, 1-5pm Mon-Fri, 10am-2pm Sat) can help you find a room, which might be a good idea because after dark the streets are quiet and the underlying charm comes out.

Note that the gaggle of Christmas shops and 'museums' are quite wiley – once in you have to walk the entire labyrinth in order to escape.

Sights

The **Rathaus on Markt** was commenced in Gothic style in the 14th century but completed in Renaissance style. The **tower** (admission €1) gives a majestic view over the town and the Tauber Valley. According to legend, the town was saved during the Thirty Years' War when the mayor won a challenge by the Imperial general Tilly and downed more than 3L of wine at a gulp. The **Meistertrunk** scene is re-enacted by the clock figures on the tourist office building (eight times daily in summer). Actors re-enact other famous scenes from the past (but not the mythical assault on the tour bus by fudge vendors) at 6.30pm Friday, May to September.

Totally uncommercial, **Jakobskirche** (☎ 700 60; Klingengasse 1; adult/child €2/1; ⌚ 9am-4pm) is sober and Gothic. Marvel at the carved *Heilige Blut Altar* (Holy Blood Altar).

The **Reichsstadt Museum** (☎ 939 043; Klosterhof 5; adult/child €3/1.50; ⌚ 9.30am-5.30pm Apr-Oct, 1-4pm Nov-Mar), in the former convent, features the superb *Rothenburger Passion* in 12 panels and the Judaica room, with a collection of gravestones with Hebrew inscriptions.

Sleeping & Eating

Resist the temptation to try a *Schneeball*, a crumbly ball of bland dough with the taste and consistency of chalk – surely one of Europe's worst 'local specialities'.

Das Lädle (☎ 6130; www.das-laedle.de; Spitalgasse 18; r €22-48) A good budget option, with light, modern rooms in a central location.

Hotel & Cafe Uhl (☎ 4895; www.hotel-uhl.de; Plölein 8; r €35-70, meals €6-10; ✗) Downstairs there's a nice bakery and café with views, upstairs the 12 rooms are bright and modern.

Altfrankische Weinstube (☎ 6404; Klosterhof 7; r €48-70; mains €7-15) Vine covered and cosy, the Altfrankische Weinstube is justifiably popular, with a varied and well-priced menu, and a fantastic atmosphere set by the wine barrels out front. The rooms are simple and comfortable.

Getting There & Away

There are hourly trains to/from Steinach, a transfer point for service to Würzburg (total journey €10, 70 minutes). Rothenburg is a cross-road for tourist buses. The Deutsche-Touring Romantic Road bus pauses here for 30 minutes. A companion bus serving the Castle Road route provides daily links May to September to Heidelberg (€46, three hours) and Nürnberg (€14, two hours).

NUREMBERG
☎ 0911 / pop 494,000

Levelled during the war, Nuremberg has spent the last few decades rebuilding itself. It's hard to sense that the town was once a half-timbered medieval wonder but that's OK, as the current version has charms of its own. The narrow backstreets reward wanderers, who can take sustenance at places grilling up the town's seductive namesake sausage. Germanisches Nationalmuseum is a reason to not just get off the train but to make the journey. In winter the famous Christmas market draws hordes.

Nuremberg played a major role during the Nazi years, as documented in Leni Riefenstahl's film *Triumph of Will* and during the war crimes trials afterwards. It has done an admirable job of confronting this ugly past with museums and exhibits.

Orientation

The main train station is just outside the city walls of the old town. The main artery, the mostly pedestrian Königstrasse, takes you through the old town and its major squares. Breite Gasse, Königsstrasse and Karolinenstrasse are the main shopping streets.

Information

Both tourist offices sell the two-day Nürnberg Card (€18), which provides free public transport and entry to all museums and attractions, including those in nearby Fürth.

Netzkultur (☎ 211 0782; 3rd fl, Maximum Bldg, Färberstrasse 11; per hr €3.50; ☼ 9-1am) Burn CDs, surf the Internet.

Post office (Bahnhofplatz 1)

Schnell und Sauber Laundry (☎ 180 9400; Sulzbacher Strasse 86; per load €4; ☼ 6am-midnight) Tram 8 to Deichslerstrasse.

Tourist offices (www.tourismus.nuernberg.de) Main office (☎ 233 6132; Königstrasse 93; ☼ 9am-7pm Mon-Sat); branch office (☎ 233 6135; Hauptmarkt 18; ☼ 9am-6pm Mon-Sat, 10am-4pm Sun May-Sep)

Sights

The stunning **Germanisches Nationalmuseum** (☎ 133 10; www.gnm.de; Kartäusergasse 1; adult/child €5/4; ☼ 10am-6pm Tue-Sun, 10am-9pm Wed) is the most important general museum of German culture. It displays works by German painters and sculptors, an archaeological collection, arms and armour, musical and scientific instruments and toys. Look for the globe dating from 1492.

Close by, the sleek and harmonious **Neues Museum** (☎ 240 200; Luitpoldstrasse 5; adult/child €4/3; ☼ 10am-8pm Tue-Fri, to 6pm Sat & Sun) contains a superb collection of contemporary art and design.

The scenic **Altstadt** is easily covered on foot. On Lorenzer Platz there's the **St Lorenzkirche**, noted for the 15th-century tabernacle that climbs like a vine up a pillar to the vaulted ceiling.

To the north is the bustling **Hauptmarkt**, where the most famous Christkindlesmarkt in Germany is held from the Friday before Advent to Christmas Eve. The church here is the ornate **Pfarrkirche Unsere Liebe Frau**; the clock's figures go strolling at noon. Near the Rathaus is **St Sebalduskirche**, Nuremberg's oldest church (dating from the 13th century), with the shrine of St Sebaldus.

Climb up Burgstrasse to the enormous 15th-century **Kaiserburg complex** (☎ 225 726; Burg 13; adult/child €5/4; ☼ 9am-6pm Apr-Sep, 10am-4pm Oct-Mar) for good views of the city. The walls spread west to the tunnel-gate of **Tiergärtnertor**, where you can stroll behind the castle to the gardens. Nearby is the renovated **Albrecht-Dürer-Haus** (☎ 231 2568; Albrecht-Dürer-Strasse 39; adult/child €5/2.50; ☼ 10am-5pm Tue-Sun, to 8pm Thu), where Dürer, Germany's renowned Renaissance draughtsman, lived from 1509 to 1528.

Nuremberg's role during the Third Reich is well known. The Nazis chose this city as their propaganda centre and for mass rallies, which were held at **Luitpoldhain**, a (never completed) sports complex of megalomaniac proportions. After the war, the Allies deliberately chose Nuremberg as the site for the trials of Nazi war criminals. Not to be missed is the **Dokumentationzentrum** (☎ 231 5666; www.museen.nuernberg.de; Bayernstrasse 110; adult/child €5/2.50; ☼ 9am-6pm Mon-Fri, 10am-6pm Sat & Sun) in the north wing of the massive unfinished Congress Hall, which would have held 50,000 people for Hitler's spectacles. The museum's absorbing exhibits trace the rise of Hitler and the Nazis and the important role Nuremberg played in the mythology. Take tram 9 or 6 to Doku-Zentrum.

Sleeping

Lette'm Sleep (☎ 992 8128; www.backpackers.de; Frauentormauer 42; dm €16-20, r with shared bathroom €44-52; ▣) Dorms are available, as well as quirky private rooms designed with colour and flair not often seen in hostels.

Pension Sonne (☎ 227 166; Königstrasse 45; s/d with shared bathroom €30/60) It's a steep climb up three flights of stairs to the cosy and bright rooms with high ceilings.

Hotel Lucas (☎ 227 845; www.hotel-lucas.de; Kaiserstrasse 22; r €50-90; ✗ ▣) Some of the 11 tidy rooms here have balconies, others have small adjoining rooms for doing work – which for you might mean scrutinising a guidebook. The location is very central.

Merian-Hotel (☎ 214 6 90; www.merian-hotel.de; Unschlittplatz 7; r €85-130) The 21 rooms here are simply decorated but that means there's no competition for your attention, which should be focused on the nearby fast-flowing Pegnitz River. The hotel has a good outdoor café in this attractive and quiet part of the old town.

Hotel Agneshof (☎ 214440; www.agneshof-nuernberg.de; Agnesgasse 10; r €100-250; ✗ ▣) In the middle of Nuremberg's well-preserved historic centre, the Agneshof has 74 bright and well-appointed rooms with wi-fi. The small sauna is a plus.

Eating

Don't leave Nuremberg without trying its famous finger-sized grilled sausages. Order 'em by the dozen with *Meerrettich* (horseradish) on the side.

Bratwursthäusle (☎ 227 695; Rathausplatz 2; meals €6-10) Here the local sausages are flame-grilled and scrumptious. Get them with *Kartoffelsalat* (potato salad). There are also nice tree-shaded tables outside.

Zwinger (☎ 220 48; Lorenzer Strasse 33; mains €6-12) Up front you can have a meal of local favourites at this popular meeting place. In back there's live music or DJs until late.

Kettensteg (☎ 221 081; Maxplatz 35; mains €7-15) Right by the river and with its own suspension bridge to the other side, this beer garden and restaurant is fine on a summer day and cosy in winter. The basic fare is tasty and absorbs lots of beer.

Lindbergh (☎ 214 25 95; Burgstrasse 1; mains €8-15) This contemporary café and bar has huge windows overlooking the St Sebalduskirche. There's a good wine list and smattering of creative continental hits on the varied menu.

Getting There & Around

Nuremberg's **airport** (NUE; www.airport-nuernberg .de) is a hub for budget carrier Air Berlin, which has service throughout Germany, as well as flights to European capitals including London, Paris and Rome. There's frequent service to the airport on the S-2 line (€1.80, 20 minutes).

The city is also a hub for train service. ICE trains run to/from Berlin-Hauptbahnhbf (€77, 4½ hours, every two hours), Frankfurt-am-Main (€39, two hours, hourly) and on the new fast line to Munich (€41, 79 minutes, hourly). Trains run hourly to Stuttgart (€28, 2¼ hours).

Tickets on the bus, tram and U-Bahn system cost €1.80 each. Day passes are €3.60.

REGENSBURG

☎ 0941 / pop 129,000

On the wide Danube River, Regensburg has relics of all periods as far back as the Romans, yet doesn't have the tourist mobs you'll find in other equally attractive German cities. Oh well, their loss. The centre escaped the war's carpet bombing and Renaissance towers that could be in Florence mix with half-timbered charm. Throngs of students keep things from getting too mouldy.

Orientation & Information

From the main train station, you walk up Maximillianstrasse for 10 minutes to reach the centre. There's Internet access at coin-operated terminals (per 15 minutes €1) on the top level of the train station.

Tourist office (☎ 507 4410; www.regensburg.de; Altes Rathaus; ☾ 9am-6pm Mon-Fri, to 4pm Sat & Sun)

Sights

Dominating the skyline are the twin spires of the Gothic **Dom St Peter** (☎ 597 1002; Domplatz; admission free; tours in German adult/child €2.50/1.50; ☾ tours 10am, 11am, 2pm Mon-Sat, 1 & 2pm Sun May-Oct; 11am Mon-Fri & 1pm Sun Dec-Apr) built during the 14th and 15th centuries from unusual green limestone.

The **Altes Rathaus** (Rathausplatz 1; guided tours €6; ☾ tours in German through the day, tours in English 3.30pm Mon-Sat May-Sep) was progressively extended from medieval to baroque times and remained the seat of the Reichstag for almost 150 years.

The **Roman wall**, with its **Porta Praetoria** arch, follows Unter den Schwibbögen onto Dr-Martin-Luther-Strasse.

Lavish **Schloss Thurn und Taxis** (☎ 504 8133; Emmeramsplatz 6; adult/child €11.50/9; ☾ 11am-5pm Mon-Fri, 10am-5pm Sat & Sun) is near the train station and includes the castle proper (Schloss) and the royal stables (Marstall). The adjoining **Basilika St Emmeram** (☎ 510 30; Emmeramsplatz; ☾ 9am-5pm) is a riot of rococo and has a perfect cloister.

Sleeping & Eating

Azur-Camping (☎ 270 025; fax 299 432; Weinweg 40; camp sites per person/site €5/6) Bus 6 from the train station goes to the entrance.

DJH Hostel (☎ 574 02; www.djh.de; Wöhrdstrasse 60; dm €17; ▢) Regensburg's modernised hostel is in a beautiful old building on Unterer Wöhrd island about a 10-minute walk north of the Altstadt. Take bus 3 from Albert-strasse to Eisstadion.

Spitalgarten Hotel (☎ 847 74; www.spitalgarten .de; St Katharinenplatz 1; s/d €23/46) Across the river is the Spitalgarten, with basic rooms in a large imposing building. A beer garden is attached.

Hotel Am Peterstor (☎ 545 45; www.hotel -am-peterstor.de; Fröliche-Türkenstrasse 12; s/d €40/55)

The 36 clean, basic rooms are simply decorated in an attractive and unfussy way.

Hotel Kaiserhof (☎ 585 350; www.kaiserhof-am -dom.de; Kramgasse 10-12; r €60-125; ☐) The best rooms at this 30-room inn face the Dom. The décor is understated, which adds to the feeling of spaciousness. Ask for a room with a new bathroom.

Roter Hahn (595 090; www.roter-hahn.com; Rote-Hahnen-Gasse 10; s/d from €80/90; ☒ ☐) Look for the namesake red cock as you penetrate the narrow cobblestone streets in the heart of the old town. The 30 rooms have an edgy contemporary feel and wi-fi. The café (mains €7 to €15) has a creative modern fusion menu.

Historische Wurstküche (☎ 466 210; Thundorferstrasse 3; meals €6) The Danube rushes past this little house that's been cooking up the addictive local version of Nuremberg sausages (slightly spicier) for centuries.

Bodega (☎ 584 0486; Vor der Grieb 1a; meals €8-16) Hidden in a little alley, this contemporary tapas bar has an array of tempting dishes on display in glass cases. Sample the long wine list while hanging out outside or settle in inside for a trip to Spain.

Getting There & Away

Regensburg is on the train line between Nuremberg (€16 to €21, one hour, hourly) and Austria. There are hourly trains to Munich (€21, 1½ hours).

AUGSBURG

☎ 0821 / pop 259,000

Originally established by the Romans, Augsburg later became a centre of Luther's Reformation. Today it's a lively provincial city, criss-crossed by little streams, that has an appealing ambience and vitality. It makes a good day trip from Munich.

The **tourist office** (☎ 502 0724; www.augsburg -tourismus.de; Maximilian Strasse 57; ☻ 9am-5pm Mon-Fri, 10am-2pm Sat) can help with accommodation.

Sights

Look for the very impressive onion-shaped towers on the **Rathaus** (☎ 3240; Rathausplatz; ☻ 10am-6pm) and the adjacent **Perlachturm**. North of here is the 11th-century **Dom Maria Heimsuchung** (Hoher Weg; ☻ 10am-6pm Mon-Sat), which has more 'modern' additions, such as the 14th-century doors showing scenes from the Old Testament.

The Fuggers – a 16th-century banking family – left their mark everywhere. They have lavish tombs inside **St Anna Kirche** (Annastrasse; ☻ 10am-12.30pm & 3-6pm Tue-Sat, noon-6pm Sun), a place also known for being a Martin Luther bolthole. The 16th-century **Fuggerei** (no laughing!) was built with banking riches to house the poor. The excellent **museum** (☎ 319 881; Mittlere Gasse 13; adult/child €2/1; ☻ 10am-6pm) shows how they lived.

Sleeping & Eating

Jakoberhof (☎ 510 030; www.jakoberhof.de; Jakoberhofstrasse 41; s/d €49/64, with shared bathroom €26/39) Rooms at this dignified inn are sparsely decorated, which makes it easier not to lose something. Look for this temple of good value under its own onion dome.

Dom Hotel (☎ 343 930; www.domhotel-augsburg .de; Frauentorstrasse 8; s/d from €67/76; ☒ ☐ ☒) The 52 comfortable rooms here are modern and have wi-fi. Some have their own solariums, while some attic rooms have open beams and great views.

König von Flandern (☎ 158 050; Karolinenstrasse 12; meals €6-10) This underground brewery is always packed. The food is tasty and goes well with the many house beers on tap. Try the piquant Alligator döppelbock.

Getting There & Away

Trains between Munich and Augsburg are frequent (€10 to €18, 40 minutes). The Deutsche-Touring Romantic Road bus stops at the train station and the Rathaus.

FÜSSEN

☎ 08362 / pop 14,000

Close to the Austrian border and the foothills of the Alps, Füssen has some splendid baroque architecture, but it is primarily visited for the two castles in nearby Schwangau associated with King Ludwig II. The **tourist office** (☎ 938 50; www.fuessen.de; Kaiser-Maximillian-Platz 1; ☻ 9am-5pm Mon-Fri, 10am-2pm Sat) is often overrun.

Sights

Neuschwanstein and **Hohenschwangau castles** provide a fascinating glimpse into the romantic king's state of mind (or lack thereof) and well-developed ego. Hohenschwangau is where Ludwig lived as a child, but more interesting is the adjacent Neuschwanstein, his own creation (albeit with the help of a

GERMANY

theatrical designer). Although it was unfinished when he died in 1886, there is plenty of evidence of Ludwig's twin obsessions: swans and Wagnerian operas. The sugary pastiche of architectural styles, alternatively overwhelmingly beautiful and just a little-too-much, reputedly inspired Disney's Fantasyland castle.

Tickets may only be bought from the **ticket centre** (☎ 930 830; www.ticket-center-hohen schwangau.de; Alpseestrasse 12; each castle adult/ child €9/free, both €17/free; ⏰ 9am-6pm mid-Apr–mid-Oct, 10am-4pm mid-Oct–mid-Apr). In summer it's worth the €1.60 surcharge to reserve ahead. To walk to Hohenschwangau takes 10 minutes while Neuschwanstein is a 30-minute steep hike. Horse-drawn carriages (€5) and shuttle buses (€2) shorten but don't eliminate the hike.

Take the bus from Füssen train station (€1.55, eight minutes, hourly) or share a taxi (☎ 7700; €8.50 for up to four people). Go early to avoid the worst of the rush.

Sleeping & Eating
A pavilion near the tourist office has a computerised list of vacant rooms in town; most of the cheapest rooms, at around €15 per person, are in private homes just a few minutes from the Altstadt. Füssen is a pretty quiet place after dark and most people will stay only long enough to see the castles. There are a couple of cafés in the centre to grab lunch at.

DJH Hostel (☎ 7754; www.djh.de; Mariahilferstrasse 5; dm €16; 💻) It gets a bit loud when the 134 beds are full, but otherwise it's quiet and only a signposted 10-minute walk from the train station.

Hotel Sonne (☎ 9080; www.hotel-sonne.de; Reichenstrasse 37; r from €80; ✗) Just across from the tourist office, the pastel-coloured Sonne is hard to miss. The 32 rooms are comfortable, if not exactly as bright as the name.

Getting There & Away
Trains to Munich (€20, two hours) run every two hours. Füssen is the start of the Romantic Rd. Deutsche-Touring buses start in Munich and are the best way to reach Wieskirche (€6, 50 minutes) if you don't have a car.

RVO bus 9606 (www.rvo-bus.de) connects Füssen, via Oberammergau, with Garmisch-Partenkirchen (€8, two hours, five to six daily).

BAVARIAN ALPS

While not quite as high as their sister summits further south in Austria and Switzerland, the Bavarian Alps (Bayerische Alpen) are really a bunch of drama queens, owing to their abrupt rise from the rolling Bavarian foothills. Stretching westward from Germany's southeastern corner to the Allgäu region near Lake Constance, the Alps take in most of the mountainous country fringing the southern border with Austria.

Getting There & Around
While the public transport network is good, the mountain geography means there are few direct routes between main centres; sometimes a short cut via Austria is quicker (such as between Füssen and Garmisch). Road rather than rail routes are often more practical. For those driving, the German Alpine Rd (Deutsche Alpenstrasse) is a scenic way to go.

BERCHTESGADEN
☎ 08652 / pop 8300

Berchtesgaden is easily the most dramatically scenic corner of the Bavarian Alps, which hang down into Austria like an appendix here. The views over the steep valleys and craggy peaks go on forever. To reach the centre from the train station, cross the footbridge and walk up Bahnhofstrasse. The helpful **tourist office** (☎ 9670; www.berchtesgaden .de; Königsseer Strasse 2; ⏰ 8am-6pm Mon-Fri, to 5pm Sat, 9am-3pm Sun mid-Jun–Sep) is just across the river from the train station.

Sights & Activities
A tour of the **Salzbergwerk** (☎ 600 220; Bergwerkstrasse 83; adult/child €13/8; ⏰ 9am-5pm May–mid-Oct, 12.30-3.30pm mid-Oct–Apr) combines history with a carnival. Visitors descend into the salt mine for a 1½-hour tour.

Nearby **Obersalzberg** is an innocent-looking place with an ugly legacy as the second seat of government for the Third Reich. Hitler, Himmler, Goebbels and the rest of the Nazi bigwigs all maintained homes here. The **Dokumentation Obersalzberg Museum** (☎ 947 960; www.obersalzberg.de; Salzbergstrasse 41; adult/child €2.50/free; ⏰ 9am-5pm April-Oct, 10am-3pm Tue-Sun Nov-Mar) documents their time in the area, as well as the horrors their policies produced, through photos, audio and film. The admission fee also gets you into the creepy **Hitler's bunker**. Catch bus 9538 (€5 return, nine minutes, hourly) from the Nazi-constructed Berchtesgaden train station to 'Dokumentation'.

Kehlstein (☎ 2969; admission €13.50; ☼ May-Oct) is a spectacular meeting house built for, but seldom used by, Hitler. Despite its reputation as the **'Eagle's Nest'**, it's a popular destination because of stunning views. Entry includes transport on special buses, which link the summit with Obersalzberg-Hintereck between 8.55am to 4.50pm, as well as the 120m lift through solid rock to the peak. Or you can make the steep ascent or descent on foot in two to three hours.

The best way to see Obersalzberg and Kehlstein is with **Eagle's Nest Tours** (☎ 649 71; www .eagles-nest-tours.com; €40), which has tours in English lasting four hours and covering the entire history of the area during WWII.

You can forget the horrors of war at the **Königssee**, a beautiful alpine lake situated 5km south of Berchtesgaden (and linked by hourly buses in summer). There are frequent boat tours across the lake to the picture-perfect chapel at St Bartholomä (€12), or all the way to Obersee (€16).

The wilds of Berchtesgaden National Park offer some of the best **hiking** in Germany. A good introduction to the area is a 2km path up from St Bartholomä beside the Königssee to the Watzmann-Ostwand, a massive 2000m-high rock face where scores of overly ambitious mountaineers have died.

Sleeping & Eating

Of the five camping grounds around Berchtesgaden, the nicest are at Königssee.

Grafenlehen (☎ 4140; www.camping-grafenlehen.de; camp sites per person/site €5.50/6) This place has a playground and mountain views.

DJH Hostel (☎ 943 70; www.djh.de; Gebirgsjägerstrasse 52; dm €14; ☼ closed Nov & Dec) Take bus 9539 to Jugendherberge and this swarming 307-bed hostel.

Hotel Floriani (☎ 660 11; www.hotel-floriani.de; Königsseer Strasse 37; s/d from €35/58) The cheerful, homey rooms all have spectacular vistas plus cable TV and access to the kitchen.

InterContinental Resort Berchtesgaden (☎ 975 50; www.ichotelsgroup.com; Hintereck 1; r from €160; ✕ ✕ ▣ ▣) You might say this beautiful new 138-room resort is a silk purse made from a sow's ear. It's built right in Obersalzberg in the Dokumentation Museum and is an ambitious attempt to reclaim the area's stunning beauty from the stain of the Nazis.

Getting There & Away

There is hourly service to Berchtesgaden from Munich (€30, 2¾ hours), which usually requires a change in Frilassing. There's direct service to nearby Salzburg in Austria (€7.60, one hour, hourly).

GARMISCH-PARTENKIRCHEN
☎ 08821 / pop 27,000

The towns of Garmisch and Partenkirchen were merged by Hitler for the 1936 Winter Olympics. Munich residents' favourite getaway spot, this often-snooty, year-round resort is also a big draw for skiers, snowboarders, hikers and mountaineers.

The **tourist office** (☎ 180 700; www.garmisch -partenkirchen.de; Richard Strauss Platz 2; ☼ 8am-6pm Mon-Sat, 10am-noon Sun) is in the centre of town. Check the Internet at **Play Maxx** (☎ 943 4086; Hindenburgstrasse 30; per 30 min €2; ☼ 10am-1am).

Sights & Activities

The huge **ski stadium** outside town hosted the Olympics. From the pedestrian Am Kurpark, walk up Klammstrasse, cross the tracks and veer left on the first path to reach the stadium and enjoy the spectacular views.

An excellent short hike from Garmisch is to the **Partnachklamm gorge**, via a winding path above a stream and underneath the waterfalls. You take the Graseck cable car and follow the signs.

An excursion to the **Zugspitze** summit, Germany's highest peak (2962m), is a popular outing from Garmisch. There are various ways up, including a return trip by the **Bayerische Zugspitzbahn rack-railway** (www .zugspitz.de; day pass from €36), just west of the main train station, summit cable car or Eibsee cable car, or you can scale it in two days. For detailed information concerning guided hiking or mountaineering courses, check with **Bergsteigerschule Zugspitze** (☎ 589 99; www.bergsteigerschule-zugspitze.de; Dreitorspitzstrasse 13, Garmisch).

Garmisch is bounded by three separate ski areas – **Zugspitze plateau** (the highest), **Alpspitze/Hausberg** (the largest) and **Eckbauer** (the cheapest). Day ski passes range from €18 for

Eckbauer to €36 for Zugspitze. The hopefully named Happy Ski Card is a pass for the entire region (from €86 for three days). A web of cross-country ski trails runs along the main valleys.

Flori Wörndle (☎ 583 00; www.skischule-woerndle.de) has ski-hire outlets at the Alpspitze and Hausbergbahn lifts. The tourist office has detailed information on the many local ski schools.

Sleeping & Eating

DJH Hostel (☎ 2980; www.djh.de; Jochstrasse 10; dm €20; closed mid-Nov–Dec) Situated in the suburb of Burgrain, this hostel has 200 beds. From the train station take bus 3 or 4 to the Burgrain stop.

Hotel Schell (☎ 957 50; www.hotel-schell.de; Partnachauenstrasse 3; s/d from €30/50; ✗) In a quaint and fairly modest house a short walk from the train station, the Schell has 25 compact well-maintained rooms.

Hotel Zugspitze (☎ 9010; www.hotel-zugspitze.de; Klammstrasse 19; r €76-105; ✗ ☺) The 48 cosy timber-lined rooms and an elegant indoor pool make you feel at home – a very nice home.

Bistro Mukkefuck (☎ 734 40; Zugspitzstrasse 3; meals €6-12) If you can get past the curious name, an outdoor beer garden and a tasty menu of salads, sandwiches and pastas awaits.

Getting There & Away

From Garmish there is train service to Munich (€16, 80 minutes, hourly) and to Innsbruck via Mittenwald (€13, 80 minutes, every two hours). RVO bus 9606, from in front of the train station, links Garmisch

---

HOT & COLD FUN IN THE ALPS

The Bavarian Alps are extraordinarily well organised for outdoor pursuits, with skiing, snowboarding and hiking being the most popular. The ski season usually runs from mid-December to April. Ski gear is available for hire in all the resorts, with the lowest daily/weekly rates including skis, boots and stocks at around €15/50. Five-day skiing courses start from €100.

During the warmer months, the activities include hiking, canoeing, rafting, biking and paragliding.

---

with Füssen (€8, two hours, five to six daily) via Oberammergau.

OBERSTDORF

☎ 08322 / pop 10,400

Over in the western Bavarian Alps, Oberstdorf sits in a pretty flat meadow below the peaks. Besides skiing, it offers superb hiking. At busy times, car use in the centre is restricted – a good thing.

The main **tourist office** (☎ 7000; www.oberstdorf .de; Bahnhofplatz 3; 8.30am-6pm Mon-Fri, 9.30am-noon Sat) is near the train station.

Savvy skiers value Oberstdorf for its friendliness, its reasonable prices and the generally uncrowded slopes. The village is surrounded by several ski areas: the **Nebelhorn** (www.dashoechste.de), **Fellhorn/Kanzelwand** (www .dashoechste.de) and **Söllereck** (www.soellereckbahn .de). Combined daily/weekly ski passes that include all three areas (plus the adjoining Kleinwalsertal lifts on the Austrian side) cost €34/174. Check with the tourist office for information on schools and equipment rental.

For an exhilarating day **hike**, ride the Nebelhorn cable car to the upper station then walk down via the Gaisalpseen, two lovely alpine lakes.

There's a **camping ground** (☎ 6525; www.camping -oberstdorf.de; Rubingerstrasse 16; camp sites per tent €3-5, per person €5-5.50) 2km north of the station beside the train line.

The **DJH Hostel** (☎ 2225; www.djh.de; Kornau 8; dm €15) is on the outskirts of town near the Söllereck chairlift – take the Kleinwalsertal bus to the Reute stop.

Hotel Kappeler Haus (☎ 96860; www.kappeler-haus .de; Am Seeler 2; s/d from €38/74) has 47 spacious rooms with nice views right near the centre. There's on-site parking and many of the rooms have wrap-around balconies. The breakfast is tops.

Südtiroler Sonnenkeller (☎ 3140; Weststrasse 5; meals €6-12) is a great basement restaurant with a large number of beers on tap and well-prepared regional foods. Try the Südtiroler Schlutzkrapfen for an amazing local take on ravioli.

There are hourly RB trains to/from Immenstadt where you connect to Lindau (€15, 1¾ hours). Munich has direct trains (€25, 2½ hours, hourly). On weekdays, bus connections to Füssen go via Pfronten (€9.30, 2½ hours, two daily).

GERMANY

BADEN-WÜRTTEMBERG

With the exception of cuckoo clocks in the Black Forest, Baden-Württemberg runs distant second in the cliché race to Bavaria. But that's really all the better, as it is a rich and varied place with just about everything that might inspire a visit to Germany – plus a few surprises.

OK, so on the top of the hour the Black Forest goes, well, cuckoo. But it is also a pretty land of hills, trees and cute villages that rewards exploration. If you want a big and quaint German village with lots of history, then there's Heidelberg. Baden-Baden is the sybaritic playground for spa-goers and Freiburg has youthful vibrance in an intriguing package. Finally, Lake Constance is a misty redoubt bordering Switzerland that has all the pleasures a large body of water can offer.

The prosperous modern state of Baden-Württemberg was created in 1951 out of three smaller regions: Baden, Württemberg and Hohenzollern (thank goodness the names stopped at two).

STUTTGART

☎ 0711 / pop 590,000

Hemmed in by grape-covered hills, residents of prosperous Stuttgart enjoy a high quality of life. Just watch them zip about in their Mercedes. Nevertheless it is Baden-Württemberg's state capital and the hub of its industries. At the forefront of Germany's economic recovery from the ravages of WWII, Stuttgart started life less auspiciously in 950 as a horse stud farm. About 80% of the city centre was destroyed in the war, but there are a few historical buildings left and – no surprise – car museums. Mostly however, it is a good hub for exploring other parts of the state.

Information

Call & Internet C@fé (☎ 259 9103; Esslingerstrasse; per hr €2; ☯ 9.30am-11pm)

Post office (Bolzstrasse 3)

Tourist office (☎ 222 80; www.stuttgart-tourist.de; Königstrasse 1a; ☯ 9am-8pm Mon-Fri, to 6pm Sat, 11am-6pm Sun) Opposite the main train station on the main pedestrian strip, the office sells the three-day StuttCard (€17.50), which allows free public transport and free entry to some museums.

Waschsalon (☎ 241 275; Hohenheimer Strasse 33; per load €7.50; ☯ 8am-6.30pm Mon-Fri, to 1pm Sat) Self-serve and drop-off.

Sights

The tower at the grotty main train station sports the three-pointed star of the Mercedes-Benz. It's also an excellent vantage point for the sprawling city and surrounding hills, and is reached via a **lift** (admission free; ☯ 10am-10pm Tue-Sun).

Stretching southwest from the Neckar River to the city centre is the **Schlossgarten**, an extensive strip of parkland divided into three sections (Unterer, Mittlerer and Oberer), complete with ponds, swans, street entertainers and modern sculptures. At their northern edge the gardens take in the **Wilhelma Zoo & Botanical Gardens** (☎ 540 20; Neckarstrasse; adult/child €11/5.50; ☯ 8.15am-6pm May-Aug, reduced hr winter). At the gardens' southern end they encompass the sprawling baroque **Neues Schloss** (Schlossplatz) and the Renaissance **Altes Schloss**, which houses a **regional museum** (☎ 279 3400; Schillerplatz 6; adult/child €3/free; ☯ 10am-5pm Tue-Sun) where exhibits include Romanera discoveries.

Next to the Altes Schloss is the city's oldest square, Schillerplatz, with its monument to the poet **Schiller**, and the 12th-century **Stiftskirche** (Stiftstrasse 12; ☯ 9am-5.30pm Mon-Wed, Fri & Sun, noon-5.30pm Thu). Adjoining the park you'll find the **Staatsgalerie** (☎ 212 4050; Konrad-Adenauer-Strasse 30; adult/child €4.50/2.50; ☯ 10am-6pm Tue-Sun, to 9pm Thu), which houses an excellent collection from the Middle Ages to the present. It's especially rich in old German masters from the surrounding Swabia region.

Next door there's the **Haus der Geschichte** (House of History; ☎ 212 3950; Urbansplatz 2; admission €3). This is an eye-catching postmodern museum that covers the past 200 years of the Baden-Württemburg area in film, photography, documents and multimedia.

MOTOR MUSEUMS

An arms race has broken out among the local auto companies, with both building new and costly monuments to themselves.

The motor car was first developed by Gottlieb Daimler and Carl Benz at the end of the 19th century. The impressive new-for-2006 **Mercedes-Benz Museum** (☎ 172 2578; Mercedesstrasse 137; admission €8; ☯ 9am-5pm Tue-Sun)

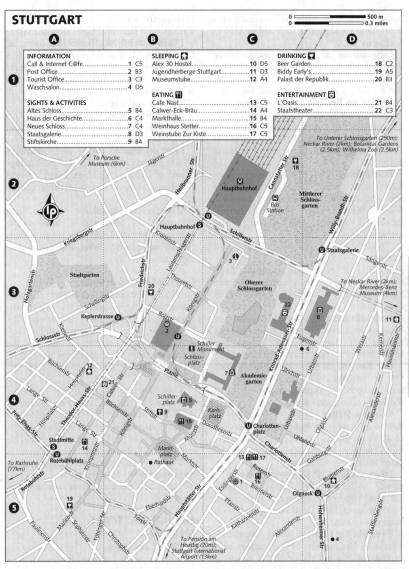

STUTTGART

0 — 500 m
0 — 0.3 miles

INFORMATION
Call & Internet C@fe....................1 C5
Post Office...................................2 B3
Tourist Office..............................3 C3
Waschsalon.................................4 D5

SIGHTS & ACTIVITIES
Altes Schloss................................5 B4
Haus der Geschichte.....................6 C4
Neues Schloss...............................7 C4
Staatsgalerie................................8 D3
Stiftskirche...................................9 B4

SLEEPING 🏠
Alex 30 Hostel............................10 D5
Jugendherberge Stuttgart...........11 D3
Museumstube.............................12 A4

EATING 🍴
Cafe Nast...................................13 C5
Calwer-Eck-Bräu.........................14 A4
Markthalle..................................15 B4
Weinhaus Stetter........................16 C5
Weinstube Zur Kiste....................17 C5

DRINKING 🍷
Beer Garden...............................18 C2
Biddy Early's..............................19 A5
Palast der Republik.....................20 B3

ENTERTAINMENT 🎭
L'Oasis.......................................21 B4
Staatstheater..............................22 C3

GERMANY

is in the suburb of Bad-Cannstatt; take S-Bahn 1 to Neckarstadion. For even faster cars, cruise over to the striking new-for-2007 **Porsche Museum** (☎ 911 5685; Porscheplatz 1; ☉ 9am-4pm Mon-Fri, to 5pm Sat & Sun); take S-Bahn 6 to Neuwirtshaus, north of the city. Admission prices for the new place were not set but expect them to rival Mercedes.

Sleeping

Alex 30 Hostel (☎ 838 8950; www.alex30-hostel.de; Alexanderstrasse 30; dm/s/d from €19/20/25; 🖥) Tidy and orderly in an interesting neighbourhood. Take U-Bahn lines 5, 6 or 7 to Olgaeck.

Jugendherberge Stuttgart (☎ 241 583; www .jugendherberge-stuttgart.de; Haussmannstrasse 27; dm €17-23) It's a steep climb to this modern hostel, which is a signposted 15-minute walk from the train station or take U9 or U14 to Staatsgalerie.

Museumstube (☎ 296 810; www.museumstube.de; Hospitalstrasse 9; s/d from €35/55) The 10 rooms are pretty much no-frills at the Museumstube but it's only a short walk to local nightlife.

Pension am Heusteig (☎ 239 300; www.central -classic.de; Heusteigstrasse 30; s/d from €59/75; ☐) Only a few minutes southeast of the city centre, the 14 rooms here are comfortable. This is a small, modest and intimate place.

InterCity Hotel (☎ 222 8233; www.intercityhotel.com; Hauptbahnhof; s/d from €70/100; ✗ ☐) Right in the train station, the 101 rooms here have wi-fi and are rather large. This is the perfect location if you plan a quick getaway or late arrival.

Eating

Stuttgart is a great place to sample Swabian specialities such as *Spätzle* (homemade noodles) and *Maultaschen* (a hearty ravioli in broth).

Markthalle (Dorotheenstrasse 4; ✆ 7am-6.30pm Mon-Fri, to 4pm Sat) An excellent Art Nouveau-style market that's jam-packed with fresh fare (often from the region) and great cafés.

Cafe Nast (☎ 238 970; Esslinger Strasse 40; snacks €2-5; ✆ 7am-6.30pm, to 3pm Sat) A vast array of tarts and other tempting treats await at this old bakery. Nice café area.

Weinhaus Stetter (☎ 240 163; Rosenstrasse 32; mains €5-8; ✆ dinner Mon-Fri, lunch Sat) The results of all those grapes you see growing in the hills line the wine list here. Locals jam the place for the *Maultaschen*.

Calwer-Eck-Bräu (☎ 222 494 40; Calwerstrasse 31; mains €7-14) The menu at this upstairs restaurant and brewery combines Bavarian and Swabian specialties. Have some *spätzle* with your *weissewurst*.

Weinstube Zur Kiste (☎ 244 002; Kanalstrasse 2; mains €8-17) Generations of Stuttgarters have patronised this old classic in the Bohnenviertel (Bean Quarter). Enjoy local chow and wines in the creaky old building or at tables outside.

Drinking & Entertainment

Though in German, *Lift Stuttgart* (€1), a comprehensive guide to local entertainment and events is useful. There's a **beer garden** (☎ 226 1274; Canstatterstr 18) in the Mittlerer

Schlossgarten northeast of the main train station, with beautiful views over the city.

L'Oasis (☎ 300 0481; Theodor-Heuss-Strasse 21) One of several trendy bars and clubs on this stretch of street. Many, like this one, have seating on the pavement. There's all sorts of seating inside and pillows are strewn about. DJs play late at night.

Biddy Early's (☎ 615 9853; Marienstrasse 28) This Irish pub is actually run by real Irish people. It has live music four nights a week.

Palast der Republik (☎ 226 4887; Friedrichstrasse 27) A legendary and tiny bar that pulls a huge crowd of laid-back drinkers. Many a world problem has been sorted at the stand-up tables.

Staatstheater (☎ 202 090; www.staatstheater .stuttgart.de; Oberer Schlossgarten 6) Home of the famous Stuttgart Ballet, this theatre holds regular symphony, ballet and opera performances.

Getting There & Around

Stuttgart's international **airport** (SGT; www .stuttgart-airport.com) is south of the city and includes service from discount carriers DBA (Germany, Nice) and Germanwings (Germany, London, Eastern Europe and the Mediterranean). It's served by S2 and S3 trains (€2.90, 30 minutes from the Hauptbahnhof).

There are frequent train departures for all major German, and many international, cities. ICE trains run to Frankfurt (€49, 1½ hours, hourly) and Munich (€39 to €46, 2¼ hours, two hourly). Trains run hourly to Nuremberg (€28, 2¼ hours).

One-way fares on Stuttgart's public transport network (www.vvs.de) are €1.80 in the central zone; a central zone day pass is €5.10.

AROUND STUTTGART
Tübingen
☎ 07071 / pop 83,000

Gliding swans set the mood for this picturesque town. It's a perfect place to spend a day wandering along winding alleys of half-timbered houses and old stone walls, and taking a boat ride down the Neckar River. Given that the local university has 22,000 students, there's an appealing edge to it all.

The **tourist office** (☎ 913 60; www.tuebingen -info.de; An der Neckarbrücke; ✆ 9am-7pm Mon-Fri, to 5pm Sat) is beside the bridge.

On **Marktplatz**, the centre of town, is the 1435 **Rathaus** with its baroque façade and astronomical clock. The nearby late-Gothic **Stiftkirche** (Am Holz-markt; ⏱ 9am-5pm Feb-Oct, to 4pm Nov-Jan) houses the tombs of the Württemberg dukes and has excellent medieval stained-glass windows. From the heights of the Renaissance **Schloss Hohentübingen** (Burgsteig 11), now part of the university, there are fine views over the steep, red-tiled rooftops of the old town. Inside, the **museum** (☎ 297 7384; ⏱ 10am-5pm Wed-Sun) covers local history.

The **Jugendherberge Tübingen** (☎ 230 02; www .djh.de; Gartenstrasse 22/2; dm €20-24; ⏱) has a delightful location by the river.

Hotel Am Schloss (☎ 929 40; www.hotelamschloss .de; Burgsteige 18; s/d from €51/86) is an attractive hotel with 37 simple and pleasant rooms. Its restaurant serves over two dozen varieties of *Maultaschen*, the local stuffed pasta (€6 to €10).

Boulanger (☎ 233 45; Collegiumsgasse 2; meals €6-10) is a classic old student bar and café. There are several more of this type nearby on Kornhausstrasse.

Neckarmuller (☎ 278 48; Gartenstrasse 4) is a brewery with a terrace on the river. It has good weisse beer.

There are hourly RE trains between Tübingen and Stuttgart (€10, one hour).

HEIDELBERG
☎ 06221 / pop 143,000

The French destroyed Heidelberg in 1693; they may have been the last visitors to dislike this charming town on the Neckar River. Its castle ruins and medieval town are irresistible drawcards for most travellers in Germany. Mark Twain recounted his succinct observations in *A Tramp Abroad*. Britain's JMW Turner loved the place and it inspired him to produce some of his finest landscape paintings. Throw in nice weather and lively pubs, and you understand why many of Heidelberg's students (attending the oldest university in the country) rarely graduate on time. But be warned: this place seethes with tourists during July and August.

Orientation

Heidelberg's captivating old town starts to reveal itself after a 15-minute walk that will interest few west of the main train station, along the Kurfürsten-Anlage. Hauptstrasse is the pedestrian way leading eastwards

through the heart of the Altstadt from Bismarckplatz via Marktplatz to Karlstor.

Information

Buchhandlung Schmitt & Hahn (☎ 845 196; Hauptstrasse 8) Classy bookshop with lots of English titles.

Post office (Sophienstrasse 8-10) Near the Altstadt.

Tourist office (☎ 194 33; www.cvb-heidelberg.de; Willy-Brandt-Platz 1; ⏱ 9am-7pm Mon-Sat year-round, 10am-6pm Sun Apr-Nov) Outside the train station. The €14 Heidelberg Card offers free public transport and free admission to many sights.

Waschtrommel (☎ 485 775; Rohrbacher Strasse 10; ⏱ 8.30am-9.30pm Mon-Fri, to 8.30pm Sat) A self-service laundry (per load €4) *and* an Internet café (per 30 min €1).

Sights

Heidelberg's imposing **Schloss** (☎ 538 421; adult/child €3/1.50, tours €4; ⏱ 10am-5.30pm) is one of Germany's finest examples of grand Gothic-Renaissance architecture. The building's half-ruined state actually adds to its romantic appeal (Twain called it 'the Lear of inanimate nature'). Seen from anywhere in the Altstadt, this striking red-sandstone castle dominates the hillside. The entry fee covers the castle, the **Grosses Fass** (Great Vat), an enormous 18th-century keg capable of holding 221,726L, and the **Deutsches Apotheken-museum** (German Pharmaceutical Museum; ☎ 258 80; Schlosshof 1; adult/child €3/1.50; ⏱ 10am-5.30pm).

You can take the **funicular railway** (adult/child return €5/4; ⏱ 9am-5pm) to the castle from lower Kornmarkt station, or enjoy an invigorating 10-minute walk up steep, stone-laid lanes. The funicular continues up to the **Königstuhl**, where there are good views.

Dominating Universitätsplatz are the 18th-century **Alte Universität** and the **Neue Universität**. Nearby there's the **Studentenkarzer** (student jail; ☎ 543 554; Augustinergasse 2; adult/child €2.50/2; ⏱ 10am-noon & 2-5pm Tue-Sat Apr-Oct, 10am-2pm Tue-Fri Nov-Mar). From 1778 to 1914 this jail was used for misbehaved students. Sentences (usually two to 10 days) were earned for 'heinous' crimes such as drinking, singing and womanising. The **Marstall** is the former arsenal, now a student *mensa*.

The **Kurpfälzisches Museum** (Palatinate Museum; ☎ 583 402; Hauptstrasse 97; adult/child €3/2; ⏱ 10am-5pm Tue-Sun, to 9pm Wed) contains paintings, sculptures and the jawbone of the 600,000-year-old Heidelberg Man.

The Heidelberg region has been a major global supplier of printing equipment, much

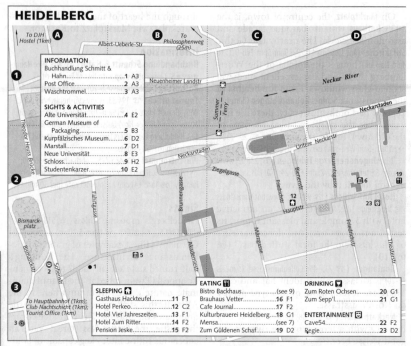

HEIDELBERG

INFORMATION
Buchhandlung Schmitt & Hahn...................1 A3
Post Office..................2 A3
Waschtrommel...................3 A3

SIGHTS & ACTIVITIES
Alte Universität...................4 E2
German Museum of Packaging...................5 B3
Kurpfälzisches Museum........6 D2
Marstall...................7 D1
Neue Universität...................8 E3
Schloss...................9 H2
Studentenkarzer...................10 E2

SLEEPING 🛏
Gasthaus Hackteufel...........11 F1
Hotel Perkeo...................12 C2
Hotel Vier Jahreszeiten.......13 F1
Hotel Zum Ritter...................14 F2
Pension Jeske...................15 F2

EATING 🍴
Bistro Backhaus...................(see 9)
Brauhaus Vetter...................16 F1
Cafe Journal...................17 F2
Kulturbrauerei Heidelberg....18 G1
Mensa...................(see 7)
Zum Güldenen Schaf...........19 D2

DRINKING 🍷
Zum Roten Ochsen............20 G1
Zum Sepp'l...................21 G1

ENTERTAINMENT 🎭
Cave54...................22 F2
Regie...................23 D2

---

of it used to create packaging for products. The **German Museum of Packaging** (Deutsches Verpackungs-Museum; ☎ 213 61; Hauptstrasse 22; adult/child €4/2; 🕐 1-6pm Wed-Fri, 11am-6pm Sat & Sun) celebrates classic packages such as the Nivea jar and the Coke bottle, all from an era when a package was *not* a plastic clamshell requiring access via a chain saw.

A stroll along the **Philosophenweg**, north of the Neckar River, gives a welcome respite from Heidelberg's tourist hordes.

Sleeping

Finding any accommodation during Heidelberg's high season can be difficult. Arrive early in the day or book ahead.

Camping Haide (☎ 802 506; www.camping-heidelberg .de; Schlierbacher Landstrasse 151; camp sites per person €5.50, tent €2.50-6) These grounds are in a pretty spot on the river. Take bus 35 to Orthopädische Klinik.

DJH Hostel (☎ 651 190; www.djh.de; Tiergartenstrasse 5; dm €15-20; 🖳) This hostel is across the river from the train station, and has 487 beds. From the station or Bismarckplatz, take bus 33 towards Ziegelhausen.

Pension Jeske (☎ 237 33; www.pension-jeske -heidelberg.de; Mittelbadgasse 2; r per person from €25) The four rooms at this backpacker favourite are squirreled away in a 250-year-old house. The Altstadt's pleasures are just outside.

Hotel Vier Jahreszeiten (☎ 241 64; www.4 -jahreszeiten.de; Haspelgasse 2; s/d from €60/100) Goethe himself reputedly once slumbered here, so you know it's old. Things have been spiffed up since, although the palette tends towards beige in the 22 rooms.

Gasthaus Hackteufel (☎ 905 380; www.hackteufel .de; Steingasse 7; s/d from €80/120; 🖳) Each of the 12 rooms is distinctive and full of character at the Hackteufel, in the middle of the romantic old town.

Hotel Perkeo (☎ 141 30; Hauptstrasse 75; s/d from €90/120; 🗙 🖳) The 24 rooms here are bright and have wi-fi. Many have views of the surrounding hills. Look for the little statue of a thirsty gatekeeper on the façade. The café is a good place to take in some of the street action.

Hotel Zum Ritter (☎ 1350; www.ritter-heidelberg .de; Hauptstrasse 178; s/d from €90/150; 🖳) Ornate Hotel Zum Ritter is close to the cathedral

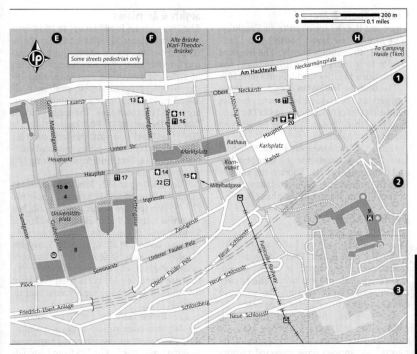

and provides grand accommodation in 39 ornate rooms. It survived the French destruction of 1693.

Eating

The Zum Güldenen Schaf is one of many Altstadt restaurants that cater exclusively to tourists. The only locals are washing dishes.

Cafe Journal (☎ 161 712; Hauptstrasse 162; meals €4-8) A classic café with a good view of the passing mobs. It's a place to linger over your own journal while enjoying coffee and a meal.

Bistro Backhaus (☎ 979 70; Im Schlosshof; meals €5-9) Worth the jaunt to the Schloss, this surprisingly hype-free place has good local favourites and at reasonable prices. There are several grilled sausages, yum.

Brauhaus Vetter (☎ 165 850; Steingasse 9; mains €5-12) A popular brewery that serves up lots of hearty fare to absorb the suds. The copper kettles gleam. Groups of six or more can order the Brewer's feast, a sausage, pretzels, radishes, meat and cheese smorgasbord.

Kulturbrauerei Heidelberg (☎ 502 980; Leyergasse 6; mains €8-15) The classic-looking Kulturbrau-erei has an excellent beer garden. It's a big, bright and airy place and is always busy.

Also useful is the **Mensa** (Universitätsplatz; meals €3), which caters to students.

Drinking & Entertainment

This being a uni town, you won't have to go far to find a happening backstreet bar. Lots of the action centres on Unterestrasse. Two ancient pubs, **Zum Roten Oschen** (☎ 209 77; Hauptstrasse 213) and **Zum Sepp'l** (☎ 230 85; Hauptstrasse 217), are now filled with tourists reliving the uni days they never had.

Regie (☎ 652 226; Theaterstrasse 2; meals €6-10) What better way to deal with the tourist invasion than with a takeaway cocktail from this stylish and large café. There are tables outside and a good menu.

Club Nachtschicht (☎ 438 550; Bergheimer Strasse 147) A classic club near the train station. There's a mix of DJs, house, pop, soul and more. Big with locals.

Cave54 (☎ 278 40; www.cave54.de; Krämerpetrolse 2; ⏲ Thu-Sun) For live jazz and blues, head to this stone cellar that oozes character. There are regular jam sessions.

Getting There & Around

There are ICE/IC trains to/from Frankfurt (€14 to €17, one hour, hourly) and Stuttgart (€21, 40 minutes, hourly) The frequent service to Mannheim (€5, 15 minutes) has connections to cities throughout Germany.

The **Deutsche-Touring bus** (www.deutsche-touring .com) serving the Castle Road route provides daily direct links to Rothenberg Ob Der Tauber (€46, three hours, May to September) from the train station.

Bismarckplatz is the main public transport hub. One-way tickets for the excellent bus and tram system are €2. Shorten the journey from the train station to the Altstadt with bus 11 or 33 to the Kornmarkt/Rathaus stop.

BADEN-BADEN

☎ 07221 / pop 54,000

Who wouldn't want to bathe naked with a bunch of strangers? That's the question at the heart of the matter in Baden-Baden, the storied and ritzy spa town. The answer of course should be anyone who wants to enjoy a truly self-indulgent experience.

And let's see, shall we call them, well, prudes, can still get a bit of the pleasure while staying suited and segregated. The natural hot springs have attracted visitors since Roman times, but this small city only really became fashionable in the 19th century. It is a stately, closely cropped and salubrious place. As noted sybarite Bill Clinton said: 'Baden-Baden is so nice you had to name it twice'.

Orientation & Information

The train station is 7km northwest of town. Leopoldplatz and Sophienstrasse are the hubs. North of here are the baths, the Stiftskirche and the Neues Schloss. Across the little river to the west you will find the Trinkhalle (pump room) and the tourist office, and past Goetheplatz both the Kurhaus and Spielhall (casino). Unless noted, everything listed below is within the centre.

The **tourist office** (☎ 275 200; www.baden-baden .com; Kaiserallee 3; ☺ 10am-5pm Mon-Sat, 2-5pm Sun) is in the Trinkhalle. There is a spa *Kurtaxe* (visitors' tax) of €3.10, entitling you to a *Kurkarte* from your hotel that brings various discounts. Drink from the source of it all here for €0.20 (it's warm and salty).

Surf the Web at **Internet & C@llshop** (☎ 398 400; Lange Strasse 54; per hr €2; ☺ 10am-10pm).

Sights & Activities

The 19th-century **Friedrichsbad** (☎ 275 920; www .roemisch-irisches-bad.de; Römerplatz 1; bathing programme €21-29; ☺ 9am-10pm Mon-Sat, noon-8pm Sun) is the reason for your journey. It's decadently Roman in style and provides a muscle-melting 16-step bathing programme. No clothing is allowed inside, and several bathing sections are mixed on most days. The more modern **Caracalla-Therme** (☎ 275 940; Römerplatz 11; per 2 hr €12; ☺ 8am-10pm) is a vast, modern complex of outdoor and indoor pools, hot- and cold-water grottoes. You must wear a bathing suit and bring your own towel.

The 2000-year-old **Römische Badruinen** (Roman Bath Ruins; ☎ 275 934; Römerplatz 1; adult/child €2/1; ☺ 11am-5pm) are worth a quick look, but for a real taste of Baden-Baden head to the **Kurhaus**, built in the 1820s, which houses the opulent **casino** (☎ 302 40; Kaiserallee 1; admission €3, guided tours adult/child €4/2; ☺ tours 9.30am-noon; gambling after 2pm), which inspired Dostoyevsky to write *The Gambler*. Wear what you want for tours, for gambling wear a coat and tie (rentals €11).

The **Merkur Cable Car** (☎ 2771; admission €4; ☺ 10am-10pm) takes you up to the 670m summit, where there are fine views and numerous walking trails (bus 204 or 205 from Leopoldplatz takes you to the cable-car station).

Sleeping & Eating

DJH Hostel (☎ 522 23; www.djh.de; Hardbergstrasse 34; dm €18-22) This modern three-storey hostel is on a hillside 3km northwest of the centre – it's a steep hike up a long flight of stairs to the entrance. Take bus 201 to Grosse Dollenstrasse then walk for 10 minutes.

Hotel Bischoff (☎ 223 78, www.hotelsbaden-baden .de; Römerplatz 2; s/d €50/70; ☐) Centrally located close to the spas, the Bischoff has 50 comfortable rooms spread over four floors, some with balconies.

Steigenberger Europäischer Hof (☎ 9330; www .steigenberger.de; Kaiserallee 2; s/d from €120/180; ☒ ☒ ☐) A true grand hotel, this regal beauty has its own little park across from the Kurhaus. Luxuries abound and the breakfast is worth an hour or two. Look for excellent off-season specials.

Hirsch's (☎ 281 110; Kaiserallee 4; mains €7-12) This candle-lit corner specialises in great Swabian dishes. It's a low-key bargain by local standards and there's a good range of beers on tap (you'll sweat them out tomorrow).

Leo's (☎ 380 81; Luisenstrasse 8; lunch special €9) A great spot for a leisurely meal. It's justifiably popular, has a varied menu and a large terrace.

Garibaldi (☎ 302 840; Luisenstrasse 4; mains €12-20) A stylish Italian bistro with pavement tables. A good wine list, pasta and fresh seafood are the features.

Getting There & Around

Baden Airpark (FKB; www.badenairpark.de) is the local airport. It has daily Ryanair service (Barcelona, Dublin, London and Rome) but like many tiny airports served by the budget carrier, getting to/from the airport can be a challenge. Consult the airport website for details on the sketchy service.

Baden-Baden is on the busy Mannheim-Basel train line. Local trains serve Karlsruhe (€7, 15 minutes) frequently and Offenburg (€8, 30 minutes, hourly), from where you can make connections to much of Germany.

Bus 201, 205 and 216 run frequently to/from Leopoldsplatz (€2).

BLACK FOREST

The Black Forest (Schwarzwald) gets its name from the dark canopy of evergreens, though it's also dotted with open slopes and farmland. Although some parts heave with visitors, a 20-minute walk from even the most crowded spots will put you in quiet countryside interspersed with enormous traditional farmhouses and patrolled by amiable dairy cows. It's not nature wild and remote, but bucolic and picturesque.

The Black Forest is east of the Rhine between Karlsruhe and Basel. It's shaped like a bean, about 160km long and 50km wide. From north to south there are four good bases for your visit: Freudenstadt, Schiltach, Triberg and Titisee. Each has good train links.

Those with a car will find their visit especially rewarding, as you can wander the rolling hills and deep valleys at will. One of the main tourist roads is the Schwarzwald-Hochstrasse (B500), which runs from Baden-Baden to Freudenstadt and from Triberg to Waldshut. Other thematic roads include Schwarzwald-Bäderstrasse (spa town route) and Schwarzwald-Panoramastrasse (panoramic

view route) and Badische Weinstrasse (wine route). Whatever you do, make certain you have an excellent commercial regional road map with you.

And, yes, there are many, many places to buy cuckoo clocks (you pay at least €150 for a good one).

Regional specialities include *Schwarzwälderschinken* (ham), which is smoked and served in a variety of ways. Rivalling those ubiquitous clocks in fame (but not price), *Schwarzwälderkirschtorte* (Black Forest cake) is a chocolate and cherry concoction. Most hotels and guesthouses have restaurants serving traditional hearty (but expensive) German fare.

FREUDENSTADT

Freudenstadt is a good base for exploring the northern Black Forest and hikes into the surrounding countryside. It's most notable feature is a vast **marketplace** that is the largest in the country. The **tourist office** (☎ 07441-8640; www.freudenstadt.de; Am Markt-platz; ☼ 10am-6pm Mon-Fri, to 2pm Sat & Sun Mar-Nov, 10am-5pm Mon-Fri, to 1pm Sat & Sun Dec-Feb) has Internet access and is especially helpful with ideas for local walks.

The **DJH Hostel** (☎ 07441-7720; www.djh.de; Eugen-Nägele-Strasse 69; dm from €18) has 138 beds in a central and classic 1960s building. **Pension Traube** (☎ 07441-917 450; fax 853 28; Markt 41; s/d €35/70) has 26 rooms right in the midst of everything. The Markt has many excellent cafés, some with wi-fi.

From Freudenstadt, train lines run south to Schiltach (€5, 30 minutes) and north to the important transfer point of Karlsruhe (€14, two hours).

SCHILTACH

The prettiest town in the Black Forest is easily Schiltach, where there is the always underlying roar of the Kinzig and Schiltach Rivers, which meet here. Half-timbered buildings lean at varying angles along the crisscrossing hillside lanes.

The **tourist office** (☎ 07836-5850; www.schiltach.de; Hauptstrasse 5; ☼ 10am-5pm Mon-Fri, to 2pm Sat) can help with accommodation and has a lot of English-language information. Be sure not to miss the **Schüttesäge-museum** (Hauptstrasse 1; ☼ 11am-5pm Tue-Sun Apr-Oct), which is part of an old mill built on the river. It shows what water power could do. The **Markt** (square) has several tiny museums that cover local

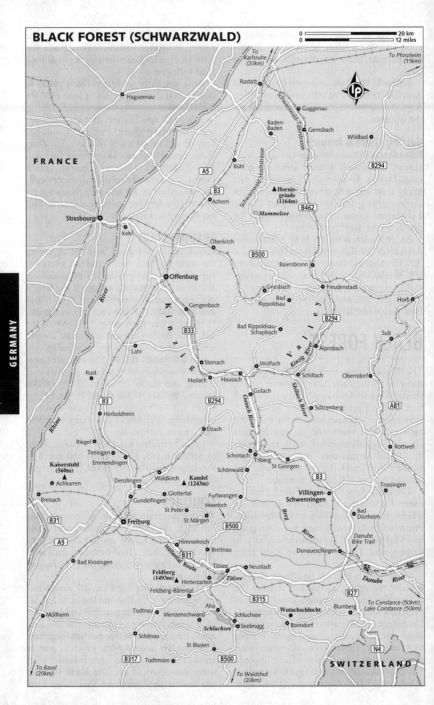

history and culture. Most are open in the afternoons during the tourist season.

There are numerous hotels and restaurants in the compact centre. **Zum Weyssen Rössle** (☎ 07836-387; www.weysses-roessle.de; Schenkenzeller Strasse 42; s/d from €47/69; 💻) dates from 1590 and has nine lovely rooms with four-poster beds and wi-fi. The excellent restaurant serves creative versions of local fare. **Zur alten Brücke** (☎ 07836-20 36; www.altebruecke.de; Schramberger Strasse 13; s/d from €35/62) is another cosy choice and has a restaurant serving various maultaschen.

Schiltach is on a small train line linking Offenburg (€8, 45 minutes) via Hausach to Freudenstadt (€5, 30 minutes) with hourly service.

Around Schiltach

Alpirsbach, 10km north of Schiltach, is a small town that is worth a trip for its 12th-century **Benedictine abbey** (adult/child €3/1.50; 🕑 10am-4.30pm Mon-Sat, 11am-4.30pm Sun). It's often uncrowded and if you find yourself alone in the large Romanesque complex it can be quite eerie. The cloisters are impressive, as is the small museum that documents the lives of those who lived here.

Alpirsbach is a stop for the hourly trains linking Schiltach and Freudenstadt.

TRIBERG

Framed by three mountains – hence the name – Triberg has two duelling cuckoo clocks that claim to be the world's largest – it's a close call on these house-sized oddities.

It has an appealing old centre and plenty of chances to go for a stroll. There's a one-hour walk to a roaring **waterfall** that starts near the **tourist office** (☎ 07722-866490; www.triberg .de; Wallfahrtstrasse 4; 🕑 10am-5pm). In the same building is the **Schwarzwaldmuseum** (☎ 07722-4434; adult/child €4/3; 🕑 10am-5pm, Sat & Sun only Nov-Apr) with displays of local crafts.

The **DJH Hostel** (☎ 07722-4110; www.djh.de; Rohrbacher Strasse 35; dm from €18) has 128 beds and spectacular views from its peak location. Take any bus from the train station to Markt and then walk 1.2km uphill.

Hotel Pfaff (☎ 07722-44 79; www.hotel-pfaff.com; Hauptstrasse 85; s/d €38/72) offers comfortable lodgings near the waterfall; some rooms have balconies with views. There is also a fine restaurant.

Triberg is midway on the Karlsruhe (€20, 1½ hours) to Konstanz (€20, 1½ hours) train

STRETCHING YOUR LEGS IN THE BLACK FOREST

With more than 7000km of marked trails, hiking possibilities during summer are, almost literally, endless. Three classic long-distance **hiking trails** run south from the northern Black Forest city of Pforzheim as far as the Swiss Rhine: the 280km Westweg to Basel; the 230km Mittelweg to Waldhut-Tiengen; and the 240km Ostweg to Schaffhausen.

The southern Black Forest, especially the area around the 1493m Feldberg summit, offers some of the best hiking; small towns such as Todtmoos or Bonndorf serve as useful bases for those wanting to get off the more heavily trodden trails. The 10km Wutach-schlucht (Wutach Gorge) outside Bonndorf is justifiably famous.

line. There's hourly service and good connections. Change at Hausach for Schiltach and Freudenstadt. The station is 1.7km from the centre, take any bus to Markt.

Around Triberg

In Furtwangen, 17km south of Triberg, visit the **Deutsches Uhrenmuseum** (German Clock Museum; ☎ 07723-920 117; Gerwigstrasse 11; adult/child €4/2.50; 🕑 9am-6pm Apr-Oct, 10am-5pm Nov-Mar) for a look at the traditional Black Forest skill of clock-making. A fun demo shows what puts the 'cuc' and the 'koo' in the namesake clock.

TITISEE

The iconic glacial **lake** here draws no shortage of visitors to the busy village of Titisee. Walking around Titisee or paddle-boating across it are major activities. But if you can drive into the surrounding rolling meadows to see some of the truly enormous traditional house-barn combos.

The **tourist office** (☎ 07651-980 40; www.titisee.de; Strandbadstrasse 4, Kurhaus; 🕑 8am-noon & 1.30-5.30pm Mon-Fri year-round, 10am-noon Sat & Sun May-Oct) can help you arrange a farm stay.

Terrassencamping Sandbank (☎ 07651-8243; fax 8286; Seerundweg; camp sites per person €5-6, site €5.50-8; 🕑 Apr-Oct) is one of four camping grounds on the Titisee.

The **DJH Hostel** (☎ 07652-238; www.djh.de; Bruderhalde 27; dm from €18) is in a huge farmhouse and is reached by bus 7300 from Titisee.

GERMANY

WORTH A TRIP: HEAVEN & HOLE

Just south of Furtwangen, look for a tiny road off to the west evocatively called the **Hexenloch** (Witch's Hole). This narrow road penetrates deep into a narrow valley of rushing white water and tall trees. It alone is worth the cost of a car rental – which is the only way to enjoy the hole. Even on warm days it's cold as a witch's... you know what, down here. The road follows the bends in the river and you'll see shaded banks of snow months after it has melted elsewhere. Look for small roadhouses with little spinning water wheels.

West of the south end of the Hexenloch road, **St Peter** is a tiny town that offers redemption with a big church. Two onion-domed towers mark the town's namesake old abbey. It's an 18th-century vision in gold, glitter and gilt that would do any Las Vegas designer proud. You can ponder your own place in heaven at the cute little cafés out front.

Hotel Sonneneck (☎ 07651-8246; fax 881 74; Parkstrasse 2; s/d €39/72) provides spacious comfort near the lake and boasts an excellent restaurant downstairs.

Titisee is linked to Freiburg by frequent train service (€9, 40 minutes). To reach Triberg to the north, there are very scenic hourly connections via Neustadt and Donaueschingen (€14, two hours).

Around Titisee

The Black Forest **ski season** runs from late December to March. While there is good downhill skiing, the area is more suited to cross-country skiing. The centre for winter sports is around Titisee, with uncrowded downhill ski runs at **Feldberg** (www.liftverbund-feldberg.de; day passes €23; rental equipment available) and numerous graded cross-country trails.

In summer you can use the lifts to reach the summit of Feldberg (1493m) for a wondrous panorama that stretches to the Alps.

Feldberg is 15km south of Titisee. It can be reached by bus 7300 from Titisee (€4, 12 minutes, hourly).

FREIBURG
☎ 0761 / pop 213,000

Nestled between hills and vineyards, Freiburg im Breisgau is a delightful place, thanks to the city's large and thriving university community. There's a sense of fun here best exemplified by the tiny medieval canals (*bächle*) running right down the middle of streets.

Founded in 1120 and ruled for centuries by the Austrian Habsburgs, Freiburg has retained many traditional features, although major reconstruction was necessary following WWII. The monumental 13th-century cathedral is the city's key landmark but the real attractions are the vibrant cafés, bars and street-life, plus the local wines. The best times for tasting are July for the four days of *Weinfest* (Wine Festival), or August for the nine days of *Weinkost* (wine tasting).

Orientation
The city centre is a convenient 10-minute walk from the train station. Walk east along Eisenbahnstrasse to the tourist office, then continue through the bustling pedestrian zone to Münsterplatz, dominated by the red-stone cathedral.

Information
Main post office (Eisenbahnstrasse 58-62)
Tourist office (☎ 388 1880; www.freiburg.de; Rotteckring 14; ☼ 9.30am-8pm Mon-Fri, to 5pm Sat, 10am-noon Sun Jun-Sep, 9.30am-6pm Mon-Fri, to 2.30pm Sat, 10am-noon Sun Nov-Apr) Amazingly helpful and loads of information on the Black Forest.
Wash & Tours (☎ 288 866; Salzstrasse 22; wash €4, Internet per 30 min €2; ☼ 9am-7pm Mon-Fri, to 6pm Sat, Sun closed) There's a drop-off laundry downstairs and an Internet café upstairs. How's that spin your web?

Sights
The major sight in Freiburg is the 700-year-old **Münster** (Cathedral; Münsterplatz; steeple adult/child €1.50/1.00; ☼ 9.30am-5pm Mon-Sat, 1-5pm Sun year-round), a classic example of both high and late-Gothic architecture that looms over Münsterplatz, Freiburg's market square. Ascend the west tower to the stunning pierced spire for great views of Freiburg and, on a clear day, the Kaiserstuhl wine region and the Vosages Mountains to the west. South of the Münster stands the picturesque **Kaufhaus**, the 16th-century merchants' hall.

The bustling **university quarter** is northwest of the **Martinstor** (one of the old city gates).

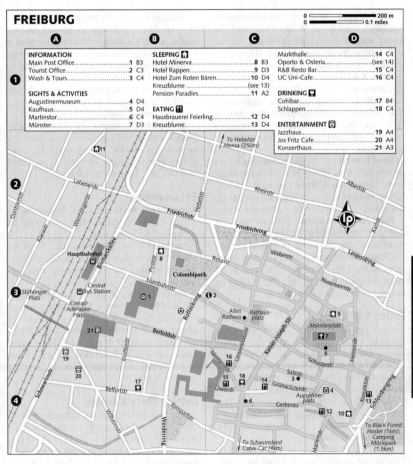

FREIBURG

INFORMATION	**SLEEPING**	Markthalle..................................**14** C4
Main Post Office..................**1** B3	Hotel Minerva.......................**8** B3	Oporto & Osteria.................(see **14**)
Tourist Office.......................**2** C3	Hotel Rappen........................**9** D3	R&B Resto Bar.......................**15** C4
Wash & Tours........................**3** C4	Hotel Zum Roten Bären.........**10** D4	UC Uni-Cafe...........................**16** C4
	Kreuzblume ....(see **13**)	
SIGHTS & ACTIVITIES	Pension Paradies....................**11** A2	**DRINKING**
Augustinermuseum...............**4** D4		Cohibar..................................**17** B4
Kaufhaus..............................**5** D4	**EATING**	Schlappen...............................**18** C4
Martinstor............................**6** C4	Hausbrauerei Feierling...........**12** D4	
Münster................................**7** D3	Kreuzblume............................**13** D4	**ENTERTAINMENT**
		Jazzhaus.................................**19** A4
		Jos Fritz Cafe..........................**20** A4
		Konzerthaus...........................**21** A3

Freiburg's main museum, the **Augustinermuseum** (☎ 201 2531; Salzstrasse 32; ☼ 10am-5pm Tue-Sun) has a fine collection of medieval art. Through 2007 the main building is being restored and much of the collection is in storage. Until completion only a few notable pieces are on exhibit and admission is free.

The popular trip by **cable car** (one way/return €7.50/10.70, concession €4.50/6.50; ☼ 9am-5pm Jan-Jun, to 6pm Jul-Sep, 9.30am-5pm Oct-Dec) to the **Schauinsland peak** (1284m) is a quick way to reach the Black Forest highlands. Numerous easy and well-marked trails make the Schauinsland area ideal for day walks. From Freiburg take tram 4 south to Günterstal and then bus 21 to Talstation.

Sleeping

Camping Möslepark (☎ 767 9333; www.camping-freiburg.com; Waldseestrasse 77; camp sites per person/tent €6/3) To reach this camping ground take tram 1 to Stadthalle (direction: Littenweiler), turn right under the road, go over the train tracks and follow the bike path.

Black Forest Hostel (☎ 881 7870; www.blackforest-hostel.de; Kartäuserstrasse 33; dm/s/d €13/23/28) Take tram 1 to Oberlinden (direction: Littenweiler) for this hostel.

Pension Paradies (☎ 273700; www.paradies-freiburg.de; Friedrich-Ebert-Platz; r €35-80; 🖳) This is a real find over the train tracks (take tram 4). The rooms are simple but stylish. There is a vast café with vegetarian specials and a large terrace.

Hotel Rappen (☎ 313 53; www.hotelrappen.de; Münsterplatz 13; s/d €60/80; ☒ ▣) This hotel has lovely rooms decorated in 'Black Forest' style with close-up views of the Münster. A good central choice.

Hotel Kreuzblume (☎ 311 9495; www.hotel -kreuzblume.de; Konviktstrasse 31; s/d €60/90) On an especially charming street, the eight-room Kreuzblume has a lovely grapevine growing right over the street. The rooms are comfortable and traditional, and the restaurant is excellent.

Hotel Minerva (☎ 386 490; www.minerva-freiburg .de; Poststrasse 8; s/d €69/90) The 26-room Minerva, only a block from the train station, has an elegant feel, with thick carpet on the floor and even thicker drapes on the walls.

Hotel Zum Roten Bären (☎ 387 870; www.roter -baeren.de; Oberlinden 12; s/d €105/145; ☒ ▣) Prices were undoubtedly more reasonable when the Roten Bären originally opened its doors early in the 12th century, but it's still good value for those looking for luxury. The restaurant is first class as well.

Eating & Drinking

There's a good selection of wurst and other quick eats from stalls set up in the market square during lunchtime.

UC Uni-Café (☎ 383 355; Niemensstrasse 7; meals €3-7) A popular hang-out that serves snacks on its see-and-be-seen outdoor terrace.

Markthalle (Grünwälderstrasse 2; meals €3-8; ☒ 7am-7pm) A huge number of stands selling ethnic food cluster around a bar selling local wine. A fun and fine deal.

Oporto (☎ 387 0038; Grünwälderstrasse 2; meals €5-10) This gorgeous wine bar and café looks like a classic from the 19th century. The bar and dining area are richly detailed. In the rear, the adjoining Osteria is all exposed brick and mimes an Italian wine cellar.

Cohibar (☎ 767 8550; Milchstrasse 9; snacks €3-5) Mellow and candlelit, this café doesn't close till 3am at weekends. At any time it's the kind of place where you may be inspired to work on your novel. Besides booze it has good coffees.

R & B Resto Bar (☎ 217 2204; Universitätstrasse; meals €6-10) In the heart of the university café district, this chic place serves fresh and creative soups, salads and sandwiches as well as pasta. In the back there's a funky bar with jazzy music. Grab a table outside and order breakfast any time.

Schlappen (☎ 334 94; Lowenstrasse 2; meals €6-9) A very old but still very happening student nightspot. It's a large, sprawling bar with a lively vibe, a budget menu and late closing.

Hausbrauerei Feierling (☎ 266 78; Gerberau 46; meals €6-12) A microbrewery in one of the most attractive preserved parts of town. In decent weather there's a huge terrace for tossing back the house product.

Restaurant Kreuzblume (☎ 311 9495; Konviktstrasse 31; meals €8-15) Traditional local meals are served in a historic setting here. All those grapes growing overhead would say – if they had voices – 'look at the wine list'.

Entertainment

Konzerthaus (☎ 388 8552; Konrad-Adenauer-Platz 1) This concert hall has an impressive range of orchestral performances.

Jazzhaus (☎ 349 73; Schnewlinstrasse 1) Jazzhaus offers live jazz alternating with dance clubs. Recommended. Admission starts at €6, depending on who's playing.

Jos Fritz Cafe (☎ 300 19; www.josfritzcafé.de; Wilhelmstrasse 15) Down a little alley past the recycling bins, this café hosts concerts of alternative bands (Bernadetee & the Suckers once brought the house down) and events such as political discussions. (Want to get things going? Say: 'That W is doing a heckuva job!')

Getting There & Around

Freiburg is on the busy Mannheim to Basel (€20, 45 minutes, hourly) train line. ICE service includes Berlin (€115, 6½ hours, every two hours), Cologne (€90, three hours, every two hours) and Frankfurt (€54, two hours, hourly). Freiburg is linked to Titisee by frequent trains (€9, 40 minutes).

Single rides on the efficient local bus and tram system cost €2. A 24-hour pass costs €4.80. Trams depart from the bridge over the train tracks.

LAKE CONSTANCE

Lake Constance (Bodensee) is an oasis in landlocked southern Germany. Even if you never make contact with the water, this giant bulge in the sinewy course of the Rhine can offer a splash of refreshment. There are many historic towns around its periphery, which can be explored by boat or bicycle and on foot. While sun is nice, the lake is best on one of the many misty days when it is shrouded in mystery.

Constance's southern side belongs to Switzerland and Austria, where the snow-capped Alps provide a perfect backdrop when viewed from the northern shore. The German side of Lake Constance features three often-crowded tourist centres in Constance, Meersburg and the island of Lindau. It's essentially a summer area, when it abounds with aquatic joy.

Getting There & Around

Trains link Lindau and Constance, and buses fill in the gaps to places like Meersburg. By car, the B31 hugs the northern shore of Lake Constance, but it can get rather busy. The Constance-Meersburg car ferry (p244) provides a vital link for those who don't want to circumnavigate the entire lake.

The most enjoyable, albeit slowest, way to get around is on the **Bodensee-Schiffsbetriebe boats** (BSB; www.bsb-online.com) which, from Easter to late October, call several times a day at the larger towns along the lake; there are discounts for rail pass-holders.

The **Erlebniskarte** (3 days/1 week €69/89) is a handy pass that allows free boat travel and free access to a host of activities around the lake. Numerous other discount cards are available. Ask at tourist information offices.

CONSTANCE

☎ 07531 / pop 81,000

Constance (Konstanz) sits right on the Swiss border. It's a tidy lake town and is a good place for gazing across the waters. Its main attraction is fittingly named Mainau Island.

It achieved historical significance in 1414, when the Council of Constance convened to try to heal huge rifts in the Catholic Church. The consequent burning at the stake of the religious reformer Jan Hus as a heretic, and the scattering of his ashes over the lake, did nothing to block the Reformation.

The **tourist office** (☎ 133 030; www.konstanz.de /tourismus; Bahnhofplatz 13; 9am-6.30pm Mon-Fri, to 4pm Sat, 10am-1pm Sun Apr-Oct; 9.30am-12.30pm, 2-6pm Mon-Fri Nov-Mar) is 150m to the right from the train station exit. **Clixworkx.net** (☎ 991 211; Bodanstrasse 21; per 15 min €1; 10am-7pm Mon-Sat) has Internet access.

WHEELING AROUND LAKE CONSTANCE

A 270km international bike track circumnavigates Lake Constance through Germany, Austria and Switzerland, tracing the often-steep shoreline beside vineyards and pebble beaches. The route is well signposted, but you may want one of the many widely sold cycling maps. The tourist booklet *Rad Urlaub am Bodensee* lists routes, rental places and a wealth of other information about the region.

In Constance, **Kultur-Rädle** (☎ 07531-273 10; Bahnhofplatz 29; bike rental per day from €10; 9am-12.30pm & 2.30-6pm Mon-Fri, 10am-4pm Sat year-round, 10am-12.30pm Sun Apr-Oct) rents out bikes and organises cycling tours.

Sights & Activities

The city's most visible feature is the Gothic spire of the cathedral, added in 1856 to a church that was started in 1052, which has excellent views over the old town. Visit the **Niederburg** quarter or relax in the parklands of the **Stadtgarten**. Head across to **Mainau Island** (☎ 3030; www.mainau.de; adult/child €12; 7am-8pm mid-Mar–Nov, 9am-6pm Nov–Mar), with its baroque castle set in vast and gorgeous gardens that include a butterfly house. Take bus 4 (€2, 25 minutes) or a BSB ferry from the harbour behind the station. Five **beaches** are open from May to September, including the Strandbad Horn, with bush-enclosed nude bathing. Take bus 5 or walk for 20 minutes around the shore.

Sleeping & Eating

Campingplatz Bodensee (☎ 33057; www.dkv-camping .de; Fohrenbühlweg 45; camp sites per person/tent €4/5) This is a lovely spot to camp. Take bus 1 to the car-ferry terminal, then walk south along the shore for 10 minutes.

Jugendherberge Konstanz (☎ 322 60; www.jugend herberge-konstanz.de; Zur Allmannshöhe 16; dm €21-24) To reach Jugendherberge Konstanz take bus 1 or 4 from the station to the Jugendherberge stop and stay in this converted water tower.

Hotel Goldener Sternen (☎ 252 28; www.hotel -goldener-sternen.de; Bodanplatz 1; s/d from €50/80) The 20 rooms are basic but comfortable at this modest place right near the train station.

Hotel Barbarossa (☎ 128 990; www.barbarossa -hotel.com; Obermarkt 8-12; s/d from €48/88;) Charming old place has been carefully restored (although the floors still creak). White walls set off beautiful wooden antiques. There's a good restaurant (mains €8 to €20) downstairs with local specialities.

Hafenalle Biergarten (☎ 211 26; Hafenstrasse 10) A perfect spot for a beer garden, Hafenalle catches the breeze off the lake. There's the usual array of pretzels and sausages.

Aran (☎ 365 2556; Marktstätte 6; meals €4-7; ☺ 7am-5pm) The current star of Constance cafés, Aran has a stylish interior where you can buy garden plants, cute décor items and excellent soups, salads and sandwiches. The bread is from its bakery.

Getting There & Away

Constance has trains to Offenburg via Triberg in the Black Forest (€26, 2¼ hours, hourly) and connections via Singen to Stuttgart (€35, 2¼ hours, hourly). There are good connections into Switzerland including Zurich (€16, one hour, hourly).

BSB Ferries on various schedules serve numerous destinations including Meersburg (€4.20, 30 minutes) and Lindau (€11.20, three to four hours).

MEERSBURG

☎ 07532 / pop 5300

Constance is the big city compared to Meersburg across the lake. The winding cobblestone streets, vine-patterned hills and a sunny lakeside promenade make it a good stop if travelling by ferry or car.

The helpful **tourist office** (☎ 440 400; www .meersburg.de; Kirchstrasse 4; ☺ 9am-noon & 2-6pm Mon-Fri, 10am-2pm Sat) is in the Altstadt and can help find accommodation if you decide to stay.

Steigstrasse is lined with delightful half-timbered houses, each boasting a gift shop. The 11th-century **Altes Schloss** (☎ 800 00; adult/child €6/4; ☺ 9am-6.30pm) is the oldest structurally intact castle in Germany.

The useful Constance to Meersburg **car ferry** (☎ 07531-803 666; person/car €2/7.20, 30 min) runs every 15 minutes year-round from the northeastern Constance suburb of Staad. BSB ferries stop on their shore-hugging voyages between Constance (€4.20, 30 minutes) and Lindau (€10.50, 2½ to three hours).

LINDAU

☎ 08382 / pop 26,500

A forgotten corner of Bavaria, most people assume the lovely little island-city is part of

Baden-Württemberg but it's not. Here you'll see the blue and white Bavarian state colours and maybe it's just us, but there's a renewed emphasis on beer compared to the wine-drinkers elsewhere on the lake.

The **tourist office** (☎ 260030; www.lindau-tourismus .de; Ludwigstrasse 68; ☺ 9am-6pm Mon-Fri, 10am-2pm Sat & Sun Jun-Sep, reduced hr winter) is directly opposite the train station. **Internet Cafe Salem** (☎ 943 1297, Bahnhofplatz 08, per 15 min €1; ☺ 10am-7pm Mon-Fri, 11am-5pm Sat & Sun) is close to the station.

Connected to the nearby lakeshore by bridges, key sights of this oh-so-charming island town have murals: **Altes Rathaus** (Reichsplatz), the **city theatre** (Barfüsser-platz) and the harbour's **Seepromenade**, with its Bavarian Lion monument and lighthouse. When the haze clears, the Alps provide a stunning backdrop for photos.

Park Camping Lindau am See (☎ 722 36; www .park-camping.de; Fraunhoferstrasse 20; camp sites per person/tent €6/2.50) is on the foreshore 3km southeast of Lindau. Take bus 1 or 2 to the bus station, then bus 3.

The attractive-looking façade of **Hotel Gasthof Goldenes Lamm** (☎ 5732; www.goldenes -lamm-lindau.de; Schafgasse 3; s/d from €47/84) is mirrored by the 21 comfortable rooms inside. The restaurant is good and has many fish dishes.

The maroon **Alte Post** (☎ 934 60; www.alte-post -lindau.de; Fischergasse 3; s/d €44/80) has 19 beautifully maintained rooms. The restaurant (mains €7 to €18) serves Bavarian/Austrian fare and has a large terrace. Guests can use bikes for free.

The personality begins over the door at **Zurtischerin Galerie und Weinstube** (☎ 5428; Ludwigstrasse 50; snacks under €4; ☺ 5pm-2am); look for the big fish. Inside there's local art on the walls and some of the characters who painted it might just let you buy them a drink. Regional wines are featured.

Lindau has trains to/from Ulm on the Munich–Stuttgart line (€20, 1¾ hours, hourly), Munich (€33, 2¼ hours, four times daily). There are hourly RB trains to/from Immenstadt where you connect to Oberstdorf (€15, 1¾ hours). Trains to nearby Bregenz (€3.20, nine minutes, hourly) let you connect to the rest of Austria.

BSB Ferries on various schedules serve destinations including Meersburg (€10.50, 2½ to three hours) and Constance (€11.20, three to four hours).

GERMANY

RHINELAND-PALATINATE

Rhineland-Palatinate (Rheinland-Pfalz) has an unsettled topography characterised by thinly populated mountain ranges and forests cut by deep river valleys. Created after WWII from parts of the former Rhineland and Rhenish Palatinate regions, its turbulent history goes all the way back to the Romans, as seen in Trier (p246). In recent centuries it was hotly contested by the French and a variety of German states.

This land of wine and great natural beauty reaches its apex in the verdant Moselle Valley towns such as Cochem, and along the heavily touristed Rhine, where rich hillside vineyards provide a backdrop for noble castles and looming medieval fortresses. For this part of Germany, focus your attention on the water and the land it courses through.

MOSELLE VALLEY

Exploring the vineyards and wineries of the Moselle (Mosel) Valley is an ideal way to get a taste of German culture and people – and, of course, the wonderful wines. Take the time to slow down and savour a glass or two.

The Moselle is bursting at the seams with historical sites and picturesque towns built along the river below steep rocky cliffs planted with vineyards (they say locals are born with one leg shorter than the other so that they can easily work the vines). It's one of the country's most romantically scenic regions, with stunning views rewarding the intrepid hikers who brave the hilly trails.

Many wine-makers have their own small *pensions* but accommodation is hard to find in May, on summer weekends or during the local wine harvest (mid-September to mid-October). Note also that much of the region – like the vines themselves – goes into a deep slumber from November to March.

Getting There & Around

The most scenic part of the Moselle Valley runs 195km northeast from Trier to Koblenz; it's most practical to begin your Moselle Valley trip from either of these two.

It is not possible to travel the banks of the Moselle River via rail. Local and fast trains run every hour between Trier and Koblenz, but the only riverside stretch of this line is between Cochem and Koblenz (however it's a scenic dandy). Apart from this run – and the scenic Moselweinbahn line taking tourists between Bullay and Traben-Trarbach – travellers must use buses, ferries, bicycles or cars to travel between most of the upper Moselle towns.

Moselbahn (☎ 0651-147 750; www.moselbahn .de) runs eight buses on weekdays (fewer at weekends) between Trier and Bullay (three hours each way), a very scenic route following the river's winding course and passing through numerous quaint villages. Buses leave from outside the train stations in Trier and Bullay.

A great way to explore the Moselle in the high season is by boat. Between May and early October, **Köln-Düsseldorfer (KD) Line** (☎ 0221-208 8318; www.k-d.com) ferries sail daily between Koblenz and Cochem (€22.40 one way, 4¾ hours). Various smaller ferry companies also operate on the Moselle from some of the towns. Eurail and German Rail passes are valid for all normal KD Line services, and travel on your birthday is free.

The Moselle is a popular area among cyclists, and for much of the river's course there's a separate 'Moselroute' bike track. Most towns have a rental shop or two, ask at the tourist offices. Many of the Moselbahn buses also carry bikes.

Koblenz

☎ 0261 / pop 109,000

Koblenz is an important ferry and train junction at the confluence of the Rhine and Moselle Rivers. The **tourist office** (☎ 303 880; www .koblenz.de; Bahnhofsplatz 7; ⊙ 9am-6pm Mon-Sat year-round, 10am-6pm Sun Apr-Oct) is in a very modern building in front of the Hauptbahnhof.

The **Deutsches Eck** is a park at the dramatic meeting point of the rivers. It's dedicated to German unity and is a good reason for a riverside stroll.

South of Koblenz, at the head of the beautiful Eltz Valley, **Burg Eltz** (☎ 02672-950 500; adult/child €6/4.50; ⊙ 9.30am-5.30pm Apr-Nov) is not to be missed. Towering over the surrounding hills, this superb medieval castle has frescoes, paintings, furniture and ornately decorated rooms. Burg Eltz is best reached by train to Moselkern, from where it's a 50-minute walk up through the forest. Alternatively, you can drive via Münster-Maifeld to the nearby car park.

In town, Altenhof and the area around Münzplatz in the Altstadt offer a variety of good eating options. The small towns in either river valley offer more salubrious accommodation than that locally.

The busy KD line ferry dock is a 10-minute walk from the train station. Trains fan out in all directions. Up the Moselle to Trier (€17, 1½ hours, hourly) via Cochem and Bullay, north along the Rhine to Cologne (€18, one hour, two hourly) and south on the Rhine to Mainz (€18, one hour, two hourly).

Cochem
☎ 02671 / pop 5400

This pretty German town has narrow alleyways and one of the most beautiful castles in the region. It's also a good base for hikes into the hills. The staff are very helpful in Cochem's **tourist office** (☎ 600 40; www.cochem.de; Endertplatz), next to the Moselbrücke bridge.

For a great view, head up to the **Pinnerkreuz** with the chairlift on Endertstrasse (€5). The stunning **Reichsburg Castle** (☎ 255; ⊗ 9am-5pm mid-Mar–mid-Nov) is just a 15-minute walk up the hill from town. There are regular daily tours (adult/child €3.50/2) and English translation sheets are available.

Cochem's **HH Hieronimi** (☎ 221; Stadionstrasse 1-3), just across the river is one of many friendly, family-run vineyards that offers tours.

Campingplatz Am Freizeitszentrum (☎ 4409; Stadionstrasse; camp sites per person/tent/car €5/4/6) is downstream from the northern bridge, alongside the river.

Moseltal-Jugendherberge (☎ 8633; www.djh.de; Klottener Strasse 9; dm €17-24) is beautifully situated on the banks of the river, the 148 beds are in spotless four-bed rooms.

Hotel-Pension Garni Villa Tummelchen (☎ 910 520; www.villa-tummelchen.com; Schlossstrasse 22; s/d from €47/80) is a bit up the hill from town and thus has sweeping Moselle views. It's worth an extra couple of euros to get a room with a balcony and a view.

This is the terminus for KD Line boats from Koblenz. Trains run twice hourly to Bullay (€4, 10 minutes), where you can pick up the Moselbahn bus.

Cochem to Trier

Take the train – or a boat – from Cochem to Bullay where you can catch the Moselbahn bus for the little river towns the rest of the way to Trier.

Full of fanciful Art Nouveau villas, the double town of **Traben-Trarbach** is a welcome relief from the 'romantic-half-timbered-town' circuit. Pick up a map of the town at the **tourist office** (☎ 839 80; www.traben-trarbach.de; Bahnstrasse 22).

The twin town of **Bernkastel-Kues** is at the heart of the middle Moselle region. On the right bank, Bernkastel has a charming **Markt**, a romantic ensemble of half-timbered houses with beautifully decorated gables. For a primer on the local vino – one of many, try Bernkastel's **Weingut Dr Willkomm** (☎ 8054; Gestade 1). Located in a lovely old arched cellar, the vineyard also distils its own brandy. The **tourist office** (☎ 4023; www.bernkastel-kues.de; Am Gestade 6) is on the Bernkastel side.

TRIER
☎ 0651 / pop 100,000

Trier is touted as Germany's oldest town and you'll find more Roman ruins here than anywhere else north of the Alps. Although settlement of the site dates back to 400 BC, Trier itself was founded in 15 BC as Augusta Treverorum, the capital of Gaul, and was second in importance only to Rome in the Western Roman Empire. Its proximity to France can be tasted in its cuisine, while its large student population injects life among the ruins.

Orientation & Information

From the main train station head west along Bahnhofstrasse and Theodor-Heuss-Allee to the Porta Nigra, where you'll find Trier's nearby **tourist office** (☎ 978 080; www.trier.de; ⊗ 9am-6pm Mon-Sat, 10am-3pm Sun May-Oct; reduced hr winter). There are good two-hour guided **city walking tours** (adult/child €6/3; ⊗ 1.30pm Sat May-Oct) in English. The Trier-Card (€12) is a combined ticket for the city's main attractions and public transport. From Porta Nigra, walk along Simeonstrasse's pedestrian zone to Hauptmarkt, the heart of the old city. Most of the sights are within this area of roughly 1 sq km. Several places around the station offer Internet access.

Sights

The town's chief landmark is the **Porta Nigra** (adult/child €2.10/1; ⊗ 9am-6pm Apr-Sep, to 5pm Mar & Oct, to 4pm Nov-Feb), the imposing city gate on

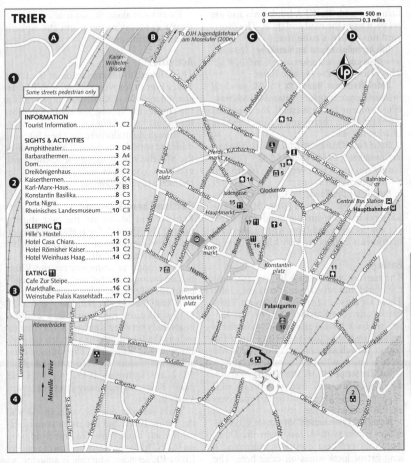

TRIER

	0	500 m
	0	0.3 miles

Some streets pedestrian only

INFORMATION
Tourist Information.....................1 C2

SIGHTS & ACTIVITIES
Amphitheater............................2 D4
Barbarathermen.........................3 A4
Dom.....................................4 C2
Dreikönigenhaus........................5 C2
Kaiserthermen..........................6 C4
Karl-Marx-Haus.........................7 B3
Konstantin Basilika....................8 C3
Porta Nigra............................9 C2
Rheinisches Landesmuseum..............10 C3

SLEEPING 🏠
Hille's Hostel........................11 D3
Hotel Casa Chiara.....................12 C1
Hotel Römisher Kaiser.................13 C2
Hotel Weinhuas Haag...................14 C2

EATING 🍴
Cafe Zur Steipe.......................15 C2
Markthalle............................16 C2
Weinstube Palais Kasselstadt..........17 C2

the northern edge of the town centre, which dates back to the 2nd century AD. The interesting **Rheinisches Landesmuseum** (Weimarer Allee 1; adult/child €2.50/0.50; 🕑 9.30am-5pm Tue-Fri, 10.30am-5pm Sat & Sun, 9.30am-5pm Mon May-Oct) puts the Roman era into context.

Trier's massive (and massively restored) Romanesque **Dom** (www.dominformation.de; Liebfrauenstrasse 12; 🕑 6.30am-6pm Apr-Oct, to 5.30pm Nov-Mar) shares a 1600-year history with the nearby and equally impressive **Konstantin Basilika** (🕾 724 68; Konstantinplatz; tours by appt €25; 🕑 10am-6pm Mon-Fri, noon-6pm Sun Apr-Oct). Also worth visiting are the Roman **Amphitheater** (Olewigerstrasse), the **Kaiserthermen** (Im Palastgarten) and **Barbarathermen** (Roman baths; Südallee). The early-Gothic **Dreikönigenhaus** (Simeonstrasse 19) was built around 1230

as a protective tower; the original entrance was on the second level, accessible only by way of a retractable rope ladder.

The **Karl Marx Haus Museum** (🕾 970 680; Brückenstrasse 10; adult/child €3/1.50; 🕑 10am-6pm Apr-Oct, to 5pm & closed Mon Nov-Mar) is the suitably modest birthplace of the man. It is a major pilgrimage stop for the growing numbers of mainland Chinese tourists to Europe.

Sleeping

Camping Treviris (🕾 869 21; Luxemburger Strasse 81; camp sites per person/tent/car €6/4/4; 🕑 Apr-Oct) This camping ground is central and beside the Moselle River.

Hille's Hostel (🕾 710 2785; www.hilles-hostel-trier.de; Gartenfeldstrasse 7; dm €15) The rooms here are

GERMANY

furnished with 25 IKEA bunk beds and are set back from the road and quiet. The courtyard now boasts a palm tree.

DJH Jugendgästehaus am Moselufer (☎ 146 620; www.djh-info.de; An der Jugendherberge 4; dm €17-24; 🖳) This place is by the Moselle River.

Hotel Weinhaus Haag (☎ 975 750; www.hotel -weinhaus-haag.de; Stockplatz 1; s/d from €47/50) A traveller favourite in the Altstadt, this hotel has a certain 1950s charm and a good selection of wine for sale.

Hotel Casa Chiara (☎ 270 730; www.casa-chiara .de; Engelstrasse 8; s/d from €50/80; 🗶 🖳) This is a family run hotel with very clean rooms and a lovely breakfast room.

Hotel Römischer Kaiser (☎ 97700;www.hotels-trier .de; Am Porta-Nigra-Platz 6; s/d €67/98; 🗶 🖳) The Kaiser is in an elegant old building. Rooms are comfortable and have wi-fi; some have balconies. Ceilings are very high and regal.

Eating

The narrow and historic Judengasse, near the Markt, has several small bars and clubs. There's a cluster of stylish places on Viehmarktplatz. The **Markthalle** (⏰ 9am-10pm Mon-Sat), set back from Palaststrasse, has places selling fresh produce and wines from the region, as well as numerous small delis and cafés where you can eat in or take away.

Cafe Zur Steipe (☎ 145 5456; Markt 14; meals €4-9; 🖳) This is a classic bakery and café with tables outside. There's wi-fi to surf while you sip the excellent coffee.

Weinstube Palais Kesselstadt (☎ 411 78; Liebfrau-enstrasse 9; mains €6-10) Across from the Dom, there's an excellent outdoor garden and a long list of local wines on offer here. The food is creative.

Getting There & Away

Trier has a train service to Koblenz (€17, 1½ hours, hourly) via Bullay and Cochem, as well as to Luxembourg (€13, 45 minutes, hourly).

RHINE VALLEY – KOBLENZ TO MAINZ

A trip along the Rhine is on the itinerary of most travellers, as it should be. The section between Koblenz and Mainz offers vistas of steep vineyard-covered mountains punctuated by scores of castles. It's really rather magical. Spring and autumn are the best times to visit; in summer it's overrun and in winter most towns go into hibernation. For information on Koblenz, see p245.

Every town along the route offers cute little places to stay or camp and atmospheric places to drink and eat.

Activities

The Koblenz-to-Mainz section of the Rhine Valley is great for wine tasting, with Bacharach, 45km south of Koblenz, being one of the top choices for sipping. For tastings in other towns just follow your instincts.

Though the trails here may be a bit more crowded with day-trippers than those along the Moselle, hiking along the Rhine is also excellent. The slopes and trails around Bacharach are justly famous.

Getting There & Around

Koblenz and Mainz are the best starting points. The Rhine Valley is also easily accessible from Frankfurt on a long day trip, but it could drive you to drink, as it were.

Each mode of transport on the Rhine has its own advantages and all are equally enjoyable. Try combining several of them. The **Köln- Düsseldorfer (KD) Line** (☎ 0221-208 83 18; www.k-d.com) runs many slow and fast boats daily between Koblenz and Mainz (as well as the less-interesting stretch between Cologne and Koblenz). The journey takes about four hours downstream and about 5½ hours upstream (€45, free with rail pass). Boats stop at many riverside towns along the way.

Train services operate on both sides of the Rhine River, but are more convenient on the left bank. You can travel nonstop on IC/EC trains or travel by slower regional RB or RE services. The ride is amazing, sit on the right heading north and on the left heading south.

Touring the Rhine Valley by car is also ideal. The route between Koblenz and Mainz is short enough for a car to be rented and returned to either city. There are no bridge crossings between Koblenz and Rüdesheim, but there are several ferry crossings.

St Goar/St Goarshausen
☎ 06741

These two towns are on opposite sides of the Rhine, St Goar is on the left bank. One of the most impressive castles on the river is **Burg Rheinfels** (☎ 383; adult/child €4/2; ⏰ 9am-6pm Apr-Oct, 11am-5pm Sat & Sun in good weather Nov-Mar) in St Goar. An absolute must-see, the labyrinthine ruins reflect the greed and ambition of Count Dieter V of Katzenelnbogen, who built the castle in 1245 to help levy tolls on passing ships ('African or European?'). Across the river, just south of St Goarshausen, is the Rhine's most famous sight, the **Loreley Cliff**. Legend has it that a maiden sang sailors to their deaths against its base. It's worth the trek to the top of the Loreley for the view.

For camping **Campingplatz Loreleyblick** (☎ 2066; camp sites per person/site €3/2.50; ◷ Mar-Oct) is on the banks of the Rhine, opposite the legendary rock.

St Goar's **Jugendherberge** (☎ 388; www.djh.de; Bismarckweg 17; dm €13) is right below the castle. You can sip the house wine here in a rural atmosphere. The **Schlosshotel Rheinfels** (☎ 8020; www.schlosshotel-rheinfels.de; s/d from €95/145; ⊠ ▢ ☎) in the castle is the top address in town. Rooms are posh and the views sublime.

Bacharach
☎ 06743 / pop 2400

Walk beneath one of its thick-arched gateways in Bacharach's medieval walls and you'll find yourself in a beautifully preserved medieval village. Drop by the **tourist office** (☎ 919 303; www.bacharach.de; Oberstrasse 45; ◷ 9am-5pm Mon-Fri, 10am-4pm Sat Apr-Oct) for information on Bacharach's sights and lodging.

Bacharach's **Jugendherberge** (☎ 1266; www.djh.de; dm €17) is a legendary facility housed in the Burg Stahleck castle. In town, **Hotel Kranenturm** (☎ 1308; www.kranenturm.com; Langstrasse 30; s/d from €40/55) is charming and offers an array of neat rooms, some with river views.

Zum Grünen Baum (☎ 1208; Oberstrasse 63; mains €6-10) is a wonderful place to sample Rhine wines.

Mainz
☎ 06131 / pop 183,000

A short train ride from Frankfurt, Mainz has an attractive old town that makes for a good day trip. Though it can't compare to the compact beauty of the nearby towns along the Rhine, Mainz impresses with its massive **Dom** (cathedral; ☎ 253 412; Domstrasse 3; ◷ 9am-6.30pm Mon-Fri, 10am-4pm Sat, 12.45-3pm Sun), which has a smorgasbord of architecture: Romanesque, Gothic and baroque. **St Stephanskirche** (Weisspetrolse 12; ◷ 10am-noon, 2-5pm) has stained-glass windows by Marc Chagall. Mainz's museums include the

RHINE TOWNS

Besides those listed in this section, here's the low-down on some other towns along the route. All have train and boat service.

Boppard Roman walls and ruins (left bank).

Oberwesel Numerous towers and walkable walls of a ruined castle (left bank).

Assmannshausen Small relatively untouristed village with nice hotels and sweeping views; good hikes (right bank).

Rüdesheim Overrated and over-visited town of trinkets and hype.

Gutenberg Museum (☎ 122 640; Liebfrauenplatz 5; adult/child €3.50/1.50; ◷ 9am-5pm Tue-Sat, 11am-3pm Sun), which contains two namesake copies of the first printed Bible. For more information on attractions in Mainz, visit the **tourist office** (☎ 286 210; www.mainz.de; Brückenturm am Rathaus; ◷ 9am-6pm Mon-Fri, 10.30am-2.30pm Sat).

Trains along the Rhine to Koblenz (€18, one hour) run twice hourly. Heidelberg (€18, one hour, hourly) is an easy trip as is Frankfurt via the Frankfurt airport (€9, 35 minutes, several per hour).

HESSE

The Hessians, a Frankish tribe, were among the first to convert to Lutheranism in the early 16th century. Apart from a brief period of unity in that same century under Philip the Magnanimous, Hesse (Hessen) remained a motley collection of principalities and, later, of Prussian administrative districts until proclaimed a state in 1945. Its main cities are Frankfurt-am-Main, Kassel and the capital, Wiesbaden.

As well as being a transport hub, Frankfurt-am-Main offers its own diversions, although you'll most likely soon leave the state entirely.

FRANKFURT-AM-MAIN
☎ 069 / pop 643,000

Called 'Mainhattan' and 'Bankfurt', and much more, Frankfurt is on the Main (pronounced 'mine') River, and, after London, it is Europe's centre of finance. Both sobriquets also refer to the city's soaring skyline of skyscrapers, a profile found nowhere else on the continent.

GERMANY

FRANKFURT-AM-MAIN

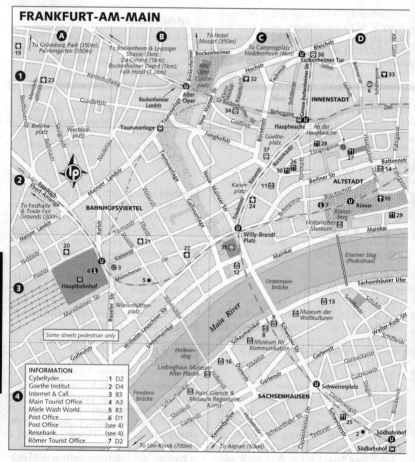

INFORMATION

CyberRyder	1 D2
Goethe Institut	2 D4
Internet & Call	3 B3
Main Tourist Office	4 A3
Miele Wash World	5 B3
Post Office	6 D1
Post Office	(see 4)
Reisebank	(see 4)
Römer Tourist Office	7 D2

But while all seems cosmopolitan, it is often just a small town at heart. Things tend to get quiet in the evenings and the long list of museums is devoid of any really outstanding stars. Then again, is has cute old pubs you would only ever find in a small town. Mind you, when a major trade fair is in town, it feels as bustling as any metropolis.

Frankfurt-am-Main is Germany's most important transport hub for air, train and road connections, so you will probably end up here at some point. Note that it is generally referred to as Frankfurt-am-Main, or Frankfurt/Main, since there is another Frankfurt (Frankfurt-an-der-Oder) located near the Polish border.

Orientation

The airport is 11 minutes by train southwest of the city centre. The Hauptbahnhof is on the western side of the city, but it's still within walking distance of the city centre.

The best route to the city centre through the sleazy train station area is along Kaiserstrasse. This leads to Kaiserplatz and on to a large square called An der Hauptwache. The area between the former prison/police station (Hauptwache), and the Römerberg, in the tiny vestige of Frankfurt's original old city, is the centre of Frankfurt. The Main River flows just south of the Altstadt, with several bridges leading to one of the city's livelier areas, Sachsenhausen. Its

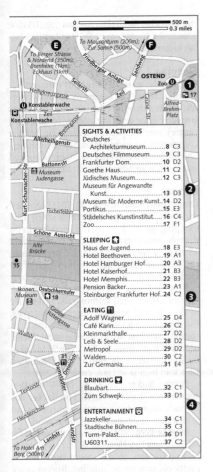

northeastern corner, known as Alt-Sachsenhausen, is full of quaint old houses and narrow alleyways.

Information
BOOKSHOPS

The Hauptbahnhof is an excellent place to go book shopping. Stores near tracks 9 and 17 have scores of English language books and periodicals, as well as guidebooks and maps.

INTERNET ACCESS

CyberRyder (☎ 396 754; Töngesgasse 31; per 30 min €2; 🕙 9am-8pm Mon-Sat) Full service shop.
Internet & Call (☎ 2424 7939; Kaiserstrasse 81; per hr €2; 🕙 9am-11pm)

LAUNDRY

Miele Wash World (Moselstrasse 17; wash/dry €4/1; 🕙 6am-11pm) Near the train station.

MEDICAL SERVICES

Doctor Referral Service (☎ 192 92; 🕙 24hr)
Uni-Klinik (☎ 630 10; Theodor Stern Kai, Sachsenhausen; 🕙 24hr)

MONEY

Reisebank Train station (🕙 6.30am-10pm); airport (Terminal 1, arrival hall B; 🕙 6am-11pm) The train station branch is near the southern exit at the head of platform 1.

POST

Post office (Zeil 90; ground fl, Karstadt department store; 🕙 9.30am-8pm) Hauptbahnhof (🕙 7am-7.30pm Mon-Fri, 8am-4pm Sat); airport (departure lounge B; 🕙 7am-9pm)

TOURIST INFORMATION

Main tourist office (☎ 212 388 00; www.frankfurt -tourismus.de; 🕙 8am-9pm Mon-Fri, 9am-6pm Sat, Sun) In the main hall of the train station. For its efficient room-finding service the charge is €3. Römer branch (Römerberg 27; 🕙 9.30am-5.30pm Mon-Fri, 10am-4pm Sat & Sun) Northwest corner of the Römerberg square. The Frankfurt-am-Main Card (one day/two days €8/12) gives 50% off admission to important attractions and unlimited travel on public transport.

Sights

About 80% of the old city was wiped off the map by two Allied bombing raids in March 1944, and postwar reconstruction was subject to the hurried demands of the new age. Rebuilding efforts were more thoughtful in the **Römerberg**, the old central area of Frankfurt west of the cathedral, where restored 14th- and 15th-century buildings provide a glimpse of the beautiful city this once was. The old town hall, or **Römer**, is in the northwestern corner of Römerberg and consists of three 15th-century houses topped with Frankfurt's trademark stepped gables.

East of Römerberg, behind the Historischer Garten (which has the remains of Roman and Carolingian foundations), is the **Frankfurter Dom** (Domplatz 14; tour adult/child €2/1; 🕙 9am-noon Mon-Thu, Sat & Sun, 2.30-6pm daily), the coronation site of Holy Roman emperors from 1562 to 1792. It's dominated by the elegant 15th-century Gothic **tower** – one of the few structures left standing after the 1944 raids.

Anyone with an interest in German literature should visit **Goethe Haus** (☎ 138 800; Grosser Hirschgraben 23-25; adult/child €5/3; ☺ 9am-6pm Mon-Fri Apr-Sep, to 4pm Mon-Fri Oct-Mar, 10am-4pm Sat & Sun year-round). Johann Wolfgang von Goethe was born in this house in 1749.

A little further afield, there's the botanical **Palmengarten** (☎ 2123 6689; Siesmayerstrasse 63; adult/child €5/2; ☺ 9am-6pm), next door to **Grüneburg Park**. The **Frankfurt Zoo** (☎ 212 337 35; Alfred-Brehm-Platz 16; adult/child €8/4; ☺ 9am-7pm, to 5pm Oct-Apr) is also a good place to unwind. It is also a nice 40-minute walk from the zoo east along the south bank of the Main River to the **lock** in Offenbach – just before it there's a good beer garden.

There's a great **flea market** (☺ 8am-2pm Sat) along Museumsufer.

MUSEUMS

Frankfurt's museum list is long but a mixed bag. To sample them all, buy a 48-hour Museumsufer ticket (€12). North of the cathedral, the excellent **Museum für Moderne Kunst** (☎ 2123 0447; Domstrasse 10; adult/child €6/3; ☺ 10am-5pm Tue & Thu-Sun, to 8pm Wed) features works of modern art by Joseph Beuys, Claes Oldenburg and many others.

For more modern art, check out the new **Portikus** (☎ 9624 4540; www.portikus.de; Alte Brücke 2 Maininsel; admission free; ☺ 11am-6pm Tue & Thu-Sun, to 8pm Wed) in a dramatic building on an island in the river.

Also on the north bank there's the **Jüdisches Museum** (Jewish Museum; ☎ 2123 5000; Untermainkai 14-15; adult/child €4/2; ☺ 10am-5pm Tue & Thu-Sun, to 8pm Wed), a huge place with exhibits on the city's rich Jewish life before WWII.

Numerous museums line the south bank of the Main River along the so-called *Museumsufer* (Museum Embankment). Pick of the crop is the **Städelsches Kunstinstitut** (☎ 605 0980; Schaumainkai 63; adult/child €8/6; ☺ 10am-5pm Tue, Fri-Sun, to 9pm Wed & Thu), with a world-class collection of paintings by artists from the Renaissance to the 20th century, including Botticelli, Dürer, Van Eyck, Rubens, Rembrandt, Vermeer, Cézanne and Renoir.

Other highlights include the **Deutsches Filmmuseum** (☎ 2123 8830; Schaumainkai 41; adult/child €2.50/1.30; ☺ 10am-5pm Tue, Thu & Fri, to 7pm Wed & Sun, 2-7pm Sat); the fascinating, design-oriented **Museum für Angewandte Kunst** (Museum of Applied Arts; ☎ 2123 4037; Schaumainkai 17; admission €5; ☺ 10am-5pm Tue & Thu-Sun, to 9pm Wed); and

the **Deutsches Architekturmuseum** (☎ 2123 8844; Schaumainkai 43; admission €6; ☺ 11am-6pm Tue & Thu-Sun, to 8pm Wed).

Sleeping

Predictably, most of Frankfurt's budget accommodation is in the grotty Bahnhofsviertel, which surrounds the station. The streets between here and the Messe (convention centre) aren't especially interesting but are convenient for early departures or meetings. During large trade fairs the town is booked out months in advance and rates soar.

BUDGET

Campingplatz Heddernheim (☎ 570 332; An der Sandelmühle 35; camp sites per site/person/car €4/6/5) This camping ground is in the Heddernheim district northwest of the city centre. It's a 15-minute ride on the U1, U2 or U3 from the Hauptwache U-Bahn station – get off at Heddernheim.

Haus der Jugend (☎ 610 0150; www.djh.de; Deutschherrnufer 12; dm €17-22) Within walking distance of the city and Sachsenhausen's nightspots, this hostel is a good choice. From the train station take bus 46 to Frankensteinerplatz, or take S-Bahn lines S3, S4, S5 or S6 to Lokalbahnhof, then walk north for 10 minutes. Check-in begins at 1pm, curfew is 2am.

Pension Backer (☎ 747 992; fax 747 900; Mendelssohnstrasse 92; s/d from €25/40) The Backer has 25 basic rooms with shared bathrooms but is in a nice residential neighbourhood.

Hotel Am Berg (☎ 612 021; www.hotel-am-berg-ffm .de; Grethenweg 23; s/d from €40/50; ✗) In pleasant Sachsenhausen, this 21-room hotel is in a pretty old sandstone building. Rooms come in all shapes and sizes.

MIDRANGE

Hotel Memphis (☎ 242 6090; www.memphis-hotel.de; Münchenerstrasse 15; s/d from €60/80; ✗ ▯) The stylish modern rooms here are fully equipped and the front desk staff are trained to assist with all your needs, business or otherwise.

Hotel Kaiserhof (☎ 256 1790; www.kaiserhof-frankfurt .de; Kaiserstrasse 62; s/d from €65/80; ✗ ▯) This remodelled hotel three minutes from the Hauptbahnhof has 42 rooms that are easy on the eyes and have wi-fi. Those on the top floor have a small terrace.

Hotel Hamburger Hof (☎ 2713 9690; www.hamburger hof.com; Poststrasse 10-12; s/d €69/79) An excellent choice, the Hamburger Hof's 60 rooms are done up in stark, contrasting colours. There's wi-fi in all and a good level of service from the staff.

Hotel Beethoven (☎ 746 091; www.hotelbeethoven .de; Beethovenstrasse 44; s/d €80/120; ✗ ▣) The elegant Beethoven is in a quiet neighbourhood north of the train station. The 31 rooms are a bit regal.

Falk Hotel (☎ 719 188 70; www.hotel-falk.de; Falkstrasse 38; r €80-180; ✗) In the fun neighbourhood of Bockenheim, this pleasant hotel has 29 rooms decorated in comfortable yet minimalist style.

TOP END

Hotel Mozart (☎ 156 8060; www.hotelmozart.de; Parkstrasse 17; s/d from €95/150; ✗ ▣) A 10-minute walk north from the Alter Opera (opera house), the Mozart is nicely furnished, has excellent breakfasts and is directly across the street from peaceful Grüneburg Park. The 35 rooms are spacious and have wi-fi.

Steigenberger Frankfurter Hof (☎ 215 02; www .steigenberger.de; Am Kaiserplatz; s/d from €150/200; ✗ ✗ ▣) Schopenhauer used to lunch here but his pessimism is unlikely to dampen your enthusiasm for this cosmopolitan and elegant 19th-century neo-Renaissance institution. The 131 rooms are traditionally luxurious.

Eating

Known to the locals as Fressgasse (Munch-Alley), the Kalbächer Petrolse and Grosse Bockenheimer Strasse area, between Opernplatz and Börsenstrasse, has some medium-priced restaurants and fast-food places with outdoor tables in summer.

The area around the main train station has lots of ethnic eating options. Baseler Strasse in particular has a Middle Eastern tone. Wallstrasse and the surrounding streets in Alt-Sachsenhausen also have lots of ethnic mid-priced restaurants.

Another good place for ravenous hunters and gatherers is the cosmopolitan Berger Strasse and Nordend areas north of the Zeil.

RESTAURANTS

Da Cimino (☎ 771 142; Abdelstrasse 28; pizza €5-9) Customers flock here for the tasty pizza, possibly the best in town.

Leib & Seele (☎ 281 529; Kornmarkt 11; mains €6-12) Modern yet old-fashioned at the same time, Leib & Seele has large windows, a terrace

and tables lit with candles. The menu extends beyond Germany and features many seasonal specials.

Eckhaus (☎ 491 197; Bornheimer Landstrasse 45; meals from €7) This is a relaxed restaurant and bar that serves well-priced salads and main dishes well into the evening. Nice outside area. Take the U-4 to Merianplatz.

CAFÉS

Walden (☎ 9288 2700; Kleiner Hirschgraben 7; meals €6-12) An über-trendy café near the centre. Breakfast is served until 5pm and you can go right from eggs to the lengthy cocktail list. At night there are DJs, soul and jazz.

Metropol (☎ 288 287; Weckmarkt 13-15; mains €7) Near the Dom, this popular place serves up café fare until late. Savour a coffee for hours with a book.

Café Karin (☎ 295 217; Grosser Hirschgraben 28; mains €9-15) Breakfast and whole-grain baked goods are the specialities at this understated place near the Zeil. The coffee is a treat as well.

APPLE-WINE TAVERNS

Apple-wine taverns are a Frankfurt's great local tradition. They serve *Ebbelwoi* (Frankfurt dialect for *Apfelwein*), an alcoholic apple cider, along with local specialities like *Handkäse mit Musik* (literally, 'hand-cheese with music'). This is a round cheese soaked in oil and vinegar and topped with onions; your bowel supplies the music. Some good *Ebbelwoi* are situated in Alt-Sachsenhausen.

Zur Germania (☎ 613 336; Textorstrasse 16; meals €7-15) This Sachsenhausen apple-wine tavern has a good outdoor area and is well-known for its huge pork roasts.

Zur Sonne (☎ 459 396; Berger Strasse 312; mains €7-16) This place has a fine yard for fair-weather imbibing in Bornheim. The schnitzels are excellent. Take the U4 to Bornheim-Mitte to get there

Adolf Wagner (☎ 612 565; Schweizer Strasse 71; meals €8-15; ☾) This old place has one of the most atmospheric interiors in Sachsenhausen. The garden is appealing as well.

SELF-CATERING

Off Hasenpetrolse, **Kleinmarkthalle** (Hasengasse 5-7; ☾ 7.30am-6pm Mon-Fri, to 3pm Sat) is a great produce market with loads of fruit, vegetables, meats and hot food.

Drinking

Many of the places listed under Eating are good for a drink, especially the apple wine joints.

Blaubart (☎ 282 229; Kaiserhofstrasse 18-20) In a large basement, the ceiling here is arched bricks. The long tables are lined with jolly beer-drinkers.

Zum Schwejk (☎ 293 166; Schäfferpetrolse 20) This is a popular gay bar. It is one of several on this street. Look for the blue mannequins out front.

Entertainment

Ballet, opera and theatre are strong features of Frankfurt's entertainment scene. Free *Frizz* has good listings (in German) of what's on in town. For information and bookings, go to **Städtische Bühnen** (☎ 134 0400; Willy-Brandt-Platz).

Forsythe Company (☎ 2123 7586; www.theforsythe company.de; Bockenheimer Depot; Carlo-Schmid-Platz 1) Easily the world's most talked-about dance company right now; the work of William Forsythe is often on tour.

Turm-Palast (☎ 281 787; Am Eschenheimer Turm) This is a multiscreen cinema with films in English.

Jazzkeller (☎ 288 537; Kleine Bockenheimer Strasse 18a) This club attracts top acts.

Mousonturm (☎ 4058 9520; Waldschmidtstrasse 4) Arty rock, dance performances and politically oriented cabaret are on tap at this converted soap factory in Bornheim.

U60311 (☎ 297 060 311; Rossmarkt 6) A top local club for techno, U60311 draws the best talent from around Europe. It's underground, literally.

Getting There & Away

AIR

Germany's largest airport is **Frankfurt airport** (FRA; ☎ 6901; www.airportcity-frankfurt.com), a vast labyrinth with connections throughout the world. It's served by most major airlines, although not many budget ones.

Only cynics like Ryanair would say that Frankfurt has another airport. **Frankfurt-Hahn airport** (HHN; www.hahn-airport.de) is 70km west of Frankfurt. Buses from Frankfurt's Hauptbahnhof take about two hours – longer than the flight from London. Given the journey time it's fitting the bus company is called **Bohr** (☎ 06543-501 90; www.bohr -omnibusse.de; adult/child €12/6; ☼ hourly).

BUS

The Deutsche-Touring Romantic Road bus (see p220) leaves from the south side of the Hauptbahnhof.

CAR

Frankfurt-am-Main features the famed Frankfurter Kreuz, the biggest autobahn intersection in the country. All the main car rental companies have offices in the main hall of the train station and at the airport.

TRAIN

The Hauptbahnhof handles more departures and arrivals than any station in Germany. Among the myriad of services: Berlin (€98, four hours, hourly), Hamburg (€93, 3½ hours, hourly) and Munich (€75, 3¾ hours). For Cologne take the fast (75 minutes) ICE line or the slower and more scenic line along the Rhine (€40, 2½ hours, hourly).

Many long-distance trains also stop at the airport. This station is beyond the S-Bahn station under Terminal 1.

Getting Around

TO/FROM THE AIRPORT

S-Bahn lines S8 and S9 run every 15 minutes between the airport and Frankfurt Hauptbahnhof (€3.35, 4.15am to 1am, 11 minutes), usually continuing via Hauptwache and Konstablerwache. Taxis (about €30) take 30 minutes without traffic jams.

The airport train station has two sections: platforms 1 to 3 (below Terminal 1, hall B) handle S-Bahn connections, while IC and ICE connections are in the long-distance train station 300m distant.

AUTHOR'S CHOICE

Why not enjoy Frankfurt's iconic apple wine while seeing the city? The **Ebbelwei-Express** (€5, apple wine extra; ☼ 1.30-5.30pm Sat & Sun) is a special tram that makes a circuit of all the city's principal sights every weekend year-round. The trams are decades old but the wood seats are the perfect venue for quaffing, munching a fresh pretzel and enjoying the sites. There's a reason every time you see one of these go by everyone on board has a huge grin. The trams stop all over town; get a schedule from the tourist offices.

GERMANY

PUBLIC TRANSPORT

Both single or day tickets for Frankfurt's excellent transport network (RMV; www .traffiQ.de) can be purchased from automatic machines at almost any train station or stop. The peak period short-trip tickets *(Kurzstrecken)* cost €1.35, single tickets cost €1.90 and a *Tageskarte* (24-hour ticket) costs €4.90 (€7.40 with the airport).

TAXI

Taxis are slow compared to public transport and expensive at €2.50 flag-fall plus a minimum of €1.60 per kilometre. There are numerous taxi ranks throughout the city, or you can book a cab (☎ 230 001, 25 00 01, 54 50 11).

NORTH RHINE-WESTPHALIA

One quarter of Germany's population, and an even larger chunk of its heavy industry, is crammed into the Rhine-Ruhr region. This is not only Germany's economic powerhouse, but also one of the most densely populated conurbations in the world. Though the area has some bleak industrial centres, Cologne and some other cities are steeped in history.

COLOGNE

☎ 0221 / pop 1 million

Cologne (Köln) seems almost ridiculously proud to be home to Germany's largest cathedral; the twin-tower shape of its weather-beaten Gothic hulk adorns the strangest souvenirs – from egg cosies and slippers to glassware and expensive jewellery. However, this bustling Rhine-side metropolis has much more to offer than its most recognisable and ubiquitous symbol. As early as the first century AD, Colonia Agrippinensis was an important Roman trading settlement. Today it's one of Germany's most multicultural spots, with a vibrant nightlife only partly fuelled by the local *Kölsch* beer.

Almost completely destroyed in WWII – except a fortuitously unscathed cathedral – Cologne has been rebuilt and meticulously restored since. *Et es, wie et es* (it is how it is) runs a familiar motto in the city dialect. Well, how is it exactly? *Joot* (good)!

Orientation

It's hard to miss the cathedral (Dom) on the doorstep of the main train station. From this, the centre of the tourist action, the pedestrianised and hideously congested Hohe Strasse runs south through the old town. Alternatively, there's a pleasant riverfront stroll 500m to the east.

The nightlife hubs of the Belgisches Viertel (tram 3, 4 or 5 to Friesenplatz) and the Zülpicher Viertel (trams 8 or 9 to Zülpicher Viertel/Bahnhof Süd) are several kilometres southwest.

Information

Future-Point (☎ 206 7251; Richmodstrasse 13; per 10 min €1; 🕑 10.30am-9pm Mon-Fri, 11.30am-8pm Sat & Sun) Internet access inside the trendy Café Lichtenberg.
Internet Café Colony (☎ 272 0630; per 10 min €0.40; Zülpicher Strasse 38-40; 🕑 10am-2am Mon-Sat, 11am-2am Sun) Wide range of services, including online laptop connection.
Köln Welcome Card (€9/14/19 for 24/48/72hr) Free public transport and discounted museum admission.
Main post office (☎ 01802-3333; WDR Centre, Breite Strasse 6-26; 🕑 9am-7pm Mon-Fri, 9am-2pm Sat)
Tourist office (☎ 2213 0400; www.koelntourismus.de; Unter Fettenhennen 19; 🕑 9am-9pm Mon-Sat, 10am-6pm Sun & hols Oct-Jun; 9am-10pm Mon-Sat, 10am-6pm Sun & hols Jul-Sep)

Sights & Activities
DOM

As easy as it is to get church-fatigue in Germany, the huge **Kölner Dom** (www.koelner-dom.de; admission free; 🕑 6am-7.30pm, no visitors during services) is one you shouldn't miss. Blackened with age, this gargoyle-festooned Gothic cathedral has a footprint of 12,470 sq metres, with twin spires soaring to 157m. Although its ground stone was laid in 1248, stop-start construction meant it wasn't finished until 1880, as a symbol of Prussia's drive for unification. Just over 60 years later it escaped WWII's heavy night-bombing largely intact. (No miracle, by the way. Allied pilots used it to navigate in an era before reliable radar.)

Sunshine filtering softly through stained-glass windows and the weak glow of candles are the only illumination in the moody, high-ceilinged interior.

Behind the altar lies the cathedral's most precious reliquary, the **Shrine of the Three Magi** (c 1150–1210), which reputedly contains the bones of the Three Wise Men.

GERMANY

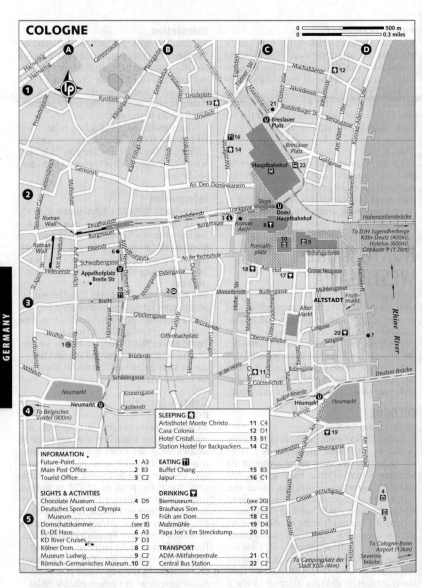

COLOGNE

INFORMATION
Future-Point..............................1 A3
Main Post Office........................2 B3
Tourist Office............................3 C2

SIGHTS & ACTIVITIES
Chocolate Museum.....................4 D5
Deutsches Sport und Olympia
  Museum..................................5 D5
Domschatzkammer..............(see 8)
EL-DE Haus...............................6 A3
KD River Cruises........................7 D3
Kölner Dom...............................8 C2
Museum Ludwig.........................9 C2
Römisch-Germanisches Museum..10 C2

SLEEPING
Artisthotel Monte Christo............11 C4
Casa Colonia..............................12 D1
Hotel Cristall..............................13 B1
Station Hostel for Backpackers.....14 C2

EATING
Buffet Chang..............................15 B3
Jaipur..16 C1

DRINKING
Biermuseum...........................(see 20)
Brauhaus Sion............................17 C3
Früh am Dom..............................18 C3
Malzmühle..................................19 D4
Papa Joe's Em Streckstump.........20 D3

TRANSPORT
ADM-Mitfahrzentrale...................21 C1
Central Bus Station......................22 C2

Brought to Cologne from Milan in the 12th century, it can just be glimpsed through the gates to the inner choir – although even this is impossible during Confession, when the entire choir is shut.

To see the shrine properly, you need to take a **guided tour** (adult/concession €4/2; 10.30am & 2.30pm Mon-Sat, 2.30pm Sun in English). Groups meet inside the main portal and tours in German (same price) are more frequent.

Alternatively, you can embark on the seriously strenuous endeavour of climbing the 509 steps of the Dom's **south tower** (adult/concession €2/1; 9am-5pm Mar-Sep, to 4pm Oct-Feb). You pass the 24-tonne **Peter Bell**, the world's largest working clanger, before emerging at 98.25m to magnificent views.

The renovated cathedral **treasury** (☎ 1794 0300; www.domschatzkammer-koeln.de; adult/concession €4/2; ☙ 10am-6pm) has a glittering collection of crowns and reliquaries.

MUSEUMS

South along the riverbank is the glass-walled **Chocolate Museum** (☎ 931 8880; www .schokoladenmuseum.de; Rheinauhafen; adult/concession €6/3.50; ☙ 10am-6pm Tue-Fri, 11am-7pm Sat & Sun, last entry 1hr before closing), famous for its fountain of liquid chocolate, whose aroma permeates the entire exhibition.

The neighbouring **Deutsches Sport und Olympia Museum** (☎ 336 090; www.sportmuseum -koeln.de, in German; Rheinauhafen 1; adult/concession €5/2.50; ☙ 10am-6pm Tue-Fri, 11am-7pm Sat & Sun) engagingly tells the history of the games with original souvenirs and multimedia displays.

Two prominent museums next to the cathedral might also take your fancy. The **Römisch-Germanisches Museum** (Roman Germanic Museum; ☎ 2212 2304; www.museenkoeln.de; Roncalliplatz 4; adult/concession €4/2; ☙ 10am-5pm Tue-Sun) displays artefacts from the Roman settlement in the Rhine Valley. The **Museum Ludwig** (☎ 2212 6165; www.museenkoeln.de; Bischofsgartenstrasse 1; adult/concession €7.50/5.50; ☙ 10am-6pm Tue-Sun, closed during Carnival) has an astoundingly good collection of 1960s Pop Art, German expressionism and Russian avant-garde painting, as well as photography.

The sombre **EL-DE Haus** (☎ 2212 6331; Appellhofplatz 23-25; adult/concession €2.50/1; ☙ 10am-4pm Tue-Fri, 11am-4pm Sat & Sun) documents Cologne's Nazi era.

Tours

Day cruises and Rhine journeys can be organised through **KD River Cruises** (☎ 208 8318; www.k-d.com; Frankenwerft 35). Day trips (10am, noon, 2pm and 6pm) cost €6.80. Sample one-way fares are €11.40 to Bonn and €35.60 to Koblenz.

Festivals & Events

Held just before Lent in late February or early March, Cologne's **Carnival** (Karneval) rivals Munich's Oktoberfest for exuberance, as people dress in creative costumes and party in the streets. Things kick off the Thursday before the seventh Sunday before

Easter and last until Monday (Rosenmontag), when there are formal and informal parades.

Sleeping

Accommodation prices in Cologne increase by at least 20% when fairs are on. For more options, the tourist office offers a room-finding service (€3).

BUDGET

Campingplatz der Stadt Köln (☎ 831 966; camp sites per person/site €4/4; ☙ Easter–mid-Oct) This place is on the riverbank on Weidenweg in Poll, 5km southeast of the city centre. There are excellent kitchen facilities and a small shop. Take the U16 to Marienburg and cross the Rodenkirchener bridge.

Jugendherberge Köln-Deutz (☎ 814 711; www .jugendherberge.de; Siegesstrasse 5a; dm €20) This is a behemoth of a hostel and while there's not much character in its green-grey rooms, those on the top floors have great views. Plus, everything feels clean and spanking new. It's a relatively easy 15-minute walk east from the main train station over the Hohenzollernbrücke.

Station Hostel for Backpackers (☎ 912 5301; www.hostel-cologne.de; Marzellenstrasse 44-56; dm €17-22, s €28-35, d €42-50, breakfast €3; ▯) Brightly patterned curtains can't quite disguise the basic quality of the dorms here. However, the place is convenient and the staff friendly and knowledgeable. It's a great spot to meet people.

Pension Jansen (☎ 251 85; www.pensionjansen .de; 2nd fl, Richard Wagner Strasse 18; s/d with shared bathroom from €40/65) This cute, well-cared-for pension has six individually decorated rooms with cheerful colours and motifs. Details like handmade wreaths hanging on aqua walls – or a big red rose screen-printed on the bed linen – convey a homey atmosphere. Book early.

MIDRANGE

Casa Colonia (☎ 160 6010; www.casa-colonia.de; Machabäerstrasse 63; s/d from €50/70) The young new owners plan to have this cosy Mediterranean charmer transformed into a cheap(ish) design hotel from early 2007, with sleek, minimalist rooms at affordable prices. Check the website for the latest details.

Artisthotel Monte Christo (☎ 277 4883; www .artisthotel-monte-christo.com; Grosse Sandkaul 24-26; s/d

€50/70) Above a club (ear-plugs provided) and with 5pm check-out, this louche hotel attracts dedicated bohemians, from Russian architecture professors to struggling DJs. The décor is camp and kitsch, with bright walls, plastic flowers, glitter-sprayed animal trophies and religious icons arranged in ways the Vatican probably wouldn't approve.

Hotel Chelsea (☎ 207 150; www.hotel-chelsea.de; Jülicher Strasse 1; s €70-160, d €80-175, ste €170-230; P) Another long-standing 'art' hotel, the Chelsea has an eye-catching roof extension. Its interior detailing is a little ordinary and nonsmokers might wish its rooms were aired more, but the overall vibe is good.

Hotel Cristall (☎ 163 00; www.hotelcristall.de; Ursulaplatz 9-11; s/d €70/90; P) The design here is a sort of womb-like, modern baroque, with low lighting and a gilt-framed romantic portrait of a woman in every room, but it also has black-and-white bathrooms and wooden floors (or black-and-white carpet tiles). Angular red, orange and purple sofas also greet you in the lobby.

Hotel Hopper et cetera (☎ 924 400; www.hopper .de; Brüsseler Strasse 26; s/d from €90/120; P) Parquet flooring, white linen and red chairs lend an elegant simplicity to this former monastery's rooms. The package is rounded off with a bar and sauna in separate parts of the vaulted cellar.

Eating
Cologne's beer halls serve meals but the city overflows with restaurants, especially around the Belgisches and Zülpicher Viertels.

Habibi (☎ 271 7141; Zülpicher Strasse 28; dishes €3-8; 11am-1am, to 3am Fri & Sat) A takeaway/restaurant with sturdy wooden tables and a smattering of decorated tiles, 'Beloved' it truly is among its young customers. Falafel joins kebabs, schawarma, halloumi cheese, hubbi (mince and almonds), mint tea on the house, and sweets.

Feynsinn (☎ 240 9210; Rathenauplatz 7; mains €5-10) The glint of artfully arranged glasses behind the mirrored bar will catch your eye from the street, as will the broken-glass chandeliers. Inside under murals, students, creative types and tourists tuck into curries, stews and other fare.

Alcazar (☎ 515 733; Bismarckstrasse 39; snacks €4-9, mains €9-15) The food and atmosphere are both hearty and warming at this old-school,

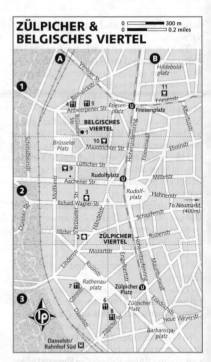

ZÜLPICHER & BELGISCHES VIERTEL

INFORMATION	
Cleanicum	1 A1

SLEEPING	
Hotel Chelsea	2 A2
Pension Jansen	3 A2

EATING	
Alcazar	4 A1
CurryCologne	5 A1
Feynsinn	6 A3
Fischermann's	7 A3
Habibi	8 B3

DRINKING	
Hallmackenreuther	9 A2
M20	10 A2
Päffgen	11 B1

slightly hippie pub. The changing menu always has one veggie option.

Hotelux (☎ 241 136; Von-Sandt Platz 10; €9-17; dinner only) Soviet leader Lenin and sailors from the Battleship Potemkin overlook the proceedings in this fun, red-lined restaurant. There's a 'metro' underground train compartment while the food runs the gamut from Russian and Georgian to Ukrainian and Armenian.

Jaipur (☎ 137 322; Marzellenstrasse 50-56; mains €9-18) The food is as authentic as the décor is excessive in Cologne's best Indian restaurant.

Fischermanns' (☎ 283 6285; Rathenauplatz 21; mains €10-17, 3-course set menu €26; ☽ dinner only) Elegant, with well-executed Eurasian cuisine, Fischermanns' is a favourite with locals celebrating a twenty- or thirty-something birthday or trying to impress a first-time date. But who needs an excuse to indulge?

Other recommendations:

CurryCologne (☎ 589 4556; Antwerperstrasse 5; dishes €2.50-6; ☽ 11am-11pm Mon-Thu, 11.30am-midnight Fri & Sat, 1-11pm Sun) A Wurst outlet goes designer and trendy.

Buffet Chang (☎ 250 9909; top fl, DuMont Carré Centre, Breite Strasse 80-90; all-you-can-eat buffet €6; ☽ 11am-9pm Mon-Sat, noon-7pm Sun) Plastic-and-formica Chinese canteen offering great value.

Drinking

As in Munich, beer in Cologne reigns supreme. More than 20 local breweries turn out a variety called *Kölsch*, which is relatively light and slightly bitter. The breweries run their own beer halls and serve their wares in skinny 200ml glasses.

BEER HALLS

Früh am Dom (☎ 258 0394; Am Hof 12-14) This three-storey beer hall and restaurant (including cellar bar) is the most central, with black-and-white flooring, copper pans and tiled ovens keeping it real, despite the souvenir shop. It's open for breakfast.

Päffgen (☎ 135 461; Friesenstrasse 64-66) Another favourite, this thrumming wood-lined room has its own beer garden. It's not far from the bars of the Belgisches Viertel.

Malzmühle (☎ 210 117; Heumarkt 6) Attracting more locals than most, possibly because of the 10L 'Pittermännchen' kegs that customers can roll home.

Brauhaus Sion (☎ 257 8540; Unter Taschenmacher 9) A traditional-looking, low-lit option, with Wurst sold by the metre.

BARS

For more options, take a tram to Zülpicher Platz and explore.

Biermuseum (☎ 257 7802; Buttermarkt 39) This is a good-time place with 18 varieties of the amber liquid on tap but not one iota of class.

Papa Joe's Em Streckstrump (☎ 257 7931; Buttermarkt 37) Live New Orleans jazz provides the

---

MY BEAUTIFUL LAUNDRETTE

No, even we can't quite believe we're enthusing about a self-service laundrette here. However, there can't be many better places to air your dirty laundry than Cologne's **Cleanicum** (www.cleanicum.de; Brusseler Strasse 74-76; loads from €3; ☽ 10am-1am Mon-Fri, 9am-1am Sat, 11am-10pm Sun). Its washing machines and dryers sit in the middle of a 'lounge' establishment that also includes sofas, magazines, a TV area, Internet terminals, a retro 1970s cocktail bar and a vibrating massage chair (€1 for 15 minutes). There's even a double bed should doing the housework make you particularly tired or frisky.

A similar, albeit less central, operation exists in Hamburg, too (p274).

---

soundtrack in this intimate pub, serving beer in larger than normal glasses for Cologne.

Hallmachenreuther (☎ 517 970; Brüsseler Platz 9) Oatmeal, white and lilacs are used in this popular café bar's retro interior. Good for a late breakfast or a late drink.

Hotelux (☎ 350 0870; Rathenauplatz 22) The little sister of the Hotelux restaurant (see Eating) serves cocktails and 'Soviet water' (ie vodka) in a similarly themed environment.

Entertainment

Gebäude 9 (☎ 814 637; Deutz-Mülheimer Strasse 127-129) Once a factory, this is now a Cologne nightlife stalwart, with clubbing, concerts, a cinema and theatre. Expect anything from drum'n'bass, indie pop, gypsy music and '60s trash to film noir and puppets.

M20 (☎ 519 666; Maastricher Strasse 20) This popular retro cocktail bar sports cube-shaped lights and brown leather sofas. Regular DJ evenings favour indie guitar rock, but some live acts play more laid-back Latin music.

Getting There & Away

AIR

Cologne-Bonn airport (CGN; www.airport-cgn.de) is growing in importance. There are now direct flights to New York, while budget airline German Wings (www.germanwings.com) uses this as its hub, notably offering cheap flights to Moscow and St Petersburg, among others.

GERMANY

CAR

The city is on a main north–south autobahn route and is easily accessible for drivers and hitchhikers. The **ADM-Mitfahrzentrale** (☎ 194 40; www.citynetz-mitfahrzentrale.de; Maximinen Strasse 2) is near the train station.

TRAIN

There are frequent RE services operating to both nearby Bonn (€6, 18 minutes) and Düsseldorf (€10 to €16, 25 to 30 minutes) as well as to Aachen (€12.50, 45 to 50 minutes). Frequent EC, IC, or ICE trains go to Hanover (€56, three hours), Frankfurt-am-Main (€55, 1¼ hours, three hourly) and Berlin (€93, 4¼ hours, hourly). Frequent Thalys high-speed services connect Cologne to Paris (€85.50, four hours) via Aachen and Brussels; rail pass-holders get only a small discount on this.

Getting Around

S-Bahn 13 runs between Cologne/Bonn airport and the main train station every 15 minutes from 5.30am to 11.20pm daily (€2.20, 20 minutes). Key in code 2000 for Köln Hauptbahnhof. Bus 670 goes to Bonn every half-hour.

Buses and trams serve the inner city, with local trains handling trips up to 50km away, including Bonn. A one-day pass costs €6 if you're staying near the city (one or two zones), €9 for most of the Cologne area (four zones); and €13.30 including Bonn (seven zones). Single city trips cost €1.20, while 1½-hour two-zone tickets are €2.20.

AROUND COLOGNE

Bonn

☎ 0228 / pop 293,000

South of Cologne on the Rhine's banks, Bonn became West Germany's temporary capital in 1949. But exactly 50 years later it was demoted when most (but not quite all) government departments returned to Berlin.

The city's brief tenure as capital, however, has left it with an excellent collection of museums. These, plus its status as Beethoven's birthplace and some 18th-century baroque architecture, make it worth a day trip.

The **tourist office** (☎ 775 000; www.bonn-regio.de; Windeckstrasse 1; ☺ 9am-6.30pm Mon-Fri, to 4pm Sat, 10am-2pm Sun) is a three-minute walk along Poststrasse from the Hauptbahnhof, and can fill you in with any extra details.

Ludwig van Beethoven fans will head straight to the **Beethoven-Haus** (☎ 981 7525; www .beethoven-haus-bonn.de; Bonngasse 24-26; adult/concession €4/3; ☺ 10am-6pm Mon-Sat, 11am-5pm Sun Apr-Oct, closing at 5pm Nov-Mar), where the composer was born in 1770. The house contains memorabilia concerning his life and music, including his last piano, with an amplified sounding board to accommodate his deafness. There's a new multimedia section and a shop selling kitschy souvenirs tinnily chiming the Ninth Symphony. The annual Beethoven Festival takes place September to October.

The **Haus der Geschichte der Bundesrepublik Deutschland** (FRG History Museum; ☎ 916 50; www.hdg .de; Willy-Brandt-Allee 14; admission free; ☺ 9am-7pm Tue-Sun) presents Germany's postwar history. It is part of the **Museumsmeile**, four museums that also includes the **Kunstmuseum** (☎ 776 260; Friedrich-Ebert-Allee 2; adult/concession €5/2.50; ☺ 10am-6pm Tue-Sun, to 9pm Wed); and the **Kunst-und Ausstellungshalle der Bundesrepublik Deutschland** (☎ 917 1200; Friedrich-Ebert-Allee 2; adult/concession €7/3.50; ☺ 10am-9pm Tue & Wed, 10am-7pm Thu-Sun).

Those wanting to go a bit further might consider combining their trip to Bonn with a visit to the spa town of Bad Godesberg.

From Cologne, it's quicker to take an RE train to Bonn (€6, 18 minutes) than a tram (€13.30 day pass, 55 minutes each way). For river trips, see p257.

DÜSSELDORF

☎ 0211 / pop 571,000

'D-Town' or 'The City D', as local magazine editors like to call Düsseldorf, is Germany's fashion capital. But that means Jil Sander and Wolfgang Joop rather than cutting-edge streetwear, as you'll soon discover observing fur-clad *Mesdames* with tiny dogs along the ritzy shopping boulevard of the Königsallee.

Indeed, this elegant and wealthy town could feel stiflingly bourgeois if it weren't for its lively old-town pubs, its position on the Rhine, its excellent art galleries and the postmodern architecture of its Mediahafen. Fortunately, those are more than enough to make up for its pretensions.

Orientation

The train station lies at the southeastern edge of the old town, about 1km west of the Rhine River. The Mediahafen and Rheinturm are much further south, on the riverbank.

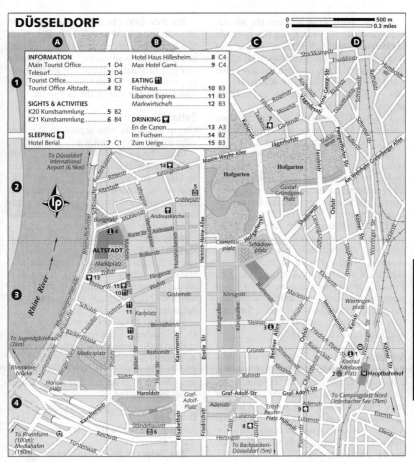

DÜSSELDORF

0 ————— 500 m
0 ————— 0.3 miles

INFORMATION
Main Tourist Office..............1 D4
Telesurf..............................2 D4
Tourist Office......................3 C3
Tourist Office Altstadt..........4 B2

SIGHTS & ACTIVITIES
K20 Kunstsammlung..............5 B2
K21 Kunstsammlung..............6 B4

SLEEPING
Hotel Berial.........................7 C1

Hotel Haus Hillesheim...........8 C4
Max Hotel Garni...................9 C4

EATING
Fischhaus............................10 B3
Libanon Express....................11 B3
Markwirtschaft......................12 B3

DRINKING
En de Canon.........................13 A3
Im Fuchsen...........................14 B2
Zum Uerige...........................15 B3

GERMANY

Information

Telesurf (Graf-Adolf-Strasse 102; per 15 min €0.50; ⏰ 10am-4am Mon-Sat, 10am-midnight Sun) Minutes left of the train station.

Tourist office (www.duesseldorf-tourismus.de) Main office (☎ 172 0222; Immermannstrasse 65B; ⏰ 10am-6pm Mon-Sat); branch office (☎ 602 5753; Burg Platz; ⏰ noon-6pm) branch office (☎ 300 4897; Sparkasse bldg, Berliner Allee 33; ⏰ 10am-6pm Mon-Sat)

Sights & Activities

Düsseldorf has a lively **Altstadt** (old town), filled with enough restaurants, beer halls and pubs to have earned it the slightly exaggerated title of the 'longest bar in the world'. In the central **Marktplatz** you'll find a statue of the former ruler, or elector, Jan Wellem.

What really sets the city apart, however, is the contemporary architecture of its **Mediahafen**. Here, in the city's south, docks have been transformed into an interesting commercial park, most notably including the **Neuer Zollhof**, three typically curved and twisting buildings by Bilbão Guggenheim architect Frank Gehry. You'll find a map of the park on a billboard behind (ie on the street side of) the red-brick Gehry building.

For a bird's-eye view of the Mediahafen, and indeed all of Düsseldorf, catch the express elevator to the 168m viewing platform of the neighbouring **Rheinturm** (adult/child €3.50/1.50; ⏰ 10am-11.30pm). There's also a revolving restaurant and cocktail bar a level above, at 172.5m.

It's a pleasant stroll between the Media-hafen and the Altstadt along the riverside **Rheinuferpromenade**. River cruises are also possible (see KD River Cruises, p257).

Alternatively, you can join the city's elite window-shopping along the **Königsallee**, or 'Kö' – Düsseldorf's answer to Rodeo Drive or the Ginza strip.

Two excellent galleries, sharing the same collection, form the backbone of Düsseldorf's reputation as a city of art.

K20 (☎ 838 10; www.kunstsammlung.de; Grabeplatz 5; adult/concession €6.50/4.50; ☙ 10am-6pm Tue-Fri, 11am-6pm Sat & Sun), containing earlier 20th-century masters, is frequently given over to blockbuster special exhibitions with lengthy queues.

K21 (☎ 838 1600; www.kunstsammlung.de; Ständehausstrasse 1; adult/concession €6.50/4.50; combination ticket €10/8) concentrates on art from 1990 onwards. Highlights include Nam June Paik's TV Garden, local artist's Katarina Fritsch's giant black mouse sitting on a sleeping man, the psychedelically decorated bar and the glassed-in roof. Sadly, there are only two panoramic photos by famous Düsseldorfer Andreas Gursky.

Sleeping

Backpackers-Düsseldorf (☎ 302 0848; www.backpackers-duesseldorf.de; Fürstenwall 180; dm €20; ☐) This modern hostel adds bright colours and table football to soft beds and great service to come out a real winner. Near the Mediahafen, it's reached from the train station by bus 725 to Kirchplatz, from where there are several trams into town.

Jugendgästehaus (☎ 557310; www.jugendherberge.de; Düsseldorfer Strasse 1; dm €22, s/d from €26/48) On the other bank of the Rhine in posh Oberkassel, this will remain open while undergoing renovation until 2008.

Hotel Haus Hillesheim (☎ 386 860; www.hotel-hillesheim.de; Jahnstrasse 19; s/d €60/70, with shared bathroom €40/55; ℗ ☐) Crammed with animal trophies, plants and all manner of bric-a-brac, this dimly lit pub has homey rooms both above it and quieter ones in the garden behind.

Hotel Berial (☎ 490 0490; Gartenstrasse 30; www.hotelberial.de; s/d €60/80; ☒ ☐) A youthful ambience reigns here, thanks to the staff and the contemporary furnishings. Décor features lots of blue, blond wood, glass bathroom doors and some bright prints.

Max Hotel Garni (☎ 386 800; www.max-hotelgarni.de; Adersstrasse 65; s/d/tr €65/75/90; ☐) With touches of lime green, up-lighting, red carpet along the wall of one hall and some squiggly original portraits, this lovely modern place has a cheerful atmosphere. Ring ahead to snaffle one of the 11 rooms.

Eating

Cheap meals are also served in the beer halls listed under Drinking.

Libanon Express (☎ 134917; Berger Strasse 19-21; café €2.50-13, restaurant €8-19) Crammed with mirrors and tiles – and with recommendations stickered on the window – this café serves great kebabs, falafel and other Middle-Eastern specialities. Belly dancers perform Wednesday to Saturday in the restaurant next door.

Marktwirtschaft (☎ 860 6848; Benrather Strasse 7; mains €6.50-14.50) With American diner–like red-leather banquettes, this neighbourhood restaurant serves comforting home-style food, ranging from a plate of steamed vegetables to Dutch *matjes*, Wiener schnitzel and Argentinean steak.

Fischhaus (☎ 854 9864; Berger Strasse 3-7; mains €9-26) This huge, glass-fronted seafood restaurant is the sort of classic affair that never goes out of fashion, and buzzes with all ages and demographics. The setting is just formal enough to make it feel special, without being intimidating.

Drinking

Alt beer, a dark and semisweet brew, is typical of Düsseldorf.

Zum Uerige (☎ 866 990; Berger Strasse 1) In this noisy, cavernous place, the trademark Uerige Alt beer flows so quickly that the waiters just carry around trays and give you a glass whenever they spy one empty.

Im Fuchsen (☎ 828 955; Ratzingerstrasse 28) The 'Little Fox' is a typically rumbustious Rheinish beer hall, with *Schweinhaxe* (knuckle of pork) and other local fare.

En de Canon (☎ 329 798; Zollstrasse 7) This centuries-old tavern is popular in summer for its beer garden.

Getting There & Away

From **Düsseldorf International** (DUS: www.duesseldorf-international.de), trains go directly to other German cities, while frequent S-Bahn services (1 and 7) head to Düsseldorf train station.

Low-cost carrier Ryanair uses **Niederrhein (Weeze) airport** (NRN; www.flughafen-niederrhein.de) and it is the usual wheeze. The **shuttle bus** (☎ 06543-501 90; www.bohr-omnibusse.de) to Düsseldorf (€11; 1¼ hours) leaves soon after the plane's scheduled arrival.

The many train services from Düsseldorf include to Cologne (€10 to €16, 25 to 30 minutes), Frankfurt-am-Main (€65, two hours), Hanover (€46 to €49, 2¾ hours) and Hamburg (€63 to €73, 3½ to four hours).

Getting Around

The metro, trams and buses are useful to cover Düsseldorf's distances. Up to three stops (*Kurzstrecke*) costs €1.10, a ticket for the centre €2 and for the greater city €3.80. Day-passes start at €4.70

AACHEN

☎ 0241 / pop 244,000

If you fancy an indulgent mini-break, Aachen has the perfect recipe. Before reaching its relaxing thermal baths, you'll find yourself wandering narrow cobbled streets past quirky fountains, shops full of gingerbread, one of Germany's most famous cafés, and a small but perfectly formed cathedral.

The town's curative thermal springs were the reason the great Frankish conqueror Charlemagne (Karl der Grosse) made this his capital in 794, and the cathedral he built consolidated its fame. Its proximity to the Netherlands and Belgium gives Aachen – Aken or Aix La Chappelle in Dutch or French – a dynamic international personality, while its large student population saves it from being too touristy and twee.

Orientation

Aachen's compact centre is contained within two ring roads roughly tracing the old city walls. The inner ring road, or Grabenring, changes names – most ending in 'graben' – and encloses the old city proper. To get to the tourist office from the Hauptbahnhof, cross Römerstrasse, follow Bahnhofstrasse north and then go left along Theaterstrasse to Kapuzinergraben.

Information

The Web (☎ 997 9210; Kleinmarschierstrasse 74-76; per 10 min €0.50; ☺ 10am-11pm Mon-Thu, to 3am Fri & Sat, 11am-10pm Sun)

Tourist office (☎ 180 2960/1; www.aachen.de; Atrium Elisenbrunnen, Kapuzinergraben; ☺ 9am-6pm Mon-Fri, to 2pm Sat year-round, plus 10am-2pm Sun Apr-Dec)

Sights

OLD TOWN & FOUNTAINS

Next to the tourist office is the **Elisenbrunnen**, the only town fountain with drinkable water; despite its sulphuric 'rotten eggs' smell, it's supposedly good for the digestion.

In the far left-hand corner of the park behind the Elisenbrunnen, you'll find the **Geldbrunnen**, which represents the circulation of money. The comical figures around the pool clutch their coins or purses while the water is sucked down the central plughole (jokingly known as 'the taxman').

Head east along the top of the park here, towards Forum M, and turn left into Buchkremerstrasse. Soon you'll reach a fountain with a scary-looking creature. This is the mythological **Bahkauv**, which was rumoured to jump on the backs of those returning late

---

THE DEVIL'S IN THE DETAIL

If the devil has all the best music, he also has the funniest myths. Aachen lore, for example, has it that you haven't really visited the town unless you've touched the thumb of hell's black prince.

The legend goes that a mysterious benefactor appeared when the town needed more money to finish its cathedral. Locals recognised him as Lucifer by his cloven hoofs, but being *lues* (cunning and crafty, in the local dialect) hatched a plan to deal with him. They agreed when he asked to be paid with the soul of the first being to enter the cathedral, and when the time came released a wolf into the building. Satan pounced on the creature, but flew into a rage on realising he'd been cheated. Storming out of the cathedral, he slammed the door so hard he trapped his thumb.

Today, a statue of the wolf (or Roman bear) stands in the cathedral's antechamber, with a hole in its chest from where its soul was ripped. Meanwhile, 'the devil's thumb' remains stuck in the main cathedral doors – between the side doors currently used. Inside the lion's head on the right-hand door, you can feel, well, a digit-shaped something.

from the pub and demand a lift all the way home.

Buchkremerstrasse becomes Buchel. Turn left just past **Leo van den Daele** (see right), then right again, you'll come to Hühnermarkt, with its **Hühnerdiebbrunnen** (Chicken thief fountain). The hasty thief hasn't noticed one of his stolen chickens is a rooster and is about to unmask him by crowing.

From here, Aachen's main **Markt** is visible just to the northeast. The 14th-century **Rathaus** (adult/concession €2/1; ☒ 10am-5pm Mon-Fri, to 1pm & 2-5pm Sat & Sun) overlooks the Markt, while a fountain statue of **Charlemagne** is in the middle.

Head back down the hill along Krämerstrasse until you come to the **Puppenbrunnen** (Puppet fountain), where you're allowed to play with the movable bronze figures.

Continuing in the same direction for 50m, you'll arrive at Aachen's famous Dom.

DOM

While Cologne's cathedral wows you with its size and atmosphere, Aachen's similarly Unesco-listed **Dom** (Kaiserdom or Münster; www .aachendom.de; ☒ 7am-7pm) impresses with its shiny neatness. The small, Byzantine-inspired **octagon** at the building's heart dates from 805 but was refurbished in 2003, so its ceiling mosaics glitter and its marble columns gleam.

The building's historical significance stems not just from Charlemagne's having ordered it built, but that 30 Holy Roman emperors were crowned here from 936 to 1531.

The brass **chandelier** hanging in the centre was donated by Emperor Friedrich Barbarossa in 1165. Meanwhile, standing at the main altar and looking back towards the door, it's just possible to glimpse Charlemagne's simple marble throne. The man himself lies in the golden **shrine** behind the altar. The cathedral became a site of pilgrimage after his death; there's a major pilgrimage at the start of June 2007.

Multilingual leaflets in the antechamber provide a concise cathedral guide.

THERMAL BATHS

The 8th-century Franks were first lured to 'Ahha' (water) for its thermal springs. And just over 1200 years later, the state-of-the-art **Carolus Thermen** (Carolus Thermal Baths; ☎ 182 740; www.carolus-thermen.de; Stadtgarten/Passstrasse 79;

without/with sauna from €9.50/19) are still reeling them in.

That's hardly surprising, for the complex is part therapeutic spa – good for rheumatism etc – and part swimming centre. Quirky currents whiz you around one pool, water jets bubble up in another and taps pour out cold water in yet another (under which single travellers might wish to shove the many canoodling couples…). Only diehard fans should pay for the sauna, as there's – bizarrely – a steam room accessible to all.

The baths are in the city garden, northeast of the centre.

Sleeping

Jugendgästehaus (☎ 711 010; www.jugendherberge .de; Maria-Theresia-Allee 260; dm €22, s/d €36.50/54; **P** 🖳) This modern DJH outpost sits on a hill overlooking the city, and gets lots of school groups. Take bus 2 to Ronheide.

Hotel Marx (☎ 375 41; www.hotel-marx.de; Hubertusstrasse 33-35; s/d €50/75, with shared bathroom from €35/60) There's a garden with pond out of the back of this traditional family-run place. Inside the rooms are decent, even if the bathrooms are a little cramped.

Hotel Domicil (☎ 705 1200; www.domicilaachen .de; Lütticher Strasse 27; s €75-85, d €100-110; **P** ✕) This elegant, neutrally decorated hotel feels like an apartment complex. It's set across two 19th-century terrace houses with its own garden in a quiet district, yet just 10 minutes on foot from the centre.

Hotel Drei Könige (☎ 483 93; www.h3k-aachen .de; Büchel 5; s €80-90, d €110-120, ste from €120; ✕ 🖳) The renovated Drei Könige has classy rooms with iron-frame beds (some four-poster) and different Mediterranean colour schemes in each, from cool pale green to sienna red.

Eating & Drinking

Aachen's students have their own 'Latin Quarter' along **Pontstrasse**, with dozens of bars and cheap eats. The street heads northeast off the Markt and runs for nearly a kilometre.

Vitaminbar (☎ 409 3912; Alexaniergraben 13-15; dishes €2.50-6.50) Exotic options like Iranian and Russian are among this café's dozens of tasty sandwich fillings. The salads are just as diverse.

Leo van den Daele (☎ 357 24; Büchel 18; dishes €4.50-8.50) A warren of 17th-century rooms linked by crooked stairs across four merchants' homes, this nationally renowned café specialises in gingerbread, or Printen. Yet you can also enjoy light meals – soups, sandwiches, quiches and *pastetchen* (vol au vents) – among its tiled stoves and antique knick-knacks.

Rose am Dom (☎ 287 82; Fischmarkt 1; mains €8-16) Being stationed in the cathedral's former kitchen gives this place a medieval atmosphere, although its partly seasonal menu is more modern and international. When mussels are on, it's hard to believe you're not in Belgium.

Getting There & Away

There are twice-hourly trains to Cologne (€12.50, 45 to 50 minutes) and Liège (€9.90, 40 minutes), as well as transfers from Düsseldorf and Köln-Bonn airports. The high-speed Thalys train passes through regularly on its way to Brussels and Paris (€80.50, 3½ hours). There's also a frequent bus to Maastricht. The bus station is at the northeastern edge of Grabenring on the corner of Kurhausstrasse and Peterstrasse.

Getting Around

Most points of interest are easily reached on foot, although the baths are a bit of a hike. Buses cost €1.45 (trip of a few stops), €2 (regular single) or €5 (day pass).

LOWER SAXONY

Lower Saxony (Niedersachsen) likes to make much of its half-timbered towns. Hamelin is certainly a true fairy-tale beauty, and leaning Lüneberg is quite unlike any other you'll see. However, the state is also home to the famous Volkswagen car company, while even the business-minded capital, Hanover, has its diversions. See also 'Bewitching Harz', p202.

HANOVER

☎ 0511 / pop 523,000

German comedians – yes, they do exist – like to dismiss Hanover as 'the autobahn exit between Göttingen and Walsrode'. However, the capital of Lower Saxony is nowhere near that grim. While it's famous for hosting trade fairs, particularly the huge CEBIT computer show in March, it also boasts acres of greenery in the Versailles-like Herrenhäuser Gärten (gardens).

Parts of the central Altstadt (old town) look medieval, but few of them are. They're mostly clever fakes built after intense WWII bombing.

Information

Hannover Tourismus (☎ information 1234 5111, ☎ room reservations 1234 555; www.hannover.de; Ernst-August-Platz 8; ☻ 9am-6pm Mon-Fri, 9am-2pm Sat)
Teleklick Hannover (Schillerstrasse 23; ☻ 10am-11pm Mon-Sat, noon-10pm Sun) Internet access.

Sights & Activities

The enormous **Grosser Garten** (Large Garden; admission €3, free in winter) is the highlight of the **Herrenhäuser Gärten** (☎ 1684 7576; www.hannover.de /herrenhausen/start.htm; ☻ 9am-sunset). It has a small maze and Europe's tallest fountain. Check the website in summer for Wasserspiele, when all fountains are synchronised, and the night-time **Illuminations**. The **Niki de Saint Phalle Grotto** is a magical showcase of the artist's work. She was French – her colourful figures adorn the famous Stravinsky fountain outside the Centre Pompidou in Paris – but developed a special relationship with Hanover. There's a popular beer garden in the Grosser Garten. Alternatively, the flora of the **Berggarten** (Mountain Garden; €2, combined entry with Grosser Garten €4) is interesting.

The **Neues Rathaus** (new town hall) was built between 1901 and 1913. Town models in the foyer reveal the extent of WWII devastation. There's a pleasant lakeside café and, if you don't mind queuing, a **curved lift** (adult/ child €2/1.50; ☻ 10am-6pm Apr-Nov) to a 98m viewing platform.

Beside the Leine River since 1974, are **Die Nanas**, three fluorescent-coloured, earth-mama sculptures by de Saint Phalle. Although major Hanover landmarks, they're best seen on Saturday, when there's a flea market at their feet.

In summer, the **Machsee** (lake) has **ferries** (crossing €3, tour €6) and numerous boats for hire. There's a free public **swimming beach** on the southeast shore.

Sleeping

The tourist office only finds private rooms during trade fairs but can arrange hotel bookings year-round for a fee.

Jugendherberge (☎ 131 7674; www.jugend herberge.de; Ferdinand-Wilhelm-Fricke-Weg 1; dm junior/ senior from €18/21; ℗ ▣) This large space-lab

MORE FAIRY-TALE TOWNS

Kids in particular will love Hamelin, just one of 60 towns situated on Germany's so-called **Märchenstrasse** (Fairytale Road; ☎ 0561-707 707; www.deutsche-maerchenstrasse.de; Obere Königsstrasse 15, Kassel). Many Grimms' fairy tales originated along this meandering route, which stretches 600km north from Hanau to Bremen. Polle boasts 'Cinderella's castle' for example, the Rapunzel tale hails from a tower in Trendelburg, and Puss in Boots first stepped out in Oedelsheim. For more details, visit the comprehensive multilingual website.

looking structure houses a modern hostel with breakfast room and terrace bar overlooking the river. Take U3 or U7 to Fischerhof, cross the Lodemannbrücke bridge and turn right.

GästeResidenz PelikanViertel (☎ 399 90; www.gaesteresidenz-pelikanviertel.de; Pelikanstrasse 11; s €40-230, d €60-260, tr €80-280; **P**) Upmarket student residence meets budget hotel, this huge complex has a wide range of plain but very pleasant rooms, all with kitchenettes. Prices fluctuate wildly, so try to avoid trade fair periods. Take U9 to Pelikanstrasse.

City Hotel Flamme (☎ 388 8004; www.cityhotel flamme.de; Lammstrasse 3; s €50-65, d €75-90; **P**) Rooms are arranged around a light-filled courtyard with a glass curtain-wall frontage, and the owners will pick you up from the nearby train station.

Lühmanns Hotel am Rathaus (☎ 326 268; www.hotelamrathaus.de; Friedrichswall 21; s €60-85, d €75-90, f €120-140; **✕ 🖥**) Arty posters and even the odd original work of art fill this comfy, tasteful choice. Although it is located on a busy street, double glazing keeps the noise at bay.

Other recommendations:

City Hotel am Thielenplatz (☎ 327 691; www.smartcity hotel.de; Thielenplatz 2; s €40-50, d €50-60; **P ✕ 🖥**) Could be fabulous when a retro 1950s conversion is finished.

Etap Hotel (☎ 235 5570; www.etaphotel.com; Runde Strasse 7; s/d €40/50; 🖥) Garish but comfortable chain hotel, right near the train station.

Eating & Drinking

Markthalle (Karmarschstrasse 49; dishes €3.50-8) This huge covered market of food stalls and gourmet delicatessens is a no-nonsense place for a quick bite – both carnivorous and vegetarian.

Maestro (☎ 300 8575; Sophienstrasse 2; mains €4.50-8) This atmospheric subterranean restaurant offers an all-you-can-eat vegetarian buffet (€7) at lunch daily. Its tucked-away courtyard beer garden (shh!) is perfect in summer.

Mr Phung Kabuki (☎ 215 7609; Friedrichswall 10; sushi €2-6, most mains €7-14) Boats bob by on the water-based sushi chain, but you can order all manner of pan-Asian and wok dishes in this airy, trendy restaurant with an enormous range of spirits.

Pier 51 (☎ 807 1800; Rudolf von Bennigsen Ufer 51; mains €6-18) This atmospheric glass-walled cube juts out into the Maschsee, and has an outside 'Piergarten' with old-fashioned covered straw seats. Cuisine is modern and international.

Brauhaus Ernst August (☎ 365 950; Schmiedestrasse 13a) A local institution, the Brauhaus Ernst August brews its own Hannöversch beer.

Getting There & Around

Hanover's **airport** (HAJ; www.hannover-airport.de) has many connections, including on low-cost carrier Air Berlin (www.airberlin.com).

There are frequent train services to Hamburg (€36, 1¼ hours), Berlin (€53, 1½ hours), Cologne (€56, three hours) and Munich (€101, five hours), among others.

U-Bahn lines from the Hauptbahnhof are boarded in the station's north (follow the signs towards Raschplatz), except the U10 and U17, which are overground trams leaving near the tourist office.

Most visitors only travel in the central 'Hannover' zone. Single tickets are €1.90 and day passes €3.60.

The S-Bahn (S5) takes 16 minutes to the airport (€3.20).

AROUND HANOVER
Hamelin

☎ 05151 / pop 59,000

Some German towns just look like they came straight from a fairy story. Thanks to the Brothers Grimm, others are even more inextricably linked. In the 19th century, the two brothers documented national folklore, and their subsequent collection of tales means the name Hamelin (Hameln in German) will be forever associated with 'the Pied Piper of'.

Of course, according to the story, this quaint, ornate town got rid of all its rats when the piper *(Der Rattenfänger)* lured them into the Weser River in the 13th century – and then lost all its children when it refused to pay him. However, you wouldn't really know it. Today, rat-shaped bread, marzipan-filled *Rattenfängertorte* (Pied Piper cake) and fluffy rat toys fill the shops, while 'the Pied Piper' himself can be seen in various tourist guide guises, mesmerising onlooking children with haunting tunes.

The train station is about 800m east of the centre. To get to **Hameln Tourist Information** (☎ 957 823; www.hameln.de/touristinfo; Diesterallee 1; ☺ 9am-6pm Mon-Fri year-round; 9.30am-4pm Sat, 9.30am-1pm Sun May-Sep, 9.30am-1pm Sat Oct-Apr) take bus 2, 3, 4, 12, 21, 33 or 34.

The best way to explore is to follow the **Pied Piper trail** – the line of white rats drawn on the pavements. There are information posts at various points. They're in German, but at least you know when to stop to admire the various restored 16th- to 18th-century half-timbered houses.

The **Rattenfängerhaus** (Rat Catcher's House; Osterstrasse 28), from 1602, is perhaps the finest example, with its steep and richly decorated gable. Also not to be missed is the **Hochzeitshaus** (1610–17) at the Markt (square) end of Osterstrasse. The **Rattenfänger Glockenspiel** at the far end chimes daily at 9.35am and 11.35am, while a **carousel of Pied Piper figures** twirls at 1.05pm, 3.35pm and 5.35pm.

Frequent S-Bahn trains (S5) head from Hanover to Hamelin (€9.10, 50 minutes). By car, take the B217 to/from Hanover.

WOLFSBURG

☎ 05361 / pop 124,000

There's no doubt in Wolfsburg that Volkswagen is king – from the huge VW emblem adorning the company's global headquarters (and a factory the size of a small country) to the insignia on almost every vehicle. 'Golfsburg', as it's nicknamed after one of it's most successful models, does a nice sideline in modern architecture. But here in 'the capital of Volkswagen', a brave-new-world theme park called Autostadt is top of the bill.

LÜNEBURG: THE WOBBLY TOWN

With an off-kilter church steeple, buildings leaning on each other and houses with swollen 'beer-belly' façades, it's as if charming Lüneburg has drunk too much of the Pilsener lager it used to brew.

Of course, the city's wobbly angles and uneven pavements have a more prosaic cause. For centuries until 1980, Lüneburg was a salt-mining town, and as this 'white gold' was extracted from the earth, ground shifts and subsidence knocked many buildings sideways. Inadequate drying of the plaster in the now-swollen façades merely added to this asymmetry.

But knowing the scientific explanation never detracts from the pleasure of being on Lüneburg's comic-book crooked streets.

Between Hanover (€23, one hour; or €17 return Niedersachsen Ticket for 1¾-hour ME services) and Hamburg (€11, 30 minutes), the city's an undemanding day trip from either. From the train station, head west into town towards the highly visible, 14th-century **St Johanniskirche**, whose 106m-high spire leans 2.2m off true. Local legend has it that the architect tried to kill himself by jumping off it. (He fell into a hay cart and was saved, but celebrating his escape later in the pub drank himself into a stupor, fell over, hit his head and died after all.)

The church stands at the eastern end of the city's oldest square, **Am Sande**, full of typically Hanseatic stepped gables. At the western end stands the beautiful black-and-white **Industrie und Handelskammer** (Trade and Industry Chamber).

Continue one block past the Handelskammer and turn right into restaurant-lined Schröderstrasse, which leads to the **Markt**, where the **ornate Rathaus** contains the **tourist office** (☎ 207 6620; www.lueneburg.de; ☺ 9am-5pm Mon-Fri, to 4pm Sat & Sun May-Sep, 9am-5pm Mon-Fri, to 2pm Sat Oct-Apr).

Admire the square, before continuing west along Waagestrasse and down our favourite Lüneburg street, **Auf dem Meere**, en route to the **St Michaeliskirche**. Here the wonky façades and wavy pavements are like something from the 1919 German expressionist movie *The Cabinet of Dr Caligari*, or out of a Tim Burton film. Just look at the steps leading to the church!

It's too late now to regain your equilibrium, so head for the pubs along **Am Stintmarkt** on the bank of the Ilmenau River.

GERMANY

Orientation & Information

Wolfsburg's centre lies just southeast of the Hauptbahnhof. Autostadt is north across the train tracks. Head through the 'tunnel' under the Phaeno science centre, and you'll see the footbridge.

Wolfsburg tourist office (☎ 899 930; www.tourismus -wolfsburg.de, for English www.wolfsburg.de; Willy Brandt-Platz 3; ☷ 9am-7pm) In the train station.

Sights & Activities

AUTOSTADT

Spread across 25 hectares, **Autostadt** (Car City; ☎ 0800-2886 782 38; www.autostadt.de; Stadtbrücke; adult/ concession/child/family €14/11/6/38; ☷ 9am-8pm Apr-Oct, 9am-6pm Nov-Mar) is a celebration of all things VW – so no muttering about the company's recent boardroom scandals up the back there, please! Exhibitions run the gamut of automotive design and engineering, the history of the Beetle and the marketing of individual marques, including VW itself, Audi, Bentley, Lamborghini, Seat and Skoda.

Included in the admission price are 45-minute shuttle **tours** (☷ 9am-6pm Mon-Fri, every 15 min, in English 1.30pm daily) of the enormous Volkswagen factory. The place is larger than Monaco, so you only get to see a snippet on the tour.

Most excitingly, there are **obstacle courses** and **safety training** (€25 each) if you have a valid licence and are comfortable with a left-hand drive car. Ring ahead to organise an English-speaking instructor.

Two hours before closing time, there's a discounted *Abendticket* (€6).

AUTOMUSEUM

For diehard fans not sated by Autostadt, the **AutoMuseum** (☎ 520 71; Dieselstrasse 35; adult/ concession/family €6/3/15; ☷ 10am-5pm) has a collection of classic VW models. The collection includes *Herbie, the Love Bug*, a beetle made of wood, one of lace iron and the original 1938 Cabriolet presented to Adolf Hitler on his 50th birthday. Take bus 208 from the main bus station to AutoMuseum.

PHAENO

The space-age building beside the train station is **Phaeno** (☎ 0180-106 0600; www.phaeno .de; Willy Brandt-Platz 1; adult/concession/family €11/7/25; ☷ 10am-6pm Tue-Sun), an expensive new science centre designed by British-based Iraqi architect Zaha Hadid and frequently

populated by hundreds of teenage school children on physics outings. Some 250 hands-on exhibits and experiments – wind up your own rocket, watch thermal images of your body – provide hours of fun. It's very physical, but also requires concentration. Instructions and explanations come in German and English.

Sleeping & Eating

DJH hostel (☎ 133 37; Lessingstrasse 60; dm junior/ senior €16.50/19.50; P ▯) Slightly cramped and fairly old, with pine furniture and checked linen, this hostel is nevertheless friendly and extremely central.

Hotel Wolf (☎ 865 60; www.alterwolf.de; Schlossstrasse 21; s/d from €35/50, f €75-85; P) While the rooms inside this attractive, black-and-white half-timbered house aren't particularly fashionable, some are huge. Handy for families, but not for the city's nightlife, it's in a quiet, leafy part of town just behind Autostadt and the city castle.

Cityhotel Journal (☎ 292662; www.cityhotel-journal .de; Kaufhofpassage 2; s/d from €40/70) Above a pub on the city's main drinking strip, this must get pretty noisy in summer. However, if you're not planning on an early night, it's friendly, homey and convenient.

Global Inn (☎ 2700; www.globalinn.de; Kleistrasse 46; s €45-65, d €90; P ✕) Some cheaper single rooms are small in this central hotel, but all are of a comfortable corporate standard. There's a very popular Italian restaurant on site, too.

Other recommendations are the **Penthouse Hotel** (☎ 2710; www.penthouse-hotel.de; Schachtweg 22; s apt €45, d apt €55-65; f apt €75), where apartments all have kitchenettes, or the five-star **Ritz Carlton** (☎ 607 000; www.ritzcarlton.com; Autostadt; r from €200; P ✕ ✕).

There are eight **Autostadt restaurants** within the park, ranging from a cheap American diner (Cylinder) to an upmarket Mediterranean (Chardonnay).

Kebab shops are dotted all along Porschestrasse and there are wall-to-wall bar/cafés along the Kaufhofpassage. Other convenient options include the Italian and pizzeria **Aalto Bistro** (☎ 891 689; Porschestrasse 1; mains €10-15; ☷ dinner Mon-Sat) and the more upmarket **Walino** (☎ 255 99; Kunstmuseum, Porschestrasse 53; mains €16-17.50 or per person 3-courses for 2 €18.50; ☷ closed Mon) located high up in the Kunstmuseum.

Getting There & Around

Frequent ICE train services go to Hanover (€19, 30 minutes) and Berlin (€39, one hour). If you use RE services from Hanover (one hour), a Niedersaschsen ticket will get you to Wolfsburg and back in a day for €17.

Most major sights are easily reached on foot, although a free shuttle bus also runs from the train station down Porschestrasse to the town centre.

For longer journeys, single bus tickets cost €1.70. A day pass costs €4. The major bus transfer point (ZOB) is at the northern end of Porschestrasse.

BREMEN

☎ 0421 / pop 550,000

Bremen is what Germans call *schön klein*, the equivalent of good things coming in small packages. You can easily travel on foot between the main attractions of its red-brick market place, Art-Deco Böttch-erstrasse and the dollhouse-sized Schnoor district.

Best known from the fairy tale of the *Town Musicians of Bremen* – four animals who ran away from their owners to find fame here – Bremen is predictably cute and pretty. But the waterfront promenade along the Weser River is a wonderful place to enjoy a drink and the student district along Ostertorsteinweg is just downright alternative.

ORIENTATION

Head south (straight ahead) from the train station to reach the centre, on banks of the Weser River. The Schlachte waterfront promenade is west of the centre; the Schnoor district lies just east. The student and nightlife district is further east still, along Ostertorsteinweg.

INFORMATION

ErlebnisCARD (adult & 2 children 1/2 days €6.50/8.50) Free public transport and discounts on sights.

Internet.Center Bremen (☎ 277 6600; Bahnhofsplatz 22-28; per hr €5; ⏰ 10am-10pm Mon-Sat, noon-8pm Sun)

Tourist office (☎ 01805-101030; www.bremen-tourism .de; Hauptbahnhof; ⏰ 9am-7pm Mon-Fri, to 6pm Sat & Sun) Organises daily city tours; branch office (Obernstrasse/ Liebfrauenkirchhof; ⏰ 10am-6.30pm Mon-Fri, to 4pm Sat & Sun)

SIGHTS & ACTIVITIES

Bremen's **Markt** is striking, particularly its ornate, gabled **Rathaus** (town hall). In front stands a 13m-tall medieval statue of the knight **Roland**, Bremen's protector. On the building's western side, you'll find a sculpture of the **Town Musicians of Bremen** (1951). Local artist Gerhard Marcks has cast them in their most famous pose, scaring the robbers who invaded their house, with the rooster atop the cat, perched on the dog, on the shoulders of the donkey.

Also on the Markt is the twin-towered **Dom St Petri** (cathedral), whose most interesting – and slightly macabre – feature is its **Bleikeller** (Lead Cellar; ☎ 365 0441; adult/concession €1.50/1; ⏰ 10am-5pm Mon-Fri, 10am-2pm Sat, noon-5pm Sun Apr-Oct) Here, open coffins reveal eight corpses that have mummified in the dry underground air. The Bleikeller has its own entrance, south of the main cathedral door.

If the Markt is memorable, then nearby **Böttcherstrasse** is unique. It's an opulent Art-Deco alley commissioned by Ludwig Roselius, the inventor of decaffeinated coffee and founder of the company Hag. He later managed to save it from the Nazis, who thought it 'degenerate'. Under the golden relief you enter a world of tall brick houses, shops, galleries, restaurants, a **Glockenspiel** and several museums (which can easily be skipped). If you can, peek in the back door of 'Haus Atlantis' (aka the Hilton hotel), for its phantasmagorical, multicoloured, glass-walled **spiral staircase**.

The maze of narrow winding alleys known as the **Schnoorviertel** was once the fishermen's quarter and then the red-light district. Now its dollhouse-sized cottages are souvenir shops and restaurants. The cute **Schnoor Teestübchen** (Teashop; Wüste Stätte 1) serves Frisian tea and cakes.

With more time, make a visit to the oyster-shaped **Universum Science Center** (☎ 334 60; www .usc-bremen.de; Wiener Strasse 2; adult/concession & child €11/7; ⏰ 9am-6pm Mon-Fri, 10am-7pm Sat & Sun, last entry 90 min before closing), or the **Beck's Brewery** (☎ 5094 5555; Am Deich 18-19; tours in German & English €7.50; ⏰ 10am-5pm Tue-Sat, to 3pm Sun, in English 2pm Tue-Sun).

SLEEPING

Camping Stadtwaldsee (☎ 841 0748; www.camping -stadtwaldsee.de; Hochschulring 1; camp sites per adult/tent/ car €7/4/1.50) Totally rebuilt in late 2005, this

GERMANY

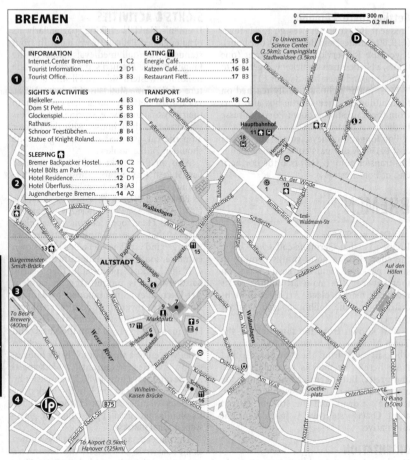

BREMEN

0			300 m
0			0.2 miles

INFORMATION
Internet.Center Bremen..............**1** C2
Tourist Information....................**2** D1
Tourist Office............................**3** B3

SIGHTS & ACTIVITIES
Bleikeller................................**4** B3
Dom St Petri............................**5** B3
Glockenspiel............................**6** B3
Rathaus...................................**7** B3
Schnoor Teestübchen................**8** B4
Statue of Knight Roland............**9** B3

SLEEPING
Bremer Backpacker Hostel........**10** C2
Hotel Bölts am Park..................**11** C2
Hotel Residence......................**12** D1
Hotel Überfluss.......................**13** A3
Jugendherberge Bremen............**14** A2

EATING
Energie Café............................**15** B3
Katzen Café.............................**16** B4
Restaurant Flett.......................**17** B3

TRANSPORT
Central Bus Station....................**18** C2

To Universum Science Center (2.5km); Campingplatz Stadtwaldsee (3.5km)

Hauptbahnhof

ALTSTADT

Weser River

GERMANY

To Beck's Brewery (400m)

Marktplatz

Schnoor

Wilhelm-Kaiser Brücke

To Airport (3.5km); Hanover (125km)

To Piano (150m)

---

camping ground features modern amenities, a supermarket and café with a lakeside terrace. By car, take the A27 to the university exit in Bremen Nord. Tram 6 will get you close and bus 28 is on the doorstep.

Jugendherberge Bremen (☎ 163 820; www.jugend herberge.de; Kalkstrasse 6; dm junior/senior €21/24, s/d €32/56; ☒ 🖳) Like a work of art from the exterior, with a yellow and orange Plexiglas façade and slit rectangular windows, this refurbished building is even better inside. Comfortable dorms are all ensuite, there's a bar/breakfast room with huge glass windows overlooking the Weser River, and a rooftop terrace. Take tram 3 or 5 to Am Brill.

Bremer Backpacker Hostel (☎ 223 8057; www .bremer-backpacker-hostel.de; Emil-Waldmannstrasse 5-6;

dm €16, s/d €27/44, bedding €3; 🅿 🖳) Five minutes from the train station, tucked away on a quiet street, you'll find simply furnished but spotless rooms, a kitchen and living room. The communal showers are all on the ground floor – thanks to low water pressure, we presume from the taps on the first floor.

Hotel Bölts am Park (☎ 346 110; www.hotel-boelts .de; Slevogtstrasse 23; s/d €50/80; 🅿) This family-run hotel in a leafy neighbourhood has real character, from the old-fashioned breakfast hall to its well-proportioned rooms. A few singles with hall showers and toilets cost €40.

Hotel Residence (☎ 348 710; www.hotelresidence .de; Hohenlohestrasse 42; s €65-100, d €80-140; 🅿 ☒)

Some rooms in this century-old terrace are a bit snug, but all are modern, comfortable and clean, while the best doubles – rooms 12 and 22 – have balconies overlooking a quiet street. A sauna, solarium and bar complete the package.

Hotel Überfluss (☎ 322 860; www.hotel-ueberfluss .com; Langenstrasse 72/Schlachte; s/d €135/180; ✗ ⚡ ⚑) Dragging quaint Bremen into the 21st century is this jaw-dropping design hotel. It's all green-tinted windows overlooking the Weser River, black bathrooms and glowing fibre-optic curtains imported from Las Vegas. However, the friendly staff prevent it from ever becoming intimidating.

EATING

The student quarter in and around Ostertorsteinweg, **Das Viertel**, is full of restaurants and cafés. The waterfront promenade, **Schlachte**, is more expensive and mainstream, but pleasant nonetheless.

Piano (☎ 785 46; Fehrfeld 64; mains €5.50-9.50) One of the most enduringly popular cafés in the student quarter, Piano serves pizza, pasta, steaks and veggie casseroles. Breakfast can also be enjoyed until 4pm.

Energie Café (☎ 277 2510; cnr Sögestrasse & Am Wall; mains €3.50-12.50; ✆ closed Sun) A delightfully upbeat café run by a local power company, this one serves delicious cut-price lunches and solid evening meals. Amuse yourself while waiting between by watching the model surfer on the wave-motion display.

Restaurant Flett (☎ 320 995; Böttcherstrasse 3-5; mains €7-15) Come here for local specialities like *Labskaus* (a hash of beef or pork with potatoes, onion and herring) or *Knipp* (fried hash and oats). Slightly touristy it might be, but it's hard to take against the photo-bedecked room, featuring first-hand snaps of celebs from Elvis to Clinton to Gerhard Schröder.

Katzen Café (☎ 326 621; Schnoor 38; mains €8.50-16.50, 3-course menu €19.50) This Moulin Rouge-style restaurant opens out into a rear sunken terrace bedecked with flowers. The menu runs the gamut from Alsatian to Norwegian, with seafood a strong theme.

GETTING THERE & AWAY

Flights from **Bremen airport** (BRE: www.airport -bremen.de) include easyJet (www.easyjet.com) flights to London-Luton.

Frequent trains go to Hamburg (€18.30 to €22, one hour), Hanover (€18.70 to €27,

one hour to one hour and 20 minutes) and Cologne (€52, three hours). Some IC trains run direct to Frankfurt-am-Main (€76, 3¾ hours) and Munich (€100, six hours) daily.

GETTING AROUND

Tram 6 leaves the airport frequently, heading to the centre (€2.05, 15 minutes). Other trams cover most of the city. With single bus/tram tickets costing €2.05, a day pass (€5 for one adult and two children) is excellent value.

HAMBURG

☎ 040 / pop 1.7 million

Water, water everywhere – Germany's leading port city has always been outward-looking. Its dynamism, multiculturalism and hedonistic red-light district, the Reeperbahn, all arise from its maritime history.

Joining the Hanseatic League trading bloc in the Middle Ages, Hamburg has been enthusiastically doing business with the rest of the world ever since. In the 1960s, it nurtured the musical talent of the Beatles. Nowadays, it's also a media capital and the wealthiest city in Germany.

The Alster Lakes, the Elbe River and the canals between the Speicherstadt warehouses are all perfect for leisure cruises. Haggling at the rowdy fish market early on a Sunday is also an unrivalled experience.

ORIENTATION

The Hauptbahnhof is quite central, near the Binnenalster and Aussenalster (Inner and Outer Alster Lakes); the Speicherstadt and port lie south/southwest of these, on the Elbe River. The nightlife districts of St Pauli (containing the Reeperbahn) and the Schanzenviertel are further west. The city's sprawl means using public transport is necessary.

INFORMATION
EMERGENCY
Police Hauptbahnhof (Kirchenallee exit); St Pauli (Davidwache, Spielbudenplatz 31; Ⓜ Reeperbahn)

INTERNET ACCESS
Internet Café (☎ 2800 3898; Adenauerallee 10; per hr €2; ✆ 10am-midnight Mon-Sat, to 1pm Sun; Ⓜ Hauptbahnhof)
Tele-Time (☎ 4131 4730; Schulterblatt 39; per hr €3; ✆ 10am-midnight; Ⓜ Feldstrasse/Sternschanze)

GERMANY

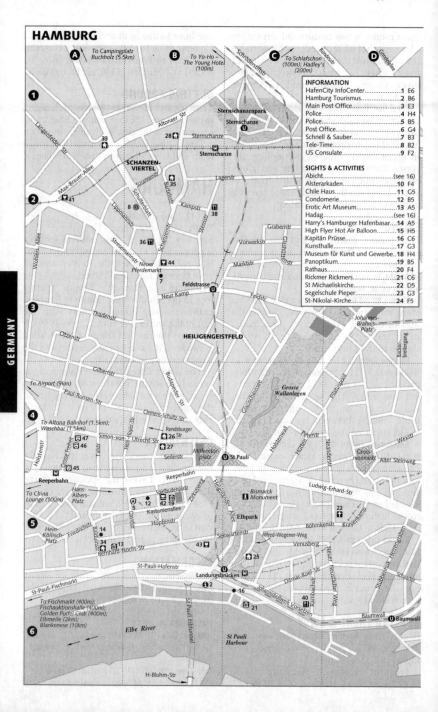

HAMBURG

GERMANY

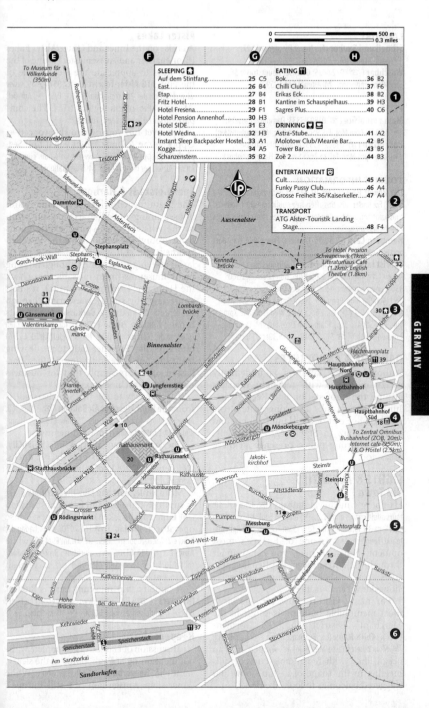

SLEEPING 🏠
Auf dem Stintfang................25 C5
East...26 B4
Etap..27 B4
Fritz Hotel.............................28 B1
Hotel Fresena.......................29 F1
Hotel Pension Annenhof......30 H3
Hotel SIDE............................31 E3
Hotel Wedina.......................32 H3
Instant Sleep Backpacker Hostel...33 A1
Kogge....................................34 A5
Schanzenstern......................35 B2

EATING 🍴
Bok...36 B2
Chilli Club..............................37 F6
Erikas Eck.............................38 B2
Kantine im Schauspielhaus...39 H3
Sagres Plus............................40 C6

DRINKING 🍸 🍺
Astra-Stube...........................41 A2
Molotow Club/Meanie Bar....42 B5
Tower Bar..............................43 B5
Zoë 2....................................44 B3

ENTERTAINMENT 🎭
Cult..45 A4
Funky Pussy Club..................46 A4
Grosse Freiheit 36/Kaiserkeller....47 A4

TRANSPORT
ATG Alster-Touristik Landing
  Stage.................................48 F4

GERMANY

LAUNDRY

Schnell und Sauber (Am Neuer Pferdemarkt 27; 6am-11pm; M Feldstrasse)

Waschbar (☎ 8972 6425; Ottenser Hauptstrasse 56; 10am-midnight; M Altona) See p259.

POST

Main post office (☎ 01802-3333; Dammtorstrasse14; 8.30am-6pm Mon-Fri, 9am-noon Sat; M Jungfernstieg)

Post office (☎ 01802-3333; Mönckebergstrasse 7; 9am-7pm Mon-Fri, to 3pm Sat; M Hauptbahnhof)

TOURIST INFORMATION

Der Power Pass (€7 for 1st day, €3 each extra day up to a week) For under-30s, this offers free public transport, reduced museums and sightseeing tours, some free club entries and a free listings magazine.

Hamburg Card (€7.50/15 1/3 days) Free public transport and museums discounts.

Tourist information Hamburg Tourismus main train station (☎ information 3005 1200, hotel bookings 3005 1300; www.hamburg-tourismus.de; Kirchenallee exit; Mon-Sat 8am-9pm, Sun 10am-6pm); Landungsbrücken, btwn piers 4 & 5 (☎ 8am-6pm Mon, Wed & Sun, to 7pm Tue, Thu-Sat Apr-Sep, 10am-6pm Oct-Mar; M Landungsbrücken); airport (☎ 5075 1010; 5.30am-11pm)

DANGERS & ANNOYANCES

Although safe, Hamburg is undeniably sleazy in parts, with red-light districts around the train station and Reeperbahn. Junkies and drunks also congregate at the Kirchenallee exit of the Hauptbahnhof and at Hansaplatz in St Georg. Fortunately, there's a strong police presence in these areas, too.

SIGHTS & ACTIVITIES
Old Town

Hamburg's medieval **Rathaus** (☎ 4283 120 10; tours adult/concession €2/1, tours in English hourly from 10.15am-3.15pm Mon-Thu, to 1.15pm Fri-Sun; M Rathaus-markt/Jungfernstieg) is one of Europe's most opulent. North of here, you can wander through the **Alsterarkaden**, the Renaissance-style arcades sheltering shops and cafés alongside a canal or 'fleet'.

For many visitors, however, the city's most memorable building is south in the Merchant's District. The 1920s, brown-brick **Chile Haus** (cnr Burchardstrasse & Johanniswall; M Mönckebergstrasse/Messberg) is shaped like an ocean liner, with remarkable curved walls meeting in the shape of a ship's bow and staggered balconies to look like decks.

Alster Lakes

A cruise on the Inner and Outer Alster Lakes (Binnenalster and Aussenalster) is one of the best ways to appreciate the elegant side of the city. **ATG Alster-Touristik** (☎ 3574 2419; www .alstertouristik.de; 2hr trip adult/child €10/5; Apr-Oct; M Jungfernstieg) offers regular trips. The company also offers 'fleet' tours.

Better yet, hire your own rowboat or canoe. Opposite the Atlantic Hotel you'll find **Seg-elschule Pieper** (☎ 247 578; www.segelschule-pieper.de; An der Alster; per hr from €12; M Hauptbahnhof).

Speicherstadt & Harbour

The beautiful red-brick, neo-Gothic warehouses lining the Elbe archipelago south of the Altstadt once stored exotic goods from around the world. Now the so-called **Speicherstadt** (M Messberg/Baumwall) is a popular sightseeing attraction. Although housing many museums (most missable, but check the Hamburg Tourismus website), it's best appreciated by simply wandering through its streets or taking a **Barkassen** boat up its canals. **Kapitän Prüsse** (☎ 313 130; www.kapitaen -pruesse.de; Landungsbrücke No 3; adult/child €12/6) offers regular Speicherstadt tours, leaving from the port (see following). Other Bar-kassen operators simply tout for business opposite the archipelago.

Another way to see the Speicherstadt is from the **High-Flyer Hot Air Balloon** (☎ 3008 6968; www.highflyer-hamburg.de; per 15 min €15; 10am-midnight, to 10pm winter) moored nearby.

The Speicherstadt merges into **HafenCity**, a major project to transform the old docks. Get details at the **InfoCenter** (☎ 3690 1799; Am Sandtorkai 30).

Meanwhile, **port and Elbe River cruises** start in summer at the St Pauli Landungsbrücken (M Landungsbrücken). The cheapest cruise operator is **Hadag** (☎ 311 7070; www.hadag.de; Brücke 2; 1hr harbour trip adult/child from €9/4.50), while **Abicht** (☎ 317 8220; www.abicht.de; Brücke 1; adult/ child €10/5; noon daily Mar-Nov) offers English commentary.

A famous ship museum here is **Rickmer Rickmers** (☎ 319 5959; www.rickmer-rickmers.de; Brücke 1; adult/concession €3/2.50; 10am-6pm).

Reeperbahn

No discussion of Hamburg is complete without mentioning St Pauli, home of the sleazy, sexadelic **Reeperbahn** (M Reeperbahn). While tamer than Amsterdam, it's still Europe's biggest red-light district – a kind of Champs Elyseés of sex shops, peep shows, dim bars and raucous clubs.

Among the 'sights' are the men-only **Herbertstrasse**, the **Erotic Art Museum** (☎ 317 4757; www.eroticartmuseum.de; Bernhard-Nocht-Strasse 69; adult/concession €8/5; ⊙ noon-10pm, to midnight Fri & Sat), and the **Condomerie** (Spielbudenplatz 18), with its extensive collection of prophylactics and sex toys.

Harry's Hamburger Hafenbasar (☎ 312482; www .hafenbasar.de; cnr Balduinstrasse & Erichstrasse; adult/child €2.50/1.50, redeemable against any purchase; ⊙ noon-6pm Tue-Sun) is bursting with African statues, Asian masks and other ephemera shipped back from abroad.

Fischmarkt

Here's the perfect excuse to stay up all Saturday night. Every Sunday between 5am and 10am, curious tourists join locals of every age and walk of life at the famous Fischmarkt in St Pauli. The market has been running since 1703, and its undisputed stars are the boisterous *Marktschreier* (market criers) who hawk their wares at full volume. Live bands also entertainingly crank out cover versions of ancient German pop songs in the adjoining *Fischauktionshalle* (Fish Auction Hall). Take bus 112 to Hafentreppe.

Blankenese

The upmarket western district of **Blankenese** (Ⓜ Blankenese, then bus 48 to Krögers Treppe or Weseberg), a former fishing village, is wonderful to explore, as are its fine houses also set on a hillside labyrinth of narrow, cobbled streets. There's a network of **58 stairways** (4864 steps total!). The best views of the broad Elbe River and the container ships putting out to sea are enjoyed from the 75m-high **Süllberg** hill.

Museums

Three of Hamburg's dozens of museums stand out. The Hamburger **Kunsthalle** (☎ 428 131 200; www.hamburger-kunsthalle.de; Glockengiesserwall; adult/concession €8.50/5; ⊙ 10am-6pm Tue-Sun, to 9pm Thu; Ⓜ Hauptbahnhof) consists of two buildings – and old one housing 20th-century art, and a new white concrete cube of contemporary works – linked by a memorable underground passage.

The **Museum für Kunst und Gewerbe** (Museum of Arts & Crafts; ☎ 428 542 732; www.mkg-hamburg .de; Steintorplatz 1; adult/concession €8/5, both from 4pm

Tue & 5pm Thu €5; ⊙ 10am-6pm Tue-Sun, to 9pm Thu; Ⓜ Hauptbahnhof) isn't quite so exalted, but its posters, ornaments and temporary exhibitions are always lots of fun.

The **Museum für Völkerkunde** (Museum of Ethnology; ☎ 01805-308 888; www.voelkerkundemuseum .com; Rothenbaumchaussee 64; adult/concession €6/3, Fri all €3; ⊙ 10am-6pm Tue-Sun, to 9pm Thu; Ⓜ Hallerstrasse) demonstrates sea-going Hamburg's acute awareness of the outside world. The giant statues from Papua New Guinea at the top of the stairs are unforgettable.

Churches

From the tower of the **St Michaeliskirche** (tower adult/concession €3/1.50; ⊙ 10am-6pm Apr-Oct, to 5pm Nov-Mar; Ⓜ Stadthausbrücke) you have panoramic views.

The WWII-damaged **St-Nikolai-Kirche** (Ost-West-Strasse; adult/child €2/1; ⊙ 11am-5pm; Ⓜ Rödingsmarkt) is now an antiwar memorial, with some chilling photos of the then-bombed-out city.

SLEEPING
Budget

For private rooms, contact **Bed & Breakfast** (☎ 491 5666; www.bed-&-breakfast.de), which has singles from €27 to €45 and doubles from €40 to €70.

Campingplatz Buchholz (☎ 540 4532; www.camping -buchholz.de; Kieler Strasse 274; camp sites per person/car €5/5, tent €8-11; Ⓜ Hamburg-Stellingen/Hagenbecks Tierpark) This small, family-run site has decent washing facilities, lots of shade and now some private hotel rooms. It's well connected to the city. When driving, take the A7/E45 and take exit 26 to Hamburg-Stellingen.

A & O Hostel (☎ 2104 0294; www.aohostel.com; Hammer Landstrasse 170; dm €12, s/d €29/32, breakfast €5, bedding €3; Ⓟ ☒ ▣ ; Ⓜ Hammer Kirche) Typical of the A & O chain – new and clean, but a trifle bland – the Hamburg branch has a slightly out-of-the-way location.

Instant Sleep Backpacker Hostel (☎ 4318 2310; www.instantsleep.de; Max-Brauer-Allee 277; dm €15-20, s/d €28/44; ▣ ; Ⓜ Sternschanze) Brightly painted murals distract you from this place's relatively spartan surrounds. It's friendly, though, and in the happening Schanzenviertel.

Auf dem Stintfang (☎ 313488; www.jugendherberge .de; Alfred-Wegener-Weg 5; dm €19-22, d €47; Ⓟ ☒ ▣ ; Ⓜ Landungsbrücken) Modern, clean and convenient (head out of the U-Bahn station, up some steps and you're at the front door),

GERMANY

this DJH hostel overlooks the Elbe and the harbour. With lots of large, noisy school groups, however, it's very keen on rules, and you're locked out part of the day.

Hotel Pension Annenhof (☎ 243 426; www.hotel annenhof.de; Lange Reihe 23; s/d €40/70; Ⓜ Hauptbahnhof) Behind the grubby façade, Annenhof's surprisingly attractive rooms have polished wooden floorboards and bright colour schemes, but no breakfast.

Other recommendations:

Schanzenstern (☎ 439 8441; www.schanzenstern.de; Bartelsstrasse 12; dm €18, s/d/tr €36/52/62; ⊠ ▢ ; Ⓜ Sternschanze) Backpackers' hostel with older rooms and healthy café.

Kogge (☎ 312 872; www.kogge-hamburg.de; Bernhard-Nocht-Strasse 59; s/d €29.50/48.50; Ⓜ Reeperbahn) Quirkily themed rock and roll pub with 5pm check-out.

Etap (☎ 306 220; www.etaphotel.com; Simon-von-Utrecht Strasse 64; s/d €44/52; ▢ ; Ⓜ St Pauli) Unusually central location for this budget chain.

Midrange

Schlafschön (☎ 4135 4949; www.schlafschoen.de; Monetastrasse 4; s with shared bathroom €55-75, d with shared bathroom €85; Ⓟ ; Ⓜ Schlump) In the same former hospital as Hadley's, you'll find this separate B&B, where sunny beach-house colours are complemented by Turkish throws and Moroccan tiles. The centrepiece is a huge breakfast room, with a courtyard balcony. Look for the door saying 'Schwesterhaus' on the left side of the street near Beim Schlump.

Hotel Fresena (☎ 410 4892; www.hotelfresena.de; Moorweidenstrasse 34; s €56-70, d €84; Ⓟ ⊠ ; Ⓜ Dammtor) Bright walls, 1970s graphic-design posters, and vaguely Oriental touches and a largely nonsmoking policy make this an excellent choice in the five-floor, five-*pension* Dammtorpalais. Breakfast is extra.

Hadley's (☎ 417 871; www.bed-&-breakfast-hamburg .de; Beim Schlump 85; s/d from €60/70; Ⓟ ; Ⓜ Schlump) This B&B's beds are set on a mezzanine platform (reached by ladder) above living areas mostly decorated in grey-blue tones. Most rooms have shared bathrooms. The place is set in a former hospital and while you can order breakfast in your room (€5 extra), we recommend heading to Hadley's warmly decorated café, just around the corner in the totally transformed ER.

Yo-Ho – The Young Hotel (☎ 284 1910; www.yoho -hamburg.de; Moorkamp 5; s/d €70/90; Ⓟ ; Ⓜ Schlump/ Christuskirche) Fashionable without being pretentious, the Yo-Ho is an exotic mix of

ascetic, vaguely Japanese rooms, a magnificent 1001-nights breakfast room and a great Syrian restaurant. Under-26s get €20 off room rates.

Hotel Wedina (☎ 280 8900; www.wedina.de; Gurlittstrasse 23; s €75-145, d €110-165; Ⓟ ; Ⓜ Hauptbahnhof) JK Rowling and Michel Houellebecq (now, that would be an interesting conversation) are just two authors who've been billeted in this arty relaxed hotel when doing public readings in the nearby Literaturhaus. There's 'urban living' in the green, blue and yellow-schemed houses. The group- and family-friendly red house also takes longer bookings.

Other recommendations:

Fritz Hotel (☎ 822 2283 0; www.fritzhotel.com; Schanzenstrasse 101-103; s/d €60/90; Ⓜ Sternschanze) This stylish townhouse hotel, decorated in white and grey with touches of red, is convenient but a tad noisy at the front.

Hotel-Pension Schwanenwik (☎ 220 0918; www.hotel -schwanenwik.de; Schwanenwik 29; s/d €70/90; Ⓟ ; Ⓜ Hauptbahnhof, then bus 6 to Mundsburger Brücke) Well-run place overlooking the Aussenalster. Also has some rooms with shared facilities (s/d €45/65).

Top End

Hamburg has many ritzy hotels, both designer and traditional, but you could do worse than starting with these.

East (☎ 309 933; Simon-von-Utrecht-Strasse 31; r €150-375; Ⓟ ⊠ ; Ⓜ St Pauli) Pillars, walls and lamps emulate organic forms in the public areas of this warm, richly decorated design hotel. Floors are themed by plants and spices.

SIDE (☎ 309 990; www.side-hamburg.de; Drehbahn 49; r €190-230; Ⓟ ⊠ ; Ⓜ Stephansplatz/Gänsemarkt) Italian designer Matteo Thun has created a space-age millionaire's bachelor pad here.

EATING

The **Schanzenviertel** (Ⓜ Feldstrasse/Schanzenstern) swarms with cheap eateries; try **Schulterblatt** for Portuguese outlets or **Susanenstrasse** for Asian and Turkish. Conversely, be aware that many fish restaurants around the Landungsbrücken are rather over-rated and quite touristy.

Erikas Eck (☎ 433 545; Sternstrasse 98; dishes €4.50-7.50; ☯ 7-2pm; Ⓜ Feldstrasse/Sternschanze) Hamburg's night-owls flock to this red-eye specialist, which starts serving breakfast at 1am.

Kantine im Schauspielhaus (☎ 2487 1239; Kirchenallee 39; lunches €4.50-7.50; ☯ noon-3pm Mon-Fri;

THE ELBMEILE

Hamburg's western riverfront from Altona to Övelgönne – the Elbmeile or Elbe Mile – is Germany's hottest dining scene. Best known is **Das Weisse Haus** (☎ 390 9016; Neumühlen 50; menus €28 & €36), owned by TV chef Tim Mälzer, a sort of local Jamie Oliver. However, serious restaurant critics tip **Le Canard** (☎ 8812 9531; www.lecanard-hamburg.de; Elbchaussee 139; mains €16-28) for an out-of-this-world experience. Both restaurants serve modern international cuisine.

More relaxed is **Lust auf Italien** (☎ 382 811; Grosse Elbstrasse 133; mains €7-17), with its communal wooden benches. The completely informal venues are the summertime 'beach' clubs. There's one along Grosse Elbstrasse not far from Lust auf Italien, or try the kiosk **Strandperle** (Schulberg 2), further west from Das Weisse Haus.

M Hauptbahnhof) There's as much theatre in this bustling basement restaurant as there is on the stage above, as waiters patrol between the tables calling out ready orders of pasta, salad or meat, and thespians gossip between rehearsals over the almost obligatory glass of house red.

Literaturhaus Café (☎ 220 1300; Schwanenwik 38; dishes €5-15; M Hauptbahnhof) With golden walls and heavy chandeliers, this stunningly baroque café positively glows, as you will too after partaking of its Mediterranean bistro fare.

Chilli Club (☎ 3570 3580; Am Sandtorkai 54; dishes €4-20; M Baumwall) This trendy noodle bar is tucked away in the industrial-looking Hafen City. Asian tapas, dim sum and sushi are also served within the restaurant's red-and-black interior.

Bok (☎ 4318 3597; Schulterblatt 3; mains €9-15; M Feldstrasse/Sternschanze) Thai, Korean and Japanese food is on the menu at this cool but casual pan-Asian restaurant in the Schanzenviertel. It's large, and if fully booked has at least three sister outlets nearby to direct you to.

DRINKING & ENTERTAINMENT

Zoë 2 (Neuer Pferdemarkt 17; ☿ from noon; M Feldstrasse) The battered sofas, rough-hewn walls and old lampshades here prove that the ad-hoc, second-hand look so popular in Berlin is a Hamburg hit, too. Bottled beers and cocktails provide all the sophistication needed.

Astra-Stube (☎ 4325 0626; www.astra-stube.de; Max-Brauer-Allee 200; ☿ from 9.30pm; M Reeperbahn) This is a lo-fi DJ bar with some live bands that pulls in curious tourists and all types and ages from the St Pauli neighbourhood or 'Kiez'.

Tower Bar (☎ 311 137 0450; Seewartenstrasse 9; ☿ from 6pm; M Landungsbrücken) For a more elegant, mature evening, repair to this 14th-floor eerie of the Hotel Hafen for unbeatable harbour views.

Meanie Bar/Molotow Club (☎ 310 845; www.molotowclub.com; Spielbudenplatz 5; ☿ from 6pm; M Reeperbahn) One of the few venues along the Reeperbahn with real local cred, the retro Meanie Bar sits above the Molotow Club, where an alternative, independent music scene thrives by hosting the likes of the White Stripes, the Hives, the Kills and the Bravery.

Cult (☎ 2982 2180; Grosse Freiheit 2; ☿ from 11pm Thu-Sat; M Reeperbahn) Claiming to be Hamburg's most beautiful club, Cult serves up an unintimidating, good-time mix of '70s and '80s music in its shiny, cathedral-like main room.

Grosse Freiheit 36/Kaiserkeller (☎ 3177 7811; Grosse Freiheit 36; ☿ from 10pm Tue-Sat; M Reeperbahn) Wedged between live sex theatres and peep shows, this is popular for live rock and pop, particularly as the Beatles played in the basement Kaiserkeller.

Funky Pussy Club (☎ 314 236; Grosse Freiheit 34; ☿ from 11pm Thu-Sat; M Reeperbahn) Despite the dreadful name, this artistically decorated place is a hit for its mainstream chart-toppers and hip-hop, dance and house. Most drinks are €1 on a Thursday.

China Lounge (☎ 3197 6622; Nobistor 14; ☿ from 11pm Thu-Sat; M Reeperbahn) This leading club has four areas playing electro, house, hip-hop and R&B – the main floor is under a huge laughing Buddha. Thursday is students' evening.

Golden Pudel Club (☎ 3197 9930; Fischmarkt 27; ☿ from 10pm; bus 112 to Hafentreppe) In a ramshackle fisherman's hut near the waterfront, this underground bar/club plays an eclectic mix of, electronica, hip-hop, R'n'B and reggae to a mixed crowd.

GERMANY

GETTING THERE & AWAY
Air
Hamburg's **airport** (HAM: www.flughafen-hamburg .de) has frequent flights to domestic and European cities, including on low-cost carrier Air Berlin (www.airberlin.com).

For flights to/from Ryanair's so-called 'Hamburg-Lübeck' see p280.

Bus
The **Zentral Omnibus Busbahnhof** (ZOB, central bus station; ☎ 247 5765; Adenauer Allee 78; ☺ 6.30am-9pm) is southeast of the Hauptbahnhof and most popular for services to central and eastern Europe. **Eurolines** (☎ 4024 7106; www .eurolines.com) has buses to Prague (one way/return €55/98) and Warsaw (one way/return €55/86), for example. However, if you call or visit, you'll find several specialist operators.

Autokraft (☎ 208 8660) travels to Berlin frequently for €24/39 one way/return. Elsewhere, **Berlin Linienbus** (☎ 030-861 9331; www.berlin linienbus.de) and **Rainbow Tours** (☎ 3209 3309; www .rainbowtours.de, in German) are both very good options for travelling to Berlin or London, respectively.

Car & Motorcycle
The A1 (Bremen–Lübeck) and A7 (Hanover–Kiel) cross south of the Elbe River.

Train
When reading train timetables, remember that there are two main train stations: Hamburg Hauptbahnhof and Hamburg-Altona. There are frequent RE/RB trains to Lübeck (€10, 45 minutes), as well as various services to Hanover (€36, 1¼ hours) and Bremen (€18.30 to €22, one hour). In addition there are EC trains to Berlin (€48 to €58, 1½ to two hours), Cologne (€68 to €78, four hours) and Munich (€111, six to nine hours). Overnight train services also travel to international destinations such as Copenhagen and Paris.

GETTING AROUND
To/From the Airport
The **Airport Express** (☎ 227 1060; www.jasper -hamburg.de) runs between the Hauptbahnhof and airport (€5; 25 minutes, every 15 to 20 minutes, ☺ 6am-11pm). You can also take the U1 or S1 to Ohlsdorf, then change to bus 110.

Public Transport
There is an integrated system of buses, U-Bahn and S-Bahn trains. Day tickets, brought from machines before boarding, cost €5.80, or €4.90 after 9am. From midnight to dawn the night-bus network takes over from the trains, converging on the main metropolitan bus station at Rathausmarkt.

SCHLESWIG-HOLSTEIN

Sandwiched between the North and Baltic seas, Schleswig-Holstein is Germany's answer to the Côte d'Azur. Of course, the northern European weather here on the Danish border often makes it a pretty funny sort of answer, as dark clouds and strong winds whip in across this flat peninsula. Still, people flock to the beaches on the coasts and the countryside in between has a stark beauty.

LÜBECK
☎ 0451 / pop 215,000
Oh, how the mighty have fallen! But Lübeck doesn't look like she cares. Once the 'queen' of the Hanseatic League – a powerful medieval trading bloc – she's now just a provincial town, yet she still boasts an extraordinary appearance.

The two pointed cylindrical towers of Lübeck's Holstentor (gate) lean towards each other across the stepped gable that joins them, behind which the streets are lined with medieval merchants' homes and spired churches forming the city's so-called 'crown'. It's hardly surprising that this 12th-century gem is on Unesco's World Heritage List. The place looks so good you could eat it – especially the colourful displays of its famous marzipan, which you actually can.

Orientation & Information
Lübeck's old town is set on an island ringed by the canalised Trave River, a 10-minute walk east of the main train station. Leaving the station, head through the bus station and veer left along Hansestrasse. The tourist office is just across the Puppenbrücke (Doll Bridge), near the Holstentor. There are billboard maps all over town and signs in English.

Lübeck Travemünde Tourismus (☎ 01805 882 233; www.lubeck-tourism.de; Holstentorplatz 1; ☺ 9.30am-7pm Mon-Fri, 10am-3pm Sat, 10am-2pm Sun Jun-Sep,

9.30am-6pm Mon-Fri, 10am-3pm Sat Oct-May) With café and Internet terminals, staff can organise city tours and sell discount cards.

Sights

The impossibly cute city gate or **Holstentor** (☎ 122 4129; adult/concession €5/3; ☼ 10am-5pm Tue-Sun Apr-Sep, 10am-4pm Tue-Sun Oct-Mar) serves as Lübeck's museum as well as its symbol. It's been under renovation, but should be out of its clever *trompe l'oeil* wraps by now. The six gabled brick buildings east of the Holstentor are the **Salzspeicher**, once used to store the salt (from Lüneburg, p267) that was pivotal to Lübeck's Hanseatic trade.

Behind these warehouses, the Trave River forms a moat around the old town, and if you do one thing in Lübeck in summer, it should be a **boat tour**. From April to September, **Maak-Linie** (☎ 706 3859; www.maak-linie .de) and **Quandt-Linie** (☎ 777 99; www.quandt-linie.de) depart regularly from either side of the Holstentorbrücke. Prices are adult/student/child €7/5.50/3.50.

Each of Lübeck's seven churches offer something different. The shattered bells of the **Marienkirche** (Schüsselbuden 13; ☼ 10am-6pm Apr-Sep, to 5pm Oct, to 4pm Tue-Sun Nov-Mar) still lie on the floor where they fell after a bombing raid. There's also a little devil sculpture outside, with an amusing fairy tale (in English). The tower lift in the **Petrikirche** (Schmiedstrasse; adult/concession €2.50/1.50; ☼ 11am-4pm Tue-Sun, to 6pm mid-Nov–mid-Dec, closed Feb) affords superb views.

The **Rathaus** (town hall; ☎ 122 1005; Breite Strasse 64; adult/concession €3/1.50; tours ☼ 11am, noon & 3pm Mon-Fri) is ornate, but the tours are in German and, frankly, most visitors will prefer a visit to **JG Niederegger** (Breite Strasse 89) opposite. This is Lübeck's mecca of chocolate-coated **marzipan**, with lots of sweet gifts and an adjoining café.

Lübeck has some 90 lovely *Gänge* (walkways) and *Höfe* (courtyards) tucked away behind its main streets, the most famous being the **Füchtingshof** (Glockengiesserstrasse 25; ☼ 9am-noon & 3-6pm) and the **Glandorps Gang** (Glockengiesserstrasse 41-51).

Both of these are near the **Günter Grass-Haus** (☎ 122 4192; www.guenter-grass-haus.de; Glockengiesserstrasse 21; adult/concession €4/2.50, 'Kombi' card with Buddenbrookhaus €7/4; ☼ 10am-6pm Apr-Dec, 11am-5pm Nov-Mar). The author of The Tin Drum (*Die Blechtrommel*) has lived in town for years.

Fellow Nobel Prize-winning author Thomas (*Death in Venice*) Mann was born in Lübeck and he's commemorated in the award-winning **Buddenbrookhaus** (☎ 122 4190; www .buddenbrookhaus.de; Mengstrasse 4; adult/concession €5/3; 'Kombi' card with Buddenbrookhaus €7/4; ☼ 10am-6pm Apr-Dec, 11am-5pm Nov-Mar).

For children, there's a fantastic **Marionettentheater** (Puppet Theatre; ☎ 700 60; cnr Am Kolk & Kleine Petersgrube; ☼ Tue-Sun). Alternatively, ask the tourist office about the nearby seaside resort of **Travemünde**.

Sleeping
BUDGET
Campingplatz Schönböcken (☎ 893 090; fax 892 287; Steinrader Damm 12; camp sites per person/tent/car €4.50/3.50/1; ☼ Apr-Oct) This modern camping ground has a kiosk, entertainment room and children's playground, although two readers have complained about the lack of shade in summer. It's 15 minutes by bus west of the city centre (take bus 7).

Jugendgästehaus Altstadt (☎ 702 0399; www .jugendherberge.de; Mengstrasse 33; dm junior/senior €18/21) If you prefer convenience, opt for this central DJH hostel. It isn't particularly new, but it's cosy and comfortable enough.

Vor dem Burgtor (☎ 334 33; www.jugendherberge.de; Am Gertrudenkirchhof 4; dm junior/senior €17/20; P 🖳) Those fussier about their furnishings might prefer the huge, modern Vor dem Burgtor, however, it's popular with school groups, and outside the old town – just.

Hotel zur Alten Stadtmauer (☎ 737 02; www.hotel stadtmauer.de; An der Mauer 57; s/d €45/75, with shared bathroom from €38/65; P) With pine furniture and splashes of red or yellow, this simple 25-room hotel is bright and cheerful. The wooden flooring means sound carries, but customers tend not to be the partying type. Back rooms overlook the river.

Two very cheap and basic places are **Sleep-Inn** (☎ 719 20; www.cvjm-luebeck.de/cvjm; Grosse Petersgrube 11; dm €12.50; ☼ mid-Jan–mid-Dec) and the **Rucksackhotel** (☎ 706 892; www.rucksackhotel-luebeck .de; Kanalstrasse 70; dm €13-15, d €34-40, bedding €3; 🖳). The latter has a vegetarian café open to the public.

MIDRANGE & TOP END
Hotel Lindenhof (☎ 872 100; www.lindenhof-luebeck .de; Lindenstrasse 1a; s €65-80, d €85-110, f €100-135; P 🗶) Its rooms are business-like and small, but a healthy breakfast buffet,

friendly service and little extras, (free biscuits, newspapers, and a 6am to midnight snack service) propel the Lindenhof into a superior league.

Hotel Jensen (☎ 702 490; www.hotel-jensen.de; An der Obertrave 4-5; s €65-85, d €85-110) Classic and romantic, this old Patrizierhaus (mansion house) is conveniently located facing the Salzspeicher across the Trave River. Its seafood restaurant, Yachtzimmer, is also excellent.

Klassik Altstadt Hotel (☎ 702 980; www-klassik -altstadt-hotel.de; Fischergrube 52; s/d €75/130, ste from €135; P X) Each room here is dedicated to a different, mostly German, writer or artist (somehow Russia's Nikolai Gogol creeps in). It's a token gesture, though, and the overwhelming impression is of a decent, traditionally furnished hotel.

Radisson SAS Senator Hotel (☎ 1420; www .senatorhotel.de, Willy-Brandt-Allee 6; s/d €135/160; P X X 🖳 🖳) The Senator's three rectangular brick wings are spectacularly cantilevered out into the Trave River, like something from *War of the Worlds*. Rooms are newly refurbished in opulent Southeast Asian colonial style, and there are wonderful restaurant views.

Eating

Suppentopf (☎ 400 8136; Fleischerstrasse 36; soups €3.50; 🕑 11am-4pm Mon-Fri, closed Jul & Aug) Join Lübeck's office workers for a stand-up lunch of delicious, often spicy soup, in this progressive modern kitchen.

Tipasa (☎ 706 0451; Schlumacherstrasse 12-14; mains €4-16) Pizzas, curries and other budget meals are served below the faux caveman frescos of animals and Australian Aboriginal dot paintings.

Nui (☎ 203 7333; Beckergrube 72; sushi €2-16, mains €9-17; 🕑 dinner only Sat, closed Sun) Tempting smells waft from the artfully organised designer plates in this trendy but relaxed Thai-cum-Japanese restaurant.

Schiffergesellschaft (☎ 767 76; Breite Strasse 2; mains €10-23) The fact it's a tourist magnet can't detract from this 500-year-old guild-hall's thrilling atmosphere. Ships' lanterns, a gilded chandelier and orange Chinese-style lamps with revolving maritime silhouettes all join 17th-century ship models in hanging from the painted, wooden-beamed ceiling. Staff in long white aprons serve fishy Frisian specialities and local beer.

Getting There & Away

Lübeck's **airport** (LBC; www.flughafen-luebeck.de) is linked to London by budget carrier Ryanair (www.ryanair.com) and to Gdansk in Poland by Hungarian low-cost carrier Wizz-Air (www.wizzair.com).

To head into town, catch scheduled bus 6 to the Hauptbahnhof and the neighbouring central bus station. If you're flying on Ryanair to 'Hamburg-Lübeck' there are synchronised shuttle buses direct to Hamburg (one way €8, 1¼ hours).

Otherwise, trains head to Hamburg at least once an hour (€10, 45 minutes) and there are frequent services to Schwerin (€11.70, 1¼ hours). Trains to/from Copenhagen also stop here.

Getting Around

Frequent double-decker buses run to Travemünde (€3.50, 45 minutes) from the central bus station. City buses also leave from here; a short journey of a few stops costs €1.40, a normal single costs €1.90 and a trip from the airport is €2.15.

NORTH FRISIAN ISLANDS

Germany's North Frisian Islands are a strange proposition. Hearing of their long grass-covered dunes, shifting sands, bird colonies and rugged cliffs, you'd imagine them as the domain of hardy nature-lovers. Instead, they're a favourite of the German jetset and actually feel more like Martha's Vineyard. Traditional reed-thatched cottages now house luxury goods stores, such as Cartier and Louis Vuitton, while car parks on Sylt are frequently crammed with Mercedes and Porsches.

Still, bicycle-riding nobodies can still be seen taking in the pure sea air in the remoter corners of glamorous Sylt. Amrum and Föhr are more peaceful still.

SYLT

☎ 04651 / pop 21,600
Even on Sylt, the most accessible and hence busiest island, it's possible to get back to nature. Admittedly not in Westerland, which is the largest town and Sylt's Miami Beach. Here high-rises obscure views of the beach, although some of the world's best **windsurfing** is off this shore.

However, even by the time you reach Kampen things are changing. Kampen might resemble St Tropez, with ritzy restaurants and celebrity guests. But it's also home to the 52.5m-tall **Uwe Dune**. Climb the wooden steps to the top for a 360-degree view.

Towards List, on the island's northern tip, is the popular **Wanderdünengebiet**, where people hike between grass-covered dunes. Or try List's **beach-side sauna**.

Inside the Westerland train station, there's an **information pavilion** (☎ 846 1029; ☺ 9am-4pm in summer, reduced hr winter) or try **Westerland Tourism** (☎ 9980 or 0180 550 9980; www.westerland.de; ☺ 9am-5pm Mon-Thu, to 2pm Fri).

Accommodation is at a premium in summer, but ask the tourist office about cheaper private rooms. Beware that credit cards are not always accepted – even in some midrange hotels. A small *Kurtaxe*, or resort tax, will be added to your bill.

Campingplatz Kampen (☎ 420 86; Möwenweg 4; camp sites per person/tent/car €3.50/4.50/1.50; ☺ Easter-Oct) Admittedly with more caravans than tents, this is still beautifully set amid dunes near Kampen, 500m from the beach.

Hostels include the Hörnum **Jugendherberge** (☎ 880 294; www.jugendherberge.de; Friesenplatz 2; dm €15.50), in the south of the island, and List's **Jugendherberge** (☎ 870 397; www.jugendherberge.de; List; dm €19). Neither is very central, but bus services bring you close.

Hotel Gutenberg (☎ 988 80; www.hotel-gutenberg.de; Friedrichstrasse 22, Westerland; s €65-75, d €115-135; ☒) Sea-green stained wood sets the tone for this clean, friendly and light-filled place. The hotel takes credit cards. The Cheaper doubles (€100) share spotless facilities.

Hotel Wünschmann (☎ 5025; www.hotelwunschmann.de; Andreas-Dirks-Strasse, Westerland; s €80-140, d €120-250; Ⓟ) The foyer has a modern designer ambience and more traditionally decorated rooms, some with seaside balconies.

Gosch (fish sandwiches €2-3.50, meals €6-10) The Gosch fast-fish chain has colonised mainland Germany, but it originated in Sylt and remains here in force.

Kupferkanne (☎ 410 10; Stapelhooger Wai, Kampen; meals €5.50-9) Giant mugs of coffee and huge slices of cake are served outdoors at this *Alice in Wonderland*-style café, where wooden tables surrounded by a maze of low bramble hedges overlook the Wadden Sea. Meals are served in the attached Frisian house.

Sansibar (☎ 964 646; Hörnumer Strasse 80; Rantum; mains €6-32) This large grass-roof pavilion on the beach north of Hörnum is ideal for a drink or dinner at sunset.

Getting There & Around

Sylt is connected to the mainland by a narrow causeway exclusively for trains. Regular services travel from Hamburg (Altona and Hauptbahnhof) to Westerland (€39, three hours).

If driving, you must load your vehicle onto a **car train** (☎ 995 0565; www.syltshuttle.de; one way €43) in Niebüll near the Danish border. There are constant crossings (usually at least once an hour) in both directions, and no reservations can be made.

There's also a **car ferry** (☎ 0180-310-3030; www.sylt-faehre.de; one way per person/car €6/38.50) from Rømøin Denmark to List in the north.

Air Berlin (www.airberlin.com) has several services a week from Berlin and Düsseldorf to **Sylt/Westerland airport** (GWT; www.flughafen-sylt.de), Hapag-Lloyd Express (www.hlx.com) flies from Hannover, Köln-Bonn and Stuttgart, and Lufthansa (www.lufthansa.com) arrives from Frankfurt, Hamburg and Munich, among others.

Sylt's two north–south bus lines run every 20 to 30 minutes, and three other frequent lines cover the rest of the island.

AMRUM & FÖHR

Tiny Amrum is renowned for its fine white *Kniepsand*. There's a 10km stroll from the tall **lighthouse** at Wittdün to the village of Norddorf, and an 8km return hike along the beach. The **tourist office** (☎ 04682-194 33; fax 04682-940 394; ferry landing, Wittdün) can provide accommodation information.

The 'green isle' of Föhr is interesting for its Frisian culture. Its main village, Wyk,

---

WALK ON WATER

Okay, that's an exaggeration. You can't quite play Jesus in the North Frisian Islands, but you can walk between the islands at low tide. The best *Wattwandern*, as this activity is called (the same as Dutch *Wadlopen*), is between the islands of Amrum and Föhr, a full-day excursion (€25.50) also involving boat and bus trips. Contact **Adler-Schiffe** (☎ 04651-987 00; www.adler-schiffe.de).

GERMANY

boasts plenty of windmills, there are 16 northern hamlets tucked behind dikes up to 7m tall, and there's the large 12th-century church of **St Johannis** in Nieblum. The **Föhr information service** (☎ 04681-3040; fax 04681-3068; Wyk harbour) can help with more details. There is no camping here.

Getting There & Around

WDR (☎ 800; www.wdr-wyk.de) has ferries to Föhr (€5.50, 45 minutes) and Amrum (€7.80, 1½ hours) from Dagebüll Hafen (change in Niebüll).

Adler-Schiffe (☎ 04651-987 00; www.adler-schiffe .de; Boysenstrasse 13, Westerland; return adult/child €22/12) offers day cruises from Hörnum harbour in Sylt, and has quicker journeys on its *Adler Express* ship.

On Amrum, there are buses between the ferry terminal in Wittdün and Norddorf.

GERMANY DIRECTORY

ACCOMMODATION

Local tourist offices are great resources for accommodation in Germany – almost all offer a *Gastgeberverzeichnis* (accommodation list) and a *Zimmervermittlung* (room-finding service), and staff will usually go out of their way to find something in your price range.

In this book, options are listed by price, with the cheapest first. Accommodation usually includes breakfast, except in camping grounds and holiday apartments. Prices include private bathrooms unless otherwise specified.

Germany has more than 2000 organised camping grounds, several hundred of which stay open throughout the year. Prices are around €3 to €5 for an adult, plus €3 to €7 for a car and/or tent. Look out for ecologically responsible camping grounds sporting the Green Leaf award from the ADAC motoring association.

Deutsches Jugendherbergswerk (DJH; www.djh .de) coordinates the official Hostelling International (HI) hostels in Germany. Guests must be members of an HI-affiliated organisation, or join the DJH when checking in. The annual fee is €12/20 for junior/senior, which refers to visitors below/above 26 years old. Bavaria is the only state that enforces a strict maximum age of 26 for visitors. A dorm bed ranges from around €15 to €20 for juniors and €16 to €25 for seniors. Camping at a hostel (where permitted) is generally half-price. Sheet hire costs from €2.50 to €4.

Private rooms and guesthouses can be excellent value, especially for lone travellers, with prices starting as low as €25. Budget hotels and *pensions* typically charge under €70 for a double room (under €50 with shared bathroom), while good-value mid-range options come in around €70 to €140. Anything over €140 can generally be considered top end, and should offer enough amenities to justify the price – spa facilities are a common extra.

Renting an apartment for a week or more is a popular option, particularly for small groups. Again, tourist offices are generally the best source of information, or have a look in newspaper classifieds under *Ferienwohnungen* (FeWo) or *Ferien-Apartments*. Rates vary widely but decrease dramatically with the length of stay. Local *Mitwohnzentralen* (accommodation-finding services) can help in finding shared houses and longer-stay rentals.

ACTIVITIES

Germany, with its rugged Alps, picturesque uplands and fairy-tale forests, is ideal for hiking and mountaineering. There are well-marked trails crisscrossing the countryside, especially in popular areas such as the Black Forest (see p237), the Harz Mountains (p202), the Saxon Switzerland area (p191) and the Thuringian Forest. The Bavarian Alps (p227) offer the most dramatic and inspiring scenery, however, and are the centre of mountaineering in Germany. Good sources of information on hiking and mountaineering are: **Verband Deutscher Gebirgs-und Wandervereine** (Federation of German Hiking Clubs; ☎ 0561-938 730; www.wanderverband .de); and **Deutscher Alpenverein** (German Alpine Club; ☎ 089-140 030; www.alpenverein.de).

The Bavarian Alps are the most extensive area for winter sports. Cross-country skiing is also good in the Black Forest and Harz Mountains. Ski equipment starts at around €15 per day, and daily ski-lift passes start at around €15. Local tourist offices are the best sources of information.

Cyclists will often find marked cycling routes, and eastern Germany has much to offer in the way of lightly travelled back roads. There's an extensive cycling trail along the Elbe River, and islands like Rügen Island (p210) are also good for cycling. For more details and tips, see Getting Around on (p287).

BOOKS

For a more detailed guide to the country, pick up a copy of Lonely Planet's *Germany*. Lonely Planet also publishes *Bavaria*, and *Berlin* and *Munich* city guides.

The German literary tradition is strong and there are many works that provide excellent background to the German experience. Mark Twain's *A Tramp Abroad* is recommended for his comical observations on German life.

For a more modern analysis of the German character and the issues that are facing Germany, dip into *Germany and the Germans* by John Ardagh.

BUSINESS HOURS

By law, shops in Germany may open from 6am to 8pm on weekdays and until 4pm on Saturday. In practice, however, only department stores and some supermarkets and fashion shops stay open until 8pm. But this is changing and in large cities more places are finding ways to stay open later and even on Sunday.

Banking hours are generally 8.30am to 1pm and 2.30pm to 4pm weekdays, but many banks remain open all day, and until 5.30pm on Thursday. government offices close for the weekend at 1pm or 3pm on Friday. Museums are often closed on Monday; opening hours vary greatly, although many are open late one evening per week.

Restaurants are usually open from 11am to midnight, with varying *Ruhetage* or closing days; many close for lunch during the day from 3pm to 6pm. Cafés often close around 8pm, though equal numbers stay open until 2am or later. Bars that don't serve food open between 5pm and 8pm and may close as late as 5am (if at all) in the larger cities.

DANGERS & ANNOYANCES

Although the usual cautions should be taken, theft and other crimes against travellers are relatively rare in Germany. Africans, Asians and southern Europeans may encounter racial prejudice, especially in eastern Germany, where they can be singled out as convenient scapegoats for economic hardship. However, the animosity is usually directed against immigrants, not tourists.

DISCOUNT CARDS

Many cities offer discount cards. These cards will usually combine up to three days' free use of public transport with free or reduced admission to major local museums and attractions. They're generally a good deal if you want to fit a lot in; see the Information section under the relevant destination and ask at tourist offices for full details.

EMBASSIES & CONSULATES

German Embassies & Consulates

Australia (☎ 02-6270 1911; 119 Empire Circuit, Yarralumla, ACT 2600)

Canada (☎ 613-232 1101; 1 Waverley St, Ottawa, Ont K2P 0T8)

France (☎ 01-53 83 45 00; 13-15 Ave Franklin Roosevelt, 75008 Paris)

Ireland (☎ 01-269 3011; 31 Trimleston Ave, Booterstown, Dublin)

New Zealand (☎ 04-473 6063; 90-92 Hobson St, Wellington)

The Netherlands (☎ 070-342 0600; Groot Hertoginnelaan 18-20, 2517 EG The Hague)

UK (☎ 020-7824 1300; 23 Belgrave Square, London SW1X 8PZ)

USA (☎ 202-298 4000; 4645 Reservoir Rd, NW Washington, DC 20007-1998)

Embassies & Consulates in Germany

The following embassies are all in Berlin. Many countries also have consulates in cities such as Frankfurt-am-Main and Munich.

Australia (Map pp170-1; ☎ 880 0800; Wallstrasse 76-78)

Canada (Map pp170-1; ☎ 203 120; Leipziger Platz 17, Tiergarten)

France (Map pp170-1; ☎ 590 039 000; Pariser Platz 5)

Ireland (Map pp170-1; ☎ 220 720; Friedrichstrasse 200)

New Zealand (Map pp170-1; ☎ 209 560; Friedrichstrasse 60)

South Africa Map pp170-1; ☎ 220 730; Tiergartenstrasse 18)

The Netherlands (Map pp170-1; ☎ 209 560; Klosterstrasse 50)

UK (Map pp170-1; ☎ 204 570; Wilhelmstrasse 70-71)

USA (Map pp170-1; ☎ 238 5174; Neustädtische Kirchstrasse 4-5)

FESTIVALS & EVENTS

January-February

Carnival season Shrovetide – also known as 'Fasching' or 'Karneval' – sees many Carnival events begin in large cities, most notably Cologne, Munich, Düsseldorf and Mainz. The partying hits a peak just before Ash Wednesday.
International Film Festival Held in Berlin (see p176).

March

Frankfurt Music Fair
Frankfurt Jazz Fair
Spring Fairs Held throughout Germany.
Bach Festival

April

Munich Ballet Days
Mannheim May Fair
Stuttgart Jazz Festival
Walpurgisnacht Festivals Held the night of 30 April/1 May in the Harz Mountains.

May

Dresden International Dixieland Jazz Festival
Dresden Music Festival Held in last week of May into first week of June.
Red Wine Festival Held in Rüdesheim.

June

Händel Festival Held in Halle.
International Theatre Festival Held in Freiburg.
Moselle Wine Week Held in Cochem.
Munich Film Festival
Sailing regatta Held in Kiel.

July

Berlin Love Parade See p176.
Folk festivals Held throughout Germany.
International Music Seminar Held in Weimar.
Kulmbach Beer Festival
Munich Opera Festival
Richard Wagner Festival Held in Bayreuth.

August

Heidelberg Castle Festival
Wine festivals Held throughout the Rhineland area.

September

Berlin Festival of Music & Drama
Oktoberfest Held in Munich (see p215).

October

Bremen Freimarkt
Berlin Jazzfest
Frankfurt Book Fair

November-December

Christmas fairs Held throughout Germany, most famously in Munich, Nuremberg, Berlin, Essen and Heidelberg.
St Martin's Festival Held throughout Rhineland and Bavaria.
Silvester New Year's Eve, celebrated everywhere.

GAY & LESBIAN TRAVELLERS

German people are generally fairly tolerant of homosexuality, but gays (Schwule) and lesbians (Lesben) still don't enjoy the same social acceptance in Germany as in some other northern European countries. Most progressive are the larger cities, particularly Berlin, Frankfurt-am-Main and Munich, which have dozens of gay and lesbian bars and meeting places. The age of consent is 18 years. Christopher Street Day, in June, is the biggest Pride festival in Germany, with events held in Berlin and many other major towns.

HOLIDAYS

Germany has many public holidays, some of which vary from state to state. Holidays include:
New Year's Day 1 January
Easter March/April
Labour Day 1 May
Ascension Day 40 days after Easter
Whitsun/Pentecost May/June
Day of German Unity 3 October
All Saints' Day 1 November
Day of Prayer & Repentance 18 November
Christmas 24–26 December

MEDIA

Magazines

Germany's most popular magazines are Der Spiegel, Focus and Stern. Die Zeit is a weekly publication about culture and the arts.

Newspapers

The most widely read newspapers in Germany are Die Welt, Frankfurter Allgemeine, Munich's Süddeutsche Zeitung and the left-leaning Die Tageszeitung (Taz). Bild is Germany's favourite sensationalist tabloid, part of the Axel Springer publishing empire.

Radio

German radio sticks to a fairly standard diet of news and discussion or Europop, inane chatter and adverts, though most regions and cities have their own stations so quality can vary. The BBC World Service (on varying AM wavelengths) broadcasts in English.

TV

Germany's two national TV channels are the government-funded ARD and ZDF. They are augmented by a plethora of regional broadcasters, plus private cable channels such as Pro7, SAT1 and RTL, which show a lot of dubbed US series and films with long ad breaks. You can catch English-language news and sports programmes on cable or satellite TV in most hotels and *pensions*.

MONEY

The easiest places to change cash in Germany are the banks or foreign exchange counters at airports and train stations, particularly those of the Reisebank. The main banks in larger cities generally have money-changing machines for after-hours use, although they don't often offer reasonable rates. Some local Sparkasse banks have good rates and low charges.

There are international ATMs virtually everywhere in Germany. Typically, withdrawals over the counter against cards at major banks cost a flat €5 per transaction. Check other fees and the availability of services with your bank before you leave home.

Travellers cheques can be cashed at any bank and the most widely accepted are Amex, Thomas Cook and Barclays. A percentage commission (usually a minimum of €5) is charged by most banks on any travellers cheque, even those issued in euros.

POST

Standard post office hours are 8am to 6pm weekdays and to noon on Saturday. Many train station post offices stay open later or offer limited services outside these hours.

Within Germany and the EU, standard-sized postcards cost €0.45 and a 20g letter is €0.55. Postcards to North America and Australasia cost €1, a 20g airmail letter is €1.55. Surface-mail parcels up to 2kg within Europe are €8.20, €12.30 to destinations elsewhere. Airmail parcels up to 1kg are €10.30/21 within Europe/elsewhere.

TELEPHONE

Calling from a private phone is most expensive between 9am and 6pm. From telephone boxes, city calls cost €0.10 per minute, calls

---

> **EMERGENCY NUMBERS**
>
> ■ Ambulance ☎ 112
> ■ Fire ☎ 112
> ■ Police ☎ 110
> ■ ADAC breakdown service ☎ 0180-222 2222

---

to anywhere else in Germany €0.20 per minute.

Expensive reverse-charge (collect) calls can be made to some countries through home-direct services. Check with your long-distance carrier or phone company before you leave home. The best bet is to have somebody at home use their cheap rates to call you.

For directory assistance within Germany call ☎ 118 33 (☎ 118 37 in English); both cost €0.25 plus €0.99 per minute. International information is ☎ 118 34 (€0.55 per 20 seconds).

Mobile Phones

Mobile phones ('handies') are ubiquitous in Germany; the main operators are T-Mobile, Vodafone, O2 and E-Plus. You can pick up a pre-pay SIM card for around €30; top-up cards are available from kiosks, various shops and vending machines. Mobile numbers generally begin with a ☎ 016 or ☎ 017 prefix. Calling from a landline costs up to €0.54 per minute.

Phone Codes

The country code for Germany is ☎ 49. To ring abroad from Germany, dial ☎ 00 followed by the country code, area code and number.

An operator can be reached on ☎ 0180-200 1033.

Phonecards

Most pay phones in Germany accept only phonecards, available for €5, €10 and €20 at post offices, news kiosks, tourist offices and banks. One call unit costs a little more than €0.06 from a private telephone and €0.10 from a public phone.

TIME

Germany runs on Western European time, one hour ahead of GMT.

TRAVELLERS WITH DISABILITIES

Germany is fair at best (but better than much of Europe) for the needs of physically disabled travellers, with access ramps for wheelchairs and/or lifts in some public buildings.

Deutsche Bahn operates a **Mobility Service Centre** (☎ 01805-512 512; ◷ 8am-8pm Mon-Fri, 8am-2pm Sat) whose operators can answer questions about station and train access. With one day's notice, they can also arrange for someone to meet you at your destination.

VISAS

Citizens of the EU and some other Western European countries can enter Germany on an official identity card. Americans, Australians, Canadians, Israelis, Japanese, New Zealanders and Singaporeans require only a valid passport (no visa). Germany is also part of the Schengen visa scheme (see p592). Three months is the usual limit of stay, less for citizens of some developing countries.

WORK

With unemployment always high, Germany offers limited prospects for employment unless you have high-level specialist skills such as IT expertise. EU citizens can work in Germany with an *Aufenthaltserlaubnis* (residency permit); non-EU citizens require a work permit as well.

TRANSPORT IN GERMANY

GETTING THERE & AWAY

Air

The main arrival and departure points in Germany used to be Frankfurt-am-Main, and Munich. But with the explosion of budget carriers, almost any town with a tarmac seems to be getting a few flights. Places such as Düsseldorf, Berlin, Nuremberg and even Baden-Baden have cheap flights to parts of Europe. See p596 for details on how you can find cheap flights within Europe.

Ryanair, easyJet, Air Berlin, DBA and Germanwings are among the foremost cheap options in Germany, but don't count Lufthansa out: it has been aggressively competing on price as well.

The following airlines all fly to/from Germany:

Air Berlin (code AB; ☎ 01805-737 800; www.airberlin.de)
Alitalia (code AZ; ☎ 01805-074 747; www.alitalia.it)
British Airways (code BA; ☎ 01805-266 522; www.britishairways.com)
Czech Airlines (code OK; ☎ 01805-006 737; www.csa.cz)
DBA (code DI; ☎ 0900 1100322; www.flydba.com)
easyJet (code BH; ☎ 01803-654 321; www.easyjet.com)
Germania Express (code ST; ☎ 01805-737 100; www.gexx.de)
Germanwings (code 4U; ☎ 01805-955 855; www.germanwings.com)
Iberia (code IB; ☎ 01803-000 613; www.iberia.es)
LOT (code LO; ☎ 01803-000 336; www.lot.com)
Lufthansa (code LH; ☎ 01803-803 803; www.lufthansa.com)
Ryanair (code FR; ☎ 0190-170 100; www.ryanair.com)
SAS (code SK; ☎ 01803-234 023; www.scandinavian.net)
Wizzair (code W6; www.wizzair.com)

Land

BUS

Travelling by bus between Germany and the rest of Europe is cheaper than by train or plane, but journeys will take a lot longer.

Eurolines is a consortium of national bus companies operating routes throughout the continent. Sample one-way fares and travel times include: London–Frankfurt (€80, 16 hours); Amsterdam–Frankfurt (€39, eight hours); Paris–Hamburg (€69, 11½ hours); Paris–Cologne (€39, 6½ hours); Prague–Berlin (€29, seven hours) and Barcelona–Frankfurt (€89, 20 hours). Eurolines has a discounted youth fare for those under-26 that saves you around 10%. Tickets can be purchased throughout Germany at most train stations. Eurolines' German arm is **Deutsche-Touring** (☎ 069-790 350; www.deutsche-touring.com).

CAR & MOTORCYCLE

Germany is served by an excellent highway system. If coming from the UK, the quickest option is the Channel Tunnel. Ferries take longer but are cheaper. You can be in Germany three hours after the ferry docks.

Within Europe, autobahns and highways become jammed on weekends in summer and before and after holidays. This is especially true where border checks are still carried out, such as going to/from the Czech Republic and Poland. For details on road rules when driving in Germany, see p288.

TRAIN

A favourite way to get to Germany from elsewhere in Europe is by train.

Long-distance trains between major German cities and other countries are called EuroCity (EC) trains. The main German hubs with the best connections for major European cities are Hamburg (Scandinavia); Cologne (Thalsys trains to France, Belgium and the Netherlands, with Eurostar connections from Brussels going on to London); Munich (southern and southeastern Europe) and Berlin (Eastern Europe).

Often longer international routes are served by at least one day train and often a night train as well.

Sea

If you're heading to/from the UK or Scandinavia, port options include Hamburg, Lübeck, Rostock, Sassnitz and Kiel. The Puttgarden–Rodbyhavn ferry to Copenhagen is popular. In eastern Germany, ferries run daily between Trelleborg (Sweden) and Sassnitz, on Rügen Island (p210).

There are daily services between Kiel and Gothenburg (Sweden) and Oslo (Norway). The Kiel–Gothenburg trip takes 13½ hours and costs from €37 to €85. A ferry between Travemünde (near Lübeck) and Trelleborg (Sweden) runs one to four times daily. The journey takes seven hours and costs from €20 to €40. Car-ferry service is good from Gedser (Denmark) to Rostock.

GETTING AROUND
Air

There are lots of flights within the country, many by budget carriers such as Air Berlin, DBA and Germanwings. See opposite for additional details. Note that with check-in times and the like, flying is often not as efficient as a fast train.

Bicycle

Radwandern (bicycle touring) is very popular in Germany. Pavements are often divided into separate sections for pedestrians and cyclists – be warned that these divisions are taken very seriously. Favoured routes include the Rhine, Moselle, Elbe and Danube Rivers and the Lake Constance area. Of course, cycling is strictly *verboten* (forbidden) on the autobahns. Hostel-to-hostel biking is an easy way to go, and route guides are

often sold at DJH hostels. There are well-equipped cycling shops in almost every town, and a fairly active market for used touring bikes.

Simple three-gear bicycles can be hired from around €10/35 per day/week, and more robust mountain bikes from €15/50. DB publishes *Bahn&Bike,* an excellent annual handbook (in German) covering bike rental and repair shops, routes, maps and other resources. **DB** (☎ 0180-515 14 14; www.bahn.de /bahnundbike) also has extensive live information on bike rentals and carriage.

A separate ticket must be purchased whenever you carry your bike on trains (generally €3 to €6). Many trains (excluding ICEs) have at least one 2nd-class carriage with a bicycle compartment.

Germany's main cycling organisation is the **Allgemeiner Deutscher Fahrrad Club** (ADFC; ☎ 0421-346 290; www.adfc.de).

Boat

Boats are most likely to be used for basic transport when travelling to or between the Frisian Islands, though tours along the Rhine, Elbe and Moselle Rivers are also popular. During summer there are frequent services on Lake Constance but, with the exception of the Constance–Meersburg and the Friedrichshafen–Romanshorn car ferries, these boats are really more tourist crafts than a transport option. From April to October, excursion boats ply lakes and rivers in Germany and can be a lovely way to see the country.

Bus

The bus network in Germany functions primarily in support of the train network. That is, they go to destinations that are not serviced by trains. Bus stations or stops are usually located near the train station in any town. Consider using buses when you want to cut across two train lines and avoid long train rides to and from a transfer point. A good example of where to do this is in the Alps, where the best way to follow the peaks is by bus.

Within Germany **Eurolines** (☎ 069-790 350) operates as Deutsche-Touring GmbH; services include the Romantic and Castle Roads buses in southern Germany, as well as organised bus tours of Germany lasting a week or more.

GERMANY

Car & Motorcycle

AUTOMOBILE ASSOCIATIONS

Germany's main motoring organisation is the Munich-based **Allgemeiner Deutscher Auto mobil Club** (ADAC; ☎ 089-767 60; www.adac.de), which has offices in all major cities.

DRIVING LICENCE

Visitors do not need an international driving licence to drive in Germany; technically you should carry an official translation of your licence with you, but in practice this is rarely necessary.

FUEL & SPARE PARTS

Prices for fuel vary from €1.30 to €1.35 per litre for unleaded regular. Avoid buying fuel at the more expensive autobahn filling stations. Petrol stations are generally easy to find, although they can be scarce in the centres of many towns.

HIRE

You usually must be at least 21 years of age to hire a car in Germany. You'll need to show your licence and passport, and make sure you keep the insurance certificate for the vehicle with you at all times.

Germany's four main rental companies are **Avis** (☎ 0180-555 77; www.avis.de), **Europcar** (☎ 0180-580 00; www.europcar.de), **Hertz** (☎ 0180-533 3535; www.hertz.de) and **Sixt** (☎ 0180-526 0250; www.sixt.de).

INSURANCE

You must have third-party insurance to enter Germany with a vehicle.

ROAD CONDITIONS

The autobahn system of motorways runs throughout Germany. Road signs (and most motoring maps) indicate national autobahn routes in blue with an 'A' number, while international routes have green signs with an 'E'. Though efficient, the autobahns are often busy, and visitors can have trouble coping with the high speeds. Secondary roads (usually designated with a 'B' number) are slower, but easier on the nerves and more scenic.

Cars are impractical in urban areas. Vending machines on many streets sell parking vouchers which must be displayed clearly behind the windscreen. Leaving your car in a central *Parkhaus* (car park) costs roughly €10 per day or €1.25 per hour.

ROAD RULES

Road rules are easy to understand and standard international signs are in use. You drive on the right, and most cars are right-hand drive. Right of way is usually signed, with major roads given priority, but on unmarked intersections traffic coming from the right always has right of way.

The usual speed limits are 50km/h in built-up areas and 100km/h on the open road. The speed on autobahns is unlimited, though there's an advisory speed of 130km/h; exceptions are clearly signposted.

The blood-alcohol limit for drivers is 0.05%. Obey rules carefully, as the police are very efficient and issue heavy on-the-spot fines. Germany also has one of the highest concentrations of speed cameras in Europe.

Local Transport

Public transport is excellent within big cities and small towns, and is generally based on buses, *Strassenbahn* (trams), S-Bahn and/or U-Bahn (underground trains). Tickets cover all forms of transit; fares are determined by zones or time travelled, sometimes both. Multiticket strips and day passes are generally available offering better value than single-ride tickets.

Make certain that you have a ticket when boarding – only buses and some trams let you buy tickets from the driver. In some cases you will have to validate it on the platform or once aboard. Ticket inspections are frequent (especially at night and on holidays) and the fine is a non-negotiable €30 or more.

Train

Operated almost entirely by Deutsche Bahn (DB; www.bahn.de), the German train system is the finest in Europe, and is generally the best way to get around the country.

Trains run on an interval system, so wherever you're heading, you can count on a service at least every two hours. Schedules are integrated throughout the country so that connections between trains are time-saving and tight, often only five minutes. Of course this means that when a train is late, connections are missed and you can find yourself stuck waiting for the next train.

CLASSES

It's rarely worth buying a 1st-class ticket on German trains; 2nd class is usually quite comfortable. There's more difference between the train classifications – basically the faster a train travels, the plusher (and more expensive) it is.

Train types include:

ICE InterCityExpress services run at speeds up to 300km/h. The trains are very comfortable and feature restaurant cars.

IC/EC Called InterCity or EuroCity, these are the premier conventional trains of DB. When trains are crowded, the open-seating coaches are much more comfortable than the older carriages with compartments.

RE RegionalExpress trains are local trains that make limited stops. They are fairly fast and run at one- or two-hourly intervals.

RB RegionalBahn are the slowest DB trains, not missing a single cow town.

S-Bahn These DB-operated trains run frequent services in larger urban areas. Not to be confused with U-Bahns, which are run by local authorities who don't honour rail passes.

EN, ICN, D These are night trains, although an occasional D may be an extra daytime train.

COSTS

Standard DB ticket prices are distance-based. You will usually be sold a ticket for the shortest distance to your destination.

Sample fares for one-way, 2nd-class ICE travel include Hamburg–Munich €115, Frankfurt-am-Main–Berlin €98 and Frankfurt-am-Main–Munich €75. Tickets are good for four days from the day you tell the agent your journey will begin, and you can make unlimited stopovers along your route during that time. In this chapter, fares given between towns are all undiscounted second class.

There are hosts of special fares that allow you to beat the high cost of regular tickets. DB is now selling tickets like airlines (ie trains with light loads may have tickets available at a discount). The key is to ask at the ticket counters. Most DB personnel are happy to help you sort through the thicket of ticket prices.

The following are among the most popular train fares offered by DB (2nd class):

BahnCard 25/50/100 Only worthwhile for extended visits to Germany, these discount cards entitle holders to 25/50/100% off regular fares and cost €50/200/3000.

Schönes Wochenende 'Good Weekend' tickets allow unlimited use of RE, RB and S-Bahn trains on a Saturday or Sunday between midnight and 3am the next day, for up to five people travelling together, or one or both parents and all their children/grandchildren for €28. They are best suited to weekend day trips from urban areas.

Sparpreis Round-trip tickets offered at major discounts.

Surf&Rail As the name implies these are bargains found online. Think €59 round-trip Munich-Berlin.

RESERVATIONS

Nearly all DB stations offer the option of buying tickets with credit cards at machines for long-haul trips; these usually have English-language options, but if in doubt consult the ticket window. Buying a ticket or supplement (*Zuschlag*) from a conductor carries a penalty (€1.50 to €4.50). If you're stuck you can *technically* use a credit card on the train, but in practice it may not be possible.

On some trains there are no conductors at all, and roving inspectors enforce compliance. If you are caught travelling without a valid ticket the fine is €30, no excuses.

During peak periods, a seat reservation (€3) on a long-distance train can mean the difference between squatting near the toilet or relaxing in your own seat. Express reservations can be made at the last minute.

SCHEDULE INFORMATION

The DB website (www.bahn.de) is excellent. There is extensive info in English and you can use it to sort out all the discount offers and schemes. In addition it has an excellent schedule feature that works not just for Germany but the rest of Europe.

For a phone schedule and fare information (available in English), call ☎ 01805-996 633 (€0.13 per minute).

TRAIN PASSES

Agencies outside Germany sell German Rail passes for unlimited travel on all DB trains for a number of days in a 30-day period. Sample 2nd-class prices for adults/under 26 are €160/130 for four days. Most Eurail and Inter-Rail passes are valid in Germany.

Hungary

Hungary's uniqueness extends beyond its incomprehensible tongue. Here's your chance to strip down to your swimmers in the midwinter minuses and loll around an open-air thermal spa, while snowy patches glisten around you. Following that, you could go to a smoky bar where a Romani band yelps while a crazed crowd whacks its boot-heels, as commanded by Hungarian tradition. Or go clubbing in an ancient bathhouse, where all dance in swimsuits, waist-deep in healing waters.

If these pursuits don't appeal, check out Roman ruins, ancient castles, Turkish minarets in baroque cities, or experience the rural pleasures of cowboys riding astride five horses, storks nesting on streetlamps, and a sea of apricot trees in bloom.

Cosmopolitan Budapest is a capital to rival any on the continent – with world-class operas, monumental historical buildings, and the Danube River flowing through the middle of it all. Prices here are somewhere in the middle: not nearly as high as Austria or nearly as reasonable as Ukraine. Having established itself as a state in the year 1000, Hungary has a long history, a rich culture and strong folk traditions that are well worth exploring. So go ahead, dive in.

FAST FACTS

- **Area** 93,000 sq km
- **Capital** Budapest
- **Currency** forint (Ft); €1 = 276Ft; US$1 = 216Ft; UK£1 = 410Ft; A$1 = 164Ft; ¥100 = 185Ft; NZ$1 = 143Ft
- **Famous for** paprika, Bull's Blood and *csárda* music
- **Official Language** Hungarian (Magyar)
- **Phrases** *jo napot kivanok* (good day); *szia* (hi/bye); *köszönöm* (thank you)
- **Population** 10 million
- **Telephone Codes** country code ☎ 36; international access code ☎ 00; intercity access code ☎ 06
- **Visa** no visa required for most countries if you stay less than 90 days; see p350

HUNGARY

HIGHLIGHTS

- Take a bath and ease your soul and your joints in Budapest's **thermal baths** (p306) and throw in a mudpack or water massage to get your blood flowing.
- See the capital city bathed in lights from atop Buda's **Castle Hill** (p305). The gothic Parliament building glows like a birthday cake.
- Taste some of Hungary's greatest wines in the alluring Valley of Beautiful Women in **Eger** (p342) and see the city's wonderful ancient castle and baroque architecture.
- Watch the cowboys ride at Bugac in **Kiskunsági Nemzeti Park** (p339) at the heart of the Hungarian *puszta* (plain) – the stuff of myth and legend.
- Feel a bit Mediterranean in the southern town of **Pécs** (p333), exploring the 16th-century Mosque Church and other Turkish sights.

ITINERARIES

- **One week** Make sure that you spend at least four days in Budapest, checking out the sights, museums and pavement cafés. On your fifth day take a day trip to a Danube Bend town. See the open-air museum in Szentendre or the cathedral at Esztergom. Day six can be spent getting a morning train to Pécs and seeing the lovely Turkish remains, and checking out the many galleries in town. Let your hair down on day seven and try some local wine in Eger, a baroque town set in red-wine country.
- **Two weeks** If you've already spent a week in Budapest, you still have time to cover a lot of ground, since all the places mentioned in this chapter are no more than five hours by train from the capital. If you are here in the summer, make sure you spend some time exploring the towns around Lake Balaton, or just chill out on the beach by the side of this popular lake. Tihany is a rambling hillside village filled with craftsmen's houses, set on a peninsula that is a protected nature zone. Keszthely is an old town with a great palace in addition to a beach. Alternatively, head south to Pécs and see more of the Great Plain. Szeged is on the Tisza River and Kecskemét is further north. Finish your trip in Eger.

CLIMATE & WHEN TO GO

Hungary has a temperate continental climate. July and August are the warmest months, and when the thermometer hits 27°C it can feel much hotter, given that most places don't have air-con. Spring is unpredictable, but usually arrives in April. November is already rainy and chilly; January and February are the coldest, dreariest months, with temperatures dropping below 0°C. September, with loads of sunshine, mild temperatures and grape-harvest festivals in the countryside, may be the best time to visit. May, with a profusion of flowers and sunshine, is a close second. See p585 for climate charts.

The busiest tourist season is July and August (Lake Balaton is especially crowded), but hotels quote high-season prices from April to October. In provincial and smaller towns, attractions are often closed, or have reduced hours, from October to May.

HISTORY
Pre-Hungarian Hungary

The plains of the Carpathian Basin attracted waves of migration, from both east and west, long before the Magyar tribes decided to settle here. The Celts occupied the area in the 3rd century BC but the Romans conquered and expelled them just before the Christian era. The lands west of the Danube (Transdanubia) in today's Hungary became part of the Roman province of Pannonia, where a Roman legion was stationed at the town of Aquincum (now

---

HOW MUCH?

- **Lángos (fried dough snack)** 120-220Ft
- **Hostel bed** 1600-3000Ft
- **Loaf of bread** 160Ft
- **Midrange double room** 8500-14,200Ft
- **Symphony ticket in Budapest** 1200-2500Ft

LONELY PLANET INDEX

- **Litre of petrol** 265Ft
- **Litre of bottled water** 150Ft
- **Beer (a bottle from grocery store)** 130Ft
- **Souvenir T-shirt** 900-2500Ft
- **Street snack (gyro)** 500Ft

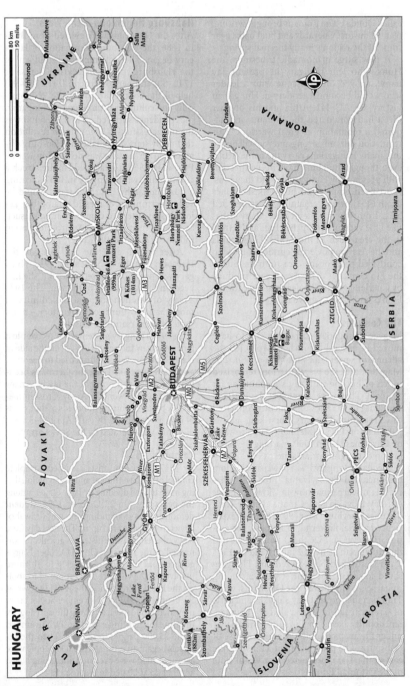

called Óbuda). The Romans brought writing, planted the first vineyards and built baths near some of the region's many thermal springs.

A new surge of nomadic tribesmen, the Huns, who lent Hungary its present-day name, arrived on the scene with a leader who would become legendary in Hungarian history. By AD 441, Attila and his brother Bleda had conquered the Romans and acquired a reputation as great warriors. This reputation still runs strong and you will notice that many Hungarians carry the name Attila, even though the Huns have no connection with present-day Hungarians, and the Huns' short-lived empire did not outlast Attila's death (453), when remaining tribesmen fled back from whence they came. Many tribes filled the vacuum left by the Huns and settled in the area, such as the Goths, Longobards and the Avars, a powerful Turkic people who controlled parts of the area from the 5th to the 8th centuries. The Avars were subdued by Charlemagne in 796, leaving space for the Franks and Slavs to move in.

The Conquest

Magyar (Hungarian) tribes are said to have moved in around 896, when Árpád led the alliance of seven tribes into the region. The Magyars, a fierce warrior tribe, terrorised much of Europe with raids reaching as far as Spain. They were stopped at the Battle of Augsburg in 955 and subsequently converted to Christianity. Hungary's first king and its patron saint, István (Stephen), was crowned on Christmas Day in 1000, marking the foundation of the Hungarian state.

Medieval Hungary was a powerful kingdom that included Transylvania (now in Romania), Transcarpathia (now in Ukraine), modern-day Slovakia and Croatia. Under King Matthias Corvinus (1458–90), Hungary experienced a brief flowering of Renaissance culture. However, in 1526 the Ottomans defeated the Hungarian army at Mohács and by 1541 Buda Castle had been seized and Hungary sliced in three. The central part, including Buda, was controlled by the Ottomans, while Transdanubia, present-day Slovakia, and parts of Transcarpathia were ruled by Hungarian nobility based in Pozsony (Bratislava) under the auspices of the Austrian House of Habsburg. The principality of Transylvania, east of the Tisza, prospered as a vassal state of the Ottoman Empire.

Habsburg Hegemony & the Wars

After the Ottomans were evicted from Buda in 1686, the Habsburg domination of Hungary began. The 'enlightened absolutism' of the Habsburg monarchs Maria Theresa (r 1740–80) and her son Joseph II (r 1780–90) helped the country leap forward economically and culturally. Rumblings of Hungarian independence surfaced off and on, but it was the unsuccessful 1848 Hungarian revolution that really started to shake the Habsburg oligarchy. After Austria was defeated in war by Prussia in 1866, a weakened empire struck a compromise with Hungary in 1867, creating a dual monarchy. The two states would be self-governing in domestic affairs, but act jointly in matters of common interest, such as foreign relations. The Austro-Hungarian monarchy lasted until WWI.

After WWI and the collapse of the Habsburg Empire in November 1918, Hungary was proclaimed a republic. But she had been on the losing side of the war. The 1920 Treaty of Trianon stripped the country of more than two-thirds of its territory – a hot topic of conversation to this day.

In 1941 Hungary's attempts to recover lost territories saw the nation in war, on the side of Nazi Germany. When leftists tried to negotiate a separate peace in 1944, the Germans occupied Hungary and brought the fascist Arrow Cross Party to power. The Arrow Cross immediately began deporting hundreds of thousands of Jews to Auschwitz. By early April 1945, all of Hungary was liberated by the Soviet army.

Communism

By 1947 the communists assumed complete control of the government and began nationalising industry and dividing up large estates among the peasantry. On 23 October 1956, student demonstrators demanding the withdrawal of Soviet troops were fired upon. The next day Imre Nagy, the reformist minister of agriculture, was named prime minister. On 28 October Nagy's government offered an amnesty to all those involved in the violence and promised to abolish the hated secret police, the ÁVH (known as ÁVO until 1949). On 4 November Soviet tanks moved into Budapest, crushing the uprising. By the time the fighting ended on 11 November, some 25,000 people were dead. Then the reprisals began: an estimated 20,000 people were arrested; 2000 were executed, including Nagy; another 250,000 fled to Austria.

By the 1970s Hungary had abandoned strict central economic control in favour of a limited market system, often referred to as 'Goulash Communism'. In June 1987 Károly Grósz took over as premier and Hungary began moving towards full democracy. The huge numbers of East Germans who were able to slip through the Iron Curtain by leaving via Hungary may have contributed to the eventual crumbling of the Berlin Wall.

The Republic

At their party congress in February 1989 the Hungarian communists agreed to give up their monopoly on power. The Republic of Hungary was proclaimed in October, and democratic elections were scheduled for March 1990. Hungary changed its political system with scarcely a murmur, and the last Soviet troops left the country in June 1991.

The painful transition to a full market economy resulted in declining living standards for most people and a recession in the early 1990s, but the end of the 20th and early years of the 21st century have seen astonishing growth. Hungary became a fully fledged member of NATO in 1999. In a national referendum during April 2003, the Hungarian people voted to join the European Union (EU), and the country became one of the newest members of the EU on 1 May 2004.

The dissolution of intra-European customs controls at airports and borders was immediate, but border restrictions with neighbouring members Austria, Slovakia and Slovenia will not be completely removed any time soon. Hungary aims to adopt the euro by 2010, providing that its high economic deficit is brought within acceptable levels.

In April 2006 the Socialist-led coalition won the parliamentary elections, becoming the first government to win consecutive terms in office since the restoration of democracy in 1990. The new prime minister, Ferenc Gyurcsany, was chosen by the Socialist Party to succeed the former prime minister, Peter Medgyessy. The coalition has been in government since the last elections in 2002.

PEOPLE

Approximately 10.6 million Magyar people live within the national borders, and another five million Hungarians and their descendants are abroad. The estimated 1.44 million Hungarians in Transylvania constitute the largest ethnic minority in Europe, and there are another 520,000 in Slovakia, 295,000 in Serbia and Montenegro, 157,000 in Ukraine and 40,600 in Austria.

Ethnic Magyars make up approximately 93% of the population. Many minority groups estimate their numbers to be significantly higher than official counts. There are 13 recognised minorities in the country, including Germans (0.6%), Slovaks (0.2%), Croatians (0.1%), Romanians (0.07%), Ukrainians (0.04%) and Rusyns (0.01%). The number of Roma is officially put at 1.9% of the population though some sources place it as high as 4%.

SPORT

The Formula One Hungarian Grand Prix, held in mid-August, is the year's biggest sporting event. The **Hungaroring** (www.hungaroring .hu) track is 19km north of Budapest, in Mogyórod, but hotels in the capital fill up and prices skyrocket.

TOP FIVE WAYS TO TAKE A BATH

- Soak in palatial elegance – tiled mosaics, stained-glass skylights – at the **Gellért Fürdő** (p306) in Buda.
- Bubble up in the jetted central section in one of the expansive outdoor thermal pools at the turn-of-the-century **Széchenyi Fürdő** (p307) in Pest.
- Float among lilies in the summer, and steam in the winter, at one of Europe's largest thermal lakes, the **Gyógytó** in Hévíz (p332).
- Go modern at the **Rába Quelle** (p323) thermal spa in Győr: slide down the waterslide and splash under the two-storey waterfall.
- Take a romantic summer evening swim in the outdoor thermal mineral pool of the **Gyógyfürdő** (p336) in Harkány; the high sulphur content might do you good.

RELIGION

Of those Hungarians declaring religious affiliation, about 52% are Roman Catholic, 16% Reformed (Calvinist) Protestant, 3% Evangelical (Lutheran) Protestant, 2.5% Greek Catholic, 1% Orthodox and 0.1% Jewish (down from a pre-WWII population of nearly 10 times the current size).

ARTS

Budapest is Hungary's artistic heart, but the provinces resound with the arts too. The country (and the capital in particular) is known for its traditional culture, with a strong emphasis on the classical – and for good reason. The history of Hungarian arts and literature includes world-renowned composers such as Béla Bartók and Franz Liszt, and the Nobel prize-winning writer Imre Kértesz and his innovative contemporary Peter Esterházy. Hungary's proximity to classically focused Vienna, as well as the legacy of the Soviet regard for the 'proper arts' means that opera, symphony and ballet are high on the entertainment agenda, and even provincial towns have decent companies.

For the more contemporary branches of artistic life, Budapest is the country's queen bee, with many art galleries, theatre and dance companies, as well as folk music and handicrafts that have grown out of village life or minority culture.

Music

As you will no doubt see from the street names in every Hungarian town and city, the country celebrates and reveres its most influential musician, composer and pianist, Franz (or Ferenc) Liszt (1811–86). The eccentric Liszt described himself as 'part Gypsy', and in his *Hungarian Rhapsodies,* as well as in other works, he does indeed weave Romani motifs into his compositions.

Ferenc Erkel (1810–93) is the father of Hungarian opera, and the stirringly nationalist *Bánk Bán* is a standard at the Hungarian State Opera House in Budapest. Béla Bartók (1881–1945) and Zoltán Kodály (1882–1967) made the first systematic study of Hungarian folk music; both integrated some of their findings into their compositions.

Hungarian folk musicians play violins, zithers, hurdy-gurdies, bagpipes and lutes on a five-tone diatonic scale. Romani (Gypsy) music, found in restaurants in its schmaltzy form (best avoided), has become a fashionable thing among the young, with Romani bands playing 'the real thing' in trendy bars till the wee hours: a dynamic, hopping mix of fiddles, bass and cymbalom (a table-top-like stringed instrument played with sticks). An instrument a Roma band would never be seen without is the tin milk bottle used as a drum, which gives Hungarian Roma music its characteristic sound, reminiscent of traditional Indian music, an influence that perhaps harks back to the Roma's Asian roots. Look out for names such as Kalyi Jag (Black Fire), Ando Drom, Kal, Silvagipsy and Parno Graszt (White Horse). The latter is a folk ensemble of musicians and dancers dedicated to preserving Romani musical traditions, who also borrow from other regional folk styles. (One of their songs sounds quite like a Jewish wedding dance.)

Klezmer music (traditional Eastern European Jewish music) has also made a comeback into the playlists of the young and trendy. Bands like Di Naye, Kapelye and the Odessza Klezmer band are popular.

You can hear classical concerts in Budapest's large, ornate halls, as well as churches, and festivals sometimes bring the music outdoors. Rock, jazz, blues, funk – just about any music you're looking for is on tap at Budapest's many night spots.

Literature

Hungary has some excellent writers, both of poetry and prose. Sándor Petőfi (1823–49) is Hungary's most celebrated poet. A line from his work *National Song* became the rallying cry for the War of Independence between 1848 and 1849, in which he fought and is commonly thought to have died. His comrade-in-arms, János Arany (1817–82), wrote epic poetry. The prolific novelist and playwright Mór Jókai (1825–1904) gave expression to heroism and honesty in works such as *The Man with the Golden Touch.* Lyric poet Endre Ady (1877–1919) attacked narrow materialism; poet Attila József (1905–37) expresses the alienation felt by individuals in the modern age; and novelist Zsigmond Móricz (1879–1942) examines the harsh reality of peasant life in Hungary.

Contemporary Hungarian writers whose work has been translated into English and are worth a read include Tibor Fischer, Péter Esterházy and Sándor Márai. The most celebrated Hungarian writer is the 2002 Nobel prize-winner, Imre Kertész, whose excellent semi-autobiographical novel *Fateless* describes the ordeal of a teenage boy sent to Nazi death camps at Auschwitz, Buchenwald and Zeitz. Kertész also wrote the screenplay for the film of the same name, directed by Lajos Koltai and nominated for the Golden Bear at the Berlin Film Festival in 2005. It is Hungary's most expensive movie production (it cost US$12 million), and one of its best. Kertész's work has been likened in its power to the writing of Primo Levi. Corvina Books publishes translations and anthologies of the above writers' works.

Visual Arts

Favourite painters from the 19th century include realist Mihály Munkácsy (1844–1900), the so-called painter of the plains, and Tivadar Kosztka Csontváry (1853–1919). Győző Vásárhelyi (1908–97), who changed his name to Victor Vasarely when he emigrated to Paris, is considered the 'father of op art'. In the 19th and early 20th century, the Zsolnay family created world-renowned decorative art in porcelain. Ceramic artist Margit Kovac (1902–1977), a Hungarian national treasure, produced a large number of statues and ceramic objects during her career. The traditional embroidery, weavings and ceramics of the nation's *népművészet* (folk art) endures and there is at least one handicraft store in every town.

ENVIRONMENT
The Land

Hungary occupies the Carpathian Basin to the southwest of the Carpathian Mountains. Water dominates much of the country's geography. The Duna (Danube River) divides the Nagyalföld (Great Plain) in the east from the Dunántúl (Transdanubia) in the west. The Tisza (597km in Hungary) is the country's longest river, and historically has been prone to flooding. Hungary has hundreds of small lakes and is riddled with thermal springs. Lake Balaton (596 sq km, 77km long), in the west, is the largest freshwater lake in Europe outside Scandinavia. Hungary's 'mountains' to the north are merely hills, with the country's highest peak being Kékes (1014m) in the Mátra Range.

Wildlife

There are plenty of common European animals (deer, wild hare, boar, otter) as well as some rarer species (wild cat, lake bat, Pannonian lizard), but three-quarters of the country's 450 vertebrates are birds, particularly waterfowl. Hungary is a premier European sight for bird-watching. Endangered or vulnerable populations include eastern imperial eagles, saker falcons and the great bustard. An estimated 70,000 cranes pass through every year and a great number of storks arrive in the northern uplands and on the Great Plain every spring.

National Parks

There are 11 national parks in Hungary. Bükk Nemzeti Park, north of Eger, is a mountainous limestone area of forest and caves. Kiskunsági Nemzeti Park (p339; www.knp.hu) and Bugac (p339), near Kecskemét, and Hortobágy Nemzeti Park (www.hnp.hu) in the Hortobágy Puszta (a World Heritage site), outside Debrecen, protect the unique grassland environment of the plains.

Environmental Issues

Pollution is a large and costly problem. Harmful emissions from low-grade fuels such as coal and the high numbers of buses and cars, especially in Budapest, affect the air quality. The overuse of nitrate fertilisers in agriculture threatens ground water beneath the plains. However, there has been a marked improvement in air and water quality in recent years as Hungary attempts to conform to EU environmental standards.

FOOD & DRINK
Staples & Specialities

The omnipresent seasoning in Hungarian cooking is paprika, a mild red pepper that appears on restaurant tables as a condiment beside the salt and black pepper, as well as in many recipes. *Pörkölt*, a paprika-infused stew, can be made from different meats, including *borju* (veal), and usually it has no vegetables. *Galuska* (small, gnocchi-like dumplings) are a good accompaniment to soak up the sauce. The well-known *paprikas csirke* (chicken paprikash) is stewed chicken in a tomato-cream-paprika sauce (not as common here as in Hungarian restaurants abroad). *Töltött káposzta* (cabbage rolls stuffed with meat and rice) is cooked in a roux made with paprika, and topped with sour cream, as is *székelygulyás* (stewed pork and sour cabbage). Another local favourite is *halászlé* (fisherman's soup), a rich mix of several kinds of poached freshwater fish, tomatoes, green peppers and...paprika.

Leves (soup) is the start to any main meal in a Hungarian home; some claim that you will develop stomach disorders if you don't eat a hot, daily helping. *Gulyás* (goulash), although served as a stew outside Hungary, is a soup here, cooked with beef, onions and tomatoes. Traditional cooking methods are far from health-conscious, but they are tasty. Frying is a nationwide obsession and you'll often find fried turkey, pork and veal schnitzels on the menu.

For dessert you might try the cold *gyümölcs leves* (fruit soup) made with sour cherries and other berries, or *palincsinta* (crepes) filled with jam, sweet cheese or chocolate sauce. A good food-stand snack is *lángos,* fried dough that can be topped with cheese and/or *tejföl* (sour cream).

Two Hungarian wines are known internationally: the sweet, dessert wine Tokaji Aszú and Egri Bikavér (Eger Bull's Blood), the full-bodied red, high in acid and tannin. But the country produces a number of other eminently drinkable wines. Hungarian beers sold nationally include Dreher and Kőbanyai; Borosodi is a decent amber brew. For the harder stuff, try *pálinka,* a strong, firewater-like brandy distilled from a variety of fruits, but most commonly plums or apricots. Zwack distillery produces Unicum, a bitter aperitif that has been around since 1790; it tastes a bit like the medicine doctors give you to induce vomiting – but it's popular.

Where to Eat & Drink

An *étterem* is a restaurant with a large selection, formal service and formal prices. A *vendéglő* is smaller, more casual and serves homestyle regional dishes. The overused term *csárda,* which originally meant a rustic country inn with Romani music, can now mean anything – including super-touristy. To keep prices down, look for *étkezde* (a tiny eating place that may have a counter or sit-down service), *önkiszolgáló* (a self-service canteen), *kinai gyorsbüfé* (Chinese fast food), *grill* (which generally serves gyros or kebabs and other grilled meats from the counter) or a *szendvicsbar* (which has open-face sandwiches to go).

There are still a number of stuffy Hungarian restaurants with condescending waiters, formal service and Romani music from another era. For the most part, avoiding places with tuxedoed waiters is a good bet.

Wine has been produced in Hungary for thousands of years and you'll find it available by the glass or bottle everywhere. There are plenty of pseudo British-Irish-Belgian pubs,

smoky *sörözö* (a Hungarian pub, often in a cellar, where drinking is taken very seriously) *borozó* (a wine bar, usually a dive) and nightclubs, but the most pleasant place to imbibe a cocktail or coffee may be in a café. A *kávéház* may primarily be an old-world dessert shop, or it may be a bar with an extensive drinks menu; either way they sell alcoholic beverages in addition to coffee. In spring, pavement tables sprout up alongside the new flowers.

Vegetarians & Vegans

Traditional Hungarian food is heavy and rich. Meat, sour cream and fat abound, and *saláta* generally means a plate of pickles (cucumbers, cabbage, beets and/or carrots). At least in Budapest, other alternatives are available, especially at Italian or Asian restaurants.

Some not-very-light, but widely available dishes for vegetarians to look for are *rántott sajt* (fried cheese), *gombafejek rántva* (fried mushroom caps), *gomba leves* (mushroom soup) and *túrós* or *káposzta csusza* (short, wide pasta with cheese or cabbage). *Bableves* (bean soup) usually contains meat.

Habits & Customs

The Magyar are a polite people and their language is filled with courtesies. To toast someone's health before drinking, say *egéségére* (egg-eh-shaig-eh-ray), and to wish them a good appetite before eating, *jo étvágat* (yo ate-vad-yaht). If you're invited to someone's home, always bring a bunch of flowers and/or a bottle of good local wine.

BUDAPEST

☎ 1 / pop 1.8 million

Budapest seductively displays its many cultural influences and historical remains: the sensible Germanic logic of its layout, the decadent opulence of its Turkish baths, the Viennese coffeehouses, the straight lines of the sober Socialist structures, the Habsburg elegance and the silent old Jewish quarter, the Balkan smokiness of its bars, and above all, the unique Magyar spirit.

Budapest can be a summer hotspot – you can walk along the Danube, go drinking and clubbing in the boat bars and get into the boho coffee-house lifestyle. During the chillier months the city transforms into a winter resort with its many bathhouses, where you can be sitting in a steaming outdoor pool while snow glistens around you. Regardless of the season, you can always plunge in and explore Budapest's rich cultural heritage of opulent architecture, fascinating and sometimes bizarre museums, art galleries and Roman ruins. But you don't have to drown yourself in culture – Budapest has some of the more exciting nightlife spots in Eastern Europe, with unusual club nights (such as dancing waist deep in thermal waters), excellent DJs, live Romani and Klezmer music, and more bars than you'll be able to crawl around.

Pest is the city's commercial centre, with culture, restaurants and nightlife, smoky bars and shady gardens, museums, cheap sleeps and high-class hotels. Buda's sleepy green hills are home to the famous Castle Hill and medieval buildings, and its peaceful neighbourhoods house the city's affluent dwellers.

Whatever you choose to sample from the offerings of Budapest, make sure you take time to enjoy it in the city's slow, relaxed pace.

HISTORY

Strictly speaking, the story of Budapest begins only in 1873 with the administrative union of three cities that had grown together: Buda, west of the Danube; Óbuda (Buda's oldest neighbourhood) to the north; and Pest on the eastern side of the river. But the area had been occupied for thousands of years before Budapest as we know it existed. The Romans built a settlement at Aquincum (Óbuda) during the first centuries of the Christian Era. In the

1500s, the Turks arrived uninvited and stayed for almost 150 years. The Habsburg Austrians helped kick the invaders out, but then made themselves at home for 200 more years.

At the turn of the 20th century, under the dual Austro-Hungarian monarchy, the population of Budapest exploded and many buildings date from that boom. The city suffered some damage in the two world wars and the 1956 revolution left structures pockmarked with bullet holes. Today many of the old buildings have been restored, and Budapest is the sophisticated capital of a proud nation, one of the newest in the EU.

ORIENTATION

The city's traditional artery, the Danube, is spanned by nine bridges that link hilly, residential Buda with bustling, commercial and very flat Pest. Two ring roads link three of the bridges across the Danube and essentially define central Pest. Important boulevards such as Rákóczi út and leafy Andrássy út fan out from these, creating large squares and circles. The most central square in Pest is Deák tér, where the three metro lines meet. Buda is dominated by Castle and Gellért Hills; the main square is Moszkva tér.

Budapest is divided into 23 kerület (districts). The Roman numeral appearing before each street address signifies the district. Central Buda is district I, central Pest is district V, and fans out to zones VI and VII. You can also tell the district by reading its postal code: the

HUNGARY

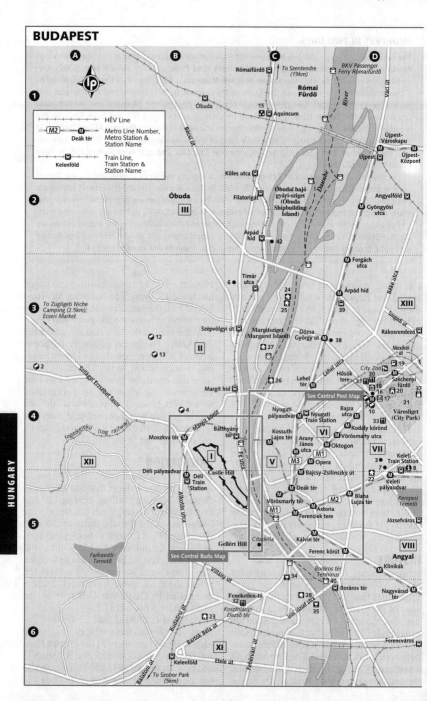

BUDAPEST

HÉV Line

Metro Line Number, Metro Station & Station Name
Deák tér

Train Line, Train Station & Station Name
Kelenföld

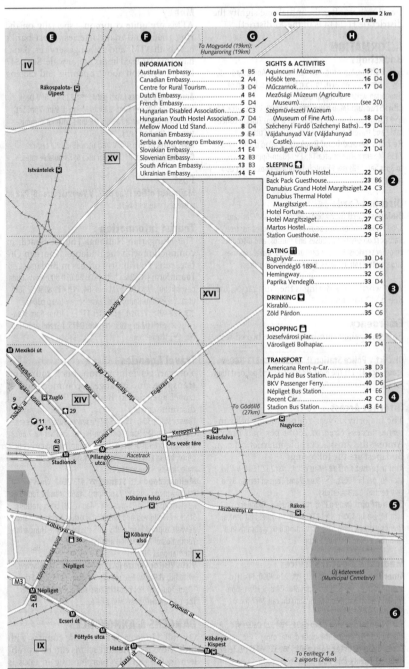

INFORMATION

Australian Embassy	**1** B5
Canadian Embassy	**2** A4
Centre for Rural Tourism	**3** D4
Dutch Embassy	**4** B4
French Embassy	**5** D4
Hungarian Disabled Association	**6** C3
Hungarian Youth Hostel Association	**7** D4
Mellow Mood Ltd Stand	**8** D4
Romanian Embassy	**9** E4
Serbia & Montenegro Embassy	**10** D4
Slovakian Embassy	**11** E4
Slovenian Embassy	**12** B3
South African Embassy	**13** B3
Ukrainian Embassy	**14** E4

SIGHTS & ACTIVITIES

Aquincumi Múzeum	**15** C1
Hősök tere	**16** D4
Műcsarnok	**17** D4
Mezősági Múzeum (Agriculture Museum)	(see 20)
Szépművészeti Múzeum (Museum of Fine Arts)	**18** D4
Széchenyi Fürdő (Széchenyi Baths)	**19** D4
Vájdahunyad Vár (Vájdahunyad Castle)	**20** D4
Városliget (City Park)	**21** D4

SLEEPING

Aquarium Youth Hostel	**22** D5
Back Pack Guesthouse	**23** B6
Danubius Grand Hotel Margitsziget	**24** C3
Danubius Thermal Hotel Margitsziget	**25** C3
Hotel Fortuna	**26** C4
Hotel Margitsziget	**27** C3
Martos Hostel	**28** C6
Station Guesthouse	**29** E4

EATING

Bagolyvár	**30** D4
Borvendéglő 1894	**31** D4
Hemingway	**32** C6
Paprika Vendeglő	**33** D4

DRINKING

Kisrabló	**34** C5
Zöld Párdon	**35** C6

SHOPPING

Jozsefvárosi piac	**36** E5
Városligeti Bolhapiac	**37** D4

TRANSPORT

Americana Rent-a-Car	**38** D3
Árpád híd Bus Station	**39** D3
BKV Passenger Ferry	**40** D6
Népliget Bus Station	**41** E6
Recent Car	**42** C2
Stadion Bus Station	**43** E4

HUNGARY

two numbers after the initial one signify the district (ie H-1114 is in the XI district).

INFORMATION
Bookshops
Irók Boltja (Map p304; ☎ 322 1645; VI Andrássy út 45; ☯ 10am-6pm Mon-Fri, to 3pm Sat) Good selection of Hungarian writers in translation.

Libri Stúdium (Map p304; ☎ 318 5680; V Váci utca 22; ☯ 10am-7pm Mon-Fri, to 3pm Sat & Sun) Tons of coffee-table and travel books, many Lonely Planet titles.

Red Bus Second-hand Bookstore (Map p304; ☎ 337 7453; V Semmelweiss utca 14; ☯ 10am-6pm Mon-Fri, to 3pm Sat) Sells used English-language books, next door to the hostel.

Discount Cards
Budapest Card (www.budapestinfo.hu; 48/72hr card 5200/6500Ft) Offers free access to many museums; free transport on city trams, buses and metros; and discounts on other services. Buy the card at hotels, travel agencies, large metro station kiosks and some tourist offices.

Also worth considering is the Hungary Card. See p347 for details.

Emergency
For emergency numbers, see the boxed text, p349.

District V Police Station (Map p304; ☎ 373 1000; V Szalay utca 11-13) The most centrally located police station in Pest.

Internet Access
The majority of year-round hostels offer internet access (free to 250Ft per half hour). Among the most accessible internet cafés in Budapest are the following.

Ami Internet Coffee (Map p304; ☎ 267 1644; V Váci utca 40; per hr 700Ft; ☯ 9am-2am) Tons of terminals; it's very central, but superbusy.

CEU NetPoint (Map p304; ☎ 328 3506; Oktober 6 utca 14; per hr 400Ft; ☯ 11am-10pm) Quiet and central. There's a dozen terminals, CD writing, fax, webcams and wi-fi connection for your laptop.

Medical & Dental Services
American Clinics (Map p303; ☎ 224 9090; I Hattyú utca 14, 5th fl; ☯ 8.30am-7pm Mon-Thu, 8.30am-6pm Fri, 8am-noon Sat, 10am-2pm Sun) On call 24/7 for emergencies.

S O S Dental Service (Map p304; ☎ 322 0602; VI Király utca 14) Around-the-clock dental care.

Teréz Gyógyszertár (Map p304; ☎ 311 4439; VI Teréz körút 41) Twenty-four-hour pharmacy.

Money
ATMs are quite common, especially on the ring roads and main arteries. Most banks have both ATMs and exchange services. Banks have standardised hours nationwide. See p347 for information about opening and closing times.

American Express (Map p304; ☎ 235 4330; V Deák Ferenc utca 10; ☯ 9am-5.30pm Mon-Fri, 9am-2pm Sat) Will change its own travellers cheques without commission; not the best rates.

K&H Bank (Map p304; V Váci utca 40) Quite central.

OTP Bank (Map p304; V Nádor utca 6) Favourable rates.

Post
Main post office (Map p304; V Városház utca 18) Pick up poste restante mail here.

Tourist Information
The Hungarian National Tourist Board, in conjunction with the Budapest Tourism Office, runs Tourinform offices in Budapest.

Tourinform (☎ 24hr hotline 06 80 630 800; www.buda pestinfo.hu); Main Office (Map p304; ☎ 438 8080; V Sütő utca 2; ☯ 8am-8pm); Liszt Ferenc Square (Map p304; ☎ 322 4098; VI Liszt Ferenc tér 11; ☯ 10am-6pm Mon-Fri); Castle Hill (Map p303; ☎ 488 0475; I Szentháromság tér; ☯ 10am-7pm)

Travel Agencies
You can get information, book tours and transport, and arrange accommodation at travel agencies in Budapest. They also sell discount cards.

Ibusz (Map p304; ☎ 485 2716; www.ibusz.hu; V Ferenciek tere 10; ☯ 9am-5pm Mon-Fri, to 1pm Sat Jul-Aug) The main branch of this national agency has an exchange office, books private rooms and pensions, and sells air and train tickets – the works.

Mellow Mood Ltd Stand (☎ 413 2062; www .mellowmood.hu; ☯ 7am-8pm) Stands can be found at Keleti (Map pp300-1) and Déli (Map p303) train stations. Staff will help you find hostel and other accommodation, as well as provide info. It's affiliated with the Hungarian Youth Hostel Association and Hostelling International (HI).

Vista Visitor Centre (Map p304; ☎ 452 3636; www .vista.hu; VI Paulay Ede utca 2; ☯ 9am-6pm Mon-Fri, 10am-3pm Sat) Book apartments and arrange tours here. There's internet access and a café.

DANGERS & ANNOYANCES
Overall, Hungary is a very safe country with little violent crime, but scams can be a problem in the capital. Overcharging in taxis is

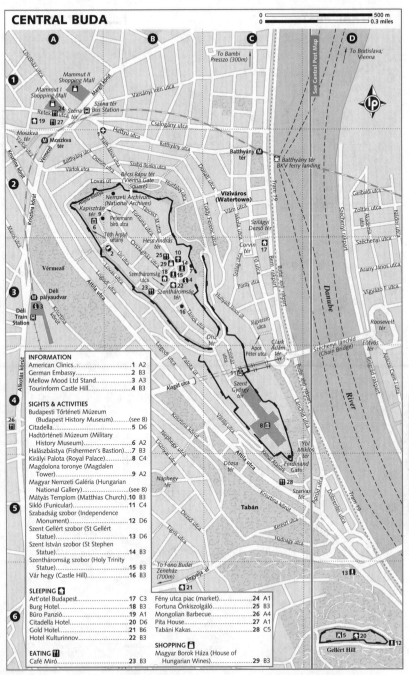

CENTRAL BUDA

0   500 m
0   0.3 miles

HUNGARY

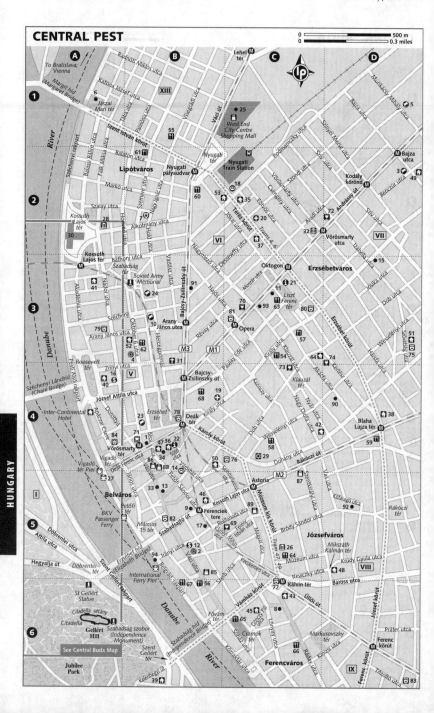

not unknown and we have received reports of unscrupulous waiters stealing credit-card information. Watch out for tricks on the street: the usual pickpocket method is for someone to distract you (by running into you, dropping something etc) while an accomplice makes off with your goods.

Guys should avoid drop-dead gorgeous women who approach them (especially around Váci utca) and offer to take them along to a local nightspot. Disreputable clubs hire these women to lure you in and then charge insane rates for drinks (upwards of €80 a pop) for you and the girls, who order refills adeptly.

There is a small but persistent neo-Nazi presence in Budapest that wants to blame Jews, Roma, Asians or blacks for the ills of the world, but for now their action seems to be limited to the staging of rallies and protests.

SIGHTS & ACTIVITIES
Buda
CASTLE HILL
Surfacing at the red line metro station of the Socialist-style Moszkva tér, continue left up Várfok utca, or cross the street and board the Vár bus (a minibus with a picture of a castle on the sign) to reach **Várhegy** (Castle Hill; Map p303) where most of Budapest's remaining medieval buildings are clustered. Várhegy is high above the glistening Danube, and wandering the old streets and enjoying the city views is part of the attraction, so get off at the first stop after the Vienna Gate and walk.

    Magdolona toronye (Magdalen Tower; Map p303; Kapisztrán tér) is all that's left of a Gothic church destroyed here during WWII. The white neoclassical building facing the square is the **Hadtörténeti Múzeum** (Military History Museum; Map p303; ☎ 356 9522; I Tóth Árpád sétány 40; admission free; ⓨ 10am-6pm Tue-Sun Apr-Sep, to 4pm Oct-Mar).

HUNGARY

For a peek into the life of the Budapest bourgeoisie, check out the mansions of the Buda Hills to the south of the ramparts promenade. Follow the third alleyway to your left and you reach Szentháromság tér and the **Szentháromság szobor** (Holy Trinity Statue; Map p303) at its centre.

Don't miss the gorgeous, neo-Gothic **Mátyás Templom** (Matthias Church; Map p303; ☎ 489 0717; I Szentháromság tér; adult/student 600/300Ft; ☯ 9am-5pm Mon-Sat, 1-5pm Sun), with a colourful tiled roof and lovely murals inside. Franz Liszt's *Hungarian Coronation Mass* was played here for the first time at the coronation of Franz Joseph and Elizabeth in 1867. Classical music concerts are still hosted here some evenings.

Sample the country's varieties of wine at the **Magyar Borok Háza** (House of Hungarian Wines; Map p303; ☎ 212 1031; www.magyarborokhaza.hu; I Szentháromság tér 6; wine tasting 3500Ft; ☯ noon-8pm) across the square, under the gaze of Hungary's first king, the equestrian **Szent István szobor** (St Stephen Statue; Map p303) to the south. Behind the monument, walk along **Halászbástya** (Fishermen's Bastion; Map p303; I Szentháromság tér; adult/student 330/160Ft; ☯ 8.30am-11pm). The fanciful, neo-Gothic arcade built on the fortification wall is prime picture-taking territory with views of the river and the parliament beyond.

Tárnok utca runs southeast to Dísz tér, past which is the entrance for the **Sikló** (Funicular; Map p303; district I Szent György tér; uphill/downhill ticket adult 600/500Ft, child 3-14yr 350Ft; ☯ 7.30am-10pm). The views from the little capsule, across the Danube and over to Pest, are glorious. The Sikló takes you down the hill to Clark Ádám tér. The massive **Királyi Palota** (Royal Palace; Map p303) occupies the far end of Castle Hill; inside are the **Magyar Nemzeti Galéria** (Hungarian National Gallery; ☎ 375 7533; I Szent György tér 6; admission free, special exhibitions adult/child/family 1500/800/3000Ft; ☯ 10am-6pm Tue-Sun) and the **Budapesti Történeti Múzeum** (Budapest History Museum; ☎ 375 7533; I Szent György tér 2; adult/student 900/450Ft; ☯ 10am-6pm daily mid-May–mid-Sep, 10am-4pm Wed-Mon mid-Sep–mid-May).

GELLÉRT HILL

The 'other peak' overlooking the Danube, south of Castle Hill, is Gellért Hill. The **Szabadság szobor** (Independence Monument), a statue of a gigantic lady with a palm leaf proclaiming freedom throughout the city, sits at its top, and is visible from almost anywhere in town. The monument was erected as a tribute to the Soviet soldiers who died liberating Hungary in 1945, but the victims' names in Cyrillic letters, that used to adorn the plinth, as well as the memorial statues of Soviet soldiers, were removed a decade ago.

West of the monument is the **Citadella** (☎ 365 6076; admission 300Ft; ☯ 8am-10pm). Built by the Habsburgs after the 1848 revolution to 'defend' the city from further Hungarian insurrection, it was never used as a fortress. Excellent views, exhibits, a restaurant and a hotel can be enjoyed in the Citadella. Take tram 19 along the riverfront from Clark Ádám tér and climb the stairs behind the waterfall and **Szent Gellért szobor** (St Gellért Statue), then follow the path through the park opposite the entrance to the Danubius Hotel Gellért. Or take bus 27 which runs almost to the top of the hill from XI Móricz Zsigmond körtér, southwest of the Gellért Hotel (and accessible using tram 19 and 49).

Bellow Gellért Hill is the city's most famous thermal spa, the **Gellért Fürdő** (Gellért Baths; Map p304; ☎ 466 6166; Danubius Hotel Gellért, XI Kelenhegyi út; thermal baths & swimming pool 2700Ft; ☯ 6am-7pm Mon-Fri, to 5pm Sat & Sun May-Sep; baths only Oct-Apr), where majestic domes arch over healing waters. This Art Nouveau palace has dreamy spas where you can soak for hours whilst enjoying its elegant and historic architecture.

SZOBOR PARK

In Buda's southwest is **Szobor Park** (Statue Park; ☎ 227 7446; www.szoborpark.hu; XXII Szabadkai út; admission 600Ft; ☯ 10am-dusk), a kind of historical dumping ground for Socialist statues deemed unsuitable since the early '90s. It's a major tourist attraction and there is a direct bus from Deák tér in Pest at 11am daily (2450Ft return, including admission). To go independently, take tram 19 from Clark Ádám tér to the XI Etele tér Terminus, then catch a yellow Volán bus to Diósd-Érd.

AQUINCUMI MÚZEUM

Seven kilometres north of Buda's centre, in Óbuda, is the **Aquincumi Múzeum** (Map pp300-1; ☎ 430 1563; III Szentendre út 139; adult/student 700/300Ft; ☯ 10am-5pm Tue-Sun Oct-Apr, to 6pm May-Sep, grounds 9am) containing the heart of the most complete ruins of a 2nd-century Roman civilian town left in Hungary. Take the HÉV from the Batthyány tér metro stop.

Pest

HŐSÖK TERE & AROUND

The leafy Andrássy út, Budapest's own Fifth Ave and Pest's northeastern artery, is the best place to start your sightseeing. At its western end, Andrassy ut turns into Bajcsy-Zsilinszky ut and touches Deak ter. Pest's central square, and its opposite end spills onto the wide, tiled **Hősök tere** (Heroes' Square; Map pp300-1) that bears a sprawling monument constructed to honour the millennial anniversary (1896) of the Magyar conquest of the Carpathian Basin.

Continental Europe's oldest underground – Budapest's M1 yellow line metro, constructed in the 19th century – runs beneath Andrássy út. Start your sightseeing almost at the end of the yellow line at Hősök tere, above the metro station of the same name. The tall green monument on the square showcases statues of important moustachioed tribal leaders, kings and statesmen. Across the street, the **Szépművészeti Múzeum** (Museum of Fine Arts; Map pp300-1; ☎ 469 7100; www2.szepmuveszeti.hu; XIV Hősök tere; admission free, temporary exhibitions adult/child 1200/600Ft; ☺ 10am-5.30pm Tue-Sun) houses a collection of foreign art, including an impressive number of El Grecos. Don't miss the **Műcsarnok** (Map pp300-1; ☎ 460 7000; www.mucsarnok.hu; XIV Hősök tere; adult/student 600/300Ft; ☺ 10am-6pm Tue-Wed & Fri-Sun, noon-8pm Thu), opposite the museum, a large contemporary art gallery that displays the work of Hungarian and international artists.

Adjacent is the oasis of **Városliget** (City Park; Map pp300-1), which has boating on a small lake in the summer, ice skating in winter, and duck-feeding year round. The park's schizophrenic **Vájdahunyad Vár** (Vájdahunyad Castle; Map pp300-1) was built in varied architectural styles typical of historic Hungary, including baroque, Romanesque, Gothic and Tudor. Originally a millennial celebration exhibit hall, the castle now contains the **Mezősági Múzeum** (Agriculture Museum; ☎ 343 0573; XIV Városliget; adult/student 500/200Ft; ☺ Tue-Fri & Sun 10am-5pm, Sat to 6pm), exciting only for those interested in Hungarian viticulture. In the park's northern corner is **Széchenyi Fürdő** (Széchenyi Baths; Map pp300-1; ☎ 363 3210; XIV Állatkerti út 11; admission 1700Ft; ☺ 6am-7pm Mon-Fri, to 5pm Sat & Sun), its cupola visible from anywhere in the park. Built in 1908, this place has an amazing outdoor pool that is open summer and winter, to cool you down or warm you up. Have a look inside all of the various entrances: the peaceful atmosphere of the indoor thermal baths, saunas and massage area contrasts with the buzzing atmosphere of the outside pool.

Walk southwest from Hősök tere on Andrássy út, to see many grand, World Heritage–listed 19th-century buildings. Stop for coffee and cake at **Lukács** (☎ 302 8747; VI Andrássy út 70; ☺ 9am-8pm Mon-Fri; 10am-8pm Sat & Sun), the old haunt of the dreaded secret police, whose headquarters have now been turned into the **Terror Háza** (Terror House; Map p304; ☎ 374 2600; www .terrorhaza.hu, Hungarian only; VI Andrássy út 60; admission foreigners 3000Ft; ☺ 10am-6pm Tue-Fri, to 7.30pm Sat & Sun), almost next door. The museum specialises in accounts of spying and atrocities, and always attracts a crowd. Although it's an interesting account of Hungary's tough times during WWII and under the Communist regime, the museum has been criticised for its lack of exhibits on the Holocaust.

Further down on Andrássy út, the opulence of the 1884 neo-Renaissance **Magyar Állami Operaház** (Hungarian State Opera House; Map p304; ☎ 332 8197; www.opera.hu; VI Andrássy út 22; tours 1200Ft; ☺ 3pm & 4pm) is a real treat; try to make it to an evening performance here. **Váci utca**, in Pest's touristy centre, is an extensive pedestrian shopping street. It begins at the southwest terminus of the yellow line, Vörösmarty tér. The **Nagycsarnok** (Great Market; Map p304; IX Vámház körút 1-3; ☺ 6am-5pm Mon, to 6pm Tue-Fri, to 2pm Sat) is a vast steel and glass structure. There are produce vendors on the ground floor, souvenirs and snacks on the 1st floor.

PARLIAMENT & AROUND

Other sights and museums are scattered about Pest. The huge, riverfront **Parlament** (Parliament; Map p304; ☎ 441 4904; www.mkogy.hu; V Kossuth Lajos tér 1-3; adult/student 1700/800Ft; ☺ 8am-6pm Mon-Fri, to 4pm Sat, to 2pm Sun for Hungarian-language tours), apparently modelled on London's Westminster, but with crazy spires, dominates Kossuth Lajos tér. English-language tours are at 10am and 2pm daily.

Across the park is the **Néprajzi Múzeum** (Ethnography Museum; Map p304; ☎ 473 2400; www.hem .hu; V Kossuth Lajos tér 12; adult/student 500/250Ft; ☺ 10am-6pm Tue-Sun), which has an extensive collection of national costumes among the permanent displays on folk life and art. Look for the mummified right hand of St Stephen in the chapel of the colossal **Szent István Bazilika** (Map p304; ☎ 311 0839; V Szent István tér; church admission free, treasury adult/ student 200/150Ft, dome 500/400Ft; ☺ 9am-7pm Mon-Sat, 1-4pm Sun) near Bajcsy-Zsilinszky út.

JEWISH QUARTER

Northeast of the Astoria metro stop is what remains of the Jewish quarter. The twin-towered, 1859 **Nagy Zsinagóga** (Great Synagogue; Map

HUNGARY

p304; ☎ 342 8949; VII Dohány utca 2; synagogue & museum adult/child 1000/400Ft; ✆ 10am-5pm Mon-Thu, 10am-2pm Fri & Sun) has a museum with a harrowing exhibit on the Holocaust, and behind the synagogue is a **Holocaust Memorial** in the shape of a weeping willow. Funded by the actor Tony Curtis, it's dedicated to those who perished in the death camps. A few blocks south along the *kis körút* (little ring road) is the **Magyar Nemzeti Múzeum** (Hungarian National Museum; Map p304; ☎ 338 2122; www .hnm.hu; VIII Múzeum körút 14-16; adult/student 800/400Ft; ✆ 10am-6pm Tue-Sun), with its historic relics from archaeological finds to coronation regalia.

BUDAPEST EYE
For a different view, rise above it all in the **Budapest Eye** (Map p304; ☎ 238 7623; www.budapesteye .hu; VI Váci út 1-3; adult/child 3000/2000Ft, extra to take photos; ✆ 10am-6pm May-Oct), a hot-air balloon tethered to the West End City Centre Shopping Mall.

TOURS
To tour the Danube, **Mahart PassNave sightseeing cruises** (☎ 484 4013; www.mahartpassnave.hu; V Vigadó tér Pier; ✆ Apr-Oct) runs 1½-hour sightseeing cruises (adult/child 1900/950Ft) and lunch and dinner buffet cruises (2800/1400Ft). On Wednesdays and Sundays from May to September, folklore evening cruises (9500Ft) include regional dishes, Romani music and folk dancing. Tickets can be purchased at the pier before departure.

For a fun way to tour the city, day or night, **Yellow Zebra Bikes** (Map p304; ☎ 266 8777; www .yellowzebrabikes.com; V Sütő utca 2, in courtyard; ✆ 8.30am-8pm May-Sep, 10am-6pm Nov-Feb, 9.30am-7.30pm Mar-Apr & Oct) offers bicycle rentals (one day 3000Ft). The office has internet access and is quite the hang-out for English speakers. The same company runs **Absolute Walking Tours** (☎ 06 30 211 8861; www.absolutetours.com), and both have tours departing from Deák tér. You could take the entertaining 3½-hour town walking tour (adult/student 4000/3500Ft), but the best tours on offer are the Hammer & Sickle and Pub Crawl (adult/student 5000/4500 Ft) tours, which give you a whiff of life under socialism, and an idea of modern Hungarian drinking habits with a lick of the strong stuff.

SLEEPING
Accommodation prices and standards are pretty reasonable in Budapest. Many year-round hostels occupy middle floors of old apartment buildings (with or without a lift) in central Pest. Come summer (July to late August), student dormitories at colleges and universities open to travellers. HI-affiliated Mellow Mood Ltd (p302) runs many summer, and a few year-round, hostels in town and has stands at Keleti and Déli train stations. Tourinform and the Hungarian Youth Hostel Association publish a youth-hostel brochure you can pick up in Tourinform's offices and various hostel receptions, or read online (www.youthhostels.hu).

Private rooms assigned by travel agents are plentiful, but not always central. Costs range from 4000Ft to 7500Ft for a single, 9000Ft to 12,000Ft for a double and 12,000Ft to 14,000Ft for a small apartment, with a supplement if you stay fewer than four nights. Ibusz (p302) has the most extensive listings in town (some with photos on its website) and Vista Visitor Centre (p302) is good for apartments. Two other private-room brokers:

Best Hotel Service (Map p304; ☎ 318 4848; www .besthotelservice.hu; V Sütő utca 2; ✆ 8am-8pm)

To-Ma Travel Agency (Map p304; ☎ 353 0819; www .tomatour.hu/beut/; V Október 6 utca 22; ✆ 9am-noon & 1-8pm Mon-Fri, 9am-5pm Sat & Sun)

Buda
BUDGET
Zugligeti Niche Camping (☎ 200 8346; www.camping niche.hu; XII Zugligeti út 101; camp sites 1/2 people 1900/ 2800Ft, caravan sites 1/2 people 2800/3700Ft; ✆ May-Oct) An excellent option for mixing a city break with a hiking holiday: the camp's location is in the Buda Hills at the bottom station of a chair lift. The camp is a bit cramped, but has good shade and there's a restaurant nearby. Take bus 158 from Moszkva tér to the terminus.

Back Pack Guesthouse (Map pp300-1; ☎ 385 8946; www.backpackbudapest.hu; XI Takács Menyhért utca 33; dm 2500-3000Ft, r 7000Ft; ✉ 💻) A hippy-ish, friendly place with an oasis-of-peace feel. There's a lush garden in the back with a hammock stretched invitingly between two trees. Dorm rooms have five to 11 beds, and there's one small double. Take bus 7 (from Erzsébet híd or Keleti train station in Pest), tram 49 from the *kis körút* in central Pest, or tram 19 from Batthyány tér in Buda.

Citadella Hotel (Map p303; ☎ 466 5794; www.citadella .hu; XI Citadella sétány, Gellért Hill; dm/r €10/51; ✉) What could be better than sleeping in a historic old fortress? Well, OK, the furniture could be newer, and the place has great views. Solo travellers may prefer somewhere more central, as it's a bit isolated and the disco can get loud.

Take bus 27 from XI Móricz Zsigmond körtér in Buda, then hike.

Martos Hostel (Map pp300-1; ☎ 209 4883; reception@ hotel.martos.bme.hu; XI Sztoczek utca 5-7; d €32, s/d with shared bathroom €16/20; ✗) Primarily student accommodation, Martos is open year-round to all. It's a few minutes' walk from Petőfi Bridge (or take tram 4 or 6).

MIDRANGE

Büro Panzió (Map p303; ☎ 212 2928/29; buro-panzio@ axelero.hu; II Dékán utca 3; s 6000-8000Ft, d 10,000-12,000Ft; ✗ 🖳) Recently revamped and redressed, Büro now wears gleaming white walls, the beds are covered in white linen and small orange lamps light up the rooms. The central Moszkva tér transportation hub – metro stop, tram stations – is barely seconds away.

Hotel Kulturinnov (Map p303; ☎ 224 8100; www.mka .hu; I Szentháromság tér 6; s/d €64/80; ✗) A small hotel sitting in the belly of the grandiose Hungarian Culture Foundation, with an L-shaped corridor leading to its 16 rooms. The feeling is relaxed and the décor longs for the '80s, but the most impressive are the surroundings: a gorgeous stately building, on top of Castle Hill, and of course the low prices.

Gold Hotel (Map p303; ☎ 209 4775; www.goldhotel .hu; I Hegyalja út 14; s €64-84, d €74-94; P ✗ 🖳 🖳) A rather odd castle-like building at Gellért Hill, with a golden yellow façade and a 'tower feature' at the front, where rooms have extra little seating areas by the window. The rooms are in terracottas and creams, with good, large beds and plenty of light. Take bus 8 from Elizabeth Bridge or bus 78 from Keleti train station in Pest.

Burg Hotel (Map p303; ☎ 212 0269; www.burghotel budapest.com; I Szentháromság tér 7-8; s €85-105, d €99-115; ✗ 🖳 🖳) A fantastic combination of location and price: the affordable Burg is at the centre of Castle Hill. Ask for a room overlooking Mátyás Templom for a truly historic wake-up view. The rooms are simple, with warm peachy walls compensating for a slight lack of light. The reception staff are friendly and informative.

TOP END

Danubius Hotel Gellért (Map p304; ☎ 889 5500; www .danubiusgroup.com/gellert; XI Szent Gellért tér 1; s €66-130, €150-210; P ✗ 🖳 🖳) This turn-of-the-(20th)-century grand dame of the Danube is worth peeking into even if you don't choose to stay here. Constructed between 1916 and 1918, its once-legendary elegance is now more on the faded side, and though it's not quite up to today's luxury standards, staying here guarantees use of big, fluffy bathrobes you can wear on your way to free access to the Gellért Baths (p306). Purr.

Art'otel Budapest (Map p303; ☎ 487 9487; www.art otel.hu; I Bem rakpart 16-19; r €198-318; P ✗ 🖳 🖳) Budapest's supermodern designer hotel, the Art'otel was dreamed up by the American Donald Sultan, and is part of a group of hotel-galleries. The rooms are a sleek mix of red, white and black, with Sultan's artworks adorning each one. The domino and needle-and-thread carpets lead you from the modern glass building through to the four old town houses in the back. Rooms for disabled travellers are available.

Pest

BUDGET

Caterina Hostel (Map p304; ☎ 269 5990; www.caterina hostel.hu; VI Teréz körút 30, 3rd fl; dm €10, r €27; ✗ 🖳) A cosy place with a clean and bright interior, excellent for travellers who want to feel at home. The only drawback is that there is no lounge, but the modern, friendly feel and accommodating owners make it a good choice. Rooms have TVs.

Museum Guest House (Map p304; ☎ 318 9508; www .budapesthostel.com; VIII Mikszáth Kálmán tér 4, 1st fl; dm 2600-3000Ft; ✗ 🖳) Wind your way through the maze of rooms. Eclectic décor includes some bunk lofts with blanket curtains and red log bedsteads. No doubles. The building is on a calm square off the main road.

Aquarium Youth Hostel (Map pp300-1; ☎ 322 0502; www.budapesthostel.com; VII Alsóerdősor utca 12, 2nd fl; dm/s/d 2800/3900/7800Ft; 🖳) Associated with the Museum Guest House, but this place has more basic bunk-bed rooms, as well as doubles.

Red Bus Hostel (Map p304; ☎ 266 0136; www .redbusbudapest.hu; V Semmelweiss utca 14, 1st fl; dm 3000Ft, r 7900Ft; ✗ 🖳) Congenial owners are part of the reason that the very central Red Bus has such a faithful following. Spacious rooms with colourful walls and wood floors are another. Next door is an associated English-language used-book store. There's a **Red Bus II** (Map p304; ☎ 321 7100; VI Szövetség utca 35; dm/s/d 2700/6500/7500Ft; ✗ 🖳) near Keleti train station.

Garibaldi Guesthouse (Map p304; ☎ 302 3457; baldi guest@hotmail.com; V Garibaldi utca 5; per person €20-45) This old building belongs to an eccentric, multilingual owner who has many apartments on several floors. Double, triple, quad and five-person guestrooms have shared kitchens and en suite bathrooms and are furnished with crazy deer-in-the-woods tapestries, plush pink draperies and odd antiques. Some small rooms with shared bath (€18) are in the inquisitive owner's flat.

Other recommended hostels:

Station Guesthouse (Map pp300-1; ☎ 221 8864; www.stationguesthouse.hu; XIV Mexikói út 36/b; dm 1900-2700Ft, r 6400Ft; ✗ ☐) This is a party house: there's a 24-hour bar, pool table and occasional live music. Take red bus 7 from Keleti train station.

Yellow Submarine Hostel (Map p304; ☎ 331 9896; www.yellowsubmarinehostel.com; VI Teréz körút 56, 3rd fl; dm/s/d 2800/7000/8000Ft; ✗ ☐) Overlooking busy ring road, near Nyugati.

Best Hostel (Map p304; ☎ 332 4934; www.best hostel.hu; VI Podmaniczky utca 27, 1st fl; dm/s/d 3000/4200/8400Ft; ✗ ☐) Closest to Nyugati train station; not too, too noisy.

Mellow Mood Central Hostel (Map p304; ☎ 411 1310; www.mellowmoodhostel.com; V Bécsi utca; dm in 4-/6-/8-bed room 4100/3600/3200Ft, tw 5700Ft; ✗ ☐)

MIDRANGE

Hostel Marco Polo (Map p304; ☎ 413 2555; www .marcopolohostel.com; VII Nyár utca 6; dm 3800-5800Ft, s 10,800-12,800Ft, d 14,200-17,000Ft; ✗ ☐) With telephones and satellite TV in the rooms, and a bar-restaurant in the cellar, this Mellow Mood Ltd hostel is more like a hotel. Pastel greens and yellows colour the nifty rooms. The neighbourhood is not the world's most polished, but it's safe.

Hotel Queen Mary (Map p304; ☎ 413 3510; www .hotelqueenmary.hu; district V Kertész utca 34; s €50-70, d €60-85; ✗ ☒) Among the trendy bars and cafés of Kertész street, this hotel, in a 19th-century building, has neat rooms with modern furniture and hanging potted plants. If you're travelling in a group, ask about the triples (€75 to €105) and quads (€84 to €112).

Leo Panzió (Map p304; ☎ 266 9041; www.leopanzio .hu; V Kossuth Lajos utca 2/A, 2nd fl; s €45-66, d €69-82; ✗ ☒) Just steps from Váci utca, the Leo is in the middle of everything. Rooms have an Art Deco-ish flair with cherry-stained beds inset with blonde wood. Some have views of Elizabeth Bridge. The tiny bathrooms sparkle.

Kálvin Ház (Map p304; ☎ 216 4635; www.kalvin house.hu; IX Gönczy Pál utca 6; s €55-62, d €65-82; ✗ ☐) One of the few historic pensions in town – the Victorian antiques and high ceilings are a standout. Laundry service and internet access are a bonus. The restored 19th-century, coral-colour building is near Kálvin tér metro station and Ráday utca nightlife.

Radio Inn (Map p304; ☎ 342 8347; www.radioinn .hu; VI Benczúr utca 19; s €52-70, d €75-86; ✗) Spacious apartments with full kitchens, sitting areas and one or two bedrooms are on offer here, and they are perfect if you wish to stay for longer and really feel at home in Budapest. Embassies are your neighbours on the quiet, tree-lined street near Bajza utca metro stop (M1 yellow line).

Other good options:

Hotel Fortuna (Map pp300-1; ☎ 288 8100; www .fortunahajo.hu; Szent István Park, waterfront; s with shared bathroom €16-20, d €24-30, tr €32-40; ℗) Float on a boat (hotel) on the Danube. Doubles with bathroom and satellite TV cost €60 to €80.

Dunaparts (☎ 225 9003; www.dunaparts.com; apt for 1-2 people €55-60) Perhaps one of the best places for renting apartments, this is an internet booking agency with one- and two-bedroom apartments in central Pest. The friendly staff come and pick you up from the airport, free of charge.

Hotel Ibis Centrum (Map p304; ☎ 215 8585; www .ibis-centrum.hu; IX Ráday utca 6; s €59-69, d €85-106; ℗ ✗ ☒ ☐) So, so near the bar and café scene. The style is chain-hotel modern and modular.

Hotel Margitsziget (Map pp300-1; ☎ 329 2949; hotelmargitsziget@axelero.hu; XIII Margitsziget; r 14,500Ft; ℗ ☒) Good-value budget resort; there are tennis courts, a swimming pool and sauna.

TOP END

Corinthia Grand Hotel Royal (Map p304; ☎ 479 4000; www.corinthiahotels.com; VII Erzsébet körút 43-49; s €140-250, d €160-350; ℗ ✗ ☒ ☒ ☒) Pest's pride and joy of five-star beauties has been carefully reconstructed in the Austro-Hungarian style of heavy drapes, sparkling chandeliers and large, luxurious ballrooms, and has won prizes for best hotel architecture.

Danubius Grand Hotel Margitsziget (Map pp300-1; ☎ 889 4700; www.danubiusgroup.com/grandhotel; XIII Margitsziget; s €131-164, d €150-184; ℗ ✗ ☒ ☒) The Margaret Island setting is a green oasis in the city, and the 1873 splendour of the hotel contrasts with the contemporary nature of its sister, the **Danubius Thermal Hotel Margitsziget** (Map pp300-1; ☎ 889 4700; www.danubiusgroup .com/thermalhotel; XIII Margitsziget; s €144-174, d €164-194; ℗ ✗ ☒ ☒). The two are connected via an underground passageway and guests at both enjoy free use of the upscale baths at the Thermal.

Four Seasons Hotel (Map p304; ☎ 268 6000; www .fourseasons.com; district V Roosevelt tér 5-6; r €270-700; ℗ ✗ ☒ ☒) Restored to Dr Seuss–esque elegance with mushroom-shaped windows, whimsical ironwork and glittering gold decorative tiles on the exterior, the Four Seasons

HUNGARY

inhabits the Art Nouveau Gresham Palace and provides superb views of the Danube through Roosevelt Park.

EATING

It's becoming more common to find both Hungarian and international cuisines on the streets of Budapest. There are restaurants so modern and trendy that they could sit proudly in the streets of Manhattan, and others that are oblivious to the concept of change, with traditional food and old-fashioned décor. Both types can be equally good (or bad), and there's no guarantee that going posh will result in better nosh. In any case, eating out is affordable in Budapest, and even on the tightest of budgets you should be able to squeeze in one upmarket restaurant.

Fast-food restaurants and take-away windows abound on the ring roads and in pedestrian areas. The train and bus stations all have food stands.

Ráday utca and Liszt Ferenc tér are the two most popular traffic-free streets. The moment the weather warms up, tables and umbrellas spring up on the pavements and the people of Budapest crowd the streets. Both areas have tons of cafés, restaurants, snack shops and bars.

Buda
BUDGET
Fény utca piac (market; Map p303; II Fény at Retek utca; 6am-5pm Mon-Fri, 6am-2pm Sat) Next to Mammut I Shopping Mall, this market has picnic supplies and produce on the ground level and food stands and butcher shops on the 1st floor.

Bambi Presszó (212 3171; II Frankel Leó út 2-4; mains 500-800Ft; 8am-9pm Mon-Fri, 9am-8pm Sat-Sun) Old plastic plants hang above your head here and plastic dominoes whack the plastic tables. This is how the old Communist *presszó* bars used to be and what makes it a cult eatery among young and old Budapestians. The food is basic, but the omelettes and sandwiches taste great. Many come just to have a beer and dream of the old times.

Fortuna Önkiszolgáló (Map p303; 375 2401; I Hess András utca 4, 1st fl; mains 500-900Ft; 11.30am-2.30pm Mon-Fri; ⊠) For a bite to eat near the castle, climb the passageway stairs to this cafeteria, which serves all the fried favourites.

Pita House (Map p303; 315 1479; II Margit körút 105; mains 500-800Ft; 8am-midnight; ⊠) This is an excellent choice if you're in Moszkva tér, with tasty gyros and falafel pitas. A helping from the salad bar costs 410Ft.

MIDRANGE
Café Miró (Map p303; 375 5458; I Úri utca 30; mains 690-2190Ft; 9am-midnight) Most restaurants on Castle Hill have surly service and are full of tourists. This arty café is no exception, but the soups and Greek salad are good. For dessert there are plenty of cakes to choose from, and the delicious *erdei gyümölcskremleves* (forest berry soup) is topped with a scoop of vanilla ice cream.

Tabáni Kakas (Map p303; 375 7165; I Attila út 27; mains 1900Ft; noon-midnight) Everything here is cooked in goose fat, and delicious it is. The place is old-fashioned and dimly lit, and the service friendly. Try the crispy goose leg with juicy, cooked red cabbage and potato and onion mash – absolutely ravishing.

TOP END
Hemingway (Map pp300-1; 381 0522; XI Kosztolányi Dezső tér 2, Feneketlen-tó; mains 1850-3100Ft; noon-midnight; ⊠) A bit of panache: dine on a terrace overlooking the Bottomless Lake. Entrées include lamb cutlet with a blue-cheese mint sauce.

Mongolian Barbecue (Map p303; 353 6363; XII Márvány utca 19/A; mains before/after 5pm 1990/3690Ft; noon-midnight; ⊠) Choose your meat and watch as it's grilled in front of you. The all-you-can-eat price includes as much house beer and wine as you can sink, too.

Pest
BUDGET
Frici Papa (Map p304; 351 0197; VII Király utca 55; mains 400-700Ft; 11am-8pm Mon-Sat) A popular place for a basic, hearty, no-frills Hungarian meal where you sit elbow-to-elbow with workers, riff-raff, families and tourists. For the price there's a surprising amount of white-meat chicken in the soup.

Kisharang (Map p304; 269 3861; V Október 6 utca 17; mains 490-850Ft; 11am-8pm Mon-Fri, 11.30am-4.30pm Sat & Sun) Lantern-like lamps hang low over chequered tablecloths in this wonderful little *étkezde* (canteen). It serves simple dishes that change daily; expect to wait for a table.

Kis Italia (Map p304; 269 3145; V Szemere utca 22; pizzas & pastas 760-990Ft; 11am-10pm Mon-Sat; ⊠) Descend into this cellar restaurant for interesting pizza combinations – such as bacon, onion and pickle – at low prices. Just ignore the cheesy synthesizer player in the corner; he's not too loud.

Ráday Étkezde (Map p304; 219 5451; IX Ráday utca 29; mains 420-650Ft; 6am-4pm Mon-Fri) Of the many takeaway windows and self-service places among the cafés and bars on Ráday utca, this is a reliable choice. The *főzelék*, a sort of creamed vegetable stew, is particularly good.

Nagycsarnok (Great Market; Map p304; IX Vámház körút 1-3; ☺ 6am-5pm Mon, to 6pm Tue-Fri, to 2pm Sat) This is Budapest's main market, selling fruit and vegetables, deli items, fish and meat. Food stalls on the upper level sell beer, sausage and tasty *lángos* among other quick eats. There's also a cafeteria – a bit of a tourist trap – with a Romani violinist and midrange prices.

Grocery-store chains are everywhere in Pest; Kaiser's has a branch facing Blaha Lujza tér and one opposite Nyugati train station on Nyugati tér.

MIDRANGE

Al-Amir (Map p304; ☎ 352 1422; VII Király utca 17; mains 700-1500Ft; ☺ noon-11pm Mon-Sat; 1-11pm Sun) Good Middle Eastern food is hard to come by in Hungary, but this place is excellent. Pictures of mysterious eyes behind veils and camels in the desert decorate the spacious, otherwise plain space. Order either a meze-type meal, combining the many starters, or try the kebabs and a nice tabbouleh. No alcohol is served.

Paprika Vendeglö (Map pp300-1; ☎ 06 70 574 6508; I Dózsa György út 72; mains 950-1600Ft; ☺ 11am-11pm) Step inside what looks like a rustic Hungarian farm house on the very urban street bordering City Park (M1 yellow line, Hősök tere). Good game dishes.

Angyalok Konyhája (Map p304; ☎ 412 0427; XIII Visegrádi utca; mains 1080-1480Ft; ☺ 11am-11pm Sun-Thu, to midnight Fri & Sat; ✗) Formerly known as Wabisabi, the food here is organic and vegan-friendly, with strong Asian influences – a rarity in meat-

---

AUTHOR'S CHOICE

Menza (Map p304; ☎ 413 1482; V Liszt Ferenc tér 2; mains 890-1990Ft; ☺ 11am-11pm; ✗) Probably the most popular restaurant in Budapest, Menza is a visual and gastronomic delight. The spacious restaurant's design is all retro shapes and colours, futuristic lampshades from the '60s and old plastic-letter wall-hanging menu boards with exquisite offerings such as pumpkin soup garnished with balsamic vinaigrette and toasted pumpkin seeds. One of the best dishes is the roast pork tenderloin with rose lentil purée and roasted potato wedges. The house wine is good. Eat at Menza, we implore you.

---

crazy Hungary. The portions are huge, although not massively delicious. The décor is a mix of Arabic and Japanese, floor seating on cushions and shoes off.

Other recommendations:
Vista Café (Map p304; ☎ 268 0888; VI Paulay Ede utca 7; mains 800-1600Ft; ☺ 9am-11pm Mon-Fri, 10am-11pm Sat & Sun) Hungarian, Mediterranean, Italian – a little of everything, including free internet access.
Kék Rózsa (Map p304; ☎ 342 8981; VII Wesselényi utca 9; mains 850-1600Ft; ☺ 11am-10pm) Three-course Hungarian menus 1200Ft to 1800Ft.
Taverna Dionysos (Map p304; ☎ 318 1222; V Belgrád rakpart 16; mains 1250-2750Ft; ☺ noon-midnight; ✗) A bit of Mediterranean sun and juicy *stifado* (a Greek stew with meat, onions and tomato).

TOP END

Fatál (Map p304; ☎ 266 2607; V Váci utca 67, cnr Pintér utca; mains 1580-2490Ft; ☺ 11.30am-2am) A whimsical menu prefaces the fun at this cellar restaurant with medieval adornment. The homy Hungarian dishes are served in gigantic portions. We've heard comment that waiters can be brusque with foreigners, but that wasn't our experience. Book ahead.

Bagolyvár (Owl's Castle; Map pp300-1; ☎ 468 3110; XIV Állatkert út 2; mains 1600-3500Ft; ☺ noon-11pm) Gundel's first sibling, the Owl's Castle, is known for Hungarian classics done impeccably. The hidden courtyard tables are a pleasant surprise.

Borvendéglő 1894 (Map pp300-1; ☎ 468 4040; XIV Állatkert út 2; mains 1650-2700Ft; ☺ 6-11pm Tue-Sat) This wine cellar is one of the two sister restaurants to the world-famous (and overpriced) Gundel restaurant around the corner. The best things about the place are the choice of wine for tasting and the traditional Hungarian drinking snacks – goose cracklings, steak tartar and *pogács* (salty, buttery biscuits).

Múzeum (Map p304; ☎ 267 0375; VIII Múzeum körút 12; mains 2400-4400Ft; ☺ 10.30am-1.30am) *Fin-de-siècle* ambience, wide lanterns hanging low from the high ceilings, the Múzeum is like an old friend to many of Budapest's diners. The Hungarian food is good and varied, the service is smooth and the place stays open late.

DRINKING

One of Budapest's ceaseless wonders is the number of bars, cellars, cafés, clubs and general places to drink. The cafés usually serve cakes, and the bars almost always have live music, and, if you can see through the smoke curtains, lovely (or at least interesting) décor.

In the spring and summer months thousands of outdoor pavement tables spring up all over the city. The best places to drink are in Pest (Buda's too sleepy to stay up all night), especially along Liszt Ferenc tér and Radáy utca; the squares are pedestrian-only and have a positively festive feel during the summer.

Buda

Kisrabló (Map pp300-1; ☎ 209 1588; XI Zenta utca 3; ☾ 11am-2am) The eclectic pub décor here resembles a boat's hull, busty masthead and all. Take tram 19 or 49 one stop past Danubius Hotel Gellért.

Zöld Párdon (Map pp300-1; XI Íríní József utca at Petőfi híd; Map pp358-9; ☾ 9am-6am mid-Apr–mid-Sep) College students on a budget flock to the big, seasonal beer garden and disco near Petőfi Bridge.

Pest

Sark (Map p304; ☎ 328 0753; VII Klauzál tér 14; ☾ 10am-2am Mon-Thu & Sun, 10am-3am Fri & Sat) A small bar on two levels with an airy ground floor and a large photo mural decorating the space. Downstairs is a smoky cellar where a Romani band plays every Tuesday (see p314) and a mix of foreigners, Hungarians and Roma jump around together. During the day it's a quiet place, nice for a coffee, but come evening time, Sark gets packed and the atmosphere is fab.

Szimpla/Dupla (Map p304; ☎ 342 8991; VII Kertész utca 48; ☾ noon-2am) Perhaps it was the espressos that inspired the name ('szimpla' means single and 'dupla' double) of these two excellent places. The café and restaurant are connected by a long, atmospheric cellar bar and make a kind of two-in-one experience. The furniture is distressed, the cutlery and crockery rescued from flea markets, and the crowd super relaxed. There's live jazz on Fridays.

Eckermann (Map p304; ☎ 374 4076; VI Andrássy út 24; ☾ 9am-11pm Mon-Sat; 10am-10pm Sun) Part of the Goethe Institut, this airy café attracts an intellectual crowd that is invariably either reading the newspapers or discussing what they've just read in the newspapers. They are apparently refugees from the now tourist-occupied Művész across the street. Try the plentiful Viennese coffee, served in bowls, and excellent pastries, perfect for breakfast. In the evenings Eckermann turns out the lights and lights up candles, and the clientele sips wine and discusses tomorrow's news.

Centrál Kávéház (Map p304; ☎ 266 4572; V Károlyi Mihály utca 9; ☾ 7am-1am) Having been closed for a long time, Centrál Kávéház is once again one of the finest coffee houses in the city. The interior has been carefully reconstructed to resemble its original 19th-century décor, with high, engraved ceilings, lace-curtained windows, tall plants, elegant, dainty coffee cups and professional service. You can have an omelette breakfast here, eat a full-on meal, or just sit down with a coffee or beer and enjoy the atmosphere.

For a cup of coffee in exquisite Art Nouveau surroundings, two places are particularly historical: **Gerbeaud** (Map p304; ☎ 429 9000; V Vörösmarty tér 7; ☾ 9am-9pm; ☒ ☒), Budapest's cake-and-coffee-culture king, serving since 1870. Or sit your bum on the same chairs where Hungary's dreaded ÁVO secret police members sat at **Lukács** (Map p304; ☎ 302 8747; VI Andrássy út 70; ☾ 9am-8pm Mon-Fri, 10am-8pm Sat & Sun), now inside the CIB Bank headquarters.

ENTERTAINMENT

Budapest has a nightlife that can keep you up for days on end. And we don't mean you trying to get to sleep in your hotel room while the club next door pounds its techno against your walls. There are nightclubs, bars, live concerts – classical and folk – Hungarian traditional dancing nights, opera treats, ballet, DJ bars and random Cinetrip (www.cinetrip.hu) club nights at the thermal spas. Yes, you heard us right. It's you, your swimsuit, your mates and a bunch of strangers, wading waist deep in thermal waters to thumping beats, and it's fantastic.

Ticket prices are quite reasonable by Western European standards, and the venues are often stunning. To find out what's on, contact Tourinform (see p302) or ticket offices, or check out the free, bimonthly *Programme Magazine* (available at tourist spots), and the free, weekly *Pesti Est* (available at restaurants and clubs). The weekly *Budapest Sun* (www.budapestsun .com) has a 10-day event calendar online, and Budapest Week Online (www.budapestweek .com) has events, music and movie listings.

Gay & Lesbian Venues

Angyal (Map p304; ☎ 351 6490; VII Szövetség utca 33; ☾ 10pm-5am Fri & Sat) Budapest's flagship gay nightclub has three bars and plays some high-energy dance mixes. Men only on Saturday (admission 800Ft).

Café Eklektika (Map p304; ☎ 266 3054; V Semmelweiss utca 21; ☾ noon-midnight Mon-Fri, 5pm-midnight Sat & Sun) The town's only real lesbian venue attracts a mixed, beat generation-type crowd.

Live Music & Theatre

Magyar Állami Operaház (Hungarian State Opera House; Map p304; ☎ 332 8197; www.opera.hu; VI Andrássy út 22) Feel a bit royal and get a box and some binoculars at this amazing, gilt-laden place that was built in 1884. Every opera performance is an event with a capital E. The ballet company performs here as well.

Liszt Ferenc Zeneakadémia (Map p304; ☎ 342 0179; www.musicacademy.hu; VI Liszt Ferenc tér 8; ⏰ 10am-2pm Mon-Fri, 2-8pm Sat & Sun for ticket office) You can hear the musicians practising outside this great Art Deco hall, where the 1907 Music Academy hosts excellent classical symphony concerts. Tickets are sold only at the onsite ticket office.

Kalamajka Táncház (Map p304; ☎ 354 3400; www .aranytiz.hu, Hungarian only; V Arany János utca 10; ⏰ 9pm-2am Sat) The Kalamajka is an excellent place to hear authentic Hungarian music, especially the Saturday night dance specials where everyone gets up and takes part.

Fonó Budai Zeneház (☎ 206 5300; www.fono.hu; XI Sztregova utca 3; concerts 700-1000Ft) The best place in Budapest for folk music of any kind, from Hungarian, Transylvanian or Balkan Romani, to Klezmer, tango and even sometimes a didgeridoo night. Check its website for upcoming events.

Sark (Map p304; ☎ 328 0753; VII Klauzál tér 14; entry 400Ft; ⏰ 10am-2am Mon-Thu & Sun, to 3am Fri & Sat) For excellent Romani music on Tuesday nights, come here and dance away to Szilvási Gipsy Folk Band (www.szilvasigipsy.hu), a band that has a little following and that gets the crowd doing impressive Hungarian-Romani dances.

Classical concerts are held regularly in the city's churches, including Mátyás Templom (p306) on Castle Hill in Buda.

Useful ticket brokers are **Music Mix** (Map p304; ☎ 266 1655; V Váci utca 33; ⏰ 10am-6pm Mon-Fri, to 3pm Sat) and **Vigadó Jegyiroda** (Map p304; ☎ 327 4322; V Vigadó tér 6; ⏰ 10am-8pm Mon-Fri).

Nightclubs

Clubbing in Budapest can mean anything from a floor-thumping techno club to a hip place to hang out and listen to jazz. Cover charges range from 200Ft to 1000Ft.

Cha Cha Cha (Map p304; V Kálvin tér metro station; ⏰ 11am-5am) Dozens of jeans and corduroy trousers were sacrificed to upholster the furniture in metro station–based Cha Cha Cha, Budapest's hippest bar-club with the city's best DJs playing records until the first morning trains start running, so the punters

can get home. Things don't get started till at least 11pm.

Gödör Klub (Map p304; ☎ 06 20 943 5463; V Erzsébet tér; ⏰ 2pm-2am) A large underground club (with a glass ceiling revealing the square above) provides the venue for truly eclectic live music – from world beat to the Doors to jazz – played to a local audience of all ages.

Trafó Bár Tangó (Map p304; ☎ 456 2049; IX Lilliom utca 41; ⏰ 6pm-1am) An arty crowd makes the scene beneath the eponymous cultural house and exhibit space. Latin, jazz and disco tunes.

SHOPPING

Apart from the usual folk arts, wines and spirits, food and music, there are a few interesting flea markets and some great young-designer shops. Tons of shops along Váci utca (p307) and stands on the top floor of the Nagycsarnok (p307) sell Hungarian souvenirs, but the real souvenir-shopper's paradise is the old town centre at Szentendre (p316), just 40 minutes away by commuter rail.

Folkart Kézmövesház (Map p304; ☎ 318 5143; V Régiposta utca 12; ⏰ 10am-7pm Mon-Fri, to 4pm Sat) Some of the most authentic handmade folk crafts available in Budapest. You can buy embroidered folk costumes from Kalocsa, leatherwork horsewhips from the plains, and woven items from across the country.

Rózsavölgyi Music Shop (Map p304; ☎ 318 3500; V Szervita tér 5; ⏰ 9.30am-7pm Mon-Fri, 10am-5pm Sat) Classical and folk music CDs and tapes are on sale here.

Retrock (Map p304; ☎ 318 1007; www.retrock .com; V Ferenc István utca 28; ⏰ 10.30am-7.30pm Mon-Fri, to 4.30pm Sat) An excellent designer/vintage clothes shop, where a bunch of young Hungarian and international designers produce kitschy, stylish and always unique clothes at affordable prices.

There's an excellent selection of Hungarian wines at the **Magyar Borok Háza** (House of Hungarian Wines; Map p303; ☎ 212 1031; www.magyarborokhaza .hu; I Szentháromság tér 6; ⏰ noon-8pm) in Buda, and of fruit brandies and wine at the **Magyar Palinka Háza** (Map p304; ☎ 235 0488; VIII Rákóczi út 17; ⏰ 9am-7pm Mon-Sat) in Pest.

Three markets take place in Budapest during the week, each a little different from the other. The closest to the city centre is **Városligeti Bolhapiac** (Map pp300-1; ⏰ 7am-2pm Sat & Sun) at Petőfi Csarnok in the City Park. There is junk and antiques, and the best things are to be found early in the morning. The real market mamma though is the **Ecseri** (XIX Nagykőrösi út 156; ⊗ 8am-4pm Mon-Fri, 7am-3pm Sat), on the western edge of town. International antiques dealers come to scout on Saturdays, so things can get pricey. Take bus 52 from Elizabeth Bridge. **Jozsefvárosi piac** (Map pp300-1; VII Kőbányai út 21-23; ⊗ 6am-6pm) is a vast Chinese goods market and a world unto itself. Take tram 28 or 37.

GETTING THERE & AWAY
Air
The main international carriers fly in and out of Budapest's **Ferihegy 2 airport** (BUD; ☎ 296 9696), 24km southeast of the centre on Hwy 4; low-cost airlines use the older **Ferihegy 1 airport** (☎ 296 7000), next door. For carriers flying within Eastern Europe, see p350; for more on getting to Budapest from outside Eastern Europe, see p596.

Boat
In addition to its hydrofoils that travel internationally to Bratislava and Vienna (p351), **Mahart PassNave** (Map p304; ☎ 484 4005; www .mahartpassnave.hu; Vigadó tér Pier) ferries depart for Szentendre, Visegrád and Esztergom in the Danube Bend daily, April to October.

Bus
Volánbusz (☎ 219 8080; www.volanbusz.hu), the national bus line, has an extensive list of destinations from Budapest. All international buses and some buses to/from southern Hungary use **Népliget bus station** (Map pp300-1; ☎ 264 3939; IX Üllői út 131). **Stadion bus station** (Map pp300-1; ☎ 252 4498; XIV Hungária körút 48-52) serves most domestic destinations. Most buses to the northern Danube Bend arrive at and leave from the **Árpád híd bus station** (Map pp300-1; ☎ 329 1450, off XIII Róbert Károly körút). All stations are on metro lines, and all are in Pest. If the ticket office is closed, you can buy your ticket on the bus.

For details of international bus services within Eastern Europe, see p350 and p599.

Car & Motorcycle
Car rental is not recommended if you are staying in Budapest. The public transportation network is extensive and cheap, whereas parking is scarce and there are more than enough cars and motor emissions on the congested streets already.

If you want to venture into the countryside, travelling by car may be the best way to go. Daily rates start around €40 per day with kilo-

metres included. If an office is not at the airport, the company will usually provide free pick-up and delivery within Budapest or at the airport during office hours. All the major international chains have branches at Ferihegy 2 airport.
Americana Rent-a-Car (Map pp300-1; ☎ 350 2542; www.americana.matav.hu; XIII Dózsa György út 65; ⊗ 8am-6pm Mon-Fri, to noon Sat) Reliable office in the Ibis Volga hotel.
Recent Car (Map pp300-1; ☎ 453 0003; www.recent car.hu; III Óbudai hajógyári-sziget 131; ⊗ 8am-8pm) One of the cheapest.

Train
The Hungarian State Railways, **MÁV** (☎ 461 5400 domestic information, 461 5500 international information; www.elvira.hu) covers the country well and has its schedule online. The **MÁV Ticket Office** (Map p304; ☎ 461 5400; VI Andrássy út 35; ⊗ 9am-6pm Mon-Fri Apr-Sep, 9am-5pm Mon-Fri Oct-Mar) provides information and sells domestic and international train tickets and seat reservations (you can also buy tickets at the busy stations). To avoid queues go to booths posted 'International Ticket Office' – you can buy domestic tickets here and there might be some English speakers.

The commuter rail, HÉV, begins at Batthyány tér in Buda and travels north through the suburbs. If you have a *turista* pass, you still need a supplemental ticket to get to Szentendre, the northern terminus, and towns outside the city limits.

Keleti train station (Eastern; ☎ 333 6342; VIII Kerepesi út 2-4) handles international trains from Vienna and many other points east, plus domestic trains to/from the north and northeast. For some Romanian, German and Slovak destinations, as well as domestic ones to/from the northwest and the Danube Bend, head for **Nyugati train station** (Western; ☎ 349 0115; VI Nyugati tér). For trains bound for Lake Balaton and the south, go to **Déli train station** (Southern; ☎ 375 6293; I Krisztina körút 37). All three train stations are on metro lines.

For details of international trains within Eastern Europe, see p351; for trains travelling to places outside Eastern Europe, see p599.

GETTING AROUND
To/From the Airport
The simplest way to get to town is to take the **Airport Minibus** (☎ 296 8555; one-way/return 2100/3600Ft; ⊗ 5am-1am) directly to the place you're staying. Buy tickets at the clearly marked stands in the arrivals halls. The cheapest way is to take the BKV Ferihegy bus (from outside the

HUNGARY

baggage claim at Ferihegy 2, or on the main road outside Ferihegy 1) to the end of its run, the Kőbánya–Kispest stop, which is at the M2 blue line metro terminus. Then ride the metro to your destination. The bus ride takes about 25 minutes, as does the metro ride to the central metro hub (Deák tér). You need a 230Ft ticket, available at newsstands or vending machines, which you can validate on the bus and in the metro. If you want to switch metro lines, you'll need a second ticket.

Boat

From May to August, the **BKV passenger ferry** (Map pp300-1; ☎ 06 20 955 3782; www.ship-bp.hu, Hungarian only) departs from Boráros tér Terminus beside Petőfi Bridge, south of the centre, and heads to Pünkösdfürdő Terminus north of Aquincum, with many stops along the way. Tickets (adult/child 500/400Ft from end to end) are usually sold on board. The ferry stop closest to the Castle District is Batthyány tér, and Petőfi tér is not far from Vörösmarty tér, a convenient place to pick up the boat on the Pest side.

Public Transport

Public transport is run by **BKV** (☎ 342 2335; www .bkv.hu). The three underground metro lines (M1 yellow, M2 red, M3 blue) meet at Deák tér in Pest. The HÉV above-ground suburban railway runs north from Batthyány tér in Buda. A *turista* transport pass is only good on the HÉV within the city limits (south of the Békásmegyer stop). There's also an extensive network of buses, trams and trolleybuses. Public transport operates from 4.30am until 11.30pm, and 18 night buses (marked with an 'É') run along main roads.

A single ticket for all forms of transport is 140Ft (60 minutes of uninterrupted travel, no metro line changes). A transfer ticket (230Ft) is valid for one trip with one validated transfer within 90 minutes. The three-day *turista* pass (2200Ft) or the seven-day pass (2600Ft) make things easier, allowing unlimited travel inside the city limits. Keep your ticket or pass handy; the fine for 'riding black' is 2000Ft on the spot, or 5500Ft if you pay later at the **BKV Office** (Map p304; ☎ 461 6544; VII Akácfa utca 22; 6am-8pm Mon-Fri, 8am-2pm Sat).

Taxi

Overcharging foreigners (rigged meters, detours…) is common. Never get into a taxi that does not have an official yellow licence plate, the

logo of the taxi firm, and a visible table of fares. If you have to take a taxi, it's best to call one; this costs less than if you flag one down. Make sure you know the number of the landline phone you're calling from as that's how the dispatcher establishes your address (though you can call from a mobile too). Dispatchers usually speak English. **City** (☎ 211 1111), **Fő** (☎ 222 2222) and **Rádió** (☎ 377 7777) are reliable companies.

THE DANUBE BEND

North of Budapest, the Danube breaks through the Pilis and Börzsöny Hills in a sharp bend before continuing into Slovakia. Here medieval kings once ruled Hungary from majestic palaces overlooking the river at Esztergom and Visegrád. East of Visegrád the river divides, with Szentendre and Vác on different branches. Today the easy access to historic monuments, rolling green scenery – and tons of souvenir craft shops – lure many day-trippers from Budapest.

SZENTENDRE

☎ 26 / pop 22,700

Once an artists' colony, now a popular day trip from Budapest (19km north), pretty little Szentendre (*sen*-ten-dreh) has narrow, winding streets and is a favourite with souvenir-shoppers. The charming old centre has plentiful cafés, art and craft galleries, and there are several Orthodox churches that are worth a peek. Expect things to get crowded in summer and at weekends. Outside town is the largest open-air village museum in the country.

Orientation & Information

From the HÉV train and bus stations, walk under the subway and up Kossuth Lajos utca to Fő tér, the centre of the Old Town. The Duna korzó and the river embankment is a block east of this square. The Mahart ferry pier is about 1km northeast on Czóbel sétány, off Duna korzó. There are no left-luggage offices at the HÉV train or bus stations.

Tourinform (☎ 317 965; Dumtsa Jenő utca 22; 9am-6.30pm Mon-Fri, 10am-2pm Sat) has information about the numerous small museums and galleries in town. The **OTP Bank** (Dumtsa Jenő utca 6) is just off Fő tér, and the **main post office** (Kossuth Lajos utca 23-25) is across from the bus and train stations. **Game Planet** (☎ 505 068; Petőfi Sándor utca

1; ☯ 10am-10pm) is an internet café with access for 300Ft per hour.

Sights

Begin your sightseeing at the colourful Fő tér, the town's main square. Here you'll find many buildings from the 18th century, including the **Emlékkereszt** (Memorial Cross; 1763) and the 1752 Serbian Orthodox **Blagoveštenska Templom** (Blagoveštenska Church; ☎ 310 554; Fő tér; admission 200Ft; ☯ 10am-5pm Tue-Sun), which is small but stunning.

All the pedestrian lanes surrounding the square burst with shops, the merchandise spilling out into displays on the streets. Downhill to the east, off a side street on the way to the Danube, is the **Margit Kovács Múzeum** (☎ 310 244; Vastagh György utca 1; adult/student 600/400Ft; ☯ 10am-6pm Feb-Oct). Kovács (1902–77) was a ceramicist who combined Hungarian folk, religious and modern themes to create her much beloved figures. Uphill to the northwest, a narrow passageway leads up from between Fő tér 8 and 9 to Várhegy (Castle Hill) and the **Szent Janos Plébánia Templom** (Parish Church of St John; Várhegy), rebuilt in 1710, from where you get great views of the town

and the Danube. Nearby, the tall red tower of the Serbian **Belgradi Székesegyház** (Belgrade Cathedral; Pátriárka utca 5), from 1764, casts its shadow. You can hear beautiful chanting wafting from the open doors during services. The **Szerb Ortodox Egyháztőrténeti Gyűjtemény** (Serbian Orthodox Ecclesiastical Art Collection; ☎ 312 399; Pátriárka utca 5; adult/student 200/100Ft; ☯ 10am-6pm Wed-Sun mid-Mar–Oct, 10am-4pm Fri-Sun Nov–mid-Mar) is in the courtyard.

Don't miss the extensive **Szabadtéri Néprajzi Múzeum** (Open-Air Ethnographic Museum; ☎ 502 500; adult/student 800/400Ft; ☯ 9am-5pm Tue-Sun Apr-Oct) 3.5km outside town. Walking through the fully furnished ancient wooden and stone homes, churches and working buildings brought here from around the country, you can see what rural life was – and sometimes still is – like in different regions of Hungary. The five reconstructed villages of this *skansen* (village museum) are not close to each other, but you can take a wagon ride (500Ft) between them. In the centre of the park stand Roman-era ruins. Frequent weekend festivals give you a chance to see folk costumes, music and dance, as well as home crafts. To get here, take the bus marked 'Skansen' from stand No 7 (100Ft, 20 minutes, hourly).

SZENTENDRE

0   300 m
0   0.2 miles

HUNGARY

Sleeping & Eating

Seeing Szentendre on a day trip from Budapest is probably your best bet. The town can be easily covered in a day, even if you spend a couple of hours at the open-air museum. For private rooms in town, head west of the centre around the Dunakanyar körút ring road, and look for 'Zimmer frei' signs. Being a tourist town, there are plenty of places to sit at an outside table and grab a bite to eat.

Pap Sziget Camping (☎ 310 697; www.pap-sziget .hu; camp sites per person €6, caravan sites €15, motel room with shared bathroom €22, 2-bedroom bungalows €32-40; ⏾ May–mid-Oct; Ⓟ) The grounds have large shady trees, a sandy beach and 120 tent and caravan sites. Bungalows are raised on stilts and there's parking below. Take bus 1, 2 or 3 – it's 2km from north of town on Szentendre Island.

Bükkös Hotel (☎ 312 021; Bükkös part 16; s/d €40/45; Ⓟ) A Maria Theresa yellow exterior and a dark-wood reception hall welcome you to this 16-room hotel in an old building. The location's good, on a stream between the HÉV station and the Old Town.

Rab Ráby (☎ 310 819; Pétér Pál utca 1A; mains 700-1200Ft; ⏾ 11am-11pm) The locals' favourite for fish.

Crowd-watch on the square at **Régimódi** (☎ 311 105; Dumtsa Jenő utca 2; mains 700-1200Ft; ⏾ 11am-11pm), but don't expect very tasty food.

Getting There & Away

The most convenient way to get to Szentendre is to take the commuter HÉV train from Buda's Batthyány tér metro station to the end of the line (497Ft one-way, 45 minutes, every 10 to 15 minutes).

From mid-May to mid-September, three Mahart PassNave ferries travel daily from Budapest's Vigadó tér Pier to Szentendre (950Ft, 1½ hours) at 9am, 10.30am and 2pm. Return trips are at 12.20pm, 4pm and 5pm. The 9am boat continues on from Szentendre to Visegrád at 10.40am. In April and October, only the daily 9am departure from Budapest (continuing on to Visegrád only on weekends) and the 4pm return to Budapest from Szentendre run.

VISEGRÁD

☎ 26 / pop 1500

The spectacular views from the ruins of Visegrád's (*vish*-eh-grahd) 13th-century citadel, high on a hill above a curve in the Danube, are what pulls visitors to this sleepy town. The first fortress here was built by the Romans as a border defence in the 4th century. Hungarian kings built a mighty citadel on the hill top, and a lower castle near the river, after the 13th-century Mongol invasions. In the 14th century a royal palace was built on the flood plain at the foot of the hills, and in 1323 King Charles Robert of Anjou, whose claim to the local throne was being fiercely contested in Buda, moved the royal household here. For nearly two centuries Hungarian royalty alternated between Visegrád and Buda.

The destruction of Visegrád came first at the hands of the occupying Turks and then at the hands of the Habsburgs, who destroyed the citadel to prevent Hungarian independence fighters from using it. All trace of the palace was lost until 1934 when archaeologists, by following descriptions in literary sources, uncovered the ruins that you can visit today.

The small town has two distinct areas: one to the north around Mahart ferry pier and another, the main town, about 1km to the south. There's a Tourinform office, and there's also a rather confusing website that discusses the town's history in English (www.visegrad .hu; click on Műemlékek).

Sights & Activities

The partial reconstruction of the **Királyi Palota** (Royal Palace; ☎ 398 026; Fő utca 29; adult/student 500/300Ft; ⏾ 9am-4.30pm Tue-Sun), 400m south of the Mahart pier, only hints at its former magnificence. Inside, a small museum is devoted to the history of the palace and its excavation and reconstruction.

The palace's original Gothic fountain, along with town-history exhibits, is in the museum at **Salamon Torony** (Solomon's Tower; ☎ 398 233; adult/child 500/300Ft; ⏾ 9am-4.30pm Tue-Sun May-Sep), a few hundred metres north of the palace. The tower was part of a lower castle controlling river traffic. From here you can climb the very steep path uphill to the **Visegrád Cittadella** (☎ 398 101; Várhegy; adult/student 800/350Ft; ⏾ 9.30am-5.30pm) directly above. While the citadel (1259) ruins themselves are not as spectacular as their history, the view of the Danube Bend from the walls is well worth the climb. From the town centre a trail leads to the citadel from behind the Catholic church on Fő tér; this is less steep than the arduous climb from Solomon's Tower. A local bus runs up to the citadel from the Mahart PassNave ferry pier three times daily (more often in July and August).

Sleeping & Eating

As with the other towns in the Danube Bend, Visegrád is an easy day trip from Budapest, so it's not necessary to stay over if you don't want to. **Visegrád Tours** (☎ 398 160; Rév utca 15; ☺ 8am-5pm), an extremely accommodating travel agency in the town centre, provides information and books private rooms for between 5500Ft and 6500Ft per person, per night.

Jurta Camping (☎ 398 217; camp sites per adult/child/tent 650/400/500Ft; ☺ May-Sep; ☐) On Mogyoróhegy (Hazelnut Hill), about 2km northeast of the citadel, this camp sight is pretty and green. There aren't any bungalows, but there are yurt tents for rent with five beds in each. The Kisvillám' bus goes to Jurta Camping from the ferry pier at 9.25am, 12.25pm and 3.25pm, June to August.

Hotel Honti Panzió (☎ 398 120; hotelhon@axelero.hu; Fő utca 66; s/d pension €30/35, s/d hotel €40/50; ☐) Honti is a friendly pension filled with homy rooms. Bigger, more expensive and newer rooms in the adjacent hotel building still have wooden furniture and rose-coloured curtains your aunt might have made.

Reneszánsz (☎ 398 081; Fő utca 11; mains 1200-2400Ft; ☺ noon-10pm) Eating in a tourist trap can be fun if you go in for men in tights and silly hats. This is the attire at this medieval banquet-style restaurant. A royal feast, with pheasant soup, roast meats and unlimited wine costs a mighty 4000Ft.

Two better, more down-to-earth options are the **Grill Udvar** (Rév utca 6; mains 500-1000Ft; ☺ 11am-11pm), for pizzas and grilled meat; and **Gulyás Csárda** (☎ 398 329; Mátyás Király utca; mains 1000-2000Ft; ☺ 11am-10pm). Both are in the town centre and known for reliable Hungarian standards and cymbalom music.

Getting There & Away

Frequent buses go to Visegrád from Budapest's Árpád híd bus station (423Ft, 1¼ hours, at least hourly), the Szentendre HÉV station (302Ft, 45 minutes, every 45 minutes) and Esztergom (302Ft, 45 minutes, hourly). No trains go to Visegrád.

On weekends in late April and during most of October, a ferry runs from Budapest to Visegrád (per person/car 280/1050Ft, 3½ hours) at 9am (via Szentendre), returning to Budapest from Visegrád at 4pm. From mid-May to mid-September that same ferry runs daily. There is an additional departure at 7.30am from late May to August, which continues on to

Esztergom at 10.50am. The return departure from Visegrád to Budapest is at 5.30pm. On weekends from June to August there is also a high-speed hydrofoil service from Budapest to Visegrád (2000Ft, one hour), departing from Budapest at 9.30am and Visegrád at 4.45pm.

ESZTERGOM

☎ 33 / pop 28,900

A town full of ecclesiastic wonders, Esztergom (*es*-ter-gohm) has been the seat of Roman Catholicism in Hungary since the 19th century. The soaring Esztergom Bazilika is home to the Primate of Hungary and surrounding museums contain many Christian treasures.

The significance of this town reaches far back into history. The 2nd-century Roman emperor-to-be Marcus Aurelius wrote his famous *Meditations* while he camped here. In the 10th century, Stephen I, founder of the Hungarian state, was born and crowned at the cathedral. From the late 10th to the mid-13th centuries Esztergom served as the Hungarian royal seat. In 1543 the Turks ravaged the town and much of it was destroyed only to be rebuilt in the 18th and 19th centuries. Many of the old buildings in the centre date from those centuries.

Orientation & Information

The train station is on the southern edge of town, about a 10-minute walk south of the bus station. From the train station, walk north on Baross Gábor út, then along Ady Endre utca to Símor János utca, past the bus station to the town centre. Don't be fooled by the run-down buildings along the walk; the town's true character reveals itself once you get to the hill below the cathedral.

K&H Bank (Rákóczi tér) does foreign exchange transactions. The **post office** (Arany János utca 2) is just off Széchenyi tér. **Gran Tours** (☎ 502 000; Rákóczi tér 25; ☺ 8am-6pm Mon-Fri) is the best source of information in town.

Sights & Activities

The country's largest church is **Esztergom Bazilika** (☎ 411 895; admission free; ☺ 7am-6pm), sitting on a hill above the Danube. The colossal building is easily spotted from the train window en route from Bratislava to Budapest. Reconstructed in the neoclassical style, much of the building dates from the 19th century; the oldest section is the white and red marble **Bakócz Kápolna** (Bakócz Chapel; 1510) that was moved here. You can climb up the winding steps to the top of the cupola for 200Ft. The **kincsház** (treasury; adult/student 450/220Ft; ☉ 9am-4.30pm mid-Mar–Oct, 11am-3.30pm Mon-Fri & 10am-3pm Sat Nov–mid-Mar) contains priceless objects, including ornate vestments and the 13th-century Hungarian coronation cross. Among those buried in the **altemplom** (crypt; admission 100Ft; ☉ 9am-5pm) under the cathedral is the controversial Cardinal Mindszenty, who was imprisoned by the communists for refusing to allow Hungary's Catholic schools to be secularised.

At the southern end of the hill is the **Vár Múzeum** (Castle Museum; ☎ 415 986; adult/student 460/240Ft; ☉ 10am-6pm Tue-Sun Apr-Oct, to 4pm Nov-Mar), inside the reconstructed remnants of the medieval royal palace (1215), which was built upon previous castles. The earliest excavated sections on the hill date from the 2nd to 3rd centuries.

Southwest of the cathedral along the banks of the Little Danube, narrow streets wind through the Víziváros (Watertown) district, home to the **Víziváros Plébánia Templom** (Watertown Parish Church; 1738) at the start of Berényi Zsigmond utca. The **Keresztény Múzeum** (Christian Museum; ☎ 413 880; Berényi Zsigmond utca 2; adult/student 400/200Ft; ☉ 10am-5.30pm Tue-Sun) is in the adjacent Primate's Palace (1882). The stunning collection of medieval religious art includes a statue of the Virgin Mary from the 11th century.

Cross the bridge south of Watertown Parish Church and about 100m further down is **Mária Valéria Bridge**. Destroyed during WWII, it once again connects Esztergom with Slovakia and the city of Štúrovo. **St István Fürdő** (☎ 312 249; Bajcsy-Zsilinszky utca 14; adult/child 550/350Ft; ☉ 9am-6pm May-Sep, indoor pool only 6am-6pm Mon & Sat, 6am-7pm Tue-Fri, 9am-4pm Sun Oct-Apr) backs up to the Little Danube promenade and has outdoor and indoor thermal baths and pools.

Sleeping & Eating

Although frequent transportation connections make Esztergom an easy day trip from Budapest, you might want to stop a night if you are going on to Slovakia. Contact Gran Tours (p319) about private rooms, for around 4000Ft per person.

Gran Camping (☎ 411 953; fortanex@alexero.hu; Nagy-Duna sétány 3; camp sites per person 1100Ft, dm/r 1700/6000Ft, bungalows 12,000-16,000Ft; ☉ May-Sep; **P**) For a camping ground this place has quite a

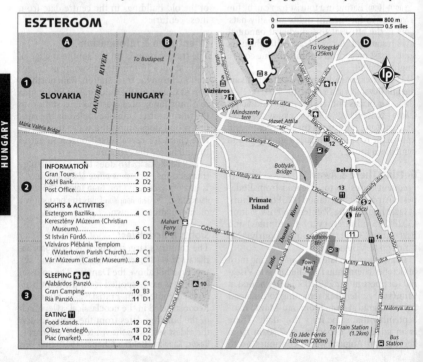

ESZTERGOM

0 — 800 m
0 — 0.5 miles

INFORMATION	
Gran Tours	1 D2
K&H Bank	2 D2
Post Office	3 D3

SIGHTS & ACTIVITIES	
Esztergom Bazilika	4 C1
Keresztény Múzeum (Christian Museum)	5 C1
St István Fürdő	6 D2
Víziváros Plébánia Templom (Watertown Parish Church)	7 C1
Vár Múzeum (Castle Museum)	8 C1

SLEEPING 🏠 🏕	
Alabárdos Panzió	9 C1
Gran Camping	10 B3
Ria Panzió	11 D1

EATING 🍴	
Food stands	12 D2
Olasz Vendeglő	13 D2
Piac (market)	14 D2

SLOVAKIA

HUNGARY

To Budapest

DANUBE RIVER

Mária Valéria Bridge

Víziváros

Pázmány

Mindszenty tere

Péter utca

József Attila tér

Gesztenye fasor

Bottyán Bridge

Belváros

Táncsics Mihály utca

Primate Island

Lőrincz utca

Rákóczi tér

Mahart Ferry Pier

Gőzhajó utca

Kis-Duna sétány

Little Danube River

Széchenyi tér

Town Hall

Arany János utca

Nagy-Duna sétány

Kossuth Lajos utca

To Jáde Forrás Étterem (200m)

To Train Station (1.2km)

Bus Station

Berényi Zsigmond utca

Máté István utca

Béttyáni Lajos utca

Bajcsy-Zsilinszky utca

Vörösmarty utca

Petőfi utca

Sándor utca

Pázmány Péter utca

Malonyai utca

To Visegrád (25km)

HUNGARY

lot of buildings: elevated bungalows sleep four to six; a dormitory houses about 100 people in four-, five- and eight-bed rooms; and the motel has serviceable doubles. It's a 10-minute walk along the Danube from the cathedral.

Alabárdos Panzió (☎ 312 640; www.alabardospanzio .hu; Bajcsy-Zsilinszky utca 49; s 7500-9500Ft; d 9500-12,000Ft; **P**) There are some lovely rooms in Alabárdos and some downright dowdy ones, with motley furnishings: some have iron beds, some modular wood veneer. Look before you choose. The location is great if you want to be close to the cathedral – the hotel is at the base of Castle Hill.

Ria Panzió (☎ 313 115; www.riapanzio.com; Batthyány Lajos utca 11; s/d €40/48; **P** **▯** **▯**) Doubles are fresh, with white walls, wood floors and royal-blue linen. Relax on the terrace or arrange an adventure through the family owners – rent a bicycle maybe, or take a water-skiing trip on the Danube in summer.

Jáde Forrás Étterem (☎ 400 949; Hősök tere 11; mains 600-1400Ft; ☯ 11am-11pm; ✖) Jáde does a mean Hunan chicken and has a reduced-price buffet at lunch. A four-course set menu is 1750Ft.

Olasz Vendeglö (☎ 312 952; Lőrincz utca 5; pizzas & pastas 700-1000Ft, mains 1000-1400Ft; ☯ 11am-10pm Sun-Thu, to midnight Fri & Sat; ✖) Pizzas and pastas at the originally named Italian restaurant are among the few vegetarian options in town. Mains include dishes such as fruit-stuffed chicken breast.

On the way to the cathedral from the bus station, the **piac** (market; Símor János utca; ☯ 7am-4pm Mon-Fri, to 1pm Sat), north of Arany János utca, has fruit and vegetables, and three **food stands** (Bajcsy-Zsilinszky utca, cnr Szent István fürdő; snacks 200-600Ft; ☯ 8am-8pm) sell burgers, gyros, falafel and the like.

Getting There & Away

Buses run to/from Budapest's Árpád híd bus station (579Ft, 1½ hours on shortest route) and to/from Visegrád (302Ft, 45 minutes) at least hourly. Two direct buses a day go from Esztergom to Győr (1160Ft, two hours).

The most comfortable way to get to Esztergom from Budapest is by rail: sleek, EC-approved cars run this route. Trains depart from Budapest's Nyugati train station (512Ft, 1½ hours) more than 20 times a day. Cross the Mária Valéria Bridge into Štúrovo, Slovakia and you can catch a train to Bratislava, which is an hour and a half away.

Mahart PassNave ferries depart from Budapest to Esztergom (via Visegrád, 1200Ft,

5½ hours) once a day from late May through August (7.30am). The daily return trip to Budapest departs from Esztergom at 3.20pm. Weekends from June to August there is also a high-speed hydrofoil service between Budapest and Esztergom (2300Ft, 2½ hours), via Visegrád, departing from Budapest at 9.30am and from Esztergom at 3.20pm. From June through August, a ferry service between Esztergom and Visegrád (700Ft, two hours) departs Esztergom at 9am and returns from Visegrád at 3.30pm.

NORTHWESTERN HUNGARY

The closer you get to the Austrian border, the more prominent the seductive atmosphere of the gilded days of the Austro-Hungarian empire becomes. Northwestern Hungary beyond the Bakony Hills is bounded by the Danube to the east and the Alps to the west. The old quarters of Sopron and Győr are brimming with what were once the residences of prosperous burghers and clerics. Fertőd, outside Sopron, is a magnificent baroque palace and Pannonhalma, outside Győr, is an early Benedictine monastery still in operation.

GYŐR

☎ 96 / pop 129,500

A sizable pedestrian centre filled with old streets and buildings make riverside Győr (pronounced, impossibly, jyeur) an inviting place for a stroll – even if there isn't one stand-out attraction. Students hang out at the many pavement cafés in this university town.

Midway between Budapest and Vienna, Győr sits at the point where the Mosoni-Danube, Rábca and Rába Rivers meet. This was the site of a Roman town named Arrabona. In the 11th century, Stephen I established a bishopric here, and in the 16th century a fortress was erected to hold back the Turks.

Orientation & Information

The large neobaroque City Hall (1898) rises up to block out all other views across from the train station. Baross Gábor utca, which leads to the old town and the rivers, lies diagonally across from City Hall. Much of central Győr is pedestrianised, making parking difficult.

HUNGARY

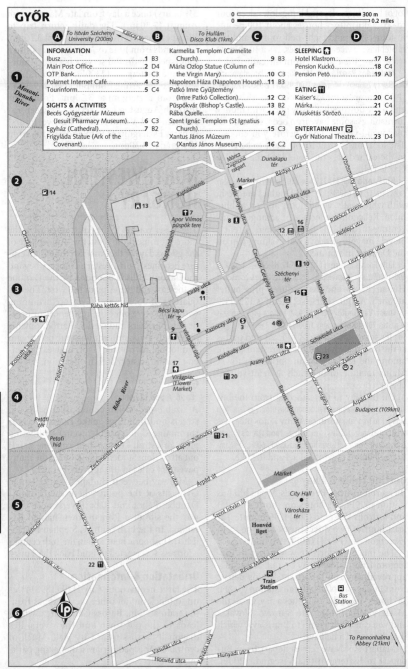

GYŐR

0	300 m
0	0.2 miles

INFORMATION
Ibusz.....................................**1** B3
Main Post Office....................**2** D4
OTP Bank..............................**3** C3
Polarnet Internet Café.........**4** C3
Tourinform............................**5** C4

SIGHTS & ACTIVITIES
Becés Gyógyszertár Múzeum
(Jesuit Pharmacy Museum)........**6** C3
Egyház (Cathedral)......................**7** B2
Frigyláda Statue (Ark of the
Covenant)..................................**8** C2

Karmelita Templom (Carmelite
Church)......................................**9** B3
Mária Ozlop Statue (Column of
the Virgin Mary)........................**10** C3
Napoleon Háza (Napoleon House)...**11** B3
Patkó Imre Gyűjtemény
(Imre Patkó Collection)..............**12** C2
Püspökvár (Bishop's Castle).............**13** B2
Rába Quelle.................................**14** A2
Szent Ignác Templom (St Ignatius
Church)......................................**15** C3
Xantus János Múzeum
(Xantus János Museum)............**16** C2

SLEEPING
Hotel Klastrom.........................**17** B4
Pension Kuckó..........................**18** C4
Pension Pető.............................**19** A3

EATING
Kaiser's....................................**20** C4
Márka......................................**21** C4
Muskétás Söröző.....................**22** A6

ENTERTAINMENT
Győr National Theatre............**23** D4

Ibusz (☎ 311 700; Kazinczy utca 3; ☯ 8.30am-4pm Mon-Fri) This travel agency arranges private rooms and area tours, including to Pannonhalma.
Main post office (Bajcsy-Zsilinszky út 46)
OTP Bank (Baross Gábor 16)
Polarnet Internet Café (Czuczor Gergely utca 6; per hr 180Ft; ☯ 9am-8pm) Above a clothing shop, with the entrance around the corner in an alleyway.
Tourinform (☎ 311 711; Árpád út 32; ☯ 8am-6pm Mon-Fri, 9am-3pm Sat) Small but helpful; offers currency exchange.

Sights & Activities

The enchanting 1725 **Karmelita Templom** (Carmelite Church; Bécsí kapu tér) and many fine baroque palaces line riverfront Bécsí kapu tér. On the northwestern side of the square are the fortifications built in the 16th century to stop the Turks. A short distance to the east is **Napoleon Háza** (Napoleon House; Király utca 4), where Bonaparte spent his only night in Hungary in 1809. Walk around the old streets and stop in at a pavement café or two.

North up Káptalandomb (Chapter Hill), in the oldest part of Győr, is the solid baroque **Egyház** (Cathedral; Apor Vilmos püspök tere; ☯ 10am-noon & 2-5pm). Situated on the hill, it was originally Romanesque, but most of what you see inside dates from the 17th and 18th centuries. Don't miss the Gothic **Héderváry Chapel** on the southern side of the cathedral, which contains a glittering 15th- century bust of King (and St) Ladislas.

West of the cathedral, the **Püspökvár** (Bishop's Castle; ☎ 312 153; adult/student 400/200Ft; ☯ 10am-6pm Tue-Sun) houses the Diocesan Treasury. The architecture represents a variety of styles; the tower was constructed in the 14th century, but the building saw a major overhaul in the 18th century. At the bottom of the hill on Jedlik Ányos utca is the **Frigyláda** (Ark of the

Covenant statue) dating from 1731. From here you can head north to a bridge overlooking the junction of the city's three rivers.

In Széchenyi tér, the heart of Győr, is the fine **Szent Ignác Templom** (St Ignatius Church; 1641) and the **Mária Ozlop statue** (Column of the Virgin Mary; 1686). Cross the square to the **Xantus János Múzeum** (Xantus János Museum; ☎ 310 588; Széchenyi tér 5; adult/student 500/250Ft; ☯ 10am-6pm Tue-Sun), built in 1743, to see exhibits on the city's history. Next door is the **Patkó Imre Gyűjtemény** (Imre Patkó Collection; ☎ 310 588; Széchenyi tér 4; adult/child 300/150Ft; ☯ 10am-6pm Tue-Sun), a fine small museum in a 17th-century house. Collections include 20th-century Asian and African art. Look out for the highly decorated baroque ceiling at the **Becés Gyógyszertár Múzeum** (Jesuit Pharmacy Museum; ☎ 320 954; Széchenyi tér 9; admission free; ☯ 7.30am-4pm Mon-Fri).

The water in the pools at thermal bath **Rába Quelle** (☎ 522 646; Fürdő tér 1; adult/student per day 1600/1000Ft; ☯ 8am-10pm) ranges from 29°C to 38°C. This place is almost an entertainment complex. One pool has a huge stone-face waterfall, another a waterslide. There's a restaurant, bar and beauty shop onsite as well as the requisite massage services.

Sleeping & Eating

For private rooms ask at Ibusz (left).
István Széchenyi University (☎ 503 447; Héderváry út 3; dm 2300Ft) Dormitory accommodation is available year-round at this huge university north of the town centre.
Pension Kuckó (☎ 316 260; fax 312 195; Arany János utca 33; s/d/apt 5900/7490/9900Ft; ☒) An old town house fitted out with bright modern trimmings. The two apartments, with small kitchens, and the café on the ground floor are especially attractive. Sister property **Pension**

WORTH THE TRIP

Take half a day and make the short trip to the ancient and impressive **Pannonhalmi Főapátság** (Pannonhalma Abbey; ☎ 570 191; www.osb.hu, no English; Vár 1; adult/student Hungarian tour 1200/500Ft, adult/ student foreign-language tour 1900/1200Ft; ☯ closed Mon Oct-May), now a Unesco World Heritage site. Most buildings in the complex date from the 13th to the 18th centuries; highlights include the Romanesque basilica (1225), the Gothic cloister (1486) and the impressive collection of ancient texts in the library. Because it's an active monastery, the abbey must be visited with a guide. From mid-March to mid-November, foreign-language tours in English, Italian, German, French and Russian are conducted at 11.20am, 1.20pm and 3.20pm.

Pannonhalma is best reached from Győr by bus as the train station is 2km southwest of the abbey. A direct bus runs daily from the Győr bus station to the abbey (Pannonhalma, vár főkapu stop) at 8am, 10am and noon (289Ft, 40 minutes), returning at 8.50am, 12.50pm and 5.35pm. Buses go hourly from Győr to the town of Pannonhalma. The abbey is a 15-minute, uphill walk from there.

HUNGARY

Petö (☎ 313 412; Kossuth Lajos utca 20; s/d 7200/8900Ft; ✕) is not far across the river.

Hotel Klastrom (☎ 516 910; www.klastrom.hu; Zechmeister utca 1; s/d/tr €55/70/80; P ✕ 💻) Sleep in a Carmelite friary that is more than 250 years old. Vaulted arch ceilings grace many of the public and guest rooms. Dark modern furniture contrasts appropriately with stark white walls. The interior courtyard looks like a formal garden.

Márka (☎ 320 800; Bajcsy-Zsilinszky út 30; mains 450-490Ft; ⏰ 11am-3.30pm Mon-Fri) Dine cafeteria-style for lunch. Enter through the pastry shop.

Muskétás Söröző (☎ 317 627; Munkácsy Mihaly utca 10; mains 630-790Ft; ⏰ 11am-midnight, bar to 1am) Eminently reasonable, this pub and eatery is especially popular with students from the nearby music college. Dine or drink downstairs in the cellar or continue through to the outdoor tables in the courtyard at the rear. The menu includes options such as turkey breast stuffed with a variety of ingredients.

A massive Kaiser's supermarket and department store takes up much of the block at Arany János utca and Aradi vértanúk útja.

Entertainment

In summer there's a month-long festival of music, theatre and dance from late June. In March, Győr hosts many events in conjunction with Budapest's Spring Festival.

Győr National Theatre (☎ 314 800; Czuczor Gergely utca 7) The celebrated Győr Ballet and the city's opera company and philharmonic orchestra all perform at the town's main, modern theatre. Tourinform (p323) can help with performance schedules.

Hullám Disco Klub (☎ 315 275; Héderváry utca 22; ⏰ 6pm-4am Fri & Sat) House music and guest DJs attracts a twenty-something crowd to this disco.

Getting There & Away

Buses travel to Budapest (1570Ft, two hours, hourly), Pannonhalma (302Ft, 30 minutes, half-hourly), Sopron (1160Ft, two hours, seven daily), Esztergom (1270Ft, two hours, one daily), Balatonfüred (1210Ft, 2½ hours, six daily) and Vienna (3790Ft, two hours, two daily).

Győr is well connected by express train to Budapest's Keleti and Déli train stations (1632Ft, 1½ hours, 15 daily) and to Sopron (1282Ft, 1½ hours, 14 daily). Six daily trains connect Győr with Vienna's Westbahnhof (4750Ft, two hours).

SOPRON

☎ 99 / pop 55,000

Sopron (*shop*-ron) is one of Hungary's most beautiful towns, with a Gothic town centre enclosed by medieval walls, narrow streets and mysterious passages. Many have called it 'little Prague', and rightly so. Sopron, although much smaller, has something of the charm of the Czech capital. Others see it as a 'dental-holiday' destination, with its surprisingly cheap dentists. Austrian day-trippers in particular come here to fix their dentures and brighten their smiles.

The Mongols and Turks never got this far, so unlike many Hungarian cities, numerous medieval buildings remain in use. The town sits on the Austrian border, only 69km south of Vienna. In 1921 the town's residents voted in a referendum to remain part of Hungary, while the rest of Bürgenland (the region to which Sopron used to belong) went to Austria. The region is known for producing good red wines such as Kékfrancos, which you can sample in local cafés and restaurants.

Orientation & Information

From the main train station, walk north on Mátyás Király utca, which becomes Várkerület, part of a loop following the line of the former town walls. Előkapu (Front Gate) and Hátsókapu (Back Gate) are the two main entrances in the walls. The bus station is northwest of the old town on Lackner Kristóf utca.

Internet Centrum Sopron (☎ 310 252; Új utca 3; per hr 400Ft; ⏰ 11am-8pm Mon-Fri, 10am-5pm Sat)

Main post office (Széchenyi tér 7-10)

OTP Bank (Várkerület 96/a)

Tourinform (☎ 338 892; www.sopron.hu; Előkapu 11; ⏰ 9am-noon & 1-5pm Mon-Fri, 9am-1pm Sat)

Sights & Activities

Fő tér is the main square in Sopron; there are several museums, monuments and churches scattered around it. Above the old town's northern gate rises the 60m-high **Tűztorony** (Fire Tower; ☎ 311 327; Fő tér; adult/student 500/250Ft; ⏰ 10am-6pm Tue-Sun), run by the Soproni Múzeum. The building is a true architectural hybrid: the 2m-thick square base, built on a Roman gate, dates from the 12th century, the middle cylindrical and arcaded balcony was built in the 16th century and the baroque spire was added in 1680. You can climb the 154 steps for views of the Alps.

HUNGARY

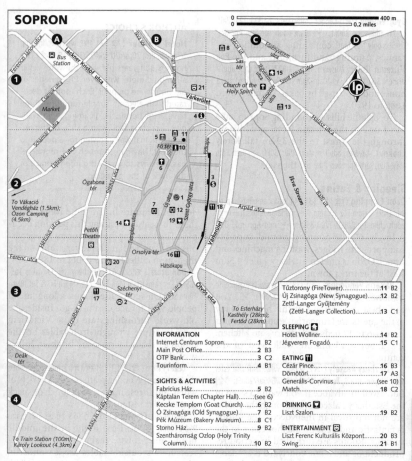

SOPRON

In the centre of Fő tér is the **Szentháromság Ozlop** (Holy Trinity Column; 1701). On the north side of the square is **Storno Ház** (☎ 311 327; Fő tér 8; adult/student 800/400Ft; ☼ 10am-6pm Tue-Sun Apr-Aug, ton2pm Tue-Sun Sep-Mar), where King Mátyás stayed in 1482 while his armies lay siege to Vienna. Today it houses a local history exhibition. Upstairs at **Fabricius Ház** (☎ 311 327; Fő tér 6; adult/student 1000/500Ft; ☼ 10am-6pm Tue-Sun Apr-Aug, to 2pm Tue-Sun Sep-Mar) walk through rooms recreated to resemble those in 17th- and 18th-century town homes. In the basement see stone sculptures and other remains from Roman times. The back rooms of the ground floor are dedicated to an archaeology exhibit.

Beyond the square is the 13th-century **Kecske Templom** (Goat Church; Templom utca 1), whose name comes from the heraldic animal of its chief benefactor. Below the church is the **Káptalan Terem** (Chapter Hall; ☎ 338 843; admission free; ☼ 10am-noon & 2-5pm Tue-Sun May-Sep), part of a 14th-century Franciscan monastery, with frescoes and stone carvings.

The **Új Zsinagóga** (New Synagogue; Új utca 11), built in the 14th century, now houses private residences and offices. The medieval **Ó Zsinagóga** (Old Synagogue; ☎ 311 227; Új utca 22; adult/student 400/200Ft; ☼ 10am-6pm Tue-Sun May-Sep), also built in the 14th century, is in better shape than many scattered around the country and contains a museum of Jewish life.

There are many other small museums in town. Two in the Ikva district, northeast of the centre, are quite interesting: the **Zettl-Langer**

Gyűjtemény (Zettl-Langer Collection; ☎ 335 123; Balfi út 11; admission 300Ft; ☒ 10am-noon Tue-Sun Apr-Oct, Fri-Sun only Nov-Mar) containing antiquities, ceramics, paintings and furniture; and the **Pék Múzeum** (Bakery Museum; ☎ 311 327; Bécsí út 5; adult/student 300/150Ft; ☒ 10am-2pm Tue-Sun May-Aug) in a house and shop used by bakers' families from 1686 to 1970.

To visit the hills surrounding Sopron, take bus 1 or 2 to the Szieszta Hotel and hike up through the forest to the 394m-tall **Károly Lookout** (Lóvérek; adult/student 250/150Ft; ☒ 9am-8pm May-Aug, 9am-4pm Sep-Apr) for the view.

Sleeping & Eating

Ózon Camping (☎ /fax 331 144; ozoncamping@sopron .hu; Erdei Malom köz 3; camp sites per large tent/small tent/adult/child 1600/800/1200/850Ft; ☒ mid-Apr–mid-Oct) A lovely, 60-site camping ground, superbly equipped with fridges, washing machines and a pool. Ózon is hidden in a leafy valley 4.5km west of the inner town.

Vákáció Vendégház (☎ 338 502; www.szallasinfo.hu /vakaciovendeghaz; Ade Endre út 31; dm 2200Ft; ☒) You can't beat the neatness at this hostel. Many of the guests are Hungarian students. Rooms have two to 12 beds each; there's no kitchen. It's about a 15-minute walk west of the centre.

Esterházy Kastély (☎ 537 640; www.castles.hu/esterhazy; Haydn utca 2, Fertőd; d/tr/q 4900/6400/7200Ft; ☒) Book well in advance if you want to sleep in the Esterházy Palace. Even though the rooms are not too royal in their décor, the setting is fantastic and beds go like hot cakes in the summer. Rooms are furnished in period reproductions and a fine courtyard is available for guests only. Breakfast is not included.

Jégverem Fogadó (☎ 510 113; www.jegverem.hu; Jégverem utca 1; s/d 5000/8000Ft) Citrus yellow walls are a backdrop to plastic plants, and non-

descript furniture in five large rooms belies the 18th-century building this pension occupies. The steaming-hot restaurant has generous portions, with multiple variations on the fried-meat cutlet (mains 850Ft to 1890Ft).

Dömötöri (☎ 506 624; Széchenyi tér 13; cakes 165-265Ft; ☒ 7am-10pm Mon-Thu, 7am-11pm Fri & Sat, 8am-10pm Sun) On sunny afternoons, a long line of people wait for ice cream-to-go. Inside, the old-world furnishings are quite Victorian; outside, white wrought-iron tables on the umbrella-shaded terrace are brighter. Either way, the cakes are great.

Cézár Pince (☎ 311 337; Hátsókapu 2; mains 480-890Ft; ☒ 11am-11pm) Wooden platters with a variety of wurst and cheese make a good lunch or snack at this cellar restaurant.

Generális-Corvinus (☎ 505 035; Fő tér 7-8; mains 990-2100Ft; ☒ 9am-11pm) Right in the middle of the inner town's main square, this café-restaurant's outside tables are a wonderful place in spring and summer for a pizza (650Ft to 1700Ft) and a drink.

For self-catering head for the **Match** (Várkerület 100) supermarket.

WORTH THE TRIP

Don't miss **Esterházy Kasthély** (☎ 537 640; Haydn utca 2, Fertőd; adult/student 1000/600Ft; ☒ 10am-6pm Tue-Sun mid-Mar–Oct, to 4pm Fri-Sun Nov–mid-Mar), a magnificent, Versailles-style baroque extravaganza 28km outside town in Fertőd. Built in 1766, this 126-room palace was owned by one of the nation's foremost families. You have to put on felt booties and slip around the marble floors under gilt chandeliers with a Hungarian guide, but information sheets in various languages are on hand. From May to October, piano and string quartets perform regularly in the frescoed concert hall where Joseph Haydn worked as court musician to the Esterházys from 1761 to 1790. The Haydn Festival takes place here in early September. The Tourinform in Győr (p323) can help you with performance schedules.

Fertőd is easily accessible from Sopron by bus (348Ft, 45 minutes, hourly); the town is dominated by the palace and its grounds.

Drinking

Liszt Szalon (☎ 323 407; Szent György utca 12; drinks 190-490Ft; ☺ 10am-10pm) A wonderful, old-world coffeehouse dedicated to Liszt (of course), with the composer's concert posters from all over the world. Good coffee and Aztec chocolate, spiced with chilli.

Entertainment

Liszt Ferenc Kulturális Központ (☎ 517 517; Liszt Ferenc tér 1; ☺ ticket office 9am-5pm Tue-Fri, to noon Sat) A concert hall, café and exhibition space all rolled into one. The information desk has the latest on classical music and other cultural events in town.

Swing (☎ 06 20 214 8029; Várkerület 15; ☺ 5pm-midnight Sun-Fri, to 2am Sat) Live jazz, country, rock or blues play nightly.

Getting There & Away

There are four buses a day to Budapest (2660Ft, four hours), nine to Győr (1160Ft, two hours). Trains to Budapest's Keleti train station (3500Ft, 2½ to three hours, eight daily) depart from Sopron, as do trains to Győr (802Ft to 1282Ft, 1½ hours, 14 daily). To get to Vienna's Südbahnhof the best way is to take the train (€12, 1½ hours, 10 daily). You clear border checks before you get on the train.

LAKE BALATON

The 77km-long Lake Balaton is Hungary's seaside. This, the largest freshwater lake in Europe outside Scandinavia, provides the Hungarians (and foreigners) with fun in both the summer and winter months. During the summer, when the place is at its peak, it's all swimming and outdoor activities, and in winter the locals get their skates on and glide on the frozen lake.

Shallow water, sandy beaches and condominiums attract visitors to the southeastern shore, where the commercialised towns are pretty characterless. More-established towns, trees and rolling hills, deeper water and less sand await on the northwestern shore. Towns on both sides are packed in July and August, and all but deserted from December to February. Many facilities such as museums, pensions and restaurants close for the winter.

Balatonfüred is easily accessed from all points; Tihany peninsula is a nature reserve and a village too cute to be true. Keszthely is really the only town that's a town in its own

right – apart from year-round lake traffic. Nearby Hévíz is a spa centre with a huge thermal *tó* (lake).

BALATONFÜRED

☎ 87 / pop 13,500

Walking the hillside streets, you catch glimpses of the easy grace that 18th- and 19th-century Balatonfüred (*bal-ah-tahn fuhr-ed*) must have enjoyed. Today many of the old buildings could use a new coat of paint and the renowned curative waters can be taken by prescription only. Stick by the lake, where a tree-filled park leads down to the waterfront, the pier and outdoor cafés. The hotels here are a bit cheaper than those on the neighbouring Tihany peninsula, making this a good base for exploring.

Orientation & Information

The adjacent bus and train stations are on Dobó István utca, 1km from the lake.

OTP Bank (Petőfi Sándor utca 8)
Post office (Zsigmond utca 14)
Tourinform (☎ 580 480; www.balatonfured.hu; Petőfi Sándor utca 68; ☺ 9am-8pm Mon-Fri & to 6pm Sat & Sun Jun-Sep, to 5pm Mon-Fri & to 1pm Sat Mar-May & Oct, to 5pm Mon-Fri Nov-Feb) The main office is inconveniently located 1km northeast of the centre; a second **Tourinform branch** (☎ 580 480; Széchenyi utca 47; ☺ 9am-5pm Mon-Fri, to 1pm Sat May-Sep; to 3pm Mon-Fri Oct-Apr) is annoyingly situated about 1.5km to the southwest.

Sights & Activities

The park along the central lakeshore, near the ferry pier, is worth a promenade. You can take a one-hour **pleasure cruise** (☎ 342 230; www.balatonihajozas.hu; Mahart ferry pier; adult/child 1200/600Ft) at 2pm and 4pm daily, May to August. The **disco hajo** (disco boat; ☎ 342 230; www.balatonihajozas.hu; Mahart ferry pier; cruises 1400Ft), a two-hour cruise with music and drinks, leaves at 9pm Tuesday through Sunday, June to August. **Kisfaludy Strand** (Aranyhíd sétány; adult/student 330/190Ft; ☺ 9am-10pm mid-Jun–mid-Sep), along the footpath 800m northeast of the pier, is a relatively sandy beach. A good way to explore the waterfront is to rent a bike from **Tempo 21** (☎ 480 671; Ady Endre utca 52; per hr/day 350/2400Ft; ☺ 9am-5pm Mon-Fri, to 1pm Sat).

North of the pier is the renovated 1846 **Kerek Templom** (Round Church; cnr Jókai Mór & Honvéd utca). **Mór Jókai Múzeum** (☎ 343 426; Honvéd utca 1; adult/child 300/150Ft; ☺ 10am-6pm Tue-Sun May-Oct) commemorates the life of the acclaimed novelist in what was once his summer house (1871). The heart of the old spa town is Gyógy

HUNGARY

tér, where **Kossuth Forrásvíz** (Kossuth Spring, 1853) dispenses slightly sulphurous water that people actually drink for health. Don't stray far from a bathroom afterwards.

Sleeping & Eating

In peak season (late May to early September) tons of guesthouses and private individuals rent rooms. Tourinform (p327) has a long list of such accommodation on its website, or you might just want to look for signs due south of the train and bus stations on Endrődi Sándor utca. **Ibusz** (www.ibusz.hu) travel agency lists private accommodation in the Balaton area on its website.

The eastern end of Tagore sétány is a strip of pleasant bars and terraced restaurants. You'll find a plethora of food stalls west along the lake and on Zákonyi Ferenc utca.

Füred Camping (☎ 580 241; cfured@balatontourist.hu; Széchenyi utca 24; camp sites per tent 1860-5300Ft, adult/child 650-1500Ft/550-1100Ft, motel r 5460-19,970Ft, bungalows 6400-19,970Ft; ⊗ Apr–mid-Oct; P) This sprawling beachfront complex 1km west of the centre has water-sport rentals, swimming pools, tennis courts, a restaurant, a convenience

shop and daily programmes. Not all tent and caravan sites have shade; site prices are determined by the size, the month and the number of people; bungalows and motel rooms are for a minimum of three persons.

Sport Panzió (☎ /fax 340 720; Horváth Mihály utca 35; s/d 3800/7600Ft; P ☒) Simple and superior. Request one of the two top-floor rooms for views out onto the lake. Honey-coloured wood is the theme in the bedrooms, restaurant and sauna. One hour on the squash court costs 1900Ft.

Hotel Blaha Lujza (☎ 581 210; www.hotelblaha.hu; Blaha Lujza utca 4; s €37, d €53-58; P) Part of this hotel was once the holiday home of the much-loved 19th-century Hungarian actress-singer Blaha Lujza. Her picture and charming old photos of the lake grace the hallway walls. There's a lot of the contemporary wood and maroon-upholstered furniture in the relatively small rooms, but it looks nice.

Stéfania Vittorlás Étterem (☎ 343 407; Tagore sétány 1; cakes 110-260Ft; ⊗ 10am-midnight; ☒) A touristy place with touristy prices but a great lakeside view. Skip the restaurant and enjoy something from the cake and ice-cream shop in the same location.

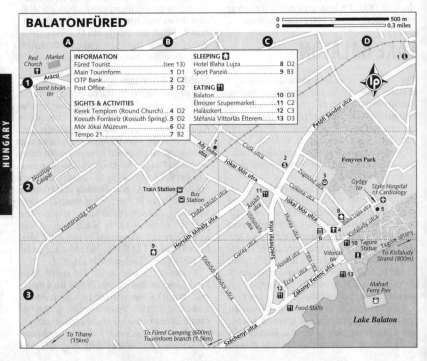

BALATONFÜRED

INFORMATION	
Füred Tourist...............................(see 13)	
Main Tourinform.............................1 D1	
OTP Bank...2 C2	
Post Office.......................................3 D2	

SIGHTS & ACTIVITIES	
Kerek Templom (Round Church)....4 D2	
Kossuth Forrásvíz (Kossuth Spring).5 D2	
Mór Jókai Múzeum..........................6 D2	
Tempo 21...7 B2	

SLEEPING	
Hotel Blaha Lujza...........................8 D2	
Sport Panzió....................................9 B3	

EATING	
Balaton..10 D3	
Élmiszer Szupermarket.................11 C2	
Halászkert.....................................12 C3	
Stéfania Vittorlás Étterem...........13 D3	

Halászkert (☎ 343 039; Zákonyi Ferenc utca 3; mains 1000-1500Ft; ⊙ 11am-10pm Apr-Sep; ✗) Come here for the *korhely halászlé* (drunkard's fish soup) and other freshwater fish dishes.

Balaton (☎ 481 319; Kisfaludy utca 5; mains 1000-2200Ft; ⊙ 11am-11pm; ✗) In the waterfront park sits a shaded terrace full of rustic tables. This may look like just a beer garden, but Balaton serves a full range of Hungarian specialities. Inside the casual restaurant a dead tree bizarrely sticks out of the floor.

Pack a picnic lunch or dinner with supplies from the **Élmiszer Szupermarket** (Jókai Mór utca 16).

Getting There & Away

Buses to Tihany (182Ft, 30 minutes) and Veszprém (302Ft, 30 minutes) leave every 15 minutes or so (except at lunch time) throughout the day. For the northwestern lakeshore towns such as Keszthely (810Ft, 1½ hours, nine daily) take the bus, since you have to switch in Tapolca with the train.

Budapest-bound buses (1390Ft) depart from Balatonfüred four times daily and take between two and three hours to get there. Trains take about the same amount of time (1690Ft, 12 daily). There are a number of towns on the train line with 'Balaton' or 'Füred' somewhere in their name, so double-check which station you're getting off at.

From April to September, **Mahart ferries** (☎ 342 230; www.balatonihajozas.hu; Mahart ferry pier) ply the water from Balatonfüred to Tihany (660Ft, 20 minutes) and Siófok (on the southeastern shore; 1200Ft, 55 minutes) eight times a day in July and August, six times a day from May to June and in September.

TIHANY

☎ 87 / pop 1200

The whole Tihany peninsula, jutting 5km into Lake Balaton, is a nature reserve. Many people consider this the most beautiful place on the lake, especially in March when the almond trees are in bloom. The quaint village of the same name sits on the eastern side of the peninsula's high plateau. Ceramics, embroidery and other folk-craft stores fill the bucolic village houses. Prices are a bargain compared to Budapest or Szentendre, and everyone knows it. You can easily shake off the tourist hordes by going hiking – maybe to the Belsőtó (Inner Lake) or the reedy (and almost dried up) Külsőtó (Outer Lake). Bird-watchers, bring your binoculars: the trails have abundant birdlife.

Orientation & Information

The harbour where ferries to/from Balatonfüred dock is a couple of kilometres downhill from the village of Tihany. Buses pull up in the heart of town, outside the post office on Kossuth Lajos utca.

Tourinform (☎ 448 804; www.tihany.hu; Kossuth Lajos utca 20; ⊙ 9am-7pm Mon-Fri & to 6pm Sat & Sun Jun-Aug, to 5pm Mon-Fri & to 3pm Sat May & Sep, to 3pm Mon-Fri Oct-Apr) sells hiking maps and film, and provides tourist information.

Sights & Activities

You can spot Tihany's twin-towered **Apátság Templom** (Abbey Church; ☎ 448 405; adult/student 500/250Ft; ⊙ 9am-6pm May-Sep, 10am-5pm Apr & Oct, 10am-3pm Nov-Mar), dating from 1754, from a long way off. Entombed in the church's crypt is the abbey's founder, King Andrew I. The Deed of Foundation for the abbey is the earliest existing document that contains Hungarian words (now stored at the Pannonhalma Abbey archives near Győr; see p323). The admission fee includes entry to the attached **Apátsági Múzeum** (Abbey Museum; ☎ 448 405; ⊙ 9am-6pm May-Sep, 10am-5pm Apr & Oct, 10am-3pm Nov-Mar). The path behind the church leads to outstanding views; it can be quite windy up there.

Follow the pathway along the ridge north from the church in the village and you pass the tiny **szabadtéri néprajzi múzeum** (open-air ethnographical museum; ☎ 714 960; Pisky sétány 10; adult/student 300/150Ft; ⊙ 10am-6pm Tue-Sun May-Sep). It's easy to miss the small cluster of fully outfitted folk houses among all the rest of the old houses that are now shops.

Back at the clearing in front of the church, there's a large hiking map with all the trails marked. Following the green trail northeast of the church for an hour will bring you to an Oroszkút (Russian Well) and the ruins of the Óvár (Old Castle), where the Russian Orthodox monks, brought to Tihany by Andrew I, hollowed out cells in the soft basalt walls.

Sleeping & Eating

This is an easy day trip from Balatonfüred. The place is pretty small, so there's no reason to stay over unless you're hiking. The Tihany Tourinform website, www.tihany.hu, lists almost 50 houses that rent private rooms, or you could look for a *'Zimmer frei'* sign in one of the windows on the small streets north of the church.

HUNGARY

Erika Hotel (☎ 448 010; fax 448 646; Batthyány utca 6; r €60; ☻ May-Sep; 🅿 🔆 🎲) The pink, 16-room inn is right in the centre of the village. The small swimming pool makes for a refreshing surprise; a cocktail from the bar completes the picture.

Stég Pub (☎ 06 70 503 0208; Kossuth Lajos utca 18; mains 750-980Ft; ☻ 10am-10pm Sun-Thu, to midnight Fri & Sat) Pizzas and salads augment the Hungarian menu at this friendly place. In nice weather, sit in the courtyard.

Of the many touristy eatery options, two have especially good views: the awning-covered back terrace at **Fogas Csárda** (☎ 448 658; Kossuth Lajos utca 9; mains 1450-2400Ft; ☻ 11am-11pm May-Oct) overlooks the Inner Lake and the peninsula's interior; and the terrace at the **Rege Café** (☎ 448 280; Kossuth Lajos utca 22; cakes 330-520Ft; ☻ 10am-6pm), where you can peer down on Lake Balaton and the harbour.

Getting There & Away

Buses travel along the 11km of mostly lakefront road between the centre of Tihany village and Balatonfüred's train station (174 Ft, 30 minutes) about 20 times a day. The advantage here is that you don't have to hike up the hill from the harbour, but the bus does stop there too.

Passenger ferries sail between Tihany and Balatonfüred from April to September (660Ft, 20 minutes, six to eight daily). The Abbey Church is high above the pier; you can follow a steep path up to the village from there.

KESZTHELY
☎ 83 / pop 21,800

Keszthely's amazing Festetics Palace, built in 1745, is a sight worth making the cross-country-and-lake trip for; stroll through the beautifully cultivated lakefront park and it's not long before you find another good reason to be here: a partying public beach. Whether you're seeking history or sun-worshipping hedonism, Keszthely (kest-hay) has at least a little of each. The town lies just over 1km northwest of the lake and with the exception of a few guesthouses, almost everything stays open year-round.

Orientation & Information

The bus and train stations, side by side at the end of Mártírok útja, are fairly close to the ferry pier. Walk northeast on Kazinczy utca and you'll see the water to your right in a few hundred metres. To get to town, turn left and head towards Kossuth Lajos utca.

Tourinform (☎ 314 144; www.keszthely.hu; Kossuth Lajos utca 28; ☻ 9am-8pm Mon-Fri & to 6pm Sat Jul-Aug, to 5pm Mon-Fri & to 1pm Sat Sep-Jun) doles out information on the whole Lake Balaton area. **Keszthely Tourist** (☎ 312 031; Kossuth Lajos utca 25; ☻ 9am-5pm Mon-Fri) puts together water-oriented sports and spa packages and represents several private accommodation businesses.

There's a huge **OTP Bank** (Kossuth Lajos utca) facing the park south of the church, and close by is the **main post office** (Kossuth Lajos utca 48).

Sights & Activities

The glimmering white, 100-room **Festetics Kastély** (Festetics Palace; ☎ 312 190; Kastély utca 1; museum adult/student 1300/700Ft; ☻ 10am-5pm Tue-Sun) was first built in 1745; the wings were extended out from the original building 150 years later. About a dozen rooms in the one-time residence have been turned into a museum. Many of the decorative arts in the gilt salons were imported from England in the mid-1800s. If you can, take one of the evening candlelight tours that are sometimes offered during summer. To reach the palace, follow Kossuth Lajos utca, the long pedestrian street in the centre of the old town. The **Helikon Könyvetár** (Helikon Library), in the baroque south wing, is known for its 900,000 volumes and its handcarved furniture, crafted by a local artisan.

In 1797 Count György Festetics, an uncle of the reformer István Széchenyi, founded Europe's first agricultural institute, the Georgikon, in Keszthely. Part of the original school is now the **Georgikon Major Múzeum** (Georgikon Farm Museum; ☎ 311 563; Bercsényi Miklós utca 67; adult/student 400/200Ft; ☻ 10am-5pm Tue-Sat, 10am-6pm Sun May-Oct).

The lakefront area centres on the long Mahart ferry pier, which has a small café near the ferry landing at the end. From April to September you can take a one-hour **pleasure cruise** (☎ 312 093; www.balatonihajozas.hu; Mahart ferry pier; adult/student 1100/500Ft) on the lake at 1pm and 3pm daily. **Városi Strand** (City Beach; Vásár tér; adult/student 500/300Ft; ☻ ticket office 8.30am-7pm, gates to midnight May-Sep) is not far west of the pier, near plenty of beer stands and food booths. There are other beaches you can explore further afield; some hotels have private shore access.

Sleeping

Like most summer-oriented tourist destinations, prices vary dramatically depending on the month. Private rooms can cost a bit more here than in the non-resort areas of Hungary;

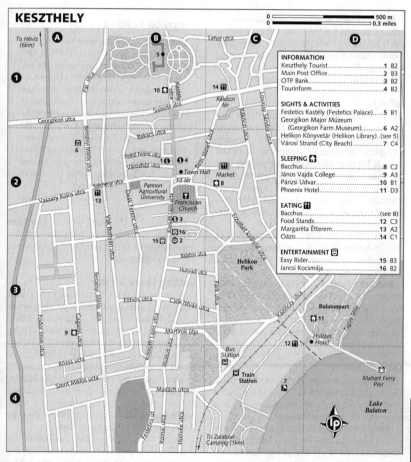

KESZTHELY

HUNGARY

Keszthely Tourist (☎ 312 031; Kossuth Lajos utca 25; ☺9am-5pm Mon-Fri) represents several private lodgings and apartment houses.

Zalatour Camping (☎ 312 782; kesztcamo@zalaszam.hu; Ernszt Géza sétány; camp & caravan sites 1450-2400Ft; bungalows 3000-4200Ft, apartments 7900-9300Ft; ☺mid-Apr–mid-Oct; P ☺) About 1km south of town, this waterfront camp has access to a rocky shore and a somewhat reedy beach. The apartments are a bit nicer than the bungalows (both sleep up to four). Don't come here for quiet; facilities include a restaurant, late-night bar, gift shop, sauna and sun beds, and a dog kennel in addition to sports stuff.

János Vajda College (☎ 311 361; Gagarin utca 4; dm 1600-3000Ft) This student dorm is open to all from July to August.

Phoenix Hotel (☎ 312 631; Balatonpart 4; s 5500-7300Ft, d 7000-8800Ft; P) This is as close as you can get to the water for as little money as you can spend if you're not camping. The low-lying wood building is in a shady grove of trees at the edge of the lakefront park. Bike rental is only 300Ft for an hour and 900Ft for the day.

Bacchus (☎ 510 450; www.bacchushotel.hu; Erzsébet királyné utca 18; s €33-47, d €40-58; P) Bacchus is positively Keszthely's best hotel. It has crisp rooms that open up to a little garden on the ground floor and balconies on the top, the staff is super-friendly and the cellar is a **wine museum** (admission free; ☺10am-11pm) where wine tastings are available (six/10 types 1500/2400Ft). Not to mention the fabulous restaurant (p332).

Párizsi Udvar (☎ 311 202; www.hotels.hu/parizsi
_udvar; Kastély utca 5; d 7900-9900Ft, tr 9600-12,600Ft, 4-
bed r 13,000-15,000Ft, 5-bed r 13,500-15,600Ft) Large basic
rooms share kitchen facilities in what was once
part of the Festetics Kastély complex. The central courtyard adds to the quiet of the place.

Eating

Open-air, self-service restaurant-stands and
bars line the trail between Kazinczy utca and
the waterfront, west of the ferry pier. In summer, places open between 8am and 10am and
close at 10pm or later. Off-season hours vary
but there's generally something open from
10am to 8pm. In town, Kossuth Lajos utca has
a number of pavement cafés in the pedestrian
area. There are a number of small grocery
shops just south on the same street.

Oázis (☎ 311 023; Rákóczi tér 3; lunches 430-520Ft;
☺ 11am-4pm Mon-Fri; ✗) A rare vegetarian eatery;
the small menu changes daily. It's not gourmet,
but it's tasty enough.

Margaréta Étterem (☎ 314 882; Bercsényi Miklós
utca 60; mains 600-1240Ft; ☺ 11am-10pm; ✗) Locals come for the good Hungarian food and
the casual, convivial vibe. Everyone here is
friendly. The patio with red-chequered tablecloths is cheery too.

Entertainment

Numerous cultural performances take place
during the Balatonfest in May and the Dance
Festival in September. Tourinform has info
on events throughout the year.

Away from the waterfront, Kossuth Lajos
utca is where to look for pubs: **Jancsi Kocsmája**
(Kossuth Lajos utca 46; ☺ noon-midnight Mon-Fri, 6pm-
midnight Sat & Sun), with tin advertising signs
hanging on the walls, is the most fun and is

mainly filled with young people. **Easy Rider**
(☎ 319 842; Kossuth Lajos utca 79; ☺ 10am-10pm Sun-
Thu, 10am-4am Fri & Sat) turns into a disco at about
10pm on weekends.

Getting There & Away

Buses to Hévíz (133Ft, 15 minutes) leave at least
every 30 minutes during the day. Other towns
served by buses include Badacsony (363Ft,
30 minutes, six daily), Balatonfüred (810Ft,
1½ hours, seven daily), Veszprém (1040Ft, two
hours, 12 daily) and Budapest (2780Ft, three
hours, six daily).

Keszthely is on a branch rail line linking
the lake's southeastern shore with Budapest
(2324Ft, three hours, eight daily). To reach
towns along Lake Balaton's northern shore by
train, you have to change at Tapolca.

From April to September, Mahart ferries
link Keszthely with Badacsonytomaj (1200Ft,
two hours, one to three daily) and other,
smaller lake towns.

SOUTH CENTRAL HUNGARY

If you've had enough of the strait-laced Habsburg influence and want something a bit more Mediterranean, head to Southern Hungary. Historically, the area bordering Croatia and Serbia and Montenegro has often been 'shared' between Hungary and these countries, and it's here that the remnants of the 150-year Turkish occupation can be most strongly felt. In the Danube village of Mohács, the Hungarian army under King Lajos II was routed by a vastly superior Ottoman force in 1526.

The region is bounded by the Danube River to the east, the Dráva River to the south and west, and Lake Balaton to the north. Generally flat, the Mecsek and Villány Hills rise up in isolation from the plain. The weather always seems to be a few degrees warmer here than in other parts of the country; the sunny clime is great for grape growing, and oak-aged Villány reds are well regarded, if highly tannic.

PÉCS

☎ 72 / pop 158,900

Pécs' (pronounced *paich*) sunny Jókai tér, paved in white marble, makes you think that the sea is close by. This lovely little town, near the southern border of Hungary, is going to be crowned European Culture Capital in 2010. This is where the Turks left their greatest monuments from 150 years of occupation; alongside are imposing churches, a lovely synagogue and more than a dozen galleries and museums, one dedicated entirely to Hungary's answer to Van Gogh, Tivadar Kosztka Csontváry. Green parks and great hiking in the Mecsek Hills only add to the appeal. Harkány is a nearby spa town that is an easy day trip.

History has far from ignored Pécs. The Roman settlement of Sopianae on this site was the capital of the province of Lower Pannonia for 400 years. Christianity flourished here in the 4th century and by the 9th century the town was known as Quinque Ecclesiae for its five churches. In 1009 Stephen I made Pécs a bishopric. The first Hungarian university was founded here in the mid-14th century. City walls were erected after the Mongol invasion of 1241, but 1543 marked the start of almost a century and a half of Turkish domination. In the 19th century the manufacture of Zsolnay porcelain and other goods, such as Pannonia sparkling wine, helped put Pécs back on the map.

Orientation & Information

The train station is a little over 1km south of the old town centre. Take bus 30 for two long stops from the station to Kossuth tér to reach the centre, or you can walk up Jókai Mór utca. The bus station is a few blocks closer, next to the market. Follow Bajcsy-Zsilinszky utca north to get to the centre.

Tourinform (☎ 213 315; www.pecs.hu; Széchenyi tér 9; ☺ 8am-5.30pm Mon-Fri, 9am-4pm Sat May-Sep, 8am-4pm Mon-Fri Oct-Mar) has internet access (per hour 100Ft) and tons of local info, including a list of museums. The **main post office** (Jókai Mór utca 10) is in a beautiful Art Nouveau building (1904) with a colourful Zsolnay porcelain roof. There are plenty of banks and ATMs scattered around town. **Ibusz** (☎ 212 157; Apáca utca 1; ☺ 8am-5pm Mon-Fri, to 2pm Sat) travel agency has a currency exchange booth, rents private rooms and books transport tickets.

Sights & Activities

The bizarrely named 'Mosque Church', which dominates the city's central square, is really quite striking. The **Mecset Templom** (Mosque Church; ☎ 321 976; Széchenyi tér; admission free; ☺ 10am-4pm Mon-Sat, 11.30am-4pm Sun mid-Apr–mid-Oct, 10am-noon Mon-Sat, 11.30am-2pm Sun mid-Oct–mid-Apr) has no minaret and has been a Christian place of worship for a long time, but the Islamic elements inside, such as the *mihrab* (prayer niche) on the southeastern wall, reveal its original purpose. Constructed in the mid-16th century from the stones of an earlier church, the mosque underwent several changes of appearance over the years – including the addition of a steeple and siding. In the late 1930s the building was restored to its medieval form.

West along Ferencesek utca at No 35, you'll pass the ruins of the 16th-century Turkish **Memi Pasa Fürdője** (Pasa Memi Bath) before you turn south on Rákóczi útca to get to the c 1540 **Hassan Jakovali Mecset** (Hassan Jakovali Mosque; ☎ 313 853; Rákóczi útca 2; adult/student 240/100Ft; ☺ 10am-1.30pm & 2-6pm Thu-Tue Apr-Sep). Though wedged between two modern buildings, this smaller mosque is more intact than its larger cousin and comes complete with a minaret. There's a small museum of Ottoman history inside.

North of Széchenyi tér, the minor **Régészeti Múzeum** (Archaeology Museum; ☎ 312 719; Széchenyi tér

HUNGARY

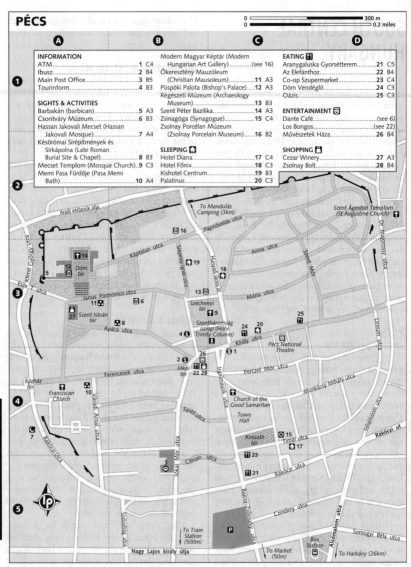

PÉCS

0 _____ 300 m
0 _____ 0.2 miles

12; adult/student 300/150Ft; 10am-4pm Tue-Sun Apr-Oct)
contains Roman artefacts found in the area.
From here, climb Szepessy Ignéc utca and
turn left (west) on Káptalan utca, which is a
street lined with museums and galleries. **Zsolnay Porcélan Múzeum** (Zsolnay Porcelain Museum; 324
822; Káptalan utca 2; adult/student 700/350Ft; 10am-4pm
Tue-Sun Apr-Oct) is on the eastern end of this strip.

English translations provide a good history of
the artistic and functional ceramics produced
from this local factory's illustrious early days
in the mid-19th century to the present. The
excellent **Modern Magyar Képtár** (Modern Hungarian Art Gallery; 324 822; Káptalan utca 4; adult/child
400/200Ft; 10am-6pm Tue-Sun Apr-Oct, to 4pm Tue-Sun
Nov-Mar) is next door, and here you can get a

comprehensive overview of Hungarian art from 1850 till today.

Continue west to Dóm tér and the walled bishopric complex containing the four-towered **Szent Péter Bazilika** (☎ 513 030; Dóm tér; complex ticket adult/student 1000/500Ft; ☺ 9am-5pm Mon-Sat, 1-5pm Sun). The oldest part of the building is the 11th-century crypt. The 1770 **Püspöki Palota** (Bishop's Palace; admission free; ☺ 2-5pm late-Jun–Aug) stands in front of the cathedral, and a 15th-century **barbakán** (barbican) is the only stone bastion to survive from the old city walls.

The early Christian cemeteries from the Roman town of Sopianae became part of the Unesco World Heritage list in 2000. Two interesting places are the 4th-century **Ókeresztény Mauzóleum** (Christian Mausoleum; ☎ 312 7190; Szent István tér 12; adult/student 350/200Ft; ☺ 10am-4pm Tue-Sun Apr-Oct) and the **Késórómai Sírépítények és Sírkápolna** (Late Roman Burial Site & Chapel; Apáca utca 8 & 14; adult/student 350/200Ft; ☺ 10am-4pm Tue-Sun Apr-Oct), which are both richly decorated.

East of the Christian Mausoleum is the **Csontváry Múzeum** (☎ 310 544; Janus Pannonius utca 11; adult/student 600/300Ft; ☺ 10am-4pm Tue-Sun Apr-Oct), displaying the dreamy work of the wonderful Tivadar Kosztka Csontváry (1853–1919), whose use of vivid colour and texture in landscape painting, as well as his tragic life, has been compared to that of Van Gogh.

Pécs' beautifully preserved 1869 **zsinagóga** (synagogue; ☎ 315 881; Kossuth tér; adult/child 300/200Ft; ☺ 10am-5pm Sun-Fri May-Oct) is south of Széchenyi tér.

Sleeping

Ibusz (☎ 212 157; Apáca utca 1; ☺ 8am-5pm Mon-Fri, to 2pm Sat) arranges private rooms for 2540Ft per person.

Mandulás Camping (☎ 515 655; Ángyán János utca 2; camp sites per person 1200Ft; motel/hotel r 3200/5800Ft; ☺ May-Oct) From the centre, take bus 33 or 34 3km up into the Mecsek Hills.

Kishotel Centrum (☎ 311 707; www.hotels.hu/centrum_kishotel; Szepessy Ignác utca 4; s/d/tr 4500/5800/8750Ft) Paintings cover just about every inch of wall space, bric-a-brac decorates shelves and the furniture is mix-and-match: it's just like staying at a Hungarian *nagymama* (grandma)'s house. The central hall on the ground floor has a small fridge and a hot plate you can use, but there aren't many other facilities.

Hotel Főnix (☎ 311 680; www.fonixhotel.hu; Hunyadi János út 2; s 5290Ft, d 7990-9490Ft) Odd angles and sloping eaves characterise the asymmetrical Hotel Főnix. Rooms are plain and those on the top floor have skylights. This hotel is second choice to the Diana.

Hotel Diana (☎ 328 594; www.dianahotel.hu, Hungarian only; Timár utca 4A; s/d 7700/11,000Ft; ☒) This small, immaculate hotel right next to the synagogue has rustic accents, such as split-wood chair rails in the guest and breakfast rooms. The rooms on the second floor are better than those on the first. Double room No 5 has a great skylight that opens.

Palatinus (☎ 889 400; palatinus.reservation@danubiusgroup.hu; Király utca 5; s €58-86, d €66-94; ℗) For some Art Nouveau glamour, Palatinus is *the* place in Pécs. An amazing, marble reception has a soaring Moorish-detailed ceiling, and the 'ballroom' makes you want to get your most expensive frock/tux on and waltz. It's a shame that the rooms are not as luxurious, but still, in Pécs, it's as good as it gets.

Eating

Pubs, cafés and fast-food eateries line pedestrian Király utca.

Aranygaluska Gyorsétterem (☎ 310 210; Irgalmasok utca 4; mains 430-640Ft; ☺ 7.30am-8pm Mon-Fri, to 5pm Sat & Sun; ☒) Working-class heroes gather here for the generously portioned, cafeteria meals – some say the best food in town. Office workers know it too: the place is packed at lunch. The *töltöt paprika* (stuffed peppers) alone fill you up.

Oázis (☎ 215 367; Király utca 17; mains 500-1000Ft; ☺ 10am-11pm) Unlike most of the kebab shops across Hungary, the owner at this take-away actually hails from the Middle East. You can taste the difference.

Az Elefánthoz (☎ 216 055; Jókai tér 6; mains 1100-2000Ft; ☺ 11am-11pm; ☒) An unatmospheric Italian restaurant that serves really good soups, pastas and pizzas. Salads, like the tuna and onions on lettuce, are meal-sized. The nonsmoking section is only three booths.

Dóm Vendéglö (☎ 210 088; Király utca 3; mains 1300-2500Ft; ☺ noon-11pm; ☒ ☒) If you like meat and Art Nouveau décor, Dóm Vendéglö is for you. Beef, venison, pork, turkey and duck, surrounded by turn-of-the-century paintings. Enter at the rear of the courtyard under the Aranyhajó Fogadó hotel.

Get self-catering supplies at **Co-op Szupermarket** (cnr Irgalmasok & Timár utcas).

Entertainment

Pécs has well-established opera and ballet companies as well as a symphony orchestra. **Tourinform** (☎ 213 315; www.pecs.hu; Széchenyi tér 9; ☺ 8am-5.30pm Mon-Fri, 9am-4pm Sat May-Sep, 8am-4pm Mon-Fri Oct-Mar) has schedule information. The free biweekly *Pécsi Est* lists what's on at nightclubs and the cinema.

Művészetek Háza (☎ 315 388; Széchenyi tér 7-8) The Artists' House is a cultural venue that hosts classical musical performances. A schedule is posted outside.

Los Bongos (☎ 06 20 468 9491; Jókai tér 6; admission 390-550Ft; ☺ 6pm-2am Mon-Sat) Fridays are a Latin fiesta, but every night sizzles. This nightclub is on the floor above Az Elefánthoz restaurant.

Dante Café (☎ 210 361; Janus Pannonius utca 11; ☺ 10am-1am) An intellectual and student crowd gathers on the ground floor below the Csontváry Múzeum. There's live jazz and other music from Thursday through Saturday.

Shopping

Cezar Winery (☎ 214 490; Szent István tér 12; ☺ 9am-5.30pm Mon-Fri) This building is where the family of Janos Pannonius made sparkling wine from 1859 to 1995. You can still buy Pannonia *pezsgő* (champagne), under new owners, in the onsite shop and view the production facilities through glass walls.

Zsolnay Bolt (☎ 310 172; Jókai tér 2; ☺ 10am-4pm Tue-Sun) You can buy a set of kooky porcelain here.

Getting There & Away

Buses for Harkány (484Ft, one hour) leave every 15 minutes throughout the day. At least four buses a day connect Pécs with Budapest (2660Ft, 4½ hours), two with Keszthely (1740Ft, three hours) and eight with Szeged (2310Ft, four hours).

Pécs is on a main rail line with Budapest's Déli train station (2610Ft, 2½ hours, eight daily). One daily train runs from Pécs (8.40pm) to Osijek (1880Ft, two hours) in Horvátország (Croatia).

AROUND PÉCS
Harkány

The hot springs at **Harkány** (www.harkany.hu, no English), 26km south of Pécs, have medicinal waters with the richest sulphuric content in Hungary. The indoor and outdoor baths and pools of **Gyógyfürdő** (☎ 480 251; www.harkanyfurdo.hu; Kossuth Lajos utca 7; adult/student 1790/1090Ft; ☺ 9am-10pm mid-Jun–Aug, to 8pm Sun-Thu & to 10pm Fri & Sat Sep–mid-

Jun) range in temperature from 26°C to 33°C in summer and from 33°C to 35°C in winter. You might consider booking a spa service, mud bath or massage. The town is basically the thermal bath complex in a 12-hectare park surrounded by holiday hotels and restaurants. Buses between Harkány and Pécs (484Ft, one hour) depart frequently, about every 15 minutes. The Harkány bus station is at the southeast corner of the park.

SOUTHEASTERN HUNGARY

The mysterious Nagyalföld (Great Plain) is an area that has been central to Hungarian myth and legend for centuries. The Plain, and its horsemen and shepherds, have represented the Hungarian ethos in poems, songs, paintings and stories. It starts at the point where Tisza River drainage basin meets the wide expanse of level *puszta* (prairie or steppe). Much of the *alföld* has been turned into farmland for growing apricots and raising geese, but other parts are little more than grassy, saline deserts sprouting juniper trees. Kiskunsági Nemzeti Park, including the Bugac Puszta, protects this unique environment.

KECSKEMÉT
☎ 76 / pop 108,180

Located about halfway between Budapest and Szeged, Kecskemét (*kech*-kah-mate) is a green, pedestrian-friendly city with interesting Art Nouveau architecture. Claims to fame include the locally produced *barack* (apricot) jam and *pálinka* (potent brandy), *libamaj* (goose liver) dishes, and the nearby Kiskunsági Nemzeti Park and horse farms.

Orientation & Information

Central Kecskemét is made up of squares that run into one another, and consequently it's hard to tell them apart. The main bus and train stations are opposite each other in József Katona Park. A 10-minute walk southwest along Nagykőrösi utca brings you to the first of the squares, Szabadság tér.

Tourinform (☎ 481 065; www.kecskemet.hu; Kossuth tér 1; ☺ 8am-5pm Mon-Fri, 9am-1pm Sat Jul-Aug) is in the northeastern corner of the large Town Hall. Staff here can help you with information about Kiskunsági Nemzeti Park. The **OTP**

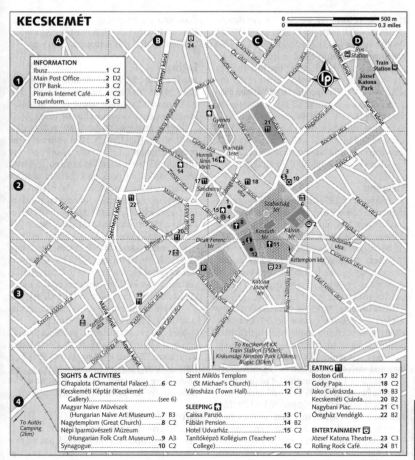

KECSKEMÉT

0   500 m
0   0.3 miles

INFORMATION	
Ibusz...............................1	C2
Main Post Office...............2	D2
OTP Bank........................3	C2
Piramis Internet Café......4	C2
Tourinform......................5	C3

SIGHTS & ACTIVITIES	
Cifrapalota (Ornamental Palace).......6	C2
Kecskeméti Képtár (Kecskemét	
Gallery)...................................(see 6)	
Magyar Naive Művészek	
(Hungarian Naive Art Museum)....7	B3
Nagytemplom (Great Church)..........8	C2
Népi Iparművészeti Múzeum	
(Hungarian Folk Craft Museum)....9	A3
Synagogue...................................10	C2

Szent Miklós Templom	
(St Michael's Church)...............11	C3
Városháza (Town Hall)...............12	C3

SLEEPING	
Caissa Panzió...............................13	C1
Fábián Pension............................14	B2
Hotel Udvarház...........................15	C2
Tanítóképző Kollégium (Teachers'	
College)...................................16	C3

EATING	
Boston Grill.................................17	B2
Gody Papa...................................18	C2
Jako Cukrászda............................19	B3
Kecskeméti Csárda.......................20	B2
Nagybani Piac..............................21	C1
Öregház Vendéglö........................22	B2

ENTERTAINMENT	
József Katona Theatre....23	C3
Rolling Rock Café..........24	B1

To Kecskemét KK
Train Station (350m);
Kiskunsági Nemzeti Park (30km);
Bugac (30km)

To Autós
Camping
(2km)

HUNGARY

Bank (Szabadság tér 1/A) is central, does foreign exchange and has an ATM. The **main post office** (Kálvin tér 10) is to the southeast. Surf the Web at **Piramis Internet Café** (☎ 418 134; Csányi utca 1-3; per hr 540Ft; 🕙 10am-8pm Mon-Fri, 1-8pm Sat & Sun), upstairs in the courtyard of a small shopping mall.

Sights

Walk around the park-like squares, starting at Szabadság tér, and admire the eclectic building styles, including the technicolour Art Nouveau of the 1902 **Cifrapalota** (Ornamental Palace; Rákóczi út 1), recently refurbished and covered in multicoloured majolica tiles. Check out the wonderful interiors of the **Kecskeméti Képtár** (Kecskemét Gallery; ☎ 480 776; Rákóczi út 1; adult/child 260/130Ft; 🕙 10am-5pm Tue-Sun). Across the street,

the Moorish building is the former **synagogue** (Rákóczi út 2), now an office building and exhibition hall called the House of Technology.

Kossuth tér is dominated by the massive 1897 Art Nouveau **Városháza** (Town Hall; admission free; 🕙 9am-5pm Mon-Fri), which is flanked by the baroque **Nagytemplom** (Great Church, 1806) and the earlier **Szent Miklós Templom** (St Michael's Church), dating from the 13th century. Nearby is the magnificent 1896 **József Katona Theatre** (☎ 483 283; Katona József tér 5; 🕙 performance times only), a neobaroque theatre with a statue of the Trinity (1742) in front of it. All of these churches are open to the public during and around mass times and are free.

The town's museums are scattered around the main squares' periphery. Go first to the

Magyar Naive Müvészek (Hungarian Naive Art Museum; ☎ 324 767; Gáspár András utca 11; adult/student 150/50Ft; ⏱ 10am-5pm Tue-Sun), in the Stork House (1730) northwest off Petőfi Sándor utca. It has an impressive small collection; the folk themes are especially noteworthy. Further to the southwest, the **Népi Iparmüvészeti Múzeum** (Hungarian Folk Craft Museum; ☎ 327 203; Serfőző utca 19a; adult/student 200/100Ft; ⏱ 10am-5pm Tue-Sun) has a definitive collection of regional embroidery, weaving and textiles, as well as some furniture, woodcarving and agricultural tools. A few handicrafts are for sale at the entrance.

Sleeping

Tourinform (p336) can help you locate the numerous colleges that offer dormitory accommodation in July and August; one good choice is the central **Tanítóképzö Kollégium** (Teachers' College; ☎ 486 977; Piaristák tere 4; s/d 2000/4000Ft; ⏱ mid-Jun–Aug; **P**). **Ibusz** (☎ 486 955; Kossuth tér 3; ⏱ 8am-5pm Mon-Fri Sep-Jun, 8am-5pm Mon-Fri, 9am-1pm Sat Jul-Aug) travel agency brokers private rooms from 2000Ft per person, with a four-night minimum.

Autós Camping (☎ 329 398; Csabai Géza körút 5; camp sites 1/2 people 1350/2100Ft, caravan sites 2200Ft, bungalows 5400Ft; ⏱ Apr-Oct) As the name implies, this place is more vehicle- than tent-camping oriented, with big treeless plots. Don't be surprised if it's jammed with caravans and Germanic speakers. Take bus 1 to get southwest of town.

Caissa Panzió (☎ 481 685; www.caissachessbooks.com; Gyenes tér 18, 4th fl; s/d/tr/q 6900/8900/10,300/11,700Ft) If you are a chess lover, stay here, at the Chess Panzió, where the manager has tournaments in the big lounge on the ground floor. The rooms are on several floors in an apartment block, and provide a slightly cheaper, shabby-chic alternative – some with shared bathrooms. There's no breakfast, but you can ask for a key and share the kitchen facilities.

Fábián Pension (☎ 477 677; www.hotels.hu/fabian; Kápolna utca 14; r 7500-9500Ft; ✗ ✗) Definitely the town's best place to stay. Fábián is a family-run place, with picture windows, clean rooms and a spacious, flowery garden. Homemade jam and sweets are served along with your cold cuts and bread at breakfast, and mum and daughter will help you plan an independent trip to the national park or to a horse farm. You can also rent bicycles here for 1500Ft per day.

Hotel Udvarház (☎ 413 912; Csányi utca 1-3; s/d/tr 11,900/14,500/17,500Ft; **P** ✗) Curvilinear blond and turquoise wood furnishings define the contemporary style of this hotel on the 1st floor above a shopping arcade (across from Piramis Internet Café). A few rooms have aircon; ask first, if this is important to you.

Eating

Jako Cukrászda (☎ 505 949; Petőfi Sándor utca 7; cakes 110-265Ft; ⏱ 7am-7pm Mon-Fri, 9am-7pm Sat & Sun) Cakes, puddings and strudels tempt from behind a long, modern glass-and-chrome case.

Öregház Vendéglö (☎ 496 973; Kölcsey utca 3; mains 600-1000Ft; ⏱ 11am-10pm; ✗) Get yourself some proper Hungarian roast: the *cigany pecsenye* (literally 'Gypsy's roast') is a mixed grill with tender cutlets of pork and chicken, a piece of bacon and a sausage. Join the friends and families who gather here for Sunday lunches. Blue-and-white *kékfestö* (indigo-dyed) tablecloths and curtains make the place homy and it's completely nonsmoking – a real rarity.

Kecskeméti Csárda (☎ 488 686; Kölcsey utca 7; mains 1290-1990Ft; ⏱ 11am-11pm; ✗) This is what a stereotypical Hungarian country inn *(csárda)* restaurant looks like – with a Romani musician and all. It may seem a bit touristy, but it's where residents go to celebrate special occasions. There's courtyard dining.

You can get some decent and cheap quick eats and a beer at **Boston Grill** (☎ 484 444; Kápolna utca 2; burgers 320-550Ft; ⏱ 11am-10pm) or **Gody Papa** (☎ 415 515; Arany János utca 3; pizzas 330-550Ft; ⏱ 11am-11pm). There is an open-air market, **Nagybani Piac** (Budai utca; ⏱ 7am-1pm Mon-Sat) for self-catering.

Entertainment

Tourinform (p336) has a list of what concerts and performances are on, or check out the free *Kecskeméti Est* (www.est.hu, Hungarian only) available at restaurants around town. Nightlife can be a little dull on weekdays outside the summer months, but you can always enjoy a coffee or a glass of wine from one of the cafés on Kossuth tér and watch the people go by.

József Katona Theatre (☎ 483 283; Katona József tér) See operettas and symphony performances in the 19th-century building.

Rolling Rock Café (☎ 506 190; Jókai utca 44; ⏱ noon-5am Thu-Sat, noon-midnight Tue-Wed) The coolest place in town for live music and a beverage.

Getting There & Away

Frequent buses depart for Budapest (1040Ft, two hours, every 40 minutes) and for Szeged (1090Ft, two hours, hourly). A direct rail line links Budapest's Nyugati train station with Kecskemét (1212Ft, 1½ hours, 12 daily) and

Kecskemét with Szeged (1844Ft, 1¼ hours, hourly except at lunch time).

KISKUNSÁG NATIONAL PARK

Totalling 76,000 hectares, **Kiskunsági Nemzeti Park** (Kiskunság National Park; www.knp.hu) consists of half a dozen 'islands' of protected land. Much of the park's alkaline ponds, dunes and grassy 'deserts' with juniper trees are off-limits. **Bugac** (*Boo*-gats) village, about 30km southwest of Kecskemét, is the most accessible part of the park. Here you can see the famous Hungarian cowboys ride at a daily horse show from May to October. The rest of the year, ask at the Kecskemét Tourinform (p336) to see if they know of a tour group you could join.

The company that owns the restaurant **Bugaci Karikás Csárda** (☎ 575 121; Nagybugac 135; mains 1200-2500Ft; ☯ 11am-11pm) runs the **horse show** (adult/student 1000/500Ft; ☯ 1.15pm May-Oct), which is the main attraction in the village. You can take a **wagon ride** (1000Ft; ☯ 12.15pm May-Oct) to go the few kilometres to the **Pásztor Múzeum** (Shepherd Museum; admission free; ☯ 10am-5pm May-Oct) first or just walk down the sand road to the staging ring. Once the show starts, the horse herders crack their whips, race one another bareback and ride 'five-in-hand', a breathtaking performance in which one *csikós* (cowboy) gallops five horses at full speed while standing on the backs of the rear two. And of course you can always stop for some wine and Romani music in the *csárda* afterwards.

The best way to get to Bugac is by bus from Kecskemét (423Ft). The 11am bus from the main terminal gets you to the park entrance around noon. Another option is to take the narrow-gauge train (326Ft) from the Kecskemét KK train station (south of the town centre) to the Móricgát stop (two after the Bugac stop) and walk across the field towards the conical-shaped roof of the Pásztor Múzeum. Departures are at 8am, 2.10pm and 7.50pm daily. After the show, the first bus back to Kecskemét passes by the park entrance at 5.15pm weekdays and 6.35pm weekends (a change at Jakabszállás is required for the last bus). The return train departs from Móricgát at 6.04pm and 11.54pm.

SZEGED

☎ 62 / pop 175,500

Szeged (*seh*-ged) is one of Hungary's best off-the-beaten-track destinations, a place that draws far fewer visitors than it should. A couple of days in this lively college town on the southern Great Plain, right on the Tisza River just before Serbia, will get you acquainted with the many ornate and colourful one-time palaces that now contain businesses or house several families. The Maros River from Romania enters the Tisza just east of the centre, and flooding is not uncommon. Much of the old town is architecturally homogeneous, as it was rebuilt after the disastrous 1879 flood destroyed large parts of the city.

Orientation & Information

The train station is south of the city centre on Indóház tér; tram 1 rides from it along Boldogasszony sugárút into the centre of town (five stops to Széchenyi tér). The bus station, on Mars tér, is to the west of the centre and is within easy walking distance via pedestrian Mikszáth Kálmán utca.

The **Tourinform** (☎ 488 699; Dugonics tér 2; ☯ 9am-5pm Mon-Fri) office is hidden in a courtyard. **Matrix Café** (☎ 423 830; Kárász utca 5; per hr 500Ft; ☯ 24hr) has dozens of internet terminals and just as many for game-addict use only.

Main post office (Széchenyi tér 1)
OTP Bank (Klauzál tér 4)

Sights & Activities

East of Széchenyi tér, the huge, neoclassical **Mórá Ferenc Múzeum** (☎ 549 040; Várkert; adult/student 400/250Ft; ☯ 10am-5pm Tue-Sun) peers down on the Tisza River. There are interesting exhibits on the Avar people (5th to 8th centuries) who lived in the area, on the area's folk life and art, as well as a room dedicated to the 1879 flood. North of the museum is a long, waterview park with walking paths and playground equipment.

To the west, the **Új Zsinagóga** (New Synagogue; ☎ 423 849; Gutenberg utca 13; adult/student 250/100Ft; ☯ 10am-noon & 1-5pm Sun-Fri Apr-Sep, 10am-2pm Sun-Fri Oct-Mar) is the most beautiful Jewish house of worship in Hungary and is still in use. An ornate, blue- and gold-painted interior graces the 1903 Art Nouveau building. Free organ concerts here are common on summer evenings. The nearby **Ó Zsinagóga** (Old Synagogue; Hajnóczy utca 12; admission free; ☯ service times) was built in 1843.

The **Szeged Open-Air Festival** is held in Dom tér from mid-July to late August. Running along three sides of the square is the **Nemzeti Emlékcsarnok** (National Pantheon), with statues and reliefs of 80 Hungarian notables. One block northeast, inside the **Szerb Ortodox Templom** (Serbian Orthodox Church; cnr Béla & Somogyi utca; adult/student 150/100Ft; ☯ 8am-8pm), have a look at

HUNGARY

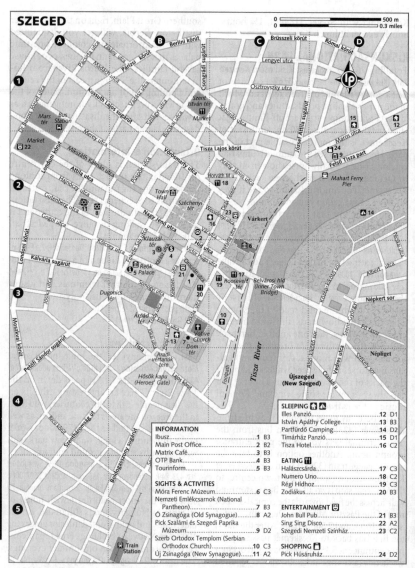

SZEGED

0 — 500 m
0 — 0.3 miles

the fantastic iconostasis – a central gold 'tree' with 60 icons hanging off its 'branches'.

Just north of the Old Town ring road is the **Pick Szalámi és Szegedi Paprika Múzeum** (☎ 421 814; Felső Tisza part 10; adult/student 320/240Ft; ☼ 3-6pm Tue-Fri & 1-4pm Sat). Two floors of exhibits and old photos show traditional methods of salami production. There's a small gift stand in

the museum and a butcher shop around the corner in this factory building.

Sleeping

Plenty of student accommodation is open to travellers in July and August, including the central **István Apáthy College** (☎ 545 896; Eötvös utca 4; r 5000Ft; ☒). Ask Tourinform (p339) for more information. **Ibusz** (☎ 471 177; www.ibusz.hu; Oroszlán utca 3; per person 4000-5000Ft; ☺ 9am-5pm Mon-Fri, to 1pm Sat) travel agency can help with private rooms.

Partfürdő Camping (☎ 430 843; Közép-kikötő sor; camp sites per person 1200Ft, bungalows 12,000Ft; ☺ mid-May–Sep; P ☒) This green, grassy camp site is across the river in New Szeged. Bungalows sleep up to four people.

Illes Panzió (☎ 315 640; www.illespanzio.fw.hu; Maros utca 37; r 5900-7900Ft; P) This newly refurbished old mansion north of the centre has fresh, clean rooms with wood panels, cool tile floors, TVs and polished woodwork.

Tímárház Panzió (☎ 425 486; Maros utca 26; s/d/tr 8200/10,000/17,600Ft; P) Boxy rooms are sparsely furnished with low-lying modern beds and flat-faced armoires.

Tisza Hotel (☎ 478 278; www.tiszahotel.hu; Wesselényi utca 1; s/d €57/67; P ☒) The classy old mamma of Szeged, this 1885 hotel has imposing marble pillars, gilded décor and vast halls with low-hanging chandeliers. You can upgrade to a 'superior' room with colonial furniture for under €20 extra. The cheapest deals are rooms with a shower, but the toilet is in a shared restroom down the hall.

Eating

Numero Uno (☎ 424 745; Széchenyi tér 5; mains 360-730Ft; ☺ 11am-11pm Mon-Sat, noon-11pm Sun; ☒) Good pizzas and calzones on the main square. There's a garden out back.

Régi Hídhoz (☎ 420 910; Oskola utca 4; mains 780-1200Ft; ☺ noon-11pm Sun-Thu, 11am-midnight Fri & Sat; ☒) This is the cheaper version of Halászcsárda (below), where many come to try Szeged's *halászlé* (fish soup). The rustic dining room has faux-treated yellow plaster walls and ceramics hanging as decorations.

Zodiákus (☎ 420 914; Oskola utca 13; mains 890-2100Ft; ☺ 11am-midnight Mon-Thu, 11am-1am Sat, 1-4pm Sun; ☒) Low lighting, barrel ceilings, amber walls and stylised zodiac-sign art make for a sultry, upscale environment. Imaginative entrées include options such as beef tenderloin topped with red currants and cheddar cheese.

Halászcsárda (☎ 555 980; Roosevelt tér 14; mains 1500-2000Ft) While in town you have to try Szegedi *halászlé*, the fish soup the area is known for. This is the place that wins all prizes for the local delicacy.

Entertainment

This being a college town means that there is a vast array of bars, clubs and other nightspots, especially around Dugonics tér. Nightclub programmes are listed in the free *Szegedi Est* magazine.

Szegedi Nemzeti Színház (☎ 479 279; Deák Ferenc utca 12-14) Since 1886, the Szeged National Theatre has been the centre of cultural life in the city. Opera, ballet and drama performances take the stage.

John Bull Pub (☎ 484 217; Oroszlán utca 6; ☺ 10am-midnight Mon-Fri, to 1am Sat & Sun) Join the 20-somethings drinking on the small patio or in the cosy pub – if you can find a free table.

Sing Sing Disco (cnr Mars tér & Dr Baross József utca; ☺ 10pm-4am Wed-Sat) A place where the youngsters let loose on weekends, with guest DJs, rave parties and occasional theme nights (let's hope none of them include prison outfits). Admission starts at 500Ft, depending on the DJ.

Shopping

Pick Húsáruház (☎ 421 879; Maros utca 21; ☺ 3-6pm Mon, 7am-6pm Tue-Fri, 6am-noon Sat) You can buy a stick of Pick salami, Szeged's brand product, as well as other meats, right from the factory store.

Getting There & Away

Buses run to Budapest (2430Ft, three hours, six daily), Kecskemét (1090Ft, two hours, hourly) and Pécs (2310Ft, four hours, eight daily), among other destinations. If you're heading to Serbia, buses make the 1½ hour run to Subotica daily at 10am (800Ft).

Szeged is on the main rail line to Budapest's Nyugati train station (2324Ft, 2½ hours, 11 daily), stopping halfway along in Kecskemét (1844Ft, 1¼ hours, 11 daily). You have to change in Békéscsaba to get to Arad (2946Ft, 3½ hours, three daily) in Romania. Two daily trains (6.35am and 4.25pm) go direct from Szeged to Subotica (1434Ft, two hours) in Serbia.

NORTHEASTERN HUNGARY

The level plains and grasslands give way to a chain of wooded hills as you head north and east. These are the foothills of the Carpathian Mountains (in modern-day Ukraine and Romania), which stretch along the Hungarian border with Slovakia. Though you'll definitely notice the rise in elevation, Hungary's highest peak of Kékes-tető is still only a proverbial bump in the road at 1014m. The microclimates

HUNGARY

in several of the hill groupings are quite conducive to wine production. Eger and Tokaj are known worldwide for their red and sweet dessert wines, respectively. Not far north of Eger is Szilvásvárad – the Hungarian home of the snow-white Lipizzaner horse makes a good day trip.

EGER

☎ 36 / pop 57,000

After Budapest, Eger (*egg*-air) is probably next on any visitor's list, and the gallons of wine that are at your disposal here definitely have something to do with it. But that's not to say there's nothing else to draw travellers here – on the contrary. This attractive baroque city has a great hilltop castle and a walkable, quaint town centre. And then, of course, there's the wine.

It was here in 1552 that Hungarian defenders temporarily stopped the Turkish advance into Western Europe and helped preserve Hungary's identity. Legend has it that István Dobó fortified his badly outnumbered soldiers with red wine while they successfully defended Eger against the siege. When the Ottomans saw the red-stained beards, rumours circulated that the Hungarians were drinking bull's blood to attain their strength. Thus the name of the region's most famous red wine came to be Egri Bikavér (Eger Bull's Blood). The Ottomans returned in 1596 and captured Eger Castle. They were evicted in 1687.

In the 18th century, Eger played a central role in Ferenc Rákóczi II's attempt to overthrow the Habsburgs, and it was then that a large part of the castle was razed by the Austrians. Credit goes to the bishops of Eger for erecting most of the town you see today. Eger has some of Hungary's finest architecture, especially examples of Copf (Zopf in Hungarian), a transitional style between late baroque and neoclassicism found only in Central Europe. Just a 20-minute walk southwest of the centre, dozens of small wine cellars are to be found carved into the sides of Szépasszony völgy (Valley of the Beautiful Women).

Orientation & Information

The main train station is a 15-minute walk south of town, on Vasút utca, just east of Deák Ferenc utca. Egervár train station, which serves Szilvásvárad and other points north, is a five-minute walk north of the castle along Vécseyvölgy utca. The bus station is west of Széchenyi István utca, Eger's main drag.

Egri Est Café (☎ 411 105; Széchenyi István utca 16; ⏰ 11am-midnight Sun-Thu, to 4am Fri & Sat) internet access for 500Ft per hour.

OTP Bank (Széchenyi István utca 2)

Post office (Széchenyi István utca 22)

Tourinform (☎ 517 715; www.eger.hu; Bajcsy-Zsilinszky utca 9; ⏰ 9am-5pm Mon-Fri, to 1pm Sat, to 6pm Mon-Fri Jul-Aug) The helpful staff here has lots of regional information on hand, including an accommodation guide.

Sights & Activities

The most striking attraction and the best views of town are from **Egri Vár** (Eger Castle; ☎ 312 744; Vár 1; adult/student combined ticket 900/450Ft; ⏰ 8am-8pm Tue-Sun Apr-Aug, to 7pm Sep, 8am-6pm Oct & Mar, to 5pm Nov-Feb), a huge walled complex at the top of the hill off Dósza tér. First fortified after an early Mongol invasion in the 13th century, the earliest ruins onsite are the foundations of St John's Cathedral, built in the 12th century and destroyed by the Turks. The excellent **István Dobó Múzeum** (admission included with castle), inside the Bishop's Palace (1470), explores the history and development of the castle and the town. Other exhibits such as the **Panoptikum** (Waxworks; adult/student 350/250Ft) and the **Éremverde** (Minting Exhibit; adult/student 240/120Ft) cost extra. Even on days when the museums are closed, you can walk around the grounds and battlements and enjoy the views if you buy a *sétaljegy* (strolling ticket, adult/child 400/200Ft).

A surprise awaits you west of the castle hill: a 40m-high **minaret** (Knézich Károly utca; admission 200Ft; ⏰ 10am-6pm Mar-Oct), minus the mosque, is allegedly Europe's northernmost remains of the Ottoman invasion in the 16th century. The **Minorita Templom** (Minorite Church; Dobó István tér; admission free; ⏰ mass times), built in 1771, is a glorious baroque building. In the square in front are statues of national hero István Dobó and his comrades-in-arms routing the Turks in 1552.

The first thing you see as you come into town from the bus or train station is the neoclassical **Egri Bazilika** (Eger Cathedral; Pyrker János tér 1), built in 1836. Directly opposite is the Copf-style **Líceum** (Lyceum; ☎ 520 400; Esterházy tér 1; admission free; ⏰ 9.30am-3.30pm Tue-Sun Apr-Sep, to 1pm Sat & Sun Oct-Mar), dating from 1765, with a 20,000-volume frescoed **könyvetár** (library; adult/student 500/350Ft) on the 1st floor and an 18th-century observatory in the **Csillagászati Múzuem** (Astronomy Museum; adult/student 500/350Ft) on the 6th floor. Climb three more floors up to

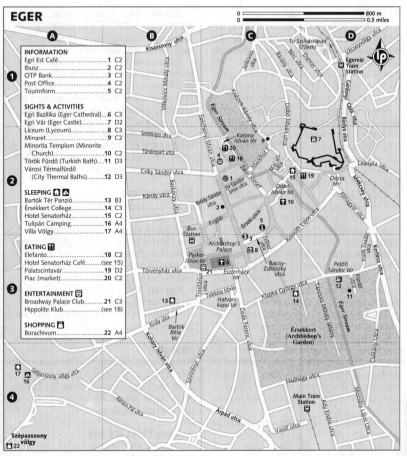

EGER

0 ____ 800 m
0 ____ 0.5 miles

INFORMATION
Egri Est Café.............................1 C2
Ibusz.......................................2 C2
OTP Bank.................................3 C3
Post Office...............................4 C2
Tourinform..............................5 C2

SIGHTS & ACTIVITIES
Egri Bazilika (Eger Cathedral)...6 C3
Egri Vár (Eger Castle)................7 D2
Líceum (Lyceum)......................8 C2
Minaret...................................9 C2
Minorita Templom (Minorite
    Church).............................10 C2
Török Fürdő (Turkish Bath)....11 D3
Városi Térmalfürdő
    (City Thermal Baths).........12 D3

SLEEPING
Bartók Tér Panzió....................13 B3
Érsekkert College....................14 C3
Hotel Senatorház.....................15 C2
Tulipán Camping.....................16 A4
Villa Völgy..............................17 A4

EATING
Elefanto.................................18 C2
Hotel Senatorház Café........(see 15)
Palatscintavár.........................19 D2
Piac (market)..........................20 C2

ENTERTAINMENT
Broadway Palace Club.............21 C3
Hippolite Klub...................(see 18)

SHOPPING
Borachivum...........................22 A4

the observation deck for a great view of the city and to try out the camera obscura, the 'eye of Eger', designed in 1776 to entertain the locals.

The Archbishop's Garden was once the private reserve of papal princes, but today the park is open to the public. Inside the park, the **Városi Térmalfürdő** (City Thermal Baths; ☎ 411 699; adult/child 500/350Ft; ✆ 6am-7.30pm Mon-Fri, 9am-7pm Sat & Sun May-Sep, 9am-6pm daily Oct-Apr) has open-air, as well as covered, pools with different temperatures (40°C being the hottest) and mineral contents. The **Török Fürdő** (Turkish Bath; Fürdő utca 3), built between 1610 and 1617, is open only to those with a doctor's order.

The prize for the most deceitful name of any attraction in the world could almost

definitely go to **Szépasszony völgy** (Valley of the Beautiful Women; off Király utca; ✆ 10am-5pm), home to dozens of small wine cellars that truck in, store and sell Bull's Blood and other regional red and white wines. Walk the horseshoe-shaped street through the valley and stop in front of one that strikes your fancy and ask ('*megkosztólhatok?*') to taste their wares (50Ft per decilitre). If you want wine to go, you can bring an empty plastic bottle and have it filled for about (600Ft per 1½ litres); they'll also sell you a kitschy little plastic barrel full. It's easy to drink a lot here, but remember that there is a zero-tolerance policy for driving in Hungary with any alcohol in your system, so walk the 20 minutes back to the centre or get a taxi (1000Ft).

HUNGARY

Sleeping

A number of colleges in town offer accommodation in July and August, including the 132-bed **Érsekkert College** (☎ 413 661; fax 520 440; Klapka György utca 12; dm 1400-2000Ft). **Ibusz** (☎ 311 451; www .ibusz.hu; Széchenyi István utca 9; ☉ 8am-4pm Mon-Fri, 9am-1pm Sat Jun-Sep) can help organise private rooms, starting at 3000Ft a night per person.

Tulipán Camping (☎ 410 580; www.home.zonnet.nl /tulipan/; Szépasszony völgy utca 71; camp sites per person 1450Ft, caravan sites with electricity per person 1950Ft, hotel r 7680Ft, 4-/5-person bungalows 5500/9900Ft; P 🐾) The five-person bungalow has one bedroom, a living room, a kitchen and a bathroom. The four-person cabin is just a room (no kitchen or bath). The hotel rooms have minifridges and include breakfast. Some of the caravan sites are in a big, treeless field. It's at a stumbling distance from the valley wine cellars and it's open year-round.

Bartók Tér Panzió (☎ 515 556; fax 515 572; Bartók Béla tér 8; s/d/tr 7000/9000/11,000Ft; ✗) A light, colourful place with basic rooms and skylights, organised around a courtyard in an old town building. The same people operate St Kristof Panzió, at the end of the square, for the same prices (contact Bartók Tér Panzió for details).

Villa Völgy (☎ 321 664; www.hotels.hu/villavolgy; Szépasszony völgy, Tulipánkert utca 5; s/d 8200/13,600Ft; P ✗) A stylish, country manor house–type hotel, in the heart of wine-tasting country. The modern interior design uses blonde wood, large colourful prints on the curtains, and graphic art rugs.

Hotel Senatorház (☎ 320 466; www.senatorhaz.hu; Dobó István tér 11; r €56-70; P 🐾) This 18th-century inn sitting on the cobblestone square, with the lights of Eger Castle glowing above, has the best location in town. The reception is cluttered with tasteful antiques, leather sofas and old photographs, and traditional wood furnishings decorate the well-equipped 11 guest rooms.

Eating

At the base of Szépasszony völgy utca there are numerous small terrace *büfé* (snack bars) that resemble food stands, but employ a waiter to serve you at your picnic table. There are also numerous restaurants and cafés along pedestrian Széchenyi István utca in town. The area is known for its *pistrang* (trout) dishes.

Piac (market; Katona István tér; ☉ 6am-6pm Mon-Fri, to 1pm Sat, to 10am Sun) Come to the covered market to get fruit, vegetables, meat and bread.

Elefanto (☎ 411 031; Katona István tér 2; mains 1350-2500Ft, pizzas 490-900Ft; ☉ 11am-midnight; ✗) Dine alfresco on the large covered terrace. This is a casual place that sometimes has light music.

Palatscintavár (☎ 413 986; Dobó István utca 9; mains around 1200Ft) This is a pancake-lover's heaven, and a wonderful vegetarian option. The restaurant seems to have been decorated by an obsessive collector of old cigarette packs and other odd and lovely things.

Hotel Senatorház Café (☎ 320 466; Dobó István tér 11; mains 1400-3000Ft; ☉ 11am-midnight; 🐾) Sitting in the main square for a meal is delightful. Even better, stop by in the evening for a candlelit dessert.

Entertainment

The Tourinform office can tell you what concerts and musicals are on at theatres in the area, the Líceum and at Eger Cathedral. The free *Egri Est* magazine has nightlife listings.

Broadway Palace Club (Pyker János tér 3; ☉ 10am-6am Wed, Fri & Sat) A good atmosphere for dancing and there are café tables outside.

Hippolite Klub (☎ 411 031; Katona István tér 2; ☉ 10am-4am) A mild-mannered restaurant by day, Hippolite turns funky disco with music starting at 9pm.

Shopping

Buy wine at the source in Szépasszony völgy. Ask a cellar to fill up your plastic jug straight from the cask, or if you insist on having a glass bottle, **Borachivum** (Szépasszony völgy utca 33; ☉ 10am-6pm) sells them.

Getting There & Away

Buses make the trip from Eger to Szilvásvárad (405Ft, 45 minutes, nine daily). Other destinations include Budapest (1500Ft, two hours, 15 daily), Kecskemét (2080Ft, 4½ hours, three daily) and also Szeged (2660Ft, 5½ hours, three daily). To get to Tokaj by bus, you have to go past it to Nyíregyháza and switch.

Eight trains a day connect Egervár station with Szilvásvárad (312Ft, one hour). Departing from the main train station, change at Füzesabony to get to Tokaj (1762Ft, two hours, seven daily). Direct trains run from Eger to Budapest's Keleti station (1968Ft, two hours) four times a day.

SZILVÁSVÁRAD

☎ 36 / pop 1850

Horse-lover? Then come this way. The quiet village of Szilvásvárad, 28km north of Eger, hides in the Bükk Hills, most of which fall within the 43,000-hectare **Bükk Nemzeti Park**. This is where you can see, ride and be pulled (in a carriage) by the precious white stallions, the Lipizzaner horses. Either make a day trip to the hills or base yourself at the park. Some 250 prize horses are kept in local stables. If you love hiking, you can base yourself at the Lipizzaner centre too, and although there's no tourist office here, the Tourinform in Eger (p342) has information and sells hiking maps.

The bus from Eger will drop you off in the centre on Egri út. Park utca is off Egri, north of the bus stop, Szalajka Völgy is to the south. You get off the train at Szilvásvárad-Szalajkavölgy, the first of the town's two stations. Follow Egri út east and then north (left) for about 10 minutes into town. At the turn, if you go right instead you'll get to the valley.

Learn more about Lipizzaner horses at the **Lipcsai Múzeum** (☎ 355 135; Park utca 8; adult/student 350/250Ft; ☼ 9am-noon & 1-4pm), which has historical exhibits and a few live animals in an 18th-century stable. Call a day ahead to arrange a carriage (from 4300/7400Ft for a two-/four-horse coach seating three people) or a horseback ride at the **Lipizzaner State Stud Farm** (Lipicai Állami Ménesgazdaság; ☎ 564 400; Fenyves utca; admission adult/child 300/200Ft; ☼ 10am-noon & 2-4pm Thu-Sun; rides 1800/2500Ft per hr in paddock/further afield).

At the beginning of Szalajka Völgy there are restaurants, souvenir shops and tracks where Lipizzaner coaches race some summer weekends. You can park here for 100Ft per hour. Hike from here further into the valley, or take a ride on a **keskeny nyomtávú vasút** (narrowgauge railway; ☎ 355 197; Szalajka völgy utca 6; one way adult/student 300/150Ft; ☼ May-Sep).

Nine daily buses connect Szilvásvárad and Eger (405Ft, 45 minutes). Trains to Egervár train station take about an hour (312Ft, eight daily).

TOKAJ
☎ 47 / pop 4650

The region has been on the Unesco World Heritage list since 2002, although grapevines have been grown in the hills surrounding Tokaj village for at least 1000 years. The volcanic soil and unique microclimate promote the growth of *Botrytis cinerea* (noble rot) on the grapes. It's these ugly, shrivelled-up grapes covered with fungus that produce Tokaji Aszú,

a world-class dessert wine. The sweetness is rated from 3 (least) to 6 (the most). Tokaj also produces less sweet wines: Szamorodni (like dry sherry), Furmint and Háslevelú (the driest of all). The village itself spreads out in a valley at the confluence of the Tisza and the Bodrog Rivers. Look for the nesting storks on telephone poles and chimneys from March through September.

Orientation & Information
Trains arrive 1200m south of the town centre; walk north on Baross Gábor utca, turn left on Bajcsy-Zsilinszky út and it turns into Rákóczi út, the main thoroughfare. The bus station is much more convenient, in town, on Seráz utca. **Tourinform** (☎ 552 070; www.tokaj.hu; Seráz utca 1; ☼ 9am-4pm Mon-Fri) is just off Rákóczi út.

Sights & Activities
Start at the **Tokaji Múzeum** (☎ 352 636; Bethlen Gábor utca 13; adult/student 400/200Ft; ☼ 10am-4pm Tue-Sun May-Nov), which leaves nothing unsaid about the history of Tokaj, the region and its wines. After you're thoroughly knowledgeable, head to the 600-year-old cellar **Rákóczi Pince** (☎ 352 408; Kossuth tér 15; ☼ 10am-6pm) for a tasting and a tour. Bottles of wine mature underground in the long cave-like corridors (one measures 28m by 10m). A flight of six Tokaj wines costs 2100Ft. The correct order of sampling Tokaj wines is: Furmint, dry Szamorodni, sweet Szamorodni and then the Aszú wines – from three to six *puttony* (the sweetest). If you only want to taste the Aszú, a three-decilitre glass costs 216Ft to 636Ft, with a minimum of four glasses to taste.

There are less formal wine cellars (*pincek*) that offer tastings. They are scattered along the roads leading into town (Tarcali) and out of (Bodorgkeresztúri) town. Look for signs on Rákóczi út, on Bem út and on Hegyalja utca (southeast of town off Bajcsy-Zsilinszky út). Other town attractions include the **Tokaji Galéria** (☎ 352 003; Bethlen Gábor utca 17; admission free; ☼ 10am-4pm May-Oct), in an 18th-century Greek Orthodox church, with works by local artists. The **Nagy Zsinagóga** (Great Synagogue; Serház utca 55), has been restored from its crumbling state.

Sleeping & Eating
Tourinform (www.tokaj.hu) lists searchable private accommodation on its website. The newest, nicest pensions are southeast of town and require at least a 20-minute walk to get to the centre.

Lux (☎ 352 145; Serház utca 14; d/tr 5400/7500Ft) This friendly six-room pension has obviously been well loved, and well used, but it is *central*. No breakfast.

Tisza Panzió (☎ 552 008; fax 552 009; Tarcali út 52; s/d 4000/6000Ft; P ✖) This *panzió* has simple and modern rooms, with TV and telephone. Tarcali út is about 25 minutes south of town along Bajcsy-Zsilinszky út (southwest of the train station).

Millennium Hotel (☎ 352 242; www.tokajmillennium .hu; Bajcsy-Zsilinszky út 34; s/d 8800/10,200Ft; P ✖) Sleek décor and up-to-date amenities, such as unlimited wireless internet connection in the guest rooms, live up to the new century name. Use of the wellbeing centre is included, but breakfast is 1100Ft extra. The hotel sits near the confluence of the Bodrog and Tisza Rivers.

Róna (☎ 352 116; Bethlen Gábor utca 19; mains 1300-1900Ft; ☯ 11am-10pm, to 9pm Nov-Feb) The speciality of the house is fish, caught in nearby rivers, but there are other Hungarian options on the menu here as well, although they are nothing fancy.

Degenfeld (☎ 553 050; Kossuth tér 1; mains 1800-2600Ft; ☯ 11.30am-10pm; ✖ ☷) Delight your tastebuds with lemon-tarragon venison or orange-ginger duck breast. The Degenfeld palace was built in 1870 and has lovely white tablecloths, fresh flowers and upholstered French imperial chairs in the dining room. A few rooms upstairs are for rent.

Shopping

You can buy wine at any of the places mentioned for tasting or stop at the **Furmint Vinotéka** (☎ 353 340; Bethlen Gábor utca 12; ☯ 9am-5pm) wineshop for a large local selection.

Getting There & Away

No direct buses connect Tokaj with Budapest or Eger. Two buses a day go to Nyíregyháza (463Ft, 40 minutes), where you can connect to either.

Four express trains a day travel to and from Budapest's Keleti station (2610Ft, two hours 45 minutes) and one local to Budapest's Nyugati (2762Ft, 4½ hours). Change at Füzesabony to get to Eger (1762Ft, two hours, five daily). Up to 18 trains a day connect Tokaj with Nyíregyháza (442Ft, 40 minutes), from where you can take a train to the Hungarian border town of Záhony and into Csop, in the Ukraine.

HUNGARY DIRECTORY

ACCOMMODATION

Budapest has the widest variety of lodging prices, but even in provincial towns you can find camping grounds, hostels and private rooms in the budget range; *panziók* (pensions), guesthouses and small hotels in the midrange; and multiamenity hotels at the top end. Reviews in this chapter are ordered according to price. Hungary's more than 400 camping grounds are listed in Tourinform's *Camping Hungary* map/brochure (www.camping.hu). Facilities are generally open May to October and difficult to reach without a car.

The **Hungarian Youth Hostel Association** (Map pp300-1; Mellow Mood Ltd; ☎ 1-413 2065; www.youth hostels.hu; VII Baross tér 15, 3rd fl, Budapest) keeps a list of year-round hostels throughout Hungary. In general, year-round hostels have a communal kitchen, laundry and internet service, sometimes a lounge, and a basic bread-and-jam breakfast may be included. Having a HI card is not required, but it may get you a 10% discount. From July to August, students vacate college and university dorms and administration opens them to travellers. Local Tourinform offices can help you locate such places.

Renting a private room in a Hungarian home is a good budget option and can be a great opportunity to get up close and personal with the culture: you generally share a bathroom with the family. Prices outside Budapest run from 2200Ft to 5500Ft per person per night.

Midrange accommodation may or may not have a private bathroom, satellite TV and in-room phone, but all top-end places do. A cold breakfast buffet is usually included in the price at pensions, and there are hot breakfasts included at hotels. A reasonable place might bill itself as a *kishotel* (small hotel) because it has satellite TV and a minibar. Air-conditioning is scarce nationwide, but you're more likely to find it at higher-priced establishments.

An engaging alternative is to stay in a rural village or farm house, but only if you have wheels – most places are truly remote. Contact Tourinform, the **National Association of Village Tourism** (Map p304; FAOS; ☎ 1-268 0592; VII Király utca 93) or the **Centre for Rural Tourism** (Map pp300-1; FTC; ☎ 1-321 4396; www.ftur.hu; VII Dohány utca 86) in Budapest.

ACTIVITIES

Hungary has more than 100 thermal baths open to the public and many are attached to hotels with wellbeing packages. Two thermal baths in Budapest, one at Harkány (p336) and the large thermal lake at Hévíz (p332) are covered in this chapter. Request the Hungarian National Tourist Office (HNTO) brochure *Water Tours in Hungary* from Tourinform; it's a gold mine of information for planning spa itineraries.

There's also a helpful HNTO *Riding in Hungary* booklet on equestrian tourism, or you could contact the **Hungarian Equestrian Tourism Association** (Map p304; MLTSZ; ☎ 1-456 0444; www.equi.hu; IX Ráday utca 8, Budapest). **Pegazus Tours** (Map p304; ☎ 1-317 1644; www.pegazus.hu; V Ferenciek tere 5, Budapest) organises horse-riding tours, and occasionally bicycle tours as well.

Hiking enthusiasts may enjoy the trails around Tihany at Lake Balaton, the Bükk Hills north of Eger or the plains at Bugac Puszta south of Kecskemét. Hiking maps usually have yellow borders. Bird-watchers could explore these same paths or take a tour with **Birding Hungary** (☎ 70-214 0261; www.birdinghungary.com; PF 4, Budapest 1511).

All admission prices in this chapter are listed as they are quoted on signs in Hungary (adult/student). Usually, children and pensioners can get into places for the same discounted price.

BOOKS

Not to be modest, an excellent overall guidebook is Lonely Planet's *Hungary*, while the *Budapest* guide takes an in-depth look at the capital. For an easy introduction to the nation's past, check out *An Illustrated History of Hungary* by István Lázár. Read László Kontler's *A History of Hungary* for a more in-depth, but easy-to-read, study.

BUSINESS HOURS

With some rare exceptions, opening hours (*nyitvatartás*) are posted on the front door of establishments; *nyitva* means 'open' and *zárva* is 'closed'. Large, chain grocery stores are usually open from 7am to 6pm Monday through Friday, and to 1pm on Saturday. Smaller ones, especially in Budapest, may be open on Sunday or holidays as well. Most towns have a 'nonstop' convenience store, and many have hypermarkets, such as Tesco, that are open 24 hours. Main post offices are open 8am to 6pm weekdays, and to noon or 1pm Saturday.

Bank hours are from 8am to 4pm Monday to Thursday and 8am to 1pm on Friday. Hospitality opening hours vary between bigger and smaller towns, but generally restaurants open from 11am to 11pm, and bars and cafés open from 8am to midnight.

COURSES

The granddaddy of all Hungarian language schools, **Debreceni Nyári Egyetem** (Debrecen Summer University; ☎ 52-489 117; www.nyariegyetem.hu; Egyetem tér 1, PO Box 35, Debrecen 4010), in eastern Hungary, is the most well known and the most well respected. It organises intensive two- and four-week courses during July and August and 80-hour, two-week advanced courses during winter. The **Debrecen Summer University Branch** (Map p304; ☎ 1-320 5751; XIII Jászai Mari tér 6) in Budapest puts on regular and intensive courses.

CUSTOMS

You can bring and take out the usual personal effects, 200 cigarettes, 1L of wine or champagne and 1L of spirits. You are not supposed to export valuable antiques without a special permit; this should be available from the place of purchase. You must declare the import/export of any amount of cash exceeding 1,000,000Ft.

DISABLED TRAVELLERS

Most of Hungary has a long way to go before it becomes accessible to the disabled, although audible traffic signals are becoming more common and there are Braille markings on the higher-denominated forint notes. For more information, contact the **Hungarian Disabled Association** (Map pp300-1; MEOSZ; ☎ 1-388 5529; meosz@matavnet.hu; III San Marco utca 76, Budapest).

DISCOUNT CARDS

Those planning extensive travel in Hungary might consider the **Hungary Card** (☎ 1-266 3741; www.hungarycard.hu), which gives 50% discounts on seven return train fares; three 33%-off one-way train trips; 50% off some bus and boat travel; free entry to some museums and attractions outside Budapest; up to 25% off selected accommodation; and 20% off the price of the Budapest Card (p302). Available at Tourinform and Volánbusz offices, larger train stations, some newsagents and petrol stations throughout Hungary, the card costs 7935Ft and is valid for one year.

HUNGARY

EMBASSIES & CONSULATES

To find out more about Hungarian embassies around the world, or foreign representation in Hungary, contact the **Ministry of Foreign Affairs** (☎ 1-458 1000; www.kum.hu).

Hungarian Embassies & Consulates

Hungarian embassies around the world include the following.

Australia (☎ 02-6282 2555; 17 Beale Cres, Deakin, ACT 2600)
Canada (☎ 613-230 9614; 299 Waverley St, Ottawa, Ontario K2P 0V9)
France (☎ 01 5636 0754; 7-9 Sq Vergennes, 75015 Paris)
Germany (☎ 030-203 100; Unter den Linden 76, 10117 Berlin)
Ireland (☎ 01-661 2902; 2 Fitzwilliam Pl, Dublin 2)
Netherlands (☎ 70-350 0404; Hogeweg 14, 2585 JD Den Haag)
UK (☎ 020-7235 5218; 35 Eaton Pl, London SW1X 8BY)
USA (☎ 202-362 6730; 3910 Shoemaker St NW, Washington, DC)

Embassies & Consulates in Hungary

Embassies in Budapest (phone code ☎ 1) include the following.

Australia (Map pp300-1; ☎ 457 9777; XII Királyhágó tér 8-9; ☺ 9am-5pm Mon-Thu, to 2pm Fri)
Austria (Map p304; ☎ 479 7010; VI Benczúr utca 16; ☺ 8am-10am Mon-Fri)
Canada (Map pp300-1; ☎ 392 3360; XII Zugligeti út 51-53; ☺ 8am-4pm Mon-Fri)
Croatia (Map p304; ☎ 269 5854; VI Munkácsy Mihály utca 15; ☺ 9am-5pm Mon-Fri)
France (Map pp300-1; ☎ 374 1100; VI Lendvay utca 27; ☺ 9am-noon Mon-Fri)
Germany (Map p304; ☎ 488 3500; I Úri utca 64-66; ☺ 9am-noon Mon-Fri)
Ireland (Map p304; ☎ 302 9600; V Szabadság tér 7-9; ☺ 9.30am-1pm & 2-4pm Mon-Fri)
Netherlands (Map pp300-1; ☎ 336 6300; II Füge utca 5-7; ☺ 10am-noon Mon-Fri)
Romania (Map pp300-1; ☎ 348 0271; XIV Thököly út 72; ☺ 9.30am-noon, closed Wed)
Serbia (Map pp300-1; ☎ 322 9838; VI Dózsa György út 92/b; ☺ 10am-1pm Mon-Fri)
Slovakia (Map pp300-1; ☎ 460 9011; IV Stefánia út 22-24; ☺ 9.30am-noon Mon-Fri)
Slovenia (Map pp300-1; ☎ 438 5600; II Cseppkő utca 68; ☺ 9am-noon Mon-Fri)
South Africa (Map pp300-1; ☎ 392 0999; II Gárdonyi Géza út 17; ☺ 9am-12.30pm Mon-Fri)
UK (Map p304; ☎ 266 2888; V Harmincad utca 6; ☺ 10.30am-1.30pm & 2.30-5.30pm Mon-Fri)
Ukraine (Map pp300-1; ☎ 422 4120; XIV Stefánia út 77; ☺ 9am-noon Mon-Wed & Fri by appointment only)

USA (Map p304; ☎ 475 4400; V Szabadság tér 12; ☺ 8.15am-5pm Mon-Fri)

FESTIVALS & EVENTS

The best annual events include the following.
Budapest Spring Festival (Mar)
Balaton Festival (May) Based in Keszthely.
Hungarian Dance Festival (late Jun) In Győr.
Sopron Festival Weeks (late Jun–mid-Jul)
Győr Summer Cultural Festival (late June-late Jul)
Hortobágy International Equestrian Days (Jul)
Szeged Open-Air Festival (Jul-Aug)
Kőszeg Castle Theatre Festival (mid-late Jul)
Pepsi Sziget Music Festival (late Jul-early Aug) On Óbudai hajógyári-sziget (Óbuda Shipbuilding Island) in Budapest.
Hungaroring Formula One Grand Prix (mid-Aug) At Mogyoród, 24km northeast of Budapest
Budapest Autumn Festival (mid-Oct-early Nov)

GAY & LESBIAN TRAVELLERS

There is no openly antigay sentiment in Hungary, but neither is there a large openly gay population. The organisations and nightclubs that do exist are generally in Budapest. For up-to-date information on venues, events, groups etc, contact **GayGuide.Net** (☎ 06 30 932 3334; http://budapest.gayguide.net).

HOLIDAYS

Hungary's 10 public holidays:
New Year's Day 1 January
1848 Revolution Day 15 March
Easter Monday March/April
International Labour Day 1 May
Whit Monday May/June
St Stephen's Day 20 August
1956 Remembrance Day 23 October
All Saints' Day 1 November
Christmas Day 25 December
Boxing Day 26 December

LANGUAGE

Hungarians speak Magyar (Hungarian), and unlike the vast majority of tongues you'll hear in Europe, it is not an Indo-European language. It is traditionally categorised as Finno-Ugric, distantly related only to Finnish and Estonian. Many older Hungarians, particularly in the western part of the country, can understand German and many young people, particularly in Budapest, speak some English. Any travel-related business will have at least one staff member who can speak English.

Hungarians always put surnames before given names, in writing and in speech. But don't worry, no one expects foreigners to reverse their names upon introduction.

MEDIA

Budapest has two English-language weeklies: the expat-oriented *Budapest Sun,* with a useful 'Style' arts and entertainment supplement, and the *Budapest Business Journal* (550Ft). Some Western English-language newspapers, including the *International Herald Tribune,* are available on the day of publication in Budapest and in other large western Hungary cities. Many more newspapers, mainly British, French and German, are sold a day late. International news magazines are also widely available.

MONEY

The unit of currency is the Hungarian forint (Ft). Coins come in denominations of one, two, five, 10, 20, 50 and 100Ft, and notes are denominated 200, 500, 1000, 2000, 5000, 10,000 and 20,000Ft. ATMs are quite common throughout the country, including train stations, and they accept most credit and cash cards. Banks usually offer exchange services as well as ATMs. Branches can be found around the main square in an Old Town centre, or on the main thoroughfare leading to it. Bank hours are from 8am to 4pm Monday to Thursday and 8am to 1pm on Friday. Visa and MasterCard are the most widely accepted credit cards, but some smaller lodgings still only accept cash. Some businesses quote prices in euros; prices in this chapter conform to quotes of individual businesses.

POST

A postcard costs 50Ft within Hungary, 110Ft within Europe, and 150Ft to the rest of the world. A *légiposta* (airmail) letter costs 190Ft within Europe, 380Ft to the rest of the world for up to 20g. Although you can buy stamps at some youth hostels and hotels, go to a post office to actually send your letter or card. If you put it in a post box on the street, it may languish for weeks. Otherwise, service is pretty speedy – a few days to Europe and about a week to the US.

Mail addressed to poste restante in any town or city will go to the main post office (*főposta*). When collecting poste-restante mail, look for the sign '*postán maradó küldemények*'. If you hold an Amex credit card or are carrying your travellers cheques, you can have your mail sent to **American Express** (Map p304; V Deák Ferenc utca 10, Budapest), where it will be held for one month.

TELEPHONE & FAX

Hungary's country code is ☎ 36. To make an outgoing international call, dial ☎ 00 first. To dial city-to-city (and all mobile phones) within the country, first dial ☎ 06 (dialling in from out of the country, leave off the 06), wait for the second dial tone and then dial the city code and phone number. All localities in Hungary have a two-digit city code, except for Budapest, whose code is ☎ 1. Mobile phone numbers all start with the prefix ☎ 06 but are countrywide numbers (ie they have no city code). Budapest numbers have seven digits, most others six digits.

The best place to make international telephone calls is from a phone box with a phone card, which you can buy at newsstands in 2000Ft and 5000Ft denominations. Some cards, such as Neophone, get you an international call for as little as 19Ft per minute. Buy a Matáv *telefonkártya* at newsstands (800Ft) to make domestic calls at card-operated machines. Some pay phones still take coins. Telephone boxes with a black-and-white arrow and red target on the door and the word '*Visszahívható*' display a telephone number, so you can be phoned back.

TOURIST INFORMATION

The HNTO has a chain of 120 **Tourinform** (☎ hotline 30 30 30 600; www.tourinform.hu, www.hungary.com) information offices across the country and is represented in 19 countries abroad. These are the best places to ask general questions and pick up brochures. The HNTO also operates a Tourinform hotline in Hungarian, English and German.

EMERGENCY NUMBERS

- General emergency ☎ 112 (English spoken)
- Police ☎ 107
- Fire ☎ 105
- Ambulance ☎ 104
- English-language crime hotline ☎ 1-438 8000
- Car assistance (24 hours) ☎ 188

If your query is about private rooms, flights or international train travel, you may have to ask a commercial travel agency; most towns have at least a couple. The oldest, Ibusz, is arguably the best for private accommodation.

VISAS

To enter Hungary, everyone needs a valid passport, or for citizens of the European Union, a national identification card. Citizens of virtually all European countries, the USA, Canada, Israel, Japan, New Zealand and Australia do not require visas to visit Hungary for stays of up to 90 days within a six-month period. UK citizens do not need a visa for a stay of up to six months. South Africans, however, do require a visa. Check with the **Ministry of Foreign Affairs** (☎ 1-458 1000; www.kum .hu) for an up-to-date list of which country nationals require visas.

Visas are issued at Hungarian consulates or missions, most international highway border crossings, Ferihegy airport and the International Ferry Pier in Budapest. However, visas are never issued on trains and rarely on buses.

WOMEN TRAVELLERS

Some Hungarian men can be very sexist in their thinking, but they are also big on being polite, so women do not suffer any particular form of harassment.

For assistance and/or information ring the **Women's Line** (Nővonal; ☎ 06 80 505 101) or **Women for Women against Violence** (NANE; ☎ 1-267 4900), which operates from 6pm to 10pm daily.

WORK

Working legally in Hungary always involved a Byzantine paper chase and it looks like it will get harder given EU membership requirements. The government has announced it will crack down on illegal workers. No-one thinks they're going to target English teachers, but the work situation for foreigners *is* in a state of flux.

TRANSPORT IN HUNGARY

GETTING THERE & AWAY
Air

From Budapest's Ferihegy 2 airport you can reach destinations in Eastern and Western Europe, the UK, Russia and connect to places beyond. Malév is the Hungarian national airline. Low-cost airlines fly from Ferihegy 1 to off-market airports in Western Europe, such as London Stansted.

Vienna's Schwechart airport is only about three hours from Budapest by bus, less to western Hungary, and often has less expensive international airfares since it handles more traffic.

Aeroflot (code SU; ☎ 318 5955; www.aeroflot.com) Flights to Russia.

Austrian Airlines (code OS; ☎ 327 9080; www.aua.com) Less than an hour's flight to Vienna.

ČSA (code OK; ☎ 318 3175; www.czech-airlines.com) At least three flights daily to/from Prague.

Lot Polish Airlines (code LO; ☎ 266 4772; www.lot.com) Budapest direct to Warsaw and connecting to other Polish and Russian cities.

Malév Hungarian Airlines (code MA; ☎ 235 3888; www.malev.hu) Flights to Vienna, Kyiv and Odesa in Ukraine, Timişoara in Romania, Split and Dubrovnik in Croatia, Varna and Sofia in Bulgaria, Prague in the Czech Republic, Kraków and Warsaw in Poland, and Moscow in Russia.

Sky Europe (code NE; ☎ 777 7000) A low-cost airline that flies daily to Warsaw and three days a week to Split and Dubrovnik.

Tarom Romanian Air Transport (code RO; ☎ 235 0809; www.tarom.ro) Direct flights to and from Bucharest.

Land

Hungary has excellent land transport connections with its neighbours. Most of the departures listed are from Budapest, though other cities and towns closer to the various borders can also be used as springboards.

BICYCLE & WALKING

Cyclists may have a problem crossing at Hungarian border stations since bicycles are banned on motorways and national highways with single-digit route numbers.

If you're heading north, there are three crossings to and from Slovakia where you should not have any problems. Bridges link Esztergom with Štúrovo and Komárom with Komárno. At Sátoraljaújhely, northeast of Miskolc, there's a highway border crossing over the Ronyva River that links the centre of town with Slovenské Nové Mesto.

BUS

Most international buses arrive at the Népliget bus station (p315) in Budapest. **Eurolines** (☎ 1-219 8080; www.eurolines.com), in conjunction with its Hungarian affiliate, **Volánbusz** (☎ 1-219 8080; www.volanbusz.hu), is the international bus company of Hungary. There's a 10% youth discount for those under 26. Useful international buses include those from Budapest to Vienna city centre (5490Ft, 3½ hours, four daily), Bratislava, Slovakia (Pozsony; 4400Ft, four hours, one daily), Subotica in Serbia (Szabatka; 3300Ft, four hours, daily), Rijeka in Croatia (7900Ft, 10 hours, one weekly), Prague in the Czech Republic (9500Ft, eight hours, five weekly), and Sofia in Bulgaria (12,500Ft, 15 hours, four weekly).

Four buses a day (7.30am, 11.15am, 5.15pm and 7.15pm) run from Vienna International Airport in Austria to the Népliget bus station in Budapest (€28). **Mitch's Tours** (☎ 06 70 588 306; www.mitchstours.com; adult/student €32/29) runs a shuttle-bus service between Deák tér or several hostels in the Budapest area and the airport or hostels in Vienna (departs Vienna 8.30am, departs Budapest 1.30pm).

CAR & MOTORCYCLE

Border controls between Hungary and her EU neighbours (as of 1 May, 2004), Slovakia and Austria, were not scheduled to be removed at the time of research, but there will be no more customs checks at these points. Third-party insurance is compulsory for driving in Hungary. If your car is registered in the EU, it's assumed you have it. Other motorists must show a Green Card or buy insurance at the border.

HITCHING

In Hungary, hitchhiking is legal except on motorways. Hitchhiking is never an entirely safe way to travel and we don't recommend it, but if you're willing, **Kenguru** (Map p304; ☎ 1-266 5837; www.kenguru.hu; VIII Kőfaragó utca 15, Budapest; ☉ 8am-6pm Mon-Fri, 10am-4pm Sat) is an agency that matches riders with drivers. Hitch a ride to Amsterdam (11,000Ft), Munich (5500Ft) or Paris (11,700Ft), among other destinations.

TRAIN

The Hungarian State Railways, **MÁV** (☎ international information 1-461 5500; www.elvira.hu Hungarian only, www.mav.hu) links up with international rail networks in all directions and its schedule is available online. MÁV sells Inter-Rail passes to European nationals (or residents of at least six months). Hungary is in Zone D along with the Czech Republic, Slovakia, Poland and Croatia. The price for any one zone is €226/158/113 for adult/youth (12-26)/child (four-12). There are big discounts on return fares only between Hungary and former communist countries: up to 65% to Slovakia, Slovenia and Croatia; 70%

to Romania; 40% to Serbia; 40% to the Czech Republic and Poland; and 50% to Ukraine, Bulgaria, Belarus and Russia. For tickets to Western Europe you'll pay the same as everywhere else unless you're aged under 26 and qualify for the 30% to 50% BIJ discount. For tickets or more information about passes and discounts, ask at the MÁV Ticket Office (p315) in Budapest.

Eurail passes are valid, but not sold, in Hungary. EuroCity (EC) and Intercity (IC) trains require a seat reservation and payment of a supplement. Most larger train stations in Hungary have left-luggage rooms open at least 9am to 5pm. There are three main train stations in Budapest, so always note the station when checking a schedule online; for more information see p315.

Some direct connections from Budapest to neighbouring countries include Vienna (6600Ft, 3½ hours, five daily); Bratislava, Slovakia (Pozsony; 5600Ft, 2½ hours, eight daily); Arad (7400Ft, 4½ hours, six daily) and Bucharest, Romania (18,600Ft, 13 to 15 hours, five daily); Csop (7600Ft, 4½ hours, two daily) and Kyiv, Ukraine (18,400Ft, 24 hours, one daily), continuing to Moscow (25,400Ft, 37 hours, one daily); Zagreb, Croatia (9000Ft, 5½ to 7½ hours, three daily); Belgrade, Serbia (9400Ft, seven hours, two daily); Ljubljana, Slovenia (13,700Ft, 8½ hours, three daily).

Other direct train destinations in Eastern Europe include Prague, Czech Republic (14,850Ft, nine hours, two daily); Kraków, Poland (13,500Ft, 10½ hours, one daily); Sofia, Bulgaria (18,200Ft, 18 to 26 hours, two daily). Fares listed are for second-class tickets without seat reservation; first-class tickets are usually 50% more. For information on international destinations outside Eastern Europe, see the main Transport chapter of this book (p596).

River

There's an international Mahart PassNave hydrofoil service on the Danube daily from April to early November between Budapest and Vienna (5½ hours), stopping in Bratislava (four hours). Adult one-way/return fares for Vienna are €75/99, for Bratislava €69/93. Students with ISIC cards pay €59/84. Boats leave from the Nemzetközi hajóállomás (International Ferry Pier), next to the **Mahart PassNave Ticket Office** (Map p304; ☎ 484 4013; www .mahartpassnave.hu; Belgrád rakpart). The ticket office in Vienna is **Mahart PassNave Wien** (☎ 01-72 92 161; Handelskai 265).

GETTING AROUND

Air

Hungary does not have any scheduled internal flights.

Bicycle

Hungary now counts 2500km of dedicated bicycle lanes around the country, with more on the way. For information and advice, contact the helpful **Hungarian Bicycle Touring Association** (MKTSZ; Map p304; ☎ 1-311 2467; mktsz@enternet.hu; VI Bajcsy-Zsilinszky út 31) in Budapest.

Boat

In summer there are regular passenger ferries on Lake Balaton and on the Danube from Budapest to Szentendre, Visegrád and Esztergom. Details of the schedules are given in the relevant destination sections.

Bus

Domestic buses, run by **Volánbusz** (☎ 1 219 8080; www.volanbusz.hu) cover an extensive nationwide network. The buses are generally relatively new, and everybody and their grandmother takes them, so they are safe. Bus fares average 1270Ft per 100km.

Timetables are posted at stations and stops. Some footnotes you could come across include *naponta* (daily), *hétköznap* (weekdays), *munkanapokon* (on work days), *munkaszüneti napok kivételével naponta* (daily except holidays), and *szabad és munkaszüneti napokon* (on Saturday and holidays). A few large bus stations have luggage rooms, or a bathroom attendant who you pay to watch your bags, but these generally close by 6pm.

Car & Motorcycle

Limited access Motorways (M1, M3, M7) require toll passes (10-day, 2000Ft) that can be purchased at petrol stations and at some motorway entrances. Check with your rental company; the car may already have an annual pass.

Many cities and towns require that you 'pay and display' when parking. The cost averages about 100Ft an hour in the countryside, and up to 180Ft on central Budapest streets.

AUTOMOBILE ASSOCIATIONS

The so-called 'Yellow Angels' of the Hungarian Automobile Club do basic breakdown repairs for free if you belong to an affiliated organisation such as AAA in the USA or AA in the UK. You can telephone 24 hours a day on ☎ 188 nationwide.

DRIVING LICENCE

Your normal, home country driving licence is sufficient for driving in Hungary.

FUEL & SPARE PARTS

Unleaded *(ólommentes)* petrol *(benzin)* in 95 and 98 octane is available all over the country and costs from 285 per litre, respectively. Most stations also have diesel fuel *(gázolaj)* costing around 240Ft per litre. You can pay by credit card. The Hungarian Automobile Club can assist with repairs.

HIRE

In general, you must be at least 21 years old and have had your licence for at least a year to rent a car. Drivers under 25 often have to pay a surcharge.

INSURANCE

Third-party insurance is compulsory. If your car is registered in the EU, it's assumed you have it. Other motorists must show a Green Card or buy insurance at the border. Rental cars come with Green Cards.

ROAD RULES

The most important rule to remember is that there's a 100% ban on alcohol when you are driving, and this rule is *very* strictly enforced. (Police even stalk the parking lots of expensive, outlying restaurants.) Do not think you will get away with one glass of wine at lunch; if caught with 0.001% alcohol in your blood, you will be fined up to 30,000Ft. If your blood alcohol level is high, you will be arrested and your licence taken away.

Using a mobile phone while driving is prohibited in Hungary. *All* vehicles must have their headlights switched on throughout the day outside built-up areas. Motorcyclists must have their headlights on at all times.

Local Transport

Public transport is efficient and extensive, with city bus and, in many towns, trolleybus services. Budapest and Szeged also have trams, and there's an extensive metro (underground or subway) and a suburban commuter railway in Budapest. Purchase tickets at newsstands before travelling and validate them once aboard. Inspectors do check tickets, especially on the metros in Budapest.

Train

MÁV (☎ domestic information 1-461 5400; www.elvira.hu Hungarian only, www.mav.hu) operates reliable train services on its 8000km of tracks. Schedules are available online and computer information kiosks are popping up at rail stations around the country. Second-class domestic train fares are 824Ft per 100km, 1st-class fares are usually 50% more. IC trains are express trains, the most comfortable and the newest. *Gyorsvonat* (fast trains) take longer and use older cars; s*zemélyvonat* (passenger trains) stop at every village along the way. Seat reservations *(helyjegy)* cost extra and are required on IC and some fast trains; these are indicated on the timetable by an 'R' in a box or a circle. (A plain 'R' means seat reservations are available.)

In all stations a yellow board indicates departures *(indul)* and a white board arrivals *(érkezik)*. Express and fast trains are indicated in red, local trains in black. In some stations, large black-and-white schedules are plastered all over the walls. To locate the timetable you need, first find the posted railway map of the country, which indexes the route numbers at the top of the schedules.

Most train stations have left-luggage offices that are open at least from 9am to 5pm.

You might consider purchasing a Hungarian Rail Pass before entering the country. The cost is US$76 for five days of 1st-class travel within 15 days and US$95 for 10 days within a month. You would, however, need to use it a lot to get your money's worth.

HUNGARY

Liechtenstein

It's true, Liechtenstein makes a fabulous wine-and-cheese-hour trivia subject – *Did you know it was the sixth smallest country?… It's still governed by an iron-willed monarch who lives in a Gothic castle on a hill… Yes, it really is the world's largest producer of dentures…* But if you're visiting this pocket-sized principality solely for the cocktail-party bragging rights, keep the operation covert. This theme-park micronation takes its independence seriously and would shudder at the thought of being considered for novelty value alone. Liechtenstein would rather be remembered for its stunning natural beauty. Measuring just 25km in length and 6km in width, the country is barely larger than Manhattan. And though it might not look like much on a map, up close it's filled with numerous hiking and cycling trails offering spectacular views of craggy cliffs, quaint villages, friendly locals and lush green forests.

FAST FACTS

- **Area** 150 sq km
- **Capital** Vaduz
- **Currency** Swiss franc (Sfr); A$1 = Sfr0.95; €1 = Sfr1.58; ¥100 = Sfr1.07; NZ$1 = Sfr0.75; UK£1 = Sfr2.34; US$1 = Sfr1.23
- **Famous for** sending postcards stamped by the country's postal service, dentures
- **Official Language** German
- **Phrases** *gruezi* (hello, good day), *merci vielmal* (thank you very much), *adieu* (goodbye), *sprechen sie Englisch?* (do you speak English?)
- **Population** 32,860
- **Telephone Codes** country code ☎ 423; international access code ☎ 00

HIGHLIGHTS

- Snap a picture of the royal castle with its stunning mountain backdrop in **Vaduz** (opposite).
- Get a souvenir **passport stamp** (opposite) and send a postcard home.
- Hit the slopes at **Malbun** (p359) to brag you've skied the Liechtenstein Alps.
- Test yourself with extreme hiking along the legendary **Fürstensteig trail** (p359).

CLIMATE & WHEN TO GO

Visit Liechtenstein from December to April for skiing, and May to October for sightseeing and hiking. Alpine resorts all but close down in late April, May and November.

HISTORY

A merger of the domain of Schellenberg and the county of Vaduz in 1712 by the powerful Liechtenstein family created the country. A principality under the Holy Roman Empire from the period 1719 to 1806, Liechtenstein finally achieved its full sovereign independence in 1866. A modern constitution was drawn up back in 1921, but even today the prince retains the power to dissolve parliament and must approve every act before it becomes law. Prince Franz Josef II was the first ruler to live in the castle above the capital city of Vaduz. He died in 1989 and was succeeded by his son, Prince Hans-Adam II.

Liechtenstein has no military service and its minuscule army (80 men!) was disbanded in 1868. It is best known for wine production, postage stamps, dentures (an important export) and its status as a tax haven. In 2000, Liechtenstein's financial and political institutions were rocked by allegations that money laundering was rife in the country. In response to international outrage, banks agreed to stop allowing customers to bank money anonymously. However, it remains under pressure to introduce more reforms.

In 2003 Hans-Adam demanded sweeping powers to dismiss the elected government, appoint judges and reject proposed laws. Opponents warned of dictatorship, but the prince threatened to stomp off back to Austria if he did not get his way, and the population – possibly worried what an empty Schloss Vaduz would do to tourism – backed him in a referendum. The following year Hans-Adam handed the day-to-day running of the country to his son Alois, although he remains head of state.

HOW MUCH?

- **Hotel bed** Sfr40-60
- **Postage stamp** Sfr1.80
- **Souvenir passport stamp** Sfr2
- **Local phone call** Sfr0.60
- **Cup of coffee** Sfr3.60

LONELY PLANET INDEX

- **1L petrol** Sfr1.75
- **1L water** Sfr2
- **500mL beer** Sfr4
- **Souvenir T-shirt** Sfr20
- **Kebab** Sfr8

LIECHTENSTEIN

IT'S LIECHTENSTEIN TRIVIA TIME

▪ If you ever meet the prince in the pub, make sure he buys a round. The royal family is estimated to be worth UK£3.3 billion.

▪ There are 8000 companies registered in the principality – that's nearly double the population of Vaduz.

▪ Liechtenstein bites into a large chunk of the false teeth market – it's the world's largest exporter of the product.

▪ Liechtenstein is the only country in the world named after the people who purchased it.

▪ In its last military engagement in 1866, none of its 80 soldiers was killed. In fact, 81 returned, including a new Italian 'friend'. The army was disbanded soon afterwards.

▪ Until 2005, when worries came to a head about the drug TCH, Liechtenstein's cows were fed hemp to keep them chilled and producing 'better' milk.

FOOD & DRINK

Liechtenstein's cuisine borrows from its larger neighbours, and it is generally good quality but expensive. Basic restaurants provide simple but well-cooked food, although budget travellers may want to live out of the supermarket fridge. Soups are popular and usually very filling, and cheeses form an important part of the diet, as do *Rösti* (fried shredded potatoes) and Wurst.

VADUZ

pop 4930

Vaduz is the kind of capital city where the butcher knows the baker – with tidy, quiet streets, lively patio cafés and a big Gothic-looking castle on a hill, it feels more like a village than anything else. It's also all most visitors to Liechtenstein see and at times it can feel like its soul has been sold to cater to the whims of tourist hordes alighting for 17 minutes on guided bus tours. Souvenir shops, tax-free luxury goods stores and cube-shaped concrete buildings dominate the small, somewhat bland town centre enclosed by Äulestrasse and the pedestrian-only Städtle.

INFORMATION

Liechtenstein Tourism (☎ 239 63 00; www.tourism us.li; Städtle 37; ⏰ 9am-noon & 1.30-5pm daily May-Oct, 9am-noon & 1.30-5pm Mon-Fri Nov-Apr) Offers souvenir passport stamps for Sfr2, plus all the usual assistance.

Main post office (Äulestrasse 38; ⏰ 7.45am-6pm Mon-Fri, 8am-11am Sat)

Telecom FL Shop (☎ 237 74 00; Austrasse 77; ⏰ 9am-noon & 1.30-6.30pm Mon-Fri, 9am-1pm Sat) Free Internet access.

SIGHTS & ACTIVITIES

Although the **Schloss Vaduz** (Vaduz Castle) is not open to the public, the exterior graces many a photograph and it is worth climbing up the hill for a closer look. At the top, there's a magnificent vista of Vaduz with a spectacular backdrop of the mountains. There's also a network of marked walking trails along the ridge. For a peek inside the castle grounds, arrive on 15 August (Liechtenstein's national day), when there are magnificent fireworks and the prince invites all 32,860 Liechtensteiners over to his place for a glass of wine or beer.

In the centre, the well-designed **Liechtensteinisches Landesmuseum** (National Museum; ☎ 239 68 20; www.landesmuseum.li; Städtle 43; adult/concession Sfr8/5; ⏰ 10am-5pm Tue-Sun, to 8pm Wed) provides a surprisingly interesting romp through the principality's history, from medieval witch-trials and burnings to the manufacture of false teeth.

Keen philatelists will lick their lips in anticipation of the **Briefmarkenmuseum** (Postage Stamp Museum; ☎ 236 61 05; Städtle 37; admission free; ⏰ 10am-noon & 1-5pm), where national stamps issued since 1912 are on display.

The national art collection is housed in a sleek modern building at the **Kunstmuseum Liechtenstein** (☎ 235 030 00; Städtle 32; www.kunst museum.li; adult/student & child Sfr8/5; ⏰ 10am-5pm Tue-Sun, to 8pm Thu). Sixteenth- to 18th-century works from the prince's private collection are among the highlights.

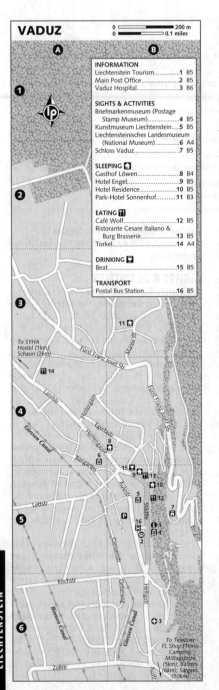

VADUZ

0 _____ 200 m
0 _____ 0.1 miles

INFORMATION
Liechtenstein Tourism...............1 B5
Main Post Office......................2 B5
Vaduz Hospital........................3 B6

SIGHTS & ACTIVITIES
Briefmarkenmuseum (Postage
    Stamp Museum).................4 B5
Kunstmuseum Liechtenstein....5 B5
Liechtensteinisches Landesmuseum
    (National Museum).............6 A4
Schloss Vaduz........................7 B5

SLEEPING
Gasthof Löwen.......................8 B4
Hotel Engel............................9 B5
Hotel Residence....................10 B5
Park-Hotel Sonnenhof...........11 B3

EATING
Café Wolf..............................12 B5
Ristorante Cesare Italiano &
    Burg Brasserie..................13 B5
Torkel..................................14 A4

DRINKING
Beat....................................15 B5

TRANSPORT
Postal Bus Station.................16 B5

SLEEPING

Ask the tourist office for a list of private rooms and chalets outside Vaduz.

Camping Mittagspitze (☎ 392 36 77, 392 23 11; camp sites per adult/child/car Sfr8.50/4.50/4, tent Sfr8; 🛁) A well-equipped camping ground in a leafy spot with a restaurant, TV lounge, playground and kiosk. It's outside Vaduz, just south of Triesen.

SYHA hostel (☎ 232 50 22; www.youthhostel.ch /schaan; Untere Rütigasse 6; dm/d Sfr30.50/82; 🕑 mid-Mar–Oct, 🕑 reception closed 10am-5pm) Renovated a few years ago, this hostel caters particularly to cyclists and families. Halfway between Schaan and Vaduz, it's within easy walking distance of either.

Hotel Engel (☎ 236 17 17; www.hotelengel.li; Städtle 13; s/d from Sfr110/165; Ⓟ ☒ ⅏ 🖳) Rooms are modern but feel soulless at this remodelled hotel. There's an Asian restaurant (Thai and Chinese) wafting tempting aromas through the hallways, and the bonus for laptop owners is free Internet in all the rooms.

Hotel Residence (☎ 239 20 20; www.residence.li; Städtle 23; s/d from Sfr195/260; Ⓟ ☒ 🖳) It's cool to see a four-star hotel doubling as a local art gallery, which is exactly what Vaduz's newest hotel does (everything on the walls is for sale). Rooms are modern, made up with lots of seagrass and muted colour schemes.

Gasthof Löwen (☎ 232 00 66; www.hotel-loewen .li; Herrengasse 35; s/d from Sfr210/265; Ⓟ) Antique furniture lends added appeal to the eight elegant and spacious rooms inside this 600-year-old guesthouse. A cosy bar, fine-dining restaurant and rear outdoor terrace, overlooking grapevines and up at the castle, are extra perks.

Park-Hotel Sonnenhof (☎ 239 02 02; www.sonnen hof.li; Mareestrasse 29; s/d from Sfr250/320; 🕑 closed Christmas-New Year; Ⓟ ⅏ 🛁) The rooms at this small luxury hotel are tip top, while the hillside views, solarium, ornate restaurant, cobbled courtyards, tinkling fountains and manicured gardens all create a privileged atmosphere.

EATING & DRINKING

Pedestrian-only Städtle street has a clutch of footpath restaurants and cafés.

Beat (☎ 236 84 84; Städtle 3; mains Sfr10-35) This spot has linen tablecloths, with a candle-lit restaurant in front and a slick bar with a lounge feel and flat-screen TVs in the back. DJs spin at night. The menu is loaded with soups, salads, pasta and plenty of Swiss-German fare.

Ristorante Cesare Italiano & Burg Brasserie (☎ 232 23 83; Städtle 15; mains Sfr15-30) Chow on pizza, burgers and salads at the downstairs café with a Parisian vibe, complete with red walls and brass fixtures. Upstairs there's a fancier Italian menu. With loads of ice-cream sundaes it's a good spot for the kids.

Torkel (☎ 232 44 10; Hintergasse 9; mains Sfr40-60) Just above the prince's vineyards is his majesty's ivy-clad restaurant. The garden terrace enjoys a wonderful perspective of the castle above, while the ancient, wood-lined interior is cosy in winter. The chef mixes classic with modern and has a couple of unusual veggie options.

AROUND VADUZ

Outside Vaduz the air is crisp and clear with a pungent, sweet aroma of cow dung and flowers. The countryside, dotted with tranquil villages and enticing churches set to a craggy Alps backdrop, is about as idyllic and relaxing as it gets.

Triesenberg, on a terrace above Vaduz, commands excellent views over the Rhine valley. It has a pretty onion-domed church and the **Heimatmuseum** (☎ 262 19 26; adult/student Sfr2/1; ⏱ 1.30-5.30pm Tue-Sat) devoted to the Walser community, whose members came from Switzerland's Valais to settle in the 13th century.

There are 400km of **hiking trails** through Liechtenstein, along with loads of well-marked **cycling routes** (look for signs with a biking symbol; distances and directions will also be included). The most famous hiking trail is the **Fürstensteig**, a rite of pas-

sage for nearly every Liechtensteiner. You must be fit and not suffer from vertigo, as in places the path is narrow, reinforced with rope handholds and/or falls away to a sheer drop. The hike, which takes up to four hours, begins at the **Berggasthaus Gaflei** (bus 30 from Triesenberg). Travel light and wear good shoes.

MALBUN
pop 100
Nestled amid the mountains in the southeast is tiny Malbun, Liechtenstein's one and only ski resort.

The road from Vaduz terminates at Malbun. There is an ATM by the lower bus stop. The **tourist office** (☎ 263 65 77; www.malbun.li; ⏱ 9am-noon & 1.30-5pm Mon-Sat, closed mid-Apr–May & Nov–mid-Dec) is on the main street, not far from Hotel Walserhof.

Although rather limited in scope – the runs are mostly novice and intermediate – the skiing is inexpensive for this part of the world and it does offer some bragging rights.

The resort has ski and snowboard schools. A one-day/-week ski pass costs Sfr37/165 for adults and Sfr31/137 for students under 28. Skis, shoes and poles cost Sfr44 for a day, and can be hired from the **sports shop** (☎ 263 37 55) in town. A chairlift at the resort operates in the summer (one way/return Sfr8/12), so you can ride up and hike down.

Hotel Gorfion-Malbun (☎ 264 18 83; www.s-hotels.com; s/d from Sfr100/160; P X 🖥 🔄) is Malbun's most spacious and upmarket hotel. It caters brilliantly to children.

LIECHTENSTEIN DIRECTORY

Liechtenstein and Switzerland share almost everything, so for more information about Liechtenstein basics check out p574.

EMERGENCY NUMBERS

The same emergency numbers apply as in Switzerland:

▪ Ambulance ☎ 144
▪ Fire ☎ 118
▪ Police ☎ 117

TRANSPORT IN LIECHTENSTEIN

GETTING THERE & AWAY

The nearest airports are Friedrichshafen (Germany) and Zürich, with train connections to the Swiss border towns of Buchs (via Romanshorn) and Sargans. From each of these towns, there are usually three buses to Vaduz (Sfr2.40/3.60 from Buchs/Sargans, Swiss Pass valid). Buses run every 30 minutes from the Austrian border town of Feldkirch; you might have to change at Schaan to reach Vaduz.

A few local Buchs–Feldkirch trains stop at Schaan (bus tickets are valid).

By road, Rte 16 from Switzerland passes through Liechtenstein via Schaan; it terminates at Feldkirch. The N13 follows the Rhine along the Swiss–Liechtenstein border.

GETTING AROUND

Postbus travel within Liechtenstein is cheap and reliable; all fares cost Sfr2.40 or Sfr3.60, with the higher rate for journeys exceeding 13km (such as Vaduz to Malbun). Grab a timetable from the Vaduz tourist office.

Poland

A flat, fertile nation in the centre of Europe, often surrounded by conquest-happy empires, can expect life to be turbulent at times. And that's been the experience of Poland, as it's grappled with centuries of war, invasion and foreign occupation. Nothing, however, has succeeded in suppressing the Poles' strong sense of nationhood and cultural identity, as exemplified by the ancient royal capital of Kraków, with its breathtaking castle, and bustling Warsaw, with its painstaking postwar reconstruction of its devastated Old Town.

Although early euphoria at joining the EU has subsided into a more realistic expectation of membership, there's a distinct sense of confidence and optimism in the big cities, and among young people in particular. As a result, regional centres such as urbane Gdańsk, cultured Wrocław and lively Poznań exude a cosmopolitan energy that's a heady mix of old and new.

Away from the cities, Poland is a diverse land, from its northern sandy beaches and magnificent southern mountains to the lost-in-time forests of the east. And everywhere there are seldom-visited towns to discover, with their own ruined castles, picturesque squares and historic churches.

Poland is still good value for travellers and has a transport system that makes it easy to get around. As Poland continues to reconcile its rediscovered European identity with its hard-won political and cultural freedoms, it's a fascinating time to visit this beautiful country.

FAST FACTS

- **Area** 312, 685 sq km
- **Capital** Warsaw
- **Currency** złoty; €1=3.98zł; US$1=3.13zł; UK£1=5.92zł; A$1=2.35zł; C$1 = 2.81zł; Ą100=2.68zł; NZ$1=2.06zł
- **Famous for** Chopin, Copernicus, Marie Curie, Solidarity, vodka
- **Official Language** Polish
- **Phrases** *dzień dobry* (good morning/afternoon), *dziękuję* (thank you), *proszę* (please), *Gdzie jest dworzec autobusowy/kolejowy?* (Where's the bus/train station?)
- **Population** 38 million
- **Telephone Codes** country code ☎ 48; international access code ☎ 00
- **Visas** not required for EU citizens; US, Canadian, New Zealand and Australian citizens do not need visas for stays of less than 90 days

POLAND

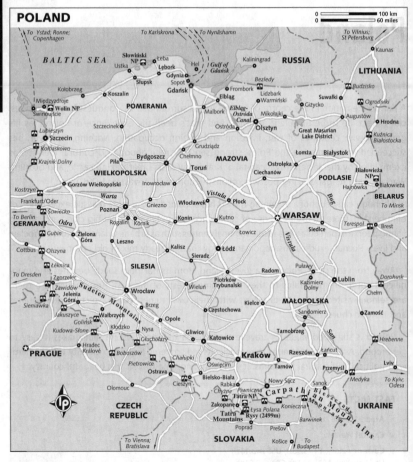

POLAND

HIGHLIGHTS

- Experience the beauty and history of Kraków's **Wawel Castle** (p389)
- Meet European bison and other magnificent fauna at **Białowieża National Park** (p387)
- Soak up the cosmopolitan vibe of **Gdańsk** (p425) and take a dip in the Baltic at nearby **Sopot** (p430)
- Enjoy the skiing or hiking life of the **Tatra Mountains** (p402)
- Discover Warsaw's tragic wartime history at the **Warsaw Rising Museum** (p381)

ITINERARIES

- **One Week** Spend a day exploring Warsaw with a stroll round the Old Town and a

stop at the Warsaw Rising Museum. The next day, head to Kraków for three days, visiting the Old Town, Wawel Castle, the former Jewish district of Kazimierz, and Wieliczka. Take a day trip to Oświęcim, then head on to Zakopane for two days.
- **Two Weeks** Follow the above itinerary, then on the eighth day travel to Wrocław for two days. Progress north to Toruń for a day, then onward to Gdańsk for two days, exploring the Old Town and visiting Westerplatte. Wind down with a couple of days at the seaside in Sopot.

CLIMATE & WHEN TO GO

Poland's weather can be unpredictable. Summer is usually warm and sunny, with July the hottest month, but it's also the season with the highest rainfall. Spring and autumn are pleasantly warm but can also be wet. Snow can fall anywhere in Poland between December and March, lingering until April or even May in the mountains.

The tourist season runs roughly from May to September, peaking in July and August. Many Polish families go on holidays during these two months, so transport is crowded and accommodation limited. Most theatres and concert halls are also closed at this time. From midautumn to midspring, outdoor activities are less prominent and many camping grounds and youth hostels are closed. See the climate charts on p586, for more information.

HISTORY

Poland's history started with the Polanians (People of the Plains). During the early Middle Ages, these Western Slavs moved into the flatlands between the Vistula and Odra Rivers. Mieszko I, Duke of the Polanians, adopted Christianity in 966 and embarked on a campaign of conquest. A papal edict in 1025 led to Mieszko's son Bolesław Chrobry (Boleslaus the Brave) being crowned Poland's first king.

Poland's early success proved fragile, and encroachment from Germanic peoples led to the relocation of the royal capital from Poznań

to Kraków in 1038. More trouble loomed in 1226 when the Prince of Mazovia invited the Teutonic Knights to help convert the pagan tribes of the north. These Germanic crusaders used the opportunity to create their own state along the Baltic coast. The south had its own invaders to contend with, and Kraków was attacked by Tatars twice in the mid-13th century.

The kingdom prospered under Kazimierz III 'the Great' (1333–1370). During this period of rebirth, many new towns sprang up, while Kraków blossomed into one of Europe's leading cultural centres.

When the daughter of Kazimierz's nephew married the Grand Duke of Lithuania, Jagiełło, Poland and Lithuania were united as the largest state in Europe, stretching from the Baltic to the Black Sea.

The Renaissance was introduced to Poland by the enlightened King Zygmunt during the 16th century, as he lavishly patronised the arts and sciences. By asserting that the Earth travelled around the sun, Nicolaus Copernicus revolutionised the field of astronomy in 1543.

The 18th century was a period of disaster and decline for Poland. First it was subject to Swedish and Russian invasions, and at century's end it faced partition by surrounding empires. In 1773 Russia, Prussia and Austria seized Polish territory in the First Partition; by the time the Third Partition was completed in 1795, Poland had vanished from the map of Europe.

Although the country remained divided through the entire 19th century, Poles steadfastly maintained their culture. Finally, upon the end of WWI the old imperial powers dissolved, and a sovereign Polish state was restored. Very soon, however, Poland was again at war. Under the command of Marshal Jozef Piłsudski, Poland defended its eastern territories from long-time enemy Russia, now transformed into the Soviet Union and determined to spread its revolution westward. After two years of impressive fighting by the outnumbered Poles, an armistice was signed, retaining Vilnius and Lviv within Poland.

Though Polish institutions and national identity flourished during the interwar period, disaster soon struck again. On 1 September 1939, a Nazi blitzkrieg rained down from the west; soon after, the Soviets invaded

---

HOW MUCH?

- **Night in a hostel** 45zł

- **Night in a midrange double room** 200zł

- **Three-course restaurant meal for two** 120zł

- **Postcard** 1zł

- **Postage stamp** 3zł

LONELY PLANET INDEX

- **Litre of petrol** 3.75zł

- **Litre of water** 2zł

- **Beer** 5-7zł

- **Souvenir T-shirt** 35zł

- **Street snack** (*zapiekanka*, a toasted roll with cheese, mushrooms and tomato sauce) 2-5zł

POLAND

TOP FIVE REMNANTS OF COMMUNISM

It's been less than two decades since the end of communist rule in Poland, but evidence of the era is fading fast. If you want to delve into the days of the Eastern Bloc, check out these remains.

- Nowa Huta – Everyone visits Kraków for its medieval splendour, but there's another side to the former royal capital that few tourists see. Catch a tram to the eastern suburb of Nowa Huta for a glimpse of the planned 'workers' paradise' district, built in the 1950s to counter the influence of the city's religious and intellectual elite.

- Stadion Dziesięciolecia – Just over the river from central Warsaw is the 10th Anniversary Stadium, constructed in the 1950s from the rubble of buildings destroyed in WWII. Initially the jewel in communist Poland's sporting crown, it was abandoned as a sporting venue in the 1980s, and now houses a huge open-air market.

- Warszawa Centralna – Opened by communist bigwigs in 1975, Warsaw's massive main train station was seen as a triumph of modern socialism over the inefficient structures of the past. However, current opinion is mixed. Many travellers have experienced the disorientating sensation of traversing its labyrinthine corridors, and Poles have pondered whether it should be torn down.

- Gdańsk Shipyards – Constructed after WWII, this sprawling industrial site north of Gdańsk's Old Town was originally known as the Lenin Shipyards. It hit the international headlines as the birthplace of the Solidarity trade union in 1980, and became the hub of the decade-long struggle to overthrow the communist system.

- Milk bars – The *bar mleczny* is a humble institution which survived the regime that founded it. Milk bars were conceived by the communist government as low-cost cafeterias for workers, serving basic vegetarian dishes. Nowadays they're a living reminder of the era, and a great place to find straightforward, unfussy Polish food.

Poland from the east, dividing the country with Germany. This agreement didn't last long, as Hitler soon transformed Poland into a staging ground for the Nazi invasion of the Soviet Union. Six million Polish inhabitants died during WWII (including the country's three million Jews), brutally annihilated in death camps. At the war's end, Poland's borders were redrawn yet again. The Soviet Union kept the eastern territories and extended the country's western boundary at the expense of Germany. These border changes were accompanied by the forced resettlement of more than a million Poles, Germans and Ukrainians.

Peacetime brought more repression. After WWII, Poland endured four decades of Soviet-dominated communist rule, punctuated by waves of protests, most notably the paralysing strikes of 1980–81, led by the Solidarity trade union. Finally, in the open elections of 1989, the communists fell from power and in 1990 Solidarity leader Lech Wałęsa became Poland's first democratically elected president.

The postcommunist transition brought radical changes, which induced new social hardships and political crises. But within a

decade Poland had built the foundations for a market economy, and reoriented its foreign relations towards the West. In March 1999, Poland was granted full NATO membership, and it joined the EU in May 2004.

Despite a strong economy, the nation swung to centre-right parties in the 2005 parliamentary elections, partly in reaction to continuing high unemployment, government spending cuts and corruption scandals. The new political tone was underlined a few weeks later by the presidential election victory of Lech Kaczyński, well known for his social conservatism.

PEOPLE

For centuries Poland was a multicultural country, home to large Jewish, German and Ukrainian communities. Its Jewish population was particularly large, and once numbered more than three million. However, after Nazi genocide and the forced resettlements that followed WWII, the Jewish population declined to 10,000 and Poland became an

(Continued on page 373)

RICHARD NEBESKY

Mitte nightlife (p180), Berlin, Germany

MARTIN MOOS

MARTIN MOOS

Mädlerpassage shopping arcade (p192), Leipzig, Germany

Sony Centre, Potsdamer Platz (p174), Berlin, Germany

King Ludwig II's Neuschwanstein Castle (p226), Füssen, Bavaria, Germany

DENNIS JOHNSON

One of Vienna's bars (p54), Austria

KunstHausWien art gallery (p49), Vienna, Austria

Grindelwald (p567), Jungfrau, Switzerland

WAYNE WALTON

Typical quaint village of Liechtenstein
(p355)

CHRIS MELLOR

Alpine town of Innsbruck (p77), Austria

The Fraumünster (p558) overlooking Limmat River,
Zürich, Switzerland

The Zeitglockenturm (p532), Bern,
Switzerland

JOHN MCLEAN

GLENN BEANLAND

Shadow of Church of St Bartholomew over the old town square, Plzeň (p130), Czech Republic

Velká Studená Valley, High Tatras (p467), Slovakia

Wooden churches (p450), Slovakia

Pravčická Brána, Bohemian Switzerland National Park (p126), Czech Republic

RICHARD NEBESKY

Skiing in the High Tatras (p467), Slovakia

Charles Bridge and Malá Strana bridge tower (p107), Prague, Czech Republic

RICHARD NEBESKY

ROBERTO SONCIN GER

Gellért Baths (p306), Budapest, Hungary

CHRISTER FREDRIKSSON

Hungarian cowboy, Kiskunság National Park (p339), Hungary

Ljubljana nightclub (p502), Slovenia

RICHARD I'ANSON

DAVID

Wine cellar, Szépasszony völgy (p343), Egar, Hungary

NEIL WILSON

Cathedral of St George (p516) overlooking the bay, Piran, Slovenia

GRANT DIXON

Hay-drying racks (p507), Bled, Slovenia

National Theatre, Pécs (p333), Hungary

MARTIN MOOS

Local bar (p396), Kraków's Old Town, Poland

Hikers taking a breather, Tatra Mountains (p402), Poland

Wawel Castle (p389), Kraków, Poland

(Continued from page 364)

ethnically homogeneous country, with some 98% of the population being ethnic Poles.

More than 60% of the citizens live in towns and cities. Warsaw is by far the largest urban settlement, followed by Łódź, Kraków, Wrocław, Poznań and Gdańsk. Upper Silesia (around Katowice) is the most densely inhabited area, while the northeastern border regions remain the least populated.

Between five and 10 million Poles live outside Poland. This émigré community, known as 'Polonia', is located mainly in the USA (particularly Chicago).

Poles are friendly and polite, but not overly formal. The way of life in large urban centres increasingly resembles Western styles and manners. In the countryside, however, a more conservative culture dominates, evidenced by traditional gender roles and strong family ties. In both urban and rural settings, many Poles are devoutly religious.

The Poles' sense of personal space may be a bit cosier than you are accustomed to – you may notice this trait when queuing for tickets or manoeuvring along city streets. When greeting each other, Polish men are passionate about shaking hands. Polish women often shake hands with men, but the man should always wait for the woman to extend her hand first.

RELIGION

Roman Catholicism is the dominant Christian denomination, adhered to by more than 80% of Poles. The Orthodox church's followers constitute about 1% of the population, mostly living along a narrow strip on the eastern frontier.

The election of Karol Wojtyła, the archbishop of Kraków, as Pope John Paul II in 1978, and his triumphal visit to his homeland a year later, significantly enhanced the status of the church in Poland. The country was proud of the late Pope: even now his image can be seen in public places and private homes throughout the country.

The overthrow of communism was as much a victory for the Church as it was for democracy. The fine line between the Church and the state is often blurred in Poland, and the Church is a powerful lobby on social issues. Some Poles have grown wary of the Church's increasing influence in society and politics, but Poland remains one of Europe's most religious countries, and packed churches are not uncommon.

ARTS

Literature

Poland has inherited a rich literary tradition dating from the 15th century, though its modern voice was shaped in the 19th century, during the long period of foreign occupation. It was a time for nationalist writers such as the poet Adam Mickiewicz (1798–1855), and Henryk Sienkiewicz (1846–1916), who won a Nobel prize in 1905 for *Quo Vadis?* This nationalist tradition was revived in the communist era when Czesław Miłosz was awarded a Nobel prize in 1980 for *The Captive Mind*.

At the turn of the 20th century, the avant-garde 'Young Poland' movement in art and literature developed in Kraków. The most notable representatives of this movement were the writer Stanisław Wyspiański (1869–1907), also famous for his stained-glass work; the playwright Stanisław Ignacy Witkiewicz (1885–1939), commonly known as Witkacy; and the Nobel laureate Władysław Reymont (1867–1925). In 1996, Wisława Szymborska (b 1923) also received a Nobel prize for her ironic poetry.

Music

The most famous Polish musician was undoubtedly Frédéric Chopin (1810–49), whose music displays the melancholy and nostalgia that became hallmarks of the national style. Stanisław Moniuszko (1819–72) injected a Polish flavour into 19th-century Italian opera music by introducing folk songs and dances to the stage. His *Halka* (1858), about a peasant girl abandoned by a young noble, is a staple of the national opera houses.

Visual Arts

Poland's most renowned painter was Jan Matejko (1838–93), whose monumental historical paintings hang in galleries throughout the country. Wojciech Kossak (1857–1942) is another artist who documented Polish history; he is best remembered for the colossal painting *Panorama of Racławicka,* on display in Wrocław (p412).

A long-standing Polish craft is the fashioning of jewellery from amber. Amber is a fossil resin of vegetable origin that comes primarily from the Baltic region, and appears in a variety of colours from pale yellow to reddish brown. The best places to buy it are Gdańsk, Kraków and Warsaw.

Polish poster art has received international recognition; the best selection of poster galleries is in Warsaw and Kraków.

Cinema

Poland has produced several world-famous film directors. The most notable is Andrzej Wajda, who received an Honorary Award at the 1999 Academy Awards. Western audiences are probably more familiar with the work of Roman Polański, who directed critically acclaimed films such as *Rosemary's Baby* and *Chinatown*. In 2002 Polański released the incredibly moving film *The Pianist,* which was filmed in Poland and set in the Warsaw Ghetto of WWII. The film went on to win three Oscars and the Cannes Palme d'Or. The late Krzysztof Kieślowski is best known for the trilogy *Three Colours Trilogy.*

ENVIRONMENT
The Land

Poland covers an area of 312,677 sq km, approximately as large as the UK and Ireland put together, and is bordered by seven states and one sea.

The northern edge of Poland meets the Baltic Sea. This broad, 524km-long coastline is spotted with sand dunes and seaside lakes. Also concentrated in the northeast are many postglacial lakes – more than any country in Europe except Finland.

The southern border is defined by the mountain ranges of the Sudetes and Carpathians. Poland's highest mountains are the rocky Tatras, a section of the Carpathian Range it shares with Slovakia. The highest peak of the Polish Tatras is Mt Rysy (2499m).

The area in between is a vast plain, sectioned by wide north-flowing rivers. Poland's longest river is the Vistula (Wisła), which winds 1047km from the Tatras to the Baltic.

Wildlife & National Parks

About 28% of Poland is covered by forest and, admirably, up to 130 sq km of new forest is planted each year. Some 60% of the forests are pine trees, but the share of deciduous species, such as oak, beech and birch, is increasing.

Poland's fauna includes hare, red deer, wild boar and, less abundantly, elk, brown bear and wildcat. European bison, which once inhabited Europe in large numbers, were brought to the brink of extinction early in the 20th century and a few hundred now live in Białowieża

National Park. The Great Masurian Lakes district attracts a vast array of bird life, such as storks and cormorants. The eagle, though rarely seen today, is Poland's national bird and appears on the Polish emblem.

Poland has 23 national parks, but they cover less than 1% of the country. No permit is necessary to visit these parks, but most have small admission fees. Camping in the parks is sometimes allowed, but only at specified sites. Poland also has a network of less strictly preserved areas called 'landscape parks'. About 105 of these parks, covering 6% of Poland, are scattered throughout the country.

FOOD & DRINK

The cheapest place to eat Polish food is a *bar mleczny* (milk bar), a no-frills, self-service cafeteria, popular with budget-conscious locals and backpackers alike. Up the scale, the number and variety of *restauracja* (restaurants) has ballooned in recent years, especially in the big cities. Pizzerias have also become phenomenally popular with Poles. And though Polish cuisine features plenty of meat, there are vegetarian restaurants to be found in most cities.

Menus usually have several sections: *zupy* (soups), *dania drugie* (main courses) and *dodatki* (accompaniments). The price of the main course may not include a side dish – such as potatoes, fries and salads – which you choose separately (and pay extra for) from the *dodatki* section. Also note that the price for some dishes (particularly fish and poultry) is often listed per 100g, so the price will depend on the total weight of the fish or meat.

Poles start their day with *śniadanie* (breakfast); and the most important and substantial meal of the day, *obiad,* is normally eaten between 2pm and 5pm. The third meal is *kolacja* (supper). Most restaurants open from midmorning until midnight, though milk bars and snack bars are open from early morning.

Staples & Specialities

Various cultures have influenced Polish cuisine, including Jewish, Ukrainian, Russian, Hungarian and German. Polish food is hearty and filling, abundant in potatoes and dumplings, and rich in meat.

Poland's most famous dishes are *bigos* (sauerkraut with a variety of meats), *pierogi* (ravioli-like dumplings stuffed with cottage cheese, minced meat, or cabbage and wild mushrooms) and *barszcz* (red beetroot soup, better known by the Russian word *borscht*).

Hearty soups such as *żurek* (sour soup with sausage and hard-boiled eggs) are a highlight of Polish cuisine. Main dishes are made with pork, including *golonka* (boiled pig's knuckle served with horseradish) and *schab pieczony* (roast loin of pork seasoned with prunes and herbs). *Gołąbki* (cabbage leaves stuffed with mince and rice) is a tasty alternative.

Placki ziemniaczane (potato pancakes) and *naleśniki* (crepes) are also popular dishes.

Drinks

Poles claim the national drink, *wódka* (vodka), was invented in their country. It's usually drunk neat and comes in a number of flavours, including *myśliwska* (flavoured with juniper berries), *wiśniówka* (with cherries) and *jarzębiak* (with rowanberries). The most famous variety is *żubrówka* (bison vodka), flavoured with grass from the Białowieża Forest. Other notable spirits include *krupnik* (honey liqueur), *śliwowica* (plum brandy) and *goldwasser* (sweet liqueur containing flakes of gold leaf).

Poles also appreciate the taste of *zimne piwo* (cold beer); the top brands, found everywhere, include Żywiec and Okocim, while regional brands are available in every city.

WARSAW

☎ 022 / pop 1.69 million

Poles and visitors alike agree: Warsaw (Warszawa in Polish, vah-*shah*-vah) is different. The business centre of Poland, its postcommunist commercial character is symbolised by capitalist towers rivalling the Stalinist-era Palace of Culture for prominence on the skyline. A spin-off from all this international trade is the city's excellent array of dining, entertainment and nightlife options.

The city's tumultuous past is reflected in its present-day appearance. The beautiful Old Town district was devastated in WWII but reconstructed with unerring accuracy, and is the most attractive part of the city. The nearby Royal Way, and the former Royal Parks, are also pleasant places to linger. Other districts feature communist-era concrete blocks and are less agreeable.

With its many museums, galleries and entertainment options, Warsaw can keep visitors

occupied for several days. As it's also Poland's central transport hub, the capital makes a good base for short trips into the surrounding countryside.

HISTORY

The Mazovian dukes were the first rulers of Warsaw, establishing it as their stronghold in the 14th century. The city's strategic central location led to the capital being transferred from Kraków to Warsaw when Poland and Lithuania were unified in 1569.

Although the 18th century was a period of catastrophic decline for the Polish state, Warsaw underwent a period of prosperity during this period. Many magnificent churches, palaces and parks were built, and cultural and artistic life blossomed. The first (short-lived) constitution in Europe was instituted in Warsaw in 1791.

In the 19th century Warsaw declined in status to became a mere provincial city of the Russian empire. Following WWI, the city was reinstated as the capital of a newly independent Poland and once more began to thrive. Following the Warsaw Rising of 1944 the city centre was devastated, and the entire surviving population forcibly evacuated. Upon war's end, the people of Warsaw returned to the capital, and set about rebuilding its historic heart.

ORIENTATION

The Vistula River divides Warsaw into two very different areas. The western left-bank sector features the city centre, including the Old Town, the historic nucleus of Warsaw. Almost all tourist attractions, as well as most tourist facilities, are on this side of the river. The eastern part of Warsaw, the suburb of Praga, has no major sights and sees few tourists.

If arriving by train, Warszawa Centralna station is, as the name suggests, within walking distance of the city centre and major attractions. If you arrive by bus at Dworzec Centralny PKS station, hop on a train from the adjoining Warszawa Zachodnia station into the centre. From the Dworzec PKS Stadion, you can catch a train to Warszawa Centralna from the Stadion train station.

INFORMATION
Bookshops

American Bookstore (Map p378; ☎ 827 48 52; ul Nowy Świat 61) Offers a wide selection of Lonely Planet titles, English publications and maps.

www.lonelyplanet.com

POLAND

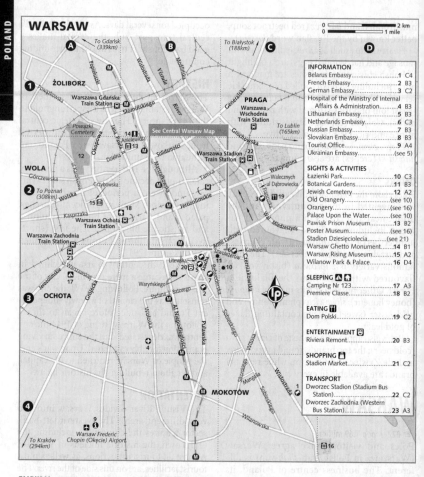

WARSAW

EMPiK Megastore Galeria Centrum (Map p378; ☎ 551 44 86; ul Marszałkowska 116/122); ul Nowy Świat (Map p378; ul Nowy Świat 15/17) For a large array of foreign newspapers and magazines, with several other branches around town.

Emergency
Ambulance ☎ 999
Fire ☎ 998
Police ☎ 997, from mobiles ☎ 112

Internet Access
Expect to pay around 9zł to 10zł per hour for internet access in Warsaw. Several convenient but dingy internet cafés are also located within Warszawa Centralna train station.
Casablanca (Map p378; ☎ 828 14 47; ul Krakowskie Przedmieście 4/6; ☼ 9am-1am Mon-Fri, 10am-2am

Sat, 10am-midnight Sun) Enter around the corner off ul Oboźna.
Internet Café (Map p378; ☎ 826 60 62; ul Nowy Świat 18/20; ☼ 9am-11pm Mon-Fri, 10am-10pm Sat & Sun)
Verso Internet (Map p378; ☎ 831 28 54; ul Freta 17; ☼ 8am-8pm Mon-Fri, 9am-5pm Sat, 10am-4pm Sun) Enter from the back of the building, off ul Świętojerska.

Medical Services
Apteka Grabowskiego (Map p378; ☎ 825 69 86; Warszawa Centralna train station) An all-night pharmacy.
CM Medical Center (Map p378; ☎ 458 70 00; 3rd fl, Marriott Hotel, al Jerozolimskie 65/79) Offers specialist doctors, carries out laboratory tests and makes house calls.
Dental-Med (Map p378; ☎ 629 59 38; ul Hoża 27) A central dental practice.

Hospital of the Ministry of Internal Affairs & Administration (Map p376; ☎ 602 15 78; ul Wołoska 137) A hospital preferred by government officials and diplomats.

Money

Foreign-exchange offices (kantors) and ATMs are easy to find around the city centre. Kantors open 24 hours can be found at the Warszawa Centralna train station, and either side of the immigration counters at the airport, but exchange rates at these places are about 10% lower than in the city centre. Avoid changing money in the Old Town, where the rates are even lower. The following places change major-brand travellers cheques, offer cash advances on Visa and MasterCard, and have ATMs that take just about every known credit card.

American Express (Map p378; Marriott Hotel, al Jerozolimskie 65/79)

Bank Pekao (Map p378; Krakowskie Przedmieście 1) Bank Pekao has a dozen branches in the city, including one next to the Church of the Holy Cross.

PBK Bank (Map p378; ground fl, Palace of Culture & Science Bldg)

PKO Bank (Map p378; plac Bankowy 2).

Post

Main post office (Map p378; ul Świętokrzyska 31/33; ☼ 24hr)

Tourist Information

Each tourist office provides free city maps and free booklets, such as the handy Warsaw in Short and the Visitor, sells maps of other Polish cities, and helps book hotel rooms. They also sell the Warsaw Tourist Card (one/three days 35/65zł), which gives free or discounted access to museums, and includes public transport and discounts at some theatres, sports centres and restaurants.

Free monthly tourist magazines worth seeking out include Poland: What, Where, When, What's Up in Warsaw and Welcome to Warsaw. The comprehensive monthly Warsaw Insider (8zł) and Warsaw in Your Pocket (5zł) are also useful.

Official tourist organisation (☎ 9431; www.warsaw tour.pl) Has several branches, including: Royal Way (Map p378; ul Krakowskie Przedmieście 39; ☼ 9am-8pm May-Sep, 9am-6pm Oct-Apr) Central office; Okęcie and Etiuda airport arrivals halls (Map p376; ☼ 8am-8pm May-Sep, 8am-6pm Oct-Apr); main hall of Warszawa Centralna train station (Map p378; ☼ 8am-8pm May-Sep, 8am-6pm Oct-Apr).

Warsaw Tourist Information Centre (Map p378; ☎ 635 18 81; www.wcit.waw.pl; pl Zamkowy 1/13; ☼ 9am-6pm Mon-Fri, 10am-6pm Sat, 11am-6pm Sun May-Sep; 9am-6pm Mon-Thu, 9am-8pm Fri, 10am-8pm Sat, 11am-8pm Sun Oct-Apr) Helpful privately-run tourist office in the Old Town.

Travel Agencies

Almatur (Map p378; ☎ 826 35 12; www.almatur.pl; ul Kopernika 23)

Orbis Travel (Map p378; ☎ 827 72 65; ul Bracka 16) Has branches all over Warsaw, as well as at the airport.

Our Roots (Map p378; ☎ 0501 23 61 17; ul Twarda 6) Warsaw's primary agency for anyone interested in tours about local Jewish heritage.

Trakt (Map p378; ☎ 827 80 68; www.trakt.com.pl; ul Kredytowa 6) Guided tours of Warsaw and beyond, in English and several other languages.

SIGHTS
Old Town

The main gateway to the Old Town is **Plac Zamkowy** (Castle Square). All the buildings here were superbly rebuilt from their foundations after WWII, earning the Old Town a place on Unesco's World Heritage List. Within the square stands the **Monument to Sigismund III Vasa**, who moved the capital from Kraków to Warsaw.

The dominant feature of the square is the massive 13th-century **Royal Castle** (Map p378;

WARSAW IN TWO DAYS

Wander through the **Old Town** (above), and tour the **Royal Castle** (above), having lunch afterwards at **Karczma Gessler** (p375). Walk along the **Royal Way** (p379), dropping into the **Chopin Museum** (p380) en route. Take the lift to the top of the **Palace of Culture & Science** (p380) for views of the city, before promenading through the nearby **Saxon Gardens** (p380).

The next day, visit the **Warsaw Rising Museum** (p381) in the morning, followed by lunch at one of the many restaurants along ul Nowy Świat. Spend the afternoon exploring **Łazienki Park** (p380), before sipping a cocktail at **Sense** (p384). Finish off the day with a visit to the nightclub district around ul Mazowiecka, or enjoy a performance at **Teatr Wielki** (p385).

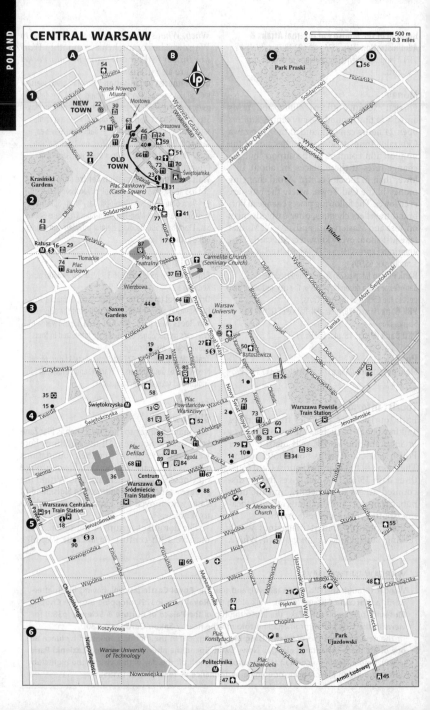

CENTRAL WARSAW

☎ 657 21 70; plac Zamkowy 4; adult/child 18/12zł; free Sun; ⌚ 10am-4pm Mon-Sat, 11am-4pm Sun, closed Mon Oct-Apr), also reconstructed after the war. The highlight of the sumptuously decorated rooms is the Senators' Antechamber, where landscapes of 18th-century Warsaw by Bernardo Bellotto (Canaletto's nephew) are on show.

From the castle, walk down ul Świętojańska to Warsaw's oldest church, the 15th-century Gothic **St John's Cathedral** (Map p378; ul Świętojańska 8; admission crypt 1zł; ⌚ 10am-1pm & 3-5.30pm Mon-Sat). This street continues to the magnificent **Rynek Starego Miasta** (Old Town Market Square).

Off the square is the **Warsaw Historical Museum** (Map p378; ☎ 635 16 25; Rynek Starego Miasta 42; adult/child 6/3zł; free Sun; ⌚ 11am-6pm Tue & Thu, 10am-3.30pm Wed & Fri, 10.30am-4.30pm Sat & Sun). At noon it shows an English-language film depicting the wartime destruction of the city.

Nearby is the **Adam Mickiewicz Museum of Literature** (Map p378; ☎ 831 76 91; Rynek Starego Miasta 20; adult/child 5/4zł; free Sun; ⌚ 10am-3pm Mon, Tue & Fri, 11am-6pm Wed & Thu, 11am-5pm Sun), featuring exhibits on Poland's most revered literary figure and other leading writers.

Walk west for one block to the **Barbican**, part of the medieval city walls. North along ul Freta is the **Marie Skłodowska-Curie Museum** (Map p378; ☎ 831 80 92; ul Freta 16; adult/child 6/3zł; ⌚ 10am-4pm Tue-Sat, 10am-2pm Sun), which features modest displays about the great lady, who, along with husband Pierre, discovered radium and polonium, and laid the foundations for radiography, nuclear physics and cancer therapy.

Heading southwest, you'll reach the **Monument to the Warsaw Rising** (Map p378; cnr ul Długa & ul Miodowa). This striking set of statuary honours the heroic Polish revolt against German rule in 1944.

Not far away, the **State Archaeological Museum** (Map p378; ☎ 831 15 37; ul Długa 52; adult/child 8/4zł; free Sun except 3rd Sun of month; ⌚ 9am-4pm Mon-Thu, 11am-6pm Fri, 10am-6pm Sun) is located in a 17th-century former arsenal.

Royal Way (Szlak Królewski)

This 4km route links the Royal Castle with Łazienki Park (see p380) via ul Krakowskie Przedmieście, ul Nowy Świat and al Ujazdowskie. Bus 180 stops at most places along this route and continues to Wilanów Park (Map p376). Bus No 100 also runs on Saturday and Sunday from May to September, between plac Zamkowy and Łazienki Park.

Just south of the Royal Castle is the ornate 15th-century **St Anne's Church** (Map p378; ul Krakowskie Przedmieście 68; ⌚ daylight hr), with impressive views from its **tower** (adult/child 3/2zł;

(✵ 10am-6pm Tue-Sun). About 300m further south is **Radziwiłł Palace** (Map p378; not open to the public), the residence of the Polish president. Opposite, **Potocki Palace** (Map p378; ☎ 421 01 25; ul Krakowskie Przedmieście 15/17; admission free; ✵ 10am-8pm) houses a contemporary art gallery.

To the west are the **Saxon Gardens** (admission free; ✵ 24hr). At the entrance is the small but poignant **Tomb of the Unknown Soldier** (Map p378), though it's not open to the public. The ceremonial changing of the guard takes place here at noon on Sunday.

South of the tomb is the **Ethnographic Museum** (Map p378; ☎ 827 76 41; ul Kredytowa 1; adult/child 8/4zł, Wed free; ✵ 9am-4pm Tue, Thu & Fri, 11am-6pm Wed, 10am-5pm Sat & Sun). It displays Polish folk costumes, and regional arts and crafts.

Back along the Royal Way is the 17th-century **Church of the Holy Cross** (Map p378; ul Krakowskie Przedmieście 3; ✵ erratic). Chopin's heart is preserved in the second pillar on the left-hand side of the main nave. It was brought from Paris, where he died of tuberculosis aged only 39. If you want to know more, head along ul Tamka to the small **Chopin Museum** (Map p378; ☎ 827 54 71; ul Okólnik 1; adult/child 10/5zł, free Wed; ✵ 10am-5pm Mon, Wed & Fri, 12-6pm Thu, 10am-2pm Sat & Sun May-Sep; 10am-2pm Mon-Wed, Fri & Sat, noon-6pm Thu Oct-Apr). On show are letters, handwritten musical scores and the great man's last piano.

East of the junction of ul Nowy Świat and al Jerozolimskie is the **National Museum** (Map p378; ☎ 621 10 31; al Jerozolimskie 3; adult/child 12/7zł, incl temporary exhibitions 19/12zł, museum free Sat; ✵ 10am-4pm Tue, Wed & Fri-Sun, 10am-6pm Thu), with an impressive collection of Greek and Egyptian antiquities, Coptic frescoes, medieval woodcarvings and Polish paintings; look out for the surrealistic fantasies of Jacek Malczewski. Next door is the **Museum of the Polish Army** (Map p378; ☎ 629 52 71; al Jerozolimskie 3; museum adult/child 6/3zł, grounds free; ✵ 10am-5pm Wed-Sun May-Sep, 10am-4pm Wed-Sun Oct-Apr), with army vehicles outside and miscellaneous militaria within.

Go south along al Ujazdowskie and cross busy ul Armii Ludowej. Over the road is the cutting-edge **Centre for Contemporary Art** (Map p378; ☎ 628 12 72; al Ujazdowskie 6; adult/child 12/6zł, free Thu; ✵ 11am-5pm Tue-Thu, Sat & Sun, 11am-9pm Fri). It's housed in the reconstructed **Ujazdów Castle** (Map p378), originally built during the 1620s. Further down (towards the south) are the small **Botanical Gardens** (Map p376; ☎ 553 05 23; adult/child 4.50/2.50zł; ✵ 10am-8pm).

Łazienki Park

This large, shady and popular **park** (admission free; ✵ daylight hr) is best known for the 18th-century **Palace upon the Water** (Map p376; ☎ 621 62 41; adult/child 12/9zł; ✵ 9am-4pm Tue-Sun). It was the summer residence of Stanisław August Poniatowski, the last king of Poland, who was deposed by the Russian army and confederation of Polish magnates in 1792. The park was once a royal hunting ground attached to Ujazdów Castle.

The **Old Orangery** (Map p376; ☎ 621 62 41; by reservation only adult/child 6/4zł) contains a sculpture gallery and an 18th-century theatre. Between noon and 4pm every Sunday from May to September, piano recitals are held among the rose gardens.

Wilanów Park

Another magnificent **park** (Map p376; ul Wisłostrada; admission free; ✵ 9.30am-dusk) lies 6km southeast of Łazienki Park. Its centrepiece is the splendid **Wilanów Palace** (Map p376; ☎ 842 07 95; adult/child 20/10zł, free Thu; ✵ 9am-4pm Mon & Thu-Sat, 9am-6pm Wed, 9am-7pm Sun May-Sep, 9am-4pm Wed-Mon Oct-May), the summer residence of King Jan III Sobieski, who ended the Turkish threat to Central Europe by defeating the Turks at Vienna in 1683. In summer, be prepared to wait. The last tickets are sold two hours before closing time.

In the well-kept park behind the palace is the **Orangery** (Map p376; admission fee varies with exhibitions; ✵ 9.30am-3.30pm Wed-Mon), which houses an art gallery. The **Poster Museum** (Map p376; ☎ 842 26 06; adult/child 8/5zł, free Wed; ✵ noon-3.30pm Mon, 10am-3.30pm Tue-Sun) in the former royal stables is a repository of Poland's world-renowned poster art.

To reach Wilanów, take bus 180 from anywhere along the Royal Way.

Palace of Culture & Science

Massive, brooding and inescapable, this **towering structure** (Map p378; ☎ 656 76 00; plac Defilad; ✵ 9am-8pm Mon-Thu, 9am-midnight Fri-Sun Jun-Aug, 9am-6pm Sep-May) has become an emblem of the city, as it's slowly rehabilitated from its Stalinist past. It has a particularly sinister aspect at dusk, though it's also a handy landmark. The Palace was built in the early 1950s as a 'gift of friendship' from the Soviet Union, and is still one of Europe's tallest buildings (234m).

The **observation terrace** (adult/child 20/15zł; ✵ 9am-6pm) on the 30th floor provides a panoramic view, though it can be very cold and windy up there.

Warsaw Rising Museum

This impressive **museum** (Map p376; ☎ 626 95 06; ul Grzybowska 79; adult/child 4/2zł, free Sun; ⏰ 10am-6pm Wed, Fri-Sun, 10am-8pm Thu) commemorates Warsaw's insurrection against its Nazi occupiers in 1944, which was destined to end in defeat and the destruction of much of the city and its population. The Rising was viciously suppressed by the Germans (while the Red Army stood by on the opposite bank of the Vistula), with more than 200,000 Poles dying by its conclusion.

The moving story of the Rising is retold here via photographs, exhibits and audiovisual displays. The centrepiece is a massive memorial wall emitting a heartbeat and selected audio recordings. At the end of the journey there's a replica 1944 café, underlining the fact that life went on, even in the worst days of the struggle. Captions are in Polish and English. Catch trams 8, 12, 22 or 24 from al Jerozolimskie, heading west.

Jewish Heritage

The suburbs northwest of the Palace of Culture & Science were once predominantly inhabited by Jewish Poles. During WWII the Nazis established a Jewish ghetto in the area, but razed it to the ground after crushing the Warsaw Ghetto Uprising in April 1943.

The **Warsaw Ghetto Monument** (Map p376; cnr ul Anielewicza & ul Zamenhofa) remembers the Nazis' victims via pictorial plaques. The nearby **Pawiak Prison Museum** (Map p376; ☎ 831 13 17; ul Dzielna 24/26; admission free; ⏰ 9am-5pm Wed, 9am-4pm Thu & Sat, 10am-5pm Fri, 10am-4pm Sun) was a Gestapo prison during the Nazi occupation. Moving exhibits include letters and other personal items.

The most poignant remainder is Europe's largest **Jewish Cemetery** (Map p376; ul Okopowa 49/51; admission 4zł; ⏰ 10am-5pm Mon-Thu, 9am-1pm Fri, 9am-4pm Sun). Founded in 1806, it has more than 100,000 gravestones. Visitors must wear a head-covering to enter, and it's accessible from the Old Town on bus 180.

The **Jewish Historical Institute** (Map p378; ☎ 827 92 21; ul Tłomackie 3/5; adult/child 10/5zł; ⏰ 9am-4pm Mon-Wed & Fri, 11am-6pm Thu) has permanent exhibits about the Warsaw Ghetto, as well as local Jewish artworks. Further south is the neo-Romanesque **Nożyk Synagogue** (Map p378; ☎ 620 43 24; ul Twarda 6; admission 3.50zł; ⏰ 10am-8pm

Sun-Thu, 10am-4pm Fri), Warsaw's only synagogue to survive WWII.

A walking tour of Jewish sites is detailed (in English and with a map) in the free pamphlet, *Jewish Warsaw*, available from tourist offices.

SLEEPING

Not surprisingly, Warsaw is the most expensive Polish city for accommodation, though there's a number of reasonably priced hostels around town. The tourist offices can help find a room.

Budget

Smolna Youth Hostel No 2 (Map p378; ☎ /fax 827 89 52; ul Smolna 30; dm 36zł, s/d 65/120zł) Very central and very popular, though there's a midnight curfew. However, the light tidy dorms have a reasonable amount of space, the tiled bathrooms are clean, and there's a lounge and kitchen area. Note that guests are separated into dorms according to gender, and reception is up four flights of stairs.

Oki Doki (Map p378; ☎ 826 51 12; www.okidoki.pl; plac Dąbrowskiego 3; dm 45zł, s/d 110/145zł) There are no drab dorms here. Each is decorated thematically using the brightest paints available; try the Communist (red with a big image of Lenin). Lower bunks have good headroom, and the shared bathrooms are clean and bright. The hostel also has a bar, free washing machine and kitchen, and hires out bikes.

Hostel Helvetia (Map p378; ☎ 826 71 08; www.hostel -helvetia.pl; ul Kopernika 36/40; dm 45zł, s/d 110/150zł; 🖳) Bright hostel with an attractive combined lounge and kitchen. Dorms have lockers available, and some rooms feature bicycle-related images in deference to the cycling-enthusiast owner. Unsurprisingly, the hostel hires out bikes. Enter from the street behind, ul Sewerynów.

Nathan's Villa Hostel (Map p378; ☎ 622 29 46; www .nathansvilla.com; ul Piękna 24/26; dm 45zł, s/d 130/160zł; 🖳) Nathan's is the standard by which all Warsaw hostels should be judged. A sunlit courtyard leads to well-organised dorms, while private rooms are comfortable and decorated with monochrome photographs of Polish attractions. The kitchen is well set up, and there's a free laundry, a book exchange, and games to while away rainy days.

Hostel Kanonia (Map p378; ☎ 635 06 76; www.kano nia.pl; ul Jezuicka 2; dm 55zł, s/d 140/180zł; 🖳) Housed in a historic building in the heart of the Old

POLAND

Town, accommodation is mostly in dorms, with only one dedicated double room. Some rooms have picturesque views onto the cobble stone streets, and there's a pleasant dining room with basic kitchen facilities.

Dom Gościnny (Map p378; ☎ 628 42 61; www.sezam .pw.edu.pl; ul Górnośląska 14; s/d 90/140zł, ste from 180zł; **P** 🖳) If you want to enjoy the pleasures of the city centre without sleeping there, this accommodation in the peaceful nearby embassy area is a good choice. Rooms have simple furnishings and plain carpets, but there's plenty of cupboard space and a kitchen.

Camping Nr 123 (Map p376; ☎ 823 37 48; ul Warszawskiej 1920r 15/17; tents 12zł, plus per person 12zł; **P** 🖳) Set in extensive grounds near the Dworzec Zachodnia bus station, cabins (40zł per person) are also available and there's a tennis court nearby.

Midrange

Hotel Praski (Map p378; ☎ 818 49 89; www.praski.pl; al Solidarności 61; s 147-210, d 160-230zł; **P**) The rooms of this inexpensive hotel vary in size, but have attractive high ceilings and comfortable beds. Bathrooms are clean, red carpets add old-fashioned charm, and some rooms have views of Praski Park. It's an easy walk across the river to the Old Town.

Premiere Classe (Map p376; ☎ 624 08 00; ul Towarowa 2; d from 179zł; **P** 🗶 🕭) If you're not bothered too much by room size, this modern hotel makes a good base. Rooms are small but bright, and neatly set up with modern furnishings. Friendly staff are a plus. Guests can use the restaurant, bar and fitness centre in the neighbouring sister hotels.

Hotel Powiśle (Map p378; ☎ 621 03 41; www.hotel powisle.oit.pl; ul Szara 10a; s/d 160/180zł; **P**) If Agatha Christie had set one of her mysteries in Poland, she would have chosen somewhere like this accommodation, pleasantly reminiscent of an old-fashioned country hotel. Although it's slightly scuffed, the generous use of wood panelling and the out-of-date carpets make for a comforting old-world feel. There's a bar and restaurant on site.

City Apartments (Map p378; ☎ 825 39 12; www.hotel inwarsaw.pl; ul Nowowiejska 1/3; apt from €60-120) A range of apartments are on offer here, from the Old Town to the city centre. They provide privacy and space, and allow for some cost-cutting via the fully equipped kitchen facilities. Although, as always happens with these places, you won't find every utensil you need.

Sofitel Victoria (Map p378; ☎ 657 80 11; www.sofi tel.com; ul Królewska 11; d/ste from €70/200; **P** 🗶 🖳 🕭) The very model of a modern business hotel, with a spacious marble foyer, and a lounge area housing a small library of books on Polish culture and history. The rooms are conservatively decorated, with gleaming bathrooms. The cheaper doubles are great value.

Old Town Apartments (Map p378; ☎ 887 98 01; www .warsawshotel.com; Rynek Starego Miasta 12/14; apt from €80) These modern renovated apartments lend you the pleasant illusion of being a local. Décor is bright and contemporary, most apartments have washing machines, and all have fully operational kitchens. Some can house up to six people.

Hotel Harenda (Map p378; ☎ 826 00 71; www.hotel harenda.com.pl; ul Krakowskie Przedmieście 4/6; s/d/ste from 250/270/460zł; **P** 🖳) Boasts a great location just off the Royal Way, although the green-and-brown colour scheme may deter some; the Harenda's rooms are neat and clean, with solid timber furniture. There's an old-fashioned feel to the hotel's interiors, and an expensive antique shop just off the foyer if retail therapy is required.

Top End

Dom Literatury (Map p378; ☎ 828 39 20; www.fundac jadl.com; ul Krakowskie Przedmieście 87/89; s/d 220/370zł) Within a grand historic building, this accommodation features rambling halls and staircases bedecked with pot plants and sizeable paintings. There are a maze of comfortable rooms, many of which have excellent views of the Old Town and the Vistula. Don't, however, expect too much English from the friendly staff.

Hotel Gromada Centrum (Map p378; ☎ 582 99 00; www.gromada.pl; plac Powstańców Warszawy 2; s/d from 320/350zł; **P** 🗶 🕭) Centrally located, the Gromada is a great launching pad for exploring the central city. Upstairs from the funky green foyer, however, the featureless brown-carpeted corridors stretch out into the distance like an optical illusion. The rooms are plain, but clean and spacious.

Hotel Le Regina (Map p378; ☎ 531 60 00; www .leregina.com; ul Kościelna 12; d/ste from €250/600; **P** 🗶 🖳 🕭) It's not cheap, but the Le Regina is a jaw-dropping combination of traditional architecture and contemporary design. The enormous rooms feature king-size beds with headboards of dark, polished wood. Deluxe rooms also have timber floors, and terraces with courtyard views. All rooms sport spectacular bathrooms with marble benchtops.

EATING

The most recent revolution to conquer the Polish capital has been a gastronomic one. A good selection of restaurants can be found in the Old Town and around ul Nowy Świat.

Polish

Bar Pod Barbakanem (Map p378; ☎ 831 47 37; ul Mostowa 27/29; mains 8-12zł; 8am-5pm) Opposite the Barbican, this popular former milk bar survived the fall of the Iron Curtain and continues to serve cheap, unpretentious food in an interior marked by tiles: on the floor, walls and tabletops. Fill up while peering out through the lace curtains at the passing tourist hordes.

Zgoda Grill Bar (Map p378; ☎ 827 99 34; ul Zgoda 4; mains 18-35zł; 10am-11pm) A bright, informal place serving up cheap and tasty Polish standards. If you're not in the mood for Polish, there are Turkish, Italian and Mexican places just along the street.

Dom Polski (Map p376; ☎ 616 24 32; ul Francuska 11; mains 26-64zł; noon-midnight) This classy restaurant, in its yellow stucco building set back from the street, is perennially popular with tour groups and out-of-towners looking for tasty food and reasonable prices. It's worth the walk over the bridge.

Restauracja Przy Zamku (Map p378; ☎ 831 02 59; plac Zamkowy 15; mains from 32-80zł; 11am-midnight) An attractive, old-world kind of place with hunting trophies on the walls and attentive, white-aproned waiters. The top-notch Polish menu includes fish and game and a bewildering array of entrées – try the excellent hare pâté served with pickles and cranberry sauce.

Karczma Gessler (Map p378; ☎ 831 44 27; Rynek Starego Miasta 21/21a; mains 50-120zł; 11am-midnight) The décor of this romantic cellar is spectacular, with exposed timber beams and lots of rustic items such as cart wheels about the place. The food is pricey but impressive. Some dishes (such as the whole goose) can be shared by three.

Café Design (Map p378; ☎ 828 57 03; ul Krakowie Przedmieście 11; mains 69-79zł; 10am-11.30pm) Classy eatery serving tradition-inspired Polish cuisine in an ultramodern venue on the Royal Way, with circular platforms supporting tables below sleek wooden panelling. English-language newspapers and magazines are at hand, and mains include dishes involving rabbit, duck, lamb and deer.

International

Dziki Ryż (Map p378; ☎ 621 50 15; ul Hoża 54; mains 18-25zł; 11am-7pm Mon-Fri, 1-5pm Sat & Sun) This hidden gem serves a range of Asian dishes, covering Chinese, Japanese, Korean and Thai cuisine. Though small (just six tables), it has loads of personality, with dark timber surfaces, bamboo place mats and Japanese newspapers plastering the walls. Red and green curries lead the way on the menu, including tofu versions, though they've been toned down for Polish palates.

Restauracja Pod Samsonem (Map p378; ☎ 831 17 88; ul Freta 3/5; mains 18-30zł; 10am-11pm) Situated in the New Town, and frequented by locals looking for inexpensive and tasty meals with a Jewish flavour. Interesting appetisers include Russian pancakes with salmon, and 'Jewish caviar'. Spot the bas relief of Samson and the lion above the next door along from the entrance.

Tam Tam (Map p378; ☎ 828 26 22; ul Foksal 18; mains from 20zł; noon-midnight) Housed in a subterranean 'African-style' place with a street-level bar. The varied menu includes pasta, goulash and kebabs, and a big list of teas and coffees. There's occasional live music in the evenings.

Podwale Piwna Kompania (Map p378; ☎ 635 63 14; ul Podwale 25; mains 21-55zł; 11am-1am) The restaurant's name (The Company of Beer) gives you an idea of the lively atmosphere in this eatery just outside the Old Town's moat. The menu features lots of grilled items and dishes such as roast duck, Wiener schnitzel, pork ribs and roasted pork knuckle. There's a courtyard for outdoor dining.

London Steakhouse (Map p378; ☎ 827 00 20; al Jerozolimskie 42; mains 32-66zł; 11am-midnight) You'll find it hard to convince yourself you're in London, but it's fun to spot the UK memorabilia among the cluttered décor, while being served by waitresses wearing Union Jack neckties and miniskirts. Steaks dominate the menu, which also includes fish and chips. There's roast beef and Yorkshire pudding on weekends.

Adler Bar & Restaurant (Map p378; ☎ 628 73 84; ul Mokotowska 69; mains 35-50zł; 8am-midnight Mon-Fri, 1pm-midnight Sat & Sun) A tiny oasis in the concrete jungle, housed within a curious circular building. Service is impeccable and a good variety of Polish and Bavarian *nouvelle cuisine* is on offer. Try the ice-meringue with strawberry mousse.

Puszkin (Map p378; ☎ 635 35 35; ul Świętojańska 2; mains 48-87zł; ☺ noon-midnight) An upmarket Russian restaurant where waiters in Cossack outfits serve up traditional dishes such as caviar, sturgeon and wild boar in opulent surrounds.

Vegetarian
Vega (Map p378; ☎ 828 64 28; ul Nowy Świat 52; soups 5zł, mains 5-20zł; ☺ 11am-8pm) Cheap and delicious vegetarian food from a place tucked away in a courtyard. Try the *naleśniki* (crepes wrapped around a variety of fillings). There's also a good number of vegan items on the menu.

Tukan Salad Bar (Map p378; ☎ 531 25 20; plac Bankowy 2; mains from 5zł; ☺ 8am-8pm Mon-Fri, 10am-6pm Sat & Sun) This place has several outlets around the capital offering possibly the widest choice of salads in Poland. As the name suggests, look for the toucan on the door. This branch is hidden from the street in the arcade running parallel.

Self-Catering
The most convenient places for groceries are the **MarcPol Supermarket** (Map p378; plac Defilad) in front of the Palace of Culture & Science building, and the **Albert Supermarket** (Map p378; Galeria Centrum, ul Marszałkowska) close by.

DRINKING
Sense (Map p378; ☎ 826 65 70; ul Nowy Świat 19; ☺ noon-1am Mon-Thu, noon-3am Fri & Sat, noon-10pm Sun) A very modern venue with a mellow atmosphere. Comfortable banquettes sit beneath strings of cube-shaped lights, and there's an extensive wine and cocktail list, with some drinks measured in a 'Palace of Culture' (a tall scientific beaker). Try the house speciality, ginger rose vodka. There's also a food menu if you're hungry.

Paparazzi (Map p378; ☎ 828 42 19; ul Mazowiecka 12; ☺ noon-1am) This is one of Warsaw's flashest venues, where you can sip a bewildering array of cocktails under blown-up photos of Hollywood stars. It's big and roomy, with comfortable seating around the central bar, and does a good line in bar food, including some tasty salads.

Pub Harenda (Map p378; ☎ 826 29 00; ul Krakowskie Przedmieście 4/6; ☺ 9am-3am) Located at the back

of Hotel Harenda, this pub is often crowded. However, it's a friendly, atmospheric place – the front section feels like a wood cabin out in the forest. There's dance music on weekends.

Demmers Teahouse (Map p378; ☎ 828 21 06; ul Krakowskie Przedmieście 61/63; ☺ 11am-7pm Mon-Fri, 11am-6pm Sat & Sun) On the Royal Way, Demmers has a staggering array of teas to try.

ENTERTAINMENT
Nightclubs
There's no shortage of good clubs in Warsaw. Explore ul Mazowiecka, ul Sienkiewicza and the area around ul Nowy Świat for more nightclub action.

Enklawa (Map p378; ☎ 827 31 51; ul Mazowiecka 12; ☺ 9pm-3am Wed-Sat) Funky red-and-orange space with comfy plush seating, mirrored ceilings, two bars and plenty of room to dance. Check out the long drinks list, hit the dance floor or observe the action from a stool on the upper balcony. Wednesday night is 'old school' night, with music from the '70s to '90s.

Foksal 19 (Map p378; ☎ 829 29 55; ul Foksal 19; ☺ bar 5pm-1am Mon-Thu, 5pm-3am Fri & Sat, nightclub 11pm-5am Fri & Sat) Ultramodern playpen for Warsaw's bright young things. Downstairs is a cool drinking zone with a backlit bar, subdued golden lighting and comfy couches. Upstairs is the nightclub – a blue-lit contemporary space with DJs playing a variety of sounds.

Hybrydy (Map p378; ☎ 822 30 03; ul Złota 7/9; ☺ 9pm-3am) This joint has been going for decades, and features all sorts of live music most nights.

Riviera Remont (Map p376; ☎ 660 91 11; ul Waryńskiego 12; ☺ Jun-Sep) A popular, cheap student club offering regular live music.

In Łazienki Park (p380), piano recitals are held every Sunday from May to September, and chamber concerts are staged in summer at its Old Orangery.

Free jazz concerts also take place in the Old Town Market Square on Saturday at 7pm in July and August.

Theatre
Advance tickets for most theatrical events can be bought at **ZASP Kasy Teatralne** (Map p378; ☎ 621 93 83; al Jerozolimskie 25; ☺ 11am-6.30pm Mon-Fri) or the **EMPiK Megastore** (Map p378; ☎ 551 44 43; ul Marszałkowska 104/122).

Teatr Ateneum (Map p378; ☎ 625 73 30; ul Jaracza 2) This place leans towards contemporary Polish-language productions.

Teatr Wielki (Map p378; ☎ 692 02 00; www.teatrwielki
.pl; plac Teatralny 1) Wielki hosts opera and ballet
in its grand premises.

Filharmonia Narodowa (Map p378; ☎ 551 71 11;
ul Jasna 5) Classical-music concerts are held
here.

Cinemas

To avoid watching Polish TV in your hotel
room, catch a film at the central **Kino Atlantic** (Map p378; ☎ 827 08 94; ul Chmielna 33) or **Kino
Relax** (Map p378; ☎ 828 38 88; ul Złota 8). Tickets cost
around 18zł.

SHOPPING

Stadion Market (Map p376; al Jerozolimskie; ☯ dawn-
around noon) This huge bazaar is situated
within a former stadium in the suburb of
Praga. It's busiest on weekends – beware of
pickpockets.

Galeria Centrum (Map p378; ul Marszałkowska 104/122)
A sprawling modern shopping mall in the
city centre.

There are also plentiful antique, arts and
crafts shops around Rynek Starego Miasta in
the Old Town, so brandish your credit card
and explore.

GETTING THERE & AWAY
Air

The **Warsaw Frédéric Chopin airport** (Map p376;
www.lotnisko-chopina.pl) is more commonly called
Okęcie airport. Domestic arrivals and departures occupy a separate part of the same
complex. The separate Etiuda terminal mostly
handles discount airlines.

The useful tourist office is on the arrivals
level of the international section. There's also
a tourist office at the Etiuda terminal.

At the arrivals level there are ATMs and
several *kantors*. There are also car-rental companies, a left-luggage room and a newsagent
where you can buy public transport tickets.

Domestic and international flights can be
booked at the **LOT office** (Map p378; ☎ 9572; al
Jerozolimskie 65/79), or at any travel agency. Other
airline offices are listed in the *Welcome to
Warsaw* magazine, and on p444.

Bus

Warsaw has two major bus terminals for PKS
buses. **Dworzec Zachodnia** (Western Bus Station; Map
p376; al Jerozolimskie 144) handles domestic buses
heading south, north and west of the capital,
including six daily to Częstochowa (30zł),

seven to Gdańsk (50zł), four to Kraków (39zł),
seven to Olsztyn (32zł), eight to Toruń (35zł),
three to Wrocław (46zł), and three to Zakopane (54zł). This complex is southwest of
the city centre and adjoins the Warszawa
Zachodnia train station. Take the commuter
train that leaves from Warszawa Śródmieście
station.

Dworzec Stadion (Stadium Bus Station; Map p376; ul
Sokola 1) adjoins the Warszawa Stadion train
station. It is also easily accessible by commuter train from Warszawa Śródmieście.
Dworzec Stadion handles some domestic
buses to the east and southeast, including 20
daily to Lublin (25zł), five to Białystok (23zł
to 29zł), 12 to Zamość (37zł), and seven to
Kazimierz Dolny (22zł).

Polski Express (Map p378; ☎ 844 55 55; www.polskiex
press.pl) operates coaches from the airport, but
passengers can get on or off and buy tickets
at the kiosk along al Jana Pawła II, next to
the Warszawa Centralna train station. Polski
Express buses travel to Białystok (34zł, one
daily), Częstochowa (50zł, two daily), Gdynia,
via Gdańsk (72zł, two daily), Kraków (67zł,
one daily), Lublin (34zł, seven daily), Szczecin
(80zł, two daily) and Toruń (48zł, 12 daily).

International buses depart from and arrive
at Dworzec Zachodnia or, occasionally, outside Warszawa Centralna. Tickets are available
from the bus offices at Dworzec Zachodnia,
from agencies at Warszawa Centralna or from
any of the major travel agencies in the city,
including Almatur.

Train

Warsaw has several train stations, but the
one that most travellers will use is **Warszawa
Centralna** (Map p378; Warsaw Central; al Jerozolimskie 54).
Refer to the relevant destination sections in
this chapter for information about services
to/from Warsaw.

Warszawa Centralna is not always where
trains start or finish; so make sure you get on
or off promptly; and guard your belongings
against pickpocketing and theft at all times.

The station's main hall houses ticket
counters, ATMs and snack bars, as well as
a post office, newsagents and a tourist office. Along the underground mezzanine level
leading to the platforms are a dozen *kantors*
(one of which is open 24 hours), a **left-luggage
office** (☯ 7am-9pm), lockers, eateries, outlets for
local public transport tickets, internet cafés
and bookshops.

Tickets for domestic and international trains are available from counters at the station (but allow at least an hour for possible queuing) or, in advance, from any major Orbis Travel office (p377). Tickets for immediate departures on domestic and international trains are also available from numerous, well-signed booths in the underpasses leading to Warszawa Centralna.

Some domestic trains also stop at Warszawa Śródmieście station, 300m east of Warszawa Centralna, and Warszawa Zachodnia, next to Dworzec Zachodnia bus station.

GETTING AROUND
To/From the Airport
The cheapest way of getting from the airport to the city centre is bus 175, which leaves every 10 to 15 minutes for the Old Town, via ul Nowy Świat and the Warszawa Centralna train station. If you arrive in the wee hours, night bus 611 links the airport with Warszawa Centralna every 30 minutes.

The taxi fare between the airport and the city centre is from 30zł to 35zł. Official taxis displaying a name, telephone number and fares can be arranged at the official taxi counters at the international arrivals level. Unauthorised 'Mafia' cabs still operate and charge astronomical rates.

Car
Warsaw traffic isn't fun, but there are good reasons to hire a car for jaunts into the countryside. Major car-rental companies are listed in the local English-language publications, and include **Avis** (☎ 650 48 72; www.avis.pl), **Hertz** (☎ 650 28 96; www.hertz.com.pl) and **Sixt** (☎ 650 20 31; www.sixt.pl). For more details about car hire see p445.

Public Transport
Warsaw's public transport operates from 5am to 11pm daily. The fare (2.40zł) is valid for one ride only on a bus, tram, trolleybus or metro train travelling anywhere in the city.

Warsaw is the only place in Poland where ISIC cards get a public-transport discount (of 48%).

Tickets are available for 60/90 minutes (3.60/4.50zł), one day (7.20zł), three days (12zł), one week (24zł) and one month (66zł). Buy tickets from kiosks (including those marked 'RUCH') before boarding, and validate them on board.

A metro line operates from the Ursynów suburb (Kabaty station) at the southern city limits to Plac Wilsona, via the city centre (Centrum), but is of limited use to visitors. Local commuter trains head out to the suburbs from the Warszawa Śródmieście station.

Taxi
Taxis are a quick and easy way to get around – as long as you use official taxis and drivers use their meters. Beware of unauthorised 'Mafia' taxis parked in front of top-end hotels, at the airport, outside Warszawa Centralna train station and in the vicinity of most tourist sights.

MAZOVIA & PODLASIE

After being ruled as an independent state by a succession of dukes, Mazovia shot to prominence during the 16th century, when Warsaw became the national capital. The region has long been a base for industry, the traditional mainstay of Poland's second largest city, Łódź. To the east of Mazovia, toward the Belarus border, lies Podlasie, which means 'land close to the forest'. The main attraction of this region is the impressive Białowieża National Park.

ŁÓDŹ
☎ 042 / pop 785,000
Łódź (pronounced woodge) became a major industrial centre in the 19th century, attracting immigrants from across Europe. Little damaged in WWII, it's a lively, likeable city with attractive Art Nouveau architecture, and the added bonus of being well off the usual tourist track. It's an easy day trip from Warsaw.

Many of the attractions – and most of the banks, *kantors* and ATMs – are along ul Piotrkowska, the main thoroughfare. You can't miss the bronze statues of local celebrities along this street, including pianist Arthur Rubenstein, seated at a baby grand. The helpful **tourist office** (☎ 638 59 55; www.cityoflodz.pl; ul Piotrkowska 87; ☻ 8.30am-4.30pm Mon-Fri, 9am-1pm Sat) hands out free tourist brochures, including the useful *1-2-3 Days in Łódź*.

The **Historical Museum of Łódź** (☎ 654 03 23; ul Ogrodowa 15; adult/child 7/4zł, free Sun; ☻ 10am-4pm Tue & Thu, 2-6pm Wed, 10am-2pm Fri-Sun) is 200m northwest of plac Wolności, at the northern end of the main drag. Also worthwhile is the **Museum of Ethnography & Archaeology** (☎ 632 84 40; plac Wolności 14; adult/child 6/4zł, free Tue; ⏰ 10am-5pm Tue, 11am-6pm Thu, 9am-4pm Wed, Fri-Sun).

Herbst Palace (☎ 674 96 98; ul Przędalniana 72; adult/child 7/4.50zł; ⏰ 10am-5pm Tue, noon-5pm Wed & Fri, noon-7pm Thu, 11am-4pm Sat & Sun) has been converted into an appealing museum. It's accessible by bus 55 heading east from the cathedral at the southern end of ul Piotrkowska. The **Jewish Cemetery** (www.jewishlodzcemetery.org; ul Bracka 40; admission 4zł, free first Sun of month; ⏰ 9am-5pm Sun-Thu, 9am-3pm Fri Apr-Oct, 9am-3pm Sun-Fri Nov-Mar) is one of the largest in Europe. It's 3km northeast of the city centre and accessible by tram 1 or 6 from near plac Wolności. Enter from ul Zmienna.

The tourist office can provide information about all kinds of accommodation. The **youth hostel** (☎ 630 66 80; www.youthhostel.lodz.wp.pl; ul Legionów 27; dm from 30zł, s/d from 45/70zł; 💻) is excellent, so book ahead. It features nicely decorated rooms in a spacious old building, with free laundry and a kitchen. It's 250m west of plac Wolności.

The **Hotel Savoy** (☎ 632 93 60; www.hotelsavoy.pl; ul Traugutta 6; s/d from 87/200zł) is well positioned just off central ul Piotrkowska. Don't be put off by the scuffed corridors and stencilled door numbers: they conceal spacious, light-filled rooms with gleaming bathrooms.

Around the corner, the **Grand Hotel** (☎ 633 99 20; www.orbis.pl; ul Piotrkowska 72; s/d from 280/357zł) offers a touch of faded, if overpriced, *fin-de-siècle* grandeur.

Opposite the Grand, **Puenta** (☎ 630 80 87: ul Piotrkowska 65: mains 14-32zł; ⏰ noon-10pm) is a brightly decorated restaurant, full of locals and visitors having a good time. The menu includes pasta, salads and a good selection of chicken and fish dishes. **Esplanada** (☎ 630 59 89; ul Piotrkowska 100; mains 35-60zł) is an excellent *belle époque*–style eatery serving quality Polish cuisine, sometimes accompanied by live folk music.

LOT (☎ 630 15 40; ul Piotrkowska 122) flies the 20-minute hop to Warsaw nine times a week. From the Łódź Kaliska train station, 1.2km southwest of central Łódź, trains go regularly to Wrocław (110 zł), Poznań (79 zł), Toruń (31 zł) and Gdańsk (46 zł). For Warsaw (29zł) and Częstochowa (23 zł), use the Łódź Fabryczna station, 400m east of the city centre. Buses go in all directions from the bus terminal, next to the Fabryczna train station.

BIAŁOWIEŻA NATIONAL PARK

☎ 085

Once a centre for hunting and timber-felling, Białowieża (Byah-wo-*vyeh*-zhah) is now Poland's oldest national park. Its significance is underlined by Unesco's unusual recognition of the reserve as both a Biosphere Reserve *and* a World Heritage Site. The forest contains 120 species of birds, along with elk, wild boars and wolves. Its major drawcard is the magnificent European bison, which was once extinct outside zoos, but has been successfully reintroduced to its ancient home.

The logical visitor base is the charming village of Białowieża. The main road to Białowieża from Hajnówka leads to the southern end of Palace Park (the former location of the Russian tsar's hunting lodge), then skirts around the park to become the village's main street, ul Waszkiewicza. At the western end of this street is the **post office** (⏰ 7am-7pm Mon-Fri, 7am-2pm Sat).

Money can be changed at the Hotel Żubrówka, but not travellers cheques or anything as exotic as Australian dollars. The hotel also has an ATM by the entrance, and public internet access for the scary rate of 10zł per half-hour.

You'll find the **PTTK (Polskie Towarzystwo Turystyczno-Krajoznawcze) office** (Polish Tourist Country Lovers Society; ☎ 681 22 95; www.pttk.bialowieza.pl; ul Kolejowa 17; ⏰ 8am-4pm) at the southern end of Palace Park. Serious hikers should contact the **National Park Office** (☎ 682 97 02; www.bpn.com.pl; ⏰ 9am-4pm) inside Palace Park. Most maps of the national park (especially the one published by PTOP – Północnopodlaskie Towarzystwo Ochrony Ptaków, North Podlasian Bird Protection Society) detail several enticing hiking trails.

Sights & Activities

A combined ticket (12zł) allows you entry to the museum, the bison reserve and the nature reserve. Alternatively, you can pay for each attraction separately.

The elegant **Palace Park** (admission free; ⏰ daylight hr) is only accessible on foot, bicycle or horse-drawn cart across the bridge from the PTTK office. Over the river is the excellent **Natural & Forestry Museum** (adult/child 10/5zł; ⏰ 9am-4.30pm Apr-Sep, 9am-4pm Tue-Sun Oct-Mar), with displays on local flora and fauna, and beekeeping.

The **European Bison Reserve** (Rezerwat Żubrów; ☎ 681 23 98; adult/child 6/3zł; ⏰ 9am-4pm) is an open-plan zoo containing many of these

POLAND

mighty beasts, as well as wolves, strange horselike tarpans and mammoth żubrońs (hybrids of bisons and cows). Entrance to the reserve is just north of the Hajnówka-Białowieża road, about 4.5km west of the PTTK office – look for the signs along the żebra żubra (bison's rib) trail, or follow the green or yellow marked trails. Alternatively, catch a local bus to the stop at the main road turn-off (2.50zł) and walk a kilometre to the entrance, but ask the driver first if the bus is taking a route past the reserve.

The main attraction is the **Strict Nature Reserve** (adult/child 6/3zł; ⊙ 9am-5pm), which starts about 1km north of Palace Park. It can only be visited on a three-hour tour with a licensed guide along an 8km trail (195zł for an English- or German-speaking guide). Licensed guides (in many languages) can be arranged at the PTTK office or any travel agency in the village. Note that the reserve does close sometimes, due to inclement weather.

A more comfortable way to visit the nature reserve is by horse-drawn cart, which costs 162zł in addition to guide and entry fees (three hours) and holds four people. Otherwise, it may be possible (with permission from the PTTK office) to visit the reserve by bicycle (with a guide).

The Dom Turysty PTTK hires out bikes (25zł per day), as do several other hotels and *pensions*.

Sleeping & Eating

There are plenty of homes along the road from Hajnówka offering private rooms for about 40/70zł for singles/doubles.

Paprotka Youth Hostel (☎ 681 25 60; www.paprotka .com.pl; ul Waszkiewicza 6; dm from 16zł, d 50zł; P ✕ 🖵) One of the best in the region: the rooms are light and spruce, with high ceilings and potted plants; the newly renovated bathrooms are clean; and the kitchen is excellent. There's a washing machine as well.

Dom Turysty PTTK (☎ 681 25 05; dm from 24zł, d/tr from 66/111zł; P) Inexpensive accommodation inside Palace Park. It has seen better days, but the position and rates are hard to beat. It has a pleasant restaurant with a bison-head motif.

Pension Gawra (☎ 681 28 04; fax 681 24 84; ul Poludn-lowa 2; d 60-120zł; P) A quiet, homely place with large rooms lined with timber in a hunting lodge style, overlooking a pretty garden just behind the Hotel Żubrówka. The doubles

with bathrooms are much more spacious than those without.

Pensjonacik Unikat (☎ 681 27 74; ul Waszkiewicza 39; s/d/tr from 80/100/160zł; P 🖮) A bit too fond of dead creatures' hides as décor, but good value with its tidy wood-panelled rooms, one of which is designed for disabled access. The restaurant offers specialities such as Belarus-style potato pancakes, and has a menu in both German and English.

Hotel Żubrówka (☎ 681 23 03; ul Olgi Gabiec 6; s/d/tr from 280/320/450zł; P ✕ 🖵) Just across the way from the PTTK office, this is the town's best hotel. It's eccentrically decorated with animal hides, a working miniature water wheel, and pseudo cave drawings along the corridors. Rooms are predictably clean and comfortable, and there's a café, restaurant and nightclub on the premises.

Getting There & Away

From Warsaw, take the express train from Warszawa Centralna to Siedlce (1½ hours), wait for a connection on the slow train to Hajnówka (two hours), and then catch one of the nine daily PKS bus services to Białowieża (5zł, one hour). Two private companies, Oktobus and Lob-Trans, also run fairly squeezy minibuses between Hajnówka and Białowieża (5zł, one hour, five to seven daily). For the latest timetable information, check out www.turystyka.hajnowka.pl/ctrpb /english/

Five buses a day travel from the Dworzec Stadion station in Warsaw to Białystok (23zł to 29zł, four hours), from where two buses travel to Białowieża (15zł, three hours). You may need to stay overnight in Białystok to catch the connecting services. Polski Express also runs one daily bus between Białystok and Warsaw (34zł, 3½ hours).

MAŁOPOLSKA

Małopolska (literally 'lesser Poland') is a historic region covering all of southeastern Poland, from the Carpathian Mountains along the nation's southern borders, to the Lublin Uplands further north. It's a beautiful area, within which the visitor can spot remnants of traditional agricultural life. The biggest attraction, however, is the former royal capital, Kraków, and the majestic Tatra Mountains to the city's south.

KRAKÓW

☎ 012 / pop 758,000

A city founded upon the defeat of a dragon is off to a promising start when it comes to attracting visitors, and Kraków doesn't disappoint. As it was the royal capital of Poland until 1596, Kraków is packed with beautiful buildings and streets dating back to medieval times. The city's centrepiece, Wawel Castle and Cathedral, is a stunning reminder of the city's luck in avoiding major damage in WWII.

Just outside the Old Town lies Kazimierz, the former Jewish quarter, its silent synagogues reflecting the tragedy of the recent past. The district's tiny streets and low-rise architecture make it an interesting place to explore.

As the nation's biggest tourist drawcard, Kraków is also replete with diversions of a more modern variety, with hundreds of restaurants, bars and other venues tucked away in its laneways and cellars. Though hotel prices are above the national average, and visitor numbers high in summer, this vibrant, cosmopolitan city is an essential part of any tour of Poland.

Information
BOOKSHOPS

EMPiK Megastore (Map p390; ☎ 429 42 34; Rynek Główny 5; ☻ 9am-10pm) Sells foreign newspapers, magazines, novels and maps.

Księgarnia Hetmańska (Map p390; ☎ 430 24 53; Rynek Główny 17) An impressive selection of English-language books, including non-fiction on Polish history and culture.

Jarden Jewish Bookshop (Map p392; ☎ 429 13 74; ul Szeroka 2) Located in Kazimierz.

Sklep Podróżnika (Map p390; ☎ 429 14 85; ul Jagiellońska 6; ☻ 11am-7pm Mon-Fri, 10am-3pm Sat) Sells a wide selection of regional and city maps, as well as Lonely Planet titles.

INTERNET ACCESS

Internet Café U Luisa (Map p390; ☎ 617 02 22; Rynek Główny 13; per hr 4zł; ☻ 10am-10pm)

Klub Garinet (Map p390; ☎ 423 22 33; ul Floriańska 18; per hr 4zł; ☻ 9am-midnight)

MONEY

Kantors and ATMs can be found all over the city centre. It's worth noting, however, that many *kantors* close on Sunday, and areas near the Rynek Główny and the main train station offer terrible exchange rates. There are also exchange facilities at the airport.

Bank Pekao (Map p390; Rynek Główny 32) Cashes travellers cheques and provides cash advances on MasterCard and Visa.

POST

Main post office (Map p390; ul Westerplatte 20; ☻ 8am-8pm Mon-Fri, 8am-2pm Sat, 9-11am Sun)

TOURIST INFORMATION

The Kraków Card (www.krakowcard.com), available from tourist offices, includes travel on public transport and entry to many museums for 45/65zł for two/three days .

Two free magazines, *Welcome to Cracow & Małopolska* and *Visitor: Kraków & Zakopane* are available at tourist offices and some travel agencies and upmarket hotels. The *Kraków in Your Pocket* booklet is also very useful.

Tourist Information Centre (Map p390; ☎ 421 77 87; www.karnet.krakow.pl; ul Św. Jana 2; ☻ 10am-6pm Mon-Sat) Central city-run agency giving assistance to visitors.

Małopolska Tourism Information Centre (Map p390; ☎ 421 77 06; www.mcit.pl; Rynek Główny 1/3; ☻ 9am-7pm Mon-Fri, 9am-4pm Sat & Sun Apr-Sep, 10am-5pm Mon-Fri, 10am-4pm Sat Oct-Mar) Helpful privately run tourist office centrally located in the Cloth Hall.

Tourist office (Map p390; ☎ 433 73 10; Rynek Główny 1; ☻ 9am-7pm Apr-Sep, 9am-5pm Oct-Mar) In the Town Hall Tower.

Tourist office (Map p390; ☎ 432 01 10; ul Szpitalna 25; ☻ 8am-8pm Mon-Fri, 9am-5pm Sat & Sun) Near the main train station, this place is smaller and less harried.

Tourist office (Map p392; ☎ 422 04 71; ul Józefa 7; ☻ 10am-4pm Mon-Fri) In Kazimierz, providing information about Jewish heritage and local attractions.

Sights & Activities
WAWEL HILL

Kraków's main draw for tourists is **Wawel Hill** (Map p390; grounds admission free; ☻ 6am-8pm May-Sep, 6am-5pm Oct-Apr). South of the Old Town, the hill is crowned with a castle and cathedral, both of which are enduring symbols of Poland.

You can choose from several attractions within the castle, each requiring a separate ticket, valid for a specific time. There's a limited daily quota of tickets for some parts, so arrive early if you want to see everything.

Within the magnificent **Wawel Castle** (Map p390; ☎ 422 51 55; www.wawel.krakow.pl) are the **State Rooms** (adult/child 14/8zł, free Mon; ☻ 9.30am-noon Mon, 9.30am-4pm Tue & Fri, 9.30am-3pm Wed, Thu & Sat,

POLAND

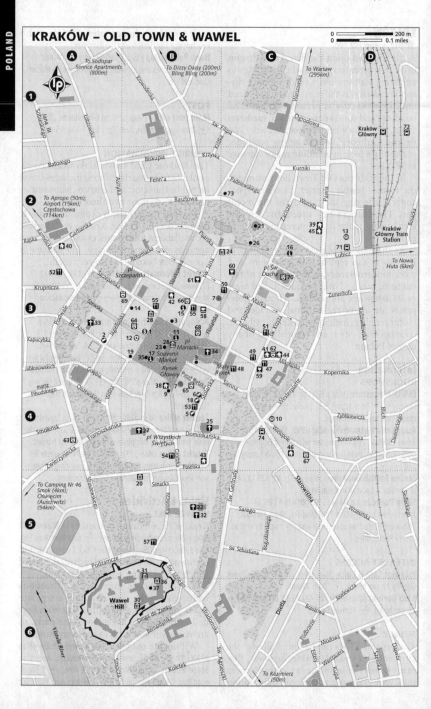

10am-3pm Sun) and the **Royal Private Apartments**
(adult/child 18/13zł; ☼ 9.30am-4pm Tue & Fri, 9.30am-3pm
Wed, Thu & Sat, 10am-3pm Sun). Entry to the latter
is only allowed on a guided tour; you may
have to accompany a Polish language tour
if it's the only one remaining for the day. If
you want to hire a guide who speaks English,
French or German, contact the onsite **guides
office** (☎ 429 33 36).

The 14th-century **Wawel Cathedral** (Map p390;
adult/child 10/5zł; ☼ 9am-3.45pm Mon-Sat, 12.15-3.45pm
Sun) was the coronation and burial place of
Polish royalty for four centuries, and houses
Royal Tombs, including that of King Kazimierz
Wielki. The **bell tower** of the golden-domed
Sigismund Chapel (1539) contains the country's
largest bell (11 tonnes).

Ecclesiastical artefacts are displayed in the
small **Cathedral Museum** (Map p390; adult/child 5/2zł;
☼ 10am-3pm Tue-Sun).

Other attractions include the **Museum of
Oriental Art** (adult/child 6/4zł, free Mon; ☼ 9.30am-noon
Mon, 9.30am-4pm Tue & Fri, 9.30am-3pm Wed, Thu & Sat,
10am-3pm Sun); the **Treasury & Armoury** (adult/child
14/8zł, free Mon; ☼ 9.30am-noon Mon, 9.30am-4pm Tue
& Fri, 9.30am-3pm Wed, Thu & Sat, 10am-3pm Sun); the
Lost Wawel (adult/child 6/4zł, free Mon; ☼ 9.30am-noon
Mon, 9.30am-4pm Tue & Fri, 9.30am-3pm Wed, Thu & Sat,

10am-3pm Sun), a well-displayed set of intriguing
archaeological exhibits; and the atmospheric
Dragon's Cave (Map p390; admission 3zł; ☼ 10am-5pm
May-Oct). Go here last, as the exit leads out onto
the riverbank.

OLD TOWN
The focus of the Old Town is **Rynek Główny**
(Main Market Square), Europe's largest medieval town square (200m by 200m). At its
centre is the 16th-century Renaissance **Cloth
Hall** (Sukiennice; Map p390). Downstairs is a
large **souvenir market** and upstairs is the **Gallery
of 19th-Century Polish Painting** (Map p390; ☎ 422 11
66; adult/child 8/5zł, free Sun; ☼ 10am-3.30pm Tue, Thu,
Sat & Sun, 10am-6pm Wed & Fri), with famous works
by Jan Matejko.

The 14th-century **St Mary's Church** (Map p390;
Rynek Główny 4; adult/child 4/2zł; ☼ 11.30am-6pm Mon-
Sat, 2-6pm Sun) fills the northeastern corner of
the square. The huge main altarpiece by Wit
Stwosz (Veit Stoss in German) of Nuremberg
is the finest Gothic sculpture in Poland, and
is opened ceremoniously each day at noon.
Every hour a *hejnał* (bugle call) is played
from the highest tower of the church. The
melody, played in medieval times as a warning call, breaks off abruptly to symbolise the

moment when, according to legend, the throat of a 13th-century trumpeter was pierced by a Tatar arrow.

West of the Cloth Hall is the 15th-century **Town Hall Tower** (Map p390; ☎ 422 99 22, ext 218; admission 4zł; ⏰ 10.30am-6pm May-Oct), which you can climb. The **Historical Museum of Kraków** (Map p390; ☎ 422 15 04; Rynek Główny 35; adult/child 5/3.50zł, free Sat; ⏰ 9am-4pm Wed & Fri-Sun, 10am-5pm Thu) has paintings, documents and oddments relating to the city.

From St Mary's Church, walk up (northeast) ul Floriańska to the 14th-century **Florian Gate**. Beyond it is the **Barbican** (Map p390; adult/child 5/3zł; ⏰ 10.30am-6pm Apr-Oct), a defensive bastion built in 1498. Nearby, the **Czartoryski Museum** (Map p390; ☎ 422 55 66; ul Św Jana 19; adult/child 9/6zł, free Thu; ⏰ 10am-6pm Tue & Thu, 10am-7pm Wed, Fri & Sat, 10am-3pm Sun) features an impressive collection of European art, including Leonardo da Vinci's *Lady with an Ermine*. Also on display are Turkish weapons and artefacts, including a campaign tent from the 1683 Battle of Vienna.

South of Rynek Główny, plac Wszystkich Świętych is dominated by two 13th-century monastic churches: the **Dominican Church** (Map p390; ul Stolarska 12; admission free; ⏰ 9am-6pm) to the east and the **Franciscan Church** (Map p390; plac Wszystkich Świętych 5; admission free; ⏰ 9am-5pm) to the west. The latter is noted for its stained-glass windows.

To the south, you'll find the **Archaeological Museum** (Map p390; ☎ 422 75 60; ul Poselska 3; adult/child 7/5zł; ⏰ 9am-2pm Mon-Wed, 2-6pm Thu, 10am-2pm Fri & Sun), with displays on local prehistory and ancient Egyptian artefacts, including animal mummies.

Continuing south along ul Grodzka is the early 17th-century Jesuit **Church of SS Peter & Paul** (Map p390; ul Grodzka 64; ⏰ dawn-dusk), Poland's first baroque church. The Romanesque 11th-century **St Andrew's Church** (Map p390; ul Grodzka 56; ⏰ 9am-6pm Mon-Fri) was the only building in Kraków to withstand the Tatars' attack of 1241.

KAZIMIERZ

Founded by King Kazimierz the Great in 1335, Kazimierz was originally an independent town. In the 15th century, Jews were expelled from Kraków and forced to resettle in a small pre-

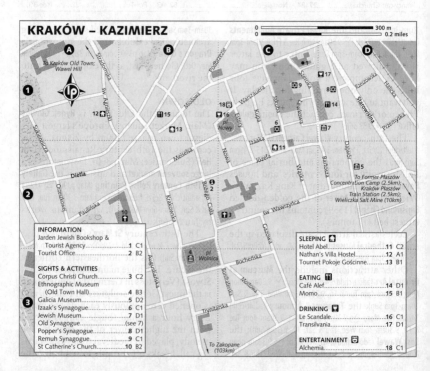

KRAKÓW – KAZIMIERZ

0 ———— 300 m
0 ———— 0.2 miles

INFORMATION
Jarden Jewish Bookshop &
   Tourist Agency...................**1** C1
Tourist Office.............................**2** B2

SIGHTS & ACTIVITIES
Corpus Christi Church...............**3** C2
Ethnographic Museum
   (Old Town Hall)...................**4** B3
Galicia Museum..........................**5** D2
Izaak's Synagogue.....................**6** C1
Jewish Museum...........................**7** D1
Old Synagogue.......................(see **7**)
Popper's Synagogue..................**8** D1
Remuh Synagogue.....................**9** C1
St Catherine's Church...............**10** B2

SLEEPING
Hotel Abel.................................**11** C2
Nathan's Villa Hostel.................**12** A1
Tournet Pokoje Gościnne.........**13** B1

EATING
Café Alef...................................**14** D1
Momo..**15** B1

DRINKING
Le Scandale..............................**16** C1
Transilvania..............................**17** D1

ENTERTAINMENT
Alchemia....................................**18** C1

To Kraków Old Town;
Wawel Hill

To Former Płaszów
Concentration Camp (2.5km);
Kraków Płaszów
Train Station (2.5 km);
Wieliczka Salt Mine (10km)

To Zakopane
(103km)

scribed area in Kazimierz, separated by a wall. The Jewish quarter later became home to Jews fleeing persecution from throughout Europe.

By the outbreak of WWII there were 65,000 Jewish Poles in Kraków (around 30% of the city's population), and most lived in Kazimierz. During the war the Nazis relocated Jews to a walled ghetto in Podgórze, just south of the Vistula River. They were exterminated in the nearby **Płaszów Concentration Camp**, as portrayed in Steven Spielberg's haunting film *Schindler's List*.

Kazimierz's western Catholic quarter includes the 14th-century Gothic **St Catherine's Church** (Map p392; ul Augustian 7; admission free; only during services), with an imposing 17th-century gilded high altar, while the 14th-century **Corpus Christi Church** (Map p392; ul Bożego Ciała 26; admission free; 9am-5pm Mon-Sat) is crammed with baroque fittings. The **Ethnographic Museum** (Map p392; 430 55 63; plac Wolnica 1; adult/child 6.50/4zł, free Sun; 10am-6pm Mon, 10am-3pm Wed-Fri, 10am-2pm Sat & Sun) in the Old Town Hall has a collection of regional crafts and costumes.

The eastern Jewish quarter is dotted with synagogues. The 15th-century **Old Synagogue** is the oldest Jewish religious building in Poland. It now houses the **Jewish Museum** (Map p392; 422 09 62; ul Szeroka 24; admission 6zł; 10am-2pm Mon, 9am-4pm Wed & Thu, Sat & Sun, 9am-5pm Fri), with exhibitions on Jewish traditions.

Not far away, the **Galicia Museum** (Map p392; 421 68 42; www.galiciajewishmuseum.org; ul Dajwór 18; adult/child 7/5zł; 9am-8pm) features an impressive photographic exhibition, depicting modern-day traces of southeastern Poland's once thriving Jewish community.

A short walk north is the small 16th-century **Remuh Synagogue** (Map p392; 422 12 74; ul Szeroka 40; adult/child 5/2zł; 9am-4pm Mon-Fri), still used for religious services. Behind it, the **Remuh Cemetery** (admission free; 9am-4pm Mon-Fri) boasts some extraordinary Renaissance gravestones. Nearby, the restored **Izaak's Synagogue** (Map p392; 430 55 77; ul Jakuba 25; admission 7zł; 9am-7pm Sun-Fri) shows documentary films about life in the Jewish ghetto.

It's easy to take a self-guided walking tour around Kazimierz with the booklet *Jewish Kazimierz Short Guide*, available from the Jarden Jewish Bookshop (see p389).

WIELICZKA SALT MINE

Wieliczka (vyeh-*leech*-kah), 15km southeast of the city centre, is famous for the **Wieliczka Salt Mine** (278 73 02; www.kopalnia.pl; ul Daniłowicza 10; adult/child 65/55zł, 20% discount after 6pm & Nov-Feb; 7.30am-7.30pm Apr-Oct, 8am-5pm Nov-Mar). It's an eerie world of pits and chambers, and every single element from chandeliers to altarpieces was hewn by hand from solid salt. The mine is included on Unesco's World Heritage List.

The highlight of a visit is the richly ornamented **Chapel of the Blessed Kinga**, a church measuring 54m by 17m, and 12m high. Construction of this underground temple took more than 30 years (1895–1927), resulting in the removal of 20,000 tonnes of rock salt.

The obligatory guided tour through the mine takes about two hours (a 2km walk). Tours in English (July to August) operate half-hourly from 8.30am to 6pm; from September to June they're approximately hourly from 9am to 5pm. There are at least two tours a day in German, and more frequently in July and August. If you're visiting independently, you must wait for a tour to start. Last admission to the mine is shortly before closing time.

THE LAJKONIK OF KRAKÓW

As you're walking through Kraków's mighty market square, you may see a street performer dressed as a man riding a richly decorated horse, with a pointed hat on his head. This is an everyday version of the Lajkonik, the central figure of an annual parade through the city.

Exact details of the Lajkonik's origin are hard to pin down, but one story involves a Tatar assault on Kraków in 1287. A group of raftsmen discovered the tent of the commanding khan on a foray outside the city walls, and dispatched the unsuspecting Tatar leader and his generals in a lightning raid. The raftsmen's leader then wore the khan's richly decorated outfit back to the city.

To commemorate the victory, each year on the first Thursday following Corpus Christi (May or June), a colourful parade takes place. Starting from the Premonstratensian monastery in Zwierzyniec, the elaborately costumed Lajkonik marches through Kraków's streets to the Main Market Square (Rynek Główny), accompanied by folk musicians. In the square, the Lajkonik prances in a lively fashion, recreating the Cracovian citizens' joy when the siege was lifted.

Minibuses to Wieliczka town depart every 10 minutes between 6am and 8pm from a location on ul Starowiślna, near the main post office in Kraków, and drop passengers outside the salt mine (2.50zł). Trains between Kraków and Wieliczka (3.80zł) leave every 45 minutes throughout the day, but the train station in Wieliczka is a fair walk from the mine.

Tours

The following companies operate tours of Kraków and surrounding areas:

Almatur (Map p390; ☎ 422 46 68; Rynek Główny 27) Arranges various outdoor activities during summer.

Cracow Tours (Map p390; ☎ 422 40 35; www.cracow tours.pl; Rynek Główny 41) Inside Orbis Travel, offering city tours, and tours of Auschwitz and the salt mines.

Crazy Guides (☎ 0888 68 68 71; www.crazyguides .com) Offers entertaining tours of the city's communist-era suburbs, in restored East German cars.

Jarden Jewish Bookshop & Tourist Agency (Map p392; ☎ 421 71 66; www.jarden.pl; ul Szeroka 2) The best agency for tours of Polish Jewish heritage. Its showpiece, 'Retracing Schindler's List' (two hours by car), costs 65zł per person. All tours require a minimum of three and must be arranged in advance. Tours are in English, but French- and German-speaking guides can be arranged.

Sleeping

Kraków is unquestionably Poland's major tourist destination, with prices to match. Booking ahead in the busy summer months is recommended.

BUDGET

Bling Bling (☎ 634 05 32; www.blingbling.pl; ul Pędzichów 7; dm 45zł, d/tr 120/180zł; 💻) Comfortable hostel north of the Old Town, offering inexpensive, good quality accommodation. High ceilings make the dorms feel spacious, though the lounge is a little dark. Laundry available.

Cracow Hostel (Map p390; ☎ 429 11 06; www.cracow hostel.com; Rynek Główny 18; dm 45-60zł; 💻) Budget accommodation is hard to find in the centre of the Old Town, but this place is perched high above the market square, with an amazing view of St Mary's Church from the roomy but comfortable lounge. There's also a kitchen and washing machine.

Greg & Tom Hostel (Map p390; ☎ 422 41 00; www .gregtomhostel.com; ul Pawia 12; dm 50zł, d/tr 120/150; 💻) This well-run hostel is spread over two locations; the private rooms are a 10-minute walk away on ul Warszawska. The staff are friendly, the rooms are clean, and laundry facilities are

included. Note that reception is up four flights of stairs, and the private rooms are above a (seemingly peaceful) massage parlour.

Nathan's Villa Hostel (☎ 422 35 45; www.nathansvilla .com; ul Św. Agnieszki 1; dm/d from 50/160zł; 🗶 💻) The best hostel in town is conveniently located between the Old Town and Kazimierz. Comfy rooms, sparkling bathrooms, free laundry and a friendly atmosphere make this place a big hit with backpackers. The addition of a cellar bar, mini-cinema and pool table have kept Nathan's ahead of the pack.

Dizzy Daisy (☎ 292 01 71; www.hostel.pl; ul Pędzichów 9; dm/d/tr 60/160/210zł; 💻) A modern chain-hostel with great facilities and light, clean rooms, frequented by an international crowd of party people. Laundry and kitchen are available.

Camping Nr 46 Smok (☎ 429 83 00; ul Kamedulska 18; per person/tent 15/19zł; 🅿) It's small, quiet and pleasantly located 4km west of the Old Town. To get here from outside the Kraków Główny train station building, take tram 2 to the end of the line in Zwierzyniec and change for any westbound bus (except No 100).

MIDRANGE

An agency offering decent rooms around town is **Jordan Tourist Information & Accommodation Centre** (Map p390; ☎ 422 60 91; www.jordan.krakow .pl; ul Pawia 8; 🕑 8am-6pm Mon-Fri, 9am-2pm Sat & Sun; s/d around 110/130zł).

Sodispar Service Apartments (☎ 0602 247 438; www.sodispar.com.pl; ul Lubelska 12; apt €30-140) Several comfortable, modern apartments sleeping up to four people, north of the Old Town. Cheaper rates are available for longer stays.

Apropo (☎ 0506 102 924; www.apropo.info; ul Karmelicka 36; d/tr 150/225zł) Set of comfortable rooms within a fully renovated old apartment, with access to shared bathrooms, a light-filled kitchen and laundry facilities. It's in a convenient location not far from the Old Town.

Tournet Pokoje Gościnne (Map p392; ☎ 292 00 88; www.accommodation.krakow.pl; ul Miodowa 7; s/d/tr from 140/180/220zł) This is a neat *pension* in Kazimierz, offering simple but comfortable and quiet rooms. The bathrooms, however, are tiny.

Hotel Royal (Map p390; ☎ 421 35 00; www.royal .com.pl; ul Św. Gertrudy 26-29; s 140-210zł, d 220-300zł, tr 300-330zł, ste 300-360zł; 🅿) Impressive Art Nouveau edifice with loads of old-world charm, just below Wawel Castle. It's split into two sections: the higher-priced two-star rooms are cosy, and far preferable to the fairly basic one-star rooms at the back.

Hotel Abel (Map p392; ☎ 411 87 36; www.hotelabel
.pl; ul Józefa 30; s/d/tr 170/230/260) Reflecting the
character of Kazimierz, this hotel has a distinctive personality, evident in its polished
wooden staircase, arched brickwork and age-
worn tiles. The comfortable rooms make a
good base for exploring the historic Jewish
neighbourhood.

Wielopole Guest Rooms (Map p390; ☎ 422 14 75;
www.wielopole.pl; ul Wielopole 3; s/d from 190/280zł;
P ⊠ ⅋) Smart and simple modern rooms
in a renovated block on the eastern edge of
the Old Town, with narrow beds but spotless
bathrooms. One room is designed for disabled
access, and breakfast is only included for stays
of two nights or more.

Hotel Wit Stwosz (Map p390; ☎ 429 60 26; www.wit
-stwosz.com.pl; ul Mikołajska 28; s/d/tr €75/86/99, ste €130) In
a historic town house belonging to St Mary's
church, and decorated in a suitably religious
theme. Rooms are compact and simply furnished, but tasteful and attractive.

TOP END

Hotel Saski (Map p390; ☎ 421 42 22; www.hotelsaski.com
.pl; ul Sławkowska 3; s/d/ste 295/360/450zł; ⊠) The Saski
occupies a historic mansion, complete with
a uniformed doorman, rattling old lift and
ornate furnishings. The rooms themselves are
comparatively plain, though some singles are
surprisingly spacious.

Hotel Wawel (Map p390; ☎ 424 13 00; www.hotel
wawel.pl; ul Poselska 22; s/d 260/380zł; ⊠) Ideally
located just off busy ul Grodzka, this is a
pleasant place offering tastefully decorated
rooms with timber highlights. It's far enough
back from the main drag to avoid most of
the noise.

Hotel Alexander (Map p390; ☎ 422 96 60; www.alex
hotel.pl; ul Garbarska 18; s/d 340/400zł; P ⊠ ⅋) The
Alexander is a bright and very modern place,
offering standard three-star comfort. It's on
a shabby but quiet street just west of the Old
Town. One room is designed for disabled
access.

Hotel Amadeus (Map p390; ☎ 429 60 70; www.hotel
-amadeus.pl; ul Mikołajska 20; s/d €156/166, ste €240;
⊠ ⅋) Everything about this hotel says
'class'. The rooms are tastefully furnished,
though singles are rather small given the
price. One room has disabled access, and
there's a sauna, a fitness centre, and a well-
regarded restaurant. While hanging around
the Amadeus' foyer, you can check out photos of famous guests.

Eating

Kraków is a food paradise, tightly packed with
restaurants serving a wide range of international cuisines.

One local speciality is *obwarzanki* (ring-
shaped pretzels powdered with poppy seeds,
sesame seeds or salt) available from street
vendors dozing next to their barrows.

POLISH

Restauracja Pod Gruszką (Map p390; ☎ 422 88 96;
ul Szczepańska 1; mains 12-55zł; ◷ noon-midnight) A
favourite haunt of writers and artists, this
upstairs establishment is the eatery that time
forgot, with its elaborate old-fashioned décor
featuring chandeliers, lace tablecloths, age-
worn carpets and sepia portraits. The menu
covers a range of Polish dishes, the most distinctive being the soups served within small
bread loaves.

Restauracja Chłopskie Jadło (Map p390; ☎ 429 51
57; ul Św. Jana 3; mains 12-80zł; ◷ noon-midnight) Arranged as an old country inn with wooden
benches and traditional music, and serving
tasty Polish food. Try the *żurek* (sour soup)
with sausage and egg, for a light but filling
meal. There are some vegetarian options on
the menu, but brace yourself for the meat
products hanging off the walls.

Nostalgia (Map p390; ☎ 425 42 60; ul Karmelicka 10;
mains 13-36zł; ◷ noon-11pm) A refined version of
the traditional Polish eatery, Nostalgia features a fireplace, overhead timber beams, uncrowded tables and courteous service. Wrap
yourself around Russian dumplings, pork
loins in green pepper sauce, or veggie options
such as potato pancakes. In warm weather
there's an outdoor dining area.

Pod Aniołami (Map p390; ☎ 421 39 99; ul Grodzka 35;
mains 25-60zł; ◷ 1pm-midnight) This eatery 'under
the angels' offers high-quality Polish food in
a pleasant cellar atmosphere, though it can
get a little smoky. Specialities include the
huntsman's smoked wild boar steak.

INTERNATIONAL

Gruzińskie Chaczapuri (Map p390; ☎ 0509 542 800; cnr ul
Floriańska & ul Św. Marka; mains 10-18zł; ◷ 10am-midnight)
Cheap and cheerful place serving up tasty
Georgian dishes. Grills, salads and steaks fill
out the menu, and there's a separate vegetar-
ian selection with items such as the traditional
Georgian cheese pie with stewed vegetables.

Bombaj Tandoori (Map p390; ☎ 422 37 97; ul Mikołajska 11; mains 11-32zł; ◷ noon-11pm) The Bombaj

Tandoori is the best curry house in Kraków, with friendly staff and a lengthy menu of Indian standards. The four-person set menu (85zł) is excellent value, and there's also a takeaway and local delivery service.

Casa della Pizza (Map p390; ☎ 421 64 98; Mały Rynek 2; mains 12-32zł; 11am-midnight) This unpretentious place is away from the bulk of the tourist traffic, with a menu of pizzas and pasta. The downstairs bar section is the Arabian-styled Shisha Club, serving Middle Eastern food.

Orient Ekspres (Map p390; ☎ 422 66 72; ul Stolarska 13; mains 15-48zł; 11am-11pm) Hercule Poirot might be surprised to find this elegant eatery here, well off the route of its railway namesake. The food is mainly Polish, with some international additions, accompanied by wine by the glass. Mellow music and candlelight make it a good place for a romantic rendezvous.

Smak Ukraiński (Map p390; ☎ 421 92 94; ul Kanonicza 15; mains 15-50zł; 11am-9pm) This Ukrainian restaurant presents authentic dishes in a cosy little cellar decorated with provincial flair. Expect lots of dumplings, *borscht* and waiters in waistcoats.

Café Alef (Map p392; ☎ 421 38 70; ul Szeroka 17; mains 16-45zł; noon-11pm) This is a quaint place in the heart of Kazimierz, with gilt-edged mirrors and lace tablecloths. It offers an array of Jewish-inspired dishes such as chicken *knedlach* (dumplings) and stuffed goose neck.

Ipanema (Map p390; ☎ 422 53 23; ul Św. Tomasza 28; mains from 16zł; noon-11pm) A banana palm as décor may seem out of place in Poland, but this bright place pulls it off. The Brazilian menu features steaks, grills and a range of interesting Afro-Brazilian dishes.

Metropolitan Restaurant (Map p390; ☎ 421 98 03; ul Sławkowska 3; mains 22-68zł; 7.30am-midnight Mon-Sat, 7.30am-10pm Sun) Attached to Hotel Saski, this place has nostalgic B&W photos of international locales plastering the walls, and is a great place for breakfast. It also serves pasta, grills and steaks, and luxurious items such as honey and orange roasted leg of duck.

VEGETARIAN

Momo (Map p392; ☎ 0609 685 775; ul Dietla 49; mains 4-12zł; 11am-8pm) Vegans will cross the doorstep of this Kazimierz restaurant with relief – the majority of the menu is completely animal-free. The space is decorated with Indian craft pieces, and serves up subcontinental soups, stuffed pancakes and rice dishes, with a great range of cakes. The Tibetan dumplings are a treat worth ordering.

Green Way Bar Wegetariański (Map p390; ☎ 431 10 27; ul Mikołajska 14; mains 10-15zł; 10am-10pm Mon-Fri, 11am-9pm Sat & Sun) The Green Way offers good value vegetarian fare such as veggie kofta, enchiladas and salads.

Drinking

There are hundreds of pubs and bars in Kraków's Old Town, many housed in ancient vaulted cellars, which get very smoky. Kazimierz also has a lively bar scene, centred on plac Nowy and its surrounding streets.

Paparazzi (Map p390; ☎ 429 45 97; ul Mikołajska 9; 11am-1am Mon-Fri, 4pm-4am Sat & Sun) If you haven't brought any reading material with you to this bar, look up – the ceiling is plastered with pages from racy tabloid newspapers. It's a bright, modern place, with black-and-white press photos covering the walls. The drinks menu includes cocktails such as the Polish Express, built around vanilla vodka. There's also inexpensive bar food.

Le Scandale (Map p392; ☎ 430 68 55; plac Nowy 9; 8am-3am) Smooth Kazimierz drinking hole with low black leather couches, ambient lighting and a gleaming well-stocked bar. Full of mellow drinkers sampling the extensive cocktail list.

Transilvania (Map p392; ☎ 0692 335 867; ul Szeroka 9; 10am-3am) The Transilvania is another convivial place in Kazimierz, with a vampire theme going on. Check out the portrait of Vlad the Impaler over the bar.

Pod Papugami (Map p390; ☎ 422 82 99; ul Św. Jana 18; 1pm-2am Mon-Sat, 3pm-2am Sun) This is a vaguely 'Irish' cellar pub decorated with old motorcycles and other assorted odds and ends. A good place to hide from inclement weather, with its pool table and tunnel-like maze of rooms.

Piwnica Pod Złotą Pipą (Map p390; ☎ 421 94 66; ul Floriańska 30; noon-midnight) Less claustrophobic than other cellar bars, with lots of tables for eating or drinking. Decent bar food and international beers on tap.

Café Camelot (Map p390; ☎ 421 01 23; ul Św. Tomasza 17; 9am-midnight) For coffee and cake, try this genteel haven hidden around an obscure street corner in the Old Town. Its cosy rooms are cluttered with lace-covered candlelit tables, and a quirky collection of wooden figurines featuring spiritual or folkloric scenes.

Entertainment

The comprehensive Polish-English booklet *Karnet* (3zł), published by the Tourist Information Centre (see p389), lists almost every event in the city.

NIGHTCLUBS

Piano Rouge (Map p390; ☎ 431 03 33; Rynek Główny 46; ☸ noon-3am) A sumptuous cellar venue decked out with classic sofas, ornate lampshades and billowing lengths of colourful silk. There's live jazz every night from Wednesday to Sunday.

Łubu-Dubu (Map p390; ☎ 423 05 21; ul Wielopole 15; ☸ 4pm-2am Sun-Thu, 5pm-4am Fri & Sat) The name of this place (*wooboo-doo*boo) is as funky as its décor. This grungy upstairs joint is an echo of the past, from the garish colours to the collection of objects from 1970s Poland. A series of rooms creates spaces for talking or dancing as the mood strikes.

Alchemia (Map p392; ☎ 421 22 00; ul Estery 5; ☸ 9am-3am) This Kazimierz venue exudes a shabby-is-the-new-cool look with rough-hewn wooden benches, candlelit tables and a companionable gloom. It hosts regular live music gigs and theatrical events through the week.

Black Gallery (Map p390; ul Mikołajska 24; ☸ noon-6am) Underground pub-cum-nightclub with a modern aspect: split levels, exposed steel frame lighting and a metallic bar. It really gets going after midnight. It also has a more civilised courtyard.

Frantic (Map p390; ☎ 423 04 83; ul Szewska 5; ☸ 6pm-4am) Occupying vast brick cellars, Frantic is trendy, attractive and popular with foreigners.

THEATRE

Stary Teatr (Map p390; ☎ 422 40 40; www.stary-teatr.pl; ul Jagiellońska 5) The best-known venue, Stary offers quality theatre.

Teatr im Słowackiego (Map p390; ☎ 422 40 22; plac Św. Ducha 1) This grand place, built in 1893, focuses on Polish classics and large productions.

Filharmonia Krakowska (Map p390; ☎ 422 94 77; ul Zwierzyniecka 1) Hosts one of the best orchestras in the country; concerts are usually held on Friday and Saturday.

CINEMAS

Two convenient cinemas are **Kino Sztuka** (Map p390; ☎ 421 41 99; cnr Św. Tomasza & Św. Jana), and the tiny **Kino Pasaż** (Map p390; ☎ 422 77 13; Rynek Główny 9). Tickets cost from 11zł.

Getting There & Away

For information on travelling from Kraków to Zakopane, Częstochowa or Oświęcim (for Auschwitz), refer to the relevant destination sections later.

AIR

The **John Paul II International airport** (www.lotnisko-balice.pl) is more often called the Balice airport, after the suburb in which it's located, about 15km west of the Old Town. The airport terminal hosts several car-hire desks, along with currency exchanges. You can buy tickets for bus 192 to the city centre from the newsagency upstairs.

LOT flies between Kraków and Warsaw several times a day, and offers direct flights from Kraków to Frankfurt and Munich. Bookings for all flights can be made at the **LOT office** (Map p390; ☎ 422 42 15; ul Basztowa 15).

A range of other airlines, including budget operators, connect Kraków to cities in Europe. There are direct flights to and from London via British Airways, Centralwings (April to October), Easyjet, Sky Europe and Ryanair. Dublin is serviced by Ryanair (May to October), Sky Europe and Aer Lingus.

BUS

If you've been travelling by bus elsewhere in Poland, Kraków's modern main **bus terminal** (Map p390; ul Bosacka 18) will seem like a palace compared to the usual facility. It's located on the other side of the main train station from the Old Town. However, bus services are limited to regional centres of minimal interest to travellers, as well as Lublin (40zł, four daily), Zamość (42zł, five daily), Warsaw (39zł, four daily), Wrocław (42zł, four daily) and Cieszyn (18zł, 10 daily) on the Czech border.

A daily Polski Express bus to Warsaw also departs from the bus terminal (67zł), but takes eight hours to reach the capital.

TRAIN

The lovely old **Kraków Główny train station** (Map p390; plac Dworcowy), on the northeastern outskirts of the Old Town, handles all international trains and most domestic rail services. The railway platforms are about 150m north of the station building.

Each day from Kraków, 10 fast trains head to Warsaw (43zł, 2¾ hours). There are also 10 fast trains daily to Wrocław (41zł, 3¾ hours), six to Poznań (48zł, six hours), two to Lublin

POLAND

(44zł, five hours), and eight to Gdynia, via Gdańsk (101zł, 7¼ hours).

Advance tickets for international and domestic trains can be booked directly at the station or from Cracow Tours (p394).

OŚWIĘCIM

☎ 033 / pop 48,000

Few place names have more impact than Auschwitz, which is seared into public consciousness as the location of history's most extensive experiment in genocide. Every year hundreds of thousands visit Oświęcim (osh-*fyen*-cheem) to learn about the infamous Nazi death camp's history, and to pay respect to the dead.

Established within disused army barracks in 1940, Auschwitz was initially designed to hold Polish prisoners, but was expanded into the largest centre for the extermination of European Jews. Two more camps were subsequently established: Birkenau (Brzezinka, also known as Auschwitz II), 3km west of Auschwitz; and Monowitz (Monowice), several kilometres west of Oświęcim. In the course of their operation, between one and 1.5 million people were murdered in these death factories – about 90% of these were Jews.

Auschwitz

Auschwitz was only partially destroyed by the fleeing Nazis, so many of the original buildings remain as a bleak document of the camp's history. A dozen of the 30 surviving prison blocks house sections of the **State Museum Auschwitz-Birkenau** (☎ 844 81 00; www .auschwitz.org.pl; admission free; 🕙 8am-7pm Jun-Aug, 8am-6pm May & Sep, 8am-5pm Apr & Oct, 8am-4pm Mar & Nov, 8am-3pm Dec-Feb).

About every half-hour, the cinema in the **visitors centre** at the entrance shows a 15-minute documentary film (admission 3.50zł) about the liberation of the camp by Soviet troops on 27 January 1945. It's shown in several languages throughout the day; check the schedule at the information desk as soon as you arrive. The film is not recommended for children under 14 years old. The visitors centre also has a cafeteria, bookshops, a *kantor* and a left-luggage room.

Some basic explanations in Polish, English and Hebrew are provided on site, but you'll understand more if you buy the small *Auschwitz Birkenau Guide Book* (translated into about 15 languages) from the visitors centre.

An English-language tour (26zł per person, 3½ hours) of Auschwitz and Birkenau leaves at 11am daily, with others starting at 10am, 1pm and 3pm if there's enough demand. Tours in German or Polish commence when a group of seven or eight can be formed; otherwise, tours in a range of languages can be arranged in advance. But make sure you receive your allotted time; some guides tell you to wander around Birkenau by yourself and to make your own way back to Auschwitz.

Birkenau

Birkenau (admission free; 🕙 8am-7pm Jun-Aug, 8am-6pm May & Sep, 8am-5pm Apr & Oct, 8am-4pm Mar & Nov, 8am-3pm Dec-Feb) was actually where the murder of huge numbers of Jews took place. This vast (175 hectares), purpose-built and grimly efficient camp had more than 300 prison barracks and four huge gas chambers complete with crematoria. Each gas chamber held 2000 people and electric lifts raised the bodies to the ovens. The camp could hold 200,000 inmates at one time.

Although much of the camp was destroyed by retreating Nazis, the size of the place, fenced off with barbed wire stretching almost as far as the eye can see, provides some idea of the scale of this heinous crime. The viewing platform above the entrance provides further perspective. In some ways, Birkenau is even more shocking than Auschwitz and there are far fewer tourists.

Sleeping & Eating

For most visitors, Auschwitz and Birkenau are an easy day trip from Kraków. The cafeteria in the visitors centre is sufficient for a quick lunch.

Centrum Dialogu i Modlitwy (☎ 843 10 00; www .centrum-dialogu.oswiecim.pl; ul Kolbego 1; camp sites from 22zł, r per person with shared bathroom from 88zł; 🖳) This place is 700m southwest of Auschwitz. It's comfortable and quiet, and the price includes breakfast. Rooms with private bathroom cost slightly more, and full board is also offered.

Getting There & Away

From Kraków Główny station, 12 mostly slow trains go to Oświęcim (10zł, 1½ hours) each day, though more depart from Kraków Płaszów station.

Far more convenient are the 16 buses per day to Oświęcim (8zł, 1½ hours), which depart from the bus station in Kraków, four of which terminate at the museum. For the others, get off at the final stop, 200m from the entrance to Auschwitz. The return bus timetable to Kraków is displayed at the Birkenau visitors centre.

Every half-hour from 11.30am to 4.30pm between 15 April and 31 October, buses shuttle passengers between the visitor centres at Auschwitz and Birkenau (buses run later to 5.30pm in May and September, and until 6.30pm from June to August). Otherwise, follow the signs for an easy walk (3km) or take a taxi. Auschwitz is also linked to the town's train station by buses 24, 25, 28 and 29 every 30 to 40 minutes.

Most travel agencies in Kraków offer organised tours of Auschwitz (including Birkenau), from 100zł to 150zł per person. Check with the operator for exactly how much time the tour allows you at Auschwitz, as some run to a very tight schedule.

CZĘSTOCHOWA

☎ 034 / pop 251,000

Częstochowa (chen-sto-*ho*-vah), 114km northwest of Kraków, is an attractive pilgrimage town, dominated by the graceful Jasna Góra monastery atop a hill at its centre. The monastery, founded by the Paulites of Hungary in 1382, is the home of the Black Madonna, and owes its fame to a miracle. In 1430 a group of Hussites stole the holy icon, slashed it and broke it into three pieces. Legend has it that the picture bled, and the monks cleaned the retrieved panel with the aid of a spring, which rose miraculously from the ground. Though the picture was restored, the scars on the Virgin's face were retained in memory of the miracle.

The Madonna was also credited with the fortified monastery's resistance to the Swedish sieges of the 1650s. In 1717 the Black Madonna was crowned Queen of Poland.

From the train station, and adjacent bus terminal, turn right (north) up al Wolności – along which are several internet cafés – to the main thoroughfare, al Najświętszej Marii Panny (simplified to al NMP). At the western end of this avenue is the monastery and at the eastern end is plac Daszyńskiego. In-between is the **tourist office** (☎ 368 22 60; al NMP 65; 🕑 9am-5pm Mon-Sat) and several banks and *kantors*.

Sights

The **Paulite Monastery on Jasna Góra** (☎ 365 38 88; www.jasnagora.pl; admission free; 🕑 dawn-dusk) retains the appearance of a hilltop fortress. Inside the grounds are three **museums** (donations welcome; 🕑 9am-5pm): the **Arsenal**, with a variety of old weapons; the **600th-Anniversary Museum** (Muzeum Sześćsetlecia), which contains Lech Wałęsa's 1983 Nobel Peace Prize; and the **Treasury** (Skarbiec), featuring offerings presented by the faithful.

The **tower** (🕑 8am-4pm Apr-Nov) is the tallest (106m) historic church tower in Poland. The baroque church beneath is beautifully decorated. The image of the Black Madonna is on the high altar of the adjacent chapel, entered from the left of the church aisle. It's hard to see, so a copy is on display in the **Knights' Hall** (Sala Rycerska) in the monastery. Note that the Madonna is sometimes concealed by a silver cover; if so, check with the on-site information office for the next scheduled uncovering. It's quite an event, as priests file in, music plays and the image slowly emerges.

On weekends and holidays expect long queues for all three museums. The crowds in the chapel may be so thick that you're almost unable to enter, much less get near the icon.

In the Town Hall the **Częstochowa Museum** (☎ 360 56 31; al NMP 45; adult/child 4/3zł; 🕑 9am-3.30pm Tue, Thu & Fri, 11am-5.30pm Wed, 10am-4pm Sat & Sun) features an ethnographic collection and modern Polish paintings.

Festivals & Events

The major Marian feasts at Jasna Góra are 3 May, 16 July, 15 August (especially), 26 August, 8 September, 12 September and 8 December. On these days the monastery is packed with pilgrims.

Sleeping & Eating

Youth Hostel (☎ 324 31 21; ul Jasnogórska 84/90; dm 20-36zł; 🕑 Jul-Aug) This hostel, two blocks north of the tourist office, has modest facilities. Look for the triangular green sign on the building's wall.

Dom Pielgrzyma (☎ 377 75 64; ul Wyszyńskiego 1/31; dm 23zł, s/d from 70/100zł) A huge place behind the monastery, it offers numerous quiet and comfortable rooms, and is remarkably good value.

Plenty of **eateries** can be found near the Dom Pielgrzyma. Better restaurants are dotted along al NMP.

Restaurant Cleopatra (☎ 368 01 01; al NMP 71; mains 10-18zł; 🕑 11am-11pm) The cheerfully out-of-place Cleopatra, near the tourist office, serves pizzas, kebabs and sandwiches among pillars painted with ancient Egyptian designs.

POLAND

Bar Viking (☎ 324 57 68; ul Nowowiejskiego 10; mains 6-40zł; ☾ 10am-10pm) About 200m south of the Częstochowa Museum is a friendly place with a good range of dishes, including vegetarian choices.

Getting There & Away

Every day from the **bus terminal** (al Wolności 45) nine buses go to Kraków (14zł to 34zł), five travel to Wrocław (21zł to 29zł), eight head for Zakopane (30zł to 41zł) and seven depart for Warsaw (30zł to 46zł).

From the impressive **train station** (al Wolności 21) five trains a day go to Warsaw (38zł, 3½ hours). There are also three daily trains to Gdynia via Gdańsk (55zł, nine hours), four to Łódź (30zł, two hours), one to Olsztyn (52zł,

7½ hours), one to Zakopane (26zł, six hours), four to Kraków (29zł, two hours) and two to Wrocław (32zł, three hours).

ZAKOPANE

☎ 018 / pop 30,000

Nestled at the foot of the Tatra Mountains, Zakopane is Poland's major winter sports centre, though it's a popular destination year-round. It may resemble a tourist trap, with its overcommercialised, overpriced exterior, but it also has a relaxed, laid-back vibe that makes it a great place to chill out for a few days, even if you're not intending to ski or hike.

Zakopane also played an important role in keeping Polish culture alive during the long years of foreign rule in the 19th century. Many

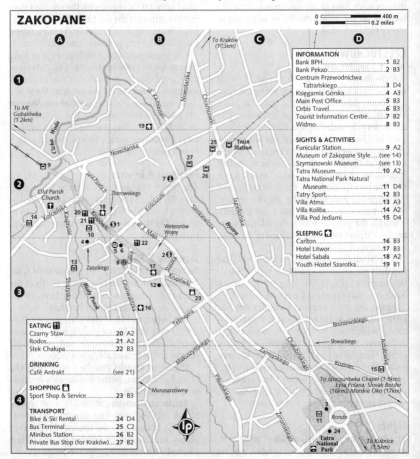

ZAKOPANE

INFORMATION
Bank BPH..............................1 B2
Bank Pekao..........................2 B3
Centrum Przewodnictwa Tatrańskiego.......................3 D4
Księgarnia Górska................4 A3
Main Post Office.................5 B3
Orbis Travel.........................6 B3
Tourist Information Centre...7 B2
Widmo..................................8 B3

SIGHTS & ACTIVITIES
Funicular Station..................9 A2
Museum of Zakopane Style....(see 14)
Szymanowski Museum..........(see 13)
Tatra Museum......................10 A2
Tatra National Park Natural Museum.............................11 D4
Tatry Sport.........................12 B3
Villa Atma.............................13 A3
Villa Koliba..........................14 A2
Villa Pod Jedlami................15 D4

SLEEPING
Carlton.................................16 B3
Hotel Litwor.........................17 B3
Hotel Sabała........................18 A2
Youth Hostel Szarotka.........19 B1

EATING
Czarny Staw.........................20 A2
Rodos...................................21 A2
Stek Chałupa.......................22 B3

DRINKING
Café Antrakt.......................(see 21)

SHOPPING
Sport Shop & Service..........23 B3

TRANSPORT
Bike & Ski Rental.................24 D4
Bus Terminal.......................25 C2
Minibus Station...................26 B2
Private Bus Stop (for Kraków)....27 B2

artistic types settled in the town, including composer Karol Szymanowski and the writer and painter, Witkacy. Witkacy's father, Stanisław Witkiewicz, was inspired by traditional local architecture to create the famous Zakopane style. Some of his buildings still stand.

Information

INTERNET ACCESS

Widmo (☎ 206 43 77; ul Galicy 6; per hr 4.50zł; ♥ 7.30am-midnight Mon-Fri, 9am-midnight Sat & Sun)

MONEY

Dozens of *kantors* can be found along the main streets. There are several banks along the pedestrian mall.

Bank Pekao (☎ 201 40 84; al 3 Maja 5)
Bank BPH (☎ 201 49 09; ul Krupówki 19)

POST

Main post office (ul Krupówki)

TOURIST INFORMATION

Tourist Information Centre (☎ 201 22 11; ul Kościuszki 17; ♥ 8am-8pm Jun-Sep, 9am-6pm Oct-May) Helpful English-speaking staff provide advice, and sell hiking and city maps. The centre can also arrange rafting trips down the Dunajec River (see p404).

TRAVEL AGENCIES

Centrum Przewodnictwa Tatrzańskiego (Tatra Guide Centre; ☎ 206 37 99; ul Chałubińskiego 42/44; ♥ 9am-3pm) Able to arrange English- and German-speaking mountain guides.

Księgarnia Górska (ul Zaruskiego 5) In the reception area of the Dom Turysty PTTK, this is the best place for regional hiking maps.

Orbis Travel (☎ 201 50 51; ul Krupówki 22) Offers the usual services, as well as accommodation in hotels and *pensions*. Also has an in-house *kantor*.

Sights & Activities

Check out exhibits about regional history, ethnography and geology at the **Tatra Museum** (☎ 201 52 05; ul Krupówki 10; adult/child 5/4zł, free Sun; ♥ 9am-4pm Tue-Sat, 9am-3pm Sun May-Oct, 9am-4pm Wed-Sat, 9am-3pm Sun Nov-Apr), along with displays on local flora and fauna. Head southwest to **Villa Koliba** (ul Kościeliska 18), the first design (1892) by Witkiewicz in the Zakopane style. Fittingly, it now houses the **Museum of Zakopane Style** (☎ 201 36 02; adult/child 5/4zł; ♥ 9am-5pm Tue-Sat, 9am-3pm Sun).

About 350m southeast is **Villa Atma** (ul Kasprusie 19) with its **Szymanowksi Museum** (☎ 201 34 93; adult/child 5/3zł, free Sun; ♥ 10am-3.30pm Wed, Thu, Sat &

Sun, 10am-6pm Fri), dedicated to the great musician who once lived there. There are piano recitals here in summer.

The **Tatra National Park Natural Museum** (☎ 206 32 03; ul Chałubińskiego 42a; admission free; ♥ 8am-3pm Mon-Sat), near the Rondo en route to the national park, has some mildly interesting exhibits about the park's natural history.

A short walk northeast up the hill leads to **Villa Pod Jedlami** (ul Koziniec 1), another splendid house built in the Zakopane style (the interior cannot be visited). Perhaps Witkiewicz's greatest achievement is the **Jaszczurówka Chapel**, about 1.5km further east along the road to Morskie Oko.

Mt Gubałówka (1120m) offers excellent views over the Tatras and is a popular destination for tourists who don't feel overly energetic. The **funicular** (tickets adult/child 8/6zł, return 14/10zł; ♥ 9am-9pm May-Sep, 8am-7pm Oct-Apr) covers the 1388m-long route in less than five minutes, climbing 300m from the funicular station just north of ul Krupówki.

Sleeping

Given the abundance of private rooms and decent hostels, few travellers actually stay in hotels. The tourist office usually knows of great bargains in guesthouses.

Some travel agencies in Zakopane can arrange private rooms, but in the peak season they may not want to offer anything for less than three nights. Expect a double room (singles are rarely offered) to cost about 70zł in the peak season in the town centre, and about 50zł for somewhere further out.

Locals offering private rooms may approach you at the bus or train stations; alternatively, just look out for signs posted in the front of private homes – *noclegi* and *pokoje* both mean 'rooms available'.

Like all seasonal resorts, accommodation prices fluctuate considerably between low season and high season (December to February and July to August). Always book accommodation in advance at these peak times, especially on weekends. The following rates are for high season.

Youth Hostel Szarotka (☎ 201 36 18; www.szarotka ptsm.republika.pl; ul Nowotarska 45; dm/d 35/90zł; **P** 🖾) This friendly, homely place gets packed in the high season. There's a kitchen and washing machine on site, and bed linen costs 5zł extra. It's on a noisy road about a 10-minute walk from the town centre.

Carlton (☎ 201 44 15; www.carlton.pl; ul Grunwaldzka 11; s/d/tr 90/180/270zł; P 🖳) Good value *pension* in a grand old house away from the main drag, featuring light-filled rooms with modern furniture. There's an impressive shared balcony overlooking the road, and a big comfy lounge lined with potted plants.

Hotel Sabała (☎ 201 50 92; www.sabala.zakopane.pl; ul Krupówki 11; s/d/ste from 275/370/480zł; P 🗶 🕿) Built in 1894 but thoroughly up-to-date, this striking timber building has a superb location overlooking the picturesque pedestrian thoroughfare. It offers cosy, attic-style rooms, and there's a sauna and solarium on the premises. A candlelit **restaurant** (mains 12-42zł) has views of street life.

Hotel Litwor (☎ 202 42 00; www.litwor.pl; ul Krupówki 40; s/d 425/575zł, ste from 600zł; P 🗶 🖳 🕿) This sumptuous four-star place, with large, restful rooms, has all the usual top-end facilities, including a gym and sauna. A discount applies to advance bookings. It also has an excellent restaurant serving classy versions of traditional dishes.

Eating & Drinking

The main street, ul Krupówki, is lined with all sorts of eateries.

Czarny Staw (☎ 201 38 56; ul Krupówki 2; mains 11-35zł; 🕘 10am-1am) Offers a tasty range of Polish dishes, including fish, much of it cooked before your very eyes on the central grill. There's a good salad bar, and live music most nights.

Rodos (ul Krupówki 6; mains 13-29zł; 🕘 9am-10pm) If you need a break from Polish food served by waiters in Tatran costume, this Greek eatery provides a good range of kebabs, gyros and pasta dishes, in a space decorated with Mediterranean scenes and the odd off-theme prop from the Middle East.

Stek Chałupa (☎ 201 59 18; ul Krupówki 33; mains 16-36zł; 🕘 11am-11pm) Big friendly barn of a place, with homely décor and waitresses in traditional garb. The menu features meat dishes, particularly steaks, though there are vegetarian choices among the salads and *pierogi*.

Café Antrakt (☎ 201 73 02; ul Krupówki 6; 🕘 11am-midnight) A mellow venue for an alcoholic or caffeine-laden drink, hidden away above Rodos with an ambient old-meets-new décor. It occasionally hosts live jazz.

Getting There & Away

From the **bus terminal** (ul Chramcówki), fast PKS buses run to Kraków every 45 to 60 minutes (13zł, 2½ hours). Two private companies, Trans Frej (www.trans-frej.com.pl, in Polish) and Szwagropol (www.szwagropol.pl, in Polish), also run comfortable buses (15zł) at the same frequency. These private buses leave from a stop along ul Kościuszki in Zakopane, and from the bus terminal in Kraków. At peak times (especially weekends), buy your tickets for the private buses in advance from counters outside the departure points in Zakopane. Tickets are also available in Kraków for Trans Frej buses from **Biuro Turystyki i Zakwaterowania Waweltur** (Map p390; ul Pawia 8) and for Szwagropol buses from **Pol-Tur** (Map p390; ul Pawia 12). The minibus station opposite the bus terminal is most useful for journeys to towns within the Tatra Mountains.

From Zakopane, PKS buses also go once daily to Lublin (57zł, six hours), Sanok (35zł, 6½ hours), Oświęcim (23zł) and Przemyśl; and four times daily to Warsaw (54zł, eight hours). At least one bus daily heads to Poprad in Slovakia (19zł). PKS buses – and minibuses from opposite the bus terminal – regularly travel to Lake Morskie Oko and on to Polana Palenica. To cross into Slovakia, get off this bus/minibus at Łysa Polana, cross the border on foot and take another bus to Tatranská Lomnica in Slovakia.

From the **train station** (ul Chramcówki), trains for Kraków (19zł, 3½ hours) leave every two hours or so, but avoid the slow train, which takes up to five hours. Between one and three trains a day go to Częstochowa, Gdynia via Gdańsk, Lublin, Łódź and Poznań, and five head to Warsaw.

TATRA MOUNTAINS

☎ 018

The Tatras, 100km south of Kraków, are the highest range of the Carpathian Mountains. Roughly 60km long and 15km wide, this mountain range stretches across the Polish–Slovak border. A quarter is in Poland and is mostly part of the Tatra National Park (about 212 sq km). The Polish Tatras contain more than 20 peaks over 2000m, the highest of which is Mt Rysy (2499m).

Cable Car to Mt Kasprowy Wierch

The **cable car** (return adult/child 30/20zł; 🕘 7am-9pm Jul-Aug, 7.30-5pm Mar-Jun & Sep-Oct, 8am-4pm Nov-Feb) from Kuźnice (3km south of Zakopane) to the summit of Mt Kasprowy Wierch (1985m) is a classic tourist experience enjoyed by Poles and foreigners alike. At the end of the trip, you can get off and stand with one foot in Poland and the other in Slovakia. The one-way journey takes 20 minutes and climbs 936m. The cable car normally shuts down for two weeks in May and November, and won't operate if the snow and, particularly, the winds are dangerous.

The view from the top is spectacular (clouds permitting). Two chairlifts transport skiers to and from various slopes between December and April. A small cafeteria serves skiers and hikers alike. In summer, many people return to Zakopane on foot down the Gąsienicowa Valley, and the most intrepid walk the ridges all the way across to Lake Morskie Oko via Pięciu Stawów, a strenuous hike taking a full day in good weather.

If you buy a return ticket, your trip back is automatically reserved for two hours after your departure, so buy a one-way ticket to the top (19zł) and another one down (14zł), if you want to stay longer. Mt Kasprowy Wierch is popular; so in summer, arrive early and expect to wait. PKS buses and minibuses to Kuźnice frequently leave from Zakopane.

Lake Morskie Oko

The emerald-green Lake Morskie Oko (Eye of the Sea) is a popular destination and among the loveliest lakes in the Tatras. PKS buses and minibuses regularly depart from Zakopane for Polana Palenica (30 minutes), from where a road (9km) continues uphill to the lake. Cars, bikes and buses are not allowed up this road, so you'll have to walk, but it's not steep (allow about two hours one way). Alternatively, take a horse-drawn carriage (32/25zł uphill/downhill, but very negotiable) to within 2km of the lake. In winter, transport is by horse-drawn four-seater sledge, which is more expensive. The last minibus to Zakopane returns between 5pm and 6pm.

Hiking

If you're doing any hiking in the Tatras get a copy of the *Tatrzański Park Narodowy* map (1:25,000), which shows all hiking trails in the area. Better still, buy one or more of the 14 sheets of *Tatry Polskie*, available at Księgarnia Górska in Zakopane (p401). In July and August these trails can be overrun by tourists, so late spring and early autumn are the best times. Theoretically you can expect better weather in autumn, when rainfall is lower.

Like all alpine regions, the Tatras can be dangerous, particularly during the snow season (November to May). Remember the weather can be unpredictable. Bring proper hiking boots, warm clothing and waterproof rain gear – and be prepared to use occasional ropes and chains (provided along the trails) to get up and down some rocky slopes. Guides are not necessary because many of the trails are marked, but can be arranged in Zakopane (see p401 for details) for about 230z³ per day.

There are several picturesque valleys south of Zakopane, including the **Dolina Strążyska**. You can continue from the Strążyska by the red trail up to **Mt Giewont** (1909m), 3½ hours from Zakopane, and then walk down the blue trail to Kuźnice in two hours.

Two long and beautiful forested valleys, the **Dolina Chochołowska** and the **Dolina Kościeliska**, are in the western part of the park, known as the Tatry Zachodnie (West Tatras). These valleys are ideal for cycling. Both are accessible by PKS buses and minibuses from Zakopane.

The Tatry Wysokie (High Tatras) to the east offer quite different scenery: bare granite peaks and glacial lakes. One way to get there is via cable car to **Mt Kasprowy Wierch**, then hike eastward along the red trail to Mt Świnica (2301m) and on to the Zawrat pass (2159m) – a tough three to four hours from Mt Kasprowy. From Zawrat, descend northwards to the Dolina Gąsienicowa along the blue trail and then back to Zakopane.

Alternatively, head south (also along the blue trail) to the wonderful **Dolina Pięciu Stawów** (Five Lakes Valley), where there is a mountain refuge 1Ľ hours from Zawrat. The blue trail heading west from the refuge passes **Lake Morskie Oko**, 1½ hours from the refuge.

Skiing

Zakopane boasts four major ski areas (and several smaller ones) with more than 50 ski lifts. **Mt Kasprowy Wierch** and **Mt Gubałówka** offer the best conditions and most challenging slopes in the area, with the ski season extending until early May. Lift tickets cost 10zł for one ride at Mt Kasprowy Wierch, and 2zł on the much smaller lift at Mt Gubałówka. Alternatively, you can buy a 10-ride card (70zł Mt Kasprowy Wierch, 18zł Mt Gubałówka) which allows you to skip the queues. Purchase your lift tickets on the relevant mountain.

Ski equipment rental is available at all facilities except Mt Kasprowy Wierch. Otherwise, stop off on your way to Kuźnice at the **ski rental** place near the Rondo in Zakopane. Other places in Zakopane, such as **Tatry Sport** (ul Piłsudskiego 4) and **Sport Shop & Service** (ul Krupówki 52a), also rent ski gear.

Sleeping

Tourists are not allowed to take their own cars into the park; you must walk in, take the cable car or use an official vehicle owned by the park or a hotel or hostel.

Camping is also not allowed in the park, but eight PTTK mountain refuges/hostels provide simple accommodation. Most refuges are small and fill up fast; in midsummer and midwinter they're invariably packed beyond capacity. No one is ever turned away, however, though you may have to crash on the floor if all the beds are taken. Do not arrive too late in the day, and bring along your own bed mat and sleeping bag. All refuges serve simple hot meals, but the kitchens and dining rooms close early (sometimes at 7pm).

The refuges listed here are open all year, but some may be temporarily closed for renovations or because of inclement weather. Check the current situation at the Dom Turysty PTTK in Zakopane or the regional **PTTK headquarters** (☎ 018-443 74 57) in Nowy Sącz.

The easiest refuge to reach from Zakopane is the large and decent **Kalatówki Hotel** (☎ 206 36 44; s/d/tr from 46/90/111zł), a 40-minute walk from the Kuźnice cable-car station. About 30 minutes beyond Kalatówki on the trail to Giewont is **Hala Kondratowa Hostel** (☎ 201 91 14; dm 20-22zł). It's in a great location and has a great atmosphere, but it is small.

Hikers wishing to traverse the park might begin at the **Roztoka Hostel** (☎ 207 74 42; dm 22-30zł), accessible by the bus or minibus to Morskie Oko. An early start from Zakopane, however, would allow you to visit Morskie Oko in the morning and stay at the **Morskie Oko Hostel** (☎ 207 76 09; dm from 40zł), or continue through to the **Dolina Pięciu Stawów Hostel** (☎ 207 76 07; dm from 25zł). This is the highest (1700m) and most scenically located refuge in the Polish Tatras.

DUNAJEC GORGE

An entertaining and leisurely way to explore the Pieniny Mountains is to go **rafting** on the Dunajec River, which winds along the Polish–Slovak border through a spectacular and deep gorge.

The trip starts at the wharf (Przystan Flisacka) in Kąty, 46km northeast of Zakopane, and finishes at the spa town of Szczawnica. The 17km (2″ hours) raft trip operates between May and October, but only starts when there's a minimum of 10 passengers.

The gorge is an easy day trip from Zakopane. In summer, 10 PKS buses to Kąty leave from the bus station. Alternatively, catch a regular bus to Nowy Targ (30 minutes) from Zakopane and one of six daily buses (one hour) to Kąty. From Szczawnica, take the bus back to Zakopane or change at Nowy Targ. Each day, five buses also travel between Szczawnica and Kraków.

To avoid waiting around in Kąty for a raft to fill up, organise a trip at any travel agency in Zakopane or at the tourist office. The cost is around 60zł to 70zł per person, and includes transport, equipment and guides.

SANOK

☎ 013 / pop 40,000

Nestled in a picturesque valley in the foothills of the Bieszczady Mountains, Sanok has been subject to Ruthenian, Hungarian, Austrian, Russian, German and Polish rule in its eventful history. Although it contains an important industrial zone, it's also a popular base for exploring the mountains.

The helpful **PTTK office** (☎ 463 21 71; www.pttk .sanok.com.pl; ul 3 Maja 2; ⏰ 8am-5pm Mon-Fri), near the market square, is the best place to find brochures on Sanok's attractions. There's also a tourist information desk inside **Orbis Travel** (☎ 463 28 59; ul Grzegorza 4; ⏰ 9am-5pm Mon-Fri, 9am-1pm Sat). There's a **Bank Pekao** (cnr ul Grzegorza & ul Kościuszki) nearby, and you can check email at **Prox** (☎ 464 22 50; ul Kazimierz Wielkiego 6; per hr 3.50zł) further west.

Sanok is noted for its unique **Museum of Folk Architecture** (☎ 463 16 72; ul Rybickiego 3; adult/child 9/6zł; ⏰ 8am-6pm May-Oct, 8am-2pm Nov-Apr), which features architecture from regional ethnic groups. Walk north from the town centre for 2km along ul Mickiewicza and ul Białogórska, then cross the bridge and turn right. The **Historical Museum** (☎ 464 13 66; ul Zamkowa 2; adult/child 10/7zł; ⏰ 9am-5pm Tue & Wed, 8am-3pm Thu & Fri, 9am-3pm Sat & Sun Apr-Oct; 8am-3pm Mon, Thu & Fri, 9am-5pm Tue & Wed, 9am-3pm Sat & Sun Nov-Mar) is housed in a 16th-century castle and contains an impressive collection of Ruthenian icons.

Sanok's surrounding villages are attractions in their own right, as many have lovely old churches. The marked **Icon Trail** takes hikers or cyclists along a 70km loop, passing by 10 village churches, as well as attractive mountain countryside. Trail leaflets and maps (in English, German and French) are available from the PTTK and Orbis offices.

Convenient budget accommodation is available at **Hotel Pod Trzema Różami** (☎ 463 09 22; trzyroze@ooh.pl; ul Jagiellońska 13; s/d/tr 80/100/120zł; P ⊕), about 300m south of the main square. Further south (another 600m) and up the scale is **Hotel Jagielloński** (☎ /fax 463 12 08; ul Jagiellońska 49; s/d/tr/ste from 90/110/130/140zł; P), with distinctive wooden furniture, parquetry floors and a very good **restaurant** (mains 14-35zł). Another comfortable option is **Hotel Sanvit** (☎ 465 50 88; www .sanvit.sanok.pl; ul Łazienna 1; s/d/tr 115/135/165zł, ste from 155zł; P ⊠ ⊕), just west of the square, with bright, modern rooms, shining bathrooms and a restaurant.

Karczma Jadło Karpackie (☎ 464 67 00; Rynek 12; mains 8-20zł; ☷ 9am-10pm) is an amenable, down-to-earth bar and restaurant on the main square. A good place to have a drink, alcoholic or otherwise, is **Weranda Caffe** (☎ 0609 741 936; ul 3 Maja 14; ☷ 10am-10pm), a cosy café-bar with a fireplace, and outdoor seating in summer.

The bus terminal and adjacent train station are about 1km southeast of the main square. Four buses go daily to Przemyśl (11zł, two hours), and one to Zakopane (35zł, 6½ hours). Buses also head regularly to Kraków and Warsaw. Train journeys to these destinations, however, may require multiple changes.

PRZEMYŚL
☎ 016 / pop 68,000

Everything about Przemyśl (*psheh*-mishl) feels big: its sprawling market square, the massive churches surrounding it, and the broad San River flowing through the city.

Luckily the area of most interest to visitors – its sloping and well-preserved **Rynek** (Market Square) – is compact and easily explored. The **tourist office** (☎ 675 16 64; www.parr.pl; Rynek 26; ☷ 8am-4pm Mon-Fri, 9am-3pm Sat) is on the northwest corner of the square as it stretches down toward the river. Check your emails at **Blue Net** (☎ 678 55 62; ul Słowackiego 14; per hr 3zł), along the main road on the eastern edge of the Old Town.

About 350m southwest of the Rynek are the ruins of a 14th-century **castle** (ul Zamkowa), built by Kazimierz Wielki. The **Regional Museum** (☎ 678 33 25; plac Czackiego 3; adult/child 5/3zł; ☷ 10.30am-5pm Tue & Fri, 10am-2pm Wed, Thu, Sat & Sun) houses a splendid collection of Ruthenian icons and Austro-Hungarian militaria, and a dry display of local archaeological finds. It's about 150m southeast of the Rynek.

For variety, visit the curious **Museum of Bells and Pipes** (☎ 678 96 66; ul Władyczne 3; adult/child 5/3zł; ☷ 10.30am-5.30pm Tue & Fri, 10am-2.30pm Wed, Thu & Sat, 12.15-3.45pm Sun Apr-Oct) in the old Clock Tower, where you can inspect several floors worth of vintage bells, elaborately carved pipes and cigar cutters (the city has long been famous across Poland for manufacturing these items). From the top of the tower, there's a great view of town.

Back in the Rynek, the **Museum of the City of Przemyśl** (☎ 678 65 01; Rynek 9; adult/child 5/3zł; ☷ 10.30am-5pm Tue & Fri, 10am-2pm Wed, Thu, Sat & Sun) showcases furniture, photographs and other items from the 19th and 20th centuries.

Przemyśl has a wide selection of inexpensive accommodation, including the central **Dom Wycieczkowy Podzamcze** (☎ 678 53 74; ul Waygarta 3; dm 20-24zł, d/tr 58/72zł), on the western edge of the Old Town. Its rooms have seen some wear, but have recently been repainted, and the largest dorm is decked out with potted plants and a TV. **Hotelik Pod Basztą** (☎ 670 82 68; ul Królowej Jadwigi 4; s/d/tr from 49/59/79zł) is just below the castle. Rooms are a little old-fashioned, with shared bathrooms, but many have castle or city views. The one 'superior' room boasts a spectacular balcony overlooking the Old Town.

More comfort is available at **Hotel Europejski** (☎ 675 71 00; ul Sowińskiego 4; s/d/tr 90/120/140zł) in a renovated old building facing the attractive façade of the train station. An impressive staircase leads to simple, light rooms with high ceilings and modern bathrooms.

Restauracja Karpacka (☎ 678 90 57; ul Kościuszki 5; mains 8-18zł; ☷ 10am-10pm), just west of the tourist office, is an old-fashioned eatery featuring bow-tied waiters, a timber ceiling and yellow stucco walls. It serves a good range of Polish standards, and Ukrainian *borscht* in a nod to the neighbours just down the road.

Another worthy place to eat is **Restauracja Piwnica Mieszczańska** (☎ 675 04 59; Rynek 9; mains 8-25zł; ☷ 11am-11pm), in the same building as the city museum. Its cellar setting is decorated with mini-chandeliers and lace tablecloths. The bourgeoisie platter (three kinds of meat) will interest ardent carnivores, and there's a reasonable selection of soups and fish dishes.

From Przemyśl, buses run to Lviv (95km) in Ukraine six times a day and regularly to all towns in southeastern Poland, including Sanok (11zl, two hours, four daily). Trains run regularly from Przemyśl to Lublin, Kraków and Warsaw, and stop here on the way to/ from Lviv. The bus terminal and adjacent train station in Przemyśl are about 1km northeast of the Rynek.

LUBLIN

☎ 081 / pop 358,000

Lublin is a city resonant with important moments in Polish history. In 1569 the Lublin Union was signed here, uniting Poland and Lithuania; and at the end of WWII, the Soviet Union set up a communist government in Lublin, prior to the liberation of Warsaw. Throughout history the city has faced numerous invasions by warlike neighbours, though today its beautifully preserved Old Town is a peaceful blend of Gothic, Renaissance and baroque architecture.

Information

Plenty of ATMs can be found on ul Krakowskie Przedmieście, and at several *kantors* along ul Peowiaków.

Bank Pekao (ul Królewska 1) Changes travellers cheques and gives cash advances on Visa and MasterCard. There's a branch at ul Krakowskie Przedmieście 64.

EMPiK Megastore (Galeria Centrum, 3rd fl, ul Krakowskie Przedmieście 16) Maps, books and international newspapers are available here.

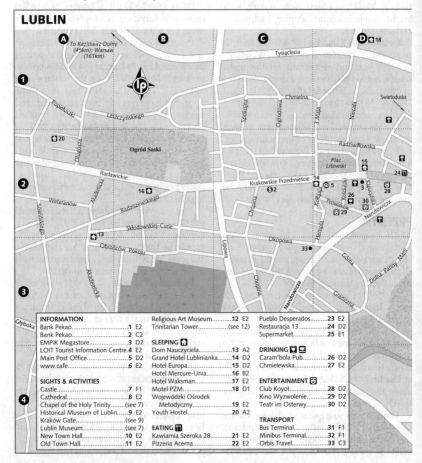

LUBLIN

LOIT Tourist Information Centre (☎ 532 44 12;
www.lublin.pl; ul Jezuicka 1/3; ☯ 10am-6pm Mon-Fri,
10am-4pm Sat, 10am-3pm Sun May-Sep, 9am-5pm Mon-
Fri, 10am-3pm Sat Oct-Apr) Has helpful English-speaking
staff, and lots of free brochures, including the city walking-
route guide *Tourist Routes of Lublin*. It also sells maps of
various Polish and Ukrainian cities.
Main post office (ul Krakowskie Przedmieście 50)
www.café (☎ 442 35 80; 3rd fl, Rynek 8; per hr 3zł;
☯ 10am-10pm)

Sights
CASTLE
The substantial castle, standing on a hill
northeast of the Old Town, has a dark history. It was built in the 14th century, then was
rebuilt as a prison in the 1820s. During the

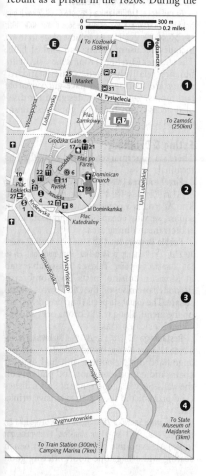

Nazi occupation, more than 100,000 people
passed its doors before being deported to
the death camps. Its major occupant is now
the **Lublin Museum** (☎ 532 50 01; www.zamek-lub
lin.pl; ul Zamkowa 9; adult/child 6.50/4.50zł; ☯ 9am-4pm
Wed-Sat, 9am-5pm Sun). On display are paintings,
silverware, porcelain, wood-carvings and
weaponry, mostly labelled only in Polish.
Check out the alleged 'devil's paw-print' on
the 17th-century table in the foyer, linked to
an intriguing local legend.

At the eastern end of the castle is the gorgeous 14th-century **Chapel of the Holy Trinity** (adult/
child 6.50/4.50zł, incl museum 10/6zł; ☯ 9am-3.45pm Mon-Sat,
9am-4.45pm Sun), accessible via the museum. Its
interior is covered with polychrome Russo-
Byzantine frescoes painted in 1418 – possibly
the finest medieval wall paintings in Poland.

OLD TOWN
The compact historic quarter is centred on
the **Rynek**, the main square surrounding the
neoclassical **Old Town Hall** (1781). The **Historical Museum of Lublin** (☎ 532 60 01; plac Łokietka 3;
adult/child 3.50/2.50zł; ☯ 9am-4pm Wed-Sat, 9am-5pm
Sun), displaying documents and photos, is inside the 14th-century **Kraków Gate**, a remnant
of medieval fortifications. Daily at noon, a
bugler plays a special tune atop the **New Town
Hall** opposite the gate. (If you're a bugling
addict, don't miss the annual **National Bugle
Contest** on 15 August.)

For an expansive view of the Old Town,
climb to the top of the **Trinitarian Tower** (1819),
which houses the **Religious Art Museum** (☎ 743 64
33; plac Katedralny; adult/child 5/3zł; ☯ 10am-5pm Apr-Oct,
10am-3pm Sat & Sun Nov-Mar). Nearby is the 16th-
century **cathedral** (plac Katedralny; ☯ dawn-dusk) and
its impressive baroque frescoes. The painting
of the Virgin Mary is said to have shed tears
in 1949, so it's a source of pride and reverence
for local believers.

MAJDANEK
About 4km southeast is the **State Museum of
Majdanek** (☎ 744 26 40; admission free; ☯ 8am-6pm
May-Sep, 8am-3pm Oct-Apr). It commemorates one
of the largest Nazi death camps, where some
235,000 people, including more than 100,000
Jews, were massacred. Barracks, guard towers
and barbedwire fences remain in place; even
more chilling are the crematorium and gas
chambers.

A short explanatory film (admission 2zł)
can be seen in the visitors centre, from which

POLAND

a marked 'visiting route' (5km) passes the massive stone **Monument of Fight & Martyrdom** and finishes at the domed **mausoleum** holding the ashes of many victims.

Trolleybus 156 from near the Bank Pekao along ul Królewska goes to the entrance of Majdanek.

Pick up the free *Tourist Routes of Lublin* guide, which includes a *Heritage Trail of the Lublin Jews* chapter, from the tourist office, if you want to walk along the marked **Jewish Heritage Trail** around Lublin.

Sleeping

BUDGET

Youth Hostel (☎ & fax 533 06 28; ul Długosza 6; dm/d/tr 19/50/75zł) Modest but well run. Simple rooms are decorated with potted plants, and there's a kitchen and a pleasant courtyard area with seating. Bed linen costs 6zł extra and it's 100m up a lane off ul Długosza.

Wojewódzki Ośrodek Metodyczny (☎ 532 92 41; www.wodn.lublin.pl; ul Dominikańska 5; dm 45zł) This place in an atmospheric Old Town building has rooms with between two and five beds. It's good value and often busy, so book ahead. Look for the sign 'Wojewódzki Ośrodek Doskonalenia Nauczycieli' outside.

Dom Nauczyciela (☎ 533 82 85; www.oupislublin .republika.pl; ul Akademicka 4; s/d/tr from 90/106/189zł) Value-packed accommodation in the heart of the university quarter, west of the Old Town. Rooms have old-fashioned décor but are clean, with good bathrooms. Some rooms have views over the city, and there are bars and eateries nearby.

Camping Marina (☎ 745 69 10; fax 744 10 70; ul Krężnicka 6; per tent 8zł, cabins from 55zł; ☯ May-Sep) Lublin's only camping ground is serenely located on a lake about 8km south of the Old Town. To get there take bus 17, 20 or 21 from the train station to Stadion Sygnał and then catch bus 25.

MIDRANGE & TOP END

Motel PZM (☎ 533 42 32; ul Prusa 8; s/d from 120/160zł; ℗ ✗) This car-friendly accommodation is housed in an uninspiring concrete pile, but it's handy for the bus station. The rooms have recently been renovated, with new furniture and freshly tiled bathrooms.

Hotel Waksman (☎ 532 54 54; www.waksman.pl; ul Grodzka 19; s/d 180/200zł, ste from 240zł; ℗ ✗ 🖳) This small gem is excellent value for its quality and location. Just within the Grodzka Gate in the

Old Town, it offers elegantly appointed rooms with different colour schemes, and an attractive lounge with tapestries on the walls. One room has a waterbed.

Hotel Europa (☎ 535 03 03; www.hoteleuropa.pl; ul Krakowskie Przedmieście 29; s/d 290/380zł; ℗ ✗ 🅿 🖳 ♿) Central hotel offering smart, thoroughly modernised rooms with high ceilings and elegant furniture, in a restored 19th-century building. Two rooms are designed for disabled access, and there's a nightclub downstairs.

Hotel Mercure-Unia (☎ 533 72 12; www.orbis.pl; al Racławickie 12; d from 245zł; ℗ ✗ 🅿 🖳) This business hotel is big, central and convenient, and offers all modern conveniences, though it's lacking in atmosphere. There's a gym, bar and restaurant on the premises.

Grand Hotel Lublinianka (☎ 446 61 00; www.lublin ianka.com; ul Krakowskie Przedmieście 56; s/d from 300/340zł; ℗ ✗ 🅿 🖳 ♿) The swankiest place in town includes free use of a sauna and Turkish bath. The cheaper (3rd floor) rooms have skylights but are relatively small, while 'standard' rooms are spacious and have glitzy marble bathrooms. One room is designed for disabled access, and there's a good restaurant downstairs.

Eating & Drinking

There's a supermarket located near the bus terminal.

Pizzeria Acerna (☎ 532 45 31; Rynek 2; mains 10-24zł; ☯ 11am-10pm Mon-Thu & Sun, 11am-midnight Fri & Sat) The Acerna is a popular eatery on the main square, serving cheap pizzas and pasta in its subterranean dining area.

Pueblo Desperados (☎ 534 61 79; Rynek 5; mains 10-27zł; ☯ 9am-10pm Mon-Thu, 9am-midnight Fri & Sat, 10am-midnight Sun) Takes a reasonable stab at Mexican cuisine in its tiny sombrero-decorated premises off the Old Town's central square. The usual suspects (burritos, tacos) are on the menu, along with Corona beer and so-called Mexican pizzas.

Restauracja 13 (☎ 532 29 19; ul Krakowskie Przedmieście 13; mains 10-26zł; ☯ 9am-midnight) Cosy orange-hued dining option with high-backed chairs and curious 'thumbprint' patterns on the walls. Serves a good range of Polish dishes (and pizzas), and there's an extensive drinks list.

Kawiarnia Szeroka 28 (☎ 534 61 09; ul Grodzka 21; mains 15-40zł; ☯ 11am-11pm Mon-Thu, 11am-midnight Fri-Sun) An evocative place with timber bench seating and a flagstone floor, offering good

Jewish and Polish cuisine. There's a terrace at the back and regular live *klezmer* bands in the evenings playing traditional Jewish music (15zł extra).

Chmielewska (☎ 743 72 96; ul Krakowskie Przedmieście 8; ☺ 10am-10pm) Charming old-fashioned café that looks like it dropped in from a bygone century. The menu is full of classic Polish cakes such as *sernik* (cheesecake) and *szarlotka* (apple pie), with a wide selection of coffee, tea and alcoholic drinks.

Caram'bola Pub (☎ 534 63 80; ul Kościuszki 8; ☺ 11am-midnight Mon-Thu, 11am-2am Fri & Sat, noon-midnight Sun) This pub is a pleasant place for a beer or two. It also serves inexpensive bar food, including the ubiquitous pizzas.

Entertainment

Club Koyot (☎ 743 67 35; ul Krakowskie Przedmieście 26; ☺ 5pm-late Sat-Thu, noon-late Fri) This club is concealed in a courtyard and features live music or DJs most nights.

Kino Wyzwolenie (☎ 532 24 16; ul Peowiaków 6; adult/child 15/13zł) If you'd prefer a movie to music, this is a classic 1920s cinema in a convenient location.

Teatr im Osterwy (☎ 532 42 44; ul Narutowicza 17) Lublin's main theatrical venue which features mostly classical plays.

Getting There & Away

From the **bus terminal** (al Tysiąclecia), opposite the castle, buses head to Białystok (24zł, three daily), Kraków (38zł to 46zł, two daily), Łódź (33zł, three daily), Olsztyn (65zł, one daily), Toruń (63zł, one daily) and Zakopane (43zł, five daily). Six buses also go daily to Przemyśl (14zł), 12 head to Zamość (13zł) and more than two dozen travel to various destinations within Warsaw (30zł, three hours). From the same terminal, Polski Express offers seven daily buses to Warsaw (34zł, three hours). Private minibuses head to various destinations, including Warsaw (30zł, 2½ hours, every half-hour), from bus stops north and west of the bus terminal.

The **Lublin Główny train station** (plac Dworcowy) is 1.2km south of the Old Town and accessible by bus 1 or 13. When leaving the station, look for the bus stop on ul Gazowa, to the left of the station entrance as you walk down the steps (not the trolleybus stop). Alternatively, trolleybus 150 from the station is handy for the university area and the youth hostel. At least a dozen fast trains go daily to Warsaw

(32zł, 2½ hours) and two fast trains travel to Kraków (46zł, five hours). Buy tickets from the station or **Orbis Travel** (☎ 532 22 56; www .orbistravel.com.pl; ul Narutowicza 33a).

Around Lublin
KOZŁÓWKA

The hamlet of Kozłówka (koz-*woof*-kah), 38km north of Lublin, is famous for its sumptuous late-baroque **palace**, which houses the **Museum of the Zamoyski Family** (☎ 852 83 00; www .muzeumzamoyskich.lublin.pl; adult/child 24/12zł; ☺ 10am-4pm Mon-Fri, 10am-5pm Sat & Sun Mar-Oct, 10am-3pm Nov-Dec). It features original furnishings, ceramic stoves and a large collection of paintings.

Even more interesting is its incongruous **Socialist-Realist Art Gallery** (adult/child 5/3zł; ☺ 10am-4pm Mon-Fri, 10am-5pm Sat & Sun Mar-Oct, 10am-3pm Nov-Dec), decked out with numerous portraits and statues of communist-era leaders. It also features many idealised scenes of farmers and factory workers striving for socialism.

You can stay in the **palace rooms** and on an 'agrotourist' **farm** (☎ 852 83 00). Contact staff in advance about availability and current costs.

From Lublin, two buses head to Kozłówka each morning, usually on the way to Michów. Only a few buses return directly to Lublin in the afternoon, so check the timetable before visiting the museum. Alternatively, you can catch one of the frequent buses to/from Lubartów, which is regularly connected by bus and minibus to Lublin.

ZAMOŚĆ

☎ 084 / pop 67,000

While most Polish cities' attractions centre on their medieval heart, Zamość (*zah*-moshch) is pure Renaissance. It was founded in 1580 by Jan Zamoyski, the nation's chancellor and commander-in-chief. Designed by an Italian architect, the city was intended as a prosperous trading settlement between Western Europe and the region stretching east to the Black Sea.

In WWII, the Nazis earmarked the city for German resettlement, sending the Polish population into slave labour or concentration camps. Most of the Jewish population of the renamed 'Himmlerstadt' was exterminated.

The splendid architecture of Zamość's Old Town escaped destruction in the war's latter stages, and was added to Unesco's World Heritage List in 1992.

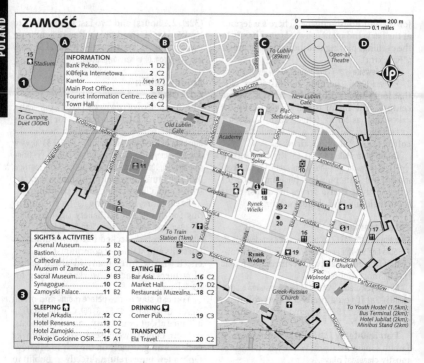

ZAMOŚĆ

INFORMATION
Bank Pekao.....................................1 D2
K@fejka Internetowa......................2 C2
Kantor...(see 17)
Main Post Office.............................3 B3
Tourist Information Centre....(see 4)
Town Hall.......................................4 C2

SIGHTS & ACTIVITIES
Arsenal Museum...............................5 B2
Bastion..6 D3
Cathedral.......................................7 B2
Museum of Zamość..........................8 C2
Sacral Museum................................9 B3
Synagogue....................................10 C2
Zamoyski Palace............................11 B2

SLEEPING
Hotel Arkadia................................12 C2
Hotel Renesans.............................13 D2
Hotel Zamojski..............................14 C2
Pokoje Gościnne OSiR....................15 A1

EATING
Bar Asia.......................................16 C2
Market Hall...................................17 D2
Restauracja Muzealna....................18 C2

DRINKING
Corner Pub....................................19 C3

TRANSPORT
Ela Travel.....................................20 C2

Information

There's a *kantor* in the Market Hall.

Bank Pekao (ul Grodzka 2) Has an ATM, cashes travellers cheques and gives advances on Visa and MasterCard.

K@fejka Internetowa (☎ 639 29 32; Rynek Wielki 10; per hr 3zł) internet access.

Main post office (ul Kościuszki) Near the cathedral.

Tourist Information Centre (☎ 639 22 92; Rynek Wielki 13; 8am-6pm Mon-Fri, 10am-6pm Sat & Sun May-Sep, 8am-5pm Mon-Fri, 9am-2pm Sat Oct-Apr) This helpful office in the town hall sells *Along the Streets of Zamość* (2zł; in English, German and Italian) and the glossy *Zamość – A Short Guidebook* (8zł), along with a good stock of maps.

Sights

Rynek Wielki is the heart of Zamość attractive Old Town. The impressive Italianate Renaissance square (exactly 100m by 100m) is dominated by the lofty, pink **Town Hall** and surrounded by colourful arcaded burghers' houses, many adorned with elegant designs. The **Museum of Zamość** (☎ 638 64 94; ul Ormiańska 30; adult/child 5/2.50zł; 9am-5pm Tue-Sun) is based in two of the loveliest buildings on the Rynek and houses interesting exhibits, including

paintings, folk costumes, archaeological finds and a scale model of the 16th-century town.

Southwest of the square is the mighty 16th-century **cathedral** (ul Kolegiacka; dawn-dusk), which hosts the tomb of Jan Zamoyski in the chapel to the right of the high altar. The **belfry** (1zł; May-Sep) can be climbed for good views of the historic cathedral bells and the Old Town. In the grounds, the **Sacral Museum** (admission 1zł; 10am-4pm Mon-Fri, 10am-1pm Sat & Sun May-Sep, 10am-1pm Sun Oct-Apr) features various robes, paintings and sculptures.

Zamoyski Palace (closed to the public) lost much of its character when it was converted into a military hospital in the 1830s. Today it's used for government offices. Nearby, the **Arsenal Museum** (☎ 638 40 76; ul Zamkowa 2; adult/child 5/2.50zł; 9am-5pm Mon-Fri) holds an unremarkable collection of cannon, swords and firearms. To the north of the palace stretches a beautifully landscaped **park**.

Before WWII, Jewish citizens accounted for 45% of the town's population (of 12,000) and most lived in the area north and east of the palace. The most significant Jewish architectural relic is the Renaissance **synagogue** (☎ 0608 409 055; ul Pereca 14; admission 2zł; ⏲ 10am-3pm Mon-Fri, 10am-5pm Sat & Sun May-Sep, by appointment Oct-Apr), built in the early 17th century. Until recently it was used as a public library, but is now empty and awaiting transformation into a museum. In the meantime you can visit and see its original wall and ceiling decoration.

On the eastern edge of the Old Town is the antiquated but bustling **Market Hall** (Hala Targowa). Behind it is the best surviving **bastion** from the original city walls.

Sleeping

BUDGET

Youth Hostel (☎ 627 91 25; ul Zamoyskiego 4; dm 12-16zł; ⏲ Jul & Aug) You can find this hostel in a school building 1.5km east of the Old Town, not far from the bus terminal. It's basic but functional and very cheap.

Pokoje Gościnne OSiR (☎ 638 60 11; ul Królowej Jadwigi 8; dm 23.50zł; s/d/s 90/125/150zł; P ✖) Located in a sprawling sporting complex a 15-minute walk west of the Old Town, and packed with old trophies and students playing table tennis. Rooms are plainly furnished, clean and comfortable, although the bathrooms fall short of the ideal.

Camping Duet (☎ 639 24 99; ul Królowej Jadwigi 14; s/d/tr 70/85/110zł; P ⏲) About 1.5km west of the Old Town, Camping Duet has neat bungalows, tennis courts, a restaurant, sauna and Jacuzzi. Larger bungalows sleep up to six.

MIDRANGE & TOP END

Hotel Arkadia (☎ 638 65 07; www.arkadia.zamosc.pl; Rynek Wielki 9; s/d/tr 100/150/180zł; P) With just seven rooms, this compact place offers a pool table and restaurant in addition to lodgings. It's charming but shabby, though its location right on the market square is hard to beat.

Hotel Jubilat (☎ 638 64 01; hoteljubilat@hoga.pl; ul Kardynała Wyszyńskiego 52; s/d 134/173zł; P ☐) An acceptable, if slightly drab, place to spend the night, right beside the bus station. It couldn't be handier for late arrivals or early departures, but it's a long way from anywhere else. It has a restaurant and fitness club.

Hotel Renesans (☎ 639 20 01; hotelrenesans@hoga.pl; ul Grecka 6; s/d 139/198zł; P ☐) It's ironic that a hotel named after the Renaissance is housed in the Old Town's ugliest building. However, it's central and the rooms are comfortable enough, if you can ignore the brown-patterned carpets.

Hotel Zamojski (☎ 639 25 16; www.orbis.pl; ul Kołłątaja 2/4/6; s/d/ste 192/285/415zł; P ✖) The best joint in town is situated within three connected old houses, just off the square. The rooms are modern and tastefully furnished, and there's a good on-site restaurant and cocktail bar, along with a fitness centre.

Eating & Drinking

There are a few cheap fast-food outlets in the Market Hall.

Bar Asia (☎ 639 23 04; ul Staszica 10; mains 5-8zł; ⏲ 8am-5pm Mon-Fri, 8am-4pm Sat) For hungry but broke travellers, this popular-style place is ideal. It serves cheap and tasty Polish food including several variants of *pierogi*, in a plain space with lace tablecloths and potted plants.

Restauracja Muzealna (☎ 638 73 00; ul Ormiańska Ormianska 30; mains 8-18zł; ⏲ 11am-10pm Mon-Sat, 11am-9pm Sun) Subterranean restaurant in an atmospheric cellar below the main square, bedecked with ornate timber furniture and portraits of nobles. It serves a better class of Polish cuisine at reasonable prices, and has a well-stocked bar.

Corner Pub (☎ 627 06 94; ul Żeromskiego 6; ⏲ 11am-11pm) This cosy Irish-style pub is a good place to have a drink. It has comfy booths and the walls are ornamented with bric-a-brac such as antique clocks, swords and model cars.

Getting There & Away

Buses are usually more convenient and quicker than trains. The **bus terminal** (ul Hrubieszowska) is 2km east of the Old Town and linked by frequent city buses, primarily route Nos 0 and 3. Daily, one or two fast buses go to Kraków (40zł, four hours), four to Warsaw (37zł, five hours) and nine to Lublin (13zł, two hours).

Quicker and cheaper are the minibuses that travel every 30 minutes between Lublin and Zamość (10zł, 1½ hours). They leave from the minibus stand opposite the bus terminal in Zamość and from a disorganised corner northwest of the bus terminal in Lublin. Check the changeable timetable for departures to other destinations, including Warsaw and Kraków.

From the train station, about 1km southwest of the Old Town, several slow trains head to Lublin (about four hours) every day and one plods along to Warsaw (six hours). **Ela Travel** (☎ 638 57 75; ul Grodzka 18) sells international bus and air tickets.

SILESIA

Silesia (Śląsk) has a history of ethnic and political flux, having been governed by Polish, Bohemian, Austrian and German rulers. After the devastating Mongol invasion of Europe in the 13th century, Silesia's rulers welcomed German immigration to rebuild population numbers, unwittingly foreshadowing future tensions between Poles and ethnic Germans. After two centuries as part of Prussia and Germany, the territory was largely included within Poland's new borders after WWII.

Nowadays Upper Silesia is the nation's industrial heart, while Lower Silesia is a fertile farming region centred on Wrocław. Along the region's southwestern edge run the Sudeten Mountains, forming the border with the Czech republic.

The industrial zone around Katowice has limited attraction for visitors. However, Wrocław is a beautiful historic city with lively nightlife, and the Sudeten Mountains draw hikers and other nature lovers.

WROCŁAW

☎ 071 / pop 639,000

When citizens of beautiful Kraków enthusiastically encourage you to visit Wrocław (*vrotswahf*), you know you're onto something good. The city's beautiful Old Town is a gracious mix of Gothic and baroque styles, and its large student population ensures a healthy number of restaurants, bars and nightclubs.

Wrocław has been traded back and forth between various rulers over the centuries, but began life in the year 1000 under the Polish Piast dynasty and developed into a prosperous trading and cultural centre. In the 1740s it passed to Prussia, under the German name of Breslau. Under Prussian rule, the city became a major textile manufacturing centre, greatly increasing its population.

Upon its return to Poland in 1945, Wrocław was a shell of its former self, having sustained massive damage in WWII. Though 70% of the city was destroyed, sensitive restoration has returned the historic centre to its former beauty.

Information

BOOKSHOPS

EMPiK Megastore (☎ 343 39 72; Rynek 50) For the widest choice of foreign-language newspapers and magazines.

Księgarnia Podróżnika (☎ 792 30 65; ul Wita Stwosza 19/20) The best place for maps and guidebooks.

INTERNET ACCESS

Dr Joystick (☎ 322 14 88; ul Staromłyńska 2a; per hr 3zł; ☺ 10.30am-10.30pm)

W Sercu Miasta (☎ 342 46 75; ul Przejście Żelaźnicie; per hr 5zł; ☺ 24hrs) Down a laneway in the middle of the Rynek.

MONEY

There are *kantors* through the city centre and a number in the bus and train stations.

Bank Pekao (ul Oławska 2) Offers the usual financial services.

POST

Main post office (Rynek 28; ☺ 6.30am-8.30pm)

TOURIST INFORMATION

Tourist office (☎ 344 31 11; www.wroclaw.pl; Rynek 14; ☺ 9am-9pm May-Sep, 9am-8pm Oct-Apr) Provides a variety of free brochures and maps and sells souvenirs.

Sights

Wrocław's pride and joy is the giant **Panorama of Racławicka** (☎ 344 23 44; ul Purkyniego 11; adult/child 20/15zł; ☺ 9am-5pm Tue-Sun May-Oct, 9am-4pm Tue-Sun Nov-Apr), a 360-degree painting of the 1794 Battle of Racławice, in which the Polish peasant army, led by Tadeusz Kościuszko, defeated Russian forces intent on partitioning Poland. Created by Jan Styka and Wojciech Kossak for the centenary of the battle in 1894, the painting is an immense 114m long and 15m high, and was brought here by Polish immigrants displaced from Lviv after WWII. Due to the communist government's uneasiness about glorifying a famous Russian defeat, however, the panorama wasn't re-erected until 1985, in a circular building east of the Old Town. Obligatory tours (with audio in English, French, German, Spanish, Russian and other languages) run every 30 minutes from 9am to 4.30pm April to November, and 10am to 3pm from December to March. The ticket also allows entry to the National Museum on the same day.

Located nearby, the **National Museum** (☎ 343 88 39; plac Powstańców Warszawy 5; adult/child 15/10zł, free Sat; ☺ 9am-4pm Wed-Fri & Sun, 10am-6pm Sat) exhibits Silesian medieval art, and a fine collection of modern Polish painting. Entry is included with a ticket to the Panorama.

In the centre of the Old Town is the **Rynek**, Poland's second-largest old market square

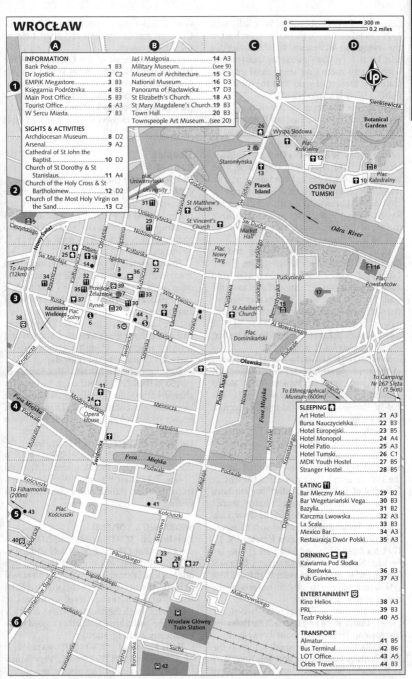

WROCŁAW

INFORMATION
Bank Pekao..........................1 B3
Dr Joystick..........................2 C2
EMPiK Megastore...............3 B3
Księgarnia Podróżnika.......4 B3
Main Post Office.................5 B3
Tourist Office.....................6 A3
W Sercu Miasta..................7 B3

SIGHTS & ACTIVITIES
Archdiocesan Museum........8 D2
Arsenal...............................9 A2
Cathedral of St John the
   Baptist............................10 D2
Church of St Dorothy & St
   Stanislaus......................11 A4
Church of the Holy Cross & St
   Bartholomew..................12 D2
Church of the Most Holy Virgin on
   the Sand.........................13 C2
Jaś i Małgosia....................14 A3
Military Museum..............(see 9)
Museum of Architecture....15 C3
National Museum...............16 D3
Panorama of Racławicka....17 D3
St Elizabeth's Church..........18 A3
St Mary Magdalene's Church.19 B3
Town Hall...........................20 B3
Townspeople Art Museum...(see 20)

SLEEPING
Art Hotel............................21 A3
Bursa Nauczycielska...........22 B3
Hotel Europejski.................23 B5
Hotel Monopol...................24 A4
Hotel Patio.........................25 A3
Hotel Tumski......................26 C1
MDK Youth Hostel..............27 B5
Stranger Hostel..................28 B5

EATING
Bar Mleczny Miś.................29 B2
Bar Wegetariański Vega.....30 B3
Bazylia...............................31 B2
Karczma Lwowska...............32 A3
La Scala.............................33 B3
Mexico Bar.........................34 A3
Restauracja Dwór Polski.....35 A3

DRINKING
Kawiarnia Pod Słodka
   Borówka.........................36 B3
Pub Guinness.....................37 A3

ENTERTAINMENT
Kino Helios.........................38 A3
PRL....................................39 B3
Teatr Polski........................40 A5

TRANSPORT
Almatur..............................41 B5
Bus Terminal......................42 B6
LOT Office..........................43 A5
Orbis Travel.......................44 B3

POLAND

(after Kraków). The beautiful **Town Hall** (built 1327–1504) on the southern side plays host to the **Townspeople Art Museum** (☎ 347 16 90; adult/child 7/5zł, free Wed; ☺ 11am-5pm Wed-Sat, 10am-6pm Sun), with stately rooms on show, and exhibits featuring the art of gold and the stories of famous Wrocław inhabitants.

In the northwestern corner of the Rynek are two small houses called **Jaś i Małgosia** (ul Św. Mikołaja) linked by a baroque gate (closed to the public). Behind them is the monumental 14th-century **St Elizabeth's Church** (ul Elżbiety 1; admission 5zł; ☺ 9am-7pm Mon-Fri, 11am-5pm Sat, 1-5pm Sun May-Oct, 10am-5pm Mon-Sat, 1-7pm Sun Nov-Apr) with its 83m-high tower, which you can climb for city views. The southwestern corner of the Rynek opens into **plac Solny** (Salt Square), once the site of the town's salt trade and now home to a 24-hour flower market.

One block east is the Gothic **St Mary Magdalene's Church** (ul Łaciarska; admission free; ☺ 9am-4pm Mon-Sat) with a Romanesque portal from 1280 incorporated into its southern external wall. Further east, the 15th-century former Bernardine church and monastery encompasses the **Museum of Architecture** (☎ 344 82 78; ul Bernardyńska 5; adult/child 7/5zł; ☺ 10am-4pm Tue, Wed, Fri & Sat, noon-6pm Thu, 11am-5pm Sun).

West of the Rynek is the **Arsenal**, a remnant of the town's 15th-century fortifications. It now houses the **Military Museum** (☎ 347 16 96; ul Cieszyńskiego 9; adult/child 7/5zł, free Wed; ☺ 11am-5pm Wed-Sat, 10am-6pm Sun), with the usual collection of old weapons.

North of the river is **Ostrów Tumski** (Cathedral Island), a picturesque area full of churches, though it's no longer an island (an arm of the Odra River was reclaimed during the 19th century). Here you'll find the Gothic **Cathedral of St John the Baptist** (plac Katedralny; ☺ 10am-8pm except during services). Uniquely, there's a lift to whisk you to the top of the **tower** (adult/child 4/3zł; ☺ 10am-6pm Mon-Sat) for superb views. Next door is the **Archdiocesan Museum** (☎ 327 11 78; plac Katedralny 16; adult/child 3/2zł; ☺ 9am-3pm Tue-Sun). Nearby are the charming **Botanical Gardens** (☎ 322 59 57; ul Sienkiewicza 23; adult/child 7/5zł; ☺ 8am-6pm), where you can chill out among the chestnut trees and tulips.

West from the cathedral is the two-storey Gothic **Church of the Holy Cross & St Bartholomew** (plac Kościelny; ☺ 9am-6pm), built between 1288 and 1350. Cross over the small bridge to the 14th-century **Church of the Most Holy Virgin Mary on the Sand** (ul Św. Jadwigi; ☺ erratic) with its lofty Gothic vaults and year-round nativity scene. Classical music concerts are often held in these two venues.

To the southeast of the Old Town is the **Ethnographical Museum** (☎ 344 33 13; ul Romualda Traugutta 111; adult/child 5/4zł, free Sat; ☺ 10am-4pm Tue, Wed & Fri-Sun, 11am-4pm Thu) and to the south is the **Church of St Dorothy & St Stanislaus** (ul Świdnicka; ☺ dawn-dusk), a massive Gothic complex built in 1351.

Sleeping

BUDGET

MDK Youth Hostel (☎ 343 88 56; mdkkopernik.wp.pl; ul Kołłątaja 20; dm/d from 22/29zł) Not far from the train station, this is a basic, recently renovated place, located in a grand mustard-coloured building. Some dorms are huge and beds are packed close together. It's almost always full, so book ahead.

Stranger Hostel (☎ 344 12 06; www.thestrangerhostel .com; ul Kołłątaja 16; dm 50zł; ☒ ⬚) A tatty old staircase leads up to Wrocław's best budget accommodation. Dorms are set in renovated apartment rooms with ornate lamps and decorative ceilings. Bathrooms are shiny clean, and guests have free access to a kitchen and washing machine. There's a games console and a DVD projector for rainy days.

Bursa Nauczycielska (☎ 344 37 81; ul Kotlarska 42; s/d/q 50/90/104zł) A basic but clean hostel with shared bathrooms, ideally located just one block northeast of the Rynek. There's a lot of brown in the colour scheme, but the rooms are quite cosy.

Camping Nr 267 Ślęza (☎ 372 55 11; ul Na Grobli 16/18; per person/tent 14/3zł, d/tr bungalows 60/90zł; Ⓟ) On the bank of the Odra, 2km east of the Old Town. Take tram 5 to plac Wróblewskiego from the train station and walk about 1km further east.

MIDRANGE & TOP END

Hotel Monopol (☎ 343 70 41; www.orbis.pl; ul Modrzejewskiej 2; s 122-182zł, d 164-264zł; ☒) Adolf Hitler was a frequent visitor, but don't let that put you off: Marlene Dietrich and Pablo Picasso stayed here too. It's an attractive old-fashioned hotel with marble pillars and carved woodwork in the foyer, though the cheapest rooms are fairly basic. The buffet breakfast makes it good value for the price and location.

Hotel Europejski (☎ 343 10 71; www.odratourist .pl; ul Piłsudskiego 88; s/d 195/205zł; ☒) Very handy for the train station. The pricier 'renovated' rooms are large and comfortable, though the décor's a bit dated.

Old Town Apartments (Map p378; ☎ 022-887 98 00; www.warsawshotel.com; Rynek Starego Miasta 12/14, Warsaw; apt 250-420zł) Warsaw-based agency with modern, fully furnished one-bedroom apartments around Wrocław's main square. Weekly rates are available.

Hotel Tumski (☎ 322 60 99; www.hotel-tumski.com .pl; Wyspa Słodowa 10; s/d/ste 230/320zł/480zł; ✗) This is a neat hotel in a peaceful setting overlooking the river, offering reasonable value for money. It's ideal for exploring the lovely ecclesiastical quarter, and there's a good restaurant attached.

Hotel Patio (☎ 375 04 00; www.hotelpatio.pl; ul Kiełbaśnicza 24; s/d/ste from 280/310/395zł; P ✗ 🖳) Pleasant lodgings a short hop from the main square, and actually within two buildings linked by a covered sunlit courtyard. Rooms are clean and light, sometimes small but with reasonably high ceilings. There's a restaurant, bar and hairdresser on site.

Art Hotel (☎ 787 71 00; www.arthotel.pl; ul Kiełbaśnicz-na 20; s/d/ste from 320/360/430zł; P ✗ 🐾 🖳) Superelegant accommodation in a renovated apartment building. Rooms feature tastefully restrained décor, quality fittings and gleaming bathrooms. Within the arched brick cellar is a top-notch restaurant, and there's a fitness room to work off the resultant calories.

Eating & Drinking

Bar Mleczny Miś (☎ 343 49 63; ul Kuźnicza 45-47; mains 3-12zł; 🕑 7am-6pm Mon-Fri, 8am-5pm Sat) In the university area, this classic cheap-eats cafeteria is basic but popular with frugal university students. Look for the bear above the sign.

Bazylia (plac Uniwersytecki; mains 4-9zł; 🕑 8am-8pm Mon-Fri, 7.30am-8pm Sat) Inexpensive and bustling modern take on the classic *bar mleczny*, in a curved space with huge plate-glass windows overlooking the venerable university buildings. The menu has a lot of Polish standards such as *bigos* and *gołąbki*, and a decent range of salads and other vegetable dishes.

Bar Wegetariański Vega (☎ 344 39 34; Rynek 1/2; mains 5-12zł; 🕑 8am-7pm Mon-Fri, 9am-5pm Sat) This is a cheap cafeteria in the centre of the Rynek, offering veggie dishes in a light green space. Good choice of soups and crepes.

Mexico Bar (☎ 346 02 92; ul Rzeźnicza 34; mains 11-39zł; 🕑 noon-midnight) Compact, warmly lit restaurant featuring sombreros, backlit masks and a chandelier made of beer bottles. There's

a small bar to lean on while waiting for a table. All the Tex-Mex standards are on the menu, but book at least two days ahead for a table on weekends.

Karczma Lwowska (☎ 343 98 87; Rynek 4; mains 20-37zł; 🕑 noon-midnight) Has a great spot on the main square, with outdoor seating in summer, and offers the usual meaty Polish standards in a space with a rustic rural look. It's worth stopping by to try the beer, served in ceramic mugs.

La Scala (☎ 372 53 94; Rynek 38; mains 23-75zł; 🕑 10am-midnight) Offers authentic Italian food and particularly good desserts. Prices are high, but you're paying for the location. There's a cheaper trattoria at ground level.

Restauracja Dwór Polski (☎ 372 48 96; Rynek 5; mains 35-45zł; 🕑 noon-midnight) This eatery is a classy place to sample good-quality Polish cuisine on the main square, in a rather grand room with silver candelabra and white table-cloths.

Pub Guinness (☎ 344 60 15; plac Solny 5; 🕑 noon-2am) No prizes for guessing what this pub serves here. A lively, fairly authentic Irish pub, spread over three levels on a busy corner. The ground-floor bar buzzes with student and traveller groups getting together, and there's a restaurant and beer cellar as well. A good place to wind down after a hard day's sightseeing.

Kawiarnia Pod Słodka Borówka (☎ 343 68 56; Rynek 45; 🕑 9am-10pm) If you're after a heart-starter, try the *kawa* (coffee) and cakes here. Nice cherry pie, and an odd collection of old hats along the wall.

Entertainment

Check out the bimonthly *Visitor* (free and in English) for details of what's on in this important cultural centre. It's available from the tourist office and upmarket hotels.

PRL (☎ 342 55 26; Rynek Ratusz 10; 🕑 noon-3am) The dictatorship of the proletariat is alive and well in this tongue-in-cheek venue inspired by communist nostalgia. Disco lights play over a bust of Lenin, propaganda posters line the walls, and red menace memorabilia is scattered through the maze of rooms. Descend to the basement – beneath the portraits of Stalin and Mao – if you'd like to hit the dance floor.

Teatr Polski (☎ 316 07 77; ul Zapolskiej 3) Wrocław's main theatrical venue stages classic Polish and foreign drama.

Filharmonia (☎ 342 20 01; www.filharmonia.wroclaw .pl; ul Piłsudskiego 19) This place hosts concerts of classical music, mostly on Friday and Saturday nights.

Kino Helios (☎ 781 55 70; www.heliosnet.pl; ul Kazimierza Wielkiego 19a) If you're after a movie head to this modern multiplex screening English-language films.

Getting There & Away

Orbis Travel (☎ 343 26 65; Rynek 29) and **Almatur** (☎ 343 41 35; ul Kościuszki 34) offer the usual services. If you're travelling to/from Wrocław at the weekend, you'll be in competition with thousands of itinerant university students, so book your ticket as soon as possible.

AIR

Every day, LOT flies four to seven times between Wrocław and Warsaw, once between Wrocław and Frankfurt-am-Main, and once to Munich. Tickets can be bought at the **LOT office** (☎ 342 51 51; ul Piłsudskiego 36). There's also a Direct Fly flight to Gdańsk on weekdays.

The airport is in Strachowice, about 12km west of the Old Town. Bus 406 links the airport with Wrocław Główny train station and bus terminal, via the Rynek.

BUS

The **bus terminal** (ul Sucha 11) is south of the main train station. Several PKS buses go daily to Warsaw (37zł, five hours), Poznań (22zł to 35zł, 2½ hours), Częstochowa (22zł, three hours) and Białystok (66zł, seven hours). For most travel, however, the train is more convenient.

TRAIN

The **Wrocław Główny station** (ul Piłsudskiego 105) was built in 1856 and is a historical monument in itself. Every day, fast trains to Kraków (42zł, 3¾ hours) depart every one or two hours, and several InterCity and express trains go to Warsaw (88zł, six hours), usually via Łódź. Wrocław is also regularly linked by train to Poznań (32zł, 3½ hours), Częstochowa (32zł, 3½ hours, four daily), Szczecin (47zł, five hours, 10 daily), and Lublin (52zł, 9½ hours, two daily).

SUDETEN MOUNTAINS

The Sudeten Mountains (Sudety) run for over 250km along the Czech–Polish border. The Sudetes feature dense forests, amazing rock formations and deposits of semiprecious stones, and can be explored along the extensive network of trails for **hiking** or **mountain biking**. The highest part of this old eroded chain is Mt Śnieżka (1602m).

Szklarska Poręba, at the northwestern end of the Sudetes, offers superior facilities for **hiking** and **skiing**. It's at the base of Mt Szrenica (1362m), and the town centre is at the upper end of ul Jedności Narodowej. The small **tourist office** (☎ 075-754 77 40; www.szklarskaporeba.pl; ul Pstrowskiego 1) has accommodation information and maps. Nearby, several trails begin at the intersection of ul Jedności Narodowej and ul Wielki Sikorskiego. The red trail goes to Mt Szrenica (two hours) and offers a peek at Wodospad Kamieńczyka, a spectacular waterfall.

Karpacz to the southeast has more nightlife on offer, though it attracts fewer serious mountaineers. It's loosely clustered along a 3km road winding through Łomnica Valley at the base of Mt Śnieżka. The **tourist office** (☎ 075-761 86 05; www.karpacz.com.pl; ul Konstytucji 3 Maja 25a) should be your first port of call. To reach the peak of Mt Śnieżka on foot, take one of the trails (three to four hours) from Hotel Biały Jar. Some of the trails pass by one of two splendid postglacial lakes; Mały Staw and Wielki Staw.

The bus is the fastest way of getting around the region. Every day from Szklarska Poręba, about five buses head to Wrocław and one train plods along to Warsaw (55zł, 12 hours). From Karpacz, get a bus to Jelenia Góra, where buses and trains go in all directions.

For the Czech Republic, take a bus from Szklarska Poręba to Jakuszyce, cross the border on foot to Harrachov (on the Czech side) and take another bus from there.

WIELKOPOLSKA

Wielkopolska (Greater Poland) is the region where Poland came to life in the Middle Ages, and is referred to as the Cradle of the Polish State. As a result of this prominent role, its cities and towns are full of historic and cultural attractions.

The royal capital moved from Poznań to Kraków in 1038, though Wielkopolska remained an important province. Its historic significance didn't save it from international conflict, however, and the region became part of Prussia in 1793. Despite intensive Germanisation, Wielkopolska rose against German rule at the end of WWI and became part of the reborn Poland. The battles of WWII later caused widespread destruction in the area.

Poznań, the region's major city, is well known for its regular trade fairs dotted throughout the calendar. It's also home to attractive architecture and museums, and the surrounding countryside is good for cycling and hiking.

POZNAŃ

☎ 061 / pop 577,000

No-one could accuse Poznań of being too sleepy. Between its regular trade fairs, student population and visiting travellers, it's a vibrant city with a wide choice of attractions.

It grew from humble beginnings, when 9th-century Polanian tribes built a wooden fort on the island of Ostrów Tumski. From 968 to 1038 Poznań was the de facto capital of Poland. Its position between Berlin and Warsaw has always underlined its importance as a trading town, and in 1925 a modern version of its famous medieval trade fairs was instituted. The fairs, filling up the city's hotels for several days at a time, are the lynchpin of the city's economy.

Poznań has a beautiful Old Town at its centre, with a number of interesting museums, and a range of lively bars, clubs and restaurants. It's both a cosmopolitan place with an active cultural scene, and a good transport hub from which to explore the region.

Information

BOOKSHOPS

EMPiK Megastore (☎ 852 66 90; plac Wolności) Offers the largest choice of foreign magazines and newspapers.

Globtroter Turystyczna (ul Żydowska) Excellent for maps and Lonely Planet guidebooks.

INTERNET ACCESS

Internet Café Bajt (☎ 853 18 08; ul Zamkowa 5; per hr 3zł; ☉ 24hr)

MONEY

A few of the *kantors* in the city centre are shown on the map; there's also one in the bus terminal and another (open 24 hours) in the train station.

Bank Pekao (ul Św. Marcin 52/56) Probably the best place for travellers cheques and credit cards. There's another branch at ul 23 Lutego.

POST

Main post office (ul Kościuszki 77; ☉ 7am-9pm Mon-Fri, 9am-5pm Sat, 10am-4pm Sun)

TOURIST INFORMATION

City Information Centre (☎ 851 96 45; ul Ratajczaka 44; ☉ 10am-7pm Mon-Fri, 10am-5pm Sat) Handles bookings for cultural events.

Tourist Information Centre (☎ 852 61 56; Stary Rynek 59; ☉ 9am-6pm Mon-Fri, 10am-4pm Sat May-Sep, 9am-5pm Mon-Fri Oct-Apr) Helpful.

Sights

OLD TOWN

If you're in the attractive **Stary Rynek** (Old Market Square) at noon, keep an eye out for the goats in the Renaissance **Town Hall** (built 1550–60). Every midday two metal goats above its clock butt their horns together 12 times, echoing an improbable centuries-old legend of two animals escaping a cook and fighting each other in the town hall tower. Inside the building, the **Poznań Historical Museum** (☎ 852 56 13; adult/child 5.50/3.50zł; ☉ 9am-4pm Mon & Tue, 11am-6pm Wed, 9am-6pm Fri, 10am-3pm Sun) displays splendid period interiors.

Also within the square are the **Wielkopolska Military Museum** (☎ 852 67 39; Stary Rynek 9; adult/child 3.50/2.20zł; ☉ 9am-4pm Tue-Sat, 10am-3pm Sun) and the **Museum of Musical Instruments** (☎ 852 08 57; Stary Rynek 45/47; adult/child 5.50/3.50zł, free Sat; ☉ 11am-5pm Tue-Sat, 10am-3pm Sun), along with the **Museum of the Wielkopolska Uprising** (☎ 853 19 93; Stary Rynek 3; adult/child 4/2zł, free Sat; ☉ 10am-5pm Tue, Thu & Fri, 10am-6pm Wed, 10am-3pm Sat & Sun), which details the conflict in the region between German and Polish fighters after WWI.

The **Archaeological Museum** (☎ 852 82 51; ul Wodna 27; adult/child 6/3zł, free Sat; ☉ 10am-4pm Tue-Fri, 10am-6pm Sat, 10am-3pm Sun) contains Egyptian mummies and displays on the prehistory of western Poland.

The 17th-century **Franciscan Church** (ul Franciszkańska 2; ☉ 8am-8pm), one block west of the Rynek, has an ornate baroque interior, complete with wall paintings and rich stucco work. Above the church, on a hill, is the **Museum of Applied Arts** (☎ 852 20 35; adult/child 5.50/3.50zł, free Sat; ☉ 10am-4pm Tue, Wed, Fri & Sat, 10am-3pm Sun), featuring glassware, ceramics, silverware and clocks.

The nearby **National Museum: Paintings & Sculpture Gallery** (☎ 856 80 00; al Marcinkowskiego 9; adult/child 10/6zł, free Sat; ☉ 10am-6pm Tue, 9am-5pm Wed, 10am-4pm Thu, 10am-5pm Fri & Sat, 10am-3pm Sun) displays mainly 19th- and 20th-century Polish paintings.

POLAND

POZNAŃ

INFORMATION
Bank Pekao.....................................1 C4
Bank Pekao.....................................2 E5
City Information Centre..............3 C4
EMPiK Megastore........................4 C4
Globtroter Turystyczna
  (Bookshop)..................................5 F5
Internet Cafe Bajt.......................6 E5
Kantor..7 D5
Kantor..8 E6
Kantor..9 E5
Main Post Office........................10 B4
Tourist Information Centre....11 E6

SIGHTS & ACTIVITIES
Archaeological Museum...........12 F6
Ethnographic Museum.............13 F5
Franciscan Church.....................14 E6
Monument to the Victims of June
  1956...15 B4
Museum of Applied Arts.........16 E5
Museum of Musical
  Instruments.............................17 F6

Museum of Poznań June
  1956...18 B4
Museum of the Wielkopolska
  Uprising....................................19 E6
National Museum: Paintings &
  Sculpture Gallery..................20 D4
Parish Church of St Stanislaus.21 F6
Poznań Historical Museum...(see 22)
Town Hall.....................................22 F6
Wielkopolska Military
  Museum.....................................23 E6

SLEEPING
Biuro Zakwaterowania
  Przemysław..............................24 A6
Dizzy Daisy..................................25 B3
Hotel Lech....................................26 B4
Hotel Mercure Poznań.............27 A4
Hotel Royal..................................28 B4
Hotel Rzymski.............................29 D4
Hotel Stare Miasto....................30 D5
Mini Hotelik................................31 B5

EATING
Bar Caritas..................................32 D4
Bar Wegetariański.....................33 E6
Gruszecki......................................34 D5
Pod Aniołem................................35 E6
Restauracja Sphinx....................36 E6
Sioux..37 F5
Tapas Bar................................(see 11)

DRINKING
Proletaryat..................................38 E6
Room 55..39 E5

ENTERTAINMENT
Czarna Owca................................40 E6
Filharmonia.................................41 B4
Lizard King..................................42 E5
Teatr Wielki................................43 B4

TRANSPORT
Bus Terminal...............................44 B6
Orbis Travel.................................45 D4

To Szczecin
(234km)

To Airport, LOT
Office (4.6km)

Cemetery
of the
Meritorious

To Poznań Citadel;
Poznań Army Museum
(500km)

Plac
Wielkopolski

Stary
Rynek

Culture
Centre

Plac
Ratajskiego

plac
Wolności

Fairgrounds

Shopping
Centre Pasaż

plac
Wiosny
Ludów

St Martin's
Church

To Park Wilsona,
Palm House (800m);
Youth Hostel No 3 (1km)

Poznań Główny
Train Station

To Rogalin
(30km)

To Kórnik (20km);
Łódź (212km)

Two blocks south of Stary Rynek is the large, pink, baroque **Parish Church of St Stanislaus** (ul Gołębia 1; ☾ erratic) with monumental altars built in the mid-17th century. A short stroll southeast is the **Ethnographic Museum** (☎ 852 30 06; ul Grobla 25; adult/child 5.50/3.50zł, free Sat; ☾ 10am-4pm Tue, Wed, Fri & Sat, 10am-3pm Sun), presenting a collection of woodcarving and traditional costumes.

The 19th-century Prussian **Poznań Citadel**, where 20,000 German troops held out for a month in February 1945, lies about 1.5km north of the Old Town. The fortress was destroyed by artillery fire but a park was laid out on the site, which incorporates the **Poznań Army Museum** (☎ 820 45 03; al Armii Poznań; adult/child 4/2zł, free Fri; ☾ 9am-4pm Tue-Sat, 10am-4pm Sun).

In a park in the new city centre, the moving **Monument to the Victims of June 1956** commemorates the dead and injured of the massive 1956 strike by the city's industrial workers, which was crushed by tanks. Next door in the Cultural Centre; there's more detail in the **Museum of Poznań June 1956** (☎ 852 94 64; ul Św. Marcin 80/82; adult/child 2/1zł; ☾ 10am-6pm Wed or by arrangement).

In **Park Wilsona**, 1km southwest of the train station, is the **Palm House** (☎ 865 89 07; ul Matejki 18; adult/child 5.50/4zł; ☾ 9am-4pm Thu-Sat, 9am-5pm Sun). This huge greenhouse (built in 1910) contains 17,000 species of tropical and subtropical plants.

Ostrów Tumski is 1km east of the Old Town (take any eastbound tram from plac Wielkopolski). This river island is dominated by the monumental, double-towered **Poznań Cathedral** (ul Ostrów Tumski), originally built in 968. The Byzantine-style **Golden Chapel** (1841) and the **mausoleums** of Mieszko I and Boleslaus the Brave are behind the high altar. Opposite the cathedral is the 15th-century Gothic **Church of the Virgin Mary** (ul Panny Marii 1/3).

Some 2.5km east of the Old Town is **Lake Malta**, a favourite weekend destination for Poles. It holds sailing regattas, outdoor concerts and other events in summer, and in winter there's a ski slope in operation. To get to the lake, take tram 1, 4 or 8 from plac Wielkopolski.

Sleeping

During trade fairs, the rates of Poznań's accommodation dramatically increases. A room may also be difficult to find, so it pays to book ahead. Prices given here are for outside trade-fair periods.

BUDGET

Check out **Biuro Zakwaterowania Przemysław** (☎ 866 35 60; www.przemyslaw.com.pl; ul Głogowska 16; ◷ 8am-6pm Mon-Fri, 10am-2pm Sat; s/d from 43/65zł, apt from 150zł), an accommodation agency not far from the train station. Rates for weekends and stays of more than three nights are cheaper than the prices quoted here.

Youth Hostel No 3 (☎ 866 40 40; ul Berwińskiego 2/3; dm 25zł) Cheap lodgings about a 15-minute walk southwest of the train station along ul Głogowska, adjacent to Park Wilsona. It's a basic 'no frills' option, but fills up fast with students and school groups. There's a 10pm curfew.

Dizzy Daisy (☎ 829 39 02; www.hostel.pl; al Niepodległości 26; dm/s/d 30/50/100zł; 🖳) This is one of the most comfortable hostels in town, with free laundry and no curfew. Outside July to August, however, it has limited places for travellers, as it's also used as student quarters.

Mini Hotelik (☎ 863 14 16; al Niepodległości 8a; s/d from 54/107zł) Like it says on the label, this is a small place in an old building between the train station and the Old Town. It's basic but clean, with colourfully painted chambers. Some rooms share a bathroom. Enter from ul Taylora.

MIDRANGE & TOP END

Hotel Lech (☎ 853 01 51; www.hotel-lech.poznan.pl; ul Św. Marcin 74; s/d 162/244zł) Hotel Lech has standard three-star décor, but rooms are relatively spacious and the bathrooms are modern. Flash your ISIC card for a discount.

Hotel Stare Miasto (☎ 663 62 42; www.hotelstaremiasto.pl; ul Rybaki 36; s/d 195/295zł; 🅿 ✗ 🖳) Elegant value-for-money hotel with a tasteful chandeliered foyer and spacious breakfast room. Rooms can be small, but are clean and bright with lovely starched white sheets. Some upper rooms have skylights in place of windows.

Hotel Rzymski (☎ 852 81 21; www.rzymskihotel.com.pl; al Marcinkowskiego 22; s/d 210/270zł) Offers the regular amenities of three-star comfort, and overlooks plac Wolności. The décor has a lot of brown, and rooms aren't quite as grand as the elegant façade suggests, but they're a decent size.

Hotel Royal (☎ 858 23 00; www.hotel-royal.com.pl; ul Św. Marcin 71; s/d 320/420zł; 🅿) This is a gorgeous place set back from the main road. Rooms have huge beds and sparkling bathrooms.

Hotel Mercure Poznań (☎ 855 80 00; www.orbis.pl; ul Roosevelta 20; s/d from €122/142; 🅿 ✗ 🛏 🖳 ♿) In a gigantic modern building just off a busy main road, this hotel offers all the expected facilities for business travellers, including a fitness centre, restaurant and bar. It's handy for the train station, and two rooms have disabled access.

Eating & Drinking

Bar Wegetariański (☎ 821 12 55; ul Wrocławska 21; mains from 5zł; ◷ 11am-6pm Mon-Fri, 11am-3pm Sat) This cheap vegetarian eatery is in a cellar off the main road, bedecked with plant life around the walls, and offers the usual meat-free dishes.

Bar Caritas (☎ 852 51 30; plac Wolności 1; mains 8-15zł; ◷ 8am-7pm Mon-Fri, 10am-5pm Sat, noon-5pm Sun) You can point at what you want without resorting to your phrasebook at this cheap and convenient milk bar. There are many variants of *naleśniki* on the menu.

Gruszecki (☎ 850 89 42; plac Wiosny Ludów 2; mains 15-38zł; ◷ 10am-9pm Mon-Sat, 11am-7pm Sun) Inside the Kupiec Poznański shopping centre, this small place serves a surprisingly wide range of dishes, including steaks, fish, pasta, fried snails and that perennial favourite, liver in raspberries. It also does more conventional breakfasts.

Pod Aniołem (☎ 852 98 54; ul Wrocławska 4; mains 16-28zł; ◷ 11am-midnight Mon-Sat, 1pm-midnight Sun) Pleasant pub with arched brick ceilings and candlelit tables, serving a range of cheap and filling Polish fare such as dumplings, salads and grilled meats.

Restauracja Restaurant Sphinx (☎ 852 80 25; Stary Rynek 77; mains 16-50zł; ◷ 11am-11pm Sun-Thu, 11am-midnight Fri & Sat) The Sphinx is a branch of the ubiquitous kebab-and-cabbage chain, offering reasonable-value grills and salads, and a menu in English. Be prepared for ancient Egyptian décor, colourful lampshades and lots of fairy lights.

Sioux (☎ 851 62 86; Stary Rynek 93; mains 22-58zł; ◷ noon-11pm) As you'd expect, this is a 'Western'-themed place, complete with waiters dressed as cowboys. Bizarrely named dishes such as 'Marinated Fist of Dancer with Wolves' (pork steak) are on the menu, along with lots of steaks, ribs, grills and tacos.

Tapas Bar (☎ 852 85 32; Stary Rynek 60; mains 28-45zł; ◷ noon-midnight) Atmospheric place dishing up authentic tapas and Spanish wine, in a room lined with intriguing bric-a-brac including jars of stuffed olives, a cactus and a model elephant. Most tapas dishes cost 16zł to 18zł, so forget the mains and share with friends.

Proletaryat (☎ 851 32 15; ul Wrocławska 9; ☼ 1pm-2am Mon-Sat, 3pm-2am Sun) Small red communist nostalgia bar with an array of socialist-era gear on the walls, including the obligatory bust of Lenin in the window, and various portraits of the great man and his comrades. Play 'spot the communist leader' while sipping a boutique beer from the Czarnków Brewery.

Room 55 (☎ 855 32 24; Stary Rynek 80/82; ☼ 9am-midnight Mon-Sat, noon-midnight Sun) One of several trendy places on the main square to enjoy a drink and something to eat. Features mellow red chairs and banquettes, with a mezzanine area for observing the beautiful people below.

Entertainment

Lizard King (☎ 855 04 72; Stary Rynek 86; ☼ noon-2am) Simultaneously happening and laid-back, this venue is easily spotted by the big guitar on its outside wall. Friendly crowds sit drinking and eating in the split-level space, casting the occasional glance at the lizard over the bar. There's live music later in the week, usually from 9pm.

Czarna Owca (☎ 853 07 92; ul Jaskółcza 13; ☼ noon-2am Mon-Fri, 5pm-2am Sat) Literally 'Black Sheep', this is a popular club with nightly DJs playing a mix of genres including R&B, house, pop and rock. There's a dance mix on weekends and a retro night on Thursday.

Teatr Wielki (☎ 852 82 91; ul Fredry 9) is the main venue for opera and ballet, while not far away, the **Filharmonia** (☎ 852 47 08; ul Św. Marcin 81) offers classical concerts at least every Friday night.

Getting There & Away

LOT flies five times a day between Warsaw and Poznań. There are flights from Poznań to Frankfurt and Munich most days; and LOT and SAS fly daily to Copenhagen. Tickets are available from the **LOT office** (☎ 849 22 61; airport) or from **Orbis Travel** (☎ 851 20 00; al Marcinkowskiego 21). The airport is in the western suburb of Ławica, 7km from the Old Town and accessible by bus 59 or 78.

The **bus terminal** (ul Towarowa 17) is a 10-minute walk east of the train station. Bus services are relatively poor, but buses do travel from Poznań five times a day to Łódź, twice a day to Toruń and twice a day to Wrocław.

The busy **Poznań Główny train station** (ul Dworcowa 1) offers services to Kraków (48zł, 6½ hours, 11 daily), Szczecin, some of which continue to Świnoujście (34zł, two hours,

18 daily), to Gdańsk and Gdynia (43zł, five hours, seven daily), Toruń (30zł, 3½ hours, three daily) and Wrocław (32zł, 3½ hours, 15 daily). More than 20 trains a day also head to Warsaw, including nine express (78zł, five hours) and eight InterCity services (86zł, three hours).

POMERANIA

Pomerania (Pomorze) had spent a millennium being fought over by Germanic and Slavic peoples, before being returned to Poland after WWII. The region covers a large swathe of territory along the Baltic coast, from the German border in the west, to the lower Vistula Valley in the east. The major urban centres are western Szczecin, and Gdańsk on Poland's northern coast. A sandy coastline stretches between them, a popular destination for holidaymakers in summer. The attractive Gothic city of Toruń lies inland, within a belt of forests and lakes.

TORUŃ

☎ 056 / pop 211,000

The first thing to strike you about Toruń is its massive red-brick churches, looking more like fortresses than places of worship. The city is defined by its striking Gothic architecture, which gives its Old Town a distinctive appearance.

Toruń is also famous as the birthplace of Nicolaus Copernicus, a figure you cannot escape as you walk the streets of his home town – you can even buy gingerbread men in his likeness. The renowned astronomer spent his youth here, and the local university is named after him.

Historically, Toruń is intertwined with the Teutonic Knights, who established an outpost here in 1233. Following the Thirteen Years' War (1454–66), the Teutonic Order and Poland signed a peace treaty here, which returned to Poland a large area of land stretching from Toruń to Gdańsk. In the following centuries, Toruń suffered a fate similar to that of the surrounding region: Swedish invasions and German domination until the early 20th century.

Toruń was fortunate to escape major damage in WWII, and as a result is the best-preserved Gothic town in Poland. The Old Town was added to Unesco's World Heritage List in 1997.

TORUŃ

INFORMATION
Bank Pekao.....................................1 E3
EMPiK Megastore.............................2 E3
Kantor..3 C3
Kantor..4 E3
Ksero Uniwerek...............................5 C2
Main Post Office..............................6 C3
PKO Bank..7 D3
Tourist Office..................................8 C3

SIGHTS & ACTIVITIES
Cathedral of SS John the Baptist &
John the Evangelist......................9 D4
Eskens' House................................10 D4
Ethnographic Museum....................11 C1
Far Eastern Art Museum..........(see 15)
Museum of Copernicus...................12 C4
Old Town Hall................................13 C3
Regional Museum....................(see 13)
St Mary's Church............................14 B3
Star House.....................................15 C3
Statue of Copernicus......................16 C3
Teutonic Castle Ruins.....................17 E3

SLEEPING 🛏
Hotel Gotyk...................................18 B3
Hotel Heban...................................19 E2
Hotel Petite Fleur...........................20 B4
Hotel Pod Orłem............................21 D3
Hotel Polonia.................................22 C2
Hotel Retman.................................23 C4

EATING 🍴
Bar Mleczny Pod Arkadami...24 C3
Gospoda Pod Modrym
Fartuchem...............................25 E2
Piwnica Artystyczna Pod
Aniołem....................................26 C3
Pizzeria Verona..............................27 C2
Sklep Kopernik.......................(see 30)
Sułtan...28 D4

DRINKING 🍷
Piwnica Ratusz...............................29 C3

ENTERTAINMENT 🎭
Dwór Artusa..................................30 C3
Jazz God.......................................31 C4
Teatr im Horzycy............................32 B2

To Camping Nr 33
Tramp (700m); Toruń
Główny Train Station (1.5km)

To Cinema City (50m);
Youth Hostel (1.6km)

To Bus Terminal (400m);
Schronisko Turystyczne
Fort IV (3km)

To Polski
Express Bus
Stop (500m)

plac
Teatralny

Rynek
Staromiejski

OLD TOWN

Church of the
Holy Spirit

Information

BOOKSHOPS
EMPiK Megastore (☎ 622 48 95; ul Wielkie Garbary 18)

INTERNET ACCESS
Ksero Uniwerek (☎ 621 92 79; ul Franciszkańska 5; per hr 3zł; 🕐 8am-7pm Mon-Fri, 9am-4pm Sat)

MONEY
ATMs can be found along ul Różana and ul Szeroka. A couple of handy *kantors* are shown on the map.
Bank Pekao (ul Wielkie Garbary 11)
PKO Bank (ul Szeroka)

POST
Main post office (Rynek Staromiejski; 🕐 7am-9pm)

TOURIST INFORMATION
The free, glossy *Toruń Tourist & Business Guide*, available from most decent hotels, advertises local eateries and nightclubs.
Tourist office (☎ 621 09 31; www.it.torun.pl; Rynek Staromiejski 25; 🕐 9am-4pm Mon & Sat, 9am-6pm Tue-Fri, 9am-1pm Sun May-Aug, 9am-4pm Mon & Sat, 9am-6pm Tue-Fri Sep-Apr) Very helpful.

Sights
The starting point for any exploration of Toruń is the **Rynek Staromiejski** (Old Town Market Square), the focal point of the Old Town. The **Regional Museum** (☎ 622 70 38; www.muzeum.torun.pl; Rynek Staromiejski 1; adult/child 10/6zł; 🕐 10am-6pm Tue-Sun May-Aug, 10am-4pm Tue-Sun Sep-Apr) sits within the massive 14th-century **Old Town Hall**, featuring a

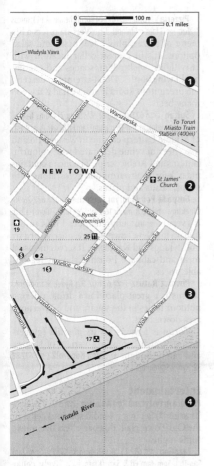

fine collection of 19th- and 20th-century Polish art. Other displays recall the town's guilds, and there's an exhibition of medieval stained glass and religious paintings. Climb the 40m-high **tower** (adult/child 10/6zł; ☺ 10am-4pm Tue-Sun Apr, 10am-7pm Tue-Sun May-Sep) for great views.

In front of the Town Hall is an elegant **statue** of Copernicus. Look for other interesting items of statuary around the square, including a dog and umbrella from a famous Polish comic strip, and a fabled violinist who saved Toruń from a plague of frogs.

The richly decorated, 15th-century **Star House**, with its baroque façade and spiral wooden staircase, contains the **Far Eastern Art Museum** (☎ 622 70 38; Rynek Staromiejski 35; adult/child 7/4zł; ☺ 10am-4pm Tue-Sun).

Just off the northwestern corner of the square is the late-13th-century **St Mary's Church** (ul Panny Marii; ☺ dawn-dusk), a Gothic building with magnificent 15th-century stalls.

In 1473, Copernicus was born in the brick Gothic house that now contains the dry **Museum of Copernicus** (☎ 622 70 38; ul Kopernika 15/17; adult/child 10/7zł; ☺ 10am-6pm Tue-Sun May-Aug, 10am-4pm Tue-Sun Sep-Apr), with replicas of the great astronomer's instruments.

One block east is the **Cathedral of SS John the Baptist & John the Evangelist** (ul Żeglarska; adult/child 2/1zł; ☺ 9am-5.30pm Mon-Sat, 2-5.30pm Sun Apr-Oct), founded in 1233 and completed more than 200 years later, with its massive **tower** (adult/child 6/4zł) and bell.

Behind the church, the **Eskens' House** (☎ 622 70 38; ul Łazienna 16; adult/child 7/4zł; ☺ 10am-4pm Tue-Sun) is a disappointing affair displaying old photographs, a few swords and archaeological finds, labelled in Polish. Further east are the ruins of the **Teutonic Castle** (☎ 622 70 39; ul Przedzamcze; adult/child 2/1zł; ☺ 9am-8pm), destroyed in 1454 by angry townsfolk protesting against the knights' oppressive regime.

In a park just north of the Old Town is the **Ethnographic Museum** (☎ 622 80 91; ul Wały Sikorskiego 19; adult/child 8/5zł; ☺ 9am-4pm Mon, Wed & Fri, 10am-6pm Tue, Thu, Sat & Sun Apr-Sep, 9am-4pm Tue-Sun Oct-Mar), showcasing traditional customs, costumes and weapons.

Sleeping

Budget lodgings are a distance from the Old Town, but in summer extra student accommodation opens its doors to travellers. Check with the tourist office for updated details.

BUDGET

Camping Nr 33 Tramp (☎ 654 71 87; www.tramp .torun.pl; ul Kujawska 14; camping per person 8zł, tents 5-10zł, d/tr/q 60/75/75zł; ☺ May-Sep) The cabins here are basic and it's alarmingly close to the train line. It's a five-minute walk west of the main train station.

Schronisko Turystyczne Fort IV (☎ 655 82 36; www .fort.torun.pl; ul Chrobrego 86; dm 17-23zł) Atmospherically located in an old Prussian fort, with long, solid brick corridors built to withstand sieges, and leading to plain, barrack-like dorms. Although inconvenient for town, it's an easy ride on bus 14 from the bus terminal or main train station.

Youth Hostel (☎ 659 61 84; ul Św. Józefa 22/24; dm 20zł) Offers plain but bright facilities overlooking parkland, 1.6km northwest of the centre. Catch bus 11 from the main train station or Old Town, to the first stop on ul Św. Jozefa. Reception closes between 10am and 5pm daily, and there's a 10pm curfew.

MIDRANGE & TOP END

Hotel Pod Orłem (☎ 622 50 24; www.hotel.torun.pl; ul Mostowa 17; s/d 110/140zł, apt 200zł; P ⊠ 🖳) This hotel is great value, and although the rooms are smallish, have squeaky wooden floors, and some contain poky bathrooms, the service is good and it's central. The foyer and corridors are fun with their jumble of framed pop-art images and old photos.

Hotel Polonia (☎ 657 18 00; www.polonia.torun.pl; plac Teatralny 5; s/d 150/180zł) The Polonia has smart, attractively furnished rooms with soothing green tones, high ceilings and good bathrooms, in a restored 19th-century building a short walk from the main square. The hotel also has its own *kantor*.

Hotel Gotyk (☎ 658 40 00; www.hotel-gotyk.com .pl; ul Piekary 20; s/d from 150/250zł) Housed in a fully modernised 14th-century building just off the main square, rooms are very neat, with ornate furniture and high ceilings, and all come with sparkling bathrooms.

Hotel Retman (☎ 657 44 60; www.hotelretman.pl; ul Rabiańska 15; s/d 160/210zł) Relatively new accommodation offering spacious, atmospheric rooms with red carpet and solid timber furniture. Downstairs is a good pub and restaurant.

Hotel Petite Fleur (☎ 663 44 00; www.petitefleur .pl; ul Piekary 25; s/d from 190/250zł; 🖳) Just opposite the Gotyk, the Petite Fleur offers fresh, airy rooms in a renovated old town house, some with exposed original brickwork and rafters. It also has a French cellar restaurant.

Hotel Heban (☎ 652 15 55; www.hotel-heban.com.pl; ul Małe Garbary 7; s/d/ste from 190/300/350zł; P ⊠ 🖳) This is a stylish, upmarket hotel occupying an historic 17th-century building in a quiet street. It also has a good restaurant, situated off a lavish foyer with painted wooden ceilings and a 24-hour bar.

Eating & Drinking

Bar Mleczny Pod Arkadami (☎ 622 24 28; ul Różana 1; mains 3-8zł; 🕑 9am-7pm Mon-Fri, 9am-4pm Sat) This classic milk bar is just off the Old Town Square, with a range of low-cost dishes. It also has a takeaway window serving a range of *zapiekanki* (toasted rolls with cheese, mushrooms and ketchup) and sweet waffles.

Pizzeria Verona (☎ 622 04 80; ul Chełmińska 11; mains 7-26zł; 🕑 11am-midnight) The Verona offers a big menu of pizzas, plus a few pasta and salad options. It's in a great cellar location with fairy lights, wicker lampshades and candles in old wine bottles. Don't attempt to descend the precipitous stairs if you've had a few too many beers.

Sułtan (☎ 621 06 07; ul Mostowa 7; mains 8-12zł; 🕑 11am-midnight Sun-Thu, 11am-1am Fri & Sat) A splash of Middle Eastern cuisine in western Poland in a cheerful venue decorated with colourful lanterns and Arabic script. The menu contains pides, kebabs, shwarma and gyros, along with soups, salads and pizzas.

Gospoda Pod Modrym Fartuchem (☎ 622 26 26; Rynek Nowomiejski 8; mains 16-29zł; 🕑 10am-10pm) This is a very pleasant, unpretentious 15th-century pub on the New Town Square, once visited by Polish kings and Napoleon. It serves the usual meat-and-cabbage Polish dishes at reasonable prices.

Piwnica Ratusz (☎ 621 02 92; Rynek Staromiejski 1) This is a great place for a drink, offering outdoor tables in the square and a cavernous area downstairs.

Toruń is famous for its *pierniki* (gingerbread), which come in a variety of shapes, and can be bought at **Sklep Kopernik** (☎ 622 88 32; Rynek Staromiejski 6).

Entertainment

Piwnica Artystyczna Pod Aniołem (☎ 622 70 39; Rynek Staromiejski 1) Set in a splendid spacious cellar in the Old Town Hall, this bar offers live music some nights.

Jazz God (☎ 652 13 08; ul Rabiańska 17; 🕑 5pm-2am Sun-Thu, 5pm-4am Fri & Sat) This is a lively cellar bar with rock DJs every night from 9pm. On Sunday there's live jazz around 8pm.

Teatr im Horzycy (☎ 622 52 22; plac Teatralny 1) The main stage for theatre performances.

Dwór Artusa (☎ 655 49 29; Artus Court, Rynek Staromiejski 6) This place often presents classical music.

Cinema City (☎ 664 64 64; ul Czerwona Droga 1; tickets 15zł) A moviehouse showing current film releases in a 12-screen multiplex.

Getting There & Away

The **bus terminal** (ul Dąbrowskiego) is a 10-minute walk north of the Old Town, though it offers surprisingly few long-distance buses. **Polski Express** (ul Mickiewicza) has 12 buses a day to Warsaw (48zł, four hours) and two a day to Szczecin.

The **Toruń Główny train station** (al Podgórska) is on the opposite side of the Vistula River and linked to the Old Town by bus 22 or 27 (get off at the first stop over the bridge). Some trains stop and finish at the more convenient Toruń Miasto train station, about 500m east of the New Town.

From the Toruń Główny station, there are fast train services to Poznań (30zł, 3½ hours, six daily), Gdańsk and Gdynia (36zł, five hours, nine daily), Kraków (50zł, 6½ hours, six daily), Łódź (32zł, eight daily), Olsztyn (32zł, eight daily), Szczecin (45zł, five hours, direct twice a week), Wrocław (43zł, 4½ hours, two daily) and Warsaw (40zł, four hours, seven daily). Trains travelling between Toruń and Gdańsk often change at Bydgoszcz, and between Toruń and Kraków you may need to get another connection at Inowrocław.

GDAŃSK
☎ 058 / pop 462,000

Few Polish cities occupy such a pivotal position in history as Gdańsk. Founded more than a millennium ago, it became the focus of territorial tensions when the Teutonic Knights seized it from Poland in 1308. The city joined the Hanseatic League in 1361, and became one of the richest ports in the Baltic through its membership of the trading organisation. Finally, the Thirteen Years' War ended in 1466 with the Knights' defeat and Gdańsk's return to Polish rule.

This to-and-fro between Germanic and Polish control wasn't over – in 1793 Gdańsk was incorporated into Prussia, and after WWI became the autonomous Free City of Danzig. The city's environs are where WWII began, when the Nazis bombarded Polish troops stationed at Westerplatte. Gdańsk suffered immense damage in the war, but upon its return to Poland in 1945, its historic centre was faithfully reconstructed.

In the 1980s, Gdańsk achieved international fame as the home of the Solidarity trade union, whose rise paralleled the fall of communism in Europe. Today it's a lively, attractive city that makes a great base for exploring the Baltic coast.

Information
BOOKSHOPS
EMPiK Megastore (☎ 301 72 44; ul Podwale Grodzkie 8) Opposite the main train station.

INTERNET ACCESS
Jazz 'n' Java (☎ 305 36 16; ul Tkacka 17/18; per hr 5zł; 🕙 10am-10pm)
Rudy Kot (ul Garncarska 18/20; per hr 4zł; 🕙 10am-10pm)

MONEY
The *kantor* at the main train station is open 24 hours.
Bank Millennium Old Town (ul Wały Jagiellońskie 14/16); Main Town (ul Długi Targ 14/16) Has more branches at central locations.
Bank Pekao (ul Garncarska 23) Will provide cash advances on Visa and MasterCard.

POST
Main post office (ul Długa 22; 🕙 8am-8pm Mon-Fri, 9am-3pm Sat)

TOURIST INFORMATION
PTTK office (☎ 301 13 43; www.pttk-gdansk.pl; ul Długa 45; 🕙 9am-5pm)

TRAVEL AGENCIES
Almatur (☎ 301 24 24; Długi Targ 11)
Orbis Travel (☎ 301 45 44; ul Podwale Staromiejskie 96/97)

Sights
MAIN TOWN
Ul Długa (Long Street) and Długi Targ (Long Market) form the city's main historic thoroughfare, and are known collectively as the **Royal Way**. Polish kings traditionally paraded through the **Upland Gate** (built in the 1770s on a 15th-century gate), onward through the **Golden Gate** (1614), and proceeded east to the Renaissance **Green Gate** (1568).

Gdańsk History Museum (☎ 767 91 00; ul Długa 47; adult/child 8/4zł, adult/child incl Artus Court Museum & Dom Uphagena 12/6zł; 🕙 noon-6pm Tue-Fri, noon-4pm Sat & Sun) is inside the towering Gothic **Main Town Hall**. On show are photos of old Gdańsk, and the damage caused during WWII.

Artus Court Museum (☎ 767 91 00; ul Długi Targ 43/44; adult/child 8/4zł, free Wed; 🕙 noon-6pm Tue-Fri, noon-4pm Sat & Sun), where merchants used to congregate, stands behind **Neptune's Fountain** (1633). The adjacent **Golden House** (1618) has a strikingly rich façade. Further west, the 18th-century **Dom Uphagena** (☎ 301 13 63; ul Długa; adult/child 8/4zł, free Sun; 🕙 noon-6pm Tue-Fri, 10am-4pm Sat, 11am-4pm Sun) features ornate furniture.

North of the Green Gate is the 14th-century **St Mary's Gate**, which houses the **State Archaeological Museum** (☎ 301 50 31; ul Mariacka 25/26;

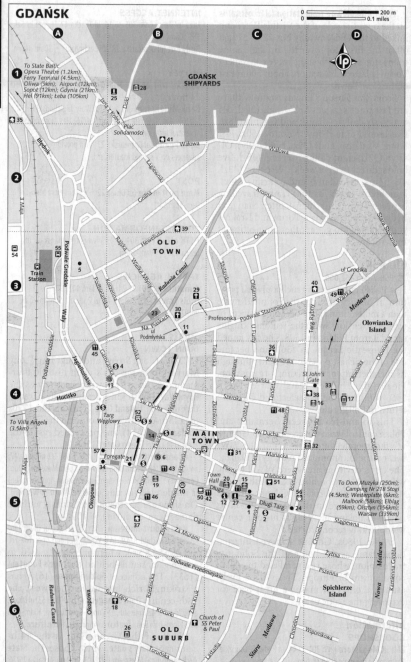

GDAŃSK

adult/child 5/4zł; 9am-4pm Tue, Thu & Fri, 10am-5pm Wed, Sat & Sun). It features an overly generous number of formerly diseased ancient human skulls, displays of amber, and river views from the adjacent **tower** (admission 2zł). Through this gate, picturesque **ul Mariacka** (St Mary's St) is lined with 17th-century burgher houses and amber shops.

At the end of ul Mariacka is the gigantic 14th-century **St Mary's Church** (adult/child 2/1zł; 8am-8pm, except during services). Watch little figures troop out at noon from its 14m-high astronomical clock, adorned with zodiacal signs. Climb the 405 steps of the **tower** (adult/child 3/1.50zł) for a giddy view over the town. West along ul Piwna (Beer St) is the Dutch Renaissance **Arsenal** (1609), now occupied by a market.

Further north along the waterfront is the 15th-century **Gdańsk Crane**, the largest of its kind in medieval Europe and capable of hoisting loads of up to 2000kg. It's now part of the **Central Maritime Museum** (301 86 11; ul Ołowianka 9-13; one section 6zł, all four sections 14zł; 10am-5pm Tue-Sun). The museum offers a fascinating insight into Gdańsk's seafaring past, including the **Sołdek Museum Ship**, built here just after WWII.

OLD TOWN

Almost totally destroyed in 1945, the Old Town has never been completely rebuilt. However, among its gems are **St Catherine's Church** (ul Wielke Młyny; 8am-6pm Mon-Sat), Gdańsk's oldest church (begun in the 1220s). Opposite, the **Great Mill** (ul Wielke Młyny) was built by the Teutonic Knights in around 1350. It

used to produce 200 tonnes of flour per day and continued to operate until 1945.

Right behind St Catherine's is **St Bridget's Church** (ul Profesorska 17; 10am-6pm Mon-Sat). Formerly Lech Wałęsa's place of worship, the church was a strong supporter of the shipyard activists in the 1980s.

The soaring **Monument to the Shipyard Workers** (plac Solidarności) stands at the entrance to the Gdańsk Shipyards to the north. It was erected in late 1980 in memory of 44 workers killed during the riots of December 1970. Down the street is the evocative **Roads to Freedom Exhibition** (Solidarity Museum; 769 29 20; ul Doki 1; adult/child 6/4zł, free Wed; 10am-4pm Tue-Sun). Look out for the section of the Berlin Wall outside.

OLD SUBURB

The **National Museum** (301 70 61; ul Toruńska 1; adult/child 9/5zł; 9am-4pm Tue-Fri, 10am-4pm Sat & Sun) is famous for its Dutch and Flemish paintings, especially Hans Memling's 15th-century *Last Judgment*.

Adjoining the museum is the former Franciscan **Church of the Holy Trinity** (ul Św. Trójcy; 10am-8pm Mon-Sat), built at the end of the 15th century.

OLIWA

Some 9km northwest is the lovely **Park Oliwski** (ul Cystersów), surrounding the towering **Oliwa Cathedral** (8am-8pm), built in the 13th century with a Gothic façade and a long, narrow central nave. The famous baroque organ is used for recitals each hour between 10am and 3pm Monday to Saturday in June, July and August. Nearby is the **Ethnographic Museum** (552 12 71;

ul Cystersów 19; adult/child 8/5zł; ⊙ 9am-4pm Tue-Fri, 10am-4pm Sat & Sun) in the Old Granary, and the **Modern Art Gallery** (☎ 552 12 71; adult/child 6/3zł; ⊙ 9am-4pm Tue-Sun) in the former Abbots' Palace.

To reach the park, take the commuter train to the Gdańsk Oliwa station (2.80zł). From there, it's a 10-minute walk; head (west) up ul Poczty Gdańsk, turn right (north) along the highway and look for the signs (in English) to 'Ethnographic Museum' and 'Cathedral'.

WESTERPLATTE

WWII began at 4.45am on 1 September 1939, when the German battleship *Schleswig-Holstein* began shelling the Polish naval post at Westerplatte, 7km north of Gdańsk's Main Town. The 182-man Polish garrison held out against ferocious attacks for a week before surrendering.

The enormity of this event is marked by a hilltop **memorial** (free; ⊙ 24hr), a small **museum** (☎ 343 69 72; ul Sucharskiego 1; admission 2zł; ⊙ 8am-7pm) and **ruins** remaining from the Nazi bombardment.

Bus 106 (25 minutes) goes to the park every 15 minutes from a stop outside the main train station in Gdańsk. Alternatively, excursion boats (23/39zł one way/return) to and around Westerplatte leave from a dock near the Green Gate in Gdańsk between 1 April and 30 October.

Sleeping

If you're having trouble finding accommodation, check with the PTTK office. Also consider staying in nearby Sopot or Gdynia.

BUDGET

Youth Hostel (☎ /fax 301 23 13; ul Wałowa 21; dm/s/d from 12/25/50zł; P ✗) Old-style hostel in a quiet, old building on the doorstep of the Gdańsk Shipyards, Lech Wałęsa's old stamping grounds. Rooms are brown and basic, but clean. Book ahead, particularly in summer. Smoking and drinking are strictly forbidden and there's a midnight curfew.

Dom Harcerza (☎ 301 36 21; www.domharcerza.prv .pl; ul Za Murami 2/10; dm 25zł, s/d/tr from 50/100/120zł) The rooms are small but cosy, and the bathrooms are clean at this place, which offers the best value and location for any budget-priced hotel. It's popular (so book ahead), and can get noisy when large groups are staying here. There's a charming old-fashioned restaurant on the ground floor.

Baltic Hostel (☎ 721 96 57; www.baltichostel.com; ul 3 Maja 25; dm 35zł, s/d 50/100zł; P ✗ 💻) Aimed at the international budget traveller, this hostel near the train and bus stations has basic, newly-furnished rooms with high ceilings. Bathrooms are clean, and there's a homely light-filled lounge area with ceramic fish on the wall. The entrance is right at the end of the long brown apartment block, around to the right.

Targ Rybny (☎ 301 56 27; www.gdanskhostel.com; ul Grodzka 21; dm from 40zł, s/d/tr from 90/140/180zł; P ✗ 💻) A popular modern hostel in a great central location overlooking the quay. It's a little cramped, but clean and sociable, with a comfy lounge area. It also offers bike rental.

Camping Nr 218 Stogi (☎ 307 39 15; www.camping-gdansk.pl; ul Wydmy 9; per person/tent 10/10zł, cabins 40-100zł; ⊙ Apr-Oct; P) This camping ground is only 200m from the beach in the seaside holiday centre of Stogi, about 5.5km northeast of the Main Town. Tidy cabins sleep between two and five people, and facilities include a volleyball court and children's playground. Take tram 8 or 13 from the main train station in Gdańsk.

MIDRANGE & TOP END

Apartments Poland (☎ 346 98 64; www.apartment poland.com; apt from €50) is an agency with renovated properties scattered through the Tri-City Area (Gdańsk/Sopot/Gdynia), including a number in central Gdańsk. Some are big enough for families or other groups. Be aware of the additional electricity charge when checking out, based on a meter reading.

Villa Angela (☎ 302 23 15; www.villaangela.pl; ul Beethowena 12; s/d/tr 175/210/285zł; P ✗ 💻) Comfortable lodgings west of the centre, with spacious recently renovated rooms (some with balconies), good furniture and gleaming bathrooms. It's accessible by buses 130, 184 or 384, or night bus N6, from the main train station.

Dom Muzyka (☎ 300 92 60; www.dom-muzyka.pl; ul Łąkowa 1/2; s/d from 180/255zł; P ✗ 📺 💻) Gorgeous white rooms with arched ceilings and quality furniture, inside the Music Academy some 300m east of the city centre. From July to August, a second wing of the building offers cheaper student-style accommodation. It's hard to spot from the street; head for the door on the city end of the courtyard within the big yellow-brick building.

Dom Aktora (☎ 301 59 01; www.domaktora.pl; ul Straganiarska 55/56; s/d/ste from 200/300/360zł) The Dom

Aktora is an historic and convenient place which is always popular, but it's a little old-fashioned in appearance.

Mercure Hevelius Gdańsk (☎ 321 00 00; www.orbis .pl; ul Heweliusza 22; s/d from 360/430zł; P ⊠ 🖳 🕭) Though the foyer still hints at its origins in the late Cold War days, this business-friendly hotel offers good quality rooms and facilities including a restaurant, bar and sauna. Two rooms are designed for disabled access, and some upper rooms have great views of the Old Town.

Hotel Hanza (☎ 305 34 27; www.hanza-hotel.com.pl; ul Tokarska 6; s/d 665/695zł; P ⊠ 🕱 🖳) The Hanza is attractively perched along the waterfront near the Gdańsk Crane, and offers elegant, tasteful rooms in a modern building. Some rooms have enviable views over the river.

Eating & Drinking

For self-catering, visit the supermarket inside the former Arsenal facing Targ Węglowy.

Bar Mleczny Neptun (☎ 301 49 88; ul Długa 33/34; mains 2-10zł; ☺ 7.30am-6pm Mon-Fri, 10am-5pm Sat, 11am-5pm Sun) This joint is a cut above your run-of-the-mill milk bar, with potted plants, lace curtains, decorative tiling and old lamps for décor.

Green Way (☎ 301 41 21; ul Garncarska 4/6; mains 7-10zł; ☺ 10am-7pm Mon-Fri, noon-7pm Sat & Sun) Popular with local vegetarians, this eatery serves everything from soy cutlets to Mexican goulash in an unfussy blue-and-yellow space.

Grand Café Rotterdam (☎ 305 45 80; Długi Targ 33/34; mains 12-27zł; ☺ 10am-2am) On the ground floor of the Dutch consulate, this café serves especially good savoury pancakes. It also has a good range of seafood dishes, including

---

AUTHOR'S CHOICE

Café Ferber (☎ 301 55 66; ul Długa 77/78; mains 14-24zł; ☺ 8am-midnight) It's startling to step straight from Gdańsk's historic main street into this very modern café, dominated by bright red panels, a suspended ceiling and boxy lighting. The scarlet décor contrasts with its comfy brown armchairs, and the menu of breakfasts, soups and sandwiches is backed up by many variants of well-made coffee. There are English-language magazines on hand, and even the bathroom is ultramodern. At the time of research, an alcohol licence was in the works.

---

stir-fried mussels. It's a pleasant spot for an alfresco beer, and has a well-stocked cellar wine bar.

Kansai (☎ 324 08 88; ul Ogarna 124/125; mains 22-36zł; ☺ noon-10pm Tue-Sun) You'd expect fish to be served in a seaport, but Kansai adds an exotic twist by serving sushi in full-on Japanese ambience. Waiters are dressed in traditional robes, there's a samurai sword on the counter, and the menu has dishes made from tuna, salmon and butterfish, along with classic California rolls.

Restauracja Kubicki (☎ 301 00 50; ul Wartka 5; mains 25-43zł; ☺ 11.30am-11.30pm) The Kubicki is a decent midpriced place to try Polish food, especially seafood. It's one of the oldest eateries in Gdańsk, established in the Danzig days of 1918, and offers appropriately old-fashioned décor and service off a scenic laneway next to the river.

Pod Łososiem (☎ 301 76 52; ul Szeroka 52/54; mains 45-95zł; ☺ noon-10pm) This is one of Gdańsk's oldest and most highly regarded restaurants, and is particularly famous for its salmon dishes. Red leather seats, brass chandeliers and a gathering of gas lamps fill out the sombre interior.

Piwinica Rajców (☎ 300 02 80; ul Długi Targ 44; mains 20-110zł; ☺ 10am-midnight) An excellent cellar-restaurant below a striking entrance that's topped by a statue of the god Mercury. The menu features some of the finest Polish cuisine to be had in Gdańsk, particularly wild boar, and extends to more exotic dishes such as springbok fillet.

U Szkota (☎ 301 49 11; ul Chlebnicka 9/12; ☺ noon-midnight) If you're in the mood to be served by buzz-cut Polish waiters dressed in kilts, this Scottish-themed venue is the place to go. The bar is small but cosy, with good-natured staff, and there's a decent selection of whiskies on the drinks list. The attached restaurant serves a largely Polish menu.

Maraska (☎ 301 42 89; ul Długa 31/32; ☺ 9am-9pm) The Maraska is a cosy teahouse with vintage wallpaper, framed pictures of yachts, and tea paraphernalia for sale. There's a good choice of desserts, and a counter selling chocolates and other sweets.

Entertainment

Yesterday (☎ 301 39 24; ul Piwna 50/51; ☺ 6pm-2am) Groovy cellar venue decked out in a 1960s theme, with colourful flower-power décor including cartoon characters and a fluorescent portrait of Chairman Mao. DJs play a variety of sounds from 9pm every night, and there's the occasional live gig. Tuesday night is British music night.

State Baltic Opera Theatre (☎ 763 49 12; www .operabaltycka.pl; al Zwycięstwa 15) This place is in the suburb of Wrzeszcz, not far from the train station at Gdańsk Politechnika.

Teatr Wybrzeże (☎ 301 70 21; ul Św. Ducha 2) Next to the Arsenal is the main city theatre. Both Polish and foreign classics (all in Polish) are part of the repertoire.

Getting There & Away

For information about international ferry services to/from Gdańsk and Gdynia, see p445.

AIR

From Gdańsk, LOT has six to seven daily flights to Warsaw, two a day to Frankfurt, and one to Hamburg and Munich. Tickets can be bought at the **LOT office** (☎ 0801 703 703; ul Wały Jagiellońskie 2/4).

BOAT

Polferries uses the **ferry terminal** (ul Przemysłowa) in Nowy Port, about 5km north of the Main Town and a short walk from the local commuter train station at Gdańsk Brzeźno. Orbis Travel and the PTTK Office in Gdańsk provide information and sell tickets.

Between 1 May and 30 September, excursion boats leave regularly from the dock near the Green Gate in Gdańsk for Sopot (35/51zł one way/return) and Gdynia (41/61zł) – and you can even go to Hel (61/92zł)! From the same dock, boats also head out to Westerplatte (23/39zł) between 1 April and 30 October.

BUS

The **bus terminal** (ul 3 Maja 12) is behind the main train station and connected to ul Podwale Grodzkie by an underground passageway. Every day there are buses to Olsztyn (26zł, seven daily), Toruń (27zł, two daily) and Warsaw (50zł, six hours, five daily), and one or two to Białystok and Świnoujście. Polski Express also offers buses to Warsaw (72zł, two daily).

TRAIN

The city's main train station, **Gdańsk Główny** (ul Podwale Grodzkie 1), is conveniently located on the western outskirts of the Old Town. Most long-distance trains actually start or finish at

Gdynia, so make sure you get on/off quickly here.

Each day more than 20 trains head to Warsaw, including eight express trains (82zł, 5½ hours) and five InterCity services (90zł, 3½ hours). There are fast trains to Olsztyn (32zł, three hours, nine daily), Kraków (115zł, eight hours, 13 daily), Poznań (45zł, five hours, seven daily), Toruń (37zł, three hours, eight daily) and Szczecin (47zł, 4½ hours, four daily). Trains also head to Białystok and Lublin three times a day.

Getting Around

The airport is in Rębiechowo, about 12km northwest of Gdańsk. It's accessible by bus 110 from the Gdańsk Wrzeszcz local commuter train station, or less frequently by bus B from outside the Gdańsk Główny train station. Taxis cost 40zł to 50zł one way.

The local commuter train, the SKM, runs every 15 minutes between 6am and 7.30pm, and less frequently thereafter, between Gdańsk Główny and Gdynia Główna stations, via Sopot and Gdańsk Oliwa stations. (Note: the line to Gdańsk Nowy Port, via Gdańsk Brzeźno, is a separate line that leaves less regularly from Gdańsk Główny.) Buy tickets at any station and validate them in the machines at the platform entrance.

AROUND GDAŃSK

Gdańsk is part of the so-called Tri-City Area including Gdynia and Sopot, which are easy day trips from Gdańsk.

Sopot

☎ 058 / pop 43,000

Sopot, 12km north of Gdańsk, has been one of the Baltic coast's most fashionable seaside resorts since the 19th century. It has an easy-going atmosphere and long stretches of sandy **beach**.

The **tourist office** (☎ 550 37 83; www.sopot.pl; ul Dworcowa 4; ☒ 9am-8pm Jun-Aug, 10am-6pm Sep-May) is about 50m from the main train station. A short walk to the east of the station is **Gamer** (☎ 555 01 83; ul Chopina 1; per hr 4zł; ☒ 9am-10pm), an internet café.

From the tourist office, head down ul Bohaterów Monte Cassino, one of Poland's most attractive pedestrian streets, and past the church to Poland's longest **pier** (515m).

Opposite Pension Wanda, **Museum Sopotu** (☎ 551 22 66; ul Poniatowskiego 8; adult/child 5/3zł;

(🕑 10am-4pm Tue-Fri, 11am-5pm Sat & Sun) has displays recalling the town's 19th-century incarnation as the German resort of Zoppot.

SLEEPING & EATING

There are no real budget options in Sopot, and prices increase during the busy summer season. Bistros and cafés serving a wide range of cuisines sprout up in summer along the promenades.

Hotel Eden (☎ 551 15 03; www.hotel-eden.com.pl; ul Kordeckiego 4/6; s 100-180zł, d 170-260zł, tr 320zł, q 340zł, ste 410zł; **P ☐**) One of the less expensive places in town. It's a quiet, old-fashioned *pension* with high ceilings and old-fashioned furniture, overlooking the town park one street from the beach. The cheaper rooms don't have private bathrooms.

Willa Karat II (☎ 550 07 42; ul 3 Maja 31; s/d/tr 150/250/270zł) Cosy budget lodgings a few blocks from the beach, with light, spacious rooms and clean bathrooms, and plants decorating the corridors. There's a kitchen and dining area for guest use. From the train station, walk right along ul Kościuszki, then left along ul 3 Maja toward the coast.

Pension Wanda (☎ 550 30 38; fax 551 57 25; ul Poniatowskiego 7; s/d/tr from 200/300/410zł, ste from 360zł; **P ✕**) The Wanda is a homely place with light, airy rooms, in a handy location about 500m south of the pier. Some rooms have sea views.

Zhong Hua Hotel (☎ 550 20 20; www.hotelchinski.pl; al Wojska Polskiego 1; s/d/ste 430/455/565zł; **✕ ☐**) Attractive accommodation in a striking wooden pavilion on the seafront. The foyer is decked out in Chinese design, with hanging lanterns and beautiful timber furniture. The theme extends to the small but pleasant rooms, with views of the water.

The classy **Café del Arte** (☎ 555 51 60; ul Bohaterów Monte Cassino 53; 🕑 10am-10pm) is a great place to enjoy coffee, cake and ice cream surrounded by artistic objects in the combined café-gallery. At the same address is **Caipirinha** (☎ 555 53 80; ul Bohaterów Monte Cassino 53; mains 12-20zł; 🕑 10am-midnight), a bar and eatery serving light meals and plenty of cocktails. Its surrealistic 'melting' architecture is what sets this building apart; you really can't miss it.

GETTING THERE & AWAY

From the **Sopot train station** (ul Dworcowa 7), local commuter trains run every 15 minutes to Gdańsk Główny (2.80zł, 15 minutes) and

Gdynia Główna (1.20zł, 10 minutes) stations. Excursion boats leave several times a day (May to September) from the Sopot pier to Gdańsk, Gdynia and Hel.

Gdynia

☎ 058 / pop 254,000

Gdynia, 9km north of Sopot, was greatly expanded as a seaport after this coastal area (but not Gdańsk) became part of Poland following WWI. Less atmospheric than Gdańsk or Sopot, it's a young city with a busy port atmosphere.

From the main Gdynia Główna train station on plac Konstytucji, where there is a **tourist office** (☎ 721 24 66; www.gdynia.pl; 🕑 8am-6pm May-Sep, 10am-5pm Oct-Apr), follow ul 10 Lutego east for about 1.5km to the pier. At the end of the pier is the **Oceanographic Museum & Aquarium** (☎ 621 70 21; adult/child 11/7zł; 🕑 10am-5pm Tue-Sun), which houses a vast array of sea creatures, both alive and embalmed.

A 20-minute walk uphill (follow the signs) from Teatr Muzyczny on plac Grunwaldzki (about 300m southwest of the start of the pier) leads to **Kamienna Góra**, a hill offering wonderful views.

SLEEPING & EATING

Gdynia is probably best visited as a day trip, but it does have a vibrant restaurant scene. There are several milk bars in the city centre, and upmarket fish restaurants along the pier.

China Town Hotel (☎ 620 92 21; www.chinahotel.pl; ul Dworca 11a; s/d 100/130zł) Inexpensive lodgings can be found here, opposite the train station. The rooms are plain but serviceable for a night, though singles are very small. There's a sushi restaurant in the same building.

Hotel Antracyt (☎ 620 12 39; ul Korzeniowskiego 19; www.hotel-antracyt.pl; s/d from 170/240zł; **P ✕ ☐**) This place is further south, on a hill in an exclusive residential area, with fine views over the water.

Willa Lubicz (☎ 668 47 40; www.willalubicz.pl; ul Orłowska 43; s/d 380/410zł; **✕**) If you're looking for style you could try this quiet, upmarket place with a chic 1930s ambience at the southern end of town; Gdynia Orłowo is the nearest train station. Third-floor rooms have views of the sea.

Bistro Kwadrans (☎ 620 15 92; Skwer Kościuszki 20; mains 9-13zł; 🕑 9am-10pm Mon-Fri, 10am-10pm Sat, noon-10pm Sun) One block north of the median strip along ul 10 Lutego, this is a great place for tasty Polish food. It also serves up pizzas, including an improbable variant involving banana and curry.

GETTING THERE & AWAY

Local commuter trains link **Gdynia Główna** station with Sopot and Gdańsk every 15 minutes (4zł, 25 minutes). From the same station, regular trains run to Hel (12zł) and Lębork (for Łeba). From the small **bus terminal** outside, minibuses also go to Hel (11zł) and Łeba, and two buses run daily to Świnoujście.

Stena Line uses the **Terminal Promowy** (ul Kwiatkowskiego 60), about 5km northwest of Gdynia. Take bus 150 from outside the main train station.

Between May and September, excursion boats leave regularly throughout the day to Gdańsk, Sopot and Hel from the Gdynia pier.

Hel

Never was a town more entertainingly named – English speakers can spend hours creating amusing twists on 'to Hel and back', or 'a cold day in Hel'. In fact, this old fishing village at the tip of the Hel Peninsula north of Gdańsk is an attractive place to visit, and a popular beach resort. The pristine, windswept **beach** on the Baltic side stretches the length of the peninsula. On the southern side the sea is popular for **windsurfing**; equipment can be rented in the villages of Władysławowo and Jastarnia.

The **Fokarium** (☎ 675 08 36; ul Morska 2; admission 1zł; ☼ 8.30am-8pm), off the main road along the seafront, is home to endangered Baltic grey seals. It also has a good souvenir shop for those 'I'm in Hel' postcards to friends back home. The 15th-century **Gothic church** (ul Nadmorksi 2), further along the esplanade, houses the **Museum of Fishery** (☎ 675 05 52; adult/child 5/3zł; ☼ 10am-4pm Tue-Sun).

Visitors often stay in **private rooms** offered within local houses (mostly from May to September), at about 90zł per double. **Captain Morgan** (☎ 675 00 91; www.captainmorgan.hel.org.pl; ul Wiejska 21; d/tr 100/140zł) also offers plain, clean rooms, and good seafood in a quirky pub stuffed with maritime memorabilia.

To Hel, minibuses leave every hour or so from the main train station in Gdynia (11zł). Several slow trains depart from Gdynia daily (12zł), and from May to September from Gdańsk. Hel is also accessible by excursion boat from Gdańsk, Sopot and Gdynia.

Łeba

☎ 059 / pop 4100

Łeba (*weh*-bah) transforms from quiet fishing village to popular seaside resort between May and September. The wide sandy **beach** and clean water is ideal if you're looking for a beach break.

From the train station, or adjacent bus stop, head east along ul 11 Listopada as far as the main street, ul Kościuszko. Then turn left (north) and walk about 1.5km to the better eastern beach via the esplanade (ul Nadmorska); if in doubt, follow the signs to the beachside Hotel Neptune.

The **tourist office** (☎ 866 25 65; ☼ 8am-4pm Mon-Fri May-Sep) is inside the train station. There are several *kantors* along ul 11 Listopada.

SŁOWIŃSKI NATIONAL PARK

Beginning just west of Łeba, this park stretches along the coast for 33km. It contains a diversity of habitats, including forests, lakes, bogs and beaches, but the main attraction is the huge number of massive (and shifting) **sand dunes** that create a desert landscape. The wildlife and birdlife is also remarkably rich.

From Łeba to the sand dunes, follow the signs from near the train station northwest along ul Turystyczna and take the road west to the park entrance in the hamlet of Rąbka. Minibuses ply this road in summer from Łeba; alternatively, it's a pleasant walk or bike ride (8km). No cars or buses are allowed beyond the park entrance.

SLEEPING & EATING

Many houses offer private rooms all year round, but finding a vacant room during summer can be tricky. There are plenty of decent eateries in the town centre and along ul Nadmorska.

Hotel Wodnik (☎ 866 13 66; www.wodnik.leba.pl; ul Nadmorska 10; s/d from 232/363zł; P ☼) One of several *pensions* along the esplanade on the eastern side of the beach.

Camping Nr 41Amber (☎ 866 24 72; www.ambre .leba.pl; ul Nadmorska 9a; per person/tent from 11/6zł; P) This is a decent camping ground, but bring mosquito repellent if you don't want to be eaten alive.

GETTING THERE & AWAY

The usual transit point is Lębork, 29km south of Łeba. In summer there are several daily trains between the two destinations (7zł). To

Lębork, slow trains run every hour or two from Gdańsk, via Gdynia, and there are buses every hour from Gdynia. In summer (June to August), two buses and two trains run directly between Gdynia and Łeba, and one train a day travels to/from Wrocław (55zł, 10 hours).

Malbork

☎ 055 / pop 42,000

Malbork Castle (☎ 647 08 00; www.zamek.malbork.pl; adult/child 25/15zł; ☼ 9am-7pm Tue-Sun May-Aug, 10am-5pm Tue-Sun Apr & Sep, 10am-3pm Tue-Sun Oct-Mar) is the centrepiece of this town, 58km southeast of Gdańsk. It's the largest Gothic castle in Europe, and was once known as Marienburg, headquarters to the Teutonic Knights. It was constructed by the Order in 1276 and became the seat of their Grand Master in 1309. Damage sustained in WWII has been repaired since the conflict's end, and it was placed on the Unesco World Heritage List in 1997.

The **Youth Hostel** (☎ 272 24 08; gimnazjum@malbork .com; ul Żeromskiego 45; dm/d 20/46zł) is a reasonable budget option in a local school about 500m south of the castle. Bed linen costs an extra 5zł per person.

Hotel & Restaurant Zbyszko (☎ 272 26 40; www .hotel.malbork.pl; ul Kościuszki 43; s/d from 140/210zł; P) is a fairly drab but conveniently located place along the road to the castle. The unremarkable rooms are serviceable for a night.

Hotel & Restaurant Zamek (☎ 272 33 67; biuro@ hotelzamek.pl; ul Starościńska 14; s/d/ste 230/300/660zł; P ✗ ✗) is inside a restored medieval building in the Lower Castle. The rooms are a bit old-fashioned, but the bathrooms are up-to-date and the restaurant has character.

The castle is 1km west of the train and bus stations. Leave the train station, turn right, cut across the highway, head down ul Kościuszki and follow the signs. Malbork is an easy day trip by train from Gdańsk (10zł, 45 minutes). There are buses every hour to Malbork from Gdynia and five daily from Gdańsk. From Malbork, trains also regularly go to Toruń and Olsztyn.

SZCZECIN

☎ 091 / pop 415,000

Szczecin (shcheh-cheen) is the major city and port of northwestern Poland. Massive damage in WWII accounts for the unaesthetic mish-mash of new and old buildings in the city centre, but enough remains to give a sense of the pre-war days. The broad streets and massive historic buildings bear a strong resemblance to Berlin, for which Szczecin was once the main port as the German city of Stettin. Szczecin may not have the seamless charm of Toruń or Poznań, but it's worth a visit if you're travelling to/from Germany.

The **tourist information office** (☎ 434 04 40; al Niepodległości 1; ☼ 9am-5pm Mon-Fri, 10am-2pm Sat Jun-Aug, 9am-5pm Mon-Fri Sep-May) is helpful, as is the **cultural & tourist information office** (☎ 489 16 30; ☼ 10am-6pm) in the castle. The **post office** and most *kantors* are along al Niepodległości, the main street. There's a handy internet café, **Portal** (☎ 488 40 66; ul Kaszubska 53; per hr 4zł; ☼ 24hr), in the side street opposite the tourist office.

The huge and austere **Castle of the Pomeranian Dukes** (ul Korsazy 34; admission free; ☼ dawn-dusk) lies 500m northeast of the tourist office. Originally built in the mid-14th century, it was enlarged in 1577 and rebuilt after WWII. Its **Castle Museum** (☎ 434 73 91; adult/child 4/3zł; ☼ 10am-6pm Tue-Sun) explains the building's convoluted history, with special exhibitions mounted from time to time.

A short walk down (south) from the castle is the 15th-century **Old Town Hall** (ul Mściwoja 8), which contains the **Museum of the City of Szczecin** (☎ 431 52 53; adult/child 6/3zł; ☼ 11am-6pm Tue, 10am-4pm Wed-Sun). Nearby is the charmingly rebuilt **Old Town** with its cafés, bars and clubs. Three blocks northwest of the castle is the **National Museum** (☎ 431 52 36; ul Staromłyńska 27; adult/child 6/3zł; ☼ 10am-6pm Tue, Wed & Fri, 10am-4pm Thu, Sat & Sun).

Sleeping & Eating

Youth Hostel PTSM (☎ 422 47 61; www.ptsm.home.pl; ul Monte Cassino 19a; dm 16-18zł, d 44zł; P ▯) This hostel has clean, spacious rooms and is located 2km northwest of the tourist office. Catch tram 1 north to the stop marked 'Piotr Skargi', then walk right one block. Bed linen costs 6zł extra.

Hotelik Elka-Sen (☎ 433 56 04; www.elkasen.szc zecin.pl; al 3 Maja 1a; s/d 120/140zł; ▯) Simple, clean rooms in a basement location in the centre of town. Just south of the tourist office, enter from the side street.

Hotel Podzamcze (☎ 812 14 04; www.podzamcze .szczecin.pl; ul Sienna 1/3; s/d 185/235zł; P) This hotel is in a charming location near the Old Town Hall, with neat, well-maintained rooms and a small restaurant.

Haga (☎ 812 17 59; ul Sienna 10; mains 10-20zł; ☼ 11am-11pm) This informal place in the Old

Town produces Dutch-style filled pancakes from a menu listing more than 400 combinations.

Restauracja Stary Szczecin (☎ 433 62 30; plac Batorego 2; mains 18-85zł; ☾ noon-midnight) A more upmarket option serving a range of traditional Polish dishes in elegant surrounds.

Camping PTTK Marina (☎ /fax 460 11 65; ul Przestrzenna 23; per person/tent 10/7.50zł, s/d/tr/q cabins 42/70/100/160zł; ☾ May-Sep; ℗) On the shore of Lake Dąbie – get off at the Szczecin Dąbie train station and ask for directions (2km).

Getting There & Away

LOT flies between Szczecin and Warsaw four times a day. Book at the **LOT office** (☎ 488 35 58; ul Wyzwolenia 17), about 200m from the northern end of al Niepodegłości.

The **bus terminal** (plac Grodnicki) and the nearby **Szczecin Główny train station** (ul Kolumba) are located 600m southeast of the tourist office. Three bus services a day head for Warsaw (61zł, six hours), two via Poznań. Fast trains travel regularly to Poznań (37zł, four hours) and Gdańsk (47zł, 3½ hours), and expresses run to Warsaw (88zł, seven hours). Slow trains plod along every two hours to Świnoujście (16zł).

Advance tickets for trains and ferries are available from **Orbis Travel** (☎ 434 26 18; plac Zwycięstwa 1), about 200m west of the main post office.

WARMIA & MASURIA

Like much of northern Poland, Warmia and Masuria have changed hands between Germanic and Polish rulers over the centuries. The countryside is a beautiful postglacial landscape dominated by 3000 lakes, linked to rivers and canals, which host aquatic activities like yachting and canoeing. This picturesque lake district has little industry, and as a result remains unpolluted and attractive, especially in summer.

OLSZTYN

☎ 089 / pop 173,000

Olsztyn (ol-shtin) is another city on the Copernicus trail, as the great astronomer once served as administrator of Warmia, commanding Olsztyn Castle from 1516 to 1520. From 1466 to 1772 the town belonged to the kingdom of Poland. With the first partition

of the nation, Olsztyn became Prussian Allenstein, until it returned to Polish hands in 1945.

Nowadays it's a pleasant city whose rebuilt Old Town is home to cobblestone streets, art galleries, cafés, bars and restaurants. As a busy transport hub, it's also the logical base from which to explore the region, including the Great Masurian Lakes district (p436).

The **tourist office** (☎ 535 35 65; www.warmia.ma zury.pl; ul Staromiejska 1; ☾ 8am-4pm Mon-Fri) is helpful. For money matters, try the **PKO Bank** (ul Pieniężnego).

For snail mail, go to the **main post office** (ul Pieniężnego); for cybermail, try **Klub Internetowy** (ul Kościuszki 26; per hr 3.50zł; ☾ 10am-9pm Mon-Sat, 11am-8pm Sun) near the train station. Books and maps are sold at **EMPiK** (ul Piłsudskiego 16) inside the Alfa Centrum shopping mall.

Sights

The **High Gate** (Upper Gate) is the remaining section of the 14th-century city walls. Further west, the 14th-century **Castle of the Chapter of Warmia** (ul Zamkowa 2) contains the **Museum of Warmia & Mazury** (☎ 527 95 96; adult/child 6/4zł; ☾ 9am-5pm Tue-Sun May-Sep, 10am-4pm Tue-Sun Oct-Apr). Its exhibits star Copernicus, who made some astronomical observations here in the early 16th century, along with coins and art.

The **Rynek** (Market Square) was rebuilt after WWII destruction. To the east, the red-brick Gothic **Cathedral of Św. Jakuba Większego** (ul Długosza) dates from the 14th century. Its 60m tower was added in 1596.

Sleeping

Hotel Wysoka Brama (☎ 527 36 75; www.hotel wysokabrama.olsztyn.pl; ul Staromiejska 1; s/d/ste 45/60/160zł) Offers cheap but basic rooms that are in a very central location next to the High Gate.

Hotel Pod Zamkiem (☎ 535 12 87; www.hotel-olsz tyn.com.pl; ul Nowowiejskiego 10; s/d 150/190zł; ℗ ▭) Cosy pension, with charmingly old-fashioned rooms, reached via an extravagant stairwell constructed of dark timber carved with German text. It's located in a convenient spot near the castle.

Polsko-Niemieckie Centrum Młodzieży (☎ 534 07 80; www.pncm.olsztyn.pl; ul Okopowa 25; s/d 190/240zł; ℗ ▭) This place is also situated next to the castle. The rooms (some with views of the castle) are plain, but have gleaming

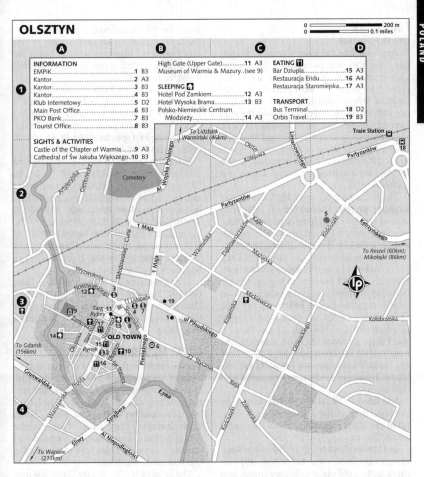

OLSZTYN

INFORMATION	
EMPiK....................................**1** B3	
Kantor..................................**2** A3	
Kantor..................................**3** B3	
Kantor..................................**4** B3	
Klub Internetowy..................**5** D2	
Main Post Office....................**6** B3	
PKO Bank..............................**7** B3	
Tourist Office.......................**8** B3	
SIGHTS & ACTIVITIES	
Castle of the Chapter of Warmia.......**9** A3	
Cathedral of Św Jakuba Większego.**10** B3	

High Gate (Upper Gate)............**11** A3	
Museum of Warmia & Mazury..(see 9)	
SLEEPING	
Hotel Pod Zamkiem................**12** A3	
Hotel Wysoka Brama..............**13** B3	
Polsko-Niemieckie Centrum	
Młodzieży...........................**14** A3	

EATING	
Bar Dziupla...........................**15** A3	
Restauracja Eridu.................**16** A4	
Restauracja Staromiejska...**17** A3	
TRANSPORT	
Bus Terminal.........................**18** D2	
Orbis Travel..........................**19** B3	

bathrooms. There's a sunlit restaurant off the foyer.

Eating

Bar Dziupla (☎ 527 50 83; Rynek 9/10; mains 11-15zł; ⏲ 8.30am-8pm Mon-Fri, 9am-8pm Sat, 9am-7.30pm Sun) This small place is renowned among locals for its tasty Polish food, such as *pierogi*. It also does a good line in soups, including Ukrainian *borscht*.

Restauracja Eridu (☎ 534 94 67; ul Prosta 3/4; mains 13-18zł; ⏲ 11am-8pm) The Eridu offers some inexpensive Middle Eastern choices in a vaguely Arabian setting. Also serves takeaway kebabs from a street window.

Restauracja Staromiejska (☎ 527 58 83; ul Stare Miasto 4/6; mains 16-36zł; ⏲ 11am-10pm) In classy premises on the Rynek, this restaurant serves quality Polish standards at reasonable prices. There's a range of *pierogi* and *naleśniki* on the menu.

Getting There & Away

From the **bus terminal** (ul Partyzantów), buses travel to Białystok (40zł, five daily), Gdańsk (30zł, three hours, six daily) and Warsaw (32zł, five hours, 10 daily).

Trains depart from the **Olsztyn Główny train station** (ul Partyzantów) to Białystok (42zł, two daily), Warsaw (38zł, three daily), Gdańsk (35zł, six daily), Poznań (44zł, three daily), Wrocław (50zł, two daily) and Toruń (32zł, seven daily). **Orbis Travel** (☎ 522 06 13; ul Piłsudskiego) sells advance train tickets.

POLAND

FROMBORK

☎ 055 / pop 2600

It may look like the town that time forgot, but Frombork was once home to Nicolaus Copernicus. It's also where he wrote his ground-breaking *On the Revolutions of the Celestial Spheres,* which established the theory that the earth travelled around the sun. Beyond the memory of its famous resident, it's a charming sleepy settlement that was founded on the shore of the Vistula Lagoon in the 13th century. It was later the site of a fortified ecclesiastical township, erected on Cathedral Hill.

The hill is now occupied by the extensive **Nicolaus Copernicus Museum** (☎ 243 72 18), with several sections requiring separate tickets. Most imposing is the red-brick Gothic **cathedral** (adult/child 4/2zł; ☾ 9.30am-5pm Mon-Sat May-Sep, 9am-3.30pm Tue-Sun Oct-Apr), constructed in the 14th century. The nearby **Bishop's Palace** (adult/child 4/2zł; ☾ 9am-4.30pm Tue-Sun May-Sep, 9am-4pm Tue-Sun Oct-Apr) houses various exhibitions on local history, while the **Belfry** (adult/child 4/2zł; ☾ 9.30am-5pm May-Sep, 9am-4pm Oct-Apr) is home to an example of Foucault's pendulum. A short distance from the main museum, the **Hospital of the Holy Ghost** (adult/child 4/2zł; ☾ 10am-6pm Tue-Sat May-Sep, 9am-4pm Tue-Sat Oct-Apr) exhibits historical medical instruments and manuscripts.

Dom Dziecka (☎ 243 72 15; ul Braniewska 11; dm 20zł) offers inexpensive accommodation about 500m east of the museum, along ul Kopernika toward Braniewo.

Dom Familijny Rheticus (☎ 243 78 00; domfamilijny@ wp.pl; ul Kopernika 10; s/d/ste 88/120/240zł; P) is a small, quaint old place with cosy rooms and good facilities, a short walk to the east of the bus stop.

The bus and train stations are along the riverfront about 300m northwest of the museum, but trains are slow and infrequent. Frombork can be directly reached by bus from Elbląg (6zł, hourly) and Gdańsk (16zł, five daily). The best place to get on and off is the bus stop directly below the museum on ul Kopernika.

ELBLĄG-OSTRÓDA CANAL

The longest navigable canal still used in Poland stretches 82km between Elbląg and Ostróda. Constructed between 1848 and 1876, this waterway was used to transport timber from inland forests to the Baltic. To over-

come the 99.5m difference in water levels, the canal utilises an unusual system of five water-powered slipways so that boats are sometimes carried across dry land on rail-mounted trolleys.

Usually, **excursion boats** (☾ mid May-late Sep) depart from both Elbląg and Ostróda daily at 8am (85zł, 11 hours), but actual departures depend on available passengers. For information, call the **boat operators** (Elbląg ☎ 055-232 43 07, Ostróda ☎ 089-646 38 71; www.zegluga.com.pl).

Hotel Młyn (☎ 055-235 04 70; www.hotelmlyn.com .pl; ul Kościuszki 132; s/d from 220/310zł; P X ▣), in Elbląg, is located in a picturesque old water mill and offers comfortable modern rooms. In Ostróda, try **Hotel Promenada** (☎ 089-642 81 00; ul Mickiewicza 3; s/d 120/180zł), 500m east of the bus and train stations. **Camping Nr 61** (☎ 055-232 43 07; www.camping-elblag.alpha.pl; ul Panieńska 14; tents 12zł, cabins 60-80zł; ☾ May-Sep), right at Elbląg's boat dock, is pleasant.

Elbląg is accessible by train and bus from Gdańsk, Malbork, Frombork and Olsztyn. Ostróda is regularly connected by train to Olsztyn and Toruń, and by bus to Olsztyn and Elbląg.

GREAT MASURIAN LAKES

The Great Masurian Lakes district east of Olsztyn has more than 2000 lakes, which are remnants of long-vanished glaciers, and surrounded by green hilly landscape. The largest lake is **Lake Śniardwy** (110 sq km). About 200km of canals connect these bodies of water, so the area is a prime destination for yachties and canoeists, as well as those who prefer to hike, fish and mountain-bike.

The detailed *Wielkie Jeziora Mazurskie* map (1:100,000) is essential for anyone exploring the region by water or hiking trail. The *Warmia i Mazury* map (1:300,000), available at regional tourist offices, is perfect for more general use.

Activities

The larger lakes can be sailed from Węgorzewo to Ruciane-Nida, while canoeists might prefer the more intimate surroundings of rivers and smaller lakes. The most popular kayak route takes 10 days (106km) and follows rivers, canals and lakes from Sorkwity to Ruciane-Nida. Brochures explaining this route are available at regional tourist offices. There's also an extensive network of **hiking** and **mountain-biking** trails around the lakes.

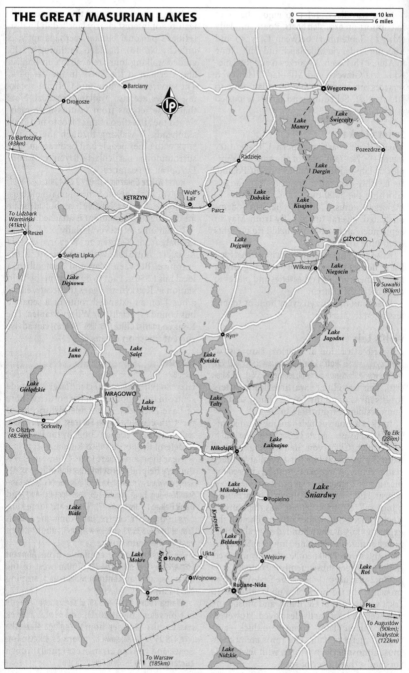

THE GREAT MASURIAN LAKES

0 — 10 km
0 — 6 miles

Barciany

Drogosze

To Bartoszyce (43km)

Węgorzewo

Lake Mamry

Lake Święcajty

Pozezdrze

Radzieje

Lake Dargin

KĘTRZYN

Wolf's Lair

Parcz

Lake Dobskie

Lake Kisajno

To Lidzbark Warmiński (41km)

Reszel

GIŻYCKO

Lake Dejguny

Lake Niegocin

Wilkasy

To Suwałki (80km)

Święta Lipka

Lake Dejnowa

Ryn

Lake Jagodne

Lake Juno

Lake Sałęt

Lake Ryńskie

Lake Giełądzkie

MRĄGOWO

Lake Juksty

Lake Tałty

To Olsztyn (48.5km)

Sorkwity

To Ełk (28km)

Lake Łuknajno

Mikołajki

Lake Śniardwy

Lake Mikołajskie

Popielno

Lake Białe

Krutynia

Lake Bełdany

Lake Mokre

Krutyń

Ukta

Wejsuny

Lake Roś

Wojnowo

Ruciane-Nida

Zgon

Pisz

To Augustów (90km); Białystok (122km)

To Warsaw (185km)

Lake Nidzkie

Most travellers prefer to enjoy the lakes in comfort on **excursion boats**. Boats run daily (May to September) between Giżycko and Ruciane-Nida, via Mikołajki; and daily (June to August) between Węgorzewo and Ruciane-Nida, via Giżycko and Mikołajki. However, services are more reliable from late June to late August. Schedules and fares are posted at the lake ports.

Święta Lipka

This village boasts a superb 17th-century **church** (🕙 7am-7pm), one of the purest examples of late-baroque architecture in Poland. Its lavishly decorated organ features angels adorning the 5000 pipes, and they dance to the organ's music. This mechanism is demonstrated several times daily from May to September, and recitals are held Friday nights from June to August.

Ask any of the regional tourist offices for a list of homes in Święta Lipka offering **private rooms**. There are several **eateries** and places to drink near the church.

Buses run to Kętrzyn every hour or so, but less often to Olsztyn.

Wolf's Lair

An eerie attraction at Gierłoż, 8km east of Kętrzyn, is the **Wolf's Lair** (Wilczy Szaniec; ☎ 089-752 44 29; www.wolfsschanze.home.pl; adult/child 8/5zł; 🕙 8am-dusk). This was Hitler's wartime headquarters for his invasion of the Soviet Union, and his main residence from 1941 to 1944.

In 1944 a group of high-ranking German officers tried to assassinate Hitler here. The leader of the plot, Claus von Stauffenberg, arrived from Berlin on 20 July for a regular military staff meeting. A frequent guest, he entered the meeting with a bomb in his briefcase. He placed it near Hitler and left to take a prearranged phone call, but the briefcase was then unwittingly moved by another officer. Though the explosion killed and wounded several people, Hitler suffered only minor injuries. Stauffenberg and some 5000 people allegedly involved in the plot were subsequently executed.

On 24 January 1945, as the Red Army approached, the Germans blew up Wolfsschanze (as it was known in German), and most bunkers were at least partly destroyed. However, huge concrete slabs – some 8.5m thick – and twisted metal remain. The ruins are at their most atmospheric in winter, with fewer visitors and a thick layer of snow.

A large map is posted at the entrance, with features of interest clearly labelled in English (Hitler's personal bunker, perhaps aptly, is unlucky No 13). Booklets outlining a self-guided walking tour are available in English and German at the kiosk in the car park. The services of English- and German-speaking guides are also available for 50zł. Note that some reports from visitors have mentioned the attraction of this place to neo-Nazi skinheads. If walking through the woods, stick with other people and be aware of your surroundings, particularly if you're of non-European appearance.

Hotel Wilcze Gniazdo (☎ 089-752 44 29; fax 752 44 92; s/d/tr 70/80/130zł), situated in original buildings within the complex, is fairly basic but adequate for one night. A restaurant is attached.

Catch one of several daily PKS buses (3.20zł) from Kętrzyn to Węgorzewo (via Radzieje, not Srokowo) and get off at the entrance. Between May and September, a local bus (2.50zł, 9am to 6pm) from the train station in Kętrzyn also goes to the site, either a bus 1 on an extended route or a separate bus bound especially for Wilczy Szaniec. The Kętrzyn **tourist office** (☎ 089-751 47 65) can advise current transport details.

Giżycko

☎ 087

Giżycko (ghee-*zhits*-ko) is the largest lakeside centre in the region, set on the northern shore of Lake Niegocin. A notable historic site is the 19th-century **Boyen Fortress** (ul Turystyczna 1; adult/child 6/3zł; 🕙 8am-7pm), built by the Prussians to defend the border with Russia.

Near the main square (plac Grunwaldzki) is the very helpful **tourist information office** (☎ 428 52 65; www.gizycko.turystyka.pl; ul Warszawska 7; 🕙 8am-5pm May-Jun, 8am-7pm Jul-Sep, 8am-4pm Oct-Apr) and **Bank Pekao** (ul Olsztyńska 17). There are some *kantors* in the town centre, including one at **Orbis Travel** (☎ 428 35 98; ul Dąbrowskiego 3), about 250m east of the main square.

Sailing boats are available from **Almatur** (☎ 428 59 71; ul Moniuszki 24), 700m west of the fortress, and at **Centrum Mazur** at Camping Nr 1 Zamek.

Wama Tour (☎ 429 30 79; ul Konarskiego 1) rents out bicycles (about 20zł), and Hotel Zamek has kayaks (8zł per hour). **Żegluga Mazurska** (☎ 428 25 78; ul Kolejowa 8) operates excursion boats, and you can arrange car rental through **Łuczany** (☎ 428 26 62; ul Suwalska 19b).

SLEEPING & EATING

Boyen Fortress Youth Hostel (☎ 428 29 59; tmtb@wp
.pl; dm 15-20zł) Has a character-packed location
within the battlements, and offers the usual
basic but clean facilities.

Hotel Zamek (☎ 428 24 19; d 144zł; ☽ May-Sep;
Ⓟ) This place provides a decent standard of
accommodation for the price.

Hotel Wodnik (☎ 428 38 71; www.cmazur.pl; ul 3 Maja
2; s/d from 180/250zł; Ⓟ ☒ ▣) A big barn of a
place just off the main square, with plain but
tidy rooms and modern bathrooms. There's
a restaurant, bar and billiards room on the
premises.

Camping Nr 1 Zamek (☎ 428 34 10; ul Moniuszki 1;
per person/tent 15/10zł; ☽ May-end Sep; Ⓟ) Just west
of the canal, this camping ground is simple
but central.

Kuchnie Świata (☎ 429 22 55; plac Grunwaldzki 1;
mains 15-40zł; ☽ 11am-11pm) A good dining choice
is this cheery red-and-orange space serving
up an eclectic range of dishes including pizza
and pasta, along with *placki ziemniaczane* and
other Polish favourites.

GETTING THERE & AWAY

From the train station, on the southern edge
of town near the lake, around seven trains
run daily to Kętrzyn and Olsztyn, and two
head to Gdańsk.

From the adjacent bus terminal, buses
travel regularly to Mikołajki (9zł, one hour),
Kętrzyn (8zł, 45 minutes) and Olsztyn. Five
buses daily head to Warsaw.

Mikołajki
☎ 087

Mikołajki (Mee-ko-*wahy*-kee), 86km east of
Olsztyn, is a great base for exploring the lakes,
and it's a picturesque little village in its own
right. The **tourist office** (☎ 421 68 50; www.mikolajki
.pl; plac Wolności 3; ☽ 9am-8pm May-Sep) is in the
town centre, though in the low season tourist advice is available at the **local government
offices** (ul Kolejowy 7; ☽ 10am-3pm Oct-Apr). There
are *kantors* and ATMs near the tourist office,
but nowhere to change travellers cheques or
get cash advances.

Sailing boats and kayaks can be hired from
Cicha Zatoka (☎ 421 50 11; al Spacerowa 1) at the waterfront on the other side of the bridge from
the town centre, and also from the appropriately named **Fun** (☎ 421 62 77; ul Kajki 82).

Lake Śniardwy and Lake Łuknajno are ideal
for **cycling**. The tourist office can provide de-

tails and maps, and bikes can be rented from
Pensionjat Mikołajki.

SLEEPING & EATING

Pensions and homes offering private rooms
are dotted along ul Kajki, the main street leading around Lake Mikołajskie; more *pensions*
can be found along the roads to Ruciane-Nida
and Ełk. There are plenty of eateries along the
waterfront and around the town square to
cater for peak-season visitors.

Pensjonat Mikołajki (☎ 421 64 37; www.pensjonat
mikolajki.prv.pl; ul Kajki 18; s/d 100/200zł) An attractive
place to stay, with timber panelling and a
prime lake-front location. Some rooms have
balconies overlooking the water.

Camping Nr 2 Wagabunda (☎ 421 60 18; ul Leśna 2;
per person/tent 15/12zł, cabins 80zł; ☽ May-Oct) Across
the bridge, this camping ground is 1km southwest of the town centre.

Pizzeria Królewska (☎ 421 63 23; ul Kajki 5; mains 8-
22zł; ☽ noon-10pm) A reasonable pizza restaurant
open year-round, in cosy cellar premises.

GETTING THERE & AWAY

From the bus terminal, next to the bridge at
plac Kościelny, six buses go to Olsztyn (13zł,
two hours) each day. Otherwise, get a bus
(hourly) to Mrągowo and change there for
Olsztyn. Several buses also go daily to Giżycko
(9zł, one hour) and three depart in summer for
Warsaw. A private company, **Agawa** (☎ 0698 256
928) runs an express service daily to Warsaw
year-round, departing from the bus terminal.

From the dozy train station, two slow trains
shuttle along daily to Olsztyn (14zł), and two
to Ełk (11zł), and one fast train heads to
Poznań via Olsztyn in summer. In quiet times,
the ticket office only opens 30 minutes (or
less) before departures.

POLAND DIRECTORY

ACCOMMODATION
Camping
Poland has hundreds of camping grounds,
and many offer good-value cabins and bungalows. Most open May to September, but
some only open their gates between June and
August.

Hostels
Schroniska młodzieżowe (youth hostels) in
Poland are operated by Polskie Towarzystwo

Schronisk Młodzieżowych (PTSM), a member of Hostelling International. Most only open in July and August, and are often very busy with Polish students; the year-round hostels have more facilities. Youth hostels are open to all, with no age limit. Curfews are common, and many hostels close between 10am and 5pm.

A number of privately-operated hostels operate in the main cities, and are geared towards international backpackers. They are usually open 24 hours and offer more modern facilities than the old youth hostels, though prices are higher. These hostels usually offer free use of washing machines, in response to the absence of laundromats in Poland.

A dorm bed can cost anything from 15zł to 50zł per person per night. Single/double rooms, if available, cost from about 80/100zł.

Hotels

Hotel prices often vary according to season, and are posted at hotel reception desks. Top-end hotels sometimes quote prices in euros, and discounted weekend rates are often available. Rooms with a private bathroom can be considerably more expensive than those with shared facilities. Most hotels offer 24-hour reception.

If possible, check the room before accepting. Don't be fooled by hotel reception areas, which may look great in contrast to the rest of the establishment. On the other hand, dreary scuffed corridors can sometimes open into clean, pleasant rooms.

Two reliable companies can arrange accommodation (sometimes with substantial discounts) over the internet through www.poland4u.com and www.hotelspoland.com.

Mountain Refuges

PTTK runs a chain of *schroniska górskie* (mountain refuges) for trekkers. They're usually simple, with a welcoming atmosphere, and serve cheap, hot meals. The more isolated refuges are obliged to accept everyone, so can be crowded in the high season. Refuges are normally open all year, but confirm with the nearest PTTK office before setting off.

Private Rooms & Apartments

Some destinations have agencies (usually called *biuro zakwaterowania* or *biuro kwater prywatnych*), which arrange accommodation in private homes. Rooms cost about 70/100zł per single/double. The most important factor to consider is location; if the home is in the suburbs, find out how far it is from reliable public transport.

During the high season, home owners also directly approach tourists. Prices are open to bargaining, but you're more likely to be offered somewhere out in the sticks. Also, private homes in smaller resorts and villages often have signs outside their gates or doors offering a *pokoje* (room) or *noclegi* (lodging).

In Warsaw, Kraków, Wrocław and Gdańsk, some agencies offer self-contained apartments, which are often an affordable alternative to hotels.

ACTIVITIES

Hikers and long-distance trekkers can enjoy marked trails across the Tatra (p403) and Sudeten Mountains (p416), around Białowieża National Park (p387) and the Great Masurian Lakes district (p436), and at places near Poznań (p417) and Œwinoujœcie. Trails are easy to follow and detailed maps are available at most larger bookshops.

As Poland is fairly flat, it's ideal for cyclists. Bicycle routes along the banks of the Vistula River are popular in Warsaw (p375), Toruń (p421) and Kraków (p389). Many of the national parks – including Tatra (near Zakopane), Wolin (near Świnoujście) and Słowiński (near Łeba) – offer bicycle trails, as does the Great Masurian Lakes district. Bikes can be rented at most resort towns and larger cities (see also p445).

Zakopane (p400) will delight skiers from December to March. Facilities are cheaper than – though not as developed as – the ski resorts of Western Europe.

Throngs of yachties, canoeists and kayakers enjoy the network of waterways in the Great Masurian Lakes district every summer; boats are available for rent from all lakeside towns. Windsurfers can head to the beaches of the Hel Peninsula (p432).

BOOKS

God's Playground: A History of Poland, by Norman Davies, offers an in-depth analysis of Polish history. The condensed version, *The Heart of Europe: A Short History of Poland,* also by Davies, has greater emphasis on the 20th century. *The Polish Way: A Thousand-Year History of the Poles and their Culture,* by Adam Zamoyski, is a superb cultural overview. The wartime Warsaw Rising is vividly brought to life in Norman Davies' *Rising '44,* and *The Polish Revolution: Solidarity 1980–82,* by Timothy Garton Ash, is entertaining and thorough. *Jews in Poland* by Iwo Cyprian Pogonowski, provides a comprehensive record of half a millennium of Jewish life.

BUSINESS HOURS

Most shops are open from 9am to 6pm Monday to Friday, and until 2pm on Saturday. Supermarkets and larger stores often have longer opening hours. Banks in larger cities are open from about 8am to 5pm weekdays (sometimes until 2pm on Saturday), but have shorter hours in smaller towns. *Kantors* generally follow shop hours.

DANGERS & ANNOYANCES

Poland is a relatively safe country, but be alert for thieves and pickpockets around major train stations, such as Warszawa Centralna. Robberies have become a problem on night trains, especially on international routes. Try to share a compartment with other people if possible. Watch out too for bogus ticket-inspectors on public transport – ask to see ID if they try to fine you.

Theft from cars is a widespread problem, so keep your vehicle in a guarded car park whenever possible. Heavy drinking is common and drunks can be disturbing, though rarely dangerous. Smoking is common in public places, especially in bars and restaurants. However, it's becoming more common for hotels and restaurants to offer nonsmoking options.

As Poland is an ethnically homogeneous nation, travellers who look racially different may attract curious stares from locals in outlying regions. Football (soccer) hooligans are not uncommon, so avoid travelling on public transport with them (especially if their team has lost!).

DISABLED TRAVELLERS

Poland is not well set-up for people with disabilities, although there have been significant improvements over recent years. Wheelchair ramps are only available at some upmarket hotels, and public transport will be a real challenge for anyone with mobility problems. However, many top-end hotels now have at least one room specially designed for disabled access – book ahead for these. There are also some low-floor trams now running on the Warsaw public transport network. Informa-

tion on disability issues is available from **Integracja** (☎ 022-635 13 30; www.integracja.org).

EMBASSIES & CONSULATES
Polish Embassies & Consulates

Australia (☎ 02-6273 1208; 7 Turrana St, Yarralumla, ACT 2600); Sydney (☎ 02-9363 9816; 10 Trelawny St, Woollhara, NSW 2025)

Canada (☎ 613-789 0468; 443 Daly Ave, Ottawa 2, Ontario K1N 6H3); Toronto (☎ 416-252 5471; 2603 Lakeshore Blvd West); Vancouver (☎ 604-688 3530; 1177 West Hastings St, Suite 1600)

France (☎ 01 43 17 34 00; 1 Rue de Talleyrand, 75007 Paris)

Germany (☎ 030-22 31 30; Lassenstrasse 19-21, 14193 Berlin); Hamburg (☎ 040-611870; Gründgensstrasse 20)

Netherlands (☎ 070-799 01 00; Alexanderstraat 25, 2514 JM The Hague)

UK (☎ 0870-774 27 00; 47 Portland Pl, London W1B 1JH); Edinburgh (☎ 0131-552 0301; 2 Kinnear Rd, EH3 5PE); Sheffield (☎ 0114- 276 6513; 4 Palmerston Rd, S10 2 TE)

USA (☎ 202-234 3800; 2640 16th St NW, Washington, DC 20009); New York (☎ 212-686 1541; 233 Madison Ave); Chicago (☎ 312-337 8166; 1530 North Lake Shore Dr); Los Angeles (☎ 310-442 8500; 12400 Wilshire Blvd)

Embassies & Consulates in Poland

All diplomatic missions listed are in Warsaw unless stated otherwise.

Australia (Map p378; ☎ 022-521 34 44; www.australia .pl; ul Nowogrodzka 11)

Belarus (Map p376; ☎ 022-742 09 90; ul Wiertnicza 58)

Canada (Map p378; ☎ 022-584 31 31; www.canada.pl; ul Matejki 1/5)

Czech Republic (Map p378; ☎ 022-628 72 21; warsaw@embassy.mzv.cz; ul Koszykowa 18)

France (Map p376; ☎ 022-529 30 00; ul Puławska 17); Kraków (Map p390; ☎ 012-424 53 00; ul Stolarska 15)

Germany (Map p376; ☎ 022-584 17 00; www.amba sadaniemiec.pl; ul Dąbrowiecka 30); Kraków (Map p390; ☎ 012-424 30 00; ul Stolarska 7)

Ireland (Map p378; ☎ 022-849 66 33; www.irlandia .pl; ul Mysia 5)

Lithuania (Map p376; ☎ 022-625 33 68; litwa.amb@ waw.pdi.net; al Szucha 5)

Netherlands (Map p376; ☎ 022-559 12 00; www.nl embassy.pl; ul Kawalerii 10)

Russia (Map p376; ☎ 022-621 34 53; ul Belwederska 49)

Slovakia (Map p376; ☎ 022-528 81 10; ul Litewska 6)

Ukraine (Map p376; ☎ 022-629 34 46; al Szucha 7)

UK (Map p378; ☎ 022-311 00 00; www.britishembassy .pl; al Róż 1); Kraków (Map p390; ☎ 012-421 70 30; ul Św. Anny 9)

USA (Map p378; ☎ 022-504 20 00; www.usinfo.pl; al Ujazdowskie 29/31); Kraków (Map p390; ☎ 012-424 51 00; ul Stolarska 9)

FESTIVALS & EVENTS

Warsaw

International Book Fair (www.bookfair.pl) Held in May.

Warsaw Summer Jazz Days (www.adamiakjazz.pl) Held in July.

Mozart Festival Held in June/July.

International Street Art Festival (www.sztukaulicy.pl) Held in July.

Warsaw Autumn Festival of Contemporary Music (www.warsaw-autumn.art.pl) Held in September.

Kraków

Organ Music Festival Held in March.

Jewish Culture Festival (www.jewishfestival.pl) Held in June/July.

International Festival of Street Theatre (www.teatrkto.pl, under 'Festiwale' link) Held in July.

Summer Jazz Festival (www.cracjazz.com) Held in July.

Czêstochowa

The major Marian feasts at Jasna Góra are 3 May, 16 July, 15 August (especially), 26 August, 8 September, 12 September and 8 December.

Wrocław

Musica Polonica Nova Festival (www.musicapolonicanova.pl, in Polish only) Held in February.

Jazz on the Odra International Festival (www.jnofestival.pl) Held in April.

Wrocław Marathon (www.wroclawmaraton.pl) Held in April.

Wrocław Non Stop (www.wroclawnonstop.pl) Held in June/July.

Wratislavia Cantans (www.wratislavia.art.pl) Held in September.

Poznań

The largest trade fairs take place in January, June, September and October.

St John's Fair Cultural event in June.

Malta International Theatre Festival (www.malta-festival.pl) Held in late June.

Gdańsk

International Organ Music Festival (www.gdanskie-organy.com, under concerts) Organ recitals are held at the Oliwa Cathedral twice a week (mid-June to late August).

International Street & Open-Air Theatre Festival (www.feta.pl) Popular event held in July.

International Organ, Choir & Chamber Music Festival (www.gdanskie-organy.com, under concerts) Every Fri in July and August, at St Mary's Church.

St Dominic's Fair (www.mtgsa.pl, under Jarmark Św. Dominika) An annual shopping fair held in August.

GAY & LESBIAN TRAVELLERS

With the Church remaining influential in social matters, and with senior government figures accused of homophobia, gay acceptance in Poland is still in development. As a result, the Polish gay and lesbian scene remains fairly discreet. Warsaw and Kraków are the best places to find gay-friendly bars, clubs and accommodation. The free tourist brochure, the *Visitor*, lists a few gay nightspots.

The best source of information on Warsaw and Kraków is online at www.gayguide.net. **Innastrona** (www.innastrona.pl) is also useful. **Lambda** (☎ 022-628 52 22; www.lambda.org.pl) is a national gay rights and information service. Newsstands and gay bars in Warsaw may also stock copies of *Nowy Men*, a gay listings magazine.

HOLIDAYS

Poland's official public holidays:

New Year's Day 1 January

Easter Monday March or April

Labour Day 1 May

Constitution Day 3 May

Corpus Christi A Thursday in May or June

Assumption Day 15 August

All Saints' Day 1 November

Independence Day 11 November

Christmas 25 and 26 December

INTERNET RESOURCES

InsidePoland (www.insidepoland.com) Current affairs and reasonable links.

Poland What Where When (www.what-where-when.pl) Online version of the handy tourist magazine.

Poland.pl (www.poland.pl) Excellent place to start surfing.

POLISHWORLD (www.polishworld.com) Directories and travel bookings.

VirtualTourist.com (www.virtualtourist.com) Poland section features postings and discussion by travellers.

VISIT.PL (www.visit.pl) Online accommodation booking service.

MEDIA

The glossy, English-language *Poland Monthly* and the *Warsaw Business Journal* are aimed at the business community, while *Warsaw Insider* has more general-interest features, listings and reviews.

The free *Welcome to…* series of magazines covers Poznań, Kraków and Warsaw monthly, with special editions released irregularly on other cities including Gdańsk and Wrocław. The free magazine *Poland: What, Where, When* covers Warsaw, Kraków and Gdańsk.

Recent newspapers and magazines from Western Europe and the USA are readily available at EMPiK bookshops, which are *everywhere*, and at newsstands in the lobbies of upmarket hotels.

The state-run Polish Radio (Polskie Radio) is the main broadcaster, while Warsaw-based Radio Zet and Kraków-based RFM are two nationwide private broadcasters.

Poland has several private TV channels, including PolSat, and two state-owned countrywide channels. Foreign-language programmes are painfully dubbed with one male voice covering all actors (that's men, women and children) and no lip-sync, so you can still hear the original language underneath. Most major hotels have access to European and US channels.

Cinemas are present in all city centres, including modern multiplexes. English-language films are usually subtitled rather than dubbed into Polish.

MONEY

The Polish currency is the złoty (*zwo*-ti), abbreviated to zł. (The currency is also sometimes referred to by its international currency code, PLN.) It's divided into 100 groszy (gr). Denominations of notes are 10, 20, 50, 100 and 200 złoty (rare), and coins come in one, two five, 10, 20 and 50 groszy, and one, two and five złoty.

ATMs

Bankomats (ATMs) accept most international credit cards and are easily found in the centre of all cities and most towns. Banks without an ATM may provide cash advances over the counter on credit cards.

Moneychangers

Private *kantors* (foreign-exchange offices) are *everywhere*. *Kantors* require no paperwork and charge no commission. Rates at *kantors* in the midst of major tourist attractions, in top-end hotels and at airports are generally poor.

The most widely accepted currencies are the euro, the US dollar and the pound sterling (in that order), though most *kantors* will change a range of other currencies. Foreign banknotes should be in perfect condition or *kantors* may refuse to accept them.

Travellers cheques are more secure than cash, but *kantors* rarely change them. Not all banks do either, and most charge 2% to 3% commission. The best place to change travellers cheques are branches of Bank Pekao or PKO Bank. In remote regions, finding an open bank that cashes travellers cheques may be tricky, especially on weekends.

POST

Postal services are operated by Poczta Polska. Most cities have a dozen or more post offices, of which the Poczta Główna (main post office) has the widest range of services.

Letters and postcards sent by air from Poland take a few days to reach a European destination and a week or so to anywhere else. The cost of sending a normal-sized letter (up to 20g) or a postcard to other European countries is 3zł, rising to 3.20zł for North America and 4.50zł for Australia.

TELEPHONE

All land-line numbers throughout Poland have seven digits. Note that it's necessary to dial both the area code and the local number, even for calls within the local area.

To call Poland from abroad, dial the country code ☎ 48, then the two-digit area code (drop the initial '0'), and then the seven-digit local number. The international access code for overseas calls from Poland is ☎ 00. If you need help, try the operators for local numbers (☎ 913), national numbers and codes (☎ 912) and international codes (☎ 908), but don't expect anyone to speak English.

Mobile Phones

The three mobile telephone providers are Orange, Era and Plus GSM. Reception is generally good and covers the whole country. Mobile numbers are often quoted as nine digits, but require an initial zero to be dialled from land-line phones.

The website www.roaming.pl has plenty of information about using a mobile in Poland.

EMERGENCY NUMBERS

■ Police ☎ 997, from mobiles ☎ 112

■ Ambulance ☎ 999

■ Fire brigade ☎ 93

■ Roadside Assistance ☎ 981

Phonecards

Most public telephones use magnetic phone-cards, available at post offices and kiosks in units of 15 (9zł), 30 (15zł) and 60 (24zł) – one unit represents one three-minute local call. The cards can be used for domestic and international calls.

VISAS

EU citizens do not need visas to visit Poland and can stay indefinitely. Citizens of Australia, Canada, Israel, New Zealand, Switzerland and USA, can stay in Poland up to 90 days without a visa. South African citizens do require a visa.

Other nationals should check with Polish embassies or consulates in their countries for current visa requirements. Updates can be found at the website of the Ministry of Foreign Affairs: www.msz.gov.pl.

TRANSPORT IN POLAND

GETTING THERE & AWAY
Air

The vast majority of international flights to Poland arrive at Warsaw's Okęcie airport (some at the Etiuda terminal), while other important airports include Kraków Balice, Gdańsk and Wrocław. The national carrier **LOT** (LO; www.lot.com; ☎ 0801 703 703) flies to all major European cities.

Other major airlines flying to Poland include the following:

Aeroflot (code SU; ☎ 022-628 25 57; www.aeroflot.com)
Air France (code AF; ☎ 022-556 64 00; www.airfrance.com)
Alitalia (code AZ; ☎ 022-692 82 85; www.alitalia.it)
British Airways (code BA; ☎ 022-529 90 00; www.ba.com)
Centralwings (code C0; ☎ 022-558 00 45; www.centralwings.com)
EasyJet (code U2; ☎ 0044 870 6 000 000; www.easyjet.com)
KLM (code KL; ☎ 022-556 64 44; www.klm.pl)
Lufthansa (code LH; ☎ 022-338 13 00; www.lufthansa.pl)
Malév (code MA; ☎ 022-697 74 72; www.malev.hu)
Ryanair (code FR; ☎ 0353-1-249 7791; www.ryanair.com)
SAS Scandinavian Airlines (code SK; ☎ 022-850 05 00; www.scandinavian.net)
SkyEurope (code NE; ☎ 022-433 07 33; www.skyeurope.com)
Wizz Air (code W6; ☎ 022-351 94 99; www.wizzair.com)

Land
BORDER CROSSINGS

Below is a list of major road border-crossings that accept foreigners and are open 24 hours.

Belarus South to north Terespol and Kuźnica Białostocka.

Czech Republic West to east Porajów, Zawidów, Jakuszyce, Lubawka, Kudowa-Słone, Boboszów, Głuchołazy, Pietrowice, Chałupki and Cieszyn.

Germany North to south Lubieszyn, Kołbaskowo, Krajnik Dolny, Osinów Dolny, Kostrzyn, Słubice, Ścwiecko, Gubin, Olszyna, Łęknica, Zgorzelec and Sieniawka.

Lithuania East to west Ogrodniki and Budzisko.

Russia (Kaliningrad) West to east Gronowo and Bezledy.

Slovakia West to east Chyżne, Chochołów, Łysa Polana, Niedzica, Piwniczna, Konieczna and Barwinek.

Ukraine South to north Medyka, Hrebenne, Dorohusk and Zosin.

If you're heading to Russia or Lithuania and your train/bus passes through Belarus, be aware that you need a Belarusian transit visa and you must obtain it in advance; see p592 for details.

BUS

International bus services are offered by dozens of Polish and international companies. They're cheaper than trains, but not as comfortable or fast.

One of the major operators is **Eurolines** (☎ 032-351 20 20; www.eurolinespolska.pl), which operates to a range of European destinations, including eastern cities such as Minsk, Brest, Vilnius, Tallinn and Riga. For more details of international bus travel into Poland, see p599.

CAR & MOTORCYCLE

To drive a car into Poland, EU citizens need their driving licence from home, while other nationalities must obtain an International Drivers Licence in their home country. Also required are vehicle registration papers and liability insurance (Green Card). If your insurance is not valid for Poland you must buy an additional policy at the border.

TRAIN

Trains link Poland with every neighbouring country and beyond, but international train travel is not cheap. To save money on fares, investigate special train tickets and rail passes (see p607). Domestic trains in Poland are significantly cheaper, so you'll save money if you buy a ticket to a Polish border destination, then take a local train.

Do note that some international trains to/from Poland have become notorious for theft. Keep a grip on your bags, particularly on the Berlin-Warsaw, Prague-Warsaw and Prague-Kraków overnight trains, and on *any* train travelling to/from Gdańsk. Some readers have reported being gassed while in their compartments and have had everything stolen while they 'slept'. Always reinforce your carriage and, if possible, sleep in a compartment with others. First-class carriages, in theory, should be safer.

Sea

Three companies operate passenger and car ferries all year:

Polferries (www.polferries.pl) Offers services between Gdańsk and Nynäshamn (18 hours) in Sweden every other day in summer (less frequently in the off season). It also has daily services from Świnoujście to Ystad (9½ hours) in Sweden, every Saturday to Rynne (six hours) in Denmark, and five days a week to Copenhagen (10½ to 11 hours).

Stena Line (www.stenaline.com) Operates between Gdynia and Karlskrona (11 hours) in Sweden.

Unity Line (www.unityline.pl) Runs ferries between Świnoujście and Ystad (eight hours).

Any travel agency in Scandinavia will sell tickets for these services. In Poland, ask at any Orbis Travel office. In summer, passenger boats ply the Baltic coast from Świnoujście to Ahlbeck, Heringsdorf, Bansin and Sassnitz in Germany.

GETTING AROUND
Air

The only domestic carrier, LOT (www.lot.com), runs flights several times a day from Warsaw to Gdańsk, Kraków, Łódź, Poznań, Szczecin and Wrocław. So, flying between, for example, Kraków and Gdańsk means a connection in Warsaw, which is not necessarily convenient.

Bicycle

Cycling is not great for getting around cities, but is often a good way to travel between villages. Major roads are busy but generally flat, while minor roads can be bumpy. If you get tired, it's easy to place your bike in the special luggage compartment of a train. These compartments are at the front or rear of slow passenger trains, but rarely found on fast or express trains, and never on InterCity or EuroCity services. You'll need a special ticket for your bike from the railway luggage office.

Bus

Buses can be useful on short routes and through the mountains in southern Poland; but usually trains are quicker and more comfortable, and private minibuses are quicker and more direct.

Most buses are operated by the state bus company, PKS. It provides two kinds of service from its bus terminals (*dworzec autobusowy PKS*): ordinary buses (marked in black on timetables), and fast buses (marked in red), which ignore minor stops.

Timetables are posted on boards inside or outside PKS bus terminals. Additional symbols next to departure times may indicate the bus runs only on certain days or in certain seasons. Terminals usually have an information desk, but it's rarely staffed with English speakers. Tickets for PKS buses are usually bought at the terminal, but sometimes from drivers.

The largest private bus operator is **Polski Express** (www.polskiexpress.pl), which operates long-distance routes to/from Warsaw (p385). Polski Express buses normally arrive and depart from PKS bus terminals – exceptions are mentioned in the relevant destination sections.

COSTS

The price of bus tickets is determined by the length, in kilometres, of the trip. Prices start at roughly 2zł for a journey of up to 5km. Minibuses charge set prices for journeys, and these are normally posted in their windows or at the bus stop.

Car & Motorcycle
FUEL & SPARE PARTS

Petrol stations sell several kinds of petrol, including 94-octane leaded, 95-octane unleaded, 98-octane unleaded and diesel. Most petrol stations are open from 6am to 10pm (from 7am to 3pm Sunday), though some operate around the clock. Garages are plentiful. Poland's roadside assistance number is ☎ 981.

HIRE

Major international car-rental companies, such as **Avis** (www.avis.pl), **Hertz** (www.hertz.pl) and **Europcar** (www.europcar.com.pl), are represented in larger cities and have smaller offices at airports. Rates are comparable to full-price rental in Western Europe.

Some companies offer one-way rentals, but no agency will allow you to drive their precious vehicle into Russia, Ukraine or Belarus.

Rental agencies will need to see your passport, your local driving licence (which must be held for at least one year) and a credit card (for the deposit). You need to be at least 21 or 23 years of age to rent a car; sometimes 25 for a more expensive car.

It's usually cheaper to prebook a car in Poland from abroad, rather than to front up at an agency inside the country. It would be even cheaper to rent a car in Western Europe (eg Berlin or Geneva), and drive it into Poland, but few rental companies will allow this. If they do, special insurance is required.

ROAD RULES

The speed limit is 130km/h on motorways, 100km/h or 110km/h on two- or four-lane highways, 90km/h on other open roads and 60km/h in built-up areas (50km/h in Warsaw). If the background of the sign bearing the town's name is white you must reduce speed to 60km/h; if the background is green there's no need to reduce speed (unless road signs indicate otherwise). Radar-equipped police are very active, especially in villages with white signs.

Unless signs state otherwise, cars may park on pavements as long as a minimum 1.5m-wide walkway is left for pedestrians. Parking in the opposite direction to traffic flow is allowed. The permitted blood alcohol level is a low 0.02%, so it's best not to drink if you're driving. Seat belts are compulsory for front seats. Motorbike helmets are also compulsory. Between 1 October and the end of February, all drivers must use headlights during the day (and night!).

Train

Trains will be your main means of transport. They're cheap, reliable and rarely overcrowded (except for July and August peak times). The **Polish State Railways** (PKP; www.pkp.pl) operates trains to almost every place listed in this chapter.

InterCity trains operate on major routes out of Warsaw, including Gdańsk, Kraków, Poznań, Wrocław and Szczecin. They only stop at major cities and are the fastest way to travel by rail. These trains require seat reservations.

Down the pecking order but still quick are *pociąg ekspresowy* (express trains) and the similar but cheaper *pociąg TLK* (TLK trains). *Pociąg pospieszny* (fast trains) are a bit slower and more crowded. *Pociąg osobowy* (slow passenger trains) stop at every tree at the side of the track and should be used only for short trips. Express and fast trains do not normally require seat reservations except at peak times; seats on slow trains cannot be reserved.

Almost all trains carry two classes: *druga klasa* (2nd class) and *pierwsza klasa* (1st class), which is 50% more expensive. The carriages on long-distance trains are usually divided into compartments: 1st-class compartments have six seats; 2nd-class ones contain eight seats.

In a couchette on an overnight train, compartments have four/six beds in 1st/2nd class. Sleepers have two/three people (1st/2nd class) in a compartment fitted with a washbasin, sheets and blankets. Most 2nd-class and all 1st-class carriages have nonsmoking compartments.

Train *odjazdy* (departures) are listed on a yellow board and *przyjazdy* (arrivals) on a white board. Ordinary trains are marked in black print, fast trains in red. An additional 'Ex' indicates an express train, and InterCity trains are identified by the letters 'IC'. The letter 'R' in a square indicates the train has compulsory seat reservation. The timetables also show which *peron* (platform) it's using. Be aware that the number applies to *both* sides of the platform. If in doubt, check the platform departure board or route cards on the side of carriages, or ask a fellow passenger.

Timetable and fare information in English is on the PKP website. *Miejsca sypialne* (sleepers) and *kuszetki* (couchettes) can be booked at special counters in larger train stations or from Orbis; pre-booking is recommended.

If a seat reservation is compulsory on your train, you will automatically be sold a *miejscówka* (reserved) seat ticket. If you do not make a seat reservation, you can travel on *any* train (of the type requested, ie slow, fast or express) to the destination indicated on your ticket on the date specified.

Your ticket will list the *klasa* (class); the *poc* (type) of train; where the train is travelling *od* (from) and *do* (to); the major town or junction the train is travelling *prez* (through); and the total *cena* (price). If more than one place is listed under the heading *prez* (via), find out from the conductor *early* if you have to change trains at the junction listed or be in a specific carriage (the train may separate later).

If you get on a train without a ticket, you can buy one directly from the conductor for a small supplement – but do it right away. If the conductor finds you first, you'll be fined for travelling without a ticket. You can always upgrade from 2nd to 1st class for a small extra fee (about 5zł), plus the additional fare.

Slovakia

A 200-year-old log cabin with perfectly preserved white geometrics just waiting to be photographed. The smell of strong coffee enjoyed midday with pastries in an old town square café. Whimsical, foot-tapping folk music punctuated by a yee! ha! yip! The crunch of fresh snow under your boot at 2000m. Slovakia is not about overwhelming sights or superlatives, it's more about the experience of a place where nature and folkways still hold sway.

Bratislava bustles these days as post-EU membership investment pours in and new restaurants seem to open daily. The rabbit-warren old town is certainly worth a day or two's distraction. Get outside the city though and you can still find ancient castles, traditional villages, well-protected nature preserves and tourist walking trails connecting the country from end to end. Dense forests cover the low hills, and remnants of fortresses top the craggy cliffs. Medieval towns sit in sight of alpine peaks. You can hike past a waterfall in a gorge one day and search out nail-less wooden churches the next.

That's not to say that Slovakia's architecture wasn't affected by communism. Industrial blight and truly ugly concrete buildings are a part of the whole. But the country's come through it all with its folksy spirit intact. So pull up a plate of dumplings with *bryndza* (sheep's cheese) and dig in.

FAST FACTS

- **Area** 49,035 sq km
- **Capital** Bratislava
- **Currency** koruna (Sk); €1 = 37Sk; US$1 = 29Sk; UK£1 = 55Sk; A$1 = 22Sk; ¥100 = 25Sk; NZ$1 = 19Sk
- **Famous for** ice hockey, beautiful women, mountain hiking, folk traditions
- **Official Language** Slovak
- **Phrases** *ahoj* (hello); *dovidenia* (goodbye); *ďakujem* (thank you); *este pivo prosím* (another beer please), *kde je WC* (veyt-say)? (where's the loo?)
- **Population** 5.4 million
- **Telephone Codes** country code ☎ + 421; international access code ☎ 00
- **Visas** citizens of the EU, USA, Canada, Australia, New Zealand and Japan can enter Slovakia for 90 days without a visa

SLOVAKIA

HOW MUCH?

- **Night in hostel** 300-600Sk

- **Double room in pension** 1500Sk

- **Day's ski hire** 300Sk

- **Pair of hiking boots** 1800Sk

- **Postcard** 6Sk

LONELY PLANET INDEX

- **Litre of petrol** 44Sk

- **Litre of bottled water** 40Sk

- **Beer** 39Sk

- **Souvenir T-shirt** 250Sk

- **Street snack (hot dog)** 15Sk

HIGHLIGHTS

- Ride one cable car then another to get to the precipitous summit of Lomnický štít in the **High Tatras** (p467).
- Turn your gaze east to the icon museum in **Bardejov** (p478), and at nearby Greek Catholic and Orthodox wooden churches.
- Delve into Slovakia's stony past at the country's largest extant fortress, now in ruins, **Spiš Castle** (p475).
- Climb the ladder- and chain-assist trails to get personal with the limestone gorges and rushing water of **Slovenský raj** (p477).

ITINERARIES

- **Three days** Spend two days wandering the pedestrian streets and stopping in the sidewalk cafés of Bratislava's old town. Climb up castle hill (or take a ride up the New Bridge elevator) for a citywide view. On day three head for one of the castles within day-trip range: Devín and Trenčín are especially stunning.
- **One week** Add on a couple of days' hiking among the alps-esque peaks of the High Tatras. Further east, Bardejov beckons with a medieval town square, wooden churches, a nearby spa town and an excellent open-air village museum.

CLIMATE & WHEN TO GO

The moderate climate averages -2°C in January and 25°C in August. Spring and autumn can be quite rainy and spring floods are not

unheard of. Snow stays on the higher slopes of the High Tatras well into June, and standing snow is common in April even in the lower ranges. See p585 for climate charts.

The tourist season is from May to September. Lodging prices are lower outside those months (except for student dorms), but many sights in outlying areas aren't open. September is still quite warm, young wine is being harvested, and the mountains are snow-free (usually), making it one of the best times to visit. Rates skyrocket for the Easter and Christmas holidays nationwide.

HISTORY

Slavic tribes wandered west into what would become Slovakia sometime round about the 5th century; by the 9th the territory was part of the short-lived Great Moravian Empire. It was about then that the Magyars (Hungarians) set up shop next door and subsequently lay claim to the whole territory. In the early 16th century, the Turks moved into Budapest pushing the Hungarian monarchs into Bratislava (then Pressburg, in German, or Pozsony, in Hungarian). Slovak intellectuals eventually cultivated ties with the Czechs, and after WWI, took their nation into the united Czechoslovakia.

The day before Hitler's troops invaded Czech territory in March 1939, leaders set up Slovakia as a fascist puppet and German ally. It was not, however, a populist move and in August 1944 Slovak partisans instigated the ill-fated Slovak National Uprising (Slovenské Národné Povstanie, or SNP), a source of ongoing national pride (and innumerable street names).

After the communist takeover in 1948, power was again centralised in Prague until 1989, when the Velvet Revolution brought down the curtains on the communists. Elections in 1992 saw the Movement for a Democratic Slovakia (HZDS) come to power and Vladimír Mečiar become prime minister. By that summer the Slovak parliament had voted to declare sovereignty, and the federation dissolved peacefully on 1 January 1993.

Mečiar's reign was characterised by antidemocratic laws and discrimination and the international community quickly turned on him. In part due to this pressure, the elections of 1998 ousted Mečiar and ushered in Mikuláš Dzurinda, leader of the right-leaning Slovak Democratic Coalition (SDK). Dzurinda

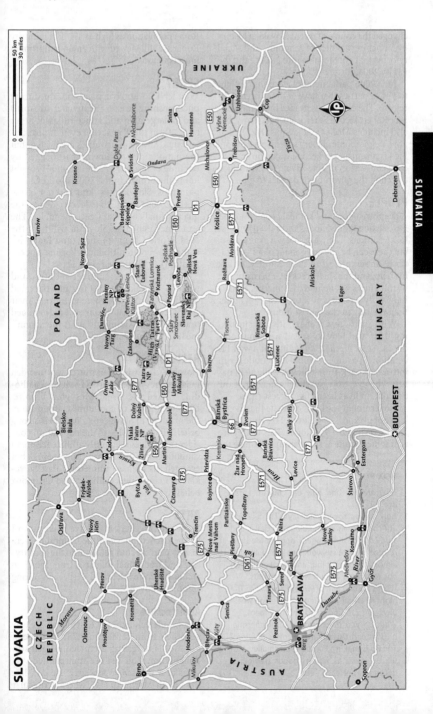

SLOVAKIA

changed the course of recent Slovakian history by launching a policy of economic and social reforms that got Slovakia into NATO and the EU by 2004.

June 2006 parliamentary elections brought to power parties that have at times been anti-reform. The coalition is headed by Prime Minister Robert Fico of Smer, a left-wing party, but also includes Mečiar's isolationist HZDS. For now, despite contradictory statements early on, Fico is promising to keep Slovakia on track to euro conversion in 2009. Time will tell which direction the government decides to go.

PEOPLE

A deeply religious and familial people, Slovaks have strong family circles and a deep sense of folk traditions. The young are warm and open, but there can be a reserve about older generations. Show interest in their country, or ask for help, and the shell cracks. Generosity and warmth lurks just behind the stoicism. Thankfully, surly service is now the exception rather than the rule in the tourist industry.

With such great scenery, it's not surprising that most Slovaks spend weekends outdoors. Isť na prechadsku (going for a walk) is a national pastime so you will doubtless run into a backpack-toting Slovak walking in nature wherever you go. About a quarter of the population lives in the five largest cities.

Government statistics estimate that Slovakia's population is 86% Slovak, 11% Hungarian, 1.2% Czech and 1.7% Roma. This last figure is in some dispute as some groups estimate the Roma population as high as 4%. The minority Roma are still viewed with an uncompromising suspicion.

SPORT

Wander into any bar or restaurant during puck-pushing season (September to April) and 12 large men and an ice rink will never be far from the TV screen, even at nice restaurants. Local club rivalries are heated, but the national team showing had flagged by the time of research. Although they brought home the bronze in the 2003 World Championships, Slovakia was knocked out of the Torino 2006 Olympic medal race during the quarter finals by rival Czech Republic. The announcement that Slovakia will host the 2011 World Championships (and Bratislava will get a new multibillion–koruna hockey stadium) surely perked up fans.

Football fills the summer months, and while the Slovaks have yet to attain the rabid fanaticism found elsewhere in Europe, their club game is a reliable source of red-blooded bravado. SK Slovan Bratislava is the nation's most successful team.

RELIGION

Slovakia's first Christian church was founded in Nitra in AD 833 after SS Cyril and Methodius visited the Great Moravian Empire. Despite 50 years of communist suppression, the majority of Slovaks retained their strong beliefs. Today, 84.1% of the population consider themselves religiously affiliated. Roman Catholics form the majority (about 60%), but evangelicals are also numerous; East Slovakia has many Greek Catholics and Orthodox believers.

ARTS

Some city dwellers may have been put off by the clichéd image of the Communist-era 'happy peasant', but get out into the countryside and traditional folk arts, from music to architecture, are celebrated – especially during summer festivals

Architecture

The wooden churches of East Slovakia, easily accessible from Bardejov (p478) are some of the most interesting architectural gems in the country. You can see transplanted versions at a skansen (open-air museum), like the one in Martin (p464), where vernacular

---

VOX POP

Who are you and how old? Martin Latal, age 29

How do you spend your days? I'm working at Accenture as a technology specialist, and studying for a manager's degree. My daily routine is of course work, but I go swimming almost every evening, and weekends I go out to a disco or pub with my friends.

What's the best part of living in Bratislava? The nightlife is really thrilling, and even on weekdays you can find good entertainment.

What do you think about EU membership, possible euro ascension and Slovakia's future? The EU is making Europe even smaller, better. Business, as well as goods trading, is getting easier each year.

village architecture is preserved. Levoča (p474) is known for its nearly complete medieval town walls and for the Gothic Church of St Jacob with a 18m-high altar carved by Master Pavol. Of course you can't miss the brutal socialist-realist architecture of the communist epoch, as evidenced by the New Bridge (Nový most, p458). Yes, it does resemble a UFO on a stick.

Cinema

Slovak cinema first made its mark as part of the Czechoslovak New Wave of the 1960s, with classic films like *Smrt si rika Engelchen* (Death Calls Itself Engelchen, 1963) directed by Ján Kádar, and *Obchod na korze* (The Shop on the Main Street, 1965) by Elmar Klos. Martin Sulík was one of Slovakia's most promising new directors, winning an Oscar nomination for *Všetko, čo mám rád* (Everything I Like, 1992), and international acclaim for *Krajinka* (The Landscape, 2000). Unfortunately, lack of funding and the closing of the Koliba movie studios has meant little serious movie making since 2000.

Music

Traditional Slovak folk instruments include the *fujara* (a 2m-long flute), the *gajdy* (bagpipes) and the *konkovka* (a strident shepherd's flute). Folk songs helped preserve the Slovak language during Hungarian rule, and in East Slovakia musical folk traditions are an integral part of village life.

In classical music, the 19th-century works of Ján L Bela and the symphonies of Alexander Moyzes receive world recognition. Slovakia's contemporary music scene is small, but vibrant. Modern musicians combine traditional lyrics or rhythms with a modern beat. Zuzana Mojžišová's music seems to have an almost Romany-like vibrancy, but stems from Slovak folk music. Marián Varga riffs on classical themes and the Peter Lipa band is granddaddy of the Bratislava Jazz Days festival.

ENVIRONMENT
The Land

Slovakia sits in the heart of Europe, straddling the northwestern end of the Carpathian Mountains. This hilly country forms a clear physical barrier between the plains of Poland and Hungary. Almost 80% of Slovakia is more than 750m above sea level, and forests, mainly beech and spruce, cover 40% of the country.

Southwestern Slovakia is a fertile lowland stretching from the foothills of the Carpathians down to the Danube River, which, from Bratislava to Štúrovo, forms the border with Hungary.

Central Slovakia is dominated by the High Tatras (Vysoké Tatry) mountains along the Polish border; Gerlachovský štít (2654m) being the highest peak. The forested ridges of the Low Tatras (Nízke Tatry) and the Malá Fatra are national park playgrounds. South are the gorges and waterfalls of Slovenský raj and the limestone caves of Slovenský kras. The longest river, the Váh, rises in the Tatras and flows 390km west and south to join the Danube at Komárno.

Wildlife & National Parks

Slovakia's national parks contain bears, marmots, wolves, lynxes, chamois, mink and otters, though they're rarely seen. Deer, pheasants, partridges, ducks, wild geese, storks, grouse, eagles and other birds of prey can be seen across the country.

National parks and protected areas make up 20% of Slovakia. The parks in the High Tatras, Slovenský raj and Malá Fatra regions should not be missed.

Environmental Issues

Slovakia is a mixed bag in environmental terms. No doubt due to most Slovaks' penchant for all things outdoorsy, large swathes of the countryside are protected parkland. On the other hand, the communist legacy left more than its fair share of grimy, industrial factories. Big centres such as Bratislava and Košice do suffer from air pollution.

The Gabčíkovo hydroelectric project, on the Danube west of Komárno, produces enough power to cover the needs of every home in Slovakia. But some believe it exacerbates the damage caused by annual floods. Events like Danube Day (www.danubeday.sk in Slovak) in June aim to raise awareness and money for river restoration.

Responsible Travel

Tens of thousands of hikers pass through Slovakia's parks and protected areas every year – try to do your bit to keep them pristine. Wherever possible, carry out your rubbish, avoid using detergents or toothpaste in or near watercourses, stick to established trails (this helps prevent erosion), cook on a kerosene stove rather than an open fire and do not engage in or encourage – by purchasing goods made from endangered species – hunting.

After the famous Schöner Náci statue in Bratislava's old town was upturned one weekend, allegedly by a group of probably inebriated English-speaking men, police presence in the old town increased. Drink responsibly.

FOOD & DRINK
Staples & Specialities
Slovak cuisine is basic central European fare: various fried meat schnitzels with fries and hearty stews with potatoes. Soups like *cesnaková polievka* (garlic soup), either creamy or clear with croutons and cheese, and *kapustnica* (cabbage soup), with a paprika and pork base, start most meals. Slovakia's national dish is *bryndzové halušky*, gnocchilike dumplings topped with soft sheep's cheese and bits of bacon fat. Don't pass up an opportunity to eat in a *salaš* or a *koliba* (rustic wooden eateries) where these traditional specialities are the mainstay.

For dessert, try *palacinka* (crepes) stuffed with jam or chocolate. *Ovocné knedličky* (fruit dumplings) are round balls filled with fruit and coated with crushed poppy seeds or breadcrumbs, dribbled with melted butter and sometimes accompanied by fruit purée and ice cream – yum.

Drinks
Slovak wine is…what do oenophiles say… highly drinkable (ie good and cheap). The Modra region squeezes dry reds, like Frankovka and Kláštorné. Slovak Tokaj, a white dessert wine from the southeast, is trying to give the Hungarian version a run for its money (though it falls short).

Slovak *pivo* (beer) is as good as the Czech stuff – try full-bodied Zlatý Bažant or dark, sweet Martiner. *Borovička* (a potent berry-based clear liquor) and *slivovice* (plum-based) are consumed as shots and are said to aid in digestion.

Where to Eat & Drink
Self-service cafeterias (called *samoobsluha reštaurácie, jedáleň* or *bufet*) cater to office workers and are great places to eat during the day (they close early). Look for food stands near train and bus stations; you can buy fruits and vegetables at the local *tržnica* (market).

All manner of trendy world food has found a foothold in Bratislava, but most Slovak towns at least have a pizzeria or a Chinese takeaway. Cafés (spelled in English) are often as much bar or restaurant as coffee shop; *kaviareň* (cafés) may only serve beverages, but that includes alcohol, a *cukráreň* (pastry or sweet shop) has the best ice cream and cakes to go with coffee.

Vegetarians & Vegans
It isn't easy being green in Slovakia. Some menus have a pasta or vegetable dish, but your only choice may be *vyprážaný syr* (fried cheese) and a *miešany šalat* (mixed salad). In this meat-lovers' haven even vegetable soups are made with chicken stock and *bezmäsa* (meatless) dishes aren't always meatless (those bacon crumbles on the dumplings apparently don't count). Things are looking up in Bratislava where a few vegetarian restaurants have sprung up. Other than that, pizzerias are always an option.

Habits & Customs
Small tips (five to 10%) are customary, but your friends are likely to say you're spoiling the waiter. At least round up the bill to the next 20Sk (50Sk if the bill is over 500Sk).

BRATISLAVA

☎ 02 / pop 421,155

Focus in on the compact historic centre and you see cobblestone roads, pedestrian plazas, pastel 18th-century rococo buildings, and sidewalk cafés galore. Expand your gaze and you can't miss the institutional housing blocks and bizarre communist constructions. An age-old castle shares the skyline with the 1970s, UFO-like New Bridge. That's Bratislava, a mixed but manageable city where both old and new merit a look.

Today the city hums as foreign investment helps upgrade roads, and beautiful people wearing black dine at the newest chichi pooh-pooh eatery. There's something a bit reckless about the development though. The old town zoning restrictions are taken lightly and weekend nights at least one gang of inebriated English-speaking blokes will likely pass by if you're out and about.

Who knows what the town will be in a few years, but for now the old centre is supremely

SLOVAKIA

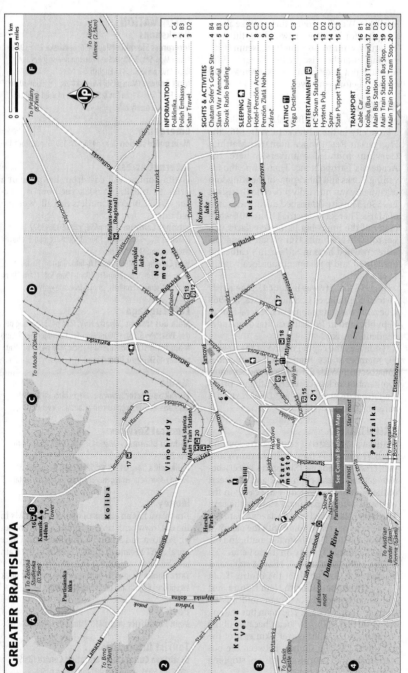

GREATER BRATISLAVA

INFORMATION	
Poliklinika...........................	1 C4
Polish Embassy...................	2 B3
Satur Travel........................	3 D2

SIGHTS & ACTIVITIES	
Chatam Sofer's Grave Site..	4 B4
Slavín War Memorial...........	5 B3
Slovak Radio Building..........	6 C3

SLEEPING	
Dopravcar...........................	7 D3
Hotel-Penzión Arcus...........	8 C3
Penzión Zlatá Noha............	9 C2
Zvárač................................	10 C2

EATING	
Vega Destination.................	11 C3

ENTERTAINMENT	
HC Slovan Stadium..............	12 D2
Hystéria Pub.......................	13 D2
Sparx..................................	14 C3
State Puppet Theatre...........	15 C3

TRANSPORT	
Cable Car............................	16 B1
Koliba (Bus No 203 Terminus).17 B2	
Main Bus Station.................	18 D3
Main Train Station Bus Stop...	19 C2
Main Train Station Tram Stop. 20 C2	

strollable. Wander around the mazelike alleys, stopping for a coffee or two along the way. You may want to pop into a museum if it's raining, but otherwise the best thing to do is just take in the different views, even as it all changes before your eyes.

HISTORY

Founded in AD 907, Bratislava was already a large city in the 12th century. In 1467 the Hungarian Renaissance monarch Matthias Corvinus founded a university here, the Academia Istropolitana. Then came the invading Turks and the capital of the Kingdom of Hungary was hurriedly moved to Bratislava in 1536. The city flourished during the reign of Maria Theresa of Austria (1740–80), when many of the imposing baroque palaces you see today were built. Hungarian monarchs were crowned here in St Martin's cathedral until 1830 and parliament met locally until 1848.

In 1918 the city was included in the newly formed Republic of Czechoslovakia, in 1969 it became the state capital of a federal Slovak Republic, and in 1993, the capital of an independent Slovakia.

Today, as the capital of one of the newest EU member states, Bratislava is a city under construction. With EU-inspired money and a proliferation of low-cost carrier flights, prices ain't what they used to be. Don't expect a bargain-basement visit.

ORIENTATION

Bratislava's pedestrian centre starts south of Hodžovo nám. Follow Poštová down and you cross Obchodná (Shopping street) before getting to the Nám SNP and the heart of the old town bounded by the castle in the west and Tesco department store in the east. The large, plazalike Hviezdoslavovo nám is a convenient reference point, with the old town to the north, the Danube to the south, and the Slovak National Theatre on its east end.

The main train station, Hlavná stanica, is located just 1km north of the centre. Tram 13 runs from the station to Nám L Štúra, just south of Hviezdoslavovo nám, and bus 93 stops at Hodžovo nám. The main bus station, called Mlynské Nivy by locals because of the street it's on, is a little over 1km east of the old town. Bus 206 shuttles between the bus station and the main train station, stopping at Hodžovo nám in between.

INFORMATION
Bookshops
Interpress Slovakia (Map p456; Sedlárska 2; ⊗ 9am-10pm Mon-Sat, 2-10pm Sun) Foreign newspapers and Bratislava periodicals in English.
Next Apache (Map p456; Panenská 28; ⊗ 9am-10pm Mon-Fri, 10am-10pm Sat & Sun) Loads of used English books and a comfy café.

Emergency
Main police station (Map p456; ☎ 159; Gunduličova 10)

Internet Access
Getting online will cost from the price of a drink to 100Sk, but 60Sk per hour is average. Small internet outlets are all over the old town.
Internet Centrum (Map p456; ☎ 0903693577; Mikalská 2; ⊗ 9am-4am) Four of the six computers have web cam and Skype access.
Wifi Café (Map p456; ground fl, Tatracentrum, Hodžovo nám; ⊗ 8am-10pm Mon-Fri, 10am-10pm Sat, 11am-10pm Sun) Flat-screen terminals, smoke-free café with wi-fi.

Left Luggage
Main bus station (Mlynské Nivy; Map p453; per bag per day 35Sk; ⊗ 5.30am-10pm Mon-Fri, 6am-6pm Sat & Sun)
Main train station (Hlavná stanica; Map p453; per bag per day 45Sk; ⊗ 6.30am-11pm)

Media
Slovak Spectator (www.slovakspectator.sk) English-language weekly, with current affairs and event listings.

Medical Services
24-hour pharmacy (Map p456; ☎ 5443 2952; Nám SNP 20)
Poliklinika (Map p453; ☎ 5296 2461; Bezručova 8) Twenty-four-hour emergency services, including dental.

Money
Bratislava has an excess of banks and ATMs in the old town, with several convenient branches on Poštova and around Kamenné nám. There are also ATMs and exchange booths in the train and bus stations, and at the airport.
Tatra Banka (Map p456; Dunajská 4) Has staff that speak exceptional English and great English signage.

Post
Main Post Office (Map p456; Nám SNP 34-35)

Tourist Information
Bratislava Culture & Information Centre (BKIS; ☎ 5249 5906; www.bkis.sk) Centre (Map p456;

Klobučnícka 2; 8.30am-6pm Mon-Fri, 9am-3pm Sat);
Main train station (Map p453; Hlavná stanica; 8am-
7.30pm Mon-Fri & 8am-5pm Sat Jun-Sep, 8am-4.30pm
Mon-Fri & 9am-2pm Sat Oct-May); Airport (MR Štefánik;
 8am-7.30pm Mon-Fri, 10am-6pm Sat) The official
central tourist point is a little sterile and the staff can seem
uninterested, but keep pressing and they'll help.
Bratislava Tourist Service (BTS; Map p456; 5464
1271; www.bratislava-info.sk; Ventúrska 9; 10am-
8pm) Tiny place, but it has a younger, more helpful staff
and lots of maps and knick-knacks.

Travel Agencies

Satur (Map p453; 5542 2828; www.satur.sk; Miletičova
1) Bratislava package trips and tours, transport tickets etc.

SIGHTS & ACTIVITIES

Bratislava Castle (Bratislavský hrad; Map p456; grounds
admission free; 9am-8pm Apr-Sep, to 6pm Oct-Mar) lords
over the west side of the old town on a hill
above the Danube. Winding ramparts and
grounds provide a great vantage point for
comparing ancient and communist Bratislava.
The castle looks a bit like a four-poster bed,
a shape that was well established by the 15th
century. During the Turkish occupation of
Budapest, this was the seat of Hungarian royalty. A fire devastated the fortress in 1811 and
most of what you see today is a reconstruction
from the 1950s (bland white interiors and all).
The saving grace of the castle's ho-hum **Historical Museum** (Historické múzeum; Map p456; 5441
1441; www.snm.sk; adult/student 100/40Sk; 9am-6pm
Tue-Sun) is that you can climb up the korunná
veža (crown tower). At the time of writing

BRATISLAVA IN TWO DAYS

Start the morning by wandering up the
ramparts of **Bratislava Castle** (left). Enter
through the **Historical Museum** (left) to
climb the veža (tower) for the highest views
of the old town. On your way back down to
town, stop at the **Museum of Jewish Culture** (below) before having lunch at **Prašná
Bašta** (p459). Spend the afternoon strolling
through the old town, stopping to drink at
as many café terraces as you dare. If you
schedule it right, you could catch an opera
at the **Slovak National Theatre** (p460) or a
band at the **Café Štúdio Club** (p459). The
following day, trip out of town to explore
Devín Castle (p461).

the tiny **treasury** (klenotnica) was closed for
reconstruction. When it reopens, the highlight
will still be the unbelievable 25,000-year-old
fertility statue of a miniature headless naked
woman carved from a mammoth tusk, the
Venus of Moravany.

To see a more historically complete castle,
take the bus beneath the bridge by Bratislava
Castle to **Devín** (p461) 9km outside the city.

A series of old homes winds down the castle
hill along Židovská in what was once the Jewish quarter. The **Museum of Clocks** (Múzeum hodín;
Map p456; 5441 1940; Židovská 1; adult/student 40/20Sk;
 10am-5pm Tue-Sun) is housed in the reputedly
skinniest house in Slovakia. Further down, the
Museum of Jewish Culture (Múzeum Židovskej kultúry;
Map p456; 5441 8507; www.chatamsofer.com; Židovská 17;
adult/student 200/20Sk; 11am-5pm Sun-Fri) displays
moving exhibits about the community lost
during WWII. Black-and-white photos show
the old ghetto and synagogue ploughed under
by the communists to make way for a highway
and bridge. The staff can help arrange a visit
to **Chatam Sofer's grave site** (Map p453; www.chatam
sofer.com; Žižkova at tram tunnel; donations accepted; by
appointment only), the resting place of the much
revered 19th-century rabbi.

A relatively modest interior belies the
elaborate history of **St Martin's Cathedral** (Dóm
sv Martina; Map p456; admission €1.25; 9-11am & 1-5pm
Mon-Sat, 1-5pm Sun). Eleven ruling monarchs (10
kings and one queen, Maria Theresa) were
crowned in this 14th century church. The
busy motorway almost touching St Martin's
follows the moat of the former city walls and
is shaking the building to its core.

MAN AT WORK

The castle? The New Bridge? Nope, the
most photo-opted sight in Bratislava ia a
bronze statue called **The Watcher** (Čumil;
Map p456). He peeps out of an imaginary
manhole at the intersection of Panská and
Sedlárska, below a 'men at work' sign. And
he's not alone. There are other quirky statues scattered around the old town. See if
you can find them: **The Frenchman** leans
on a park bench, **The Photographer** stalks
his subject paparazzi-style around a corner
and the **Schöner Náci** tips his top hat on
a square. Look up for other questionable
characters, like a timepiece-toting monk
and a rather naked imp, decorating building façades.

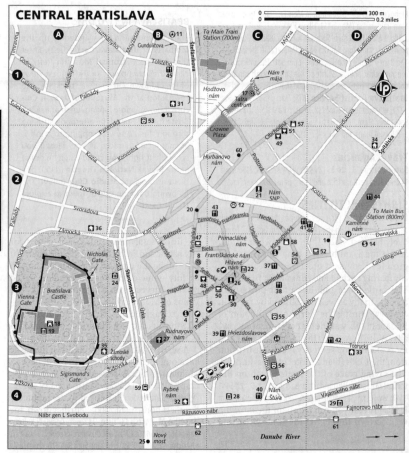

CENTRAL BRATISLAVA

Further east along the Danube, the 1st-floor exhibits of the **Slovak National Museum** (Slovenské Národné múzeum; Map p456; ☎ 5934 9122; www.snm.sk; Vajanského nábrežie 2; adult/student 60/20Sk; 9am-5pm Tue-Sun) provide a super overview of the folk cultures and customs of Slovakia's regions. Skip the tired natural-history stuff upstairs.

An 18th-century palace and a Stalinist-modernist make interesting cohosts for the **Slovak National Gallery** (Slovenská Národná Galéria; Map p456; ☎ 5443 4587; www.sng.sk; Rázusovo nábrežie 2; adult/student 80/40Sk; 10am-5pm Tue-Sun) and the nation's eclectic art collection – from Gothic to graphic design.

The old town's two opulent theatres are off Hviezdoslavovo nám, a broad, tree-lined plaza. The gilt neobaroque 1914 **Reduta Palace**

(see Slovak Philharmonic on p460) hosts the nation's symphony, and the ornate 1886 **Slovak National Theatre** (see p460) is the city's opera house. Neither is open for tours, but tickets are cheap if you want to see a show.

Bustling, narrow **Rybárska brána** runs through the pedestrian zone to Hlavné nám (Main Square), which is filled with café tables in summer, and a craft market at Easter and Christmas times. **Roland's Fountain** (Map p456) at the centre may have been built in 1572 as an old-fashioned fire hydrant. Flanking one side of the square is the 1421 **town hall** *(radnica)* containing the **Municipal Museum** (Mestské múzeum; Map p456; ☎ 5920 5130; Hlavné nám; adult/student 50/20Sk; 10am-5pm Tue-Fri, 11am-6pm Sat & Sun). Buzz past the tedious archaeological cases and look for the stairs down to the cellar torture chambers, complete with illustrated murals.

The focal point of the Nám SNP is the **Monument to the Slovak National Uprising** and the heroes who fought fascism in WWII. On 31 December 2002, hundreds of thousands gathered here to ring in the new year – and a new nation – when separation from the Czech Republic became official.

Hiking

To get out of the city and into the forest, take trolley bus 203 northeast from Hodžovo nám to the end of the line at Koliba, then walk up the road for about 20 minutes to the **TV tower** (Map p453) on Kamzík Hill (440m). Posted maps outline the many hiking possibilities in the forest surrounds and there are a couple of hotels with restaurants in the park. A **cable car** (lanovka; Map 000; ☎ 4425 9188; adult/student round-trip 90/60Sk; ☺ 10am-4pm Oct-May) makes the 15-minute journey downhill to the picnic areas and playgrounds of Železná studienka.

FESTIVALS & EVENTS

Bratislava's best events are arts related. From June to September the **Cultural Summer Festival** (Kultúrne leto; ☎ 5441 3063) brings a smorgasbord of operas, plays and performances to the streets and venues around town. Classical music takes centre stage at the **Bratislava Music Festival** (Bratislavské hudobné slávnosti; ☎ 5443 4546;

www.bhsfestival.sk in Slovak), which runs from late September to mid-October. **Bratislava Jazz Days** (Bratislavských jazzových dní; ☎ 5293 1572; www.bjd.sk) swings for three days in September. Twenty-sixth of November is the usual start to the **Christmas market** on Hlavné nám.

SLEEPING

Bratislava's no-longer-dirt-cheap lodging market is still cheaper than London, but don't expect comparable services. Bratislava Culture & Information Service (p454) can help with private rooms (from 1100Sk per person) and student dormitories (July and August, from 300Sk per person). To book an apartment, check out www.bratislavahotels.com.

Budget

Patio Hostel (Map p456; ☎ 5292 5797; www.patio hostel.com; Špitalska 35; dm 450-550Sk, d per person 860-900Sk; P X 🖵) Clean and fresh and dorm-like (100 beds) – that is if you were allowed to paint the concrete block walls with bright colours and stylised graffiti at college. Each floor has a kitchenette and there's a courtyard patio in addition to the computer room and basement rec room (TV, fussball).

Downtown Backpackers (Map p456; ☎ 5464 1191; www.backpackers.sk; Panenská 31; dm 500-600Sk, d per person 1000Sk; X 🖵) If you'd rather have lively conversation and laid-back Bohemian charm (exposed brick, red common-area walls) than

SLOVAKIA

COMMUNIST BRATISLAVA

Forty-five years of communist rule was bound to leave a mark. An obsession with modern functionalism led to many heinous buildings. The whole **Petržalka** (Map p453) concrete jungle housing estate is a key example. (We couldn't find any studies calculating how many people go to the wrong flat in an identical building down the road after a drink or two...) The adjacent **New Bridge** (Nový most; Map p456; ☎ 6252 0300; www.u-f-o.sk; Viedenská cesta; observation deck 100Sk; ☽ 10am-11pm), or the UFO (pronounced ew-fo) bridge, is a modernist marvel from 1972. After a three-year renovation it reopened in 2006 with an overhyped nightclub aloft, in addition to the prerequisite overpriced restaurant and viewing platform. And no, you're not seeing things, there is an upside down pyramid in the new town; that's the **Slovak Radio building** (Slovenský rozhlas; Map p453; cnr Mýtna & Štefanovičova).

On Slavín Hill, northwest of the old town, the **Slavín War Memorial** (Map p453) is one of the few remaining testaments to socialist realism as an art. It honours the Soviet soldiers who battled for Bratislava in 1945.

If you're nostalgic for the good old days, down a brewsky or two with Stalin, Lenin and the boys (or at least their statues) at the **KGB bar** (opposite).

---

a lock on your door, you've found your place. Some of the eight- and 10-bed dorm rooms act as a corridor to another. The gathering room has a bar. Take bus 93 two stops from the train station.

Other options:

Doprastav (Map p453; ☎ 5557 4313; www.dopra stav.sk/otherservices; Košická 52; dm 280-360Sk, s/d 625/952Sk) Hotel and dorm rooms near a shopping complex.

Zvárač (Map p453; ☎ 4924 6000; www.vuz.sk; Pionierska 17; s 700-900Sk, d 1100-1400Sk) Perfectly functional workers' hostel with attached bathrooms.

Midrange

Penzión Zlatá Noha (Map p453; ☎ 5477 4922; www .zlata-noha.sk; Bellova 2, Koliba hill; s 1350Sk, d 1700-1900Sk; ⓟ ✗ ▣) Tranquillity and family-run attention make up for distance at this homy, modern guesthouse above town. If you want to use the wi-fi, ask for a room near the reception. Take bus 203 from Hodžovo nám and ring for the fifth stop, Jeséniova.

Hotel-Penzión Arcus (Map p453; ☎ 5557 2522; www .hotelarcus.sk; Moskovská 5; s 1400-1800Sk, d 2600Sk; ⓟ ✗) This friendly, popular hotel near the bus station is only 15 minutes' walk from the old town. Though updated in 2001, the varied rooms (some with balcony, some with courtyard views) still seem a little outmoded. But all the bathrooms are sparkly white.

Pension Castle Club (Map p456; ☎ 5464 1472; www .stayslovakia.com; Zámocké schody 4; s/d with shared bathroom €60/75, q €120; ✗) It's quite an uphill hike to this townhouse B&B near the castle. The few basic rooms book up fast. An attic quad (more

stairs!) has a bathroom, high-speed internet connection and two double beds.

Penzión Chez David (Map p456; ☎ 5441 3824; www .chezdavid.sk; Zámocká 13; s €64-74, d €78-88; ⓟ ✗) A cool blue colour scheme, great old photos of synagogues on the walls, and a primo location. You'll hardly even notice the building's boxy functionalism (though the rooms are small).

Top End

Hotel Marrol's (Map p456; ☎ 5778 4600; www.hotelmarrols .sk; Tobrucká 4; s 7000Sk, d 7300-9600Sk; ⓟ ✗ ✗ ▣ ▣) Black-and-white movie stills, clubby leather chairs, sumptuous fabrics; Hotel Marrol's is straight off the silver screen – c 1940. Hard to imagine more retro refinement packed into one cultural landmark building.

Hotel Danube (Map p456; ☎ 5934 0000; www.hotel danube.com; Rybné nám 1; s €189-225, d €209-250; ⓟ ✗ ✗ ▣ ▣) A business behemoth, the Danube dominates the trade sector with serious services and a can-do staff. Oh, the riverfront location doesn't hurt either. Weekend rates and online packages bring the price way down.

EATING

The old town certainly isn't lacking in dining options and tables pop up all along the pedestrian byways as soon as warm weather allows. Many of the restaurants are tourist- or expat-oriented, with correspondingly spiked prices (foreign language names are a giveaway). Student eateries line Obchodná, at the northern end of the pedestrian zone.

Budget

Downtown Tesco (Map p456; ☎ 4446 4057; Kamenné nám; ⏰ 8am-9pm Mon-Fri, 9am-7pm Sat & Sun) has a supermarket in the basement and a 2nd-floor cafeteria, tucked behind the garden department.

Old Market (Stara Tržnica; Map p456; Nám SNP 25; ⏰ 7am-9pm Mon-Fri, 7am-6pm Sat, 1-6pm Sun) Fresh fruit-and-veggie vendors in the centre, hot food stands around the edge and a cafeteria upstairs.

U Jakubu (Map p456; ☎ 5441 7951; Nám SNP 24; mains 59-65Sk; ⏰ 8am-6pm Mon-Fri) All the standard Slovak dishes lie before you; it's self-service at U Jakuba, where a soup-and-main costs as little as 90Sk.

Divesta diétna jedáleň (Map p456; Laurinská 8; mains 60-80Sk; ⏰ 11am-3pm Mon-Fri) The big queues speak volumes about the veggie tucker at this central buffet.

Midrange

Prašná Bašta (Map p456; ☎ 5443 4957; Zámočnicka 11; mains 105-215Sk) Good, reasonable Slovak food. The round, vaulted interior oozes old Bratislava charm.

Archa (Map p456; ☎ 5443 0865; Uršuľí Chicken sautéed with avocado? This is Slovak cuisine gone contemporary, with loads of vegetables. The interior is decorated to look like an ark.

Also recommended:

Pizza Mizza (Map p456; ☎ 5296 5034; Tobrucká 5; mains 99-160Sk) City's best slice.

Vega Destination (Map p453; ☎ 3352 6994; Malý trh 2; mains 120-180Sk; ✗) Space-age vegetarian.

Top End

Traja Mušketieri (Map p456; ☎ 5443 0019; Sládkovičova 7; mains 350-600Sk) A stylised, upmarket version of a medieval tavern comes complete with a poetic menu. The waiters really know how to treat you well.

Of the many spiffy global food alternatives in the old town, **Kogo** (Map p456; ☎ 5464 5094; Hviezdoslavovo nám 21; mains 260-650Sk), for Italian seafood, is among the newest; and **Malecón** (Map p456; ☎ 0910274583; Nám L Štúra 4; mains 269-459Sk) has the most-praised Latin fare.

DRINKING

From mid-April to October, just about any sidewalk café will do for a drink.

Čokoládovňa (Map p456; ☎ 5433 3945; Michalská 6; ⏰ 9am-9pm) This tiny 'chocolate café' has cocktails, coffees and desserts made with the dark ambrosia.

Roland Café (Map p456; ☎ 5443 1372; Hlavné nám 5; ⏰ 9am-1am) Was this Roland ever not on the main square? This institution has a full menu as well as cocktails and coffee and cakes.

Kréma Gurmánov Bratislavy (KGB; Map p456; ☎ 5273 1279; Obchodná 52; ⏰ 10am-2am Mon-Fri, 4pm-3am Sat, 4pm-midnight Sun) Drink a dark and smoky toast to a statue of Stalin under a Soviet flag at KGB bar.

If you want to meet up and yarn with other English speakers, head to **Dubliner** (Map p456; ☎ 5441 0706; Sedlárska 6; ⏰ 11am-3am Mon-Sat, to 1am Sun) or to **Slovak Pub** (Map p456; ☎ 5441 0706; Obchodná 62; ⏰ 10am-midnight Mon-Thu, 10am-1am Fri & Sat, noon-midnight Sun). Otherwise, you may want to avoid them.

ENTERTAINMENT

Clubs

Café Štúdio Club (Map p456; ☎ 5443 1796; cnr Laurinská & Radničná; ⏰ 10am-1am Mon-Wed; to 3am Thu & Fri, 4pm-3am Sat) Bop to the oldies, or chill out to jazz; most nights there's live music of some sort. A 1950s vibe prevails.

Hysteria Pub (Map p453; ☎ 0910447744; Odbojárov 9; ⏰ 10am-1am Mon-Thu; to 5am Fri & Sat, 11am-midnight Sun) Comical murals depict inebriated

SLOVAKIA

AUTHOR'S CHOICE

Thermal waters bubble under much of the country and Slovakia's premier spa site, **Piešťany** (☎ 33-775 7733; www.spa-piestany.sk; Kúpeľe ostrov), is only 87km north of Bratislava. Until recently most Slovak spas were medical facilities requiring a doctor's note. Not so today. OK, there's still a slightly antiseptic look about treatment rooms, but many of Piešťany's lovely 19th-century buildings sport a new coat of Maria Theresa yellow paint and others are under reconstruction. On Kúpelne ostrov (Spa Island) you can swim in thermal pools, breathe seaside-like air in a New Age salt cave and be wrapped naked in hot mud. Head to the *kasa* (cashier) at Napoleon 1 to book a service, or go online. There are several hotels on the island. Trains from Bratislava take 1¼ hours (130Sk, 12 daily) and you can continue on the same line to Trenčín (76Sk, 45 minutes).

cowboys downing tequila at this fun-loving restaurant-bar-disco. It's multigeneration-ally popular.

Sparx (Map p453; ☎ 0903403097; Cintorínska 32; ⌚ 11am-midnight Mon-Wed, to 1am Thu, to 3am Fri & Sat) This cavernous bar (once a big beer hall) has live music Thursdays and becomes a disco at weekends.

Gay & Lesbian Venues

U Anjelov (Map p456; ☎ 5443 2724; Laurínská 19; ⌚ 9am-midnight Mon-Thu, until 1.30am Fri, 1pm-1.30am Sat, 1pm-midnight Sun) Bratislava's gay café serves creative mixed drinks, sometimes garnished with a candied marshmallow, while Frank Sinatra croons overhead.

Apollon Club (Map p456; ☎ 09-15-48 00 31; www .apollon-gay-club.sk; Panenská 24; ⌚ 6pm-3am Mon-Thu & Sun, 6pm-5am Fri & Sat) The main gay dance club in town (not that there are many) with two bars and three stages. Boys only Thursdays.

Sport

You can buy tickets online at www.ticket portal.sk.

HC Slovan (Map p453; ☎ 4445 6500; www.hcslovan .sk in Slovak; Odbojárov 3) Bratislava's hallowed ice-hockey team plays at a stadium northeast of the old town.

SK Slovan (☎ 4437 3083; Junácka 2) The home football team kicks it around nearby.

Theatre & Concerts

Slovak National Theatre (Slovenské Národné Divadlo; Map p456; www.snd.sk; Hviezdoslavovo nám) Opera and ballet are performed at this ornate theatre. Get tickets ahead of time at the booking office (*pokladňa*; Map p456; ☎ 5443 3764) located behind the theatre, at the corner of Jesen-ského and Komenského. It's open from 8am to 5.30pm Monday to Friday, and from 9am to 1pm on Saturday.

Slovak Philharmonic (Slovenská Filharmónia; Map p456; ☎ 5920 8233; www.filharmonia.sk; cnr Nám L Štúra & Medená; ticket office ⌚ 1-7pm Mon, Tue, Thu & Fri, 8am-2pm Wed) This state orchestra plays at a theatre in the Reduta Palace.

State Puppet Theatre (Štátne Bábkové Divadlo; Map p453; ☎ 5292 3668; www.babkovedivadlo.sk; Dunajská 36) Puts on puppet shows, usually at 10am and sometimes again at 2pm.

Folk dance and music ensembles, like **Sľuk** (☎ 6285 9125; www.sluk.sk) and **Lúčnica** (☎ 5292 0068; www.lucnica.sk), perform at various venues around town.

SHOPPING

There are several crystal, craft and jewellery stores in and around Hlavné nám.

Úľuv (Map p456; ☎ 5273 1351; www.uluv.sk; Obchodná 64) For serious folk art shopping head to Úľuv, where there are two stores and a courtyard filled with artisans' studios. There's even a small restaurant serving folksy specials.

Vinotéka Sv Urbana (Map p456; ☎ 5433 2573; Klobučnícka 4) Has wines for sample and sale.

GETTING THERE & AWAY
Air

Bratislava's **MR Štefánika airport** (BTS; ☎ 3303 3353; www.airportbratislava.sk) is 7km northeast of the centre. **Sky Europe** (☎ 4850 4850; www.skyeurope .com) has two to three daily flights to Košice (50 minutes, three daily) for as little as 190Sk (plus 300Sk in taxes) if you book ahead. For more on flying within Eastern Europe, see this chapter's Transport section (p487). For more on getting to Slovakia from further afield, see the Transport chapter (p596).

Vienna International airport (VIE; www.viennaair port.com) is only 60km from Bratislava, and is connected by near-hourly buses.

Boat

Floating down the Danube River is a cruisy way to get between Bratislava and Vienna (€21 one way, 1½ hours) or Budapest (€69 one way, four hours). From mid-April to September, **Slovenská plavba a prístavy** (☎ 5293 2226; www.lod.sk) runs at least one hydrofoil to Vienna and one to Budapest daily from the **hydrofoil terminal** (Map p456; Fajnorovo nábrežie 2). From June to October the **Twin City Liner** (☎ 09-03-61 07 16; www.twincityliner.com) operates three boats a day between the Bratis-lava **propeller terminal** (Map p456; Rázusovo nábrežie), in front of the Hotel Devin, and Vienna.

Bus

The **main bus station** (autobusová stanica, AS; Map p453; reservations ☎ 5556 7349; www.eurolines.sk), is 1.5km east of the old town. Locals call it Mlynské Nivy, after the street it's on. Buses leave from here heading to towns across Slovakia, includ-ing Žilina (203Sk, three hours, seven daily), Poprad (345Sk, seven hours, four daily), Košice (441Sk, eight hours, nine daily) and Bardejov (491Sk, nine to 11 hours, three daily).

Eurolines (☎ 5556 7349; www.eurolines.sk) runs international buses from Bratislava to Prague (420Sk, four hours, three daily), Budapest (560Sk, four hours, one daily) and Kraków.

For more on getting to Bratislava by bus from outside Eastern Europe, see (p599).

Train

At least 12 daily trains leave the **main train station** (Hlavná stanica; www.zsr.sk), 1km north of the centre, to Košice (518Sk, 5½ to nine hours), most via Žilina (268Sk, 2¾ to four hours) and Poprad (420Sk, 4¾ to eight hours).

GETTING AROUND
To/From the Airport

Bus 61 links the airport with the main train station (18Sk; 20 minutes). To get to town by taxi shouldn't cost much more than 500Sk – make sure the meter is used.

Bus & Tram

Dopravný Podnik Bratislava (DPB; ☎ 5950 5950; www.dpb .sk) runs an extensive tram, bus and trolleybus network. You can buy tickets (14/18/22Sk for 10/30/60 minutes) at the **DPB office** (Map p456; Obchodná 14; ☼ 9am-5.30pm Mon-Fri) and at newsstands. Validate on board. One-/two-/three-/seven-day *turistické cestovné lístky* (tourist travel tickets) cost 90/170/270/310Sk and are sold at the DPB office and train and bus stations. Check routes and schedules at www.imhd.sk.

Bratislava Culture & Information Centres (p454) sell the **Bratislava City Card** (1/2/3 days 200/300/370Sk), which covers city transport and provides discounted museum admissions among other benefits.

Car

Numerous international rental agencies have offices at the airport; **Alimex** (☎ 5564 1641; www .alimex.sk) charges from 699Sk per day. **Avis** (Map p456; ☎ 5341 6111; www.avis.sk; Rybné nám 1) has a desk in the Hotel Danube, but prices are high (from 1200Sk per day).

Taxi

Bratislava's taxis have meters, but they can be set to run at different rates. Cheating is becoming less common; within the old town a trip should cost no more than 300Sk. Call **Transtel Taxi** (☎ 16 301) or **Super Taxi** (☎ 16 616).

AROUND BRATISLAVA

Hardcore castle aficionados should don their daypack and head to **Devín Castle** (☎ 6573 0105; Muranská; adult/student 80/30Sk; ☼ 10am-5pm Tue-Fri, to 6pm Sat & Sun mid-Apr-Oct), 9km west of Bratislava. Once the military plaything of 9th-century warlord

Prince Ratislav, the castle withstood the Turks but was blown up in 1809 by the French. Peer at the older bits that have been unearthed and tour a reconstructed palace museum. Bus 29 links Devín with Bratislava's New Bridge stop, under the bridge. Austria is just across the river.

WEST SLOVAKIA

Snaking along the Small Carpathians on the main route northeast of Bratislava, watch for hilltop castle ruins high above the Váh River. Trenčín's magnificent, reconstructed castle is one of the most impressive along this once heavily fortified stretch.

TRENČÍN

☎ 032 / pop 56,850

A mighty castle looms above the 18th- and 19th-century buildings in this lively university town. Roman legionnaires fancied the site, establishing a military post, Laugaricio, in the 2nd century AD. A rock inscription recalls the 2nd legion's victory over the Germanic Kvad tribes. Trenčín Castle was first noted in a Viennese chronicle of 1069, but today's structure dates from around the 15th century. An excellent art museum rounds out the city's offerings.

Orientation & Information

From the adjacent bus and train stations walk west through Park MR Štefánika and beneath the highway past the Hotel Tatra, where a street bears left uphill to Mierové nám, the main square. The whole centre is easily walkable.

EMERGENCY
Police station (☎ 159; Štúrovo nám 10)

INTERNET ACCESS
Mike Studio (Mierové nám 25; ☼ 9am-10pm Mon-Sat, 10am-10pm Sun; per min 1Sk) Just internet, no café.

MONEY
VUB Banka (Mierové nám 37) ATM and exchange.

POST
Main post office (Mierové nám 21)

TOURIST INFORMATION
Cultural Information Centre (☎ 161 86; www.trencin .sk; City Office, Sládkovičova; ☼ 8am-6pm May-Sep, 8am-5pm Mon-Fri Oct-Apr) The helpful, well-informed staff can recommend one of the many local pensions.

SLOVAKIA

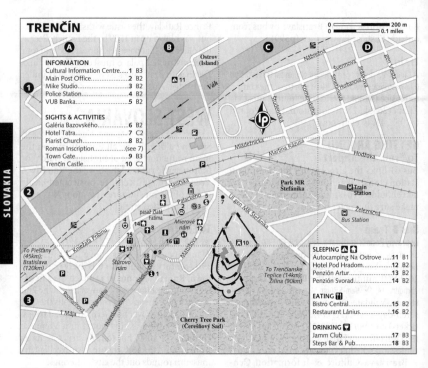

TRENČÍN

0 ————— 200 m
0 ————— 0.1 miles

INFORMATION	
Cultural Information Centre.....**1** B3	
Main Post Office......................**2** B2	
Mike Studio............................**3** B2	
Police Station.........................**4** B2	
VUB Banka.............................**5** B2	

SIGHTS & ACTIVITIES	
Galéria Bazovského.................**6** B2	
Hotel Tatra............................**7** C2	
Piarist Church........................**8** B2	
Roman Inscription................(see 7)	
Town Gate.............................**9** B3	
Trenčín Castle......................**10** C2	

SLEEPING	
Autocamping Na Ostrove **11** B1	
Hotel Pod Hradom...............**12** B2	
Penzión Artur........................**13** B2	
Penzión Svorad.....................**14** B2	

EATING	
Bistro Central.......................**15** B2	
Restaurant Lánius.................**16** B2	

DRINKING	
Jamm Club............................**17** B3	
Steps Bar & Pub....................**18** B3	

Sights

Sitting astride a rocky crag above the town squares, **Trenčín Castle** (Trenčiansky hrad; ☎ 7435 657; adult/student 80/40Sk; ⏰ 9am-5.30pm May-Oct, to 3.30pm Nov-Apr) would be hard to miss. At night, the castle is lit with green and purple lights. From up top you have sweeping views of the Váh River plain. Much of the castle you see is post-1950s reconstruction; a fire in the 1800s left the place in ruins. The Well of Love, purportedly dug by a man trying to win his lover back from servitude in the castle, is 70m deep. To go inside the palace, you have to join one of the frequent tours (in Slovak only, call two days ahead to arrange an English-speaking guide). The best time to visit is on summer evenings when two-hour **medieval night tours** (adult/student 100/50Sk) entertain you with sword fighting, minstrels, fun and staged frolics.

The famous **Roman inscription** of AD 179 is on the cliff behind the **Hotel Tatra** (☎ 6506 111; www.hotel-tatra.sk; Ulica gen MR Štefánika 2) and can only be seen through a viewing window on the hotel's staircase – ask at reception for permission to see it. The translation reads: 'To the victory of the emperor and the army

which, numbering 855 soldiers, resided at Laugaricio. By order of Maximianus, legate of the 2nd auxiliary legion.'

The **Galéria Bazovského** (☎ 7436 858; http:// gmab.scot.sk in Slovak; Palackého 27; adult/student 40/10Sk; ⏰ 9am-5pm Tue-Sun), in a restored 19th-century palace, houses a collection of works by local painter Miloš Bazovský (1899–1968). Temporary exhibits represent some of the best of 20th-century Slovak and Czech art.

At the western end of Mierové nám are the baroque **Piarist Church** (Piaristický kostol) and a 16th-century **town gate** (mestská brána).

Sleeping

Trenčín has tonnes more pensions than we can list here, ask at the tourist office if the ones below are full.

Autocamping na Ostrove (☎ 7434 013; http://web .viapvt.sk/autocamping.tn; per car/tent 50/70Sk, per person in hut 200Sk; ⏰ May–mid-Sep) On an island in the Váh River, walking distance from the city centre, this decent camping ground also has two five-bed *chaty* (huts).

Penzión Svorad (☎ 7430 322; www.svorad-trencin .sk; Palackého 4; s 450-800Sk, d 700-1200Sk; ⊠) Frayed curtains, peeling linoleum – but oh, the castle views. It's clear this is in part of a grammar school; the staff is quite rule-oriented.

Penzión Artur (☎ 7481 029; www.arturtn.sk; Palackého 23; s/d/tr 1200/1500/2000Sk) Modular modern furniture in a colourful old town building. The wine restaurant and sidewalk café add to the appeal.

Hotel Pod Hradom (☎ 7442 507; www.podhradom .sk in Slovak; Matúšova 12; r 2300-2950Sk) On a winding wee street en route to the castle, this pretty little lodging has a prime location and patio. All rooms have minibars and broadband, many have sloped ceilings and skylights, some have a *mažleska postel* (literally 'marriage bed', with one continuous queen-sized mattress).

Eating & Drinking

Bistro Central (Štúrovo nám 10; mains 42-86Sk; ☺ 9am-7pm Mon-Thu, 9am-4am Fri, 7pm-4am Sat) You can nosh kebab meat in *langoš* (fried bread) from this food stand after the clubs let out.

Restaurant Lánius (☎ 7441 978; Mierové nám 20; mains 90-190Sk) Creaking beams, wood fires and wood floors; the rustic set up matches the hearty Slovak fare. Pass the dining room in the front; the one up the stairs at the rear of the courtyard is more fun.

Steps Bar & Pub (☎ 7446 252; Sládkovičova 4-6; ☺ 10.30am-1am Sun-Thu, to 4am Fri & Sat) The ground-floor pub has imports on tap. Upstairs the bar attracts a beautiful, college-age crowd.

Jamm Club (Štúrovo nám 5; ☺ noon-1am Mon-Thu, to 3am Fri, 2pm-3am Sat, 2pm-1am Sun) Red and black painted walls make this cellar club seem extra dark. Live jazz and blues alternates with '70s and '80s disco nights.

Getting There & Away

Trains are the quickest and most cost-efficient way to get here from Bratislava (180Sk, two hours, seven daily). Most continue on to Košice (420Sk, four hours). Twenty trains a day travel to Žilina (180Sk, 1½ hours) from here.

CENTRAL SLOVAKIA

The rolling hills and forested mountain ranges of Central Slovakia are home to the shepherding tradition that defines Slovak culture. Watch roadside for farmers selling local sheep's cheese. The beautiful Malá Fatra mountain range is where this nation's Robin Hood, Juraj Jánošík, once roamed.

ŽILINA

☎ 041 / pop 85,268

A Slavic tribe in the 6th century was the first to recognize Žilina's advantageous location on the Váh River at the intersection of several important trade routes. Today it makes a convenient base for exploring the Malá Fatra National Park, as well as the area's fortresses, towns and folk villages. There isn't much to see in town besides the old palace-castle on the outskirts.

Orientation

The train station is on the northeastern side of the old town, near the Váh River. A 700m walk along Národná takes you past Nám A Hlinku up to Mariánské nám, the main square. From the south end of the bus station, follow Jána Milca northeast to Národná.

Information

CK Selinan (☎ 5620 789; www.zilina.sk; Burianova medzierka 4; ☺ 8am-5pm Mon-Fri) Located in a lane off the western side of Mariánské nám, this travel agency is an official tourist office representative. It can also arrange accommodation in the Malá Fatras.

Internet Caffe (☎ 0903522226; Bottova 12; per min 1.5Sk; ☺ 10am-10pm Mon-Fri, 2-10pm Sat & Sun) Also has a full bar.

Main post office (Sládkovičova 1) Three blocks north of Mariánské nám.

Tatra Banka (cnr Mariánské nám & Farská) Has an ATM and change facility.

Sights

North across the Váh River, the **Budatín Castle** (Budatínsky zámok; ☎ 5620 033; Topoľová 1; adult/student 50/30Sk; ☺ 9am-5.15pm Tue-Sun Jul & Aug, to 4pm Apr-Jun, Sep & Oct) is more mansion than stronghold. Inside, the **Považské Museum** contains exhibits of 18th- and 19th-century decorative arts as well as wire figures made by area tinkers. Other than that, you're left to a stroll through the pleasant old town.

Sleeping

CK Selinan (above) can help with private rooms from 300Sk per person.

Velký Diel (☎ 5005 249; kadorova@dorm.utc.sk; Žilinská univerzita, Vysokoškolákov 20; dm 300-500Sk; ⊠) A student dorm open to travellers in July and August only, Velký Diel is worth contacting year-round just in case it has a vacancy. Take tram 1 from the bus or the train stations to get here.

Penzión Majovey (☎ 5624 152; fax 5624 239; Jána Milca 3; s/d 1000/1750Sk) The deep coral outside is more interesting than the stark white inside but bathrooms are huge and tile floors keep things cool throughout. Breakfast is an extra 100Sk.

Hotel Grand (☎ 5626 809; www.hotelgrand.sk; Sládkovičova 1; s/d 1590/2630Sk; **P**) Floor-to-ceiling windows brighten up the bland rooms in this 90-year-old hotel off the main square. Go deluxe and ask for one with whirlpool tub and air-con (3180Sk).

Eating & Drinking

Voyage Voyage (☎ 5640 230; Mariánské nám 191; mains 100-175Sk) With sleek neon and chrome, this is not your typical Slovak eatery. Dishes are as updated as the scene. Try one of the milk shakes.

Pizzeria Carolina (☎ 5003 030; Národná 5; pizzas 98-137Sk) Tables are filled weekdays to weekend; Carolina's is especially popular with college students. There's a mixed salad bar of sorts.

Boston (☎ 0905481214; Mariánské 24; ⏰ 9am-midnight Sun-Thu, to 2am Fri & Sat) Live jazz Tuesday at 8pm; bar action nightly.

Getting There & Away

Žilina is on the main railway line from Bratislava to Košice. Trains head to Trenčín (180Sk, one hour, 20 daily), Bratislava (268Sk, 2¾ hours, 12 daily), Poprad (200Sk, two hours, 17 daily) and Košice (316Sk, three hours, 10 daily).

AROUND ŽILINA

A few folk culture sights within an hour of Žilina are well worth exploring. The nearby town of **Martin** (☎ tourist information 4234 776; www .tikmartin.sk; Štefánika 9A) is industrial, but it also has the country's biggest *skansen* (open-air

village museum), complete with working *krčma* (pub). Traditional plaster-and-log buildings from all over the region have been moved to the **Museum of the Slovak Village** (Múzeum Slovenské Dediny; ☎ 043-4239 491; adult/student 50/30Sk; ⏰ 9am-6pm Mon-Sun). Take the bus to Martin (40Sk, 40 minutes, half-hourly), 35km south of Žilina. The village museum is 4km southeast of the city. Take bus 10 from the bus station to the last stop, Ľadovaň, and walk the remaining 1km up through the forest.

Dark log homes painted with contrasting patterns fill the traditional village of **Čičmany** (www.cicmany.viapvt.sk in Slovak), which is 50 minutes south of Žilina by bus (destination Čičmany, 47Sk, five daily). If you've seen a brochure or postcard of Slovakia, you've probably seen a photograph of a Čičmany house. Most are private residences, but **Radenov House** (No 42; adult/ student 40/20Sk; ⏰ 10am-4pm Tue-Sun) is a museum and **Penzión Katka** (☎ 041-5492 132; www.penzionkatka .sk; No 50; r per person 370-430Sk) rents rooms. Return bus times allow lots of hours to wander.

MALÁ FATRA NATIONAL PARK
☎ 041

Sentinel-like formations stand watch at the rocky gorge entrance to the valley and precipitous peaks top the pine-clad slopes above. The Malá Fatra National Park (Národný park Malá Fatra) incorporates a chocolate box–pretty, 200-sq-km swathe of its namesake mountain range. The Vrátna Valley (Vrátna dolina), 25km east of Žilina, lies at the heart of the park. From here you can access the trailheads, ski lifts and a cable car to start your exploration. The long, one-street town of Terchová is at the lower end of the valley, Chata Vrátna is at the top. The village of Štefanová sits to the east, 1km uphill from Terchová.

WORTH A TRIP

Bojnice Castle (Bojnice zámok; ☎ 5430 633; www.bojnicecastle.sk; adult/child 200/70Sk; ⏰ 9am-5pm Tue-Sun May, Jun & Sep, daily Jul & Aug, 10am-3pm Tue-Sun Oct-Apr) comes straight out of a fairy-tale dream. The original 12th-century fortification got an early 20th-century redo by the Pálffy family, who modelled it on French romantic castles. (Original Gothic and Renaissance parts do survive within.) The time to visit is during one of the many festivals and night-time tours. The biggest is the **International Festival of Ghosts and Ghouls** in May, which attracts thousands daily. Costumed guides re-enact legends and put on shows throughout the castle and grounds. The place also gets decked out for Christmas, Valentine's Day and medieval events, among others; check the website for schedules. A bus from Žilina to Prievidza takes 1½ hours (80Sk, eight daily), from Bratislava it's 3½ hours (198Sk, eight daily). Bojnice is 3km from Prievidza (via local bus 3). It's not on a main train line.

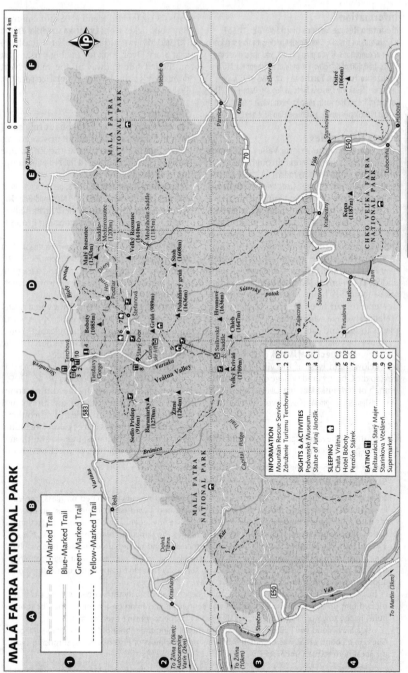

MALÁ FATRA NATIONAL PARK

- – – – Red-Marked Trail
- – - – Blue-Marked Trail
- – - – Green-Marked Trail
- ····· Yellow-Marked Trail

INFORMATION
Mountain Rescue Service	1 D2
Združenie Turizmu Terchová	2 C1

SIGHTS & ACTIVITIES
Podvanské Museum	3 C1
Statue of Juraj Janošík	4 C1

SLEEPING
Chata Vrátna	5 C2
Hotel Boboty	6 D2
Penzión Stárek	7 D2

EATING
Reštaurácia Starý Majer	8 C2
Starinkova Vceláreň	9 C1
Supermarket	10 C1

SLOVAKIA

Information

Mountain Rescue Service (Horská služba; ☎ 5695 232; http://his.hzs.sk/; Štefanová) Check with this service for trail conditions. If you plan to hike, you should get the VKÚ's 1:50,000 *Malá Fatra – Vrátna* map (sheet No 110).

Združenie Turizmu Terchová (☎ 5695 307; www .ztt.sk in Slovak; Sv Cyrila a Metoda 96; 🕙 9am-6pm) The tourist office on the main road in Terchová. It has internet access (100Sk per hour), and there's an ATM next door.

Sights & Activities

The road enters the Vrátna Valley just south of Terchová, where it runs through the crags of **Tiesňavy Gorge** (Tiesňavy roklina). A **cable car** (kabínkova lanovka; ☎ 5993 049; Chata Vrátna; adult/student one way 250/170Sk; 🕙 8am-4pm) runs from above the hut at the top of the valley to **Snilov Saddle** (Snilovské sedlo; 1524m) below two peaks, **Chleb** (1647m) and **Velký Kriváň** (1709m). Both are on the red, ridge trail, one of the most popular in the park. A hike northeast from Chleb over **Poludňový grúň** (1636m), **Hromové** (1636m) and **Stoh** (1608m) to **Medziholie Saddle** (1185m) takes about 5½ hours. From there you can descend for an hour on the green trail to **Štefanová** village where there's a bus stop, places to stay and eat.

Above the village of Terchová is an immense aluminium **statue of Juraj Jánošík** (see the boxed text below), and west of the village bus stop next to the Obecný úrad (village office) is a little branch of **Podvanské Museum** (adult/student 20/10Sk; 🕙 9am-1pm & 1.30-3pm Mon-Sun) devoted to him.

SKIING

The Vrátna Valley has plenty of tows and lifts are open from December to April. A day pass costs 680Sk for adults and 480Sk for children. Buy your ticket from **Lyžiarska stredisko Vrátna** (☎ 5695 055; www.vratna.sk). The *kasa* (cashier) is at Starý Dvor, look for the big parking lot on the left side midway up the valley. Next door there's a shack with **ski rental** (per pair 300Sk; 🕙 8am-4pm).

Sleeping

Places to stay book up fast both during summer and ski season. Ask about private rooms (from 300Sk per person) at the Združenie Turizmu Terchová office (left). No wild camping is allowed in the park.

Autocamp Varín (☎ 5621 478; per person/tent/car 75Sk each, 4-person hut 1000Sk; 🕙 May–mid-Oct; 🖢) Fifteen kilometres west of the Vrátna Valley, Varín is one of the closest camping grounds to the park.

Chata Vrátna (☎ 5695 739; www.vratna.sk/chata vratna/; dm 220Sk, d with shared bathroom 760Sk; 🅿) Muddy hikers, giggling children and a fragrant wood-smoke aroma fill this well-worn, chalet-style outfit at the top of Vrátna Valley.

Penzión Stárek (☎ 5695 359; www.penzionstarek .sk; Štefanová 124; d per person 400-540Sk; 🗙) A warm and welcoming eight-room log cabin. You'll often find the owner's family gathered at the restaurant's outdoor picnic tables.

Hotel Boboty (☎ 5695 228; www.hotelboboty.sk in Slovak; Nový Dvor; s 800Sk, d 900-1900Sk; 🅿 🗙 💻 🖢) Skyscraping windows in the dining room create tremendous vistas of the forests and mountains beyond in a clean-line contemporary style. Expect services galore, including sauna, massage, billiards, free ski shuttle and some in-room internet connections. From

---

SLOVAKIA'S ROBIN HOOD

Juraj Jánošík has been written about, sung about, painted on canvas, etched on glass, carved in wood; he's been made the subject of three movies and a card game, there's even an opera. It's hard to imagine a bigger national character. But like any legend, Jánošík is a mix of fact and fiction. Born into a peasant family in Terchová in 1688, he joined up with Ferenc Rákóvczi II in 1703 to fight the Habsburgs. While away his mother died and his father was beaten to death by their landlord for taking time off to bury her. Jánošík took to the hills and spent years robbing from the rich and giving to the poor (although some say he didn't make much of a distinction about who he stole from and didn't give it away).

In 1713 he was captured in a pub; the story goes that an old lady threw down some peas that tripped him up as he tried to escape. He was sentenced and hung on a hook by the ribs (gory huh?) in the town of Liptovský Mikuláš. But where in the town isn't even certain.

Ask a Slovak and you'll likely hear what sensational thing the robber did in their home village. Guess in a country that was dominated by foreigners for most of history, it's not surprising that the local hero was an underdog.

the bus stop at Nový Dvor, walk five minutes' uphill in the direction of Štefanová.

Eating

The food situation in the park is pretty bleak; most Slovaks bring their own. There are takeaway stands at Starý Dvor and there's a **supermarket** *(potraviny)* at the valley turnoff in Terchová. Most hotels have restaurants. There's a pizzeria in Penzión Stárek (opposite).

Starinkova Včeláreň (☎ 5993 130; A Hlinku 246; snacks 20-50Sk) A friendly tearoom has scones and homemade honey to go with its brew.

Reštaurácia Starý Majer (☎ 5695 419; mains 1000-200Sk; ⏱ 10am-9pm) Farm implements decorate the walls and hearty *halušky* top the menu.

Getting There & Around

At least every two hours, more often on weekdays, buses link Žilina with Terchová (40Sk, 45 minutes) and Chata Vrátna (50Sk, one hour). Or you can change in Terchová for local buses that make multiple stops in the valley.

Ask at the Terchová information centre (opposite) about bicycle rental.

EAST SLOVAKIA

Majestic? Ancient? Sublime? No one adjective well describes East Slovakia with its alpine peaks, old towns and even older castles. In one compact region you can hike the High Tatras, explore a medieval town square in Levoča, conquer the Špis Castle ruins, visit the Renaissance era in Bardejov and get back to city life in Košice. Though it's a distance from Bratislava, once you get here, the area is easy to traverse by bus. And Poland's just the other side of the mountains.

HIGH TATRAS

☎ 052

When you first see the alpine, snow-strewn High Tatras (Vysoké Tatry) jutting out of the valley floor north of Poprad, you may do a double take. This isn't Switzerland after all. But Gerlachovský štít (2654m) is the highest in the Carpathian range, and the Tatras tower over most of Eastern Europe. The massif is only 25km wide, adding to the sense that some alien plopped these huge mountains here. The photo opportunities at higher elevations will get you fantasising about a career with *National Geographic* –

pristine snowfields, ultramarine mountain lakes, crashing waterfalls. Sadly, a massive windstorm in late 2004 uprooted the dense pine forest that surrounded the resort towns of Starý Smokovec and Tatranská Lomnica. Huge swathes will look barren and war ravaged for years to come. Trunks have been cleared leaving fields full of giant upturned stumps and dirt. This hasn't stopped the crowds from showing up.

Since 1949 most of the Slovak part of this jagged range has been included in the Tatra National Park (Tanap), complementing a similar park in Poland. A 600km network of hiking trails reaches all the alpine valleys and some peaks, with *chaty* (mountain huts) to stop at along the way. Routes are colour coded and easy to follow. Park regulations require you to keep to the marked trails and to refrain from picking flowers.

Climate & When to Go

When planning your trip, keep in mind that the higher trails are closed from November to mid-June to protect the environment, and avalanches may close lower portions as well. There's snow by November that lingers at least until May. Always wear hiking boots and layer clothing. Know that the assistance of the Mountain Rescue Service is not free and beware of sudden thunderstorms on ridges and peaks where there's no protection. June and July are especially rainy. July and August are the warmest (and most crowded) months. Hotel prices and crowds are at their lowest from October to April.

For the latest weather and trail conditions stop by the **Mountain Rescue Service** (Horská Záchranná Služba; ☎ emergency 18 300; http://his.hzs.sk/; Starý Smokovec 23).

Orientation

Starý Smokovec, a 20th-century resort town, is roughly central along the High Tatras chain, with Tatranská Lomnica, the smallest and quaintest resort, 5km to the east. Lakeside, development-crazy Štrbské Pleso, 11km to the west, was the only one of the big three resorts villages left with trees after the storm, and in some ways is the prettiest now. A narrow-gauge electric train connects Poprad with Štrbské Pleso via Starý Smokovec, where you have to change to get to Tatranská Lomnica. Roads lead downhill from the resorts to less expensive villages.

HIGH TATRAS

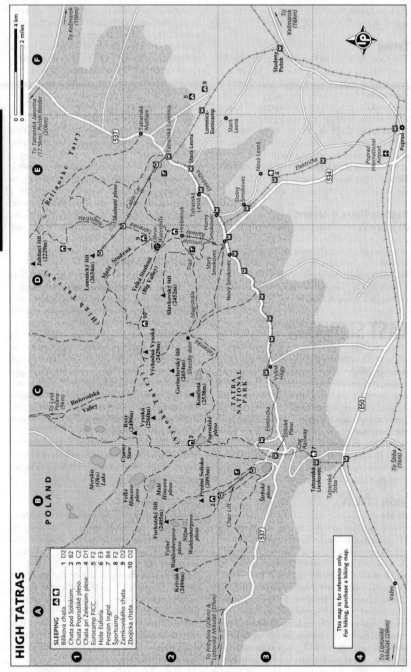

SLEEPING
Bilíkova chata	1 D2
Chata pod Soliskom	2 B2
Chata Popradské pleso	3 C2
Chata pri Zelenom plese	4 D1
Eurocamp FICC	5 F2
Hotel Eufória	6 E3
Penzión Ingrid	7 B4
Sportcamp	8 F2
Zamkovského chata	9 D2
Zbojnícka chata	10 D2

This map is for reference only.
For hiking, purchase a hiking map.

MAPS
Our High Tatras map is intended for orientation only, not as a hiking guide. Buy a proper VKÚ 1:25,000 (sheet No 2) or 1:50,000 *Vysoké Tatry* (sheet No 113) trail map when you arrive – both cost around 120Sk. They're usually available at hotels, shops and newsstands, as well as information offices. Green maps list summer *hiking turistka* (hiking trails) and the blue ones show winter ski routes.

Information
INTERNET ACCESS
Hotel FIS (☎ 4492 221; Areál FIS, Štrbské Pleso; per hr 100Sk; ◷ 24hr) Two lobby computers are available for general rental.
Townson Travel (☎ 4782 731; Tatranská Lomnica 94; per hr 80Sk; ◷ 9am-5pm Mon-Fri) This travel agency has one computer with access, but it closes sporadically.
U Michalka Café (Starý Smokovec 4; per hr 80Sk; ◷ 11am-10pm) One terminal in the corner.

MONEY
All three main resorts have ATMs.
Slovenská Sporiteľňa (Cesta Slobody 24, Starý Smokovec) On the main road, has an ATM and exchange.

POST
Post Office (off Cesta Slobody) Above Starý Smokovec train station.

TOURIST INFORMATION
Tatra Information Office (TIK) Starý Smokovec (☎ 4423 440; www.tatry.sk; Dom služieb 24; ◷ 8am-8pm Mon-Fri, to 1pm Sat); Tatranská Lomnica (☎ 4468 118; Cesta Slobody; ◷ 10am-6pm Mon-Fri, 9am-1pm Sat) Oodles of info.
Tatra National Park Info Centrum (☎ 4492 391; www.tanap.sk; Štrbské Pleso; ◷ 9am-4pm) Next to Toliar department store; staff knows a lot about trails.

TRAVEL AGENCIES
T-Ski Travel (☎ 4423 200; www.slovakiatravel.sk; Starý Smokovec 46; ◷ 9am-4pm Mon-Thu, to 5pm Fri-Sun) Books lodging, including some huts, and arranges ski and sport programmes. It's at the funicular station.

Sights & Activities
STARÝ SMOKOVEC
From Starý Smokovec a **funicular railway** (pozemná lanovka; ☎ 4467 618; www.tldtatry.sk; adult/student return 100/60Sk; ◷ 7.30am-7pm), or a 55-minute hike on the green trail, takes you up to **Hrebienok** (1280m). From here you have a great view of the Velká Studená Valley and a of couple

hiking options. The red trail, past the Bilíkova chata to **Obrov Waterfalls** (Obrovsky vodopad), takes about an hour. This is part of the **Tatranská Magistrála Trail** that follows the southern slopes of the High Tatras for 65km. Continuing on from the falls, it's a 35-minute hike to Zamkovského chata, and Skalnaté pleso (see below), with its cable car and trails down to Tatranská Lomnica.

TATRANSKÁ LOMNICA
An extremely popular **cable car** (kabínková lanovka; www.tldtatry.sk; adult/student return 390/270Sk; ◷ 8.30am-7pm Jul-Aug, to 3.30pm Sep-Jun) links Tatranská Lomnica with the bustling lake and winter sports area of **Skalnaté pleso** (1751m). From there, another **cable car** (adult/student return 550/350Sk; ◷ 8.30am-7pm Jul-Aug, to 3.30pm Sep-Jun) goes on to the precipitous 2634m summit of **Lomnický štít** – bring a jacket. And queues are long during peak season, so get there early.

Alternatively, you can yomp it up to Skalnaté (2½ hours), where there is also an ordinary **chairlift** (adult/student 150/90Sk; ◷ 8.30am-5.30pm Jul-Aug, 8.30am-4.30pm Sep-Jun) running up to **Lomnické sedlo**, a 2190m saddle below the summit.

Is it a rollercoaster? Is it a summer bobsled? Both, it's **Tatrabob** (☎ 4467 951; Tatranská Lomnica 29; per ride 50Sk; ◷ 9am-10pm Jul & Aug, 9am-7pm Sep-Jun). Individual riders get hauled up on a track and then let go to control their own undulating descent.

ŠTRBSKÉ PLESO
From the modern ski resort of Štrbské Pleso and its glacial lake (1346m), follow the red-marked Magistrála Trail (uphill from the train station) for about an hour up to **Popradské pleso**, an even more idyllic lake at 1494m. From Popradské pleso the Magistrála zigzags steeply up the mountainside then traverses east towards **Sliezsky dom** and **Hrebienok** (four hours).

There is also a year-round **chairlift** (☎ 4492 343; www.parksnow.sk; adult/student return 200/140Sk; ◷ 8am-3.30pm) to **Solisko**, from where it's a one-hour walk north along the red trail to the 2093m summit of **Predné Solisko**.

There's usually a guy hawking rides on a **snowmobile** (snižký skooter; 10 min 600Sk) in the field on the side of the road to the chairlift and Areál FIS.

MOUNTAIN CLIMBING
You can reach the top of **Slavkovský štít** (2452m) via the blue trail from Starý Smokovec (seven

to eight hours return), but to scale the peaks without marked hiking trails (Gerlachovský štít included) you must hire a mountain guide (members of recognised climbing clubs excluded). Contact the **Mountain Guides Society Office** (☎ 4422 066; www.tatraguide.sk; Starý Smokovec 38; ☺ 10am-6pm Mon-Fri, noon-6pm Sat & Sun Jun-Sep, 10am-6pm Mon-Fri Oct-May), by the Hotel Smokovec. It runs classes too.

SKIING, SNOWBOARDING & MOUNTAIN BIKING

Štrbské Pleso is probably the most poplar ski and snowboard area, but Starý Smokovec and Tatranská Lomnica both have lifts and runs. You can hire skis, snowboards, even mountain bikes, (all about 300Sk a day) from **Crystal Ski** (☎ 4492 834; www.crystalski.sk; Areál FIS; ☺ 8.30am-4.30pm) in Štrbské Pleso and from **Tatrasport** (☎ 4425 241; www.tatry.net/tatrasport; ☺ 8am-noon & 1-6pm) in Starý Smokovec, above the bus station parking lot.

Sleeping

No wild camping is permitted within the national park, but there are a couple of camping grounds near Tatranská Lomnica. Lodging rates are high in the three main resorts; if you're looking for bargains you have to go downhill to towns like Nová Lesná, Stará Lesná and Tatranská Štrba. It's best to book private rooms ahead of time via the internet (www.tatry.sk and www.tanap.sk/homes.html) as tourist offices up here don't do bookings.

Up on the trails, a *chata* (mountain hut) can be anything from a shack to chalet. A bed goes for 300Sk to 500Sk; all may be full midsummer. Food is usually available, but you may want to bring some of your own supplies. A stay in a *chata* is one of the best mountain experiences the Tatras have to offer. Contact the *chata* directly to book ahead, essential in July and August. Someone usually speaks enough English to communicate.

STARÝ SMOKOVEC & AROUND
Pension Vesna (☎ 4422 774; vesna@stonline.sk; Nový Smokovec 69; r per person 600Sk; P) Both family-orientated and friendly. Most of the seven rooms at this guesthouse have three beds and a separate living area. Vesna's below Nový Smokovec train stop, behind the sanatorium.

Hotel Euforia (☎ 4783 061; www.hoteleuforia.sk; Nová Lesná 399; s/d 1150/1550Sk; P) With blond wood and cobalt blue rugs, Euforia is fresher and

brighter (and newer) than most of what's up the hill. It's 3km south of Starý Smokovec, near the Nová Lesná train stop. A big terrace closes off with windows for winter.

Grand Hotel (☎ 4870 000; www.grandhotel.sk; Starý Smokovec 38; s/d 2300/3900Sk; P ✗ ☮) More than 100 years of history are tied up in this full-service property front and centre in Starý Smokovec. It's a biggie.

Some mountain huts above:

Bilíkova chata (1220m; ☎ 4422 439; fax 4422 267) Hotel-like chalet with restaurant and one-, two- and three-bed rooms with shared bathrooms.

Zbojnícka chata (1960m; ☎ 0903638000; www .zbojnickachata.sk) Sixteen beds, dorm style, restaurant (breakfast included).

Zamkovského chata (1475m; ☎ 4422 636; www .zamka.sk) Twenty-four beds in four-bed rooms; board available.

TATRANSKÁ LOMNICA & AROUND
Eurocamp FICC (☎ 4467 741; www.eurocamp-ficc.sk; per person/tent/car 110/80/80Sk, 2-/3-/4-bed bungalows 1200/1400/1600Sk; ☺ year-round; P ☮) Row upon row of caravans line up at this 1500-capacity ground. On site there are two restaurants, a bar, billiards, a supermarket, a swimming pool and sauna, and ball courts. It's five minutes' northeast of the Lomnica–Eurocamp train station on the line to Studený Potok.

Športcamp (☎ 4467 288; http://sportcamp.host.sk in Slovak; per person/tent/car 80/80/50Sk) Two kilometres south of Eurocamp FICC is a less hyper, 100-site camping ground with tennis and volleyball courts

Penzión Encian (☎ 4467 520; penzion.encian@sinet.sk; s/d 1000/1500Sk; P) You couldn't ask for better hosts than Zdenka and Štefan Unák. They've warmed up the small restaurant with a fire in the hearth and old skiing memorabilia on display. Eave-top room 13 has a great view of Lomnický štít.

Grandhotel Praha (☎ 4467 941; www.grandhotel praha.sk; s/d 2900/3900Sk; P ✗ ▢ ☮) Remember when train travel was elegant? OK, so we're too young, but the 1899 Grandhotel isn't. Rooms are appropriately classic, if uninspired, and there's a new spa.

Take the cable car up from Tatranská Lomnica to Skalnaté pleso, and hike west to the huts above Starý Smokovec (above), or you can make the strenuous 2½-hour red-trail trek from Skalnaté pleso to **Chata pri Zelenom plese** (1540m; ☎ 4467 420; www.zelenepleso.sk). The lakeside hut has 50 beds.

ŠTRBSKÉ PLESO & AROUND

Penzión Pleso (☎ 4492 160; Nové Štrbské Pleso 11; www
.penzionpleso.sk; r per person 650Sk, ste per person 800Sk; P)
The inside of this refurbishment-in-progress
is well ahead of the outside. Go for contemporary suite 11 because of the views from corner,
full-length windows. Breakfast is 90Sk.

Penzión Ingrid (☎ 0905108088; www.ingrid.sk; Tatranská Štrba 1121; apt per person 400–800Sk; P ✗) This
tidy new accommodation opened 500m from
the Tatranská Štrba zubačka (cog railway) in
late 2005. Apartments each have a two-burner
cooktop, a small fridge and an electric kettle.

Mountain huts above Štrbské Pleso:

Chata pod Soliskom (1800m; ☎ 0905652036; www
.chatasolisko.sk) Nine beds, nice terrace and no hiking
required (it's next to the chairlift).

Chata Popradské pleso (1500m; ☎ 4492 177; www
.popradskepleso.sk) Sizeable chalet with restaurant and
132 beds in two eight-bed rooms. The attic floor sleeps 25
in sleeping bags.

Eating & Drinking

The villages are close enough that it's easy to
eat in one and sleep in another. All of the hotels, and some of the *penzións* (homy hotels),
have restaurants; the grand ones have bars and
discos. Look for the local *potraviny* (supermarket) on the main road in each village.

Samoobslužná Reštaurácia (☎ 4781 011; Hotel Toliar, Štrbské Pleso 21; mains 40–70Sk; ⊙ 7am-10pm) This
self-service cafeteria has one-dish meals (goulash, chicken stir-fry) and some vegetarian
options.

Reštaurácia Stará Mama (☎ 4467 216; shopping centre Sintra, Tatranská Lomnica; mains 65–172Sk) Substantial
soups and homemade dumplings are the main
reason hikers frequent this rustic fave; but the
menu is actually quite extensive.

Pizzéria Albas (☎ 4423 460; Albas, Starý Smokovec;
pizzas 100–170Sk) Everyone you talk to seems to
recommend this big, antiseptic pizzeria. It's
the pizza, not the place.

Zbojnícka Koliba (Tatranská Lomnica; mains 150–350Sk)
Musicians play gypsy songs on the cimbalon
while your chicken roasts over the open fire.
Sit back, order some *bryndza* to spread on
bread, have some hot spiced wine and wait,
it'll take an hour to cook. The Koliba is on the
road up to the Grand Hotel Praha.

Tatry Pub (☎ 4422 448; Starý Smokovec; ⊙ 1-11pm
Mon-Thu, 11am-midnight Fri-Sun) Refresh yourself at
the official watering hole of the Mountain
Guide Club. It's on the main road west and
up from the car park.

Getting There & Away

To reach the Tatras from most destinations
you need to switch in Poprad (p472).

BUS

Buses from Poprad travel to Starý Smokovec
(18Sk, 20 minutes, every half hour), Tatranská Lomnica (25Sk, 35 minutes, hourly) and
Štrbské Pleso (45Sk, 50 minutes, every 45
minutes). One daily, early-morning bus links
Bratislava with Starý Smokovec (346Sk, 6½
hours) directly.

From Tatranská Lomnica buses leave for
Kežmarok (22Sk, 30 minutes) at least every
1½ hours.

TRAIN

To reach the High Tatras by train you'll have
to change at Poprad (p472). There are frequent narrow-gauge electric trains between
Poprad and the High Tatras (see Getting
Around). All three main train stations have
left-luggage offices.

WALKING INTO POLAND

There's a highway border crossing at Lysá
Poľana, 2.5km north of Tatranská Javorina,
which is accessible by bus from Tatranská
Lomnica (30Sk, 45 minutes, at least five daily).
From the Polish side there are regular public
buses and private minibuses to Zakopane
(26km).

Getting Around

Tatra electric train service (Tatranská elekrická
železnica, TEZ) links most of the towns and
villages in the Tatras at least hourly. One line
runs from Poprad via Starý Smokovec (30
minutes) to Štrbské Pleso (one hour), with
frequent stops in between. Another line connects Starý Smokovec to Tatranská Lomnica
(15 minutes). A third route is from Tatranská
Lomnica through Studeny Potok (15 minutes) looping round to Poprad (25 minutes).
A 20Sk ticket covers a six to 14km ride. It's
easier to buy a one-/three-/seven-day pass for
100/200/360Sk. If there's not a ticket window
at your stop, buy one from the conductor.
Validate it on board.

A cog railway connects Tatranská Štrba (on
the main Žilina–Poprad railway line) with
Štrbské Pleso (30Sk, 15 minutes, hourly).

Local buses run between the resorts every
20 minutes and tend to be quicker than the
train – they have fewer stops though. Starý

Smokovec to Tatranská Lomnica (10Sk) takes 10 minutes, and to Štrbské Pleso (28Sk) takes 30 minutes.

The main road through the Tatras resorts is Rte 537, or Cesta Slobody (Freedom Way). You can connect to it from the E50 motorway through Tatranská Štrba, Poprad or Velká Lomnica.

Hire mountain bikes from Tatrasport in Starý Smokovec and Crystal Ski in Štrbské Pleso, which both also rent skis (see p470).

POPRAD

☎ 052 / pop 55,400

Poprad is an important transportation transfer point for the High Tatras and Slovenský raj National Parks, and a possible base for seeing Levoča and surrounding towns if you have a car. Otherwise, skip the modern, industrial city. From the adjacent train and bus stations the central pedestrian square, Nám sv Egídia, is a five-minute walk south on Alžbetina.

Information

City Information Centre (☎ 7721 700; www.poprad .sk; Nám sv Egídia 15; ☿ 8am-6pm Mon-Fri, 9am-noon Sat Jul-Aug, 8.30am-5pm Mon-Fri, 9am-noon Sat Sep-Jun) Has information about the Tatras and can help with accommodation.

Sinet (Nám sv Egídia 28; per hr 40Sk; ☿ 9am-9pm Mon-Sat, from 1pm Sun). Internet and email available.

Sleeping

The old Germanic village of Spišská Sobota, 2km northeast of the centre, is now a Poprad adjunct. There are more than 10 lodging options on or near its medieval square.

Hotel Sobota (☎ 4663 121; www.hotelsobota.sk; Kežmarská 15; s/d 1750/2200Sk; ⓟ ⊠ ⌧ ⌨) One of the newer lodging options; it has great slate and timber construction. It's near the road connecting Kežmarok and Levoča.

Eating

Numerous restaurants and cafés line Nám sv Egídia.

Pizzeria Utopia (☎ 7732 222; Dostojevského 23; pizzas 100-200Sk) For eclectic antiques and pizza head south across the E18 to Utopia. Salami, blue cheese and corn is an interesting combination, don't you think?

Getting There & Away

Bus 12 travels between the Poprad city centre and **Poprad-Tatry International airport** (☎ 7763 875;

www.airport-poprad.sk; Na Letisko 100), 5km west of the centre. The only flights that use this airport are the ones to and from London (see p596).

Intercity (IC) or Eurocity (EC) trains are the quickest way to get in and out of Poprad; four a day run to Bratislava (420Sk, 4¼ hours) and Košice (154Sk, 1¼ hours). For more on the electric trains that traverse the 13km or so to the High Tatras resorts, see p471.

To cities in Western and Central Slovakia, trains are generally better than buses (quicker, comparable cost). For more on transferring to the High Tatras resorts by bus, see p471. To get to Poland, you can take a bus from Poprad to Tatranska Javorina (58Sk, 1¼ hours, four daily), near the border at Lysá Poľana. Walk across to the buses waiting to take you to Zakopane.

KEŽMAROK

☎ 052 / pop 12,740

Snuggled beneath the broody peaks of the High Tatras, Kežmarok may not seem dramatic, but it is a truly pleasant place. The numerous architecturally distinct churches, the pocket-sized old town square with resident castle, all the ice-cream shops…

Ever since it was colonised by Germans back in the 13th century, Kežmarok has been treading a subtly different path from the rest of the country. The residents even declared themselves an independent republic, albeit infinitesimally, in 1918. Though the Germanic settlers moved on, they left behind something of their character on the town buildings. On the second weekend in July, the **European Folk Craft Market** attracts artisans from all across the country to demonstrate and sell their wares. Plenty of food and drink to be had then too.

Orientation & Information

Kežmarok is 14km east of Tatranská Lomnica and 16km northeast of Poprad – easy day-tripping distances. The bus and train stations are side by side, northwest of the old town, just across the Poprad River, via Dr Alexandra, to the main square, Hlavné nám.

The extremely useful **Kežmarok Information Agency** (☎ 4524 047; www.kezmarok.net; Hlavné nám 46; ☿ 8am-noon & 1-5pm Mon-Fri, 9am-2pm Sat, 9am-2pm Sun Jun-Sep) stocks heaps of brochures and souvenirs. The staff can help with info about the Tatras too. One of the best bookstore map selections in the country is at **Alter Ego** (☎ 4525 432; Hlavné nám 3).

Sights

The huge red-and-green, 1894 pseudo-Moorish **New Evangelical Church** (cnr Toporcerova & Hviezdoslavovo; 10am-noon & 2-4pm May-Sep) dominates the south end of town. Next door, the **Old Wooden Evangelical Church** (10am-noon & 2-4pm Mon-Sat May-Sep) was built in 1717 without a single nail and has an amazing interior of carved and painted wood. A 30Sk ticket covers entry to both.

The wooden altars in the 15th-century Gothic **Basilica of the Holy Cross** (Bazilika sv Kríža; Nám Požárnikov; donation 10Sk; 9am-5pm Mon-Fri Jun-Sep) were supposedly carved by students of Master Pavol of Levoča. Small, mansionlike **Kežmarok Castle** (4522 618; Hradné nám 45; adult/student 60/30Sk; 9am-noon & 1-5pm Tue-Sun May-Sep) dates back to the 15th century and is now a museum with local history, archaeology and period furniture exhibits. Entry from October to April is with a tour that leaves on the hour from 8am to 3pm, Monday to Friday.

Sleeping & Eating

Penzión U Jakubu (4526 314; www.penzionujakuba .sk; Starý trh 39; d 880-1190Sk) An authentic, folksy Slovakness pervades this *penzión* and restaurant. Take a seat at a big wooden bench table near the open fire and be waited on by servers in area folk dress. Remember to call a day ahead if you want a whole roast pig. Rooms are simply dressed in pine.

Sidewalk cafés abound in the pedestrian area around Hlavné nám. There are no fewer than six *cukráreň* serving pastries and ice cream, or you could stop at the tables on the square run by **Pizza Classica** (4523 693; cnr Hviezdoslavova & Hlavné nám; pizzas 90-170Sk).

Getting There & Away

Buses are the way to get around locally – they run hourly to/from Poprad (22Sk, 30 minutes) and every 1½ hours to/from Tatranská Lomnica (22Sk, 30 minutes). From Monday to Friday, there are three buses a day to Červený Kláštor (58Sk, 1″ hours), only one on Saturday and Sunday).

PIENINY NATIONAL PARK

 052

Gently bubbling water flows between impressive 500m-tall sheer cliffs: the 21 sq km **Pieniny National Park** (Pieninský Národný Park) was created to protect the 9km **Dunajec Gorge**. The park combines with a similar one on the Polish side of the river and extends between the Slovak village of Červený Kláštor and Szczawnica, Poland. River rafting is the main attraction here, but there are also hiking trails and an ancient monastery. Pick up VKÚ's 1:25,000 *Pieninský Národný Park* map (sheet No 7) for detailed exploring.

At the mouth of the gorge is the fortified **Red Monastery** (Červený Kláštor; 4822 955; adult/student 50/25Sk; 9am-5pm May-Oct). Built in the 14th century, it's now used as a park administrative centre and museum with a collection of statuary and old prints of the area. Two kilometres west of the monastery is a small **information centre** (4822 122; Rte 543; www.pieniny .sk; 9am-5pm May-Oct).

There are two departure points along Rte 243 for a **river float trip** (adult/child 250/100Sk; daylight May-Oct) on a *plte* (shallow, flat-bottom wood rafts): one opposite the monastery, and another 1km upriver west of the village. A raft may wait to set out until it has as many passengers as possible (capacity 12). Don't be expecting white-water thrills – the Dunajec is a rather sedate 1½-hour experience terminating near the Slovak village of Lesnica.

To return to Červený Kláštor you can hike back the way you came, roughly southwest, along the river-side trail through the gorge, in a little over an hour. It's an interesting walk even if you don't do water. Or, walk 500m southeast of the river to Chata Pieniny in Lesnica. The hiker's lodge rents out bicycles (one way 100Sk) and runs a shuttle bus (50Sk) to take you the 22km over-mountain distance by road. Follow the yellow trail north of Lesnica (1.5km) and you reach a pedestrian border crossing into Poland for tourists, open from 9am to 4pm from May to October.

Sleeping & Eating

Cheap and cheerful **Chata Pieniny** (4397 530; www.chatapieniny.sk; Lesnica; dm 280Sk) is an old log lodge with two- to six-bed rooms at the terminus of the raft trip. There's a restaurant, a minimarket and bike rental available. It's located 500m south of the river landing terminus, at the far north end of Lesnica.

Copious *privaty* and *zimmer frei* ('private', or 'free' room in Slovak and German respectively) and *pension* signs line the one long road in Červený Kláštor. The not-so-youthful **Hotel Pltník** (4822 525; www.hotelpltnik.sk; s/d 720/870Sk;) also has camping (per person/tent 60/50Sk) in the big river-front field next door.

SLOVAKIA

Food stalls stand between the monastery and the river launch.

Getting There & Away

Getting here is a challenge unless you have a car. Buses run to Červený Kláštor from Poprad (89Sk, 1⅓ hours) three times a day Monday to Saturday and once on Sunday. From Košice (152Sk, 3″ hours) there's one direct afternoon bus, otherwise you have to change in Stará Ľubovňa (120Sk, 2″ hours, five daily) for the connecting service to Červený Kláštor (40Sk, 35 minutes, six daily).

LEVOČA

☎ 053 / pop 14,604

Medieval walls stand stolid and defensive, protecting the age-old centre from onslaught. Thank goodness no hyper-mart developer is getting in here. Levoča is one of the few Slovak cities to have her ancient old town defences largely intact. The pride of Slovakia's religious art collection, an 18m-high altar carved by renowned artist Master Pavol of Levoča, resides within the centre square's Church of St Jacob.

In the 13th century the king of Hungary invited Saxon Germans to colonise the eastern frontiers of his kingdom as a protection against Tatar incursions. Levoča was one of the main towns comprising what came to be known as the Spiš region.

Orientation & Information

Levoča is on the main E50 motorway between Poprad (28km) and Košice (94km). The centre is 1km north of the train and bus stations. Both banks and post are on the small main square, Nám Majstra Pavla.

Levonet Internet Café (Nám Majstra Pavla 38; per hr 80Sk; ☼ 10am-midnight) Check your email.

Tourist information office (☎ 4513 763; www .levoca.sk; Nám Majstra Pavla 58; ☼ 9am-5pm Mon-Sat, 10am-2pm Sun May-Oct, 9am-4.30pm Mon-Fri Nov-Apr) Ask staff for the free photocopied map they keep under the counter if you want one.

Sights

The spindles-and-spires **Church of St Jacob** (Chrám sv Jakuba; ☎ 4512 347; www.chramsvjakuba.sk; adult/student 50/30Sk; ☼ 11.30am, 1, 2, 3 & 4pm Tue-Sat Sep-Jun, 11am-5pm Mon, 9am-5pm Tue-Sat Jun-Aug), built in the 14th and 15th centuries, elevates your spirit with its soaring arches, precious art and rare furnishings. Everyone comes to see the splen-

did golden Gothic altar (1517) created by Master Pavol of Levoča. On it he carved and painted representations of the Last Supper and the Madonna and Child. (This Madonna's face appears on the 100Sk banknote.) Buy tickets at the **cashier** (kasa; ☼ 11am-5pm) inside the **Municipal Weights House** across the street from the north door. Once inside, drop a 5Sk coin in the machine at the back for a recorded description in English.

The square is choc-a-bloc with Gothic and Renaissance eye candy. No 20 is the **Master Pavol Museum** (☎ 4513 496; adult/student 40/20Sk; ☼ 9am-5pm) dedicated to the city's most celebrated son. The 15th-century **town hall** (radnica) houses a lacklustre **Spiš Museum** (☎ 4512 449; adult/student 40/20Sk; ☼ 9am-5pm). The adjacent 16th-century **cage of shame** is for naughty boys and girls.

From town you can see the **Church of Mariánska hora**, 2km north, where the largest Catholic pilgrimage in Slovakia takes place in early July.

Sleeping

Recreačné Zariadenie (☎ 4512 705; www.rz-levoca .web2001.cz; Levočská Dolina; per person/tent 85/70Sk, 2-bed hut 380Sk; P) A good camping option, Recreačné Zariadenie is 5km northwest of the centre and bikes can be rented. Relax in the sauna after all that pedalling.

Oáza (☎ 4514 511; www.ubytovanieoaza.sk; Nová 65; per person 300Sk) Two-bed rooms with shared bathroom, and four-bed rooms with bathroom and kitchen, are just what the budget doctor ordered. There's a big garden (with lawn, caged chickens and vegetables) between the two parts of the house.

On the main square, choose between the self-catering friendly apartments (with a new lift) at **Penzión U Leva** (☎ 4502 311; www.uleva.sk; Nám Majstra Pavla 24; s/d 1100/2000Sk; P) or the swishy luxury of **Hotel Satel** (☎ 4512 943; www.hotelsatel .com; Nám Majstra Pavla 55; s/d 1765/2730Sk; P) in a 14th-century building.

Eating

Vegetarián (☎ 4514 576; Uhoľná 137; mains 45-90Sk; ☼ 10am-3.15pm Mon-Fri) Wholesome smells and a no-fuss menu make this basic veggie haunt a hit.

Reštaurácia u Janusa (☎ 4514 592; Klaštorská 22; mains 70-120Sk) Choose from all the fried pork favourites at this, the locals' pick for best Slovak food.

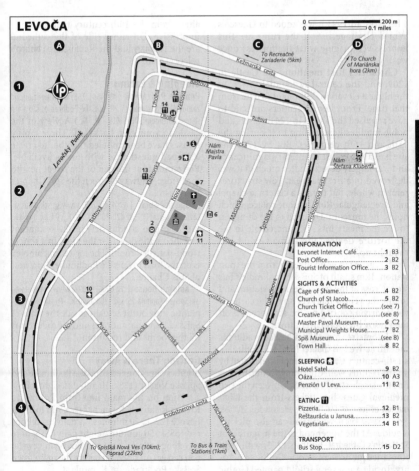

LEVOČA

	0	200 m
	0	0.1 miles

SLOVAKIA

INFORMATION	
Levonet Internet Café...........................1	B3
Post Office..2	B2
Tourist Information Office..................3	B2

SIGHTS & ACTIVITIES	
Cage of Shame.....................................4	B2
Church of St Jacob..............................5	B2
Church Ticket Office...................(see 7)	
Creative Art.................................(see 8)	
Master Pavol Museum........................6	C2
Municipal Weights House...................7	B2
Spiš Museum................................(see 8)	
Town Hall...8	B2

SLEEPING	
Hotel Satel...9	B2
Oáza..10	A3
Penzión U Leva..................................11	B2

EATING	
Pizzeria...12	B1
Reštaurácia u Janusa........................13	B2
Vegetarián..14	B1

TRANSPORT	
Bus Stop..15	D2

Pizzeria (☎ 0905396528; Vetrová 4; pizzas 100-160Sk)
For such a smoky, nameless place, the pizza's
really not bad.

Getting There & Away

Bus travel is pretty practical in the area as
there are frequent services to Spišské Podhradie (22Sk, 20 minutes, 11 daily) and to Poprad (40Sk, 30 minutes, 21 daily), which has
onward train connections. Two to five buses
a day wend their way to/from Košice (128Sk,
two hours). Buses also run to Spišská Nová
Ves (18Sk, 20 minutes, every 30 minutes),
where you can switch to the main Bratislava
to Košice train line. The local bus stop at Nám
Štefana Kluberta is a little closer to town than
the station, and most routes stop there.

SPIŠSKÉ PODHRADIE

☎ 053

Slovakia's most grandiose castle sits above a
bedraggled little town (big village). Not much
reason to come here except for Spiš Castle and
the Spiš Chapter ecclesiastical settlement on
either side.

Sights

From the motorway you catch glimpses of
eerie outlines and stony ruins crowning the
ridge on the eastern side of Spišské Podhradie. Can it really be that big? Indeed, **Spiš
Castle** (Spišský hrad; ☎ 4541 336; www.spisskyhrad.com
in Slovak; adult/student 100/60Sk; ☯ 9am-6pm May-Oct,
by appointment Nov-Apr), among the largest in
Eastern Europe, spreads over more than

SLOVAKIA

4 hectares. In 1993 it was added to Unesco's World Heritage list. If the ruins are this impressive, imagine what the fortress once was.

Chronicles first mention Spiš Castle in 1209, and the central residential tower, at the highest elevation, is thought to date from that time. From here defenders are said to have repulsed the Tatars in 1241. Rulers and noble families kept adding to it during the 15th and 16th centuries. But by 1780 the site had already lost its military significance and was largely deserted after much of it was destroyed in a fire that year. Few structures remain whole, but there's a cistern, a chapel and a rectangular Romanesque palace, which holds the museum. Descend to the dungeon to see the meaty bits – it's incredible to see the torture devices the human mind has thought up.

The castle is a good hike up from the train station, 1km south of Spišské Podhradie's bus stop. Cross at the tracks near the station and follow the yellow markers up to the castle. If you're driving or cycling, the access road is off the Prešov highway east of town.

A kilometre west of Spišské Podhradie sits the still active **Spiš Chapter** (Spišská Kapitula), a 13th-century Catholic complex encircled by a 16th-century wall. Charming Gothic houses line the single street running between the two medieval gates. Buy tickets from the **information office** (☎ 0907388411; adult/student 20/10Sk; ⏱ 11.15am-2.45pm), where you can also pick up a guide. At the upper end is the magnificent **St Martin's Cathedral**, built in 1273, with twin Romanesque towers and a Gothic sanctuary. Inside are several trifold painted Gothic altars from the 15th century that are quite impressive. On either side of the cathedral are the **seminary** and the Renaissance **bishop's palace** (1652).

Sleeping & Eating

Penzión Podzámok (☎ 4541 755; www.penzionpod zamok.sk; Podzámková 28, Spišské Podhradie; s/d with shared bathroom 300/650Sk; Ⓟ ⚘) A view of the castle in your own backyard. Three family houses have been cobbled together to create a 42-bed guesthouse with meals available. Podzámok is at the end of the street next to the bridge, halfway between the Spiš Chapter and Castle.

Spišsky Salaš (☎ 4541 202; www.spisskysalas.sk; Levočská cesta 11; s/d 420/800Sk; Ⓟ) What rustic fun! Dig into a lamb stew in the restaurant and then settle down for the night in a simple wood-panelled room. The log cabin complex is on the road to Spišské Podhradie, 3km west of Spiš Chapter.

Kolping House (☎ 0905790097; www.hotelkolping .sk; Spišská Kapitula 15; s/d 1100/1600Sk; Ⓟ ▣) A romantic little outfit actually inside the walls of Spišská Kapitula; antiques and reproductions fill the rooms and restaurant.

Getting There & Away

A railway line connects Spišské Podhradie and Spišské Vlachy (12Sk, 10 minutes, eight daily), a station on the main line from Poprad to Košice. Relatively frequent buses run to/from Levoča (22Sk, 20 minutes, 11 daily) and Poprad (55Sk, 50 minutes, eight daily). If you're travelling to Spiš Chapter by bus from Levoča, you can get off one stop before the main town Spišské Podhradie, at Kapitula.

TOP FIVE FORTRESSES

Castles and ruins abound in Slovakia. Pick up a national map, look for the ruin symbols and start hiking. You may find only a hearth, or you may find a room's outlines, but you're sure to have a good work-out and great views once you reach the crest. Here are the top-five formal castle sights to tour:

▪ This was the big one; the ruins of **Spiš Castle** (p475) spread out for what seems like forever.

▪ Walt Disney couldn't have invented a dreamier sight than **Bojnice Castle** (p464).

▪ **Devín Castle** (p461) has stood at the intersection of Slovakia, Austria and Hungary for a millennium.

▪ Be led by torch light by a medieval guide on a night tour of **Trenčín Castle** (p462)

▪ Climb up the tower of **Bratislava Castle** (p455) and you're at the highest vantage point in the old town.

SLOVENSKÝ RAJ
☎ 053

Rumbling waterfalls, steep gorges, sheer rock-faces, thick forests and hilltop meadows: **Slovenský raj** (Slovak Paradise; www.slovenskyraj.sk; admission 20Sk) is a national park for the passionately outdoorsy. Easier trails exist, but the one-way, ladder- and chain-assist ascents are the most dramatic. You cling to a metal rung headed straight up a precipice while an icy waterfall splashes and sprays a metre away, that's after you've scrambled horizontally across a log ladder to cross the stream down below. Pure exhilaration.

Orientation & Information
The nearest town of any size is the unattractive but almost unavoidable Spišská Nová Ves, 23km southeast of Poprad. The main trailheads on the northern edge of the national park are at Čingov, 5km west of Spišská Nová Ves and Podlesok, 1km southwest of Hrabušice. There are lodgings and eateries near northern trailheads, but for full town services, go into Spišská Nová Ves or Hrabušice. Dedinky, at the south end of the park, is a regular village with pub, supermarket, a lake and houses. Before you go trekking, make sure to buy VKÚ's 1:25,000 *Slovenský raj* hiking map (No 4), available at many tourist offices and bookshops countrywide.

EMERGENCY
Mountain Rescue Service (Horská Služba; emergency ☎ 183 00)

INTERNET ACCESS
Internet Klub (☎ 4414 402; Letná 4, Spišská Nová Ves; per hr 50Sk; ⏱ 9am-9pm)
Ascona Café (Hlavná 99, Hrabušice; per hr 25Sk; ⏱ 1pm-midnight Sun-Thu, to 3am Fri & Sat)

MONEY
It's best to procure money before you get to the park unless you're planning to stop in Spišská Nová Ves, where there's an ATM at the train station and at banks on the main square.

TOURIST INFORMATION
Your lodging place is usually your best source of information; orientation maps are posted near trailheads. **Tourist Information Centre** (☎ 4428 292; www.slovenskyraj.sk; Letná 49, Spišská Nová Ves; ⏱ 8am-5pm Mon-Fri, 9.30am-1.30pm Sat Jun-Sep, 8am-

4.30pm Mon-Fri Oct-May) Hit-or-miss help with area accommodation and info.
Tourist information (☎ 4299 854; Hlavná, Hrabušice; ⏱ 8am-6pm Jul & Aug, 8am-4pm Mon-Fri Sep-Jun) Small, summertime office.

Sights & Activities
Trails that include a one-way *roklina* (gorge) take at least a half day: the shortest, **Zejmarska Gorge** hike on a blue trail, starts at Biele Vody (25 minutes northeast of Dedinky on the red trail). The physically fit can run, clamber and climb up in 50 minutes; others huff and puff up in 90 minutes. To get back, you can follow the green trail down to Dedinky, or there's a **chairlift** (adult/student 30/15Sk; ⏱ 9am-5pm) that, if it's working, goes on the hour.

From Čingov a green trail leads up the **Hornád River Gorge** to **Letanovský mlyn** (1½ hours), from there the blue trail continues along the river to the base of the green, one-way, technically aided **Kláštorisko Gorge** hike (one hour). At **Kláštorisko chata** (☎ 4493 307; cabins per person 250Sk), there's a restaurant and small cabins (book ahead to make sure you have a place). From Kláštorisko you can follow another green trail back along the ridge towards Čingov. Allow at least six hours for the circuit, lunch at Kláštorisko included.

From Podlesok, an excellent day's hike heads up the **Suchá Belá Gorge** (with several steep ladders), then east to Kláštorisko on a yellow then red trail. From here, take the blue trail down to the Hornád River, then follow the river gorge upstream to return to Podlesok. Six to seven hours.

Six kilometres west of Dedinky is **Dobšinská Ice Cave** (Dobšinská Ľadová Jaskyňa; ☎ 7881 470; adult/student 150/130Sk; ⏱ 9am-4pm Tue-Sun Jun-Aug, 9.30am-2pm Tue-Sun May & Sep). The frozen formations are most dazzling in May, before they start to melt. Tours leave every hour or so.

Sleeping & Eating
Surrounding towns also have private rooms and pensions (a lot of which are listed at www.slovenskyraj.sk); those below are closer to the trails. All the park's lodgings have restaurants. From May to September there are food stands near the Podlesok trailhead parking lot; a Bila supermarket sits next to the bus station in Spišska Nová Ves.

Autocamp Podlesok (☎ 4299 165; slovrajbela@stonline .sk; Podlesok; per person/tent 60/60Sk, huts per person 230Sk; Ⓟ) Big, big, big. Pitch a tent in the field or

SPIŠSKÁ NOVÁ VES & SLOVENSKÝ RAJ

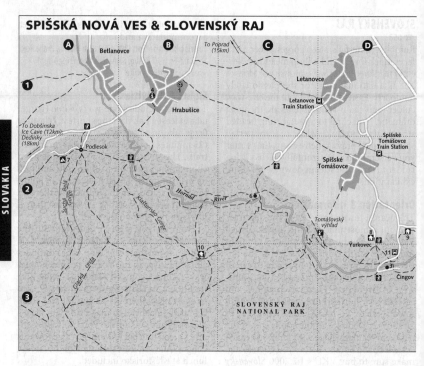

SLOVAKIA

choose from the A-frames, small huts or cottages with two to 12 beds and a bathroom. It's a 2km walk from Hrabušice.

Autocamping Tatran (☎ 4297 105; www.durkovec.sk; per person/tent 80/60Sk; dm 220Sk, 2-person hut with shared bathroom 190Sk; ⓟ ⒭) Tents crowd together in the pasture surrounded by tiny huts, a big dormitory and multiroom rental houses with satellite TV (2500Sk). Tromp 2km west of the Čingov bus stop.

Hotel Flora (☎ 4491 129; www.hotelfloraslovenskyraj .sk; Čingov; s/d 750/1200Sk; ⓟ) A renovation made the lobby and restaurant of this mountain hotel fabulous: stone fireplace, leather chairs, big windows. Food's good too. Pity the rooms didn't come along for the ride. It's 1km before the village.

Penzión Pastierňa (☎ 058-798 1175; Dedinky 42; per person from 300Sk; ⓟ) Small wooden guesthouse at the edge of Dedinky, near the forest and green trailhead.

Getting There & Around

You may want to consider springing for a car in Košice; connections aren't great. A few buses run directly from Poprad to Dedinky

(53Sk, 1¼ hours, three daily) and to Hrabušice (25Sk, 40 minutes, five on weekdays, one on weekends). Other than that, Spišska Nová Ves is the main transfer point for the Slovenský raj region; most buses go in the morning. There's a bus service to/from Poprad (40Sk, 45 minutes, eight daily), Levoča (18Sk, 20 minutes, every half hour) and Košice (117Sk, two to three hours, two daily).

From Spišska Nová Ves, two buses a day run to Hrabušice (22Sk, 35 minutes), two to the trailheads of Čingov (10Sk, 12 minutes) and three to Dedinky (53Sk, one hour).

BARDEJOV
☎ 054 / pop 33,400

All steep roofs and flat fronts, each main-square Gothic-Renaissance burgher's house is set apart by its particular pastel hue and intricate paint-and-plaster details. It may as well be the 15th century, this town has been so enthusiastically well preserved (there's always some scaffolding signalling upkeep somewhere). Unesco thought so too, adding it to the World Heritage list in 2000. Today the quiet square is the tourist draw, but there's

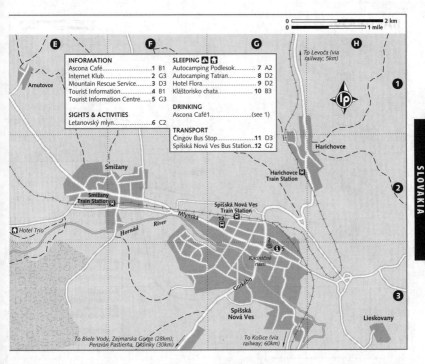

INFORMATION
Ascona Café...........................1 B1
Internet Klub.........................2 G3
Mountain Rescue Service........3 D3
Tourist Information...............4 B1
Tourist Information Centre......5 G3

SIGHTS & ACTIVITIES
Letanovský mlyn....................6 C2

SLEEPING
Autocamping Podlesok............7 A2
Autocamping Tatran...............8 D2
Hotel Flora............................9 D2
Kláštorisko chata..................10 B3

DRINKING
Ascona Café1......................(see 1)

TRANSPORT
Čingov Bus Stop....................11 D3
Spišská Nová Ves Bus Station..12 G2

Map labels: To Levoča (via railway; 5km); Arnutovce; Harichovce; Smižany; Harichovce Train Station; Smižany Train Station; Spišská Nová Ves Train Station; Mlynská; Hotel Trio; Hornád River; Radničné nám; Gorkého; Spišská Nová Ves; Lieskovany; To Biele Vody, Zejmarska Gorge (28km); Penzión Pastierňa, Dedinky (30km); To Košice (via railway; 60km)

SLOVAKIA

also an excellent icon museum that sheds light on this region's eastern-facing religion. A couple of kilometres north of town in Bardejovské Kúpele there's a hot spring spa inviting you to take a cure, and an open-air village museum waiting to be explored. Wooden churches in the area reflect the Carpatho-Rusyn heritage that the area shares with neighbouring parts of the Ukraine and Poland.

History

Bardejov received its royal charter in 1376, and grew rich on trade between Poland and Russia. After an abortive 17th-century revolt against the Habsburgs, Bardejov's fortunes declined. In late 1944 heavy WWII fighting took place at the Dukla Pass on the Polish border, 54km northeast of Bardejov, near Svidník (preserved WWII Soviet and German tanks still sit on the roadside and there's a military museum).

Orientation

The main square, Radničné nám, is a 600m walk southwest of the bus and train station. Some old town walls still encircle the city, enter through the gate off Slovenská at Baštová.

Information

ČSOB (Radničné nám 7) Bank and ATM.
Golem Internet Café (Radničné nám 25; per hr 25Sk; 9am-11pm Mon-Fri, 1-11pm Sat & Sun)
Main post office (Dlhý rad 14)
Tourist information centre (☎ 4744 003; www.e-bardejov.sk; Radničné nám 21; 9am-5.30pm Mon-Fri, 11.30am-3.30pm Sat & Sun May-Sep) Info, souvenirs and guide service.

Sights

There are two branches of the **Šariš Museum** (☎ 4724 966; www.muzeumbardejov.sk; adult/student 40/20Sk; 8am-noon & 12.30-4pm Tue-Sun) Housing altarpieces and a historical collection, the **town hall** (*radnica*) was built in 1509 and was the first Renaissance building in Slovakia. More than 130 dazzling icons from the 16th to 19th century make up the **Icon Exposition** (Expozícia ikony; Radničné nám 27). Originally they decorated Greek Catholic and Orthodox churches east of here.

The interior of the 15th-century **Basilica of St Egídius** (Bazilika Sv Egídia; adult/student 30/20Sk, tower 40/20Sk; 10am-3pm Mon-Fri, to 2pm Sat) is packed with no less than 11 Gothic altarpieces, built from 1460 to 1510.

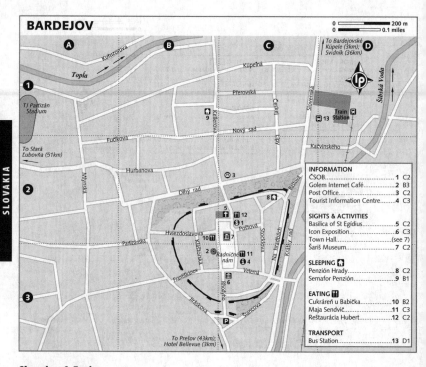

BARDEJOV

0 ——— 200 m
0 ——— 0.1 miles

To Bardejovské
Kúpele (3km);
Svidník (36km)

TJ Partizán
Stadium

To Stará
Ľubovňa (51km)

Kutuzovova

Topľa

Kúpeľná

Prerovská

Slovenská

Kellerova

České

Lipy

Kačvinského

Train
Station

Šibská Voda

Nový sad

Hurbanova

Dlhý rad

Fučíkova

Mlynská

Partizánska

Hviezdoslavova

Kláštorská

Poštová

Stöcklova

Na hradbách

Krátky rad

Radničné
nám

Veterná

Rhody

Frantíškov

Jiraškova

Stanova

To Prešov (43km);
Hotel Bellevue (3km)

INFORMATION	
ČSOB..	1 C2
Golem Internet Café........................	2 B3
Post Office..	3 C2
Tourist Information Centre............	4 C3

SIGHTS & ACTIVITIES	
Basilica of St Egídius......................	5 C2
Icon Exposition................................	6 C3
Town Hall....................................	(see 7)
Šariš Museum..................................	7 C2

SLEEPING	
Penzión Hrady..................................	8 C2
Semafor Penzión..............................	9 B1

EATING	
Cukráreň u Babička..........................	10 B2
Maja Sendvič....................................	11 C3
Reštaurácia Hubert..........................	12 C2

TRANSPORT	
Bus Station.......................................	13 D1

Sleeping & Eating

Ask at the information office about private rooms (from 300Sk a night).

Penzión Hrady (☎ 0903211865; www.penzionivana.sk; Stocklova 8; s/d/tr 495/750/880Sk; P) Want your hair cut? There's a salon across the hall in this busy building. Basic rooms, basic prices.

Penzión Semafor (☎ 0905830984; www.penzion semafor.sk; Kellerova 13; s/d 700/900Sk, ste 800/1100Sk; P) If the large, bright doubles are good, the 'apartments' (bigger rooms) are even better. All share a communal kitchen in this family-run guesthouse.

Hotel Bellevue (☎ 4728 404; www.bellevuehotel.sk; Mihalov 2503; s/d 2600/1900Sk; P ☒ ☒ ☐ ☒) This hotel on a hill is as close as the town comes to swank. From here you have a view from above, cherrywood beds, a pool and a full-service restaurant. It's 3km south of the city; take bus 8 from the train station.

Reštaurácia Hubert (Radničné nám 4; mains 100-169Sk; ☒ 10am-10pm Mon-Fri, 11am-3pm Sat & Sun) Game dishes and other meaty fare top the list in this cellar restaurant.

On the main square **Cukráreň u Babička** (Radničné nám 49; cakes 30-100Sk), back in a Renais-

sance arcade, serves pastries and cakes like your Slovak grandma used to make, and **Maja Sendvič** (☎ 091941064; Radničné nám 15; sandwiches 40-50Sk; ☒ 8am-8pm Mon-Thu, 8am-midnight Fri, 3-11pm Sat & Sun) has baguette sandwiches to go.

Getting There & Away

Buses run between Bardejov and Košice (100Sk, 1¾ hours, eight daily) and to/from Poprad (135Sk, 2½ hours, 12 daily).

AROUND BARDEJOV

Three short kilometres to the north, with frequent local bus connections, is the parklike spa town of **Bardejovské Kúpele**. If you want to book a service (mineral bath 200Sk, 15-minute massage 170Sk), you have to go in person to the **Spa House** (Kúpelny dom; ☎ 4774 225; ☒ 8am-noon & 1-5pm Mon-Sat) at the top of the main pedestrian street. Across the way is the **Museum of Folk Architecture** (Múzeum Ľudovej Architektúry; ☎ 4722 070; adult/student 40/20Sk; ☒ 9am-5pm Tue-Sun, to 3pm Oct-Apr). One of the nail-less wooden churches is among the many traditional buildings moved to this *skansen* (open-air village museum). Peer into the simple dwellings and see how rural folk lived. If you have a car, park in the lot by the bus station at the base of the village and walk up; the whole place is pedestrian-only.

Buy a *Wooden Churches Around Bardejov* booklet at the tourist information centre (p479) in Bardejov if you want to explore more of the area's Eastern vernacular architecture.

KOŠICE

☎ 055 / pop 235,006

Wander among the midday work crowd down the long town square, crane your neck to admire the massive Cathedral of St Elizabeth then head underground to explore the ancient city's archaeology. Come evening, gather with the rest of Košice on the benches near the musical fountain. With so many people out and about, Slovakia's second city has a real sense of cohesion and community that's missing in the capital. You get the feeling if you sat down for a beer at one of the many street festivals, you might actually make friends. Old town buildings range from 12th-century Gothic to 20th-century Art Nouveau. Why not spend a day or two and check it out?

History

Košice received its city coat of arms in 1369 and for many years was the eastern stronghold of the Hungarian Kingdom. Transylvanian prince Ferenc Rákóczi II had his headquarters at Košice during the Hungarian War of Independence against the Habsburgs (1703–11). On 5 April 1945 the Košice Government Program – which made communist dictatorship in Czechoslovakia a virtual certainty – was announced here. Today US Steel girders form the backbone of the city; you can't miss the company's influence – from the flare stacks to the brand new ice-hockey stadium it sponsored.

Orientation

The adjacent bus and train stations are just east of the old town. A five-minute walk along Mlynská brings you into Hlavná, which broadens to accommodate the squares of Nám Slobody and Hlavné nám.

Information

BOOKSHOPS

Art Forum (☎ 6232 677; Mlynská 6) Coffee-table pictorials and fiction in English, some even by Slovak authors.

BP Press (Hlavná 102; ☻ 7am-8pm Mon-Fri, 8am-8pm Sat & Sun) Foreign magazines and newspapers.

EMERGENCY

Police station (☎ 159; Pribinova 6)

INTERNET ACCESS

City Information Centre (☎ 6258 888; Hlavná 59; per hr 30Sk; ☻ 9am-6pm Mon-Fri, 9am-1pm Sat)

Net Club (Hlavná 9; per hr 50Sk; ☻ 9am-10pm) Fast connections.

MEDICAL SERVICES

Fakultná Nemocnica L Pasteura (☎ 6153 111; Rastislavova 45) Hospital.

MONEY

Ľudová Banka (Mlynská 29) ATM and exchange; between the centre and transport stations.

POST

Main post office (Poštová 18)

TOURIST INFORMATION

The train station and airport also have information stands.

Municipal Information Centre (MIC; ☎ 16 168; www.mickosice.sk) Tesco Department Store (Hlavná 111; ☻ 8am-8pm Mon-Fri, 8am-4.30pm Sat); Dargov Department Store (Hlavná 2; ☻ 8am-7pm) Small and personal, with a vibrant staff and tonnes of knick-knacks for sale.

City Information Centre (☎ 6258 888; www.kosice .sk; Hlavná 59; ☻ 9am-6pm Mon-Fri, 9am-1pm Sat) Large and busy; books galore. Runs information stands at the airport and train station with the same hours.

Sights

The dark and brooding 14th-century **Cathedral of St Elizabeth** (Dóm sv Alžbety; ☎ 0908667093; adult/student 70/35Sk; ☻ 1-5pm Mon, 9am-5pm Tue-Fri, 9am-1pm Sat) wins the prize for sight most likely to grace your Košice postcard home. You can't miss Europe's easternmost Gothic cathedral dominating the square. Below the church a **crypt** contains the tomb of Duke Ferenc Rákóczi, who was exiled to Turkey after the failed 18th-century Hungarian revolt against Austria. Don't forget to climb the church's **tower** for city views. To the south of the cathedral is the 14th-century **St Michael's Chapel** (adult/student 30/15Sk; ☻ 1-5pm Mon, 9am-5pm Tue-Fri, 9am-1pm Sat).

Get lost in the mazelike passages and tunnels of the **archaeological excavations** (☎ 6228393; adult/child 25/10Sk; ☻ 10am-6pm Tue-Sun), discovered

SLOVAKIA

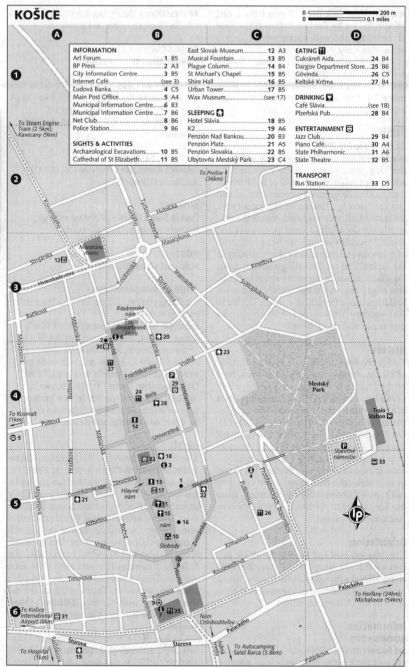

KOŠICE

0 — 200 m
0 — 0.1 miles

INFORMATION
Art Forum.............................. 1 B5
BP Press............................... 2 A3
City Information Centre........... 3 B5
Internet Café.....................(see 3)
Ľudová Banka....................... 4 C5
Main Post Office................... 5 A4
Municipal Information Centre...6 B3
Municipal Information Centre...7 B6
Net Club............................... 8 B6
Police Station........................ 9 B6

SIGHTS & ACTIVITIES
Archaeological Excavations....... 10 B5
Cathedral of St Elizabeth.......... 11 B5

East Slovak Museum............. 12 A3
Musical Fountain................... 13 B5
Plague Column...................... 14 B4
St Michael's Chapel............... 15 B5
Shire Hall............................. 16 B5
Urban Tower......................... 17 B5
Wax Museum....................(see 17)

SLEEPING
Hotel Slávia.......................... 18 B5
K2....................................... 19 A6
Penzión Nad Bankou............. 20 B3
Penzión Platz........................ 21 A5
Penzión Slovakia................... 22 B5
Ubytovňa Mestský Park......... 23 C4

EATING
Cukráreň Aida...................... 24 B4
Dargov Department Store...... 25 B6
Góvinda............................... 26 C5
Keltské Krčma....................... 27 B4

DRINKING
Café Slávia........................(see 18)
Plzeňská Pub........................ 28 B4

ENTERTAINMENT
Jazz Club.............................. 29 B4
Piano Café............................ 30 A4
State Philharmonic................ 31 A6
State Theatre........................ 32 B5

TRANSPORT
Bus Station........................... 33 D5

during building work in 1996. These are the buried remains of medieval Košice: defence chambers, fortifications and waterways.

To check out the **Urban Tower** (built in the 14th century, rebuilt in the 1970s) you have to buy entry to the cheesy **Wax Museum** (Múzeum voskových figurín; ☎ 6232 534; www.waxmuseum.sk; Hlavná 3; adult/student 120/80Sk; ⓥ noon-4pm Tue-Sun).

Don't miss the intriguing gold treasure in the basement vault of the **East Slovak Museum** (Východoslovenské múzeum; ☎ 6220 309; Hviezdoslavovo 3; adult/student 40/20Sk; ⓥ 9am-5pm Tue-Sat, 9am-1pm Sun). A secret stash of 2920 gold coins, dating from the 15th to 18th centuries, was discovered during the renovation of the house at Hlavná 68 in 1935. Anyone have a shovel?

Young and old gather on the benches in front of the **musical fountain** by the 1899 **State Theatre** (right).

North of the theatre is a large baroque **plague column** from 1723. The 1945 Košice Government Program was proclaimed from the 1779 **Shire Hall** (Župný dom; Hlavná 27); today there's a minor art gallery inside.

Sleeping

For available accommodation, the City Information Centre puts out a booklet that includes summer dorms and private rooms (both from 300Sk).

Kosmalt (☎ 6423 572; www.kosmalt.sk; Kysucká 16; s/d 590/630Sk; 🖳 Ⓟ) It's usually possible to find a room in this big apartment-block hostel with common game room, bar and restaurant. Antique elevators, tolerable rooms. Take tram 6 from the train/bus station to the Kino Družba stop.

Penzión Slovakia (☎ 7289 820; www.penzionslovakia .sk; Orlia 6; s 950-1150Sk, d 1350-1750) This small city guesthouse has loads of charm. Named after Slovak towns, the rooms have wood-panelled ceilings, skylights and midcentury mod furnishings in the apartments. Rosto Steakhouse grill restaurant, downstairs, is worth visiting in its own right.

Penzión Nad Bankou (☎ 6838 221; www.penzion nadbankou.holiday.sk; Kováčska 63; s/d 1000/1400Sk; Ⓟ) Whitewashed walls and pine furniture characterise the simple pension 'above a bank'. Through the owners you can arrange a light-aeroplane ride for 1950Sk.

Hotel Slávia (☎ 6224 395; www.hotelslavia.sk; Hlavná 63; s 2100-3050Sk, d 2700-3900Sk; Ⓟ 🍴 🖳) Colourful mosaic murals are the icing on this 1902 Art Nouveau cake. The flourish continues

inside with serpentine, flower-shape lights and candy-coloured pastels. Other options:

Ubytovňa Mestský Park (☎ 6333 904; www.uby tovna-ke.sk; Mestský Park 13; dm 220Sk) Workers hostel, mostly male guests.

K2 (☎ 6255 948; Štúrova 32; s/d with shared bathroom 350/700Sk) Hostel with bed-only singles and doubles that book up fast.

Penzión Platz (☎ 6223 450; www.platz.sk; Dominikán-ske nám 23; r 1500-1800Sk) It's a modular veneer world behind the pretty plaster façade.

Eating & Drinking

Dargov Department Store (Hlavná 2; mains 20-80Sk; ⓥ 7am-7pm Mon-Fri, 9am-5pm Sat, 9am-3pm Sun) The ground-floor cafeteria serves hot dishes – sausages, stuffed cabbage rolls – as well as sandwiches and salads. There's a supermarket too.

Góvinda (☎ 6200 428; Puškinova 8; mains 80-120Sk ⓥ noon-7pm Mon-Sat) Dive in to divine vegetarian Indian food at this small Hare Krishna eatery.

Keltské Krčma (Celtic Pub; ☎ 6225 328; Hlavná 80; mains 160-300Sk; ⓥ 10am-11.30pm Mon-Thu, to 1am Fri & Sat, 3-11.30pm Sun) Vaulted ceilings, ancient-looking masks and wood booths create a scene conducive to leisurely eating or drinking Celt style. The eclectic menu includes Slovak pork in an apricot sauce, English roast beef and Mexican enchiladas.

Plzeňská Pub (☎ 6220 402; Hlavná 92; ⓥ noon-midnight Mon-Thu, to 1am Fri-Sun) Czech beer on tap and roast pork and dumplings in the kitchen. Eat it in the beer garden out back.

Drink your coffee or cocktail in turn-of-the-20th-century style at **Café Slaviá** (☎ 6233 190; Hotel Slaviá, Hlavná 63; ⓥ 7am-11pm) or indulge in a creamy cake with your java down the street at **Cukráreň Aida** (☎ 6256 649; Hlavná 81; snacks 30-100Sk; ⓥ 8am-10pm). Ice cream for breakfast, yum.

Entertainment

The monthly publication *Kam do Mesta* (www.kamdomesta.sk) lists in Slovak the whats, wheres and whens of Košice's entertainment scene.

State Theatre (Štátne Divadlo Košice; ☎ 6221 231; www.sdke.sk; Hlavná 58; box office ⓥ 9am-5.30pm Mon-Fri, 10am-1pm Sat) This 1899 neobaroque theatre stages operas, ballets and dramas from September to May.

State Philharmonic Košice (Štátna Filharmónia Košice; ☎ 6224 514; www.sfk.sk; Moyzesova 66) The city's principal orchestra has extra performances in May during the spring music festival.

SLOVAKIA

DJs spin house most nights at both at the **Jazz Club** (☎ 6224 237; Kováčska 39; ☼ 11am-midnight Mon-Thu, 11am-2am Fri, 4pm-2am Sat, 4pm-midnight Sun) and at the **Piano Café** (☎ 0915517339; Hlavná 92; ☼ 10am-midnight Mon-Thu, 10am-1am Fri, 3pm-1am Sat, 3pm-midnight Sun). But each occasionally has live jazz.

Shopping

Wander onto the alleylike Hrnčiarska for some truly unique shopping. Along this 'craftsman' street there's a potter's shop, an iron-works master, a herbalist and a gemstone artist, among others.

Getting There & Away

AIR

Košice International airport (KSC; ☎ 6221 093; www .airportkosice.sk) is about 6km southwest of the centre. **Sky Europe** (☎ reservations 02-4850 4850; www .skyeurope.com) has two or three daily flights to/ from Bratislava (one hour) that may set you back as little as 500Sk oneway with tax, if you book ahead. **Czech Airlines** (ČSA; ☎ 6782 490; www .czechairlines.com) has three daily flights to and from Prague. For more on getting to Košice from outside Eastern Europe see (p596)

BUS

Buses wend their way to/from Levoča (117Sk, 2½ hours, two daily), Bardejov (98Sk, 1¾ hours, eight daily) and Poprad (134Sk, 2½ hours, four daily). Buses also travel to Uzhhorod in Ukraine (140Sk, 2½ hours) at least once a day (twice from Tuesday to Sunday) and to Nowy Targ in Poland (180Sk, four hours) Thursday and Saturday. A bus goes from Košice to Miskolc (120Sk, two hours), in Hungary, on Wednesday, Friday and Saturday.

CAR

There are several big international chain car rental representatives at the airport, but **Alimex** (☎ 7290 100; www.alimex.sk; Košice International airport) is cheaper, especially if you're willing to drive around with adverts painted on the car (as little as 699Sk per day, unlimited kilometres).

TRAIN

Express trains run to/from Poprad (154Sk, 1¼ hours, up to 10 daily) and Žilina (316Sk, 2¾ hours, 14 daily). If you're commuting all the way to/from Bratislava, an IC or EC train (518Sk, 5½ hours, four daily) is your best bet; otherwise you could crawl along for more than seven hours with no dining car. For domestic schedules visit www.zsr.sk.

A sleeper train leaves Košice every morning for Kyiv in Ukraine (913Sk, 22½ hours), stopping at Čop (193Sk, 2½ hours), 14km from Uzhhorod. Two trains (one overnight) a day head for Prague in the Czech Republic (1140Sk, 11 hours), two for Budapest in Hungary (967Sk, four hours) and three for Kraków in Poland (844Sk, 6½ hours).

Getting Around

Transport tickets (12Sk, one zone) are good for buses and trams in most of the city; buy them from newsstands and public transport kiosks and validate on board. Bus 23 between the airport and the train station requires a two-zone ticket (19Sk).

SLOVAKIA DIRECTORY

ACCOMMODATION

For every season there is a price: May to September is considered tourist season, but prices top out around the Christmas/New Year and Easter holidays. From October to April, rates drop dramatically (10% to 50%). We quote tourist season prices. Reviews in this chapter are ordered according to price. There's a tourist tax of 30Sk.

For more lodging options in Bratislava, see www.lonelyplanet.com. Note that non-smoking rooms are not yet common outside the capital.

Camping

Most camping grounds open from May to September and are often accessible on public transport. Many have a restaurant and assorted cheap cabins. Wild camping is generally prohibited in national parks.

Hostels

Outside Bratislava there are no backpacker-style hostels in Slovakia. Student dormitories throughout the country open to tourists in July and August. If you're looking for cheap sleeps outside those months, *ubytovňa* is the word to know. These are hostels for workers (in cities) or Slovak tourists (near natural attractions) that usually have basic, no-nonsense shared-bathroom singles and doubles or bunks.

Private Rooms, Pensions & Hotels

Tourist towns usually have private rooms for rent; look for signs reading '*privát*' or '*zimmer frei*' (from 1100Sk in Bratislava, 300Sk elsewhere). Information offices may have lists of renters.

Pensions are family-run B&Bs, or bigger inns, that have fewer services but more character than hotels. Outside the capital, hotels are often still institutional, communist leftovers. At both, breakfast is usually either included in the rate or can be added on for 80Sk to 200Sk.

ACTIVITIES

Slovakia is one of Eastern Europe's best areas for hiking: see the Malá Fatra (p464), High Tatras (p467) and Slovenský raj (p477). There's also excellent rock climbing and mountain biking in the High Tatras. See the Starý Smokovec section (p469).

The country has some of Europe's cheapest ski resorts. The season runs from December to April in the High Tatras and Malá Fatra. Ski hire starts at 299Sk per day.

BUSINESS HOURS

Restaurants nationwide are generally open from 10am to 10pm. Stand-alone shops open around 9am and close at 5pm or 6pm weekdays and at noon on Saturday. The local *potraviny* (supermarket) hours are from 6.30am or 7am until 5pm or 6pm Monday to Friday and from 7am to noon on Saturday. Big-name chain grocery and department stores (Tesco, Billa etc) have longer hours, typically until 9pm for downtown branches and 24 hours for suburban hyper-markets.

Bank hours are open from about 8am to 5pm Monday to Thursday, and until 4pm Friday. Post offices work from about 8am to 7pm Monday to Friday and until 11am Saturday.

Most museums and castles are closed on Monday. Many tourist attractions outside the capital open only from May to September.

DANGERS & ANNOYANCES

Crime is low compared with the West, but pickpocketing does happen. Just be aware. Never leave anything on the seat of an unattended vehicle, even a locked one; apparently that's just advertising that you don't want it any more.

DISABLED TRAVELLERS

Slovakia is behind many EU countries in terms of facilities for the disabled. Few hotels and restaurants have ramps or barrier-free rooms.

Slovak Union for the Disabled (Slovenský zväz telesne postihnutých; ☎ 02-6381 4478; www.sztp.sk) is fighting to change the status quo.

EMBASSIES & CONSULATES
Slovak Embassies & Consulates

Australia (☎ 02 6290 1516; www.slovakemb-aust.org; 47 Culgoa Circuit, O'Malley, Canberra, ACT 2606)

Austria (☎ 01-318 905 5200; www.vienna.mfa.sk; Armbrustergasse 24, 1-1190 Wien)

Canada (☎ 613-749 4442; www.ottawa.mfa.sk; 50 Rideau Terrace, Ottawa, Ontario K1M 2A1)

Czech Republic (☎ 233 113 051; www.praha.mfa.sk; Pod Hradbami 1, 160 00 Praha 6)

France (☎ 01-44 14 56 00; www.amb-slovaquie.fr; 125 Rue de Ranelagh, 75016 Paris)

Germany (☎ 030-8892 6 200; www.botschaft-slowakei .de; Fredrichstrasse 60, Berlin 10707)

Hungary (☎ 01-460 9010; www.budapest.mfa.sk; Stéfania út 22-24, H-1143 Budapest XIV)

Ireland (☎ 01-660 0012; www.dublin.mfa.sk; 20 Clyde Rd, Ballsbridge, Dublin 4)

UK (☎ 020-7313 6470; www.slovakembassy.co.uk; 25 Kensington Palace Gardens, London W8 4QY)

USA (☎ 202-237 1054; www.slovakembassy-us.org; 3523 International Court NW, Washington, DC 20008)

Embassies & Consulates in Slovakia

Australia and New Zealand do not have embassies in Slovakia; the nearest are in Vienna and Berlin respectively. The following are all in Bratislava (area code ☎ 02).

Austria (Map p456; ☎ 5443 1443; www.embassy austria.skwww.mzv.cz/bratislava/; Ventúrska 10)

Czech Republic (Map p456; ☎ 5920 3303; Hviezdoslavovo nám 8)

France (Map p456; ☎ 5934 7111; www.france.sk; Hlavné nám 7)

Germany (Map p456; ☎ 5920 4400; www.german embassy.sk; Hviezdoslavovo nám 10)

Ireland (Map p456; ☎ 5930 9611; bratislava@iveagh .irlgov.ie; Carlton Savoy Bldg, Mostová 2)

Poland (Map p453; ☎ 5441 3174; Hummelova 4)

UK (Map p456; ☎ 5998 2000; www.polskevelyys lanectvo.sk; Panská 16)

USA (Map p456; ☎ 5443 0861; www.britishembassy.sk; www.usembassy.sk; Hviezdoslavovo nám 4)

FESTIVALS & EVENTS

During summer months folk festivals take place all over Slovakia. In late June or early

July folk dancers and musicians from all over Slovakia gather at the biggest, the **Východná Folklore Festival** (www.obec-vychodna.sk in Slovak), 32km west of Poprad. The two-week **Bratislava Music Festival** (Bratislavské hudobné slánosti; ☎ 02-5443 4546; www.bhsfestival.sk in Slovak) is held in late September to early October, and the **Bratislava Jazz Days** (Bratislavských jazzových dní'; ☎ 02-5293 1572; www .bjd.sk) swings one weekend in September. The **Slovak Spectator** (www.slovakspectator.sk) newspaper lists events countrywide.

HOLIDAYS

New Year's & Independence Day 1 January
Three Kings Day 6 January
Good Friday & Easter Monday March/April
Labour Day 1 May
Victory over Fascism Day 8 May
Cyril & Methodius Day 5 July
SNP Day 29 August
Constitution Day 1 September
Our Lady of Sorrows Day 15 September
All Saints' Day 1 November
Christmas 24 to 26 December

INTERNET RESOURCES

The **Slovak Tourism Board's website** (www.slova kiatourism.sk) boasts about the country's attractions. **Slovakia Document Store** (www.panorama.sk) contains links to a wealth of Slovakia-related stuff; including books you can buy from abroad. **What's On Slovakia** (www.whatsonslovakia .com) lists events. You can check on the news from Slovakia at www.slovensko.com, get the low-down on exhibits nationwide at www .muzeum.sk and find yourself at the Slovak map site www.kompas.sk.

MONEY

Slovakia's currency is the Slovak crown, or Slovenská koruna (Sk), containing 100 halier (hellers). There are coins of 50 hellers, and one, two, five and 10 crowns (Sk). Banknotes come in denominations of 20, 50, 100, 200, 500, 1000 and 5000 crowns.

Almost all banks have exchange desks and there are usually branches in or near a town's old town square. ATMs are quite common even in smaller towns, but shouldn't be relied upon in villages. Main banks include the **Všeobecná úverová banka** (VUB; General Credit Bank; www.vub.sk) and the **Slovenská sporiteľňa** (Slovak Savings Bank; www.slsp.sk).

In Bratislava, credit cards are widely accepted. Elsewhere, Visa and MasterCard are accepted at most hotels, at some shops and at higher category restaurants (if you announce before requesting the bill that you plan to pay with credit).

If you stay in hostels, eat your meals in local pubs and take local transport, and you can expect to spend €25 to €45 a day in Bratislava (€20 to €30 elsewhere). Double this amount if you are looking to bed down in pensions and dine in smarter eateries. Some businesses quote prices in euros; prices in this chapter reflect the quotes of individual businesses.

POST

Poste restante sent to Bratislava (c/o Poste restante, 81000 Bratislava 1), can be picked up at the Main Post Office (p454) and will be kept for one month.

TELEPHONE
Phone Codes

Slovakia's country code is ☎ 421. When dialling from abroad, you need to drop the zero on city area codes and mobile phone numbers. To dial internationally from inside Slovakia, dial ☎ 00, the country code and the number.

Mobile phone numbers are often used for business and generally start with ☎ 09. If you are calling a Slovak mobile phone from abroad, drop the initial zero.

Phonecards

Most payphones require *telefónna karta* (telephone cards), which you can purchase from newsagents, for local calls. International phone cards, like **EZ Phone** (www.ezcard.sk; per min to UK & USA 2Sk) can also be bought there. Both of these cards are easy to mistake for mobile phone credit, so pay attention to what you're buying.

TOURIST INFORMATION

The **Association of Information Centres of Slovakia** (AiCES; ☎ 16 186; www.aices.sk) is an extensive network of city information centres. There's no Slovakiawide information office; your best bet is to go online to the **Slovak Tourist Board** (www .slovakiatourism.sk).

EMERGENCY NUMBER

■ Ambulance, Fire, Police ☎ 112

VISAS

Slovakia joined the EU in May 2004. Citizens of other EU countries, Australia, New Zealand, Canada, Japan and the US can enter visa-free for up to 90 days. South Africans do need a visa. For a full list, see www.mzv .sk, under Ministry and then Travel. If you do require a visa, it must be bought in advance – they are not issued on arrival.

TRANSPORT IN SLOVAKIA

GETTING THERE & AWAY

Air

Bratislava's small airport receives flights from more than 20 cities across the Continent. **Czech Airlines** (ČSA; ☎ 02-5296 1042; www.czechairlines .com) flies to Prague three times per day. **Slovak Airlines** (☎ 02-4870 4870; www.slovakairlines.sk) flies to Moscow weekly in conjunction with Aeroflot. **SkyEurope Airlines** (☎ 02-4850 4850; www .skyeurope.com) connects Bratislava a couple of times a week to Split, Zadar and Dubrovnik in Croatia, Sofia and Burgas in Bulgaria, and Bucharest in Romania.

For more on getting to Slovakia from outside Eastern Europe, see the Regional Directory chapter (p596).

Vienna's international airport is just 60km from Bratislava, and is served by a vast range of international flights. Buses connect to Bratislava hourly.

Land

BUS

Eurolines (☎ 02-5556 7349; www.eurolines.sk) runs buses between Bratislava and Prague (410Sk, four hours, three daily) and Bratislava and Budapest (570Sk, 3½ hours, one daily). Other international lines heading east do so from Košice (p484).

For more on getting to Bratislava by bus from further afield see the Regional Directory chapter (p599).

CAR & MOTORCYCLE

As well as your vehicle's registration papers, you need a 'green card', which shows you are covered by at least third-party liability insurance. Your vehicle must display a nationality sticker and carry a first-aid kit and warning triangle.

TRAIN

Direct trains connect Bratislava with Prague (655Sk, 4½ hours, six daily), Budapest (486Sk, three hours, seven daily) and Vienna (297Sk, one hour, 30 daily). Night departure trains link Bratislava with Moscow (2738Sk, 32½ hours, one daily) and Warsaw (1410Sk, 10½ hours, one daily). A daily train to Kyiv (1913Sk, 21 hours, one daily) passes through Košice on its way from Budapest.

River

For more on the boats that link Bratislava with Vienna and Budapest from April to September, see p460.

GETTING AROUND

Bicycle

Roads are often narrow and potholed and in towns cobblestones and tram tracks can prove dangerous. Theft's a problem, so a lock is a must. You can hire bikes in popular biking areas like the High Tatras. The cost of transporting a bike by rail is usually 10% of the train ticket.

Bus

National buses run by **Slovenská autobusová doprava** (SAD; www.eurolines.sk) are comparably priced to trains, but less convenient for the bigger cities in this chapter. Buses are quite useful in East Slovakia, however. To search for schedules, go to www.busy.sk; it's in Slovak, but is decipherable if you remember *odkiaľ* means 'from', *kam* means 'to', and *vyhľadať* means 'search' (click it a second time after the error-looking message comes up). When looking at bus schedules in terminals, beware of the footnotes (many fewer buses go on weekends). It's helpful to know that *premáva* means 'it operates' and *nepremáva* means 'it doesn't operate'.

Car & Motorcycle

DRIVING LICENCE

All foreign driving licences with photo ID are valid in Slovakia.

HIRE

Both Bratislava and Košice airports have several international and local car rental agencies.

ROAD RULES

In order to use Slovakia's motorways (denoted by green signs) all vehicles must have a motorway sticker (*nálepka*), which should be displayed in the windscreen. Rental cars

SLOVAKIA

come with them. You can buy stickers at border crossings, petrol stations or Satur offices (100Sk for 15 days, 600Sk for a year, both for vehicles up to 1.5 tonnes).

Parking restrictions are eagerly enforced with bright orange tyre boots. Always buy a ticket, either from a machine, or from the attendant wandering around with a waist pack, and put it on your dashboard.

Local Transport

City buses and trams operate from around 4.30am to 11.30pm daily. Tickets are sold at public transport offices and at newsstands. In Bratislava, some stops have ticket-vending machines. Validate tickets in the red machines on board or you could face a fine of up to 1400Sk.

Train

Slovak Republic Railways (Železnice Slovenskej Republiky or ŽSR; ☎ 18 188; www.zsr.sk) provides a cheap and efficient rail service. Most of the places covered in this chapter are on or near the main railway line between Bratislava and Košice.

Slovenia

It's a tiny place – there's no doubt about that – with a surface area of just over 20,000 sq km and only 2 million people. But 'good things come in small packages', and never was that old chestnut more appropriate than in describing Slovenia (Slovenija), an independent republic bordering Italy, Austria, Hungary and Croatia.

Slovenia has been dubbed a lot of different things by its PR machine – 'Europe in Miniature', 'The Sunny Side of the Alps', 'The Green Piece of Europe' – and they're all true. Slovenia has everything, from beaches, snowcapped mountains, hills awash in grapevines and wide plains blanketed in sunflowers, to Gothic churches, baroque palaces and Art Nouveau civic buildings. Its incredible mixture of climates brings warm Mediterranean breezes up to the foothills of the Alps, where it can snow in summer. And with more than half of its total area covered in forest, Slovenia truly is one of the 'greenest' countries in the world. And in recent years it really has become Europe's activities playground.

Among Slovenia's greatest assets, though, are the Slovenes themselves – welcoming, generous, multilingual and broad-minded.

SLOVENIA

FAST FACTS

- **Area** 20,273 sq km
- **Capital** Ljubljana
- **Currency** euro (€); A$1 = €0.58; ¥100 = €0.67; NZ$1 = €0.47; UK£1 = €1.44; US$1 = €0.78
- **Famous for** mountain sports, Lipizzaner horses, ruby red Teran wine
- **Official Language** Slovene; English, Italian and German widely spoken
- **Phrases** *dober dan* (hello), *živijo* (hi), *prosim* (please), *hvala* (thank you), *oprostite* (excuse me), *nasvidenje* (goodbye)
- **Population** 2 million
- **Telephone Codes** country code ☎ 386; international access code ☎ 00; ☎ toll free ☎ 080
- **Visas** not required for most nationalities; see p522

HIGHLIGHTS

- Experience the architecture, hilltop castle, green spaces and vibrant nightlife of **Ljubljana** (p493), Slovenia's 'Beloved' capital.
- Be astounded at the impossibly picture-postcard setting of **Bled** (p504): the lake, the island, the hilltop castle as backdrop.
- Get outdoors in the majestic mountain scenery at **Bovec** (p509), arguably the country's best outdoor-activities centre.
- Explore theThe series of karst cave at **Škocjan** (p512) that look straight out of Jules Verne's *A Journey to the Centre of the Earth*.
- Swoon in the romantic Venetian port of **Piran** (p515), with great restaurants, and the nearby resort of **Portorož** (p518).

ITINERARIES

- **Three days** Enjoy a long weekend in Ljubljana, sampling the capital's museums and nightlife, with an excursion to Bled.
- **One week** Spend a couple of days in Ljubljana, then head northward to unwind in Bohinj or romantic Bled beside idyllic mountain lakes. Depending on the season take a bus or drive over the hair-raising Vršič Pass into the valley of the vivid blue Soča River and take part in some extreme sports in Bovec or Tolmin before returning to Ljubljana.
- **Two weeks** As above, adding a trip to the coast – Koper and, of course, Piran – via Škocjan or perhaps a journey to both Postojna and Predjama.

CLIMATE & WHEN TO GO

The ski season lasts mainly from December to March, though avalanche risks can keep the Vršič Pass closed as late as May. Lake Bled freezes over in winter, but the short coastline has a mild, almost Mediterranean climate. April is often wet, but accommodation is cheaper then, and the flower-carpeted meadows and forests are at their scenic best. May and June are warmer, but during summer hotel prices start to rise, peaking in August, when rooms can be hard to come by at any price in certain parts of the country. Moving into autumn, warm September days are calm and ideal for hiking and climbing, while October and November can be damp. See climate charts on p586.

HOW MUCH?

- **100km by bus/train** €9/5.50
- **Bicycle rental (one day)** €4.7020 to €5.45
- **Bottle of ordinary/quality Slovenian wine** €4.20/8.35
- **Cup of coffee in a café** €0.85
- **Ski pass (one day)** €20.20

LONELY PLANET INDEX

- **Litre of petrol** €1 to €1.05
- **Litre of water** €0.6045 to €0.70
- **Half-litre of local beer** €0.9575 to €1.10 (shop), €1.70 to €2.30 (bar)
- **Souvenir T-shirt** € 10€8.35 to €12.50
- **Street snack (burek)** €1.90 to €2.2050

HISTORY

Slovenes can make a credible claim to have invented democracy. By the early 7th century their Slavic forebears had founded the Duchy of Carantania based at Krn Castle (now Karnburg in Austria). Ruling dukes were elected by ennobled commoners and invested with power before ordinary citizens. This model was noted by the 16th-century French political theorist Jean Bodin, whose work was a key reference for Thomas Jefferson when writing the American Declaration of Independence. Carantania (later Carinthia) was fought over by Franks and Magyars from the 8th to 10th centuries, and later divided up among Austro-Germanic nobles and bishops, who protected themselves within ever-multiplying castles. By 1335 Carantania and most of present-day Slovenia, with the exception of the Venetian-controlled coastal towns, were dominated by the Habsburgs.

Indeed, Austria ruled what is now Slovenia until 1918, apart from a brief but important interlude when Napoleonic France claimed the area among its half-dozen 'Illyrian Provinces' (1809–13) and made Ljubljana the capital. Though he razed many castles, Napoleon proved a popular conqueror, as his relatively liberal regime de-Germanised the education system. Slovene was taught in schools for the first time, leading to a blossoming of national

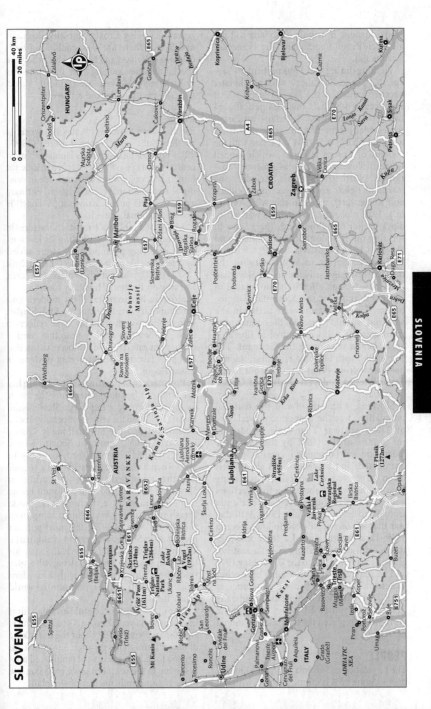

consciousness. In tribute, Ljubljana still has a French Revolution Square (Trg Francoske Revolucije).

Fighting during WWI was particularly savage along the Soča Valley – what would later become known as the Isonzo Front, which was occupied by Italy then dramatically retaken by German-led Austrian-Hungarian forces. Many fighters' tunnels are still visible around Kobarid (p510). WWI ended with the collapse of Austria-Hungary, which handed western Slovenia to Italy as postwar reparations. Northern Carinthia, including the towns of Beljak and Celovec (now Villach and Klagenfurt), voted to stay with Austria in a 1920 plebiscite. What little was left of Slovenia joined fellow south (*jug*) Slavs in forming the Kingdom of Serbs, Croats and Slovenes, later Yugoslavia.

Nazi occupation in WWII was for the most part courageously resisted by Slovenian partisans, though after Italy capitulated in 1943 the anti-partisan Slovenian Domobranci (Home Guards) were active in the west and, in a bid to prevent the communists from gaining political control in liberated areas, began supporting the Germans. The war ended with Slovenia regaining Italian-held areas from Piran to Bovec, but losing Trst (Trieste) and part of divided Gorica (Gorizia).

Slovenia, with only 8% of the national population, was the economic powerhouse of Tito's postwar Yugoslavia, producing up to 20% of the GDP. By the 1980s the federation was becoming increasingly Serb-dominated, and Slovenes, who already felt taken for granted economically, feared losing their political autonomy. After free elections and careful planning, Slovenia broke away from Yugoslavia on 25 June 1991. A 10-day war that left 66 people dead followed; rump Yugoslavia swiftly signed a truce in order to concentrate on bashing Croatia instead. Slovenia was admitted to the UN in May 1992 and in May 2004, together with nine other 'accession' countries, became a member of the EU. In January 2007 Slovenia became the first of these 10 new EU states to adopt the euro, which replaced the tolar as the national currency.

PEOPLE

The population of Slovenia is largely homogeneous. Some 83% is ethnic Slovene, with the remainder being Croats, Serbians, Bosnians and Roma; there are also small, long-term enclaves of Italians and Hungarians, who have special deputies looking after their interests in Parliament. Slovenes are ethnically Slavic, typically multilingual and extroverts.

ARTS

Far and away Slovenia's best-loved writer is the Romantic poet France Prešeren (1800–49), whose statue commands Ljubljana's most central square (p498). Prešeren's patriotic yet humanistic verse was a driving force in raising Slovene national consciousness. Fittingly a stanza of his poem *Zdravljica* (A Toast) is now the national anthem.

Many of Ljubljana's most characteristic architectural features, including its idiosyncratic recurring pyramid motif, were added by celebrated Slovenian architect Jože Plečnik (1872–1957), who cut his professional teeth working on Prague's Hradčany Castle.

Slovenia has some excellent modern and contemporary artists, including Rudi Skočir, whose Klimt-with-muscles style reflects a taste for Viennese Art Nouveau that continues to permeate day-to-day Slovenian interior design. A favourite sculptor-cum-designer is Oskar Kogoj.

Postmodernist painting and sculpture has been more or less dominated since the 1980s by the multimedia group Neue Slowenische Kunst (NSK) and the artists' cooperative Irwin. It also spawned the internationally known industrial-music group Laibach, whose leader, Tomaž Hostnik, died tragically in 1983 when he hanged himself from a *kozolec* (see the boxed text, p507), the traditional Slovenian hayrack. Slovenia's vibrant music scene embraces rave, techno, jazz, punk, thrash-metal and *chanson* (torch songs from the likes of Vita Mavrič); the most popular rock band in Slovenia at present is Siddharta. There's also a folk-music revival: listen for the groups Katice and Katalena, who play traditional Slovene music with a modern twist. Terra Folk is the quintessential world music band.

One of the most successful Slovenian films in recent years was Damjan Kozole's *Rezerni Deli* (Spare Parts; 2003) about the trafficking of illegal immigrants through Slovenia from Croatia to Italy by a couple of embittered misfits living in the southern town of Krško, site of the nation's only nuclear power plant.

ENVIRONMENT

Slovenia is amazingly green; indeed, 57% of its total surface area is covered in forest. It is home to some 3200 plant species – some 70 of which are endemic. Triglav National Park (p504) is particularly rich in indigenous flowering plants. Living deep in karst caves, the endemic 'living fossil' *Proteus anguinus* is a blind salamander that can survive for years without eating (see the boxed text, p511).

FOOD & DRINK

It's relatively hard to find such archetypal Slovenian foods as *žlikrofi* ('ravioli' filled with cheese, bacon and chives) served with *bakalca*, a lamb-based goulash, *mlinci* (corn pancakes) often served with goose and *ajdovi žganci z ocvirki* (buckwheat porridge with the savoury pork crackling/scratchings). An inn (*gostilna* or *gostišče)* or restaurant (*restavracija)* more frequently serves pizza, *rižota* (risotto), *klobasa* (sausage), *zrezek* (cutlet/steak), *golaž* (goulash) and *paprikaš* (piquant chicken or beef 'stew'). Fish (*riba*) is usually priced by the *dag* (100gdecagram or 0.1kg). Freshwater trout (*postrv)* generally costs half the price of other sea fish, though grilled squid (*lignji na žaru*) doused in garlic butter is a ubiquitous bargain at around €6.25 per plate.

Also common are Balkan favourites, such as *cevapčiči* (spicy meatballs of beef or pork), *pleskavica* (meat patties) and *ražnjiči* (shish kebabs). Add €1.50 to €2.10 for the *krompir* (potatoes).

You can snack cheaply on takeaway pizza slices or slabs of *burek* (€1.90 to €2.50), flaky pastry sometimes stuffed with meat but more often cheese or even apple. Alternatives include *štruklji* (cottage-cheese dumplings) and *palačinke* (thin sweet pancakes).

Some restaurants have bargain-value *dnevno kosilo* (four-course lunch menus), including *juha* (soup) and *solata* (salad), for around €6.25. This can be less than the price of a cheap main course, and usually one option will be vegetarian.

Tap water is safe to drink; people drink it everywhere. Distinctively Slovenian wines (*vino*) include peppery red Teran made from Refošk grapes in the Karst region and Cviček, a dry light red – almost rosé – wine from eastern Slovenia. Slovenes are justly proud of their top vintages, but cheaper bar-standard 'open wine' (*odprto vino*) sold by the decilitre (0.1L) are often pure rot-gut.

TOP FIVE CAFÉS

- **Café Teater**, Piran (p518)
- **Kavarna Cacao**, Portorož (p518)
- **Kavarna Zvezda**, Ljubljana (p501)
- **Loggia Café**, Koper (p515)
- **Slaščičarna Šmon**, Bled (p506)

Beer (*pivo*), whether *svetlo* (lager) or *temno* (dark), is best on draught (*točeno*).

There are dozens of kinds of *žganje* (fruit brandy) available, including *češnovec* (made with cherries), *sadjavec* (mixed fruit), *brinjevec* (juniper), *hruška* (pears, also called *viljamovka*) and *slivovka* (plums).

Na zdravje! (Cheers!).

LJUBLJANA

☎ 01 / pop 254,200

Ljubljana is by far and away Slovenia's largest and most populous city. It is also the nation's political, economic and cultural capital. In many ways, though, the city whose name almost means 'beloved' (*ljubljena*) in Slovene does not feel like an industrious municipality of national importance but a pleasant, self-contented town with responsibilities only to itself and its citizens. You might think that way, too, especially in spring and summer when café tables fill the narrow streets of the Old Town and street musicians entertain passers-by on Čopova ul and Prešernov trg. Then Ljubljana becomes a little Prague without the heavy crowds or a Paris without the attitude. The Slovenian capital may lack the grandeur or big-name attractions of those two cities, but the great museums and galleries, atmospheric bars and varied, accessible nightlife make it a great place to visit and stay awhile.

HISTORY

If Ljubljana really was founded by Jason and the Golden Fleece–stealing Argonauts as the city would have you believe, they left no proof of their stay. However, legacies of the Roman city of Emona – remnants of walls, dwellings and early churches – can still be seen throughout the city. Ljubljana more or less took its present form as Laibach under the Austrian Habsburgs,

SLOVENIA

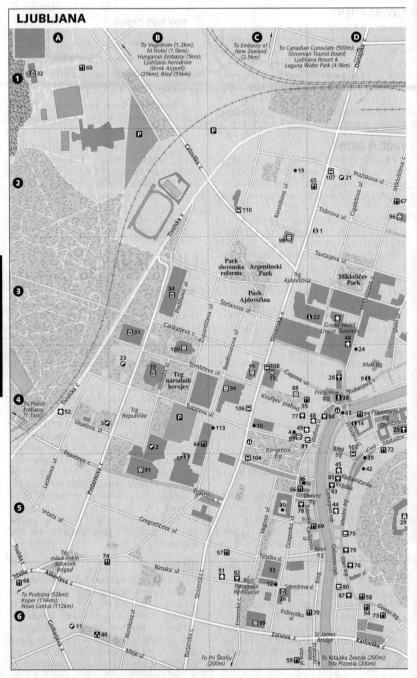

LJUBLJANA

To Vegedrom (1.2km);
M Hotel (1.5km);
Hungarian Embassy (5km);
Ljubljana Aerodrom
(Brnik Airport)
(25km); Bled (55km)

To Embassy of
New Zealand
(2.5km)

To Canadian Consulate (500m);
Slovenian Tourist Board;
Ljubljana Resort &
Laguna Water Park (4.5km)

Park
slovenske
reforme

Argentinski
Park

Park
Ajdovščina

Trg
Ajdovščina

Miklošičev
Park

Grand Hotel
Union Business

Trg
narodnih
herojev

Mali trg

Prešernov
trg

Knafljev prehod

Trg
Republike

Kongresni
trg

Ribji
trg

Pogačarjev
trg

Gornji
trg

Dvorni
trg

Novi
trg

Trg
mladinskih
delovnih
brigad

To Polish
Embassy
(1.1km)

To Postojna (52km);
Koper (116km);
Novo Gorica (112km)

Trg
Francoske
Revolucije

St James
Bridge

To Pri Škofju
(200m)

To Kitajska Zvezda (200m);
Trta Pizzeria (200m)

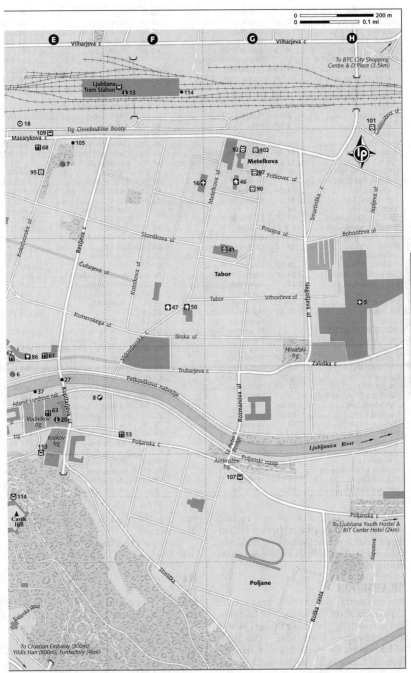

SLOVENIA

but it gained regional prominence in 1809, when it became the capital of Napoleon's short-lived Illyrian Provinces. Some fine Art Nouveau buildings filled up the holes left by a devastating earthquake in 1895.

ORIENTATION

Prešernov trg, on the left bank of the Ljubljanica River, is the heart of Ljubljana. Just across delightful Triple Bridge (p498) is the picturesque – if bite-sized – Old Town, which follows the north and west flanks of looming Castle Hill. The bus and train sta-tions are 800m north of Prešernov trg up Miklošičeva c.

The airport, Ljubljana Aerodrom, is at Brnik near Kranj, some 27km north of Ljubljana.

Maps

Excellent free maps, some of which show the city's bus network, are available from the various tourist offices. The more de-tailed 1:20,000-scale *Mestni Načrt Ljubljana* (Ljubljana City Map; €7.05) published by Kod & Kam is available at newsstands and bookshops.

INFORMATION
Bookshops

Geonavtik (☎ 252 70 27; www.geonavtik.com; in Slovene; Kongresni trg 1; ☺ 8.30am-8.30pm Mon-Fri, 8.30am-4pm Sat) Stocks Lonely Planet guides and books about Slovenia.

Kod & Kam (☎ 200 27 32; www.kod-kam.si; Trg Francoske Revolucije 7; ☺ 9am-8pm Mon-Fri, 8am-1pm Sat) Map specialist.

Internet Access

Web connection is available at virtually all hostels and hotels, the **Slovenian Tourist Information Centre** (right; €1.05 per half-hour) and **STA Ljubala café** (right; €1.05 per 20 minutes), as well as the following:

Cyber Café Xplorer (☎ 430 19 91; Petkovškovo nabrežje 23; per 30min/hr/5hr €2.40/4/11; ☺ 10am-10pm Mon-Fri, 2-10pm Sat & Sun) Ljubljana's best internet café, with 10 superfast computers and wi-fi.

DrogArt (☎ 438 72 70; Kolodvorska ul 20; per 15min/hr free/€1.70; ☺ 10am-6pm Mon-Fri) Opposite the train station.

Portal.si Internet Kotiček (☎ 090 42 30; Trg OF 4; per hr €3.75; ☺ 7am-8.30pm) Located in the bus station.

Laundry

Washing machines are available, even to non-guests, at the **Celica Hostel** (☎ 230 97 00; www.hostelcelica.com; Metelkova ul 8) for €5 per load, including washing powder. Commercial laundries, including **Chemo Express** (☎ 251 44 04; Wolfova ul 12; ☺ 7am-6pm Mon-Fri), charge from €3.75 per kg.

Left Luggage

Bus station (Trg OF 4; per day €1.80; ☺ 5am-9.30pm)
Train station (Trg OF 6; per day €2.10; ☺ 24hr) Coin lockers on platform No 1.

Ljubljana Card

The excellent-value Ljubljana Card (€12.50), valid for three days (72 hours) and available from the tourist offices, offers free admission to many museums, unlimited city bus travel, and discounts on organised tours, accommodation and restaurants, hire cars etc.

Medical Services

Clinic – Emergency Medical Assistance Clinic (Klinični Centre – Urgenca; ☎ 232 30 60; Bohoričeva ul 9; ☺ 24hr)

Medical Centre (Zdravstveni Dom Center; ☎ 472 37 00; Metelkova ul 9; ☺ 7.30am-7pm) For nonemergencies.

Money

There are ATMs at every turn, including in both the train and bus stations, where you'll also find **bureaux de change** (☺ 6am-10pm) that will change cash for no commission but not travellers cheques.

Abanka (☎ 471 81 00; Slovenska c 50; ☺ 9am-5pm Mon-Fri, 9am-noon Sat)

Nova Ljubljanska Banka (☎ 425 01 55; Trg Republike 2; ☺ 8am-6pm Mon-Fri) Headquarters of the nation's biggest bank.

Post

Main post office (Slovenska c 32; ☺ 8am-7pm Mon-Fri, 8am-1pm Sat) Holds poste restante for 30 days.

Post office branch (Trg OF 5; ☺ 7am-9pm Mon-Fri, 7am-6pm Sat) Due west of the train station.

Toilets

Two convenient public toilets (€0.20) are in the **Plečnikov podhod**, the underpass/subway below Slovenska c linking Kongresni trg with Plečnikov trg, and on **Hribarjevo nabrežje** below Pločnik (p502) on Prešernov trg.

Tourist Information

Ljubljana Tourist Information Centre (TIC; ☎ 306 12 15; www.ljubljana-tourism.si) Stritarjeva ul (Kresija Bldg, Stritarjeva ul; ☺ 8am-9pm Jun-Sep, 8am-7pm Oct-May); Train Station (☎ 433 94 75; Trg OF; ☺ 8am-10pm Jun-Sep, 10am-7pm Oct-May)

Slovenia Tourist Information Centre (STIC; ☎ 306 45 76; www.slovenia-tourism.si; Krekov trg 10; ☺ 8am-9pm Jun-Sep, 8am-7pm Oct-May) Internet and bicycle hire also available.

Travel Agencies

Erazem (☎ 430 55 37; www.erazem.net; basement, Miklošičeva c 26; ☺ 10am-5pm Mon-Fri, 10am-1pm Sat Jun-Sep, noon-5pm Mon-Fri Oct-May) Popular with backpackers and students. Staff make flight and train bookings, and sell ISIC, ITIC and IYTC cards.

STA Ljubljana (☎ 439 16 90; www.staljubljana.com, in Slovene; 1st fl, Trg Ajdovščina 1; ☺ 10am-1pm & 2-5pm Mon-Fri) Offers discount airfares for students and its café has internet access.

SIGHTS

Ljubljana Castle crowns a wooded hill that forms the city's focal point. It's an architectural mish-mash, including fortified walls dating from the early 16th century, a 1489 chapel and a 1970s concrete café. Admission to the central court-yard and some north-facing ramparts is free, but there are even better 360-degree views from

LJUBLJANA IN TWO DAYS

Begin your first day at **Ljubljana Castle** (p497) to get an idea of the lay of the land. After a seafood lunch at **Ribca** (p501), explore the Old Town then cross the Ljubljanica via St James Bridge and walk north along bust-lined Vegova ul to **Kongresni trg** and **Prešernov trg** (below). Over a fortifying libation at **Pločnik** (p502), plan your evening: low key at **Jazz Club Gajo** (p503), raucous at **Funfactory** (p502) or **D'Place** (p502), or alternative at one of the **Metelkova** (p502) venues.

On your second day check out some of the city's excellent **museums** and **galleries** (p497), and then stroll through **Park Tivoli** (below) to the **Museum of Contemporary History** (below) before returning to dine at **Aska in Volk** (p501) in the Old Town.

the 19th-century **Belvedere** (adult/student & senior €3.30/2; 9am-9pm May-Sep, 10am-6pm Oct-Apr); admission includes a visit to the Virtual Museum, a 20-minute 3-D video tour of Ljubljana and its history. The fastest way to reach the castle is via the new **funicular** (not yet open at the time of writing), which ascends from Vodnikov trg, though you can also take the hourly **tourist train** (adult/child €2.50/1.70; 9am-9pm mid-Jun–Sep, 11am-6pm Apr–mid-Jun, 9am-7pm Oct, 11am-3pm Nov-Mar) from Prešernov trg. You can also reach it on foot in about 15 minutes from the Old Town.

Central Prešernov trg is dominated by the salmon pink **Franciscan Church of the Annunciation** (1660; 6.40am-12.30pm & 3-8pm) and the **Prešeren monument** (1905), in honour of the national poet France Prešeren. Furtively observing Prešeren from a terracotta window at Wolfova ul 4 is a bust of his unrequited love (and poetic inspiration), Julija Primic. Wander north of the square to admire the fine **Art Nouveau buildings** along Miklošičeva c, including the **Grand Hotel Union Executive** (p500) at No 1, built in 1905, and the colourful **former Cooperative Bank** (1922) at No 8.

Leading southward from Prešernov trg is the small but perfectly formed **Triple Bridge**; prolific architect Jože Plečnik (p492) added two side bridges to the original span (1842) in 1931 to create something truly unique. The recently renovated baroque **Robba Fountain** stands before the Gothic **Town Hall** (1718) in **Mestni trg**, the 'City Sq', that leads into two more: **Stari trg** (Old Sq) and **Gornji trg** (Upper Sq), which have become something of a centre for Slovenian fashion boutiques. The squares wind picturesquely around the castle bluff and are sprinkled with inviting cafés and restaurants.

East of the Triple Bridge, the 18th-century **Cathedral of St Nicholas** (10am-noon & 3-6pm) is filled with pink marble, white stucco, gilt and a panoply of baroque frescoes. Behind the cathedral is a lively open-air **market** (p501)

selling both foodstuffs and dry goods, the magnificent riverside **Plečnik Colonnade** and the **Dragon Bridge** (Zmajski Most; 1901), a span guarded by four of the mythical creatures that have become the city's mascots.

The grand if rather pompous main building of **Ljubljana University** (Kongresni trg 12) was the regional parliament (1902) under Habsburg rule. The more restrained **Philharmonic Hall** (Filharmonija; Kongresni trg 10) dates from 1898 and is home to the Slovenian Philharmonic Orchestra, founded in 1701. South of the university building is the **National and University Library** (Gosposka ul 14; 8am-8pm Mon-Fri, 9am-2pm Sat), Plečnik's masterpiece completed in 1941, and its stunning **main reading room**. Diagonally opposite is the excellent **City Museum** (241 25 00; www.mm-lj.si; Gosposka ul 15; adult/child €2.10/1.25; 10am-6pm Tue-Sun), which focuses on Ljubljana's history and culture. The reconstructed Roman street in the basement is worth a visit in itself.

Of several major galleries and museums west of Slovenska c, the best are the impressive **National Gallery** (241 54 34; www.ng-slo.si; Prešernova c 24; adult/student & senior €2.90/4.20, free admission 2-6pm Sat & 1st Sun of month; 10am-6pm Tue-Sun), which contains the nation's historical art collection; the vibrant and inspiring (but outwardly drab) 1940s **Modern Art Museum** (241 68 00; www.mg-lj.si; Cankarjeva cesta 15; adult/student & senior €4.20/2.10; 10am-6pm Tue-Sun); and the fascinating **Museum of Contemporary History** (300 96 10; www.muzej-nz.si; Celovška c 23; adult/student €2.10/1.25; 10am-6pm Tue-Sat) in **Park Tivoli**, with its imaginative look at 20th-century Slovenia, via the milk carton. The latter museum also plunges you unexpectedly into a WWI trench.

The **National Museum** (241 44 04; www.narmuz-lj.si; Muzejska ul 1; adult/student & senior €4.60/3.35, admission 1st Sun of month free; 10am-6pm Fri-Wed, 10am-8pm Thu) occupies an elegant 1888 building. It has rich archaeological and coin collections, but at the time of writing only temporary exhibitions and the natural history section were accessible, while the main galleries were closed for a protracted renovation.

The **Slovenian Ethnographic Museum** (☎ 300 87 45; www.etno-muzej.si; Metelkova ul 2; adult/student & senior €3.35/2.10; ☺ 10am-6pm Tue-Sun), housed in the 1886 Belgian Barracks on the southern edge of Metelkova (see Metelkova Mesto, p502), has a permanent collection on the 3rd floor with traditional Slovenian trades and crafts – everything from beekeeping and blacksmithing to glass-painting and pottery making – and some excellent exhibits directed at children. Temporary exhibits are on the 1st and 2nd floors.

TOURS

A two-hour guided **walking tour** (adult/student & senior €6.25/2.90; ☺ 10am daily Apr-Sep, 11am Fri-Sun Oct Mar) in English and organised by the TIC departs from the **Town Hall** (Mestni trg 1) year-round. Ask the TIC about its cycle, boat and balloon tours.

SLEEPING

Ljubljana is not overly endowed with accommodation choices, especially at the midrange level, but things are changing. In fact, the following selection includes the lion's share of central budget and midrange options available at the time of research. The tourist offices have comprehensive details of other hotels further out in the suburbs, of similarly inconvenient private rooms and of the half-dozen other central top-end hotels.

Budget

Ljubljana Resort (☎ 568 39 13; www.ljubljanaresort.si; Dunajska c 270; camp sites per adult €7.10-12.10, per child €5.30-9.10; ☺ year-round; 🖳 🖳) It's got a pretty grandiose name, but wait till you see the facilities at this attractive seven-hectare camping ground-cum-resort 5km north of the city centre. Along with a 62-room hotel (singles/doubles from €54.25 to €75.10) and five chalets (rooms €75.10), there's

the Laguna water park (open from June to September), with outdoor swimming pools, fitness studio with sauna, and badminton and volleyball courts. Take bus 8 to its terminus or the more frequent bus 6 (stop Ježica).

Dijaški Dom Tabor (☎ 234 8840; www2.arnes.si /~ssljddta4; dm/s/d €10/26/38; ☺ late Jun-late Aug; ✗) From sometime in June until to August five colleges open their dormitories (*dijaški dom*) to foreigner travellers, but only this 300-bed one, a 10-minute walk southeast of the bus and train stations, is really central. Enter from Kotnikova ul.

Ljubljana Youth Hostel (☎ 548 00 55; www.yh -ljubljana.com; Litijska c 57; dm HI member/nonmember €16.50/17.50; 🖳) This HI-affiliated hostel has six rooms with shared facilities at the BIT Center Hotel (below). While not in the most central location, 3km east of the city centre, the hostel is easily reached on bus 5, 9 or 13 (stop Emona). A boon is the attached sports centre (open 7am to 11pm), where guests get a 50% discount.

Alibi Hostel (☎ 251 12 44; www.alibi.si; Cankarjevo nabrežje 27; dm/d €20/60; ✗ 🖳 🖳) This unbelievably well-situated 110-bed hostel is changing the face of budget accommodation in Ljubljana. It's right on the Ljubljanica in the former headquarters of the British Council, and has brightly painted, airy dorms with six to 12 wooden bunks and five doubles on four floors.

Midrange

Vila Veselova (☎ 059-926 721, 041-678 000; www.v-v .si; Veselova ul 14; dm €20-25, d/tr €70/90; ✗ 🖳 🖳) This very attractive freestanding villa, with its own garden and 40 beds in the centre of the museum district, offers mostly hostel accommodation in three rooms with four to eight beds, but a double and an apartment with en suite facilities make it an attractive midrange option. Some rooms face Park Tivoli across busy Tivolska c.

BIT Center Hotel (☎ 548 00 55; www.bit-center.net; Litijska c 57; s/d/tr €34/50/54; 🖳) The Bit Center

SLOVENIA

AUTHOR'S CHOICE

Celica Hostel (☎ 230 97 00; www.hostelcelica.com; Metelkova ul 8; dm €17, s/d/tr cell €44/46/57, 4-to 5-bed room per person €24, 6-to 7-bed room per person €19; 🅿 ✗ 🖳 ♿) This stylishly revamped former prison (1882) in Metelkova has 20 designer 'cells', complete with original bars, both rooms and apartments with three to seven beds, and a packed-full, popular 12-bed dorm. The ground floor is home to three cafés (set lunch €3 to €5.25; open 7.30am to midnight): a traditional Slovenian *gostilna*, a Western-style café (with two internet stations) and the Oriental Café, with cushions, water pipes and shoes strictly outside. Celica has become such a landmark that there are guided tours daily at 2pm.

offers one of the best-value deals in Ljubljana, although at 3km east of the city centre (bus 5, 9 or 13 to Emona stop), it's a bit far from the action. Its 33 rooms are spartan but bright and comfortable.

Park Hotel (☎ 300 25 00; www.hotelpark.si; Tabor 9; s €39-55, d €48-71; ☒ ☐) A partial face-lift inside and out has made this 145-room tower-block hotel an even better-value midrange choice in central Ljubljana. Pleasant, well-renovated standard rooms are bright and unpretentiously well equipped. Cheaper rooms have en suite toilet but share showers. Students with ISIC cards get a 10% discount.

Hotel Emonec (☎ 200 15 20; www.hotel-emonec.com; Wolfova ul 12; s €53, d €60-70, tr €83; ☒ ☐) The décor is simple and coldly modern at this 26-room hotel, but everything is spotless and you can't beat the central location – only steps away from Prešernov trg at the back of a courtyard.

Pri Mraku (☎ 421 96 00; www.daj-dam.si; Rimska c 4; s €60-74.50, d €95-112, tr €116-125; ☒ ☒ ☐) Although it calls itself a *gostilna*, the 'At Twilight' is really just a smallish hotel (36 rooms) in an old building with no lift. Almost opposite the Križanke on Trg Francoske Revolucije, it's ideally located for culture vultures. Only some rooms have air-con.

M Hotel (☎ 513 70 00; www.m-hotel.si; Derčeva ul 4; s €62-83, d €95-115; ☒ ☐ ☒) This hotel 2km northwest of the city center and set back from noisy Celovška c (bus 1, 5, 8 or 15 to Kino Šiška stop) is not much to look at from the outside, but the 154 rooms are comfortable and airy, with all the basic mod-cons.

Top End

Grand Hotel Union Executive (☎ 308 1270; www.gh -union.si; Miklošičeva c 1; s €149-179, d €159-212, ste €350-420; ☒ ☒ ☐ ☒) This 187-room hotel, the Art Nouveau southern wing of a two-part hostelry, was built in 1905 and remains the most desirable address for visitors to Ljubljana. It has glorious public areas, including a cellar restaurant, Unionska Klet, which moves to the Unionski Vrt (Union Garden) restaurant in summer. Guests can use the indoor swimming pool, sauna and fitness centre on the 8th floor of adjacent Grand Hotel Union Business.

EATING

The Old Town has plenty of appealing restaurants, though the choice of bona fide restaurants isn't quite as overwhelming as that of cafés. For cheaper options, try the dull but functional snack bars around the bus and train stations and both on and in the shopping mall below Trg Ajdovščina.

Restaurants

Kitajska Zvezda (☎ 425 88 24; Hrenova ul 19; entrées €1.50-2.45, mains €5-6.45; ☺ 11am-11pm) If you're looking for a fix of rice or noodles, try the 'Chinese Star' on the river just south of the Old Town. Szechuan dishes, including the *ma po doufu* (tofu with garlic and chilli), are quite good.

Vegedrom (☎ 513 26 42; Vodnikova c 35; soups & salads €2.10-3.35, dishes €4.20-9.80; ☺ 9am-10pm Mon-Fri, noon-10pm Sat) This appealing, if somewhat pricey, vegan restaurant is at the northeastern edge of Park Tivoli. The platters for two are good value at €17.50 to €20.90, and there's a salad bar.

Cantina Mexicana (☎ 426 93 25; Knafljev prehod 3; entrées €2.70-3.75, mains €7.10-13.80; ☺ 11am-midnight Sun-Thu, 11am-1am Fri & Sat) The capital's most stylish Mexican restaurant has an eye-catching red and blue exterior, and hacienda-like décor, sofas and lanterns inside. The fajitas (€7.50 to €11.70) are great.

Harambaša (☎ 041-843 106; Vrtna ul 8; dishes €2.70-4; ☺ 10am-10pm Mon-Fri, noon-10pm Sat, noon-6pm Sun) Here you'll find authentic Bosnian – Sarajevan to be precise – cuisine served at low tables in a charming modern cottage atmosphere, with quiet Balkan music and a lively crowd.

Yildiz Han (☎ 426 57 17; Karlovška c 19; entrées €2.70-5, mains €6.90-10.20; ☺ noon-midnight Tue-Sun) If Turkish is your thing, head for this mum and dad-run restaurant, which features belly dancing and/or live Turkish music on Friday night.

Gostilna Pri Pavli (☎ 425 92 75; Stari trg 1; entrées €4.10-5.40, mains €5.80-10.85; ☺ 8am-11pm) A wonderful holdover from the socialist era, 'Paula's Place' is an attractive, country-style inn in an enviable location that has managed to retain its old-school style and prices. The Farmer's Feast (€22.10) is a two-person feast.

Pri Škofju (☎ 426 45 08; Rečna ul 8; entrées €4.20-6.25, mains €4.60-13.35; ☺ 8am-midnight Mon-Thu, noon-midnight Sat & Sun) This wonderful little place in tranquil Krakovo south of the city centre serves some of the best prepared local dishes and salads in Ljubljana, with an ever-changing menu. Set lunches are a snip at €5 to €6.70.

Julija (☎ 425 64 63; Stari trg 9; entrées €5-7.50, mains €7.50-15.85; ☺ 8am-midnight Mon-Thu & Sat, 8am-1am Fri, 10am-11pm Sun) Julija serves decent risotto and pasta dishes either outside on the pavement terrace or in a Delft-tiled backroom behind a café decorated with 1920s prints.

Taverna Tatjana (☎ 421 00 87; Gornji trg 38; entrées €5-8.35, mains €8.35-20.90; ⌚ 5pm-midnight) Looking like an old-world wooden-beamed cottage pub with a nautical theme, this is actually a rather exclusive fish restaurant with a lovely (and protected) back courtyard for the warmer months.

Sokol (☎ 439 68 55; Ciril Metodov trg 18; entrées €4.10-9.50, mains €5.80-11.20; ⌚ 7am-11pm Mon-Sat, 10am-11pm Sun) In this old vaulted house, traditional Slovenian food is served on heavy tables by costumed waiters. Pizza is available if traditional dishes like *obara* (veal stew; €5.40) and Krvavica sausage with cabbage (€5.80) don't appeal.

Pri Vitezu (☎ 426 60 58; Breg 18-20; entrées €6.70-14.20, mains €11.70-20;, ⌚ noon-11pm Mon-Sat) Located directly on the left bank of the Ljubljanica, 'At the Knight' is the place for a special meal (Mediterranean-style grills and Adriatic fish dishes), whether in the vaulted cellar dining rooms or adjoining wine bar.

Ali Baba (☎ 230 17 87, 051-234 066; Poljanska c 11; mains €7.10-7.75; ⌚ 7am-11pm Mon-Fri, 10am-10pm Sat) Carpets and low brass tables decorate this cosy little restaurant, whose Iranian and Indian dishes are popular with journalists and students.

Aska in Volk (☎ 251 10 69; Gornji trg 4; mains €7.10-13.80; ⌚ noon-10pm Sun-Thu, noon-11pm Fri & Sat) The 'Lamb and Wolf', which takes its name from a Bosnian novel, is a very stylish choice for South Slav specialities, including roast lamb.

Like most European capitals today, Ljubljana is awash in pizzerias, where pizza routinely costs €4 to €6.50. The pick of the crop includes **Foculus Pizzeria** (☎ 251 56 43; Gregorčičeva ul 3; ⌚ 10am-midnight Mon-Fri, noon-midnight Sat & Sun), which boasts a vaulted ceiling painted with spring and autumn leaves; **Trta** (☎ 426 50 66; Grudnovo nabrežje 21; ⌚ 11am-10.30pm Mon-Fri, noon-10.30pm Sat), on the right bank of the Ljubljanica; and **Mirje** (☎ 426 60 15; Tržaška c 5; ⌚ 10am-10pm Mon-Fri, noon-10pm Sat), southwest of the city centre, which does some excellent pasta dishes, too.

Quick Eats

Delikatesa Ljubljanski Dvor (☎ 426 93 27; Kongresni trg 11; pizza slices €1.20-1.70; ⌚ 9am-midnight Mon-Sat) Locals queue for huge, bargain slices of pizza, salads and grilled vegetables sold by weight, and braised veggies to take away or eat on the spot.

Nobel Burek (Miklošičeva c 30; burek €1.90, pizza slice €1.50; ⌚ 24hr) This round-the-clock hole-in-the-wall serves Slovenian-style fast food.

Paninoteka (☎ 059-018 445, 041-529 824; Jurčičev trg 3; soups & toasted sandwiches €2.10-3.35; ⌚ 8am-1am Mon-Sat, 9am-11pm Sun) Healthy sandwich creations on a lovely little square by the river.

Hot Horse Trubarjeva c 31 (snacks & burgers €2.50-3.35; ⌚ 8am-1am Mon-Sat, noon-1am Sun) Park Tivoli branch (Park Tivoli; ⌚ 24hr) These two places exist to supply Ljubljančani with a favourite treat: horse burgers. The branch in Park Tivoli is just down the hill from the Museum of Contemporary History (p498).

Ribca (☎ 425 15 44; Adamič-Lundrovo nabrežje 1; dishes €2.70-6.70; ⌚ 7am-4pm Mon-Fri, 7am-2pm Sat) This basement seafood bar below the Plečnik Colonnade in Pogačarjev trg serves tasty fried squid, sardines and herrings to hungry market-goers.

Self-Catering

Handy supermarkets and convenience stores include **Mercator** (Slovenska c 55; ⌚ 7am-9pm) and, opposite the train and bus stations, **Noč in Dan** (☎ 234 79 62; Trg OF 13; ⌚ 24hr), a variety store open 'Day and Night'. The **Maximarket supermarket** (☎ 476 68 00; basement, Trg Republike 1; ⌚ 9am-9pm Mon-Fri, 8am-5pm Sat) below the department store of that name has the largest selection of food and wine in the city centre, as well as a bakery.

The open-air **market** (Pogačarjev trg & Vodnikov trg; ⌚ 8am-6pm Mon-Fri, 6am-5pm Sat Jun-Sep, 6am-4pm Mon-Sat Oct-May) opposite the cathedral sells mostly fresh fruit and vegetables.

DRINKING

Few cities have central Ljubljana's concentration of fabulously inviting cafés and bars, the vast majority with outdoor seating.

Cafés & Teahouses

Kavarna Zvezda (☎ 421 90 90; Kongresni trg 4 & Wolfova ul 14; ⌚ 7am-11pm Mon-Sat, 10am-8pm Sun) The Star Café is celebrated for its shop-made cakes, especially *skutina pečena* (€2), an eggy cheesecake.

Café Antico (☎ 425 13 39; Stari trg 17; ⌚ 10am-midnight Mon-Sat, 11am-10am Sun) With Frescoed ceilings and retro-style furniture, this is *the* place for a quiet tête-à-tête over a glass of wine.

Čajna Hiša (☎ 421 24 44; Stari trg 3; ⌚ 9am-11pm Mon-Fri, 9am-3pm & 6-10pm Sat) If you take your cuppa seriously, come here; the appropriately named 'Teahouse' offers a wide range of green and black teas and fruit tisanes for €1.60 to €3.15 a pot, and sells the leaves, too.

Le Petit Café (☎ 426 14 88; Trg Francoske Revolucije 4; ⌚ 7.30am-11pm Sun-Thu, 9am-midnight Fri & Sat) Just opposite the Križanke, this pleasant, studenty

SLOVENIA

place offers great coffee and a wide range of breakfast goodies (€2.90 to €4.20).

Kafeterija Lan (Gallusovo nabrežje 27; ☙ 9am-midnight Mon-Thu, 9am-1am Fri & Sat, 10am-1am Sun) This little greener-than-green café-bar on the river below Cobbler Bridge is something of a hipster-gay magnet.

Slaščičarna Pri Vodnjaku (☎ 425 07 12; Stari trg 30; ☙ 8am-midnight) For all kinds of chocolate of the ice cream and drinking kind, the 'Confectionery by the Fountain' will surely satisfy – there are 32 different flavours (€0.85 per scoop), as well as teas (€1.50) and fresh juices (€1.05 to €3.35)

Pubs & Bars

Pločnik (Prešernov trg 1; ☙ 7am-1am Apr-Oct) This roped-off café-bar on the southern side of Prešernov trg, with the distinctive name of 'Pavement', is one of the most popular places for a drink if you just want to sit outside and watch the passing parade. There's often live music.

Maček (☎ 425 37 91; Krojaška ul 5; ☙ 9am-1am) *The* place to be seen on a sunny summer afternoon, the 'Cat' is Pločnik's rival on the right bank of the Ljubljanica. Happy hour is between 4pm and 7pm daily.

Cutty Sark (☎ 425 14 77; Knafljev prehod 1; ☙ 9am-1am Mon-Sat, noon-1am Sun) A pleasant and well-stocked nautically themed pub in the courtyard behind Wolfova ul 6, the Cutty Sark is a congenial place for a *pivo* or glass of *vino*.

Dvorni Bar (☎ 251 12 57; Dvorni trg 1; ☙ 8am-1am) This wine bar is an excellent place to taste Slovenian vintages; it stocks 100 varieties, and frequently schedules promotions and wine tastings.

Pr'skelet (☎ 252 77 99; Ključavničarska ul 5; ☙ 10am-3am) OK, it might be something of a one-joke wonder, but you'll shake, rattle and roll at this skeleton-themed basement bar, where cocktails are two for one throughout the day.

Salon (☎ 439 87 64; Trubarjeva c 23; ☙ 9am-1am Mon & Tue, 9am-3am Wed-Sat, 10am-1am Sun) Salon is a dazzling designer-kitsch cocktail bar featuring gold ceilings, faux leopard armchairs, heavy burgundy and gold drapes, and excellent cocktails (€4.20 to €6.25) and shooters (€3.75 to €4.20).

Žmavc (☎ 251 03 24; Rimska c 21; ☙ 7.30am-1am Mon-Sat, 8am-1am Sun) A super-popular student hang-out west of Slovenska c, with comic-strip scenes and figures running halfway up the walls. It's owned by the same people who run the Vila Veselova (p499).

ENTERTAINMENT

The free quarterly magazine **Ljubljana Life** (www .ljubljanalife.com) has practical information and listings. It's distributed free at the airport and in hotels and the tourist offices.

Where to? in Ljubljana, available from the tourist offices, lists cultural and sporting events.

Nightclubs

D'Place (☎ 040-626 901; www.club-dplace.com, in Slovene; Šmartinska c 152; ☙ 10pm-6am Thu-Sat) This new club, with different themed evenings (eg hip-hop and R 'n' B on Saturday), has been making quite a splash since it's recent opening. It's in the Kolosej multiplex cinema at BTC City Shopping Centre.

Funfactory (☎ 428 96 90; Jurčkova c 224; ☙ 9pm-dawn Thu-Sat) Ljubljana's biggest club is hidden in a shopping centre opposite the Leclerc Hypermarket (take bus 3 to the end) in the far southeastern suburbs

Global (☎ 426 90 20; www.global.si, in Slovene; Tomšičeva ul 2; ☙ 9am-5am 5pm Mon-Sat) This retro cocktail bar on the 6th floor of the Nama department store becomes a popular dance venue nightly and attracts a chi-chi crowd. Take the bouncer-guarded lift in the passageway linking Cankarjeva ul and Tomšičeva ul.

Klub K4 (☎ 438 03 04; www.klubk4.org; Kersnikova ul 4; ☙ 10pm-4am) This evergreen club in the basement of the Student Organisation of Ljubljana University (Študentska Organizacija Univerze Ljubljani; ŠOU) features rave-electronic music Friday and Saturday, with other styles of music on weeknights, and a popular gay and lesbian night on Sunday. It closes when the university breaks up.

Bacchus Center Club (☎ 241 82 44; Kongresni trg 3; ☙ 10pm-5am Mon-Sat) This place has something for everyone (it also has a restaurant and bar-lounge) and attracts a mixed crowd.

As Pub (☎ 425 88 22; Knafljev prehod 5a; ☙ 7am-3am Wed-Sat) DJs transform this candlelit basement bar, hidden beneath an incongruously upmarket fish restaurant, into a pumping, crowd-pulling nightclub four nights a week.

Metelkova Mesto (Metelkova ul; www.metelkova .org) 'Metelkova Town', an ex-army garrison taken over by squatters after independence, is now a free-living commune – a miniature version of Copenhagen's Christiania. In this two-courtyard block, half a dozen idiosyncratic venues hide behind gaily tagged doorways, coming to life generally after midnight Thursday to Saturday. Entering the main 'city gate' from Masarykova c, the building to the right houses Gala Hala, with live bands and club nights, Channel Zero (punk, hardcore) and 100% Mizart. Easy to miss in the first building to the left are Klub Tiffany for gay men and Klub Monokel for lesbians. Beyond the first courtyard to the southwest, well-hidden Klub Gromka (folk, live concerts) is beneath the body-less heads. Next door is Menza pri Koritu (performance) and the idiosyncratic Čajnica pri Mariči (psycho-blues). Cover charges and midweek openings are rare but erratic for all Metelkova venues.

Live Music
ROCK, POP & JAZZ

Orto Bar (☎ 232 16 74; www.orto-bar.com; Grabaličeva ul 1; ☼ 6pm-4am Mon-Thu, 6pm-5am Fri & Sat, 6pm-2am Sun) A popular bar for late-night drinking and dancing with occasional live music, Orto is just five minutes' walk from Metelkova.

Jazz Club Gajo (☎ 425 32 06; www.jazzclubgajo.com; Beethovnova ul 8; ☼ 11am-2am Mon-Fri, 7pm-midnight Sat & Sun) Gajo is the city's premier venue for live jazz, and attracts both local and international talent, usually midweek or on Friday at 8.30pm (jam sessions at 8.30pm Monday).

CLASSICAL

Cankarjev Dom (☎ 241 71 00; www.cd-cc.si, in Slovene; Prešernova c 10) Ljubljana's premier cultural and conference centre has two large auditoriums (the Gallus Hall has perfect acoustics) and a dozen smaller performance spaces offering a remarkable smorgasbord of performance arts. The ticket office (☎ 241 72 99; open 11am to 1pm and 3pm to 8pm Monday to Friday, 11am to 1pm Saturday and one hour before performance) is in the subway below Maximarket supermarket on the opposite side of Trg Republike.

Philharmonic Hall (Filharmonija; ☎ 241 08 00; www.filharmonija.si; Kongresni trg 10) Head on down to the attractive Philharmonic Hall for classical concerts.

Opera House (☎ 241 17 40; www.opera.si; Župančičeva ul 1) Opera and ballet are performed at the neo-Renaissance 1882 Opera House.

Križanke (☎ 241 60 00, 241 60 26; Trg Francoske Revolucije 1-2) Hosts events of the Ljubljana Summer Festival (p520) in what was a sprawling monastic complex dating back to the 13th century.

Cinema

Kinoteka (☎ 434 25 20; www.kinoteka.si, in Slovene; Miklošičeva c 28) The 'Slovenian Cinematheque' screens archival art and classic films.

Kino Dvor (Court Cinema; ☎ 434 25 44; www.kinodvor.si, in Slovene; Kolodvorska ul 13; ☼ 6pm, 8pm & 10pm) Kinoteka's sister-cinema shows more contemporary films.

GETTING THERE & AWAY

The shedlike **bus station** (☎ 234 46 01, information 090 42 30; www.ap-ljubljana.si; Trg OF 4; ☼ 5.30am-10.30pm Mon-Sat, 8am-8pm Sun) opposite the train station has bilingual info-phones, and its timetable is useful once you get the hang of it. Frequent buses serve Bohinj (€8, two hours, 86km, hourly) via Bled (€6.15, 1¼ hours, 57km). Most buses to Piran (€11.70, three hours, 140km, up to seven daily) go via Koper (€10.75, 2½ hours, 122km, up to 11 daily) and Postojna (€5.75, one hour, 53km, up to 24 daily). All bus services are much less frequent on weekends.

Ljubljana's **train station** (☎ 291 33 32; www.slo-zeleznice.si; Trg OF 6; ☼ 5am-10pm) has daily services to Koper (€7.30 to €8.70, 2½ hours, 153km, four times daily). Alternatively take the Sežana-bound train (5.55am) and change (rapidly – you've got seven minutes!) at Divača (1¾ hours). For international services, see p523.

GETTING AROUND

The cheapest way to **Ljubljana Aerodrom** (LJU; www.lju-airport.si) at Brnik is by city bus from stop 28 (€3.70, 50 minutes, 27km) at the bus station. These run hourly from 6.10am to 8.10pm Monday to Friday; on the weekend there's a bus at 6.10am and then one every two hours from 9.10am to 7.10pm. A **private airport van** (☎ 04-252 63 19, 041-792 865) also links Trg OF near the bus station with the airport up to 10 times daily between 5.20am and 10.30pm (€8, 30 minutes).

You can park on the street (€0.40 to €0.50 per hour) in Ljubljana, though not always easily in the museum area and near Metelkova. Once you've found a space it's generally most efficient to walk.

Ljubljana has an excellent network (21 lines) of city buses; the main lines operate every five to 15 minutes from 3.15am to midnight. However, the central area is perfectly walkable, so buses are really only necessary if you're staying out of town. Buy little metal tokens (žetoni; €0.80) in advance from newsstands, or pay €1.25 on board.

Ljubljana Bike (☎ 051-441 900; per 2hr/day €0.85/4.20; ☺ 8am-8pm Apr-Oct) has bikes available from some 10 locations around the city, including the train station, the STIC office (p497), the Celica Hostel (p499) and at the at the start of Miklošičeva c.

JULIAN ALPS

The Julian Alps – named in honour of Caesar himself – form Slovenia's dramatic northwest frontier with Italy. Triglav National Park, established in 1924, includes almost all of the alps lying within Slovenia. The centrepiece of the park is, of course, Mt Triglav (2864m), Slovenia's highest mountain, but there are many other peaks here reaching above 2000m, as well as ravines, canyons, caves, rivers, streams, forests and alpine meadows. Along with an embarrassment of fauna and flora, the area offers a wide range of adventure sports at very affordable prices.

KRANJ
☎ 04 / pop 34,850

Situated at the foot of the Kamnik-Savinja Alps, with the snow-capped peak of Storžič (2132m) and others looming to the north, Kranj is Slovenia's fourth-largest city. The attractive Old Town, perched on an escarpment above the confluence of the Sava and Kokra Rivers, barely measures 1km by 250m.

The frequent weekday buses between Kranj and Ljubljana Aerodrom at nearby Brnik make it possible to head straight from the plane to the Julian Alps without diverting to the capital. While waiting for your onward bus to Bled or Kranjska Gora, have a look at the Old Town, starting with the Art Nouveau **former post office** (Maistrov trg), a 600m walk south

from the bus station past the eyesore 87-room **Hotel Creina** (☎ 281 75 00; www.hotel-creina.si; Koroška c 5; s/d €60/80; ☒ ☐), the only game in town and where most airline crews stay while overnighting in Slovenia. Most places of interest are along just three south-bound pedestrianised streets – Prešernova ul, Tavčarjeva ul and Tomišičeva ul – two of which lead to the **Church of St Cantianus**, with impressive frescoes and stained glass. Another 300m further south, the Old Town dead-ends behind the Serbian Orthodox **Plague Church**, built during a time of pestilence in 1470, and a 16th-century **defence tower**. **Mitnica** (☎ 040-678 778; Tavčarjeva ul 35; ☺ 7am-11pm Mon-Wed, 7am-1am Thu, 7am-3am Fri & Sat), a lovely café-bar in the basement of a 16th-century toll house with a huge terrace backing on to the river, is just the place to relax in Kranj on a warm afternoon.

From Kranj it's an easy excursion to **Škofja Loka**, whose main square, **Mestni Trg**, is one of Slovenia's most beautiful and whose fine **Loka Castle** (Grajska pot 13) contains a decent **ethnographical museum** (☎ 517 04 00; adult/child €2.90/2.10; ☺ 9am-6pm Tue-Sun Apr-Oct, 9am-5pm Sat & Sun Nov-Mar). Buses depart hourly from Kranj (€2.10, 25 minutes, 13km).

BLED
☎ 04 / pop 5250

With its emerald-green lake, picture-postcard church on an islet, medieval castle clinging to a rocky cliff, and some of the highest peaks of the Julian Alps and the Karavanke as backdrops, Bled seems too to good to be true, designed, it would seem, by some god of tourism. As it is Slovenia's most popular destination it can get pretty crowded in summer, but it's small, convenient and a delightful base from which to explore the mountains.

HIKING MT TRIGLAV

The Julian Alps offer some of Europe's finest hiking. In summer some 167 mountain huts (planinska koča or planinski dom) operate, none more than five hours' walk from the next. These huts get very crowded, especially on weekends, so booking ahead is wise. If the weather turns bad, however, you won't be refused refuge.

At €20 per person in a private room or half that amount in a dormitory in a Category I hut (Category II huts charge €13.35 and €7.50 respectively), the huts aren't cheap, but as they serve meals you can travel light. Sturdy boots and warm clothes are indispensable, even in midsummer. Trails are generally well marked with a white-centred red circle, but you can still get lost and it's very unwise to trek alone. It's best to engage the services of a qualified (and licensed) guide.

The tourist offices in Bled, Bohinj, Kranjska Gora and Bovec all have lots of hiking information, sell maps in a variety of useful scales and can help book huts in their regions.

Information

3glav adventures (☎ 041-683 184, 041-819 636; www.3glav-adventures.com; Ljubljanska c 1; ☽ 9am-7pm Apr-Oct)

À Propos Bar (☎ 574 40 44; Bled Shopping Centre, Ljubljanska c 4; per 15/30/60min €1.25/2.10/4.20; ☽ 8am-midnight) Offers internet access.

Gorenjska Banka (C Svobode 15; ☽ 9-11.30am & 2-5pm Mon-Fri, 8-11am Sat) In the Park Hotel shopping complex.

Kompas (☎ 572 75 00; www.kompas-bled.si; Bled Shopping Centre, Ljubljanska c 4; ☽ 8am-7pm Mon-Sat, 8am-noon & 4-8pm Sun Jul & Aug, 8am-7pm Mon-Sat, 8am-noon & 4-7pm Sun Sep-Jun) Rents private rooms and bicycles.

Tourist Information Centre Bled (☎ 574 11 22; www .bled.si; C Svobode 10; ☽ 8am-10pm Mon-Sat, 10am-10pm Sun Jul & Aug, 8am-8pm Mon-Sat, 10am-6pm Sun Jun & Sep,

8am-7pm Mon-Sat, 9am-5pm Sun Oct & Mar-May, 9am-5pm Mon-Sat, 9am-2pm Sun Nov-Feb)

Sights

On its own tiny island, the baroque **Church of the Assumption** (☽ 8am-dusk) is Bled's icon. Getting there by a piloted **gondola** (pletna; ☎ 041 293 424) is the archetypal tourist experience. Gondola prices (return per person €10) are standard from any jetty, and you'll stay on the island long enough to ring the 'lucky' bell; all in all, it's a 1½-hour trip. Ordinary row-yourself boats for three to four people cost €10.50 per hour.

Perched atop a 100m-cliff, **Bled Castle** (☎ 578 05 25; Grajska c 25; adult/student/child €5/4.60/3.10; ☽ 8am-8pm May-Oct, 8am-5pm Nov-Apr) is the perfect backdrop to a lake view. One of many access

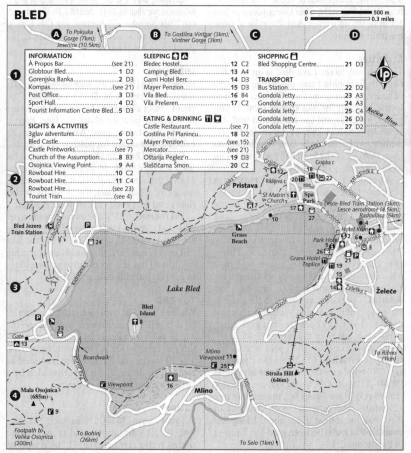

footpaths leads up from behind the Bledec Hostel (right). Admission includes entry to the **museum collection** as well as **Castle Printworks**. The fabulous views are 'free' if you have a meal or sunset beer on the superbly situated terrace of the Castle Restaurant (opposite).

A short distance southeast of Bled and well served by bus (€1.70, 15 minutes, 7.5km, half-hourly), the town of **Radovljica** appears at first glance to be an amorphous, modern sprawl. However, it has a particularly delightful square called **Linhartov trg** in its Old Town, where there's a restored, painted **manor house**, an interesting **gallery** and the fascinating **Beekeeping Museum** (☎ 532 05 20; Linhartov trg 1; adult/student €2.10/1.90; ☼ 10am-1pm & 3-6pm Tue-Sun May-Oct, 10am-noon & 3-5pm Wed, Sat & Sun Mar, Apr, Nov & Dec). The square starts 400m southeast of Radovljica bus station via Gorenjska c or just 100m north up narrow Kolodvorska ul from the train station.

Activities
The best way to see Lake Bled is on foot; the 6km stroll shouldn't take more than a couple of hours, including the short (but steep) climb to the brilliant **Osojnica viewing point**. If you prefer, jump aboard the **tourist train** (adult/child €2.50/1.70; ☼ 9.30am-9.30pm May–mid-Oct) for the 45-minute twirl around the lake, which departs from in front of the **Sport Hall** (Ljubljanska c 5) up to 20 times daily in summer.

A popular and easy walk is to **Vintgar Gorge** (adult/student/child €2.90/2.50/2.10; ☼ 8am-7pm late Apr-Oct) some 4km from the town centre to the northwest. The highlight is the 1600m-long wooden walkway, erected in 1893 and continually rebuilt, that criss-crosses the swirling Radovna River for the first 700m or so. Thereafter the scenery becomes tamer, passing a tall railway bridge and a spray-spouting weir, and ending at the anticlimactic 13m-high **Šum Waterfall**. The easiest way to get to the gorge is via the appealing Gostilna Vintgar, an inn just three well-signed kilometres away on quiet, attractive roads from the Bledec Hostel.

For something tougher, join one of the **rafting** or **kayaking** (€23 to €38) or **paragliding** (€70) trips on offer from **3glav adventures** (☎ 041-683 184, 041-819 636; www.3glav-adventures.com; Ljubljanska c 1; ☼ 9am-7pm Apr-Oct), the number one adventure- and extreme-sport specialist in Bled. Ask the tourist office about **hiking** and **mountain-bike routes** between road-less hamlets in the mountains.

Sleeping
BUDGET
Private rooms are offered by dozens of homes in the area. Both Kompas (p505) and **Globtour Bled** (☎ 575 13 00; www.globtour-bled.com; Ljubljanska c 7; ☼ 8am-8pm Mon-Sat, 8am-noon & 4-8pm Sun Jul & Aug, 8am-7pm Mon-Fri, 9am-2pm Sat Sep-Jun) in the Hotel Krim have extensive lists, with prices for singles/doubles starting at €20/30.

Bledec Hostel (☎ 574 52 50; Grajska c 17; HI members/nonmembers high season dorm €17.5/20, low season €15.50/18, d high season €23.50/26, low season €21.50/24; ✗ ▣) This well-organised hostel has four-bed dorms with private bathrooms, a bar and an inexpensive restaurant. Laundry (€8.35 per load €8.35) and internet access (€2.10 per half-hour €2.10) are available.

Camping Bled (☎ 575 20 00; www.camping.bled.si; Kidričeva c 10c; adult €8.50-11, child €6-7.70; ☼ Apr–mid-Oct) This popular 6.5-hectare site fills a rural valley behind a waterside restaurant at the western end of the lake.

MIDRANGE
Mayer Penzion (☎ 574 10 58; www.mayer-sp.si; Želeška c 7; d/q €70/90, apt €65-75; ✗ ▣) This delightful 13-room inn in a renovated 19th-century house is in a quiet location above the lake. Even if you're not staying here, have a meal at its excellent restaurant (opposite).

Garni Hotel Berc (☎ 576 56 58; www.berc-sp.si; Pod Stražo 13; s €40, d €65-70; ✗ ▣) Just opposite the Mayer, this new purpose-built *penzion*, reminiscent of a Swiss chalet, has 15 rooms on two floors and gets good reviews from readers.

Vila Prešeren (☎ 578 08 00; www.vila.preseren.s5.net; Kidričeva c 1; s lake view €58-64, park view €50-55, d lake view €78-88, park view €67-72, ste €112-154) Facing the lake just west of Spa Park, this positively charming mini-hotel has just six rooms and two suites in a lovely old villa dating from 1865.

TOP END
Vila Bled (579 15 00; www.vila-bled.com; C Svobode 26; s €130-150, d €170-190, ste lake view €210-240, park view €190-210; ▣ ▨) Now a Relais & Chateaux property, this place started life as Tito's summer retreat. The 10 rooms and 20 suites are furnished in retro 1950s décor, and it is surrounded by a large park and has its own beach.

Eating
Slaščičarna Šmon (☎ 574 16 16; Grajska c 3; ☼ 7.30am-9pm) Bled's culinary speciality is *kremna snežna rezina* (cream cake; €1.70), a layer of

vanilla custard topped with whipped cream and sandwiched neatly between two layers of flaky pastry, and this is the place to try it.

Gostilna Pri Planincu (☎ 574 16 13; Grajska c 8; entrées €4.20-8, mains €5.85-15; ⊙ noon-10pm) 'At the Mountaineers' is a homey pub-restaurant just down the hill from the Bledec Hostel, with simple Slovenia mains and grilled Balkan specialities, like *čevapčiči* (spicy meatballs of beef or pork; €5.65) and tasty *pljeskavica z kajmakom* (Serbian-style meat patties with mascarpone-like cream cheese; €6.25).

Ostarija Peglez'n (☎ 574 42 18; C Svobode 19a; entrées €4.60-7.50, mains €6.25-16.25; ⊙ 11am-midnight) Our new favourite restaurant in Bled, the 'Iron Inn' is just opposite the landmark Grand Hotel Toplice, with fascinating retro décor and serving some of the best fish dishes in town.

Mayer Penzion (☎ 574 10 58; www.mayer-sp.si; Želeška c 7; entrées €7-8, mains €9.20-18.80; ⊙ 5pm-midnight Tue-Fri, noon-midnight Sat & Sun) The restaurant at this delightful inn (above) serves such tasty Slovenian fare such as sausage, trout, roast pork and *skutini štruklji* (cheese curd pastries). The list of Slovenian wines is a cut above.

Castle Restaurant (☎ 579 44 24; entrées €5-10.85, mains €10.85-18.80; ⊙ 10am-10pm) You can't beat the views from this place and the wine list – all Slovenian – is exceptional.

You'll find a **Mercator** (Ljubljanska c 4; ⊙ 7am-7pm Mon-Sat, 8am-noon Sun) at the eastern end of Bled Shopping Centre.

Getting There & Away

Frequent buses to Bohinj (€3.50, one hour, 26km, hourly), Ljubljana (€6.10, 1¼ hours, 57km, hourly) and Radovljica (€1.70, 15 minutes, 7.5km, half-hourly) use the central bus station.

Bled has no central train station. Trains to Bohinjska Bistrica (€1.45, 20 minutes, 18km, seven daily) and Nova Gorica (€5.05, 2¼ hours, 79km, seven daily) use little Bled Jezero train station, which is 2km west of central Bled – handy for the camping ground but little else. Trains for Ljubljana (€3.90 to €5.30, 55 minutes, 51km, up to 17 daily) use Lesce-Bled train station, 4km to the east of town.

BOHINJ

☎ 04 / pop 5260

Bohinj, a larger and much less-developed glacial lake 26km to the southwest, is a world apart from Bled. Triglav itself is visible from the lake and there are activities galore – from kayaking and mountain biking to trekking up Triglav via one of the southern approaches.

Bohinjska Bistrica, the area's largest village, is 6km east of the lake and useful mainly for its train station. The main tourist hub on the lake is **Ribčev Laz**, at the lake's eastern end. Its miniscule commercial centre contains a supermarket, post office with ATM and the obliging **Tourist Information Centre Bohinj** (☎ 574 60 10; www.bohinj.si; Ribčev Laz 48; ⊙ 8am-8pm Jul & Aug, 8am-6pm Mon-Sat, 9am-3pm Sun Sep-Jun), which changes money, sells **fishing licences** (€25 to €50.50 per day) and can help with accommodation. Central **Alpinsport** (☎ 572 34 86; www.alpinsport.si; Ribčev Laz 53; ⊙ 9am-7pm Jun-Aug, 10am-6pm Sep-May) organises a range of activities, and hires kayaks, canoes, bicycles and other equipment from a kiosk near the stone bridge. Next door is the **Church of St John the Baptist**, which contains splendid 15th- and 16th-century frescoes, but is undergoing a protracted renovation.

A nearby village called **Stara Fužina** has an appealing little **Alpine Dairy Museum** (☎ 572 30 95;

SLOVENIA

A NATIONAL ICON

Nothing is as Slovenian as the *kozolec*, the hayrack seen almost everywhere in the country, except on the far northeastern plain and in the Karst region. Because the ground in Alpine and hilly areas can be damp, wheat and hay are hung from racks, allowing the wind to do the drying faster and more thoroughly.

Until the late 19th century the *kozolec* was looked upon as just another tool to make a farmer's work easier and the land more productive. Then the artist Ivan Grohar made it the centrepiece of many of his impressionist paintings, and the *kozolec* became as much a part of the cultural landscape as the physical one. Today it has become virtually a national icon.

There are many different types of Slovenian hayracks: single ones standing alone or 'goat hayracks' with sloped 'lean-to' roofs, parallel and stretched ones and double hayracks (*toplarji*), often with roofs and storage areas on top. Simple hayracks are not unknown in other parts of Alpine central Europe, but *toplarji*, decorated or plain, are unique to Slovenia.

Stara Fužine 181; adult/child €1.70/1.25; ⏰ 11am-7pm Tue-Sun Jul & Aug, 10am-noon & 4-6pm Tue-Sun Jan-Jun, Sep & Oct). Just opposite is a cheesemonger called **Planšar** (☎ 572 30 95; Stara Fužina 179; ⏰ 10am-8pm Tue-Sun Jun-Oct, 10am-8pm Sat & Sun Dec-May), which specialises in home-made dairy products: hard Bohinj cheese, a soft, strong-tasting cheese called *mohant*, cottage cheese, curd pie, sour milk and so on. Just 2km east is **Studor**, a village famed for its *toplarji*, the double-linked hayrack with barns or storage areas at the top, some of which date from the 18th and 19th centuries.

Depending on the season, **Tourist boats** (☎ 041-434 986; adult/child one-way €6.25/4.60, return €7.45/5.45; ⏰ 10am-6pm) depart from the pier just opposite the Alpinsport kiosk every half-hour to an hour, terminating 15 minutes later at the Ukanc jetty at the lake's far western west end. Just 300m up from the Ukanc jetty and 5km west of Ribčev Laz, a **cable car** (adult/child return €10/7; ⏰ every 30min 7am-7pm Jul & Aug, 8am-6pm Sep-Jun) will whisk you up a vertical kilometre to 1540m; from here, paths continue up **Mt Vogel**.

Sleeping

Private rooms (per person €9.20-15.10) are available through the tourist office.

Penzion Rožič (☎ 572 33 93; rozic@siol.net; Ribčev Laz 42; per person €20-25; 🖵) This unpretentious chalet-style guesthouse with 20 rooms and a popular restaurant is just 200m east of the tourist office.

Hotel Bellevue (☎ 572 33 31; www.alpinum.net; Ribčev Laz 65; s €39-52, d €55-89; 🖵) The shabby, 59-room Bellevue has a beautiful (if somewhat isolated) location on a hill about 800m south of the Hotel Jezero. Whodunit fans take note: Agatha Christie stayed here for three weeks in 1967. Thirty-eight of the rooms are in the unattractive Savica Annexe.

Hotel Jezero (☎ 572 91 00; www.bohinj.si/alpinum /jezero; Ribčev Laz 51; s €52-86, d €69-141; 🖵 🏊) This recently renovated 63-room place is the closest hotel to the lake, just opposite the stone bridge in Ribčev Laz. It has a lovely indoor swimming pool, two saunas and a fitness centre.

Autokamp Zlatorog (☎ 572 34 82; www.alpinum .net; Ukanc 2; per person €5.85-10; ⏰ May-Sep) This pine-shaded 2.5-hectare camping ground accommodating 500 guests is on the lake at its western end.

Getting There & Around

Buses run regularly from Ukanc to Ljubljana (€8.50, two hours, 91km, hourly) via Ribčev

Laz, Bohinjska Bistrica and Bled (€4, one hour, 34km), with six extra buses daily between Ukanc and Bohinjska Bistrica (€2.20, 20 minutes, 12km). Buses headed as far as Ukanc are marked to 'Bohinj Zlatorog'. From Bohinjska Bistrica, passenger trains to Novo Gorica (€4.50, 1½ hours, 61km, up to seven daily) make use of a century-old tunnel under the mountains that provides the only direct option for reaching the Soča Valley. In addition there are six daily auto trains (*avtovlaki*) to Podbrdo (€7.10, eight minutes, 7km) and Most na Soči (€10.85, 25 minutes, 28km).

KRANJSKA GORA

☎ 04 / pop 1420

Kranjska Gora, lying in the Sava Dolinka Valley that separates the Karavanke range of mountains from the Julian Alps, is the largest and best-equipped ski resort in the country. It's at its most perfect under a blanket of snow, but its surroundings are wonderful to explore in warmer months as well. There are endless possibilities for hiking and mountaineering in Triglav National Park on the town's southern outskirts, and few travellers will not be impressed by a trip over the Vršič Pass (1611m), the gateway to the Soča Valley.

As ski resorts go, compact Kranjska Gora is relatively cute and sits right beside the ski lifts. There are world record-setting ski jumps 4km west at Planica. Needless to say, there are a lot of places offering ski tuition and equipment hire, including **ASK Kranjska Gora Ski School** (☎ 588 53 00; www.ask-kg.com; Borovška c 99a) in the same building as SKB Banka.

Borovška c, 400m south of where buses arrive and depart, is the heart of the village, with the endearing **Liznjek House** (☎ 588 19 99; Borovška 63; adult/child €2.30/1.70; ⏰ 10am-8pm Tue-Sat, 10am-5pm Sun May-Oct & Dec-Mar), an 18th-century museum house with a good collection of household objects and furnishings peculiar to this area of Gorenjska province. At its western end is the **Tourist Information Centre Kranjska Gora** (☎ 588 17 68; www.kranjska-gora.si; Tičarjeva c 2; ⏰ 8am-7pm Mon-Sat, 9am-6pm Sun Jun-Sep & mid-Dec–Mar, 8am-3pm Mon-Fri, 9am-6pm Sat, 9am-1pm Sun Apr, May, Oct–mid-Dec).

Sleeping & Eating

Accommodation costs peak from December to March and in midsummer. April is the cheapest time to visit, though some hotels close for renovations and redecorating at this time. **Private rooms** (s €15.50-20.50, d €21-35) can be arranged through the tourist office and **Globtour** (☎ 582 02 00; www.globtour-kranjskagora.com; Borovška c 92; ☺ 9am-7pm daily Jul, Aug, Dec-Mar, 9am-7pm Mon-Sat Sep-Nov & Apr-Jun).

Hostel Nika (☎ 588 10 00; zvone.oreskovic@s5.net; Čičare 2; dm €11, s/d €16/28; ☒ ☐) This somewhat institutional hostel, with 66 beds in a large village, is about 800m northeast of the town centre and just across the main road from the TGC Shopping Centre.

Hotel Miklič (☎ 588 16 35; www.hotelmiklic.com; Vitranška ul 13; s €45-66, d €70-112; ☒ ☐) This pristine *penzion* south of the town centre is surrounded by luxurious lawns and flowerbeds, and boasts an excellent restaurant. It's definitely a cut above most other accommodation options in Kranjska Gora.

Hotel Kotnik (☎ 588 15 64; hotel@hotel-kotnik.si; Borovška c 75; s €48-62, d €56-84; ☒) If you're not into big high-rise hotels with hundreds of rooms, choose this charming, bright yellow property. It has 15 cosy rooms, a great restaurant and pizzeria, and it couldn't be more central.

Gostilna Pri Martinu (☎ 582 03 00; Borovška c 61; entrées €4.20-5.85, mains €5.85-10; ☺ 10am-11pm) This atmospheric tavern-restaurant in an old house opposite the fire station is one of the best places in town to try local specialities, such as venison, trout and *telečja obara* (veal stew,; €3.75).

Getting There & Away

Buses run hourly to Ljubljana (€8.50, two hours, 91km) via Jesenice (€3, 30 minutes, 23km), where you should change for Bled (€2.60, 20 minutes, 16km). There are just two direct departures to Bled (€4.90, one hour, 40km) on weekdays at 9.15am and 1.10pm. A service to Bovec (€5.50, two hours, 46km) via the spectacular Vršič Pass departs daily in July and August, and on Saturday and Sunday in June and September.

SOČA VALLEY

The region of the Soča Valley stretches from Triglav National Park to Nova Gorica. It is dominated by the 96km-long Soča River coloured a deep – almost artificial – turquoise. The valley has more than its share of historical sights, but most people come here for rafting, hiking and skiing.

Bovec

☎ 05 / pop 1650

The effective capital of the Soča Valley, Bovec has a great deal to offer adventure-sports en-

thusiasts. With the Julian Alps above, the Soča River below and Triglav National Park at the back door, you could spend a week hiking, kayaking, mountain biking and, in winter, skiing at Mt Kanin, Slovenia's highest ski station, without ever doing the same thing twice.

The compact village square, **Trg Golobarskih Žrtev**, has everything you need. There are cafés, a hotel, the extremely helpful **Tourist Information Centre Bovec** (☎ 384 19 19; www.bovec .si; Trg Golobarskih Žrtev 8; ☺ 9am-8pm daily Jul & Aug, 9am-5pm Mon-Fri, 9am-noon & 4-6pm Sat, 9am-noon Sun Sep-Jun) and a handful of adrenaline-raising adventure-sports companies, including: **Avantura** (☎ 041-718 317; bovecavantura@hotmail.com); **Soča Rafting** (☎ 389 62 00; www.socarafting.si); **Outdoor Freaks** (☎ 389 64 90, 041-553 675; www.freakoutdoor .com); **Sport Mix** (☎ 389 61 60, 031-871 991; traft@siol .net); and **Top Extreme** (☎ 330 00 90, 041-620 636; www .top.si). Following are just some of the activities on offer:

Canyoning Two hours at Sušec costs €33.70 to €39.

Hydrospeed Like riding down a river on a boogie board; you'll pay €30 to €35 for an 8km ride.

White-water rafting Available only from April to October, it costs around €27 to €37 for a 10km trip, €34.60 to €40 for 21km.

Kayaking A guided 10km paddle costs from €30 per person, or two-day training courses from €77.

Caving A trip costs from €25.50 per person with guide.

In winter you can take a tandem paraglider flight (ie as a passenger accompanied by a qualified pilot) from the top of the Kanin cable car, 2000m above the valley floor. AThe cost of a flight costs from €100; ask the Avantura agency for details.

Private rooms (per person €12-25) are easy to come by in Bovec, and the tourist office and other agencies have hundreds on their lists.

Camping facilities are generally better in Kobarid, but **Kamp Polovnik** (☎ 388 60 69; www.camp -polovnik.com; adult/child €6.70/4.80; ☺ Apr-Oct) about 500m southeast of the town centre is in an attractive setting and much more convenient.

The 103-room **Alp Hotel** (☎ 388 60 40; www.bovec .net/hotelalp; Trg Golobarskih Žrtev 48; s €37-48, d €57.50-78; ☒ ☐) is fairly good value and as central as you are going to find in Bovec.

Dobra Vila (☎ 389 64 00; www.dobra-vila-bovec.com, Mala Vas 112; s/d €55/72; ☐) is a positive stunner of a 12-room boutique hotel housed in the former telephone exchange building. It has its own small cinema, library and vine cellar, as well as a fabulous restaurant.

Kobarid

☎ 05 / pop 1250

Some 21km south of Bovec, quaint Kobarid (Caporetto in Italian) lies in a broad valley on the west bank of the Soča River. Although it's surrounded by mountain peaks higher than 2200m, Kobarid feels more Mediterranean than alpine, and the Italian border at Robič is only 9km to the west.

On the town's main square is the extreme-sports agency, **XPoint** (☎ 388 53 08, 041-692 290; www.xpoint.si; Trg Svobode 6; ☼ 9.30am-5pm Apr-Oct), which can organise rafting, canyoning, canoe-ing and paragliding in Kobarid and Tolmin, 16km to the southeast. The **Tourist Information Centre Kobarid** (☎ 380 04 90; www.lto-sotocje .si; Gregorčičeva ul 8; ☼ 9am-8pm Mon-Fri, 9am-12.30pm & 3.30-8pm Sat & Sun Jul & Aug, 9am-12.30pm & 1.30-7pm Mon-Fri, 9am-1pm Sat Sep-Jun) is next door to the award-winning **Kobarid Museum** (☎ 389 00 00; Gregorčičeva ul 10; adult/student/child €4/2.90/2.10; ☼ 9am-6pm Mon-Fri, 9am-7pm Sat & Sun Apr-Oct, 10am-5pm Mon-Fri, 10am-6pm Sat & Sun Nov-Mar), devoted almost entirely to the Isonzo (Soča) Front of WWI (p492), which formed the backdrop to Ernest Hemingway novel's *A Farewell to Arms*. A free pamphlet titled *The Kobarid Historical Walk* outlines a 5km-long route that will take you past remnant WWI troop emplacements to the impressive Kozjak Stream Waterfalls.

The oldest camping ground in the Soča Valley, **Kamp Koren** (☎ 389 13 11; www.kamp-koren.si; Drežniške Ravne 33; per person €6.50-8.50; ☼ mid-Mar–Oct) is a small, one-hectare site, with wheelchair access, about 500m north of Kobarid on the left bank of the Soča River and just before the turnoff to Drežniške Ravne, a lovely village with traditional farmhouses.

The welcoming little **Apartma-Ra** (☎ 389 10 07; apartma-ra@siol.net; Gregorčičeva ul 6c; per person €15-25; ✗ ✗) between the museum and Trg Svobode is entirely nonsmoking. Some rooms have terraces, and bicycles are available for hire to guests for €6/9 per half-/full day.

In the centre of Kobarid you'll find two of Slovenia's best provincial restaurants, both of which specialise in fish and seafood: the incomparable **Topli Val** (☎ 389 93 00; Trg Svobode 1; entrées €7.50-10.85, mains €6.75-25; ☼ noon-10pm) and **Kotlar** (☎ 389 11 10; Trg Svobode 11; entrées €5.40-10.40, mains €6.25-16.70; ☼ noon-11pm Thu-Mon).

Getting There & Away

Weekday buses from Bovec via Kobarid go to Novo Gorica (€5.75, 1½ hours, 55km, five daily) and to Ljubljana (€6.95, three hours, 130km, up to four daily) passing Most na Soči train station for Bled and Bohinj. A bus crosses over the spectacular Vršič Pass to Kranjska Gora (€6.65, three hours, 68km) daily in July and August.

Novo Gorica

☎ 05 / pop 12,600

Novo Gorica is a green university town strad-dling the Italian border. When the town of Gorica, capital of the former Slovenian prov-ince of Goriška, was awarded to the Italians after WWII, the new socialist government in Yugoslavia set itself to building a model town on the eastern side of the border. They called it 'New Gorica' and erected a chain-link bar-rier between the two towns. This mini-'Berlin Wall' was pulled down to great fanfare in 2004, leaving the anomalous Piazza Transalp-ina (Trg z Mozaikom) straddling the border right behind Novo Gorica train station, where you'll now find the rather esoteric **Museum of the Border** (☎ 333 44 00; admission free; ☼ 1-5pm Mon-Fri, 9am-7pm Sat, 10am-7pm Sun).

With no barrier remaining, there's really nothing to stop you wandering across to the Italian side, where the Italian bus 1 will whisk you to Gorizia train station. However, this is still not a *legal* border crossing and won't become one until Slovenia joins the Schengen Convention. Meanwhile EU citizens may use a less direct shuttle bus (€1, 25 minutes, hourly) between the two train stations, or cross on foot at the **Gabrielle border crossing** (☎ 8am-8pm), some 500m south at the end of Erjavčeva ul, which becomes Via San Gabriele in Italy.

Other passport-holders are expected to use the 24-hour **Rožna Dolina-Cassa Rosa border cross-ing**. That's reached by half-hourly buses (any number) from Novo Gorica bus station, or by walking 20 minutes south from the train sta-tion: follow the railway line through the cycle tunnel, from where you immediately cross the tracks on a footbridge and continue along Ul Pinka Tomažiča and Pot na Pristavo. From Cassa Rosa take Italian bus 8 northbound along its convoluted route, which loops back to Gorizia bus/train stations.

The helpful **Tourist Information Centre Nova Gorica** (☎ 333 46 00; www.novagorica-turizem.si; Bev-kov trg 4; ☼ 8am-8pm Mon-Fri, 9am-1pm Sat & Sun Jul & Aug, 8am-6pm Mon-Fri, 9am-1pm Sat & Sun Sep-Jun) is in the lobby of the Kulturni Dom (Cultural House).

Novo Gorica's only inexpensive accommodation option, **Prenočišče Pertout** (☎ 330 75 50, 041-624 452; www.prenociscepertout.com; Ul 25 Maja 23; s/d/tr €22.50/36/48), is a five-room B&B in Rožna Dolina, south of the town centre and scarcely 100m northeast of the Italian border.

The Italian restaurant **Marco Polo** (☎ 302 97 29; Kidričeva ul 13; entrées €5.85-12.50, mains €7.50-1500; ☷ 11am-11pm Sun-Thu, 11am-midnight Fri & Sat, noon-midnight Sun), 250m east of the tourist office, is one of the town's best places to eat, serving both pizza (€3.75 to €6.25) and more ambitious dishes, and with a delightful back terrace.

Buses travel hourly between Novo Gorica and Ljubljana (€10.35, 2½ hours, 116km) via Postojna (€5.75, one hour, 53km), and up to six times daily to Bovec (€7.30, two hours, 77km) via Kobarid (€5.75, 1½ hours, 55km).

Trains link Novo Gorica with Bohinjska Bistrica (€4.50, 1½ hours, 61km, up to seven daily) and Bled or via Sežana and Divača to Postojna and Ljubljana (€7.30, 3½ hours, 153km, up to six daily).

KARST & COAST

Slovenia's short coast (47km) on the Adriatic is not renowned for its fine beaches, though the southernmost resort of Portorož has some decent ones. Three important towns full of Venetian Gothic architecture – Koper, Piran and Izola – are the drawing card here and will keep even the most indefatigable of sightseers busy. En route from Ljubljana you'll cross the Karst, a huge limestone plateau and a land of olives, ruby-red Teran wine, *pršut* (air-dried ham), old stone churches and deep subterranean caves. In fact, Slovenia's two most famous caverns – theme park–like Postojna and awesome Škocjan – are here.

POSTOJNA
☎ 05 / pop 8670

Slovenia's most popular natural tourist attraction, **Postojna Cave** (☎ 700 01 00; www.postojnska-jama .si; adult/student/child €16.65/12.50/13.80; ☷ tours hourly 9am-6pm May-Sep, 10am, noon, 2pm & 4pm Apr & Oct, 10am, noon & 2pm Mon-Fri, 10am, noon, 2pm & 4pm Sat & Sun Nov-Mar) is about 2km northwest of the town of Postojna. The 5.7km-long cavern is visited on a 1½-hour tour, but about 4km of it is covered by an electric train. The remaining 1700m is on foot. Inside, impressive stalagmites and stalactites stretch almost endlessly in all directions, as do the chattering crowds who pass them. The tour culminates with a quick encounter (in a tank) with the endemic *Proteus anguinus* (below). Dress warmly or rent a woollen cape (€2); even on summer days it's only 10°C (50°F) inside the cave.

Close to the cave's entrance is the **Proteus Vivarium** (adult/student/child €5/3.50/2.90; ☷ 8.30am-6.30pm May-Sep, 9.30am-4.30pm Apr & Oct, 9.30am-2.30pm Mon-Fri, 9.30am-4pm Sat & Sun Nov-Mar), a speliobiological research station with a video introduction to underground zoology. A 45-minute tour then leads you into a small, darkened cave to peep at some of the shy creatures you've just learned about. Don't expect monsters

SLOVENIA

THE HUMAN FISH

Proteus anguinus is one of the most mysterious creatures in the world. A kind of salamander, but related to no other amphibian, it is the largest known permanent cave-dwelling vertebrate. The blind little fellow lives hidden in the pitch black for up to a century and can go for years without food. It was discovered by the 17th-century Slovenian polymath Janez Vajkard Valvasor, who named it after the protector of Poseidon's sea creatures in Greek mythology and the Latin word for 'snake'.

Proteus anguinus is 25cm to 30cm long and is a bundle of contradictions. It has a long tail fin that it uses for swimming, but can also propel itself with its four legs (the front pair have three small 'fingers' and the back have two 'toes'). Though blind, *Proteus anguinus* has an excellent sense of smell and is sensitive to weak electric fields in the water. It uses these to move around in the dark, locate prey and communicate. It breathes through frilly, bright-red gills at the base of its head when submerged, but also has rudimentary lungs for breathing when outside the water. The human-like skin has no pigmentation whatsoever, but looks pink in the light due to blood circulation.

The question that scientists have asked themselves for three centuries is: how do they reproduce? The salamander's reproduction has never been witnessed in a natural state, and they haven't been very cooperative in captivity. It is almost certain that they hatch their young from eggs and don't reach sexual maturity until the (almost human) age of 16 or 18 years.

of the deep; most are so minuscule you can hardly see them.

Predjama, a village 9km northwest of Postojna, consists of half a dozen houses, an inn, a mock-medieval jousting course and the remarkable **Predjama Castle** (☎ 751 60 15; adult/student/ child €5/3.50/2.90; ☺ 9am-7pm May-Sep, 10am-6pm Apr & Oct, 10am-4pm Nov-Mar), which actually appears to grow out of a yawning cave. The partly furnished interior boasts costumed wax mannequins, one of which dangles from the dripping rock-roofed torture chamber. Beneath are stalactite-adorned **caves** (adult/student/child €5/3.50/2.90, cave & castle combination ticket €9/6.30/5.20), which lack Postojna's crowds but also much of its grandeur.

Sleeping & Eating

Lots of houses in Postojna rent out **private rooms** (per person €13.90-15.80). Your best contact is **Kompas Postojna** (☎ 721 14 80; info@kompas-postojna.si; Titov trg 2a; ☺ 8am-8pm Mon-Fri, 9am-1pm Sat Jun-Aug, 8am-7pm Mon-Fri, 9am-1pm Sat May, Sep & Oct, 8am-5pm Mon-Fri, 9am-1pm Sat Nov-Apr).

Hotel & Hostel Sport (☎ 720 622 44; www.sport-hotel .si; Kolodvorska c 1; dm €13-15, s €34-38, d €43-56; ☒ ☐) This recent arrival, with 37 spic-and-span and very comfortable rooms, including 40 hostel beds, is just 300m north of the centre of Postojna. True to its name, it can arrange all sorts of activities, including mountain-biking trips in nearby Notranjska Regional Park.

Pizzeria Minutka (☎ 720 36 25; Ljubljanska c 14; pizza €4.20-5.85; ☺ 10am-11pm) A pizzeria with a terrace, Minutka is a favourite with locals and is just south of the Hotel & Hostel Sport.

Getting There & Away

Buses from Ljubljana to Koper, Piran or Novo Gorica all stop in Postojna (€5.75, one hour, 54km, half-hourly). The train is less useful, as the train station is 1km east of town near the bypass (ie 3km from the caves).

As close as you'll get by local bus from Postojna to Predjama (€1.70, 15 minutes, 9km, five daily Monday to Friday) and during the school year only is Bukovje, a village about 2km northeast of Predjama. A taxi from Postojna, including an hour's wait at Predjama Castle, will cost €25, which staff at Kompas Postojna can arrange.

ŠKOCJAN CAVES

☎ 05

The immense **Škocjan Caves** (☎ 763 28 40, 708 21 10; www.park-skocjanske-jame.si; Škocjan 2; adult/student/child

€10.85/7.50), a Unesco World Heritage site since 1986, are far more captivating than the larger one at Postojna, and for many travellers a visit here will be one of the highlights of their trip to Slovenia – a page right out of Jules Verne's *A Journey to the Centre of the Earth*. With relatively few stalactites, the attraction is the sheer depth of the awesome underground chasm, which you cross by a dizzying little footbridge. To see this you must join a shepherded two-hour walking tour, involving hundreds of steps and ending with a rickety funicular ride. Tours depart hourly from 10am to 5pm from May to September, and 10am, 1pm and 3.30pm in April, May and October, and 10am and 1pm Monday to Saturday, and 10am, 1pm and 3pm Sunday from November to March.

The nearest town with accommodation is **Divača** (population 1300), 5km to the northwest. Here **Gostilna Malovec** (☎ 763 02 00; Kraška 30a; s/d €20/40) has a half-dozen basic but comfortable renovated rooms in a building beside its popular restaurant (entrées €3.35 to €5.85, mains €5 to €9.10; open 7am to 10pm). For something a bit more, well, 21st century, cross the road to **Orient Express** (☎ 763 30 10; Kraška c 67; pizza €5-10.85; ☺ 11am-11pm Sun-Fri, 11am-2am Sat), a lively pizzeria and pub.

Buses from Ljubljana to Koper and the coast stop at Divača (€7.60, 1½ hours, 82km, half-hourly), as do trains (€5.90, 1½ hours, 104km, hourly). Staff at both the train station and at helpful **Kraški Turist** (☎ 041-573 768; kraskiturist@gmail.com; ☺ 8am-5pm Apr-Oct) next to the small café at the station can provide you with a photocopied route map for walking to the caves. Alternatively, Kraški Turist has bicycles for hire (€1.25/8.35 per hour/day) and can arrange transport for around €5 per person.

LIPICA

☎ 05 / pop 130

Lipica is where Austrian Archduke Charles, son of Ferdinand I, established a stud farm to breed horses for the Spanish Riding School in Vienna in 1580.

The snow-white beasties are still bred here at the **Lipica Stud Farm** (☎ 739 15 80; www.lipica.org; Lipica 5; adult/student from €7/3.50), which offers equestrian fans a variety of tours, as well as rides and lessons. Tour times are too complex and varied to list here, please contact the farm for details.

The 68-room **Hotel Maestoso** (☎ 739 15 80; www .lipica.org; s €53-68, d €82-106; ☐ ☒) has excellently appointed modern rooms looking over the golf links–like landscape.

KOPER

☎ 05 / pop 23,270

By far the largest town on the Slovenian coast, Koper (Capodistria in Italian) is a workaday port city that at first glance scarcely seems to give tourism a second thought. Yet its central core is delightfully quiet, quaint and much less touristy than its ritzy cousin Piran, 17km down the coast.

Koper grew rich as a key port trading salt, and was the capital of Istria under the 15th- and 16th-century Venetian Republic. At that time it was an island commanding a U-shaped bay of saline ponds, something hard to imagine now, given the centuries of land reclamation that have joined it very firmly to the mainland.

Orientation

The joint bus and train station is 1.4km southeast of central Titov trg. To walk into town, just head north along Kolodvorska c in the direction of the cathedral's distinctive campanile (bell tower). Alternatively, take bus 1, 2 or 3 to Muda Gate.

Information

Banka Koper (Kidričeva ul 14; ☉ 8.30am-noon & 3-5pm Mon-Fri, 8.30am-noon Sat)

Kompas (☎ 663 05 82; Pristaniška ul 17; ☉ 8am-7.30pm Mon-Fri, 8am-1pm Sat) Has private rooms.

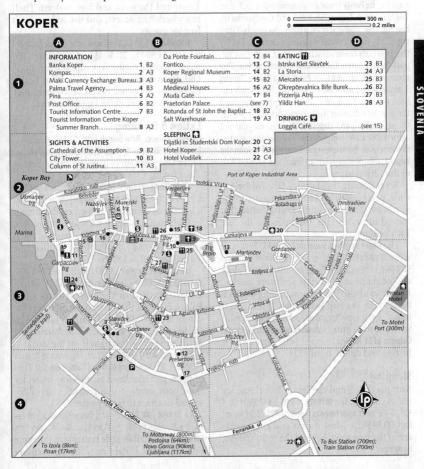

KOPER

INFORMATION	Da Ponte Fountain...................12 B4	**EATING**
Banka Koper...........................1 B2	Fontico....................................13 C3	Istrska Klet Slavček...............23 B3
Kompas..................................2 A3	Koper Regional Museum........14 B2	La Storia................................24 A3
Maki Currency Exchange Bureau..3 A3	Loggia....................................15 B2	Mercator................................25 B3
Palma Travel Agency...............4 B3	Medieval Houses....................16 A2	Okrepčevalnica Bife Burek....26 B2
Pina.......................................5 A2	Muda Gate.............................17 B4	Pizzerija Atrij.........................27 B3
Post Office..............................6 B2	Praetorian Palace...............(see 7)	Yildiz Han...............................28 A3
Tourist Information Centre.......7 B3	Rotunda of St John the Baptist...18 B2	
Tourist Information Centre Koper	Salt Warehouse......................19 A3	**DRINKING**
Summer Branch.....................8 A2		Loggia Café.......................(see 15)
	SLEEPING	
SIGHTS & ACTIVITIES	Dijaški in Študentski Dom Koper.20 C2	
Cathedral of the Assumption....9 B2	Hotel Koper...........................21 A3	
City Tower..............................10 B3	Hotel Vodišek........................22 C4	
Column of St Justina...............11 A3		

SLOVENIA

Maki Currency Exchange Bureau (Pristaniška ul 13; ☼ 7.30am-7.30pm Mon-Fri, 7.30am-1pm Sat)

Palma Travel Agency (☎ 663 36 60; Pristaniška ul 21; ☼ 8am-7pm Mon-Fri, 8am-noon Sat) Can arrange private rooms.

Pina (☎ 627 80 72; Kidričeva ul 43; adult/student per hr €3.75/1.25; ☼ 9am-9pm Mon-Fri) Central internet café with 10 terminals.

Tourist Information Centre main branch (☎ 664 64 03; tic@koper.si; Praetorian Palace, Titov trg 3; ☼ 8am-9pm Jul & Aug, 9am-5pm Sun Sep-Jun); summer branch (☎ 663 20 10; Ukmarjev trg 7; ☼ 8am-9pm Jul & Aug)

Sights

The greatest attraction of Koper is aimless wandering. You change centuries abruptly passing through the **Muda Gate** (1516). Continue north past the **Da Ponte Fountain** (Prešernov trg), erected in 1666, and up Župančičeva ul and Čevljarska ul, the narrow commercial artery, to reach Titov trg. This fine central square is dominated by the 1480 **City Tower** attached to the part-Gothic, part-Renaissance **Cathedral of the Assumption**. The renovated 15th-century **Praetorian Palace** (Titov trg 3; admission free) contains the town hall, with exhibits on the 1st floor and an old pharmacy and the tourist office on the ground floor. Opposite, the splendid 1463 **Loggia** is now an elegant yet affordable café (opposite). To the east of it is the circular Romanesque **Rotunda of St John the Baptist**, a baptistery dating from the second half of the 12th century.

Several more fine façades face **Trg Brolo**, a wide, peacefully Mediterranean square to the southeast. One is the shield-dotted **Fontico** that started life as a grain warehouse in the late 14th century.

The **Koper Regional Museum** (☎ 663 35 70; Kidričeva ul 19; adult/child €1.70/1.25; ☼ 10am-6pm Tue-Fri, 9am-1pm Sat & Sun) is inside the Belgramoni-Tacco Palace and contains an Italianate sculpture garden. Kidričeva ul also has a few appealing **medieval houses** with beamed overhangs. It leads west into Carpacciov trg, the former fish market with a 15th-century **salt warehouse** and a stone **Column of St Justina**, topped with a statue of St Justina and dating from 1571.

Sleeping

Kompas (p513) and the Palma Travel Agency (above) can arrange **private rooms** (s €12.50-14.60, d €20.85-25) and **apartments** (apt for 2 €29.20-35.40, apt for 4 €43.80-54.20). Most rooms and apartments are in the new town beyond the train station, however.

Motel Port (☎ 639 32 60; motel.port@siol.net; Ankaranska c 7; dm €14, rm for up to 3/4 €46/65; ✕ 🖳) Hidden on the top floor of a Mondrianesque shopping centre south of the Old Town, this place has excellent en suite rooms, but its location beside a truck terminal results in a deep traffic rumble and the mainly male, lorry-driver clientele may discourage single women.

Dijaški in Študentski Dom Koper (☎ 662 62 50; www.d-dom.kp.edus.si, in Slovene; Cankarjeva ul 5; dm €15; ☼ late Jun-late Aug; ✕) In summer this relatively central student dormitory becomes a hostel. Try to arrive early, as it gets booked up fast.

Hotel Vodišek (☎ 639 24 68; www.hotel-vodisek.com; Kolodvorska c 2; s/d/tr €40/60/75; ✕ 🖳 🛗) This tiny hotel, with 32 reasonably priced rooms is in a shopping centre halfway between the Old Town and the train and bus stations. TheIt has wheelchair access, and use of bicycles is free for guests.

Hotel Koper (☎ 610 05 00; www.terme-catez.si; Pristaniška ul 3; s €60, d €100-110; 🖳 🛗) This pleasant, 65-room property on the very edge of the historic Old Town is the only central hotel in Koper. RatesIt has wheelchair access, and rates include entry to Aquapark at the Hotel Žusterna.

Eating & Drinking

Okrepčevalnica Bife Burek (☎ 271 347; Kidričeva ul 8; snacks €1.50-2.10; ☼ 7am-10pm) Buy good-value *burek* and pizza slices here and enjoy them at Titov trg for a take-away snack.

Yildiz Han (☎ 626 14 60; Pristaniška ul 2; entrées €2.70-5, mains €6.90-10.20; ☼ noon-midnight) 'Star House', a branch of a similarly named establishment in Ljubljana, has all our Turkish favourites, including *sigara böreği* (filo parcels filled with cheese) and *yaprak dolmasi* (stuffed vine leaves), as well as kebabs.

Istrska Klet Slavček (☎ 627 67 29; Župančičeva ul 39; dishes €3.35-10.85; ☼ 7am-10pm Mon-Fri) This 'Istrian Cellar', situated in the 18th-century Carli Palace, is one of the most colourful places for a meal in the Old Town. Filling set lunches go for less than €10, and there's Malvazija and Teran wine drawn straight from the barrel.

Pizzerija Atrij (☎ 626 28 03; Triglavska ul 2; pizza €4.20-6.05; ☼ 9am-10pm Mon-Fri, 10am-10pm Sat) This popular pizzeria down an alleyway no wider than your average quarterback's shoulder spread has a small back garden.

La Storia (☎ 031-769 079; Pristaniška ul 3; entrées €4.80-6.70, mains €5-10; ☼ 11am-9pm Mon-Fri, noon-5pm Sat & Sun) This Italian-style trattoria in the same building as the Hotel Koper focuses on pasta dishes and salads, and has outside seating in the warmer months. The salad bar (small/large €2.30/3.35) is good value.

Mercator (Titov trg 2; 7am-8pm Mon-Fri, 7am-1pm Sat, 8am-noon Sun) This small supermarket branch in the Old Town also opens on weekends.

Loggia Café (621 32 13; Titov trg 1; 7.30am-10pm Mon-Sat, 10am-10pm Sun) This lovely café in the exquisite 15th-century Loggia is the best vantage point for watching the crowds on Titov trg.

Getting There & Away

Buses run to Piran (€2.60, 30 minutes, 18km) half-hourly on weekdays and every 40 minutes on weekends. Up to 15 buses daily run to Ljubljana (€10.35, 1¾ to 2½ hours, 120km), though the train is more comfortable, with IC services (€8.70, 2¼ hours) at 5.55am and 2.45pm, and local services (€7.30, 2½ hours) at 10.03am and 7.12pm.

Buses to Trieste (€3, one hour, 23km, up to 13 daily) run along the coast via Ankaran and Muggia on weekdays only. Destinations in Croatia include Rijeka (€7.60, two hours, 84km, 10.10am Monday to Friday), Rovinj (€11.10, 129km, three hours, 3.55pm daily July and August) via Poreč (€8, two hours, 88km), plus two or three to Poreč only, notably at 8.30am Monday to Friday.

IZOLA

☎ 05 / pop 10,425

Overshadowed by much-more genteel Piran, Izola (Isola in Italian) is bypassed by most foreign visitors and, frankly, the locals don't seem to give a damn. This also-ran place does have a certain Venetian charm, a few narrow old streets, and some nice waterfront bars and restaurants. Ask the helpful **Tourist Information Centre Izola** (640 10 50; tic.izola@izola .si; Sončno nabrežje 4; 9am-9pm Mon-Sat, 10am-5pm Sun Jun-Sep, 8am-7pm Mon-Fri, 8am-5pm Sat Oct-May) about private rooms, or in summer check out the 174-bed **Dijaški Dom Izola** (662 1740; branko .miklobusec@guest.arnes.si; Prekomorskih Brigad ul 7; dm from €20; Jul & Aug;), which overlooks the marina and offers about the cheapest beds you'll find within striking distance of Piran. Because of the lack of tourists Izola is a good place to enjoy a seafood meal, especially at **Ribič** (641 83 13; Veliki trg 3; entrées €4.20-8.75, mains €8-17.50; 8am-1am), a venue much loved by locals. Out in Izola's industrial suburbs, **Ambasada Gavioli** (641 8212; www.ambasada-gavioli.com; Industrijska c; midnight-6am Sat) remains Slovenia's

top nightrave club, featuring a procession of international star DJs.

Frequent buses between Koper (€1.70, 15 minutes, 6km) and Piran (€1.70, 20 minutes, 9.5km) go via Izola, and there's a catamaran service to Venice (p523).

PIRAN

☎ 05 / pop 4050

Everyone's favourite town on the Slovenian coast, picturesque little Piran (Pirano in Italian) sits on the tip of a narrow peninsula, the westernmost point of Slovenian Istria. Strunjan Bay is to the north; Piran Bay and Portorož, Slovenia's largest beach resort, lie to the south. Piran's Old Town is a gem of Venetian Gothic architecture and is full of narrow streets. In summer the town gets pretty overrun by tourists, but in April or October it's hard not to fall in love with the winding Venetian-Gothic alleyways and tempting seafood restaurants. It's thought that the town's name comes from the Greek word for fire (*pyr*). In ancient times fires were lit at Punta, the very tip of the peninsula, to guide ships to the port at Aegida (now Koper).

Orientation

Buses from everywhere except Portorož arrive at the bus station, just a 300m stroll along the portside Cankarjevo nabrežje from central Tartinijev trg. Be warned that a car is an encumbrance, not a help in Piran. Vehicles are stopped at a tollgate 200m south of the bus station, where the sensible choice is to use the huge Fornače car park (€0.80/7.70 per hour/day €0.80/7.70). You could take a ticket and drive on into the town centre (first hour free, then €2.70 per hour) but old Piran is so small, parking is so limited and its alleyways so narrow (mostly footpaths) that you're likely to regret it.

Information

Banka Koper (Tartinijev trg 12; 8.30am-noon & 3-5pm Mon-Fri, 8.30am-noon Sat)

Cyber Point Piran (671 00 22; http://cyberpoint .ksop-cscp.si, in Slovene; 4th fl, Študentek Bldg, Župančičeva ul 14; per hr €4.20; 1-9pm Mon-Fri) Internet access on five terminals.

Maona Tourist Agency (673 45 20; www.maona .si; Cankarjevo nabrežje 7; 9am-7pm Mon-Fri, 10am-1pm & 5-7pm Sat, 10am-1pm Sun) Unstintingly helpful travel agency can organise anything from private rooms to activities and cruises.

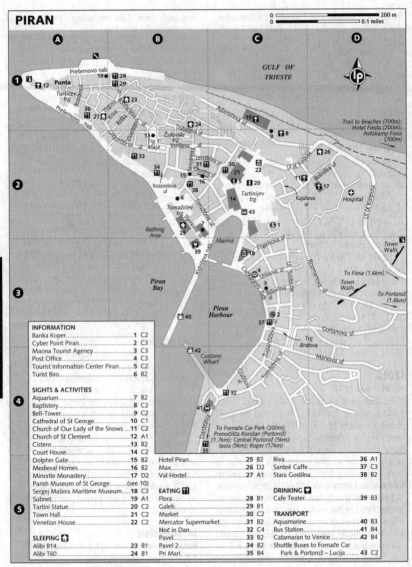

PIRAN

GULF OF TRIESTE

Trail to Beaches (700m);
Hotel Fiesta (700m);
Avtokamp Fiesa (700m)

Piran Bay

Piran Harbour

To Fiesa (1.6km)

To Portorož (1.8km)

To Fornače Car Park (200m);
Prenočišča Korotan (Portorož)
(1.7km); Central Portorož (5km);
Izola (9km); Koper (17km)

INFORMATION		
Banka Koper	1	C2
Cyber Point Piran	2	C3
Maona Tourist Agency	3	C3
Post Office	4	C3
Tourist Information Center Piran	5	C2
Turist Biro	6	B2

SIGHTS & ACTIVITIES		
Aquarium	7	B2
Baptistery	8	C2
Bell-Tower	9	C2
Cathedral of St George	10	C1
Church of Our Lady of the Snows	11	C2
Church of St Clement	12	A1
Cistern	13	B2
Court House	14	C2
Dolphin Gate	15	B2
Medieval Homes	16	B2
Minorite Monastery	17	D2
Parish Museum of St George	(see 10)	
Sergej Mašera Maritime Museum	18	C3
Subnet	19	A1
Tartini Statue	20	C2
Town Hall	21	C2
Venetian House	22	C2

SLEEPING		
Alibi B14	23	B1
Alibi T60	24	B1

Hotel Piran	25	B2
Max	26	D2
Val Hostel	27	A1

EATING		
Flora	28	B1
Galeb	29	B1
Market	30	C2
Mercator Supermarket	31	B2
Noč in Dan	32	C4
Pavel	33	B2
Pavel 2	34	B2
Pri Mari	35	B4

Riva	36	A1
Santeé Caffe	37	C3
Stara Gostilna	38	B2

DRINKING		
Cafe Teater	39	B3

TRANSPORT		
Aquamarine	40	B3
Bus Station	41	B4
Catamaran to Venice	42	B4
Shuttle Buses to Fornače Car Park & Portorož – Lucija	43	C2

Tourist Information Center Piran (☎ 673 02 20;
www.piran.si; Tartinijev trg; ❧ 9am-1.30pm & 3-9pm
mid-Jun–mid-Sep, 10am-5pm mid-Sep–mid-Jun) Located
in the impressive Town Hall.

Sights & Activities

Piran is continuously watched over by the **Cathedral of St George** (Adamičeva ul 2). If time weighs

on your hands, visit the attached **Parish Museum
of St George** (☎ 673 34 40; admission €1; ❧ 11am-
5pm), which contains church plate, paintings
and a lapidary. The cathedral's freestanding
bell tower (1608) was clearly modelled on the
campanile at San Marco's Basilica in Venice,
and its octagonal **baptistery** dating from the
mid-17th century has imaginatively recycled

a 2nd-century Roman sarcophagus for use as a baptismal font. The **Minorite Monastery** (☎ 673 44 17; Bolniška ul 20) on the way down to Tartinijev trg has a delightful cloister, and in the **Church of Our Lady of the Snows** almost opposite is a superb 15th-century arch painting of the Crucifixion. The **Sergej Mašera Maritime Museum** (☎ 671 00 40; Cankarjevo nabrežje 3; adult/student €2.50/2.10; ☽ 9amnoon & 6-9pm Tue-Sun Jul & Aug, 9am-noon & 3-6pm Tue-Sun Sep-Jun) has 2000-year-old Roman amphorae beneath the glass ground floor, and lots of impressive antique ships' models and ex-voto offerings upstairs.

One of Piran's most eye-catching structures is the red 15th-century **Venetian House** (Tartinijev trg 4), with its tracery windows and stone lion relief. When built this would have overlooked Piran's inner port, which was filled to form Tartinijev trg in 1894. The square is named in honour of the violinist and composer Giuseppe Tartini (1692–1770), who was born in what is now the house at Tartinijev trg 7 and whose **statue** stands in the middle of the square. The square is dominated to the north by the porticoed 19th-century **Town Hall**, which houses the tourist office, and to the west by the **Court House**. The **Aquarium** (☎ 673 25 72; Kidričevo nabrežje 4; adult/child €2.50/1.70; ☽ 10am-noon & 2-7pm late Mar–mid-Jun, Sep–mid-Oct, 9am-10pm mid-Jun–Aug), south of the square along the harbour, has a tremendous variety of sea life packed into its two-dozen tanks.

Behind the market north of Tartinijev trg, **medieval homes** have been built into an ancient defensive wall along Obzidna ul, which passes under the 15th-century **Dolphin Gate**. **Trg 1 Maja** (1st May Sq) may sound like a socialist parade ground, but in fact it's one of Piran's most attractive squares, with a **cistern** dating from the late 18th century. Rainwater from the surrounding roofs flowed into it through the fish borne by the two stone putti in the back.

Punta, the historical 'snout' of Piran, still has a **lighthouse**, but today's is small and modern. Just behind it, however, the round, serrated tower of 18th-century **Church of St Clement** evokes the ancient beacon from which Piran likely got its name.

Most water-related activities take place in Portorož, but if you want to give diving a go, **Subnet** (☎ 673 22 18; www.sub-net.si; Prešernovo nabrežje 24; shore/boat dive €25/40; ☽ 9am-noon & 2-6pm Sun-Fri, 9am-noon & 2-7pm Sat) organises shore and boatguided dives, gives PADI open-water courses (around €150) and hires equipment. Don't expect Red Sea–style coralcorals in these parts,

though. The most unusual underwater sight hereabouts is the wreck of a WWII seaplane in Portorož Bay.

Sleeping

Private rooms (s €15.85-25, d €23-35) and **apartments** (apt for 2 people €36.30-44.20, for 4 €56-72) are available through Maona Tourist Agency (p515) and the **Turist Biro** (☎ 673 25 09; www.turistbiro-ag.si; Tomažičeva ul 3; ☽ 10am-1pm & 4-7pm Mon-Fri, 10am-1pm Sat & sun), opposite the Hotel Piran.

Avtokamp Fiesa (☎ 674 62 30, 031-487 255; autocamp .fiesa@siol.net; adult €8.35-10, child €2.50; ☽ May-Sep) The closest camping ground to Piran is at Fiesa, 4km by road but less than 1km if you follow the coastal trail east of the Cathedral of St George. It's tiny and becomes very crowded in summer.

Val Hostel (☎ 673 25 55; www.hostel-val.com; Gregorčičeva ul 38a; with/without HI card €20/24 Jun-Aug, €18/23 Sep-May; ✕ ▯) This central partially renovated hostel has 22 rooms, with shared shower, free internet access, kitchen and washing machine. It's a great favourite with backpackers.

Alibi B14 (☎ 031-363 666; www.alibi.si; Bonifacijeva ul 14; per person €20-25; ✕ ▯) The most welcome arrival on the budget/midrange accommodation scene in Piran in years is this upbeat and colourful four-floor party hostel, with six rooms, each with four to six beds, kitchenette and bath. It's in ancient townhouse on a narrow street, and there's a washing machine and free internet access.

Alibi T60 (Trubarjeva ul 60; per person €30; ✕ ▧ ▯) Even better is Alibi B14's sister-hostel, the more subdued Alibi T60, to the east, with a fully equipped double on each of its five floors. The top room's view terrace view is priceless. Reception is at Alibi B14.

Hotel Fiesa (☎ 671 22 00; www.hotel-fiesa.com; Fiesa 57; s €53-70, d €75-98) Although not in Piran itself, this 22-room hotel overlooking the sea near the Avtokamp Fiesa camping ground is one of the most atmospheric places to stay in the area.

Max (☎ 673 34 36, 041-692 928; www.maxpiran.com; Ul IX Korpusa 26; s/d €50/60; ✕ ▯) Piran's most romantic accommodation option has rooms, each named rather than numbered, in a delightful, very pink townhouse just down from the cathedral.

Hotel Piran (☎ 676 21 00; www.hoteli-piran.si; Stjenkova ul 1; s €57-84, d €70-123, ste €131-181; ✕ ▧ ▯) The Hotel Piran has 80 rooms and 10 apartments, and is right on the water.

Eating & Drinking

One of Piran's attractions is its plethora of fish restaurants, especially along Prešernovo nabrežje, though don't expect any bargains. Virtually all charge around €6.25 for a plate of grilled squid and from €33.40 per kg for fish.

Pavel (☎ 674 71 01; Gregorčičeva ul 3; 🕙 11am-11pm) This fish restaurant – the granddaddy of them all – and its sister-eatery nearby, **Pavel 2** (☎ 674 71 02; Kosovelova ul 1; 🕙 11am-midnight), cater to the tourist trade and are somewhat overpriced; expect to pay about €25 per person with house wine.

Flora (☎ 673 12 58; Prešernovo nabrežje 26; pizza €3.35-5.85; 🕙 8am-1am Jul & Aug, 10am-10pm Sep-Jun) The terrace of this simple pizzeria east of the Punta lighthouse has uninterrupted views of the Adriatic.

Pri Mari (☎ 673 47 35, 041-616 488; Dantejeva ul 17; entrées €3.75-8.30, mains €6.25-14.60; 🕙 noon-10pm Tue-Sat, noon-6pm Sun) This very stylish restaurant south of the bus station makes an ambitious (and successful) attempt at combining Mediterranean and Slovenian food. Service is slow, so go with time on your hands.

Stara Gostilna (☎ 673 31 65; Savudrijska ul 2; entrées €4.20-7, mains €5.85-14.60; 🕙 9am-11pm) This delightful bistro in the Old Town serves both meat and fish dishes, and offers some of the best and most welcoming service in town.

Riva (☎ 673 22 25; Gregorčičeva ul 43; entrées €5-8.30, mains €5-16.60; 🕙 9am-midnight) Our new favourite (and very classy) seafood restaurant on Prešernovo nabrežje has the best sea views, décor and a pizzeria (pizza €4.20 to €5.40) next door for ichthyphobes.

Galeb (☎ 673 32 25; Pusterla ul 5; meals from €14.60; 🕙 11am-4pm & 6pm-midnight Wed-Mon) This excellent family-run restaurant is east of the Punta lighthouse. It's totally nonsmoking.

Santeé Caffe (☎ 051-309 980; Cankarjevo nabrežje 11; sandwiches from €1.25, salads €4.20; 🕙 7am-midnight) The hyperfriendly Santeé Caffe has sandwiches (€1.25 to €3.10) and salads (€4.20), and walls painted in colours as vivid as its excellent ice creams.

Café Teater (☎ 041-638 933; Stjenkova ul 1; 🕙 7am-3am Mon-Fri, 9am-3am Sat & Sun) Anyone who's anyone in Piran can be found at this café, with a waterfront terrace and antique furnishings.

There's an outdoor **market** (Zelenjavni trg; 🕙 7am-2pm Mon-Sat) in the small square behind the Town Hall. There's a small **Mercator** (Levstikova ul 3; 🕙 7am-8pm Mon-Fri, 7am-1pm Sat, 8-11am Sun) supermarket in the Old Town, and a **Noč**

in Dan (☎ 671 57 52; Tomšičeva ul 41; 🕙 7am-midnight) branch opposite the bus station.

Getting There & Away

From the bus station buses run every 30 to 40 minutes to Koper (€2.60, half-hour, 18km) via Izola, while five daily (Monday to Friday only) head for Trieste (€4.60, 1¾ hours, 36km) and up to eight daily to Ljubljana (€11.70, 2½ to three hours, 140km) via Divača and Postojna.

From Tartinijev trg, shuttle buses (€1) travel to Portorož–Lucija (bus 1) and Portorož via Strunjan (bus 3).

Piran and Izola despatch catamarans to Venice (p523) at least once a week.

PORTOROŽ

☎ 05 / pop 2800

Portorož (Portorose in Italian), Slovenia's biggest resort, can be a bit honky-tonk, especially along Obala, the main drag, but it isn't all bad. Its sandy beaches are the largest on the coast and are relatively clean, there are pleasant spas and wellness centres where you can take the waters or cover yourself in curative mud, and the list of other activities is endless. At the same time the vast array of accommodation options makes Portorož a useful fall back if everything's full in nearby Piran. Full listings are available at the **Tourist Information Centre Portorož** (☎ 674 02 31; www.portoroz.si; Obala 16; 🕙 9am-1.30pm & 3-9pm mid-Jun–mid-Sep, 10am-5pm mid-Sep–mid-Jun). Just off the main road between Piran and the centre of Portorož, the unusually upmarket, summeronly hostel **Prenočišča Korotan** (☎ 674 5400; www.sd .upr.si/sdp/prenocisca; Obala 11; s/d/tr €29/41/55; 🕙 Jul & Aug; 🖵) in Korotan has en suite rooms and its internet computers are open to nonguests year-round. Most of Portorož is high-rise city. For something on a more human scale, check out the lovely 48-room **Hotel Marco** (☎ 617 40 00; www .hotel-marko.com; Obala 28; s €54-83, d 67-104), with lovely gardens and just opposite the beach.

The pleasant cantina **Papa Chico** (☎ 677 93 10; Obala 26; entrées €3.75-5.45, mains €4.60-8.75; 🕙 9am-2am Mon-Sat, 10am-2am Sun) serves 'Mexican fun food' (go figure), including fajitas (€7.50 to €9.20).

The über-designer café **Kavarna Cacao** (☎ 674 10 35; Obala 14; 🕙 8am-3am) wins the award as the most stylish on the coast, with a fabulous terrace.

There are dozens of decent pizzerias all along Obala, but the place of choice is **Pizzeria Figarola** (☎ 674 22 00; Obala 14a; pizza €5.65-7.50; 🕙 10am-10pm), with a huge terrace just up from the main pier, serving pizza and pasta dishes.

Every 20 minutes, shuttle bus 1 (€1) from Piran trundles right along Obala to Lucija, passing by Prenočišča Korotan.

SLOVENIA DIRECTORY

ACCOMMODATION

Accommodation listings throughout this guide have been ordered by price – from the cheapest to the most expensive. Very, very roughly, budget accommodation means a double room under €50, midrange is €51 to €100 and top end is anything over €101.

Camping grounds generally charge per person, whether you're in a tent or caravan. Rates always include hot showers. Almost all sites close from mid-October to mid-April. Camping 'rough' is illegal in Slovenia, and this is enforced, especially around Bled. Seek out the Slovenian Tourist Board's *Camping in Slovenia*.

Slovenia's growing stable of hostels includes Ljubljana's trendy Celica and the Alibi hostels found both in the capital and at Piran. Throughout the country there are student dorms moonlighting as hostels in July and August. Unless stated otherwise hostel rooms share bathrooms. They typically cost €13 to €21; prices are at their highest in midsummer, when it can sometimes be difficult to find accommodation at any price.

Tourist information offices can help you access extensive networks of private rooms, apartments and tourist farms, or they can recommend private agencies that will. Such accommodation can appear misleadingly cheap if you carelessly overlook the 30% to 50% surcharge levied on stays of less than three nights. Also beware that many such properties are in outlying villages with minimal public transport, and that the cheapest one-star category rooms with shared bathroom are actually very rare, so you'll often pay well above the quoted minimum. Depending on the season you might save a little money by going directly to any house with a sign reading *sobe* (rooms).

Guesthouses, known as a *penzion, gostišče,* or *prenočišča,* are often cosy and better value than full-blown hotels, some of which are unattractive if well-renovated socialist-era holdovers. Nonetheless it can be difficult to find a double room in a hotel for under €50. Beware that locally listed rates are usually quoted per person assuming double occupancy. A tourist tax – routinely €0.65 to €1 per person and a

hefty single-occupancy supplement – often lurk in the footnotes. Unless otherwise indicated, room rates include en suite toilet, shower with towels and soap, and breakfast.

ACTIVITIES

Slovenia is a very well-organised place for all outdoor activities.

Extreme Sports

Several areas specialise in adrenaline-rush activities, the greatest range being available at Bovec, famous for white-water rafting, hydro-speed, kayaking and canyoning – ie sliding down and through waterfalls and gullies in a neoprene wetsuit with the assistance of a well-trained (and licensed) guide. Bovec is also a great place for paragliding; in winter you ascend Mt Kanin (below) via ski lift and then jump off. Gliding costs are very reasonable from Lesce near Bled. Scuba diving from Piran is also good value.

Hiking

Hiking is extremely popular, with the **Alpine Association of Slovenia** (www.pzs.si) counting some 55,000 members and Ljubljančani flocking in droves to Triglav National Park on weekends. There are around 7000km of waymarked paths, and in summer 167 mountain huts offer comfortable trailside refuge. Several shorter treks are outlined in the Sunflower Guide *Slovenia* (www.sunflowerbooks.co.uk), now in its 2nd edition.

Skiing

Skiing is a Slovenian passion, with slopes particularly crowded over the Christmas holidays and early in February; see **Slovenia – Official Travel Guide** (www.slovenia-tourism.si/skiing) for much more information.

Just west of Maribor in eastern Slovenia (the country's second-largest city) is a popular choice and the biggest downhill skiing area in the country. Although relatively low (336m to 1347m), it's easily accessible, with very varied downhill pistes and relatively short lift queues.

Kranjska Gora (up to 1291m) has some challenging runs, and the world record for ski-jumping was set at nearby Planica. Above Lake Bohinj, Vogel (up to 1800m) is particularly scenic, as is Kanin (up to 2300m) above Bovec, which can have snow as late as May. Being relatively close to Ljubljana, Krvavec (up to 1970m), northeast of Kranj, can have particularly long lift queues.

Other Activities

Mountain bikes are available for hire from travel agencies at Bovec, Bled and Bohinj. The hire season is usually limited to May to October, however.

The Soča River near Kobarid and the Sava Bohinjka near Bohinj are great for fly-fishing (season April to October). Licences (per day €5, catch and release €34) are sold at tourist offices and certain hotels.

Spas and wellness centres are very popular in Slovenia; see **Slovenia Spas** (www.terme-giz.si) for more information. Most towns have some sort of spa complex, and hotels often offer free or bargain-rate entry to their guests. One of the most celebrated spa towns in the country is Rogaška Slatina, close to the Croatian border about 40km east of Celje.

BUSINESS HOURS

All businesses post their opening times (*delovni čas*) on the door. Many shops close Saturday afternoons. Sundays are still 'holy'; although a handful of grocery stores open, including some branches of the ubiquitous Mercator chain. Most museums close on Monday. Banks often take lunch breaks from 12.30pm to 2pm and only a few open on Saturday morning.

Restaurants typically open for lunch and dinner until at least 10pm, and bars until midnight, though they may have longer hours on the weekend and shorter ones on Sunday.

EMBASSIES & CONSULATES
Slovenian Embassies & Consulates

Slovenian representations abroad are fully listed on **Government of the Republic of Slovenia – Ministry of Foreign Affairs** (www.mzz.gov.si) and include the following embassies:**Australia** (☎ 02-6243 4830; vca@gov.si; 6th fl, St George's Bldg, 60 Marcus Clarke St, Canberra ACT 2601)

Austria (☎ 01-586 13 09; vdu@gov.si; Nibelungengasse 13, A-1010 Vienna)

Canada (☎ 613-565 5781; vot@gov.si; Ste 2101, 150 Metcalfe St, Ottawa K2P 1P1)

Croatia (☎ 01-63 11 000; vzg@gov.si; Savska c 41, 10000 Zagreb)

Hungary (☎ 01-438 5600; vbp@gov.si; Cseppkő út 68, 1025 Budapest)

Ireland (☎ 01-670 5240; vdb@gov.si; 2nd fl, Morrison Chambers, 32 Nassau St, Dublin 2)

Italy (☎ 06-80 914 310; vri@gov.si; Via Leonardo Pisano 10, 00197 Rome)

Netherlands (☎ 070-310 86 90; vhg@gov.si; Anna Paulownastraat 11, 2518 BA Den Haag)

UK (☎ 020-7222 5400; vlo@gov.si; 10 Little College St, London SW1P 3SH)

USA (☎ 202-667 5363; vwa@gov.si; 1525 New Hampshire Ave NW, Washington, DC 20036)

Embassies & Consulates in Slovenia

Following are among the embassies and consulates in Ljubljana:**Australia** Consulate (☎ 01-425 42 52; 12th fl, Trg Republike 3; ☾ 9am-1pm Mon-Fri)

Austria Embassy (☎ 01-479 07 00; Prešernova c 23; ☾ 8am-noon Mon-Thu, 8-11am Fri) Enter from Veselova ul.

Canada Consulate (☎ 01-430 35 70; Dunajska c 22; ☾ 9am-noon Mon-Fri)

Croatia Embassy (☎ 01-425 62 20; Gruberjevo nabrežje 6; ☾ 10am-1pm Mon-Fri)

Hungary Embassy (☎ 01-512 18 82; ul Konrada Babnika 5; ☾ 9am-noon Mon, Wed & Fri)

Ireland Embassy (☎ 01-300 89 70; Poljanski nasip 6; ☾ 9am-12.30pm & 2.30-4.30pm Mon-Fri)

Italy Embassy (☎ 01-426 21 94; Snežniška ul 8; ☾ 9-11am Mon-Fri)

Netherlands Embassy (☎ 01-420 14 61; Poljanski nasip 6; ☾ 9am-noon Mon-Fri)

New Zealand Consulate (☎ 01-580 30 55; Verovškova ul 57; ☾ 8am-3pm Mon-Fri)

South Africa Consulate (☎ 01-200 63 00; Pražakova ul 4; ☾ 3-4pm Tue)

UK Embassy (☎ 01-200 39 10; 4th fl, Trg Republike 3; ☾ 9am-noon Mon-Fri)

USA Embassy (☎ 01-200 55 00; Prešernova c 31; ☾ 9-11.30am Mon-Fri)

FESTIVALS & EVENTS

Major cultural and sporting events are listed under 'Events' on the website of the **Slovenian Tourist Board** (www.slovenia-tourism.si) and in the STB's annual *Calendar of Major Events in Slovenia*. Among the most important and/or colourful are **Kurentovanje** (www.kurentovanje.net) in Ptuj, a 'rite of spring' celebrated for 10 days up to Shrove Tuesday (February or early March) and the most popular Mardi Gras celebration in Slovenia; the three-day **Ski Jumping World Cup Championships** (www.planica.info) at Planica near Kranjska Gora in March; **Druga Godba** (www.druga godba.si), a festival of alternative and world music at the Križanke in Ljubljana in late May/early June; the **Festival Lent** (http://lent.slov enija.net), a two-week extravaganza of folklore and culture in Maribor's Old Town in late June/early July; the **Ljubljana Summer Festival** (www.festival-lj.si), the nation's premier cultural event (music, theatre and dance) held from early July to late August; **Rock Otočec** (www.rock-otocec.com), a three-day rock concert in early

July at Prečna airfield, 5km northwest of Novo Mesto and Slovenia's biggest open-air rock concert; the **Cows' Ball** at **Bohinj** (www.bohinj.si), a zany weekend of folk dance, music, eating and drinking in September to mark the return of the cows from their high pastures to the valleys; and the **Ljubljana Marathon** (http://maraton .slo-timing.com) in late October.

GAY & LESBIAN TRAVELLERS

The typical Slovenian personality is quietly conservative but deeply self-confident, re-markably broad-minded and particularly tolerant. **Roza Klub** (☎ 01-430 47 40; Kersnikova ul 4) in Ljubljana is made up of the gay and les-bian branches of ŠKUC (Študentski Kulturni Center or Student Cultural Centre).

GALfon (☎ 01-432 40 89; ✆ 7-10pm) is a hotline and source of general information for gays and lesbians. The websites of **Slovenian Queer Resources Directory** (www.ljudmila.org/siqrd) and **Out in Slovenia** (www.outinslovenija.com) are both exten-sive and partially in English.

HOLIDAYS

Slovenia celebrates 14 holidays (*prazniki*) a year. If any of the following fall on a Sunday, then the Monday becomes the holiday.
New Year 1 & 2 January
Prešeren Day (Slovenian Culture Day) 8 February
Easter & Easter Monday March/April
Insurrection Day 27 April
Labour Days 1 & 2 May
National Day 25 June
Assumption Day 15 August
Reformation Day 31 October
All SaintsSaints' Day 1 November
Christmas Day 25 December
Independence Day 26 December

INTERNET ACCESS

There is internet access in towns and cities throughout the county but most cyber-cafés usually have only a handful of terminals. In some places you may have to resort to the local library, school or university. Be advised that Slovenian keyboards are neither qwerty nor azerty but qwertz, reversing the y and z keys, but otherwise following the Anglophone norm.

INTERNET RESOURCES

The website of the **STB** (www.slovenia-tourism.si) is tremendously useful, as is that of **Mat'Kurja** (www.matkurja.com), a directory of Slovenian web resources. Most Slovenian towns and cities have a website accessed by typing www.town name.si or www.townname-tourism.si. Es-pecially good are **Ljubljana** (www.ljubljana-tourism .si) and **Piran-Portorož** (www.portoroz.si).

LANGUAGE

Closely related to Croatian and Serbian, Slov-ene (*slovenščina*) is written in the Latin alpha-bet and consonants are generally pronounced as in English, with some notable exceptions: c=ts, č=ch, and j=y (though a 'j' is silent at the end of a word), š=sh and ž=zh (as the 's' in 'pleasure'). On toilets an 'M' (*Moški*) indicates 'men', and 'Ž' (*Ženske*) is 'women'. Virtually everyone in Slovenia speaxks at least one other language; restaurant menus and ATMs are commonly in Italian, German and English, as well as Slovene. See the Language chapter (p613) for key phrases and words.

MONEY

Slovenia exchanged its 15-year-old currency, the tolar (SIT), for the euro in January 2007, the first of the 10 so-called accession coun-tries that joined the EU in 2004 to do so. Exchanging cash is simple at banks, major post offices, travel agencies and *menjalnice* (bureaux de change), although some of the latter don't accept travellers cheques. Prices listed in this chapter are in euros, for the most part converted from prices quoted in tolars at the time of research, so expect some slight variations. Major credit and debit cards are accepted almost everywhere, and ATMs are ubiquitous.

POST

Local mail costs €0.20 for up to 20g, while an international airmail stamp costs €0.45. Poste restante is free; address it to and pick it up from the main post office at Slovenska c 32, 1101 Ljubljana.

TELEPHONE

Public telephones require a phonecard (*telefonska kartica* or *telekartica*), available at post offices and some newsstands. The cheapest card (€3, 25 unit) gives about 20 minutes' calling time to other European countries. Most locals have a mobile phone; SIM cards with around €4 credit are avail-able for €12 from **SiMobil** (www.simobil.si) and €15.40 from **Mobitel** (www.mobitel.si). In fact, even certain businesses only quote mobile

EMERGENCY NUMBERS

- Police ☎ 113
- Ambulance ☎ 112
- Fire brigade ☎ 112
- Road emergency or towing ☎ 1987

numbers, identified by the prefix 031, 040, 041 and 051.

TOILETS

Toilets are free in restaurants, but usually incur a €0.20 charge at bus stations and other public sites.

TOURIST INFORMATION

The Ljubljana-based **Slovenian Tourist Board** (☎ 01-589 18 40; www.slovenia-tourism.si; Dunajska c 156) has dozens of tourist information centres (TICs) in Slovenia and branches in a half-dozen cities abroad; see its 'Representations of STB Abroad' on its website for details. Request its free *Next Exit: Guide to Slovenia's Byways*, which contains coupons for 5% to 15% savings on various hotels, activities and sights, including the Škocjan Caves.

VISAS

Citizens of virtually all European countries, as well as Australia, Canada, Israel, Japan, New Zealand and the USA, do not require visas to visit Slovenia for stays of up to 90 days. Holders of EU and Swiss passports can enter using a national identity card.

Those who do require visas (including South Africans) can get them at any Slovenian embassy or consulate (see p520) for up to 90 days. They cost €35 regardless of the type or length of validity. You'll need confirmation of a hotel booking plus one photo, and may have to show a return or onward ticket.

WOMEN TRAVELLERS

Travelling as a single woman in Slovenia is no different from travelling in most Western European countries. If you can handle yourself in the very occasional less-than-comfortable situation, you'll be fine.

In the event of an emergency call the **police** (☎ 113) any time or the **SOS Helpline** (☎ 080-11 55; www.drustvo-sos.si; ☺ noon-10pm Mon-Fri, 6-10pm Sat & Sun).

TRANSPORT IN SLOVENIA

GETTING THERE & AWAY
Air

Slovenia's only international airport receiving regular scheduled flights is **Ljubljana Aerodrom** (LJU; www.lju-airport.si) at Brnik, 27km north of Ljubljana. From its base here, the Slovenian flag-carrier, Adria Airways, serves up to two-dozen European destinations depending on the season. Adria flights can be remarkably good value, but with the inauguration of easyJet and Wizzair flights between the Slovenian capital and London, most British visitors are now weekend visitors on budget airlines. Adria flights include useful connections to Pristina (Kosovo), Ohrid (Macedonia) and Tirana (Albania). Flight frequency drops in winter.

The following airlines travel to and from Slovenia:

Adria Airways (code JP; ☎ 01-231 33 12; www.adria-airways.com)

Air France (code AF; ☎ 01-244 34 47; www.airfrance.com) Daily flights to Paris (CDG).

Austrian Airlines (code OS; ☎ 01-202 01 22; www.aua.com) Multiple daily flights to Vienna.

ČSA Czech Airlines (code OK; ☎ 04-206 17 50; www.csa.cz) Flights to Prague.

easyJet (code EZY; ☎ 04-206 16 77; www.easyjet.com) Low-cost flights to London Stansted.

JAT Airways (code JU; ☎ 01-231 43 40; www.jat.com) Daily flights to Belgrade.

LOT Polish Airlines (code LO; ☎ 04-202 01 22; www.lot.com) Flights to Warsaw.

Malév Hungarian Airlines (code MA; ☎ 04-206 16 76; www.malev.hu) Daily flights Budapest.

Turkish Airlines (code TK; ☎ 04-206 16 80; www.turkishairlines.com) Flights to Istanbul.

Wizz Air (code W6; ☎ 04-206 19 81; www.wizzair.com) Budget flights to London Luton and Brussels (Charleroi).

An alternative budget option to Slovenia, especially if you want to concentrate on the coast, is **Ryanair** (www.ryanair.com), which links London Stansted with **Ronchi dei Legionari airport** (www.aeroporto.fvg.it) at Trieste. Trieste may (still) be in Italy but it's much closer to Koper, Piran and the Soča Valley than Ljubljana's airport at Brnik. From the Trieste airport terminal there is a daily bus (single/return €15/25) at 2.40pm to Koper (1½ hours, 56km), Izola (two hours, 61km), Portorož and Piran (2½ hours, 69km). Check **Terravision**

Airport Bus Transfer (www.lowcostcoach.com) for this service.

Land

BUS

International bus destinations from Ljubljana include Frankfurt (€80, 12½ hours, 777km, 7.30pm Sunday to Friday, 9.30pm Saturday) via Munich (€35.40, 6¾ hours, 344km); Sarajevo (€35.65, 9½ hours, 570km, 7.15pm Monday, Wednesday and Friday); Split (€34.20, 10½ hours, 528km, 7.40pm daily) via Rijeka (€11.43, 2½ hours, 136km); and Zagreb (€13.20, 2¾ hours, 154km, 2.30am, 7.30am and 8pm).

There are regular buses on weekdays only between Trieste and Koper (see p515) plus a direct year-round Ljubljana–Trieste service (€11.50, 2½ hours, 105km, 6.25am Monday to Saturday), with an additional departure at 8.15am on Saturday between June and mid-October.

TRAIN

Ljubljana–Vienna trains (€57, 6¼ hours, 385km, twice daily) via Graz (€30, 200km, 3½ hours) are expensive, although SparSchiene fares as low as €29 apply on certain trains at certain times. Otherwise save money by going first to Maribor (€7.30 to €12.30, 2½ hours, 156km, up to two dozen daily), where you can buy a Maribor–Graz ticket (€11, 1¼ hours, three daily) and then continue on domestic tickets from Graz to Vienna (€13.50, 2¾ hours, 201km). Similar savings apply via Jesenice and Villach and/or Klagenfurt.

Three trains depart daily from Ljubljana for Munich (€66, 6½ hours, 405km). The 8.17pm departure has sleeping carriages available.

Ljubljana–Venice trains (€25, four hours, 244km) depart at 1.47am (via Trieste; €15, 99km), 10.28am and 4.16pm. It's cheaper to go first to Novo Gorica (€7.30, three hours, 153km, six daily), walk to Gorizia and then take an Italian train to Venice (€7.90, 2¼ hours).

For Zagreb there are eight trains daily from Ljubljana (€11.90, two hours, 154km) via Zidani Most. Several trains from the capital serve Rijeka (€11.40, two hours, 136km) via Postojna.

Ljubljana–Budapest trains (€58.60, 8¾ hours, 451km, three daily) go via Ptuj and Hodoš; there are Budapest Spezial fares available for as low as €39 on certain trains at cer-

tain times. The 9.05pm train to Thessaloniki (€83.80, 25 hours, 1159km, one daily) goes via Belgrade (€39.40, 10 hours, 535km).

Seat reservations, compulsory on trains to and from Italy and on InterCity (IC) trains, cost €3, but it is usually included in the ticket price.

Sea

From Piran **Venezia Lines** (☎ 05-674 70 29; www .topline.si) catamarans sail to Venice (one way/ return €49/60.50, 2¼ hours) from May to mid-September. The **Prince of Venice** (☎ 05-617 80 00; portoroz@kompas.si) catamaran from nearby Izola also serves Venice (€42 to €67, 2½ hours) from mid-April to September. Both operate between once and four times a week, generally returning the same evening.

GETTING AROUND

Trains are usually cheaper but less frequent than buses. Be advise that the frequency on both forms of transport drops off very significantly on weekends and during school holidays.

Bus

It's worth booking long-distance buses ahead of time, especially for travel on Friday afternoon. If your bag has to go in the luggage compartment below the bus, it will cost €1.25 extra. The online bus timetable, **Avtobusna Postaja Ljubljana** (www.ap-ljubljana.si), is extensive, but generally only for buses that use Ljubljana as a hub.

Car & Bicycle

Hiring a car is recommended, and can even save you money as you can access cheaper out-of-centre hotels and farm or village homestays. Daily rates usually start at €45/245 per day/week, including unlimited mileage, collision-damage waiver and theft protection. Unleaded 95-octane petrol *(bencin)* costs €1.03 to €1.05 per litre, with diesel at €0.98. You must keep your headlights illuminated throughout the day.

Bicycles are available for hire at some train stations, tourist offices, travel agencies and hotels. You'll find mountain bikes easiest to hire in Bovec, Bled and Bohinj.

Hitching

Hitchhiking is fairly common and legal, except on motorways and a few major highways. Even young women hitch in Slovenia, but it's

SLOVENIA

never totally safe and Lonely Planet doesn't recommend it.

Train

The national railway, **Slovenske Železnice** (Slovenian Railways; ☎ 01-291 33 32; www.slo-zeleznice.si) has a useful online timetable that's easy to use. Buy tickets before boarding or you'll incur a €2.10 supplement. Be aware that InterCity (IC) trains carry a surcharge of €1.40 to €1.70 on top of standard quoted fares.

A useful and very scenic rail line from Bled Jezero station via Bohinjska Bistrica near Lake Bohinj cuts under the mountains to Most na Soči (for Kobarid), then down the Soča Valley to Nova Gorica. Cars are carried through the tunnel section on a special auto train (avtovlak).

Switzerland

Switzerland is an easy country to swallow; it melts in your mouth as smoothly as the rich chocolates and creamy cheeses it is famous for. With a kind of slap-you-in-the-face natural beauty Hollywood filmmakers salivate over and a reputation as a summer and winter sports paradise, it's pretty hard to not get hooked. Switzerland is where people first skied for fun, and along with heavenly powder pistes and ultraglam resorts (think St Moritz), the country dishes up enough adrenalin-pumping fuel to keep your inner junkie satiated for weeks (think out-of-this-world hiking or flying through the sky on a pair of manmade wings).

Okay, so all the clichés you've heard about Switzerland are likely true. It's pretty damn easy to envision rosy-faced goat herders yodelling to a clinking cowbell melody amid sky-scraping peaks. But even though they've perfected the whole G-rated Matterhorn look, don't mistake the Swiss for a bunch of Goody Two-Shoes. This is the country, after all, that invented absinthe and LSD. It's as well known for secret bank accounts and shady business deals as for fondue and droopy-roofed chalets. Small, fiercely independent and culturally complex (there are four official languages, Swiss German, French, Italian and Romansch), the Swiss have expensive tastes. Cities like Geneva (the most cosmopolitan), Zürich (the most outrageous), Bern (the most charming) and Lucerne (the most beautiful) heave with heady artistic activity, legendary nightlife and some of the planet's highest living standards.

FAST FACTS

- **Area** 41,285 sq km
- **Capital** Bern
- **Currency** Swiss franc (Sfr); A$1 = Sfr0.91; €1 = Sfr1.56; ¥100 = Sfr1.07; NZ$1 = Sfr0.75; UK£1 = Sfr2.26; US$1 = Sfr1.22
- **Famous for** cheese, the Matterhorn, banking
- **Official Languages** French, German, Italian, Romansch
- **Phrases** *gruezi* (hello, good day), *merci vielmal* (thank you very much), *adieu* (goodbye), *sprechen sie Englisch?* (do you speak English?)
- **Population** 7.4 million
- **Telephone Codes** country code ☎ 41; international access code ☎ 00

SWITZERLAND

HIGHLIGHTS

■ Gasp at gargantuan mountain vistas, partake in white-knuckle adrenalin adventures or spend a night in the hay in the gorgeous **Jungfrau region** (p567).

■ Play in the mighty Matterhorn's shadow in everyone's favourite Swiss ski town, **Zermatt** (p548).

■ Immerse yourself in **Bern**'s (p531) elegant medieval charm and pulsating party scene.

■ Soak up seriously sexy ambience sipping wine at a lakeside café in Switzerland's sultry Italian canton, **Ticino** (p550).

■ Eat lunch in the revolving restaurant at the top of the **Schilthorn** (p569), dominated by mammoth Eiger, Mönch and Jungfrau (Ogre, Monk and Virgin) mountain views.

ITINERARIES

■ **One week** Start in vibrant Zürich. Shop famous Bahnhofstrasse or hit a hip new martini bar. Head to the Jungfrau region next, and explore some kick-ass (think James Bond racing an avalanche down a sheer snowy rock face) Alpine scenery. Take a pit stop in beautiful Lucerne before finishing up in fabulously medieval Bern.

■ **Two weeks** As above, then head west for French immersion lessons in international Geneva or cosmopolitan Lausanne. Spend a few nights in Neuchâtel and Freiburg cantons, stopping to taste *the*

HOW MUCH?

■ **Hostel dorm bed** Sfr28

■ **Bottle of absinthe** Sfr50

■ **100km by train** Sfr30

■ **City bus ride** Sfr2-3

■ **Local telephone call** Sfr0.60

LONELY PLANET INDEX

■ **1L petrol** Sfr1.74

■ **1L bottled water** Sfr2

■ **Half-pint of beer** Sfr4

■ **Souvenir T-shirt** Sfr20

■ **Kebab** Sfr9

---

cheese in Gruyères. Zip down to Zermatt or across to St Moritz to partake in a little skiing. Loop east to experience Switzerland's Italian side.

CLIMATE & WHEN TO GO

Although there are plenty of crystal clear, sunny days, winters in Switzerland can be cold, snowy and sometimes (especially around Zürich) rather grey, with temperatures between 2°C and 6°C. Summers mix sunshine with rain. Temperatures range from 20°C to 25°C, except in Ticino, which has a hotter, Mediterranean climate. You will need to be prepared for a range of temperatures, depending on your altitude.

Visit Switzerland from December to April for winter sports, and May to October for general sightseeing and hiking. Alpine resorts all but close down in late April, May and November. See also Climate Charts (p585).

HISTORY

The first inhabitants of the region were a Celtic tribe, the Helvetii. The Romans arrived in 107 BC via the Great St Bernard Pass, but were gradually driven back by the Germanic Alemanni tribe, which settled in the region in the 5th century AD. Burgundians and Franks also came to the area, and Christianity was gradually introduced.

The territory was united under the Holy Roman Empire in 1032, but central control was never tight, and neighbouring nobles fought each other for local influence. Rudolph I spearheaded the Germanic Habsburg expansion and gradually brought the squabbling nobles to heel.

The Swiss Confederation

Upon Rudolph's death in 1291, local leaders saw a chance to gain independence. The forest communities of Uri, Schwyz and Nidwalden formed an alliance on 1 August 1291, which is seen as the origin of the Swiss Confederation (their struggles against the Habsburgs are idealised in the legend of William Tell). This union's success prompted other communities to join: Lucerne (1332), followed by Zürich (1351), Glarus and Zug (1352), and Bern (1353).

Encouraged by successes against the Habsburgs, the Swiss acquired a taste for

SWITZERLAND

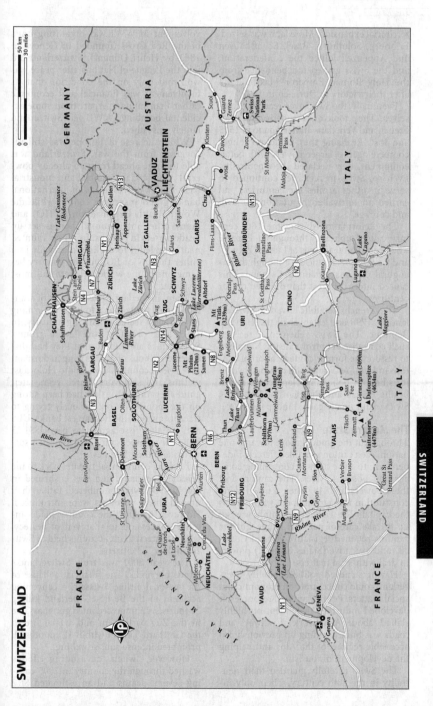

SWITZERLAND

territorial expansion. More land was seized. Fribourg, Solothurn, Basel, Schaffhausen and Appenzell joined the confederation, and the Swiss gained independence from the Holy Roman Emperor Maximilian I after their victory at Dornach in 1499.

Eventually, the Swiss over-reached themselves. They took on a superior force of French and Venetians at Marignano in 1515 and lost. Realising they could no longer compete against larger powers with better equipment, they declared their neutrality. Even so, Swiss mercenaries continued to serve in other armies for centuries, and earned an unrivalled reputation for skill and courage.

The Reformation during the 16th century caused upheaval throughout Europe. The Protestant teachings of Luther, Zwingli and Calvin spread quickly, although the inaugural cantons remained Catholic. This caused internal unrest that dragged on for centuries.

The French Republic invaded Switzerland in 1798 and established the Helvetic Republic. The Swiss vehemently resisted such centralised control, causing Napoleon to restore the former confederation of cantons in 1803. Yet France still retained overall jurisdiction. Following Napoleon's defeat by the British and Prussians at Waterloo, Switzerland finally gained independence.

The Modern State

Throughout the gradual move towards one nation, each canton remained fiercely independent, to the extent of controlling coinage and postal services. The cantons lost these powers in 1848, when a new federal constitution was agreed upon, with Bern as the capital. The Federal Assembly was set up to take care of national issues, but the cantons retained legislative (Grand Council) and executive (States Council) powers to deal with local matters.

Having achieved political stability, Switzerland could concentrate on economic and social matters. Poor in mineral resources, it developed industries dependent on highly skilled labour. A network of railways and roads was built, opening up previously inaccessible regions of the Alps and helping the development of tourism.

The Swiss carefully guarded their neutrality in the 20th century. Their only involvement in WWI was organising units of the Red Cross (founded in Geneva in 1863 by Henri Dunant). Switzerland did join the League of Nations after peace was won, but only on the condition that its involvement was financial and economic rather than military. Apart from some accidental bombing, WWII left Switzerland largely unscathed.

While the rest of Europe was still recovering from the war, Switzerland was able to forge ahead from an already powerful commercial, financial and industrial base. Zürich developed as an international banking and insurance centre, while the World Health Organization (WHO) and many other international bodies set up headquarters in Geneva. Its much-vaunted neutrality led it to decline to actually join either the UN or EU, but the country became one of the world's richest and most respected.

Then, in the late 1990s, a series of scandals forced Switzerland to begin reforming its famously secretive banking industry. In 1995, after pressure from Jewish groups, Swiss banks announced that they had discovered millions of dollars lying in dormant pre-1945 accounts, belonging to Holocaust victims and survivors. Three years later, amid allegations that they had been sitting on the money without seriously trying to trace its owners, the two largest banks, UBS and Credit Suisse agreed to pay US$1.25 billion in compensation to Holocaust survivors and their families.

Banking confidentiality dates back to the Middle Ages here, and was enshrined in law in 1934, when numbered, rather than named, bank accounts were introduced. However, in 2004, the country made another concession to that veil of secrecy, when it agreed to tax accounts held in Switzerland by EU citizens.

The year 2001 was truly Switzerland's annus horribilis. The financial collapse of the national airline Swissair, a canyoning accident in the Bernese Oberland killing 21 tourists, an unprecedented gun massacre in the Zug parliament and a fatal fire in the Gotthard Tunnel within 12 months all prompted intense soul-searching.

However, when devastating floods washed through the country in 2005 causing several deaths and an estimated Sfr2

IT ALL HAPPENED IN SWITZERLAND

▪ Albert Einstein came up with his theories of relativity and the famous formula '$E=MC^2$' in Bern in 1905.

▪ Switzerland gave birth to the World Wide Web at the acclaimed CERN (European Centre for Nuclear Research) institute outside Geneva.

▪ Val de Travers, near Neuchâtel, claims to be the birthplace of the mythical green alcohol absinthe.

▪ The first acid trip took place in Switzerland. In 1943, chemist Albert Hofmann was conducting tests for a migraine cure in Basel when he accidentally absorbed the lysergic acid diethylamide, or LSD, compound through his fingertips.

▪ Of the 800-or-so films a year produced by India's huge movie-making industry, more are shot in Switzerland than in any other foreign country. 'For the Indian public, Switzerland is the land of their dreams', film star Raj Mukherjee has said. Favourite destination shoots include the Berner Oberland, Central Switzerland and Geneva.

▪ Switzerland's central Alpine region possesses one of Europe's richest traditions of myth and legend. Pontius Pilate is said to rise out of the lake on Mt Pilatus, near Lucerne, every good Friday (the day he condemned Jesus Christ) to wash blood from his hands – and anybody who witnesses this event will allegedly die within the year. Tiny 'wild folk' with supernatural powers, called Chlyni Lüüt, were once reputed to inhabit Mt Rigi, also near Lucerne. Their children's spleens were removed at birth, giving them the ability to leap around mountain slopes.

---

billion damage, there were fewer anguished cries about what was going wrong with Switzerland and more pragmatic debate on what should be done.

Switzerland swung to the conservative right in its parliamentary government in 2003, and today recognises that it's facing universal challenges; it has begun to reach out more to the world. In 2002 it finally became the 190th member of the UN. In 2005 it joined Europe's 'Schengen' passport-free travel zone (effective 2007) and, in theory, opened its borders to workers from the 10 new EU members.

It still isn't a member of the EU itself and, although the French-speaking regions would like it, doesn't look like becoming one anytime soon. However, in many ways Switzerland no longer views isolation as quite so splendid.

PEOPLE

Switzerland's name may stand for everything from knives to watches, but don't expect this nation to take a stand for anyone other than itself. Militarily neutral for centuries, and armed to the teeth to make sure it stays that way, in Switzerland it's the Swiss Way or the highway.

With a population of 7.4 million, Switzerland averages 174 people per square kilometre. Zürich is the largest city (population 338,794) followed by Geneva (179,426), Basel (161,800) and Bern (120,596). Most people are of Germanic origin, as reflected in the breakdown of the four national languages. Around 20% of the population are residents but not Swiss citizens.

The Swiss are polite, law-abiding people who usually see no good reason to break the rules. Living quietly with your neighbours is a national obsession. Good manners infuse the national psyche, and politeness is the cornerstone of all social intercourse. Always shake hands when being introduced to a Swiss, and kiss on both cheeks to greet and say goodbye to friends. Don't forget to greet shopkeepers when entering shops. When drinking with the Swiss, always wait until everyone has their drink and toast each of your companions, looking them in the eye and clinking glasses. Drinking before the toast is unforgivable, and will lead to seven years of bad sex…or so the superstition goes. Don't say you weren't warned.

In a few mountain regions such as Valais, people still wear traditional rural costumes, but dressing up is usually reserved for festivals. Yodelling, playing the alp horn and Swiss wrestling are also part of the Alpine tradition.

RELIGION

The country is split pretty evenly between Protestantism (40%) and Roman Catholicism (46%). Most of the rest of the population are recorded as 'unaffiliated'. The dominant faith varies between cantons. Strong Protestant areas are Bern, Vaud and Zürich, whereas Valais, Ticino and Uri are mostly Catholic. Most Swiss pay a *kirchensteur* (church tax) – a percentage of their income tax that the government distributes to the churches through state subsidies.

ARTS

Many foreign writers and artists, such as Voltaire, Byron, Shelley and Turner have visited and settled in Switzerland. Local and international artists pouring into Zürich during WWI spawned the dadaist movement there.

Paul Klee (1879–1940) is the best-known native painter. He created bold, hard-lined abstract works. The writings of philosopher Jean-Jacques Rousseau (1712–78), in Geneva, played an important part in the development of democracy. Critically acclaimed postwar dramatists and novelists, Max Frisch (1911–91) and Friedrich Dürrenmatt (1921–90), entertained readers with their dark satire, tragi-comedies and morality plays. On the musical front, Arthur Honegger (1892–1955) is Switzerland's most recognised composer.

The Swiss have made important contributions to graphic design and commercial art. Anyone who's ever used a computer will have interacted with their fonts, from Helvetica to Fruitiger to Univers. The father of modern architecture, Le Corbusier (1887–1965), who designed Notre Dame du Haut chapel at Ronchamps in France, Chandigarh in India and the UN headquarters in New York, was Swiss. One of the most-acclaimed contemporary architectural teams on earth, Jacques Herzog and Pierre de Meuron, live and work in Basel. Winners of the prestigious Pritzker Prize in 2001, this pair created London's acclaimed Tate Modern museum building.

Gothic and Renaissance architecture are prevalent in urban areas, especially Bern. Rural Swiss houses vary according to region, but are generally characterised by ridged roofs with wide, overhanging eaves, and balconies and verandas enlivened by colourful floral displays, especially geraniums.

To the chagrin of many, Switzerland also sports some pretty artistic graffiti. Giant intricately spray-painted patterns (along with less savoury pieces) grace buildings scattered along railway tracks near train stations.

ENVIRONMENT

Mountains make up 70% of Switzerland's 41,285 sq km. Farming of cultivated land is intensive and cows graze on the upper slopes as soon as the retreating snow line permits.

The Alps occupy the central and southern regions of the country. The Dufourspitze (4634m), a peak on the Monte Rosa Mountains, is the highest point, although the Matterhorn (4478m) is more famous.

Glaciers account for a 2000-sq-km area. The Aletsch Glacier is Europe's largest valley glacier at 169 sq km.

The St Gotthard Mountains, in the centre of Switzerland, is the source of many lakes and rivers, including the Rhine and the Rhône. The Jura Mountains straddle the border with France, and peak at around 1700m. Between the two systems is the Mittelland, also known as the Swiss Plateau, a region of hills crisscrossed by rivers, ravines and winding valleys.

The most distinctive Alpine animal in Switzerland is the ibex, a mountain goat that has huge curved and ridged horns. There are about 12,000 of them left in the country.

Switzerland has just one national park, the Swiss National Park. At just 169 sq km it is quite small but offers opportunities for walking and ibex viewing.

Switzerland has long been an environmentally aware nation. Its citizens diligently recycle household waste and cities encourage the use of public transport. The policy in the mountains is to contain rather than expand existing resorts.

Global warming could have a serious impact on Switzerland because of the effect on

Alpine glaciers. Since the 1950s the federal government has introduced various measures to protect forests, lakes and marshland from environmental damage and, in 1991, it signed the Alpine Convention, which seeks to reduce damage caused by motor traffic and tourism.

FOOD & DRINK

Lactose intolerants will struggle in this dairy-obsessed country, where cheese is a way of life. The best-known Swiss dish is fondue, in which melted Emmental and gruyère are combined with white wine, served in a large pot and eaten with bread cubes. Another popular artery-hardener is *raclette*, melted cheese served with potatoes. *Rösti* (fried, buttery, shredded potatoes) is German Switzerland's national dish, and is served with everything.

Many dishes are meaty, and veal is highly rated throughout the country. In Zürich it is thinly sliced and served in a cream sauce *(Gschnetzeltes Kalbsfleisch). Bündnerfleisch* is dried beef, smoked and thinly sliced. Like their northern neighbours, the Swiss also munch on a wide variety of Wurst (sausage).

Wine is considered an essential accompaniment to lunch and dinner. Local vintages are generally good quality, but you might never have heard of them, as they are rarely exported. The main growing regions are Italian- and French-speaking areas, particularly in Valais and by Lakes Neuchâtel and Geneva.

Buffet-style restaurant chains, such as Manora, have a huge selection of freshly cooked food at low prices. Migros and Coop are the main supermarket chains. Street stalls are a good place to pick up cheap eats – you'll find kebabs and sandwiches everywhere. If you're fond of kebabs (as we are), the stalls on Zürich's Niederdorfstrasse (p559) are some of our favourites in the country. Bratwurst and pretzel stands (sometimes the pretzels are even stuffed with meats and cheeses) also abound in German cantons.

Restaurants sometimes close between meals (generally from 3pm to 5pm), although this is becoming rare in large cities, and tend to have a closing day, often Monday. Cafés usually stay open all day. Bars are open from lunch time until at least midnight. Clubs get going after 10pm and close around 4am.

In cities and larger towns there are dedicated vegetarian restaurants. Most eateries also will offer a small selection of nonmeat options, including large salad plates.

Finally, Switzerland makes some of the most delectable chocolate in the world – don't miss it!

BERN

pop 120,596

One of the planet's most underrated capitals, Bern is a fabulous find. With the genteel, old soul of a Renaissance man and the heart of a high-flying 21st-century gal, the city is at once medieval and modern. The 15th-century old town is gorgeous enough to sweep you off your feet and make you forget the century (it's definitely worthy of its 1983 Unesco World Heritage site protection order). But edgy vintage boutiques, artsy-intellectual bars and raging nightlife will slam you back into the present.

Bern was founded in 1191 by Berchtold V and named for the unfortunate bear (*bärn* in local dialect) that was his first hunting victim. The bear remains the heraldic mascot of the city today. Attractions include checking out Paul Klee's, visiting Einstein's home and taking a swift float down the Aare River's blue-green waters.

ORIENTATION

The compact centre of old town is contained within a sharp U-bend of the Aare River. The train station is on the western edge within easy reach of all the main sights, and offers bike rental and airline check-in.

INFORMATION
Bookshops

Stauffacher (☎ 031 311 24 11; Neuengasse 25; 🕑 8am-6.30pm Mon-Fri, to 4pm Sat) English-language bookshop.

Discount Card

BernCard (per 24/48/72hr Sfr17/27/33) Admission to the permanent collections of all museums, plus free public transport and discounts on city tours.

Emergency

Police station (☎ 031 321 21 21; train station)

Internet Access

Inside Internet Bar (☎ 031 313 81 91; Aarbergergasse 46; per hr Sfr7-9; ☺ 11am-12.30am Mon-Sat, noon-10pm Sun) Fully stocked bar and groovy atmosphere.

Medical Services

Emergency doctor, dentist, pharmacist (☎ 090 057 67 47; ☺ 24hr)

University hospital (☎ 031 632 21 11; Fribourg-strasse; ☺ 24hr) West of the centre, has a casualty department.

Post

Main post office (Schanzenstrasse; ☺ 7.30am-6.30pm Mon-Fri, 8am-noon Sat)

Tourist Information

Bern tourist office (☎ 031 328 12 28; www.berne tourism.ch; train station; ☺ 9am-8.30pm daily Jun-Sep, 9.30am-6.30pm Mon-Sat & 10am-5pm Sun Oct-May) Offers two-hour city tours by coach (Sfr25, daily April to October, Saturday November to March) and foot (Sfr14, daily June to September) in summer. Its free booklet, *Bern aktuell*, has plenty of useful information. There's another tourist office by the bear pits.

Bern Youth Guide (www.youthguide.ch) This online service has some excellent tips and links.

Travel Agencies

STA Travel (☎ 031 302 03 12; Falkenplatz 9; ☺ 9.30am-6pm Mon-Fri, 10am-1pm Sat) Budget and student travel agency.

SIGHTS
Old Town

Pick up a city map from the tourist office (Sfr1) and start exploring. Don't pay too much attention to the map though. The best places are often found on detours down skinny side alleys. Stumble into a funky

---

BERN IN TWO DAYS

Stroll around **old town** (above). Check out the clock tower and ogre fountain, duck into the myriad cellar shops. Lunch at the popular **Altes Tramdepot** (p535), then visit the **Einstein museum** (right). At night bar-hop around town.

Spend morning number two looking at paintings; try the **Paul Klee Centre** (right) and the **Kunstmuseum** (p534). If it's warm, go swimming in the **Marzili pools** (p534) or float down the swift **Aare River** (p534).

---

retro cellar shop, selling penis-shaped peppermint candies alongside chunky silver rings. Keep an eye out for a gallery selling all sorts of shells and bright beaded necklaces or a hideaway bar of the trendiest proportions.

Classic not-to-be-missed stops on your conventional map include the **ogre fountain**, in Kornhausplatz, depicting a giant enjoying a meal of wriggling children. The **Zeitglockenturm**, dividing Marktgasse and Kramgasse, is a colourful clock tower with revolving figures that herald the chiming hour.

The unmistakably Gothic, 15th-century cathedral **Münster** (☺ 10am-5pm Tue-Sat, 11.30am-5pm Sun) is worth stepping into. It features imposing, 12m-high, stained-glass windows and an elaborate main portal.

Just across the Aare River are the **bear pits** (Bärengraben). Though bears have been the entertainment at this site since 1857, it's really depressing to see such majestic beasts doing tricks for treats in such a cramped, concrete environment – this author had to turn away pretty quickly.

Einstein Museum

The world's most famous scientist developed his theory of relativity in Bern in 1905, and the small **Einstein Haus** (☎ 031 312 00 91; www.einstein-bern.ch; Kramgasse 49; adult/student & senior Sfr6/4.50; ☺ 10am-7pm Apr-Oct, 1-5pm Tue-Fri, noon-4pm Sat Feb, Mar & Nov–mid-Dec, closed mid-Dec–Jan) has been given a facelift recently to celebrate the centenary of that discovery.

The humble apartment where Einstein lived with his young family while working as a low-paid clerk in the Bern patent office has been redecorated in the style of the time. Numerous multimedia displays now flesh out the story of the subsequent general equation – $E=MC^2$, or energy equals mass multiplied by the speed of light squared – which fundamentally changed humankind's understanding of space, time and the universe.

Paul Klee Centre

Renzo Piano's remarkable building, the **Zentrum Paul Klee** (☎ 031 359 01 01; www.zpk.org; adult/concession/child Sfr14/12/6, extra Sfr2 for special exhibitions; ☺ 10am-5pm Tue, Wed & Fri-Sun, to 9pm Thu) is Bern's Guggenheim. Curving up and down

SWITZERLAND

BERN

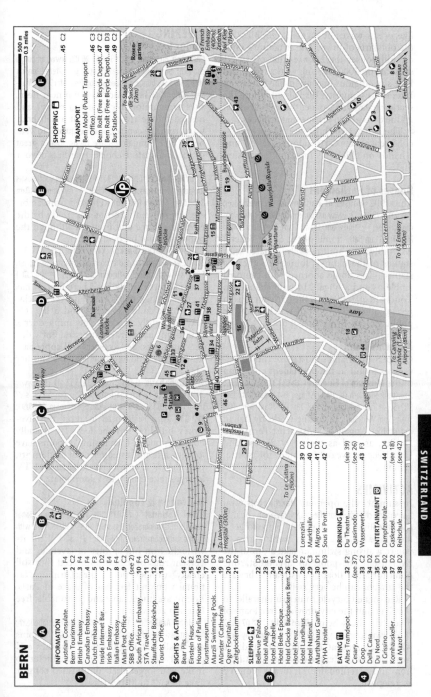

INFORMATION
Austrian Consulate.................1 F4
Bern Tourismus.......................2 C2
British Embassy........................3 F4
Canadian Embassy...................4 F4
Dutch Embassy.........................5 D2
Inside Internet Bar....................6 D2
Irish Embassy.............................7 E4
Italian Embassy.........................8 F4
Main Post Office........................9 C2
SBB Office...........................(see 2)
South African Embassy..........10 F4
STA Travel...............................11 D2
Stauffacher Bookshop...........12 C2
Tourist Office...........................13 F2

SIGHTS & ACTIVITIES
Bear Pits.................................14 F2
Einstein Haus.........................15 E2
Houses of Parliament............16 D3
Kunstmuseum.........................17 D2
Marzili Swimming Pools.........18 D4
Münster (Cathedral)...............19 E3
Ogre Fountain.........................20 D2
Zeitglockenturm.....................21 D2

SLEEPING
Bellevue Palace......................22 D3
Hotel Allegro..........................23 B1
Hotel Arabelle........................24 B1
Hotel Belle Epoque................25 E2
Hotel Glocke Backpackers Bern.26 D2
Hotel Kreuz............................27 D2
Hotel Landhaus......................28 F2
Hotel National........................29 C3
Marthahaus Garni...................30 D1
SYHA Hostel............................31 D3

EATING
Altes Tramdepot.....................32 F2
Cesary................................(see 37)
Coop......................................33 C2
Della Casa..............................34 D2
Du Nord.................................35 D1
Il Grissino..............................36 D2
Kornhauskeller.......................37 D2
Le Mazot................................38 D2
Lorenzini................................39 D2
Markthalle..............................40 C2
Migros...................................41 D2
Sous le Pont...........................42 C1

DRINKING
Du Theatre........................(see 39)
Quasimodo........................(see 26)
Wasserwerk...........................43 F3

ENTERTAINMENT
Dampfzentrale.......................44 D4
Gaskessel.........................(see 18)
Reitschule..........................(see 42)

SHOPPING
Fizzen....................................45 C2

TRANSPORT
Bern Mobil (Public Transport
   Office)................................46 C3
Bern Rollt (Free Bicycle Depot).47 C2
Bern Rollt (Free Bicycle Depot).48 D3
Bus Station.............................49 C2

0   500 m
0   0.3 miles

SWITZERLAND

like ocean waves, it forms three 'hills' on the outskirts of town. The structure's middle hill houses the main exhibition space, showcasing 4000 rotating works from Paul Klee's prodigious and often-playful career. Interactive computer displays built into the seating mean you can get the low-down on all the Swiss-born artist's major pieces.

The other two 'hills' are given over to conferences, concerts, administration and a hands-on children's museum (admission Sfr15).

Houses of Parliament

The 1902 **Houses of Parliament** (Bundeshäuser; ☎ 031 332 85 22; www.parliament.ch; Bundesplatz; admission free; ☉ tours 9am, 10am, 11am, 2pm, 3pm & 4pm Mon-Fri, 11am Sat), home of the Swiss Federal Assembly, are impressively ornate, with statues of the nation's founding fathers, a stained-glass dome adorned with cantonal emblems and a huge, 214-bulb chandelier. Tours are offered when the parliament is in recess, otherwise you can watch from the public gallery. Bring a passport.

Kunstmuseum

One of Switzerland's most prized art collections is found in the permanent collection of the **Museum of Fine Art** (☎ 031 328 09 44; www .kunstmuseumbern.ch; Hodlerstrasse 8-12; adult/student Sfr7/5, special exhibitions Sfr8-18; ☉ 10am-9pm Tue, 10am-5pm Wed-Sun), including works by Italian artist Fra Angelico, Swiss artist Ferninand Hodler, as well as pieces by Picasso and Dalí. Keep an eye out for interesting special exhibits.

ACTIVITIES

In summer the open-air **Marzili pools** (www .aaremarzili.ch; admission free; ☉ May-Sep), beside the **Aare River**, are the perfect place to get a tan; there's even a topless bathing area. If you're a strong swimmer take a dip in the river itself. The pools are a good starting point for a fast float downstream – beware the current can be very swift.

Red-signed bicycle routes run parallel to the river and the city provides free loans of bikes, via the scheme **Bern Rollt** (☎ 079 277 28 57; www.bernrollt.ch; ☉ 7.30am-9.30pm May-Oct), which has huts at Bahnhofplatz and the western end of Zeughausgasse. Identification and a refundable Sfr20 are required as a deposit.

SLEEPING
Budget

Camping Eichholz (☎ 031 961 26 02; www.campingei cholz.ch; Strandweg 49; camp sites per site/person/car Sfr9/7.50/3.50, bungalows per person from Sfr18; ☉ May-Sep; ☐) The best place to camp near Bern, sites are comfortable (not too rocky) and nestled by the river. It's about a half-hour walk from the centre (or take tram 9 to Wabern). The bungalows are basic, but a great get-back-to-nature choice regardless of your budget.

SYHA hostel (☎ 031 311 63 16; www.youthhostel .ch/bern; Weihergasse 4; dm Sfr35; ☉ reception 7-10am & 3-10pm, 5-10pm Dec-Feb) Removed from ambient city noise, this hostel sits pretty by the river. It is large and friendly, although the building is not particularly new.

Hotel Glocke Backpackers Bern (☎ 031 311 37 71; www.bernbackpackers.com; Rathausgasse 75; dm Sfr36, s/d with shared bathroom Sfr70/125; ☐ ☒ ☐) Backpackers usually head here first. It has a great lounge that's cosy and very sociable (think comfy couches and a big TV playing nightly movies). The simple dorms and rooms have firm mattresses, fluffy duvets and sinks. Self-caterers will appreciate the kitchen. The bar downstairs is another plus.

Marthahaus Garni (☎ 031 332 41 35; www .marthahaus.ch; Wyttenbachstrasse 22a; dm Sfr39, s/d/ tr Sfr110/125/155, s/d with shared bathroom Sfr65/95; ☒ ☐) In a residential location, this five-storey building has the feel of a friendly boarding house. Clean, simple rooms have lots of white and a smattering of modern art, plus there's a communal kitchen and TV lounge. Take tram 9 to Viktoriaplatz.

Midrange & Top End

Hotel National (☎ 031 381 19 88; www.national bern.ch; Hirschengraben 24; s/d/f Sfr85/130/180, s/d with shared bathroom from Sfr55/100; ☐ ☐) With its wrought-iron lift, springs of lavender and Persian rugs over newly surfaced (but still creaky) wooden floors, the charming National wouldn't feel out of place in Paris. Rooms are impeccable and personable; free Internet access is a plus.

Hotel Arabelle (☎ 031 301 03 05; www.arabelle.ch; Mittelstrasse 6; s/d from Sfr120/135; ☒ ☐) Rooms are small, but bright colour schemes and parquet floors lend enough character to make you forget their diminished stature. Take bus 12 to Mittelstrasse.

Hotel Kreuz (☎ 031 329 95 95; www.hotelkreuz -bern.ch in German; Zeughausgasse 26; s/d from Sfr120/170) This very modern hotel has smart rooms with all the creature comforts, a tiny bar with unique metal and stained-glass light fixtures and a restaurant serving Swiss-German fare (mains Sfr15 to Sfr30).

Hotel Belle Epoque (☎ 031 311 43 36; www.belle -epoque.ch; Gerechtigkeitsgasse 18; s/d from Sfr195/280; ☒ ⬜) Standards are very high at this lovely and romantic old-town hotel with opulent Art Deco furnishings. Check out the TV tucked into steamer-trunk–style cupboard.

Hotel Allegro (☎ 031 339 55 00; www.allegro-hotel .ch; Kornhausstrasse 3; s/d from Sfr220/260; ☒ ☒ ⬜) Décor ranges from sleek 'Asiatic' to brassy 'Broadway' and there's even a Paul Klee–themed suite at this unpretentious hotel. It's in a great location, just above old town, with fabulous views from its front rooms.

Bellevue Palace (☎ 031 320 45 45; www.bellevue -palace.ch; Kochergasse 3-5; s/d Sat & Sun from Sfr260/350, Mon-Fri Sfr350/460; ☒ ☒ ☒ ⬜) Bern's only five-star hotel is the first choice address for Bern's power brokers and international statesmen such as Nelson Mandela.

EATING

Wall-to-wall cafés and restaurants line the popular meeting places of Bärenplatz and Theaterplatz, as well as the more upmarket Gerechtigkeitsgasse. The restaurants listed here do not close between meals.

Restaurants

Le Mazot (☎ 031 311 70 88; Bärenplatz 5; mains Sfr11-30) Very cosy with dark wood panels, this place is a well-known specialist in Swiss food. There is a massive *rösti, raclette* and fondue menu. For those with small stomachs, half-portions are available. Sit outside in the glassed-in patio on warm days.

Il Grissino (☎ 031 311 00 59; Waisenhausplatz 28; mains Sfr12-25) With 'bump knees with your neighbour'–style seating (claustrophobics beware), this oft-packed pizza and pasta joint emits a boisterous vibe. Choose from more than 30 different pizzas; the large is big enough for two (unless you're super hungry).

Altes Tramdepot (☎ 031 368 14 15; Am Bären-graben; mains Sfr15-25) Locals don't let the touristy bear pit location keep them away and neither should you. This cavernous brewery

is a Bern favourite, serving Swiss specialities along with a variety of international dishes. The atmosphere is as inviting as the cuisine.

Cesary (☎ 031 318 93 83; Kornhausplatz 11; mains Sfr15-30) New and trendy, this super-swank Italian restaurant and lounge attracts a well-dressed crowd. After work it's all about the suits and ties, but when dark descends so do the little black dresses and Gucci purses. Stop by for an aperitif and people watching from the comfort of a suave white leather stool.

Du Nord (☎ 031 332 23 38; Lorrainestrasse 2; mains Sfr17-35) A trendy and alternative crowd flocks to this laid-back, gay-friendly restaurant in the Lorraine quarter for well-prepared, modern international cuisine, drinks at the bar and occasional gigs.

Lorenzini (☎ 031 310 50 67; Hotelgasse 10; mains Sfr20-55) A bit of a Bern institution, the Lorenzini complex of wine bars and an Italian restaurant is popular with young professionals looking for coffee and salad or a full meal of homemade pasta. The patio is perfect for people watching.

Della Casa (☎ 031 311 21 42; Schauplatzgasse 16; mains Sfr28-40; ☒ 8am-11.30pm Mon-Fri, to 3pm Sat) One of the best, albeit meat-obsessed, places in town, it is an old, cosy eatery with floral curtains, leadlight lamps and traditional Swiss specialities.

Kornhauskeller (☎ 031 327 72 72; Kornhausplatz 18; mains from Sfr32) Dine under tall vaulted arches covered in frescos in the stunning subterranean restaurant or sip cocktails with Bern's beautiful people in the bar on the mezzanine level – make sure to check out the historic stained-glass windows.

Quick Eats & Self-Catering

Markthalle (Bubenbergplatz 9; mains Sfr5-8) Slurp down pizza, kebabs and spaghetti standing at a Formica table or perched on bar stools in this buzzing central arcade filled with all sorts of cheap eateries.

Sous le Pont (☎ 031 306 69 55; Schützenmatte; snacks & light meals Sfr5-15; ☺ 11.30am-2pm & 6pm-midnight Tue-Fri; 6pm-2am Sat) Organic meat and lots of vegetarian options are offered in the semichaotic surrounds of Reitschule. Every Wednesday, there's a speciality evening showcasing a different cuisine.

Self-caterers can buy up big at **Coop** (Neuengasse; ☺ 8am-8pm Mon-Sat) and **Migros** (Marktgasse 46; ☺ 8am-8pm Mon-Sat), which also have cheap self-service restaurants (Sfr3 to Sfr7).

DRINKING

See the *Bern Guide* available from the tourist office, for details on Bern nightlife.

Du Theatre (☎ 031 311 17 71; Hotelgasse 10) Part of the upmarket Lorenzini complex, this chic lounge bar has a cool 30-something crowd parked on its plump 1970s leather sofas.

Quasimodo (☎ 031 311 13 81; Rathausgasse 75) Backpackers staying at the Hotel Glocke will like the convenience of this techno bar-club downstairs. Arrive after 10pm and you'll find the small dance floor packed with swaying, sweaty revellers from all parts of the globe, including Switzerland.

Wasserwerk (☎ 031 312 12 31; www.wasserwerk club.ch; Wasserwerkgasse 5) The main techno venue in town, this has a bar, club and sometimes live music. It boasts that both Moby and the Prodigy played here in their heyday.

ENTERTAINMENT

Gaskessel (☎ 031 372 49 00; www.gaskessel.ch; Sandrainstrasse 25) Inside this graffiti-covered domed building in Marzili is a countercultural centre, with lots of trance, rap and some popular gay evenings.

Dampfzentrale (☎ 031 311 63 37; www.dampfzent rale.ch; Marzilistrasse 47) This refined performing arts centre combines jazz, funk and soul music gigs with avant-garde art exhibitions and dance. It's in a pleasant riverside spot and serves a brilliant Sunday brunch.

Reitschule (☎ 031 306 69 52; www.reitschule.ch; Schützenmatte) While determinedly cleaning up its act and trying to keep the drugs out, this infamous – and ramshackle – centre for alternative arts, music and theatre still retains a bit of its old charisma, attracting local slackers, students and curious tourists.

Sports

Bern's new 32,000-seat **Stade de Suisse** (www .stadedesuisse.ch) was built over the demolished former Wankdorf Stadium. It will be one of the four Swiss venues when Austria and Switzerland co-host football's Euro 2008 championship.

SHOPPING

From luxury boutiques to family-run tobacco stores selling Cuban cigars and creative flasks, Bern has its shopping bases covered. There are loads of stores in old town – check out the area around Kornhausplatz as well as Marktgasse and Spietgasse. Some of the most unique boutiques (for men and women) are hidden in underground cellars, so be sure to wander down at least a few flights of stairs.

Fizzen (☎ 031 311 1116; Bollwerk 17) For decent second-hand garb (along with loads of crazy coloured condoms) visit this locally recommended place.

There is an open-air market on Bärenplatz each Tuesday and Saturday (daily in summer). On the first Saturday of the month there is a craft market in front of the cathedral.

If truly local souvenirs interest you, grab a Toblerone chocolate – it's made in Bern.

GETTING THERE & AWAY

There are daily flights to Lugano, London, Paris, Amsterdam and other European destinations from Bern-Belp airport. Postbuses depart from the western side of the train station.

Three motorways intersect in the northern part of the city. The N1 runs from Neuchâtel in the west and Basel and Zürich in the northeast. The N6 connects Bern with Thun and the Interlaken region in the southeast. The N12 is the route from Geneva and Lausanne in the southwest.

Trains connect to most Swiss towns, including Basel (Sfr36, 70 minutes, hourly),

Geneva (Sfr49, 1¾ hours, hourly), Interlaken (Sfr25, 50 minutes, hourly) and Zürich (Sfr47, 70 minutes, hourly).

GETTING AROUND

Bern-Belp airport (BRN; ☎ 031 960 21 11; www.alpar.ch) is 9km southeast of the city centre. A frequent bus links the airport to the train station (Sfr15, 20 minutes).

Bus and tram tickets cost Sfr1.90 (maximum six stops) or Sfr2.80. A city day pass and regional network is Sfr12. If you're planning on clubbing, **Moonliner** (www.moonliner.ch) night buses depart Friday and Saturday nights from Bahnhofplatz at 12.45am, 2am and 3.15am; passes aren't valid and fares start at Sfr5. Tickets can be purchased at all bus tops.

Many taxis wait by the train station. They charge Sfr6.50 plus Sfr3.10 per kilometre (Sfr4 after 8pm and on Sunday).

From May to October there are free loans of city bikes outside the train station. Bring ID and a Sfr20 deposit.

FRIBOURG, NEUCHÂTEL & THE JURA

From the evocative medieval cantonal capitals of Fribourg and Neuchâtel to the mysterious green hills and deep dark forests of the Jura, the country's northwest corner proffers a wealth of sights and escapes well off the beaten track, yet is still an easy day trip from Bern. Be it marvelling at majestic ice creations or following the call of the devilish green fairy into the wayward Val de Travers, travelling here promises a brilliant sensory experience.

NEUCHÂTEL

pop 31,004

Spend an afternoon cruising Neuchâtel's open-air cafés, walking along its glittering lake and feasting your eyes on the charming sandstone elegance of its old town and your stress will melt away. The canton's compact capital is really just a laid-back French-style resort surrounded by vineyards. If you're looking to do a little shopping, the central pedestrian zone is packed with all sorts of souvenir shops and funky, reasonably priced boutiques. The pedestrian zone and

Place Pury (the local bus hub) are about 1km from the train station; walk down the hill along Ave de la Gare.

The **tourist office** (☎ 032 889 68 90; www.ne.ch/tourism; Place du Port; ⏰ 9am-noon & 1.30-5.30pm Mon-Fri, to noon Sat Sep-Jun, to 7pm Mon-Sat, 4-7pm Sun Jul & Aug) is in the main post office by the lake.

Sights & Activities

The 12th-century **Chateau de Neuchâtel** (☎ 032 889 60 00; 45min tours free; ⏰ 10am-4pm Apr-Sep) and the adjoining **Collegiate Churches** are the centrepieces of old town. The striking cenotaph of 15 statues dates from 1372. Nearby, the **prison tower** (☎ 032 717 76 02; Rue J de Hochberg 5; admission Sfr1; ⏰ 8am-6pm Apr-Aug) offers broad views of the town and lake.

Visit the **Musée d'Art et d'Histoire** (Museum of Art & History; ☎ 032 717 79 20; Esplanade Léopold-Robert 1; adult/student Sfr9/6, free Wed; ⏰ 10am-6pm Tue-Sun), on the waterfront, to see 18th-century beloved clockwork figures.

Sleeping

Oasis Neuchâtel (☎ 032 731 31 90; auberge.oasis@bluewin.ch; Rue du Suchiez 35; dm/d Sfr24/60; ⏰ Apr-Oct) Glorious views and friendly accommodation are this independent hostel's trademarks. It's about 2km from the centre; take bus 1 (Cormondréche) to Vauseyon and follow the signs towards Centre Sportive.

Hôtel de l'Ecluse (☎ 032 729 93 10; www.hoteldelecluse.ch; Rue de l'Ecluse 24; s/d from Sfr100/150; P 🖳) Elegant rooms in this fine house sport brass beds and kitchenettes. Breakfast is served in the bar and there are a couple of terraces for guests to lounge on.

Hôtel Alpes et Lac (☎ 032 723 19 19; www.alpesetlac.ch; Place de la Gare 2; s/d from Sfr125/180; P 🍴 🖳) A stately 19th-century hotel across from the train station. Digs are comfortable enough to chill in and offer mod cons such as wi-fi (Sfr5/11 per 30 minutes/24 hours). There are two restaurants (one Swiss, one Chinese).

Eating

Local specialities include fresh trout, tripe and *tome neuchâteloise chaude*, a baked cheese starter.

La Creperie (☎ 032 725 17 71; Rue de Hôpital 7; crepes from Sfr6.50) Tables are practically piled on top of each other at this cluttered little spot in the heart of town. It's nearly always

SWITZERLAND

THE GREEN FAIRY

It was in the deepest darkest depths of Couvet in the Val de Travers – otherwise dubbed the Pays des Fées (Fairyland) – that absinthe was first distilled in 1740 and produced commercially in 1797. (However, it was a Frenchman called Pernod who made the bitter green liqueur known with the distillery he opened just a few kilometres across the French–Swiss border in Pontarlier.)

From 1910, following Switzerland's prohibition of the wickedly alcoholic and ruthlessly bitter aniseed drink, distillers of the so-called 'devil in the bottle' in the Val de Travers moved underground. In 1990 the great grandson of a preprohibition distiller in Môtiers came up with Switzerland's first legal aniseed liqueur since 1910 – albeit one which was only 45% proof alcohol (instead of 50% to 75%) and which scarcely contained *thujone* (the offensive chemical found in wormwood, said to be root of absinthe's devilish nature). But in March 2005, Switzerland lifted its absinthe ban and the **Blackmint – Distillerie Kübler & Wyss** (☎ 032 861 14 69; www.blackmint.ch; Rue du Château 7, Môtiers) distilled its first true and authentic batch of the mythical *fée verte* (green fairy) from valley-grown wormwood. Mix one part crystal-clear liqueur with five parts water to make it green. When we got a group of friends together back home to sample the stuff, reports of trails and light and floaty feelings started coming in after the first glass.

---

full. There are dozens upon dozens of sweet and savoury crepes, including one with absinthe. The coffee is strong and as French as the ambience.

Le Brasserie Jura (☎ 032 725 14 10; Rue de la Treille 7; lunch menu Sfr16.50, mains Sfr15-35) With a name like Jura Brasserie, this hot spot couldn't be more local. Food is cooked to fill. *Tripes à la Neuchâteloise* (tripe) is the menu star and vegetarians are well catered for with vegetable *rösti*, veg-stuffed ravioli or six-cereal ravioli doused in goat-cheese sauce.

Appareils de Chauffage (☎ 032 721 43 96; Rue des Moulins 37; mains from Sfr15) Grab a board game from the bar and settle in for a few hours at this funky café serving quality coffee and a range of spirits and beer. There are Swiss and international dishes on the menu.

Cafe des Halles (☎ 032 724 31 41; Rue du Trésor 4; pizzas Sfr 20, mains Sfr35) In an impressive historic house dating back to 1569, this place is the gourmet's central choice. The cooking is mainly French, but also includes scrumptious pizzas and pastas. Dine outside on the large shaded terrace overlooking the main square. The set three-course dinners for Sfr45 are good value.

Coop (Rue de la Treille 4) Self-caterers can stock up on local wine, cheeses and absinthe at this branch of the Coop chain.

Entertainment

La Case à Chocs (☎ 032 721 20 56; www.case-a-chocs .ch; Quai Philippe Godet 16; concerts Sfr10-15; ✆ Thu-Sun) An alternative venue in a converted brewery with live music, occasional cinema and art shows. Check the website for details.

Getting There & Around

There are fast trains to Geneva (Sfr42, 70 minutes, hourly) and Bern (Sfr19, 35 minutes, hourly). Postbuses heading to the Jura leave from the station.

Local buses cost Sfr1.80 to Sfr2.80 per trip.

VAL DE TRAVERS

Hikers come to Val de Travers to marvel at the enormous **Creux du Van** abyss. This spectacular crescent-moon wall, a product of glacial erosion, interrupts the habitually green rolling countryside in startling fashion – it is just 1km long, but plunges 440m to the bottom (the first 200m is a sheer stony drop). The Creux is most easily reached on foot from Noiraigue, which can be reached by hourly train from Neuchâtel (Sfr6.60, 20 minutes). The round-trip hike can take up to five hours depending on the route.

If you're in search of the truth about absinthe, visit the distillery in **Môtiers** (see the boxed text, above). Trains run from Neuchâtel (Sfr10.40, 35 minutes).

FRIBOURG

pop 32,553

Medieval Fribourg (dating back to the 12th century) boasts the usual cathedrals and art museums, but for something different focus on the beer.

With two great breweries in town you can't go wrong. Head to **Brasserie du Cardinal** (☎ 058 123 16; www.cardinal.ch; Passage du Cardinal; tours Sfr10; �} 8.30-3pm Mon-Thu) to sample one of Switzerland's best-known lagers, brewed here since 1788. Tours demonstrate how water, malt and hops are turned into nine different types of Cardinal beer.

Small-time microbrewery **Brasserie Artisanale de Fribourg** (☎ 026 322 80 88; Rue de la Samaritaine 19; �} 8am-5pm Sat) is run by a couple of mates who began the enterprise as an amusing pastime (and now run it as a Saturday hobby!). The one-room brewery produces just 50 hectolitres a year. Pay Sfr4 for a bottle of its golden German-style Barbeblanche or Barberousse with subtle caramel and honey aromas.

Imaginative and luxurious **Auberge aux 4 Vents** (☎ 026 347 36 00; www.aux4vents.ch; Res Balzli Grandfrey 124; s/d Sfr120/170, s/d/tr/q with shared bathroom from Sfr50/100/140/160; ☐ ☒), just outside the city limits, is our sleeping pick. The eight rooms are individually designed. We especially liked room 'bleue', featuring dreamy blue flowery period furnishings and a tub on rails that rolls out through the window for a bath beneath stars. The highly recommended conservatory-style restaurant overlooks a stunning medieval Fribourg panorama. To get to the '4 Winds', 2km north in Grandfrey, drive north along Rue de Morat and turn right immediately before the train bridge.

Fribourg is easily accessible by train from Bern (Sfr14, 30 minutes, hourly).

GRUYÈRES

Known above all for the cheese by the same name, beautiful **Gruyères** attracts busloads of tourists who gawk at the fine 15th- to 17th-century homes and the 13th-century fairytale castle on the hill. We'd suggest you follow their example.

The secret behind gruyère cheese is revealed at the **Maison du Gruyère** (☎ 026 921 84 00; www.lamaisondugruyere.ch; adult/student/child Sfr5/4/2; �} 9am-7pm Apr-Sep, to 6pm Oct-Mar) in Pringy, 1.5km from Gruyères. Cheese-making takes place four times daily between 9am and 3pm and can be watched through glass windows.

Cheese is produced in a couple of traditional mountain chalets along the **Sentier des Fromageries**, a trail leading through green Gruyère pastures. Ask at the Maison du Gruyère for the brochure outlining the two-hour walk (about 8km).

The **Musée HR Giger** (☎ 026 921 22 00; adult/child Sfr10/5; �} 10am-6pm Apr-Oct, 10am-5pm Tue-Sun Nov-Mar), housed in a 16th-century mansion, is a shrine to HR Giger's expansive imagination – fans of the *Alien* movies will especially relish the place – along with all things occult and bizarre. Be sure to check out the very Giger-style bar across the road afterwards.

A restored 19th-century manor, **Le Pâquier** (☎ 026 912 20 25; www.lepatchi.ch; Rue de la Gare 10, Le Pâquier; s/d/tr Sfr60/90/120; ☐ ☐), 3.5km northwest of Gruyères, is a good sleeping bet.

The cosy, cowbell-strewn **Chalet de Gruyères** (☎ 026 921 21 54; www.chalet-gruyeres.ch; Rue du Château 53; fondues & raclettes Sfr28) serves a great *croûte en fromage* (hot, open-faced cheese sandwich); meringues come with the thickest gruyère double cream ever.

There are trains from Fribourg (Sfr16.80, 40 minutes, hourly). The town is a 10-minute walk uphill from its station.

JURA CANTON

Its grandest towns are little more than enchanting villages and this northwestern corner of the country remains undiscovered. Deep, mysterious forests and impossible green clearings succeed one another across the low mountains of the Jura and some 1200km of marked paths across the canton give hikers plenty of scope.

The capital is Delémont, but there is little reason to linger. Instead, head west to the delightful medieval village of **St Ursanne** instead. Along with a 12th-century Gothic church, there are clusters of ancient houses, a 16th-century town gate and lovely stone bridge. The town is on the Doubs River's banks and kayaking is popular in summer. **Le Clip** (☎ 032 461 37 22; Place du Mai 1, St Ursanne; trips Sfr45) runs exciting half-day trips.

Hôtel Demi-Lune (☎ 032 461 35 31; www.hotels-suisse.ch/demi-lune in French; Rue Basse 2, St Ursanne; s/d from Sfr75/125) has classy rooms overlooking the river.

Trout is the local speciality and you can get a good version at **La Cicogne** (☎ 032 461 35 45; St Ursanne; mains from Sfr20), an unpretentious spot opposite the church.

From Delémont there are trains to St Ursanne (Sfr6.60, 17 minutes, hourly).

GENEVA

pop 179,426

If one city on the planet could truly say it fits the whole world on its hand, surely it would be Geneva (Genève in French, Genf in German). Strung along the sparkling shores of Europe's largest Alpine lake, this is about as international as it gets. Its people chatter in every language under the sun (in fact almost 40% of them are not Swiss) and this cosmopolitan city of bankers, diplomats and transients likes to boast that 'it belongs not so much to Switzerland as to the world'. This rings pretty true: the UN, WHO, International Red Cross, International Labour Organisation…you name them, they're in Geneva. In fact, the place is home to some 200-odd top-dog governmental and nongovernmental international organisations.

ORIENTATION

The Rhône River runs through Geneva, dividing it into *rive droite* (right bank) and *rive gauche* (left bank). On the northern side is the main train station, Gare de Cornavin; south of the river lies the old town. In summer, Geneva's most visible landmark is the Jet d'Eau, a giant fountain on the southern shore.

INFORMATION
Emergency
Police Station (☎ 117; Rue de Berne 6)

Internet Access
For a list of free-access public wi-fi terminals in Geneva, see www.espritdegeneve.ch.
Internet Café de la Gare (☎ 022 731 51 87; per 10/30mins Sfr2/4, per hr Sfr6; ♥ 8.30am-10pm Mon-Thu, 9.30am-11pm Fri & Sat, 9.30am-10pm Sun) In the train station, on the Place de Montbrillant side.

Internet Resources
City of Geneva (www.ville-ge.ch)
International Geneva Welcome Centre (www .cagi.ch)

Medical Services
Cantonal hospital (☎ 022 372 33 11; Rue Micheli-du-Crest 24)
Permanence Médico Chirurgicale (☎ 022 731 21 20; Rue de Chantepoulet 1-3) A private 24-hour clinic.

Servette Clinique (☎ 022 733 98 00; Ave Wendt 60) Emergency dental treatment.
Telephone advice service (☎ 111) For medical information.

Post
Main post office (Rue du Mont-Blanc 18; ♥ 7.30am-6pm Mon-Fri, 8.30am-noon Sat)

Tourist Information
Genève tourist office (☎ 022 909 70 00; www.gen eve-tourisme.ch; Rue du Mont-Blanc 18; ♥ 10am-6pm Mon, 9am-6pm Tue-Sat)

Travel Agencies
American Express (Amex; ☎ 022 731 76 00; Rue du Mont-Blanc 7; ♥ 8.30am-5.45pm Mon-Fri, 9am-noon Sat)
STA Travel (☎ 022 329 97 33; Rue Vignier Leschol 3; ♥ 9.15am-6pm Mon-Fri, 9am-noon Sat)

SIGHTS & ACTIVITIES
City Centre
The city centre is so compact it's easy to see many of the main sights on foot. Start a scenic walk through the old town at the **Île Rousseau**, home to a statue in honour of the celebrated freethinker. Head west along the southern side of the Rhône until you reach the 13th-century **Tour de L'Île**, once part of the medieval city fortifications. Then walk south down the narrow, cobbled Rue de la Cité until it becomes Grand-Rue. **Rousseau's birthplace** is at No 40.

A short detour off Grand-Rue leads you to the part-Romanesque, part-Gothic **Cathédrale St Pierre**, where John Calvin preached from 1536 to 1564. The cathedral rests on a significant **archaeological site** (☎ 022 311 75 74; Cour de St Pierre 6; adult/student Sfr5/3; ♥ 10-11.30am & 2-4.30pm Mon-Fri, 10am-5pm Sat, noon-5pm Sun). A visit reveals some fine 4th-century mosaics and a 5th-century baptismal font.

You'll find the **Jet d'Eau** on the lake's southern shore. Calling this a fountain is an understatement. The water shoots up with incredible force (200km/h, 1360HP), to create a 140m-high plume. At any one time there are seven tonnes of water in the air, and much of it falls on spectators who venture out on the pier.

United Nations
The Art Deco **Palais des Nations** (☎ 022 907 48 96; Ave de la Paix 9-14; tours adult/student Sfr8.50/6.50;

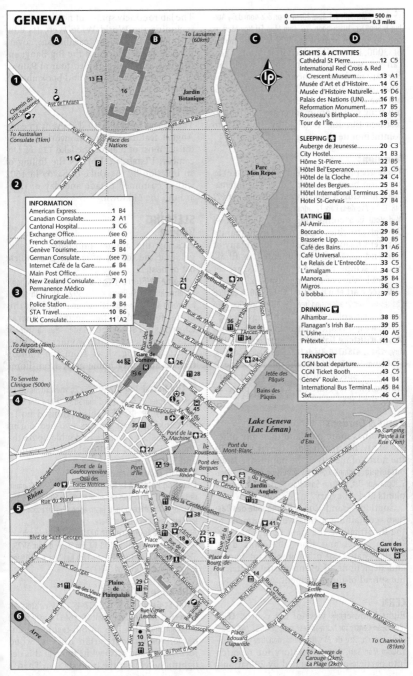

GENEVA

0 — 500 m
0 — 0.3 miles

INFORMATION
American Express.................**1** B4
Canadian Consulate..............**2** A1
Cantonal Hospital.................**3** C6
Exchange Office...................(see 6)
French Consulate...................**4** B6
Genève Tourisme...................**5** B4
German Consulate.................(see 7)
Internet Café de la Gare..........**6** B4
Main Post Office.................(see 5)
New Zealand Consulate...........**7** A1
Permanence Médico
Chirurgicale.....................**8** B4
Police Station........................**9** B4
STA Travel..........................**10** B6
UK Consulate......................**11** A2

SIGHTS & ACTIVITIES
Cathédral St Pierre................**12** C5
International Red Cross & Red
Crescent Museum.............**13** A1
Musée d'Art et d'Histoire.......**14** C6
Musée d'Histoire Naturelle....**15** D6
Palais des Nations (UN).........**16** B1
Reformation Monument.........**17** B5
Rousseau's Birthplace...........**18** B5
Tour de l'Île.........................**19** B5

SLEEPING
Auberge de Jeunesse............**20** C3
City Hostel..........................**21** B3
Hôme St-Pierre....................**22** B5
Hôtel Bel'Esperance.............**23** C5
Hôtel de la Cloche................**24** C4
Hôtel des Bergues................**25** B4
Hôtel International Terminus.**26** B4
Hotel St-Gervais **27** B4

EATING
Al-Amir...............................**28** B4
Boccacio.............................**29** B6
Brasserie Lipp......................**30** B4
Café des Bains.....................**31** A6
Café Universal.....................**32** B6
Le Relais de L'Entrecôte........**33** C5
L'amalgam..........................**34** C3
Manora...............................**35** B4
Migros................................**36** C3
ù bobba..............................**37** B5

DRINKING
Alhambar............................**38** B5
Flanagan's Irish Bar..............**39** B5
L'Usine...............................**40** A5
Prétexte.............................**41** C5

TRANSPORT
CGN boat departure..............**42** C5
CGN Ticket Booth.................**43** C5
Genev' Roule......................**44** B4
International Bus Terminal......**45** B4
Sixt....................................**46** C4

SWITZERLAND

⊗ 9am-6pm daily Jul-Aug, 10am-noon & 2-4pm daily Apr-Jun & Sep-Oct, 10am-noon & 2-4pm Mon-Fri Nov-Mar) is the European arm of the UN and the home of 3000 international civil servants. You can see where decisions about world affairs are made on the hour-long tour (bring your passport to get in). Afterwards check out the extensive gardens – don't miss the towering grey monument coated with heat-resistant titanium donated by the USSR to commemorate the conquest of space.

Museums

There are plenty of museums (many free) to keep you busy on a rainy day. The **International Red Cross & Red Crescent Museum** (☎ 022 748 95 25; Ave de la Paix 17; admission free; ⊗ 10am-5pm Wed-Mon) is a compelling multimedia trawl through atrocities perpetuated by humanity in recent history. Against the long litany of war and nastiness, documented in films, photos, sculptures and soundtracks, are set the noble aims of the organisation.

Musée d'Art et d'Histoire (☎ 022 418 26 00; Rue Charles-Galland 2; admission free; ⊗ 10am-5pm Tue-Sun) has a vast collection of paintings, sculptures, weapons and archaeological displays. **Musée d'Histoire Naturelle** (Museum of Natural History; ☎ 022 418 63 00; Rte de Malagnou 1; admission free; ⊗ 9.30am-5pm Tue-Sun) is the place to check out every species of tiger known to man, stuffed for perpetuity. It's a good place to bring the kids.

Parks & Gardens

Geneva has more parkland than any other Swiss city, much of it along the lakefront. In the north of the city is the impressive **Jardin Botanique** (Botanic Gardens; admission free; ⊗ 8am-7.30pm Apr-Oct, 9.30am-5pm Nov-Mar) with exotic plants and an aviary.

South of Grand-Rue is **Promenade des Bastions**, containing a massive monument to the Reformation: the giant figures of Bèze, Calvin, Farel and Knox are flanked by smaller statues of other important figures and depictions of events instrumental in the spread of the movement.

CERN

Eight kilometres west of the centre, **CERN** (European Centre for Nuclear Research; ☎ 022 767 84 84; www.cern.ch; Rte de Meyrin; admission free; ⊗ 9am-5.30pm Mon-Sat), is a laboratory for research into particle physics funded by 20 nations.

The lab routinely spins out new creations – including the World Wide Web. Its educational Microcosm exhibition covers particle accelerators and the Big Bang; enthusiasts can take a guided tour at 9am or 2pm (take your passport and book ahead). Take bus 9.

FESTIVALS & EVENTS

The **Geneva Festival**, a 10-day event in early August, features parades, fireworks and live music, most of it along the lake. On 11 December, **L'Escalade** celebrates the foiling of an invasion by the Duke of Savoy in 1602 with a costumed parade and day of races around the old town.

SLEEPING
Budget

Pick up the annual *Info-Jeunes Genève* guide at the tourist office for a complete list of hostels.

Hôme St-Pierre (☎ 022 310 37 07; www.home stpierre.ch; Cour St-Pierre 4; dm Sfr27, s/d with shared bathroom Sfr40/60; ▣) It's women only at this hostel founded by the German Lutheran Church in 1874. The place sees a lot of returning guests – little wonder considering its amazing views from the rooftop terrace and cosy home-away-from-home persona.

City Hostel (☎ 022 901 15 00; www.cityhostel.ch; Rue de Ferrier 2; 3- or 4-bed dm Sfr31, 2-bed dm Sfr35, s/d Sfr58/85; Ⓟ ✗ ▣) This organised hostel is spanking clean and its two-bed dorms give travellers a chance to double up on the cheap. Facilities include kitchen, laundry and TV room.

Also recommended:

Camping Pointe á la Bise (☎ 022 752 12 96; Chemin de la Bise 19; camp sites per adult/tent/car Sfr7.50/7/6.50; ⊗ Apr-Oct) Camping spots in an appealing lakeshore location. Take bus E to get there.

Auberge de Jeunesse (☎ 022 732 62 60; www.yh -geneva.ch; Rue Rothschild 28-30; dm Sfr26, d from Sfr75; ⊗ reception 6.30-10am & 2pm-1am Jun-Sep, 6.30-10am & 4pm-midnight Oct-May; ▣)

Midrange & Top End

Hotel St-Gervais (☎ 022 732 45 72; www.stgervais -geneva.ch; Rue des Corps-Saint 20; r Sfr115, with shared bathroom Sfr85) Just like an old-fashioned auberge, rooms tout tartan carpets, wood furnishings and crisp white linen at this delightful hotel near the train station. There's wi-fi available and it's stumbling distance from the train station.

Hôtel International Terminus (☎ 022 906 97 77; www.international-terminus.ch; Rue des Alpes 20; s/d/tr from Sfr120/160/180; P ✗ ⬛) This three-star hotel has absurdly low rates for Geneva, making it one of the best-value places near the train station (in winter a double room can go for even less). Rooms are well appointed, some come with swanky red carpets, and all come with cable TV.

Hôtel Bel'Esperance (☎ 022 818 37 37; www.hotel-bel-esperance.ch; Rue de la Vallée 1; s/d from Sfr120/160; ✗) This hotel is small, simple and slightly worn, but rooms are quiet and clean, there's a shared kitchen and the place is just a few minutes' walk from the old town. The flower-filled rooftop terrace, with table and chairs for lounging, is a delight when it's warm and sunny.

Auberge de Carouge (☎ 022 342 22 88; Rue Ancienne 39; s/d/tr/q Sfr130/180/210/250; P) With its tree-shaded garden and the artsy scene of Théâtre de Carouge around the corner, this hotel oozes old-world appeal. Its room count is just a couple over a dozen, so get in quick.

Hôtel des Bergues (☎ 022 908 70 00; www.hotel desbergues.com; Quai des Bergues 33; s/d from Sfr600/730; P ✗) Even the most basic rooms at this national monument drip marble and are decorated with copies of works by Claude Monet. The Suite Royal (a serious steal at just Sfr6600 per night!) is a sight to behold – a 134-sq-metre apartment with Jacuzzi,

DVD, private terraces, dressing room, dining room and, just in case, bullet-proof windows.

EATING

Geneva is the cuisine capital of Switzerland, with a wide range of choices.

Restaurants

In the old town, terrace cafés and restaurants crowd along the medieval Place du Bourg-de-Four.

Boccaccio (☎ 022 329 45 22; blvd Georges-Favon 45; mains Sfr14-25) This popular Geneva restaurant is done up like an Italian village with murals on the walls. A business crowd packs the place at lunch. The menu focuses on pizza, pasta and salads. Sit outside during summer.

L'amalgam (Rue de L'Ancien-Port 13; mains Sfr15-20) Locals flock to this locals'-favourite café for its rotating menu of simple food; decorations include African art, palms and ochre tones. The mood is decidedly mellow. It's a tiny joint with no phone.

Café Universal (☎ 022 781 18 81; blvd du Pont d'Arve 26; mains Sfr15-30) With heavy chandeliers, monster mirrors and 1920s posters, this place is chic and French. It draws an arty crowd into its tightly packed interior.

ù bobba (☎ 022 310 53 40; Rue de la Corraterie 21; mains Sfr15-42) A cultured crowd gathers at this dining spot, decked in red and gold and oozing attitude. Particularly hot is its u jardinù bobba, one of Geneva's best roof terraces. Inventive mains range from veal medallions with pistachio nuts (Sfr42) to Gorgonzola-dunked gnocchi (Sfr25).

Café des Bains (☎ 022 321 57 98; www.cafedesbains .com; Rue des Bains 26; mains Sfr20-40) Beautiful objects and an eye for design are trademarks of this fusion restaurant where Genevan beauties flock. The king prawns pan-fried with green pepper, sweet Thai basil and mango and served with a mint and apricot mousse certainly won our hearts. Veggie options are plentiful and excellent.

Le Relais de L'Entrecôte (☎ 022 310 60 04; Rue du Rhône 49; starters/mains Sfr10/25) If entrecôte and fries (some say the best steak and chips in Geneva) are your cup of tea then this busy bistro wedged between designer shops is for you. Try to snag the table with lake view.

Brasserie Lipp (☎ 022 311 10 11; Rue de la Confédération 8; plat du jour Sfr20-28, mains Sfr35) Eternal favourite with the Genevois; come for a drink and snack or full meal – everything from oysters to a perch fillet. There's an outdoor terrace in summer. It's on the 2nd floor of the shopping arcade.

Quick Eats & Self-Catering

Rue de Fribourg, Rue de Neuchâtel, Rue de Berne and the northern end of Rue des Alpes are loaded with kebab, falafel and quick-eat joints. Eat in or take away at the following places:

Migros (Rue des Pâquis; 8am-7pm Mon-Fri, 8am-6pm Sat) Head to this supermarket to stock up on supplies. You'll also find baguettes (Sfr2) and sandwiches (Sfr4) in its self-service restaurant.

Manora (Rue de Cornavin 4; mains Sfr5-15) Rather tasty buffet food, including extensive salad and dessert bars, are served at this quick-eat Swiss chain.

Al-Amir (Rue de Berne 22; kebabs Sfr8) This hole-in-the wall Lebanese takeaway serves the best kebab in town.

DRINKING & ENTERTAINMENT

The latest nightclubs, live-music venues and theatre events are well covered in the weekly *Genève Agenda* (free from the tourist office). Try strolling around the Quartier des Pâquis (between the train station and the lake); it's packed with pubs and bars.

La Plage (☎ 022 342 20 98; Rue Vautier 19) The Beach in Carouge is a timeless watering hole with bare wood tables, checked lino floor, green wood shutters and tables outside.

Alhambar (☎ 022 312 13 13; www.alhambar.com; Rue de la Rôtisserie 10; noon-2pm Mon, noon-2pm & 5pm-1am or 2am Tue-Fri, 5pm-2am Sat, 11am-midnight Sun) With a buzzing atmosphere, an eclectic music programme and the best Sunday brunch in town, Alhambar provides an oasis of theatricality in an otherwise staid shopping district.

Flanagan's Irish Bar (☎ 022 310 13 14; Rue du Cheval-Blanc 4) Popular with the city's English-speakers and expats, this pub keeps Guinness flowing into the wee hours.

L'Usine (☎ 022 328 08 18; Place des Volontaires 4) In a converted factory, it's something of a city party-base. The drinking is fairly cheap and the entertainment ranges from dance nights and concerts to cabaret, theatre and other nocturnal diversions.

Prétexte (☎ 022 310 14 28; Rue du Prince 9; admission Sfr10; 11pm-5am Thu-Sat) With a healthily kitsch décor, two bars and a dance floor, this opulent place is the main gay club.

GETTING THERE & AWAY

Geneva airport (GVA; ☎ 022 717 71 11; www.gva.ch) is an important transport hub and has frequent connections to every major European city. **EasyJet** (code EZ; ☎ 084 888 82 22; www.easyjet .com) is a popular budget carrier with flights to many European destinations.

Next to Jardin Anglais is a ticket booth for **Compagnie Générale de Navigation** (CGN; ☎ 022 312 52 23; www.cgn.ch), which operates a May to September steamer service to all towns and major villages bordering Lake Geneva (Lac Léman), including those in France. Destinations include Lausanne (Sfr30, 3½ hours, hourly) and Montreux (Sfr42, 4½ hours, hourly). Eurail and Swiss Pass holders are valid on CGN boats or there are CGN boat day passes for Sfr55.

International buses depart from **Place Dorcière** (☎ 022 732 02 30; Place Dorciére), off Rue des Alpes. There are buses to London (Sfr145, 17 hours, twice weekly) and Barcelona (Sfr100, 10 hours, twice weekly).

An autoroute bypass skirts Geneva, with major routes intersecting southwest of the city: the N1 from Lausanne joins with the E62 to Lyon (130km) and the E25 heading southeast towards Chamonix.

Sixt (☎ 022 732 90 90; Place de la Navigation 1) generally has the best daily rates for last-minute car hire.

Trains run to most Swiss towns including Zürich (Sfr78, three hours, hourly) and Interlaken (Sfr65, three hours, hourly).

There are regular international trains to Paris (Sfr105 by TGV, 3½ hours, eight times daily), Hamburg (Sfr285, 10 hours, daily), Milan (Sfr84, four hours, daily) and Barcelona (Sfr105, nine hours, daily).

GETTING AROUND

Getting from the airport is easy with regular trains into Gare de Cornavin (Sfr2.60, six minutes). Bus No 10 (Sfr2.20) does the same 5km trip. A taxi costs Sfr25 to Sfr35.

There are free bikes available from **Genève Roule** (☎ 022 740 13 43; www.geneveroule.ch; Place de Montbrillant 17; 7.30am-9.30pm May-Oct). Bring your ID and Sfr20 for a deposit.

Buses, trams, trains and boats service the city, and ticket dispensers are found at all stops. Tickets cost Sfr1.80 (within one zone, 30 minutes) and Sfr2.20 (two zones, one hour). A day pass costs Sfr6 for the city or Sfr12 for the whole canton. Tickets and passes are also valid for CGN boats that travel along the city shoreline.

LAKE GENEVA REGION

Switzerland's Riviera lines the shores of Europe's largest lake – known to many as Lake Geneva, to Francophones as Lac Léman – and rivals its French counterpart as a magnet for the rich and famous. Amid a climate mild enough for palm trees to grow, are swanky yet charming little resort towns such as Vevey and Montreux. There's also the marvellous emerald spectacle of tightly ranked vineyards spreading in terraces up the steep hillsides.

LAUSANNE
pop 115,916

In a fabulous location overlooking Lake Geneva, Lausanne is an enchanting beauty with several distinct personalities: the former fishing village, Ouchy, with its summer beach-resort feel; Place St-François, with stylish, cobblestone shopping streets; and Flon, a warehouse district of bars, galleries and boutiques. It's also got a few amazing sights. One of the country's grandest Gothic cathedrals dominates its medieval centre.

The **tourist office** (☎ 021 613 73 21; www .lausanne-tourisme.ch; Place de la Navigation 4; �9am-6pm) is next door to the Ouchy metro station. You can buy the Lausanne Card here (Sfr15, valid two days), which allows unlimited travel anywhere in the city by bus and train.

Sights & Activities
MUSÉE DE L'ART BRUT

Perhaps the most alluring **museum** (☎ 021 647 54 35; www.artbrut.ch in French; Ave de Bergiéres 11; adult/student Sfr8/5; � 11am-1pm & 2-6pm Tue-Fri, 11am-6pm Sat & Sun) in the country, the collection here is a fascinating amalgam of 15,000 works of art created by untrained artists – psychiatric patients, eccentrics and incarcerated criminals. The works offer a striking

variety, at times a surprising technical capacity and in some cases an inspirational world-view. Biographies and explanations are in English. The museum is about 600m northwest of the Place St Francois.

CATHEDRALE DE LAUSANNE

This glorious Gothic **cathedral** (☉ 7am-7pm Mon-Fri, 8am-7pm Sat & Sun Apr-Sep, to 5.30pm Oct-Mar) is arguably the finest in Switzerland. Built in the 12th and 13th centuries, highlights include the stunningly detailed carved portal, vaulted ceilings and archways, and carefully restored stained-glass windows.

MUSÉE OLYMPIQUE

Lausanne is home to the International Olympic Committee, and sports aficionados can immerse themselves in archival footage, interactive computers and memorabilia at the information-packed **Musée Olympique** (☎ 021 621 65 11; www.olympic.org; Quai d'Ouchy 1; adult/student/child Sfr14/9/7; ☉ 9am-6pm Mon-Wed & Fri-Sun, 9am-8pm Thu May-Sep, closed Mon Oct-Apr).

Sleeping

Camping de Vidy (☎ 021 622 50 00; www.campin glausannevidy.ch; Chemin du Camping 3; camp sites per site/tent/car Sfr8/12/3.50) This camping ground is on the lake just to the west of the Vidy sports complex. Sites are well maintained and it's popular with families in summer. Get off bus 2 at Bois de Vaux.

Jeunotel SA (☎ 021 626 02 22; www.jeunotel.ch; Chemin du Bois-de-Vaux 36; dm Sfr30, s/d with shared bathroom Sfr60/80; [P] [🖳] ; bus 2) The cheaper rooms feel rather dismal with exposed block walls, but the place caters to young Swiss staying for weeks at a time and the bar can become lively at night, making it a good spot to practice another language.

Lausanne Guesthouse & Backpacker (☎ 021 601 80 00; www.lausanne-guesthouse.ch; Chemin des Epinettes 4; dm Sfr35, s/d with shared bathroom Sfr81/88; [✕] [🖳]) This tastefully renovated 1894 townhouse perched high on a hill has stunning views. The garden terrace is great for summertime chilling and meeting other backpackers. The entire place is nonsmoking. Parking costs Sfr10.

Le Château d'Ouchy (☎ 021 616 74 51; www .chateaudouchy.com; Place du Port 2; s/d from Sfr125/240; [P] [✕] [🖳]) A whimsical castle (mostly built in the 19th century around the original medieval tower, complete with dungeon) with

SWITZERLAND

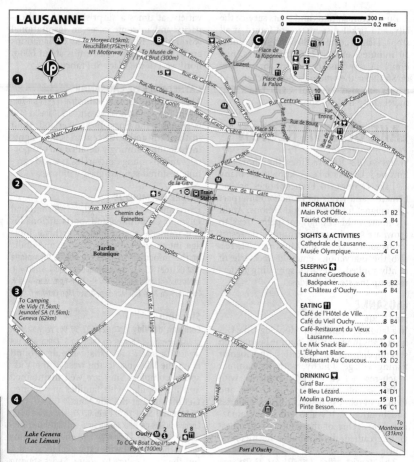

LAUSANNE

SWITZERLAND

rooms furnished in Louis XIII style but, sadly, showing signs of age.

Eating

Le Mix Snack Bar (☎ 078 808 79 68; Rue Central 29; mains from Sfr4.50) Small and smoky with cheery orange walls, this low-key place fills up at lunch when locals flock in for a sandwich, kebab, burger or coffee.

Café de l'Hôtel de Ville (☎ 021 312 10 12; Place de la Palud 10; mains from Sfr10) This café tempts you to linger over steamy cups of coffee and trashy French tabloids for hours on end. It's a favourite with students and travellers chowing on organic dishes surrounded by the buzz of animated conversation. At night come for drinks.

L'Éléphant Blanc (☎ 021 312 71 77; Rue Cité-Devant 4; mains Sfr18-25; ☽ Mon-Fri) On warm days tables spill out of the restaurant and onto the footpath in front of this tiny and popular student haunt. It's a good place to fill your stomach before boozing.

Café du Vieil Ouchy (☎ 021 616 21 94; Place du Port 3, Ouchy; mains Sfr18-37; ☽ Thu-Mon) The sunny terrace is the perfect spot for a summer meal of *rösti* and other Swiss classics. In winter linger over a creamy fondue inside cosy timber environs.

Café-Restaurant du Vieux Lausanne (☎ 021 323 53 90; Rue Pierre Viret 6; mains from Sfr20; ☽ lunch & dinner Tue-Fri, dinner only Sat) The French and Swiss cooking comes in generous portions at this old stalwart, although meat is the central theme. In summer you can sit beneath the narrow pergola out the back.

Drinking & Entertainment

Lausanne is one of the country's busier cities for nightlife. Look for the free listings booklet *What's Up* in many bars.

Le Bleu Lézard (☎ 021 321 38 35; Rue Enning 10) World-music jam sessions and film nights make this cavelike basement bar a happening spot. Cure your Sunday hangover with the all-day brunch.

Pinte Besson (☎ 021 312 59 69; Rue de l'Ale 4) The city's oldest tavern has been serving local wines to Lausannois punters since 1780. The place oozes the atmosphere of another age and makes no concessions to modern modishness.

Giraf Bar (☎ 021 323 53 90; Escaliers du Marché; ☽ closed Sun & Mon) This tiny smoke-filled bar fills up on a Friday or Saturday night. The giraffe-skin motif is repeated inside on lampshades and the music can reach back to the 1980s.

Mad – Moulin a Danse (☎ 021 312 11 22; www .mad.ch in French; Rue de Genève 23; admission Thu-Sun Sfr20; ☽ Wed-Sun) A typical large club that's generally packed on weekends, it relies on music theme nights to keep things interesting. The downstairs cellar bar has free admission on Wednesday. On Sunday's the club hosts Trixx Club for gays and lesbians.

Getting There & Around

Buses service most destinations (Sfr1.80 for up to three stops, or Sfr2.80 one-hour unlimited stops in central Lausanne). The metro connects Ouchy with the train station and costs the same as the buses.

There are trains to/from Geneva (Sfr20, 50 minutes, three hourly), Bern (Sfr30, 70 minutes, one or two hourly) and Interlaken Ost (Sfr55, two hours, two hourly). For boat services see p544.

VEVEY

pop 15,400

It's easy to see why Charlie Chaplin chose to spend the last 25 years of his life in Vevey. The swanky little place (one of Switzerland's two main Riviera resorts), with a colourful old square bumped up against the lake, is located in beautiful country. It also has a number of unique shops and lazy-day cafés. On summer Saturdays the sprawling square turns into a bustling marketplace with traditionally dressed merchants selling local handicrafts and wines.

For sleeping try the **Riviera Lodge** (☎ 021 923 80 40; www.rivieralodge.ch; Place du Marché; dm Sfr26, d with shared bathroom Sfr80; P ☒) in a hip 19th-century townhouse near the waterfront. The hostel's rooftop terrace has great views. The futuristic lounge makes a good reading nook. At the time of research guests received free bus tickets to the Château de Chillon and 50% off admission.

Le National (☎ 021 923 76 25; Rue du Torrent 9; mains Sfr10-20) is a great place to eat and drink. Chill at the cool bar with leaning glass-topped tables and stools or, for the more lounge-inclined, spots by the window. The restaurant serves a mix of international dishes.

MONTREUX

pop 22,800

In 1971 Frank Zappa was doing his thing in the Montreux casino when the building caught fire, casting a pall of smoke over Lake Geneva and inspiring the members of Deep Purple to pen their classic rock number *Smoke on the Water*.

The showpiece of the Swiss Riviera has been an inspiration to writers, artists and musicians for centuries. Famous one-time residents include Lord Byron, Ernest Hemingway and the Shelleys. It's easy to see why – Montreux not only boasts stunning Alps views and tidy rows of pastel buildings, it's also home to Switzerland's most extraordinary castle, the ever-popular Château de Chillon.

Each year the town hosts the **Montreux Jazz Festival** (☎ 021 963 82 82; www.montreuxjazz .com) in early July. It runs for two weeks. Free concerts take place every day, but count on Sfr40 to Sfr100 for one of the big gigs.

Sights

Switzerland's most popular fortress, **Château de Chillon** (☎ 021 966 89 10; www.chillon.ch; adult/student/child Sfr8.50/6.50/4; ☽ 9am-7pm Apr-Sep, 9.30am-5pm Mar & Oct, 10am-4pm Nov-Feb) was originally constructed on the shores of Lake Geneva in the 11th century. It caught the public imagination when Lord Byron wrote *The Prisoner of Chillon* about Bonivard, a prior chained in the dungeons for almost four years in the 16th century.

You can easily spend a couple of hours touring the tower, courtyards, dungeons and staterooms containing weapons, frescoes and furniture.

The castle is a pleasant 45-minute walk along the lakefront from Montreux. Otherwise take trolley bus 1 (Sfr2.60, Veytaux stop), which passes by every 10 minutes.

Sleeping & Eating

Auberge de Jeunesse (☎ 021 963 49 34; Passage de l'Auberge 8, Territet; dm from Sfr32; ☿ mid-Feb–mid-Nov) This waterfront hostel has a cheery atmosphere and simple rooms. Dorms come with as few as two beds. Catch bus No 1 from the train station.

Hôtel Masson (☎ 021 966 00 44; www.hotelmasson .ch; Rue Bonivard 5; s/d Sfr150/230; P) In the hills just west of Montreux, this one-time vintner's mansion is on the Swiss Heritage list of the country's most beautiful hotels. The grounds are luxurious, and the place reeks of old-world European charm. A small sauna and Jacuzzi are extra perks.

La Rose des Sables (☎ 021 961 15 46; Ave des Alps; mains from Sfr3; ☿ lunch) Inexpensive sandwiches, croissants, quiches and a mouthwatering chocolate selection make this charming patisserie a lovely lunch option.

Café du Grütli (☎ 021 963 42 65; Rue du Grand Chêne 8; mains Sfr20-30; ☿ Tue-Sat) Head to this eatery, hidden away in the old part of town, for good home cooking – ranging from *rösti* with ham to hearty meat dishes and the inevitable fondue.

Getting There & Away

There are trains to Geneva (Sfr26, 70 minutes, hourly) and Lausanne (Sfr9.80, 25 minutes, three hourly). Make the scenic journey to Interlaken via the GoldenPass Panoramic, with changes at Zweisimmen and Spiez (Sfr60, three hours, daily; rail passes valid).

GRYON & LEYSIN

Leave the beaten track and soak up the Swiss Alpine experience in untouristy **Gryon** (1130m), southeast of Montreux. It's close to the ski fields of Villars, some great meadow hiking trials and home to the fantastic **Swiss Alp Retreat** (☎ 024 498 33 21; Chalet Martin; www.gryon.com; dm/d from Sfr18/52; P 🖳). The hostel, run by a Swiss-Australian couple, has a laid-back vibe and gets rave reviews from travellers. It runs a number of popular excursions, including summer glacier skiing trips (Sfr125). Ask about ski-and-stay packages in winter.

To reach Gryon you will need to take a train from Lausanne to Bex (Sfr18, 40 minutes, hourly) and then the cogwheel train to the village (Sfr5.80, 30 minutes, hourly). The hostel is a five-minute walk from the train stop. Follow the signs.

Another tranquil Alpine spot, **Leysin** attracts skiers, snowboarders, hikers and meditators. In a 19th-century guesthouse the **Hiking Sheep** (☎ 024 494 35 35; www.hiking sheep.com; dm/d with shared bathroom from Sfr27/74; P ☒ 🖳) is another longtime favourite with backpackers. It has breathtaking views from its balconies, a pine-forested backyard and great vibes. Don't miss the hammocks. All sorts of activities can be arranged.

Leysin is accessible by a cogwheel train from Aigle (Sfr8.40, 30 minutes, hourly); there are trains to Aigle from Lausanne (Sfr29, 30 minutes, hourly).

VALAIS

It's pretty hard not to be seduced in Matterhorn country, where endless panoramic vistas and breathtaking views win over even the toughest critics. An area of extraordinary natural beauty, the Valais boasts the 10 highest mountains in Switzerland – all over 4000m. It's also home to one of the most popular, and best, skiing and boarding destinations in Europe, Zermatt. When the snow melts and the valleys turn lush and green the opportunities for hiking are boundless.

ZERMATT

pop 5500

One word says it all: Matterhorn. Synonymous with Switzerland, the Alps' most famous peak (4478m) keeps solitary vigil over this skiing, mountaineering and hiking hotspot.

On 13 July 1865 Edward Whymper led the first successful ascent of the mountain. The climb took 32 hours but the descent was marred by tragedy when four team members crashed to their deaths in a 1200m fall down the North Wall.

Skiers and snowboarders prefer going down to climbing up. The town doubled in size during the ski boom of the 1960s and '70s. For the rich and stylish, Zermatt is a place to see (as well as ski) and be seen (skiing or otherwise).

Orientation & Information

Zermatt is small, easy to navigate and car-free. The main street is Bahnhofstrasse, but street names are rarely used.

You can go online for free (or bring your laptop for a wi-fi moment) at **Papperla Pub** (right). The **tourist office** (☎ 027 966 81 00; www .zermatt.ch; Bahnhofplatz 5; ☒ 8.30am-noon & 1.30-6pm Mon-Fri, 9.30am-noon & 4-6pm Sat & Sun late Sep–mid-Jun, 8.30am-6pm Mon-Sat, 8.30am-noon & 1.30-6pm Sun mid-Jun–Sep) has all the local info.

Sights & Activities

Views from the cable cars and gondolas are pretty much uniformly breathtaking. The cogwheel train to **Gornergrat** (3090m) is one of the highlights. The mountain railway (Sfr36 one way) takes 25 to 43 minutes and there are two to three departures an hour. For the best views of the Matterhorn sit on the right-hand side. Alternatively, it takes around five hours to walk up from Zermatt to Gornergrat.

A walk in the **cemetery** is a sobering experience for any would-be mountaineer, as numerous monuments tell of untimely deaths on Monte Rosa and the Matterhorn.

Alpin Center (☎ 027 966 24 60; www.zermatt .ch/alpincenter; Bahnhofstrasse 58; ☒ 8am-noon & 2-6pm mid-Nov–Apr & Jul-Sep) contains the ski and snowboard school and the mountain-guides office (*Bergführerbüro*). For climbing the Matterhorn guides recommend previous experience, one week's preparation, and the small matter of Sfr1130 per person. Also ask here about Haute Route ski touring and heli-skiing. In the off-season you can reach them by phone only (between 9am and 11am and 2pm and 5pm Monday to Friday).

SKIING & SNOWBOARDING

Zermatt has numerous demanding slopes to test the experienced and intermediate skier in three main skiing areas: **Rothorn**, **Stockhorn** and **Matterhorn Glacier Paradise** (formerly Klein Matterhorn). In all, there are 245km of ski runs and free ski buses sim-

plify transferring between areas. February to April is peak time but in early summer the snow is still good and the lifts are less busy. Beginners have fewer options on the slopes.

The Klein Matterhorn is topped by the highest cable car station in Europe (3820m), providing access to the highest skiing on the Continent. It also has the most extensive summer skiing in Switzerland (up to 21km of runs) and is the starting point for skiing at the Italian resort of Cervinia. The No 7 run down from the border is an exhilarating, broad avenue, great for intermediates and above. Be aware bad weather can close the lifts leading up to the Klein Matterhorn on either side. Runs can be icier on the Italian side too (the skiing in Cervinia is best in March), but there are plenty of options. Don't leave it too late to get the lifts back up, or you could find yourself staying overnight!

A day pass for all ski lifts in Zermatt (excluding Cervinia) costs Sfr67/57/34 for adults/seniors & students/children and Sfr75/64/38 including Cervinia.

Sleeping & Eating

Be warned, many hotels and restaurants close between seasons.

Hotel Bahnhof (☎ 027 967 24 06; www.hotel bahnhof.com; dm Sfr33, s/d with shared bathroom from Sfr67/88; ☒ closed around mid-Oct–mid-Dec) A long-time mountaineers' mecca, the hotel has an impressive industrial-size kitchen, large dorms, and doubles with balconies facing the Matterhorn. It is directly opposite the station and gets good marks for cleanliness and service.

Hotel Blauherd (☎ 027 967 22 91; www.hotels -suisse.ch/blauherd; Wiestistrasse; s/d Sfr95/190; ☒) Rooms are clean and cosy at this friendly chalet-style hotel. The buffet breakfast is generous and you can use the pool in the nearby Hotel Cristiania. Staff will pick you up at the train station – it's a bit of a walk from the centre of town.

Restaurant Weisshorn (☎ 027 967 57 52; Am Bach 6; fondue Sfr25-28; meal Sfr40-50; ☒ mid-Jun–Sep & mid-Nov–Apr) The garish mural of Chichenitza, the Mexican temple, contrasts with the glowing orange Matterhorn table lamps. The food range is just as odd, from nachos and *quesadillas* (flour tortillas with savoury fillings) to fondue.

Drinking & Entertainment

Papperla Pub (☎ 027 967 40 40; Steinmattstrasse 34; ☯ 2.30pm-2am year-round) This is *the* après-ski pub in Zermatt, especially during the slow season (like January). Around the circular bar arranged on a couple of levels are high tables with stools or, if you prefer, low lounges. A DJ is usually in action and there's no shortage of ski resort drinking hijinks.

Broken Bar Disco (☎ 027 967 19 31; Bahnhofstrasse 41; ☯ 10pm-4am year-round) Down in a vaulted cellar of the Hotel Post, this is a popular dance dive where you can jive on a keg and expend any energy leftover after the day on the slopes. The Hotel Post is home to various other bars and eateries.

Getting There & Around

Zermatt is car-free. Dinky little electric vehicles are used to transport goods and serve as taxis and so on around town. Leave your vehicles in the huge open parking area in Täsch (Sfr7.50 per day), or one of the several covered garages there and take the train (Sfr7.80, 12 minutes) into Zermatt.

Trains depart from Brig, stopping at Visp en route. It's a steep, scenic journey (one way/return Sfr37/65, 80 minutes, hourly). Swiss Passes are valid. There is no discount for Eurail Pass holders. The only way out is to backtrack, but if you're going to Saas Fee you can divert there from Stalden-Saas. The popular and scenic *Glacier Express* travels between St Moritz and Zermatt (see p555).

LEUKERBAD

If you're looking for a little thermal rest and relaxation, this is the place to get it. Leukerbad, west of Brig, is home to Europe's largest thermal centre. The majestic mountain walls encasing the village like an amphitheatre grander than anything the Romans could have conceived make an awe-inspiring backdrop for outdoor bathing meditations.

There are no less than 10 different places to take to the waters, but the biggest and best is **Burgerbad** (☎ 027 472 20 20; www.burger bad.ch; Rathausstrasse; admission Sfr21; ☯ 8am-8pm Sun-Thu, to 9pm Fri & Sat) with indoor and outdoor pools, whirlpools and water massage jets. If you tire of soaking, ride the cable car up the sheer side of the northern ridge of

mountains to Gemmi Pass (2350m; one way/return Sfr15.50/24). It's a good area for hiking. To walk to the top of the pass takes two hours.

Weisses Rössli (☎ 027 470 33 77; off Dorfplatz; s/d with shared bathroom Sfr50/100) is an attractive place with a helpful friendly host. There is a restaurant serving Valais specialities on the ground floor.

Leukerbad is 16km north of Leuk, which is on the main rail route from Lausanne to Brig. A blue postbus goes from outside the Leuk train station to Leukerbad (Sfrfr10.40, 30 minutes, hourly) usually at 42 minutes past the hour; last departure is 7.42pm.

TICINO

Sip chardonnay in a colourful piazza café in the late afternoon and shiver as the Mediterranean air whips hot and spicy across your sun-speckled head. Check out the peacock-proud posers, clad in a style that is so *this* season, propelling their scooters in and out of frenetic village traffic. Melodic notes and lots of hand gestures, steaming plates of pasta, creamy gelatos. Did you cross the border into Italy? No, this is just the Switzerland Heidi failed to mention.

South of the Alps, Ticino (Tessin in German) has a distinct look. The canton manages to perfectly fuse Swiss cool with Italian passion, as evidenced by a lusty love for Italian comfort food and full-bodied wines that's balanced by a healthy respect for rules and regulations.

BELLINZONA

pop 17,100

Ticino's capital is a quiet stunner. Strategically placed at the conversion point of several valleys leading down from the Alps, Bellinzona is visually unique. Inhabited since Neolithic times, it is dominated by three grey-stone, fairy-tale medieval castles that have attracted everyone from Swiss invaders to painters such as JMW Turner. Turner may have liked the place, but Bellinzona has a surprisingly low tourist profile, in spite of its castles together forming one of only six Unesco World Heritage sites in Switzerland.

The **tourist office** (☎ 091 825 21 31; fax 091 825 38 17; www.bellinzonaturismo.ch; Viale Stazione 18; ☯ 9am-

6.30pm Mon-Fri, 9am-noon Sat), in the post office, can provide information on Bellinzona and the whole canton.

You can roam the ramparts of the two larger castles, **Castelgrande** or **Castello di Montebello**, both of which are still in great condition and offer panoramic views of the town and countryside.

The rooms at the **Hotel San Giovanni** (☎ 091 825 19 19; www.hotelzimmer.ch; Via San Giovanni 7; s/d with shared bathroom Sfr50/90) feel cluttered and bland, but it's the cheapest decent option around town.

The only place to sleep just inside the old town (part of the city wall stands menacingly behind it) is the pleasant **Albergo Croce Federale** (☎ 091 825 16 67; fax 091 826 25 50; Viale Stazione 12; s/d Sfr100/150). Rooms are straightforward but light, and the restaurant downstairs is cheerful.

Osteria Ticinese (☎ 091 825 16 73; Via Orico 3; pasta Sfr11-15, mains Sfr13-16) dishes up hearty portions of standard Italian fare in cheerful environs. It gets really crowded around lunch.

Bellinzona is on the train route connecting Locarno (Sfr7.20, 25 minutes, twice hourly) and Lugano (Sfr11.40, 30 minutes, twice hourly).

LOCARNO
pop 14,400

The rambling red enclave of Italianate townhouses, piazzas and arcades ending at the northern end of Lake Maggiore, coupled with more hours of sunshine than anywhere else in Switzerland, give this laid-back town a summer resort atmosphere. Locarno gained notoriety when it hosted the 1925 Peace Conference intended to bring stability to Europe after WWI.

Piazza Grande is the centre of town. You can gulp down shots and smoke Cuban cigars while checking your email at the Latino-style **Pardo Bar** (☎ 091 752 21 23; Via della Motta 3; per hr Sfr20; ⌚ 11am-1am). In the nearby casino complex is the **tourist office** (☎ 091 751 03 33; locarno@ticino.com; ⌚ 9am-6pm Mon-Fri, 10am-5pm Sat, 10am-2pm Sun).

Sights & Activities

Don't miss the formidable **Madonna del Sasso**, up on the hill with panoramic views of the lake and town. The sanctuary was built after the Virgin Mary allegedly appeared in a vision in 1480. It features a church with 15th-century paintings, a small museum and several distinctive statues. There is a funicular from the town centre, but the 20-minute climb is not demanding (take Via al Sasso off Via Cappuccini) and you pass some shrines on the way.

In August more than 150,000 film buffs hit town for the two-week **Festival Internazionale di Film** (International Film Festival; ☎ 091 756 21 21; www.pardo.ch; Via Luini 3). Cinemas are used during the day but at night films are shown in the open-air on a giant screen in the Piazza Grande.

Sleeping & Eating

Vecchia Locarno (☎ 091 751 65 02; www.hotel-vecchia-locarno.ch; Via della Motta 10; s/d with shared bathroom Sfr50/95) Rooms are gathered around a sunny internal courtyard, evoking Mediterranean flavours. The simply furnished digs are comfortable. Ask for one with views over the old town and hills.

Grand Hotel Locarno (☎ 091 743 02 82; ww.grand-hotel-locarno.ch; Via Sempione 17; s/d Sfr160/340; P ⌘ ▢) Grand in name and looks, this is an old-style relic of *belle époque* proportions. Rooms in this historic building are a trifle faded but the best of them still retain the elegance of a bygone era.

Lake Maggiore has a great variety of fresh and tasty fish. Look out for *persico* (perch) and *corigone* (whitefish).

Osteria Chiara (☎ 091 743 32 96; Vicolo della Chiara 1; mains Sfr15-30) Tucked away on a cobbled lane, this has all the cosy feel of a grotto. Sit at tables beneath the pergola or by the fireplace for chunky dishes of, say, *malfatti con zucca al timo* (big gnocchi-style pasta with pumpkin and thyme). From the lake follow the signs up Vicolo dei Nessi.

For self-caterers on Piazza Grande there's a Coop supermarket and a Migros De Gustibus snack bar.

Drinking

Sport Bar (Via della Posta 4) A fairly run-of-the-mill place by day, this rough-and-tumble bar with a red-walled dance space out the back and beer garden on the side is an extremely popular hangout with Locarno's young and restless.

Getting There & Away

The St Gotthard Pass provides the road link (N2) to central Switzerland. There are trains

SWITZERLAND

from Brig (Sfr50, 2½ hours, hourly) that pass through Italy en route. You change trains at Domodóssola across the border, so take your passport.

LUGANO

pop 26,100

Switzerland's southernmost tourist town is a sophisticated slice of Italian life, with colourful markets, upmarket shops, pedestrian-only piazzas and lakeside parks. Resting on the shore of Lake Lugano, with Mounts San Salvatore and Bré rising on either side, it's also a great base for lake trips, water sports and hillside hikes.

The old town is a 10-minute walk down the hill to the east. On the lake side of the Municipio building is the **tourist office** (☎ 091 913 32 32; info@lugano-tourism.ch; Riva Albertolli; ☼ 9am-6.30pm Mon-Fri, to 12.30pm & 1.30-5pm Sat, 10am-3pm Sun, closed Sat & Sun Dec-Feb).

Sights & Activities

Wander through the mostly porticoed lanes woven around the busy main square, Piazza della Riforma (which is even more lively when the Tuesday and Friday morning markets are held). Via Nassa is the main shopping street and indicates there is no shortage of cash in this town.

The simple Romanesque **Chiesa di Santa Maria degli Angioli** (St Mary of the Angels; Piazza Luini; ☼ 8am-5pm), against which a now-crumbling former hotel was built, contains two frescoes by Bernardino Luini dating from 1529. Covering the entire wall that divides the church in two is a grand didactic illustration of the Crucifixion. The closer you look, the more scenes of Christ's Passion are revealed, along with others of him being taken down from the cross and the Resurrection. The power and vivacity of the colours are astounding.

Chomp into some cocoa culture at the **Museo del Cioccolato Alprose** (☎ 091 611 88 56; www.alprose.ch; Via Rompada 36, Casalano; adult/child Sfr4/1; ☼ 9am-6pm Mon-Fri, to 5pm Sat & Sun). As well as getting a chocolate-coated history lesson, you can watch the sugary substance being made. Get there by the Ferrovia Ponte Tresa train (Sfr6).

Alternatively, take a **boat trip** to one of the many photogenic villages hugging the shoreline of Lake Lugano. One of the most popular is car-free **Gandria**, a tiny hillside village with historic homes and shops, and narrow winding alleyways right down to the water. If you hit town at meal times you can tuck into a traditional Ticinese dish in one of the many **grotti**.

Sleeping

Many hotels close for at least part of the winter.

Hotel & Hostel Montarina (☎ 091 966 72 72; www.montarina.ch; Via Montarina 1; dm Sfr25, s/d Sfr80/120; ☼ mid-Mar–Oct; P 🛋) Behind the train station is this charming hotel, whose best rooms are airy, with timber floors and antiques. The nearby hostel has rooms with four to 16 bunk beds. A buffet breakfast is available for Sfr12.

Hotel Pestalozzi (☎ 091 921 46 46; www.attuale.com/pestalozzi.html; Piazza Independenza 9; s/d from Sfr85/160; ✄) A renovated Art Nouveau building, this is a good central deal. Rooms have a fresh feel, with crisp whites and blues dominating the decoration. The cheapest share bathrooms and don't have air-con.

Hotel Federale (☎ 091 910 08 08; www.hotel-federale.ch; Via Regazzoni 8; s Sfr160, d Sfr190-260; P 🖥) If you can afford the grand top-floor doubles with lake views, this place beats many multi-stellar places hands-down. A short luggage-laden stumble from the train station, it is in a quiet spot with immaculately kept rooms and friendly staff. There is wi-fi in the lobby.

Eating & Drinking

Head to the pedestrian-only piazzas to tempt the tastebuds, with *panini* (bread rolls; Sfr5) and gelati (Sfr3) from street stalls, or larger meals in the pizzerias and cafés spilling onto the streets.

L'Antica Osteria del Porto (☎ 091 971 42 00; Via Foce 9; mains Sfr25-35) Savour local fish and Ticinese dishes such as *brasato di manzo al Merlot con polenta gratinata e legume* (grilled beef with polenta and vegetables). The terrace overlooking the Cassarate stream is pleasant, and you also have lake views.

Soho Café (☎ 091 922 60 80; Corso Pestalozzi 3; ☼ 10am-1am Mon-Fri, 4pm-1am Sat) This place is buzzing and chill at the same time. Filled with Lugano's beautiful people, stop by the orange-lit bar for a drink before slipping into a chair for catch-up chat with friends. DJs keep the music loud enough to groove too, but quiet enough to have a conversation.

Entertainment

Desperados (☎ 091 921 11 97; Via al Forte 4; ⏰ 10pm-5am) This late-night disco bar is hot, cramped and sweaty – in other words the perfect nightclub. The entrance is on a tiny square off Vicolo Orfanotrofio.

Getting There & Around

Lugano is on the same road and rail route as Bellinzona. Two postbuses run to St Moritz (Sfr74, four hours, daily in summer but only Friday, Saturday and Sunday in winter). Swiss Pass holders will still pay Sfr11 and everyone needs to reserve their seats the day before at the bus station, the train information office or by calling ☎ 091 807 85 20. Buses leave from the bus station on Via Serafino Balestra, though the St Moritz bus also calls at the train station.

GRAUBÜNDEN

Rural charm, untamed beauty and some of the world's most haute couture skiing are on the menu in Graubünden (Grisons, Grigioni, Grishun). It's easy to get off the trodden path here. The roads are mostly narrow, winding and often pocked. Great carpets of deep green felt seem to have been draped over the valleys and lower hills of this, the country's biggest canton. An outdoor adventurer's paradise, the region features more than 11,000km of walking trails, more than 600 lakes and 1500km of downhill ski slopes – including super swanky St Moritz and backpacker mecca Flims-Laax.

CHUR

pop 31,900

Chur, the canton's capital and largest town, is one of the oldest settlements in Switzerland, tracing its history back some 3000 years. Today it serves as a gateway for the region, although it's not a very obvious tourist attraction – buildings are stark and grey. For a town map see the **tourist office** (☎ 081 252 18 18; Grabenstrasse 5; ⏰ 1.30-6pm Mon, 8.30am-noon & 1.30-6pm Tue-Fri, 9am-noon Sat).

The **Kunstmuseum** (☎ 081 257 28 68; Postplatz; admission Sfr12; ⏰ 10am-noon & 2-5pm Tue, Wed & Fri-Sun, 10am-noon & 2-8pm Thu) has a collection of artwork by the three Giacomettis (Alberto, Augusto and Giovanni), and exhibits by local sci-fi artist HR Giger (of *Alien* fame).

The **Hotel Franziskaner** (☎ 081 252 12 61; fax 081 252 12 79; Kupfergasse 18; s/d from Sfr65/110) is located right on the old town square and can get a little rowdy on weekends but we think that just adds to its charm. Rooms are clean and plenty comfortable with simple pine furniture. The cheapest share bathrooms.

Easily Chur's most atmospheric old-time eatery, **Speiserestaurant Zum Alten Zollhaus** (☎ 081 252 33 98; Malixerstrasse 1; mains Sfr30) is the kind of place where black-and-white–clad waitresses bustle beneath centuries-old timber beams and serve up local and Swiss German dishes, including lots of fresh game meat in autumn.

A restless student population has led to high-density bar activity in the old town. The scene is on Untere Gasse, basically a row of bars. **Street Café** (☎ 081 253 714; Grabenstrasse 47) is one of the trendier hangouts for the earlier part of the evening.

Chur is connected to Zürich (Sfr40, 85 minutes, hourly) and St Moritz (Sfr38, two hours, hourly).

FLIMS-LAAX

They say if the snow ain't falling anywhere else, you'll surely find some around Flims-Laax. These towns, along with tiny Falera, 20km west of Chur, form a single ski area known as the Weisses Arena (White Arena), with 220km of slopes catering for all levels. Laax in particular is known as a mecca for snowboarders, who spice up the local nightlife too. The resort is barely two hours by train and bus (less by car) from Zürich airport.

There main **tourist office** (☎ 081 920 92 00; www.alpenarena.ch; Via Nova; ⏰ 8am-6pm Mon-Fri, to 4pm Sat May-Oct, to 5pm Mon-Sat Nov-Apr) is in Flims-Dorf.

The ski slopes range as high as 3000m and are mostly intermediate or easy, although there are some 45km of more challenging runs. A one-day ski pass includes ski buses and costs Sfr62 (plus Sfr5 for the KeyCard that you use to access the lifts).

Laax was the first Swiss resort to allow snowboarders to use the lifts back in 1985, and remains a mecca for snowsurfers, with two huge half-pipes (one said to be the biggest in the world) and a freestyle park huddled around the unfortunately named Crap Sogn Gion peak. The season starts in late October on the glacier and, depending on snowfalls, in mid-December elsewhere.

In summer try your hand at **river rafting** on a turbulent 17km stretch of the Vorder-rhein between Ilanz and Reichenau. It will take you through the **Rheinschlucht** (Rhine Gorge), somewhat optimistically dubbed Switzerland's Grand Canyon, but impressive enough for all that. **Swissraft** (☎ 081 911 52 50; www.swissraft.ch) offers half-/full-day rafting for Sfr109/160.

It may resemble an awful 1970s housing estate, but **Riders Palace** (☎ 081 927 97 00; www .riderspalace.ch; Laax Murschetg; dm Sfr30-60; d to Sfr200 per person; 🖳) is actually a curious bit of designer cool for the snow party animal (hotel motto: sleeping is for dreamers). You can go for basic but comfortable bunk-bed accommodation or stylish rooms (with baths by Philippe Starck). The pricing system is a trifle complicated, and can include your ski pass. The so-called Multimedia rooms are doubles/triples with Playstation, DVD player and Dolby surround sound. The whole place is wi-fi wired and located 200m from the Laax lifts. Its lobby bar is open to the general public and picks up après-ski traffic that continues until well into the night, occasionally with live acts.

Postbuses run to Flims and the other villages in the White Arena area hourly from Chur (Sfr12.40 to Flims-Dorf, 30 minutes). A local free shuttle bus connects the three villages.

ST MORITZ
pop 4900

Just like rolled jeans and big sunglasses, ski resorts are constantly going into and out of style. A few years ago it was all about Aspen, but this season the name on everyone's lips in the rich-famous-royal (or maybe just young and super fabulous) clique is St Moritz. The place is definitely hot. And with its smugly perfect lake and aloof mountains, the town also looks a million dollars.

Orientation & Information

Hilly St Moritz Dorf is above the train station, with luxury hotels, restaurants and shops. To the southwest, 2km around the lake is the more downmarket St Moritz Bad; buses run between the two. St Moritz is

seasonal and becomes a ghost town during November and from late April to early June.

The train station near the lake rents out bikes in summer and changes money from 6.50am to 8.10pm daily. The **St Moritz tourist office** (☎ 081 837 33 33; stmoritz.ch; Via Maistra 12; 🕙 9am-5pm Mon-Fri) has all the usual traveller info.

Activities

Skiers and snowboarders will revel in the 350km of runs on the slopes of **Corviglia-Marguns** (☎ 081 830 00 00; www.bergbahnenengadin.ch; day lift ticket Sfr63, ski & boot rental Sfr45). The choice for beginners is limited. There are also 160km of **cross-country trails** (equipment rental Sfr20) and 120km of marked **hiking paths**.

You can also try golf (including on the frozen lake in winter), tennis, in-line skating, fishing, horse riding, sailing, windsurfing and river rafting, to mention just a few. The tourist office has a list of prices and contacts.

Sleeping & Eating

Youth Hostel St Moritz Bad (☎ 081 833 39 69; www .youthhostel.ch/st.moritz; Via Surpunt 60; dm with half-board Sfr46; 🖳) Backing on to the forest and cross-country ski course, this large, modern hostel has excellent facilities. There's mountain bike rental, compulsory half-board and a TV lounge. From the train station take the bus towards Maloja and get off at the Hotel Sonne. From here it is a six-minute walk.

Chesa Chantarella (☎ 081 833 33 55; www.chesa -chantarella.ch; Via Salastrains; s/d Sfr95/190; 🕙 Jun-Sep & Dec-Apr; 🅿) High up over town, this is a charming, knock-about sort of place that also happens to house one of the town's better-value eateries for local cooking and fondue.

Hotel Waldhaus am See (☎ 081 836 60 00; www .waldhaus-am-se.ch; s/d Sfr170/320; 🅿 🖳) Brilliantly located in grounds overlooking the lake and a short walk from the train station, this place has pleasant rooms, many with enticing views. It has its own sizzling restaurant too, with grilled meat specialities.

Jöhri's Talvo (☎ 081 833 44 55; Via Gunels 15; mains Sfr10-20) This place, beyond Bad in nearby Champfér, is the best valley restaurant, serving up fish and local dishes in rustic surroundings.

Engiadina (☎ 081 833 32 65; Plazza da Scuola 2; fondue from Sfr32 per person) This comfortable, cosy spot is famous for fondue, and that's the best thing to eat here (it's Sfr38.50 per person with champagne). It's open year-round.

Drinking

Around 20 bars and clubs have dancing and/or music. While you bop to the beat your wallet might also be waltzing itself wafer-thin, because nights out in St Moritz can be nasty on the banknotes.

Bobby's Pub (☎ 081 834 42 83; Via dal Bagn) This vaguely pub-type place with undulating bar and a wide selection of beers attracts young snowboarding types in season, and just about everyone in town out of season, being one of the few places open year-round.

Getting There & Away

Two postbuses run to Lugano (Sfr74, four hours, daily summer; Friday, Saturday and Sunday winter). You must reserve a seat the day before. Call ☎ 081 837 67 64. The bus costs Sfr10 for those holding Swiss Travel passes.

The *Glacier Express* plies one of Switzerland's most famous scenic train routes, connecting St Moritz to Zermatt (Sfr138, 7½ hours, daily) via the 2033m Oberalp Pass. It covers 290km and crosses 291 bridges. Novelty drink glasses in the dining car have sloping bases to compensate for the hills – remember to keep turning them around!

SWISS NATIONAL PARK

The road west from Müstair stretches 34km over the Ofenpass (Pass dal Fuorn, 2149m), through the thick woods of Switzerland's only **national park** (www.nationalpark.ch; ☷ Jun-Oct) and on to **Zernez**, which is home to the **Chasa dal Parc Naziunal Svizzer** (National Park House; ☎ 081 856 13 78; www.nationalpark.ch; ☷ 8.30am-6pm, to 10pm Tue Jun-Oct). It is on the main road just as it leaves the east end of town and is open the same months as the park. It provides hiking details with locations to see particular animals.

There's no charge to enter the park and parking is free. Walkers can enter by trails from Zernez, S-chanf and Scuol. Deviating from the paths is not permitted. Regulations prohibit camping, littering, lighting fires, cycling, picking flowers, bringing dogs into the park, or disturbing the animals in any way. Fines of up to Sfr500 may be imposed for violations.

Sleeping & Eating

There are several hotel and restaurant options in Zernez and a couple in the park itself.

Il Fuorn (☎ 081 856 12 26; www.ilfuorn.ch; dm Sfr19, s/d from Sfr75/140, half-board extra Sfr30; ☷ Jun-Oct) In the middle of the national park by the

---

A LITTLE ANIMAL MAGIC *Sarah Johnstone*

If you'd like a break from people and their playthings, the Swiss National Park provides an ideal spot far from the madding crowd. It's a place to enjoy the vast, untrammelled countryside.

The park was established in 1914, the first such park to be created in Europe. At 172.4 sq km, it is smaller than most American and Canadian national parks, but the command of conservation is more rigorously adhered to. The key principle is to keep things natural. This even means holding down the number of paths to a minimum, to lessen the impact of human curiosity.

Such care has led to a flourishing of flora and fauna. You can view a number of animals that are not usually seen – ibex, marmot, chamois and deer roam through the park at will.

A three-hour walk from S-chanf to Trupchun is especially popular in October, when you can get close to large deer. The Naturlehrpfad circuit near Il Fuorn gives an opportunity to see bearded vultures, released into the wild since 1991.

In summer 2005, one of the descendants of the handful of Slovenian brown bears released into the wild in northern Italy since the 1990s caused a storm by, er, wandering over the border into the Val Müstair near the Ofenpass (Pass dal Fuorn). He came to join the small number of wolves that have again been roaming the east of the canton since 2002. The appearance of the bear attracted floods of animal-spotters, but the hullabaloo was short-lived, as the bear wandered back into Italy. In September he was back and upsetting locals by killing a dozen or more sheep to keep hunger at bay.

SWITZERLAND

main road, it is a handy hulk of a place with surprisingly pleasant rooms (unless you want to opt for the very basic dorm with huddled-together mattresses). Trout is big on the menu.

Hotel Bär & Post (☎ 081 851 55 00; www.baer-post .ch; s/d Sfr90/160) In business since 1905, this is one of the town's choicest options. The best rooms are really spacious, local stone pine predominates and there is also a sauna on the premises. The restaurant, decked out in typical timber style for the region, is a good place to sample local cooking (mains Sfr20 to Sfr40).

Getting There & Away

Train services regularly run from Zernez to St Moritz (Sfr16.80, 50 minutes), with stops at S-chanf, Zuoz and Celerina. Change trains at Samedan for the latter and for St Moritz.

ZÜRICH

pop 338,794

If you haven't actually visited Switzerland's most populous city, you are more likely to associate its name with being a boring banking capital than an up-and-coming urban hot-spot. That is a real shame, because contemporary Zürich has a kind of pulsating energy not readily found elsewhere in Switzerland. Now that its Street Parade has overtaken London's Notting Hill Carnival, Zürich is host to Europe's largest yearly street party. In addition to this its former industrial quarter has been transformed into a hip nightlife venue catering to a youngish crowd, and this happening 'Züri-West' district has the same buzz as Berlin's Prenzlauerberg or Mitte. The infamous 'gnomes', as the British like to call Zürich's bankers, are still in evidence, but sometimes they can astonish you by whizzing by on a Segway scooter.

ORIENTATION

Zürich is at the northern end of Lake Zürich (Zürichsee), with the city centre split by the Limmat River. Like most Swiss cities it is compact and easy to navigate. The main train station (Hauptbahnhof) is on the western bank of the river, close to the old centre.

INFORMATION

Bookshops

Orell Füssli Bookshop (☎ 044 211 04 44; Bahnhofstrasse 70) Great source of fiction and travel books in English.

Travel Book Shop (☎ 044 252 38 83; Rindermarkt 20) Sells English-language travel books and maps.

Discount Card

ZürichCard (per 24/72hr Sfr15/30) Available from the tourist office and the airport train station, this provides free public transport, free museum admission and more.

Internet Access

Quanta (☎ 01 260 72 66; cnr Niederdorfstrasse & Mühlegasse; per hr Sfr10; ☼ 9am-midnight)

Medical Services

Bellevue Apotheke (☎ 044 252 56 00; Theaterstrasse 14) A 24-hour chemist.

Cantonal University Hospital (☎ 044 255 11 11; Rämistrasse 100) Casualty department.

Post

Main post office (☎ 044 296 21 11; Kasernenstrasse 95-97; ☼ 7.30am-8pm Mon-Fri, 8am-4pm Sat) There's a more convenient location at the main train station.

Tourist Information

Zürich tourist office (☎ 044 215 30 00; www.zurich tourism.ch; train station; ☼ 8.30am-8.30pm Mon-Fri, to 6.30pm Sat & Sun) Arranges hotels, car rentals and excursions.

SIGHTS

Many things to see and do in Zürich don't cost a cent. In addition to the sights listed here there are numerous art galleries.

Old Town

Allocate at least a couple of hours to explore the cobbled streets of the pedestrian-only old town lining both sides of the river. You never know what a turn down an intimate alleyway might reveal – perhaps a 16th-century guildhall, a tiny boutique, cosy café or maybe courtyards and fountains.

Elegant **Bahnhofstrasse** is simply perfect for window-shopping and affluent Züricherwatching. The bank vaults beneath the street are said to be crammed with gold and silver. Above ground, you'll find luxury shops selling the best Switzerland can offer – from watches and clocks to chocolates, furs, porcelain and fashion labels galore.

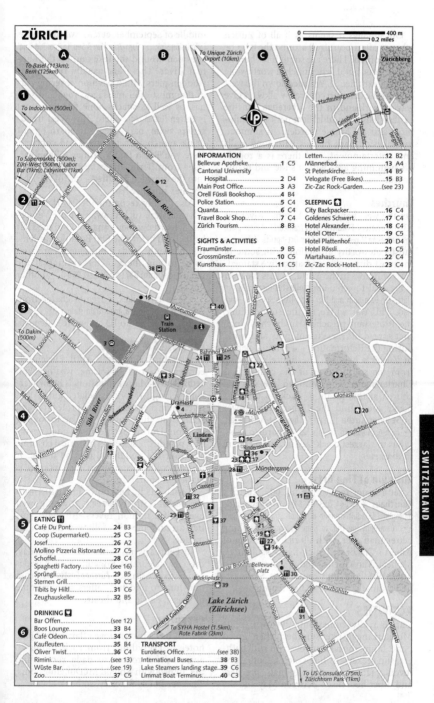

ZÜRICH

INFORMATION
Bellevue Apotheke..................1 C5
Cantonal University
  Hospital..............................2 D4
Main Post Office.....................3 A3
Orell Füssli Bookshop..............4 B4
Police Station........................5 C4
Quanta.................................6 C4
Travel Book Shop....................7 C4
Zürich Tourism.......................8 B3

SIGHTS & ACTIVITIES
Fraumünster..........................9 B5
Grossmünster.......................10 C5
Kunsthaus...........................11 C5

Letten...............................12 B2
Männerbad..........................13 A4
St Peterskirche.....................14 B5
Velogate (Free Bikes).............15 B3
Zic-Zac Rock-Garden...........(see 23)

SLEEPING
City Backpacker.....................16 C4
Goldenes Schwert..................17 C4
Hotel Alexander.....................18 C4
Hotel Otter...........................19 C5
Hotel Plattenhof....................20 D4
Hotel Rössli..........................21 C5
Martahaus...........................22 C4
Zic-Zac Rock-Hotel.................23 C4

EATING
Café Du Pont.......................24 B3
Coop (Supermarket)..............25 C3
Josef.................................26 A2
Mollino Pizzeria Ristorante......27 C5
Schoffel..............................28 C4
Spaghetti Factory...............(see 16)
Sprüngli..............................29 B5
Sternen Grill........................30 C5
Tibits by Hiltl.......................31 C6
Zeughauskeller.....................32 B5

DRINKING
Bar Offen........................(see 12)
Boos Lounge........................33 B4
Café Odeon.........................34 B4
Kaufleuten..........................35 B4
Oliver Twist.........................36 C4
Rimini............................(see 13)
Wüste Bar.......................(see 19)
Zoo...................................37 C5

TRANSPORT
Euronlines Office................(see 38)
International Buses.................38 B3
Lake Steamers landing stage...39 C6
Limmat Boat Terminus...........40 C3

SWITZERLAND

On Sundays it seems as if all of Zürich takes an afternoon stroll around the lake; be sure to join in. There are sometimes human traffic jams, but it is definitely a worthwhile cultural experience. Wander down the west bank of the lake and concrete walkways give way to parkland in the **Arboretum**. On the eastern bank, the **Zürichhorn** park has sculptures and a Chinese Garden. In summer, the lakeside park buzzes with food stalls and entertainment, and there is a roped-off swimming area with a slide and diving board.

Churches

On the west bank of the Limmat River the 13th-century **Fraumünster** (cathedral; Münsterplatz; 9am-6pm May-Sep, 10am-5pm Oct-Apr) is Zürich's most noteworthy attraction, with some of the most distinctive and attractive stained-glass windows in the world. Across the river is the dual-towered **Grossmünster** (Grossmünsterplatz; 9am-6pm mid-Mar–Oct, 10am-5pm Nov–mid-Mar). This was where, in the 16th century, the Protestant preacher Huldrych Zwingli first spread his message of 'pray and work' during the Reformation – a seminal period in Zürich's history. The figure glowering from the south tower of the cathedral is Charlemagne, who founded the original church at this location. Back on the west bank, you'll find the 13th-century tower of **St Peterskirche** (St Peter's Church; St-Peterhofstatt; 8am-6pm Mon-Fri, to 3pm Sat) is hard to miss. It has the largest clock face in Europe (8.7m in diameter).

Museum of Fine Arts

After a major renovation in 2005, Zürich's **Kunsthaus** (044 253 84 84; www.kunsthaus.ch; Heimplatz 1; adult/student & senior Sfr12/7, free Sun; 10am-9pm Tue-Thu, to 5pm Fri-Sun) is looking better than ever, with its rich collection of Alberto Giacometti stick-figure sculptures, Monets, Van Goghs, Rodin sculptures and other 19th- and 20th-century art. Swiss artist Ferdinand Hodler is also represented.

ACTIVITIES

Zürich really comes into its own in its Mediterranean-like summer when green parks lining the lake are overrun with bathers, sun seekers, in-line skaters, footballers, lovers, picnickers, party animals, preeners and other hedonists. Between May and the middle of September, **outdoor swimming areas** (admission Sfr6; 9am-7pm May & Sep, to 8pm Jun-Aug) are open around the lake and up the Limmat River. These are usually rectangular wooden piers with a pavilion covering part of the; most offer massages, yoga and saunas, as well as snacks. One favourite spot is **Letten** (Lettensteg), where Züri-West trendsetters swim, barbecue, skateboard or just drink and chat on the grass and concrete. Here you'll also find a former S-Bahn carriage from Berlin that's been transformed into the crowded **Bar Offen** – one of Zürich's premier summer bars.

Also highly recommended is **Männerbad** (Schanzengraben), tucked away on the Venice-like Schanzengraben canal, behind the Hallenbad and below the Old Botanic Gardens. It's men-only by day; but women are welcome to join them in the evening at the fantastic **Rimini Bar** (044 211 95 94) – another hot spot.

Use of city bikes is free of charge from **Velogate** (platform 18, main train station; 7.30am-9.30pm). Bring photo ID and a Sfr20 deposit.

FESTIVALS & EVENTS

On the third Monday in April, Zürich celebrates the arrival of warmer weather with **Sechseläuten**. Many professionals in Switzerland belong to work-associated guilds that offer them a certain level of protection and security in their jobs – similar to joining a union. During Sechseläuten guild members parade the streets in historical costume and tour the guildhalls, playing music. A fireworks-filled 'snowman' (the Böögg) is ignited at 6pm.

Zürich lets its hair down in August with the techno **Street Parade**, attracting well over half a million ravers. All-night parties around the city follow a three-hour parade.

In February, just after Ash Wednesday, the city celebrates **Fasnacht**, with parades and festive costumes. **Zürcher Festspiele**, from mid-June to mid-July, offers a programme of music, dance and theatre.

SLEEPING

Zürich has a bizarre love affair with theme hotels – everything from rock rooms to animal-print rooms to dada rooms and the 'in bed with Ronald McDonald' rooms. Cheaper hotels fill early, so book ahead.

SWITZERLAND

Budget

City Backpacker (☎ 044 251 90 15; www.city-back packer.ch; Niederdorfstrasse 5; dm Sfr31, s/d Sfr66/92) You climb a hell of a lot of stairs to reach reception in this bustling favourite, but it's worth the trek. Smack in the middle of old town, the hostel offers sparkling dorms and doubles, self-catering kitchen and coin laundry. With lounge chairs and sky-scraping city views, the summer rooftop terrace is the best spot in Zürich to wind down at sunset with a few cold beers.

SYHA Hostel (☎ 043 399 78 00; www.youthhos tel.ch; Mütschellenstrasse 114, Wollishofen; dm Sfr38, s/d Sfr99/116; ☐) Expensively overhauled in 2005, this huge hostel now features a swish reception/dining hall and sparkling modern bathrooms. Dorms remain quite small, though. Take tram 7 to Morgental or S-Bahn to Wollishofen.

Martahaus (☎ 044 251 45 50; www.martahaus .ch; Zähringerstrasse 36; dm Sfr 38, s/d Sfr115/150, with shared bathroom Sfr85/100) With 1970s black leather lounges in the spacious breakfast room–cum-lounge and a roof terrace, this is a fun, friendly place to stay. Other features include a bar, laundry and gym. Negatives include street noise and tiny, shared bathrooms.

Dakini (☎ 044 291 42 20; www.dakini.ch; Brauerstrasse 87; s/d from Sfr65/90; ☐) This relaxed B&B attracts a bohemian crowd of artists and performers, academics and trendy tourists who don't bat an eyelid at its location near the red-light district. Five bedrooms in two apartments share kitchen and bathroom. Take tram 8 to Bäckeranlange.

Midrange & Top End

Hotel Alexander (☎ 044 251 82 03; www.hotel -alexander.ch; Niederdorfstrasse 40; s/d from Sfr95/140; P ✴) It's smack in the centre of old town, and the rooms are sparkling clean with polished floorboards, white walls and nice touches like chocolates on the pillows. The bathrooms stand out with huge showers and a Mediterranean tile motif. Breakfast is included, there's wi-fi and an attached takeaway spot to quell late night munchies.

Hotel Otter (☎ 044 251 22 07; www.wueste.ch; Oberdorfstrasse 7; s/d Sfr100/130) This flamboyantly quirky hotel is by far our favourite place to stay in town. The 17 rooms are each fantastically unique – one's a safari lodge, another a

religious grotto, and then there's the Arabian-themed room. Not to be missed. The location, on fashionable Oberdorfstrasse, is very central, too.

Hotel Plattenhof (☎ 044 251 19 10; www.plattenhof .ch; Plattenstrasse 26; s/d from Sfr165/205; P) This place manages to be cool without looking pretentious. It features a youthful, vaguely Japanese style, with low beds and mood lighting in its newest rooms. Even the older rooms are stylishly minimalist. Take tram 6 to Platte.

Hotel Rössli (☎ 044 256 70 50; www.hotelroessli.ch; Rössligasse 7; s/d from Sfr180/210) There's a calming, ascetic quality to this boutique hotel with its white walls and furnishings only occasionally disrupted by greys, mint greens or pale blues. It also has an elegant bar.

Also recommended:

Goldenes Schwert (☎ 044 250 70 80; www.gayhotel .ch; Marktgasse 14; s/d from Sfr130/165) Gay hotel with some elaborately themed rooms; the top floor gets the least noise from the downstairs disco.

Zic-Zac Rock-Hotel & Zic-Zac Rock-Garden (☎ 044 261 21 81; www.ziczac.ch in German; Marktgasse 17; d Sfr160, with shared bathroom Sfr75/120; ☐) Novelty place featuring rock-star rooms in bold colours and an attached restaurant that is a slice of Americana in Switzerland (mains Sfr15 to Sfr25).

EATING

Zürich has a thriving café culture and hundreds of restaurants serving all types of local and international cuisine. A good place to start exploring is Niederdorfstrasse and the backstreets nearby, which are filled with wall-to-wall cafés, restaurants and bars of every description. Most restaurants stay open from early morning to late evening.

Restaurants

Spaghetti Factory (☎ 044 251 94 00; Niederdorfstrasse 5; pasta Sfr15-22) With a fun, buzzing atmosphere, this restaurant serves delicious bowls of its namesake dish (22 choices). The spaghetti with pesto sauce is delicious. The place often has long lines. Portions are just right.

Zeughauskeller (☎ 044 211 26 90; Bahnhofstrasse 28a; mains Sfr15-30) The menu at this huge, atmospheric beer hall offers 20 different kinds of sausages in eight languages, as well as numerous other Swiss specialities of carnivorous and vegetarian varieties.

Mollino Pizzeria Ristorante (☎ 044 261 01 17; Limmatquai 16; mains Sfr18-25) Head to this lively restaurant for mouth-watering pizzas, delicious cappuccino and exquisite lake views. Sit outside when it's warm, inside amid the cheery frescos when it's blustery.

Sprüngli (☎ 044 244 47 11; Bahnhofstrasse 21; chocolates from Sfr2, mains Sfr19-28) The mother of all chocolate shops, it's a Zürich legacy and must for chocoholics. Choose from a huge range of truffles and cakes from downstairs display cases, or mingle with the well-heeled crowd in the elegant 1st-floor tearooms for a rather special experience.

Café Du Pont (☎ 044 211 66 77; Beatenplatz 4; mains Sfr20-30) There's no question this is a kitschy spot that takes the movie scene a little overboard – all the entrées are named for classic films and TV screens periodically play previews. Still the cavernous place (think industrial) has a feisty vibe. The mostly American menu serves lots of Tex-Mex, pasta, burger and seafood dishes with better than average results. A favourite with the expat community, it's also a good (and noisy) spot to bring the family.

Josef (☎ 044 271 65 95; Gasometerstrasse 24; mains Sfr20-48) A Züri-West stalwart, Josef frequently changes it décor and Swiss-Italian menu, but always has a good wine list and remains constantly popular with the 'in' set, even if just for a drink.

Quick Eats

Cheap eats abound around the train station, especially in the underground Shopville. Niederdorfstrasse has a string of snack bars offering pizza, kebabs and Asian food for about Sfr9.

Sternen Grill (Bellevueplatz/Theatrestrasse 22; snacks Sfr5-8) This is the city's most famous – and busiest – sausage stand; just follow the crowds streaming in for a tasty grease fest.

Tibits by Hiltl (☎ 044 260 32 22; Seefeldstrasse 2; dishes per 100g Sfr3.70) Tibits is where with-it, health-conscious Zürchers head for a light bite when meeting friends. There's a tasty vegetarian buffet, as well as fresh fruit juices, coffees and cake.

Schoffel (☎ 044 261 20 70; Schoffelgasse 7; mains Sfr8-16) On weekend mornings, locals flock to this café for a leisurely coffee and newspaper read within the cheery yellow modern-art–filled walls. Soups, salads and big bowls of yogurt and fruit are on the menu.

DRINKING

Late-night pubs, clubs and discos clutter Niederdorfstrasse and adjoining streets. Zürich's former industrial area has become one of its hippest neighbourhoods: the much-vaunted 'Züri-West' quarter starts roughly west of the train station. Langstrasse, directly behind the station, is a minor red light district with loads of popular bars clustered along its side streets. Its safe to wander through, although you may be offered drugs or sex.

Wüste Bar (☎ 044 251 22 07; Oberdorfstrasse 7) One of our top choices, this small and groovy spot underneath the Otter Hotel has plush red seats and a cowhide bar. There's sometimes live music.

Oliver Twist (☎ 044 252 47 10; Rindermarkt 6) English-speakers gravitate towards this pub, which serves Irish, British, Australian and South African beers. It's a smoky, noisy place, often standing-room-only and somewhat of a meat market.

Café Odeon (☎ 044 251 16 50; Am Bellevue) Lenin and James Joyce once downed drinks at this swish, smoky bar with marble walls and chandeliers. Come for the Art Nouveau interior, but ignore the quite ordinary food.

Boos Lounge (Schweizergasse 6) This place was packed when we stopped by, and it was early on a Monday afternoon. Slick and modern, it's a top choice for an after-work cocktail amid mod red walls, multihued lighting and a disco ball.

ENTERTAINMENT

Züritipp is the city's events magazine, available around town and from the tourist office. Generally dress well and expect to pay Sfr15 to Sfr30 admission to enter Zürich's clubs.

Supermarket (☎ 044 440 20 05; www.supermarket .li; Geroldstrasse 17; admission from Sfr15) Zürich's number one club is smaller than the name suggests, but boasts three cosy lounge bars around the dance floor, a covered back courtyard and an interesting roster of DJs playing house music.

Indochine (☎ 044 448 11 11; www.club-indochine .ch; Limmatstrasse 275; ☒ from 10pm Thu-Sat) Models and rich kids mingle between the dimly lit fat Buddhas of this faux opium den. Zürich's equivalent to London's Chinawhite or Paris' Buddha Bar.

SWITZERLAND

Labyrinth (☎ 044 440 59 80; Pfingstweidstrasse 70) Zürich's top gay club features half-naked pole-dancing narcissists flaunting their six packs and lots of eye-candy at the bar. Take tram 4 to Förrlibuckstrasse.

Kaufleuten (☎ 044 225 33 22; www.kaufleuten.com in German; Pelikanstrasse 18) A club with a long history and hot reputation at the top end of the market. Dress to impress, as everyone in here looks like they walked out of a model shoot or film set. The place boasts that Prince and Madonna were once guests. Tram 2 or 9 to Sihlstrasse will get you there.

Labor Bar (☎ 044 272 44 02; www.laborbar.ch; Schiffbaustrasse 3; ⏰ from 10pm Fri & Sat, from 9pm Sun) The set for local celebrity Kurt Aeschbacher's TV show, this is the epitome of retro chic, with lots of Plexiglas and diffused coloured light. It's always filled with beautiful people; Friday is Celebreighties and Sunday 'for gays and friends'.

Rote Fabrik (☎ 044 481 91 43; www.rotefabrik.ch in German; Seestrasse 395) A long-standing Zürich institution, this club has managed to hold its own throughout the years. It stages everything from rock concerts to original-language films, theatre and dances, and has a bar and restaurant. Take bus 161 or 165 from Bürkliplatz.

GETTING THERE & AWAY

Unique Zürich airport (ZRH; ☎ 043 816 22 11; www .zurich-airport.com) is 10km north of the city centre. It's a small international hub with two terminals.

The N3 approaches Zürich from the south along the shore of Lake Zürich. The N1 is the fastest route from Bern and Basel and is the main entry point from the west.

There are direct trains to Stuttgart (Sfr61, three hours, daily), Munich (Sfr86, 4½ hours, daily), Innsbruck (Sfr66, four hours) and Milan (Sfr72, four hours, daily), as well as many other international destinations. There also are departures to most of the Swiss towns, including Lucerne (Sfr22, 50 minutes, hourly), Bern (Sfr48, 70 minutes, hourly) and Basel (Sfr32, 65 minutes, hourly).

GETTING AROUND

Trains make the 10-minute trip from the airport to the main train station (Sfr5.40) around every 10 minutes. Taxis cost around Sfr50.

There is a comprehensive, unified bus, tram and S-Bahn service in the city, which includes boats plying the Limmat River. Short trips under five stops are Sfr2.30. A 24-hour pass, including travel to and from the airport, is Sfr10.80. For unlimited travel within the canton, including extended tours of the lake, a day pass costs Sfr28.40, or Sfr20 after 9am (9-Uhr-Pass).

Lake steamers depart from Bürkliplatz from early April to late October (Swiss Pass and Eurail valid, Inter-Rail 50% discount). Taxis in Zürich are expensive, even by Swiss standards, at Sfr6 plus Sfr3.50 per kilometre.

CENTRAL SWITZERLAND & BERNER OBERLAND

Welcome to the fairy-tale Alpine creation they call the Berner Oberland, a region so silver-screen perfect that you'll think you have conjured it up. Pretending that you are James Bond in *On her Majesty's Secret Service* pursuing villains down the sheer face of the Schilthorn, kicking plumes of white fluffy powder up into a deep-water blue sky – that can't be real! Well, Mark Twain *did* once write that no opiate compared with walking through the Berner Oberland…but super-hero fantasies aside, it *is* real. Travelling through the Berner Oberland is a lot like having your cake and eating it too. Not only are you able to spend endless mesmerizing hours staring at the sheer, outrageous beauty of those snow-white, jagged, craggy, so-big-they're-going-to-swallow-you-whole mountains that are found everywhere, but you can also play in them.

In summer the region turns into a recreation of Heidi's turf – all sparkling mountain lakes and tinkling cowbells. Sleep in the hay in tiny Gimmelwald or go hiking around eye-catching Mürren. Thrill-seekers and backpackers congregate around Interlaken (although it's also got loads for all types of travellers), with a reputation for offering every adventure sport under the sun. When you have had your fill of outdoor adventures, spend some time in soul soothing Lucerne.

LUCERNE

pop 58,600

Lapped by a scenic lake and surrounded by mountains of myth, a picture of this once small fishing village and its wooden Kapellbrücke (Chapel Bridge) is enough to connote the very essence of Switzerland. One of Switzerland's major draw cards Lucerne is a collage of medieval bridges, old squares and watery vistas. Legend has it that an angel with a light showed Lucerne's first settlers where to build a chapel, and in good weather even an atheist might describe the city's location as heaven-sent.

Orientation & Information

The mostly pedestrian-only old town is on the northern bank of the Reuss River. The train station is centrally located on the southern bank. The **Internet Shop** (☎ 041 211 21 31; cnr Pilatustrasse & Seebrücke; per hr Sfr10; ☺ 9am-10pm Mon-Sat, to 8pm Sun) is across from the train station. Beside platform three is **Luzern tourist office** (☎ 041 227 17 17; www.luzern.org; Zentralstrasse 5; ☺ 8.30am-7.30pm Mon-Fri, 9am-7.30pm Sat & Sun Apr-Oct, to 6pm Nov-Mar).

Sights

If you plan to visit several of Lucerne's many museums, consider purchasing the Sfr29 Museum Pass, valid for one month. It lets you into all museums as often as you want.

OLD TOWN

Your first port of call should be the medieval old town with ancient rampart walls and towers, 15th-century buildings with painted façades and the two much-photographed covered bridges. **Kapellbrücke**, dating from 1333, is Lucerne's best-known landmark. It's famous for its distinctive water tower and the spectacular 1993 fire that nearly destroyed it. Though it has been rebuilt, fire damage is still obvious on the 17th-century pictorial panels under the roof. In better condition, but rather dark and dour, are the *Dance of Death* panels under the roofline of **Spreuerbrücke** (Spreuer Bridge).

PICASSO MUSEUM

You'll find yourself face-to-face with the artist at this **museum** (☎ 041 410 35 33; Furrengasse 21; adult/student Sfr8/6; ☺ 10am-6pm Apr-Oct, 11am-1pm & 2-4pm Nov-Mar). The main attraction is nearly 200 photographs by David Douglas Duncan that show an impish Picasso at work and play in his Cannes home during the last 17 years of his life. The intimate black-and-white photos also portray his muse, Jacqueline, and his children. Don't expect to find much of Picasso's own work, other than a few ceramics and sketches, however.

ROSENGART COLLECTION

By contrast, the **Sammlung Rosengart** (☎ 041 220 16 60; www.rosengart.ch; Pilatusstrasse 10; adult/student Sfr15/9, combined with Picasso Museum Sfr18/16; ☺ 10am-6m Apr-Oct, 11am-5pm Nov-Mar) *does* contain a significant amount of Picasso's art. Showcasing the works retained by Angela Rosengart, a Swiss art dealer and friend of Picasso's, its ground floor is entirely devoted to the Spanish master. In the basement, there's a selection of sketches and small paintings by Paul Klee; upstairs you'll find works by Cezanne, Kandinsky, Miró, Modigliani, and a fine handful of works by Marc Chagall.

VERKEHRSHAUS

Planes, trains and automobiles are the name of the game in the huge, family-oriented **Transport Museum** (☎ 041 370 44 44; Lidostrasse 5; adult/student/child Sfr24/22/10; ☺ 10am-6pm Apr-Oct, to 5pm Nov-Mar), east of the city centre, that's devoted to Switzerland's proud transport history. Space rockets, a communications display, simulators, a planetarium and an **IMAX theatre** (Sfr16 extra) all help make this Switzerland's most popular museum. For unrivalled views of the town and lake, take off 140m above the complex in the Hi-Flyer, a captive balloon you can ride for an extra Sfr20 (15 minutes' duration). Take bus 6, 8 or 24 from Bahnhofplatz.

Activities

If you're ready to face your fear factor contact **Outventure** (☎ 041 611 14 41; www.outventure .ch; Hansmatt 5, CH-6362, Stansstad), which has the usual adrenalin-junkie fixes on offer, including bungy jumping (Sfr160), tandem paragliding (Sfr150), canyoning (Sfr170) and glacier trekking (Sfr170). There's a daily shuttle from tourist office.

In addition there are options for scenic cruises on the lake, including aboard old-fashioned paddle steamers. Check out

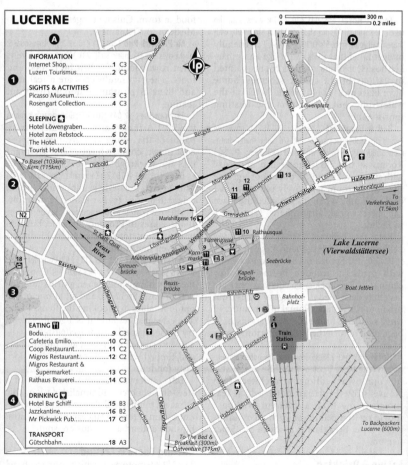

LUCERNE

0 — 300 m
0 — 0.2 miles

INFORMATION
Internet Shop.....................1 C3
Luzern Tourismus................2 C3

SIGHTS & ACTIVITIES
Picasso Museum..................3 C3
Rosengart Collection............4 C3

SLEEPING
Hotel Löwengraben...............5 B2
Hotel zum Rebstock..............6 D2
The Hotel........................7 C4
Tourist Hotel....................8 B2

EATING
Bodu.............................9 C3
Cafeteria Emilio................10 C2
Coop Restaurant.................11 C2
Migros Restaurant...............12 C2
Migros Restaurant &
    Supermarket.................13 C2
Rathaus Brauerei................14 C3

DRINKING
Hotel Bar Schiff................15 B3
Jazzkantine.....................16 B2
Mr Pickwick Pub.................17 C3

TRANSPORT
Gütschbahn......................18 A3

SWITZERLAND

www.lakelucerne.ch (in German) for more
information or stop by the tourist office.

Festivals & Events

Lucerne's six-day **Fasnacht** celebrations are
more boisterous and fun than Basel's carnival. The party kicks off on 'Dirty Thursday'
with the emergence of the character 'Fritschi'
from a window in the town hall, when bands
of musicians and revellers take to the streets.
The carnival moves through raucous celebrations climaxing on Mardi Gras (Fat Tuesday), and is over on Ash Wednesday.

Sleeping

Lucerne has some great budget options, most
of which are nicer than midrange places.

Backpackers Lucerne (☎ 041 360 04 20; www
.backpackerslucerne.ch; Alpenquai 42; dm Sfr28, d Sfr66;
reception 7-10am & 4-11pm) Backpackers love
this lively, longtime favourite, with balconies overlooking the lake in a leafy spot.
Clean and friendly, its facilities include
kitchen and laundry. It's a 15-minute walk
southeast of the train station.

Hotel Löwengraben (☎ 041 417 12 12; www
.loewengraben.ch; Löwengraben 18; dm Sfr30, s/d from
Sfr120/165;) In a converted prison with
basic, whitewashed, 'cell-like' rooms and
some fancier suites (albeit with bars on
the windows), the hotel is good for novelty value. There's also a trendy bar and
nightclub. In the winter, prices drop by
about Sfr20.

Tourist Hotel (☎ 041 410 24 74; www.touristho tel.ch; St Karliquai 12; dm Sfr35, s/d from Sfr90/120, with shared bathroom from Sfr70/100; ⊠ ▣) A friendly budget hotel that feels more like an upmarket hostel, it offers spotless rooms painted in various bright colour schemes. Some have balconies. Look for the hotel on the waterfront, but away from the bustling tourist zone.

Bed & Breakfast (☎ 041 310 15 14; www.the BandB.ch; Taubenhausstrasse 34; s/d with shared bathroom Sfr80/120; ☙ reception closed noon-3pm; ℗ ⊠) Rooms at this B&B are stylish and cosy with white walls and parquet flooring. The shared bathroom is a lovely old-fashioned deal with tub. When it's crowded the place can have a great atmosphere. Take bus 1 to Eichof.

Hotel zum Rebstock (☎ 041 410 35 81; www .hereweare.ch; St Leodegar-Strasse 3; s/d & tr from Sfr160/260; ℗) Spread over two houses – one with medieval wooden beams and low ceilings – Rebstock's excellent rooms are tastefully decorated in a range of styles from urban to rustic and colonial to romantic. In three of them, funky tile decorations have been used to turn the bathrooms into works of art.

Hotel (☎ 041 226 86 86; www.the-hotel.ch; Sem pacherstrasse 14; ste Sfr350-540; ⊠) Be a film star in your own bedtime in architect Jean . Nouvel's low-lit design hotel, which features a scene from a different art-house movie on the ceiling of each sleek matt-black suite. Breakfast is an extra Sfr25 per person.

Eating & Drinking

Many places in Lucerne double as bars and restaurants. Places open for breakfast and stay open until late in the evening. Self-caterers should head to Hertensteinstrasse, where cheap eats are plentiful. There's a Coop restaurant, two Migros restaurants and a supermarket.

Cafeteria Emilio (☎ 041 410 28 10; Ledergasse 8; mains Sfr6-14) You'll be rubbing shoulders with other diners at this tiny place, but it has a certain charm and you won't find cheaper pizzas, pastas and salads.

Rathaus Bräuerei (☎ 041 410 52 57; Unter der Egg 2; mains Sfr8-30) Sit outside by the water or inside amid the shiny copper beer tanks. This atmospheric restaurant serves big glasses of home brews and some of the most delicious

food in town. Cuisine ranges from local to Mexican to Vietnamese.

Mr Pickwick Pub (☎ 041 410 59 27; Rathausquai 6; sandwiches Sfr6.50, mains Sfr10-23) Visit this lively, often rowdy joint, for Brit beer, food and footy. The pub sandwiches are a real steal and there is pleasamt outdoor riverfront seating.

Jazzkantine (☎ 041 410 73 73; Grabengasse 8; mains from Sfr15) A funky, arty and rather smoky haunt of the young and creative. There's cool music, counter meals, Saturday-night gigs and weeknight jazz workshops.

Bodu (☎ 041 410 01 77; Kornmarkt 5; mains Sfr18-45) This French brasserie is a local institution, celebrated for its Parisian-café interior, Bordeaux wines and excellent river views. It specialises in Provençal cuisine, but also branches out into dishes from Piedmont and even the Antilles.

Hotel Bar Schiff (☎ 041 418 52 52; Unter der Egg 8; soups & sandwiches Sfr8-12, mains Sfr20-40) Come for the daily happy hour when a drink and appetizer costs Sfr12.50, and sit at one of the outdoor tables overlooking the Reuss River. The esteemed restaurant is a good place to try the local speciality, *Kügelipastetli* – vol-au-vents stuffed with meat and mushrooms and topped with a rich sauce. It also does tasty fondue.

Loft (Haldenstrasse 21; ☙ Wed-Sun) With a steel-and-concrete minimalist design, this attracts a trendy, well-dressed but unpretentious young crowd. Danceable house, Latin, hip-hop and urban sounds are spun.

Getting There & Around

The N2/E9 motorway, which connects Basel and Lugano, passes by Lucerne. The N14 is the road link to Zürich. Trains connect Lucerne to Bern (Sfr30, 1½ hours, hourly), Geneva (Sfr70, 3¼ hours, hourly), Interlaken (Sfr26, two hours, hourly), Lugano (Sfr56, 2½ hours) and Zürich (Sfr19, 50 minutes, hourly).

INTERLAKEN

pop 15,000

Flanked by the stunning Lakes Thun and Brienz, and within yodelling distance of the mighty peaks of the Jungfrau, Mönch and Eiger, is ever-popular Interlaken. It's a great base for exploring the delights of the Jungfrau region. As it caters to backpackers like nowhere else in Switzerland, many budget travellers make this their main stop in the country. Solo travellers looking to meet like-minded individuals will have a field day here. Interlaken also is a mecca for thrill seekers. Many a traveller leaves with a much lighter wallet after blowing mind-boggling amounts of cash on a range of white-knuckle, high-adrenalin sports. Most are not disappointed. If you're not into the backpacker scene, don't fear, the town is also home to a range of charming guesthouses and modern hotels.

Orientation & Information

Most of Interlaken lies between its two train stations, Interlaken Ost and West, which both offer bike rental and daily money-exchange facilities. The main shopping street, Höheweg, runs between the stations, and you can walk from one to the other in 20 minutes.

Near Interlaken West is the **main post office** (cnr Marktgasse & Höheweg) and **Interlaken tourist office** (☎ 033 826 53 00; www.interlakentourism.ch in German; Höheweg 37; ⊕ 8am-6.30pm Mon-Fri, to 5pm Sat, 10am-noon & 4-6pm Sun Jul & Aug, 8am-noon & 1.30-6pm Mon-Fri, to noon Sat Sep-May).

Sights & Activities
EXTREME SPORTS

Interlaken is the world's second-biggest adventure sports destination, just behind New Zealand, and everything you can think of in this regard is offered from here (although the activities take place in the greater Jungfrau region). Options include skydiving (Sfr380); paragliding (Sfr150); night sledding past frozen waterfalls followed by a fondue dinner (Sfr95); skiing or snowboarding including transport, lift ticket and appropriate clothing and gear rental (Sfr165); and fly-in, drink a glass of champagne then hit the virgin powder glacier skiing (Sfr250). In summer there's canyoning, where you jump, slide and rappel down rocks and waterfalls (from Sfr125) and rafting on the class III–IV Lütschine River (Sfr95).

The vast majority of excursions occur without incident, but there's always a small risk of injury. Two tragically fatal accidents (canyoning in the Saxetet Gorge and bungee jumping off the Stechelberg-Mürren cable car) about five years ago fortunately have not been repeated, but it is always a

good idea to ask about safety records and procedures.

Those without lots of cash should check out the hiking trails, all with signposts giving average walking times, that dot the area.

The major operators, each able to arrange most sports, include the following:

Alpin Center (☎ 033 823 55 23; www.alpincenter.ch; Hauptstrasse 16)

Alpin Raft (☎ 033 823 41 00; www.alpinraft.ch; Hauptstrasse 7)

Outdoor Interlaken (☎ 033 826 77 19; www.outdoor -interlaken.ch; Hauptstrasse 15)

Swissraft (☎ 033 823 02 10; www.swissraft.ch; Obere Jungfraustrasse 72)

MYSTERY PARK

For something a little less extreme (especially if you have the kids along) head to **Mystery Park** (☎ 033 827 57 57; Hauptstrasse 43; adult/child Sfr48/28; ⊕ 10am-6pm). The latest brainchild of Erich von Däniken, the out-there author of the 1970s best-seller *Chariots of the Gods*, this theme park features replicas of Aztec pyramids and more space-aged buildings, where virtual reality/computer technology will invite you to consider Mr Däniken's theory that human beings descended from aliens.

Sleeping

Balmer's Herberge (☎ 033 822 19 61; www.balmers .ch; Hauptstrasse 23; dm Sfr27, s/d/q with shared bathroom Sfr33/76/132; ⌨) Young Americans have flocked to this cosy Swiss chalet with a raucous summer-camp feel for more than 50 years – it's a great place to meet people and party. On the negative side you're locked out of your room (even the doubles) during the day, you'll be constantly harassed to partake in the adventure sports and the staff even charges you to use the kitchen. If you can resist the temptation to buy, however, it's a good deal.

River Lodge (☎ 033 822 44 34; www.riverlodge .ch; Brienzstrasse 24; dm from Sfr28, s/d Sfr62/84; ⌨) Originally a camping area, this place was destroyed in the 2005 floods and rebuilt as a more upmarket joint, although a few dorms bed are available. River views are featured from each of the bungalows lining the waterfront, which house between one and four people in bunks. In summer the hosts encourage you to bring the feather

SWITZERLAND

AUTHOR'S CHOICE

Hotel Lötschberg/Susi's B&B (☎ 033 822 25 45; www.lotschberg.ch; General Guisan Strasse 31; B&B s/d Sfr105/135, hotel s/d from Sfr120/165; P ✗) This place has received consistently positive reviews over its 100 years of continuous operation, for its personal service and friendly hosts. Rooms here are spotless, and each is individually and thoughtfully decorated with homemade art on the walls. The attached B&B offers the cheapest digs, although these are still quite comfortable. In the main house, rooms come in a variety of sizes. A few are quite small, so ask when booking if you're claustrophobic. If you can nab it, grab the attic 'honeymoon' room. It has a huge slanted window that boasts in-you-face mountain views. In summer the place gets really full, and the outdoor patio with sturdy wooden benches and tables is a great place to chill out and meet other travellers.

The hotel arranges quite a few activities for guests. 'Cooking with Fritz' (Sfr 30) is its latest endeavour. Well worth the price, the host teaches you how to make traditional Swiss fondue and *rösti* from scratch. Fritz also takes guests paragliding (Sfr130) and for night sledding and fondue (Sfr75). Both cost less than going through the in-town companies, but are only open to guests.

---

duvet outside and sleep under the stars by the water. A communal kitchen and bikes and kayaks for guests are extra perks.

Backpackers Villa Sonnenhof (☎ 033 826 71 71; www.villa.ch; Alpenstrasse 16; dm/d from Sfr33/98; ☺ reception 7.30-11am & 4-9pm, to 10pm Jun-Aug; ▣) Widely regarded as the cleanest and most genteel of Interlaken's hostels, this place still has plenty going on – in the corner somewhere you're likely to find at least a few folks reliving their last skydive over pints of beer. Spacious, renovated rooms have nice touches such as steamer trunks and balconies, some with Jungfrau views. There's a small kitchen, a lounge and table tennis in the garden.

Funny Farm (☎ 079 652 61 27; www.funny-farm .ch; Hauptstrasse; dm Sfr35; ▨) Another budget powerhouse, Funny Farm has a raucous feel and draws in hordes of Australians. It revels in its anarchic, ramshackle premises – somewhere halfway between a squat and an island shipwreck. There's a ramshackle house surrounded by makeshift bars and a swimming pool, but guests don't care; they're here for the party.

Hotel-Gasthof Hirschen (☎ 033 822 15 45; www .hirschen-interlaken.ch; Hauptstrasse 11; s/d from Sfr90/180) Following a Sfr400,000 renovation in 2004, this 16th-century heritage-listed Swiss chalet is enjoying a new lease of life. Rooms are now 'rustic modern', with parquet floors, bathroom pods and wireless LAN (local area network).

Victoria-Jungfrau Grand Hotel & Spa (☎ 033 828 28 28; www.victoria-jungfrau.ch; Höheweg 41; s/d Sfr510/620) The granddaddy of Interlaken hotels, the Victoria easily outclasses everything else in town. From its swanky lobby and pampering spa to its old-world rooms, this 1865 landmark is the last word in Swiss style.

Eating & Drinking

Balmer's has the town's hottest after-dark scene (especially when its club is open), with Funny Farm a close second, and guests rarely leave at night. Self-caterers can stock up on beer (and food) at the **Coop Pronto** (Höheweg 11).

Balmer's Café & Grill (☎ 033 822 19 61; www.balmers .ch; Hauptstrasse 23; mains Sfr10-12) The American-style food (think big juicy burgers and greasy fries) served here is quite good and fairly priced, making it an option even if you're not staying at the hostel. The lounge-like atmosphere with wooden tables and a roaring fire is appealing. There's local beer on tap and fondue for Sfr16 per person. The downstairs club, Metro Bar, rocks the house Sunday through Wednesday nights. It gets going after 11pm.

Per Bacco (☎ 033 822 97 92; Rugenparkstrasse 2; mains Sfr12-15; ☺ 9am-1am Mon-Sat) With a quaint wine-cellar feel, this sophisticated place has a sophisticated wine list to match. It tends to attract a well-dressed older crowd, but anyone looking for cosy atmosphere, good wine and hearty bowls of yummy pasta won't be disappointed.

Des Alpes (☎ 033 822 23 23; Höeweg 115; mains Sfr12-25) With priceless Jungfrau sunset views, this restaurant is deservedly popular. If the weather is clear at least pop in for a coffee or cocktail. The food is good too, with a variety of Swiss dishes and meat fondue.

Top o'Met (☎ 033 828 66 66; 18th fl, Metropole Hotel, Höheweg 37; buffet from Sfr10.50, mains from Sfr18) Sip on a cocktail and enjoy the sweeping mountain views. Or stop by for an ice-cream sundae, meal or coffee during the day.

Bären (☎ 033 822 7676; Marktgasse 19; mains from Sfr20) *Rösti* and Bratwurst are the house specialities at this locally recommended restaurant. It also does very good fondue, salads with homemade dressing and other delicious Swiss dishes. Sit outside when it's warm.

Golder Anker (☎ 033 822 16; Marktgasse 57; mains Sfr20-40) The junkie, the banker, the tourist and the hotel proprietor – meet them all at the Golder Anker. Rebuilt after the 2005 floods, this well-respected establishment serves interesting dishes, ranging from chicken fajitas and red snapper to ostrich steaks. It also has a roster of live bands and international artists.

Getting There & Away

Main roads go east to Lucerne and west to Bern, but the only way south for vehicles, without a detour around the mountains, is the car-carrying train from Kandersteg, south of Spiez. Trains to Grindelwald (Sfr9.80, 40 minutes, hourly), Lauterbrunen (Sfr8, 20 minutes, hourly) and Lucerne (Sfr30, two hours, hourly) depart from Interlaken Ost. Trains to Brig (Sfr40, 1½ hours, hourly) and Montreux via Bern (Sfr92, two hours, hourly) leave from either Interlaken West or Ost.

JUNGFRAU REGION

Dominated by the famous Eiger, Mönch and Jungfrau (Ogre, Monk and Virgin) mountains, the Jungrfrau Region boasts the country's highest density of dramatic scenery. In winter, the Jungfrau is a magnet for skiers and snowboarders, with 200km of pistes. A one-day ski pass for Kleine Scheidegg-Männlichen, Grindelwald-First, or Mürren-Schilthorn costs Sfr56.

The Lauterbrunnen Valley branches out from Interlaken with sheer rock faces and towering mountains on either side, attracting an army of hikers and mountain bikers. Cowbells echo in the valley and every house and hostel has a postcard-worthy view. Many visitors choose to visit this valley on a day trip from Interlaken.

Grindelwald

Picturesque Grindelwald was once a simple farming village. Today it's the largest ski resort in the Jungfrau, nestled in a valley under the north face of the Eiger.

Grindelwald tourist office (☎ 033 854 12 12; www.grindelwald.ch in German; ☼ 8am-7pm Mon-Fri, to 6pm Sat, 9am-noon & 2-5pm Sun Jul-Sep, shorter hr & closed Sun btwn seasons) is located in the centre at the Sportzentrum, 200m from the train station.

The First is the main **skiing** area in winter, with runs stretching from **Oberjoch** at 2486m to the village at 1050m. In the summer it caters to **hikers** with 90km of trails about 1200m, 48km of which are open year-round. You can catch the longest **cable car** in Europe from Grindelwald-Grund to Männlichen, where there are more extraordinary views and hikes (one way/return Sfr29/46).

The cosy wooden chalet housing the excellent **SYHA hostel** (☎ 033 853 10 09; www.youth hostel.ch/grindelwald; Terrassenweg; dm from Sfr31, d from Sfr76; ☼ reception from 3.30pm Mon-Sat, from 5pm Sun) is perched high on a ridge with magnificent views. Avoid the 20-minute slog from the train station by taking the Terrassenweg-bound bus to the Gaggi Säge stop. The hostel closes between seasons.

Near the Männlichen cable-car station, the modern **Mountain Hostel** (☎ 033 854 3838; www.mountainhostel.ch; dm/d with shared bathroom from Sfr35/88; P) is a good base for sports junkies. Cyclists are especially welcomed. Rates include free ice-skating and swimming at a nearby facility.

The **Residence** (☎ 033 854 55 55; www.residence -grindelwald.ch; s/d from Sfr90/150; P X) is in quiet location on the eastern side of the village. Family-run, cosy and modern it has a terrace restaurant and allows you free access to a nearby hotel's swimming pool. There's a terrace restaurant overlooking the Wetterhorn.

On the way out of town, **Onkel Tom's Hütte** (☎ 033 853 52 39; Im Graben 4; pizzas Sfr13-30; ☼ 4-10.30pm Tue, noon-2pm & 4pm-midnight Wed-Sun) is an atmospheric place serving good pizzas in three sizes (to suit any appetite). It's very popular and usually requires a wait.

For steaks, sandwiches and burgers along with good views, try **Memory** (☎ 033 854 31 31; mains Sfr15-25) inside the Eiger Hotel. It also does tasty *rösti* and fondue.

Self-caterers can stock up at Coop supermarket opposite the tourist office.

The village is easily reached by road. There is a train to Interlaken Ost (Sfr9.40, 40 minutes, hourly).

Lauterbrunnen

Tiny Lauterbrunnen, with its attractive main street cluttered with Swiss chalet architecture, is friendly and down-to-earth. It's known largely for the impressive **Trümmelbach Falls** (admission Sfr10; ⏰ 9am-5pm Apr-Nov), 4km out of town, where, inside the mountain, up to 20,000L of water per second corkscrews through a series of ravines and potholes shaped by the swirling waters. A bus from the train station (Sfr3) takes you to the falls.

Camping Jungfrau (☎ 033 856 20 10; adult/tent Sfr9/6, cabins per person Sfr25), at the end of Main St, has excellent facilities and awesome views of towering peaks and sheer cliffs.

Just a two-minute walk from the train station, the **Valley Hostel** (☎ 033 855 20 08; www .valleyhostel.ch; dm/d from Sfr18/44; P ✗ ▣) offers up comfy rooms (many of them have balconies), a communal kitchen and a mellow environment.

When it comes to culinary matters, Lauterbrunnen has few options. Stock up at the Coop near the tourist office, or try the restaurant at the **Hotel Oberland** (☎ 033 855 12 41; Main St; mains from Sfr17). It has a big menu of *rösti*, pasta and salads.

Gimmelwald

Decades ago an anonymous backpacker scribbled these words in the Mountain Hostel's guest book: 'If heaven isn't what it's cracked up to be, send me back to Gimmelwald.' Enough said. When the sun is out in Gimmelwald, the place will take your breath away. Once a secret bolthole for hikers and adventurers looking to escape the region's worst tourist excesses, tiny Gimmelwald is seeing a lot more foot traffic these days. But even increasing crowds can't diminish its scintillating, textbook Swiss scenery and charm.

The hamlet is particularly enchanting in winter, when weathered wooden cha-

lets peep out from a thick blanket of snow and the mountains feel close enough to touch.

After a long summer hike, bed down in the barn at **Esther's Guesthouse** (☎ 033 855 54 88; www.esthersguesthouse.ch; barn accommodation Sfr22, s/d with shared bathroom Sfr40/80). Offered June to October, sleeping in the straw is surprisingly comfortable. A generous breakfast of organic food and a shower are included. If you'd rather not roll in the hay, there are lovely rooms in the main house (the place was expanding when we stopped by). If you can't stay, stop in to pick up homemade beef jerky (some of the best we've ever tasted), cheeses and other organic products.

The **Mountain Hostel** (☎ 033 855 17 04; www .mountainhostel.com; dm Sfr23; ▣) recently added an outdoor hot tub, so now you can *literally* soak up their jaw-dropping mountain views. The simple, rustic place does snacks and sells beer, and the super-friendly owners have loads of area tips.

Restaurant-Pension Gimmelwald (☎ 033 855 17 30; mains Sfr18) has hearty cooking, including fondue and farmers' barley soup. Don't miss the 'Gimmelwalder Horse-Shit Balls' for Sfr4. You'll have to visit to find out what they're made from.

To reach Gimmelwald hike up a steep trail (it's sometimes closed in winter due to avalanche danger) for about an hour and a half from Stechelberg or get a lift on the cable car (one way Sfr8). A great way to get to Stechelberg from Lauterbrunnen is to hike along a flat path for about 1½ hours. The trail passes through dramatic scenery. From Mürren, Gimmelwald is a pleasant 40-minute walk downhill, or catch the cable car (one way Sfr8).

Mürren

Arrive in Mürren on a clear evening, when the sun hangs low on the horizon, and you'll think you've died and gone to heaven. The peaks feel so close you're sure you can touch them, and staring slack-jawed at the towering masses of rock (some of the best views in the region) could be considered an activity in itself.

In summer, the **Allmendhubel funicular** (one way/return Sfr12/7.40) takes you above Mürren to a panoramic restaurant. From here, you can set out on many hikes, including the famous **Northface Trail** (2½ hours), via Schiltalp to the west, which offers outstanding views across the Lauterbrunnen valley. There's also an easier **Children's Adventure Trail** (one hour).

Sleeping options within Mürren include **Eiger Guesthouse** (☎ 033 856 54 60; eigerguest house@muerren.ch; dm from Sfr50, d with shared bathroom Sfr120), by the train station, which has a bar, restaurant and games room. There's also **Hotel Edelweiss** (☎ 033 855 13 12; edelweiss@muerren .ch; s/d Sfr95/190), which is perched right on the edge of a cliff and has vertiginous views, particularly through the large windows of its lounge and indoor restaurant. Try for a room with a balcony.

Tham's Snacks & Drinks (☎ 033 856 01 10; mains Sfr15-28; ☺ noon-9pm Jul & Aug) serves Thai, Singaporean, Malaysian and other Asian dishes cooked by a former five-star chef who's literally taken to the hills to escape the rat race. Tham's keeps irregular hours during the low season, so call ahead. Try the Hotel Blumental's rustic **Restaurant La Grotte** (☎ 033 855 18 26; mains Sfr16.50-35) for highly regarded fondues and flambés, although it's becoming slightly touristy in summer. Both it and Tham's are along the lower main thoroughfare.

One of the best parts about Mürren is getting there. From Lauterbrunnen take a cable car to Grütschalp, then switch to the train (Sfr9.40 total). The ride yields tremendous unfolding views across the valley to the Jungfrau, Mönch and Eiger peaks.

Schilthorn

There's a fantastic 360-degree panorama from the 2970m **Schilthorn** (www.schilthorn.ch) one that's possibly even better than from Jungfraujoch. On a good day, you can see from Titlis around to Mont Blanc, and across to the German Black Forest. Yet, some visitors seem more preoccupied with practising their delivery of the line, 'The name's Bond, James Bond', than taking in the 200 or so mountains. That's because a few scenes from *On Her Majesty's Secret Service* were shot here in late 1968/early 1969. You can watch them on a 180-degree panoramic screen at the free **Touristorama** in the cable car building.

The revolving **Piz Gloria Restaurant** (mains Sfr15-35) is really quite amazing. The food

(pasta, burgers, etc) is reasonably priced; and the views come with million-dollar smiles.

In winter there is a gnarly but heavenly **ski run** down to Mürren. You will need to be a pretty advanced rider to try it – it's long and steep and the moguls can be massive. If you know what you are doing, however, you will have a blast – think deep powder and places to catch lots of air. A day pass to Schilthorn-Mürren costs Sfr65 (you won't have to pay again for the cable cars).

If you are not skiing, you will need a Sfr115 excursion trip (Half-Fare Card and Swiss Pass, 50% off, Eurail Pass 25%) going to Lauterbrunnen, Grütschalp, Mürren, Schilthorn and returning through Stechelberg to Interlaken. A return from Lauterbrunnen (via Grütschalp), and Mürren costs about Sfr100, as does the journey up and back via the Stechelberg cable car.

Jungfraujoch

The train trip to Jungfraujoch (3454m) is touristy and expensive, but you do it anyway because (a) it's generally an once-in-a-lifetime experience and (b) you have to see it for yourself. Plus, there is a reason why about two million people a year visit this, the highest train station in Europe. On a clear day the outlook is indisputably spectacular. Good weather is essential so call ☎ 033 855 10 22 for taped forecasts in multiple languages before leaving.

From Interlaken Ost the journey is 2½ hours each way (Sfr169 return). Trains go via Grindelwald or Lauterbrunnen to Kleine Scheidegg. From here the line is less than 10km long but took 16 years to build. Opened in 1912, the track powers through both the Eiger and the Mönch, pausing briefly for travellers to take happy snaps of views from two windows blasted in the mountainside, before terminating at Jungfraujoch.

There's a cheaper 'good morning ticket' of Sfr145 if you can drag yourself out of bed for the early train (6.35am from Interlaken) and leave the summit by noon. From 1 November to 30 April the discount applies to the 6.35am and 7.35am trains, and there's no noon restriction. Eurail pass-holders get 25% off, Swiss Pass holders slightly more.

SWITZERLAND

NORTHERN SWITZERLAND

This region is left off most people's Switzerland itineraries, which is why you should visit. Sure, it is known for industry and commerce, but it also has some great attractions. Breathe in the sweet (okay slightly stinky) odours of black-and-white cows as you roll through the bucolic countryside. Take time to explore the tiny rural towns set among green rolling hills and on Lake Constance (Bodensee) and the Rhine River on the German border.

BASEL

pop 161,800

Visit Basel in the summer. Strangely, given its northerly location, the city has some of the hottest weather in the country. When the mercury starts rising the city sheds its notorious reserve and just cuts loose. As locals bob along in the fast-moving Rhine (Rhein) River, cool off in the city's numerous fountains, whiz by on motor scooters and dine and drink on overcrowded pavements, you could almost be in Italy, rather than on the dual border with France and Germany.

Basel's (Bâle in French) idyllic old town and many enticing galleries and museums are top draws at any time of year. The famous Renaissance humanist, Erasmus of Rotterdam, was associated with the city and his tomb rests in the cathedral.

Orientation & Information

The pedestrian-only old town and most popular sights are all on the south bank in Grossbasel (Greater Basel). **Internet Pub** (☎ 084 489 19 91; Steinentorstrasse 11; per hr Sfr8; ☻ 9am-10pm Mon-Thu, to 8pm Fri, to 5pm Sat) is a smoky joint where you can down a beer and surf the Web. The **main post office** (Rudengasse 1; ☻ 7.30am-6.30pm Mon-Fri, 8am-noon Sat) is in the city centre. The **main tourist office** (☎ 061 268 68 68; www.baseltourismus.ch; Stadtcasino, Barfüsserplatz; ☻ 8.30am-6pm Mon-Fri, 10am-5pm Sat, 10am-4pm Sun) is at this address until 2007; afterwards check the website for new office location. There is another branch of the **tourist office** (☎ 061 268 68 68; ☻ 8.30am-6.30pm Mon-Fri, 9am-2pm Sat & Sun) at the train station.

Sights & Activities

With its cobbled streets, colourful fountains, medieval churches and stately buildings, the old town is a wonderful place to wander. In Marktplatz check out the impressive rust-coloured **Rathaus** (town hall), with frescoed courtyard. The 12th-century **Münster** (cathedral), southeast from Marktplatz, is another highlight, with Gothic spires and Romanesque St Gallus doorway.

Theaterplatz is a crowd-pleaser, with a curious **fountain**, designed by Swiss sculptor Jean Tinguely. His madcap scrap-metal machines perform a peculiar water dance, delighting children and weary travellers alike. Also check out the 700-year-old **Spalentor** gate tower, a remnant of the town's old city walls, with a massive portal and grotesque gargoyles.

Art lovers should head to the **Kunstmuseum** (☎ 061 206 62 62; www.kunstmuseumbasel.ch; St Albangraben 16; adult/student Sfr10/5, free 1st Sun of month; ☻ 10am-5pm Tue-Sun). It holds the largest art collection in Switzerland, including works by Klee and Picasso.

Of the private Swiss art collections made public, Hildy and Ernst Beyeler's is probably the most astounding. In the **Beyeler Collection** (☎ 061 645 97 00; www.beyeler.com; Baselstrasse 101; adult/student/child under 10 Sfr21/12/free; ☻ 10am-6pm Thu-Tue, to 8pm Wed) the quality of the 19th- and 20th-century paintings is matched only by the way Miró and Max Ernst sculptures are juxtaposed with similar tribal figures. All are fabulously displayed in Italian architect Renzo Piano's open-plan building. Take tram 6 to Riehen.

Festivals & Events

Basel makes much of its huge **Fasnacht** spring carnival, even though many people prefer Lucerne's exuberant celebrations. The festival kicks off at 4am exactly on the Monday after Ash Wednesday with the **Morgestraich**. The streetlights are suddenly extinguished and the large procession starts to wend its way through the central district. Participants wear elaborate costumes and masks, restaurants and bars stay open all night and the streets are packed with revellers. The main parades are on the Monday and Wednesday afternoons, with Tuesday afternoon reserved for the children's parade.

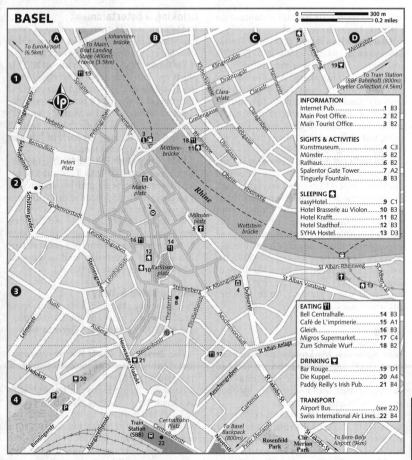

BASEL

INFORMATION
Internet Pub...........................1 B3
Main Post Office....................2 B2
Main Tourist Office................3 B2

SIGHTS & ACTIVITIES
Kunstmuseum.......................4 C3
Münster................................5 B2
Rathaus................................6 B2
Spalentor Gate Tower............7 A2
Tinguely Fountain.................8 B3

SLEEPING
easyHotel.............................9 C1
Hotel Brasserie au Violon.....10 B3
Hotel Krafft........................11 B3
Hotel Stadthof.....................12 B3
SYHA Hostel.......................13 D3

EATING
Bell Centralhalle..................14 B3
Café de L'imprimerie.............15 A1
Gleich.................................16 B3
Migros Supermarket.............17 C4
Zum Schmale Wurf...............18 B2

DRINKING
Bar Rouge...........................19 D1
Die Kuppel..........................20 A4
Paddy Reilly's Irish Pub........21 B4

TRANSPORT
Airport Bus.....................(see 22)
Swiss International Air Lines..22 B4

Sleeping

Hotels are often full during Basel's numerous trade fairs and conventions, so book ahead.

easyHotel (www.easyhotel.com; Riehenring 109; r from Sfr30; ✕) What's plastic and orange and cheap all over? Yep, after the no-frills airline easyJet, here's the second instalment in Stelios Haji-Ioannou's hotel empire. Rooms are functional, clean, modern and, if not especially aesthetically appealing, slightly better than in the London outlet. Variable pricing sees costs rise at busy times (up to Sfr140 when we looked, but could go above that). Book well ahead, and if possible get a room with air-conditioning so you won't have to open a window on to the noisy street.

Basel Backpack (☎ 061 333 00 37; www.baselback pack.ch; Dornacherstrasse 192; dm Sfr31, s/d/f Sfr80/96/144; ✕ 🖳) This friendly independent hostel in a converted factory building has cheerful, colour-coded eight-bed dorms and more sedate doubles and family rooms. Breakfast is extra.

SYHA hostel (☎ 061 278 97 39; www.youthhos tel.ch/basel; St Alban Kirchrain 10; dm Sfr35, s/d from Sfr80/82; 🅿 🖳) This is the older of the two official hostels in town, less conveniently but more attractively located in a quiet, leafy spot.

Hotel Stadthof (☎ 061 261 87 11; www.stadthof .ch; Gerbergasse 84; s/d with shared bathroom Sfr80/120; ✕) Tucked into a corner of buzzing Barfüsserplatz, this hotel has rudimentary but very clean rooms. Its bar and restaurant do a roaring trade. Book ahead.

Hotel Brasserie au Violon (☎ 061 269 87 11; www .au-violon.com; Im Lohnhof 4; s/d from Sfr100/150) The doors are one of the few remaining hints that quaint, atmospheric Au Violon was once a prison. Its understated rooms are decently sized (most comprise two former cells) and decorated in relaxing neutral tones. The hotel overlooks the city from its quiet, leafy hilltop location and has a well-respected restaurant.

Hotel Krafft (☎ 061 690 91 30; www.hotelkrafft.ch; Rheingasse 12; s/d from Sfr145/230) The renovated Krafft will appeal to design-savvy urbanites. Sculptural modern chandeliers have been added to its creaky-floored dining room overlooking the Rhine, and minimalist tea bars (all stainless steel, grey and Japanese teapots) now adorn each landing of the spiral stairs. Rooms have a tasteful 1950s retro feel and classic furniture from the likes of Charles and Ray Eames. The river bank is popular at night, however, so in summer this won't suit light sleepers.

Eating

For a quick, cheap bite on the run, the daily market on Marktplatz has tasty Bratwurst (Sfr5) and delicious breads (Sfr3 to Sfr7). Alternatively, there's pedestrian-only Steinenvorstadt, with its countless fast-food outlets, cafés and restaurants.

Zum Schmale Wurf (☎ 061 683 33 25; Rheingasse 10; mains Sfr10-30) Delicious smells and an air of intergenerational bonhomie waft over this Italian antipasto, pasta and meat heaven on the river. Lunch menus (Sfr18.50) occasionally branch out into global cuisine, with *merguez* (French spicy beef) sausages or jambalaya.

Café de L'imprimerie (☎ 061 262 36 06; St Johanns Vorstadt 19; 2-course menu Sfr14.50-16.50) An unpretentious bistro offering filling meals at affordable prices; locals like to lounge over pints at the sturdy wood tables.

Gleich (☎ 061 261 48 83; Leonhardsberg 1; mains Sfr18) Anticarnivores cherish the large vegetarian menu and minimalist décor at this longtime favourite haunt.

For self-caterers, there's the local **Migros** (Sternengasse 17). Or for a huge selection of organic local produce (including 200 different cheeses) try the **Bell Centralhalle** (cnr Streitgasse & Weisse Gasse).

Drinking & Entertainment

In Steinenvorstadt, there's a string of cinemas with latest-release movies. There's also a bar/café/restaurant to suit every taste.

Bar Rouge (☎ 061 361 30 31; Messeplatz 10) This plush red bar with panoramic views from the 31st floor of the *Messeturm* (or convention tower) is the city's most memorable. Hipsters and (early on weekday evenings) a few suits come to appreciate the regular DJs and films. It closes for parts of July and August, so ring ahead then.

Paddy Reilly's Irish Pub (☎ 061 281 33 36; Steinentorstrasse 45; mains Sfr5-12.50) This pub entices expats with Brit beers and big-screen TV. It's a cosy spot to kick back with a Guinness and watch the sport.

Die Kuppel (☎ 061 270 99 39; www.kuppel.ch; Binningerstrasse 14) An atmospheric wooden dome, with a dance floor and cocktail bar, in a secluded park; salsa, soul, house and '70s/'80s are regularly on the bill.

Getting There & Away

By motorway, the E25/E60 heads from Strasbourg and passes by the EuroAirport, and the E35/A5 hugs the German side of the Rhine.

The **EuroAirport** (BSL or MLH; www.euroairport .com), 5km northwest of town, in France, is the main airport for Basel.

Basel is a major European rail hub with two main train stations, the SBB and the BBF (on the northern bank). The SBB has two sections, one servicing destinations within Switzerland, and the SNCF section, which services France. Trains to Germany leave from the BBF station.

Destinations include Paris (Sfr69, five hours, seven times daily). Local trains to the Black Forest stop only at BBF, though fast EC services stop at SBB, too. Main destinations along this route are Amsterdam (Sfr180, eight hours, daily), Frankfurt (Sfr80, three hours, daily) and Hamburg (Sfr198, 6½ hours, daily). Services within Switzerland leave from SBB. There are fast trains to Geneva (Sfr71, three hours, twice hourly) and Zürich (Sfr30, 70 minutes, twice hourly).

Getting Around

For the EuroAirport catch bus No 50 from in front of the SBB Station (Sfr6.60). City buses and trams run every six to 10 minutes

(Sfr1.80 for four or fewer stops, Sfr2.80 for central zone, or Sfr8 for a day pass). By the SBB station is a hut offering free bike loans in summer.

SCHAFFHAUSEN

pop 32,900

On the northern bank of the Rhine, Schaffhausen has a quaint medieval old town, filled with beautiful oriel windows, painted façades and ornamental fountains. It's a pleasant day trip from Zürich.

The **Schaffhausen tourist office** (☎ 052 625 51 41; tourist@swissworld.com; Fronwagturm; 🕙 9am-5pm Mon-Fri, 10am-noon Sat, to 4pm Sat & 10am-1pm Sun Jun-Aug) is in the heart of the old town.

The best views around are found at the 16th-century hilltop **Munot fortress** (admission free; 🕙 8am-10pm May-Sep, 9am-5pm Oct-Apr). The summit is a 15-minute walk from the centre of town. **Rheinfall** (Rhine Falls) is a 40-minute stroll westward along the river, or take bus 1 to Neuhausen. Though the drop is only 23m, the waterfall is considered the largest in Europe, with an extraordinary amount of water thundering over it. The 45km of the Rhine from Schaffhausen to Constance is one of the river's most stunning stretches. It passes by meadows, castles and ancient villages, including **Stein am Rhein**, 20km to the east, where you could easily wear out your camera snapping pictures of the buildings in the picture-perfect Rathausplatz.

The **SYHA hostel** (☎ 052 625 88 00; fax 052 624 59 54; Randenstrasse 65; dm Sfr24; 🕙 Mar-Oct) is in an impressive 16th-century former manor house (although the place does smell a bit musty). Take bus No 3 to Breite. The **Fischerzunft** (☎ 052 632 05 05; www.fischerzunft.ch; Bahnhofstrasse 46; s/d from Sfr142/215), one of Switzerland's most opulent hotels away from the big city, has a subtle Oriental theme, with printed silks in the bedrooms and a sinfully expensive restaurant (menus up to Sfr265!).

Check out **Fass-Beiz** (☎ 052 625 46 10; Webergasse 13; dishes Sfr7.50-25) for food and drinks. An alternative bar-café, it has a laid-back atmosphere and serves tasty sit-down dishes with an excellent vegetarian selection. There are music gigs and theatre performances in the cellar below.

Schaffhausen has good roads in all directions. Trains run to Zürich (Sfr17.20, 50 minutes, hourly).

APPENZELLERLAND

Just as Tasmania is to Australians and Appalachia to Americans, Appenzellerland is the butt of many a Swiss joke – its people the country's bumpkins, reputedly slow on the uptake. The roots of this backward reputation are fairly easy to divine. To use just one example, Innerhoden, one of the two semicantons that make up Appenzellerland, unusually still holds a yearly open-air parliament and it didn't permit women to vote until 1991. Even then, the Supreme Court had to intervene.

In a general sense, however, many foreigner visitors find the Appenzellers' devotion to rural tradition immensely charming and just what they expected from Switzerland. Appenzellerland has beautiful villages, mostly untouched by modern times. Life moves along at an enviably relaxed pace – the contented locals may know more than they are credited with.

The pastel hued village of **Appenzell** is a feast both for the eyes and the stomach. Behind the highly decorative façades of its traditional Swiss buildings lie numerous cafés, confiseries, cheese shops, delicatessens, butchers and restaurants all offering local specialities. (Inevitably, given Appenzell's popularity with guided bus tours, there are plenty of shops selling tacky trinkets, too.)

It's suitable for lunch and a wander on a Sunday afternoon, or you could come for longer and explore the surrounding hills. Whichever you choose, remember to come hungry and with enough space in your luggage for chocolate, cheese and alcoholic souvenirs.

The train station is 400m from the town centre. The **tourist office** (☎ 071 788 96 41; www.appenzellerland.ch in German; Hauptgasse; 🕙 8am-noon & 2-5pm Mon-Fri, 9am-noon & 2-4pm Sat) is in the centre.

Gasthaus Traube (☎ 071 787 14 07; www.hotel-traube.ch; s Sfr85-110, d Sfr150-180; 🕙 closed Feb) is the most charming place to sleep in town (look for it just off Landsgemeindeplatz behind Hotel Santis). The rooms are small, but feature wooden beds and new bathrooms with sliding frosted glass doors. The on-site restaurant feels like a traditional tavern and serves good fondue.

There is a train to St Gallen (Sfr12, 30 minutes, twice hourly).

SWITZERLAND DIRECTORY

ACCOMMODATION

Switzerland caters to all budgets – you can camp, sleep in a barn, stay in a hostel or live it up in a five-star hotel. However, prices may seem steep at even the most inexpensive places compared with other parts of Europe. Tourist offices always have brochures listing prices and facilities of local accommodation.

Hostels, hotels and pensions most often include breakfast in their price, and while many rooms are tiny, most are of quite high standard and almost all include wonderful feather duvets. In budget places breakfast is basic: generally just a beverage with bread rolls, cheese spread, butter and jam.

Most hostels and budget hotels have two classes of rooms – cheaper rooms with shared bathroom and shower facilities and more expensive rooms with private bathroom. For budget rooms expect to pay under Sfr100, while midrange places will set you back anywhere from Sfr100 to Sfr200. Top-end places will cost anything from Sfr200.

Barns

When their cows are out to pasture in the summer, Swiss farmers have habitually put their empty barns to good use, allowing travellers to sleep in them for a very small fee of about Sfr20. It's a unique experience that disappoints few. **Aventure sur la paille** (☎ 041 678 1286; www.aventure-sur-la-paille .ch) produces a booklet listing participating farmers.

Hostels

Switzerland has two types of hostels: official Swiss Youth Hostels (SYHA), affiliated with Hostelling International (HI), where nonmembers pay an additional 'guest fee' of Sfr6, and the independent hostels. Independent hostels tend to be more charismatic and better bets for solo travellers or anyone looking to meet other backpackers. Prices listed in this book for SYHA hostels do not include the guest fee. On average a dorm bed in either type of hostel costs between Sfr20 and Sfr30.

ACTIVITIES

There are dozens of ski resorts throughout the Alps, the pre-Alps and the Jura, and some 200 different ski schools. Equipment hire is available at resorts and ski passes allow unlimited use of mountain transport.

There is simply no better way to enjoy Switzerland's spectacular scenery than to walk through it. There are 50,000km of designated paths, often with a convenient inn or café located en route. Yellow signs marking the trail make it difficult to get lost, and each provides an average walking time to the next destination. Slightly more strenuous mountain paths have white-red-white markers. The **Schweizer Alpen-Club** (SAC; ☎ 031 370 1818; www.sac-cas.ch in German; Monbijousstrasse 61, Bern) maintains huts for overnight stays at altitude and can also help with extra information.

Lonely Planet's *Walking in Switzerland* contains track notes for walking in the Swiss countryside.

You can water-ski, sail and windsurf on most lakes. And there are more than 350 lake beaches. Rafting is possible on many Alpine rivers, including the Rhine and the Rhône.

Bungy jumping, paragliding, canyoning and other high-adrenalin sports are widely available throughout Switzerland, especially in the Interlaken area.

BUSINESS HOURS

Most shops are open from 8am to 6.30pm Monday to Friday, with a 90-minute or two-hour break for lunch at noon. In towns there's often a late shopping day till 9pm, typically on Thursday or Friday. Closing times on Saturday are usually 4pm or 5pm. At some places, such as large train stations, you may find shops are open daily. Banks are open 8.30am to 4.30pm Monday to Friday, with some local variations. Eating and drinking establishments are open for lunch and dinner unless otherwise noted in our reviews.

EMBASSIES & CONSULATES
Swiss Embassies & Consulates

For a comprehensive list of Swiss embassies overseas, visit www.eda.admin.ch.
Australia (☎ 02-6162 8400; www.eda.admin.ch/ australia; 7 Melbourne Ave, Forrest, Canberra, ACT 2603)

Canada (☎ 613-235 1837; www.eda.admin.ch/canada; 5 Marlborough Ave, Ottawa, Ontario K1N 8E6)
Ireland (☎ 01-218 6382; www.eda.admin.ch/dublin; 6 Ailesbury Rd, Ballsbridge, Dublin 4)
New Zealand (☎ 04-472 1593; vertretung@wel.rep .admin.ch; 22 Panama St, Wellington)
South Africa (☎ 012-452 06 60; www.eda.admin.ch /pretoria; 225 Veale St, Parc Nouveau, New Muckleneuk 0181, Pretoria)
UK (☎ 020-7616 6000; www.eda.admin.ch/london; 16-18 Montague Pl, London W1H 2BQ)
USA (☎ 202-745 7900; www.eda.admin.ch/washington; 2900 Cathedral Ave NW, Washington DC 20008-3499)

Embassies & Consulates in Switzerland

All embassies are found in Bern. Consulates can be found in several other cities, particularly in Zürich and Geneva. Australia and New Zealand have no embassy in Switzerland, but each has a consulate in Geneva. Most of Bern's embassies are located southeast of the Kirchenfeldbrücke. For a comprehensive list, go to www.eda .admin.ch.

Australia (☎ 022 799 91 00; www.australia.ch; Chemin des Fins 2, Grand-Saconnex, Geneva)
Austria (☎ 031 356 52 52; bern-ob@bmaa.gv.at; Kirchenfeldstrasse 77-79, Bern)
Canada (Bern ☎ 031 357 32 00; www.canada -ambassade.ch; Kirchenfeldstrasse 88; Geneva ☎ 022 919 92 00; 5 Ave de l'Ariana)
France (Bern ☎ 031 359 21 11; www.ambafranch-ch .org; Schosshaldenstrasse 46; Geneva ☎ 022 319 00 00; www.consulfrance-geneve.org; 11 Rue J Imbert Galloix)
Germany (Bern ☎ 031 359 41 11; www.deutsche -botschaft.ch; Willadingweg 83; Basel ☎ 061 693 33 03; Schwarzwaldallee 200)
Ireland (☎ 031 352 14 42; Kirchenfeldstrasse 68, Bern)
Italy (☎ 031 350 07 77; Elfenstrasse 14, Bern)
Netherlands (☎ 031 350 87 00; www.nlembassy.ch; Kollerweg 11, Bern)
New Zealand (☎ 022 929 03 50; Chemin des Fins 2, Grand-Saconnex, Geneva)
UK (Bern ☎ 031 359 77 00; www.britain-in-switzerland .ch; Thunstrasse 50; Geneva ☎ 022 918 24 00; Rue de Vermont 37-39; Zürich ☎ 01 383 65 60; Hegibachstrasse 47)
USA (Bern ☎ 031 357 70 11; http://bern.usembassy.gov; Jubiläumsstrasse 93; Geneva ☎ 022 840 51 60; Rue Versonnex 7; Zürich ☎ 043 499 29 60; Dufourstrasse 101)

FESTIVALS & EVENTS

Many events take place at a local level throughout the year (check with the local tourist offices as dates often vary from year to year). Following is just a brief selection.

February
Fasnacht A lively spring carnival of wild parties and parades is celebrated countrywide, but with particular enthusiasm in Basel and Lucerne.

March
Combats de Reines From March to October, the lower Valais stages traditional cow fights known as the Combats de Reines.

April
Landsgemeinde On the last Sunday in April, the people of Appenzell gather in the main square to take part in a unique open-air parliament.

July
Montreux Jazz Festival Big-name rock/jazz acts hit town for this famous festival (www.montreuxjazz.com) held during the first two weeks of July.

August
National Day On 1 August, celebrations and fireworks mark the country's National Day.
Street Parade Zürich lets its hair down in the second week of August with an enormous techno parade with 30 lovemobiles and more than half a million excited ravers.

October
Vintage Festivals Down a couple in wine-growing regions such as Neuchâtel and Lugano in early October.

November
Onion Market Bern takes on a carnival atmosphere for a unique market day held on the fourth Monday of November.

December
L'Escalade This historical festival held in Geneva on 11 December celebrates deliverance from would-be conquerors.

GAY & LESBIAN TRAVELLERS

Attitudes toward homosexuality are reasonably tolerant in Switzerland and the age of consent is 16. Zürich has a lively gay scene and hosts the Christopher Street Day march in late June. It is also home to **Cruiser magazine** (www.cruiser.ch in German), which lists significant gay and lesbian organisations, and has extensive listings of bars and events in Switzerland (Sfr4.50).

Take a look at **Pink Cross** (www.pinkcross.ch in German) for more insights into gay life in Switzerland.

HOLIDAYS

New Year's Day 1 January
Easter March/April – Good Friday, Easter Sunday and Monday
Ascension Day 40th day after Easter
Whit Sunday & Pentecost 7th week after Easter
National Day 1 August
Christmas Day 25 December
St Stephen's Day 26 December

INTERNET RESOURCES

Switzerland has a strong presence on the Internet, with most tourist-related businesses having their own website; a good place to start is **Switzerland Tourism** (www.my switzerland.com), with many useful links.

LANGUAGE

Located in the corner of Europe where Germany, France and Italy meet, Switzerland is a linguistic melting pot with three official federal languages: German (spoken by 64% of the population), French (19%) and Italian (8%). A fourth language, Rhaeto-Romanic, or Romansch, is spoken by less than 1% of the population, mainly in the canton of Graubünden. Derived from Latin, it's a linguistic relic that has survived in the isolation of mountain valleys. Romansch was recognised as a national language by referendum in 1938 and given federal protection in 1996.

English-speakers will have few problems being understood in the German-speaking parts. However, it is simple courtesy to greet people with the Swiss-German *grüezi* and to inquire *Sprechen Sie Englisch?* (Do you speak English?) before launching into English.

In French Switzerland you shouldn't have too many problems either, though the locals' grasp of English probably will not be as good as the German-speakers'. Italian Switzerland is where you will have the greatest difficulty. Most locals speak some French and/or German in addition to Italian. English has a lower priority, but you'll still find that the majority of hotels and restaurants have at least one English-speaking staff member.

MONEY

Swiss francs (Sfr, written CHF locally) are divided into 100 centimes (called *rappen* in German-speaking Switzerland). There are notes for 10, 20, 50, 100, 200, 500 and 1000 francs, and coins for five, 10, 20 and 50 centimes, and one, two and five francs.

All major travellers cheques and credit cards are accepted. Nearly all train stations have currency-exchange facilities open daily. Commission is not usually charged for changing cash or cheques but it's gradually creeping in. Shop around for the best exchange rates. Hotels usually have the worst rates.

There are no restrictions on the amount of currency that can be brought in or taken out of Switzerland.

There's no need to tip in Switzerland, unless you feel the service was really superlative. Tips are included in meal prices.

ATMs are widespread throughout the country.

POST

Postcards and letters to Europe cost Sfr1.30/1.20 priority/economy; to elsewhere they cost Sfr1.80/1.40. The term poste restante is used nationwide or you could use the German term, *Postlagernde Briefe*. Mail can be sent to any town with a post office and is held for 30 days; show your passport to collect mail. Amex also holds mail for one month for people who use its cheques or cards.

Post office opening times vary but typically they are open from 7.30am to noon and from 2pm to 6.30pm Monday to Friday and until 11am Saturday.

TELEPHONE

The privatised Swisscom is the main telecommunications provider. The minimum charge in Swisscom payphones is Sfr0.60, though per-minute rates are low. Swisscom charges the same rate for national or local calls. During the day it's Sfr0.08 per minute, and during evenings and weekends it drops

LANGUAGE AREAS

- Romansch
- German
- French
- Italian

Basel   Zürich
Bern   Lucerne   Chur
Lausanne   St Moritz
Geneva   Bellinzona

EMERGENCY NUMBERS

- **Ambulance** ☎ 144
- **Fire** ☎ 118
- **Motoring breakdown assistance**
  ☎ 140
- **Police** ☎ 117
- **REGA air rescue** ☎ 1414

---

to Sfr0.04. Regional codes no longer exist in Switzerland. Although the numbers for a particular city or town all start with the same two or three digits (for example Zürich ☎ 01, Geneva ☎ 022) numbers must always be dialled in full (ie always include telephone codes), even when you're calling from within the same town.

International call prices have dropped substantially in recent years. A standard-rate call to the USA/Australia/UK costs Sfr0.12/0.25/0.12 per minute. Standard rates apply on weekdays (day or night), and there are reduced rates on weekends and public holidays. Many telephone boxes no longer take coins; the prepaid *taxcard* comes in values of Sfr5, Sfr10 and Sfr20, and is sold in post offices, kiosks and train stations.

You can purchase a SIM card from Swisscom for your mobile phone as well as prepaid cards. Calls are not cheap, however. The SIM card costs about Sfr40 and then calls are almost Sfr1 per minute, although they're cheaper at nights and weekends. Mobile service in Switzerland is generally excellent – even in the mountains.

Hotels can charge as much as they like for telephone calls, and they usually charge a lot, even for direct-dial calls.

TOURIST INFORMATION

Local tourist offices are extremely helpful. They have reams of literature to give out, including maps (nearly always free). Offices can be found everywhere tourists are likely to go and will often book hotel rooms and organise excursions. If you are staying in resorts, ask the local tourist office whether there's a Visitor's Card, which is excellent for discounts.

Switzerland Tourism also sells the **Swiss Museum Passport** (www.museumspass.ch; adult/stu-

dent Sfr30/25), which will save you big bucks if you plan to visit more than a handful of museums. Note that if you've purchased a Swiss Pass, entrance to all Swiss museums is free.

VISAS

Visas are not required for passport holders from Australia, Canada, New Zealand, South Africa, the UK or the USA. A maximum three-month stay applies, although passports are rarely stamped.

TRANSPORT IN SWITZERLAND

GETTING THERE & AWAY
Air

The busiest international airports are **Unique Zürich** (ZUR; ☎ 043 816 22 11; www.uniqueairport.com) and **Geneva International Airport** (GEN; ☎ 022 717 71 11; www.gva.ch/en), each with several nonstop flights a day to major transport hubs such as London, Paris and Frankfurt. Most international airlines fly into Switzerland, as do a few budget operators. EasyJet offers regular services from London to/from Basel and Geneva, while bmibaby flies from East Midlands, in the UK, to Geneva. Switzerland's international carrier is Swiss International Airlines (known as Swiss).

Airport departure taxes are always included in the ticket price.

Air Berlin (code AB; ☎ 084 873 78 00; www.airberlin .com)

Air France (code AF; ☎ 01 439 18 18; www.airfrance .com)

American Airlines (code AA; ☎ 01 654 52 57; www .americanairlines.com)

bmibaby (code BD; ☎ 041 900 00 13 00; www .bmibaby.com)

British Airways (code BA; ☎ 0848 845 845; www .britishairways.com)

Delta Airlines (code DL; ☎ 0800 55 20 36; www.delta .com)

easyJet (code EZ; ☎ 0848 888 222; www.easyjet.com)

flybe (code BEE; ☎ 1392 268 500; www.flybe.com)

Helvetic (code OAW; ☎ 043 557 90 99; www.helvetic .com)

Lufthansa (code LH; ☎ 01 447 99 66; www.lufthansa .com)

SkyEurope (code NE; ☎ 043 557 90 99; www.sky europe.com)

Swiss International Airlines (code LX; ☎ 0848 853 00 00; www.swiss.com)
United Airlines (code UA; ☎ 01 212 47 17; www .united.com)

Lake

Lake steamers from Germany and Austria traverse Lake Constance (Bodensee) to Switzerland. For boat information contact the operators based in Switzerland (☎ 071 463 34 35), Austria (☎ 055 744 28 68) or Germany (☎ 075-3128 1398).

From Italy you can catch a steamer across Lake Maggiore into Locarno. Contact **Navigazione Lago Maggiore** (NLM; ☎ 084 881 11 22, 091 751 18 65) for more information.

France can be reached from Geneva via Lake Geneva (Lac Léman); contact **Compagnie Générale de Navigation** (CGN; ☎ 022 08 48 81 18 48) for more information.

Land
BUS

With such cheap flights available, there are few people who travel to Switzerland by bus these days. **Eurolines** (☎ 090 057 37 47; www .eurolines.com) has services to Eastern Europe, Austria, Spain, Germany and Portugal, but distances are long.

If you want to visit several countries by bus, the UK-based **Busabout** (☎ in UK 020 7950 1661; www.busabout.com) operates summer services from Bern to Paris, and from Lauterbrunnen (for Interlaken) to Paris and Venice. See the Busabout website for details. Prices start at UK£219 for a two-week consecutive pass.

CAR & MOTORCYCLE

Roads into Switzerland are good despite the difficulty of the terrain, but special care is needed to negotiate mountain passes. Some, such as the N5 route from Morez (France) to Geneva, are not recommended if you have not had previous mountain-driving experience.

Upon entering Switzerland you will need to decide whether you wish to use the motorways (there is a one-off charge of Sfr40). Arrange to have some Swiss francs ready, as you might not always be able to change money at the border. Better still, pay for the tax in advance through Switzerland Tourism or a motoring organisation. The sticker (called a *vignette*) you receive is valid for a year and must be displayed on the windscreen. A separate fee must be paid for trailers and caravans (motorcyclists must pay too). Some Alpine tunnels incur additional tolls.

TRAIN

Located in the heart of Europe, Switzerland is a hub of train connections to the rest of the Continent. Zürich is the busiest international terminus. It has two direct day trains and one night train to Vienna (nine hours). There are several trains daily to both Geneva and Lausanne from Paris (three to four hours by superfast TGV). Travelling from Paris to Bern takes 4½ hours by TGV. Most connections from Germany pass though Zürich or Basel. Nearly all connections from Italy pass through Milan before branching off to Zürich, Lucerne, Bern or Lausanne. Reservations on international trains are subject to a surcharge of Sfr5 to Sfr30, which depends upon the date and the service.

GETTING AROUND
Air

Internal flights are not of great interest to most visitors, owing to the short distances and excellent ground transport. **Swiss International Air Lines** (www.swiss.com) is the local carrier, linking major towns and cities several times daily, including Zürich, Geneva, Basel, Bern and Lugano.

Bicycle

Despite the hilly countryside, many Swiss choose to get around on two wheels. You can hire bikes from most train stations (adult/child Sfr30/25 per day) and return to any station with a rental office, though this incurs a Sfr6 surcharge. Bikes can be transported on most trains; SBB (the Swiss rail company) rentals travel free (maximum five bikes per train). If you have your own wheels you'll need a bike pass (one day Sfr15, with Swiss travel pass Sfr10). Local tourist offices often have good cycling information. Bern, Basel, Geneva and Zürich offer free bike loans from their train stations.

Bus

Yellow postbuses are a supplement to the rail network, following postal routes and

PASSES & DISCOUNTS

Swiss public transport is an efficient, fully integrated and comprehensive system, which incorporates trains, buses, boats and funiculars. Convenient discount passes make the system even more appealing.

The **Swiss Pass** (www.swisstravelsystem.ch) is the best deal for people planning to travel extensively, offering unlimited travel on Swiss Federal Railways, boats, most Alpine postbuses, and trams and buses in 35 towns. Reductions of 25% apply to funiculars and mountain railways. These passes are available for four days (Sfr262), eight days (Sfr362), 15 days (Sfr430), 22 days (Sfr495) and one month (Sfr545); prices are for 2nd-class tickets. The **Swiss Flexi Pass** allows free, unlimited trips for three to eight days within a month and costs Sfr270 to Sfr460 (2nd class). With either pass, two people travelling together get 15% off. Both passes now allow you free admission to all Swiss museums, making them an even better bargain.

The **Swiss Card** allows a free return journey from your arrival point to any destination in Switzerland, 50% off rail, boat and bus excursions, and reductions on mountain railways. It costs Sfr165 (2nd class) or Sfr240 (1st class) and it is valid for a month. The **Half-Fare Card** is a similar deal minus the free return trip. It costs Sfr99 for one month.

Except for the Half-Fare Card, these passes are best purchased before arrival in Switzerland from **Switzerland Tourism** (www.myswitzerland.com) or a travel agent. The **Family Card** gives free travel for children aged under 16 if they're accompanied by a parent and is available free to pass purchasers.

There are also passes valid for any four days of unlimited travel in Switzerland and either Austria or France (Sfr391) within two months.

---

linking towns to the more inaccessible regions in the mountains. In all, routes cover some 8000km of terrain. Services are regular, and departures tie in with train arrivals. Postbus stations are next to train stations, and offer destination and timetable information.

Car

The **Swiss Touring Club** (Touring Club der Schweiz; ☎ 022 417 27 27; www.tcs.ch; Chemin de Blandonnet, Case postale 820, CH-1214, Venier/Geneva) is the largest motoring organisation in Switzerland. It is affiliated with the AA in Britain and has reciprocal agreements with motoring organisations worldwide.

You do not need an International Driving Licence to operate a vehicle in Switzerland. A licence from your home country is sufficient. There are numerous petrol stations and garages throughout Switzerland if you break down.

For the best deals on car hire you have to prebook. Some of the lowest rates are found through **Auto Europe** (www.autoeurope .com). One-way drop-offs are usually free of charge within Switzerland, although a collision-damage waiver costs extra.

Be prepared for winding roads, high passes and long tunnels. Normal speed limits are 50km/h in towns, 120km/h on motorways, 100km/h on semimotorways (designated by roadside rectangular pictograms showing a white car on a green background) and 80km/h on other roads. Mountain roads are well-maintained but you should stay in low gear whenever possible and remember that ascending traffic has the right of way over descending traffic, and postbuses always have right of way. Snow chains are recommended during winter. Use dipped lights in *all* road tunnels. Some minor Alpine passes are closed from November to May – check with the local tourist offices.

Switzerland is tough on drink-driving; if your blood alcohol level is over 0.05% you face a large fine or imprisonment.

Train

The Swiss rail network covers 5000km and is a combination of state-run and private lines. Trains are clean, reliable, frequent and as fast as the terrain will allow. Prices are high, and if you plan on taking more than one or two train trips it's best to purchase a travel pass (above). All fares quoted in this chapter are for 2nd class; 1st-class fares are about 65% higher. All major stations are connected by hourly departures,

SWITZERLAND

but services stop from around midnight to 6am.

Most train stations offer luggage storage, either at a counter (usually Sfr5 per piece) or in 24-hour lockers (Sfr2 to Sfr7). They also have excellent information counters that give out free timetable booklets and

advise on connections. Train schedules are revised yearly, so double-check details before travelling. For train information, consult the excellent website for the **Schweizerische Bundesbahnen** (SBB; www.sbb .ch) or call ☎ 090 030 03 00 (Sfr1.19 per minute).

Regional Directory

CONTENTS

In addition to the country-specific information included at the end of each of this book's country chapters, we present you with this Regional Directory, chock-full of useful information about Central Europe as a whole and sage advice for travellers to the region. This chapter should satisfy many of your questions or doubts as you go about planning your trip.

ACCOMMODATION

All of the accommodation listings in this book are presented according to price range, from budget to midrange listings and then top-end reviews detailing the destination's most expensive choices axnd best splurges. As the prices among different countries in Central Europe vary so greatly, there is no absolute price for each category; price range is a relative concept! Still, the cheapest places in which to rest your travel-weary head throughout the region are camping grounds, followed by hostels and university accommodation. Guesthouses, *pensions*, private rooms and cheap hotels can also be good value.

Accommodation can be hard to find during peak holiday periods and in popular tourist destinations, and it's advisable to book ahead where possible. You can always change places once you get there – the important thing is that you aren't left wandering around a city or town with all your bags while translating 'No Vacancy' signs.

If you arrive in a country by air, there is often an accommodation-booking desk at the airport, although it rarely covers the lower strata of hotels. Tourist offices often have extensive accommodation lists, and the more helpful ones will go out of their way to find you something suitable. In most countries the fee for this service is very low, and if the accommodation market is tight, it can save you a lot of running around. This is also an easy way to get around any language problems. Agencies offering private rooms can be good value; staying with a local family doesn't always mean that you'll lack privacy, but you'll probably have less freedom than in a hotel.

Apartment Rental

While this may not at first glance appear the most economically viable option for budget-conscious travellers, apartment rental is an increasingly popular option in Central Europe, particularly in the eastern part of the region. It may make sense to rent an apartment if you're travelling with a family or a group of up to four persons, or planning to stay in one place for a week or longer. You have the freedom of coming and going when you like without worrying about curfews and check-out times, plus a feeling of coming 'home' after a hard day of sightseeing.

All apartments should be equipped with kitchens (or at least a kitchenette), which will save on the dining bill and allow you to peruse the neighbourhood markets and shops, and so eat like the locals do. Some apartments are a little more upscale, with laundry facilities, parking, daily cleaning services and even a concierge. Apartments can be rented from €40 to €100 per day and can usually accommodate from two to four or five persons.

Check with local tourist offices in the individual country chapters for a list of rental properties. Doing a Web search will come up with an array of choices too, often with photos of the apartments themselves.

Camping

Camping is immensely popular and provides the cheapest accommodation across the region. It's particularly well catered for in the western part of the region (especially Germany and Austria), slightly less so in the eastern countries. There's usually a charge per tent or site, per person and per vehicle. In the countries in the west, there are well-maintained areas at national parks and reserves for tent-pitching, and some grounds offer bungalows or wooden cabins. In the east, cabins are the norm, and local people often think only of them when they hear the word 'camping'; these cabins cost double or triple the cost for pitching a tent on grounds that have minimal services.

In large cities, most camping grounds will be some distance from the centre. For this reason, camping is most popular with people who have their own transport. If you're on foot, the money you save by camping can quickly be eaten up by the cost of commuting to/from a town centre. You may also need a tent, sleeping bag and cooking equipment, unless you stay in wooden cabins.

Pitching a tent in nondesignated areas is tolerated much more in eastern Central Europe than in the western part, where it's to all intents and purposes illegal to camp anywhere but in designated areas or, with permission, on private property. This does not mean it is tolerated or even legal everywhere in the eastern countries – in the Czech Republic, for example, it is illegal to pitch a tent on public property.

Camping grounds may be open from April to October, May to September, or perhaps only June to August, when they are usually filled to capacity. Few private camping grounds are open year-round.

Farmhouses

'Village tourism', which means staying at a farmhouse, is quite popular in the more eastern countries, particularly in Slovenia and Hungary. It's like staying in a private room or *pension*, except that the participating farms

are in picturesque rural areas and may offer nearby activities such as horse riding, kayaking, skiing and cycling. Not to mention fresh milk straight from the cow! It's highly recommended. Swiss farmers usually open up some barn space (p574) for travellers come summer.

Guesthouses & Pensions

Small private *pensions* (guesthouses) are common in all parts of Central Europe. Priced somewhere between hotels and private rooms, *pensions* typically have less than a dozen rooms and there's sometimes a small restaurant or bar on the premises. You'll get much more personal service at a *pension* than you would at a hotel at the expense of a wee bit of privacy. Although the majority of *pensions* are simple affairs, there are more expensive ones where you'll find bathrooms with en suites and other luxuries.

Homestays & Private Rooms

A homestay means renting a room in a private home and is not as common in the western countries of Central Europe as in the eastern ones, where it can be a rewarding way to experience daily life. Travel agencies sometimes arrange accommodation in private rooms in local homes, though you're better off asking at local tourist information bureaus. You might also be approached at train and bus stations with offers of a room. Conditions vary – try to see photos first or ask for a visit.

Hostels

Hostels offer the cheapest (secure) roof over your head in Central Europe, and you do not have to be a youngster to take advantage of them. Most hostels are part of each country's Youth Hostel Association (YHA). The YHA is affiliated with Hostelling International (HI), which has moved away from an emphasis on 'youth' in an effort to attract a wider clientele.

Technically, you're supposed to be a YHA or HI member to use affiliated hostels, but you can often stay by paying an extra charge and this will usually be set against the cost of future membership. Stay enough nights as a nonmember and you automatically become a member. Note that in a few areas (Bavaria in Germany, for example), the strict maximum age for anyone, except group leaders or parents accompanying a child, is 26.

Hostels vary widely in character, but the growing number of travellers and the increased competition from other forms of accommodation, particularly private 'backpacker hostels', have prompted many hostels to improve their facilities and cut back on rules and regulations. Increasingly, hostels are open all day, curfews are disappearing (with, unfortunately, some notable exceptions, as in Poland, where many shut their doors between 10pm and 5am) and 'wardens' with sergeant-major mentalities are an endangered species. Hostels tend to favour smaller dorms, with just four to six beds, and many also provide single and double rooms.

At a hostel, you get a bed for the night, plus use of communal facilities, which often include a kitchen where you can prepare your own meals. You are sometimes required to have a sleeping sheet, but can usually rent one for a small fee if required. They are still by and large the best places to meet fellow travellers and crash inexpensively for the night.

The following websites are recommended as resources for hostellers; all of them have booking engines, helpful advice from fellow travellers and excellent tips for novice hostellers.

Hostel Planet (www.hostelplanet.com)
Hostels.com (www.hostels.com)
Hostelz (www.hostelz.com)

Hotels

At the bottom of the price range, hotels may be no more expensive than private rooms or guesthouses, while at the other extreme they extend to luxurious five-star hotels with price tags to match. Categorisation varies from country to country and the hotels recommended in this book cater for every budget. We have endeavoured, where possible, to provide a range of price options for accommodation in each city or town.

The cheapest rooms sometimes have a washbasin but no bathroom, which means you'll have to go down the corridor to use the toilet and shower. Breakfast may be included in the price of a room or be extra – and mandatory.

Check your hotel room and the bathroom before you agree to take it, and make sure to ask about discounts, which are often available for groups or for longer stays. If you think a hotel room is too expensive, ask if there's anything cheaper; often hotel owners may try to steer you into more expensive rooms. In the eastern countries in particular, hotel owners may be open to a little bargaining if times are slack.

The definition of 'nonsmoking room' in some hotels, particularly in Poland and Hungary, can vary. Some rooms designated as nonsmoking appear to have been so designated only the previous day – a smell may remain, and ashtrays might be provided. Care has been taken in this book to identify, with a nonsmoking icon, those places that follow stricter guidelines.

University Accommodation

Some universities rent out space in student halls in July and August. Accommodation will sometimes be in single rooms but more commonly in doubles or triples, and cooking facilities may be available. Toilets and showers are usually shared. Inquire directly at local colleges or universities, at student information services or at local tourist offices.

ACTIVITIES

In a word: unlimited. While the cities of Central Europe offer nonstop entertainment, it's in the region's forests, on its lakes and rivers and atop its mountains where you'll get the biggest thrills – and lungfuls of fresh air! Check with tourist information offices for more details on what's available, including the websites listed on p592.

Refer to the boxed text on p586 for info on spas and saunas, which are a great way to relax after a solid day of outdoor activities.

Canoeing, Kayaking & Rafting

Some of the region's best places for paddling include:

Bavarian Alps Germany (p227)
Dunajec River Poland (p404)
Great Masurian Lakes Poland (p436)
Lake Balaton region Hungary (p327)
Soča River Slovenia (p509)
Swiss Alps Switzerland (p565)
Tisza River Kiskunság National Park, Hungary (p339)
Vltava River Český Krumlov, Czech Republic (p136)

Cycling

Cycling allows you to get up close to the scenery and the local people, keeping you fit in the process. It's a good way to get around many cities and towns and to see remote corners of a country you wouldn't ordinarily get to.

Much of Central Europe is ideally suited to cycling. In the mountainous regions it can be heavy going, but this is offset by the dense concentration of things to see. Particularly challenging – and rewarding – are the upper reaches of the Danube in southern Germany, and anywhere in the Alps (for those fit enough). Physical fitness is not a major prerequisite for cycling on the plains of eastern Hungary (they're flatter than French crêpes) but the persistent wind might slow you down. Other popular holiday cycling areas include the Danube Bend (p316) in Hungary, most of eastern Slovakia (p467), and Slovenia's Karst region (p511).

See p600 for details on bringing a bike by air. Most long-distance bus companies transport bicycles. In the country chapters of this guide you'll find places listed where you can hire a bike.

See under Getting Around in the Transport section at the end of each country chapter for more specifics on riding and renting bicycles and for tips on places to go.

Hiking

Keen hikers can spend a lifetime exploring Central Europe's many exciting trails. Probably the most spectacular are to be found in the Alps in Switzerland, Austria and Germany. The Alps are crisscrossed with clearly marked trails and offer rewarding challenges for everyone from beginners to experts; food and accommodation are available along the way in season. There's also excellent hiking in the eastern part of the region, with well-maintained trails traversing forests, mountains and national parks.

Particularly recommended are:

Bavarian Alps Germany (p227)
Feldkirch to Hainburger Pforte via Hohe Tauern National Park Austria
High Tatra Mountains Poland (p403) and Slovakia (p467)
Julian Alps Slovenia (p504)
Lake Constance to Vienna Austria
Malá Fatra Slovakia (p464)
Saxon Switzerland area Germany (p191)
Szilvásvárad area Hungary (p344)
Valais region Switzerland (p548)

Public transport will often take you to the trailheads, and chalets or mountain huts. Hikers can find dorm accommodation and basic meals in almost all of these places. The best months for hiking are from June to September, especially late August and early September, when the summer crowds will have largely disappeared.

Mountain paths have direction indicators and often markers indicating their level of difficulty. Those with a red-white-red marker mean you need sturdy hiking boots and a pole; a blue-white-blue marker indicates the need for mountaineering equipment.

Horse Riding

There are many places throughout the region to strap on a saddle, go horse riding through lovely terrain and then walk with a funny waddle after dismounting. Horse riding is particularly well-organised in Hungary, where a local folk saying claims that Hungarians 'were created by God to sit on horseback'. The best centres are at Szilvásvárad (p344) and Kecskemét (p336). Horse riding is also very popular (and affordable) in the Czech Republic, Poland and Slovenia. In Switzerland, the area of choice is in St Moritz (p554), and in Germany, head to tiny Sylt and Amrum in the North Frisian Islands (p280).

Skiing & Snowboarding

Central Europe is the continent's ski capital. The country chapters are brimming with details on how to get your downhill and cross-country thrills in the region.

The skiing season usually lasts from early December to late March, though at higher altitudes it may extend an extra month either way. Snow conditions can vary greatly from year to year and region to region, but January and February tend to be the best (and busiest) months.

A general rule of thumb as far as prices go is that the further east you go, the less expensive is the skiing. Of course, no place in the region can compete with the vistas of Switzerland; if you can afford it, a visit there is a must for any avid skier or fearless snowboarder. Zermatt (p548) and other resorts in the Valais region are among the best in the world.

Other areas with much to offer include:
Bavarian Alps Germany (p227)
Central and High Alps, including the Carinthia region Austria
High Tatra Mountains Slovakia (p467) and Poland (p403)
Julian Alps Slovenia (p504)

Dependable snow falls can also be found in Germany's Black Forest (p240) and Harz Mountains (p202), and around the Pohorje district in eastern Slovenia (p519), where night-time torch parties are held on the slopes.

A skiing holiday can be expensive due to the costs of ski lifts, accommodation and the inevitable après-ski drinking sessions. Equipment hire (or even purchase), on the other hand, can be relatively cheap if you follow the tips outlined in the country chapters of this guidebook, and the hassle of bringing your own skis may not be worth it. Skiing holidays in Europe often work out twice as expensive as a summer holiday of the same length. Cross-country skiing generally costs less than downhill since you don't rely as much on ski lifts.

Snowboarding is especially popular in Slovakia, as is cross-country skiing in the Czech Republic.

CHILDREN

Central Europe is a great place to bring the young ones along – and keep them interested (and tired) enough to usually avoid complaints. The region has well-established attractions geared towards children of all ages, though this is truer of the more western countries. In countries such as Switzerland and Austria, it's also easy to find facilities for children in restaurants and hotels. In the more eastern countries of the region, such as Slovakia, finding such services is more of a challenge.

Most car-rental firms in the region have children's safety seats for hire at a small cost, but it is essential that you book them in advance. The same goes for high chairs and cots (cribs); they're standard in many restaurants and hotels but numbers are limited. The choice of baby food, infant formulas, soy and cow's milk, disposable nappies (diapers) and the like is generally good, though this is more true of large cities than smaller ones and especially towns and villages. If your baby or child requires special medicines or food, bring more than you think might be necessary, as availability when needed might be limited, particularly in the eastern countries of the region.

This book mentions places of interest to children (or their parents!) throughout the country chapters. Lonely Planet's *Travel with*

Children, by Cathy Lanigan, is an excellent source of information and includes topics ranging from children's health to games that will keep the kids amused.

CLIMATE CHARTS

The following climate charts provide a snapshot of Central Europe's weather patterns. See p22 for suggestions on when to visit the region.

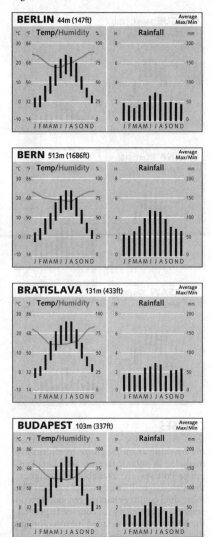

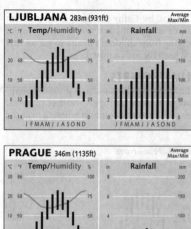

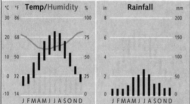

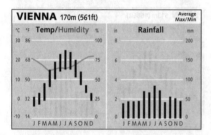

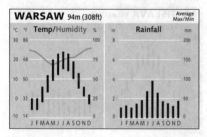

COURSES

In Central Europe you can enrol in courses on anything from language to alternative medicine to organic farming to skiing. Language courses are available to foreigners through universities or private schools. The individual country chapters give pointers on where to start looking for courses. In general, the best sources of detailed information are the cultural institutes maintained by many European countries around the world; failing that, try their national tourist offices or embassies. Student-exchange organisations, student travel agencies and organisations such as the YMCA/YWCA and HI can also help you.

CUSTOMS

Duty-free goods are no longer sold to those travelling from one EU country to another. For goods that are purchased at airports or on ferries outside the EU, the usual allowances apply for tobacco (200 cigarettes, 50 cigars or 250g of loose tobacco), alcohol (1L of spirits or 2L of liquor with less than 22% alcohol by volume; and 2L of wine) and perfume (50g of perfume and 0.25L of eau de toilette).

Do not confuse these allowances with duty-*paid* items (including alcohol and tobacco) bought at normal shops and supermarkets in another EU country. If bought for personal use, the allowances in this case are more than generous: 800 cigarettes, 200 cigars or 1kg of loose tobacco; 10L of spirits (more than 22% alcohol by volume), 20L of fortified wine or aperitif, 90L of wine or 110L of beer; and unlimited quantities of perfume. Within the eastern part of Central Europe, you are generally unlikely to be subjected to a search at the few border points that still exist, but do not be lulled into a false sense of security.

THERMAL BATHS & SAUNAS

While there are many attractive and comfortable saunas throughout Switzerland, Austria and especially Germany to relax in after winter activities or on cool summer evenings, the eastern countries in the region take the prize when it comes to elegant, opulent thermal baths. Any trip will be improved by, for example, a visit to the thermal and Turkish baths of Budapest (p306), the spa town of Harkány (p336) and the thermal lake at Hévíz (p332), all in Hungary; the *fin-de-siécle* spas of Karlovy Vary (Karlsbad; p126) in the Czech Republic; and the spas at Rogaška Slatina (p520) in Slovenia. These are generally cavernous, often multi-roomed extravaganzas with steam rooms, pools and several kinds of saunas, plus fearsome-looking masseurs.

DANGERS & ANNOYANCES

Central Europe is as safe – or unsafe – as any other part of the developed world. If you can handle yourself in the big cities of Western Europe, North America or Australia, you'll have little trouble dealing with the less pleasant sides of travel to the region. In the ex-communist countries to the east, some locals will regale you with tales of how dangerous their city is and how you need to exercise utmost caution. Take note of what they say, but know that mostly they're comparing the present situation with that before the end of communism when the crime rate was almost zero or, more usual, went unreported in the press.

Whatever you do, don't leave friends and relatives worrying about how to get in touch with you in case of emergency. If possible, work out a list of places where they can contact you or, best of all, phone home now and then, or email. For those planning to go hiking or skiing, it's best to leave plenty of clues as to your planned destination and date, as well as an expected return date or a time for people to go looking for you in case you run into trouble in the wild. This is best done at national-park headquarters or at your hotel or resort.

Drugs

Always treat drugs with a great deal of caution. There may be a lot of drugs available in some of the places you'll visit, but that doesn't mean they're legal. Even a little harmless hashish can cause a great deal of trouble in some places.

Don't even think about bringing drugs home with you either: if you have what energetic customs officials may think are stamps in your passport from 'suspect' places, they may well decide to take a closer look.

Racism

Nonwhite travellers should be aware that in some of these countries there are negative attitudes to immigrants and that you may be mistaken for one and therefore a target for misguided discontent. Skinheads and neo-Nazis in parts of former East Germany and other areas have singled out the resident Roma (sometimes called Gypsies), blacks, Asians and people of Middle Eastern descent as scapegoats for their own problems. In these days of 'War on Terror' alarm, people of African, Middle Eastern or Arab descent should be aware that some locals may harbour knee-jerk negative feelings towards them.

Theft

Theft is definitely a problem in Europe and your wariness should extend to other travellers. The most important things to guard are your passport, papers, tickets and money – in that order. Carry your own padlock for hostel lockers. Be especially careful on overnight trains to keep your bags under your bed bunk or locked. It's also a good idea to keep your wallet and documents under your pillow or, better yet, on your person as you sleep. Make copies of all important documents, such as your passport; see p593 for more on this topic.

Be aware of pickpockets. They strike on crowded transport and at touristed areas such as major train stations – prime attractions such as Prague Castle are also favourite haunts of thieves.

Parked cars, particularly cars with foreign number plates and/or rental-agency stickers, are prime targets for petty criminals in most cities, so avoid leaving luggage and other items in plain view. In case of theft or loss, always report the incident to the police and ask for a statement; otherwise, your travel-insurance company won't pay up.

DISABLED TRAVELLERS

In the western countries of Central Europe, you will find wheelchair ramps a common feature of midrange hotels and certainly of upmarket hotels, as well as most museums and many restaurants and cafés. Trains that accept Eurail passes in Germany and Switzerland are fitted for wheelchair access; these need prebooking but usually at no extra cost. In the eastern countries, the lack of a dedicated infrastructure geared towards disabled travellers, plus the poorer state of many roads and pavements, make them more challenging destinations. In these countries, you're unlikely to find any services outside of tourist destinations and hotels.

If you have a physical disability, get in touch with your national support organisation and ask about the countries you plan to visit. These organisations often have complete libraries devoted to travel, and they can put you in touch with travel agents who specialise in tours for the disabled. Other excellent sources for helpful information and travel tips include **Disability World** (www.disabilityworld.com), the **Royal Association for Disability & Rehabilitation** (RADAR; www.radar.org.uk), **Access-Able Travel Source** (www.access-able.com) and the **Society for Accessible Travel & Hospitality** (www.sath.org).

DISCOUNT CARDS
Camping Card International
The Camping Card International (CCI) is a camping-ground ID valid for a year that can be used instead of a passport when checking into camping grounds and includes third-party insurance. Many camping grounds will offer a small discount (usually 5% to 10%) if you have one. CCIs are issued by automobile associations, camping federations and, sometimes, at camping grounds. The CCI is also useful as it can sometimes serve as a guarantee, so that you don't have to leave your passport at reception.

Hostel Cards
A hostelling card is useful – if not always mandatory – for those staying at hostels. Many hostels in Central Europe don't require that you be a hostelling association member, but they often charge less if you have a card. Many hostels will issue one on the spot or after a few stays, though this might cost a bit more than getting it in your home country. Alternatively, you can contact the local **HI** (www.hihostels.com) and purchase one there.

Senior Cards
Museums and other sights, public swimming pools and spas, and transport companies frequently offer discounts to retired people or those aged over 60 or 65 (sometimes as low as 55 for women). Local and long-distance travel is often cheaper as well. It's best to bring proof of age. European residents over 60 are eligible for the Railplus Card, which provides discounts of around 25% for train travel.

Student, Youth & Teacher Cards
The most useful of the available student/youth discount cards is the International Student Identity Card (ISIC), a plastic ID-style card with your photograph that provides discounts on various forms of transport (including air travel and local public transport), cheap or free admission to a variety of museums and sights, and inexpensive meals in some student caféterias and some restaurants. Teachers can get the International Teachers Identity Card (ITIC).

If you're aged under 26 but are not a student, you can apply for a Euro26 card, or an International Youth Travel Card (IYTC, formerly GO25) which is issued by the Federation of International Youth Travel Organisations (FIYTO). Both cards go under different names in different countries and give much the same discounts and benefits as an ISIC.

All these cards are issued by student unions, hostelling organisations or youth-oriented travel agencies, or you can download an application and purchase them online at www .isiccard.com or www.euro26.org.

ELECTRICITY
All the countries of Central Europe run on 220V, 50Hz AC. Check the voltage and cycle (usually 50Hz) used in your home country. Most appliances that are set up for 220V will handle 240V quite happily without modifications (and vice versa); the same goes for 110V and 125V combinations. It's preferable to adjust your appliance to the exact voltage if you can (some modern battery chargers and radios will do this automatically). Don't mix 110/125V with 220/240V without a transformer, which will be built in if the appliance can, in fact, be adjusted.

Several countries outside Europe (the USA and Canada, for instance) have 60Hz AC, which will affect the speed of electric motors even after the voltage has been adjusted, so CD players (where motor speed is all-important) will be useless. But appliances such as electric razors, hair dryers, irons and radios will work fine.

Plugs throughout Central Europe are the standard round two-pin variety, sometimes called the 'europlug'. If your plugs are of a different design, you'll need an adaptor.

EMBASSIES & CONSULATES
See the individual country chapters for the addresses of embassies and consulates both in Central Europe and in your home country.

It's important to realise what your embassy can and cannot do to help you if you get into trouble while abroad. Generally speaking, it won't be much help in emergencies if the trouble you're in is remotely your own fault. Remember that you are bound by the laws of the country you are visiting.

In genuine emergencies you might get some assistance, but only if other channels have been exhausted. For example, if you need to get home urgently, a free ticket home is exceedingly unlikely – the embassy would expect you to have insurance. If you have all your money and documents stolen, it might assist with getting a new passport, but a loan for onward travel is almost always out of the question.

GAY & LESBIAN TRAVELLERS

Homosexual activities are legal in every country covered by this book though local attitudes towards it, and especially to public displays of same-sex affection, vary widely among them, and between large, urban centres and smaller, rural areas. Wherever possible this guide lists contact addresses under individual country Directory sections, as well as reviews of gay and lesbian venues in the Entertainment listings for major cities. While Berlin, Munich and Vienna have large, vibrant and active gay scenes, it's a different story in the eastern countries of the region: while most capital cities have small gay scenes, these are usually centred on one or two bars and clubs. Outside large population centres, gay and lesbian venues are almost nonexistent.

Following are a few notable websites with up-to-date information for the European gay and lesbian community:

365Gay (www.365gay.com) A worldwide, daily gay and lesbian newspaper with a round-up of current events and articles.

Gay Journey (www.gayjourney.com) A mishmash of gay travel-related information including forums, booking engines, travel packages, regional bars and clubs, and write-ups of gay-friendly destinations.

International Gay & Lesbian Travel Association (www.iglta.org) Gay and lesbian-friendly businesses (including accommodation and services) throughout the world, as well as a current newsletter and travel agency.

Mi Casa Su Casa (www.gayhometrade.com) The international home-exchange network service for gay and lesbian travellers. Membership is US$60 for three years, and it provides listings for home-swapping vacation rentals around the world.

Spartacus International Gay Guide (www.spartacus world.com) A male-only directory of gay entertainment venues in Europe and the rest of the world.

INSURANCE

A travel insurance policy to cover theft, loss and medical problems is a good idea. The policies issued by STA Travel and other student travel organisations are usually good value. Some policies offer lower and higher medical-expense options; the higher ones are chiefly for countries such as the USA that have extremely expensive medical costs. For this region it's best to take out the higher cover. There is a wide variety of policies available, so check the fine print.

Note that some insurance policies will specifically exclude 'dangerous activities', which can include scuba diving, motorcycling and even trekking. You may prefer a policy that pays doctors or hospitals directly rather than you having to pay on the spot and claim later. If you have to make a claim later make sure you keep all documentation. Some policies ask you to call back (reverse charges) to a centre in your home country where an immediate assessment of your problem is made. Check that the policy covers ambulances and also an emergency flight home.

If you're an EU citizen, the European Health Insurance Card (EHIC) covers you for most medical care. The form is available from health centres. However, the E111 will not cover you for non-emergencies or emergency repatriation. Citizens from other countries should find out if there is a reciprocal arrangement for free medical care between their country and the countries being visited.

For information on car insurance see p602.

INTERNET ACCESS

Every city and almost any decent-sized town in Central Europe has internet access of some sort, though the same can't be said about all rural areas.

Wi-fi (WLAN in Germany) is increasingly becoming available across Central Europe, most commonly in cafés, libraries, train stations and, of course, top-end and business hotels. Often you'll find access is through large providers such as **t-mobile** (hotspot.t-mobile.com), which charge €6 or more per hour. To find wi-fi hot spots, try sites such as www.jiwire.com.

Some internet cafés may not serve coffee or other drinks, and sometimes you'll be limited to a monitor in a dark, smelly room full of teenage boys playing war games. But especially in the more-developed cities, internet cafés can be a social hub and a great way of meeting locals as well as fellow travellers. Make sure you have a Web-based email account so that you can send and receive email along the road if you don't have a laptop or other Web-enabled device with you.

If you're travelling with a notebook or a hand-held computer, be aware that your modem may not work once you leave your home country. The safest option is to buy a reputable 'global' modem before you leave home, or buy a local PC-card modem if you're spending an extended time in any one country. For more information on travelling with a portable computer, see www.teleadapt.com.

MONEY

At the time of publication, the only countries in Central Europe using the euro as their currency are Austria, Germany and Slovenia, though several eastern countries with EU membership were contemplating the adoption of the euro. Every other country uses its own currency, but major international currencies such as the euro and the US dollar are easy to exchange. Even in the eastern part of the region, the local currencies are easily convertible, stable and reliable.

Some exchange rates are given in the Fast Facts boxes at the start of each country chapter. A useful internet site for calculating exchange rates is www.oanda.com/convert/classic.

ATMs & Credit Cards

The hassle of trying to change travellers cheques at the weekend and dealing with rip-off bureaux de changes are a thing of the past throughout Central Europe due to the onslaught of ATMs that accept most credit and cash cards.

Visa and MasterCard remain the most popular credit cards in the region, followed by Amex, which has offices in every country. While they are accepted at an ever-growing number of places in the eastern part of the region, credit and cash cards are not as widely accepted there as in the more western countries.

Cash

This is, of course, the easiest way to carry money, but obviously not the most secure. The two most favoured currencies throughout the region are the euro and the US dollar. It is, however, easy to exchange virtually any other major world currency in big cities, though the exchange rates may be poor.

Travellers Cheques

The main advantage of carrying travellers cheques rather than cash is the protection they offer from theft, though they have lost their once enormous popularity as more and more travellers – including those on tight budgets – withdraw cash through ATMs as they go along.

Banks usually charge from 1% to 2% commission to change travellers cheques. Amex

---

---

and Thomas Cook representatives cash their own travellers cheques without commission, but both give rather poor rates of exchange. If you're changing more than US$20, you're usually better off going to a bank and paying the standard commission to change the cheques there.

Western Union

If all goes horribly wrong – your money, travellers cheques and credit cards are all stolen – then don't despair. As long as you know the phone number of a friend or relative back home, they will be able to get money wired to you anywhere in Central Europe via Western Union. We do not even bother listing Western Union representatives in this guide, as there are literally thousands of them. Just look for the distinctive yellow and black sign. The sender will be given a code that they then communicate to you and you take to the nearest office, along with your passport, to receive your cash.

PHOTOGRAPHY & VIDEO

If shooting with 35mm film, bring a range of films with you, from 100ASA for nice, sunny days and outdoor locations, to 400ASA for cloudy days and indoor shots, and even 800ASA to capture Prague's Charles Bridge at night time. Film may well be more costly in Central Europe than it would be in your home country, so it's advisable to bring extra rolls with you. Films can safely pass through most airport X-Ray machines, supposedly up to at least 16 times (so says Kodak) without any loss of quality.

Film and camera equipment are available everywhere in Central Europe, but obviously shops in larger cities and towns have a wider selection. Avoid buying film at tourist sites; it may have been stored badly (by a window), or for a long time (perhaps even having reached its use-by date), and it will certainly be expensive.

For digital camera users, try to bring as much memory as you can (if you don't have your laptop to download photos onto regularly); memory cards and sticks are often expensive to buy, especially when you need to get one quick! Otherwise, many of the internet cafés listed throughout this book will be able to download your photos and burn them onto a CD for a small fee. Just to be on the safe side, bring along your USB cable and your camera's driver on a CD – unless the internet café runs XP on its computers (or uses Macs), they will likely need to download your camera's driver onto their system before being able to download your masterpieces.

Lonely Planet's *Travel Photography*, by Richard I'Anson, is a useful guide for people who want to get their shots just right.

Video camera users should make sure they keep their batteries charged and have the correct charger, plugs and European transformer, if necessary. In most countries in Central Europe it is possible to obtain video cartridges easily in large towns and cities, but make sure you buy one with the correct operating system. Like Australia and most of the rest of Europe, Central Europe usually uses the PAL format, which is incompatible with the North American and Japanese NTSC system. It is usually worth buying at least a few cartridges duty-free at the start of your trip. Similarly, if you want to buy prerecorded videotapes to play back home, you won't get the picture if the systems are different.

POST

Postal services can be considered reliable throughout Central Europe. See the individual country chapters for details of postage costs.

Poste restante (having letters sent to you care of local post offices) is still available across the region but is not the most reliable way of receiving letters, and seems rather redundant in the age of email and SIM cards. Express services such as **DHL** (www.dhl.com) are best for essential deliveries.

You can also have mail sent to you at Amex offices as long as you have an Amex card or are carrying its travellers cheques. When you buy Amex cheques, ask for a booklet listing all its office addresses worldwide. Amex will forward mail for a small fee, but what it won't do is accept parcels, registered letters, notices for registered letters, answer telephone inquiries about mail or hold mail longer than 30 days.

SOLO TRAVELLERS

There are a number of obvious advantages to solo travel: you do exactly what you want to do, see what you want to see and are more likely to meet locals and socialise with people you'd otherwise never speak to. However, it can also be lonely and less fun when things get frustrating. Fortunately, the European backpacking infrastructure is tailored to people travelling alone and hostels are great places to meet others. Indeed, you may find you'll spend a few days here and there with others you've met in hostels and who are heading in your direction, or keen to share the cost of a day trip or two. Most big cities in Central Europe also have expat bars for those missing a slice of ersatz-home.

There are no specific dangers for solo travellers in Central Europe, though you may get a

---

DVDS

You might be tempted to buy some unlicensed DVDs, which are still sold (illegally) in some parts of the eastern countries of Central Europe. This can result in great bargains for those who don't mind buying pirated copies, although you should also realise that unlicensed DVDs are illegal in most countries – that said, you're unlikely to be caught bringing a few cheap DVDs home.

DVDs are encoded with a regional code (for America and Canada this is 1, for Europe and South Africa 2 and for Australia and New Zealand 3). If you buy a disc in Europe check that its code corresponds with that of your DVD player at home as a player coded 1 or 3 will not play a disc that is coded 2. A way round this is to look for universally compatible players and discs carrying a 0 code.

few odd looks in the eastern part of the region, where people are less used to seeing independent travel. Be aware that you can be charged higher single supplement fees for a room when staying at some places, and you might find that you're not at the best table in restaurants as a lone diner. Women travelling solo should also check out the advice on opposite.

TELEPHONE

You can ring abroad from almost any phone box in Central Europe. Public telephones accepting stored-value phonecards (available from post offices, telephone centres, newsstands and retail outlets) are virtually the norm now; in some countries coin-operated phones are almost impossible to find. In the countries in the east of the region you'll also find call centres – increasingly the domain of entrepreneurs who offer discounted rates, although there are also the state-run call centres, which are often in the same building as the main post office. At these places you can often make your call from one of the booths inside an enclosed area, paying the cashier as you leave.

Mobile Phones

Mobile phones have become essential communication devices throughout Central Europe, which means you'll likely see a Slovenian farmer chatting on a mobile while leaning on a hayrack, and a grannie thumbing a text message to her grandchildren while tottering down a laneway in rural Hungary. If you plan to spend more than a week or so in one country, seriously consider buying a SIM card to slip into your phone (but check before you leave with your provider at home that your handset has not been blocked). SIM cards can cost as little as €10 and can be topped up with cards available at supermarkets and any mobile-phone dealers. Alternatively, if you have roaming, your phone will usually switch automatically over to a local network. This can be expensive if you use the phone a great deal, but can be very useful for ad hoc use on the road. Check with your provider for any possible extra costs associated with *receiving* calls when in the region.

Phone Codes

International dialling codes and international access codes are given in the Fast Facts boxes at the beginning of each country chapter. Every town has its local area code within the country listed directly underneath its chapter heading.

TIME

All the countries covered in this book are on GMT+1 hour. They all employ daylight savings. Clocks are usually put forward an hour on the last Sunday in March. They are set back one hour on the last Sunday in October.

TOURIST INFORMATION

The availability of tourist information is widespread throughout Central Europe, with booths or offices set up in main cities and towns, usually in the tourist city centres but also at airports, train stations and sometimes bus stations. The services offered will differ but most of these places provide details of accommodation and other practical help – for example, basic town maps showing where to find toilets and internet cafés (among the most frequently asked questions!). In smaller towns in Poland, Hungary and Slovakia, it's best not to count on fully-fledged tourist booths, but wherever they are missing, duck into a major hotel, where the reception staff will likely be happy to assist.

In each country chapter, tourist contacts are provided under various city, town and village sections. Following is a list of official country websites that endeavour to provide up-to-date travel information:

Austria (www.austria-tourism.at)
Czech Republic (www.czechtourism.com)
Germany (www.visits-to-germany.com)
Hungary (www.tourinform.hu; www.hungary.com)
Liechtenstein (www.tourismus.li)
Poland (www.polandtour.org)
Slovakia (www.slovakiatourism.sk)
Slovenia (www.slovenia-tourism.si)
Switzerland (www.myswitzerland.com)

VISAS

Travellers from EU countries, the USA, Canada, New Zealand and Australia need only a valid passport to enter any of the countries covered by this book. Non-EU citizens, however, are usually allowed only a three-month stay within any six-month period. Nationals of some other countries may need a visa in order to enter a specific country. Detailed visa regulations are given under Visas in the Directory section of each country chapter. If you are not certain whether you need a visa or not, check at a local embassy or consulate (see under Embassies & Consulates in each country chapter's Directory section).

In line with the Schengen Agreement, many countries in Central Europe have no border crossings between them. Also, since EU enlargement in 2004, many – but not all – of the border posts between the eastern countries of the region and the original EU member states have disappeared. This book notes in the relevant chapter where border posts are likely to still exist. Considering this inconsistency, and the fact that Switzerland and Liechtenstein are not members of the Schengen Agreement, you may still be required to show your passport at some checkpoints. Also remember that the countries comprising the Schengen zone are treated as one collective country in terms of the standard three-month stay – in other words, make certain that you leave the Schengen zone before your 90 days are up (say by a jaunt to the Czech Republic) and then return, getting a new entrance stamp in your passport.

For those who do require visas, it's important to remember that these will have a 'use-by' date, and you'll be refused entry after that period has elapsed. It may not be checked when entering these countries overland, but major problems can arise if it is requested during your stay or on departure and you can't produce a visa that's current.

Consulates sometimes issue visas on the spot, although some levy a 50% to 100% surcharge for 'express service'. If there's a choice between getting a visa in advance and on the border, go for the former option if you have the time. You can either do this in your home country, or, more conveniently, while on the road. Getting a visa from a neighbouring country, with the help of a travel agent, often saves headaches and bureaucracy. Also remember that many countries do not issue visas on their borders, or change their mind frequently about it. Carry spare passport photos; you may need from one to four photos every time that you apply for a visa.

Copies

The hassles created by losing your passport can be considerably reduced if you have a record of its number and issue date or, even better, photocopies of the relevant data pages. A photocopy of your birth certificate can also be useful.

Also take written note of the serial numbers of any travellers cheques (and cross them off as

you cash them) and take photocopies of your credit cards, air ticket, insurance policy and other travel documents. Keep all this emergency material separate from your passport, cheques and cash, and leave extra photocopies with someone you can rely on at home. If you do lose your passport, notify the police immediately to get a statement, and contact your nearest consulate/embassy.

Passport

Your most important travel document is your passport, which should remain valid until well after you return home. If it's just about to expire, renew it before you travel. Some countries insist your passport remain valid for a specified period (usually three months) beyond the expected date of your departure from that country. In practice, this is rarely checked.

Once you start travelling, carry your passport (or a copy of it) at all times and guard it carefully.

WEIGHTS & MEASURES

The metric system is in use throughout Central Europe. In Germany, cheese and other food items are often sold per *Pfund* (500g).

Decimals are shown with commas and thousands with full stops. There's a metric conversion chart on the inside cover of this book.

WOMEN TRAVELLERS

Frustrating though it is, women travellers continue to face more challenging situations when travelling than men do. If you are a solo woman traveller, you may find it helpful to familiarise yourself with the status of local women to better understand the responses you elicit from locals. Hopes of travelling inconspicuously, spending time alone and absorbing the surroundings are often thwarted by men who assume a woman on her own desires company, or who seemingly find it impossible to divert their gaze. Bear in mind that most of this behaviour, which can come across as threatening, is more often than not harmless. Try not to let it deter you. Hopefully the more women that travel, whether alone, in pairs, or in groups, the less unwanted attention lone female travellers in the region will attract.

Women travellers, in general, will find Central Europe relatively enlightened and shouldn't often have to invent husbands that will be joining them soon or boyfriends that will be back any minute. If you do find yourself in an uncomfortable situation or area, jump in a taxi if you possibly can (and worry about the cost later), or pipe up and make a racket.

Despite feminism's influence on many European countries and the progress made in elevating the status of women in recent years, women remain under-represented in positions of power in both governmental and corporate spheres – in many areas you will notice the glut of women in low-paid, menial jobs. Rather, as is the case worldwide, women remain over-represented among the illiterate and unemployed.

WORK

European bosses aren't keen on giving jobs to foreigners when unemployment rates are what they are in some areas, particularly in the eastern part of the region. Officially, EU citizens are allowed to work in any other EU country, but the paperwork isn't always straightforward for long-term employment and after three months they will probably need to apply for a residency permit. Other nationalities require special work permits that can be almost impossible to arrange, especially for temporary work. However, that doesn't prevent enterprising travellers from occasionally topping up their funds by working in the hotel or restaurant trades at beach or ski resorts or teaching a little English, and they don't always have to do this illegally either.

Teaching English is the easiest way to make some extra cash in the ex-communist countries, but the market is saturated in places such as Prague and Budapest. You'll probably be much more successful in less popular places such as Ljubljana or smaller towns and cities throughout the region. If you do find a temporary job in Central Europe, though, the pay is likely to be abysmally low. Do it for the experience – not to earn your fortune – and you won't be disappointed. Other typical tourist jobs (for example washing dishes in Alpine resorts) often come with board and lodging, and you'll probably have a good time partying with other travellers, although the pay often amounts to little more than pocket money.

Students will find that their national student-exchange organisations may be able to arrange temporary work permits to several countries through special programmes. Call your local university or college for more information. For more details on working as a foreigner, see under Work in the individual country chapter Directory sections.

If you have a parent or grandparent who was born in an EU country, you may have certain rights you never knew about. Get in touch with that (and your) country's embassy and ask about dual citizenship (some countries may not allow this) and work permits – if you go for citizenship, also ask about any obligations, such as military service and residency.

If you play an instrument or have other artistic talents, you could try working the streets. As every Peruvian pipe player (and his fifth cousin) still knows, busking is fairly common in major Central European cities such as Prague, Budapest, Frankfurt and Ljubljana. In most places, however, you are likely to require municipal permits for this sort of thing. It is illegal in some parts of Switzerland and Austria and not always well tolerated in Germany. Talk to other street artists before you start.

Selling goods on the street is generally frowned upon and can be tantamount to vagrancy, apart from at flea markets. It's also a hard way to make money if you're not selling something special. Most countries require permits for this sort of thing.

There are several references and websites that publicise specific positions across Central Europe. **Transitions Abroad** (www.transitionsabroad.com) publishes *Work Abroad: The Complete Guide to Finding a Job Overseas* and the *Alternative Travel Directory: The Complete Guide to Studying, Traveling and Living Overseas*, as well as a colour magazine called *Transitions Abroad*. Its website lists paid positions and volunteer and service programmes.

Action Without Borders (www.idealist.org) and **GoAbroad.com** (www.goabroad.com) list hundreds of jobs and volunteer opportunities.

Work Your Way Around the World, by Susan Griffith, gives good, practical advice on a wide range of issues. The publisher, **Vacation Work** (www.vacationwork.co.uk), has many other useful titles, including *Summer Jobs Abroad,* edited by David Woodworth and Victoria Pybus.

Volunteer Work

Organising a volunteer work placement is a great way to gain a deeper insight into local culture. If you're staying with a family, or working alongside local colleagues, you'll probably learn much more about life here than you would if you were continually on the move through the country.

In some instances volunteers are paid a living allowance and sometimes they work for their keep, while other programmes require the volunteer to pay.

There are several websites that can help you search for volunteer work opportunities in Central Europe. As well as the websites mentioned earlier, try **WorkingAbroad** (www .workingabroad.com) – it's a good resource for researching possibilities and applying for positions. The **Coordinating Committee for International Voluntary Service** (www.unesco.org/ccivs) is an umbrella organisation with over 140 member organisations worldwide. It's useful if you want to find out about your country's national volunteer-placement agency.

The **International Willing Workers on Organic Farms** (WWOOF; www.wwoof.org) is an association of organisations in the western countries of Central Europe. If you join a WWOOF organisation, you can arrange to live and work on a host's organic farm.

Transport in Central Europe

CONTENTS

GETTING THERE & AWAY

Figuring how best to reach your desired destination/s can be one of the biggest headaches of travelling, but it can also be one of its more interesting and stimulating aspects. A well-planned entry to the region can literally set the mood for your Central European explorations.

Central Europe is well connected to the rest of the world by air. Germany is a major international hub and is likely to be the place where many incoming travellers will begin their journey. However, despite western Central Europe being the traditional starting point for destinations further east, several hubs in the east of the region such as Prague, Budapest and Warsaw are becoming more established as regional gateways. With intense competition between numerous long-haul airlines and no-frills carriers in both Europe and the USA, there are plenty of cheap tickets available to a variety of gateway cities.

Taking the train (northwards from Turkey or Greece for example, or eastwards from France or Spain) is essentially a more invigorating and scenic way to enter Central Europe than flying. Trains are an especially excellent (though not always cheaper) option for the thrill of crossing over from Western to Eastern Europe – through the psychological boundary that still exists, despite EU enlargement effectively making the experience just another border crossing.

Bus, bicycle and car are other popular modes of transport that can be used to enter the region, each with their own distinct advantages. Whichever transport method you choose, you will find helpful practical information in the following sections. Also refer to the Transport sections at the end of each country chapter for more destination-specific details.

AIR

Air travel to Central Europe has rarely been more competitively priced, with the national carriers of the UK, Czech Republic, Poland and Hungary all offering regular flights. Remember to reconfirm your onward or return bookings at least 72 hours before departure on international flights; otherwise you'll risk missing your flight if it is rescheduled or overbooked.

Airlines

The following is a list of most of the major airlines servicing Central Europe. See the Transport sections at the end of each country chapter for more information.
Adria Airways (www.adria-airways.com)
Air Berlin (www.airberlin.com)
Air France (www.airfrance.com)
Austrian Airlines (www.aua.com)
British Airways (www.britishairways.com)

THINGS CHANGE...

The information in this chapter is particularly vulnerable to change. Check directly with the airline or a travel agent to make sure you understand how a fare (and ticket you may buy) works and be aware of the security requirements for international travel. Shop carefully. The details given in this chapter should be regarded as pointers and are not a substitute for your own careful, up-to-date research.

ČSA (www.czechairlines.com)
easyJet (www.easyjet.com)
Germania Express (www.gexx.de)
LOT Polish Airlines (www.lot.com)
Lufthansa (www.lufthansa.com)
Malév Hungarian Airlines (www.malev.hu)
Ryanair (www.ryanair.com)
SkyEurope Airlines (www.skyeurope.com)
Slovak Airlines (www.slovakairlines.sk)
Swiss International Airlines (www.swiss.com)

Tickets

For long-term travel, there are plenty of discount tickets that are valid for 12 months, allowing multiple stopovers with open dates. For short-term travel, cheaper fares are often available by travelling midweek, staying away at least one Saturday night or taking advantage of promotional offers.

The internet is obviously a great resource for bargain air fares. Airlines may sell seats by auction (for example, www.priceline.com) or simply cut prices to reflect the reduced cost of electronic selling. Unlike the full-service airlines, no-frills carriers often make one-way tickets available at around half the return fare, meaning that it is easy to put together an open-jaw ticket (flying to one place but leaving from another). Shop around but always make sure that the price you are quoted includes the relevant taxes. Some of the most frequently used online sites are included in the 'Online Tickets' boxed text on right.

Though the internet offers some highly convenient ticketing options, there is still something to be said for reliable travel agents who know all about special deals, have strategies for avoiding inconvenient stopovers and can offer advice on everything from which airline has the best vegetarian food to the best travel insurance to bundle with your ticket. Companies such as STA Travel, which has offices worldwide, are most likely not going to disappear overnight and they offer good prices to most destinations.

AIR PASSES

The **Europebyair FlightPass** (www.europebyair.com) gives travellers from countries such as the USA, Canada, Australia and New Zealand one-way nonstop fares throughout Europe for only US$99 per flight, with no blackout dates. Passes are good for 120 days.

The **British Midland Discover Europe Airpass** (www.flybmi.com/bmi/en-gb/planandbook/tourEurope.aspx)

> **ONLINE TICKETS**
>
> Here are some of the more popular online sites for airline purchases:
> **Ebookers** (www.ebookers.com)
> **Expedia** (www.expedia.com)
> **FlyBudget.Com** (www.flybudget.com)
> **Kayak** (www.kayak.com)
> **LastMinute.Com** (www.lastminute.com)
> **Opodo** (www.opodo.com)
> **Orbitz** (www.orbitz.com)
> **STA Travel** (www.statravel.com)
> **Travelocity** (www.travelocity.com)

allows non-European travellers a two-tiered travel pass, with reservations required only for the first sector and no limit on the amount of flights purchased.

The **Star Alliance European Airpass** (www.staralliance .com) offers between three and 10 flight passes to be used within a three-month period starting at US$65 each, but cities can only be visited once (unless changing flights).

COURIER FLIGHTS

Courier tickets are a great bargain if you're lucky enough to find one. You get cheap passage in return for accompanying packages or documents through customs and delivering them to a representative at the destination airport. You are permitted to bring along a carry-on bag, but that's often all. Be aware that this type of ticket is usually very restricted, so check carefully before purchasing.

Courier flights are occasionally advertised in newspapers, or you could contact air-freight companies listed in the phone book.

The **International Association of Air Travel Couriers** (IAATC; www.courier.org) offers access to its website and booking service for US$45.

SECONDHAND TICKETS

You'll occasionally see advertisements on youth-hostel bulletin boards and in newspapers from people who want to sell the unused portion of their air tickets. Don't ever shell out money for such tickets – if used for international travel they're usually worthless, as the name on the ticket must match the name on the passport of the person checking in.

STUDENT & YOUTH FARES

Full-time students and people aged under 26 sometimes have access to better deals than

---

CLIMATE CHANGE & TRAVEL

Climate change is a serious threat to the ecosystems that humans rely upon, and air travel is the fastest-growing contributor to the problem. Lonely Planet regards travel, overall, as a global benefit, but believes we all have a responsibility to limit our personal impact on global warming.

Flying & Climate Change

Pretty much every form of motor transport generates CO_2 (the main cause of human-induced climate change) but planes are far and away the worst offenders, not just because of the sheer distances they allow us to travel, but because they release greenhouse gases high into the atmosphere. The statistics are frightening: two people taking a return flight between Europe and the US will contribute as much to climate change as an average household's gas and electricity consumption over a whole year.

Carbon Offset Schemes

Climatecare.org and other websites use 'carbon calculators' that allow travellers to offset the greenhouse gases they are responsible for with contributions to energy-saving projects and other climate-friendly initiatives in the developing world – including projects in India, Honduras, Kazakhstan and Uganda.

Lonely Planet, together with Rough Guides and other concerned partners in the travel industry, supports the carbon offset scheme run by climatecare.org. Lonely Planet offsets all of its staff and author travel.

For more information check out our website: www.lonelyplanet.com.

---

other travellers. The better deals may not always be cheaper fares but can include more flexibility to change flights and/or routes. You have to show a document proving your date of birth and a valid International Student Identity Card (ISIC) or an International Youth Travel Card (IYTC) when buying your ticket and boarding the plane. See www.istc .org for more information.

From Asia

The cheapest option from Asia will likely be a low-cost flight to Western Europe from one of the discount air-fare capitals of Asia: Hong Kong, Singapore and Bangkok.

In Singapore **STA Travel** (☎ 6737 7188; www .statravel.com.sg) has competitive fares. In Hong Kong try either **STA Travel** (☎ 2736 1618; www .statravel.com.hk) or **Four Seas Tours** (☎ 2200 7760; www.fourseastravel.com).

In India, cheap tickets can be bought from the bucket shops around Connaught Place in Delhi. **STIC Travels** (in Delhi ☎ 11-233 57 468, in Mumbai ☎ 22-221 81 431; www.stictravel.com) has offices in dozens of Indian cities.

From Australia

Cheap flights from Australia to Europe generally go via Southeast Asia, involving stopovers at Kuala Lumpur, Bangkok or Singapore.

There are quite a few travel agents that specialise in discount air tickets. Some, particularly smaller travel agents, advertise cheap air fares to Europe in the travel sections of weekend newspapers such as the *Age* in Melbourne and the *Sydney Morning Herald*.

STA Travel (Australia-wide ☎ 1300 733 035; www.sta travel.com.au), which has offices in all major cities and on many university campuses, and **Flight Centre** (Australia-wide ☎ 133 133; www.flightcentre.com .au), which has over 100 offices throughout the country, are major dealers in cheap air fares in Australia.

From Canada

Canadian discount ticket agents are known as consolidators and their fares tend to be at least 10% higher than those sold in the USA. The *Globe & Mail, Toronto Star, Montreal Gazette* and *Vancouver Sun* carry travel agents' ads and are a good place to look out for cheap airfares. Often the best way to reach Central European destinations from Canada is via New York City or London, where cheap and direct air fares can often be found.

Travel CUTS (☎ 800-667-2887; www.travelcuts.com) is Canada's national student travel agency and has offices in all major cities.

From Continental Europe

Some recommended travel agencies in France include **OTU Voyages** (www.otu.fr) and **Nouvelles Frontières** (☎ 0825 000 747; www.nouvelles-frontieres.fr), both of which specialise in student fares and have country-wide branches.

In Spain, recommended agencies include **Barcelo Viajes** (☎ 902 116 226) and **Nouvelles Frontières** (☎ 902 170 979; www.nouvelles-frontieres.es).

See also the Transport sections in the individual country chapters in this book.

From New Zealand

STA Travel (☎ 0508 782 872; www.statravel.co.nz) and **Flight Centre** (☎ 0800 243 544; www.flightcentre.co.nz) are popular travel agents in New Zealand. The cheapest fares to Europe are routed through Southeast Asia and cost about the same as from Australia.

From the UK & Ireland

London is Europe's major centre for discounted fares. You can often find fares from here that either match or beat land-based alternatives in terms of cost. However, beware of the taxes, which can be very high.

Plenty of budget travel agencies advertise in the travel sections of weekend newspapers and also in the entertainment listings magazine *Time Out* (www.timeout.com) and the Web-based TNT Magazine Online (www.tntmagazine.com).

STA Travel (☎ 0870 163 0026; www.statravel.co.uk) has some 70 branches throughout the UK and Ireland and sells tickets to all travellers but caters especially to young people and students.

Other recommended travel agencies to check out are **Trailfinders** (☎ 0845 058 5858; www.trailfinders.co.uk) and **Travelbag** (☎ 0800 082 5000; www.travelbag.co.uk).

From the USA

Discount travel agents in the USA are known as consolidators. San Francisco is the ticket consolidator capital of America, although some cheap deals can be found in Los Angeles, New York and other big cities. Consolidators can be tracked down through the phone book or daily newspapers. **Priceline** (www.priceline.com) is a 'name-your-price' auction service on the Web.

STA Travel (☎ 800-781-4040; www.statravel.com) has offices in all major cities.

You should be able to fly between New York and Europe very cheaply, especially outside of the high season. There are also direct flights to countries in eastern Central Europe, such as on ÈSA to Prague, LOT to Warsaw and Malév to Budapest.

On a stand-by basis, one-way fares can work out to be remarkably cheap. New York–based **Airhitch** (www.airhitch.org) might get you a great deal on a flight to/from Europe.

LAND
Border Crossings

As almost every country covered in this book is an EU member (the exceptions are Switzerland and Liechtenstein), there will be few border crossings to deal with if entering from other EU countries to the west or from the north (from Lithuania to Poland for example). However, some border posts may remain when you travel between Poland, Slovakia, Hungary and Slovenia and the countries to the west. These are noted in the relevant country chapters but the situation will likely change over the lifetime of this book. These still-existing borders have more to do with immigration control – and to the bureaucracy involved in slowly dismantling borders – and travellers with valid passports should face no problems (see p593 for more information).

Travellers crossing between Belarus or Ukraine and Poland, Slovakia or Hungary can expect tight border controls; make certain you have valid visas for Belarus and/or Ukraine. Crossing from Romania, Yugoslavia or Croatia involves no great problems as long as you have the necessary visas and documents.

Bus

Every major (and most minor) urban centres in the region are well connected to destinations outside Central Europe by a plethora of international bus companies. Even if coming from far-flung locations such as London, Istanbul or Moscow, bus travel to the heart of Europe is easy (though hard on the backside and nerves) with a connection or two. See the Transport and Getting There & Away sections of individual country chapters for specific routes and prices.

Train

There are regular train services connecting Central Europe with practically every corner of the continent. Train travel could end up more expensive than bus travel, but it is generally more comfortable. See the Transport and

Getting There & Away sections of individual country chapters for information on train travel throughout the region.

SEA

Though not the most common way of getting to Central Europe, the ports of Germany and Poland make alternative gateways to and from the region. In Germany, there are ports in Hamburg, Lübeck, Rostock, Sassnitz and Kiel that are serviced from the UK and Scandinavia; see p287 for a complete rundown of possible services. In Poland, the port cities of Gdańsk and Gdynia can connect you via ferry to Sweden and Denmark; see p445 for more details.

GETTING AROUND

AIR

Air travel is best viewed as a means to get you to the starting point of your itinerary rather than as your main means of travel within Central Europe. Flying lacks the flexibility and scenery of ground transport and generally can be expensive for short trips, unless you rely on no-frills airlines. However, remember that budget air travel usually involves a lack of creature comforts on flights and you may be deposited at a small airport with limited and lengthy transport connections to your destination city. See p596 for a list of major airlines operating in the region.

BICYCLE

In a word: doable. Of course, the landscape is so varied throughout Central Europe – which encompasses some of Europe's highest mountain peaks and some of the flattest land this side of Kansas – that getting around by bike will depend on your own skill and endurance levels. See p584 for some tips on recommended places to cycle in the region. For information on bicycle tours, see p605.

The key to a successful trip is to travel light. What you carry should be largely determined by your destination and type of trip. It's worth carrying the tools necessary for repairing a puncture even for the shortest and most basic trip. Other things you might want to consider packing are spare brake and gear cables, spanners, Allen keys, spare spokes and strong adhesive tape. Before you set off ensure that you are competent at carrying out basic

repairs – there's no point in weighing yourself down with equipment that you haven't got a clue how to use. Always check over your bike thoroughly each morning and again at night when the day's touring is over. Take a good lock and always use it when you leave your bike unattended.

The wearing of helmets is not compulsory but is certainly advised.

While pollution and noxious exhaust fumes can taint any bike trip anywhere, you'll find the exhaust coming out of trucks and heavy vehicles in the east of the region especially hard to take! You might find yourself gasping in a cloud of blue or black smoke as these vehicles lumber along quiet country roads.

Purchase

For major cycling tours, it's best to have a bike you're familiar with, so consider bringing your own (see the boxed text on below) rather than buying on arrival. If you can't be bothered with the hassle then there are plenty of possibilities for purchasing bikes in Central Europe: from shops selling new and secondhand bicycles, to private vendors advertising in local papers. If you're just interested in biking around a certain area and do not need an expensive bike, consider purchasing a pre-loved model from a secondhand shop or sporting goods store that sells bikes – it might be cheaper than paying for several days' rental.

Rental

It is relatively easy to rent bicycles in the western countries, especially in Austria, Germany

---

TRANSPORTING A BICYCLE

If you want to bring your bicycle to Central Europe, you should be able to take it on the plane. You can either take it apart and pack the pieces in a bike bag or box, or simply wheel it to the check-in desk, where it should be treated as a piece of luggage. You may have to remove the pedals and turn the handlebars sideways so that it takes up less space in the aircraft's hold. Be sure to check all this with the airline well in advance, before you pay for your ticket. If your bicycle and other luggage exceed the weight allowance, ask about alternatives or you may suddenly find yourself being charged a fortune for excess baggage.

and Switzerland, and you can often negotiate good deals. Local tourist offices will carry information on rental outlets. However, there may be a dearth of bicycle-hire opportunities in the east of the region, where the best hunting grounds will often be camping grounds and resort hotels in season. You might be able to drop the bicycle off at a different location so you don't have to double back on your route. See individual country chapters for more details.

In smaller towns and villages in the Eastern European countries, you can often find a bike the old-fashioned, informal way – by asking around. Locals may be happy to lend their bike for a small fee.

BUS

Buses generally have the edge over trains in terms of costs, sometimes quite substantially, but are slower and less comfortable, especially if you get stuck with an old clunker (as can happen sometimes in the eastern part of the region). Buses tend to be best for shorter hops such as getting around cities and reaching remote rural villages and are often the only option in mountainous regions.

Europe's biggest network of international buses is provided by a group of bus companies that operates under the name of **Eurolines** (www .eurolines.com). Eurolines has dozens of offices throughout the region, and in almost every case its head office is located in a city's main bus station. See the Transport and Getting There & Away sections in individual country chapters for more information about domestic and long-distance buses.

Bus Passes

Eurolines offers various bus passes. These passes are cheaper than rail passes, but not as extensive or as flexible, and if you're sticking to the Central Europe region you might be better off buying single tickets as you go along. Most trips must be international, though a few internal journeys are possible between major cities in Germany and Austria.

Busabout (UK ☎ 020-7950 1661; www.busabout .com) operates buses that complete set circuits around a number of European countries – including Austria, Czech Republic, Germany and Switzerland – and stop at major cities. You get unlimited travel per sector and can 'hop-on, hop-off' at any scheduled stop, then resume with a later bus. Buses are often over-

subscribed, so prebook each sector to avoid being stranded. Departures are every two days from April/May to October. Passes allowing you to cover a lot of territory start at under US$500.

CAR & MOTORCYCLE

Travelling with your own vehicle allows increased flexibility and the option to get off the beaten track. Unfortunately, cars can be inconvenient in city centres when you have to negotiate strange one-way systems or find somewhere to park in a confusing concrete jungle.

Camper Van

A popular way to tour Europe is for two to four people to band together to buy or rent a camper van. The main advantage of going by camper van is flexibility, with transportation, accommodation and storage all taken care of. Disadvantages include the cramped conditions, parking, the risk of breakdowns and repairs, and having to leave your gear inside when you are exploring.

Prices and facilities in camper vans vary considerably and it's certainly worth getting advice (if not a mechanical check) from a mechanic to see if you are being offered a fair price.

Driving Licence & Documentation

Proof of ownership of a private vehicle should always be carried when touring the region. An EU driving licence is acceptable for driving throughout Central Europe, as are North American and Australian ones. But to be on the safe side – or if you have any other type of licence – you should obtain an International Driving Permit (IDP) from your local motoring organisation. It's easy to get and could save you much hassle later on. Holders of old-style green UK licences must be backed up with a German translation in Austria.

Fuel & Spare Parts

Fuel prices can vary enormously from country to country and may bear little relation to the general cost of living. Unleaded petrol of 95 or 98 octane as well as diesel is widely available throughout Central Europe.

Ireland's Automobile Association maintains a good web page of European fuel prices at www.aaroadwatch.ie/eupetrolprices.

Hire & Lease

Hiring a vehicle is a relatively straightforward procedure. The big international firms will give you reliable service and a good standard of vehicle. Usually you will have the option of returning the car to a different outlet at the end of the rental period. Prebook for the lowest rates – if you walk into an office and ask for a car on the spot, you will pay more, even allowing for special weekend deals. Costs in the eastern areas of Central Europe tend to be higher than in the western areas.

Fly/drive combinations and other packages are worth looking into. If you're coming from North America, Australia or New Zealand, ask your airline if it has any special deals for rental cars in Europe, or check the ads in the weekend travel sections of major newspapers.

You can make advance reservations with the following international companies online:

Avis (www.avis.com)
Budget (www.budget.com)
Europcar (www.europcar.com)
Hertz (www.hertz.com)

If you haven't booked in advance, look for the national or local firms which often undercut the big companies. Nevertheless, you need to be wary of dodgy deals where they take your money and point you towards some clapped-out wreck. Also, when comparing rates of these companies, beware of printed tariffs intended only for local residents, which may be lower than the prices foreigners are charged. If in doubt, ask. And get advice from fellow travellers about the best companies.

No matter where you rent, it is imperative to understand exactly what is included in your rental agreement (collision waiver, unlimited mileage etc). Make sure you are covered with an adequate insurance policy. Ask in advance if you are allowed to drive a rented car across borders.

The minimum rental age is usually 21 and you'll probably need a credit card. Prices at airport rental offices are usually higher than at branches in the city centres.

Motorcycle and moped rental is not very common in Central Europe. It is, however, sadly common to see inexperienced riders leap on rented bikes and very quickly fall off them again, leaving a layer or two of skin on the road in the process.

Leasing a vehicle has none of the hassles of purchasing and could work out cheaper than hiring over longer periods. The **Renault Eurodrive** (www.franceatleisure.com/renault_eurodrive.asp) scheme provides new cars for non-EU residents for a period of between 17 and 170 days. Its offices are based in several cities in France but the company offers a drop-off and pick-up service (for an extra fee) in Zürich, Munich and Frankfurt. In the USA, **Kemwel Holiday Autos** (☎ 877-820-0668; www.kemwel.com) arranges excellent European leasing deals.

Insurance

Third-party motor insurance is compulsory throughout Europe.

In general you should get the insurer of your private vehicle to issue a Green Card (which may cost extra), an internationally recognised proof of insurance, and check that the card lists all the countries you intend to visit. You'll need this in the event of an accident outside the country where the vehicle is insured. The European Accident Statement (known as the 'Constat Amiable' in France) is available from your insurance company and is copied so that each party at an accident can record the identical information for insurance purposes. Never sign statements you can't read or understand – insist on a translation and sign that only if it's acceptable.

Taking out a European breakdown assistance policy, such as the Five Star Service offered by **AA** (in UK ☎ 0800 085 2840; www.theaa.com) or the European Motoring Assistance offered by **RAC** (in UK ☎ 0800 550 055; www.rac.co.uk), is a good investment. Non-Europeans might find it cheaper to arrange for international coverage with their own national motoring organisation before leaving home. Ask your motoring organisation for details about free and reciprocal services offered by affiliated organisations around Europe.

Every vehicle travelling across an international border should display a sticker that shows the country of registration. It's compulsory to carry a red reflector warning triangle almost everywhere in Europe, which must be displayed in the event of a breakdown. Recommended accessories are a first-aid kit (compulsory in Slovenia), a spare bulb kit and a fire extinguisher. Contact the RAC or the AA for more information about what is required in specific countries. Refer also to the Transport sections of individual country chapters in this book.

Motorcycle Touring

Europe is ideal for motorcycle touring, with good-quality winding roads, stunning scenery and an active motorcycling scene. The weather is not always reliable, though, so make sure your wet-weather gear is up to scratch. The wearing of helmets for rider and passenger is compulsory throughout Central Europe. See the Transport sections in the country chapters for additional rules.

Take note of local customs about parking motorcycles on footpaths (pavements). Though this is illegal in some countries, the police often turn a blind eye as long as the vehicle doesn't obstruct pedestrians.

For useful tips from other motorcyclists who have crossed the region, check out the website of **Ride the World** (www.ridetheworld.com). Travellers interested in more adventurous biking activities can scan **Horizons Unlimited** (www.horizonsunlimited.com).

Road Conditions

Conditions and types of roads vary across the region, but it is possible to make some generalisations. The fastest routes are four- or six-lane dual carriageways/highways (motorways, autobahns, autoroutes etc). These roads are great for speed and comfort but driving can be dull, with little or no interesting scenery. Some of these roads incur a general tax for usage (Germany, Switzerland and Austria), but there will usually be an alternative route you can take. Motorways and other primary routes are almost always in very good condition.

Road surfaces on minor routes are not perfect in some countries (eg Poland, Slovakia), although normally they will be more than adequate. These roads are narrower and progress is generally much slower. To compensate, you can expect much better scenery and plenty of interesting villages along the way. Though it's a gross generalisation, minor roads tend to be in better condition in the western half of the region compared with the newer EU member states.

Road Rules

Motoring organisations are able to supply their members with country-by-country information on motoring regulations, or they may produce motoring guidebooks for sale. The **RAC** (in UK ☎ 08705 722 722; www.rac.co.uk) provides comprehensive destination-specific notes with a summary of national road rules and regulations.

You drive on the right-hand side of the road throughout the region and overtake on the left. Keep right except when overtaking, and use your indicators for any change of lane and when pulling away from the kerb.

Driving in the countries in eastern Central Europe is more dangerous than in the western countries such as Switzerland. Driving at night can be especially hazardous in rural areas as the roads are often narrow and winding, and you may encounter horse-drawn vehicles, cyclists, pedestrians and domestic animals. In the event of an accident you're supposed to notify the police and file an insurance claim. If your car has significant body damage from a previous accident, point this out to customs upon arrival and have it noted somewhere, as damaged vehicles may only be allowed to leave the country with police permission.

You may be surprised at the apparent disregard of traffic regulations in some places, but as a visitor it is always best to be cautious. In many countries, driving infringements are subject to an on-the-spot fine; always ask for a receipt.

Take care with speed limits, as they vary from country to country. Speed limits are signposted, and are generally 110km/h or 120km/h on motorways, 100km/h on other highways, 80km/h on secondary and tertiary roads and 50km/h or 60km/h in built-up areas. Motorcycles are usually limited to 90km/h on motorways, and vehicles with trailers to 80km/h. In towns you may only sound the horn to avoid having an accident. There is usually no speed limit on autobahns; exceptions are clearly signposted.

Everywhere in Central Europe, the use of seat belts is mandatory. In most countries, children aged under 12 and intoxicated passengers are not permitted in the front seat. Driving after drinking any alcohol is a very serious offence – Central European countries have between a 0% to 0.8% blood-alcohol-concentration (BAC) limit. See the individual country chapters for more details on legal blood-alcohol limits.

Throughout Europe, when two roads of equal importance intersect, the vehicle coming from the right has right of way unless signs indicate otherwise. In many countries this also applies to cyclists, so take care. On roundabouts (traffic circles) vehicles already in the roundabout have the right of way. Public transport vehicles pulling out from a stop also have right of way. Stay out of lanes marked 'bus' except when you're making a right-hand turn. Pedestrians have the right of way at marked crossings and whenever you're making a turn. In Europe it's prohibited to turn right against a red light even after coming to a stop.

It's usually illegal to stop or park at the top of slopes, in front of pedestrian crossings, at bus or tram stops, on bridges or at level crossings. You must use a red reflector warning triangle when parking on a highway (in an emergency). If you don't use the triangle and another vehicle hits you from behind, you will be held responsible.

Watch out for trams (streetcars) as these have priority at crossroads and when they are turning right (provided they signal the turn). Don't pass a tram that is stopping to let off passengers until everyone is out and the tram doors have closed again (unless, of course, there's a safety island). Never pass a tram on the left or stop within 1m of tram tracks. A police officer who sees you blocking a tram route by waiting to turn left will flag you over.

HITCHING

Hitching is never entirely safe in any country, and we don't recommend it. Travellers who decide to hitch should understand that they are taking a small but potentially serious risk. People who do choose to hitch will be safer if they travel in pairs and let someone know where they plan to go.

That said, hitching can be a rewarding – or very frustrating – way of getting around. Rewarding because you get to meet and interact with local people and are forced into unplanned detours that may yield unexpected highlights off the beaten track. Frustrating because you may get stuck on the side of the road to nowhere with nowhere cheap (or just plain nowhere) to stay. Then it begins to rain…

Hitchers can end up making good time, but obviously your plans need to be flexible in case a trick of the light makes you appear invisible to passing motorists. A man and woman travelling together is probably the best combination. Two or more men must expect some delays; two women together will make good time and should be relatively safe. A woman hitching on her own is taking on added risks. Three people will have a very hard time getting a lift.

A few simple rules should be followed by all hitchers, particularly women: don't accept a ride with two or more men, never let your pack be put in the boot (trunk), only sit next to a door that can be opened, ask drivers where they are going before you say where you're going etc. Don't hesitate to refuse a ride if you feel at all uncomfortable, and insist on being let out at the first sign of trouble. Best of all, try to find a travelling companion.

Don't try to hitch from city centres; take public transport to suburban exit routes. Hitching is usually illegal on motorways (freeways) – stand on the slip roads or approach drivers at petrol stations and truck stops. Look presentable and cheerful and make a cardboard sign indicating your intended destination in the local language. Never hitch where drivers can't stop in good time or without causing an obstruction. At dusk, give up and think about finding somewhere to stay. If your itinerary includes a ferry crossing, it might be worth trying to score a ride before the ferry rather than after, since vehicle tickets sometimes include all passengers free of charge.

In the eastern part of the region, hitching is still a popular mode of transport, mostly among poor students. There, you can offer to pay your driver a small fee (in communist times, paying roughly the equivalent of a bus fare, or less, was common; the expectation to do so may still be there). If you look like a foreigner your chances of getting a ride might improve. Remember to use the local name for the town or city on your sign: 'Praha' not 'Prague'; 'Wien' not 'Vienna'.

It is often possible to arrange a lift in advance: scan student notice boards in colleges, contact car-sharing agencies or click into chat rooms based in your destination city/country and post a request.

For general facts, destination-based information and ride-share options, http://europe .bugride.com may be helpful. The useful www .hitchhikers.org connects hitchhikers and drivers worldwide.

LOCAL TRANSPORT
Bus & Minibus

Local buses are convenient for getting around, and are more flexible when choosing destinations as they travel not only around the cities, but to outlying towns. One form of transport (both city- and nation-wide) that sadly doesn't exist in Central Europe's western countries is the shared minibus (sometimes called maxi-taxis). These convenient but cramped mini-buses are used throughout the eastern countries of the region as a form of both intercity and city transport. They often cost slightly more than a bus but get you to your destination faster.

Taxi

Taking a taxi in Switzerland, Austria and Germany will cost you a pretty penny for the ride. There might also be supplements (depending on the country) for things such as luggage, the time of day, whether you booked it by phone or not, the location from which you boarded and for extra passengers. Where they exist, good bus, rail, tram and underground (subway/metro) train networks make the use of taxis all but unnecessary.

Lower fares in Poland, Hungary, Slovakia and other countries in the east of the region make taxis a much more viable option there, but take care when catching taxis from airports or bus and train stations. Certain taxi companies have a monopoly on such places and either have a higher per-kilometre fare or indulge in all sorts of interesting tricks to make the meter speed up as soon as foreign accents are heard.

Train

Metros or trains such as the U- and S-bahns in Berlin and also Vienna (involving travel under- and over-ground respectively) are a great way to cover vast city distances for a small flat fare.

Tram

Trams are also popular, mainly in the east of the region, and vary hugely in their speed and modernity. Some older models are noisy clunkers, while Prague's fleet of sleek trams have everything from electronic destination displayers to an endemic pickpocketing problem.

Trolleybus

You might also encounter trolleybuses, another phenomenon of the old Soviet bloc. Despite their slowness and general high level of discomfort, they are environmentally friendly (being powered by electricity and having no emissions).

TOURS

National tourist offices in most countries offer organised trips to points of interest, be they within cities or in rural areas. They often work out more expensive than going it alone, but are sometimes worth it if you are pressed for time. A short city tour, for example, will give you a quick overview of the place and can be a good way to begin your visit; afterwards, you'll know more precisely where you want to go again and where you want to avoid.

A package tour is worth considering only if your time is very limited or you have a special interest such as skiing, canoeing, sailing, horse riding, cycling or spa treatments. Most tour prices are for double occupancy, which means singles have to share a double room with a stranger of the same sex or pay a supplement to have the room to themselves.

Paul Laifer Tours (☎ 973-887-1188; www.laifertours .com), based in New Jersey and a Central European specialist, offers excellent, complete package tours out of the USA to Central Europe. Another US-based company offering 1st-class (read: not cheap) package tours is **Homeric Tours** (☎ 212 753 1100; www.homerictours .com), which has a focus on Greece but also specialises in Central and Eastern European destinations.

A British company highly experienced in travel to Eastern Europe is **Regent Holidays** (☎ 0117-921 1711; www.regent-holidays.co.uk). Other British companies worth considering are **Exodus** (☎ 0870 240 5550; www.exodus.co.uk) and **Exploreworld-wide** (☎ 0870 333 4001; www.exploreworldwide.com).

In Australia, a good-value option is **Intrepid Travel** (☎ 1300 360 887; www.intrepidtravel.com). You can also obtain a detailed brochure that outlines dozens of upmarket tours mainly of Eastern Europe from the **Eastern Europe Travel Bureau** (☎ 02-9262 1144; www.eetbtravel.com).

Young (18- to 35-year-old) revellers can make merry on Europe-wide bus tours. **Contiki** (☎ 020-8290 6422; www.contiki.com) and **Top Deck** (☎ 0208 879 6789; www.topdecktravel.co.uk) offer camping and hotel-based bus tours throughout Central Europe. They usually last for several weeks and can be a lot of fun – if a bit hard on the liver.

For people aged over 50, **Saga Holidays** (in UK ☎ 0800 096 0074; www.sagaholidays.com) offers holidays that range from cheap coach tours to luxury cruises (and it has cheap travel insurance).

Bicycle Tours

There are many travel agencies or sporting organisations that organise bicycle trips throughout central Europe. Your best bet is to ask at a cycling club or travel agency specialising in activity-based tours of the region. A good US-based outfit is **CBT Tours** (☎ 800-736-2453; www.cbttours.com). For biking in Germany, see **Nature Park Travel** (www.natureparktravel.com). Also check out **Velofahren.de** (www.velofahren.de) for some excellent tips about cycling throughout Germany and other Central European countries, with many postings and helpful hints from avid cyclists.

TRAIN

Trains are the most atmospheric, comfortable and fun way to make long overland journeys in Central Europe. All of the major cities are on the rail network, and it's perfectly feasible for train travel to be your only form of intercity transport. Overnight trains have the added benefit of saving you a night's accommodation. Trains are also a great way to meet the locals – it's not unusual to be invited to stay for a night or two with the people you shared your couchette with. That plus the stunning scenery you'll see in places such as Switzerland and Austria make train travel in this region very enticing.

If you plan to travel extensively by train, it might be worth getting hold of the *Thomas Cook European Timetable*, which gives a complete listing of train schedules and indicates where supplements apply or where reservations are necessary. It is updated monthly and is available from **Thomas Cook** (www.thomascook .com) outlets in the UK (online elsewhere in the world).

If you intend to stick to one or a handful of countries it might be worthwhile getting hold of the national timetable(s). A particularly useful online resource for timetables in Central Europe is the **Deutsche Bahn** (www.bahn.de) website. Train fares and schedules in US and Canadian dollars on the most popular routes in Europe, including information on rail and youth passes, can be found at www.raileurope .com. For fares in UK pounds go to www .raileurope.co.uk. If all that isn't enough, check out the **European Rail Guide** (www.europeanrailguide .com) website for current timetables and fares.

Classes

While seats on trains in Germany, Austria, Switzerland and Liechtenstein usually just come in 1st- and 2nd-class varieties, in the eastern countries of the region there are generally three classes of sleeping accommodation

on trains – each country has a different name for them, but for the sake of simplicity, we'll call them 3rd, 2nd and 1st class. However, short trips, or longer ones that don't involve sleeping on the train, will usually be seated like a normal train – benches or seats (on suburban trains) or aeroplane-style seats (on smarter intercity services). For more details on sleeping on overnight trains, see the boxed text on opposite.

EXPRESS TRAINS

Fast trains, or those that make few stops, are identified by the symbols EC (EuroCity) or IC (InterCity). The German ICE trains are even faster. Supplements can apply on fast trains, and it is a good idea (sometimes obligatory) to make seat reservations at peak times and on certain lines.

Costs

While reasonable, train travel is generally pricier than bus travel. First-class tickets are about double the price of 2nd-class tickets, which are in turn approximately twice the price of 3rd class. Costs are significantly lower in the eastern part of the region for both international and domestic journeys. Prices for train travel within Germany are particularly expensive.

Reservations

It is always advisable to buy a ticket in advance. Seat reservations are also advisable but only necessary if the letter 'R' is posted on the timetable next to your desired route. Out of peak season, reservations can be made pretty much up to an hour before departure, but never count on this. On busy routes and during the summer, always try to reserve a seat several days in advance. For peace of mind, you may prefer to book tickets via travel agencies before you leave home, although this will be more expensive than booking on arrival in the region. You can book most routes in the region from any main station in Central Europe.

Safety

Be aware that trains, while generally very safe, are favoured haunts of petty criminals. Carry your valuables on you at all times – don't even go to the bathroom without taking your cash, wallet and passport. If you are sharing a compartment with others, you'll have to decide

OVERNIGHT TRAINS

When you'll be travelling overnight (nearly always the case when going between the west and the east of the region) you'll get a bed reservation included in the price of your ticket, although you may have to pay a few euros extra for the bedding once on board. Each wagon is administered by a steward or stewardess who will look after your ticket and – crucially, if you arrive during the small hours – will make sure that you get off at the correct stop. Each wagon has a toilet and washbasin at either end, although their state of cleanliness can vary massively. Be aware that toilets can be closed while the train is stopping in a station. Also be aware that overnight trains in Poland have a reputation as targets for theft. Note that European trains sometimes split en route to service two destinations, so even if you're on the right train, make sure you're also in the correct carriage.

Western Central Europe

In these countries trains will usually offer a choice of couchette or sleeper if you don't fancy sleeping in your seat with somebody else's elbow in your ear. Again, reservations are advisable as sleeping options are allocated on a first-come, first-served basis.

Couchette bunks are comfortable enough, if lacking a bit in privacy. There are four per compartment in 1st class or six in 2nd class. A bunk costs around €22 on top of the price of your ticket for most international trains, irrespective of the length of the journey.

Sleepers are the most comfortable option, offering beds for one or two passengers in 1st class, and two or three passengers in 2nd class. Charges vary depending on the journey, but they are significantly more expensive than couchettes. Most long-distance trains have a dining (buffet) car or an attendant who wheels a snack trolley through carriages. If possible buy your food before travelling as on-board prices tend to be high.

Eastern Central Europe

Third-class sleeping accommodation is not available everywhere, but it's the cheapest way to sleep, although you may feel your privacy has been slightly invaded. The accommodation consists of six berths in each compartment.

Second class has four berths in a closed compartment. If there are three in your group, you'll often not be joined by anyone.

First class is a treat, although you are paying for space rather than décor or unsurly service in most countries. Here you'll find two berths in a compartment, usually adorned with plastic flowers to remind you what you've paid for.

whether or not you trust them. If there's any doubt, be cautious with your belongings when leaving the compartment. At night, make sure your door is locked from the inside. If you have a compartment to yourself, you can ask the steward(ess) to lock it while you go to the dining car or go for a wander outside when the train is stopped. However, be aware that most criminals strike when they can easily disembark the train.

Train Passes

European rail passes are worth buying if you plan to do a reasonable amount of intercountry travelling within a short space of time. Research your options before committing to a particular pass – find the one out there that most fits your plans and budget. Many passes also grant reductions on other modes of travel as well as entry to some tourist sites.

Try to plan your itinerary carefully. Don't overdo the overnight travelling. Although it can work out to be a great way of saving time and money, you don't want to be too tired to enjoy the next day of sightseeing: remember, even intercountry distances are relatively small in Central Europe and many of these overnight train rides are only five to seven hours long. After a few sleepless nights in a row, all the art on the walls of those museums you visit will start to look like Impressionism.

When weighing up options, consider the cost of other cheap ticket deals, including advance-purchase reductions, one-off promotions or special circular-route tickets.

TRANSPORT IN
CENTRAL EUROPE

International tickets are usually valid for two months, and you can make as many stops as you like en route; make your intentions known when purchasing and inform train conductors how far you're going before they punch your ticket.

Not all countries in Central Europe are covered by rail passes, but most passes include a number of destinations and so are worthwhile if you are concentrating your travels on the region. Pour yourself a cuppa or favourite drink and check out the excellent summary of available passes at www.seat61.com/railpass .htm – there's a lot of information to digest before deciding on the pass that's best for you.

An agency that sells a multitude of passes, including the ones mentioned below, is **Rail Europe** (in USA ☎ 877-257-2887; www.raileurope.com; in UK ☎ 08708 371 371; www.raileurope.co.uk).

EURAIL

Eurail (www.eurail.com) passes are valid for unlimited travel on national railways and some private lines between many European countries. The Eurailpass is the standard pass for travellers 26 years and over. It provides unlimited 1st-class travel only: 15 days to three months costs US$605 to US$1703. This is the best pass for those who want to spend most of their time on trains.

The Eurailpass Flexi is also for travellers 26 and over. It offers 1st-class travel for any chosen days within a two-month period: 10/15 days US$715/940. This is a better option for most people.

The Eurailpass Youth pass offers the same options as the standard Eurailpass, but for those aged under 26 years, and for 2nd-class travel only. Passes cover periods from 15 days to three months for US$394 to US$1108. This is the classic backpacker's pass.

The Eurailpass Youth Flexi offers the same options as the standard Eurailpass Flexi, but for those aged under 26, and for 2nd-class travel only: 10/15 days for US$465/611.

Two to five people travelling together can get a 'saver' version of all passes mentioned above, saving about 15%.

Also for non-Europeans is the Eurail Selectpass, which gives buyers the option of choosing which countries it covers and for how long. Options are myriad and can offer significant savings over the above passes if, for example, you are only going to three or four countries.

EURODOMINO

There is a Eurodomino pass for some of the countries covered in the Inter-Rail pass (see below), and it's worth considering if you're homing in on a particular region. These passes are sold in Europe to European residents. Adults (travelling 1st or 2nd class) and those under 26 can opt for three to eight days valid travel within one month. An example is unlimited 2nd-class travel in Germany for three days for UK£140.

EUROPEAN EAST PASS

The European East Pass can be purchased by anyone not permanently resident in Europe (including the UK). The pass is valid for travel in Austria, Hungary, Czech Republic, Slovakia and Poland, also giving the holders additional offers especially in Austria and Hungary (for example discounted Danube River trips with DDSG Blue Danube).

This pass is sold by travel agents in North America, Australia and the UK. In the USA, **Rail Europe** (www.raileurope.com) charges US$124/172 for five days of 1st/2nd-class travel within one month; extra rail days (maximum five) cost US$29/23 each. The European East Pass can also be bought via **RailChoice** (www.railchoice .co.uk), which charges UK£124 (2nd class) for five days plus approximately an extra UK£15 per extra day of validity.

INTER-RAIL

These passes are available to European residents (and to nationals of Turkey, Morocco, Tunisia and Algeria) of more than six months' standing (passport identification is required). Terms and conditions vary slightly from country to country, but when travelling in the country where you bought the pass, there is only a discount of around 50% on normal fares.

The **Inter-Rail pass** (www.interrailnet.com) is split into a number of zones: Zone C includes Germany, Switzerland and Austria; Zone D is Hungary, Slovakia, Poland and the Czech Republic; and Zone G includes Slovenia. This pass is not valid on some high-speed services.

The Inter-Rail pass is available in two classes: adult and youth (under 26). Prices for any one zone for 16 days are UK£215/145; two zones for 22 days UK£295/205; and the all-zone global pass for one month UK£405/285. This is the classic European backpacker's pass.

NATIONAL RAIL PASSES

If you intend to travel extensively within one country, check whether national rail passes are available. These might save you a bit of money and also the time and hassle of having to buy individual tickets. Some details can be found in the country chapters; also check out www.raileurope.com. You need to plan ahead if you intend to take this option, as some passes can only be purchased prior to arrival in the country concerned. Some national flexipasses, near-equivalents to the Eurodomino passes mentioned above, are only available to non-Europeans.

Health

CONTENTS

Travel health depends on your predeparture preparations, your daily health care while travelling in Central Europe and how you handle any medical problem that does develop. Few prepared travellers experience anything more than an upset stomach.

BEFORE YOU GO

Prevention is the key to staying healthy while abroad. A little planning before departure will save trouble later: see your dentist before a long trip and carry a spare pair of contact lenses or glasses. Bring medications in their original, clearly labelled, containers. A signed and dated letter from your physician describing your medical conditions and medications, including generic names, is also a good idea. If carrying syringes or needles, be sure to have a physician's letter documenting their necessity.

HEALTH INSURANCE

Make sure that you have adequate health insurance. See p589 for general information.

RECOMMENDED VACCINATIONS

The World Health Organization (WHO) recommends that all travellers should be covered for diphtheria, tetanus, measles, mumps, rubella and polio. Travellers should also be aware that most vaccines don't produce immunity until at least two weeks after they're given.

IN TRANSIT

DEEP VEIN THROMBOSIS (DVT)

Blood clots may form in the legs during plane flights, chiefly because of prolonged immobility. The longer the flight, the greater the risk. The chief symptom of DVT is swelling or pain of the foot, ankle, or calf, usually but not always on just one side. When a blood clot travels to the lungs, it may cause chest pain and breathing difficulties. Travellers with any of these symptoms should immediately seek medical attention.

To prevent the development of DVT on long flights you should walk about the cabin, contract the leg muscles while sitting, drink plenty of fluids and avoid alcohol and tobacco.

IN CENTRAL EUROPE

AVAILABILITY & COST OF HEALTH CARE

Good basic health care is readily available and for minor illnesses pharmacists can give valuable advice and sell over-the-counter medication. They can also advise when more specialised help is required. The standard of dental care is usually good.

In the east of the region, medical care is not always readily available outside of major cities but embassies, consulates and five-star hotels can usually recommend doctors or clinics. In

---

INTERNET RESOURCES & BOOKS

The WHO's publication *International Travel and Health* is revised annually and is available online at www.who.int/ith/. Other useful websites include www.mdtravelhealth .com (travel health recommendations for every country, updated daily) and www .mariestopes.org.uk (information on women's health and contraception).

Lonely Planet's *Travel with Children* includes advice on travel health for younger children. A recommended reference is *Travellers' Health* by Dr Richard Dawood.

some cases, medical supplies required in hospital may need to be bought from a pharmacy and nursing care may be limited.

INFECTIOUS DISEASES
HIV & AIDS

Infection with the human immunodeficiency virus (HIV) may lead to acquired immune deficiency syndrome (AIDS), which is a fatal disease. Any exposure to blood, blood products or body fluids may put the individual at risk. The disease is often transmitted through sexual contact or dirty needles – vaccinations, acupuncture, tattooing and body piercing can be potentially as dangerous as intravenous drug use. If you do need an injection, ask to see the syringe unwrapped in front of you, or take a needle and syringe pack with you.

Fear of HIV infection should never preclude treatment for serious medical conditions.

Sexually Transmitted Diseases

HIV/AIDS and hepatitis B can be transmitted through sexual contact. Other STDs include gonorrhoea, herpes and syphilis; sores, blisters or rashes around the genitals and discharges or pain when urinating are common symptoms. In some STDs, such as wart virus or chlamydia, symptoms may be less marked or not observed at all, especially in women. Chlamydia infection can cause infertility in men and women before any symptoms have been noticed. Syphilis symptoms eventually disappear completely but the disease continues and can cause severe problems in later years. While abstinence from sexual contact is the only 100% effective prevention, using condoms is also effective. The treatment of gonorrhoea and syphilis is with antibiotics. The different sexually transmitted diseases each require specific antibiotics.

ENVIRONMENTAL HAZARDS
Altitude Sickness

Lack of oxygen at high altitudes (over 2500m) affects most people to some extent. The effect may be mild or severe and occurs because less oxygen reaches the muscles and the brain at high altitude, requiring the heart and lungs to compensate by working harder. Symptoms of Acute Mountain Sickness (AMS) usually develop during the first 24 hours at altitude but may be delayed up to three weeks. Mild symptoms include headache, lethargy, dizziness, difficulty sleeping and loss of appetite. AMS may become more severe without warning and can be fatal. Severe symptoms include breathlessness, a dry cough (which may progress to the production of pink, frothy sputum), severe headache, lack of coordination and balance, confusion, irrational behaviour, vomiting, drowsiness and unconsciousness. There is no hard-and-fast rule as to what is too high: AMS has been fatal at 3000m, although 3500m to 4500m is the usual range.

Treat mild symptoms by resting at the same altitude until recovery, usually a day or two. Paracetamol or aspirin can be taken for headaches. If symptoms persist or become worse, however, *immediate descent is necessary*; even 500m can help. Drug treatments should never be used to avoid descent or to enable further ascent. The risk of getting AMS can be reduced by taking the following measures:

- Ascend slowly. Have frequent rest days, spending two to three nights at each rise of 1000m. If you reach a high altitude by trekking, acclimatisation takes place gradually and you are less likely to be affected than if you fly directly to high altitude. It is always wise to sleep at a lower altitude than the greatest height reached during the day if possible. Also, once above 3000m, care should be taken not to increase the sleeping altitude by more than 300m per day.
- Drink extra fluids. The mountain air is dry and cold and moisture is lost as you breathe. Evaporation of sweat may occur unnoticed and result in dehydration.
- Eat light, high-carbohydrate meals for more energy.
- Avoid alcohol as it may increase the risk of dehydration.
- Avoid sedatives.

Hypothermia

Hypothermia occurs when the body loses heat faster than it can produce it and the core temperature of the body falls. It is surprisingly easy to progress from very cold to dangerously cold due to a combination of wind, wet clothing, fatigue and hunger, even if the air temperature is above freezing. It is best to dress in layers; silk, wool and some of the new artificial fibres are all good insulating materials. A hat is important, as a lot of heat is lost through the head. A strong, waterproof outer layer (and a 'space' blanket for emergencies) is essential. Carry basic supplies, including food containing simple sugars to generate heat quickly and fluid to drink.

Symptoms of hypothermia are exhaustion, numb skin (particularly toes and fingers), shivering, slurred speech, irrational or violent behaviour, lethargy, stumbling, dizzy spells, muscle cramps and violent bursts of energy. Irrationality may take the form of sufferers claiming they are warm and trying to take off their clothes.

To treat mild hypothermia, first get the person out of the wind and/or rain, remove their clothing if it's wet and replace it with dry, warm clothing. Give them hot liquids – not alcohol – and some high-kilojoule, easily digestible food. Do not rub victims: instead, allow them to slowly warm themselves. This should be enough to treat the early stages of hypothermia. The early recognition and treatment of mild hypothermia is the only way to prevent severe hypothermia, which is a critical condition.

TRAVELLERS DIARRHOEA

Simple things such as a change of water, food or climate can all cause a mild bout of diarrhoea, but a few rushed toilet trips with no other symptoms is not indicative of a major problem.

Dehydration is the main danger with any diarrhoea, particularly in children or the elderly as dehydration can occur quite quickly. Under all circumstances *fluid replacement* (at least equal to the volume being lost) is the most important thing to remember. Weak black tea with a little sugar, soda water, or soft drinks allowed to go flat and diluted 50% with clean water are all good. With severe diarrhoea a rehydrating solution is preferable to replace minerals and salts lost.

Gut-paralysing drugs such as loperamide or diphenoxylate can be used to bring relief from the symptoms, although they do not actually cure the problem. Only use these drugs if you do not have access to toilets, eg if you *must* travel. Note that these drugs are not recommended for children aged under 12 years.

CUTS, BITES & STINGS

Wash well and treat any cut with an antiseptic such as povidone-iodine. Where possible avoid bandages and Band-Aids, which can keep wounds wet.

Bee and wasp stings are usually painful rather than dangerous. However, in people who are allergic to them severe breathing difficulties may occur and require urgent medical care. Calamine lotion or a sting relief spray will give relief and ice packs will reduce the pain and swelling.

Rabies

Rabies is spread through bites or licks on broken skin from an infected animal. It is always fatal unless treated promptly. Animal handlers should be vaccinated, as should those travelling to remote areas where a reliable source of postbite vaccine is not available within 24 hours. Three injections are needed over a month. If you have not been vaccinated, you will need a course of five injections starting 24 hours or as soon as possible after the injury. If you have been vaccinated, you will need fewer injections and have more time to seek medical help.

SEXUAL HEALTH

The **International Planned Parent Federation** (www .ippf.org) can advise about the availability of contraception in different countries. Contraception, including condoms, is widely available in the western part of the region. However, emergency contraception, which needs to be taken less than 24 hours after unprotected sex, may not be available throughout all of the region. When buying condoms, look for a European CE mark, which means they have been rigorously tested.

Language

CONTENTS

This language guide contains basic vocabulary and pronunciation guidelines to help you get around Central Europe. For a more detailed guide to all the languages included here, get a copy of Lonely Planet's *Eastern Europe Phrasebook* and *German Phrasebook*.

CZECH

PRONUNCIATION

Many Czech letters are pronounced the same as their English counterparts. Accents lengthen vowels and stress is always on the first syllable. Words are pronounced as they're written, so if you follow the guidelines below you'll have no trouble being understood. In indexes on Czech maps, **ch** comes after **h**.

c	as the 'ts' in 'bits'
č	as the 'ch' in 'church'
ch	as in Scottish *loch*
ď	as the 'd' in 'duty'
ě	as the 'ye' in 'yet'
j	as the 'y' in 'you'
ň	as the 'ni' in 'onion'
ř	as the sound 'rzh'
š	as the 'sh' in 'ship'
ť	as the 'te' in 'stew'
ž	as the 's' in 'pleasure'

ACCOMMODATION

hotel	hotel
guesthouse	penzión
youth hostel	ubytovna
camping ground	kemping
private room	privát
single room	jednolůžkový pokoj
double room	dvoulůžkový pokoj
Do you have any rooms available?	Máte volné pokoje?
How much is it?	Kolik to je?
Does it include breakfast?	Je v tom zahrnuta snídane?

CONVERSATION & ESSENTIALS

Hello/Good day.	Dobrý den. (pol)
Hi.	Ahoj. (inf)
Goodbye.	Na shledanou.
Yes.	Ano.
No.	Ne.
Please.	Prosím.
Thank you.	Dekuji.
That's fine/You're welcome.	Není zač/Prosím.
Sorry.	Promiňte.
I don't understand.	Nerozumím.
What's it called?	Jak se to jmenuje?
How much is it?	Kolik to stojí?

EMERGENCIES – CZECH

Help!	Pomoc!
Call a doctor/ ambulance/police!	Zavolejte doktora/ sanitku/policii!
Go away!	Běžte pryč!
I'm lost.	Zabloudil jsem. (m)
	Zabloudila jsem. (f)

SHOPPING & SERVICES

the bank	banka
the chemist	lékárna
the church	kostel
the market	trh
the museum	muzeum
the post office	pošta
the tourist office	turistickáinformační kancelář
travel agency	cestovní kancelář

TIME, DAYS & NUMBERS

What time is it?	Kolik je hodin?
today	dnes
tonight	dnes večer
tomorrow	zítra
yesterday	včera
in the morning	ráno
in the evening	večer

SIGNS – CZECH

Vchod	Entrance
Východ	Exit
Informace	Information
Otevřeno	Open
Zavřeno	Closed
Zakázáno	Prohibited
Policie	Police Station
Záchody/WC/Toalety	Toilets
Páni/Muži	Men
Dámy/Ženy	Women

Monday	pondělí
Tuesday	úterý
Wednesday	středa
Thursday	čtvrtek
Friday	pátek
Saturday	sobota
Sunday	neděle

0	null
1	jeden
2	dva
3	tři
4	čtyři
5	pět
6	šest
7	sedm
8	osm
9	devět
10	deset
100	sto
1000	tisíc

TRANSPORT

What time does the ... leave/arrive?	Kdy odjíždí/přijíždí ...?
boat	loď
city bus	městský autobus
intercity bus	meziměstský autobus
train	vlak
tram	tramvaj
arrival	příjezdy
departure	odjezdy
timetable	jízdní řád
Where is the bus stop?	Kde je autobusová zastávka?
Where is the station?	Kde je nádraží?
Where is the left luggage room?	Kde je úschovna zavazadel?
Please show me on the map.	Prosím, ukažte mi to na mapě.

Directions

Where is it?	Kde je to?
left	vlevo
right	vpravo
straight ahead	rovně

GERMAN

PRONUNCIATION

Unlike English or French, German has no silent letters: you pronounce the **k** at the start of the word *Knie* (knee), the **p** at the start of *Psychologie* (psychology), and the **e** at the end of *Ich habe* (I have).

Vowels

As in English, vowels can be pronounced long, as the 'o' in 'pope', or short, as in 'pop'. As a rule, German vowels are long before one consonant and short before two consonants, eg the **o** is long in *Dom* (cathedral), but short in *doch* (after all).

a	short, as the 'u' in 'cut', or long as in 'father'
au	as the 'ow' in 'vow'
ä	short as in 'cat', or long as in 'care'
äu	as the 'oy' in 'boy'
e	short as in 'bet', or long as in 'obey'
ei	as the 'ai' in 'aisle'
eu	as the 'oy' in 'boy'
i	short as in 'it', or long as in 'marine'
ie	as in 'brief'
o	short as in 'not', or long as in 'note'
ö	as the 'er' in 'fern'
u	as in 'pull'
ü	like **u** but with lips stretched back

Consonants

Most German consonants sound similar to their English counterparts. One important difference is that **b**, **d** and **g** sound like 'p', 't' and 'k' at the end of a word.

b	as in 'be'; as 'p' when word-final
ch	as in Scottish *loch*
d	as in 'do'; as 't' when word-final
g	as in 'go'; as 'k' when word-final
j	as the 'y' in 'yet'
qu	as 'k' plus 'v'
r	can be trilled or guttural, depending on the region
s	as in 'sun'; as the 'z' in 'zoo' when followed by a vowel

sch	as the 'sh' in 'ship'
sp/st	as 'shp/sht' when word-initial
-tion	the 't' is pronounced as the 'ts' in 'its'
v	as the 'f' in 'fan'
w	as the 'v' in 'van'
z	as the 'ts' in 'its'

ACCOMMODATION

hotel	Hotel
guesthouse	Pension/Gästehaus
youth hostel	Jugendherberge
camping ground	Campingplatz
a single room	ein Einzelzimmer
a double room	ein Doppelzimmer
one night	eine Nacht
two nights	zwei Nächte
Do you have any rooms available?	Haben Sie noch freie Zimmer?
How much is it per night/person?	Wieviel kostet es pro Nacht/Person?
Is breakfast included?	Ist Frühstück inbegriffen?

CONVERSATION & ESSENTIALS

Good day.	Guten Tag.
Hello.	Grüss Gott. (in Bavaria & Austria)
Goodbye.	Auf Wiedersehen.
Bye.	Tschüss. (inf)
Yes.	Ja.
No.	Nein.
Please.	Bitte.
Thank you.	Danke.
You're welcome.	Bitte sehr.
Excuse me/ Forgive me.	Entschuldigung.
Do you speak English?	Sprechen Sie Englisch?
How much is it?	Wieviel kostet es?
What's your name?	Wie heissen Sie?
My name is ...	Ich heisse ...

SHOPPING & SERVICES

| What time does it open/close? | Um wieviel Uhr macht es auf/zu? |

SIGNS – GERMAN

Eingang	Entrance
Ausgang	Exit
Auskunft	Information
Offen	Open
Geschlossen	Closed
Zimmer Frei	Rooms Available
Voll/Besetzt	Full/No Vacancies
Polizeiwache	Police Station
Verboten	Prohibited
Toiletten (WC)	Toilets
Herren	Men
Damen	Women

a bank	eine Bank
the chemist/ pharmacy	die Apotheke
the ... embassy	die ... Botschaft
the market	der Markt
the newsagents	der Zeitungshändler
the post office	das Postamt
the stationers	der Schreibwarengeschäft
the tourist office	das Verkehrsamt

TIME, DAYS & NUMBERS

What time is it?	Wie spät ist es?
today	heute
tomorrow	morgen
yesterday	gestern
in the morning	morgens
in the afternoon	nachmittags
Monday	Montag
Tuesday	Dienstag
Wednesday	Mittwoch
Thursday	Donnerstag
Friday	Freitag
Saturday	Samstag, Sonnabend
Sunday	Sonntag
0	null
1	eins
2	zwei/zwo
3	drei
4	vier
5	fünf
6	sechs
7	sieben
8	acht
9	neun
10	zehn
100	hundert
1000	tausend

LANGUAGE

TRANSPORT

What time does ... (leave/arrive)?	*Wann (fährt ... ab/kommt ... an)?*
the boat	*das Boot*
the bus (city)	*der Bus*
the bus (intercity)	*der (überland) Bus*
the tram	*die Strassenbahn*
the train	*der Zug*
What time is the next boat?	*Wann fährt das nächste Boot?*
I'd like to hire a car/bicycle.	*Ich möchte ein Auto/Fahrrad mieten.*
I'd like a one-way/ return ticket.	*Ich möchte eine Einzel-karte/ Rückfahrkarte.*
1st class	*erste Klasse*
2nd class	*zweite Klasse*
left luggage locker	*Schliessfächer*
timetable	*Fahrplan*
bus stop	*Bushaltestelle*
tram stop	*Strassenbahnhaltestelle*
train station	*Bahnhof (Bf)*
ferry terminal	*Fährhafen*

Directions

Where is the ...?	*Wo ist die ...?*
Go straight ahead.	*Gehen Sie geradeaus.*
Turn left.	*Biegen Sie links ab.*
Turn right.	*Biegen Sie rechts ab.*
near/far	*nahe/weit*

HUNGARIAN

PRONUNCIATION

Hungarian consonants can be simplified by pronouncing them much the same as in English; the exceptions are listed below. Double consonants **ll**, **tt** and **dd** are lengthened so you can almost hear them as separate letters. The letters **cs**, **dz**, **dzs**, **gy**, **ly**, **ny**, **sz**, **ty** and **zs** (consonant clusters) are separate letters in Hungarian and appear that way in telephone books and other alphabetical listings, so *cukor* (sugar) appears in the dictionary before *csak* (only).

c	as the 'ts' in 'hats'
cs	as the 'ch' in 'church'
dz	as in 'adze'
dzs	as the 'j' in 'jet'
gy	as the 'du' in 'endure'
j	as the 'y' in 'yes'
ly	as the 'y' in 'yes'
ny	as the 'ni' in 'onion'
r	like a slightly rolled Scottish 'r'
s	as the 'sh' in 'ship'
sz	as the 's' in 'set'
ty	as the 'tu' in British English 'tube'
w	as 'v' (found in foreign words only)
zs	as the 's' in 'pleasure'

Vowels are a bit trickier, and the semantic difference between **a**, **e** or **o** with and without an accent mark is great. For example, *hát* means 'back' while *hat* means 'six'.

a	as the 'o' in hot
á	as in 'father'
e	a short 'e' as in 'set'
é	as the 'e' in 'they' with no 'y' sound
i	as in 'hit' but shorter
í	as in 'police'
o	as in 'open'
ó	a longer version of **o** above
ö	as the 'u' in 'fur' with no 'r' sound
ő	a longer version of **ö** above
u	as in 'pull'
ú	as the 'ue' in 'blue'
ü	similar to the 'u' in 'flute'; purse your lips tightly and say 'ee'
ű	a longer, breathier version of **ü** above

ACCOMMODATION

hotel	*szálloda*
guesthouse	*panzió*
youth hostel	*ifjúsági szálló*
camping ground	*kemping*
private room	*fizetővendégszoba*
single room	*egyágyas szoba*
double room	*kétágyas szoba*
Do you have rooms available?	*Van szabad szobájuk?*
How much is it per night/person?	*Mennyibe kerül éjszakánként/ személyenként?*
Does it include breakfast?	*Az ár tartalmazza a reggelit?*

EMERGENCIES – HUNGARIAN

Help!	*Segítség!*
Call a doctor!	*Hívjon egy orvost!*
Call an ambulance!	*Hívja a mentőket!*
Call the police!	*Hívja a rendőrséget!*
Go away!	*Menjen innen!*
I'm lost.	*Eltévedtem.*

SIGNS – HUNGARIAN

Bejárat	Entrance
Kijárat	Exit
Információ	Information
Nyitva	Open
Zárva	Closed
Tilos	Prohibited
Rendőrőr-	Police Station
Kapitányság	
Toalett/WC	Toilets
Férfiak	Men
Nők	Women

CONVERSATION & ESSENTIALS

Hello.	*Jó napot kivánok.* (pol)
	Szia/Szervusz. (inf)
Goodbye.	*Viszontlátásra.* (pol)
	Szia/Szervusz. (inf)
Yes.	*Igen.*
No.	*Nem.*
Please.	*Kérem.*
Thank you.	*Köszönöm.*
Sorry/Forgive me.	*Sajnálom/Elnézést.*
Excuse me.	*Bocsánat.*
What's your name?	*Mi a neve/neved?* (pol/inf)
My name is ...	*A nevem ...*
I don't understand.	*Nem értem.*
Do you speak English?	*Beszél angolul?*
What's it called?	*Hogy hívják?*
How much is it?	*Mennyibe kerül?*

SHOPPING & SERVICES

Where is ...?	*Hol van ...?*
a bank	*bank*
a chemist	*gyógyszertár*
the market	*a piac*
the museum	*a múzeum*
the post office	*a posta*
a tourist office	*turistairoda*
What time does it open/close?	*Mikor (nyit ki/zár be)?*

TIME, DAYS & NUMBERS

What time is it?	*Hány óra?*
today	*ma*
tonight	*ma este*
tomorrow	*holnap*
yesterday	*tegnap*
in the morning	*reggel*
in the evening	*este*
Monday	*hétfő*
Tuesday	*kedd*
Wednesday	*szerda*
Thursday	*csütörtök*
Friday	*péntek*
Saturday	*szombat*
Sunday	*vasárnap*
0	*nulla*
1	*egy*
2	*kettő*
3	*három*
4	*négy*
5	*öt*
6	*hat*
7	*hét*
8	*nyolc*
9	*kilenc*
10	*tíz*
100	*száz*
1000	*ezer*

TRANSPORT

What time does the ... leave/arrive?	*Mikor indul/érkezik a ...?*
boat/ferry	*hajó/komp*
city/intercity bus	*város/varosközi*
plane	*repülőgép*
train	*vonat*
tram	*villamos*
Where is ...?	*Hol van ...?*
the bus stop	*az autóbuszmegálló*
the station	*az állomás*
the left-luggage office	*a csomagmegőrző*
arrival	*érkezés*
departure	*indulás*
timetable	*menetrend*

Directions

Turn left.	*Forduljon balra.*
Turn right.	*Forduljon jobbra.*
Go straight ahead.	*Menyen egyenesen elore.*
Please show me on the map.	*Kérem, mutassa meg a térképen.*
near/far	*közel/messze*

POLISH

PRONUNCIATION

Written Polish is phonetically consistent, which means that the pronunciation of letters or clusters of letters doesn't vary from word to word. The stress almost always goes on the second-last syllable.

Vowels

a	as the 'u' in 'cut'
e	as in 'ten'
i	like the 'ee' in 'feet' but shorter
o	as in 'lot'
u	a bit shorter than the 'oo' in 'book'
y	similar to the 'i' in 'bit'

There are three vowels unique to Polish:

ą	a nasal vowel sound like the French *un*, similar to 'own' in 'sown'
ę	also nasalised, like the French *un*, but pronounced as 'e' when word-final
ó	similar to Polish **u**

Consonants

The consonants **b**, **d**, **f**, **k**, **l**, **m**, **n**, **p**, **t**, **v** and **z** are pronounced more or less as they are in English. The following consonants and clusters of consonants sound distinctly different to their English counterparts:

c	as the 'ts' in 'its'
ch	as the 'ch' in Scottish *loch*
cz	as the 'ch' in 'church'
ć	much softer than Polish **c** ('tsi' before vowels)
dz	similar to the 'ds' in 'suds' but shorter
dź	as **dz** but softer ('dzi' before vowels)
dż	as the 'j' in 'jam'
g	as in 'get'
h	as **ch**
j	as the 'y' in 'yet'
ł	as the 'w' in 'wine'
ń	as the 'ny' in 'canyon' ('ni' before vowels)
r	always trilled
rz	as the 's' in 'pleasure'
s	as in 'set'
sz	as the 'sh' in 'show'
ś	as **s** but softer ('si' before vowels)
w	as the 'v' in 'van'
ź	softer version of **z** ('zi' before vowels)
ż	as **rz**

ACCOMMODATION

hotel	hotel
youth hostel	schronisko młodzieżowe
camping ground	kemping
single room	pokój jednoosobowy
double room	pokój dwuosobowy
private room	kwatera prywatna
Do you have any rooms available?	Czy są wolne pokoje?

How much is it?	Ile to kosztuje?
Does it include breakfast?	Czy śniadanie jest wliczone?

CONVERSATION & ESSENTIALS

Hello.	Cześć. (inf)
Hello/Good morning.	Dzień dobry.
Goodbye.	Do widzenia.
Yes.	Tak.
No.	Nie.
Please.	Proszę.
Thank you.	Dziękuję.
Excuse me/Sorry.	Przepraszam.
I don't understand.	Nie rozumiem.
What is it called?	Jak to się nazywa?
How much is it?	Ile to kosztuje?

EMERGENCIES – POLISH

Help!	Pomocy!/Ratunku!
Call a doctor/ an ambulance!	Proszę wezwać lekarza/ karetkę!
Call the police!	Proszę wezwać policję!
I'm lost.	Zgubiłem się. (m)
	Zgubiłam się. (f)

SHOPPING & SERVICES

the bank	bank
the chemist	apteka
the church	kościół
the city centre	centrum miasta
the market	targ/bazar
the museum	muzeum
the post office	poczta
the tourist office	informacja turystyczna

What time does it open/close?	O której otwierają/zamykają?

TIME, DAYS & NUMBERS

What time is it?	Która jest godzina?
today	dzisiaj
tonight	dzisiaj wieczorem
tomorrow	jutro
yesterday	wczoraj
in the morning	rano
in the evening	wieczorem

Monday	poniedziałek
Tuesday	wtorek
Wednesday	środa
Thursday	czwartek
Friday	piątek
Saturday	sobota
Sunday	niedziela

0	zero
1	jeden
2	dwa
3	trzy
4	cztery
5	pięć
6	sześć
7	siedem
8	osiem
9	dziewięć
10	dziesięć
11	jedenaście
20	dwadzieścia
100	sto
1000	tysiąc

TRANSPORT

What time does the ... leave/arrive?	O której godzinie przychodzi/ odchodzi ...?
boat	statek
bus	autobus
plane	samolot
train	pociąg
tram	tramwaj
arrival	przyjazd
departure	odjazd
timetable	rozkład jazdy
Where is the bus stop?	Gdzie jest przystanek autobusowy?
Where is the station?	Gdzie jest stacja kolejowa?
Where is the left-luggage office?	Gdzie jest przechowalnia bagażu?

Directions

Please show me on the map.	Proszę pokazać mi to na mapie.
straight ahead	prosto
left	lewo
right	prawo

SLOVAK

PRONUNCIATION

The 43 letters of the Slovak alphabet have similar pronunciation to those of Czech. In words of three syllables or less the stress falls on the first syllable. Longer words also have a secondary accent on the third or fifth syllable. There are 13 vowels (**a, á, ä, e, é, i, í, o, ó, u, ú, y, ý**), three semi-vowels (**l, ĺ, r**) and five diphthongs (**ia, ie, iu, ou, ô**).

c	as the 'ts' in 'its'
č	as the 'ch' in 'church'
dz	as the 'ds' in 'suds'
dž	as the 'j' in 'judge'
ia	as the 'yo' in 'yonder'
ie	as the 'ye' in 'yes'
iu	as the word 'you'
j	as the 'y' in 'yet'
ň	as the 'ni' in 'onion'
ô	as the 'wo' in 'won't'
ou	as the 'ow' in 'know'
š	as the 'sh' in 'show'
y	as the 'i' in 'machine'
ž	as the 'z' in 'azure'

ACCOMMODATION

hotel	hotel
guesthouse	penzion
youth hostel	mládežnícka ubytovňa
camping ground	kemping
private room	privat
single room	jednolôžková izba
double room	dvojlôžková izba
Do you have any rooms available?	Máte voľné izby?
How much is it?	Koľko to stojí?
Is breakfast included?	Sú raňajky zahrnuté v cene?

CONVERSATION & ESSENTIALS

Hello.	Ahoj.
Goodbye.	Dovidenia.

LANGUAGE

SIGNS – SLOVAK

Vchod	Entrance
Východ	Exit
Informácie	Information
Otvorené	Open
Zatvorené	Closed
Zakázané	Prohibited
Polícia	Police Station
Záchody/WC/Toalety	Toilets
Páni	Men
Dámy)	Women

Yes.	Áno.
No.	Nie.
Please.	Prosím.
Thank you.	D'akujem.
Excuse me/	Prepáčte mi/
Forgive me.	Odpuste mi.
I'm sorry.	Ospravedlňujem sa.
I don't understand.	Nerozumiem.
What is it called?	Ako sa do volá?
How much is it?	Koľko to stojí?

SHOPPING & SERVICES

the bank	banka
the chemist	lekárnik
the church	kostol
the city centre	stred (centrum) mesta
the market	trh
the museum	múzeum
the post office	pošta
the telephone centre	telefónnu centrálu
the tourist office	turistické informačné centrum

TIME, DAYS & NUMBERS

What time is it?	Koľko je hodín?
today	dnes
tonight	dnes večer
tomorrow	zajtra
yesterday	včera
in the morning	ráno
in the evening	večer

Monday	pondelok
Tuesday	utorok
Wednesday	streda
Thursday	štvrtok
Friday	piatok
Saturday	sobota
Sunday	nedeľa

0	nula
1	jeden
2	dva
3	tri
4	štyri
5	päť
6	šesť
7	sedem
8	osem
9	deväť
10	desať
100	sto
1000	tisíc

TRANSPORT

What time does the ... leave/arrive?	Kedy odchádza/prichádza ...?
boat	loč
city bus	mestský autobus
intercity bus	medzimestský autobus
plane	lietadlo
train	vlak
tram	električka

arrival	príchod
departure	odchod
timetable	cestovný poriadok

Where's the bus stop?	Kde je autobusová zastávka?
Where's the station?	Kde je vlaková stanica?
Where's the left-luggage office?	Kde je úschovňa batožín?

Directions

Please show me on the map.	Prosím, ukážte mi to na mape.
left	vľavo
right	vpravo
straight ahead	rovno

SLOVENE

PRONUNCIATION

Slovene pronunciation isn't difficult as most letters are very similar to English. The alphabet has 25 letters – 'q', 'w', 'x' and 'y' don't exist but the following letters have been added: ê, é, ó, ò, č, š and ž. Each letter represents one sound only. The letters l and v are both pronounced like the English 'w' when they occur at the end of syllables and before vowels.

c	as the 'ts' in 'its'
č	as the 'ch' in 'church'
ê	as the 'a' in 'apple'
e	as the 'a' in 'ago'

é	as the 'e' in 'they'
j	as the 'y' in 'yellow'
ó	as the 'a' in 'water'
ò	as the 'o' in 'soft'
r	a rolled 'r'
š	as the 'sh' in 'ship'
u	as in 'put'
ž	as the 's' in 'treasure'

ACCOMMODATION

hotel	*hotel*
guesthouse	*gostišče*
camping ground	*kamping*

Do you have a ...?	*Ali imate prosto ...?*
bed	*posteljo*
cheap room	*poceni sobo*
single room	*enoposteljno sobo*
double room	*dvoposteljno sobo*

How much is it ...?	*Koliko stane ...?*
per night/person	*za eno noč/osebo*
for one/two nights	*za eno noč/za dve noči*

Is breakfast included? *Ali je zajtrk vključen?*

CONVERSATION & ESSENTIALS

Hello.	*Pozdravljeni.* (pol)
	Zdravo/Živivo. (inf)
Good day.	*Dober dan!*
Goodbye.	*Nasvidenje!*
Yes.	*Da* or *Ja.* (inf)
No.	*Ne.*
Please.	*Prosim.*
Thank you.	*Hvala.*
You're welcome.	*Prosim/Ni za kaj!*
Excuse me.	*Oprostite.*
What's your name?	*Kako vam je ime?*
My name is ...	*Jaz sem ...*
Where are you from?	*Od kod ste?*
I'm from ...	*Sem iz ...*

SHOPPING & SERVICES

Where is the/a ...?	*Kje je ...?*
bank/exchange	*banka/menjalnica*
embassy	*konzulat/ambasada*
post office	*pošta*
tourist office	*turistični informa-cijski urad*

SIGNS – SLOVENE

Vhod	Entrance
Izhod	Exit
Informacije	Information
Odprto	Open
Zaprto	Closed
Prepovedano	Prohibited
Stranišče	Toilets
Moški	Men
Ženske	Women

TIME, DAYS & NUMBERS

today	*danes*
tonight	*nocoj*
tomorrow	*jutri*
in the morning	*zjutraj*
in the evening	*zvečer*

Monday	*ponedeljek*
Tuesday	*torek*
Wednesday	*sreda*
Thursday	*četrtek*
Friday	*petek*
Saturday	*sobota*
Sunday	*nedelja*

0	*nula*
1	*ena*
2	*dve*
3	*tri*
4	*štiri*
5	*pet*
6	*šest*
7	*sedem*
8	*osem*
9	*devet*
10	*deset*
100	*sto*
1000	*tisoč*

TRANSPORT

What time does ... leave/arrive?	*Kdaj odpelje/pripelje ...?*
boat/ferry	*ladja/trajekt*
bus	*avtobus*
plane	*avion*
train	*vlak*

timetable	*spored*
train station	*železniška postaja*
bus station	*avtobusno postajališče*
one-way/return	*enosmerna/povratna*

Can you show me on the map?	*A mi lahko pokažete na mapi?*

Behind the Scenes

THIS BOOK

Central Europe is part of Lonely Planet's Europe series, which includes *Western Europe*, *Eastern Europe*, *Mediterranean Europe*, *Scandinavian Europe* and *Europe on a Shoestring*. Lonely Planet also publishes phrasebooks to these regions.

This book was commissioned in Lonely Planet's London office, and produced by the following:

Commissioning Editor Janine Eberle
Coordinating Editor Trent Holden
Coordinating Cartographer Jolyon Philcox
Coordinating Layout Designer Steven Cann
Managing Editor Suzannah Shwer
Managing Cartographer Mark Griffiths
Proofreader Alan Murphy
Cover Designer Pepi Bluck
Colour Designer Yvonne Bischofberger
Project Managers Ray Thomson, Glenn van der Knijff
Language Content Coordinator Quentin Frayne

Thanks to Celia Wood, Dave Burnett, Jennifer Garrett, Josh Geoghegan, Indra Kilfoyle, Mark Germanchis, Nick Stebbing, Rebecca Lalor, Trent Paton, Sally Darmody

THANKS

Aaron Anderson Thanks to Becca, the love of my life, my motivator, and sometimes devil's advocate. Thanks to my mum (Joyce); grandma (Pauline); Uncle Joe; John (my Austrian Dad) plus family – Liz, Tommy and Sebastian; and Becca's parents – David and Patricia Blond. All my friends who listen to my stories about weird places they may never give a crap to see. My Peeps from Memphis: Jered,

Bramlett, Jerry, Jeff Green, Brian @ Outdoors, Sydney and the Cannons. *Mi amigo*, Juan Carlos. My neighbours Russell, Brett, Nan and kids. Big thanks to Major Freedom who always keeps me pumped up about life…and finally to H.S.T. aka Dr Gonzo (1937-2005), I hope the cannon shot got you far enough along.

Brett Atkinson Thanks to Tomáš and Kateřina for overwhelming me with hospitality (long may the chicken fly, and see you in Enzed guys). Hi and thanks to Greg and the crew in Olomouc, and to Oldřiška in Český Krumlov. In LP'ville, thanks to Judith Bamber and Janine Eberle for their support and giving me this opportunity. To Will Gourlay, Sarah Johnstone and Tom Masters, thanks for answering my questions with grace. *Dobrý den* and *děkuji* to all the tourism offices around the Czech Republic that provided me with information, often meeting me halfway with the challenges of language. Back in New Zealand, thanks to Mum and Dad for their unconditional support, and love and special thanks to Carol – my partner in travel adventures and life. Long may the adventures continue.

Becca Blond Thanks to my sister Jessica for making research in Zurich and Liechtenstein heaps more fun. Big thanks to Bernd Fasching at City Backpacker in Zurich for the hospitality and all the helpful tips. In Interlaken, thanks to Susi and Fritz for the skiing, fondue and hospitality. On the home front, thanks to my fabulous boyfriend Aaron and my dog Duke, I love you both. As always

THE LONELY PLANET STORY

The story begins with a classic travel adventure: Tony and Maureen Wheeler's 1972 journey across Europe and Asia to Australia. There was no useful information about the overland trail then, so Tony and Maureen published the first Lonely Planet guidebook to meet a growing need.

From a kitchen table, Lonely Planet has grown to become the largest independent travel publisher in the world, with offices in Melbourne (Australia), Oakland (USA) and London (UK). Today Lonely Planet guidebooks cover the globe. There is an ever-growing list of books and information in a variety of media. Some things haven't changed. The main aim is still to make it possible for adventurous travellers to get out there – to explore and better understand the world.

At Lonely Planet we believe travellers can make a positive contribution to the countries they visit – if they respect their host communities and spend their money wisely. Every year 5% of company profit is donated to charities around the world.

thanks to my family and friends – you know who you are by now.

Lisa Dunford Dearest Saša, what would I have done without you and your family, Fero, Šimon, Sara and Mom & Dad Augustin – thank you doesn't seem to cover it. You are a true friend. To Magda, and your son, Martin: you've been helping me as long as I can remember. You're in my thoughts. Olga, Easter breakfast with champagne was magnificent. Thanks too to the Lonely Planet readers like the students I met on the train to Velky Meder, to the random strangers who tolerated my Slovak and put me on the right bus, and to the Lonely Planet editors, copy editors and cartographers who made all this possible. Oh, and Billy, you're the best travelling companion ever; ICAU.

Steve Fallon A number of people assisted in the research and writing of the Slovenia chapter, in particular my two dear friends and fonts-of-all-knowledge, Verica Leskovar and Tatjana Radovič at the Ljubljana Tourist Board. Others to whom I'd like to say *najlepša hvala* for assistance, sustenance and/or inspiration along the way include Valburga Baričević of Hoteli Piran; Tjaša Borštnik of the Ljubljana Tourist Board; Jelena Dašič of the Bovec Tourist Information Centre; Majda Rozina Dolenc of the Slovenian Tourist Board, Ljubljana; Marino Fakin of Slovenian Railways, Ljubljana; Darjono Husodo and Maja Tratar-Husodo of the Antiq Hotel, Ljubljana; Aleš Hvala of the Hvala hotel, Kobarid; Lado Leskovar of Unicef and RTV, Ljubljana; Vojko Anzeljc and Tone Plankar at the Ljubljana bus station; Aleksander Riznič of Radio Odeon, Črnomelj; Petra Stušek of the Ljubljana Tourist Board; Eva Štravs of the Bled Tourist Information Centre; Brigita Zorec of Ljubljana Aerodrom; and Olga Žvanut of Slovenian Railways, Ljubljana. As always, my efforts here are dedicated to my partner, Michael Rothschild, an 'honest' man at last.

Sarah Johnstone Thanks to all the usual suspects, plus Nicole Röbel at Berlin Tourismus Marketing, Doris Annette Schütz of Lübeck und Travemünde Tourist-Service, Christine Lambrecht, Dr Annette Zehnter, Paul Gronert and Nadine in Dessau and everyone else who helped out. I'm grateful to fellow author Ryan for covering, ahem, the bird-flu zone, and indebted to the night-porter in my Cologne hotel for saving me from the *amokläufer* incanting loud death threats in the wee hours…who turned out to be merely an inconsiderate gangsta rapper. Finally, thanks to Richard Priest for being the only one to truly appreciate the ridiculous humour of that story!

623

Da
Big
tor, t
editors
train, an
I waited fo
to the Hung
Sopor who w
communicatio

Tim Richards Dzię
helpful Polish tourist of
their ears on all matters inv
pecially Tom in Kraków; Agnies
Monika in Warsaw; Karolina in Łóu
Wrocław; Antoni in Lublin; Joanna in Z
Maciej in Toruń; Monika in Poznań; Ewa in
zecin; and Anna in Giżycko. Amy Doidge and he
colleagues at the Australian Embassy in Warsaw
also provided useful assistance, as did Aussie
expat Darren Haines-Powell. Thanks to my former
teaching colleagues Magda Fijałkowska and Ewa
Bandura for their friendship across the years and

SEND US YOUR FEEDBACK

We love to hear from travellers – your comments keep us on our toes and help make our books better. Our well-travelled team reads every word on what you loved or loathed about this book. Although we cannot reply individually to postal submissions, we always guarantee that your feedback goes straight to the appropriate authors, in time for the next edition. Each person who sends us information is thanked in the next edition – and the most useful submissions are rewarded with a free book.

To send us your updates – and find out about Lonely Planet events, newsletters and travel news – visit our award-winning website: **www.lonelyplanet.com/contact**.

Note: we may edit, reproduce and incorporate your comments in Lonely Planet products such as guidebooks, websites and digital products, so let us know if you don't want your comments reproduced or your name acknowledged. For a copy of our privacy policy visit www.lonelyplanet.com/privacy.

nd Gosia Grabarczyk
er! Thanks (and con-
aj' manufacturer Beata
to the barstaff at U Sz-
ept the *goldwasser* coming
Thanks also to the PKP staff
trains running on time, no
weather. A final thanks to the
n who talked with me in Polish
a tram stop below Wawel Castle,
eriences as a slave labourer for the
it's personal stories like his that make
nlightening.

r Berkmoes Thanks to my old friend Clau-
hle who helped immeasurably – and found
away coffee when my life depended on it. One
you're cooking in Thailand, the next you're lost
the Witch's Hole. Thanks also to my long-ago
colleague Angela Cullen who taught me many language skills. I'd call Carsten Ivers tow-headed, but
he might weep. Rather I'll thank him on behalf of
the thousands of German dowagers whose feet are
as soft and smooth as a virgin's. And thanks to Stefi
Graf whose mythical smelly tennis shoes launched
my career. At Lonely Planet, the indefatigable Mark
Griffiths, delightful Tashi Wheeler and patient Kim
Noble made this yet another fun project. My fellow authors made it a delight too, especially Sarah,
who cracked me up. Finally kudos to my Munich

shopper and partner Erin Corrigan for, well, everything. Oh, and Cake for Nugget. Says it all.

OUR READERS

Many thanks to the travellers who used the last
edition and wrote to us with helpful hints, useful
advice and interesting anecdotes:

B Leyla Bagloul, Petr Bohac, Linde Butterhoff, **C** John Chapman,
George Chatziargyris, Michael Cwach, **D** Emmanuelle de Mer,
Klara Debeljak, Julieanne & Stephen Dimitrios, **F** David Fagundes,
G Patrick Gallagher, Chloe Groom, **H** Ronald Hakenberg, Ina
Hoetzsch, Ilona Hofman, Steve Hollis, **I** Alex Isaac, **J** Joyce Jeffery,
Barry Johnston, Alex Johnstone, **K** Martina Kamenikova, Richard
Keeling, Christian Kirsch, Melissa Kluger, Floris Kortie, Jan Kotuc,
L Audrey Langlois, Rupert Lory, **M** Dee Macpherson, Robyn
Matthews, Gerry Mcgilvray, Gabi McNicol, Gordon Milward, Paul
Mollatt, Heather Monell, Pauline Moreno, Rich Morgan, **N** Marc
Nadeau, Carrie Ng, Jonathan Newton, **P** Stephen Paylor, Karen
Playfair, **R** Miriam Raftery, Thomas Reydon, Juliet Richters,
Eva Romo, David Route, **S** Seumas Sargent, Noelle Siri, Hamon
Stewart, John Streets, Ernest Stricker, Jana Svitkova, **T** Lauren
Thompson, Fab Tomlin, Maria Tripska, **W** Claire Wells, Liz
Wightwick, Amber Wilkin,

ACKNOWLEDGMENTS

Many thanks to the following for the use of their
content:

Map data contained in colour highlights map
© Mountain High Maps 1993 Digital Wisdom, Inc.

Index